Peterson's Study Abroad

2005

THOMSON

PETERSON'S

Australia • Canada • Mexico • Singapore • Spain • United Kingdom • United States

About Thomson Peterson's

Thomson Peterson's (www.petersons.com) is a leading provider of education information and advice, with books and online resources focusing on education search, test preparation, and financial aid. Its Web site offers searchable databases and interactive tools for contacting educational institutions, online practice tests and instruction, and planning tools for securing financial aid. Thomson Peterson's serves 110 million education consumers annually.

For more information, contact Thomson Peterson's, 2000 Lenox Drive, Lawrenceville, NJ 08648; 800-338-3282; or find us on the World Wide Web at www.petersons.com/about.

Editor: Joseph Krasowski; Production Editor: L. A. Wagner; Copy Editor: Sally Ross; Research Project Manager: Christine Lucas; Research Associate: Amy L. Weber; Programmer: Alex Lin; Manufacturing Manager: Ivona Skibicki; Composition Manager: Gary Rozmierski; Client Relations Representatives: Mimi Kaufman, Lois Regina Milton, Mary Ann Murphy, Jim Swinarski, and Eric Wallace.

ISBN 0-7689-1562-7

Printed in the United States of America

10 9 8 7 6 5 4 3 2 1   07 06 05

Twelfth Edition

CONTENTS

A Note from the Peterson's Editors

If you're planning to become one of the estimated 200,000 American students who annually spend a semester or year studying abroad, you've probably begun to collect brochures on various programs and examined the beautiful travel posters that cover bulletin boards across your campus. At this point you may also be wondering how you will ever sort out which program is best for you, how you will afford it, how you will convince your parents and advisers to let you go, and how you will finalize all the details involved.

Many students abandon the idea of going abroad when faced with these issues. You don't have to be one of them! *Peterson's Study Abroad 2005* is designed to walk you step-by-step through the process of selecting a program and preparing for what may be the most enriching time of your academic life.

This guide is divided into three main parts:

THE INS AND OUTS OF STUDYING ABROAD section provides insight into:

- How to decide if you are a good candidate for a study-abroad program

- Avoiding culture shock, traveling smart, and living within your budget

- Transferring credits and finding and securing financial aid

- Obtaining passports and visas

- What nontraditional destinations have to offer

- Exchange programs for students with disabilities

The "How to Use This Guide" article provides in-depth explanations about each element contained in the profiles, the criteria used to select the programs, and data collection procedures.

The **PROFILES OF STUDY-ABROAD PROGRAMS** section lists nearly 1,900 programs. These profiles contain all the details you'll need to make a list of preliminary program choices.

Finally, the three **INDEXES** contained in this guide—Field of Study, Program Sponsors, and Host Institutions—are invaluable resources for narrowing your choice of programs.

Peterson's publishes a full line of resources to help guide you through the college search and selection process. Peterson's publications can be found at your local bookstore, library, and high school guidance office or online at www.petersons. com.

Like anything worthwhile, you'll get out of your study-abroad experience what you put into it. Peterson's is dedicated to helping you gather all the information you need to make a sound decision. We wish you the best of luck in your search for the perfect study-abroad program for you!

The Ins and Outs of Studying Abroad

Credit for Study Abroad

Stephen Cooper, Ph.D.

Former Director of Academic Programs Abroad, Louisiana State University

Parents encourage it. The financial aid office insists on it. The United States Congress even authorizes money for students who go for it—college credit.

It increasingly matters to students that they earn maximum credit for an overseas experience as the costs of a college education increase. While it may be tempting to set up your own trip or sign up for an adventurous tour, most students seek an international experience that will strengthen their academic record. Credit programs provide significant structure, educational gains, and other benefits, not the least of which is the academic credit itself.

This guide includes only credit-granting study-abroad programs. Here we'll discuss the kinds of credit possible and the best ways to ensure that you get the credit you want. Unless you are going on a program run by your own university, you will probably earn credit *by transfer.* That means your home university will evaluate the courses you took and decide whether to accept them and then how to put them on your transcript.

CREDIT FOR WHAT?

Depending on your home university, you could earn credit in general education courses, electives, your major and minor subjects, and foreign languages (possibly even for languages not taught at your home school). While you may be able to get credit that will appear on your transcript, you may also want to know if that credit can be applied toward your degree.

Also consider the personal benefits of taking a course that won't satisfy any degree requirement but that could provide you with rewarding cultural enrichment. For example, an engineering major who has already "maxed out" in electives might find the value of an art history course in Paris, a political science course in Germany, or a theater course in London too rich a treat to pass up—a healthy attitude for a student who might not return overseas for decades.

WHO GIVES THE CREDIT?

Be certain of the source of the credit offered before you sign up for a program. If you are going on your own school's program, find out if the courses actually appear in your college course catalog. If they are extramural courses, verify that your academic advisers will accept them and that you will not exceed any limits on taking such courses.

If you decide to join a program set up by another U.S. university, more care is required. You'll probably need more information than appears in the program brochure. Will the sponsoring U.S. school issue the transcript, or will a foreign university or some agency do so? *Find this out before you sign up!* Either way, you may need more details on the courses offered to satisfy your college's academic counselors that you can earn *credit by transfer.*

HOW MUCH CREDIT CAN I EARN?

The amount of credit you can earn will depend on policies of the host institution and your school as well as what you take abroad and (often) whether or not you get written prior approval. Of course, *you have to pass all those courses.* In fact, your home school may require that you earn a C or better in a course before accepting the credits.

Your home advisers may require a lot of information on the courses you want to take to help estimate how much credit you will earn. If a foreign university will issue your final transcript, some admissions officers and registrars will look closely at the number of contact hours in a particular course—that is, the actual number of

hours you will have in lectures, labs, field experiences, and tutorials. If a U.S. university will provide the official transcript, the transfer may be simpler because of similarities in credit systems here.

As you look at programs offered by other U.S. universities, remember that some offer credit on the *quarter system,* others on a *semester credit* basis. If your college and the sponsoring school differ, another transfer issue may arise. For example, some U.S. universities use a ratio of 3:2 in transferring quarter credit hours to semester credits. How would this affect you? Get your admissions office or registrar to help you calculate credit-hour transfer potential.

Many U.S. students choose *direct enrollment* in foreign universities for a semester or a year, some going on exchanges. Again, it is important to get course descriptions in advance and, sometimes just as important, to demonstrate to your home school that the foreign university has some kind of accreditation or official standing with the country's ministry of education.

Getting course information in adequate detail sometimes proves difficult, for example, in Europe, where the U.S. practice of publishing comprehensive course catalogs is rare. However, with persistence, the right contacts, help from your study-abroad adviser, and the use of faxes and e-mails, you can usually get enough advance information to determine if you will be able to earn desired credit, again by transfer, from the overseas school. Even if the descriptive course material given is in the language of the host country, you can usually get it translated for your school officials who will rule on its acceptability.

PRIOR APPROVAL—GET IT IN WRITING!

Most students should know before they take off for a particular study-abroad experience whether or not they will earn credit. In fact, many universities require a process of prior approval and will not accept any credit earned abroad that was not authorized beforehand. Indeed, part of the process of obtaining financial aid via your home school for your overseas study may include seeking signatures from persons who can approve your anticipated selections. Usually, your study-abroad adviser, registrar, or admissions office will guide you through the process. Keep in mind that if you fail to get that approval in writing, you could return with little to show for your academic efforts abroad.

You might also have to seek from the host university such items as course outlines and reading lists, information on the level of the course (first year, advanced, etc.), prerequisites, the number of contact hours, and the format of the course, such as lecture, seminar, lab, or field study.

Different universities in the United States handle the acceptance or transfer of credit in different ways. Some have already set up exact matches or direct equivalents, which pair foreign university courses with courses in your home school's catalog. More commonly, though, the home university will receive the overseas courses as substitutes for some of your required courses or as electives that can still fulfill degree requirements. Find out in each case how your institution will handle each of your chosen courses.

DOCUMENTING CREDIT EARNED ABROAD

Note that some overseas institutions do not create transcripts; instead, you may have to get other kinds of documentation, including letters from the professors who taught you. Find out in advance what to expect and how to get what you will need. Also, be sure that the transcript or other materials are sent to the proper person at your home school. At some U.S. colleges, a good way to handle this is to have everything sent to your study-abroad adviser, as that person will know how to route everything to avoid delays or loss. Find out before you leave so you can tell your host school authorities.

Upon return, in addition to the transcript, be prepared to show your home school other items related to the courses you took, including course syllabi, reading lists, exams returned, papers you did, your lecture notes, and the like. These can

help document the nature and level of the course work and ensure that you earn full credit.

OTHER CREDIT OPTIONS

So far, we have focused on traditional course work. But some students earn credit for study abroad in other ways. Some colleges offer what is called credit for experiential education, sometimes for work experience, for public service projects, and sometimes for travel abroad. If this is a possibility at your school, find out what is required to document the experience to earn credit.

More and more U.S. universities encourage internships and may give credit for them alone or in combination with course work taken abroad. Check with your home school in advance to see if credit applies. See the article on "International Internships" in this guide to explore this possibility.

Many U.S. schools give credit by exam, especially in foreign languages but also in other

subjects. It works like this: You take a course abroad, return home, and sit for a formal examination on your campus to see how much knowledge you gained. The exam might be oral, written, or both and is almost always designed by your own home campus faculty. You can find out before departure if this is an option and how to prepare for the exam.

Independent study provides another avenue for credit. An independent study or readings course is an individualized course for credit agreed upon between a student and a professor, one that usually allows the student to pursue some special research topic or do selected work in depth in a specialized area, usually in the student's major field of study. Some students set up independent readings or project courses with cooperative host or home campus faculty members prior to leaving on an overseas study program. You may also get to take such courses in the host university's program. Doing so may be limited in terms of credits that may be earned and will usually require formal enrollment in those courses. Nevertheless, independent study for credit provides valuable possibilities for carrying out research projects and doing work that could not be done for credit in an overseas institution or program offered by another U.S. school. If you can take advantage of this option, be sure to make precise arrangements with your sponsoring professor(s) so that you meet required deadlines and satisfy expectations established. Then, keep in touch with your sponsoring faculty members while you are abroad to advise them of your progress and to seek guidance. Save copies of

anything you mail back to them, as not all foreign postal systems are perfect, nor is our own!

Graduate students may need credit for their overseas study. In addition to the options discussed above, some graduate schools in the United States allow thesis or dissertation credit for research done abroad. In fact, some universities will enroll graduate students for credit concurrently with the foreign experience, and indeed this may be a requirement for maintaining fellowships or other awards from the home school.

Now, you may also have the option of telecommunication course work or using e-mail, the Internet, and television via satellite transmission.

CREDIT AND FINANCIAL AID

The federal government has made it clear that U.S. college students who are eligible for federal loans, grants, and scholarships may use their aid in overseas programs approved by their home universities, but the programs have to be for credit. Carefully read the article "Paying for Study Abroad" for details, and study your home school's rules.

WHAT ABOUT GRADES?

In addition to granting credits for courses taken abroad, many U.S. colleges accept grades and post them on the home transcript. Specialists in your office of admissions or your registrar will know how to do this, but you will want to understand what will happen, too.

Different universities have different grading systems. In some countries, numbers are used rather than letter grades. Some foreign universities give comments but no grades of any kind. Your home university may or may not convert the grades received to your own school's grading scale, post the foreign grades on your transcript, or average the grades into your personal grade point average.

Furthermore, some overseas university systems tend to grade more severely than those in the United States. For that reason, many U.S. students take advantage of a pass/fail grading option in order to protect their averages. If you seek that option, do so officially, in writing, and before departure to ensure acceptability by your home school; you may have to petition your dean in writing. Once abroad, it is difficult to change a course to pass/fail.

If you get a foreign university transcript or one from the U.S. institution that provided your program abroad, save original copies or find out how to get them; you may decide to apply to graduate or a professional school after graduation, and you will probably have to provide original transcripts from all the institutions you have attended.

SOLVING PROBLEMS

Clearly, the best way to avoid difficulty in earning credit for your experience abroad is to seek formal prior approval of the course work you want to take. On most campuses, this requires patience, legwork, research, diplomacy, and attention to detail. Your study abroad adviser and other personnel will assist you as much as they can, but you will have full responsibility for providing what is needed before you go and when you return.

Once abroad, expect surprises. You may have to change some courses, and you may run into other unanticipated difficulties. Act quickly and resourcefully. Use e-mail and faxes as well as the telephone to keep in touch with your advisers back home. This contact will pay for itself when you get back home and the final credit evaluation begins. Also, provide your home university with your foreign address once you get settled.

Students who understand the kinds of credit available in study abroad and how to arrange for that credit usually do quite well, returning home not only with fond memories, increased global awareness, and personal growth but also with a vital addition to their academic records. I hope that all of this happens to you, and more!

_____

Stephen Cooper, Ph.D., was Director of Academic Programs Abroad at Louisiana State University from 1980–1990. A frequent presenter at professional conferences, he has also written articles and chapters on study abroad for various publications. He coedited Financial Aid for Study Abroad: A Manual for Advisers and Administrators *(NAFSA, 1989). In 1993 he received the Lily von Klemperer Award from the study abroad section of NAFSA for his service to the field.*

Paying for Study Abroad

Nancy Stubbs

Director of Study Abroad Programs, University of Colorado at Boulder

So, you've found the perfect study-abroad program, and you have the information you need. You even found out that the credit earned abroad will transfer back to your home institution. What's next? Paying for it. This article is designed to help you get the most for your money as well as guide you through the financial aid issues that may concern you.

HOW MUCH WILL IT REALLY COST?

Study-abroad costs vary greatly from program to program. Even at the same site, three or four different programs can charge different fees. There are a variety of reasons for this. When shopping around for the best price, you should think about what the program offers.

When you study abroad (as opposed to enrolling directly in a foreign institution to pursue a degree), you pay for a certain amount of service and expertise. A faculty member at the sponsoring U.S. institution may be hired as program director. He or she will speak the language of the country, be familiar with the educational system and local customs, and be on-site during the program to help you get oriented, fill out forms, register for courses, and deal with emergencies.

The program may schedule special events that aren't open to others at the program site. Field trips, special orientations, or language classes are good examples. The cost of these events could be built into the fee you pay. Or, they might be optional events, allowing you to choose and pay for those that interest you. It's important to have a good idea of *all* costs, since it is impossible to create a reasonable budget if you keeping running across unexpected expenses.

You may also pay tuition to the sponsoring institution as a way of allowing the course work to be transferred and transcripted. Normally, at least part of this tuition is used to pay program costs; some of it may be kept by the sponsor to cover the cost of administering the program.

As you can see, the cost of programs can vary even at the same site because of the number of persons hired to assist you, the cost of extra events planned for the program, administrative costs at the home institution, or even things like the type of housing available. You've probably figured out that study abroad will cost more in a country with a higher cost of living. But, you can also pay a lot in a country where living costs are low if you choose to attend a private school with no subsidized tuition.

WHY DO I NEED A BUDGET?

There are several reasons to assemble a good estimate of your program costs. Most obvious is the need to know how much money you will need. Unless you have been abroad on your own before, you will probably not think of all costs associated with study abroad.

For instance, you don't need to worry about passport and visa costs, airport taxes, customs fees, the cost of changing currency, currency fluctuations, and so on to be a college student in the U.S. All of these could be part of your budget for study abroad.

While vacation travel, shopping, or recreational activities may not fit the definition of "required educational costs," you will surely want to have enough money for some fun while you are abroad. If you do succeed in finding an outside source of funding, you may need a budget so that the aid administrator can determine your award. It is in your best interest to be sure that all reasonable costs are included in this budget.

Always ask for an estimate of total costs for the program, preferably broken down into categories. The program administrator should be able to provide this for you. If not, ask for a list of alumni willing to speak to interested persons. You can ask them what they spent. Be sure to check with your home school study-abroad adviser, too. He or she may have information about budgets and transferring funds that will help you determine the real

cost of study abroad. Here are typical categories for the study-abroad budget:

- Tuition and fees at the study-abroad site

- Tuition due to the institution administering the program

- Books, paper, and other school supplies

- Room and meal costs, including those during vacation periods

- Typical living costs, including local commuting, laundry, telephone, postage, and entertainment

- Medical and other insurance (lost baggage, trip cancellation, etc.)

- Passport, visa, and airport tax fees

- Round-trip transportation to and from the program site

- Travel on weekends and vacation

- Optional program activities, such as field trips and cultural events

HOW CAN I PAY FOR IT?

There is, unfortunately, no huge source of private scholarships available for undergraduate study abroad. Most private funding is dedicated to graduate, or even postgraduate, study and research. Still, there are a variety of places you can look for outside help:

- Federal or state financial aid

- Institutional, private, and other types of government aid for education

- Scholarships for undergraduate study abroad

FEDERAL AND STATE FINANCIAL AID

By far the largest pool of funding available to U.S. college students is federal and state financial aid. Federal financial aid is money supplied through the Higher Education Act of 1965 to assist students in getting a college education. State aid is similar but comes from your state's tax funds. You may be using financial aid already. If so, you might be able to use that aid to study abroad.

Federal and state aid is divided into three categories:

- **Grants and scholarships,** which do not have to be repaid. The most common federal grants are Federal Pell Grants and Federal Supplemental Educational Opportunity Grants. State grants can include various diversity grants for nontraditional students and state-funded scholarship programs for residents who attend public or private institutions.

- **Work-study funds,** which partially pay your salary for certain jobs. Work-study programs can be funded by both the federal and state governments.

- **Educational loans,** which you can obtain without a credit rating, and which usually do not have to be repaid until you graduate. Some of the loans have an added advantage— the government pays the interest while you are in school. The Federal Perkins Loan program is one of the most familiar of these. The federal government also offers the Stafford Loan, the PLUS Loan for parents, and Direct Loans. Some states also have loan programs for students attending state institutions.

Check with your financial aid office to determine which state aid programs are available at your institution. This office can also assist you in learning about federal aid, institutional scholarships, and often even private scholarships.

CAN I USE MY FINANCIAL AID TO STUDY ABROAD?

The answer is—sometimes. Federal aid can legally be used to study abroad as long as the program you attend has been approved for credit by your home institution.

Many state aid programs follow the same rules and regulations as the federal government. If your state does this, you should be able to use state aid for study-abroad programs approved by your home campus. In some cases, state grants or scholarships may be restricted to use in that state.

If you already get federal or state aid, you know that both are governed by a multitude of rules and regulations. Each institution is allowed some latitude in deciding how aid programs will be administered and how certain things, like the cost of attending school, will be determined. This is good—it allows aid administrators to take into account special circumstances when awarding aid. Here are some things to know if you are investigating whether state or federal aid can be used for study abroad:

1. It is legal to use federal grants, work-study, or loans for study abroad, but you can only get aid from a school where you are enrolled in a degree program, and you must be enrolled at least half-time (or full-time in some cases) while you get the aid. So, you have to maintain enrollment at your "home" campus (where you plan to get your degree), and your home campus must agree that the credit earned abroad is "approved." Under these circumstances, your home campus can award federal aid even if you are going abroad on a program sponsored by another U.S. school or by a foreign institution.

2. It may not be possible to use your work-study award abroad because of restrictions on where you can work and how your time must be reported.

3. You will find it easiest to use federal or state aid if you go on a study-abroad program run by your school. The programs are already academically approved, and your school has devised some mechanism to keep you enrolled while you study abroad. The credit does not have to satisfy major requirements, but you need to be able to use it for general education or elective credit.

4. If your perfect program is administered by another U.S. institution or if you wish to enroll directly in a foreign school's program, you can still arrange to use your federal or state aid. Your home school must have a mechanism for examining the courses you will take and for approving them for transfer. Again, the credit does not have to satisfy major requirements, but you need to be able to use it for general education or elective credit.

5. Once the program is approved by your home institution, it is necessary to have a written agreement between your school and the school or organization that administers it. Ask your home school study-abroad office or your financial aid office about this agreement.

6. Your financial aid office may require a budget for your study-abroad program to ensure that you are not awarded too much aid (more than the cost of your education). Federal law allows the use of aid to cover all "reasonable" costs of study abroad, including round-trip transportation, tuition and fees for the program, living costs, passport and visa fees, health insurance, etc.

7. If your study-abroad program costs more than what you normally pay, ask your financial aid office to consider the higher costs and give you more aid. If studying abroad costs less, you should expect the normal aid award to be reduced.

8. If you have never applied for a federal loan, federal law requires that you attend school for at least thirty days before you can get your loan money. You are also required to have special counseling about borrowing money for college; your first loan cannot be disbursed to you until you have received this counseling.

9. You have extra responsibilities if you receive federal or state aid for study abroad. You may have to gather information about the cost of your program. You must take responsibility for ensuring that all forms, documents, and other materials are filled out and turned in so you can get your aid award. You will have to arrange for someone you trust to "watch over" your aid, perhaps pick up refund checks, and contact your financial aid officer if problems arise, since it is very hard to sort out problems when you are away from your campus. This can often be done with a "power of attorney." Most importantly,

to approve the program so credit can be transferred back toward your degree. You will undoubtedly have to make extra arrangements to ensure that the benefits are properly awarded and tracked.

Many universities award institutional aid to their students. This may be a tuition scholarship, a merit award for good grades, or some other nongovernment scholarship or loan. If you plan to go on a study-abroad program run by your institution, ask if you can use these funds. If the answer is "no," ask why, since you are going on a program that is an extension of your institution. Some institutions will not allow such scholarships to be used for programs sponsored by others, but some will. Again, it never hurts to ask.

You can look for private aid that is awarded to you to be used wherever you go to school. You have undoubtedly heard about the "millions of dollars in private aid" that can be located by various scholarship search companies. It isn't necessary to pay someone to look for scholarships. Most college reference libraries have private funding sourcebooks that list hundreds of scholarships. This is especially useful if you are a member of an ethnic minority or if you are a "nontraditional" (i.e., older, married, disabled, etc.) student. An excellent resource for this type of information is *Peterson's Scholarships, Grants & Prizes 2005*. You can also search for scholarships on the Internet at www.petersons.com/finaid.

you must be sure you take enough courses and earn satisfactory grades while abroad.

10. If you think you might be eligible for state or federal financial aid, talk to your study-abroad adviser and your financial aid officer. Find out what policies exist for using aid to study abroad, and be sure you follow instructions so you won't be denied aid at the last minute or have difficulties getting the money that has been awarded.

INSTITUTIONAL, PRIVATE, AND OTHER TYPES OF GOVERNMENT AID FOR EDUCATION

You may be receiving other assistance for your education that can be used for a study-abroad program. For instance, if you are in an ROTC program or if you receive veteran's benefits or vocational-rehabilitation benefits, it may be possible to use these funds for study abroad. Since these are all government programs, you must work carefully with your campus representative to see how the benefits might be applied to study abroad. It will be important for your home school

SCHOLARSHIPS FOR UNDERGRADUATE STUDY ABROAD

There are a few scholarships specifically for undergraduate study abroad. You must apply at least a year in advance for some, so it is wise to plan ahead if you want to apply for these scholarships.

Perhaps the best-known undergraduate scholarships are provided by Rotary International. This service organization has a yearly nationwide competition for high school, graduate, and undergraduate students. Awards range from travel grants to full-cost grants. The application deadline for the national competition is usually in the early fall preceding the year that you will study abroad. Check with your local Rotary Club.

The U.S. government now provides scholarships specifically for undergraduate and graduate study abroad. The National Security Education Program (NSEP) provides scholarships for study in nontraditional countries. Awards are made after a highly competitive national process. If you get a scholarship from NSEP, you will be expected to complete a service requirement. Your campus should have an NSEP representative who can give you more information about this program. Check with your study-abroad office for details.

Other scholarships for study abroad will not cover all costs but can be used to supplement other funding. Some study-abroad programs have scholarships for their students. Your campus might provide scholarships if you go on an approved program or one run by your institution. A few scholarships are provided to U.S. students by foreign governments, and there is an increasing number of scholarships available to minority and nontraditional students. Information about these types of scholarships can be found by contacting your study-abroad office.

WHERE DO I START?

Begin your search by taking a realistic look at the cost of your perfect program. Compare that to your own resources. How much money can you or your family devote to study abroad? Don't assume you can earn money while you study; it is illegal for foreign students to work in many countries. Don't decide you can sell all your earthly possessions if it means you will return home destitute and unable to continue your education. Also, think about owing thousands in student loans if you plan to borrow your way abroad. Is it realistic to think you can repay all of those loans, or would it be better to wait a semester or year so funds can be saved?

After you have a clear picture of the program's costs and your ability to pay them, begin to look for other sources of money. Check with your study-abroad and financial aid offices to see if you might qualify for federal, state, or institutional aid. Look at private funding resource books to see if there are scholarships you can use. Ask your study-abroad office about the NSEP and Rotary scholarships or any other source of funding for study-abroad, and ask the program sponsor if you qualify for scholarships, work, or other types of assistance.

Most students still fund study abroad with individual or family funds. An increasing number of people, however, are finding support from the aid sources mentioned above. If you will need help funding your study-abroad program, begin early, look carefully, and remember that you won't get funding if you don't ask. Good luck!

Nancy Stubbs is Director of Study Abroad Programs at the University of Colorado at Boulder, where she has worked since 1979. She is coeditor of Financial Aid for Study Abroad: A Manual for Advisers and Administrators. *She has written many articles and given presentations on funding for study abroad. She is past chair of a subcommittee of study abroad professionals who work to make federal financial aid available to students who study abroad.*

The Essentials: Passports, Visas, ID Cards, Money, and More

Stephanie Orange

Former Director of Public Relations, Council on International Educational Exchange

L eaving the United States to study in another country isn't as easy as grabbing a backpack and buying a plane ticket. You'll have to deal with a lot of details—passports, visas, and traveler's checks. As soon as you decide to study outside the United States, start getting the formalities out of the way. Careful preparation and planning is an important part of any successful trip abroad.

PASSPORTS

U.S. citizens need a passport to enter just about any foreign country and return to the United States. Exceptions include short-term travel between the United States and Mexico, Canada, and most Caribbean countries. Even when it's not specifically required, however, a valid U.S. passport is the best travel documentation available.

Passports for U.S. citizens 16 years of age or older are valid for ten years and cost $55 plus a $30 fee for processing first-time applications. Between March and August the demand is heaviest, so processing your application during these months will take longer. Apply several months before your departure date; if you're going to need visas, allow yourself even more time.

If you have never applied for a passport before, you must apply in person at a post office authorized to accept passport applications; at a federal, state, or county courthouse; or at one of the thirteen passport agencies located around the United States. To apply, bring proof of U.S. citizenship (such as a certified copy of a birth certificate, naturalization certificate, or consular report of birth abroad) and proof of identity (such as a valid driver's license, *not* a Social Security or credit card). You'll also need two recent identical photographs two inches square. Photographs can be black-and-white or color, but they must be taken

against a white background. Most photo shops will know exactly what you need. Finally, you must complete the passport application form.

You may apply by mail and avoid the $30 processing fee if you have had a passport within fifteen years of the new application, you submit your most recent passport with the application, and your previous passport was not issued before your sixteenth birthday. To apply this way, get the special mail-in application form, which can be obtained from a post office, courthouse, or passport agency. Attach your previous passport and two new passport photographs, and mail all the materials to the address on the application.

Authorities may require you to show your passport for identification at any time you are abroad, so it's a good idea to keep it with you. It's also a good idea to keep it safe from loss or theft. To do this, carry your passport in a pouch that is tied at the neck or worn around the waist like a belt. The pouch can also hold traveler's checks and other valuables and should always be kept inside your clothing. Loss, theft, or destruction of a valid passport is a serious matter and should be reported immediately to local police and to the nearest U.S. embassy or consulate. If you lose your passport in another country, you will need to get a replacement at a U.S. embassy or consulate. For more information about passports, contact the Office of Passport Services, Department of State at 877-487-2778.

VISAS

Depending on the country you visit and the length and purpose of your stay, you may also need a visa. A visa is an endorsement or stamp placed in your passport by a foreign government; it permits you to visit the country for a specified purpose and for a limited time. To study in a particular country, you often need a special student visa. In most cases, you'll have to obtain visas before you leave the United States. Apply directly to the embassies or consulates of the countries you plan to visit, or check with your study abroad adviser. The Department of State *cannot* help you get a visa. Since a visa is usually stamped directly onto one of the blank pages in your passport, you'll need to fill out a form and send your passport to the appropriate foreign embassy or consulate. You'll have to pay for most visas, and you may need one or two photos. (Have extras made when you're having passport pictures taken.) The whole process can take several weeks, so start early.

INTERNATIONAL STUDENT IDENTITY CARD

The International Student Identity Card is a basic travel document for students going abroad. The Card—issued to more than 4.5 million students each year by student travel organizations in eighty-two countries—is the product of the International Student Travel Confederation (www. istc.org), which is based in Copenhagen, Denmark. The Council on International Educational Exchange (Council) is the U.S. sponsor of the Card. The International Student Identity Card provides internationally recognized proof of student status; with it, you gain access to any student discounts available where you decide to study or travel. In addition to these discounts, students with the International Student Identity Card get special discounts on airfares, international phone calls, international money transfers, lodging in the United States, and more. Perhaps the best-known discounts are for student fares on international flights; cardholders can save up to 50 percent over commercial fares on the same routes. These fares—the result of special negotiations between the airlines and the Council (and other student travel organizations around the world)—are *not* available from the airline directly; they are only offered through specially authorized student travel offices such as Council Travel.

In addition to student discounts, the International Student Identity Cards issued in the United States provide basic medical and accident insurance. Students who obtain the Card in the United States receive coverage while traveling outside of the United States for as long as their Card is valid. Also available to cardholders is a toll-free hotline for travelers in need of assistance in a legal, medical, or financial emergency.

The International Student Identity Card is valid from September 1st until December 31st each year. There is no age limit, although age restrictions may apply on some discounts. A free benefit guide to all Card purchasers provides detailed information on insurance, emergency traveler's assistance, student airfares, and cardholder discounts in the United States and abroad.

The Card is available at all Council Travel offices and at issuing offices at hundreds of U.S. colleges and universities. You can also order the Card by mail from Council, 633 Third Avenue, New York, NY 10017. You can also call 800-781-4040 or 800-592-2887 toll-free for more information, for an application form, or for the location of the issuing office nearest you.

MONEY

The safest way to carry your money abroad is in the form of traveler's checks, which can be replaced if lost or stolen. Most traveler's checks cost 1 percent of the total amount you're buying. Traveler's checks in U.S. dollars are widely accepted around the world. It is also possible to purchase traveler's checks in other major currencies, such as the Euro, British pounds, and Japanese yen. While it is hard to predict the course of the international currency market, you can insulate yourself from its fluctuations by purchasing traveler's checks in the currency of the country where you will be staying.

Overseas, you can change dollars into other currencies at most banks and at a variety of other types of exchange bureaus. Because currency dealers take a commission and often add a service charge as well, exchange rates differ from one place to another. Be sure to investigate all options for the best rate of exchange, especially if you're going to be changing large amounts of money. Whatever you do, be wary of currency exchange with money changers on the street; in most countries this type of transaction is illegal.

If you run short of money, traveler's checks or cash can be quickly cabled to you from the United States through companies such as Western Union. An emergency cash transfer like this, however, is usually quite expensive.

The proliferation of automated teller machines (ATMs) around the world provides one of the best ways of transferring money and exchanging currency. Many ATMs in the United States and abroad are connected to international networks such as Cirrus® and Plus System®. This means that you can get cash in the local currency directly from your bank account in the United States. Usually you'll get a very favorable rate of exchange—the same one banks use when exchanging money among themselves. Contact your bank for more information.

BE INFORMED

In order to get the most out of your experience abroad, you'll want to do some research on the country you'll be visiting. Guidebooks, novels, movies, histories, and social, economic, and political studies are some of the materials you might want to take a look at before leaving. Investigate your library, ask professors what they recommend, and check to see what your local bookstore has in stock.

No matter where you go, you'll be asked questions about U.S. foreign policy—especially about matters that directly affect the country you're visiting. The best thing to do is to prepare yourself a little in advance by reading newspapers like *The New York Times*, *Washington Post*, and *Christian Science Monitor*, which are known for their coverage of international affairs. Especially valuable are the publications of the Foreign Policy Association, a nonprofit, nonpartisan organization dedicated to informing the public of the complexities of foreign policy issues. You can get information about their publications, including the annual *Great Decisions*, from the Foreign Policy Association, 470 Park Avenue North, New

York, NY 10016-6819; telephone: 212-481-8100 or on the Web at www.fpa.org.

CUSTOMS

When you come back to the United States, you'll have to go through customs. The U.S. government prohibits Americans from bringing back certain articles and imposes import fees or duties on other items. In general, the first $400 worth of goods is duty-free, but for more than $400 of goods, whether items are for personal or commercial use,

expect to pay a duty of 2 percent to 40 percent depending on the type of merchandise. Everything that you'll need to know about customs regulations for your return to the United States can be found in *Your Trip Abroad* a pamphlet available from the Consumer Information Center, P.O. Box 100, Pueblo, CO 81002.

_____

Stephanie Orange is the former Director of Public Relations for the Council on International Educational Exchange.

Options in International Educational Exchange for People with Disabilities

Mobility International USA and the National Clearinghouse on Disability and Exchange

There are few things in life as exciting, challenging, and transforming as studying, living, working, or volunteering abroad. While relatively few people with disabilities take advantage of these life-changing opportunities, more and more people with all types of disabilities are becoming aware that they too can participate in international programs. People who use wheelchairs or crutches, are blind or partially sighted, are deaf or hard of hearing, or learning disabled have all been successful participants in international exchange, volunteer, and work programs.

People with disabilities benefit from international programs by being able to share experiences with others. At the same time, international exchange, volunteer, and work programs create leadership skills essential in our increasingly global society.

With the passage of the Americans with Disabilities Act in 1990, international exchange programs, study-abroad offices, and international community service projects are now mandated to offer the same services to people with disabilities as they do to nondisabled individuals. Although this does not mean they can guarantee accessible services and sites abroad, it does mean that they need to assist qualified disabled applicants in making international programs as accessible as possible. A world of opportunities awaits people with disabilities!

Including people with disabilities in international programs creates a multicultural atmosphere for all participants. Encouraging and facilitating the participation of people with disabilities is as important to diversity as including people with a range of economic, social, and ethnic backgrounds in international programs. These types of experiences also provide participants with the opportunity to share their unique perspective with others around the world.

It is the mission of Mobility International USA (MIUSA) and the National Clearinghouse on Disability and Exchange to promote the inclusion of individuals with disabilities in international programs and assist international exchange organizations in the process of increasing general program accessibility.

The Clearinghouse provides information and referral services free of charge for anyone with a disability who is interested in academic, volunteer, or work opportunities abroad. MIUSA and the Clearinghouse also can provide consultation and training to international organizations interested in including more people with disabilities in exchange, volunteer, and work programs.

STUDY ABROAD

As more universities around the world are learning about accommodating students with disabilities, an increasing number of accessible study-abroad programs are becoming available for students. In England, for instance, Lancaster University actively recruits international students with disabilities to its program. Many other universities also provide fully accessible programs for foreign students.

Universities and independent exchange organizations should not wait until they have disabled applicants to reach out to students with disabilities. Programs can prepare in advance to include people with disabilities by making simple modifications. These adaptations might include building ramps, arranging for notetakers or interpreters, and linking international students with disabled peers on campus.

Some ways in which international programs can work toward accommodating students with disabilities include program modifications (such as making classrooms more accessible), building ramps, arranging for notetakers or interpreters, and linking international students with other students with disabilities on campus.

Advance planning and good communication are essential to organizing a successful experience abroad. Providing advisers with information about specific accessibility requirements well in advance is the key to finding an appropriate program. People with disabilities need to be advocates for themselves at every step in the process, as well as being creative and flexible in approaching international experiences.

WORK AND VOLUNTEER ABROAD

Work and volunteer programs are other types of international opportunities available for students with disabilities. International community service projects are a great way to volunteer in another country and participate in a wide variety of projects. They offer a wide range of opportunities and last from a few weeks to as long as one or two years.

Each individual has his or her own unique skills to contribute, and with a little creativity, many sites and activities can be adapted to suit anyone.

General volunteer opportunities range from working with homeless children in Peru to participating in environmental projects in Nepal. Exciting volunteer opportunities also exist, which are directly related to disability issues—for example, helping to build wheelchairs in Latin America or teaching sign language in Malaysia.

Many long-term service activities are also open to people with disabilities. The Peace Corps, for example, has placed a number of disabled individuals in two-year assignments throughout the world.

Work opportunities are available through organizations like the Council on International Educational Exchange (Council). Work programs often include assistance in identifying an employment location, securing work permits, and adapting to a new environment.

SURVIVAL ABROAD

People with disabilities often need to be innovative in solving problems of accessibility and communication when traveling or living abroad. It is very helpful to contact disability- related organizations in your host country well in advance. These organizations can provide information on local services such as wheelchair repair, accessible lodging, sign language interpreters, and mobility training, as well as firsthand information about conditions for people with disabilities in specific countries.

FINANCIAL AID

Financing an international experience can be a challenge for anyone. People with disabilities can take advantage of general scholarships as well as financial aid directly related to disability. Other resources include service clubs like Rotary International, as well as vocational rehabilitation departments and friends and family.

Contact the National Clearinghouse on Disability and Exchange for a list of international and disability-related scholarships and grants.

AIRLINE AND RAIL TRAVEL

Those traveling on U.S. airlines are covered by the Air Carriers Access Act, as well as the Americans with Disabilities Act. On non-U.S. carriers, check the policy with the airline and let them know about your needs in advance. Gathering a little information before you fly can make problem solving much easier. Give foreign airlines as much information as necessary on your disability well in advance.

Train travel in Europe is easier than ever for people with disabilities, but, again, be proactive about your needs. Contact local disability organizations in advance for information on how to best navigate each country's transportation system.

GO FOR IT!

Many people with disabilities have found that international programs provide tremendously enriching experiences. Those willing to be assertive about finding an accessible program will discover that there are many interesting options available for people with disabilities.

Where in the World? Nontraditional Destinations

Karen Jenkins

President, Brethen Colleges Abroad

If you are interested in studying in a nontraditional location, you have nearly the whole world to choose from. You can study in Asia, Africa, Latin America, the Caribbean, the Middle East, or the nations and territories of the South Pacific. More than 80 percent of the world's population resides in these areas, with many of the countries showing striking contrasts between rich and poor and modern and traditional.

These areas also boast cultures that are among the oldest, including many that have cradled some of the great religions of the world and provided the basis for modern learning and technology. These countries reveal the global interconnectedness of problems once thought to be national—from the environment, population growth, and immigration to human rights and the use of force and weapons of warfare.

Perhaps you think that the most difficult part of a study-abroad experience in a nontraditional location is leaving the familiar, stepping into the unknown, and traveling to a remote place where every aspect of life seems different. But it is that very difference that makes study in a nontraditional location so exciting and attractive. You can examine political change in South Africa, rural health care in India, wildlife conservation in Botswana, economic development in Japan, Arabic in Egypt, agriculture in Cuba, or urban planning in Mexico City. If you know some French, why not study it in Morocco? If you are interested in learning about post-colonial nations, Ghana and Indonesia are living laboratories. What better place than Jordan to study early Christianity, Islam, or Judaism? The art collection at your college or university may be excellent, but imagine viewing Chinese art in its intended lodgings—the imperial palace in Beijing.

Your desire to study in a nontraditional location may require additional preparatory work, from finding a suitable program to predeparture reading.

Remember that there are fewer academic programs in nontraditional locations than in Western Europe, where the overwhelming majority of American undergraduates study abroad.

According to the book, *Open Doors 2003*, more than 160,000 students studied abroad in Western Europe during the 2001–02 academic year—63 percent from the U.S. The remaining 37 percent studied throughout the rest of the world. For instance, only 3,911 students from U.S. colleges studied in China, a country with the largest population in the world and one of the most rapidly growing economies. Although Mexico and Latin America have a direct impact on U.S. immigration and labor practices, only 14,023 students chose to study in these countries in 2001–02. Forty-two countries in Africa, which is working hard to improve the quality of life for people, served as home to only 4,692 students. The connection with U.S. foreign policy and long-term relations with other nations becomes apparent when you consider the importance of studying Arabic and learning about Islam, yet only 1,310 U.S. students studied in the Middle East in 2001.

HOW CAN I FIND AN ACADEMIC PROGRAM OUTSIDE OF WESTERN EUROPE?

Over the past decade more colleges, universities, and educational exchange organizations have been offering an increasing array of programs in parts of the world beyond Europe; this guide lists many such programs. Start by visiting your campus study-abroad office for information about programs, admission requirements, and application deadlines. Seek out faculty members who specialize in your country or geographic area of interest. They are likely to have traveled in that part of the world, maintained contacts with colleagues at universities, and have information about academic programs for international students.

WHY DO I WANT TO STUDY IN THIS KIND OF PLACE?

Perhaps you are adventuresome and seek a study experience that offers independence. Or you want to test yourself by going somewhere different. Maybe you're a romantic with the desire to see Ankara, Lima, or Mbabane instead of Paris, London, or Geneva. That spirit of adventure and independence will reward you when you learn to speak Swahili in Kenya, study agricultural development in India, or visit the Buddhist temple of Borobudur in Java, Indonesia.

WILL THE PROGRAM FIT MY MAJOR?

Early planning is important when pursuing any study-abroad program, no matter what the academic discipline or geographic location. The sooner you decide you want to study abroad, the more likely you are to find a program that either fits your major or fulfills core requirements. Talk to your faculty academic adviser about what courses you can take abroad, what courses can be accepted toward graduation requirements, and what additional expenses to anticipate. Early planning is especially important if you are a science major with limited options for the number of classes you can take away from your campus. You may be able to fulfill art, history, or language requirements in a program abroad.

DO I NEED TO SPEAK THE LANGUAGE?

If language is not a requirement for admission to a program, don't let your lack of knowledge of a specific language stop you from applying. Undoubtedly, your access to people and their culture is best facilitated by fluency in their language, which will allow you to learn about your hosts and to share in their lives and customs. Many good programs, however, will offer a language component. While you may only acquire "survival" language skills, with diligence you should be able to learn to communicate your basic needs in a short time. Your sincere attempt to learn and use the language of your chosen country will be appreciated and applauded by your hosts. You are likely to be rewarded by sincere gestures of friendship and with more opportunities to gain even greater language proficiency.

WHOM DO I TALK TO ONCE I'VE FOUND A PROGRAM?

Support for international study programs varies from campus to campus. If you are enrolled at a college or university that sends a large number of students abroad, there is likely to be a study-abroad office on campus that is staffed by advisers who will answer questions on issues such as transferring academic credit, financial aid, and required immunizations. If your campus does not have a study-abroad office, your faculty academic adviser, department chair, and registrar should all be consulted. You will want to talk to the registrar at your school to ensure that credit you earn abroad will be accepted by your school.

Next, check with the financial services office for information about how the program will be financed, especially if you are receiving any type of financial assistance. Some colleges and universities charge full tuition and make payments to programs abroad on behalf of their students. Others expect students to be responsible for making financial arrangements once they are accepted into a program. Many institutions allow students to apply part of their financial aid to study abroad, so be sure to ask. However the finances are arranged, it is usually preferable to remain a registered student at your institution during the time you are studying abroad.

HOW DEEPLY WILL I BE INVOLVED WITH OTHER PEOPLE AND CULTURES?

It may be difficult for you to find a program that offers practical applications of your classroom work. First, you will be on a student visa, which will prohibit you from engaging in paid employment. Second, it is unlikely that you will possess the skills needed by the host country, such as animal husbandry, engineering, teaching, or auto mechanics. A well-designed study-abroad program, however, might include field trips, volunteer work projects, or language instruction, all of which will provide you with opportunities to interact with people outside of the classroom. Look for a program that is affiliated with a university in the host country. That will enable you to learn about a different educational system, take classes taught by local professors, and make friends with students. Many countries have a rich tradition of learning and higher education. Studying at a university or institute in Japan or Mali will prove to be a unique experience that will involve you with another people and culture.

WHAT MIGHT THE PROGRAM STRUCTURE BE LIKE IN A NONTRADITIONAL COUNTRY?

Programs will be different, but you should still look for a few standard elements. A knowledgeable and experienced on-site coordinator who oversees the academic program, coordinates the logistics, and negotiates the local bureaucracy can make the program run smoothly and allay concerns of your family and friends. If English is not the national language, look for a language component in the program. Acquiring even limited language ability will enable you to enjoy your experience more fully and to learn much more about the culture.

Be sure that the program has a strong academic focus. Do not be misled by descriptions that emphasize the experiential nature of the program at the expense of the academic work. The experiential aspect of any program abroad should be integrated into academic objectives. In a developing country where more hours may be spent outside of the classroom, there should be a structured academic schedule for that time.

WHAT SHOULD I DO WHEN PEOPLE SAY "YOU WANT TO GO WHERE?"

Your family and friends may be reluctant to see you enroll in a program in a nontraditional location, since you will more than likely be living in a developing nation. These are places that few Americans know anything about except through sensational and often unflattering news stories. If you are a member of an ethnic minority, going to a nontraditional location—an African American in China, a Korean American in Ecuador, a Native American in South Africa, or a Hispanic American in Russia—may seem doubly complicated.

However, none of these are insurmountable obstacles, yet all require extra planning, research, and persistence. Your determination will be rewarded when you embark on your adventure better prepared for an encounter with a different culture, when your college or university opens its doors to a different type of program, and when your family and friends help you engage in preparations and become more knowledgeable about the place you will be living. Furthermore, when you seek your first professional position after completing your education, the time you spent in a nontraditional location will prove to be an asset. Employers are always looking for young people who are adaptable but focused, and a successful experience abroad, especially in a place not many other students have been, is evidence of that.

Most important, you will spend part of your college years participating in a community that few Americans visit. You will attach names and faces to the news stories you've heard and will be able to decide for yourself how accurate they are. You will learn that many of the world's problems can be solved by knowledgeable citizens willing to actively engage their friends and neighbors in the search for creative solutions, no matter where they live.

If you have chosen your program for sound academic reasons, your family is likely to be more accepting. They should also be reassured if the program is well organized and supervised. Their surprise at your chosen location is probably because of one-sided information and scanty knowledge about your chosen country. If you are from a racial minority in the United States, your family may believe you will be subjected to discrimination while abroad. Or perhaps you are from a family of recent immigrants who do not understand why you would want to go to a place they left because of conflict or harsh economic conditions.

Use your family's skepticism as an opportunity not only to prepare for your departure but also to help inform and educate them about another part of the world and its changing conditions. Involve them by sharing program literature, maps, encyclopedia articles, newspaper stories, novels, and tourist information. Your family and friends will appreciate knowing that you are preparing seriously for your journey and will enjoy learning about the people and culture of your destination.

If you have chosen a place that is not often in the news, your task may be easier than if you'd decided to go somewhere that has received a lot of negative attention. Start by asking your family what they know about the country. If all their knowledge is from provocative and disturbing news reports, try to provide information to help them understand that the majority of people in the country work hard and are proud of their culture and national achievements. Take the concerns of your family and friends seriously, and work in an informed and determined way to overcome them.

HOW DO I GET READY TO GO? ARE THERE ANY SPECIAL HEALTH ISSUES TO CONSIDER ONCE I'M THERE?

While you are obtaining your passport and any required visas, you should also be preparing for different food, customs, climate, and time zones to help you stay safe and healthy. Check with your physician about required immunizations such as yellow fever and recommendations for medication if you are traveling in an area where, for instance, malaria is prevalent. If you live near a large city or university, you may find a travel

clinic staffed by physicians and health-care workers who specialize in tropical medicine. You can find valuable information on the Web site of the Centers for Disease Control and Prevention (CDC) at www.cdc.gov. There is a link to "Travelers' Health" which gives up-to-date information and advice on health conditions as well as immunizations and medications for specific countries. Also be sure to read "Safety in Study Abroad" on page 43.

Staying safe and healthy, even in a developing country, is not impossible. Prepare, remain alert, and follow the advice of friends who live there or who have traveled there.

Perhaps the biggest danger to your health and safety is a motor vehicle accident. Traffic patterns and driving habits are different all over the world, and you must be aware of them. Don't rent a motor scooter in a city where thousands are on the street if you are not an experienced driver and prepared to observe the country's driving rules. The enforcement of motor vehicle standards may be lax and, in some places, it is not uncommon for operators to overcrowd buses. It is important that you remain alert when you are walking and when choosing your mode of transportation.

Always try to get plenty of rest and, if you drink alcohol, do not drive! Remember, too, that alcohol can affect your mental control even on foot. Be careful, or you'll make the common mistake of looking in the wrong direction when crossing a street in a country where the traffic flows in the opposite direction.

Much is often made of what not to eat or drink in a tropical country. You will miss an important aspect of your experience if you are afraid to consume the food; you'll also spend needless time looking for something familiar. Some of the best food in the world is outside the United States, recently picked, harvested with little chemical preservatives, and prepared fresh from the market.

It is important that you consume adequate liquids to remain healthy. Get in the habit of looking around and observe what others are drinking. Throughout Indonesia, for instance, where in some places the water supply is undrinkable, Indonesians drink bottled water, which is cheap and easily obtainable. Hotels and restaurants routinely boil water, wash their vegetables in it, and offer bottled water. Indonesians at home do likewise. If you are unsure about the food or water supply, find local students and friends and do as they do. Your friends and their families will be just as concerned about their health as you are about yours.

WHAT IF THERE IS A CRISIS IN THE COUNTRY WHERE I'M TRAVELING?

Remember that your family may be concerned about your safety while you're away from home, especially when you are in place that seems so different and remote. This is especially true during times of heightened international tension. The possibility of war or terrorist attacks is a growing concern. Therefore, it is important that you pay close attention to the organizers of your program and read all materials they send before your departure. Upon arrival, you should receive an on-site orientation with information on how to travel, where to travel, what precautions to take, and the importance of taking responsibility for good decision-making when it comes to your personal safety.

The officials of your program and your host university will be experienced and sensitive to student concerns. They will provide accurate updates in the event of a crisis situation. They will also be familiar with local security procedures and be in close contact with the civil authorities and health professionals. Should a crisis arise or a situation deteriorate, the staff will advise you on appropriate actions to take.

You can take responsibility for your safety by being aware of your local surroundings just as you would if you were in the U.S. or on your home campus. You should keep a low profile and not call unnecessary attention to yourself. Do not carry a large backpack, an expensive camera, or computer equipment and do not wear excessive or expensive jewelry. Your behavior is just as important to keeping a low profile.

- Avoid speaking on a cell phone in public places. Not only is it impolite, but you will call unnecessary attention to yourself.

- When talking in public, do not speak in a loud voice with expansive gestures.

- Do not espouse your political views either about the U.S. or your host country. You do not want to easily distinguish yourself from local students and young people.

In the unlikely event that the U.S. government recommends an evacuation of students, the first concern of your program providers will be to ensure that arrangements are made for you and your fellow students to travel to a secure location. Every effort will be made to facilitate the completion of the academic program in cooperation with the students' home institution.

CAN I LIVE IN A PLACE THAT SEEMS SO REMOTE AND FAR FROM HOME?

Today, no place is really remote. E-mail, cell phones, satellite communication, and air transpor-

tation make it easy to communicate and travel quickly over long distances. There are familiar fast-food stores in Beijing, Rio de Janeiro, and Abidjan. Yet many parts of the world retain their distinctive character and confront visitors with what may seem like overwhelming differences in culture and customs. These differences are exactly what you are seeking!

Moving to any new place requires a period of adjustment, especially if you are faced with new food, customs, language, and climate. Be prepared for "culture shock," which can range from homesickness to extreme feelings of dislike for your new place of residence. It is normal to miss the familiar but you can overcome such feelings by reading as much as possible about your destination and talking with students, faculty or friends who have been there before you depart. Once you have arrived, keep in contact with family and friends back home. E-mail and inexpensive calling cards makes that easy!

Make friends with other students and their families in your new host country. The best way to learn about others is to spend time with them. Keep a journal and record your feelings and observations. Most importantly go out and experience the people and culture. You wanted to study in a nontraditional destination because it is different! That is what you sought, so let the differences hit you; soak them up, enjoy them, and learn from them!

HOW WILL I COPE IN A POOR COMMUNITY?

If you expect to observe extreme poverty for the first time in your life when abroad, then you certainly haven't been inquisitive or observant enough about the United States. Extreme poverty exists here, although its location off well-built interstate highways, in segregated inner cities, and in rural areas may make it easy to miss. Poverty in developing countries will be more apparent, as the majority of people live below the standards of the average American. Many developing countries have initiated innovative programs to deter deforestation, alleviate hunger, improve crop yields, lower the birth rate, bring health care to rural areas, increase literacy, introduce appropriate technologies, or make microbusiness loans available. Your quiet and respectful observations will be more appropriate to people working hard to overcome poverty. You might also learn some useful techniques that are adaptable to your community in the United States.

Your respectful observation should also include dressing neatly. American students often assume that jeans, T-shirts, and sandals are appropriate in poor and developing countries. They are often surprised that people abroad tend to dress very neatly, with men rarely in shorts and women rarely in short tops or sleeveless dresses. People in developing countries are very proud of their progress in literacy and education, alleviation of disease and poverty, stable governments, and rural development. So be respectful of the issues impacting the country in which you choose to study.

WHAT DO I DO WHEN IN A COUNTRY WITH A REPUTATION FOR OPPRESSION OR HUMAN RIGHTS VIOLATIONS?

You are traveling to another country to learn, and your objectives should be to just that. If you have selected a country because you want to try to change conditions or to encourage others to take action against conditions you think are objectionable, you should reconsider your choice. If after you've been in a country for a period of time you encounter social, political, environmental, or economic conditions that offend you, remember that it's not your place to express opposition or disapproval. That doesn't mean you're not entitled to your opinion—just keep it to yourself. Write down your feelings in a journal or discuss them with those in your academic program. You

don't want to embarrass your hosts or create a situation that could get them into trouble by speaking inappropriately. Nor do you want to jeopardize your study program. When you return home your observations and firsthand accounts might provide the basis for an independent study project. You may decide to work for an organization with a mission to alleviate the conditions you observed, and your experience abroad could prove to be invaluable.

WILL I BE DIFFERENT WHEN I RETURN?

You will meet people who will welcome you to their countries and teach you a new definition of hospitality, friendship, and beauty. Victoria Falls between Zambia and Zimbabwe is majestic, the variety of flora and fauna in Indonesia overwhelming, the food in Thailand exquisite, the rain forests of Brazil magnificent, the blueness of the Caribbean Sea awesome, and the religious architecture of Turkey inspiring.

Whether you are different when you return to your campus and familiar surroundings after studying and living in a nontraditional destination will depend on your willingness to embrace new places, people, and customs with openness and enthusiasm.

_____

Karen Jenkins is the President of Brethren Colleges Abroad. Brethren Colleges Abroad offers study-abroad programs around the world for undergraduate students and is committed to global education with an emphasis on studying issues of peace and justice. Ms. Jenkins has lived, worked, and traveled extensively in southern Africa; has taught graduate-level courses; and has undertaken development consultant contracts with international agencies in more than twenty developing nations.

International Internships

Charles A. Gliozzo

Assistant to the Dean of International Studies and Programs at Michigan State

A report of The American Council of Education, *Educating Americans for a World In Flux*, listed ten ground rules for internationalizing educational institutions. Ground rule number five is "to expand study-abroad and internship opportunities for all students." The Council concluded, "international internships are among the most valuable educational experience any student can receive."

WHAT IS AN INTERNATIONAL INTERNSHIP?

An international internship is an academic and organizational off-campus learning experience that maximizes the cross-cultural and professional development of students, practitioners, employers/employees, and faculty with respective institutions, government agencies, and private sector organizations. International internships cannot be underestimated. They will acquaint you with career options in your field of study, offering practical activities that supplement academic work.

An international internship allows you to test the validity of academic or career choices while making a contribution to an organization. You will obtain greater marketability in the future, and your employer will benefit in the short term with additional assistance, as well as in the long term through early identification and training of a potential future employee.

International internships offer the opportunity to learn about the role of the United States in the world. Your internship is a bridge between your education and preparation for career opportunities. Internships in other countries allow you to understand firsthand how our society is part of a larger world system encompassing economics, education, business, and politics.

If these opportunities sound inviting or if you have been considering the possibility of interning overseas, there are a lot of questions to ask yourself and many issues to consider. The information that follows will help you sort out whether an international internship is right for you and how to go about finding the right one. Don't try to go it alone! Talk to your study-abroad adviser, your teachers, and career guidance counselors who are professionally trained and can help you make the right choices and avoid many pitfalls.

BEGINNING YOUR SEARCH

As the popularity of international internships increases every year, so does competition for the limited number of openings. A careful and thorough search is important, not only to find an internship, but to identify one that will be enjoyable and challenging. If you are fairly convinced you want to pursue an internship abroad, your next step is to answer these questions:

- What realistic expectations do you have?

- Is it worth your time and effort to carry out the necessary preliminary work, such as processing the application, writing cover letters, completing your résumé, filling out forms, writing follow-up letters, and numerous other tasks?

- Are you able to afford going overseas?

- Does your academic institution endorse participation in an international internship program? If it does, does your school have its own program or does it allow you to obtain an international internship with another university or organization?

- Will you receive academic credit for the internship and how will your internship be evaluated for credit?

- Do you need a visa or work permit?

- Where are internships and how do you obtain information about them? (A guide to reference works, Web sites, etc., appears at the end of this article.)

- Would your objectives be better served by pursuing an internship in the United States?

Once you have answered these questions, make a list of your preferences and goals. Be as realistic and honest with yourself as possible, as you consider these questions:

- What is your preferred internship location?

- How many hours are you willing to work?

- What is the exact nature of the work you are seeking?

- What specific working conditions would be acceptable? Close supervision or independent work? A structured or relaxed environment? A social atmosphere or a solitary one?

- What do you need to earn, if anything? Salary? Stipend? Room and board? College credit?

- Are job contacts or permanent employment priorities available?

An international internship could be a rewarding experience, but consider both the benefits and disadvantages.

THE BENEFITS

Following are some benefits of international internships:

- **A cross-cultural exposure.** An international internship will give you a living-learning experience in another society.

- **The possibility of obtaining academic credit to satisfy graduation requirements.** Many institutions will supplement their internship programs with academic courses on the history/culture, etc., of the host country. Note, not all international internships give academic credit.

- **Develop foreign language competency.** Many international jobs require knowledge of a foreign language. Foreign language competency is gaining significance as more students seek overseas positions in the face of a restrictive U.S. job market.

- **Increase your chances for career placement in multinational and international companies, in government agencies, and in educational institutions.**

- **Establish contacts for developing future career goals.** In today's competitive job market, knowing key individuals is a plus.

- **Challenges of adapting to a variety of environments; this skill will be very useful in any international job you'll undertake in the future.**

BE AWARE OF THE DISADVANTAGES

Following are some disadvantages of international internships:

- **Restrictions that an intern may encounter in an international setting.** Linguistic and cultural barriers may limit expectations. For example, you may assume that the internship is an entry-level career position only to discover that it provides substantially less work.

- **The expense of travel, housing, and overseas administration and other fees.** Some international internships are paid, but many do not offer stipends.

- **Accommodations, which may be difficult to secure or are substandard.**

FINDING THE RIGHT INTERNSHIP

Once you know what you want from your internship, it is important to find the right internship. Examine your personal job-related strengths and weaknesses. Be sure to analyze your past academic and work performances. If you want to emphasize your strong points to a prospective internship sponsor, you have to know what they are. Are your skills analytical, verbal, or quantitative? Are you a self-starter with initiative? Are you qualified to do a research project requiring organization and attention to detail? Are you better working on a group project, where communication skills are essential?

This guide lists many study-abroad programs that offer internships. Once you have narrowed your search to a particular geographic region, you can use the **Field of Study Index** to identify programs that interest you. When you develop your "short list" of possibilities, you can begin to contact institutions and organizations to request more information. Learn about the structure of the program and whether the program is well organized.

An internship can consist of one specific job or many. In any case, you should closely examine the internship requirements. You must be prepared to make whatever adjustments are necessary to comply with the policies, regulations, and standards of the host organization and country. What may seem like the perfect internship may end up being a job filling out forms in triplicate. To avoid this problem, your duties should be decided in advance. A good way to learn about the quality of the internship is to contact previous

interns. The organization to which you are applying, in most cases, will give you the names of former interns if you request them.

EVALUATION

The evaluation process is important in any internship. Content and quality must be monitored closely by the sponsoring organization to preserve the integrity of the program and ensure maximum learning experience.

You may be required to keep a journal or write an evaluative paper. If an academic project is required, it will be evaluated by the faculty supervisor. Your intern coordinator should contact the host employer during your internship to assess your progress. A formal evaluation should be completed by the employer, and debriefing meetings should be held with all parties involved in your internship.

CONCLUSION

You should not jump haphazardly into an internship, whether it's in the United States or abroad. Interns should be motivated and self-directed to complete a series of assignments in preparing for an internship. Interns must have the qualifications required by the host organization, language competency, and an understanding of the culture. You should work closely with the intern coordinator to determine internship goals and to identify organizations. This process requires serious thought and commitment.

Remember, you will be investing your time and energy—often with no financial compensation—so it pays to do some research. Your search for the best internship should follow the basic approaches of looking for a full-time job. College career placement and overseas study offices are invaluable resources in assisting you.

Charles A. Gliozzo is a Professor and Assistant to the Dean of International Studies and Programs at Michigan State University and Director Emeritus of the Office of Overseas Study.

Volunteering Abroad

Gina Chase

Director of International Voluntary Service, Council on International Educational Exchange

If you're looking for a way to learn by doing, to expand your awareness of another population and culture while making a worthwhile contribution, then volunteering abroad may be for you. There's a lot to gain. By helping out in another country, you'll get to learn firsthand about local issues, lifestyles, and politics. You'll get to develop the kind of cross-cultural communication and language skills many international businesses now seek. You'll get practical experience working with others and accomplishing goals through teamwork. And, most important, you'll get the opportunity to contribute and play a role in something that has meaning and importance.

How can you help? Plant trees to slow erosion in South America. Dig for archaeological treasures in the Middle East. Help a medical team distribute food and medicine in Africa. Build a school, community center, or irrigation system in Asia. Whatever your interest, chances are there's a community service project somewhere in the world that needs your time, energy, and commitment.

FINDING THE RIGHT PROGRAM

The study-abroad office on your campus is a good place to start. Even if staff members don't have information on volunteer programs, they can help you prepare for life in another country. As you do your research, keep in mind that many volunteer activities are also called unpaid internships. The career services office may be helpful in finding opportunities related to your area of study.

Ask around. Professors and faculty advisers can help you evaluate programs, as well as your own motivation and expectations. Here are some questions to help you choose a program that's right for you:

- Who is the sponsoring organization and how long has it run the program?

- With whom and for whom will you be working?

THE RIGHT STUFF?

Volunteering abroad isn't for everyone. Flexibility and the ability to take initiative and work independently are important traits in a volunteer, as is the willingness to work with others with different views.

International projects present special challenges. If you're considering this type of work, you'll need to have realistic expectations of what you can accomplish and what you will get in return. To give you a better idea about the stops and starts you'll likely encounter, imagine that you have gone to Ghana to help build a water irrigation system in a rural village. There aren't enough shovels for all the volunteers, so you take turns digging and shoveling. The project progresses rapidly, but to complete the job, the team will need pipes. Halfway through your stay, you find out that the needed pipes will not arrive in time for you to see the project to its end. You spend the rest of your time playing games with the village children and helping the women carry water in buckets from the nearest stream.

In this scenario, you may not have completed the irrigation system, but you did demonstrate the ability to adapt to a difficult situation. You got to join in the daily lives of people very different from yourself. Although you didn't accomplish the stated goal of building an irrigation system, the village is that much closer to having a completed solution and you came away with an experience that will stay with you forever.

- What kind of supervision will be provided? This varies widely from program to program, and it's important to be clear about the resources you can depend on while out of the country.

- What are the living arrangements? On most projects, you can't expect luxury, but you'll want to be prepared. Are room and board provided, included in the program fee, or something you'll have to provide for yourself when you get there? Again, what you must cover varies greatly from program to program.

- Is health insurance provided or must you provide your own? Either way is acceptable, but you must be sure you're covered.

- What do former participants say about the program? Contacting former participants is probably the best way to get a feel for the program, and most organizations are willing to provide a list to you.

- Will you be able to get academic credit for your participation? On some programs the academic credit is built in. If it's not, you might still want to check with your advisers on campus to see if you can work out an independent study credit.

- What is the total cost to you for participating in the program? Before signing up, find out about airfare and ground transportation costs, recommended pocket money, etc. It's important to get a sense of all the resources you will need for the experience.

Getting There and Getting Around on a Budget

Morissa Pawl

While studying in another country for a year or semester, you'll have many opportunities to meet new people, encounter different cultures, and travel. But to take full advantage of your travel opportunities, you'll need to arm yourself with the facts. Here are some tips that can help stretch your travel dollars and prepare you for the unexpected.

Start with a flexible round-trip airline ticket. If you're like most students, you'll be hard pressed to pick a return date a half year or year in advance. You may decide to take off and explore the country after your program ends. To keep your options open, ask for a ticket that allows you to change travel dates. First, find out if the ticket has an expiration date. Many fares offered by airlines or consolidators are good only for three to six months. If you try to use the ticket after this date, you may get stuck with a higher fare, or even worse, you may have to buy another ticket. Student fares are usually the most flexible. Offered by organizations that specialize in student travel, such as STA Travel or Council Travel, these tickets may be valid for as long as one year.

You'll also want to look for tickets that allow you to return from a different city. If you know your travel plans beforehand, shop for a ticket that accommodates your itinerary without costing a small fortune. One way to stretch your travel dollars is to buy a ticket that allows for extra stopovers en route for little or no additional cost. The most common stopover is available in the airline's hub city. For example, a student ticket to Athens on Air France may let you stop over in Paris in either direction. But remember to ask about this option before you make your arrangement—many tickets won't allow you to add stopovers once you've begun to travel.

You may be tempted to make one-way arrangements and book the return trip later. *Forget it!* Most countries make it extremely difficult for travelers to enter without a return ticket. A few may even turn you away. Avoid the risk and

THE INS AND OUTS OF STUDYING ABROAD

WHAT IF YOU LOSE YOUR AIRLINE TICKETS?

If you bought your ticket directly from an airline, you'll need to call one of their offices. You'll be asked to purchase a new ticket and file a lost ticket claim. You can expect to receive a refund for the cost of the replacement ticket, less a fee of $50-$75, about six months after you file your claim.

To replace Student Tickets, issued by agencies such as STA Travel, contact the closest office. You'll pay a $25 reissue fee, and your ticket will be reissued at no extra cost.

purchase a round-trip ticket that can be changed or refunded. Before you purchase the ticket, ask if an unused portion will have any refund value. Many tickets are only partially refundable if canceled.

Explore the alternatives for getting around in the country in which you'll travel before you leave. Buying rail or bus tickets in country can be expensive. Visitors can often get much better deals. Ask your travel adviser about rail passes such as Britrail, Eurail, and Japan Rail, and bus passes such as Eurobus before you leave.

Ask about budget accommodations. If you know you'll be doing a lot of travel on your own, consider staying in youth hostels. Your travel adviser can give you information on this low-cost housing, as well as budget hotels, pensions, and hotel pass packages in your destinations.

Purchase an International Student Identity Card (ISIC). The ISIC offers full-time students a wide variety of discounts. It may be purchased on college and university campuses across the U.S. and from organizations such STA Travel and Council on International Educational Exchange.

Find out about luggage restrictions before you pack. You'll undoubtedly have a lot of stuff you want to bring with you for a half year or year away, but most international flights restrict you to two pieces of checked luggage. Some flights may restrict the weight of each bag to as little as 20 pounds. What to do if you really have to bring your skis, three seasons worth of clothes, and a small army of appliances? Ship the extras! Several companies provide shipping at very low cost. But ask about delivery times. Some services may take a few months. You can find shipping companies listed in newspapers and your phone book.

Before you leave the U.S., leave a photocopy of your passport and important travel documents with a family member or friend. You'll want to carry a copy of the originals and a list of document numbers, issue dates, and places —separate from the real thing—with you as well.

Once you arrive in a foreign city, especially one off the beaten path, let the American Consulate or Embassy know you're there. If you misplace or have your passport stolen, contact the closest Embassy or Consulate for a replacement.

Consider using traveler's checks and credit cards—they're safer than traveling with cash. Stick with companies that offer extensive services in the country you're visiting. Because you'll have to head to one of their offices if your cards or checks are lost or stolen, you'll want to choose a company with a nearby branch. American Express, Thomas Cook, and VISA have networks around the world, but ask about local preferences too. If you decide to use traveler's checks, remember to keep the check registers up to date and store these records separately from the checks themselves. You'll need this information if the checks are lost or stolen.

Staying Healthy Abroad

Joan Elias Gore

Director for Institutional Relations at Denmark's International Study Program

Study abroad is an adventure of the mind and spirit. It is also an adventure of and for the body. Traveling overseas is an exhilarating experience—it should be a healthy one, too.

In most regions there are no special health procedures about which you should be concerned. Health-care systems and facilities in many overseas locations are quite similar to what we have in the United States. In other regions, however, there are differences and specifically recommended health procedures that you should know about.

The following will acquaint you with health matters related to the different phases of your study abroad experience. Although help is available both in the United States and abroad, you must take an active and responsible role in planning for and maintaining a healthful approach to your overseas experience.

HEALTH AND YOUR STUDY-ABROAD APPLICATION

Application forms will ask you about your current health status. They will probably ask for a doctor's recommendation. Be honest in your application forms and with your doctor. The information being sought will determine how best to provide you with service and support in your overseas program.

Housing forms can also be important for health. Remember to include information about any allergies, physical challenges, or other health issues that might affect where you can live comfortably.

Students should ask program operators about any health or safety concerns they may have.

PREDEPARTURE HEALTH CHECKLIST

Once you've been accepted into a program, you will need to take appropriate health measures as dictated by your overseas location. Although many countries

require no special procedures, you should find out if any apply in the area(s) in which you will be traveling and studying. L. Robert Kohls' *Survival Kit for Overseas Living: For Americans Planning to Live and Work Abroad* (Intercultural Press, 2001) includes an excellent checklist that discusses many of the items that follow.

Predeparture medical appointments. Make all medical appointments well in advance of your travel date. Begin at least three months ahead to allow for completion of immunizations, for gamma globulin shots (a preventive against hepatitis A), and for assessments of any special medical problems you may have. You can consult your doctor, your public health service office, or your school's international health advisory service to find out what immunizations you'll need for the areas to which you're traveling. Also ask about the advisability of hepatitis B protection. Note that children and pregnant women often receive different recommendations than the rest of the population.

Health records. Update your health records, including eyeglass and contact lens prescriptions and prescriptions for any medications you routinely take. Have prescriptions written using generic names to facilitate getting them filled overseas, where U.S. brand names might not be available. If relevant to your medical condition, EKGs and X-rays should also be included in these updated records. A doctor's statement about your prescriptions and how they are to be used, along with statements about any special medical conditions you have, should also be included. Dental records should be included if special procedures

or medications are indicated for you. You should carry all of these records in a safe place during travel.

Routine check-ups. Prior to departure, complete all routine medical examinations such as gynecological and dental checkups that might fall within your time abroad.

Prescription drugs. Take extra prescription drugs. Pack them in different places, but avoid putting them in luggage that might get misplaced or stolen. It's best to put them in carry-on luggage.

Instruments for self-administered medication. Take instruments necessary for self-administration of medications. Diabetic persons should carry a supply of disposable syringes and needles to help protect against HIV infection and other communicable diseases in areas where medical personnel do not use disposable materials. If you plan to study in an area where AIDS is endemic, ask about the advisability of carrying a supply of needles and syringes (even if you do not need them for routine medication) in the event of an accident or illness that requires injections.

Extra appliances. Take extra glasses or contact lenses and extra dental appliances if you use them.

Medical kit. Take a medical kit containing such items as bandages, adhesive tape, gauze, sterile cleansers, antibacterial ointment and antiseptic cream, sunburn ointment, aspirin or other pain-killers, and anti-diarrheal medicine. Depending on the region, take water purification tablets, antihistamines for allergy relief, salt tablets, skin moisturizers, and insect repellants. Check with your doctor or health service about the best insect repellant to take for the region.

HEALTH ADVISORIES

If you have special medical needs or if you are going to an area where there may be special medical requirements, it is important to seek authoritative advice. Your family physician, student health service, public health service, and school may have specializations in geographic medicine or may operate travel clinics. Contact one of these offices and ask which vaccinations are indicated—both the recommended and the required—prior to your departure. In addition, ask your doctor to help you determine if any special conditions apply to your travel overseas because of any particular health needs.

Regional problems. Are there particular health problems in the region to which you're going? You can phone the U.S. State Department's Overseas Citizens Services at 202-647-5225 between 8 a.m. and 5 p.m. Eastern Standard Time Monday–Saturday and at 202-647-4000 after hours for information on current health conditions worldwide. The U.S. Department of Health and Human Services Centers for Disease Control publishes *Health Information for International Travel* every other year with updates on vaccinations and other health issues. For a fee, the information can be ordered by calling toll-free 877-252-1200. You can also find much of this information online by visiting the Web site for the Centers for Disease Control at www.cdc.gov.

Medical insurance. Check with your insurance company to determine whether your insurance policy covers you when you are outside the United States. Medical insurance policies do not always provide this coverage. If you are going overseas through a U.S.–operated study-abroad program, check with the program to determine what health and accident coverage is provided.

The International Student Identity Card provides accident and sickness insurance for travel outside the United States, as well as discounts on transportation and housing accommodations. This insurance is in effect for overseas travel from the time of purchase until the expiration date. The card includes a toll-free emergency number as well as other information. You may obtain this card by contacting the Council on International Educational Exchange. You may be able to obtain the card at your school or at any Council Travel office in the United States.

REGIONAL HEALTH ISSUES

In areas of the world where there are special health issues, you need to be informed in advance

about what to expect. The following list should help you anticipate these issues and prepare you to deal with them.

Medical requirements for admission to the country. Find out if any exist. Many countries have very strict requirements, and you may experience serious delays if you have not met them.

Regional diseases. Ask about the nature, prevention, and treatment of the region's specific illnesses. You will find that malaria and diarrhea are the two most prevalent diseases afflicting travelers, particularly in developing regions. You should take an antidiarrheal medication with you on your travels. Ask your physician about which one is appropriate for you. If you are going to an area where malaria is prevalent, you may be advised to begin a program of antimalarial medication, which begins before you leave the United States and continues for a short period after you return.

Regions where AIDS is prevalent. Know how to handle injections, emergencies, and blood transfusions in regions affected by AIDS.

Diet and eating patterns. Inquire about local diet and eating patterns, including the need for and availability of nutritional supplements.

Laws about medications. Find out about laws regulating the import and possession of medications, hypodermic needles and syringes, and condoms and other contraceptives.

Recommended medical kit items. Research any recommended medications and materials that you should take along in a medical kit.

Health-care delivery systems. Find out about the health-care delivery in the region, especially if it differs from that in the United States. Ask how patients are likely to be treated, what kinds of facilities will be found, how payments for services are handled, and what your legal right will be to obtain services in the country.

Jet lag. Ask your physician about ways you can anticipate and possibly reduce the effects of jet lag. Some precautions are dietary; no alcohol en route but drinking plenty of other fluids is a good example.

All the above information should be available from the advisory service where you are inquiring about predeparture immunizations. Your study-abroad program director should also be able to provide you with answers to these questions.

HEALTH QUESTIONS ON-SITE
Taking the following basic health precautions once you arrive in the country you're traveling to will complete your efforts to have a healthy and happy experience overseas.

How to get medical help. Learn how to find a doctor overseas. If you are with a study-abroad program, your director should be able to tell you where to find a reliable doctor. There may be a specific doctor serving your group. Acquaint yourself with emergency phone numbers (some countries have systems similar to 911 in the United States), special medical services for which you may be eligible in the country, and information about organizations that can provide you with assistance for special medical needs.

Prior to your arrival, you should let program directors know about any special requirements you might have so that you can be accommodated upon arrival. If you find yourself traveling alone in a developing area, you might contact a Western-style hotel and ask for the doctor to whom guests are referred. You might also go to a university hospital or contact a U.S. Consulate office for a list of doctors. The International

Association for Medical Assistance to Travelers (IAMAT) provides a list of English-speaking doctors all over the world. There is no fee, but donations to this nonprofit organization are welcomed.

Jet lag and culture shock. As surprising as it may seem, jet lag and culture shock are real health issues. Traveling through time zones and traveling for long periods of time, facing new values, habits, and methods of daily life—all this can leave travelers impatient, bewildered, and depressed. Your study-abroad program director should provide you with information about how to function in your new culture—how to make phone calls, how to make travel arrangements within the country, how to receive basic services, and how to get information and assistance.

Armed with all this information, you may still find yourself alternately exhilarated and exasperated, thrilled at the experiences the new culture offers you and frustrated with the culture's differences from your own. In the first few weeks of your experience, you will likely experience these ups and downs. The feelings you experience are natural. If you are angry, impatient, homesick, or depressed your first few days, remind yourself that these things will pass once you have rested and are eating normally. If homesickness or depression persists, however, look upon them as the medical problems that they indeed may be and seek professional assistance from counselors or doctors.

Diet. Food overseas may be quite different from what you are used to in the United States. They may be "healthier" in some instances (more vegetables and fruits) or "less healthy" in others (more fried foods than you may usually eat), but most often they will just be different from what you are used to—eel soup, for example! Make sure that you take special dietary needs into account, if you have any, and make arrangements in advance with your program director so that your special needs will be met.

Follow recommended precautions if there are any. For example, in some areas you will be told to avoid eating foods at public stands on the street or to avoid eating uncooked or unwashed foods. Listen closely to precautions given in the health advisories you gather before departure and on site in your region from program directors.

Exercise. Exercise is important for both physical and mental health. You will probably find yourself walking more while overseas than in America, partly because you may not be driving a car, but also because student housing overseas is often not as close to class meeting places as it is in the United States. Find out in advance from program directors about safe routes to class, and follow the recommendations. Try to exercise. It is an excellent counterbalance to dietary change and to the emotional ups and downs associated with culture shock.

Substance abuse problems. One of the most typical health problems students can experience overseas is alcohol abuse. Alcohol may be more readily available overseas; laws regarding minimum age are more lenient, and traditions concerning alcohol consumption as a part of everyday social life are different from those in the United States. Students often find themselves with accustomed rules gone and new rules unknown. The damage from alcohol abuse to the body can be considerable but moreover, legal implications can be quite severe in some countries. Drunk driving laws, for example, may be far more severe abroad than they are in the United States.

The same precautions apply to drug use. Not only is drug abuse damaging to the body but it can also have legal consequences that will affect you as a student visiting another country. Some countries provide very stiff penalties for drug use; these penalties are not any less severe simply because the offender is a student.

Emotional problems. If you are experiencing emotional problems in the United States, you will find that overseas travel and study will not do away with your condition. *Do not* plan to go abroad to "get away from it all"! Rarely does genuine emotional illness lessen overseas, where culture shock and different dietary and exercise patterns exist. Indeed, study overseas may exacerbate a condition. It is not unusual for people at some time in their lives to need professional counseling. If you find yourself experiencing emotional stress while overseas, take advantage of counseling and support systems. Organizations such as Alcoholics Anonymous exist worldwide, as do other groups with various emotional and development goals. Your program director should be able to help you locate such groups and give you information about them.

Sexually transmitted diseases and AIDS. Diseases such as gonorrhea, herpes, and syphilis continue to pose health threats for travelers in virtually all countries in the world. HIV, the virus responsible for AIDS, can be transmitted sexually and presents grave health risks everywhere. HIV is also transmitted by poor medical practices, such as the use of unsterilized needles for vaccinations, allergy shots, medications, and blood transfusions and by use of contaminated blood in transfusions. Take the same precautions you would in the United States to avoid exposure to sexually transmitted diseases. Follow health advisories, especially in areas where AIDS is endemic. If you feel it is appropriate, take latex condoms with you overseas, as those available abroad may be inferior or offer poor protection. If you become pregnant while overseas, consult a physician immediately.

Accidents. Accidents can be a matter of concern for travelers, who should take special precautions overseas. To help avoid them you should, of course, follow traffic rules and use seat belts whenever possible. Make sure the equipment you use (bicycles, mopeds, motorcycles, or cars) is operationally safe. Inquire about driving regulations, and make sure you can legally drive in the country. Study symbols and signs so that you can drive safely. Be very cautious while swimming, especially in large bodies of water. Find out about tides and currents before you jump in. Electrical appliances overseas may operate differently than those in the United States. Be aware of the different voltages in other countries, and make sure the equipment you use is suited to the local voltage.

International medical differences. Health-care delivery in many countries is different from what you'll find in the United States. Try to get information about health-care delivery in the country in which you'll be studying. Keep in mind that value differences can play a part in medical practice abroad; in some countries patients are expected simply to follow the doctor's advice and never to question what they are told, while in other countries patients are invited to ask questions.

The hotline number on your student ID can help you get information on services overseas, as can emergency numbers you obtain from your own insurance program. You may also be able to call your physician in the United States to get advice.

BEFORE YOU LEAVE THE U.S.

The U.S. State Department has a Web site that monitors travel, health, and crime and security issues and reports on unusual immigration practices, unusual currency and entry regulations, drug possession and use penalties, and terrorist activity for every country in the world. It is a good idea to check this site before you leave so that you'll know what to expect when you arrive (or whether or not you should go at all). Visit www.state.gov for more information.

RE-ENTRY ISSUES

Many students returning from overseas study fail to consider jet lag and the culture shock associated with returning to the United States to be potential health issues and are surprised to find themselves drained emotionally and enervated physically shortly after they return. You need to adjust to your own native culture, just as

you did to the foreign. Your body will need to adjust to the time difference, too. Take time to relax and absorb all the changes.

Returning home may result in other emotional stresses, too. You may find that problems you left behind when you went overseas have not been resolved. You may find it a little hard to fit back into a social group that has gone on without you for some time. You may find that friends have changed. The bad feelings associated with these things are usually temporary. But if you continue to feel stress because of them, you should seek professional counseling.

CONCLUSION

Your health is partly an issue of where you are and, in many regions of the world, health issues are no different than those in the United States. But your health is equally an issue of your own responsibility. Take reasonable precautions before you go, seek advice from authoritative sources about special health needs you might face, concern yourself with how to care for yourself, and take care of yourself when you return home. These things will all add up to a healthy experience in most parts of the world.

Joan Elias Gore is the Director for Institutional Relations at Denmark's International Study Program. Over the span of her career, she has worked with agencies that have developed and managed programs worldwide, functioned as resident director for overseas programs, and worked as a study-abroad adviser and administrator within the university setting.

Safety in Study Abroad

William L. Gertz

Executive Vice President, American Institute for Foreign Study Worldwide Marketing

Every year, hundreds of thousands of U.S. citizens travel abroad for business, pleasure, or study. For most people, travel abroad is a positive, rewarding, and educational experience. For the few who experience safety-related problems, a lack of planning and general awareness are often contributing factors. Whether you are an experienced traveler or traveling abroad for the first time you should pay special attention to your personal safety and security. This will make your study-abroad experience satisfying and rewarding. Don't lose any sleep over sensational headlines. You probably face as much danger on your home campus as in any major westernized city in the world. The real danger when traveling abroad is casting off all inhibitions and ignoring normal precautions that common sense dictates no matter where you are.

Cautious students may say to themselves, "I'm staying home!" However, the reality is that the risks of studying abroad are small compared to the benefits of the overseas experience. If you prepare adequately for your study-abroad experience, you will greatly minimize the risks associated with foreign travel. At the very least, your research on safety should include the following:

General country conditions. Learn about the place where you plan to study. The U.S. State Department issues periodic Travel Warnings, which may recommend that Americans defer travel to a particular country. Public Announcements are a means to disseminate information about terrorist threats and other significant risks to the security of American travelers. Check all-news channels, such as CNN, frequently to keep abreast of international events.

Local laws and customs. Although you are an American citizen, you are subject to the laws of the country in which you are studying. This cannot be stressed enough. What you consider to be your basic rights is an American concept that does not necessarily apply abroad. Don't assume that what is acceptable in the U.S. is acceptable abroad.

The study-abroad program. As you search through this book for a study-abroad program, ask yourself these questions:

- What kind of track record does the program have?

- Is there information available on health and safety issues?

- Are the medical facilities acceptable and what currency will they accept?

- Is your medical insurance valid?

- Are local excursions well planned and are third-party providers, such as bus companies, selected with care?

- Is there a homestay option? Have the families been carefully screened?

- In a university residence, is security adequate and are there locks on the doors?

- How safe is the neighborhood where you will be living?

- What is the attitude of the local police toward visiting students?

Don't be shy! Ask these questions before you enroll in a program.

As you carefully consider the country and the local environment, there is still one more piece to the safety in study-abroad puzzle. That piece is you! How will you act in your new environment? Here is some advice given to students enrolled in programs offered by the American Institute for Foreign Study.

Blend in. It is not a good idea to attract undue attention to yourself. For example, don't wear a baseball cap backwards—it says "American." Women often receive more than their fair share of unwanted attention. Dressing conservatively is the best way to play it safe from the start. Leave provocative

clothing at home. In some places, you may be harassed, pinched, or even grabbed. Observe the strategy of local women for fending off unwanted attention.

Exercise caution. Always be aware of your surroundings and remain alert. Don't stumble through unknown streets alone. Would you do this in New York or Boston?

Drink wisely. If you are going to drink alcohol, do so only with trusted friends and make sure one friend remains sober. Of course, never drink and drive.

Be aware of cultural behavior. What may be customary in the U.S. may send the wrong signals abroad.

Avoid illegal drugs. If you are caught, you are subject to local laws.

Watch your bags. Don't carry or flash large sums of money, and leave your valuables at

semesteratsea®

A Voyage of Discovery

Institute for Shipboard Education

···▸ spring
···▸ summer
···▸ fall

Imagine a semester where you travel the globe, experiencing a diversity of cultures and meeting people around the world, while earning credits toward your degree. Each fall, spring and summer semester up to 650 undergraduate students live and learn together aboard *Explorer*, Semester at Sea's floating campus. On our 100-day fall and spring voyages visit countries such as **Venezuela, Brazil, South Africa, Tanzania, India, Thailand, Vietnam, China and Japan.** On our 65-day summer program, visit **Spain, Ireland, England, Belgium, Poland, Russia, Norway, and Iceland.** Study global issues, interact with people around the world and have the most exciting and rewarding semester of your college experience.

designed by **media27.com**

www.semesteratsea.com
info@semesteratsea.com

Toll Free 800-854-0195

412-648-7490

home. Never leave your wallet or purse unattended. Passports are a primary target for pickpockets.

Protect your passport. The passport is the most significant identification you carry so take extra precautions, since passport theft is on the rise. Use discretion when displaying it since it can draw unwanted attention. If it is lost or stolen, report it immediately.

Use the "buddy" system. Whenever possible, travel with a friend or a group. If you are out at night, walk on well-lighted, heavily traveled streets and never go out alone. Avoid high crime areas, parks, and shortcuts through alleys and side streets. Use caution as a pedestrian, especially in countries where they drive on the "other" side of the road.

Choose vehicles wisely. Use only official taxis and agree on the rate before you drive off.

Exercise. If you plan to exercise, do it in daylight. Be careful of local drivers who may not be used to people running along the road.

Avoid civil disturbances. Avoid demonstrations, rallies, and other disputes with local citizens. Should violence break out, arrests are sometimes made indiscriminately. You don't want to be arrested or detained as an "innocent bystander."

If you feel you are in a dangerous situation, head for a hotel or restaurant and ask for help.

_A_dditional
Study-Abroad Resources

The following list provides the names of the organizations mentioned in the preceding articles. For your convenience, we have created one comprehensive list, along with contact information.

DISABILITY AND EXCHANGE

Disability Rights and Education Defense Fund (DREDF) provides information on the Americans with Disabilities Act.

> 2212 Sixth Street
> Berkeley, CA 94710
> Phone: 510-644-2555
> Fax: 510-841-8645
> Web site: www.dredf.org

Mobility International USA/National Clearinghouse on Disability and Exchange empowers people with disabilities around the world through international exchange and international development to achieve their human rights.

> P.O. Box 10767
> Eugene, OR 97440
> Phone: 541-343-1284
> Fax: 541-343-6812
> Web site: www.miusa.org

Service Civil International (SCI) provides information on volunteer and work camp opportunities.

> 5474 Walnut Level Road
> Crozet, VA 22932
> Phone: 434-823-9003
> Fax: 206-350-6585
> Web site: www.sci-ivs.org

Society for Accessible Travel & Hospitality (SATH) provides travel and accessibility information for people with disabilities.

> 347 Fifth Avenue, Suite 610
> New York, NY 10016
> Phone: 212-447-7284
> Fax: 212-725-8253
> Web site: www.sath.org

University of New Orleans Training, Resource, and Assistive-Technology Center provides quality services to persons with disabilities, rehabilitation professionals, educators, and employers.

> P.O. Box 1051
> Lakefront Campus
> New Orleans, LA 70148
> Phone: 504-280-5707
> Web site: www.uno.edu/~trac

Volunteers for Peace offers information on a variety of volunteer opportunities.

> 1034 Tiffany Road
> Belmont, VT 05730
> Phone: 802-259-2759
> Fax: 802-259-2922
> Web site: www.vfp.org

FINANCIAL AID

Council on International Educational Exchange offers exchange, volunteer, and work opportunities throughout the world.

> 7 Custom House Street, Third Floor
> Portland, ME 04101
> Phone: 800-40-STUDY
> Fax: 207-553-7699
> Web site: www.ciee.org

Institute of International Education offers information on international study and volunteer opportunities.

> 1400 K Street, NW
> Washington, D.C. 20005
> Phone: 800-618-NSEP
> Fax: 202-326-7835
> Web site: www.iie.org

The Rotary Foundation of Rotary International is a worldwide organization of business and professional leaders that provides humanitarian service, encourages high ethical standards in all vocations, and helps build goodwill and peace in the world.

> One Rotary Center
> 1560 Sherman Avenue
> Evanston, IL 60201
> Phone: 847-866-3000
> Fax: 847-328-8554
> Web site: www.rotary.org

HEALTH AND SAFETY

Association for Safe International Road Travel (road travel reports for 150 countries) promotes road travel safety through education and advocacy and provides travelers with road safety information, enabling them to make informed travel choices.

> 11769 Gainsborough Road
> Potomac, MD 20854
> Phone: 301-983 5252
> Fax: 301-983-3663
> Web site: www.asirt.org

Cultural Insurance Services International offers 24-hour telephone help with medical, legal, financial, language, and other travel-related problems. It also offers group and individual insurance plans for study abroad, including medical, accident, accidental death, baggage, etc.

> River Plaza
> 9 West Broad Street
> Stamford, CT 06902-3788
> Phone: 800-303-8120
> Fax: 203-399-5596
> Web site: www.culturalinsurance.com

CultureGrams is a widely used cultural reference product in the education, government, and nonprofit arenas.

> 333 South 520 West, Suite 360
> Lindon, UT 84042
> Phone: 800-528-6279
> Fax: 801-847-0127
> Web site: www.culturegrams.com

International Association for Medical Assistance to Travelers (IAMAT) advises travelers about health risks, the geographical distribution of diseases worldwide, and immunization requirements for all countries.

> 417 Center Street
> Lewiston, NY 14092
> Phone: 716-754-4833
> Web site: www.iamat.org

NAFSA: Association of International Educators promotes the exchange of students and scholars to and from the United States.

> 1307 New York Avenue, NW, 8th Floor
> Washington, D.C. 20005
> Phone: 202-737-3699
> Fax: 202-737-3657
> Web site: www.nafsa.org

U.S. Center for Disease Control and Prevention (travel health advisories) provides warnings about potential health risks in foreign countries.

> 1600 Clifton Road
> Atlanta, GA 30333
> Phone: 404-639-3311
> Web site: www.cdc.gov/travel

U.S. State Department (for advisories) issues travel warnings when the State Department recommends that Americans avoid a certain country.

> 2201 C Street, NW
> Washington, D.C. 20520
> Phone: 202-647-4000
> Web site: http://www.travel.state.gov/travel/warnings.html

INTERNATIONAL VOLUNTEER ORGANIZATIONS

American Friends Service Committee carries out service, development, social justice, and peace programs throughout the world.

> 1501 Cherry Street
> Philadelphia, PA 19102
> Phone: 215-241-7000
> Fax: 215-567-7275
> Web site: www.afsc.org

Amigos de las Americas creates opportunities for young people to excel in leadership roles promoting public health, education, and community development.

> 5618 Star lane
> Houston, TX 77057
> Phone: 800-231-7796
> Fax: 713-782-9267
> Web site: www.amigoslink.org

Community Service Volunteers works to reconnect people to their community through volunteering and training.

> 237 Pentonville Road
> London N1 9NJ
> United Kingdom
> Web site: www.csv.org.uk

Earthwatch engages people worldwide in scientific field research and education to promote the understanding and action necessary for a sustainable environment.

> 3 Clock Tower Place, Suite 100
> Box 75
> Maynard, MA 01754
> Phone: 800-776-0188
> Fax: 978-461-2332
> Web site: www.earthwatch.org

Global Volunteers provides short-term service opportunities on community development programs in host communities abroad.

> 375 East Little Canada Road
> Saint Paul, MN 55117-1628
> Phone: 651-407-6100
> Fax: 651-482-0915
> Web site: www.globalvolunteers.org

Habitat for Humanity International is a nonprofit, nondenominational Christian housing organization that builds simple, decent, affordable houses in partnership with those who lack adequate shelter.

> 121 Habitat Street
> Americus, GA 31709-3498
> Phone: 229-924-6935
> Web site: www.habitat.org

The International Partnership for Service Learning unites academic study and volunteer service, giving students a fully integrated study abroad experience.

> 815 Second Avenue, Suite 315
> New York, NY 10017
> Phone: 212-986-0989
> Fax: 212-986-5039
> Web site: www.ipsl.org

Lisle, Inc. broadens global awareness and cultural understanding worldwide through opportunities that integrate learning with experience.

> 900 Country Road
> Leander, TX 78641
> Phone: 800-477-1538
> Fax: 512-259-0392
> Web site: www.lisle.utoledo.edu

University Research Expeditions Program (UREP) invites students to explore new intellectual and professional worlds, with hundreds of classes, workshops, seminars, and specialized training for schools, organizations, individuals, and businesses.

> University of California
> One Shields Avenue
> Davis, CA 95616
> Web site: http://www.extension.ucdavis.
>   edu/urep

INTERNSHIPS

AIESEC/US facilitates international exchange of thousands of students and recent graduates each year.

> 127 West 26th Street, 10th Floor
> New York, NY 10001
> Phone: 212-757-3774
> Fax: 212-757-4062
> Web site: www.aiesec.org

American Scandinavian Foundation promotes international understanding through educational and cultural exchange between the United States and Denmark, Finland, Iceland, Norway, and Sweden.

> 58 Park Avenue
> New York, NY 10016
> 212-879-9779
> Web site: www.amscan.org

Association for International Practical Training (AIPT) provides international human resource development through practical training programs.

> 10400 Little Patuxent Parkway, Suite 250
> Columbia, MD 210044-3519
> Phone: 410-997-2200
> Fax: 410-992-3924
> Web site: www.aipt.org

CARE works with poor communities in more than 70 countries around the world to find lasting solutions to poverty.

> 151 Ellis Street
> Atlanta, GA 30303
> Phone: 404-681-2552
> Fax: 404-589-2651
> Web site: www.careusa.org

CDS International is a non-profit organization committed to the advancement of international practical training opportunities for young professionals, students, educators, as well as labor, business, and government representatives.

> 871 United Nations Plaza
> New York, NY 10017-1814
> Phone: 212-497-3500
> Fax: 212-497-3535
> Web site: www.cdsintl.org

InterExchange, Inc. provides valuable cross-cultural life and work experiences for young adults.

> 161 Sixth Avenue
> New York, NY 10013
> Phone: 212-924-0446
> Fax: 212-924-0575
> Web: www.interexchange.org

International Cooperative Education (ICE) provides American college and university students with the opportunity to gain practical work experience abroad. Each summer ICE arranges for students to travel to Europe, Australia, Asia, and South America to work as paid interns.

> 15 Spiros Way
> Menlo Park, CA 94025
> Phone: 650-323-4944
> Fax: 650-323-1104
> Web site: www.icemenlo.com

U.S. Department of State Internship Coordinator, Student Intern Program enables students to obtain job experience in a foreign affairs environment. Students work in Washington, D.C., while others have the opportunity to work at U.S. embassies and consulates abroad.

> 2401 E Street NW, Suite 518 H
> Washington, D.C. 22520
> Web site: www.careers.state.gov/student

PASSPORTS, VISAS, AND STUDENT ID CARDS

Council Travel

> 633 Third Avenue
> New York, NY 10017
> Phone: 800-781-4040

Foreign Policy Association provides independent publications, programs, and forums to increase public awareness of, and foster popular participation in, matters relating to those policy issues.

> 470 Park Avenue, North
> New York, NY 10016-6819
> Phone: 212-481-8100
> Web site: www.fpa.org

TRAVEL

STA Travel

> Phone: 888-427-5639
> Web site: www.statravel.ca

Searching for Study-Abroad Programs Online

Thinking about studying abroad? The Internet can be a great tool for gathering information about institutions and their study-abroad programs. There are many worthwhile sites that are ready to help guide you through the various aspects of the selection process, including Peterson's Study-Abroad Channel at www.petersons.com/stdyabrd.

HOW PETERSON'S STUDY-ABROAD CHANNEL CAN HELP

If you want to see the world and get college credit for it, Peterson's has everything you need to know about studying overseas at leading universities.

Choosing a study-abroad program involves a serious commitment of time and resources. Therefore, it is important to have the most up-to-date information about prospective institutions and their programs at your fingertips. That is why Peterson's Study-Abroad Channel is a great place to start the process!

STUDY-ABROAD PROGRAMS DETAILED SEARCH

Explore more than 1,900 programs! To search by sponsoring institution, select a letter from the alphabetical list of sponsor names. If you're interested in studying in a certain country, scroll through the list of countries to find the institutions that sponsor a program in your country of interest. If field of study is your top priority, scroll through the list of major areas of study to find out who is sponsoring programs in that area.

Once you have found a program of your choice, simply click on it to get more in-depth information, including venue, admission requirements, costs, financial aid, contact information, and more.

E-mail This Program

If, after looking at the information provided on Peterson's Study-Abroad Channel, you still have questions, you can send an e-mail directly to the school. Just click on "E-mail This Program" and send your message. In most instances, if you keep your questions short and to the point, you will receive an answer in no time at all.

Web Site Visit

For programs that have provided their Web sites, simply click on "Web Site Visit" and you will be taken directly to that program's Web page.

USE THE TOOLS TO YOUR ADVANTAGE

Choosing to study abroad is an important decision. The tools available to you at www. petersons.com/stdyabrd can help you make an informed decision. So, what are you waiting for? Fire up your computer; a study-abroad program is just a click away!

How to Use This Guide

Before you start to use this book to search for a program, you'll want to understand some of the terms commonly applied to study-abroad programs. There are many different ways that study-abroad programs are organized—in some cases you can apply to the *same* program through several different institutions—and even pay several different costs!

Let's take one example: You'd like to spend a semester at the University of Oxford in England. In this case, several U.S. colleges and universities send students to Oxford. The program arrangements, offerings, and costs may be different for each. The institutions offering these program arrangements are commonly referred to as *sponsors*. In this case, Oxford is called the *host* institution. If Oxford enrolls students directly (you don't have to go through any U.S. institution), then it is operating as both the sponsor and the host. You'll want to check out all the programs that take place at Oxford to find the one that best suits your needs.

Some sponsors have their own facilities in another country or simply book space for classes or living accommodations without involving a foreign university. In this case, there is no "host" institution.

Sometimes an organization or institution operates as what is called here a program *facilitator*—that is, it handles enrollment administration stateside for other schools' programs, especially those sponsored by foreign schools.

You are probably aware of whether or not your school is part of a *consortium*. Schools in a consortium share any number of resources or have made cooperative arrangements so that students from one member institution have some privileges at another member institution. Consortia commonly sponsor study-abroad programs for all of the students of their member institutions.

PROFILES OF STUDY-ABROAD PROGRAMS

Profiles of more than 1,900 study-abroad programs are divided into two sections: **Country-to-Country Programs** and **Programs by Country.** These profiles contain all the details you'll need to make a list of preliminary program choices.

The **Country-to-Country Programs** section lists those academic programs that incorporate traveling as a major emphasis of the curriculum. For example, students might spend a few weeks in each of several European countries visiting museums as part of an art program or corporations for a business class. This section is organized alphabetically by the sponsoring institution.

The **Programs by Country** section contains most of the study-abroad programs in the guide. This section is divided alphabetically by country in which the programs take place. Country listings are further subdivided alphabetically by city. If a program takes place in more than one city, it appears at the beginning of the country listing under the City to City heading.

Note that for ease of use, this book divides the United Kingdom into its constituent countries—England, Scotland, and Wales. Also note that this book contains two separate sections for Ireland and Northern Ireland.

INDEXES

Field of Study. Consult this index if you want to know which colleges or universities offer course work in the academic area you're pursuing. Each subject area is subdivided by country; all relevant programs and their profile page numbers are listed. By using this index you can find out, for example, which Spanish programs are available in Mexico or where you can study African art and culture.

Program Sponsors. This index lists each program in the book by its sponsoring institution. Use this index to find out about your school's offerings as well as those of any other school.

Host Institutions. Perhaps you've always wanted to study at the American University in Cairo or LaTrobe University in Australia. These institutions act as "hosts," and a U.S. school makes arrangements for students to take courses at these foreign institutions. The index lists host institutions alphabetically by country.

DATA COLLECTION PROCEDURES

Peterson's obtained program information through a questionnaire sent to study-abroad directors in spring and summer 2004. While the editors believe the information in this book is accurate, Peterson's does not assume responsibility for the quality of the programs or the practices of the sponsoring institutions. You are encouraged to obtain as much information as possible from the sponsors themselves.

CRITERIA FOR INCLUSION IN THIS GUIDE

The programs in this book have met the following criteria:

The sponsoring college, university, or group of schools (consortium) has been accredited by one of the national, regional, or international organizations that review undergraduate and graduate degree–granting institutions in the United States and abroad. The guide also lists programs sponsored by third-party organizations who have arranged for an accredited college or university to transfer credit.

The program must be regularly accepted for undergraduate credit at U.S. colleges and universities. You will still need to get approval from your own school, however, to receive credit for the program you choose.

The program's enrollment cannot be limited to students from the sponsoring school; students from other schools must be able to participate. This means that you should also check with your own school to see if they offer limited-enrollment programs that do not appear in this guide.

Profiles of Study-Abroad Programs

Country-to-Country Programs

ACIE (ACTR/ACCELS)
ACIE (ACCELS) CENTRAL EUROPEAN LANGUAGE STUDY PROGRAMS

Hosted by Debrecen Summer School (Debrecen, Hungary), Palacky University, Masaryk University, Eötvös Loránd University Budapest (ELTE), Comenius University in Bratislava, CERGE-EI

Academic Focus • Czech, Hungarian, Slavic languages.

Program Information • Students attend classes at Palacky University (Olomouc, Czech Republic), Masaryk University (Brno, Czech Republic), CERGE-EI (Prague, Czech Republic), Eötvös Loránd University Budapest (ELTE) (Budapest, Hungary), Debrecen Summer School (Debrecen, Hungary), Comenius University in Bratislava (Bratislava, Slovakia).

Sessions • Fall, spring, yearlong.

Eligibility Requirements • Minimum age 18; open to freshmen, sophomores, juniors, seniors, graduate students, adults; 3 letters of recommendation; good academic standing at home school; 1 year of college course work in Czech, Slovak or Hungarian.

Living Arrangements • Students live in host institution dormitories, locally rented apartments. Quarters are shared with students from other programs. Meals are taken on one's own, in residences, in central dining facility.

Costs (2002-2003) • One term: contact sponsor for cost. Yearlong program: contact sponsor for cost. $35 application fee. $500 nonrefundable deposit required. Financial aid available for all students: scholarships.

For More Information • Nurhan Kocaoglu, Russian and Eurasian Program Manager, ACIE (ACTR/ACCELS), 1776 Massachusetts Avenue, NW, Suite 700, Washington, DC 20036; *Phone:* 202-833-7522; *Fax:* 202-833-7523. *E-mail:* outbound@actr.org. *World Wide Web:* http://www.actr.org/

ACIE (ACTR/ACCELS)
ACIE (ACTR) NIS REGIONAL LANGUAGE TRAINING PROGRAM

Academic Focus • Cultural studies, language studies.

Program Information • Program takes place in Yerevan, Armenia; Baku, Azerbaijan; Minsk, Belarus; Tbilisi, Georgia; Almaty, Kazakhstan; Bishkek, Kyrgyzstan; Chisinau, Moldova; Russia; Ashgabat, Turkmenistan; Ukraine; Uzbekistan. Faculty members are local instructors hired by the sponsor. Optional travel at an extra cost.

Sessions • Fall, spring, yearlong.

Eligibility Requirements • Minimum age 18; open to sophomores, juniors, seniors, graduate students, adults; 3 letters of recommendation; good academic standing at home school; 1 year of college course work in Russian or regional language.

Living Arrangements • Students live in host institution dormitories, host family homes. Quarters are shared with students from other programs. Meals are taken on one's own, with host family, in residences, in central dining facility, in restaurants.

Costs (2002-2003) • One term: contact sponsor for cost. Yearlong program: contact sponsor for cost. $35 application fee. $500 nonrefundable deposit required. Financial aid available for all students: scholarships.

For More Information • Ms. Margaret Stephenson, Russian and Eurasian Program Officer, ACIE (ACTR/ACCELS), 1776 Massachusetts Avenue, NW, Suite 700, Washington, DC 20036; *Phone:* 202-833-7522; *Fax:* 202-833-7523. *E-mail:* outbound@actr.org. *World Wide Web:* http://www.actr.org/

AMERICAN UNIVERSITY
ANDES TO THE RAINFORESTS

Hosted by University of Diego Portales

Academic Focus • Environmental science/studies, Latin American studies, political science and government, Spanish language and literature.

Program Information • Students attend classes at University of Diego Portales (Santiago, Chile). Scheduled travel to southern Chile, Rio de Janeiro, Brazilia, Salvador da Bahia, Lima, Cuzco.

Sessions • Fall.

Eligibility Requirements • Open to juniors, seniors, graduate students; 2.75 GPA; 1 letter of recommendation; 2 years of college course work in Spanish.

Living Arrangements • Students live in host family homes, hotels. Meals are taken as a group, on one's own, with host family, in residences, in restaurants.

Costs (2003) • One term: $18,126; includes tuition, housing, some meals, excursions, student support services. $35 application fee. $300 deposit required. Financial aid available for all students: scholarships, loans.
For More Information • Dr. David C. Brown, Dean, Washington Semester and World Capitals Program, American University, Tenley Campus–Constitution Building, Washington, DC 20016-8083; *Phone:* 800-424-2600; *Fax:* 202-895-4960. *E-mail:* travel@american.edu. *World Wide Web:* http://www.worldcapitals.american.edu/

AMERICAN UNIVERSITY
SEMESTER IN AUSTRALIA AND NEW ZEALAND
Hosted by Australian Catholic University–Sydney
Academic Focus • Full curriculum.
Program Information • Students attend classes at Australian Catholic University–Sydney (Sydney, Australia). Scheduled travel to New Zealand, the Great Barrier Reef.
Sessions • Spring.
Eligibility Requirements • Open to sophomores, juniors, seniors; 2.75 GPA; 1 letter of recommendation; good academic standing at home school; second semester sophomore status.
Living Arrangements • Students live in host institution dormitories, host family homes. Meals are taken on one's own, in residences, in restaurants.
Costs (2003) • One term: $16,634; includes tuition, housing, some meals, excursions, student support services. $35 application fee. $300 nonrefundable deposit required. Financial aid available for all students: scholarships, loans.
For More Information • Dr. David C. Brown, Dean, Washington Semester and World Capitals Program, American University, Tenley Campus–Constitution Building, Washington, DC 20016-8083; *Phone:* 202-895-4900; *Fax:* 202-895-4960. *E-mail:* travel@american.edu. *World Wide Web:* http://www.worldcapitals.american.edu/

AMERICAN UNIVERSITY
SEMESTER IN SOUTHERN AFRICA
Hosted by The University of Venda for Science and Technology
Academic Focus • African studies, ecology, international affairs, peace and conflict studies.
Program Information • Students attend classes at The University of Venda for Science and Technology (Thohoyandou, South Africa). Classes are also held on the campus of Cape Technikon (Cape Town, South Africa). Scheduled travel to Victoria Falls, Harare, game parks, Mutare, Greater Zimbabwe and surrounding areas; field trips to areas surrounding Cape Town and Zimbabwe.
Sessions • Fall.
Eligibility Requirements • Open to sophomores, juniors, seniors, graduate students; 2.75 GPA; 1 letter of recommendation; recommendation of advisor; no foreign language proficiency required.
Living Arrangements • Students live in host institution dormitories, locally rented apartments, host family homes. Meals are taken as a group, on one's own, with host family, in residences, in restaurants.
Costs (2003) • One term: $16,534; includes tuition, housing, some meals, excursions, books and class materials, student support services. $35 application fee. $300 nonrefundable deposit required. Financial aid available for all students: scholarships, loans.
For More Information • Dr. David C. Brown, Dean, Washington Semester and World Capitals Programs, American University, Tenley Campus–Constitution Building, Washington, DC 20016-8083; *Phone:* 800-424-2600; *Fax:* 202-895-4960. *E-mail:* travel@american.edu. *World Wide Web:* http://www.worldcapitals.american.edu/

AMERICAN UNIVERSITY
SEMESTER IN THE MEDITERRANEAN
Hosted by University of Alcalá de Henares
Academic Focus • Full curriculum.
Program Information • Students attend classes at University of Alcalá de Henares (Madrid, Spain). Scheduled travel to Madrid, Turkey, Rome; field trips to Athens, islands; optional travel at an extra cost.
Sessions • Fall.

Eligibility Requirements • Open to sophomores, juniors, seniors, graduate students; 2.75 GPA; 1 letter of recommendation; no foreign language proficiency required.
Living Arrangements • Students live in host family homes, hotels. Meals are taken as a group, on one's own, with host family, in residences, in central dining facility, in restaurants.
Costs (2002) • One term: $17,484; includes tuition, housing, some meals, excursions, student support services. $35 application fee. $300 deposit required. Financial aid available for all students: scholarships, loans.
For More Information • Dr. David C. Brown, Dean, Washington Semester and World Capitals Program, American University, Tenley Campus–Constitution Building, Washington, DC 20016; *Phone:* 800-424-2600; *Fax:* 202-895-4960. *E-mail:* travel@american.edu. *World Wide Web:* http://www.worldcapitals.american.edu/

ANTIOCH COLLEGE
COMPARATIVE WOMEN'S STUDIES IN EUROPE
Academic Focus • Anthropology, bisexual studies, Central European studies, community service, comparative history, cultural studies, Eastern European studies, European studies, German studies, intercultural studies, interdisciplinary studies, international affairs, Jewish studies, lesbian studies, liberal studies, Polish studies, political science and government, public policy, social sciences, social services, social work, sociology, visual and performing arts, women's studies.
Program Information • Program takes place in Brussels, Belgium; Berlin, Germany; Utrecht, Netherlands; Crakow, Poland; Warsaw, Poland; London, England. Faculty members are drawn from the sponsor's U.S. staff and local instructors hired by the sponsor. Scheduled travel to Utrecht, Amsterdam, Berlin, Krakow, Warsaw, London, Antwerp, Brussels; field trips to Auschwitz-Birkenau concentration camp, Ravensbruck Women's Work Camp.
Sessions • Fall.
Eligibility Requirements • Minimum age 18; open to sophomores, juniors, seniors; course work in women's studies; 2 letters of recommendation; good academic standing at home school; no foreign language proficiency required.
Living Arrangements • Students live in host institution dormitories, host family homes, hotels. Meals are taken as a group, on one's own, with host family, in residences, in central dining facility, in restaurants.
Costs (2003-2004) • One term: $13,645; includes tuition, housing, some meals, excursions, books and class materials, international student ID, intercontinental travel. $35 application fee. $150 nonrefundable deposit required. Financial aid available for students from sponsoring institution: scholarships, loans.
For More Information • Ms. Karin Heisecke, Director, Women's Studies in Europe, Antioch College, Antioch Education Abroad, 795 Livermore Street, Yellow Springs, OH 45387-1697; *Phone:* 937-769-1015; *Fax:* 937-769-1019. *E-mail:* aea@antioch-college.edu. *World Wide Web:* http://www.antioch-college.edu/aea/

ANTIOCH COLLEGE
EUROPE IN TRANSITION: INTEGRATION AND POST-INDUSTRIAL CHANGE
Hosted by Budapest University of Economic Sciences and Public Administration, Charles University, University of Tübingen, Jagiellonian University
Academic Focus • Central European studies, comparative history, economics, European studies, German studies, Hungarian studies, Polish studies, political science and government, social sciences, sociology, urban studies.
Program Information • Students attend classes at Charles University (Prague, Czech Republic), University of Tübingen (Tübingen, Germany), Budapest University of Economic Sciences and Public Administration (Budapest, Hungary), Jagiellonian University (Krakow, Poland). Classes are also held on the campus of Central European University (Budapest, Hungary). Scheduled travel to Tübingen, Berlin, Warsaw, Prague, Olomonc, Budapest, Pecs; field trips to parliaments/government offices, housing associations/refugee centers, Auschwitz concentration camp, economic development/enterprise associations.
Sessions • Spring.

Eligibility Requirements • Minimum age 18; open to sophomores, juniors, seniors; course work in social science; 2 letters of recommendation; good academic standing at home school; no foreign language proficiency required.

Living Arrangements • Students live in host institution dormitories, host family homes, hotels. Quarters are shared with students from other programs. Meals are taken as a group, on one's own, with host family, in residences, in central dining facility, in restaurants.

Costs (2003-2004) • One term: $13,645; includes tuition, housing, all meals, excursions, international airfare, books and class materials, international student ID, intercontinental travel. $35 application fee. $150 nonrefundable deposit required. Financial aid available for students from sponsoring institution: scholarships, loans.

For More Information • Dr. Dale Gardner, Assistant Director, Antioch College, Antioch Education Abroad, 795 Livermore Street, Yellow Springs, OH 45387; *Phone:* 937-769-1015; *Fax:* 937-769-1019. *E-mail:* aea@antioch-college.edu. *World Wide Web:* http://www.antioch-college.edu/aea/

ASSOCIATED COLLEGES OF THE MIDWEST
ACM LONDON AND FLORENCE: ARTS IN CONTEXT PROGRAM

Held at Linguaviva Italian School

Academic Focus • Architecture, art history, drama/theater, history, Italian language and literature, literature, Renaissance studies.

Program Information • Classes are held on the campus of Linguaviva Italian School (Florence, Italy). Faculty members are drawn from the sponsor's U.S. staff and local instructors hired by the sponsor. Scheduled travel to Rome; field trips to Pisa, Salisbury, Bath, Venice; optional travel to Europe at an extra cost.

Sessions • Spring.

Eligibility Requirements • Open to sophomores, juniors, seniors; 3 letters of recommendation; good academic standing at home school; no foreign language proficiency required.

Living Arrangements • Students live in host family homes. Meals are taken on one's own, with host family, in residences, in restaurants.

Costs (2003) • One term: contact sponsor for cost. $400 nonrefundable deposit required.

For More Information • Program Associate, ACM London and Florence Program, Associated Colleges of the Midwest, 205 West Wacker Drive, Suite 1300, Chicago, IL 60606; *Phone:* 312-263-5000; *Fax:* 312-263-5879. *E-mail:* acm@acm.edu. *World Wide Web:* http://www.acm.edu/

BELOIT COLLEGE
ESTONIA/MOROCCO PROGRAM IN CROSS-CULTURAL PSYCHOLOGY

Hosted by Arabic Language Institute in Fez, University of Tartu

Academic Focus • Arabic, area studies, interdisciplinary studies, language studies, psychology.

Program Information • Students attend classes at University of Tartu (Tartu, Estonia), Arabic Language Institute in Fez (Fez, Morocco). Scheduled travel to Latvia, Lithuania, the Sahara desert; field trips to the medieval city of Tallinn, a Russian Orthodox Convent, Old Cities outdoor markets, the Atlas Mountains, Meknes, Marrakech; optional travel to regional destinations (weekends) at an extra cost.

Sessions • Fall, program runs every other year.

Eligibility Requirements • Open to sophomores, juniors, seniors; course work in psychology; 4 letters of recommendation; preference is given to students who have completed a course in statistics and in research methods; preference is given to students with background in Arabic, Estonian, French or Russian.

Living Arrangements • Students live in host institution dormitories, host family homes. Meals are taken with host family, in residences.

Costs (2002-2003) • One term: $14,232; includes tuition, housing, all meals, excursions. $100 nonrefundable deposit required. Financial aid available for all students: loans.

For More Information • Office of International Education, Beloit College, 700 College Street, Beloit, WI 53511; *Phone:* 608-363-2269; *Fax:* 608-363-2689. *World Wide Web:* http://www.beloit.edu/~oie/

BEMIDJI STATE UNIVERSITY
EUROSPRING

Hosted by Wycliffe Hall

Academic Focus • Architecture, art, biological/life sciences, comparative history, drama/theater, English, history, international affairs, medicine, music, music education, music history, performing arts, political science and government, religious studies, visual and performing arts.

Program Information • Students attend classes at Wycliffe Hall (Oxford, England). Scheduled travel to Paris, Florence, Lucerne, Venice, Pisa, Salzburg, Rome, Vienna, Prague; field trips to Bath, Stonehenge, Avebury, Portsmouth, Salisbury, Stratford-upon-Avon; optional travel to student-arranged destinations at an extra cost.

Sessions • Spring.

Eligibility Requirements • Open to sophomores, juniors, seniors, graduate students, adults; 2.0 GPA; good academic standing at home school; no foreign language proficiency required.

Living Arrangements • Students live in host institution dormitories, hotels. Quarters are shared with students from other programs. Meals are taken as a group, in central dining facility, in restaurants.

Costs (2002) • One term: $4730; includes housing, all meals, excursions, international airfare, student support services, Continental tour travel. $150 nonrefundable deposit required. Financial aid available for students from sponsoring institution: scholarships, loans, grants.

For More Information • Ms. LaMae Hawk, Director, International Program Center, Bemidji State University, Deputy Hall 103, Box 13, 1500 Birchmont Drive, NE, Bemidji, MN 56601-2699; *Phone:* 218-755-4096; *Fax:* 218-755-2074. *E-mail:* lhawk@bemidjistate.edu. *World Wide Web:* http://www.bemidjistate.edu/international/study_abroad.htm

BOWLING GREEN STATE UNIVERSITY
ACADEMIC YEAR/SEMESTER IN FRANCE AND AFRICA

Hosted by Alliance Française, Institut d'Etudes Françaises de Touraine

Academic Focus • African studies, French studies.

Program Information • Students attend classes at Alliance Française (Paris, France), Institut d'Etudes Françaises de Touraine (Tours, France). Classes are also held on the campus of University of Ouagadougou (Ouagadougou, Burkina Faso). Scheduled travel to Dordogne, Normandy, La Rochelle, Strasbourg, Mont-Saint-Michel; field trips to various sites in and around Ouagadougou, Chartres, châteaux of the Loire Valley.

Sessions • Fall, spring, yearlong.

Eligibility Requirements • Minimum age 17; open to freshmen, sophomores, juniors, seniors; 2.5 GPA; 1 letter of recommendation; good academic standing at home school; essay; no foreign language proficiency required.

Living Arrangements • Students live in host family homes. Meals are taken with host family.

Costs (2004-2005) • One term: $7769 for Ohio residents; $11,423 for nonresidents (plus $635 for optional Paris session). Yearlong program: $15,848 for Ohio residents; $23,156 for nonresidents (includes Paris session); includes tuition, housing, all meals, excursions, books and class materials, student support services, round-trip airfare to Africa from France, local transportation, airport pick-up. $25 application fee. Financial aid available for students from sponsoring institution: scholarships, loans, travel grants from Center for International Programs.

For More Information • Ms. Heather Gabel, Director, AYA France/Burkina Faso, Bowling Green State University, Department of Romance Languages, Bowling Green, OH 43403; *Phone:* 419-372-7146; *Fax:* 419-372-7332. *E-mail:* ayafran@bgnet.bgsu.edu. *World Wide Web:* http://www.bgsu.edu/

COLLEGE OF WOOSTER
WOOSTER IN GREECE

Held at Athens Centre

Academic Focus • Ancient history, archaeology, classics and classical languages, history.

Program Information • Classes are held on the campus of Athens Centre (Athens, Greece). Faculty members are drawn from the sponsor's U.S. staff and local instructors hired by the sponsor. Scheduled travel to cities in Greece and Greek islands (Crete,

Santorini), Istanbul, Turkey; field trips to cities in Greece and Greek islands (Crete, Santorini), Istanbul, Turkey; optional travel to a destination of the student's choice at an extra cost.
Sessions • Fall, program runs every 3 years.
Eligibility Requirements • Open to sophomores, juniors; 2.5 GPA; good academic standing at home school; no foreign language proficiency required.
Living Arrangements • Students live in locally rented apartments. Quarters are shared with host institution students. Meals are taken on one's own, in restaurants.
Costs (2003) • One term: contact sponsor for cost. $500 nonrefundable deposit required. Financial aid available for students from sponsoring institution: scholarships.
For More Information • Dr. Thomas Falkner, Professor of Classics, College of Wooster, Department of Classics, Wooster, OH 44691; *Phone:* 330-263-2000. *E-mail:* tfalkner@wooster.edu. *World Wide Web:* http://www.wooster.edu/ipo/

EASTERN MICHIGAN UNIVERSITY
ASIAN CULTURAL HISTORY TOUR

Academic Focus • Art, history, literature, political science and government, religious studies.
Program Information • Program takes place in Beijing, China; Hong Kong, China; Shanghai, China; Agra, India; Delhi, India; Varanasi, India; Laos; Vientiane, Laos; Kuala Lumpur, Malaysia; Kathmandu, Nepal; Nagarkot, Nepal; Singapore, Singapore; Bangkok, Thailand; Da Nang, Vietnam; Hue, Vietnam; Saigon, Vietnam. Faculty members are drawn from the sponsor's U.S. staff. Scheduled travel to over 50 cities; field trips to museums, nature preserves, monuments, religious communities, temples, ruins, government centers.
Sessions • Fall.
Eligibility Requirements • Minimum age 18; open to sophomores, juniors, seniors; 2.5 GPA; 2 letters of recommendation; good academic standing at home school; no foreign language proficiency required.
Living Arrangements • Students live in hotels, hostels, pensions. Meals are taken as a group, in restaurants.
Costs (2003) • One term: $9760; includes housing, some meals, insurance, excursions, international student ID, student support services, travel in Asia. $200 refundable deposit required. Financial aid available for students from sponsoring institution: scholarships, loans.
For More Information • Academic Programs Abroad, Eastern Michigan University, 103 Boone Hall, Ypsilanti, MI 48197; *Phone:* 800-777-3541; *Fax:* 734-487-4377. *E-mail:* programs.abroad@emich.edu. *World Wide Web:* http://www.emich.edu/abroad/

EASTERN MICHIGAN UNIVERSITY
EUROPEAN CULTURAL HISTORY TOUR

Academic Focus • Art, history, literature, political science and government.
Program Information • Program takes place in Salzburg, Austria; Vienna, Austria; Prague, Czech Republic; Berlin, Germany; Munich, Germany; Aswan, Egypt; Cairo, Egypt; Luxor, Egypt; Helsinki, Finland; Paris, France; Athens, Greece; Crete, Greece; Delphi, Greece; Israel; Florence, Italy; Rome, Italy; Venice, Italy; Bergen, Norway; Oslo, Norway; Cracow, Poland; Moscow, Russia; St. Petersburg, Russia; Stockholm, Sweden; Istanbul, Turkey; Selcuk, Turkey; London, England. Faculty members are drawn from the sponsor's U.S. staff. Scheduled travel to over 50 cities; field trips to museums, concerts, theatre performances, monuments and ruins, historic sites, government centers.
Sessions • Fall.
Eligibility Requirements • Minimum age 18; open to sophomores, juniors, seniors; 2.5 GPA; 2 letters of recommendation; good academic standing at home school; no foreign language proficiency required.
Living Arrangements • Students live in hotels, hostels, pensions. Meals are taken as a group, in restaurants.
Costs (2003) • One term: $9760; includes housing, some meals, insurance, excursions, international student ID, student support services, travel in Europe. $200 refundable deposit required. Financial aid available for students from sponsoring institution: scholarships, loans.

For More Information • Academic Programs Abroad, Eastern Michigan University, 103 Boone Hall, Ypsilanti, MI 48197; *Phone:* 800-777-3541; *Fax:* 734-487-4377. *E-mail:* programs.abroad@emich.edu. *World Wide Web:* http://www.emich.edu/abroad/

FLORIDA INTERNATIONAL UNIVERSITY
UNIVERSITY OF THE WEST INDIES, JAMAICA, BARBADOS, AND TRINIDAD AND TOBAGO

Hosted by University of the West Indies, St. Augustine Campus, University of the West Indies, Cave Hill Campus, University of the West Indies
Academic Focus • Full curriculum.
Program Information • Students attend classes at University of the West Indies, Cave Hill Campus (Bridgetown, Barbados), University of the West Indies (Kingston, Jamaica), University of the West Indies, St. Augustine Campus (Saint Augustine, Trinidad and Tobago).
Sessions • Fall, spring.
Eligibility Requirements • Open to sophomores, juniors, seniors, graduate students; 3.0 GPA; no foreign language proficiency required.
Living Arrangements • Students live in host institution dormitories.
Costs (2004) • One term: $5000; includes housing, all meals, international airfare, books and class materials, student support services. $150 application fee. Financial aid available for students from sponsoring institution: scholarships, loans.
For More Information • Office of International Studies, Florida International University, University Park Campus-TT100, Miami, FL 33199; *Phone:* 305-348-1913; *Fax:* 305-348-1941. *E-mail:* ois@fiu.edu. *World Wide Web:* http://ois.fiu.edu/

INTERNATIONAL HONORS PROGRAM
CHALLENGES OF A GLOBAL CULTURE

Academic Focus • Anthropology, economics, history, international affairs, Nepali, political science and government.
Program Information • Program takes place in Nepal; Tibet. Faculty members are drawn from the sponsor's U.S. staff and local instructors hired by the sponsor. Scheduled travel to Nepal, Tibet; field trips to villages, shrines; optional travel to Nepal at an extra cost.
Sessions • Fall.
Eligibility Requirements • Minimum age 18; open to sophomores, juniors, seniors, adults; 2 letters of recommendation; good academic standing at home school; no foreign language proficiency required.
Living Arrangements • Students live in host institution dormitories, host family homes. Meals are taken as a group, on one's own, with host family, in residences.
Costs (2004) • One term: $19,700; includes tuition, housing, all meals, excursions, international airfare, books and class materials, international student ID. $45 application fee. $2500 nonrefundable deposit required. Financial aid available for all students: scholarships, loans, need-based grants, some federal and home institution aid.
For More Information • Mr. David Lamitie, Assistant Director, Admissions, International Honors Program, Boston University, 232 Bay State Road, Fifth Floor, Boston, MA 02215; *Phone:* 617-353-9888; *Fax:* 617-353-5402. *E-mail:* info@ihp.edu. *World Wide Web:* http://www.ihp.edu/

INTERNATIONAL HONORS PROGRAM
CITIES IN THE 21ST CENTURY 2

Academic Focus • Anthropology, economics, environmental science/studies, interdisciplinary studies, international affairs, political science and government, sociology, urban studies, urban/regional planning.
Program Information • Program takes place in Rio de Janiero, Brazil; Paris, France; Cape Town, South Africa. Faculty members are drawn from the sponsor's U.S. staff and local instructors hired by the sponsor. Scheduled travel; field trips to national parks, cities, NGOs, public/government agencies; optional travel to South Africa at an extra cost.
Sessions • Spring.

Eligibility Requirements • Minimum age 18; open to sophomores, juniors, seniors, adults; 2 letters of recommendation; good academic standing at home school; no foreign language proficiency required.
Living Arrangements • Students live in host institution dormitories, host family homes. Meals are taken as a group, on one's own, with host family, in residences.
Costs (2004-2005) • One term: $19,700; includes tuition, housing, all meals, excursions, international airfare, books and class materials, international student ID. $45 application fee. $2500 nonrefundable deposit required. Financial aid available for all students: scholarships, loans, need-based grants, some federal and home institution aid.
For More Information • Mr. David Lamitie, Assistant Director, Admissions, International Honors Program, Boston University/International Honors Program, 232 Bay State Road, Fifth Floor, Boston, MA 02215; *Phone:* 617-353-9888; *Fax:* 617-353-5402. *E-mail:* info@ihp.edu. *World Wide Web:* http://www.ihp.edu/

INTERNATIONAL HONORS PROGRAM
CITIES IN THE 21ST CENTURY 1

Academic Focus • Anthropology, economics, environmental science/studies, interdisciplinary studies, international affairs, political science and government, sociology, urban studies, urban/regional planning.
Program Information • Program takes place in Beijing, China; Shanghai, China; Bangalore, India; Auckland, New Zealand. Faculty members are drawn from the sponsor's U.S. staff and local instructors hired by the sponsor. Scheduled travel to India, South Africa, Brazil; field trips to national parks, cities, NGOs, public/government agencies; optional travel at an extra cost.
Sessions • Spring.
Eligibility Requirements • Minimum age 18; open to sophomores, juniors, seniors, adults; 2 letters of recommendation; good academic standing at home school; no foreign language proficiency required.
Living Arrangements • Students live in host institution dormitories, host family homes. Meals are taken as a group, on one's own, with host family, in residences.
Costs (2004-2005) • One term: $19,700; includes tuition, housing, all meals, excursions, international airfare, books and class materials, international student ID. $45 application fee. $2500 nonrefundable deposit required. Financial aid available for all students: scholarships, loans, need-based grants, some federal and home institution aid.
For More Information • Mr. David Lamitie, Assistant Director, Admissions, International Honors Program, Boston University/International Honors Program, 232 Bay State Road, Fifth Floor, Boston, MA 02215; *Phone:* 617-353-9888; *Fax:* 617-353-5402. *E-mail:* info@ihp.edu. *World Wide Web:* http://www.ihp.edu/

INTERNATIONAL HONORS PROGRAM
GLOBAL HEALTH AND COMMUNITY

Academic Focus • Anthropology, biological/life sciences, cultural studies, economics, environmental health, health-care management, international affairs, political science and government, public health, sociology.
Program Information • Program takes place in Cuba; India; South Africa. Faculty members are drawn from the sponsor's U.S. staff and local instructors hired by the sponsor. Scheduled travel; field trips to villages, NGOs, public/government agencies; optional travel at an extra cost.
Sessions • Spring.
Eligibility Requirements • Minimum age 18; open to sophomores, juniors, seniors, graduate students, adults; 2 letters of recommendation; good academic standing at home school; no foreign language proficiency required.
Living Arrangements • Students live in host institution dormitories, host family homes. Meals are taken as a group, on one's own, with host family, in residences.
Costs (2004-2005) • One term: $19,700; includes tuition, housing, all meals, excursions, international airfare, books and class materials, international student ID. $45 application fee. $2500 nonrefundable deposit required. Financial aid available for all students: scholarships, loans, need-based grants, some federal and home institution aid.

For More Information • Mr. David Lamitie, Assistant Director, Admissions, International Honors Program, 232 Bay State Road, Fifth Floor, Boston, MA 02215; *Phone:* 617-353-9888; *Fax:* 617-353-5402. *E-mail:* info@ihp.edu. *World Wide Web:* http://www.ihp.edu/

INTERNATIONAL HONORS PROGRAM
INDIGENOUS PERSPECTIVES

Academic Focus • Aboriginal studies, anthropology, ecology, environmental science/studies, intercultural studies, interdisciplinary studies, political science and government, sociology.
Program Information • Program takes place in India; Mexico; New Zealand. Faculty members are drawn from the sponsor's U.S. staff and local instructors hired by the sponsor. Scheduled travel to local villages; field trips to national parks, small villages, rainforests, fisheries; optional travel at an extra cost.
Sessions • Fall.
Eligibility Requirements • Minimum age 18; open to sophomores, juniors, seniors, adults; 2 letters of recommendation; good academic standing at home school; no foreign language proficiency required.
Living Arrangements • Students live in host institution dormitories, host family homes. Meals are taken as a group, on one's own, with host family, in residences.
Costs (2004-2005) • One term: $19,700; includes tuition, housing, some meals, excursions, international airfare, books and class materials, international student ID. $45 application fee. $2500 nonrefundable deposit required. Financial aid available for all students: scholarships, loans, need-based grants, some federal and home institution aid.
For More Information • Mr. David Lamitie, Assistant Director, Admissions, International Honors Program, Boston University, 232 Bay Side Road, Fifth floor, Boston, MA 02215; *Phone:* 617-353-9888; *Fax:* 617-353-5402. *E-mail:* info@ihp.edu. *World Wide Web:* http://www.ihp.edu/

INTERNATIONAL HONORS PROGRAM
RETHINKING GLOBALIZATION: NATURE, CULTURE, JUSTICE

Academic Focus • Anthropology, conservation studies, ecology, economics, environmental science/studies, interdisciplinary studies, international affairs, political science and government, science, sociology.
Program Information • Program takes place in India; Mexico; New Zealand; Tanzania; England. Faculty members are drawn from the sponsor's U.S. staff and local instructors hired by the sponsor. Scheduled travel to England, New Zealand, Tanzania, India, Mexico; field trips to national parks, small villages, rainforests, fisheries; optional travel to India, Mexico, New Zealand at an extra cost.
Sessions • Yearlong.
Eligibility Requirements • Minimum age 18; open to sophomores, juniors, seniors, adults; 2 letters of recommendation; good academic standing at home school; no foreign language proficiency required.
Living Arrangements • Students live in host institution dormitories, host family homes. Meals are taken as a group, on one's own, with host family, in residences.
Costs (2002-2003) • Yearlong program: $34,500; includes tuition, housing, all meals, excursions, international airfare, books and class materials, international student ID. $45 application fee. $2500 nonrefundable deposit required. Financial aid available for all students: scholarships, loans, need-based grants, some federal and home institution aid.
For More Information • Mr. David Lamitie, Assistant Director, Admissions, International Honors Program, Boston University, 232 Bay State Road, Fifth Floor, Boston, MA 02215; *Phone:* 617-353-9888; *Fax:* 617-353-5402. *E-mail:* info@ihp.edu. *World Wide Web:* http://www.ihp.edu/

THE INTERNATIONAL PARTNERSHIP FOR SERVICE LEARNING
MASTER'S DEGREE IN INTERNATIONAL SERVICE

Hosted by University of Surrey Roehampton, Autonomous University of Guadalajara, University of Technology
Academic Focus • Community service, public administration, social services.

Program Information • Students attend classes at University of Technology (Kingston, Jamaica), Autonomous University of Guadalajara (Guadalajara, Mexico), University of Surrey Roehampton (London, England). Field trips.
Sessions • Fall in Jamaica, fall in Mexico, England in spring.
Eligibility Requirements • Open to graduate students; 2 letters of recommendation; 2 years college course work in Spanish (for Mexico term only).
Living Arrangements • Students live in host institution dormitories, host family homes. Meals are taken with host family, in residences.
Costs (2003-2004) • Yearlong program: $32,400; includes tuition, housing, some meals, excursions, student support services, service placement and supervision. $50 application fee. $250 refundable deposit required. Financial aid available for all students: scholarships, federal financial aid.
For More Information • Ms. Ilana Golin, Coordinator of Student Programs, The International Partnership for Service Learning, 815 Second Avenue, Suite 315, New York, NY 10017-4594; *Phone:* 212-986-0989; *Fax:* 212-986-5039. *E-mail:* info@ipsl.org. *World Wide Web:* http://www.ipsl.org/

INTERNATIONAL STUDIES ABROAD
MULTI-COUNTRY PROGRAM

Hosted by International University 'Menéndez Pelayo'–Seville, University of Belgrano, University of Guanajuato
Academic Focus • History, international business, Spanish language and literature.
Program Information • Students attend classes at University of Belgrano (Buenos Aires, Argentina), International University 'Menéndez Pelayo'–Seville (Seville, Spain), University of Guanajuato (Guanajuato, Mexico). Scheduled travel to Mexico City, Madrid, Toledo, Colonia del Sacramento, Leon; field trips to El Tigre, Colonia del Sacramento, Jerez de la Frontera, Italica, Granada, San Miguel de Ateude, Teotihuacan.
Sessions • Fall, spring.
Eligibility Requirements • Minimum age 18; open to freshmen, sophomores, juniors, seniors, adults; 2.5 GPA; 1 letter of recommendation; good academic standing at home school; transcript; minimum 2.5 GPA or 2 letters of recommendation; 1 year of college course work in Spanish.
Living Arrangements • Students live in host family homes, hotels. Quarters are shared with host institution students. Meals are taken with host family, in residences.
Costs (2004-2005) • One term: $11,000; includes tuition, housing, all meals, insurance, excursions, laundry service, ground transportation, tutors, Internet access. $200 deposit required. Financial aid available for all students: scholarships, loans, U.S. federal financial aid.
For More Information • Ms. Krista House, Study Abroad Coordinator, International Studies Abroad, 901 West 24th Street, Austin, TX 78705; *Phone:* 800-580-8826; *Fax:* 512-480-8866. *E-mail:* isa@studiesabroad.com. *World Wide Web:* http://www.studiesabroad.com/

LAKE FOREST COLLEGE
PROGRAM IN GREECE AND TURKEY

Held at Arcadia Center for Mediterranean and Balkan Studies and Research
Academic Focus • Archaeology, art, classics and classical languages, cultural studies, Greek studies.
Program Information • Classes are held on the campus of Arcadia Center for Mediterranean and Balkan Studies and Research (Athens, Greece). Faculty members are drawn from the sponsor's U.S. staff and local instructors hired by the sponsor. Scheduled travel to Seljuk, Turkey, Santorini, Peloponnese, Crete, Thessaloniki; field trips to Delphi, Mykonos.
Sessions • Spring.
Eligibility Requirements • Open to sophomores, juniors, seniors; course work in classics, literature, art or fine arts; 2.7 GPA; 2 letters of recommendation; good academic standing at home school; statement; prerequisite course for students with no previous background in classical studies; no foreign language proficiency required.

Living Arrangements • Students live in hotels. Meals are taken on one's own, in restaurants.
Costs (2003) • One term: $14,200 ($18,800 with prerequisite course); includes tuition, housing, all meals, excursions, books and class materials. $20 application fee. $250 nonrefundable deposit required. Financial aid available for students from sponsoring institution: scholarships, loans.
For More Information • Prof. Janet McCracken, Chairperson, Program in Greece and Turkey, Lake Forest College, 555 North Sheridan Road, Lake Forest, IL 60045-2399; *Phone:* 847-735-5185; *Fax:* 847-735-6291. *E-mail:* greece@lfc.edu. *World Wide Web:* http://www.lakeforest.edu/

LONG ISLAND UNIVERSITY
FRIENDS WORLD PROGRAM IN COMPARATIVE RELIGION AND CULTURE

Hosted by Friends World Center, Friends World Center, Friends World Center, Friends World Center, Friends World Center
Academic Focus • Cultural studies, East Asian studies, Indian studies, interdisciplinary studies, Middle Eastern studies, peace and conflict studies, religious studies.
Program Information • Students attend classes at Friends World Center (Jerusalem, Israel), Friends World Center (Jerusalem, Israel), Friends World Center (Jerusalem, Israel), Friends World Center (Jerusalem, Israel), Friends World Center (Jerusalem, Israel). Scheduled travel to yoga ashrams, monasteries, meditation centers, intentional communities; field trips to local religious sites, cultural sites; optional travel to Thailand, Nepal.
Sessions • Yearlong.
Eligibility Requirements • Minimum age 18; open to sophomores, juniors, seniors, adults; 2.8 GPA; good academic standing at home school; interview; essay; no foreign language proficiency required.
Living Arrangements • Students live in host institution dormitories, hotels. Quarters are shared with host institution students. Meals are taken as a group, on one's own, in restaurants.
Costs (2003-2004) • Yearlong program: $31,000 (estimated); includes tuition, housing, all meals, excursions, international airfare, books and class materials, student support services. $30 application fee. $200 deposit required. Financial aid available for students from sponsoring institution: scholarships, loans, need-based grants.
For More Information • Friend's World Admissions, Long Island University, 239 Montauk Highway, Southampton, NY 11968; *Phone:* 631-287-8474; *Fax:* 631-287-8463. *E-mail:* fw@liu.edu. *World Wide Web:* http://www.southampton.liu.edu/fw/

NORTHWOOD UNIVERSITY
TERM IN EUROPE

Academic Focus • Full curriculum.
Program Information • Program takes place in Prague, Czech Republic; Stuttgart, Germany; Paris, France; Athens, Greece; Budapest, Hungary; Florence, Italy; Rome, Italy. Faculty members are drawn from the sponsor's U.S. staff. Scheduled travel to museums, historic sites, cultural sites; field trips; optional travel to a venue of the student's choice at an extra cost.
Sessions • Fall.
Eligibility Requirements • Open to juniors, seniors; 3.0 GPA; 1 letter of recommendation; good academic standing at home school; no foreign language proficiency required.
Living Arrangements • Students live in host family homes, hotels. Meals are taken on one's own, in restaurants.
Costs (2003) • One term: $8500; includes tuition, housing, some meals, international airfare, books and class materials, student support services, some excursions. $200 refundable deposit required. Financial aid available for students from sponsoring institution: scholarships, loans, state and federal financial aid.
For More Information • Dr. Robert Serum, Vice President, Academics, Northwood University, 4000 Whiting Drive, Midland, MI 48640; *Phone:* 989-837-4327; *Fax:* 989-837-4247. *E-mail:* dickl@northwood.edu. *World Wide Web:* http://www.northwood.edu/scr/studyabroad/

O'NEILL NATIONAL THEATER INSTITUTE
O'NEILL NATIONAL THEATER INSTITUTE

Hosted by National Theatre Institute–Moscow (Moscow, Russia), National Theatre Institute–Stratford-upon-Avon (Stratford-upon-Avon, England)

Academic Focus • Creative writing, dance, drama/theater, performing arts.

Program Information • Students attend classes at National Theatre Institute–Moscow (Moscow, Russia), National Theatre Institute–Stratford-upon-Avon (Stratford-upon-Avon, England). Scheduled travel to Moscow, England; field trips to Bath, Birmingham, London.

Sessions • Fall, spring.

Eligibility Requirements • Minimum age 18; open to freshmen, sophomores, juniors, seniors, graduate students, adults; major in theater studies; course work in theater; 2.5 GPA; 2 letters of recommendation; good academic standing at home school; personal interview; résumé; essay; no foreign language proficiency required.

Living Arrangements • Students live in host institution dormitories. Quarters are shared with host institution students. Meals are taken as a group, in central dining facility, in restaurants.

Costs (2004) • One term: $14,200; includes tuition, housing, all meals, excursions, international airfare, student support services. $40 application fee. $800 nonrefundable deposit required. Financial aid available for all students: scholarships, loans.

For More Information • Kato McNickle, Director of College Relations and International Programs, O'Neill National Theater Institute, 305 Great Neck Road, Waterford, CT 06385; *Phone:* 860-443-7139; *Fax:* 860-443-9653. *E-mail:* kjmcn@conncoll.edu. *World Wide Web:* http://nti.conncoll.edu/

ST. OLAF COLLEGE
GLOBAL SEMESTER

Hosted by Yonsei University Seoul, The Chinese University of Hong Kong, American University in Cairo

Academic Focus • Art, economics, history, interdisciplinary studies, religious studies, sociology.

Program Information • Students attend classes at The Chinese University of Hong Kong (Hong Kong, China), American University in Cairo (Cairo, Egypt), Yonsei University Seoul (Seoul, Korea). Classes are also held on the campus of Ecumenical Christian Centre (Bangalore, India). Scheduled travel to Geneva, Istanbul, Shanghai, Beijing, Bangkok, Mumbai, New Delhi; field trips to Luxor, Mysore, Mumbai; optional travel to Israel at an extra cost.

Sessions • Fall.

Eligibility Requirements • Open to sophomores, juniors, seniors; 3 letters of recommendation; good academic standing at home school; interview; no foreign language proficiency required.

Living Arrangements • Students live in host institution dormitories, locally rented apartments, hotels. Meals are taken as a group, in central dining facility.

Costs (2003) • One term: $21,125; includes tuition, housing, some meals, excursions, international airfare, international student ID, transportation between program locations. $75 application fee. $150 nonrefundable deposit required. Financial aid available for students from sponsoring institution: scholarships, loans.

For More Information • Mr. Patrick Quade, Director, International and Off-Campus Studies, St. Olaf College, 1520 St. Olaf Avenue, Northfield, MN 55057; *Phone:* 507-646-3069; *Fax:* 507-646-3789. *E-mail:* quade@stolaf.edu. *World Wide Web:* http://www.stolaf.edu/services/iso/

ST. OLAF COLLEGE
TERM IN ASIA

Hosted by Vietnam National University, The Chinese University of Hong Kong, Chiang Mai University

Academic Focus • Art, history, political science and government, sociology, Thai.

Program Information • Students attend classes at The Chinese University of Hong Kong (Hong Kong, China), Chiang Mai University (Chiang Mai, Thailand), Vietnam National University (Hanoi, Vietnam). Scheduled travel to Shanghai, Beijing, Xi'an, Guilin, Bangkok, Vietnam; field trips to the hill tribes in Thailand; optional travel to Cambodia at an extra cost.

Sessions • Fall.

Eligibility Requirements • Open to sophomores, juniors, seniors; 3 letters of recommendation; good academic standing at home school; interview; no foreign language proficiency required.

Living Arrangements • Students live in host institution dormitories, locally rented apartments, host family homes, hotels, hostels. Meals are taken with host family.

Costs (2003) • One term: $18,725; includes tuition, housing, some meals, excursions, international airfare, international student ID, travel between program locations. $75 application fee. $150 nonrefundable deposit required. Financial aid available for students from sponsoring institution: scholarships, loans.

For More Information • Mr. Patrick Quade, Director, International and Off-Campus Studies, St. Olaf College, 1520 St. Olaf Avenue, Northfield, MN 55057; *Phone:* 507-646-3069; *Fax:* 507-646-3789. *E-mail:* quade@stolaf.edu. *World Wide Web:* http://www.stolaf.edu/services/iso/

ST. OLAF COLLEGE
TERM IN THE MIDDLE EAST

Hosted by University Cadi Ayyad Marrakech, Bosphorus University, American University in Cairo

Academic Focus • History, interdisciplinary studies, political science and government, religious studies, sociology.

Program Information • Students attend classes at American University in Cairo (Cairo, Egypt), University Cadi Ayyad Marrakech (Marrakech, Morocco), Bosphorus University (Istanbul, Turkey). Classes are also held on the campus of Lutheran Hostel (Jerusalem, Israel). Scheduled travel to Sinai, Rabat, Morocco, Cappadocia; field trips to Alexandria.

Sessions • Fall.

Eligibility Requirements • Open to sophomores, juniors, seniors; 3 letters of recommendation; interview; no foreign language proficiency required.

Living Arrangements • Students live in host institution dormitories, locally rented apartments, hostels. Meals are taken as a group, in central dining facility, in restaurants.

Costs (2003) • One term: $21,025; includes tuition, housing, some meals, excursions, international airfare, international student ID. $75 application fee. $150 nonrefundable deposit required. Financial aid available for students from sponsoring institution: scholarships, loans.

For More Information • Mr. Patrick Quade, Director, International Studies, St. Olaf College, 1520 St. Olaf Avenue, Northfield, MN 55057; *Phone:* 507-646-3069; *Fax:* 507-646-3789. *E-mail:* quade@stolaf.edu. *World Wide Web:* http://www.stolaf.edu/services/iso/

SANN RESEARCH INSTITUTE
SEMESTER IN ASIA

Hosted by International College Beijing (Beijing, China), Eastern Asia University, South-East Asia University, Sann Research Institute

Academic Focus • Art, Buddhist studies, Chinese studies, Nepali, Nepali studies, political science and government, religious studies.

Program Information • Students attend classes at International College Beijing (Beijing, China), Sann Research Institute (Kathmandu, Nepal), Eastern Asia University (Patum Thani, Thailand), South-East Asia University (Bangkok, Thailand). Classes are also held on the campus of (Banaras, India). Scheduled travel to villages, trekking, a safari, Tibet; field trips to historic, traditional, and cultural sites related to study; optional travel to Thailand, other Asian "in-between" countries at an extra cost.

Sessions • Fall, spring.

Eligibility Requirements • Minimum age 18; open to freshmen, sophomores, juniors, seniors, graduate students, adults; 2.5 GPA; good health; no foreign language proficiency required.

Living Arrangements • Students live in host institution dormitories, host family homes. Meals are taken as a group, with host family, in residences.

Costs (2003-2004) • One term: $11,500; includes tuition, housing, all meals, excursions, international airfare. $475 application fee. $500 refundable deposit required.

For More Information • Narayan Shrestha, President, Sann Research Institute, 948 Pearl Street, Boulder, CO 80302; *Phone:* 303-449-4279; *Fax:* 303-440-7328. *E-mail:* info@sannr.com. *World Wide Web:* http://www.sannr.com/

SCHOOL FOR INTERNATIONAL TRAINING, SIT STUDY ABROAD
THE BALKANS: GENDER, TRANSFORMATION, AND CIVIL SOCIETY

Academic Focus • Croatian, economics, European studies, history, international affairs, peace and conflict studies, political science and government, Serbian, social sciences, women's studies.
Program Information • Program takes place in Zagreb, Croatia. Faculty members are drawn from the sponsor's U.S. staff and local instructors hired by the sponsor. Scheduled travel to Slovenia, Bosnia, Serbia; field trips.
Sessions • Fall, spring.
Eligibility Requirements • Open to sophomores, juniors, seniors; 2.5 GPA; 2 letters of recommendation; good academic standing at home school; no foreign language proficiency required.
Living Arrangements • Students live in host family homes, hotels. Meals are taken as a group, on one's own, with host family, in residences, in restaurants.
Costs (2003-2004) • One term: $12,050; includes tuition, housing, all meals, insurance, excursions, international student ID. $50 application fee. $400 nonrefundable deposit required. Financial aid available for all students: scholarships.
For More Information • School for International Training, SIT Study Abroad, Kipling Road, Brattleboro, VT 05302-0676; *Phone:* 888-272-7881; *Fax:* 802-258-3296. *E-mail:* studyabroad@sit.edu. *World Wide Web:* http://www.sit.edu/studyabroad/

SCHOOL FOR INTERNATIONAL TRAINING, SIT STUDY ABROAD
TIBETAN STUDIES

Academic Focus • Anthropology, Buddhist studies, economics, geography, history, liberal studies, political science and government, refugee studies, religious studies, Tibetan, visual and performing arts.
Program Information • Program takes place in Dharmsala, India; Kathmandu, Nepal. Faculty members are drawn from the sponsor's U.S. staff and local instructors hired by the sponsor. Scheduled travel to Tibet, Dolpo/Mustang region; field trips to monasteries, art performances, government offices, sacred sites.
Sessions • Fall, spring.
Eligibility Requirements • Open to sophomores, juniors, seniors; 2.5 GPA; 2 letters of recommendation; good academic standing at home school; no foreign language proficiency required.
Living Arrangements • Students live in host family homes, hotels, campsites. Meals are taken as a group, on one's own, with host family, in residences, in restaurants.
Costs (2003-2004) • One term: $12,825; includes tuition, housing, all meals, insurance, excursions. $50 application fee. $400 nonrefundable deposit required. Financial aid available for all students: scholarships.
For More Information • School for International Training, SIT Study Abroad, Kipling Road, Brattleboro, VT 05302-0676; *Phone:* 888-272-7881; *Fax:* 802-258-3296. *E-mail:* studyabroad@sit.edu. *World Wide Web:* http://www.sit.edu/studyabroad/

SEMESTER AT SEA, INSTITUTE FOR SHIPBOARD EDUCATION
SEMESTER AT SEA

Held aboard the S.S. Universe Explorer
Academic Focus • Anthropology, art, biological/life sciences, economics, English, geography, history, marine sciences, music, performing arts, philosophy, political science and government, psychology, religious studies, sociology.
Program Information • Classes are held aboard the S.S. Universe Explorer (At Sea). Faculty members are drawn from the sponsor's U.S. staff. Scheduled travel to Osaka, Shanghai, Hong Kong, Rangoun, Madras, Mombasa, Cape Town, Salvador; field trips to museums, local universities, businesses, religious sites, historical sites; optional travel to the Taj Mahal, Madras, pyramids in Egypt, Shanghai, Hong Kong, Cambodia, Ho Chi Minh City at an extra cost.
Sessions • Fall, spring.
Eligibility Requirements • Minimum age 18; open to freshmen, sophomores, juniors, seniors, adults; good academic standing at

home school; essay; completion of 1 full-time college term; no foreign language proficiency required.
Living Arrangements • Students live in the S. S. Universe Explorer. Meals are taken on one's own, in central dining facility.
Costs (2003-2004) • One term: $14,975; includes tuition, housing, some meals, insurance, student support services. $35 application fee. $1000 refundable deposit required. Financial aid available for all students: scholarships, work study, loans, grants.
For More Information • Mr. Paul Watson, Director of Enrollment Management, Semester at Sea, Institute for Shipboard Education, 811 William Pitt Union, Pittsburgh, PA 15260; *Phone:* 800-854-0195; *Fax:* 412-648-2298. *E-mail:* info@semesteratsea.com. *World Wide Web:* http://www.semesteratsea.com/

UNIVERSITY OF ILLINOIS AT URBANA-CHAMPAIGN
ART AND DESIGN IN GREAT BRITAIN

Hosted by Goldsmiths College, University of London, Central Saint Martins College of Art and Design, Glasgow School of Art, University of Wolverhampton, University of Northumbria at Newcastle, Norwich School of Art and Design, Camberwell College of Arts
Academic Focus • Art, art history, ceramics and pottery, commercial art, costume design, design and applied arts, drawing/painting, fashion design, fine/studio arts, industrial design, interior design, photography.
Program Information • Students attend classes at Goldsmiths College, University of London (London, England), Central Saint Martins College of Art and Design (London, England), University of Wolverhampton (Wolverhampton, England), University of Northumbria at Newcastle (Newcastle upon Tyne, England), Norwich School of Art and Design (Norwich, England), Camberwell College of Arts (London, England), Glasgow School of Art (Glasgow, Scotland).
Sessions • Fall, spring, yearlong.
Eligibility Requirements • Open to sophomores, juniors, seniors, graduate students; major in art, design; course work in foundation courses in art or design; 3.0 GPA; 2 letters of recommendation; good academic standing at home school; slides of work.
Living Arrangements • Students live in host institution dormitories, locally rented apartments. Quarters are shared with host institution students. Meals are taken on one's own, in residences, in central dining facility, in restaurants.
Costs (2003-2004) • One term: $5963–$9615 for fall term; $5963–$15,399 for spring. Yearlong program: $10,100–$23,354; includes tuition, housing, student support services, medical emergency evacuation insurance. $55 application fee. $500 nonrefundable deposit required. Financial aid available for students from sponsoring institution: scholarships, loans.
For More Information • Ms. Fiona Griswold, Assistant Director, Programs in the U.K. and Ireland, University of Illinois at Urbana-Champaign, Study Abroad Office, 910 South Fifth Street, #115, Champaign, IL 61820; *Phone:* 217-333-6322; *Fax:* 217-244-0249. *E-mail:* sao@uiuc.edu. *World Wide Web:* http://www.ips.uiuc.edu/sao/index.shtml

UNIVERSITY OF KANSAS
HUMANITIES AND WESTERN CIVILIZATION IN FLORENCE, ITALY AND PARIS, FRANCE

Held at ACCENT Paris Center, ACCENT Florence Center
Academic Focus • Art history, civilization studies, European studies.
Program Information • Classes are held on the campus of ACCENT Paris Center (Paris, France), ACCENT Florence Center (Florence, Italy). Faculty members are drawn from the sponsor's U.S. staff. Scheduled travel to Rome, Brittany, Normandy; field trips to Siena, Chartres, Ravenna, Amiens.
Sessions • Fall, spring.
Eligibility Requirements • Minimum age 18; open to sophomores, juniors, seniors; 2.75 GPA; 2 letters of recommendation; good academic standing at home school; autobiographical essay; statement of purpose essay; no foreign language proficiency required.
Living Arrangements • Students live in host institution dormitories, locally rented apartments. Meals are taken on one's own, in residences, in central dining facility, in restaurants.

Costs (2003-2004) • One term: $10,290; includes tuition, housing, some meals, excursions, international student ID, student support services, 5-day rail pass, emergency evacuation and repatriation services, Metro Pass for Paris, rental of some required texts. $38 application fee. $300 nonrefundable deposit required. Financial aid available for students from sponsoring institution: scholarships, loans.

For More Information • Mr. Roland Pritchett, Senior Program Coordinator, University of Kansas, Office of Study Abroad, Lippincott Hall, 1410 Jayhawk Boulevard, Room 108, Lawrence, KS 66045-7515; *Phone:* 785-864-3742; *Fax:* 785-864-5040. *E-mail:* osa@ku.edu. *World Wide Web:* http://www.ku.edu/~osa/

UP WITH PEOPLE
WORLDSMART LEADERSHIP PROGRAM

Academic Focus • Communications, international affairs, peace and conflict studies, speech pathology.

Program Information • Faculty members are drawn from the sponsor's U.S. staff. Scheduled travel to Japan, Europe; field trips to tourist sites.

Sessions • Fall, spring.

Eligibility Requirements • Minimum age 18; open to freshmen, sophomores, juniors, seniors, graduate students, adults; 2 letters of recommendation; good academic standing at home school; leadership experience, community service/volunteer experience; no foreign language proficiency required.

Living Arrangements • Students live in host family homes. Meals are taken with host family, in residences.

Costs (2005) • One term: $14,500–$14,900; includes tuition, housing, some meals, excursions, student support services, ground transportation during program, international airfare during program. $50 application fee. $1000 nonrefundable deposit required. Financial aid available for all students: scholarships, loans.

For More Information • Program Admissions, Up With People, 1675 Broadway, Suite 1460, Denver, CO 80202; *Phone:* +303 460-7100 Ext. 108; *Fax:* +303 225-4649. *E-mail:* apply@worldsmart.org. *World Wide Web:* http://www.worldsmart.org/

WHITWORTH COLLEGE
BRITISH ISLES STUDY PROGRAM

Academic Focus • Art, British studies, history, literature.

Program Information • Program takes place in Ireland; England; Northern Ireland; Scotland; Wales. Faculty members are drawn from the sponsor's U.S. staff. Scheduled travel to the Lake District, North Devon, London, Oxford, Ireland.

Sessions • Fall, next offered in fall 2005.

Eligibility Requirements • Open to sophomores, juniors, seniors, adults; 2.5 GPA; 2 letters of recommendation.

Living Arrangements • Students live in host family homes, hotels, bed-and-breakfast facilities. Meals are taken as a group, in residences, in restaurants.

Costs (2003) • One term: contact sponsor for cost. $200 nonrefundable deposit required. Financial aid available for students from sponsoring institution: scholarships, loans.

For More Information • Ms. Sue Jackson, Director, Off-Campus Programs, Whitworth College, Center for International and Multicultural Education, 300 West Hawthorne Road, Spokane, WA 99251-2702; *Phone:* 509-777-4596; *Fax:* 509-777-3723. *E-mail:* sjackson@whitworth.edu. *World Wide Web:* http://www.whitworth.edu/

WHITWORTH COLLEGE
CENTRAL AMERICA SERVICE AND STUDY PROGRAM

Academic Focus • History, Latin American studies, political science and government, Spanish language and literature.

Program Information • Program takes place in Costa Rica; Guatemala; Honduras; Nicaragua. Faculty members are drawn from the sponsor's U.S. staff.

Sessions • Spring, program runs every 3 years.

Eligibility Requirements • Open to sophomores, juniors, seniors; 2.5 GPA; 2 letters of recommendation; 2 years of college course work in Spanish.

Living Arrangements • Students live in host family homes, hotels, bed-and-breakfast facilities. Meals are taken as a group, in residences, in restaurants.

Costs (2004) • One term: contact sponsor for cost. $200 nonrefundable deposit required. Financial aid available for students from sponsoring institution: scholarships, loans.

For More Information • Ms. Sue Jackson, Director, Off-Campus Programs, Whitworth College, Center for International and Multicultural Education, 300 West Hawthorne Road, Spokane, WA 99251-2702; *Phone:* 509-777-4596; *Fax:* 509-777-3723. *E-mail:* sjackson@whitworth.edu. *World Wide Web:* http://www.whitworth.edu/

Programs by Country

AT SEA

CITY TO CITY

SEA EDUCATION ASSOCIATION
SEA SEMESTER—WOODS HOLE, MA

Held aboard the Research Vessel Robert C. Seamans, SSV, Research Vessel Corwith Cramer
Academic Focus • American studies, biological/life sciences, conservation studies, earth sciences, ecology, environmental science/studies, fisheries studies, history, interdisciplinary studies, marine sciences, oceanography, physical sciences, public policy.

Woods Hole SEA Semester

17 ACADEMIC CREDITS

Sea Education Association
P.O. Box 6, Woods Hole, MA 02543
1-800-552-3633
http://www.sea.edu

Program Information • Classes are held aboard the Research Vessel Corwith Cramer (), Research Vessel Robert C. Seamans, SSV (). Faculty members are drawn from the sponsor's U.S. staff. Scheduled travel to the north and south Pacific, the Caribbean, a 6 week stay as crew on an oceanographic research vessel in the North Atlantic; field trips to New Bedford Whaling Museum, Nantucket Whaling Museum.
Sessions • Fall, spring, winter, fall II; spring II.
Eligibility Requirements • Minimum age 18; open to freshmen, sophomores, juniors, seniors, graduate students, adults; 2 letters of recommendation; good academic standing at home school; must be able to remain afloat in water for 30 minutes; no foreign language proficiency required.
Living Arrangements • Students live in program-owned houses, on 134 foot sailing/research vessels. Quarters are shared with host institution students. Meals are taken as a group, in residences.
Costs (2004-2005) • One term: $19,840; includes tuition, housing, some meals, books and class materials, student support services. $35 application fee. $500 nonrefundable deposit required. Financial aid available for all students: scholarships, loans, grants.
For More Information • Ms. Judith M. Froman, Dean of Enrollment, Sea Education Association, Box 6, 171 Woods Hole Road, Woods Hole, MA 02543; *Phone:* 508-540-3954 Ext. 10; *Fax:* 508-457-4673. *E-mail:* admission@sea.edu. *World Wide Web:* http://www.sea.edu/

SEA-MESTER PROGRAMS
SEA-MESTER PROGRAMS

Academic Focus • Community service, marine sciences, oceanography, speech communication.
Program Information • Faculty members are drawn from the sponsor's U.S. staff. Scheduled travel to British Virgin Islands, St. Barts, Saba, St. Kitts, Nevis, Antigua, Montserrat, Guadeloupe, Dominica, Martinique, St. Lucia, St. Vincent, Tobago Cays, Grenadines, Grenada; field trips to British Virgin Islands, St. Barts, Saba, St. Kitts, Nevis, Antigua, Montserrat, Guadeloupe, Dominica, Martinique, St. Lucia, Tobago Cays, Grenadines, Grenada.
Sessions • Fall, spring.
Eligibility Requirements • Minimum age 17; open to freshmen, sophomores, juniors, seniors; 2 letters of recommendation; no foreign language proficiency required.
Living Arrangements • Students live in on an 88 foot schooner or 50 foot sailing yachts. Meals are taken as a group, in central dining facility.
Costs (2004-2005) • One term: $13,500-$14,000; includes tuition, housing, all meals, excursions, books and class materials, lab equipment. $50 application fee. $1200 refundable deposit required.
For More Information • Mr. Mike Meighan, Program Director, Sea-mester Programs, PO Box 5477, Sarasota, FL 34277; *Phone:* 941-924-6789; *Fax:* 941-924-6075. *E-mail:* info@seamester.com. *World Wide Web:* http://www.seamester.com/

ARGENTINA
CITY TO CITY
FLORIDA INTERNATIONAL UNIVERSITY
EXCHANGE PROGRAM WITH UNIVERSITY OF BELGRANO– ARGENTINA

Hosted by University of Belgrano
Academic Focus • Full curriculum.
Program Information • Students attend classes at University of Belgrano (Buenos Aires). Optional travel to anywhere in the country at an extra cost.
Sessions • Fall, spring.

Eligibility Requirements • Open to sophomores, juniors, seniors, graduate students, adults; 3.0 GPA; fluency in Spanish.

Living Arrangements • Students live in host family homes. Meals are taken with host family, in residences.

Costs (2002-2003) • One term: $4800 (estimated); includes housing, all meals, insurance, student support services. $150 application fee. Financial aid available for all students: scholarships, loans.

For More Information • Office of International Studies, Florida International University, University Park Campus–TT100, Miami, FL 33199; *Phone:* 305-348-1913; *Fax:* 305-348-1941. *E-mail:* ois@fiu.edu. *World Wide Web:* http://ois.fiu.edu/

UNIVERSITY OF MIAMI
UNIVERSIDAD DE SAN ANDRÉS

Hosted by San Andrés University

Academic Focus • Business administration/management, communications, economics, international affairs, political science and government, social sciences, Spanish language and literature.

Program Information • Students attend classes at San Andrés University (Victoria).

Sessions • Fall, spring, yearlong.

Eligibility Requirements • Minimum age 18; open to sophomores, juniors, seniors; 3.0 GPA; 2 letters of recommendation; language evaluation; personal interview; fluency in Spanish.

Living Arrangements • Students live in locally rented apartments, program-owned apartments, host family homes. Quarters are shared with host institution students, students from other programs. Meals are taken on one's own, in central dining facility, in restaurants.

Costs (2003-2004) • One term: $12,919. Yearlong program: $25,838; includes tuition, student support services. $40 application fee. $500 nonrefundable deposit required. Financial aid available for students from sponsoring institution: scholarships, loans.

For More Information • Mr. Chris Tingue, Assistant Director, University of Miami, International Education and Exchange Programs, 5050 Brunson Drive, Allen Hall 212, PO Box 248005, Coral Gables, FL 33124-1610; *Phone:* 305-284-3434; *Fax:* 305-284-4235. *E-mail:* ieep@miami.edu. *World Wide Web:* http://www.studyabroad.miami.edu/

BUENOS AIRES

AMERICAN INSTITUTE FOR FOREIGN STUDY (AIFS)
UNIVERSITY OF BELGRANO, ARGENTINA

Hosted by University of Belgrano

Academic Focus • Art history, economics, history, literature, political science and government, Spanish language and literature.

Program Information • Students attend classes at University of Belgrano. Field trips to Colonia, Iguazú Falls, Uruguay.

Sessions • Fall, spring, yearlong.

Eligibility Requirements • Open to freshmen, sophomores, juniors, seniors; 2.5 GPA; 1 year of college course work in Spanish.

Living Arrangements • Students live in host family homes. Meals are taken with host family, in residences.

Costs (2004-2005) • One term: $8995. Yearlong program: $17,390; includes tuition, housing, some meals, excursions, student support services, outbound flight. $75 application fee. $350 nonrefundable deposit required.

For More Information • Mr. David Mauro, Admissions Advisor, American Institute For Foreign Study (AIFS), 9 West Broad Street, Stamford, CT 06902-3788; *Phone:* 800-727-2437 Ext. 5163; *Fax:* 203-399-5597. *E-mail:* dmauro@aifs.com. *World Wide Web:* http://www.aifsabroad.com/

AMERICAN UNIVERSITY
SEMESTER IN BUENOS AIRES

Hosted by University of Belgrano

Academic Focus • Argentine studies, history, international affairs, international business, Latin American studies, political science and government, Spanish language and literature.

Program Information • Students attend classes at University of Belgrano. Scheduled travel to Patagonia, Uruguay, Iguazú Falls; field trips to Colonia.

Sessions • Fall.

Eligibility Requirements • Open to sophomores, juniors, seniors, graduate students; 2.75 GPA; 1 letter of recommendation; second semester sophomore status; recommendation of advisor; 2 years of college course work in Spanish.

Living Arrangements • Students live in host family homes. Meals are taken with host family, in residences.

Costs (2001) • One term: $16,734; includes tuition, housing, some meals, excursions, books and class materials, international student ID, student support services. $35 application fee. $300 nonrefundable deposit required. Financial aid available for all students: scholarships, loans.

For More Information • Dr. David C. Brown, Dean, Washington Semester and World Capitals Programs, American University, Tenley Campus–Constitution Building, Washington, DC 20016-8083; *Phone:* 800-424-2600; *Fax:* 202-895-4960. *E-mail:* travel@american.edu. *World Wide Web:* http://www.worldcapitals.american.edu/

CIEE
CIEE STUDY CENTER, BUENOS AIRES, ARGENTINA

Hosted by Catholic University of Argentina, University of Buenos Aires, Facultad Latinoamericana de Ciencias Sociales FLACSO

Academic Focus • Communications, economics, education, history, international affairs, library science, literature, political science and government, sociology, Spanish language and literature.

Program Information • Students attend classes at Catholic University of Argentina, University of Buenos Aires, Facultad Latinoamericana de Ciencias Sociales FLACSO. Scheduled travel to Córdoba; field trips to Tigre, city tours, museums, concerts; optional travel to Iguazú Falls, Jujuy, Chile, Montevideo, Patagonia at an extra cost.

Sessions • Fall, spring, yearlong.

Eligibility Requirements • Minimum age 18; open to sophomores, juniors, seniors, graduate students, adults; course work in social science, Latin American studies; 2.75 GPA; 2 letters of recommendation; 3 years of college course work in Spanish.

Living Arrangements • Students live in host institution dormitories, host family homes. Quarters are shared with host institution students. Meals are taken on one's own, with host family, in residences, in central dining facility.

Costs (2004-2005) • One term: $9600. Yearlong program: $17,500; includes tuition, housing, some meals, insurance, excursions, student support services, computer and library access at host institution, pre-departure advising. $30 application fee. $300 deposit required. Financial aid available for all students: minority student scholarships, travel grants.

For More Information • Ms. Ellen Whitman, Admissions Officer, Spain and Latin America, CIEE, 7 Custom House Street, 3rd Floor, Portland, ME 04101; *Phone:* 800-40-STUDY; *Fax:* 207-553-7699. *E-mail:* studyinfo@ciee.org. *World Wide Web:* http://www.ciee.org/isp/

COLLEGE CONSORTIUM FOR INTERNATIONAL STUDIES–CENTRAL WASHINGTON UNIVERSITY
ARGENTINA PROGRAM

Hosted by University of Belgrano

Academic Focus • Argentine studies, comparative history, economics, political science and government, Spanish language and literature.

Program Information • Students attend classes at University of Belgrano. Field trips to local museums, Teatro Colon, La Boca, markets; optional travel to Iguazú Falls, Patagonia at an extra cost.

Sessions • Fall, spring.

Eligibility Requirements • Open to sophomores, juniors, seniors; 2.5 GPA; 3 letters of recommendation; good academic standing at home school; essay; transcript; 0.5 years of college course work in Spanish.

Living Arrangements • Students live in host family homes. Meals are taken with host family, in residences.

ARGENTINA
Buenos Aires

Costs (2005) • One term: $3300; includes tuition, insurance, student support services, airport transfer, half-day city tour. $85 application fee. $300 deposit required. Financial aid available for students from sponsoring institution: scholarships, loans.

For More Information • Ms. Heather Barclay Hamir, Director, Study Abroad and Exchange Programs, College Consortium for International Studies–Central Washington University, OISP/Central Washington University, 400 East 8th Avenue, Ellensburg, WA 98926-7408; *Phone:* 509-963-3612; *Fax:* 509-963-1558. *E-mail:* goabroad@cwu.edu. *World Wide Web:* http://www.ccisabroad.org/. Students may also apply through College Consortium for International Studies, 2000 P Street NW, Suite 503, Washington, DC 20036.

COLLEGE CONSORTIUM FOR INTERNATIONAL STUDIES–CENTRAL WASHINGTON UNIVERSITY
PROGRAM IN BUENOS AIRES, ARGENTINA

Hosted by University of Belgrano

Academic Focus • Latin American studies, Spanish language and literature.

Program Information • Students attend classes at University of Belgrano. Field trips to Teatro Colon, La Boca, markets; optional travel to sites in and around Argentina at an extra cost.

Sessions • Fall, spring.

Eligibility Requirements • Open to sophomores, juniors, seniors; 2.5 GPA; 2 letters of recommendation; good academic standing at home school; 0.5 years of college course work in Spanish.

Living Arrangements • Students live in host family homes. Meals are taken with host family, in residences.

Costs (2005) • One term: $3600; includes tuition, insurance, excursions, student support services, fees. $85 application fee. $300 refundable deposit required. Financial aid available for students from sponsoring institution: scholarships, loans.

For More Information • Ms. Heather Barclay Hamir, Director, Study Abroad and Exchange Programs, College Consortium for International Studies–Central Washington University, 400 East University Way, Ellensburg, WA 98926-7408; *Phone:* 509-963-3612; *Fax:* 509-963-1558. *E-mail:* goabroad@cwu.edu. *World Wide Web:* http://www.ccisabroad.org/

IES, INSTITUTE FOR THE INTERNATIONAL EDUCATION OF STUDENTS
IES–BUENOS AIRES

Hosted by Institute for the International Education of Students (IES)–Buenos Aires, University of Torcuato di Tella–Buenos Aires, University of Buenos Aires

Academic Focus • Argentine studies, business administration/management, economics, history, international affairs, international business, Latin American studies, literature, political science and government, sociology, Spanish language and literature.

Program Information • Students attend classes at University of Torcuato di Tella–Buenos Aires, University of Buenos Aires, Institute for the International Education of Students (IES)–Buenos Aires. Scheduled travel to Fiesta del Ternero, Ayacucho, Chascómus, Luján, Tandil, Colonia; field trips; optional travel to La Rioja, Córdoba at an extra cost.

Sessions • Fall, spring, yearlong.

Eligibility Requirements • Minimum age 18; open to sophomores, juniors, seniors, graduate students, adults; 3.0 GPA; 1 letter of recommendation; good academic standing at home school; no foreign language proficiency required.

Living Arrangements • Students live in host family homes. Meals are taken with host family, in residences, in central dining facility.

Costs (2003-2004) • One term: $9500. Yearlong program: $17,100; includes tuition, housing, some meals, excursions, student support services, partial insurance coverage. $50 application fee. $500 nonrefundable deposit required. Financial aid available for all students: scholarships, institutional partner need-based grants.

For More Information • International Education Representative, IES, Institute for the International Education of Students, 33 North La Salle Street, 15th Floor, Chicago, IL 60602; *Phone:* 800-995-2300; *Fax:* 312-944-1448. *E-mail:* info@iesabroad.org. *World Wide Web:* http://www.IESabroad.org/

INSTITUTE FOR STUDY ABROAD, BUTLER UNIVERSITY
ARGENTINE UNIVERSITIES PROGRAM

Hosted by Catholic University of Argentina, University of Torcuato di Tella–Buenos Aires, Salvador University Buenos Aires, University of Buenos Aires

Academic Focus • Full curriculum.

Program Information • Students attend classes at Catholic University of Argentina, University of Torcuato di Tella–Buenos Aires, Salvador University Buenos Aires, University of Buenos Aires. Field trips to Colonia, Mar del Plata, San Martin de los Andes, Argentina.

Sessions • Fall, spring, yearlong, US academic year.

Eligibility Requirements • Open to sophomores, juniors, seniors; 3.0 GPA; 1 letter of recommendation; good academic standing at home school; enrollment at an accredited American college or university; Spanish language evaluation; 2 years of college course work in Spanish.

Living Arrangements • Students live in host family homes. Meals are taken with host family, in residences.

Costs (2003) • One term: $9445. Yearlong program: $16,695; includes tuition, housing, some meals, excursions, international student ID, student support services, cultural and sporting events, pre-departure advising. $40 application fee. $500 nonrefundable deposit required. Financial aid available for all students: scholarships, travel grants.

For More Information • Institute for Study Abroad, Butler University, 1100 West 42nd Street, Suite 305, Indianapolis, IN 46208-3345; *Phone:* 800-858-0229; *Fax:* 317-940-9704. *E-mail:* copa@butler.edu. *World Wide Web:* http://www.ifsa-butler.org/

INTERNATIONAL STUDIES ABROAD
BUENOS AIRES, ARGENTINA–COURSES WITH ARGENTINE STUDENTS

Hosted by University of Belgrano

Academic Focus • Full curriculum.

Program Information • Students attend classes at University of Belgrano. Field trips to El Tigre, La Plata, Iguazú Falls, Colonia del Sacramento; optional travel to Estancia in Córdoba, Peninsula Valdes, the Andean Northwest, Bariloche.

Sessions • Fall, spring, yearlong, fall 4; spring 4; year 4.

Eligibility Requirements • Minimum age 18; open to freshmen, sophomores, juniors, seniors, graduate students, adults; 2.5 GPA; 1 letter of recommendation; good academic standing at home school; transcript; 2 years of college course work in Spanish.

Living Arrangements • Students live in locally rented apartments, host family homes. Quarters are shared with host institution students. Meals are taken with host family, in residences.

Costs (2004-2005) • One term: $7900–$8900. Yearlong program: $14,950–$15,450; includes tuition, housing, some meals, insurance, excursions, student support services, excursion transportation, Internet access, tutoring, laundry service. $200 deposit required. Financial aid available for all students: scholarships, work study, U.S. federal financial aid.

For More Information • Argentina Site Specialist, International Studies Abroad, 901 West 24th Street, Austin, TX 78705; *Phone:* 800-580-8826; *Fax:* 512-480-8866. *E-mail:* isa@studiesabroad.com. *World Wide Web:* http://www.studiesabroad.com/

INTERNATIONAL STUDIES ABROAD
BUENOS AIRES, ARGENTINA; COURSES WITH ARGENTINE STUDENTS

Hosted by University of Belgrano

Academic Focus • Argentine studies, history, Latin American studies.

Program Information • Students attend classes at University of Belgrano. Field trips to La Plata, Uruquay, Iguazú Falls; optional travel to Bariloche-Patagonia, Peninsula Valdes, Estancia in Córdoba at an extra cost.

Sessions • Fall, spring, yearlong, fall II.

Eligibility Requirements • Minimum age 18; open to freshmen, sophomores, juniors, seniors, graduate students, adults; 2.5 GPA; 1 letter of recommendation; good academic standing at home school; transcript; 2 years of college course work in Spanish.

Living Arrangements • Students live in locally rented apartments, host family homes. Meals are taken with host family, in residences.
Costs (2004-2005) • One term: $7900. Yearlong program: $14,950; includes tuition, housing, all meals, insurance, excursions, student support services, laundry service, tutorial assistance, ground transportation on excursions and from/to airport, Internet access. $200 deposit required. Financial aid available for all students: scholarships, loans, U.S. federal financial aid.
For More Information • Argentina Site Specialist, International Studies Abroad, 901 West 24th Street, Austin, TX 78705; *Phone:* 800-580-8826; *Fax:* 512-480-8866. *E-mail:* isa@studiesabroad.com. *World Wide Web:* http://www.studiesabroad.com/

INTERNATIONAL STUDIES ABROAD
BUENOS AIRES, ARGENTINA–INTENSIVE SPANISH LANGUAGE
Hosted by University of Belgrano
Academic Focus • Spanish language and literature.
Program Information • Students attend classes at University of Belgrano. Field trips to El Tigre, La Plata, Iguazú Falls, Colonia del Sacramento; optional travel to Estancia in Córdoba, Peninsula Valdes, the Andean Northwest.
Sessions • Fall, spring.
Eligibility Requirements • Minimum age 18; open to freshmen, sophomores, juniors, seniors, graduate students, adults; 2.5 GPA; 1 letter of recommendation; good academic standing at home school; transcript; no foreign language proficiency required.
Living Arrangements • Students live in locally rented apartments, host family homes. Quarters are shared with host institution students. Meals are taken with host family, in residences.
Costs (2004-2005) • One term: $6950; includes tuition, housing, some meals, insurance, excursions, student support services, excursion transportation, Internet access, laundry service. $200 deposit required. Financial aid available for all students: scholarships, work study, federal financial aid.

For More Information • Argentina Site Specialist, International Studies Abroad, 901 West 24th Street, Austin, TX 78705; *Phone:* 880-580-8826; *Fax:* 512-480-8866. *E-mail:* isa@studiesabroad.com. *World Wide Web:* http://www.studiesabroad.com/

KNOX COLLEGE
BUENOS AIRES PROGRAM
Hosted by Palermo University Buenos Aires
Academic Focus • Environmental science/studies, history, international affairs, journalism, Latin American studies, peace and conflict studies, political science and government, popular culture, social sciences, Spanish language and literature.
Program Information • Students attend classes at Palermo University Buenos Aires. Scheduled travel to Iguazú Falls, Patagonia, Puerto Madryn; field trips to haciendas, Tigre.
Sessions • Fall.
Eligibility Requirements • Minimum age 18; open to sophomores, juniors, seniors; course work in social sciences (2 courses); 2.5 GPA; 4 letters of recommendation; good academic standing at home school; 2 years of college course work in Spanish.
Living Arrangements • Students live in host family homes. Meals are taken with host family.
Costs (2004-2005) • One term: $10,455; includes tuition, housing, all meals, insurance, excursions, international airfare, student support services, lectures, tickets to opera, theatre, movies and sporting events. $650 nonrefundable deposit required. Financial aid available for all students: scholarships, loans.
For More Information • Prof. Jessie Dixon, Professor of Spanish, Knox College, Box 71, Galesburg, IL 61401-4999; *Phone:* 309-341-7331; *Fax:* 309-341-7824. *E-mail:* argentina@knox.edu. *World Wide Web:* http://www.knox.edu/offcampus/

ARGENTINA
Buenos Aires

LEXIA INTERNATIONAL
LEXIA IN BUENOS AIRES

Hosted by University of Buenos Aires
Academic Focus • Anthropology, area studies, Argentine studies, art, art history, business administration/management, civilization studies, comparative history, cultural studies, drawing/painting, environmental science/studies, ethnic studies, film and media studies, fine/studio arts, geography, history, interdisciplinary studies, international affairs, international business, Latin American literature, Latin American studies, liberal studies, literature, music, music history, music performance, philosophy, political science and government, psychology, religious studies, social sciences, sociology, Spanish language and literature, urban studies, visual and performing arts.
Program Information • Students attend classes at University of Buenos Aires. Field trips to Colonia, La Plata, Montevideo, Estancia.
Sessions • Fall, spring, yearlong.
Eligibility Requirements • Minimum age 18; open to sophomores, juniors, seniors, graduate students, adults; 2.5 GPA; 2 letters of recommendation; no foreign language proficiency required.
Living Arrangements • Students live in host institution dormitories, host family homes. Quarters are shared with host institution students. Meals are taken on one's own, with host family, in residences, in central dining facility, in restaurants.
Costs (2003-2004) • One term: $10,950. Yearlong program: $20,550; includes tuition, housing, some meals, insurance, excursions, international student ID, student support services, computer access, transcript. $35 application fee. $300 refundable deposit required. Financial aid available for all students: scholarships, work study.
For More Information • Lexia International, 23 South Main Street, Hanover, NH 03755; *Phone:* 800-775-3942; *Fax:* 603-643-9899. *E-mail:* info@lexiaintl.org. *World Wide Web:* http://www.lexiaintl. org/

MIDDLEBURY COLLEGE SCHOOLS ABROAD
SCHOOL IN LATIN AMERICA–ARGENTINA PROGRAM

Hosted by University of Torcuato di Tella–Buenos Aires, University of Buenos Aires, Salvador University Buenos Aires
Academic Focus • Full curriculum.
Program Information • Students attend classes at University of Torcuato di Tella–Buenos Aires, University of Buenos Aires, Salvador University Buenos Aires. Field trips.
Sessions • Fall, spring, yearlong.
Eligibility Requirements • Open to sophomores, juniors, seniors; 2.7 GPA; 2 letters of recommendation; 2.5 years college course work in Spanish, including 1 content course at the 300-level.
Living Arrangements • Students live in host family homes. Meals are taken on one's own, with host family.
Costs (2004-2005) • One term: $7200. Yearlong program: $14,400; includes tuition, student support services. $50 application fee. $300 nonrefundable deposit required. Financial aid available for students from sponsoring institution: scholarships, loans.
For More Information • Mr. Jamie Northrup, University Relations Coordinator, Middlebury College Schools Abroad, Office of Off-Campus Study, Sunderland Language Center, Middlebury, VT 05753; *Phone:* 802-443-5745; *Fax:* 802-443-3157. *E-mail:* schoolsabroad@ middlebury.edu. *World Wide Web:* http://www.middlebury.edu/ msa/

SCHOOL FOR INTERNATIONAL TRAINING, SIT STUDY ABROAD
SOUTHERN CONE: REGIONAL INTEGRATION, DEVELOPMENT, AND SOCIAL CHANGE

Academic Focus • Economics, international affairs, Latin American studies, political science and government, sociology, Spanish language and literature.
Program Information • Faculty members are drawn from the sponsor's U.S. staff and local instructors hired by the sponsor. Scheduled travel to Posadas, Argentina, Encarnacion, Ciudad del Este, Paraguay; field trips to Iguazú Falls, Curitiba, Brazil, Colonia, Montevideo, Uruguay.
Sessions • Fall, spring.
Eligibility Requirements • Open to sophomores, juniors, seniors; course work in economics, political economy, or development

studies; 2.5 GPA; 2 letters of recommendation; good academic standing at home school; 1.5 years of college course work in Spanish.
Living Arrangements • Students live in host family homes, hotels. Meals are taken as a group, on one's own, with host family, in residences, in restaurants.
Costs (2003-2004) • One term: $12,800; includes tuition, housing, all meals, insurance, excursions. $50 application fee. $400 nonrefundable deposit required. Financial aid available for all students: scholarships.
For More Information • School for International Training, SIT Study Abroad, Kipling Road, Brattleboro, VT 05302-0676; *Phone:* 888-272-7881; *Fax:* 802-258-3296. *E-mail:* studyabroad@sit.edu. *World Wide Web:* http://www.sit.edu/studyabroad/

STATE UNIVERSITY OF NEW YORK AT PLATTSBURGH
LATIN AMERICAN SOUTHERN CONE PROGRAMS, BUENOS AIRES, WITH MIDDLEBURY COLLEGE

Hosted by Salvador University Buenos Aires
Academic Focus • Full curriculum.
Program Information • Students attend classes at Salvador University Buenos Aires. Field trips to neighborhoods of Buenos Aires; optional travel to Brazil, Iguazú Falls, Patagonia, Punta del Este at an extra cost.
Sessions • Fall, spring, yearlong, South American academic year.
Eligibility Requirements • Minimum age 18; open to sophomores, juniors, seniors, graduate students, adults; 2.5 GPA; 3 letters of recommendation; intermediate-level Spanish.
Living Arrangements • Students live in locally rented apartments, host family homes. Meals are taken on one's own, with host family, in residences, in restaurants.
Costs (2003-2004) • One term: New York residents contact sponsor for cost; $6,995 for nonresidents. Yearlong program: New York residents contact sponsor for cost; $12,995 for nonresidents; includes tuition. $20 application fee. $200 nonrefundable deposit required. Financial aid available for all students: scholarships, loans.
For More Information • Ms. Liz Ross, C.V. Starr-Middlebury School in Latin America, State University of New York at Plattsburgh, Middlebury College, Middlebury, VT 05753; *Phone:* 802-443-5745. *E-mail:* schoolsabroad@middlebury.edu. *World Wide Web:* http:// www.plattsburgh.edu/studyabroad/

UNIVERSITY OF MIAMI
SALVADOR UNIVERSITY, ARGENTINA

Hosted by Salvador University Buenos Aires
Academic Focus • Business administration/management, communications, education, liberal studies, social sciences, Spanish language and literature.
Program Information • Students attend classes at Salvador University Buenos Aires.
Sessions • Fall, spring, yearlong.
Eligibility Requirements • Minimum age 18; open to sophomores, juniors, seniors; 3.0 GPA; 2 letters of recommendation; language evaluation; personal interview; fluency in Spanish.
Living Arrangements • Students live in host institution dormitories, program-owned apartments, host family homes. Quarters are shared with host institution students, students from other programs. Meals are taken on one's own, in central dining facility, in restaurants.
Costs (2003-2004) • One term: $12,919. Yearlong program: $25,838; includes tuition, student support services. $40 application fee. $500 nonrefundable deposit required. Financial aid available for students from sponsoring institution: scholarships, loans.
For More Information • Mr. Chris Tingue, Assistant Director, University of Miami, International Education and Exchange Programs, 5050 Brunson Drive, Allen Hall 212, PO Box 248005, Coral Gables, FL 33124-1610; *Phone:* 305-284-3434; *Fax:* 305-284-4235. *E-mail:* ieep@miami.edu. *World Wide Web:* http://www.studyabroad. miami.edu/

UNIVERSITY OF MIAMI
TORCUATO DI TELLA UNIVERSITY

Hosted by University of Torcuato di Tella–Buenos Aires

Academic Focus • Business administration/management, communications, economics, international affairs, political science and government, social sciences, Spanish language and literature.
Program Information • Students attend classes at University of Torcuato di Tella–Buenos Aires.
Sessions • Fall, spring, yearlong.
Eligibility Requirements • Minimum age 18; open to sophomores, juniors, seniors; 3.0 GPA; 2 letters of recommendation; language evaluation; personal interview; fluency in Spanish.
Living Arrangements • Students live in program-owned apartments, host family homes. Quarters are shared with host institution students, students from other programs. Meals are taken on one's own, in central dining facility, in restaurants.
Costs (2003-2004) • One term: $12,919. Yearlong program: $25,838; includes tuition, student support services. $40 application fee. $500 nonrefundable deposit required. Financial aid available for students from sponsoring institution: scholarships, loans.
For More Information • Mr. Chris Tingue, Assistant Director, University of Miami, International Education and Exchange Programs, 5050 Brunson Drive, Allen Hall 212, PO Box 248005, Coral Gables, FL 33124-1610; *Phone:* 305-284-3434; *Fax:* 305-284-4235. *E-mail:* ieep@miami.edu. *World Wide Web:* http://www.studyabroad. miami.edu/

UNIVERSITY OF MINNESOTA
LANGUAGE AND CULTURE IN BUENOS AIRES

Hosted by Fundación José Ortega y Gasset
Academic Focus • Area studies, economics, history, political science and government, Spanish language and literature.
Program Information • Students attend classes at Fundación José Ortega y Gasset. Field trips to San Isidro, San Antonio de Areco, Luján, Colonia del Sacramento.
Sessions • Fall, spring.
Eligibility Requirements • Minimum age 18; open to freshmen, sophomores, juniors, seniors; 2.5 GPA; no foreign language proficiency required.
Living Arrangements • Students live in locally rented apartments. Quarters are shared with students from other programs. Meals are taken as a group, on one's own, in residences, in central dining facility, in restaurants.
Costs (2004-2005) • One term: contact sponsor for cost. $150 application fee. $400 nonrefundable deposit required. Financial aid available for students from sponsoring institution: scholarships, loans.
For More Information • Learning Abroad Center, University of Minnesota, 230 Heller Hall, 271 19th Avenue South, Minneapolis, MN 55455; *Phone:* 888-700-UOFM; *Fax:* 612-626-8009. *E-mail:* umabroad@umn.edu. *World Wide Web:* http://www.umabroad.umn. edu/

CÓRDOBA
FLORIDA INTERNATIONAL UNIVERSITY
EXCHANGE PROGRAM WITH CATHOLIC UNIVERSITY OF CÓRDOBA

Hosted by Catholic University of Córdoba
Academic Focus • Full curriculum.
Program Information • Students attend classes at Catholic University of Córdoba. Optional travel to anywhere in the country at an extra cost.
Sessions • Fall, spring.
Eligibility Requirements • Open to sophomores, juniors, seniors, graduate students, adults; 3.0 GPA; fluency in Spanish.
Living Arrangements • Students live in host family homes. Meals are taken with host family, in residences.
Costs (2002-2003) • One term: $5600 (estimated); includes housing, all meals, insurance, international airfare, books and class materials, international student ID. $150 application fee. Financial aid available for all students: scholarships, loans.
For More Information • Office of International Studies, Florida International University, University Park Campus–TT100, Miami, FL 33199; *Phone:* 305-348-1913; *Fax:* 305-348-1941. *E-mail:* ois@fiu. edu. *World Wide Web:* http://ois.fiu.edu/

ENTRE RIOS
WALLA WALLA COLLEGE
ADVENTIST COLLEGES ABROAD

Hosted by Rio Plata Adventist University
Academic Focus • Full curriculum, Spanish language and literature.
Program Information • Students attend classes at Rio Plata Adventist University. Scheduled travel to Peru, Buenos Aires, Iguazú Falls, Rio de Janeiro; optional travel at an extra cost.
Sessions • Yearlong.
Eligibility Requirements • Open to freshmen, sophomores, juniors, seniors; 2.5 GPA; 3 letters of recommendation; good academic standing at home school; minimum 3.0 GPA in Spanish; 1 year of college course work in Spanish.
Living Arrangements • Students live in host institution dormitories. Quarters are shared with host institution students, students from other programs. Meals are taken as a group, in central dining facility.
Costs (2002-2003) • Yearlong program: contact sponsor for cost. $100 refundable deposit required. Financial aid available for all students: scholarships, loans.
For More Information • Mr. Jean-Paul Grimaud, Chair of Modern Language Department, Walla Walla College, 204 South College Avenue, College Place, WA 99324; *Phone:* 509-529-7769; *Fax:* 509-527-2253. *E-mail:* grimje@wwc.edu

MENDOZA
INSTITUTE FOR STUDY ABROAD, BUTLER UNIVERSITY
INTERMEDIATE LATIN AMERICAN STUDIES

Hosted by National University of Cuyo
Academic Focus • Latin American studies, Spanish language and literature.
Program Information • Students attend classes at National University of Cuyo. Field trips.
Sessions • Fall, spring.
Eligibility Requirements • Open to sophomores, juniors, seniors; 3.0 GPA; 1 letter of recommendation; good academic standing at home school; enrollment at an accredited American college or university; Spanish language evaluation; 1 year of college course work in Spanish.
Living Arrangements • Students live in host family homes. Meals are taken with host family, in residences.
Costs (2003) • One term: $8035; includes tuition, housing, all meals, excursions, international student ID, student support services, cultural and sporting events, pre-departure advising. $40 application fee. $500 nonrefundable deposit required. Financial aid available for all students: scholarships, travel grants.
For More Information • Institute for Study Abroad, Butler University, 1100 West 42nd Street, Suite 305, Indianapolis, IN 46208-3345; *Phone:* 800-858-0229; *Fax:* 317-940-9704. *E-mail:* copa@butler.edu. *World Wide Web:* http://www.ifsa-butler.org/

INSTITUTE FOR STUDY ABROAD, BUTLER UNIVERSITY
UNIVERSIDAD NACIONAL DE CUYO

Hosted by National University of Cuyo
Academic Focus • Argentine studies, geography, history, philosophy, visual and performing arts.
Program Information • Students attend classes at National University of Cuyo. Field trips.
Sessions • Fall, spring, yearlong, US academic year.
Eligibility Requirements • Open to sophomores, juniors, seniors; 3.0 GPA; 1 letter of recommendation; good academic standing at home school; enrollment at an accredited American college or university; Spanish language evaluation; 2 years of college course work in Spanish.
Living Arrangements • Students live in host family homes. Meals are taken with host family.
Costs (2003) • One term: $8035. Yearlong program: $14,470; includes tuition, housing, all meals, excursions, international student ID, student support services, cultural and sporting events, pre-

ARGENTINA
Mendoza

departure advising. $40 application fee. $500 nonrefundable deposit required. Financial aid available for all students: scholarships, travel grants.

For More Information • Institute for Study Abroad, Butler University, 1100 West 42nd Street, Suite 305, Indianapolis, IN 46208-3345; *Phone:* 800-858-0229; *Fax:* 317-940-9704. *E-mail:* copa@butler.edu. *World Wide Web:* http://www.ifsa-butler.org/

ROSARIO

AHA INTERNATIONAL AN ACADEMIC PROGRAM OF THE UNIVERSITY OF OREGON
ROSARIO ARGENTINA: NORTHWEST COUNCIL ON STUDY ABROAD

Hosted by National University of Rosario
Academic Focus • Argentine studies, art history, business administration/management, history, international business, Latin American literature, Latin American studies, literature, marketing, Spanish language and literature.
Program Information • Students attend classes at National University of Rosario. Scheduled travel to Buenos Aires, Patagonia; field trips to local attractions, Espinillo Island, local "estancia," museums, parks, monuments.
Sessions • Fall, spring.
Eligibility Requirements • Open to sophomores, juniors, seniors; 2.5 GPA; 2 letters of recommendation; good academic standing at home school; 1 term college course work in Spanish or 2 years of high school Spanish.
Living Arrangements • Students live in host family homes. Meals are taken with host family.
Costs (2003-2004) • One term: $6015; includes tuition, housing, all meals, insurance, excursions, books and class materials, student support services, local bus pass. $50 application fee. $200 refundable deposit required. Financial aid available for all students: scholarships, loans, grants.
For More Information • Ms. Amy Hunter, Associate Director for University Programs, AHA International An Academic Program of the University of Oregon, 741 SW Lincoln Street, Portland, OR 97201; *Phone:* 503-295-7730; *Fax:* 503-295-5969. *E-mail:* mail@aha-intl.org. *World Wide Web:* http://www.aha-intl.org/

SAN MIGUEL DE TUCUMÁN

MIDDLEBURY COLLEGE SCHOOLS ABROAD
SCHOOL IN LATIN AMERICA–TUCUMÁN PROGRAM

Hosted by National University of Tucumán
Academic Focus • Full curriculum.
Program Information • Students attend classes at National University of Tucumán. Field trips.
Sessions • Fall, spring, yearlong.
Eligibility Requirements • Open to sophomores, juniors, seniors; 2.7 GPA; 2 letters of recommendation; B average in both Spanish and major; B- average overall; 2.5 years of college course work in Spanish.
Living Arrangements • Students live in host family homes. Meals are taken on one's own, with host family, in residences.
Costs (2004-2005) • One term: $7200. Yearlong program: $14,400; includes tuition. $50 application fee. $300 nonrefundable deposit required. Financial aid available for students from sponsoring institution: scholarships, loans.
For More Information • Mr. Jamie Northrup, University Relations Coordinator, Middlebury College Schools Abroad, Office of Off-Campus Study, 129 Sunderland Language Center, Middlebury, VT 05753; *Phone:* 802-443-5745; *Fax:* 802-443-3157. *E-mail:* schoolsabroad@middlebury.edu. *World Wide Web:* http://www.middlebury.edu/msa/

ARMENIA

CITY TO CITY
ACIE (ACTR/ACCELS)
ACIE–NIS REGIONAL LANGUAGE TRAINING PROGRAM–ARMENIA

Hosted by Yerevan State University
Academic Focus • Cultural studies, language studies.
Program Information • Students attend classes at Yerevan State University (Yerevan).
Sessions • Fall, spring, yearlong.
Eligibility Requirements • Minimum age 18; open to sophomores, juniors, seniors, graduate students, adults; 3 letters of recommendation; good academic standing at home school; 1 year of college course work in Russian or Armenian.
Living Arrangements • Students live in host institution dormitories, locally rented apartments, host family homes. Quarters are shared with students from other programs. Meals are taken on one's own, with host family, in residences, in restaurants.
Costs (2002-2003) • One term: contact sponsor for cost. Yearlong program: contact sponsor for cost. $35 application fee. $500 nonrefundable deposit required. Financial aid available for all students: scholarships.
For More Information • Ms. Margaret Stephenson, Russian and Eurasian Program Officer, ACIE (ACTR/ACCELS), 1776 Massachusetts Avenue, NW, Suite 700, Washington, DC 20036; *Phone:* 202-833-7522; *Fax:* 202-833-7523. *E-mail:* outbound@actr.org. *World Wide Web:* http://www.actr.org/

AUSTRALIA

CITY TO CITY
FLORIDA INTERNATIONAL UNIVERSITY
EXCHANGE PROGRAM WITH VICTORIA UNIVERSITY

Hosted by Victoria University
Academic Focus • Full curriculum.
Program Information • Students attend classes at Victoria University (Melbourne). Optional travel to anywhere in the country at an extra cost.
Sessions • Spring, winter.
Eligibility Requirements • Open to sophomores, juniors, seniors, graduate students, adults; 3.0 GPA.
Living Arrangements • Students live in host institution dormitories. Quarters are shared with host institution students. Meals are taken on one's own, in central dining facility.
Costs (2002-2003) • One term: $8000 (estimated); includes housing, all meals, international airfare, books and class materials, student support services. $150 application fee. Financial aid available for all students: scholarships, loans.
For More Information • Office of International Studies, Florida International University, University Park Campus–TT100, Miami, FL 33199; *Phone:* 305-348-1913; *Fax:* 305-348-1941. *E-mail:* ois@fiu.edu. *World Wide Web:* http://ois.fiu.edu/

ITHACA COLLEGE
ITHACA COLLEGE WALKABOUT DOWN UNDER

Hosted by Murdoch University, University of Tasmania, La Trobe University, Griffith University
Academic Focus • Aboriginal studies, Australian studies, communications, environmental science/studies, history, interdisciplinary studies, literature.
Program Information • Students attend classes at Murdoch University (Perth), University of Tasmania (Hobart), La Trobe University (Melbourne), Griffith University (Brisbane). Scheduled travel; field trips to class-related sites; optional travel at an extra cost.
Sessions • Fall, spring, yearlong.

Eligibility Requirements • Open to sophomores, juniors, seniors; 2.5 GPA; 2 letters of recommendation; good academic standing at home school; judicial review.

Living Arrangements • Students live in host institution dormitories, locally rented apartments, hotels. Quarters are shared with host institution students, students from other programs. Meals are taken on one's own, in residences, in central dining facility, in restaurants.

Costs (2003-2004) • One term: $16,800. Yearlong program: $33,600; includes tuition, housing, all meals, insurance, excursions, international airfare, books and class materials, student support services. $50 application fee. $500 nonrefundable deposit required. Financial aid available for all students: scholarships, loans.

For More Information • Ms. Rachel Cullenen, Associate Director for Study Abroad, Ithaca College, International Programs, Ithaca, NY 14850-7150; *Phone:* 607-274-3306; *Fax:* 607-274-1515. *E-mail:* rcullenen@ithaca.edu. *World Wide Web:* http://www.ithaca.edu/oip/

MICHIGAN STATE UNIVERSITY
THE PEOPLE, GOVERNMENT, JUSTICE SYSTEM, AND PUBLIC POLICIES OF AUSTRALIA

Academic Focus • Criminal justice, political science and government, social sciences.

Program Information • Faculty members are drawn from the sponsor's U.S. staff. Field trips to national/state parliaments, trial and supreme courts, an Aboriginal reserve at Jervis Bay, Goulburn Prison.

Sessions • Spring.

Eligibility Requirements • Minimum age 18; open to freshmen, sophomores, juniors, seniors; 2.5 GPA; good academic standing at home school; approval of faculty directors.

Living Arrangements • Students live in host institution dormitories. Meals are taken as a group, on one's own, in central dining facility, in restaurants.

Costs (2003) • One term: $2850 (estimated); includes housing, some meals, insurance, excursions, books and class materials, student support services. $100 application fee. $200 nonrefundable deposit required. Financial aid available for students from sponsoring institution: scholarships, loans.

For More Information • Ms. Sherry Martinez-Bonilla, Office Assistant, Michigan State University, Office of Study Abroad, 109 International Center, East Lansing, MI 48824-1035; *Phone:* 517-353-8920; *Fax:* 517-432-2082. *E-mail:* marti269@msu.edu. *World Wide Web:* http://studyabroad.msu.edu/

RUTGERS, THE STATE UNIVERSITY OF NEW JERSEY
STUDY ABROAD IN AUSTRALIA

Hosted by Macquarie University, University of Melbourne, University of Queensland

Academic Focus • Full curriculum.

Program Information • Students attend classes at Macquarie University (Sydney), University of Melbourne (Melbourne), University of Queensland (Brisbane). Optional travel to the Great Barrier Reef, the Outback, rainforests at an extra cost.

Sessions • Fall, spring, yearlong.

Eligibility Requirements • Open to sophomores, juniors, seniors; 3.0 GPA; 2 letters of recommendation; good academic standing at home school.

Living Arrangements • Students live in host institution dormitories, program-owned apartments. Quarters are shared with host institution students, students from other programs. Meals are taken on one's own, in residences, in central dining facility.

Costs (2003-2004) • One term: $8671 for New Jersey residents; $11,321 for nonresidents. Yearlong program: $16,642 for New Jersey residents; $21,942 for nonresidents; includes tuition, housing, insurance, student support services. $20 application fee. $750 nonrefundable deposit required. Financial aid available for students from sponsoring institution: scholarships, loans.

For More Information • Ms. Karin Bonello, Regional Coordinator, Rutgers, The State University of New Jersey, 102 College Avenue, New Brunswick, NJ 08901-8543; *Phone:* 732-932-7787; *Fax:* 732-932-8659. *E-mail:* ru_abroad@email.rutgers.edu. *World Wide Web:* http://studyabroad.rutgers.edu/

THE SCHOOL FOR FIELD STUDIES
AUSTRALIA: TROPICAL RAINFOREST MANAGEMENT STUDIES

Held at Center for Rainforest Studies

Academic Focus • Australian studies, biological/life sciences, conservation studies, ecology, economics, environmental science/studies, forestry, natural resources.

Program Information • Classes are held on the campus of Center for Rainforest Studies (Tropical North Queensland). Faculty members are drawn from the sponsor's U.S. staff and local instructors hired by the sponsor. Scheduled travel to Chillagoe, Aboriginal lands, Mission Beach; field trips to Atherton Tablelands rainforest, Lake Tinaroo, local farms; optional travel to the Great Barrier Reef at an extra cost.

Sessions • Fall, spring.

Eligibility Requirements • Minimum age 18; open to freshmen, sophomores, juniors, seniors; course work in biology or ecology; 2.7 GPA; 2 letters of recommendation; personal statement; no foreign language proficiency required.

Living Arrangements • Students live in cabins in the rainforest. Quarters are shared with host institution students. Meals are taken as a group, in central dining facility.

Costs (2002-2003) • One term: $13,670; includes tuition, housing, all meals, excursions, lab equipment. $45 application fee. $500 nonrefundable deposit required. Financial aid available for all students: scholarships, loans.

For More Information • Admissions Department, The School for Field Studies, 10 Federal Street, Salem, MA 01970-3853; *Phone:* 800-989-4418; *Fax:* 978-741-3551. *E-mail:* admissions@fieldstudies.org. *World Wide Web:* http://www.fieldstudies.org/

ADELAIDE

AMERICAN UNIVERSITIES INTERNATIONAL PROGRAMS (AUIP)
UNIVERSITY OF SOUTH AUSTRALIA, AUSTRALIA

Hosted by University of South Australia

Academic Focus • Full curriculum.

Program Information • Students attend classes at University of South Australia. Optional travel to South Island of New Zealand (in early February), Kangaroo Island (March), the Flinders Ranges (July) at an extra cost.

Sessions • Fall, spring, yearlong.

Eligibility Requirements • Minimum age 18; open to sophomores, juniors, seniors, adults; 2.5 GPA; 2 letters of recommendation; good academic standing at home school; essay; original transcript; no foreign language proficiency required.

Living Arrangements • Quarters are shared with host institution students, students from other programs. Meals are taken on one's own, in residences, in restaurants.

Costs (2003) • One term: $5195. Yearlong program: $9890; includes tuition, insurance, student support services, university fees. $50 application fee. $500 nonrefundable deposit required.

For More Information • Ms. Linda Detling, Program Coordinator, American Universities International Programs (AUIP), PMB 221, 305 West Magnolia Street, Fort Collins, CO 80521; *Phone:* 970-495-0869; *Fax:* 970-484-2028. *E-mail:* info@auip.com. *World Wide Web:* http://www.auip.com/

AUSTRALEARN: NORTH AMERICAN CENTER FOR AUSTRALIAN AND NEW ZEALAND UNIVERSITIES
UNIVERSITY OF ADELAIDE

Hosted by University of Adelaide

Academic Focus • Full curriculum.

Program Information • Students attend classes at University of Adelaide. Scheduled travel to a pre-trip excursion to the Great Barrier Reef and an Aboriginal Cultural Park; optional travel to Ayers Rock, coastal region, Sydney, Perth at an extra cost.

Sessions • Fall, spring, yearlong, alternate year.

Eligibility Requirements • Minimum age 18; open to sophomores, juniors, seniors, graduate students; 2.5 GPA; 1 letter of recommendation; good academic standing at home school.

AUSTRALIA
Adelaide

Living Arrangements • Students live in host institution dormitories, locally rented apartments. Quarters are shared with host institution students. Meals are taken on one's own, in residences, in central dining facility.
Costs (2004) • One term: $11,420. Yearlong program: $20,565; includes tuition, housing, all meals, insurance, excursions, international student ID, student support services. $30 application fee. $300 refundable deposit required. Financial aid available for all students: scholarships, loans.
For More Information • AustraLearn: North American Center for Australian and New Zealand Universities, 12050 North Pecos Street, Suite 320, Westminster, CO 80234; *Phone:* 800-980-0033; *Fax:* 303-446-5955. *E-mail:* studyabroad@australearn.org. *World Wide Web:* http://www.australearn.org/

AUSTRALEARN: NORTH AMERICAN CENTER FOR AUSTRALIAN AND NEW ZEALAND UNIVERSITIES
UNIVERSITY OF SOUTH AUSTRALIA

Hosted by University of South Australia
Academic Focus • Full curriculum.
Program Information • Students attend classes at University of South Australia. Scheduled travel to a pre-trip excursion to the Great Barrier Reef and an Aboriginal Cultural Park; optional travel to Ayers Rock, coastal regions, Sydney, Perth at an extra cost.
Sessions • Fall, spring, yearlong, alternate year.
Eligibility Requirements • Minimum age 18; open to sophomores, juniors, seniors, graduate students; 2.5 GPA; 1 letter of recommendation; good academic standing at home school.
Living Arrangements • Students live in locally rented apartments. Quarters are shared with host institution students. Meals are taken on one's own, in residences.
Costs (2004) • One term: $7385. Yearlong program: $13,200; includes tuition, insurance, excursions, international student ID, student support services. $30 application fee. $300 deposit required. Financial aid available for all students: scholarships, loans.
For More Information • AustraLearn: North American Center for Australian and New Zealand Universities, 12050 North Pecos Street, Suite 320, Westminster, CO 80234; *Phone:* 800-980-0033; *Fax:* 303-446-5955. *E-mail:* studyabroad@australearn.org. *World Wide Web:* http://www.australearn.org/

CENTER FOR INTERNATIONAL STUDIES
UNIVERSITY OF SOUTH AUSTRALIA

Hosted by University of South Australia
Academic Focus • Full curriculum.
Program Information • Students attend classes at University of South Australia. Scheduled travel to the south coast, the Flinders Range; field trips to city tours; optional travel at an extra cost.
Sessions • Fall, spring, yearlong.
Eligibility Requirements • Minimum age 18; open to sophomores, juniors, seniors, graduate students, adults; 2.5 GPA; 1 letter of recommendation; good academic standing at home school; personal essay.
Living Arrangements • Quarters are shared with host institution students, students from other programs. Meals are taken on one's own, in residences, in restaurants.
Costs (2003) • One term: $5975. Yearlong program: $10,000; includes tuition, insurance, excursions, international student ID, student support services, airport reception. $50 application fee. $500 nonrefundable deposit required. Financial aid available for all students: scholarships.
For More Information • Mr. Jeff Palm, Program Director, Center for International Studies, 17 New South Street, #105, Northampton, MA 01060; *Phone:* 413-582-0407; *Fax:* 413-582-0327. *E-mail:* jpalm@cisabroad.com. *World Wide Web:* http://www.cisabroad.com/

CULTURAL EXPERIENCES ABROAD (CEA)
STUDY LIBERAL ARTS AND SCIENCES IN ADELAIDE

Hosted by The Flinders University of South Australia
Academic Focus • Full curriculum.
Program Information • Students attend classes at The Flinders University of South Australia. Scheduled travel to the Outback, Melbourne; field trips to Kangaroo Island, Flinders Banges, Fleurieu Peninsula, Cleland, Handerf, Coorong National Park and Game Reserve; optional travel to Ayers Rock, an Outback Tour at an extra cost.
Sessions • Fall, spring, yearlong.
Eligibility Requirements • Minimum age 18; open to sophomores, juniors, seniors; 2.5 GPA; 1 letter of recommendation; good academic standing at home school.
Living Arrangements • Students live in host institution dormitories. Quarters are shared with host institution students, students from other programs. Meals are taken on one's own, in residences, in central dining facility, in restaurants.
Costs (2003-2004) • One term: $10,495–$10,695. Yearlong program: $18,995; includes tuition, housing, some meals, excursions, international student ID, student support services, University ID card, e-mail access, airport reception, social activities. $50 application fee. $400 nonrefundable deposit required.
For More Information • Cultural Experiences Abroad (CEA), 1400 East Southern Avenue, Suite B-108, Tempe, AZ 85282-8011; *Phone:* 480-557-7900; *Fax:* 480-557-7926. *E-mail:* petersons@gowithcea.com. *World Wide Web:* http://www.gowithcea.com/

THE FLINDERS UNIVERSITY OF SOUTH AUSTRALIA
STUDY ABROAD

Hosted by The Flinders University of South Australia
Academic Focus • American studies, archaeology, art, Asian studies, Australian studies, biological/life sciences, biomedical sciences, chemical sciences, commerce, computer science, drama/theater, earth sciences, economics, education, electrical engineering, engineering, English, environmental health, environmental science/studies, film and media studies, fisheries studies, French language and literature, geography, Greek, history, Indonesian, international affairs, international business, Italian language and literature, labor and industrial relations, law and legal studies, marine sciences, mathematics, nursing, nutrition, philosophy, physics, political science and government, psychology, religious studies, social sciences, social work, sociology, Spanish language and literature, speech communication, statistics, tourism and travel, women's studies.
Program Information • Students attend classes at The Flinders University of South Australia. Field trips to Cleland Wildlife Park; optional travel to Kangaroo Island, the Flinders Ranges at an extra cost.
Sessions • Fall, spring, yearlong.
Eligibility Requirements • Minimum age 18; open to freshmen, sophomores, juniors, seniors, graduate students, adults; 2.5 GPA.
Living Arrangements • Students live in host institution dormitories, locally rented apartments. Quarters are shared with host institution students, students from other programs. Meals are taken as a group, on one's own, in residences, in central dining facility.
Costs (2003) • One term: A$7369. Yearlong program: A$14,525; includes tuition, insurance, student support services, student fees, airport reception.
For More Information • Ms. Helen Stephenson, Study Abroad and Exchange Officer, The Flinders University of South Australia, International Office, GPO Box 2100, Adelaide, South Australia 5001, Australia; *Phone:* 800-686-3562; *Fax:* +61 8-8201-3177. *E-mail:* study.abroad@flinders.edu.au. *World Wide Web:* http://www.flinders.edu.au/international/students/. Students may also apply through Butler University, Institute for Study Abroad, 1100 West 42nd Street, Suite 305, Indianapolis, IN 46208-3345; CEA, Cultural Experiences Abroad, 1400 East Southern Avenue, Suite B-108, Tempe, AZ 85282-8011.

IDP EDUCATION AUSTRALIA
ADELAIDE UNIVERSITY PROGRAM

Hosted by University of Adelaide
Academic Focus • Full curriculum.
Program Information • Students attend classes at University of Adelaide.
Sessions • Fall, spring, yearlong.
Eligibility Requirements • Open to sophomores, juniors, seniors, graduate students; 2.8 GPA.

Living Arrangements • Students live in host institution dormitories, locally rented apartments.

Costs (2004) • One term: contact sponsor for cost. Yearlong program: contact sponsor for cost. $100 deposit required.

For More Information • Ms. Deborah Brown, Senior Manager, Study Abroad, IDP Education Australia, 1400 16th Street, NW, Suite 101, Washington, DC 20036-2219; *Phone:* 866-STUDYOZ; *Fax:* 202-332-3297. *E-mail:* studyabroad@washington.idp.com. *World Wide Web:* http://www.idp.com/

IDP EDUCATION AUSTRALIA
FLINDERS UNIVERSITY PROGRAM

Hosted by The Flinders University of South Australia
Academic Focus • Full curriculum.
Program Information • Students attend classes at The Flinders University of South Australia.
Sessions • Fall, spring, yearlong.
Eligibility Requirements • Open to freshmen, sophomores, juniors, seniors, graduate students; 2.5 GPA.
Living Arrangements • Students live in host institution dormitories, locally rented apartments.
Costs (2004) • One term: contact sponsor for cost. Yearlong program: contact sponsor for cost. $100 deposit required.
For More Information • Ms. Deborah Brown, Senior Manager, Study Abroad, IDP Education Australia, 1400 16th Street, NW, Suite 101, Washington, DC 20036-2219; *Phone:* 866-STUDYOZ; *Fax:* 202-332-3297. *E-mail:* studyabroad@washington.idp.com. *World Wide Web:* http://www.idp.com/

IDP EDUCATION AUSTRALIA
UNIVERSITY OF SOUTH AUSTRALIA PROGRAM

Hosted by University of South Australia
Academic Focus • Aboriginal studies, education, film and media studies, graphic design/illustration, information science, international affairs, parks and recreation, social sciences, teaching, tourism and travel.
Program Information • Students attend classes at University of South Australia.
Sessions • Fall, spring, yearlong.
Eligibility Requirements • Open to freshmen, sophomores, juniors, seniors; 2.5 GPA.
Costs (2004) • One term: contact sponsor for cost. Yearlong program: contact sponsor for cost. $100 deposit required.
For More Information • Ms. Deborah Brown, Senior Manager, Study Abroad, IDP Education Australia, 1400 16th Street, NW, Suite 101, Washington, DC 20036-2219; *Phone:* 866-STUDYOZ; *Fax:* 202-332-3297. *E-mail:* studyabroad@washington.idp.com. *World Wide Web:* http://www.idp.com/

IES, INSTITUTE FOR THE INTERNATIONAL EDUCATION OF STUDENTS
IES–ADELAIDE

Hosted by University of Adelaide
Academic Focus • Full curriculum.
Program Information • Students attend classes at University of Adelaide. Scheduled travel to central Australia; field trips to Kangaroo Island.
Sessions • Fall, spring, yearlong, calendar year.
Eligibility Requirements • Minimum age 18; open to juniors, seniors, graduate students, adults; 3.0 GPA; 1 letter of recommendation; good academic standing at home school.
Living Arrangements • Students live in host institution dormitories, locally rented apartments. Meals are taken on one's own, in residences, in central dining facility.
Costs (2003-2004) • One term: $10,600. Yearlong program: $19,080; includes tuition, housing, all meals, excursions, student support services, partial insurance coverage. $50 application fee. $500 nonrefundable deposit required. Financial aid available for all students: scholarships, institutional partner need-based grants.
For More Information • International Education Representative, IES, Institute for the International Education of Students, 33 North LaSalle Street, 15th Floor, Chicago, IL 60602; *Phone:* 800-995-2300; *Fax:* 312-944-1448. *E-mail:* info@iesabroad.org. *World Wide Web:* http://www.IESabroad.org/

INSTITUTE FOR STUDY ABROAD, BUTLER UNIVERSITY
FLINDERS UNIVERSITY

Hosted by The Flinders University of South Australia
Academic Focus • Full curriculum.
Program Information • Students attend classes at The Flinders University of South Australia. Scheduled travel to farms; optional travel to Kangaroo Island at an extra cost.
Sessions • Fall, spring, yearlong, US academic year.
Eligibility Requirements • Open to sophomores, juniors, seniors; 2.5 GPA; 1 letter of recommendation; good academic standing at home school; enrollment at an accredited American college or university.
Living Arrangements • Students live in host institution dormitories, locally rented apartments. Quarters are shared with host institution students. Meals are taken as a group, on one's own, in residences, in central dining facility.
Costs (2003) • One term: $9375. Yearlong program: $14,475; includes tuition, housing, insurance, excursions, international student ID, student support services, cultural and sporting events, pre-departure advising. $40 application fee. $500 nonrefundable deposit required. Financial aid available for all students: scholarships, travel grants.
For More Information • Institute for Study Abroad, Butler University, 1100 West 42nd Street, Suite 305, Indianapolis, IN 46208-3345; *Phone:* 800-858-0229; *Fax:* 317-940-9704. *E-mail:* study-abroad@butler.edu. *World Wide Web:* http://www.ifsa-butler. org/

INSTITUTE FOR STUDY ABROAD, BUTLER UNIVERSITY
UNIVERSITY OF ADELAIDE

Hosted by University of Adelaide
Academic Focus • Full curriculum.
Program Information • Students attend classes at University of Adelaide. Scheduled travel to farms; optional travel to a Kangaroo Island Excursion at an extra cost.
Sessions • Fall, spring, yearlong, US academic year.
Eligibility Requirements • Open to sophomores, juniors, seniors; 2.8 GPA; 1 letter of recommendation; good academic standing at home school; enrollment at an accredited American college or university.
Living Arrangements • Students live in host institution dormitories. Quarters are shared with host institution students. Meals are taken as a group, in residences, in central dining facility, in restaurants.
Costs (2003) • One term: $9375. Yearlong program: $15,375; includes tuition, housing, insurance, excursions, international student ID, student support services, cultural and sporting events, pre-departure advising. $40 application fee. $500 nonrefundable deposit required. Financial aid available for all students: scholarships, travel grants.
For More Information • Institute for Study Abroad, Butler University, 1100 West 42nd Street, Suite 305, Indianapolis, IN 46208-3345; *Phone:* 800-858-0229; *Fax:* 317-940-9704. *E-mail:* study-abroad@butler.edu. *World Wide Web:* http://www.ifsa-butler. org/

STATE UNIVERSITY OF NEW YORK COLLEGE AT BUFFALO
SOUTH AUSTRALIA EXCHANGE/STUDY ABROAD

Hosted by University of South Australia
Academic Focus • Full curriculum.
Program Information • Students attend classes at University of South Australia. Optional travel to the Flinders Range, Kangaroo Island at an extra cost.
Sessions • Fall, spring, yearlong.
Eligibility Requirements • Open to sophomores, juniors, seniors; 2.75 GPA; 2 letters of recommendation.
Living Arrangements • Students live in host institution dormitories, locally rented apartments. Quarters are shared with host institution students, students from other programs. Meals are taken on one's own, in residences.

AUSTRALIA
Adelaide

Costs (2003-2004) • One term: $7585–$9310 for New York residents; $12,035 for nonresidents. Yearlong program: $13,085–$16,535 for New York residents; $21,985 for nonresidents; includes tuition, housing, all meals, insurance, international airfare, books and class materials, adminstrative, passport, visa, and college fees. $10 application fee. $250 nonrefundable deposit required. Financial aid available for students from sponsoring institution: scholarships, loans.

For More Information • Dr. Lee Ann Grace, Director, International Education, State University of New York College at Buffalo, 1300 Elmwood Avenue, Buffalo, NY 14222-1095; *Phone:* 716-878-4620; *Fax:* 716-878-3054. *E-mail:* intleduc@buffalostate.edu. *World Wide Web:* http://www.buffalostate.edu/intnated/

STATE UNIVERSITY OF NEW YORK COLLEGE AT BROCKPORT
UNIVERSITY OF ADELAIDE PROGRAM

Hosted by University of Adelaide
Academic Focus • Full curriculum.
Program Information • Students attend classes at University of Adelaide. Field trips to sites throughout Sydney (during orientation).
Sessions • Fall, spring, yearlong.
Eligibility Requirements • Minimum age 18; open to juniors, seniors; course work in area of internship, if applicable; 2.8 GPA; 2 letters of recommendation; ability to do upper-division course work in chosen subject; résumé required for internship option.
Living Arrangements • Students live in locally rented apartments, residential colleges. Quarters are shared with host institution students. Meals are taken as a group, on one's own, in residences, in central dining facility.
Costs (2003-2004) • One term: $9950 for fall term; $10,050 for spring. Yearlong program: $18,150; includes tuition, housing, excursions, international student ID, student support services, meals if staying in Residential Colleges. $350 nonrefundable deposit required. Financial aid available for all students: scholarships, loans, regular financial aid, grants.
For More Information • Dr. John J. Perry, Director, Office of International Education, State University of New York College at Brockport, 350 New Campus Drive, Brockport, NY 14420; *Phone:* 800-298-SUNY; *Fax:* 585-637-3218. *E-mail:* overseas@brockport.edu. *World Wide Web:* http://www.brockport.edu/studyabroad/

UNIVERSITY OF MIAMI
FLINDERS UNIVERSITY, AUSTRALIA

Hosted by The Flinders University of South Australia
Academic Focus • Australian studies, biological/life sciences, chemical sciences, education, engineering, English, history, political science and government.
Program Information • Students attend classes at The Flinders University of South Australia.
Sessions • Fall, spring, yearlong.
Eligibility Requirements • Minimum age 18; open to sophomores, juniors, seniors; 3.0 GPA; 2 letters of recommendation; official transcripts.
Living Arrangements • Students live in host institution dormitories. Quarters are shared with host institution students. Meals are taken on one's own, in central dining facility.
Costs (2003-2004) • One term: $12,919. Yearlong program: $25,838; includes tuition, student support services. $40 application fee. $500 nonrefundable deposit required. Financial aid available for students from sponsoring institution: scholarships, loans.
For More Information • Ms. Glenda Hayley, Assistant Director, University of Miami, International Education and Exchange Programs, 5050 Brunson Drive, Allen Hall 212, PO Box 248005, Coral Gables, FL 33124-1610; *Phone:* 305-284-3434; *Fax:* 305-284-4235. *E-mail:* ieep@miami.edu. *World Wide Web:* http://www.studyabroad.miami.edu/

ARMIDALE
IDP EDUCATION AUSTRALIA
UNIVERSITY OF NEW ENGLAND PROGRAM

Hosted by University of New England
Academic Focus • Full curriculum.

Program Information • Students attend classes at University of New England.
Sessions • Fall, spring, yearlong.
Eligibility Requirements • Open to freshmen, sophomores, juniors, seniors.
Costs (2004) • One term: contact sponsor for cost. Yearlong program: contact sponsor for cost. $100 deposit required.
For More Information • Ms. Deborah Brown, Senior Manager, Study Abroad, IDP Education Australia, 1400 16th Street, NW, Suite 101, Washington, DC 20036-2219; *Phone:* 866-STUDYOZ; *Fax:* 202-332-3297. *E-mail:* studyabroad@washington.idp.com. *World Wide Web:* http://www.idp.com/

STATE UNIVERSITY OF NEW YORK AT NEW PALTZ
STUDY ABROAD AT ARMIDALE, AUSTRALIA

Hosted by University of New England
Academic Focus • Full curriculum.
Program Information • Students attend classes at University of New England.
Sessions • Fall, spring, yearlong.
Eligibility Requirements • Minimum age 18; open to sophomores, juniors, seniors; 2.5 GPA; 2 letters of recommendation; good academic standing at home school.
Living Arrangements • Students live in host institution dormitories. Quarters are shared with host institution students, students from other programs. Meals are taken on one's own, in residences, in central dining facility, in restaurants.
Costs (2003-2004) • One term: $5012 for New York residents; $5663 for nonresidents. Yearlong program: $10,024 for New York residents; $11,326 for nonresidents; includes tuition, insurance, student support services, administrative fee. $25 application fee. $300–$600 nonrefundable deposit required. Financial aid available for students from sponsoring institution: scholarships, loans.
For More Information • Center for International Programs, State University of New York at New Paltz, 75 South Manheim Boulevard, Suite 9, New Paltz, NY 12561; *Phone:* 845-257-3125; *Fax:* 845-257-3129. *E-mail:* international@newpaltz.edu. *World Wide Web:* http://www.newpaltz.edu/studyabroad/

BALLARAT
IDP EDUCATION AUSTRALIA
UNIVERSITY OF BALLARAT PROGRAM

Hosted by University of Ballarat
Academic Focus • Asian studies, Australian studies, business administration/management, ecology, education, environmental science/studies, geology, graphic design/illustration, information science, nursing, psychology, social sciences, sports management, teaching, visual and performing arts.
Program Information • Students attend classes at University of Ballarat.
Sessions • Fall, spring, yearlong.
Eligibility Requirements • Open to sophomores, juniors; 2.5 GPA.
Costs (2004) • One term: contact sponsor for cost. Yearlong program: contact sponsor for cost. $100 deposit required.
For More Information • Ms. Deborah Brown, Senior Manager, Study Abroad, IDP Education Australia, 1400 16th Street, NW, Suite 101, Washington, DC 20036-2219; *Phone:* 866-STUDYOZ; *Fax:* 202-332-3297. *E-mail:* studyabroad@washington.idp.com. *World Wide Web:* http://www.idp.com/

STATE UNIVERSITY OF NEW YORK COLLEGE AT CORTLAND
UNIVERSITY OF BALLARAT

Hosted by University of Ballarat
Academic Focus • Full curriculum.
Program Information • Students attend classes at University of Ballarat. Field trips to local sites of cultural and historic importance; optional travel to Melbourne, Sydney, Adelaide, Great Ocean Road, Kangaroo Island, Uluro, Alice Springs at an extra cost.
Sessions • Fall, spring, yearlong, alternate year.

Eligibility Requirements • Minimum age 18; open to sophomores, juniors, seniors; 2.5 GPA; 2 letters of recommendation; good academic standing at home school.

Living Arrangements • Students live in host institution dormitories, locally rented apartments. Quarters are shared with host institution students, students from other programs. Meals are taken on one's own, in residences.

Costs (2003-2004) • One term: $9500. Yearlong program: contact sponsor for cost; includes tuition, housing, all meals, insurance, excursions, international airfare, books and class materials, international student ID, student support services, passport and visa fees. $20 application fee. $200 refundable deposit required. Financial aid available for students from sponsoring institution: scholarships, loans.

For More Information • Ms. Liz Kopp, Assistant Director, International Programs, State University of New York College at Cortland, PO Box 2000, Cortland, NY 13045; *Phone:* 607-753-2209; *Fax:* 607-753-5989. *E-mail:* cortlandabroad@cortland.edu. *World Wide Web:* http://www.studyabroad.com/suny/cortland/

BRISBANE

ARCADIA UNIVERSITY
GRIFFITH UNIVERSITY

Hosted by Griffith University: Queensland College of Art, Griffith University, Griffith University Gold Coast University College

Academic Focus • Biological/life sciences, fine/studio arts, liberal studies, social sciences.

Program Information • Students attend classes at Griffith University: Queensland College of Art, Griffith University, Griffith University Gold Coast University College.

Sessions • Fall, spring, yearlong, US academic year.

Eligibility Requirements • Open to sophomores, juniors, seniors; 3.0 GPA; 1 letter of recommendation.

Living Arrangements • Students live in host institution dormitories, locally rented apartments, program-owned apartments, host family homes. Quarters are shared with host institution students. Meals are taken on one's own, in residences, in central dining facility.

Costs (2003-2004) • One term: $8290. Yearlong program: $13,990–$14,290; includes tuition, housing, insurance, international student ID, student support services, transcripts, pre-departure guide. $35 application fee. $500 nonrefundable deposit required. Financial aid available for all students: scholarships, loans.

For More Information • Arcadia University, Center for Education Abroad, 450 South Easton Road, Glenside, PA 19038-3295; *Phone:* 866-927-2234; *Fax:* 215-572-2174. *E-mail:* cea@arcadia.edu. *World Wide Web:* http://www.arcadia.edu/cea/

ARCADIA UNIVERSITY
UNIVERSITY OF QUEENSLAND

Hosted by University of Queensland

Academic Focus • Full curriculum.

Program Information • Students attend classes at University of Queensland. Optional travel at an extra cost.

Sessions • Fall, spring, yearlong, US academic year.

Eligibility Requirements • Open to sophomores, juniors, seniors; 2.7 GPA; 1 letter of recommendation.

Living Arrangements • Students live in host institution dormitories, locally rented apartments, program-owned apartments. Quarters are shared with host institution students, students from other programs. Meals are taken as a group, on one's own, in residences.

Costs (2003-2004) • One term: $10,725. Yearlong program: $17,990 for Australian academic year; $18,350 for US academic year; includes tuition, housing, insurance, international student ID, student support services, transcripts, pre-departure guide. $35 application fee. $500 nonrefundable deposit required. Financial aid available for all students: scholarships, loans.

For More Information • Arcadia University, Center for Education Abroad, 450 South Easton Road, Glenside, PA 19038-3295; *Phone:* 866-927-2234; *Fax:* 215-572-2174. *E-mail:* cea@arcadia.edu. *World Wide Web:* http://www.arcadia.edu/cea/

AUSTRALEARN: NORTH AMERICAN CENTER FOR AUSTRALIAN AND NEW ZEALAND UNIVERSITIES
GRIFFITH UNIVERSITY

Hosted by Griffith University Gold Coast University College, Griffith University–Brisbane Campus
Academic Focus • Full curriculum.
Program Information • Students attend classes at Griffith University Gold Coast University College, Griffith University–Brisbane Campus. Scheduled travel to a pre-trip excursion to the Great Barrier Reef and an Aboriginal Cultural Park; optional travel to Sydney, the Outback, Gold Coast, the Great Barrier Reef at an extra cost.
Sessions • Fall, spring, yearlong, alternate year.
Eligibility Requirements • Minimum age 18; open to sophomores, juniors, seniors, graduate students; 2.5 GPA; 1 letter of recommendation; good academic standing at home school.
Living Arrangements • Students live in host institution dormitories, locally rented apartments. Quarters are shared with host institution students. Meals are taken on one's own, in residences, in central dining facility.
Costs (2004) • One term: $10,065. Yearlong program: $18,545; includes tuition, housing, all meals, insurance, excursions, books and class materials, international student ID, student support services. $30 application fee. $300 deposit required. Financial aid available for all students: scholarships, loans.

For More Information • AustraLearn: North American Center for Australian and New Zealand Universities, 12050 North Pecos Street, Suite 320, Westminster, CO 80234; *Phone:* 800-980-0033; *Fax:* 303-446-5955. *E-mail:* studyabroad@australearn.org. *World Wide Web:* http://www.australearn.org/

AUSTRALEARN: NORTH AMERICAN CENTER FOR AUSTRALIAN AND NEW ZEALAND UNIVERSITIES
QUEENSLAND UNIVERSITY OF TECHNOLOGY

Hosted by Queensland University of Technology
Academic Focus • Full curriculum.
Program Information • Students attend classes at Queensland University of Technology. Scheduled travel to a pre-trip excursion to the Great Barrier Reef and an Aboriginal Cultural Park; optional travel to the Great Barrier Reef, Sydney, New Zealand, Ayers Rock at an extra cost.
Sessions • Fall, spring, yearlong, alternate year.
Eligibility Requirements • Minimum age 18; open to sophomores, juniors, seniors, graduate students; 2.5 GPA; 1 letter of recommendation; good academic standing at home school.
Living Arrangements • Students live in locally rented apartments. Quarters are shared with host institution students. Meals are taken on one's own, in residences.
Costs (2004) • One term: $10,895. Yearlong program: $20,115; includes tuition, housing, insurance, excursions, international student ID, student support services. $30 application fee. $300 deposit required. Financial aid available for all students: scholarships, loans.
For More Information • AustraLearn: North American Center for Australian and New Zealand Universities, 12050 North Pecos Street, Suite 320, Westminster, CO 80234; *Phone:* 800-980-0033; *Fax:* 303-446-5955. *E-mail:* studyabroad@australearn.org. *World Wide Web:* http://www.australearn.org/

AUSTRALEARN: NORTH AMERICAN CENTER FOR AUSTRALIAN AND NEW ZEALAND UNIVERSITIES
UNIVERSITY OF QUEENSLAND

Hosted by University of Queensland
Academic Focus • Full curriculum.
Program Information • Students attend classes at University of Queensland. Scheduled travel to a pre-trip excursion to the Great Barrier Reef and an Aboriginal Cultural Park; optional travel to the Great Barrier Reef, Sydney, New Zealand at an extra cost.
Sessions • Fall, spring, yearlong, alternate year.
Eligibility Requirements • Minimum age 18; open to sophomores, juniors, seniors, graduate students; 3.0 GPA; 1 letter of recommendation; good academic standing at home school.
Living Arrangements • Students live in host institution dormitories, locally rented apartments. Quarters are shared with host institution students, students from other programs. Meals are taken on one's own, in residences, in central dining facility.
Costs (2004) • One term: $11,805. Yearlong program: $21,395; includes tuition, housing, all meals, insurance, excursions, international student ID, student support services. $30 application fee. $300 deposit required. Financial aid available for all students: scholarships, loans.
For More Information • AustraLearn: North American Center for Australian and New Zealand Universities, 12050 North Pecos Street, Suite 320, Westminster, CO 80234; *Phone:* 800-980-0033; *Fax:* 303-446-5955. *E-mail:* studyabroad@australearn.org. *World Wide Web:* http://www.australearn.org/

FAIRFIELD UNIVERSITY
FAIRFIELD UNIVERSITY BRISBANE CAMPUS

Hosted by Australian Catholic University–McAuley Campus
Academic Focus • Full curriculum.
Program Information • Students attend classes at Australian Catholic University–McAuley Campus. Optional travel to cultural/historic and natural sites at an extra cost.
Sessions • Fall, spring, yearlong.
Eligibility Requirements • Minimum age 18; open to sophomores, juniors, seniors; 2.8 GPA; 2 letters of recommendation; good academic standing at home school; transcript.
Living Arrangements • Students live in locally rented apartments. Quarters are shared with host institution students. Meals are taken on one's own, in residences.
Costs (2002-2003) • One term: $14,580. Yearlong program: $29,160; includes tuition, insurance, international student ID, student support services, airport pick-up. $50 application fee. $1000 refundable deposit required. Financial aid available for students from sponsoring institution.
For More Information • Office of International Education, Fairfield University, Dolan House, 1073 North Benson Road, Fairfield, CT 06824; *Phone:* 203-254-4332; *Fax:* 203-254-4261. *E-mail:* studyabroadoffice@mail.fairfield.edu. *World Wide Web:* http://www.fairfield.edu/sce/studyabroad/

HARDING UNIVERSITY
HARDING UNIVERSITY IN BRISBANE, AUSTRALIA

Held at Harding University in Brisbane
Academic Focus • Liberal studies, religious studies.
Program Information • Classes are held on the campus of Harding University in Brisbane. Faculty members are drawn from the sponsor's U.S. staff. Scheduled travel to the Outback, Alice Springs, the Great Barrier Reef; field trips to Moreton Bay, the Australian woodshed, Brisbane; optional travel to New Zealand.
Sessions • Fall.
Eligibility Requirements • Open to sophomores, juniors, seniors; 2.0 GPA; good academic standing at home school.

Living Arrangements • Students live in locally rented apartments. Quarters are shared with host institution students. Meals are taken as a group, in residences.

Costs (2003) • One term: $13,000; includes tuition, housing, some meals, excursions, international airfare, international student ID. $200 application fee. Financial aid available for students from sponsoring institution: scholarships, work study, loans.

For More Information • Dr. Jeffrey T. Hopper, Dean of International Programs, Harding University, 900 East Center Street, Box 10754, Searcy, AR 72149; *Phone:* 501-279-4529; *Fax:* 501-279-4184. *E-mail:* intlprograms@harding.edu

IDP EDUCATION AUSTRALIA
GRIFFITH UNIVERSITY PROGRAM

Hosted by Griffith University
Academic Focus • Full curriculum.
Program Information • Students attend classes at Griffith University.
Sessions • Fall, spring, yearlong.
Eligibility Requirements • Open to freshmen, sophomores, juniors, seniors; 2.5 GPA.
Living Arrangements • Students live in host institution dormitories, locally rented apartments.
Costs (2004) • One term: contact sponsor for cost. Yearlong program: contact sponsor for cost. $100 deposit required.
For More Information • Ms. Deborah Brown, Senior Manager, Study Abroad, IDP Education Australia, 1400 16th Street, NW, Suite 101, Washington, DC 20036-2219; *Phone:* 866-STUDYOZ; *Fax:* 202-332-3297. *E-mail:* studyabroad@washington.idp.com. *World Wide Web:* http://www.idp.com/

IDP EDUCATION AUSTRALIA
QUEENSLAND UNIVERSITY OF TECHNOLOGY PROGRAM

Hosted by Queensland University of Technology
Academic Focus • Full curriculum.
Program Information • Students attend classes at Queensland University of Technology.
Sessions • Fall, spring, yearlong.
Eligibility Requirements • Open to sophomores, juniors, seniors, graduate students, adults; 2.5 GPA.
Living Arrangements • Students live in locally rented apartments.
Costs (2004) • One term: contact sponsor for cost. Yearlong program: contact sponsor for cost. $100 deposit required.
For More Information • Ms. Deborah Brown, Senior Manager, Study Abroad, IDP Education Australia, 1400 16th Street, NW, Suite 101, Washington, DC 20036-2219; *Phone:* 866-STUDYOZ; *Fax:* 202-332-3297. *E-mail:* studyabroad@washington.idp.com. *World Wide Web:* http://www.idp.com/

IDP EDUCATION AUSTRALIA
UNIVERSITY OF QUEENSLAND PROGRAM

Hosted by University of Queensland
Academic Focus • Full curriculum.
Program Information • Students attend classes at University of Queensland.
Sessions • Fall, spring, yearlong.
Eligibility Requirements • Open to sophomores, juniors, seniors; 3.0 GPA; current enrollment at an accredited college or university.
Living Arrangements • Students live in host institution dormitories, locally rented apartments.
Costs (2004) • One term: contact sponsor for cost. Yearlong program: contact sponsor for cost. $100 deposit required.
For More Information • Ms. Deborah Brown, Senior Manager, Study Abroad, IDP Education Australia, 1400 16th Street, NW, Suite 101, Washington, DC 20036-2219; *Phone:* 866-STUDYOZ; *Fax:* 202-332-3297. *E-mail:* studyabroad@washington.idp.com. *World Wide Web:* http://www.idp.com/

INSTITUTE FOR STUDY ABROAD, BUTLER UNIVERSITY
GRIFFITH UNIVERSITY

Hosted by Griffith University
Academic Focus • Full curriculum.
Program Information • Students attend classes at Griffith University. Scheduled travel to farms; optional travel at an extra cost.
Sessions • Fall, spring, yearlong, US academic year.
Eligibility Requirements • Open to sophomores, juniors, seniors; 2.5 GPA; 1 letter of recommendation; good academic standing at home school; enrollment at an accredited American college or university.
Living Arrangements • Students live in host institution dormitories, locally rented apartments. Quarters are shared with host institution students. Meals are taken as a group, on one's own, in residences.
Costs (2003) • One term: $8975. Yearlong program: $13,775; includes tuition, housing, excursions, international student ID, student support services, cultural and sporting events, pre-departure advising. $40 application fee. $500 nonrefundable deposit required. Financial aid available for all students: scholarships, travel grants.
For More Information • Institute for Study Abroad, Butler University, 1100 West 42nd Street, Suite 305, Indianapolis, IN 46208-3345; *Phone:* 800-858-0229; *Fax:* 317-940-9704. *E-mail:* study-abroad@butler.edu. *World Wide Web:* http://www.ifsa-butler.org/

INSTITUTE FOR STUDY ABROAD, BUTLER UNIVERSITY
UNIVERSITY OF QUEENSLAND

Hosted by University of Queensland
Academic Focus • Full curriculum.
Program Information • Students attend classes at University of Queensland. Scheduled travel to farms; optional travel to Moreton Bay, Stradbroke Island at an extra cost.
Sessions • Fall, spring, yearlong, US academic year.
Eligibility Requirements • Open to sophomores, juniors, seniors; 3.0 GPA; 1 letter of recommendation; good academic standing at home school; enrollment at an accredited American college or university.
Living Arrangements • Students live in host institution dormitories, locally rented apartments, program-owned houses. Quarters are shared with host institution students. Meals are taken as a group, on one's own, in residences, in central dining facility.
Costs (2003) • One term: $10,475. Yearlong program: $16,975; includes tuition, housing, insurance, excursions, international student ID, student support services, cultural and sporting events, pre-departure advising. $40 application fee. $500 nonrefundable deposit required. Financial aid available for all students: scholarships, travel grants.
For More Information • Institute for Study Abroad, Butler University, 1100 West 42nd Street, Suite 305, Indianapolis, IN 46208-3345; *Phone:* 800-858-0229; *Fax:* 317-940-9704. *E-mail:* study-abroad@butler.edu. *World Wide Web:* http://www.ifsa-butler.org/

INTERNATIONAL STUDIES ABROAD
BRISBANE, AUSTRALIA–SEMESTER/YEAR AT THE UNIVERSITY OF QUEENSLAND

Hosted by University of Queensland
Academic Focus • Full curriculum.
Program Information • Students attend classes at University of Queensland. Field trips to Stradbroke Island; optional travel to Coolum and Blackall Range, Noosa at an extra cost.
Sessions • Fall, spring, yearlong.
Eligibility Requirements • Minimum age 18; open to freshmen, sophomores, juniors, seniors, adults; 3.0 GPA; 1 letter of recommendation; good academic standing at home school; transcript.
Living Arrangements • Students live in host institution dormitories, locally rented apartments. Quarters are shared with host institution students, students from other programs. Meals are taken as a group, on one's own, in residences, in central dining facility, in restaurants.

Costs (2004-2005) • One term: $12,500. Yearlong program: $22,500; includes tuition, housing, all meals, insurance, excursions, student support services, tutoring, airport pick-up. $200 deposit required. Financial aid available for all students: loans, U.S. federal financial aid.

For More Information • Australia Site Specialist, International Studies Abroad, 901 West 24th Street, Austin, TX 78705; *Phone:* 512-480-8522; *Fax:* 512-480-8866. *E-mail:* isa@studiesabroad.com. *World Wide Web:* http://www.studiesabroad.com/

QUEENSLAND UNIVERSITY OF TECHNOLOGY
PROGRAM IN AUSTRALIA

Hosted by Queensland University of Technology
Academic Focus • Full curriculum.
Program Information • Students attend classes at Queensland University of Technology. Field trips to forests, lakes, islands, local industries in the southeast Queensland region, mining centers, cultural centers, coastal regions, Queensland National Parks; optional travel to the Great Barrier Reef, Sydney, Cairns, Port Douglas, Snowy Mountains, Gold Coast, the Outback, whale watching (Hervey Bay), Moreton Bay Island at an extra cost.
Sessions • Fall, spring, yearlong.
Eligibility Requirements • Open to sophomores, juniors, seniors, graduate students, adults; 2.5 GPA.
Living Arrangements • Students live in locally rented apartments, host family homes. Quarters are shared with host institution students, students from other programs. Meals are taken on one's own, with host family, in residences, in restaurants.
Costs (2004) • One term: A$7776. Yearlong program: A$15,537; includes tuition, insurance, lab equipment, student support services, Guild fees.
For More Information • QUT Study Abroad, Queensland University of Technology, International Relations Unit, GPO Box 2434, Brisbane, Queensland 4001, Australia; *Phone:* +61 7-3864-4300; *Fax:* +61 7-3864-1216. *E-mail:* studyabroad@qut.edu.au. *World Wide Web:* http://www.international.qut.edu.au/courses/studyabroad. jsp/. Students may also apply through AustraLearn, North American Center for Australian and New Zealand Universities, 12050 North Pecos Street, Suite 320, Westminster, CO 80234; Arcadia University, Center for Education Abroad, 450 South Easton Road, Glenside, PA 19038-3295; Study Australia, 54515 State Road 933 North, Notre Dame, IN 46556-1004.

STATE UNIVERSITY OF NEW YORK AT OSWEGO
QUEENSLAND UNIVERSITY OF TECHNOLOGY

Hosted by Queensland University of Technology
Academic Focus • Full curriculum.
Program Information • Students attend classes at Queensland University of Technology. Optional travel to Fraser Island, the Great Barrier Reef, Australia, New Zealand, south Pacific at an extra cost.
Sessions • Fall, spring, yearlong.
Eligibility Requirements • Open to sophomores, juniors, seniors; 2.5 GPA; 3 letters of recommendation; good academic standing at home school; program of study statement.
Living Arrangements • Students live in host institution dormitories, locally rented apartments, host family homes. Quarters are shared with host institution students, students from other programs. Meals are taken as a group, on one's own, in residences, in restaurants.
Costs (2003-2004) • One term: $6020. Yearlong program: $12,040; includes tuition, insurance, student support services. $250 nonrefundable deposit required. Financial aid available for students: home university financial aid, loan processing and scholarships for Oswego students.
For More Information • Ms. Nefertitti Saheed, Program Specialist, State University of New York at Oswego, 122A Swetman Hall, Oswego, NY 13126; *Phone:* 888-4-OSWEGO; *Fax:* 315-312-2477. *E-mail:* intled@oswego.edu. *World Wide Web:* http://www.oswego. edu/intled/

STATE UNIVERSITY OF NEW YORK AT PLATTSBURGH
STUDY IN AUSTRALIA, BRISBANE

Hosted by University of Queensland
Academic Focus • Anthropology, Australian studies, biological/life sciences, business administration/management, drama/theater, economics, English, information science, interdisciplinary studies, journalism, marketing, psychology, religious studies, sociology.
Program Information • Students attend classes at University of Queensland.
Sessions • Fall, spring, yearlong.
Eligibility Requirements • Minimum age 18; open to sophomores, juniors, seniors; 3.0 GPA; 2 letters of recommendation; SUNY and UQ applications; essay; transcript.
Living Arrangements • Students live in locally rented apartments. Quarters are shared with host institution students, students from other programs. Meals are taken on one's own, in residences, in central dining facility, in restaurants.
Costs (2003-2004) • One term: $11,570. Yearlong program: $23,140; includes tuition, housing, some meals, insurance, international student ID, student support services, program fee. $20 application fee. $350 nonrefundable deposit required. Financial aid available for students from sponsoring institution: scholarships, loans.
For More Information • Ms. Jo Ann Mackie, Study Abroad Coordinator, State University of New York at Plattsburgh, Study Abroad Office, 101 Broad Street, Plattsburgh, NY 12901; *Phone:* 518-564-2321; *Fax:* 518-564-2326. *E-mail:* international@plattsburgh. edu. *World Wide Web:* http://www.plattsburgh.edu/studyabroad/

STATE UNIVERSITY OF NEW YORK COLLEGE AT CORTLAND
GRIFFITH UNIVERSITY

Hosted by Griffith University
Academic Focus • Full curriculum.
Program Information • Students attend classes at Griffith University. Optional travel to the Great Barrier Reef, Sydney, the Great Ocean Road, Uluru, Alice Springs, the Blue Mountains at an extra cost.
Sessions • Fall, spring, yearlong, alternate year.
Eligibility Requirements • Minimum age 19; open to sophomores, juniors, seniors; 2.5 GPA; 2 letters of recommendation; good academic standing at home school.
Living Arrangements • Students live in host institution dormitories, locally rented apartments. Quarters are shared with host institution students, students from other programs. Meals are taken on one's own, in residences.
Costs (2003-2004) • One term: $9000. Yearlong program: contact sponsor for cost; includes tuition, housing, all meals, insurance, excursions, international airfare, books and class materials, international student ID, student support services, passport and visa fees. $20 application fee. $250 nonrefundable deposit required. Financial aid available for students from sponsoring institution: scholarships, loans.
For More Information • Ms. Liz Kopp, Assistant Director, Office of International Programs, State University of New York College at Cortland, PO Box 2000, Cortland, NY 13045; *Phone:* 607-753-2209; *Fax:* 607-753-5989. *E-mail:* cortlandabroad@cortland.edu. *World Wide Web:* http://www.studyabroad.com/suny/cortland/

STUDY AUSTRALIA
QUEENSLAND UNIVERSITY OF TECHNOLOGY

Hosted by Queensland University of Technology
Academic Focus • Full curriculum.
Program Information • Students attend classes at Queensland University of Technology. Scheduled travel to Sydney; field trips to the Blue Mountains; optional travel to the Great Barrier Reef, the Outback, Tasmania, Fiji, New Zealand at an extra cost.
Sessions • Fall, spring, yearlong.
Eligibility Requirements • Minimum age 18; open to freshmen, sophomores, juniors, seniors.
Living Arrangements • Students live in host institution dormitories, locally rented apartments, host family homes. Quarters are

AUSTRALIA
Brisbane

shared with host institution students, students from other programs. Meals are taken on one's own, in residences, in central dining facility.
Costs (2003) • One term: $9825. Yearlong program: $18,390; includes tuition, housing, insurance, excursions, student support services, travel discounts. $500 refundable deposit required. Financial aid available for all students: scholarships, loans.
For More Information • Mr. Chris Shepherd, Director of Programs and Services, Study Australia, 54515 State Road 933 North, Notre Dame, IN 46556-1004; *Phone:* 800-585-9658; *Fax:* 509-357-9457. *E-mail:* info@study-australia.com. *World Wide Web:* http://www.study-australia.com/

STUDY AUSTRALIA
UNIVERSITY OF QUEENSLAND
Hosted by University of Queensland
Academic Focus • Full curriculum.
Program Information • Students attend classes at University of Queensland. Scheduled travel to Sydney; field trips to the Blue Mountains; optional travel to the Great Barrier Reef, the Outback, Tasmania, Fiji, New Zealand at an extra cost.
Sessions • Fall, spring, yearlong.
Eligibility Requirements • Minimum age 18; open to sophomores, juniors, seniors; 3.0 GPA; good academic standing at home school; enrollment at an accredited American college or university.
Living Arrangements • Students live in host institution dormitories, locally rented apartments, program-owned apartments, host family homes. Quarters are shared with host institution students, students from other programs. Meals are taken on one's own, in residences, in central dining facility.
Costs (2003) • One term: $9825. Yearlong program: $18,390; includes tuition, housing, insurance, excursions, student support services, travel discounts. $500 refundable deposit required. Financial aid available for all students: scholarships, loans.
For More Information • Mr. Chris Shepherd, Director of Programs and Services, Study Australia, 54515 State Road 933 North, Notre Dame, IN 46556-1004; *Phone:* 800-585-9658; *Fax:* 509-357-9457. *E-mail:* info@study-australia.com. *World Wide Web:* http://www.study-australia.com/

UNIVERSITY OF MIAMI
GRIFFITH UNIVERSITY, AUSTRALIA
Hosted by Griffith University
Academic Focus • Art, Asian studies, economics, environmental science/studies, international affairs, international business, political science and government, science.
Program Information • Students attend classes at Griffith University.
Sessions • Fall, spring, yearlong.
Eligibility Requirements • Minimum age 18; open to freshmen, sophomores, juniors, seniors; 3.0 GPA; 2 letters of recommendation; official transcripts.
Living Arrangements • Students live in host institution dormitories, host family homes. Quarters are shared with host institution students, students from other programs. Meals are taken on one's own, in residences, in central dining facility.
Costs (2003-2004) • One term: $12,919. Yearlong program: $25,838; includes tuition, student support services. $40 application fee. $500 nonrefundable deposit required. Financial aid available for students from sponsoring institution: scholarships, loans.
For More Information • Ms. Glenda Hayley, Assistant Director, University of Miami, International Education and Exchange Programs, 5050 Brunson Drive, Allen Hall 212, PO Box 248005, Coral Gables, FL 33124-1610; *Phone:* 305-284-3434; *Fax:* 305-284-4235. *E-mail:* ieep@miami.edu. *World Wide Web:* http://www.studyabroad.miami.edu/

UNIVERSITY OF QUEENSLAND
STUDY ABROAD PROGRAM
Hosted by University of Queensland
Academic Focus • Full curriculum.
Program Information • Students attend classes at University of Queensland. Optional travel to Heron Island, Lamington National Park, Stradbroke Island, Gold Coast hinterland at an extra cost.

Sessions • Fall, spring, yearlong, Australian academic year.
Eligibility Requirements • Open to sophomores, juniors, seniors, graduate students; 3.0 GPA; good academic standing at home school; no foreign language proficiency required.
Living Arrangements • Students live in host institution dormitories, locally rented apartments. Quarters are shared with host institution students, students from other programs. Meals are taken as a group, in residences, in central dining facility.
Costs (2004) • One term: A$8200. Yearlong program: A$16,400; includes tuition, lab equipment, student support services.
For More Information • Ms. Cecile McGuire, Marketing Officer, Study Abroad, University of Queensland, International Education Directorate, Brisbane, Queensland 4072, Australia; *Phone:* +61 7-3365-7962; *Fax:* +61 7-3365-3591. *E-mail:* studyabroad@uq.edu.au. *World Wide Web:* http://www.uq.edu.au/studyabroad/. Students may also apply through Butler University, Institute for Study Abroad, 1100 West 42nd Street, Suite 305, Indianapolis, IN 46208-3345; AustraLearn, North American Center for Australian and New Zealand Universities, 12050 North Pecos Street, Suite 320, Westminster, CO 80234; Australian Education Office, 1601 Massachusetts Avenue, NW, Washington, DC 20036; Arcadia University, Center for Education Abroad, 450 South Easton Road, Glenside, PA 19038-3295; International Studies Abroad, 901 West 24th, Austin, TX 78705; Study Australia, 54515 State Road 933 North, Notre Dame, IN 46556-1004.

BYRON BAY
SCHOOL FOR INTERNATIONAL TRAINING, SIT STUDY ABROAD
AUSTRALIA: CONSERVATION AND RESOURCE MANAGEMENT
Academic Focus • Aboriginal studies, anthropology, Australian studies, conservation studies, environmental science/studies, ethics, ethnic studies, geography, natural resources, public policy, social sciences.
Program Information • Faculty members are drawn from the sponsor's U.S. staff and local instructors hired by the sponsor. Scheduled travel to Tasmania, Fraser Island; field trips to national parks, rural areas.
Sessions • Fall, spring.
Eligibility Requirements • Open to sophomores, juniors, seniors; 2.5 GPA; 2 letters of recommendation; good academic standing at home school.
Living Arrangements • Students live in host family homes, hotels, campsites. Meals are taken as a group, on one's own, with host family, in residences, in restaurants.
Costs (2003-2004) • One term: $12,825; includes tuition, housing, all meals, insurance, excursions. $50 application fee. $400 nonrefundable deposit required. Financial aid available for all students: scholarships.
For More Information • School for International Training, SIT Study Abroad, Kipling Road, Brattleboro, VT 05302-0676; *Phone:* 888-272-7881; *Fax:* 802-258-3296. *E-mail:* studyabroad@sit.edu. *World Wide Web:* http://www.sit.edu/studyabroad/

CAIRNS
INSTITUTE FOR STUDY ABROAD, BUTLER UNIVERSITY
JAMES COOK UNIVERSITY
Hosted by James Cook University–Cairns Campus
Academic Focus • Full curriculum.
Program Information • Students attend classes at James Cook University–Cairns Campus. Scheduled travel to farms; optional travel to reef scuba diving at an extra cost.
Sessions • Fall, spring, yearlong, US academic year.
Eligibility Requirements • Open to sophomores, juniors, seniors; 2.5 GPA; 1 letter of recommendation; good academic standing at home school; enrollment at an accredited American college or university.
Living Arrangements • Students live in host institution dormitories. Quarters are shared with host institution students. Meals are taken as a group, on one's own, in residences, in central dining facility.

Costs (2003) • One term: $9575. Yearlong program: $15,175; includes tuition, housing, insurance, excursions, international student ID, student support services, cultural and sporting events, pre-departure advising. $40 application fee. $500 nonrefundable deposit required. Financial aid available for all students: scholarships, travel grants.

For More Information • Institute for Study Abroad, Butler University, 1100 West 42nd Street, Suite 305, Indianapolis, IN 46208-3345; *Phone:* 800-858-0229; *Fax:* 317-940-9704. *E-mail:* study-abroad@butler.edu. *World Wide Web:* http://www.ifsa-butler.org/

SCHOOL FOR INTERNATIONAL TRAINING, SIT STUDY ABROAD
AUSTRALIA: NATURAL AND CULTURAL ECOLOGY

Academic Focus • Aboriginal studies, anthropology, Australian studies, biological/life sciences, botany, conservation studies, ecology, environmental science/studies, ethnic studies, marine sciences, natural resources, social sciences, wildlife studies.

Program Information • Faculty members are drawn from the sponsor's U.S. staff and local instructors hired by the sponsor. Scheduled travel to the Daintree Rainforest, an Aboriginal camping trip, Atherton Tablelands, Brisbane; field trips to the Great Barrier Reef, research centers.

Sessions • Fall, spring.

Eligibility Requirements • Open to sophomores, juniors, seniors; course work in environmental studies, biology, ecology, or related field; 2.5 GPA; 2 letters of recommendation; good academic standing at home school.

Living Arrangements • Students live in host family homes, hotels, campsites. Meals are taken as a group, on one's own, with host family, in residences, in restaurants.

Costs (2003-2004) • One term: $12,825; includes tuition, housing, all meals, insurance, excursions. $50 application fee. $400 nonrefundable deposit required. Financial aid available for all students: scholarships.

For More Information • School for International Training, SIT Study Abroad, Kipling Road, Brattleboro, VT 05302-0676; *Phone:* 888-272-7881; *Fax:* 802-258-3296. *E-mail:* studyabroad@sit.edu. *World Wide Web:* http://www.sit.edu/studyabroad/

STATE UNIVERSITY OF NEW YORK AT OSWEGO
JAMES COOK UNIVERSITY

Hosted by James Cook University–Cairns Campus, James Cook University–Townsville Campus

Academic Focus • Full curriculum.

Program Information • Students attend classes at James Cook University–Cairns Campus, James Cook University–Townsville Campus. Optional travel to Australia, New Zealand, the South Pacific at an extra cost.

Sessions • Fall, spring, yearlong.

Eligibility Requirements • Open to sophomores, juniors, seniors; 2.5 GPA; 3 letters of recommendation; good academic standing at home school; program study statement.

Living Arrangements • Students live in host institution dormitories, locally rented apartments, host family homes. Quarters are shared with host institution students. Meals are taken on one's own, in residences, in central dining facility, in restaurants.

Costs (2003-2004) • One term: $6520. Yearlong program: $13,040; includes tuition, insurance, student support services. $250 nonrefundable deposit required. Financial aid available for students: home university financial aid, loan processing and scholarships for Oswego students.

For More Information • Ms. Nefertitti Saheed, Program Specialist, State University of New York at Oswego, 122A Swetman Hall, Oswego, NY 13126; *Phone:* 888-4-OSWEGO; *Fax:* 315-312-2477. *E-mail:* intled@oswego.edu. *World Wide Web:* http://www.oswego.edu/intled/

CALLAGHAN
COLLEGE CONSORTIUM FOR INTERNATIONAL STUDIES–ST. BONAVENTURE UNIVERSITY AND TRUMAN STATE UNIVERSITY
UNIVERSITY OF NEWCASTLE, CALLAGHAN, AUSTRALIA

Hosted by University of Newcastle

Academic Focus • Full curriculum.

Program Information • Students attend classes at University of Newcastle. Optional travel at an extra cost.

Sessions • Fall, spring, yearlong.

Eligibility Requirements • Minimum age 18; open to sophomores, juniors, seniors, graduate students, adults; 2.5 GPA; 3 letters of recommendation; good academic standing at home school; transcript; essay.

Living Arrangements • Students live in host institution dormitories, program-owned apartments. Quarters are shared with host institution students. Meals are taken on one's own, in residences.

Costs (2004-2005) • One term: $6465. Yearlong program: $12,930; includes tuition, insurance, administrative fees. $30 application fee. $200 nonrefundable deposit required. Financial aid available for students from sponsoring institution: scholarships, loans.

For More Information • Center for International Education Abroad, College Consortium for International Studies–St. Bonaventure University and Truman State University, Truman State University, Kirk Building 114, Kirksville, MO 63501; *Phone:* 660-785-4076; *Fax:* 660-785-7473. *E-mail:* ciea@truman.edu. *World Wide Web:* http://www.ccisabroad.org/. Students may also apply through St. Bonaventure University, St. Bonaventure, NY 14778.

IDP EDUCATION AUSTRALIA
UNIVERSITY OF NEWCASTLE PROGRAM

Hosted by University of Newcastle

Academic Focus • Full curriculum.

Program Information • Students attend classes at University of Newcastle.

Sessions • Fall, spring, yearlong.

Eligibility Requirements • Open to freshmen, sophomores, juniors, seniors, graduate students; 2.5 GPA.

Living Arrangements • Students live in host institution dormitories, locally rented apartments.

Costs (2004) • One term: contact sponsor for cost. Yearlong program: contact sponsor for cost. $100 deposit required.

For More Information • Ms. Deborah Brown, Senior Manager, Study Abroad, IDP Education Australia, 1400 16th Street, NW, Suite 101, Washington, DC 20036-2219; *Phone:* 866-STUDYOZ; *Fax:* 202-332-3297. *E-mail:* studyabroad@washington.idp.com. *World Wide Web:* http://www.idp.com/

CANBERRA
ARCADIA UNIVERSITY
AUSTRALIAN NATIONAL UNIVERSITY

Hosted by Australian National University

Academic Focus • Full curriculum.

Program Information • Students attend classes at Australian National University. Field trips; optional travel at an extra cost.

Sessions • Fall, spring, yearlong, US academic year.

Eligibility Requirements • Open to juniors, seniors; 3.0 GPA; 1 letter of recommendation.

Living Arrangements • Students live in host institution dormitories, program-owned apartments, program-owned houses, residential colleges. Quarters are shared with host institution students, students from other programs. Meals are taken as a group, on one's own, in residences, in central dining facility.

Costs (2003-2004) • One term: $9790. Yearlong program: $16,650 for Australian academic year; $16,980 for US academic year; includes tuition, housing, insurance, international student ID, student support services, pre-departure guide, transcript. $35 application fee. $500 nonrefundable deposit required. Financial aid available for all students: scholarships, loans.

For More Information • Arcadia University, Center for Education Abroad, 450 South Easton Road, Glenside, PA 19038-3295; *Phone:*

866-927-2234; *Fax:* 215-572-2174. *E-mail:* cea@arcadia.edu. *World Wide Web:* http://www.arcadia.edu/cea/

AUSTRALEARN: NORTH AMERICAN CENTER FOR AUSTRALIAN AND NEW ZEALAND UNIVERSITIES
THE AUSTRALIAN NATIONAL UNIVERSITY

Hosted by Australian National University
Academic Focus • Full curriculum.
Program Information • Students attend classes at Australian National University. Scheduled travel to a pre-trip excursion to the Great Barrier Reef and an Aboriginal Cultural Park; optional travel to Sydney, Melbourne, the Outback, the coast at an extra cost.
Sessions • Fall, spring, yearlong, alternate year.
Eligibility Requirements • Minimum age 18; open to sophomores, juniors, seniors, graduate students; 3.0 GPA; 1 letter of recommendation; good academic standing at home school.
Living Arrangements • Students live in host institution dormitories, locally rented apartments. Quarters are shared with host institution students. Meals are taken as a group, on one's own, in residences, in central dining facility.
Costs (2004) • One term: $11,395. Yearlong program: $20,875; includes tuition, housing, all meals, insurance, excursions, international student ID, student support services. $30 application fee. $300 deposit required. Financial aid available for all students: scholarships, loans.
For More Information • AustraLearn: North American Center for Australian and New Zealand Universities, 12050 North Pecos Street, Suite 320, Westminster, CO 80234; *Phone:* 800-980-0033; *Fax:* 303-446-5955. *E-mail:* studyabroad@australearn.org. *World Wide Web:* http://www.australearn.org/

AUSTRALEARN: NORTH AMERICAN CENTER FOR AUSTRALIAN AND NEW ZEALAND UNIVERSITIES
UNIVERSITY OF CANBERRA

Hosted by University of Canberra
Academic Focus • Full curriculum.
Program Information • Students attend classes at University of Canberra. Scheduled travel to a pre-trip excursion to the Great Barrier Reef and an Aboriginal Cultural Park; optional travel to coastal regions, ski fields, Melbourne, Sydney at an extra cost.
Sessions • Fall, spring, yearlong, alternate year.
Eligibility Requirements • Minimum age 18; open to sophomores, juniors, seniors, graduate students; 2.5 GPA; 1 letter of recommendation; good academic standing at home school.
Living Arrangements • Students live in host institution dormitories, locally rented apartments. Quarters are shared with host institution students. Meals are taken on one's own, in residences, in central dining facility.
Costs (2004) • One term: $6755. Yearlong program: $11,845; includes tuition, housing, some meals, insurance, excursions, international student ID, student support services. $30 application fee. $300 deposit required. Financial aid available for all students: scholarships, loans.
For More Information • AustraLearn: North American Center for Australian and New Zealand Universities, 12050 North Pecos Street, Suite 320, Westminster, CO 80234; *Phone:* 800-980-0033; *Fax:* 303-446-5955. *E-mail:* studyabroad@australearn.org. *World Wide Web:* http://www.australearn.org/

AUSTRALIAN NATIONAL UNIVERSITY
STUDY ABROAD AT THE AUSTRALIAN NATIONAL UNIVERSITY

Hosted by Australian National University
Academic Focus • Aboriginal studies, anthropology, art history, Asian studies, Australian studies, biological/life sciences, computer science, economics, fine/studio arts, forestry, full curriculum, music, political science and government, psychology, science.
Program Information • Students attend classes at Australian National University.
Sessions • Fall, spring, yearlong.

Eligibility Requirements • Open to sophomores, juniors, seniors; 3.0 GPA; 2 letters of recommendation; good academic standing at home school; must have completed at least 3 semesters of college course work.
Living Arrangements • Students live in host institution dormitories. Quarters are shared with host institution students. Meals are taken as a group, on one's own, in residences, in central dining facility.
Costs (2004) • One term: A$8273 (estimated). Yearlong program: A$16,526 (estimated); includes tuition, insurance, lab equipment, student support services, student union fees. A$5250 deposit required.
For More Information • Ms. Linda Losanno, Coordinator, Visiting Student Program, Australian National University, International Education Office, Canberra, Australian Capital Territory 0200, Australia; *Phone:* +61 6-249-4643; *Fax:* +61 6-249-5550. *E-mail:* studyabroad.info@anu.edu.au. *World Wide Web:* http://online.anu.edu.au/ieo/. Students may also apply through Butler University, Institute for Study Abroad, 1100 West 42nd Street, Suite 305, Indianapolis, IN 46208-3345; IDP Education Australia, 1616 P Street NW,Suite #150, Washington, DC 20036; Australian Education Office, 1601 Massachusetts Avenue, NW, Washington, DC 20036; AustraLearn, North American Center for Australian and New Zealand Universities, 12050 North Pecos Street, Suite 320, Westminster, CO 80234; Arcadia University, Center for Education Abroad, 450 South Easton Road, Glenside, PA 19038-3295; Australian Education Connection, 5722 South Flamingo Road, #303, Ft. Lauderdale, FL 33330.

IDP EDUCATION AUSTRALIA
AUSTRALIAN NATIONAL UNIVERSITY PROGRAM

Hosted by Australian National University
Academic Focus • Full curriculum.
Program Information • Students attend classes at Australian National University.
Sessions • Fall, spring, yearlong.
Eligibility Requirements • Open to sophomores, juniors, seniors; 3.0 GPA; minimum 3.4 GPA for internships; portfolio or videotape for National Institute of the Arts.
Living Arrangements • Students live in host institution dormitories, locally rented apartments.
Costs (2004) • One term: contact sponsor for cost. Yearlong program: contact sponsor for cost. $100 deposit required.
For More Information • Ms. Deborah Brown, Senior Manager, Study Abroad, IDP Education Australia, 1400 16th Street, NW, Suite 101, Washington, DC 20036-2219; *Phone:* 866-STUDYOZ; *Fax:* 202-332-3297. *E-mail:* studyabroad@washington.idp.com. *World Wide Web:* http://www.idp.com/

IDP EDUCATION AUSTRALIA
UNIVERSITY OF CANBERRA PROGRAM

Hosted by University of Canberra
Academic Focus • Full curriculum.
Program Information • Students attend classes at University of Canberra.
Sessions • Fall, spring, yearlong.
Eligibility Requirements • Open to sophomores, juniors, seniors; good academic standing at home school.
Living Arrangements • Students live in host institution dormitories, locally rented apartments.
Costs (2004) • One term: contact sponsor for cost. Yearlong program: contact sponsor for cost. $100 deposit required.
For More Information • Ms. Deborah Brown, Senior Manager, Study Abroad, IDP Education Australia, 1400 16th Street, NW, Suite 101, Washington, DC 20036-2219; *Phone:* 866-STUDYOZ; *Fax:* 202-332-3297. *E-mail:* studyabroad@washington.idp.com. *World Wide Web:* http://www.idp.com/

INSTITUTE FOR STUDY ABROAD, BUTLER UNIVERSITY
AUSTRALIAN NATIONAL UNIVERSITY

Hosted by Australian National University
Academic Focus • Full curriculum.

Program Information • Students attend classes at Australian National University. Scheduled travel to farms; optional travel to Jervis Bay, Manly Beach, Sydney at an extra cost.
Sessions • Fall, spring, yearlong, US academic year.
Eligibility Requirements • Open to sophomores, juniors, seniors; 3.0 GPA; 1 letter of recommendation; good academic standing at home school; enrollment at an accredited American college or university.
Living Arrangements • Students live in host institution dormitories. Quarters are shared with host institution students. Meals are taken as a group, on one's own, in residences, in central dining facility.
Costs (2003) • One term: $8775. Yearlong program: $14,775; includes tuition, housing, insurance, excursions, international student ID, student support services, cultural and sporting events, pre-departure advising. $40 application fee. $500 nonrefundable deposit required. Financial aid available for all students: scholarships, travel grants.
For More Information • Institute for Study Abroad, Butler University, 1100 West 42nd Street, Suite 305, Indianapolis, IN 46208-3345; *Phone:* 800-858-0229; *Fax:* 317-940-9704. *E-mail:* study-abroad@butler.edu. *World Wide Web:* http://www.ifsa-butler.org/

STATE UNIVERSITY OF NEW YORK COLLEGE AT BROCKPORT
AUSTRALIAN NATIONAL UNIVERSITY PROGRAM

Hosted by Australian National University
Academic Focus • Full curriculum.
Program Information • Students attend classes at Australian National University. Field trips to various sites throughout Sydney.
Sessions • Fall, spring, yearlong.
Eligibility Requirements • Minimum age 18; open to juniors, seniors; course work in area of internship, if applicable; 3.0 GPA; 2 letters of recommendation; good academic standing at home school; ability to do upper-division course work in chosen subject; résumé for internship option.
Living Arrangements • Students live in host institution dormitories, residential colleges. Quarters are shared with host institution students. Meals are taken as a group, on one's own, in residences, in central dining facility.
Costs (2003-2004) • One term: $9950 for fall term; $10,050 for spring. Yearlong program: $18,150; includes tuition, housing, excursions, international student ID, student support services. $350 nonrefundable deposit required. Financial aid available for all students: scholarships, loans, regular financial aid, grants.
For More Information • Dr. John J. Perry, Director, Office of International Education, State University of New York College at Brockport, 350 New Campus Drive, Brockport, NY 14420; *Phone:* 800-298-SUNY; *Fax:* 585-637-3218. *E-mail:* overseas@brockport.edu. *World Wide Web:* http://www.brockport.edu/studyabroad/

STATE UNIVERSITY OF NEW YORK COLLEGE AT BROCKPORT
UNIVERSITY OF CANBERRA PROGRAM

Hosted by University of Canberra
Academic Focus • Full curriculum.
Program Information • Students attend classes at University of Canberra. Field trips to sites in Sydney (during orientation).
Sessions • Fall, spring, yearlong.
Eligibility Requirements • Minimum age 18; open to juniors, seniors; 3.0 GPA; 2 letters of recommendation; good academic standing at home school; ability to do upper-division course work in chosen subject.
Living Arrangements • Students live in host institution dormitories. Quarters are shared with host institution students. Meals are taken on one's own, in residences.
Costs (2003-2004) • One term: $9750 for fall term; $9850 for spring. Yearlong program: $17,750; includes tuition, housing, excursions, international student ID, student support services. $350 nonrefundable deposit required. Financial aid available for all students: scholarships, loans, regular financial aid, grants.
For More Information • Dr. John J. Perry, Director, Office of International Education, State University of New York College at Brockport, 350 New Campus Drive, Brockport, NY 14420; *Phone:*

800-298-SUNY; *Fax:* 585-637-3218. *E-mail:* overseas@brockport.edu. *World Wide Web:* http://www.brockport.edu/studyabroad/

DARWIN
IDP EDUCATION AUSTRALIA
NORTHERN TERRITORY UNIVERSITY PROGRAM

Hosted by Charles Darwin University
Academic Focus • Full curriculum.
Program Information • Students attend classes at Charles Darwin University. Scheduled travel to Kakadu; optional travel.
Sessions • Fall, spring, yearlong.
Eligibility Requirements • Open to freshmen, sophomores, juniors, seniors; minimum 2.5 GPA or recommendation from home institution.
Living Arrangements • Students live in host institution dormitories, locally rented apartments.
Costs (2004) • One term: contact sponsor for cost. Yearlong program: contact sponsor for cost. $100 deposit required.
For More Information • Ms. Deborah Brown, Senior Manager, Study Abroad, IDP Education Australia, 1400 16th Street, NW, Suite 101, Washington, DC 20036-2219; *Phone:* 866-STUDYOZ; *Fax:* 202-332-3297. *E-mail:* studyabroad@washington.idp.com. *World Wide Web:* http://www.idp.com/

STATE UNIVERSITY OF NEW YORK COLLEGE AT BROCKPORT
CHARLES DARWIN UNIVERSITY

Hosted by Charles Darwin University
Academic Focus • Full curriculum.
Program Information • Students attend classes at Charles Darwin University. Field trips to various sites throughout Sydney (during orientation).
Sessions • Fall, spring, yearlong.
Eligibility Requirements • Minimum age 18; open to juniors, seniors; 2.5 GPA; 2 letters of recommendation; good academic standing at home school; ability to do upper-division course work in chosen subject.
Living Arrangements • Students live in host institution dormitories. Quarters are shared with host institution students. Meals are taken on one's own, in residences.
Costs (2003-2004) • One term: $9150 for fall term; $9250 for spring. Yearlong program: $16,550; includes tuition, housing, excursions, international student ID, student support services. $350 nonrefundable deposit required. Financial aid available for all students: scholarships, loans, regular financial aid, grants.
For More Information • Dr. John Perry, Director, Office of International Education, State University of New York College at Brockport, 350 New Campus Drive, Brockport, NY 14420; *Phone:* 800-298-SUNY; *Fax:* 585-637-3218. *E-mail:* overseas@brockport.edu. *World Wide Web:* http://www.brockport.edu/studyabroad/

FREMANTLE
IDP EDUCATION AUSTRALIA
UNIVERSITY OF NOTRE DAME AUSTRALIA PROGRAM

Hosted by University of Notre Dame Australia
Academic Focus • Asian studies, Australian studies, business administration/management, communications, ecology, environmental science/studies, finance, health and physical education, human resources, international business, marketing, natural resources, Pacific studies, tourism and travel.
Program Information • Students attend classes at University of Notre Dame Australia.
Sessions • Fall, spring, yearlong.
Eligibility Requirements • Open to freshmen, sophomores, juniors, seniors, graduate students; 3.0 GPA.
Living Arrangements • Students live in locally rented apartments, host family homes, hostels.
Costs (2004) • One term: contact sponsor for cost. Yearlong program: contact sponsor for cost. $100 deposit required.
For More Information • Ms. Deborah Brown, Senior Manager, Study Abroad, IDP Education Australia, 1400 16th Street, NW, Suite

101, Washington, DC 20036-2219; *Phone:* 866-STUDYOZ; *Fax:* 202-332-3297. *E-mail:* studyabroad@washington.idp.com. *World Wide Web:* http://www.idp.com/

STUDY AUSTRALIA
UNIVERSITY OF NOTRE DAME
Hosted by University of Notre Dame Australia
Academic Focus • Full curriculum.
Program Information • Students attend classes at University of Notre Dame Australia. Scheduled travel to Sydney; field trips to the Blue Mountains; optional travel to Hawaii, New Zealand, Tasmania, the Great Barrier Reef at an extra cost.
Sessions • Fall, spring, yearlong.
Eligibility Requirements • Minimum age 18; open to freshmen, sophomores, juniors, seniors; 2.5 GPA; 2 letters of recommendation; good academic standing at home school.
Living Arrangements • Students live in host institution dormitories, locally rented apartments, host family homes, locally rented houses. Quarters are shared with host institution students, students from other programs. Meals are taken on one's own, in restaurants.
Costs (2003) • One term: $8295. Yearlong program: $15,090; includes tuition, housing, insurance, excursions, student support services. $500 refundable deposit required. Financial aid available for all students: scholarships, loans.
For More Information • Mr. Chris Shepherd, Director of Programs and Services, Study Australia, 54515 State Road 933 North, Notre Dame, IN 46556-1004; *Phone:* 800-585-9638; *Fax:* 509-357-9457. *E-mail:* info@study-australia.com. *World Wide Web:* http://www.study-australia.com/

GOLD COAST
ARCADIA UNIVERSITY
BOND UNIVERSITY
Hosted by Bond University
Academic Focus • Business administration/management, communications, film and media studies, law and legal studies, liberal studies, social sciences.
Program Information • Students attend classes at Bond University.
Sessions • Fall, spring, yearlong.
Eligibility Requirements • Open to freshmen, sophomores, juniors, seniors, graduate students; 3.0 GPA; 1 letter of recommendation.
Living Arrangements • Students live in host institution dormitories, locally rented apartments. Quarters are shared with host institution students. Meals are taken on one's own, in residences.
Costs (2003-2004) • One term: $9990. Yearlong program: $18,200; includes tuition, housing, insurance, international student ID, student support services, transcripts, pre-departure guide. $35 application fee. $500 nonrefundable deposit required. Financial aid available for all students: scholarships, loans.
For More Information • Arcadia University, Center for Education Abroad, 450 South Easton Road, Glenside, PA 19038-3295; *Phone:* 866-927-2234; *Fax:* 215-572-2174. *E-mail:* cea@arcadia.edu. *World Wide Web:* http://www.arcadia.edu/cea/

AUSTRALEARN: NORTH AMERICAN CENTER FOR AUSTRALIAN AND NEW ZEALAND UNIVERSITIES
BOND UNIVERSITY
Hosted by Bond University
Academic Focus • Full curriculum.
Program Information • Students attend classes at Bond University. Scheduled travel to a pre-trip excursion to the Great Barrier Reef and an Aboriginal Cultural Park; optional travel to Brisbane, the Outback, Sydney, the Great Barrier Reef at an extra cost.
Sessions • Fall, spring, yearlong.
Eligibility Requirements • Minimum age 18; open to sophomores, juniors, seniors, graduate students; 2.5 GPA; 1 letter of recommendation; good academic standing at home school.
Living Arrangements • Students live in host institution dormitories, locally rented apartments. Quarters are shared with host institution students. Meals are taken on one's own, in residences, in central dining facility.

Costs (2004) • One term: $12,275. Yearlong program: $22,895; includes tuition, housing, all meals, insurance, excursions, international student ID, student support services. $30 application fee. $300 deposit required. Financial aid available for all students: scholarships, loans.
For More Information • AustraLearn: North American Center for Australian and New Zealand Universities, 12050 North Pecos Street, Suite 320, Westminster, CO 80234; *Phone:* 800-980-0033; *Fax:* 303-446-5955. *E-mail:* studyabroad@australearn.org. *World Wide Web:* http://www.australearn.org/

CENTER FOR INTERNATIONAL STUDIES
BOND UNIVERSITY
Hosted by Bond University
Academic Focus • Full curriculum.
Program Information • Students attend classes at Bond University. Field trips to a hinterland excursion; optional travel to the Great Barrier Reef at an extra cost.
Sessions • Fall, spring, yearlong.
Eligibility Requirements • Minimum age 18; open to sophomores, juniors, seniors, graduate students, adults; 2.5 GPA; 1 letter of recommendation; good academic standing at home school; personal essay.
Living Arrangements • Students live in host institution dormitories. Quarters are shared with host institution students, students from other programs. Meals are taken on one's own, in central dining facility.
Costs (2003) • One term: $9550. Yearlong program: $17,400; includes tuition, housing, some meals, insurance, international student ID, student support services, airport pick-up. $50 application fee. $500 nonrefundable deposit required. Financial aid available for all students: scholarships.
For More Information • Mr. Jeff Palm, Program Director, Center for International Studies, 17 New South Street, #105, Northampton, MA 01060; *Phone:* 413-582-0407; *Fax:* 413-582-0327. *E-mail:* jpalm@cisabroad.com. *World Wide Web:* http://www.cisabroad.com/

COLLEGE CONSORTIUM FOR INTERNATIONAL STUDIES–ST. BONAVENTURE UNIVERSITY AND TRUMAN STATE UNIVERSITY
SEMESTER IN AUSTRALIA
Hosted by Bond University
Academic Focus • Full curriculum.
Program Information • Students attend classes at Bond University. Field trips to a nearby camp (during orientation); optional travel to New Zealand, New Caledonia, the Great Barrier Reef, Fiji at an extra cost.
Sessions • Fall, spring, yearlong.
Eligibility Requirements • Minimum age 18; open to freshmen, sophomores, juniors, seniors, adults; 2.5 GPA; 3 letters of recommendation; statement of purpose.
Living Arrangements • Students live in host institution dormitories, program-owned apartments. Quarters are shared with host institution students, students from other programs. Meals are taken as a group, on one's own, in residences.
Costs (2004-2005) • One term: $8950. Yearlong program: $17,900; includes tuition, insurance, instructional and administrative fees. $30 application fee. $200 nonrefundable deposit required. Financial aid available for students from sponsoring institution: loans.
For More Information • Center for International Education Abroad, College Consortium for International Studies, Truman State University, Kirk Building 114, Kirksville, MO 63501; *Phone:* 660-785-4079; *Fax:* 660-785-7476. *E-mail:* ciea@truman.edu. *World Wide Web:* http://www.ccisabroad.org/. Students may also apply through St. Bonaventure University, St. Bonaventure, NY 14778.

IDP EDUCATION AUSTRALIA
BOND UNIVERSITY PROGRAM
Hosted by Bond University
Academic Focus • Full curriculum.

Program Information • Students attend classes at Bond University. Field trips to Byron Bay, Stradbroke Island; optional travel to Byron Bay, Stradbroke Island at an extra cost.
Sessions • Fall, spring, 3rd trimester.
Eligibility Requirements • Minimum age 18; open to sophomores, juniors, seniors, graduate students; 2.5 GPA; 1 letter of recommendation; good academic standing at home school.
Living Arrangements • Students live in host institution dormitories, locally rented apartments. Quarters are shared with host institution students, students from other programs. Meals are taken as a group, on one's own, in central dining facility.
Costs (2004) • One term: A$10,000; includes tuition. A$100 deposit required.
For More Information • Ms. Deborah Brown, Senior Manager, Study Abroad, IDP Education Australia, 1400 16th Street, NW, Suite 101, Washington, DC 20036-2219; *Phone:* 866-STUDYOZ; *Fax:* 202-332-3297. *E-mail:* studyabroad@washington.idp.com. *World Wide Web:* http://www.idp.com/

STATE UNIVERSITY OF NEW YORK AT PLATTSBURGH
STUDY IN AUSTRALIA, GOLD COAST

Hosted by Bond University
Academic Focus • Australian studies, business administration/management, communications, film and media studies, information science, international affairs, international business, journalism, law and legal studies, liberal studies, psychology.
Program Information • Students attend classes at Bond University. Optional travel to the Great Barrier Reef, Ayers Rock, Sydney, New Zealand at an extra cost.
Sessions • Fall, spring, yearlong.
Eligibility Requirements • Minimum age 18; open to sophomores, juniors, seniors, adults; 2.6 GPA; 2 letters of recommendation; SUNY application; essay; transcript.
Living Arrangements • Students live in host institution dormitories, locally rented apartments. Quarters are shared with host institution students, students from other programs. Meals are taken as a group, on one's own, in central dining facility, in restaurants.
Costs (2003-2004) • One term: $11,700 for New York residents; nonresidents contact sponsor for cost. Yearlong program: $23,400 for New York residents; nonresidents contact sponsor for cost; includes tuition, housing, some meals, insurance, international student ID, student support services, program fees. $20 application fee. $350 nonrefundable deposit required. Financial aid available for students from sponsoring institution: scholarships, loans.
For More Information • Ms. Jo Ann Mackie, Study Abroad Coordinator, State University of New York at Plattsburgh, Study Abroad Office, 101 Broad Street, Plattsburgh, NY 12901; *Phone:* 518-564-2321; *Fax:* 518-564-2326. *E-mail:* international@plattsburgh.edu. *World Wide Web:* http://www.plattsburgh.edu/studyabroad/

STUDY AUSTRALIA
BOND UNIVERSITY

Hosted by Bond University
Academic Focus • Full curriculum.
Program Information • Students attend classes at Bond University. Scheduled travel to Sydney; field trips to the Blue Mountains; optional travel at an extra cost.
Sessions • Fall, spring, winter, yearlong.
Eligibility Requirements • Minimum age 18; open to freshmen, sophomores, juniors, seniors; 2.5 GPA; good academic standing at home school.
Living Arrangements • Students live in host institution dormitories, locally rented apartments, host family homes. Quarters are shared with host institution students, students from other programs. Meals are taken on one's own, in central dining facility.
Costs (2003) • One term: $9825. Yearlong program: $18,295; includes tuition, housing, insurance, student support services. $500 refundable deposit required. Financial aid available for all students: scholarships, loans.
For More Information • Mr. Chris Shepherd, Director of Programs and Services, Study Australia, 54515 State Road 933 North, Notre Dame, IN 46556-1004; *Phone:* 800-585-9658; *Fax:* 509-357-9457. *E-mail:* info@study-australia.com. *World Wide Web:* http://www.study-australia.com/

UNIVERSITY STUDIES ABROAD CONSORTIUM
FULL CURRICULUM STUDIES IN GOLD COAST, AUSTRALIA

Hosted by Griffith University–Nathan Campus, Griffith University–Logan Campus, Griffith University Gold Coast University College
Academic Focus • Full curriculum.
Program Information • Students attend classes at Griffith University Gold Coast University College, Griffith University–Logan Campus, Griffith University–Nathan Campus.
Sessions • Fall, spring, yearlong.
Eligibility Requirements • Minimum age 18; open to freshmen, sophomores, juniors, seniors, graduate students, adults; 2.5 GPA.
Living Arrangements • Students live in host institution dormitories, locally rented apartments. Quarters are shared with host institution students. Meals are taken on one's own, in residences, in central dining facility, in restaurants.
Costs (2005) • One term: $5980. Yearlong program: $11,780; includes tuition, insurance, student support services. $50 application fee. $150 refundable deposit required. Financial aid available for all students: scholarships, loans.
For More Information • University Studies Abroad Consortium, USAC/323, Reno, NV 89557-0093; *Phone:* 775-784-6569; *Fax:* 775-784-6010. *E-mail:* usac@unr.edu. *World Wide Web:* http://usac.unr.edu/

HOBART

AUSTRALEARN: NORTH AMERICAN CENTER FOR AUSTRALIAN AND NEW ZEALAND UNIVERSITIES
UNIVERSITY OF TASMANIA

Hosted by University of Tasmania
Academic Focus • Full curriculum.
Program Information • Students attend classes at University of Tasmania. Scheduled travel to a pre-trip excursion to the Great Barrier Reef and an Aboriginal Cultural Park; optional travel to Melbourne, other areas of Tasmania, New Zealand at an extra cost.
Sessions • Fall, spring, yearlong, alternate year.
Eligibility Requirements • Minimum age 18; open to sophomores, juniors, seniors, graduate students; 2.5 GPA; 1 letter of recommendation; good academic standing at home school.
Living Arrangements • Students live in locally rented apartments. Quarters are shared with students from other programs. Meals are taken on one's own, in residences.
Costs (2004) • One term: $8870. Yearlong program: $15,695; includes tuition, housing, insurance, excursions, international student ID, student support services. $30 application fee. $300 deposit required. Financial aid available for all students: scholarships, loans.
For More Information • AustraLearn: North American Center for Australian and New Zealand Universities, 12050 North Pecos Street, Suite 320, Westminster, CO 80234; *Phone:* 800-980-0033; *Fax:* 303-446-5955. *E-mail:* studyabroad@australearn.org. *World Wide Web:* http://www.australearn.org/

IDP EDUCATION AUSTRALIA
UNIVERSITY OF TASMANIA PROGRAM

Hosted by University of Tasmania
Academic Focus • Full curriculum.
Program Information • Students attend classes at University of Tasmania.
Sessions • Fall, spring, yearlong.
Eligibility Requirements • Open to sophomores, juniors, seniors; 2.5 GPA.
Costs (2004) • One term: contact sponsor for cost. Yearlong program: contact sponsor for cost.
For More Information • Ms. Deborah Brown, Senior Manager, Study Abroad, IDP Education Australia, 1400 16th Street, NW, Suite 101, Washington, DC 20036-2219; *Phone:* 866-STUDYOZ; *Fax:* 202-332-3297. *E-mail:* studyabroad@washington.idp.com. *World Wide Web:* http://www.idp.com/

AUSTRALIA
Hobart

INSTITUTE FOR STUDY ABROAD, BUTLER UNIVERSITY
UNIVERSITY OF TASMANIA–HOBART

Hosted by University of Tasmania
Academic Focus • Full curriculum.
Program Information • Students attend classes at University of Tasmania. Scheduled travel to farms; optional travel to beaches, wilderness parks, chocolate factory, breweries, sporting events at an extra cost.
Sessions • Fall, spring, yearlong, US academic year.
Eligibility Requirements • Open to sophomores, juniors, seniors; 2.5 GPA; 1 letter of recommendation; good academic standing at home school; enrollment at an accredited American college or university.
Living Arrangements • Students live in host institution dormitories, locally rented apartments. Quarters are shared with host institution students, students from other programs. Meals are taken as a group, on one's own, in residences, in central dining facility, in restaurants.
Costs (2003) • One term: $8875. Yearlong program: $12,975; includes tuition, housing, insurance, excursions, international student ID, student support services, cultural and sporting events, pre-departure advising. $40 application fee. $500 nonrefundable deposit required. Financial aid available for all students: scholarships, travel grants.
For More Information • Institute for Study Abroad, Butler University, 1100 West 42nd Street, Suite 305, Indianapolis, IN 46208-3345; *Phone:* 800-858-0229; *Fax:* 317-940-9704. *E-mail:* study-abroad@butler.edu. *World Wide Web:* http://www.ifsa-butler.org/

STATE UNIVERSITY OF NEW YORK AT OSWEGO
UNIVERSITY OF TASMANIA

Hosted by University of Tasmania–Launceston Campus, University of Tasmania
Academic Focus • Full curriculum.
Program Information • Students attend classes at University of Tasmania–Launceston Campus, University of Tasmania. Optional travel to Australia, New Zealand, the South Pacific at an extra cost.
Sessions • Fall, spring, yearlong.
Eligibility Requirements • Open to sophomores, juniors, seniors; 2.5 GPA; 3 letters of recommendation; good academic standing at home school; program of study statement.
Living Arrangements • Students live in host institution dormitories, locally rented apartments. Quarters are shared with host institution students. Meals are taken on one's own, in residences, in restaurants.
Costs (2003-2004) • One term: $5320. Yearlong program: $10,640; includes tuition, insurance, student support services. $250 nonrefundable deposit required. Financial aid available for students: home university financial aid, loan processing and scholarships for Oswego students.
For More Information • Ms. Nefertitti Saheed, Program Specialist, State University of New York at Oswego, 122A Swetman Hall, Oswego, NY 13126; *Phone:* 888-4-OSWEGO; *Fax:* 315-312-2477. *E-mail:* intled@oswego.edu. *World Wide Web:* http://www.oswego.edu/intled/

LAUNCESTON

INSTITUTE FOR STUDY ABROAD, BUTLER UNIVERSITY
UNIVERSITY OF TASMANIA–LAUNCESTON

Hosted by University of Tasmania–Launceston Campus
Academic Focus • Full curriculum.
Program Information • Students attend classes at University of Tasmania–Launceston Campus. Scheduled travel to farms; optional travel to beaches, wilderness parks, achocolate factory, breweries, sporting events at an extra cost.
Sessions • Fall, spring, yearlong, US academic year.

Eligibility Requirements • Open to sophomores, juniors, seniors; 2.5 GPA; 1 letter of recommendation; good academic standing at home school; enrollment at an accredited American college or university.
Living Arrangements • Students live in host institution dormitories. Quarters are shared with host institution students, students from other programs. Meals are taken as a group, on one's own, in residences, in central dining facility, in restaurants.
Costs (2003) • One term: $8875. Yearlong program: $12,975; includes tuition, housing, insurance, excursions, international student ID, student support services, cultural and sporting events, pre-departure advising. $40 application fee. $500 nonrefundable deposit required. Financial aid available for all students: scholarships, travel grants.
For More Information • Institute for Study Abroad, Butler University, 1100 West 42nd Street, Suite 305, Indianapolis, IN 46208-3345; *Phone:* 800-858-0229; *Fax:* 317-940-9704. *E-mail:* study-abroad@butler.edu. *World Wide Web:* http://www.ifsa-butler.org/

LISMORE

AUSTRALEARN: NORTH AMERICAN CENTER FOR AUSTRALIAN AND NEW ZEALAND UNIVERSITIES
SOUTHERN CROSS UNIVERSITY

Hosted by Southern Cross University
Academic Focus • Full curriculum.
Program Information • Students attend classes at Southern Cross University. Scheduled travel to the Great Barrier Reef and an Aboriginal Cultural park (pre-trip excursion); optional travel to Brisbane, the Outback, Sydney, Gold Coast, Ayers Rock (Uluru), Byron Bay at an extra cost.
Sessions • Fall, spring, yearlong, alternate year.
Eligibility Requirements • Minimum age 18; open to sophomores, juniors, seniors, graduate students; 2.5 GPA; 1 letter of recommendation; good academic standing at home school.
Living Arrangements • Students live in host institution dormitories, locally rented apartments. Quarters are shared with host institution students, students from other programs. Meals are taken on one's own, in residences.
Costs (2004) • One term: $8310. Yearlong program: $15,000; includes tuition, housing, insurance, excursions, international student ID, student support services. $30 application fee. $300 deposit required. Financial aid available for all students: scholarships, loans.
For More Information • AustraLearn: North American Center for Australian and New Zealand Universities, 12050 North Pecos Street, Suite 320, Westminster, CO 80234; *Phone:* 800-980-0033; *Fax:* 303-446-5955. *E-mail:* studyabroad@australearn.org. *World Wide Web:* http://www.australearn.org/

IDP EDUCATION AUSTRALIA
SOUTHERN CROSS UNIVERSITY PROGRAM

Hosted by Southern Cross University
Academic Focus • Full curriculum.
Program Information • Students attend classes at Southern Cross University.
Sessions • Fall, spring, yearlong.
Eligibility Requirements • Open to freshmen, sophomores, juniors, seniors; 2.7 GPA.
Living Arrangements • Students live in host institution dormitories, locally rented apartments.
Costs (2004) • One term: contact sponsor for cost. Yearlong program: contact sponsor for cost. $100 deposit required.
For More Information • Ms. Deborah Brown, Senior Manager, Study Abroad, IDP Education Australia, 1400 16th Street, NW, Suite 101, Washington, DC 20036-2219; *Phone:* 866-STUDYOZ; *Fax:* 202-332-3297. *E-mail:* studyabroad@washington.idp.com. *World Wide Web:* http://www.idp.com/

INSTITUTE FOR STUDY ABROAD, BUTLER UNIVERSITY
SOUTHERN CROSS UNIVERSITY

Hosted by Southern Cross University
Academic Focus • Aboriginal studies, art, computer science, forestry, geography, music, psychology, sociology, teaching, telecommunications.
Program Information • Students attend classes at Southern Cross University. Scheduled travel to farms; optional travel to central Australia, Fraser Island at an extra cost.
Sessions • Fall, spring, yearlong, US academic year.
Eligibility Requirements • 2.5 GPA; 1 letter of recommendation; good academic standing at home school; enrollment at an accredited American college or university.
Living Arrangements • Students live in host institution dormitories, locally rented apartments. Quarters are shared with host institution students. Meals are taken on one's own, in residences.
Costs (2003) • One term: $8575. Yearlong program: $12,975; includes tuition, housing, insurance, excursions, international student ID, student support services, cultural and sporting events, pre-departure advising. $40 application fee. $500 deposit required. Financial aid available for all students: scholarships, travel grants.
For More Information • Institute for Study Abroad, Butler University, 1100 West 42nd Street, Suite 305, Indianapolis, IN 46208-3345; *Phone:* 800-858-0229; *Fax:* 317-940-9704. *E-mail:* study-abroad@butler.edu. *World Wide Web:* http://www.ifsa-butler.org/

STATE UNIVERSITY OF NEW YORK COLLEGE AT BROCKPORT
SOUTHERN CROSS UNIVERSITY PROGRAM

Hosted by Southern Cross University
Academic Focus • Full curriculum.
Program Information • Students attend classes at Southern Cross University. Field trips to locations throughout Sydney during orientation; optional travel.
Sessions • Fall, spring, yearlong.
Eligibility Requirements • Minimum age 18; open to juniors, seniors; 2.75 GPA; 2 letters of recommendation; ability to do upper-division course work in chosen subject.
Living Arrangements • Students live in host institution dormitories, program-owned houses. Quarters are shared with host institution students. Meals are taken on one's own, in residences.
Costs (2003-2004) • One term: $9150 for fall term; $9250 for spring. Yearlong program: $16,550; includes tuition, housing, excursions, international student ID, student support services. $350 nonrefundable deposit required. Financial aid available for all students: scholarships, loans, regular financial aid, grants.
For More Information • Dr. John Perry, Director, Office of International Education, State University of New York College at Brockport, 350 New Campus Drive, Brockport, NY 14420; *Phone:* 800-298-SUNY; *Fax:* 585-637-3218. *E-mail:* overseas@brockport.edu. *World Wide Web:* http://www.brockport.edu/studyabroad/

MAROOCHYDORE
UNIVERSITY OF IDAHO
AUSTRALIAN STUDIES–UNIVERSITY OF THE SUNSHINE COAST

Hosted by University of the Sunshine Coast
Academic Focus • Accounting, Australian studies, business administration/management, communications, design and applied arts, ecology, international business, marine sciences, public health, sports management, tourism and travel.
Program Information • Students attend classes at University of the Sunshine Coast. Field trips to a local Aboriginal Cultural Center, Fraser Island, Hervey Bay (whale watching), Brisbane Southbank Parklands; optional travel to the Great Barrier Reef at an extra cost.
Sessions • Fall, spring, yearlong.
Eligibility Requirements • Open to sophomores, juniors, seniors, graduate students; 2.75 GPA.
Living Arrangements • Students live in host institution dormitories, program-owned apartments. Quarters are shared with host

institution students, students from other programs. Meals are taken on one's own, in residences, in central dining facility.
Costs (2003-2004) • One term: $4500. Yearlong program: $9000; includes tuition, student support services. $100 application fee. $200 refundable deposit required. Financial aid available for students from sponsoring institution: scholarships, loans, grants.
For More Information • Ms. Amy Bergmann, Advisor, University of Idaho, 209 Morrill Hall, Moscow, ID 83844-3013; *Phone:* 208-885-7870; *Fax:* 208-885-2859. *E-mail:* abroad@uidaho.edu. *World Wide Web:* http://www.ets.uidaho.edu/ipo/abroad/

MELBOURNE
ARCADIA UNIVERSITY
MONASH UNIVERSITY

Hosted by Monash University
Academic Focus • Biological/life sciences, business administration/management, commerce, economics, engineering, fine/studio arts.
Program Information • Students attend classes at Monash University. Field trips; optional travel at an extra cost.
Sessions • Fall, spring, yearlong, US academic year.
Eligibility Requirements • Open to sophomores, juniors, seniors; 3.0 GPA; 1 letter of recommendation.
Living Arrangements • Students live in host institution dormitories, locally rented apartments, program-owned apartments, residential colleges. Quarters are shared with host institution students, students from other programs. Meals are taken on one's own, in residences.
Costs (2003-2004) • One term: $9525. Yearlong program: $15,790 for Australian academic year; $16,100 for US academic year; includes tuition, housing, insurance, international student ID, student support services, transcript, pre-departure guide. $35 application fee. $500 nonrefundable deposit required. Financial aid available for all students: scholarships, loans.
For More Information • Arcadia University, Center for Education Abroad, 450 South Easton Road, Glenside, PA 19038-3295; *Phone:* 866-927-2234; *Fax:* 215-572-2174. *E-mail:* cea@arcadia.edu. *World Wide Web:* http://www.arcadia.edu/cea/

ARCADIA UNIVERSITY
UNIVERSITY OF MELBOURNE

Hosted by University of Melbourne
Academic Focus • Agriculture, biological/life sciences, business administration/management, engineering, liberal studies, premedical studies, social sciences.
Program Information • Students attend classes at University of Melbourne. Field trips; optional travel at an extra cost.
Sessions • Fall, spring, yearlong, US academic year.
Eligibility Requirements • Open to sophomores, juniors, seniors; 3.0 GPA; 1 letter of recommendation.
Living Arrangements • Students live in host institution dormitories, locally rented apartments, program-owned apartments, residential colleges. Quarters are shared with host institution students, students from other programs. Meals are taken as a group, on one's own, in residences, in central dining facility.
Costs (2003-2004) • One term: $11,590. Yearlong program: $19,490–$19,890; includes tuition, housing, insurance, international student ID, student support services, transcripts, pre-departure guide. $35 application fee. $500 nonrefundable deposit required. Financial aid available for all students: scholarships, loans.
For More Information • Arcadia University, Center for Education Abroad, 450 South Easton Road, Glenside, PA 19038-3295; *Phone:* 866-927-2234; *Fax:* 215-572-2174. *E-mail:* cea@arcadia.edu. *World Wide Web:* http://www.arcadia.edu/cea/

AUSTRALEARN: NORTH AMERICAN CENTER FOR AUSTRALIAN AND NEW ZEALAND UNIVERSITIES
LA TROBE UNIVERSITY

Hosted by La Trobe University, La Trobe University
Academic Focus • Full curriculum.
Program Information • Students attend classes at La Trobe University, La Trobe University. Scheduled travel to a pre-trip

excursion to the Great Barrier Reef and an Aboriginal Cultural Park; optional travel to Adelaide, Outback, Sydney at an extra cost.

Sessions • Fall, spring, yearlong, alternate year.

Eligibility Requirements • Minimum age 18; open to sophomores, juniors, seniors, graduate students; 2.5 GPA; 1 letter of recommendation; good academic standing at home school.

Living Arrangements • Students live in host institution dormitories, locally rented apartments. Quarters are shared with host institution students. Meals are taken as a group, on one's own, in residences, in central dining facility.

Costs (2004) • One term: $10,010. Yearlong program: $18,075; includes tuition, housing, insurance, excursions, international student ID, student support services. $30 application fee. $300 deposit required. Financial aid available for all students: scholarships, loans.

For More Information • AustraLearn: North American Center for Australian and New Zealand Universities, 12050 North Pecos Street, Suite 320, Westminster, CO 80234; *Phone:* 800-980-0033; *Fax:* 303-446-5955. *E-mail:* studyabroad@australearn.org. *World Wide Web:* http://www.australearn.org/

AUSTRALEARN: NORTH AMERICAN CENTER FOR AUSTRALIAN AND NEW ZEALAND UNIVERSITIES
MONASH UNIVERSITY

Hosted by Monash University

Academic Focus • Full curriculum.

Program Information • Students attend classes at Monash University. Scheduled travel to a pre-trip excursion to the Great Barrier Reef and an Aboriginal Cultural Park; optional travel to Sydney, Adelaide at an extra cost.

Sessions • Fall, spring, yearlong, alternate year.

Eligibility Requirements • Minimum age 18; open to sophomores, juniors, seniors, graduate students; 3.0 GPA; good academic standing at home school.

Living Arrangements • Students live in host institution dormitories, locally rented apartments. Quarters are shared with host institution students. Meals are taken on one's own, in residences, in central dining facility.

Costs (2004) • One term: $8445. Yearlong program: $15,305; includes tuition, housing, insurance, international student ID, student support services. $30 application fee. $300 deposit required. Financial aid available for all students: scholarships, loans.

For More Information • AustraLearn: North American Center for Australian and New Zealand Universities, 12050 North Pecos Street, Suite 320, Westminster, CO 80234; *Phone:* 800-980-0033; *Fax:* 303-446-5955. *E-mail:* studyabroad@australearn.org. *World Wide Web:* http://www.australearn.org/

BENTLEY COLLEGE
BUSINESS PROGRAM ABROAD IN MELBOURNE, AUSTRALIA

Hosted by RMIT University

Academic Focus • Accounting, business administration/management, computer science, cultural studies, economics, finance, marketing.

Program Information • Students attend classes at RMIT University. Scheduled travel; field trips to Great Ocean Road, cultural sites; optional travel to Grampions, New South Wales, Queensland, Ayres Rock at an extra cost.

Sessions • Fall, spring.

Eligibility Requirements • Open to juniors, seniors; 3.0 GPA; 1 letter of recommendation; good academic standing at home school; essay; no foreign language proficiency required.

Living Arrangements • Students live in host institution dormitories, locally rented apartments. Quarters are shared with host institution students, students from other programs. Meals are taken on one's own, in residences, in restaurants.

Costs (2002-2003) • One term: $15,600; includes tuition, housing, some meals, insurance, excursions, international student ID, student support services, airport pick-up. $35 application fee. $500 nonrefundable deposit required. Financial aid available for students from sponsoring institution: scholarships, loans.

For More Information • Mr. Andrew Dusenbery, Education Abroad Advisor, Bentley College, 175 Forest Street, Waltham, MA 02452; *Phone:* 781-891-3474; *Fax:* 781-891-2819. *E-mail:* study_abroad@bentley.edu. *World Wide Web:* http://ecampus.bentley.edu/dept/sa/

CENTER FOR INTERNATIONAL STUDIES
LA TROBE UNIVERSITY

Hosted by La Trobe University

Academic Focus • Full curriculum.

Program Information • Students attend classes at La Trobe University. Optional travel at an extra cost.

Sessions • Fall, spring, yearlong.

Eligibility Requirements • Minimum age 18; open to sophomores, juniors, seniors, graduate students, adults; 2.5 GPA; 1 letter of recommendation; good academic standing at home school; personal essay.

Living Arrangements • Students live in host institution dormitories, program-owned apartments. Quarters are shared with host institution students. Meals are taken on one's own, in residences, in central dining facility.

Costs (2003) • One term: $7370. Yearlong program: $13,000; includes tuition, housing, insurance, international student ID, student support services, airport reception. $50 application fee. $500 nonrefundable deposit required. Financial aid available for all students: scholarships.

For More Information • Mr. Jeff Palm, Program Director, Center for International Studies, 17 New South Street, #105, Northampton, MA 01060; *Phone:* 413-582-0407; *Fax:* 413-582-0327. *E-mail:* jpalm@cisabroad.com. *World Wide Web:* http://www.cisabroad.com/

CIEE
CIEE STUDY CENTER, MELBOURNE, AUSTRALIA

Hosted by La Trobe University, University of Melbourne

Academic Focus • Full curriculum.

Program Information • Students attend classes at La Trobe University, University of Melbourne. Field trips to sites around Melbourne; optional travel to Sydney, Tasmania, Great Ocean Road at an extra cost.

Sessions • Fall, spring, yearlong, alternate year.

Eligibility Requirements • Open to sophomores, juniors, seniors; 3.0 GPA; 2 letters of recommendation; good academic standing at home school.

Living Arrangements • Students live in host institution dormitories, locally rented apartments. Quarters are shared with host institution students, students from other programs. Meals are taken on one's own, in residences, in restaurants.

Costs (2004-2005) • One term: $10,950 for La Trobe; $12,950 for Melbourne. Yearlong program: $19,900 for La Trobe; $22,000 for Melbourne; includes tuition, housing, insurance, excursions, student support services, pre-departure advising, cultural activities. $30 application fee. $300 deposit required. Financial aid available for all students: scholarships, minority student scholarships, travel grants.

For More Information • Mr. Adam Rubin, Admissions Officer, Asia Pacific, CIEE, 7 Custom House Street, 3rd Floor, Portland, ME 04101; *Phone:* 800-40-STUDY; *Fax:* 207-553-7699. *E-mail:* studyinfo@ciee.org. *World Wide Web:* http://www.ciee.org/isp/

IDP EDUCATION AUSTRALIA
DEAKIN UNIVERSITY PROGRAM

Hosted by Deakin University–Melbourne Campus

Academic Focus • Full curriculum.

Program Information • Students attend classes at Deakin University–Melbourne Campus.

Sessions • Fall, spring, yearlong.

Eligibility Requirements • Open to sophomores, juniors, seniors; 2.6 GPA.

Living Arrangements • Students live in host institution dormitories, locally rented apartments.

Costs (2004) • One term: contact sponsor for cost. Yearlong program: contact sponsor for cost. $100 deposit required.

For More Information • Ms. Deborah Brown, Senior Manager, Study Abroad, IDP Education Australia, 1400 16th Street, NW, Suite 101, Washington, DC 20036-2219; *Phone:* 866-STUDYOZ; *Fax:* 202-332-3297. *E-mail:* studyabroad@washington.idp.com. *World Wide Web:* http://www.idp.com/

IDP EDUCATION AUSTRALIA
LA TROBE UNIVERSITY PROGRAM

Hosted by La Trobe University
Academic Focus • Full curriculum.
Program Information • Students attend classes at La Trobe University. Field trips.
Sessions • Fall, spring, yearlong.
Eligibility Requirements • Open to freshmen, sophomores, juniors, seniors; 2.5 GPA.
Costs (2004) • One term: contact sponsor for cost. Yearlong program: contact sponsor for cost. $100 deposit required.
For More Information • Ms. Deborah Brown, Senior Manager, Study Abroad, IDP Education Australia, 1400 16th Street, NW, Suite 101, Washington, DC 20036-2219; *Phone:* 866-STUDYOZ; *Fax:* 202-332-3297. *E-mail:* studyabroad@washington.idp.com. *World Wide Web:* http://www.idp.com/

IDP EDUCATION AUSTRALIA
MONASH UNIVERSITY PROGRAM

Hosted by Monash University
Academic Focus • Australian studies, business administration/management, design and applied arts, economics, education, engineering, fine/studio arts, information science, library science, science, teaching, visual and performing arts.
Program Information • Students attend classes at Monash University.
Sessions • Fall, spring, yearlong.
Eligibility Requirements • Open to sophomores, juniors, seniors; 3.0 GPA.
Living Arrangements • Students live in host institution dormitories.
Costs (2004) • One term: contact sponsor for cost. Yearlong program: contact sponsor for cost. $100 deposit required.

For More Information • Ms. Deborah Brown, Senior Manager, Study Abroad, IDP Education Australia, 1400 16th Street, NW, Suite 101, Washington, DC 20036-2219; *Phone:* 866-STUDYOZ; *Fax:* 202-332-3297. *E-mail:* studyabroad@washington.idp.com. *World Wide Web:* http://www.idp.com/

IDP EDUCATION AUSTRALIA
RMIT UNIVERSITY PROGRAM

Hosted by RMIT University
Academic Focus • Full curriculum.
Program Information • Students attend classes at RMIT University.
Sessions • Fall, spring, yearlong.
Eligibility Requirements • Open to freshmen, sophomores, juniors, seniors, graduate students; good academic standing at home school; personal statement; involvement in extracurricular activities.
Living Arrangements • Students live in locally rented apartments.
Costs (2004) • One term: contact sponsor for cost. Yearlong program: contact sponsor for cost. $100 deposit required.
For More Information • Ms. Deborah Brown, Senior Manager, Study Abroad, IDP Education Australia, 1400 16th Street, NW, Suite 101, Washington, DC 20036-2219; *Phone:* 866-STUDYOZ; *Fax:* 202-332-3297. *E-mail:* studyabroad@washington.idp.com. *World Wide Web:* http://www.idp.com/

IDP EDUCATION AUSTRALIA
SWINBURNE UNIVERSITY OF TECHNOLOGY PROGRAM

Hosted by Swinburne University of Technology
Academic Focus • Art, business administration/management, computer science, engineering, film and media studies, graphic design/illustration, information science, social sciences, tourism and travel.

AUSTRALIA
Melbourne

Program Information • Students attend classes at Swinburne University of Technology.
Sessions • Fall, spring, yearlong.
Eligibility Requirements • Open to sophomores, juniors, seniors; 2.5 GPA.
Costs (2004) • One term: contact sponsor for cost. Yearlong program: contact sponsor for cost. $100 deposit required.
For More Information • Ms. Deborah Brown, Senior Manager, Study Abroad, IDP Education Australia, 1400 16th Street, NW, Suite 101, Washington, DC 20036-2219; *Phone:* 866-STUDYOZ; *Fax:* 202-332-3297. *E-mail:* studyabroad@washington.idp.com. *World Wide Web:* http://www.idp.com/

IDP EDUCATION AUSTRALIA
UNIVERSITY OF MELBOURNE PROGRAM

Hosted by University of Melbourne
Academic Focus • Full curriculum.
Program Information • Students attend classes at University of Melbourne.
Sessions • Fall, spring, yearlong.
Eligibility Requirements • Open to sophomores, juniors, seniors; 3.0 GPA.
Living Arrangements • Students live in host institution dormitories, locally rented apartments.
Costs (2004) • One term: contact sponsor for cost. Yearlong program: contact sponsor for cost. $100 deposit required.
For More Information • Ms. Deborah Brown, Senior Manager, Study Abroad, IDP Education Australia, 1400 16th Street, NW, Suite 101, Washington, DC 20036-2219; *Phone:* 866-STUDYOZ; *Fax:* 202-332-3297. *E-mail:* studyabroad@washington.idp.com. *World Wide Web:* http://www.idp.com/

IDP EDUCATION AUSTRALIA
VICTORIA UNIVERSITY PROGRAM

Hosted by Victoria University
Academic Focus • Full curriculum.
Program Information • Students attend classes at Victoria University.
Sessions • Fall, spring, yearlong.
Eligibility Requirements • Open to freshmen, sophomores, juniors, seniors; 2.5 GPA.
Costs (2004) • One term: contact sponsor for cost. Yearlong program: contact sponsor for cost. $100 deposit required.
For More Information • Ms. Deborah Brown, Senior Manager, Study Abroad, IDP Education Australia, 1400 16th Street, NW, Suite 101, Washington, DC 20036-2219; *Phone:* 866-STUDYOZ; *Fax:* 202-332-3297. *E-mail:* studyabroad@washington.idp.com. *World Wide Web:* http://www.idp.com/

IES, INSTITUTE FOR THE INTERNATIONAL EDUCATION OF STUDENTS
IES–MELBOURNE

Hosted by University of Melbourne
Academic Focus • Full curriculum.
Program Information • Students attend classes at University of Melbourne. Scheduled travel to New Zealand (Semester I), Tasmania (Semester II).
Sessions • Fall, spring, yearlong, calendar year.
Eligibility Requirements • Minimum age 18; open to sophomores, juniors, seniors, graduate students, adults; 3.0 GPA; 1 letter of recommendation; good academic standing at home school.
Living Arrangements • Students live in host institution dormitories, locally rented apartments, host family homes. Quarters are shared with host institution students. Meals are taken on one's own, with host family, in residences, in central dining facility.
Costs (2002-2003) • One term: $11,700. Yearlong program: $21,060; includes tuition, housing, some meals, excursions, student support services, partial insurance coverage. $50 application fee. $500 nonrefundable deposit required. Financial aid available for all students: scholarships, institutional partner need-based grants.
For More Information • International Education Representative, IES, Institute for the International Education of Students, 33 North

LaSalle Street, 15th Floor, Chicago, IL 60602; *Phone:* 800-995-2300; *Fax:* 312-944-1448. *E-mail:* info@iesabroad.org. *World Wide Web:* http://www.IESabroad.org/

INSTITUTE FOR STUDY ABROAD, BUTLER UNIVERSITY
MONASH UNIVERSITY

Hosted by Monash University
Academic Focus • Full curriculum.
Program Information • Students attend classes at Monash University. Scheduled travel to farms; field trips to Great Ocean Road; optional travel to Kangaroo Island, Great Ocean Road at an extra cost.
Sessions • Fall, spring, yearlong, US academic year.
Eligibility Requirements • Open to sophomores, juniors, seniors; 3.0 GPA; 1 letter of recommendation; good academic standing at home school; enrollment at an accredited American college or university.
Living Arrangements • Students live in host institution dormitories. Quarters are shared with host institution students. Meals are taken as a group, on one's own, in residences, in central dining facility.
Costs (2003) • One term: $9275. Yearlong program: $14,975; includes tuition, housing, insurance, excursions, international student ID, student support services, cultural and sporting events, pre-departure advising. $40 application fee. $500 nonrefundable deposit required. Financial aid available for all students: scholarships, travel grants.
For More Information • Institute for Study Abroad, Butler University, 1100 West 42nd Street, Suite 305, Indianapolis, IN 46208-3345; *Phone:* 800-858-0229; *Fax:* 317-940-9704. *E-mail:* study-abroad@butler.edu. *World Wide Web:* http://www.ifsa-butler.org/

INSTITUTE FOR STUDY ABROAD, BUTLER UNIVERSITY
UNIVERSITY OF MELBOURNE

Hosted by University of Melbourne
Academic Focus • Full curriculum.
Program Information • Students attend classes at University of Melbourne. Scheduled travel to farms; field trips to Great Ocean Road; optional travel at an extra cost.
Sessions • Fall, spring, yearlong, US academic year.
Eligibility Requirements • Open to sophomores, juniors, seniors; 3.0 GPA; 1 letter of recommendation; good academic standing at home school; enrollment at an accredited American or Canadian college or university.
Living Arrangements • Students live in host institution dormitories, locally rented apartments, program-owned houses. Quarters are shared with host institution students. Meals are taken as a group, on one's own, in residences, in central dining facility.
Costs (2003) • One term: $10,875. Yearlong program: $16,975; includes tuition, housing, insurance, excursions, international student ID, student support services, cultural and sporting events, pre-departure advising. $40 application fee. $500 nonrefundable deposit required. Financial aid available for all students: scholarships, travel grants.
For More Information • Institute for Study Abroad, Butler University, 1100 West 42nd Street, Suite 305, Indianapolis, IN 46208-3345; *Phone:* 800-858-0229; *Fax:* 317-940-9704. *E-mail:* study-abroad@butler.edu. *World Wide Web:* http://www.ifsa-butler.org/

MONASH UNIVERSITY
PROGRAM IN AUSTRALIA

Hosted by Monash University
Academic Focus • Aboriginal studies, full curriculum.
Program Information • Students attend classes at Monash University. Optional travel to Sydney, Canberra, the Outback at an extra cost.
Sessions • Fall, spring, yearlong.
Eligibility Requirements • Open to sophomores, juniors, seniors, graduate students; 3.0 GPA; 2 letters of recommendation.

Living Arrangements • Students live in host institution dormitories, locally rented apartments, host family homes. Quarters are shared with host institution students. Meals are taken as a group, on one's own, with host family, in residences, in central dining facility.

Costs (2005) • One term: A$9500. Yearlong program: A$19,000; includes tuition, student support services, amenities fees, excursions during orientation, airport transfer.

For More Information • Ms. Robyn Masters, Acting Manager, Monash Abroad, Monash University, International Centre, Building 73, Wellington Road, Clayton, Victoria 3800, Australia; *Phone:* +61 3-9905-8311; *Fax:* +61 3-9905-5856. *E-mail:* monash.abroad@monint. monash.edu. *World Wide Web:* http://www.monash.edu/international/

NORTHERN ILLINOIS UNIVERSITY
POLITICAL INTERNSHIPS IN MELBOURNE, AUSTRALIA

Hosted by University of Melbourne

Academic Focus • Political science and government.

Program Information • Students attend classes at University of Melbourne. Optional travel to Australia at an extra cost.

Sessions • Fall, spring.

Eligibility Requirements • Open to juniors, seniors; course work in political science (1.5 years); 3.0 GPA; 2 letters of recommendation; good academic standing at home school; essay; résumé.

Living Arrangements • Students live in host institution dormitories, locally rented apartments. Quarters are shared with host institution students, students from other programs. Meals are taken as a group, on one's own, in central dining facility.

Costs (2003-2004) • One term: $9175; includes tuition, housing, some meals, insurance, placement, room and board monthly refund. $45 application fee. $800 refundable deposit required. Financial aid available for students from sponsoring institution: regular financial aid.

For More Information • Ms. Clare Foust, Program Assistant, Northern Illinois University, Study Abroad Office, Williston Hall 417, DeKalb, IL 60115-2854; *Phone:* 815-753-0420; *Fax:* 815-753-0825. *E-mail:* niuabroad@niu.edu. *World Wide Web:* http://www.niu.edu/niuabroad/

ST. OLAF COLLEGE
ENVIRONMENTAL SCIENCE IN AUSTRALIA

Hosted by Global Educational Designs

Academic Focus • Anthropology, ecology, environmental science/studies, marine sciences.

Program Information • Students attend classes at Global Educational Designs. Scheduled travel to Eastern Australia; field trips.

Sessions • Spring, program runs every other year.

Eligibility Requirements • Open to sophomores, juniors, seniors; course work in biology or environmental studies; good academic standing at home school.

Living Arrangements • Students live in host institution dormitories, locally rented apartments, hotels, research centers, campsites. Meals are taken as a group, in central dining facility.

Costs (2004) • One term: $19,765; includes tuition, housing, some meals, excursions, international airfare, international student ID. $75 application fee. $150 nonrefundable deposit required. Financial aid available for students from sponsoring institution: scholarships, loans.

For More Information • Mr. Patrick Quade, Director, International Studies, St. Olaf College, 1500 St. Olaf Avenue, Northfield, MN 55057; *Phone:* 507-646-3069; *Fax:* 507-646-3789. *E-mail:* bakko@stolaf.edu. *World Wide Web:* http://www.stolaf.edu/services/iso/

SCHOOL FOR INTERNATIONAL TRAINING, SIT STUDY ABROAD
AUSTRALIA: THE MULTICULTURAL SOCIETY

Academic Focus • Aboriginal studies, anthropology, economics, geography, history, liberal studies, political science and government, social sciences, sociology, urban studies, visual and performing arts.

Program Information • Faculty members are drawn from the sponsor's U.S. staff and local instructors hired by the sponsor. Scheduled travel to south Australia, the Northern Territory, Sydney;

field trips to museums, cattle and sheep stations, wildlife sanctuaries, Aboriginal performances.

Sessions • Fall, spring.

Eligibility Requirements • Open to sophomores, juniors, seniors; 2.5 GPA; 2 letters of recommendation; good academic standing at home school.

Living Arrangements • Students live in host family homes, hotels, hostels, campsites. Meals are taken as a group, on one's own, with host family, in residences, in restaurants.

Costs (2003-2004) • One term: $12,675; includes tuition, housing, all meals, insurance, excursions, international student ID. $50 application fee. $400 nonrefundable deposit required. Financial aid available for all students: scholarships.

For More Information • School for International Training, SIT Study Abroad, Kipling Road, Brattleboro, VT 05302-0676; *Phone:* 888-272-7881; *Fax:* 802-258-3296. *E-mail:* studyabroad@sit.edu. *World Wide Web:* http://www.sit.edu/studyabroad/

STATE UNIVERSITY OF NEW YORK AT BUFFALO
MONASH UNIVERSITY STUDY ABROAD PROGRAM

Hosted by Monash University

Academic Focus • Full curriculum.

Program Information • Students attend classes at Monash University. Field trips to a farmstay.

Sessions • Fall, spring, yearlong.

Eligibility Requirements • Minimum age 18; open to sophomores, juniors, seniors, graduate students; 3.0 GPA; 3 letters of recommendation; good academic standing at home school.

Living Arrangements • Students live in host institution dormitories. Quarters are shared with host institution students, students from other programs. Meals are taken on one's own, in central dining facility.

Costs (2003) • One term: $4400. Yearlong program: $8800; includes tuition, insurance, excursions, student support services, administrative fees, airport pick-up. $300 nonrefundable deposit required. Financial aid available for all students: scholarships, federal and New York State financial aid.

For More Information • Dr. Sandra J. Flash, Director of Study Abroad Programs, State University of New York at Buffalo, 210 Talbert Hall, Box 601604, Buffalo, NY 14260-1604; *Phone:* 716-645-3912; *Fax:* 716-645-6197. *E-mail:* studyabroad@buffalo.edu. *World Wide Web:* http://www.buffalo.edu/studyabroad/

STATE UNIVERSITY OF NEW YORK AT NEW PALTZ
STUDY ABROAD IN MELBOURNE, AUSTRALIA

Hosted by Victoria University

Academic Focus • Full curriculum.

Program Information • Students attend classes at Victoria University.

Sessions • Fall, spring, yearlong.

Eligibility Requirements • Minimum age 18; open to sophomores, juniors, seniors; 2.5 GPA; 2 letters of recommendation; good academic standing at home school; no foreign language proficiency required.

Living Arrangements • Students live in host institution dormitories. Quarters are shared with host institution students, students from other programs. Meals are taken on one's own, in central dining facility.

Costs (2003-2004) • One term: $4234 for New York residents; $5664 for nonresidents. Yearlong program: $8468 for New York residents; $11,328 for nonresidents; includes tuition, insurance, administrative fee. $25 application fee. $300–$600 nonrefundable deposit required. Financial aid available for students from sponsoring institution: scholarships, loans.

For More Information • Center for International Programs, State University of New York at New Paltz, 75 South Manheim Boulevard, Suite 9, New Paltz, NY 12561; *Phone:* 845-257-3125; *Fax:* 845-257-3929. *E-mail:* international@newpaltz.edu. *World Wide Web:* http://www.newpaltz.edu/studyabroad/

AUSTRALIA
Melbourne

STATE UNIVERSITY OF NEW YORK AT OSWEGO
LA TROBE UNIVERSITY

Hosted by La Trobe University
Academic Focus • Full curriculum.
Program Information • Students attend classes at La Trobe University. Optional travel to Australia, New Zealand, the South Pacific at an extra cost.
Sessions • Fall, spring, yearlong.
Eligibility Requirements • Open to freshmen, sophomores, juniors, seniors; 2.5 GPA; 3 letters of recommendation; good academic standing at home school; program study statement.
Living Arrangements • Students live in host institution dormitories, locally rented apartments. Quarters are shared with host institution students. Meals are taken on one's own, in residences, in restaurants.
Costs (2003-2004) • One term: $6120. Yearlong program: $12,240; includes tuition, insurance, student support services. $250 nonrefundable deposit required. Financial aid available for students: home university financial aid, loan processing and scholarships for Oswego students.
For More Information • Ms. Nefertitti Saheed, Program Specialist, State University of New York at Oswego, 122A Swetman Hall, Oswego, NY 13126; *Phone:* 888-4-OSWEGO; *Fax:* 315-312-2477. *E-mail:* intled@oswego.edu. *World Wide Web:* http://www.oswego.edu/intled/

STATE UNIVERSITY OF NEW YORK COLLEGE AT BUFFALO
RMIT EXCHANGE/STUDY ABROAD

Hosted by RMIT University
Academic Focus • Full curriculum.
Program Information • Students attend classes at RMIT University.
Sessions • Fall, spring, yearlong.
Eligibility Requirements • Open to sophomores, juniors, seniors; 3.0 GPA; 2 letters of recommendation.
Living Arrangements • Students live in locally rented apartments, host family homes. Quarters are shared with host institution students, students from other programs. Meals are taken on one's own, in residences.
Costs (2003-2004) • One term: $8065-$9975 for New York residents; $11,605-$12,515 for nonresidents. Yearlong program: $13,825-$17,645 for New York residents; $20,905-$22,725 for nonresidents; includes tuition, housing, all meals, insurance, international airfare, books and class materials, administrative, college, and passport fees. $10 application fee. $250 nonrefundable deposit required. Financial aid available for students from sponsoring institution: scholarships, loans.
For More Information • Dr. Lee Ann Grace, Director, International Education, State University of New York College at Buffalo, 1300 Elmwood Avenue, Buffalo, NY 14222-1095; *Phone:* 716-878-4620; *Fax:* 716-878-3054. *E-mail:* intleduc@buffalostate.edu. *World Wide Web:* http://www.buffalostate.edu/intnated/

STATE UNIVERSITY OF NEW YORK COLLEGE AT BROCKPORT
SWINBURNE UNIVERSITY OF TECHNOLOGY PROGRAM

Hosted by Swinburne University of Technology
Academic Focus • Full curriculum.
Program Information • Students attend classes at Swinburne University of Technology. Field trips to various sites throughout Sydney (during orientation).
Sessions • Fall, spring, yearlong.
Eligibility Requirements • Minimum age 18; open to sophomores, juniors, seniors; 2.5 GPA; 2 letters of recommendation; good academic standing at home school; ability to do upper-division coursework in chosen subject; must be at least a second semester sophomore.
Living Arrangements • Students live in host institution dormitories. Quarters are shared with host institution students. Meals are taken on one's own, in residences.
Costs (2003-2004) • One term: $9150 for fall term; $9250 for spring. Yearlong program: $16,550; includes tuition, housing, excursions, international student ID, student support services. $350

nonrefundable deposit required. Financial aid available for all students: scholarships, loans, regular financial aid, grants.
For More Information • Dr. John J. Perry, Director, Office of International Education, State University of New York College at Brockport, 350 New Campus Drive, Brockport, NY 14420; *Phone:* 800-298-SUNY; *Fax:* 585-637-3218. *E-mail:* overseas@brockport.edu. *World Wide Web:* http://www.brockport.edu/studyabroad/

STATE UNIVERSITY OF NEW YORK COLLEGE AT BROCKPORT
UNIVERSITY OF MELBOURNE PROGRAM

Hosted by University of Melbourne
Academic Focus • Full curriculum.
Program Information • Students attend classes at University of Melbourne. Field trips to sites throughout Sydney (during orientation).
Sessions • Fall, spring, yearlong.
Eligibility Requirements • Minimum age 18; open to juniors, seniors; course work in area of internship, if applicable; 3.0 GPA; 2 letters of recommendation; good academic standing at home school; ability to do upper-division course work in chosen subject; résumé required for internship option.
Living Arrangements • Students live in host institution dormitories, college square, residential colleges. Quarters are shared with host institution students. Meals are taken on one's own, in residences.
Costs (2003-2004) • One term: $11,125 for fall term; $11,325 for spring. Yearlong program: $20,600; includes tuition, housing, excursions, international student ID, student support services, airport pick-up upon arrival. $350 nonrefundable deposit required. Financial aid available for all students: scholarships, loans, regular financial aid, grants.
For More Information • Dr. John J. Perry, Director, Office of International Education, State University of New York College at Brockport, 350 New Campus Drive, Brockport, NY 14420; *Phone:* 800-298-SUNY; *Fax:* 585-637-3218. *E-mail:* overseas@brockport.edu. *World Wide Web:* http://www.brockport.edu/studyabroad/

STUDY AUSTRALIA
DEAKIN UNIVERSITY

Hosted by Deakin University–Melbourne Campus
Academic Focus • Full curriculum.
Program Information • Students attend classes at Deakin University–Melbourne Campus. Scheduled travel to Sydney; field trips to the Blue Mountains, Great Ocean Road or Grampians National Park; optional travel to Hawaii, New Zealand, Tasmania, the Great Barrier Reef at an extra cost.
Sessions • Fall, spring, yearlong.
Eligibility Requirements • Minimum age 18; open to freshmen, sophomores, juniors, seniors; 2.75 GPA; good academic standing at home school.
Living Arrangements • Students live in host institution dormitories, locally rented apartments, host family homes. Quarters are shared with host institution students, students from other programs. Meals are taken on one's own, in restaurants.
Costs (2003) • One term: $8890. Yearlong program: $16,280; includes tuition, housing, insurance, excursions, student support services. $500 refundable deposit required. Financial aid available for all students: scholarships, loans.
For More Information • Mr. Chris Shepherd, Director of Programs and Services, Study Australia, 54515 State Road 933 North, Notre Dame, IN 46556-1004; *Phone:* 800-585-9638; *Fax:* 509-357-9457. *E-mail:* info@study-australia.com. *World Wide Web:* http://www.study-australia.com/

STUDY AUSTRALIA
MONASH UNIVERSITY

Hosted by Monash University
Academic Focus • Full curriculum.
Program Information • Students attend classes at Monash University. Scheduled travel to Sydney; field trips to the Blue Mountains; optional travel to Hawaii, New Zealand, Tasmania, the Great Barrier Reef at an extra cost.
Sessions • Fall, spring, yearlong.

Eligibility Requirements • Minimum age 18; open to freshmen, sophomores, juniors, seniors; 3.0 GPA; good academic standing at home school.

Living Arrangements • Students live in host institution dormitories, locally rented apartments, host family homes. Quarters are shared with host institution students, students from other programs. Meals are taken on one's own, in restaurants.

Costs (2003) • One term: $8990. Yearlong program: $16,480; includes tuition, housing, insurance, excursions, student support services. $500 refundable deposit required. Financial aid available for all students: scholarships, loans.

For More Information • Mr. Chris Shepherd, Director of Programs and Services, Study Australia, 54515 State Road 933 North, Notre Dame, IN 46556-1004; *Phone:* 800-585-9638; *Fax:* 509-357-9457. *E-mail:* info@study-australia.com. *World Wide Web:* http://www.study-australia.com/

STUDY AUSTRALIA
ROYAL MELBOURNE INSTITUTE OF TECHNOLOGY

Hosted by RMIT University
Academic Focus • Full curriculum.
Program Information • Students attend classes at RMIT University. Scheduled travel to Sydney; field trips to the Blue Mountains; optional travel to Fiji, New Zealand, Tasmania, the Great Barrier Reef at an extra cost.
Sessions • Fall, spring, yearlong.
Eligibility Requirements • Minimum age 18; open to freshmen, sophomores, juniors, seniors; 2.75 GPA; good academic standing at home school; enrollment at an accredited American college or university.
Living Arrangements • Students live in host institution dormitories, locally rented apartments, host family homes. Quarters are shared with host institution students, students from other programs. Meals are taken on one's own, in residences, in central dining facility.
Costs (2003) • One term: $9675. Yearlong program: $17,850; includes tuition, housing, insurance, excursions, international student ID, student support services, travel discounts. $500 refundable deposit required. Financial aid available for all students: scholarships, loans.
For More Information • Mr. Chris Shepherd, Director of Programs and Services, Study Australia, 54515 State Road 933 North, Notre Dame, IN 46556-1004; *Phone:* 800-585-9658; *Fax:* 509-357-9457. *E-mail:* info@study-australia.com. *World Wide Web:* http://www.study-australia.com/

UNIVERSITY OF MELBOURNE
STUDY ABROAD PROGRAM AT THE UNIVERSITY OF MELBOURNE

Hosted by University of Melbourne
Academic Focus • Full curriculum.
Program Information • Students attend classes at University of Melbourne. Optional travel to an Aboriginal habitation, Great Ocean Road, Bell's Beach, Mt. Buller (ski trip), the Red Centre Desert at an extra cost.
Sessions • Fall, spring, yearlong.
Eligibility Requirements • Open to freshmen, sophomores, juniors, seniors, graduate students; 3.0 GPA; 2 letters of recommendation; good academic standing at home school.
Living Arrangements • Students live in host institution dormitories, locally rented apartments, program-owned apartments, residential colleges. Quarters are shared with host institution students, students from other programs. Meals are taken as a group, in residences.
Costs (2003) • One term: A$8500. Yearlong program: A$17,000; includes tuition, insurance, student support services.
For More Information • Mr. Chris Downes, General Manager, Marketing and Recruitment Offshore, University of Melbourne, International Centre, Parkville, Victoria 3010, Australia; *Phone:* +61 3-8344-9958; *Fax:* +61 3-8344-0130. *E-mail:* studyabroad@international.unimelb.edu.au. *World Wide Web:* http://www.unimelb.edu.au/international/sabroad.html. Students may also apply through Butler University, Institute for Study Abroad, 1100 West 42nd Street, Suite 305, Indianapolis, IN 46208-3345; Arcadia University, Center for Education Abroad, 450 South Easton Road, Glenside, PA

19038-3295; Marymount College, Office of Study Abroad, 100 Marymount Avenue, Tarrytown, NY 10591-3796; CIEE, 7 Customs House Street, 3rd Floor, Portland, ME 04101; IES, Institute for the International Education of Students, 33 North LaSalle Street, 15th Floor, Chicago, IL 60602; State University of New York at Brockport, Office of International Education, 350 New Campus Drive, Brockport, NY 14420; Rutgers University, Study Abroad, 102 College Avenue, New Brunswick, NJ 08901-8543.

UNIVERSITY OF MIAMI
MONASH UNIVERSITY, AUSTRALIA

Hosted by Monash University
Academic Focus • Asian studies, economics, engineering, environmental science/studies, international affairs, international business, law and legal studies, political science and government, science.
Program Information • Students attend classes at Monash University.
Sessions • Fall, spring, yearlong.
Eligibility Requirements • Minimum age 18; open to sophomores, juniors, seniors; 3.0 GPA; 2 letters of recommendation; official transcripts.
Living Arrangements • Students live in host institution dormitories, host family homes. Quarters are shared with host institution students, students from other programs. Meals are taken on one's own, in residences, in central dining facility.
Costs (2003-2004) • One term: $12,919. Yearlong program: $25,838; includes tuition, student support services. $40 application fee. $500 refundable deposit required. Financial aid available for students from sponsoring institution: scholarships, loans.
For More Information • Ms. Glenda Hayley, Assistant Director, University of Miami, International Education and Exchange Programs, 5050 Brunson Drive, Allen Hall 212, PO Box 248005, Coral Gables, FL 33124-1610; *Phone:* 305-284-3434; *Fax:* 305-284-4235. *E-mail:* ieep@miami.edu. *World Wide Web:* http://www.studyabroad.miami.edu/

UNIVERSITY STUDIES ABROAD CONSORTIUM
FULL CURRICULUM STUDIES: MELBOURNE, AUSTRALIA

Hosted by Deakin University–Melbourne Campus, Deakin University–Warrnambool Campus, Deakin University–Geelong Campus
Academic Focus • Full curriculum.
Program Information • Students attend classes at Deakin University–Melbourne Campus, Deakin University–Warrnambool Campus, Deakin University–Geelong Campus.
Sessions • Fall, spring, yearlong.
Eligibility Requirements • Minimum age 18; open to freshmen, sophomores, juniors, seniors, graduate students, adults; 2.6 GPA; 1 letter of recommendation.
Living Arrangements • Students live in host institution dormitories, locally rented apartments. Quarters are shared with host institution students. Meals are taken on one's own, in residences, in central dining facility, in restaurants.
Costs (2005) • One term: $5180. Yearlong program: $10,180; includes tuition, insurance, student support services. $50 application fee. $150 refundable deposit required. Financial aid available for all students: scholarships, loans.
For More Information • University Studies Abroad Consortium, USAC/323, Reno, NV 89557-0093; *Phone:* 775-784-6569; *Fax:* 775-784-6010. *E-mail:* usac@unr.edu. *World Wide Web:* http://usac.unr.edu/

NEWCASTLE
AUSTRALEARN: NORTH AMERICAN CENTER FOR AUSTRALIAN AND NEW ZEALAND UNIVERSITIES
UNIVERSITY OF NEWCASTLE

Hosted by University of Newcastle
Academic Focus • Full curriculum.
Program Information • Students attend classes at University of Newcastle. Scheduled travel to a pre-trip excursion to the Great

Barrier Reef and an Aboriginal Cultural Park; optional travel to Sydney, the coast, Brisbane, the Outback at an extra cost.
Sessions • Fall, spring, yearlong, alternate year.
Eligibility Requirements • Minimum age 18; open to sophomores, juniors, seniors, graduate students; 2.5 GPA; 1 letter of recommendation; good academic standing at home school.
Living Arrangements • Students live in host institution dormitories, locally rented apartments. Quarters are shared with host institution students. Meals are taken on one's own, in residences, in central dining facility.
Costs (2004) • One term: $10,475. Yearlong program: $18,130; includes tuition, housing, some meals, insurance, excursions, international student ID, student support services. $30 application fee. $300 deposit required. Financial aid available for all students: scholarships, loans.
For More Information • AustraLearn: North American Center for Australian and New Zealand Universities, 12050 North Pecos Street, Suite 320, Westminster, CO 80234; *Phone:* 800-980-0033; *Fax:* 303-446-5955. *E-mail:* studyabroad@australearn.org. *World Wide Web:* http://www.australearn.org/

CENTER FOR INTERNATIONAL STUDIES
UNIVERSITY OF NEWCASTLE

Hosted by University of Newcastle
Academic Focus • Full curriculum.
Program Information • Students attend classes at University of Newcastle. Optional travel at an extra cost.
Sessions • Fall, spring, yearlong.
Eligibility Requirements • Minimum age 18; open to freshmen, sophomores, juniors, seniors, graduate students, adults; 2.5 GPA; 1 letter of recommendation; good academic standing at home school; personal essay.
Living Arrangements • Students live in locally rented apartments, program-owned apartments. Quarters are shared with host institution students, students from other programs. Meals are taken as a group, on one's own, in residences, in restaurants.
Costs (2003-2004) • One term: $7100. Yearlong program: $12,400; includes tuition, housing, insurance, excursions, international student ID, student support services, airport reception. $50 application fee. $500 nonrefundable deposit required. Financial aid available for all students: scholarships, work study.
For More Information • Mr. Jeff Palm, Program Director, Center for International Studies, 17 New South Street, #105, Northampton, MA 01060; *Phone:* 413-582-0407; *Fax:* 413-582-0327. *E-mail:* jpalm@cisabroad.com. *World Wide Web:* http://www.cisabroad.com/

STATE UNIVERSITY OF NEW YORK COLLEGE AT BUFFALO
NEWCASTLE EXCHANGE/STUDY ABROAD

Hosted by University of Newcastle
Academic Focus • Full curriculum.
Program Information • Students attend classes at University of Newcastle.
Sessions • Fall, spring, yearlong.
Eligibility Requirements • Open to sophomores, juniors, seniors; 3.0 GPA; 2 letters of recommendation.
Living Arrangements • Students live in host institution dormitories, locally rented apartments. Quarters are shared with host institution students, students from other programs. Meals are taken on one's own, in residences.
Costs (2003-2004) • One term: $7345-$8528 for New York residents; $10,898-$11,795 for nonresidents (undergraduate). Yearlong program: $12,605-$14,971 for New York residents; $19,711-$21,505 for nonresidents (undergraduate); includes tuition, housing, all meals, insurance, international airfare, books and class materials, adminstrative, passport, college, and immigration fees. $10 application fee. $250 nonrefundable deposit required. Financial aid available for students from sponsoring institution: scholarships, loans.
For More Information • Dr. Lee Ann Grace, Director, International Education, State University of New York College at Buffalo, 1300 Elmwood Avenue, Buffalo, NY 14222-1095; *Phone:* 716-878-4620; *Fax:* 716-878-3054. *E-mail:* intleduc@buffalostate.edu. *World Wide Web:* http://www.buffalostate.edu/intnated/

PERTH
AHA INTERNATIONAL AN ACADEMIC PROGRAM OF THE UNIVERSITY OF OREGON
AHA AT CURTIN UNIVERSITY OF TECHNOLOGY

Hosted by Curtin University of Technology
Academic Focus • Full curriculum.
Program Information • Students attend classes at Curtin University of Technology.
Sessions • Fall, spring, yearlong.
Eligibility Requirements • Open to sophomores, juniors, seniors, graduate students; 2 letters of recommendation; good academic standing at home school; college transcripts.
Living Arrangements • Students live in host institution dormitories, locally rented apartments. Quarters are shared with host institution students. Meals are taken on one's own, in residences, in central dining facility.
Costs (2003-2004) • One term: $5500 (estimated). Yearlong program: $11,000 (estimated); includes tuition, insurance, international student ID, student support services. $50 application fee. $200 refundable deposit required.
For More Information • Ms. Carlotta Troy, Associate Director for University Programs, AHA International An Academic Program of the University of Oregon, 741 SW Lincoln Street, Portland, OR 97201; *Phone:* 503-295-7730; *Fax:* 503-295-5969. *E-mail:* mail@aha-intl.org. *World Wide Web:* http://www.aha-intl.org/

ARCADIA UNIVERSITY
UNIVERSITY OF WESTERN AUSTRALIA

Hosted by University of Western Australia
Academic Focus • Agriculture, biological/life sciences, commerce, economics, education, engineering, law and legal studies, liberal studies, mathematics, medicine.
Program Information • Students attend classes at University of Western Australia. Field trips; optional travel to destinations arranged by UWA.
Sessions • Fall, spring, yearlong, US academic year.
Eligibility Requirements • Open to sophomores, juniors, seniors; 3.0 GPA; 1 letter of recommendation.
Living Arrangements • Students live in host institution dormitories, locally rented apartments, residential colleges. Quarters are shared with host institution students, students from other programs. Meals are taken as a group, on one's own, in residences, in central dining facility.
Costs (2003-2004) • One term: $9490. Yearlong program: $16,290 for Australian academic year; $16,600 for US academic year; includes tuition, housing, insurance, international student ID, student support services, transcript, pre-departure guide. $35 application fee. $500 nonrefundable deposit required. Financial aid available for all students: scholarships, loans.
For More Information • Arcadia University, Center for Education Abroad, 450 South Easton Road, Glenside, PA 19038-3295; *Phone:* 866-927-2234; *Fax:* 215-572-2174. *E-mail:* cea@arcadia.edu. *World Wide Web:* http://www.arcadia.edu/cea/

AUSTRALEARN: NORTH AMERICAN CENTER FOR AUSTRALIAN AND NEW ZEALAND UNIVERSITIES
EDITH COWAN UNIVERSITY

Hosted by Edith Cowan University
Academic Focus • Full curriculum.
Program Information • Students attend classes at Edith Cowan University. Scheduled travel to a pre-trip excursion to the Great Barrier Reef and an Aboriginal Cultural Park; optional travel to the Outback, the coast, other parts of Australia at an extra cost.
Sessions • Fall, spring, yearlong, alternate year.
Eligibility Requirements • Minimum age 18; open to sophomores, juniors, seniors, graduate students; 2.5 GPA; 1 letter of recommendation.
Living Arrangements • Students live in host institution dormitories, locally rented apartments. Quarters are shared with host institution students. Meals are taken on one's own, in residences, in central dining facility.

Costs (2004) • One term: $8445. Yearlong program: $15,305; includes tuition, housing, insurance, excursions, international student ID, student support services. $30 application fee. $300 deposit required. Financial aid available for all students: scholarships, loans.

For More Information • AustraLearn: North American Center for Australian and New Zealand Universities, 12050 North Pecos Street, Suite 320, Westminster, CO 80234; *Phone:* 800-980-0033; *Fax:* 303-446-5955. *E-mail:* studyabroad@australearn.org. *World Wide Web:* http://www.australearn.org/

AUSTRALEARN: NORTH AMERICAN CENTER FOR AUSTRALIAN AND NEW ZEALAND UNIVERSITIES
MURDOCH UNIVERSITY

Hosted by Murdoch University
Academic Focus • Full curriculum.
Program Information • Students attend classes at Murdoch University. Scheduled travel to a pre-trip excursion to the Great Barrier Reef and an Aboriginal Cultural Park, a 10-day trip through the Outback; optional travel to the Outback, Asia, other parts of Australia at an extra cost.
Sessions • Fall, spring, yearlong, alternate year.
Eligibility Requirements • Minimum age 18; open to sophomores, juniors, seniors, graduate students; 2.75 GPA; 1 letter of recommendation; good academic standing at home school.
Living Arrangements • Students live in host institution dormitories, locally rented apartments. Quarters are shared with host institution students. Meals are taken on one's own, in residences, in central dining facility.
Costs (2004) • One term: $9270. Yearlong program: $16,675; includes tuition, housing, insurance, excursions, international student ID, student support services. $30 application fee. $300 deposit required. Financial aid available for all students: scholarships, loans.
For More Information • AustraLearn: North American Center for Australian and New Zealand Universities, 12050 North Pecos Street, Suite 320, Westminster, CO 80234; *Phone:* 800-980-0033; *Fax:* 303-446-5955. *E-mail:* studyabroad@australearn.org. *World Wide Web:* http://www.australearn.org/

CENTER FOR INTERNATIONAL STUDIES
MURDOCH UNIVERSITY

Hosted by Murdoch University
Academic Focus • Full curriculum.
Program Information • Students attend classes at Murdoch University. Scheduled travel to Outback Australia (10-day northwest trip).
Sessions • Fall, spring, yearlong.
Eligibility Requirements • Minimum age 18; open to sophomores, juniors, seniors, graduate students; 2.75 GPA; 1 letter of recommendation; good academic standing at home school; personal essay.
Living Arrangements • Students live in program-owned apartments. Quarters are shared with host institution students, students from other programs. Meals are taken on one's own, in residences, in central dining facility, in restaurants.
Costs (2003) • One term: $7760. Yearlong program: $13,450; includes tuition, housing, insurance, excursions, international student ID, student support services, airport reception. $50 application fee. $500 nonrefundable deposit required. Financial aid available for all students: scholarships.
For More Information • Mr. Jeff Palm, Program Director, Center for International Studies, 17 New South Street, #105, Northampton, MA 01060; *Phone:* 413-582-0407; *Fax:* 413-582-0327. *E-mail:* jpalm@cisabroad.com. *World Wide Web:* http://www.cisabroad.com/

CIEE
CIEE STUDY CENTER AT MURDOCH UNIVERSITY, PERTH, AUSTRALIA

Hosted by Murdoch University
Academic Focus • Full curriculum.
Program Information • Students attend classes at Murdoch University. Scheduled travel to sailing in Fremantle, the Margaret River; field trips to museums, Parliament, Rottnest Island, southwest coast; optional travel to the Outback, Shark Bay, Karijini National Park, Ningaloo Reef, Thailand at an extra cost.
Sessions • Fall, spring, yearlong, alternate year.
Eligibility Requirements • Open to sophomores, juniors, seniors, adults; 3.0 GPA; 2 letters of recommendation; good academic standing at home school.
Living Arrangements • Students live in university apartments. Quarters are shared with host institution students, students from other programs. Meals are taken on one's own, in residences, in restaurants.
Costs (2004-2005) • One term: $9900. Yearlong program: $18,100; includes tuition, housing, insurance, excursions, student support services, pre-departure advising, cultural activities. $30 application fee. $300 deposit required. Financial aid available for all students: scholarships, minority student scholarships, travel grants.
For More Information • Mr. Adam Rubin, Admissions Officer, Asia Pacific, CIEE, 7 Custom House Street, 3rd Floor, Portland, ME 04101; *Phone:* 800-40-STUDY; *Fax:* 207-553-7699. *E-mail:* studyinfo@ciee.org. *World Wide Web:* http://www.ciee.org/isp/

IDP EDUCATION AUSTRALIA
CURTIN UNIVERSITY OF TECHNOLOGY PROGRAM

Hosted by Curtin University of Technology
Academic Focus • Business administration/management, engineering, health, science.
Program Information • Students attend classes at Curtin University of Technology.
Sessions • Fall, spring, yearlong.
Eligibility Requirements • Open to sophomores, juniors, seniors, graduate students; 2.75 GPA.
Living Arrangements • Students live in locally rented apartments.
Costs (2004) • One term: contact sponsor for cost. Yearlong program: contact sponsor for cost. $100 deposit required.
For More Information • Ms. Deborah Brown, Senior Manager, Study Abroad, IDP Education Australia, 1400 16th Street, NW, Suite 101, Washington, DC 20036-2219; *Phone:* 866-STUDYOZ; *Fax:* 202-332-3297. *E-mail:* studyabroad@washington.idp.com. *World Wide Web:* http://www.idp.com/

IDP EDUCATION AUSTRALIA
EDITH COWAN UNIVERSITY PROGRAM

Hosted by Edith Cowan University
Academic Focus • Full curriculum.
Program Information • Students attend classes at Edith Cowan University.
Sessions • Fall, spring, yearlong.
Eligibility Requirements • Open to freshmen, sophomores, juniors, seniors; 2.5 GPA.
Living Arrangements • Students live in host institution dormitories, locally rented apartments.
Costs (2004) • One term: contact sponsor for cost. Yearlong program: contact sponsor for cost. $100 deposit required.
For More Information • Ms. Deborah Brown, Senior Manager, Study Abroad, IDP Education Australia, 1400 16th Street, NW, Suite 101, Washington, DC 20036-2219; *Phone:* 866-STUDYOZ; *Fax:* 202-332-3297. *E-mail:* studyabroad@washington.idp.com. *World Wide Web:* http://www.idp.com/

IDP EDUCATION AUSTRALIA
MURDOCH UNIVERSITY PROGRAM

Hosted by Murdoch University
Academic Focus • Aboriginal studies, Asian studies, Australian studies, biological/life sciences, biomedical sciences, business administration/management, ecology, economics, environmental science/studies, information science, marine sciences, psychology, veterinary science, women's studies.
Program Information • Students attend classes at Murdoch University.
Sessions • Fall, spring, yearlong.
Eligibility Requirements • Open to sophomores, juniors, seniors, graduate students; 2.75 GPA; good academic standing at home school.

AUSTRALIA
Perth

Living Arrangements • Students live in host institution dormitories, locally rented apartments.
Costs (2004) • One term: contact sponsor for cost. Yearlong program: contact sponsor for cost. $100 deposit required.
For More Information • Ms. Deborah Brown, Senior Manager, Study Abroad, IDP Education Australia, 1400 16th Street, NW, Suite 101, Washington, DC 20036-2219; *Phone:* 866-STUDYOZ; *Fax:* 202-332-3297. *E-mail:* studyabroad@washington.idp.com. *World Wide Web:* http://www.idp.com/

IDP EDUCATION AUSTRALIA
UNIVERSITY OF WESTERN AUSTRALIA PROGRAM

Hosted by University of Western Australia
Academic Focus • Aboriginal studies, anthropology, Australian studies, biological/life sciences, earth sciences, ecology, environmental science/studies, history, interdisciplinary studies, international affairs.
Program Information • Students attend classes at University of Western Australia.
Sessions • Fall, spring, yearlong.
Eligibility Requirements • Open to juniors, seniors, graduate students; 3.0 GPA; current enrollment at home institution.
Living Arrangements • Students live in host institution dormitories, locally rented apartments.
Costs (2004) • One term: contact sponsor for cost. Yearlong program: contact sponsor for cost. $100 deposit required.
For More Information • Ms. Deborah Brown, Senior Manager, Study Abroad, IDP Education Australia, 1400 16th Street, NW, Suite 101, Washington, DC 20036-2219; *Phone:* 866-STUDYOZ; *Fax:* 202-332-3297. *E-mail:* studyabroad@washington.idp.com. *World Wide Web:* http://www.idp.com/

INSTITUTE FOR STUDY ABROAD, BUTLER UNIVERSITY
MURDOCH UNIVERSITY

Hosted by Murdoch University
Academic Focus • Full curriculum.
Program Information • Students attend classes at Murdoch University. Scheduled travel to a farm; optional travel to surfing, the Margaret River Valley, white water rafting, sporting and cultural events, diving at an extra cost.
Sessions • Fall, spring, yearlong, US academic year.
Eligibility Requirements • Open to sophomores, juniors, seniors; 2.7 GPA; 1 letter of recommendation; good academic standing at home school; enrollment at an accredited American college or university.
Living Arrangements • Students live in host institution dormitories, locally rented apartments. Quarters are shared with host institution students, students from other programs. Meals are taken on one's own, in residences.
Costs (2003) • One term: $9475. Yearlong program: $14,375; includes tuition, housing, insurance, excursions, international student ID, student support services, cultural and sporting events, pre-departure advising. $40 application fee. $500 nonrefundable deposit required. Financial aid available for all students: scholarships, travel grants.
For More Information • Institute for Study Abroad, Butler University, 1100 West 42nd Street, Suite 305, Indianapolis, IN 46208-3345; *Phone:* 800-858-0229; *Fax:* 317-940-9704. *E-mail:* study-abroad@butler.edu. *World Wide Web:* http://www.ifsa-butler.org/

INSTITUTE FOR STUDY ABROAD, BUTLER UNIVERSITY
UNIVERSITY OF WESTERN AUSTRALIA

Hosted by University of Western Australia
Academic Focus • Full curriculum.
Program Information • Students attend classes at University of Western Australia. Scheduled travel to farms; optional travel to surfing, the Margaret River Valley, sporting events, a winery, diving spots at an extra cost.
Sessions • Fall, spring, yearlong, US academic year.

Eligibility Requirements • Open to sophomores, juniors, seniors; 3.0 GPA; 1 letter of recommendation; good academic standing at home school; enrollment at an accredited American or Canadian college or university.
Living Arrangements • Students live in host institution dormitories, program-rented houses. Quarters are shared with host institution students, students from other programs. Meals are taken as a group, on one's own, in residences, in central dining facility, in restaurants.
Costs (2003) • One term: $9975. Yearlong program: $15,975; includes tuition, housing, insurance, excursions, international student ID, student support services, cultural and sporting events, pre-departure advising. $40 application fee. $500 nonrefundable deposit required. Financial aid available for all students: scholarships, travel grants.
For More Information • Institute for Study Abroad, Butler University, 1100 West 42nd Street, Suite 305, Indianapolis, IN 46208-3345; *Phone:* 800-858-0229; *Fax:* 317-940-9704. *E-mail:* study-abroad@butler.edu. *World Wide Web:* http://www.ifsa-butler.org/

MURDOCH UNIVERSITY
STUDY ABROAD PROGRAMME

Hosted by Murdoch University
Academic Focus • Full curriculum.
Program Information • Students attend classes at Murdoch University. Scheduled travel to the northwest of the state; field trips to areas around Perth; optional travel to northwest Australian Outback at an extra cost.
Sessions • Fall, spring, yearlong.
Eligibility Requirements • Open to sophomores, juniors, seniors, adults; 2.75 GPA; 2 letters of recommendation; good academic standing at home school.
Living Arrangements • Students live in host institution dormitories, locally rented apartments, host family homes. Quarters are shared with host institution students, students from other programs. Meals are taken on one's own, with host family, in residences, in central dining facility, in restaurants.
Costs (2004) • One term: A$7200. Yearlong program: A$14,400; includes tuition, student support services, $300 towards the Northwest Outback excursion. Financial aid available for all students: emergency loans.
For More Information • Ms. Natasha Hicks, Student Advisor, Murdoch University, Student Support, South Street, Perth, Western Australia 6150, Australia; *Phone:* +61 8-9360-6778; *Fax:* +61 8-9360 6559. *E-mail:* studyabroad@central.murdoch.edu.au. *World Wide Web:* http://www.murdoch.edu.au/international/. Students may also apply through CIEE, 7 Customs House Street, 3rd Floor, Portland, ME 04101; Butler University, Institute for Study Abroad, 1100 West 42nd Street, Suite 305, Indianapolis, IN 46208-3345; AustraLearn, North American Center for Australian and New Zealand Universities, 12050 North Pecos Street, Suite 320, Westminster, CO 80234; CIS–Centre for International Studies, 17 New South Street, #105, Northampton, MA 01060.

SOUTHERN METHODIST UNIVERSITY
SMU IN AUSTRALIA

Hosted by Curtin University of Technology
Academic Focus • Aboriginal studies, anthropology, cultural studies, history, political science and government, social sciences, sociology.
Program Information • Students attend classes at Curtin University of Technology. Field trips.
Sessions • Spring.
Eligibility Requirements • Open to juniors, seniors; 2.8 GPA; 2 letters of recommendation; good academic standing at home school; essay; personal interview; no foreign language proficiency required.
Living Arrangements • Students live in host institution dormitories, program-owned apartments. Quarters are shared with host institution students, students from other programs. Meals are taken on one's own, in residences, in central dining facility.
Costs (2003) • One term: $15,235; includes tuition, housing, some meals, excursions, student support services, Asian Study Tour, SMU

student fee. $40 application fee. $500 nonrefundable deposit required. Financial aid available for students from sponsoring institution: scholarships, loans.

For More Information • Ms. Nancy Simmons, Assistant to the Director, Southern Methodist University, PO Box 750391, Dallas, TX 75275-0391; *Phone:* 214-768-2338; *Fax:* 214-768-1051. *E-mail:* intlpro@mail.smu.edu. *World Wide Web:* http://www.smu.edu/studyabroad/

STATE UNIVERSITY OF NEW YORK AT BINGHAMTON
MURDOCH UNIVERSITY EXCHANGE PROGRAM

Hosted by Murdoch University
Academic Focus • Full curriculum.
Program Information • Students attend classes at Murdoch University. Optional travel to a subsidized camping trip to the Outback, Asia at an extra cost.
Sessions • Fall, spring, yearlong.
Eligibility Requirements • Open to sophomores, juniors, seniors; 3.0 GPA; 3 letters of recommendation.
Living Arrangements • Students live in host institution dormitories, locally rented apartments, program-owned apartments. Quarters are shared with students from other programs. Meals are taken on one's own, in residences.
Costs (2003-2004) • One term: $8500 for New York residents $11,000 for nonresidents. Yearlong program: $16,000 for New York residents $21,000 for nonresidents; includes tuition, housing, all meals, insurance, international airfare, books and class materials, international student ID, student support services. $250 nonrefundable deposit required. Financial aid available for students from sponsoring institution: scholarships, loans.
For More Information • Dr. Katherine Krebs, Director, State University of New York at Binghamton, Office of International Programs, Binghamton, NY 13902-6000; *Phone:* 607-777-2336; *Fax:* 607-777-2889. *E-mail:* oip@binghamton.edu. *World Wide Web:* http://oip.binghamton.edu/

STATE UNIVERSITY OF NEW YORK AT NEW PALTZ
STUDY ABROAD IN PERTH, AUSTRALIA: CURTIN UNIVERSITY

Hosted by Curtin University of Technology
Academic Focus • Full curriculum.
Program Information • Students attend classes at Curtin University of Technology. Optional travel at an extra cost.
Sessions • Fall, spring, yearlong.
Eligibility Requirements • Minimum age 18; open to sophomores, juniors, seniors; 2.75 GPA; 2 letters of recommendation.
Living Arrangements • Students live in host institution dormitories. Quarters are shared with host institution students. Meals are taken on one's own, in residences, in restaurants.
Costs (2003-2004) • One term: $5959 for New York residents; $6114 for nonresidents. Yearlong program: $11,918 for New York residents; $12,228 for nonresidents; includes tuition, insurance, student support services, administrative fee. $25 application fee. $300 nonrefundable deposit required. Financial aid available for students from sponsoring institution: scholarships, loans.
For More Information • Center for International Programs, State University of New York at New Paltz, 75 South Manheim Boulevard, Suite 9, New Paltz, NY 12561; *Phone:* 845-257-3125; *Fax:* 845-257-3129. *E-mail:* international@newpaltz.edu. *World Wide Web:* http://www.newpaltz.edu/studyabroad/

STATE UNIVERSITY OF NEW YORK AT OSWEGO
EDITH COWAN UNIVERSITY

Hosted by Edith Cowan University
Academic Focus • Full curriculum.
Program Information • Students attend classes at Edith Cowan University. Optional travel to Australia, New Zealand, the South Pacific at an extra cost.
Sessions • Fall, spring, yearlong.

Eligibility Requirements • Open to sophomores, juniors, seniors; 2.5 GPA; 3 letters of recommendation; good academic standing at home school; personal statement.
Living Arrangements • Students live in host institution dormitories, locally rented apartments. Quarters are shared with host institution students. Meals are taken on one's own, in residences, in restaurants.
Costs (2003-2004) • One term: $5920. Yearlong program: $11,840; includes tuition, insurance, student support services. $250 nonrefundable deposit required. Financial aid available for students: home university financial aid, loan processing and scholarships for Oswego students.
For More Information • Ms. Nefertitti Saheed, Program Specialist, State University of New York at Oswego, 122A Swetman Hall, Oswego, NY 13126; *Phone:* 888-4-OSWEGO; *Fax:* 315-312-2477. *E-mail:* intled@oswego.edu. *World Wide Web:* http://www.oswego.edu/intled/

STATE UNIVERSITY OF NEW YORK COLLEGE AT BROCKPORT
UNIVERSITY OF WESTERN AUSTRALIA PROGRAM

Hosted by University of Western Australia
Academic Focus • Full curriculum.
Program Information • Students attend classes at University of Western Australia. Field trips to sites throughout Sydney (during orientation).
Sessions • Fall, spring, yearlong.
Eligibility Requirements • Minimum age 18; open to juniors, seniors; 3.0 GPA; 2 letters of recommendation; ability to do upper-division course work in chosen subject.
Living Arrangements • Students live in locally rented apartments, residential colleges. Quarters are shared with host institution students. Meals are taken as a group, on one's own, in residences, in central dining facility.
Costs (2003-2004) • One term: $9750 for fall term; $10,000 for spring. Yearlong program: $17,900; includes tuition, housing, excursions, international student ID, student support services, meals in residential colleges. $350 nonrefundable deposit required. Financial aid available for all students: scholarships, loans, regular financial aid, grants.
For More Information • Dr. John J. Perry, Director, Office of International Education, State University of New York College at Brockport, 350 New Campus Drive, Brockport, NY 14420; *Phone:* 800-298-SUNY; *Fax:* 585-637-3218. *E-mail:* overseas@brockport.edu. *World Wide Web:* http://www.brockport.edu/studyabroad/

STUDY AUSTRALIA
MURDOCH UNIVERSITY

Hosted by Murdoch University
Academic Focus • Full curriculum.
Program Information • Students attend classes at Murdoch University. Scheduled travel to a 10-day northwest excursion, Sydney; field trips to the Blue Mountains; optional travel to Fifi, New Zealand, Tasmania, the Great Barrier Reef at an extra cost.
Sessions • Fall, spring, yearlong.
Eligibility Requirements • Minimum age 18; open to freshmen, sophomores, juniors, seniors; 2.5 GPA; good academic standing at home school; enrollment at an accredited American college or university.
Living Arrangements • Students live in host institution dormitories, locally rented apartments, program-owned apartments, host family homes. Quarters are shared with host institution students, students from other programs. Meals are taken on one's own, in residences, in central dining facility.
Costs (2003) • One term: $8295. Yearlong program: $15,090; includes tuition, housing, insurance, excursions, student support services, travel discounts, 10-day northwest camping trip. $500 refundable deposit required. Financial aid available for all students: scholarships, loans.
For More Information • Mr. Chris Shepherd, Director of Programs and Services, Study Australia, 54515 State Road 933 North, Notre Dame, IN 46556-1004; *Phone:* 800-585-9658; *Fax:* 509-357-9457. *E-mail:* info@study-australia.com. *World Wide Web:* http://www.study-australia.com/

AUSTRALIA
Perth

STUDY AUSTRALIA
UNIVERSITY OF WESTERN AUSTRALIA

Hosted by University of Western Australia
Academic Focus • Full curriculum.
Program Information • Students attend classes at University of Western Australia. Scheduled travel to Sydney; field trips to the Blue Mountains; optional travel to Fiji, New Zealand, Tasmania, the Outback, the Great Barrier Reef at an extra cost.
Sessions • Fall, spring, yearlong.
Eligibility Requirements • Minimum age 18; open to sophomores, juniors, seniors; 3.0 GPA; good academic standing at home school; enrollment at an accredited American college or university.
Living Arrangements • Students live in host institution dormitories, locally rented apartments, host family homes. Quarters are shared with host institution students, students from other programs. Meals are taken on one's own, in residences, in central dining facility.
Costs (2003) • One term: $9290. Yearlong program: $17,080; includes tuition, housing, insurance, excursions, student support services, travel discounts. $500 refundable deposit required. Financial aid available for all students: scholarships, loans.
For More Information • Mr. Chris Shepherd, Director of Programs and Services, Study Australia, 54515 State Road 933 North, Notre Dame, IN 46556-1004; *Phone:* 800-585-9658; *Fax:* 509-357-9457. *E-mail:* info@study-australia.com. *World Wide Web:* http://www.study-australia.com/

UNIVERSITY OF MIAMI
EDITH COWAN UNIVERSITY

Hosted by Edith Cowan University
Academic Focus • Biomedical sciences, business administration/management, education, engineering, information science, marine sciences, physical sciences.
Program Information • Students attend classes at Edith Cowan University.
Sessions • Fall, spring, yearlong.
Eligibility Requirements • Minimum age 18; open to juniors, seniors; 3.0 GPA; 2 letters of recommendation; official transcripts.
Living Arrangements • Students live in host institution dormitories. Quarters are shared with host institution students, students from other programs. Meals are taken on one's own, in central dining facility.
Costs (2003-2004) • One term: $12,919. Yearlong program: $25,838; includes tuition, student support services. $40 application fee. $500 nonrefundable deposit required. Financial aid available for students from sponsoring institution: scholarships, loans.
For More Information • Ms. Glenda Hayley, Assistant Director, University of Miami, International Education and Exchange Programs, 5050 Brunson Drive, Allen Hall 212, PO Box 248005, Coral Gables, FL 33124-1610; *Phone:* 305-284-3434; *Fax:* 305-284-4235. *E-mail:* ieep@miami.edu. *World Wide Web:* http://www.studyabroad.miami.edu/

UNIVERSITY OF MIAMI
MURDOCH UNIVERSITY

Hosted by Murdoch University
Academic Focus • Australian studies, biological/life sciences, business administration/management, chemical sciences, English, history, political science and government.
Program Information • Students attend classes at Murdoch University.
Sessions • Fall, spring, yearlong.
Eligibility Requirements • Minimum age 18; open to sophomores, juniors, seniors; 3.0 GPA; 2 letters of recommendation; official transcripts.
Living Arrangements • Students live in host institution dormitories. Quarters are shared with host institution students. Meals are taken on one's own, in central dining facility.
Costs (2003-2004) • One term: $12,919. Yearlong program: $25,838; includes tuition, student support services. $40 application fee. $500 nonrefundable deposit required. Financial aid available for students from sponsoring institution: scholarships, loans.
For More Information • Ms. Glenda Hayley, Assistant Director, University of Miami, International Education and Exchange Programs, 5050 Brunson Drive, Allen Hall 212, PO Box 248005, Coral Gables, FL 33124-1610; *Phone:* 305-284-3434; *Fax:* 305-284-4235. *E-mail:* ieep@miami.edu. *World Wide Web:* http://www.studyabroad.miami.edu/

UNIVERSITY OF MINNESOTA, DULUTH
STUDY IN AUSTRALIA

Hosted by Curtin University of Technology
Academic Focus • Full curriculum.
Program Information • Students attend classes at Curtin University of Technology.
Sessions • Fall, spring, yearlong.
Eligibility Requirements • Open to sophomores, juniors, seniors; 2.75 GPA; must be at least a second semester sophomore.
Living Arrangements • Students live in host institution dormitories, locally rented apartments. Quarters are shared with host institution students, students from other programs. Meals are taken on one's own, in residences, in central dining facility.
Costs (2003) • One term: contact sponsor for cost. Yearlong program: contact sponsor for cost. $50 application fee. $400 nonrefundable deposit required.
For More Information • Ms. Carol Michealson, Program Coordinator, University of Minnesota, Duluth, International Education, 110 Cina, 1123 University Drive, Duluth, MN 55812; *Phone:* 218-726-8229; *Fax:* 218-726-6386. *E-mail:* ints@d.umn.edu. *World Wide Web:* http://www.d.umn.edu/ieo/

UNIVERSITY OF WESTERN AUSTRALIA
STUDY ABROAD PROGRAM

Hosted by University of Western Australia
Academic Focus • Full curriculum.
Program Information • Students attend classes at University of Western Australia. Field trips to Western Australia; optional travel to western and other parts of Australia at an extra cost.
Sessions • Fall, spring, yearlong.
Eligibility Requirements • Open to sophomores, juniors, seniors; 3.0 GPA; enrollment at an accredited American college or university.
Living Arrangements • Students live in host institution dormitories, locally rented apartments. Quarters are shared with host institution students, students from other programs. Meals are taken as a group, in residences.
Costs (2004) • One term: A$7750. Yearlong program: A$15,500; includes tuition, student support services.
For More Information • Ms. Milly Ingate, Manager, Student Exchange and Study Abroad, University of Western Australia, International Centre, Sterling Highway, Crawley, Western Australia 6009, Australia; *Phone:* +618 9-3808199; *Fax:* +618 9-3824071. *E-mail:* studyabroad@admin.uwa.edu.au. *World Wide Web:* http://www.international.uwa.edu.au/. Students may also apply through Butler University, Institute for Study Abroad, 1100 West 42nd Street, Suite 305, Indianapolis, IN 46208-3345; University of Arizona, Center for Global Student Programs, 915 North Tyndall Avenue, Tuscon, AZ 85721; Duke University, Office of Study Abroad, 2016 Campus Drive, Box 90057, Durham, NC 27708-0586; Connecticut College, 270 Mohegan Avenue, New London, CT 06320; State University of New York at Brockport, Office of International Education, 350 New Campus Drive, Brockport, NY 14420; Australian Education Connection, 5722 South Flamingo Road, #303, Ft. Lauderdale, FL 33330; Arcadia University, Center for Education Abroad, 450 South Easton Road, Glenside, PA 19038-3295; Cornell University, Cornell Abroad, 474 Uris Hall, Ithaca, NY 14853.

QUEENSLAND
IDP EDUCATION AUSTRALIA
UNIVERSITY OF THE SUNSHINE COAST PROGRAM

Hosted by University of the Sunshine Coast
Academic Focus • Accounting, art, Australian studies, business administration/management, civilization studies, communications, computer science, cultural studies, design and applied arts, ecology, education, environmental science/studies, international affairs, international business, science, sociology, teaching.
Program Information • Students attend classes at University of the Sunshine Coast.
Sessions • Fall, spring, yearlong.

Eligibility Requirements • Open to sophomores, juniors, seniors; 2.5 GPA.

Living Arrangements • Students live in host institution dormitories, locally rented apartments.

Costs (2004) • One term: contact sponsor for cost. Yearlong program: contact sponsor for cost. $100 deposit required.

For More Information • Ms. Deborah Brown, Senior Manager, Study Abroad, IDP Education Australia, 1400 16th Street, NW, Suite 101, Washington, DC 20036-2219; *Phone:* 866-STUDYOZ; *Fax:* 202-332-3297. *E-mail:* studyabroad@washington.idp.com. *World Wide Web:* http://www.idp.com/

STATE UNIVERSITY OF NEW YORK COLLEGE AT CORTLAND
UNIVERSITY OF THE SUNSHINE COAST

Hosted by University of the Sunshine Coast
Academic Focus • Full curriculum.
Program Information • Students attend classes at University of the Sunshine Coast. Field trips to Brisbane (Queensland Art Gallery), the Gold Coast (Sea World), Hervey Bay (whale watching), Aboriginal Culture Center, Mt. Ceolum, Steve Irwin's Australia Zoo; optional travel to Cairns, Fraser Island, Sydney, Gold Coast, Moreton Bay, Uluro, Alice Springs, Outback at an extra cost.
Sessions • Fall, spring, yearlong.
Eligibility Requirements • Minimum age 19; open to freshmen, sophomores, juniors, seniors; 2.5 GPA; 2 letters of recommendation; good academic standing at home school.
Living Arrangements • Students live in locally rented apartments, student accommodations adjacent to campus. Quarters are shared with host institution students, students from other programs. Meals are taken on one's own, in residences.
Costs (2003-2004) • One term: $9500. Yearlong program: contact sponsor for cost; includes tuition, housing, all meals, insurance, excursions, international airfare, books and class materials, international student ID, student support services, passport and student visa fees, full social/activities program designed for international and study abroad students. $20 application fee. $250 nonrefundable deposit required. Financial aid available for students from sponsoring institution: scholarships, loans.
For More Information • Ms. Liz Kopp, Assistant Director, Office of International Programs, State University of New York College at Cortland, PO Box 2000, Cortland, NY 13045; *Phone:* 607-753-2209; *Fax:* 607-753-5989. *E-mail:* cortlandabroad@cortland.edu. *World Wide Web:* http://www.studyabroad.com/suny/cortland/. Students may also apply through University of the Sunshine Coast, Maroochydore, DC, Queensland 4558, Australia.

ROCKHAMPTON
AUSTRALEARN: NORTH AMERICAN CENTER FOR AUSTRALIAN AND NEW ZEALAND UNIVERSITIES
CENTRAL QUEENSLAND UNIVERSITY

Hosted by Central Queensland University
Academic Focus • Full curriculum.
Program Information • Students attend classes at Central Queensland University. Scheduled travel to a pre-trip excursion to the Great Barrier Reef and an Aboriginal Cultural Park, the Whitsunday Islands; optional travel to the Great Barrier Reef, the Outback, the Whitsunday Islands, Brisbane at an extra cost.
Sessions • Fall, spring, yearlong, alternate year.
Eligibility Requirements • Minimum age 18; open to sophomores, juniors, seniors, graduate students; 2.5 GPA; 1 letter of recommendation; good academic standing at home school.
Living Arrangements • Students live in host institution dormitories, locally rented apartments. Quarters are shared with host institution students. Meals are taken as a group, on one's own, in residences, in central dining facility.
Costs (2004) • One term: $9285. Yearlong program: $13,955; includes tuition, housing, all meals, insurance, excursions, international student ID, student support services. $30 application fee. $300 deposit required. Financial aid available for all students: scholarships, loans.

For More Information • AustraLearn: North American Center for Australian and New Zealand Universities, 12050 North Pecos Street, Suite 320, Westminster, CO 80234; *Phone:* 800-980-0033; *Fax:* 303-446-5955. *E-mail:* studyabroad@australearn.org. *World Wide Web:* http://www.austr.learn.org/

IDP EDUCATION AUSTRALIA
CENTRAL QUEENSLAND UNIVERSITY PROGRAM

Hosted by Central Queensland University
Academic Focus • Full curriculum.
Program Information • Students attend classes at Central Queensland University.
Sessions • Fall, spring, yearlong.
Eligibility Requirements • Open to sophomores, juniors, seniors; 2.5 GPA.
Living Arrangements • Students live in host institution dormitories.
Costs (2004) • One term: contact sponsor for cost. Yearlong program: contact sponsor for cost. $100 deposit required.
For More Information • Ms. Deborah Brown, Senior Manager, Study Abroad, IDP Education Australia, 1400 16th Street, NW, Suite 101, Washington, DC 20036-2219; *Phone:* 866-STUDYOZ; *Fax:* 202-332-3297. *E-mail:* studyabroad@washington.idp.com. *World Wide Web:* http://www.idp.com/

STATE UNIVERSITY OF NEW YORK COLLEGE AT BUFFALO
CENTRAL QUEENSLAND EXCHANGE

Hosted by Central Queensland University
Academic Focus • Full curriculum.
Program Information • Students attend classes at Central Queensland University.
Sessions • Fall, spring, yearlong.
Eligibility Requirements • Open to sophomores, juniors, seniors; 3.0 GPA; 2 letters of recommendation.
Living Arrangements • Students live in host institution dormitories, locally rented apartments. Quarters are shared with host institution students, students from other programs. Meals are taken on one's own, in residences.
Costs (2003-2004) • One term: $8412 for New York residents; $12,862 for nonresidents. Yearlong program: $14,519 for New York residents; $23,419 for nonresidents; includes tuition, housing, all meals, insurance, international airfare, books and class materials, adminstrative, passport, college, and immigration fees; linen; security deposit. $10 application fee. $250 nonrefundable deposit required. Financial aid available for students from sponsoring institution: scholarships, loans.
For More Information • Dr. Lee Ann Grace, Director, International Education, State University of New York College at Buffalo, 1300 Elmwood Avenue, Buffalo, NY 14222-1095; *Phone:* 716-878-4620; *Fax:* 716-878-3054. *E-mail:* intleduc@buffalostate.edu. *World Wide Web:* http://www.buffalostate.edu/intnated/

SYDNEY
AHA INTERNATIONAL AN ACADEMIC PROGRAM OF THE UNIVERSITY OF OREGON
UNIVERSITY OF SYDNEY PROGRAM

Hosted by University of Sydney
Academic Focus • Full curriculum.
Program Information • Students attend classes at University of Sydney.
Sessions • Fall, spring, yearlong.
Eligibility Requirements • Open to sophomores, juniors, seniors, graduate students; 3.25 GPA; 2 letters of recommendation; good academic standing at home school; college transcripts.
Living Arrangements • Students live in host institution dormitories, locally rented apartments. Quarters are shared with host institution students. Meals are taken on one's own, in residences, in central dining facility.

AUSTRALIA
Sydney

Costs (2003-2004) • One term: $5700 (estimated). Yearlong program: $11,400; includes tuition, insurance, international student ID, student support services. $50 application fee. $200 deposit required.

For More Information • Ms. Carlotta Troy, Associate Director for University Programs, AHA International An Academic Program of the University of Oregon, 741 SW Lincoln Street, Portland, OR 97201; *Phone:* 503-295-7730; *Fax:* 503-295-5969. *E-mail:* mail@aha-intl.org. *World Wide Web:* http://www.aha-intl.org/

AMERICAN INSTITUTE FOR FOREIGN STUDY (AIFS)
MACQUARIE UNIVERSITY

Hosted by Macquarie University
Academic Focus • Aboriginal studies, anthropology, Australian studies, biological/life sciences, chemical sciences, Chinese language and literature, economics, English literature, finance, geography, geology, history, language studies, law and legal studies, linguistics, mathematics, philosophy, physics, political science and government, psychology, sociology.
Program Information • Students attend classes at Macquarie University. Field trips to Melbourne.
Sessions • Fall, spring, yearlong.
Eligibility Requirements • Minimum age 17; open to sophomores, juniors, seniors; 2.5 GPA; 1 letter of recommendation; good academic standing at home school.
Living Arrangements • Students live in host institution dormitories. Quarters are shared with host institution students. Meals are taken as a group, on one's own, in central dining facility.
Costs (2004-2005) • One term: $11,995. Yearlong program: $23,490; includes tuition, housing, some meals, excursions, student support services. $75 application fee. $350 nonrefundable deposit required. Financial aid available for all students: scholarships.
For More Information • Mr. David Mauro, Admissions Advisor, American Institute For Foreign Study (AIFS), 9 West Broad Street, Stamford, CT 06902-3788; *Phone:* 800-727-2437 Ext. 5163; *Fax:* 203-399-5597. *E-mail:* dmauro@aifs.com. *World Wide Web:* http://www.aifsabroad.com/

ARCADIA UNIVERSITY
MACQUARIE UNIVERSITY

Hosted by Macquarie University
Academic Focus • Biological/life sciences, business administration/management, communications, liberal studies, political science and government, social sciences.
Program Information • Students attend classes at Macquarie University. Field trips; optional travel to sites arranged by Macquarie University at an extra cost.
Sessions • Fall, spring, yearlong, US academic year.
Eligibility Requirements • Open to sophomores, juniors, seniors; 3.0 GPA; 1 letter of recommendation.
Living Arrangements • Students live in host institution dormitories, locally rented apartments. Quarters are shared with host institution students. Meals are taken on one's own, in residences.
Costs (2003-2004) • One term: $9990. Yearlong program: $16,890 for Australian academic year; $17,200 for US academic year; includes tuition, housing, insurance, international student ID, student support services, transcripts, pre-departure guide. $35 application fee. $500 nonrefundable deposit required. Financial aid available for all students: scholarships, loans.
For More Information • Arcadia University, Center for Education Abroad, 450 South Easton Road, Glenside, PA 19038-3295; *Phone:* 866-927-2234; *Fax:* 215-572-2174. *E-mail:* cea@arcadia.edu. *World Wide Web:* http://www.arcadia.edu/cea/

ARCADIA UNIVERSITY
SYDNEY SEMESTER INTERNSHIP

Academic Focus • Australian studies.
Program Information • Faculty members are local instructors hired by the sponsor. Field trips to Darwin/Broome.
Sessions • Fall, spring.
Eligibility Requirements • Open to juniors, seniors; 3.0 GPA; 1 letter of recommendation; 3 prior courses which relate to the internship.

Living Arrangements • Students live in locally rented apartments. Quarters are shared with students from other programs. Meals are taken as a group, on one's own, in residences.
Costs (2003-2004) • One term: $8450; includes tuition, housing, insurance, excursions, international student ID, student support services, pre-departure guide, transcript. $35 application fee. $500 nonrefundable deposit required. Financial aid available for all students: scholarships, loans.
For More Information • Arcadia University, Center for Education Abroad, 450 South Easton Road, Glenside, PA 19038-3295; *Phone:* 866-927-2234; *Fax:* 215-572-2174. *E-mail:* cea@arcadia.edu. *World Wide Web:* http://www.arcadia.edu/cea/

ARCADIA UNIVERSITY
UNIVERSITY OF NEW SOUTH WALES

Hosted by University of New South Wales
Academic Focus • Full curriculum.
Program Information • Students attend classes at University of New South Wales. Field trips; optional travel at an extra cost.
Sessions • Fall, spring, yearlong, US academic year.
Eligibility Requirements • Open to sophomores, juniors, seniors; 3.0 GPA; 1 letter of recommendation; good academic standing at home school.
Living Arrangements • Students live in host institution dormitories, locally rented apartments, program-owned apartments, residential colleges. Quarters are shared with host institution students. Meals are taken as a group, on one's own, in residences, in central dining facility.
Costs (2003-2004) • One term: $10,925. Yearlong program: $18,450 for Australian academic year; $18,850 for US academic year; includes tuition, housing, insurance, international student ID, student support services, transcripts, pre-departure guide. $35 application fee. $500 nonrefundable deposit required. Financial aid available for all students: scholarships, loans.
For More Information • Arcadia University, Center for Education Abroad, 450 South Easton Road, Glenside, PA 19038-3295; *Phone:* 866-927-2234; *Fax:* 215-572-2174. *E-mail:* cea@arcadia.edu. *World Wide Web:* http://www.arcadia.edu/cea/

ARCADIA UNIVERSITY
UNIVERSITY OF SYDNEY

Hosted by University of Sydney
Academic Focus • Full curriculum.
Program Information • Students attend classes at University of Sydney.
Sessions • Fall, spring, yearlong, US academic year.
Eligibility Requirements • Open to sophomores, juniors, seniors; 3.0 GPA; 1 letter of recommendation; good academic standing at home school.
Living Arrangements • Students live in host institution dormitories, locally rented apartments, program-owned apartments, residential colleges. Quarters are shared with host institution students, students from other programs. Meals are taken as a group, on one's own, in residences, in central dining facility.
Costs (2003-2004) • One term: $10,890. Yearlong program: $18,350 for Australian academic year; $18,690 for US academic year; includes tuition, housing, some meals, insurance, international student ID, student support services, transcripts, pre-departure guide. $35 application fee. $500 nonrefundable deposit required. Financial aid available for all students: scholarships, loans.
For More Information • Arcadia University, Center for Education Abroad, 450 South Easton Road, Glenside, PA 19038-3295; *Phone:* 866-927-2234; *Fax:* 215-572-2174. *E-mail:* cea@arcadia.edu. *World Wide Web:* http://www.arcadia.edu/cea/

AUSTRALEARN: NORTH AMERICAN CENTER FOR AUSTRALIAN AND NEW ZEALAND UNIVERSITIES
MACQUARIE UNIVERSITY

Hosted by Macquarie University
Academic Focus • Full curriculum.
Program Information • Students attend classes at Macquarie University. Scheduled travel to a pre-trip excursion to the Great

Barrier Reef and an Aboriginal Cultural Park; optional travel to Canberra, Brisbane, Melbourne, the coast, the Blue Mountains at an extra cost.

Sessions • Fall, spring, yearlong, alternate year.

Eligibility Requirements • Minimum age 18; open to sophomores, juniors, seniors, graduate students; 2.5 GPA; 1 letter of recommendation; good academic standing at home school.

Living Arrangements • Students live in host institution dormitories, locally rented apartments. Quarters are shared with host institution students. Meals are taken on one's own, in residences.

Costs (2004) • One term: $10,050. Yearlong program: $18,075; includes tuition, housing, insurance, excursions, international student ID, student support services. $30 application fee. $300 deposit required. Financial aid available for all students: scholarships, loans.

For More Information • AustraLearn: North American Center for Australian and New Zealand Universities, 12050 North Pecos Street, Suite 320, Westminster, CO 80234; *Phone:* 800-980-0033; *Fax:* 303-446-5955. *E-mail:* studyabroad@australearn.org. *World Wide Web:* http://www.australearn.org/

BOSTON UNIVERSITY
SYDNEY INTERNSHIP PROGRAM

Held at Boston University Sydney Center

Academic Focus • Advertising and public relations, art, art administration, art history, Australian studies, business administration/management, communications, economics, film and media studies, health-care management, journalism, literature, political science and government, public policy, radio.

Program Information • Classes are held on the campus of Boston University Sydney Center. Faculty members are local instructors hired by the sponsor. Scheduled travel to Canberra, the Snowy Mountains; field trips to historic sites, museums.

Sessions • Fall, spring.

Eligibility Requirements • Open to sophomores, juniors, seniors, adults; 2 letters of recommendation; good academic standing at home school; essay; approval of participation; transcript; minimum 3.0 GPA in major.

Living Arrangements • Students live in host institution dormitories. Meals are taken on one's own, in residences, in restaurants.

Costs (2004-2005) • One term: $12,000; includes tuition, housing, internship placement. $50 application fee. $400 nonrefundable deposit required. Financial aid available for all students: scholarships, work study, loans, resident assistant positions.

For More Information • Division of International Programs, Boston University, 232 Bay State Road, Boston, MA 02215; *Phone:* 617-353-9888; *Fax:* 617-353-5402. *E-mail:* abroad@bu.edu. *World Wide Web:* http://www.bu.edu/abroad/

BRETHREN COLLEGES ABROAD
BCA PEACE AND JUSTICE PROGRAM IN SYDNEY, AUSTRALIA

Hosted by Macquarie University

Academic Focus • Aboriginal studies, full curriculum.

Program Information • Students attend classes at Macquarie University. Field trips to the Blue Mountains.

Sessions • Fall, spring, yearlong.

Eligibility Requirements • Minimum age 18; open to sophomores, juniors, seniors; 2.6 GPA; 3 letters of recommendation; good academic standing at home school.

Living Arrangements • Students live in host institution dormitories. Meals are taken on one's own, in residences, in central dining facility.

Costs (2003-2004) • One term: $11,500. Yearlong program: $19,900; includes tuition, housing, all meals, insurance, excursions, international student ID, student support services. $50 application fee. $100 nonrefundable deposit required.

For More Information • Ms. Natalya Latysheva-Derova, Program Officer, Brethren Colleges Abroad, 50 Alpha Drive, Elizabethtown, PA 17022; *Phone:* 866-222-6188; *Fax:* 717-361-6619. *E-mail:* info@bcanet.org. *World Wide Web:* http://www.bcanet.org/

CENTER FOR INTERNATIONAL STUDIES
MACQUARIE UNIVERSITY

Hosted by Macquarie University

Academic Focus • Full curriculum.

Program Information • Students attend classes at Macquarie University. Optional travel to the Great Barrier Reef, the Outback at an extra cost.

Sessions • Fall, spring, yearlong.

Eligibility Requirements • Minimum age 18; open to sophomores, juniors, seniors, graduate students, adults; 2.5 GPA; 1 letter of recommendation; good academic standing at home school; personal essay.

Living Arrangements • Students live in locally rented apartments, program-owned apartments. Quarters are shared with host institution students. Meals are taken as a group, on one's own, in residences, in central dining facility, in restaurants.

Costs (2003) • One term: $8700. Yearlong program: $15,700; includes tuition, housing, insurance, excursions, international student ID, student support services, airport reception. $50 application fee. $500 nonrefundable deposit required. Financial aid available for all students: scholarships.

For More Information • Mr. Jeff Palm, Program Director, Center for International Studies, 17 New South Street, #105, Northampton, MA 01060; *Phone:* 413-582-0407; *Fax:* 413-582-0327. *E-mail:* jpalm@cisabroad.com. *World Wide Web:* http://www.cisabroad.com/

CIEE
CIEE STUDY CENTER, SYDNEY, AUSTRALIA

Hosted by Macquarie University, University of Sydney

Academic Focus • Full curriculum.

Program Information • Students attend classes at Macquarie University, University of Sydney. Scheduled travel to the Blue Mountains, local towns; field trips to sites around Sydney; optional travel to Melbourne, Tasmania at an extra cost.

Sessions • Fall, spring, yearlong, alternate year.

Eligibility Requirements • Open to sophomores, juniors, seniors; 3.0 GPA; 2 letters of recommendation; good academic standing at home school.

Living Arrangements • Students live in host institution dormitories, locally rented apartments. Quarters are shared with host institution students, students from other programs. Meals are taken on one's own, in residences, in restaurants.

Costs (2004-2005) • One term: $11,500 for Macquarie; $12,950 for Sydney. Yearlong program: $19,900 for Macquarie; $22,000 for Sydney; includes tuition, housing, insurance, excursions, student support services, pre-departure advising, cultural activities. $30 application fee. $300 deposit required. Financial aid available for all students: scholarships, minority student scholarships, travel grants.

For More Information • Mr. Adam Rubin, Admissions Officer, Asia Pacific, CIEE, 7 Custom House Street, 3rd Floor, Portland, ME 04101; *Phone:* 800-40-STUDY; *Fax:* 207-553-7699. *E-mail:* studyinfo@ciee.org. *World Wide Web:* http://www.ciee.org/isp/

COLLEGE CONSORTIUM FOR INTERNATIONAL STUDIES–ST. BONAVENTURE UNIVERSITY AND TRUMAN STATE UNIVERSITY
MACQUARIE UNIVERSITY–SEMESTER IN AUSTRALIA

Hosted by Macquarie University

Academic Focus • Full curriculum.

Program Information • Students attend classes at Macquarie University. Optional travel to the Great Barrier Reef, the Outback, New Zealand at an extra cost.

Sessions • Fall, spring, yearlong.

Eligibility Requirements • Minimum age 18; open to sophomores; 2.5 GPA; 3 letters of recommendation; good academic standing at home school; essay.

Living Arrangements • Students live in host institution dormitories, program-owned apartments. Quarters are shared with host institution students, students from other programs. Meals are taken as a group, on one's own, in residences, in restaurants.

Costs (2004-2005) • One term: $6975. Yearlong program: $13,950; includes tuition, insurance, administration fees. $30 application fee.

AUSTRALIA
Sydney

$200 nonrefundable deposit required. Financial aid available for students from sponsoring institution: loans.

For More Information • Ms. Alice Sayegh, Director, International Studies, College Consortium for International Studies–St. Bonaventure University and Truman State University, Saint Bonaventure University, St. Bonaventure, NY 14778; *Phone:* 716-375-2574; *Fax:* 716-375-7882. *E-mail:* asayegh@sbu.edu. *World Wide Web:* http://www.ccisabroad.org/. Students may also apply through Truman State University, Center for International Education Abroad, 100 East Normal, Kirk Building #120, Kirksville, MO 63501.

COLLEGE CONSORTIUM FOR INTERNATIONAL STUDIES–TRUMAN STATE UNIVERSITY
MACQUARIE UNIVERSITY

Hosted by Macquarie University
Academic Focus • Full curriculum.
Program Information • Students attend classes at Macquarie University. Scheduled travel; optional travel at an extra cost.
Sessions • Fall, spring, yearlong.
Eligibility Requirements • Minimum age 18; open to sophomores, juniors, seniors, graduate students, adults; 3 letters of recommendation; good academic standing at home school; transcript; no foreign language proficiency required.
Living Arrangements • Students live in host institution dormitories, locally rented apartments. Quarters are shared with host institution students. Meals are taken on one's own.
Costs (2002-2003) • One term: $4560. Yearlong program: $9120; includes tuition, insurance. $200 nonrefundable deposit required. Financial aid available for students from sponsoring institution: scholarships, loans.
For More Information • Center for International Education Abroad, College Consortium for International Studies–Truman State University, Truman State University, Kirk Building 114, Kirksville, MO 63501; *Phone:* 660-785-4076; *Fax:* 660-785-7473. *E-mail:* ciea@truman.edu. *World Wide Web:* http://www.ccisabroad.org/. Students may also apply through St. Bonaventure University, St. Bonaventure, NY 14778.

IDP EDUCATION AUSTRALIA
AUSTRALIAN CATHOLIC UNIVERSITY PROGRAM

Hosted by Australian Catholic University–Sydney
Academic Focus • Full curriculum.
Program Information • Students attend classes at Australian Catholic University–Sydney. Field trips.
Sessions • Fall, spring, yearlong.
Eligibility Requirements • Open to sophomores, juniors, seniors; current enrollment at home institution.
Living Arrangements • Students live in host institution dormitories, program-owned apartments, host family homes.
Costs (2004) • One term: contact sponsor for cost. Yearlong program: contact sponsor for cost. $100 deposit required.
For More Information • Ms. Deborah Brown, Senior Manager, Study Abroad, IDP Education Australia, 1400 16th Street, NW, Suite 101, Washington, DC 20036-2219; *Phone:* 866-STUDYOZ; *Fax:* 202-332-3297. *E-mail:* studyabroad@washington.idp.com. *World Wide Web:* http://www.idp.com/

IDP EDUCATION AUSTRALIA
MACQUARIE UNIVERSITY PROGRAM

Hosted by Macquarie University
Academic Focus • Full curriculum.
Program Information • Students attend classes at Macquarie University.
Sessions • Fall, spring, yearlong.
Eligibility Requirements • Open to freshmen, sophomores, juniors, seniors, graduate students; 2.5 GPA.
Living Arrangements • Students live in host institution dormitories, locally rented apartments.
Costs (2004) • One term: contact sponsor for cost. Yearlong program: contact sponsor for cost. $100 deposit required.
For More Information • Ms. Deborah Brown, Senior Manager, Study Abroad, IDP Education Australia, 1400 16th Street, NW, Suite 101, Washington, DC 20036-2219; *Phone:* 866-STUDYOZ; *Fax:* 202-332-3297. *E-mail:* studyabroad@washington.idp.com. *World Wide Web:* http://www.idp.com/

IDP EDUCATION AUSTRALIA
UNIVERSITY OF SYDNEY PROGRAM

Hosted by University of Sydney
Academic Focus • Aboriginal studies, agriculture, architecture, Australian studies, business administration/management, economics, education, fine/studio arts, health, law and legal studies, music, nursing, teaching, veterinary science.
Program Information • Students attend classes at University of Sydney.
Sessions • Fall, spring, yearlong.
Eligibility Requirements • Open to sophomores, juniors, seniors, graduate students; course work in related field; 3.0 GPA.
Living Arrangements • Students live in host institution dormitories, locally rented apartments.
Costs (2004) • One term: contact sponsor for cost. Yearlong program: contact sponsor for cost. $100 deposit required.
For More Information • Ms. Deborah Brown, Senior Manager, Study Abroad, IDP Education Australia, 1400 16th Street, NW, Suite 101, Washington, DC 20036-2219; *Phone:* 866-STUDYOZ; *Fax:* 202-332-3297. *E-mail:* studyabroad@washington.idp.com. *World Wide Web:* http://www.idp.com/

IDP EDUCATION AUSTRALIA
UNIVERSITY OF TECHNOLOGY SYDNEY PROGRAM

Hosted by University of Technology Sydney
Academic Focus • Full curriculum.
Program Information • Students attend classes at University of Technology Sydney.
Sessions • Fall, spring, yearlong.
Eligibility Requirements • Open to sophomores, juniors, seniors, graduate students; 3.0 GPA.
Living Arrangements • Students live in host institution dormitories, locally rented apartments.
Costs (2004) • One term: contact sponsor for cost. Yearlong program: contact sponsor for cost. $100 deposit required.
For More Information • Ms. Deborah Brown, Senior Manager, Study Abroad, IDP Education Australia, 1400 16th Street, NW, Suite 101, Washington, DC 20036-2219; *Phone:* 866-STUDYOZ; *Fax:* 202-332-3297. *E-mail:* studyabroad@washington.idp.com. *World Wide Web:* http://www.idp.com/

IDP EDUCATION AUSTRALIA
UNIVERSITY OF WESTERN SYDNEY PROGRAM

Hosted by University of Western Sydney
Academic Focus • Aboriginal studies, Asian studies, communications, ecology, economics, environmental science/studies, film and media studies, finance, graphic design/illustration, nutrition, tourism and travel.
Program Information • Students attend classes at University of Western Sydney.
Sessions • Fall, spring, yearlong.
Eligibility Requirements • Open to freshmen, sophomores, juniors, seniors; 2.5 GPA.
Living Arrangements • Students live in host institution dormitories, locally rented apartments.
Costs (2004) • One term: contact sponsor for cost. Yearlong program: contact sponsor for cost. $100 deposit required.
For More Information • Ms. Deborah Brown, Senior Manager, Study Abroad, IDP Education Australia, 1400 16th Street, NW, Suite 101, Washington, DC 20036-2219; *Phone:* 866-STUDYOZ; *Fax:* 202-332-3297. *E-mail:* studyabroad@washington.idp.com. *World Wide Web:* http://www.idp.com/

INSTITUTE FOR STUDY ABROAD, BUTLER UNIVERSITY
MACQUARIE UNIVERSITY

Hosted by Macquarie University
Academic Focus • Full curriculum.

Program Information • Students attend classes at Macquarie University. Scheduled travel to farms; optional travel to a surf safari, Outback trips at an extra cost.

Sessions • Fall, spring, yearlong, US academic year.

Eligibility Requirements • Open to sophomores, juniors, seniors; 2.5 GPA; 1 letter of recommendation; good academic standing at home school; enrollment at an accredited American college or university.

Living Arrangements • Students live in host institution dormitories, locally rented apartments. Quarters are shared with host institution students, students from other programs. Meals are taken as a group, on one's own, in residences, in central dining facility, in restaurants.

Costs (2003) • One term: $9975. Yearlong program: $15,775; includes tuition, housing, insurance, excursions, international student ID, student support services, cultural and sporting events, pre-departure advising. $40 application fee. $500 nonrefundable deposit required. Financial aid available for all students: scholarships, travel grants.

For More Information • Institute for Study Abroad, Butler University, 1100 West 42nd Street, Suite 305, Indianapolis, IN 46208-3345; *Phone:* 800-858-0229; *Fax:* 317-940-9704. *E-mail:* study-abroad@butler.edu. *World Wide Web:* http://www.ifsa-butler. org/

INSTITUTE FOR STUDY ABROAD, BUTLER UNIVERSITY
UNIVERSITY OF NEW SOUTH WALES

Hosted by University of New South Wales

Academic Focus • Full curriculum.

Program Information • Students attend classes at University of New South Wales. Scheduled travel to farms, the Blue Mountains; optional travel to a surf safari, local wilderness areas, sporting and local cultural events, beaches at an extra cost.

Sessions • Fall, spring, yearlong, US academic year.

Eligibility Requirements • Open to sophomores, juniors, seniors; 3.0 GPA; 1 letter of recommendation; good academic standing at home school; enrollment at an accredited American college or university.

Living Arrangements • Students live in host institution dormitories, locally rented apartments. Quarters are shared with students from other programs. Meals are taken as a group, on one's own, in residences, in central dining facility, in restaurants.

Costs (2003) • One term: $11,375. Yearlong program: $17,775; includes tuition, housing, insurance, excursions, international student ID, student support services, cultural and sporting events, pre-departure advising. $40 application fee. $500 nonrefundable deposit required. Financial aid available for all students: scholarships, travel grants.

For More Information • Institute for Study Abroad, Butler University, 1100 West 42nd Street, Suite 305, Indianapolis, IN 46208-3345; *Phone:* 800-858-0229; *Fax:* 317-940-9704. *E-mail:* study-abroad@butler.edu. *World Wide Web:* http://www.ifsa-butler. org/

INSTITUTE FOR STUDY ABROAD, BUTLER UNIVERSITY
UNIVERSITY OF SYDNEY

Hosted by University of Sydney

Academic Focus • Full curriculum.

Program Information • Students attend classes at University of Sydney. Scheduled travel to farms, the Blue Mountains; optional travel to a surf safari, Outback trips at an extra cost.

Sessions • Fall, spring, yearlong, US academic year.

Eligibility Requirements • Open to sophomores, juniors, seniors; 3.0 GPA; 1 letter of recommendation; good academic standing at home school; enrollment at an accredited American college or university.

Living Arrangements • Students live in host institution dormitories, locally rented apartments, program-owned houses. Quarters are shared with host institution students. Meals are taken on one's own, in residences, in central dining facility.

Costs (2003) • One term: $11,375. Yearlong program: $17,575; includes tuition, housing, insurance, excursions, international student ID, student support services, cultural and sporting events,

pre-departure advising. $40 application fee. $500 nonrefundable deposit required. Financial aid available for all students: scholarships, travel grants.

For More Information • Institute for Study Abroad, Butler University, 1100 West 42nd Street, Suite 305, Indianapolis, IN 46208-3345; *Phone:* 800-858-0229; *Fax:* 317-283-9704. *E-mail:* study-abroad@butler.edu. *World Wide Web:* http://www.ifsa-butler. org/

INSTITUTE FOR STUDY ABROAD, BUTLER UNIVERSITY
UNIVERSITY OF TECHNOLOGY, SYDNEY

Hosted by University of Technology Sydney

Academic Focus • Full curriculum.

Program Information • Students attend classes at University of Technology Sydney. Scheduled travel to farms; optional travel to a surf safari, Outback trips at an extra cost.

Sessions • Fall, spring, yearlong, US academic year.

Eligibility Requirements • Open to sophomores, juniors, seniors; 3.0 GPA; 1 letter of recommendation; good academic standing at home school; enrollment at an accredited American college or university.

Living Arrangements • Students live in locally rented apartments. Quarters are shared with students from other programs. Meals are taken on one's own, in residences.

Costs (2003) • One term: $10,375. Yearlong program: $16,575; includes tuition, housing, insurance, excursions, international student ID, student support services, cultural and sporting events, pre-departure advising. $40 application fee. $500 nonrefundable deposit required. Financial aid available for all students: scholarships, travel grants.

For More Information • Institute for Study Abroad, Butler University, 1100 West 42nd Street, Suite 305, Indianapolis, IN 46208-3345; *Phone:* 800-858-0229; *Fax:* 317-940-9704. *E-mail:* study-abroad@butler.edu. *World Wide Web:* http://www.ifsa-butler. org/

INTERNATIONAL STUDIES ABROAD
SYDNEY, AUSTRALIA–UNIVERSITY OF SYDNEY SEMESTER/ YEAR

Hosted by University of Sydney

Academic Focus • Full curriculum.

Program Information • Students attend classes at University of Sydney. Scheduled travel to the Tugalong Outback Station; field trips to the Blue Mountains; optional travel to Hunter Valley, Jervis Bay, the Snowy Mountains at an extra cost.

Sessions • Fall, spring, yearlong.

Eligibility Requirements • Minimum age 18; open to freshmen, sophomores, juniors, seniors, adults; 3.0 GPA; 1 letter of recommendation; good academic standing at home school; transcript.

Living Arrangements • Students live in host institution dormitories, locally rented apartments. Quarters are shared with host institution students, students from other programs. Meals are taken on one's own, in residences, in restaurants.

Costs (2004-2005) • One term: $12,900. Yearlong program: $24,500; includes tuition, housing, insurance, excursions, student support services, tutoring, airport pick-up. $200 deposit required. Financial aid available for all students: loans, U.S. federal financial aid.

For More Information • Australia Site Specialist, International Studies Abroad, 901 West 24th Street, Austin, TX 78705; *Phone:* 512-480-8522; *Fax:* 512-480-8866. *E-mail:* isa@studiesabroad.com. *World Wide Web:* http://www.studiesabroad.com/

MARIST COLLEGE
AUSTRALIAN INTERNSHIP PROGRAM

Hosted by Australian Catholic University–Sydney

Academic Focus • Business administration/management, education, environmental science/studies, information science, liberal studies, religious studies, social sciences.

Program Information • Students attend classes at Australian Catholic University–Sydney. Field trips to Sydney environs.

Sessions • Fall, spring, yearlong.

Eligibility Requirements • Open to sophomores, juniors, seniors; 2.8 GPA; 2 letters of recommendation; good academic standing at home school.

Living Arrangements • Students live in host family homes. Meals are taken with host family.

Costs (2003-2004) • One term: $12,500. Yearlong program: $25,000; includes tuition, housing, some meals, insurance, excursions, student support services, internship. $35 application fee. $300 nonrefundable deposit required. Financial aid available for students from sponsoring institution: scholarships, loans.

For More Information • Ms. Carol Toufali, Coordinator, Marist Abroad Program, Marist College, 3399 North Road, Poughkeepsie, NY 12601-1387; *Phone:* 845-575-3330; *Fax:* 845-575-3294. *E-mail:* international@marist.edu. *World Wide Web:* http://www.marist.edu/international/

MICHIGAN STATE UNIVERSITY
CIC/AESOP INTERNSHIPS IN AUSTRALIA

Hosted by University of New South Wales
Academic Focus • Full curriculum.
Program Information • Students attend classes at University of New South Wales.
Sessions • Fall, spring.
Eligibility Requirements • Minimum age 18; open to juniors, seniors, graduate students; 3.0 GPA; 2 letters of recommendation; good academic standing at home school; approval of faculty director; resumé; personal statement.

Living Arrangements • Students live in host institution dormitories, locally rented apartments, host family homes. Quarters are shared with host institution students. Meals are taken on one's own, in residences, in restaurants.

Costs (2002-2003) • One term: $8700; includes tuition, housing, insurance, student support services, administration fees. $100 application fee. $200 nonrefundable deposit required. Financial aid available for students from sponsoring institution: scholarships, loans.

For More Information • Ms. Sherry Martinez-Bonilla, Office Assistant, Michigan State University, Office of Study Abroad, 109 International Center, East Lansing, MI 48824-1035; *Phone:* 517-353-8920; *Fax:* 517-432-2082. *E-mail:* marti269@msu.edu. *World Wide Web:* http://studyabroad.msu.edu/

STATE UNIVERSITY OF NEW YORK AT NEW PALTZ
STUDY ABROAD IN SYDNEY, AUSTRALIA

Hosted by University of Technology Sydney
Academic Focus • Full curriculum.
Program Information • Students attend classes at University of Technology Sydney.
Sessions • Fall, spring, yearlong.
Eligibility Requirements • Minimum age 18; open to sophomores, juniors, seniors; 3.0 GPA; 2 letters of recommendation; good academic standing at home school.

Living Arrangements • Students live in locally rented apartments. Quarters are shared with students from other programs. Meals are taken on one's own, in residences, in restaurants.

Costs (2003-2004) • One term: $5346 for New York residents; $5663 for nonresidents. Yearlong program: $10,692 for New York residents; $11,324 for nonresidents; includes tuition, insurance, student support services, administrative fee. $25 application fee. $300-$600 nonrefundable deposit required. Financial aid available for students from sponsoring institution: scholarships, loans.

For More Information • Center for International Programs, State University of New York at New Paltz, 75 South Manheim Boulevard, Suite 9, New Paltz, NY 12561; *Phone:* 845-257-3125; *Fax:* 845-257-3129. *E-mail:* international@newpaltz.edu. *World Wide Web:* http://www.newpaltz.edu/studyabroad/

STATE UNIVERSITY OF NEW YORK AT OSWEGO
ACU NATIONAL UNIVERSITY

Hosted by Australian Catholic University–Melbourne, Australian Catholic University–Canberra, Australian Catholic University–McAuley Campus, Australian Catholic University–Sydney

Academic Focus • Full curriculum.
Program Information • Students attend classes at Australian Catholic University–Melbourne, Australian Catholic University–Canberra, Australian Catholic University–McAuley Campus, Australian Catholic University–Sydney. Optional travel to Australia, New Zealand, the South Pacific at an extra cost.
Sessions • Fall, spring, yearlong.
Eligibility Requirements • Open to sophomores, juniors, seniors; 2.5 GPA; 3 letters of recommendation; good academic standing at home school; personal statement.

Living Arrangements • Students live in host institution dormitories, locally rented apartments, host family homes. Quarters are shared with host institution students, students from other programs. Meals are taken on one's own, with host family, in residences, in restaurants.

Costs (2003-2004) • One term: $5720. Yearlong program: $11,440; includes tuition, insurance, student support services. $250 nonrefundable deposit required. Financial aid available for students: home university financial aid, loan processing and scholarships for Oswego students.

For More Information • Ms. Nefertitti Saheed, Program Specialist, State University of New York at Oswego, 122A Swetman Hall, Oswego, NY 13126; *Phone:* 888-4-OSWEGO; *Fax:* 315-312-2477. *E-mail:* intled@oswego.edu. *World Wide Web:* http://www.oswego.edu/intled/

STATE UNIVERSITY OF NEW YORK AT OSWEGO
OSWEGO SYDNEY INTERNSHIP PROGRAM

Hosted by Centers for Academic Programs Abroad (CAPA)
Academic Focus • Aboriginal studies, art, Australian studies, history, international business, political science and government.
Program Information • Students attend classes at Centers for Academic Programs Abroad (CAPA). Field trips to the Blue Mountains.
Sessions • Fall, spring.
Eligibility Requirements • Open to sophomores, juniors, seniors; 2.5 GPA; 3 letters of recommendation; good academic standing at home school; study statement.

Living Arrangements • Students live in host institution dormitories. Quarters are shared with students from other programs. Meals are taken as a group, on one's own, in residences, in restaurants.

Costs (2004) • One term: $6995; includes tuition, housing, some meals, insurance, excursions, student support services, internship placement, airport pick-up, social events. $250 nonrefundable deposit required. Financial aid available for students: home university financial aid, loan processing and scholarships for Oswego students.

For More Information • Ms. Nefertitti Saheed, Program Specialist, State University of New York at Oswego, 122A Swetman Hall, Oswego, NY 13126; *Phone:* 888-4-OSWEGO; *Fax:* 315-312-2477. *E-mail:* intled@oswego.edu. *World Wide Web:* http://www.oswego.edu/intled/

STATE UNIVERSITY OF NEW YORK AT PLATTSBURGH
STUDY IN AUSTRALIA, SYDNEY

Hosted by University of New South Wales
Academic Focus • Architecture, Australian studies, biological/life sciences, business administration/management, engineering, environmental science/studies, fine/studio arts, liberal studies.
Program Information • Students attend classes at University of New South Wales.
Sessions • Fall, spring, yearlong.
Eligibility Requirements • Minimum age 18; open to sophomores, juniors, seniors; 3.0 GPA; 2 letters of recommendation; SUNY and UNSW applications; essay; transcript.

Living Arrangements • Students live in locally rented apartments. Quarters are shared with host institution students, students from other programs. Meals are taken on one's own, in residences, in central dining facility, in restaurants.

Costs (2003-2004) • One term: $11,570. Yearlong program: $23,140; includes tuition, housing, some meals, insurance, international student ID, student support services, program fee. $20 application fee. $350 nonrefundable deposit required. Financial aid available for students from sponsoring institution: scholarships, loans.

For More Information • Ms. Jo Ann Mackie, Study Abroad Coordinator, State University of New York at Plattsburgh, Study Abroad Office, 101 Broad Street, Plattsburgh, NY 12901; *Phone:* 518-564-2321; *Fax:* 518-564-2326. *E-mail:* international@plattsburgh. edu. *World Wide Web:* http://www.plattsburgh.edu/studyabroad/

STATE UNIVERSITY OF NEW YORK COLLEGE AT BROCKPORT
MACQUARIE UNIVERSITY PROGRAM

Hosted by Macquarie University
Academic Focus • Full curriculum.
Program Information • Students attend classes at Macquarie University. Scheduled travel to Sydney, for orientation; field trips; optional travel at an extra cost.
Sessions • Fall, spring, yearlong.
Eligibility Requirements • Minimum age 18; open to sophomores, juniors, seniors; 2.5 GPA; 2 letters of recommendation; must be at least a second semester sophomore; ability to do upper-division coursework in chosen subject; no foreign language proficiency required.
Living Arrangements • Students live in host institution dormitories, residential colleges, university apartments. Quarters are shared with host institution students. Meals are taken as a group, on one's own, in residences, in central dining facility.
Costs (2003-2004) • One term: $9300 for fall term; $9450 for spring. Yearlong program: $16,900; includes tuition, housing, excursions, international student ID, student support services, all meals if living in residential colleges. $350 nonrefundable deposit required. Financial aid available for all students: scholarships, loans, regular financial aid, grants.

For More Information • Dr. John Perry, Director, Office of International Education, State University of New York College at Brockport, 350 New Campus Drive, Brockport, NY 14420; *Phone:* 800-298-SUNY; *Fax:* 585-637-3218. *E-mail:* overseas@brockport.edu. *World Wide Web:* http://www.brockport.edu/studyabroad/

STATE UNIVERSITY OF NEW YORK COLLEGE AT BROCKPORT
UNIVERSITY OF SYDNEY PROGRAM

Hosted by University of Sydney
Academic Focus • Full curriculum.
Program Information • Students attend classes at University of Sydney. Field trips to destinations throughout Sydney and environs.
Sessions • Fall, spring, yearlong.
Eligibility Requirements • Minimum age 18; open to sophomores, juniors, seniors; course work in area of internship, if applicable; 3.0 GPA; 2 letters of recommendation; good academic standing at home school; must be at least a second semester sophomore; ability to do upper-division course work in chosen subject; résumé required for internship option.
Living Arrangements • Students live in Sydney University Village. Quarters are shared with host institution students. Meals are taken on one's own, in residences, in central dining facility.
Costs (2003-2004) • One term: $10,925 for fall term; $11,050 for spring. Yearlong program: $20,425; includes tuition, housing, excursions, international student ID, student support services. $350 nonrefundable deposit required. Financial aid available for all students: scholarships, loans, regular financial aid, grants.
For More Information • Dr. John J. Perry, Director, Office of International Education, State University of New York College at Brockport, 350 New Campus Drive, Brockport, NY 14420; *Phone:* 800-298-SUNY; *Fax:* 585-637-3218. *E-mail:* overseas@brockport.edu. *World Wide Web:* http://www.brockport.edu/studyabroad/

AUSTRALIA
Sydney

MORE ABOUT THE PROGRAM
Through SUNY College at Brockport, participants have the opportunity to spend a semester or year in Sydney, Australia, studying at the University of Sydney. Participants are able to choose from a wide range of courses available at the University while living in accommodations located within walking distance of the campus. At the University of Sydney, students are ensured of a world-class educational experience. The University is a leading teaching and research institution, and many of its faculty members are distinguished scholars and researchers and leaders in their fields.

STATE UNIVERSITY OF NEW YORK COLLEGE AT BROCKPORT
UNIVERSITY OF WESTERN SYDNEY PROGRAM

Hosted by University of Western Sydney
Academic Focus • Full curriculum.
Program Information • Students attend classes at University of Western Sydney. Field trips to various destinations throughout Sydney and the surrounding area.
Sessions • Fall, spring, yearlong.
Eligibility Requirements • Minimum age 18; open to juniors, seniors; 2.5 GPA; 2 letters of recommendation; good academic standing at home school; ability to do upper-division level coursework in chosen subject; résumé for internship option.
Living Arrangements • Students live in host institution dormitories. Quarters are shared with host institution students. Meals are taken on one's own, in residences.
Costs (2005) • One term: contact sponsor for cost. Yearlong program: contact sponsor for cost. $350 deposit required. Financial aid available for all students: scholarships, loans, regular financial aid, grants.
For More Information • Dr. John Perry, Director, Office of International Education, State University of New York College at Brockport, 350 New Campus Drive, Brockport, NY 14420; *Phone:* 800-298-SUNY; *Fax:* 585-637-3218. *E-mail:* overseas@brockport.edu. *World Wide Web:* http://www.brockport.edu/studyabroad/

STUDY AUSTRALIA
MACQUARIE UNIVERSITY

Hosted by Macquarie University
Academic Focus • Full curriculum.
Program Information • Students attend classes at Macquarie University. Scheduled travel to Sydney; field trips to the Blue Mountains, Melbourne; optional travel to the Great Barrier Reef, the Outback, Tasmania, Fiji, New Zealand at an extra cost.
Sessions • Fall, spring, yearlong.
Eligibility Requirements • Minimum age 18; open to sophomores, juniors, seniors; 2.5 GPA; good academic standing at home school; enrollment at an accredited American college or university.
Living Arrangements • Students live in host institution dormitories, locally rented apartments, program-owned apartments, host family homes. Quarters are shared with host institution students, students from other programs. Meals are taken on one's own, in residences, in central dining facility.
Costs (2003) • One term: $9250. Yearlong program: $17,250; includes tuition, housing, insurance, excursions, student support services, travel discounts. $500 refundable deposit required. Financial aid available for all students: scholarships, loans.
For More Information • Mr. Chris Shepherd, Director of Programs and Services, Study Australia, 54515 State Road 933 North, Notre Dame, IN 46556-1004; *Phone:* 800-585-9658; *Fax:* 509-357-9457. *E-mail:* info@study-australia.com. *World Wide Web:* http://www.study-australia.com/

STUDY AUSTRALIA
UNIVERSITY OF NEW SOUTH WALES

Hosted by University of New South Wales
Academic Focus • Full curriculum.
Program Information • Students attend classes at University of New South Wales. Scheduled travel to Sydney; field trips to the Blue Mountains; optional travel to the Great Barrier Reef, the Outback, Tasmania, Fiji, New Zealand at an extra cost.
Sessions • Fall, spring, yearlong.
Eligibility Requirements • Minimum age 18; open to sophomores, juniors, seniors; 3.0 GPA; good academic standing at home school; enrollment at an accredited American college or university.
Living Arrangements • Students live in host institution dormitories, locally rented apartments, program-owned apartments, program-owned houses, host family homes. Quarters are shared with host institution students, students from other programs. Meals are taken on one's own, in residences, in central dining facility.
Costs (2003) • One term: $10,375. Yearlong program: $19,450; includes tuition, housing, insurance, excursions, student support services, travel discounts. $500 refundable deposit required. Financial aid available for all students: scholarships, loans.
For More Information • Mr. Chris Shepherd, Director of Programs and Services, Study Australia, 54515 State Road 933 North, Notre Dame, IN 46556-1004; *Phone:* 800-585-9658; *Fax:* 509-357-9457. *E-mail:* info@study-australia.com. *World Wide Web:* http://www.study-australia.com/

STUDY AUSTRALIA
UNIVERSITY OF SYDNEY

Hosted by University of Sydney
Academic Focus • Full curriculum.
Program Information • Students attend classes at University of Sydney. Scheduled travel to Sydney; field trips to the Blue Mountains; optional travel to the Great Barrier Reef, the Outback, Tasmania, Fiji, New Zealand at an extra cost.
Sessions • Fall, spring, yearlong.
Eligibility Requirements • Minimum age 18; open to sophomores, juniors, seniors; 2.8 GPA; good academic standing at home school; enrollment at an accredited American college or university.
Living Arrangements • Students live in host institution dormitories, locally rented apartments, program-owned apartments, program-owned houses, host family homes. Quarters are shared with host institution students, students from other programs. Meals are taken on one's own, in residences, in central dining facility.
Costs (2003) • One term: $10,375. Yearlong program: $19,450; includes tuition, housing, insurance, excursions, student support services, travel discounts. $500 refundable deposit required. Financial aid available for all students: scholarships, loans.
For More Information • Mr. Chris Shepherd, Director of Programs and Services, Study Australia, 54515 State Road 933 North, Notre Dame, IN 46556-1004; *Phone:* 800-585-9658; *Fax:* 509-357-9457. *E-mail:* info@study-australia.com. *World Wide Web:* http://www.study-australia.com/

UNIVERSITY OF MIAMI
UNIVERSITY OF TECHNOLOGY–SYDNEY

Hosted by University of Technology Sydney
Academic Focus • Art, Asian studies, economics, environmental science/studies, international affairs, international business, law and legal studies, political science and government, science.
Program Information • Students attend classes at University of Technology Sydney.
Sessions • Fall, spring, yearlong.
Eligibility Requirements • Minimum age 18; open to sophomores, juniors, seniors; 3.0 GPA; 2 letters of recommendation; official transcripts.
Living Arrangements • Students live in host institution dormitories, host family homes. Quarters are shared with host institution students, students from other programs. Meals are taken on one's own, in residences, in central dining facility.
Costs (2003-2004) • One term: $12,919. Yearlong program: $25,838; includes tuition, student support services. $40 application fee. $500 nonrefundable deposit required. Financial aid available for students from sponsoring institution: scholarships, loans.
For More Information • Ms. Glenda Hayley, Assistant Director, University of Miami, International Education and Exchange Programs, 5050 Brunson Drive, Allen Hall 212, PO Box 248005, Coral Gables, FL 33124-1610; *Phone:* 305-284-3434; *Fax:* 305-284-4235. *E-mail:* ieep@miami.edu. *World Wide Web:* http://www.studyabroad.miami.edu/

UNIVERSITY OF MINNESOTA
STUDY AND INTERSHIPS IN SYDNEY

Academic Focus • Australian studies.
Program Information • Faculty members are local instructors hired by the sponsor. Field trips to the Blue Mountains.
Sessions • Fall, spring.
Eligibility Requirements • Open to freshmen, sophomores, juniors, seniors; 2.5 GPA.
Living Arrangements • Students live in program-owned apartments. Meals are taken as a group, on one's own, in residences, in central dining facility.
Costs (2004-2005) • One term: contact sponsor for cost. $50 application fee. $400 nonrefundable deposit required. Financial aid available for students from sponsoring institution: scholarships, loans.
For More Information • Learning Abroad Center, University of Minnesota, 230 Heller Hall, 271 19th Avenue South, Minneapolis, MN 55455; *Phone:* 888-700-UOFM; *Fax:* 612-626-8009. *E-mail:* umabroad@umn.edu. *World Wide Web:* http://www.umabroad.umn.edu/

UNIVERSITY OF WESTERN SYDNEY
STUDY ABROAD AT UNIVERSITY OF WESTERN SYDNEY

Hosted by University of Western Sydney
Academic Focus • Full curriculum.
Program Information • Students attend classes at University of Western Sydney. Field trips to the inner city, the Blue Mountains; optional travel to tourist sites predominantly in New South Wales (bushwalking, snow skiing, wine tasting) at an extra cost.
Sessions • Fall, spring, yearlong.
Eligibility Requirements • Minimum age 18; open to freshmen, sophomores, juniors, seniors, graduate students; 2.5 GPA; 2 letters of recommendation; good academic standing at home school.
Living Arrangements • Students live in host institution dormitories, locally rented apartments, program-owned apartments, program-owned houses. Quarters are shared with host institution students, students from other programs. Meals are taken as a group, on one's own, in residences, in restaurants.
Costs (2004-2005) • One term: A$6600 (A$8200 with internship). Yearlong program: A$13,200 (A$16,400 with internship); includes tuition, student support services, overseas student health coverage. Financial aid available for all students: loans.
For More Information • Ms. Wendy Spinks, Study Abroad Coordinator, University of Western Sydney, UWS International, Locked Bag 1797, Penrith South DC, New South Wales 1797, Australia; *Phone:* +61 2-47-360-928; *Fax:* +61 2-47-360-922. *E-mail:* studyabroad@uws.edu.au. *World Wide Web:* http://www.uws.edu.au/international/. Students may also apply through CIEE, 7 Customs House Street, 3rd Floor, Portland, ME 04101.

UNIVERSITY OF WISCONSIN–STEVENS POINT
SEMESTER IN THE SOUTH PACIFIC

Hosted by Macquarie University
Academic Focus • Anthropology, cultural studies, economics, history, literature, natural resources.
Program Information • Students attend classes at Macquarie University. Scheduled travel to Fiji, New Zealand (South Island); field trips to the Outback (White Cliffs), the Blue Mountains; optional travel to Tahiti, the Cook Islands, Hawaii, the Great Barrier Reef at an extra cost.
Sessions • Fall, spring.
Eligibility Requirements • Minimum age 18; open to sophomores, juniors, seniors, adults; 2.25 GPA; 3 letters of recommendation; good academic standing at home school.
Living Arrangements • Students live in host institution dormitories, locally rented apartments, host family homes. Quarters are shared with students from other programs. Meals are taken as a group, in central dining facility.
Costs (2003-2004) • One term: $9350 for Wisconsin residents; $15,000 for nonresidents (estimated); includes tuition, housing, all meals, excursions, international airfare, books and class materials. $15 application fee. $250 nonrefundable deposit required. Financial aid available for all students: scholarships, work study, loans.

For More Information • Mr. Mark Koepke, Associate Director, University of Wisconsin–Stevens Point, International Programs Office, Stevens Point, WI 54481; *Phone:* 715-346-2717; *Fax:* 715-346-3591. *E-mail:* intlprog@uwsp.edu. *World Wide Web:* http://www.uwsp.edu/studyabroad/

TOOWOOMBA
CENTER FOR INTERNATIONAL STUDIES
UNIVERSITY OF SOUTHERN QUEENSLAND

Hosted by University of Southern Queensland
Academic Focus • Full curriculum.
Program Information • Students attend classes at University of Southern Queensland. Field trips to a city tour; optional travel to an Australian farm, the Great Barrier Reef, the Outback at an extra cost.
Sessions • Fall, spring, yearlong.
Eligibility Requirements • Minimum age 18; open to sophomores, juniors, seniors, graduate students, adults; 2.5 GPA; 1 letter of recommendation; good academic standing at home school; personal essay.
Living Arrangements • Students live in host institution dormitories, program-owned apartments. Quarters are shared with host institution students, students from other programs. Meals are taken on one's own, in residences, in central dining facility, in restaurants.
Costs (2003) • One term: $6575-$7600. Yearlong program: $11,300-$13,350; includes tuition, housing, all meals, insurance, international student ID, student support services, airport reception. $50 application fee. $500 nonrefundable deposit required. Financial aid available for all students: scholarships.
For More Information • Mr. Jeff Palm, Program Director, Center for International Studies, 17 New South Street, #105, Northampton, MA 01060; *Phone:* 413-582-0407; *Fax:* 413-582-0327. *E-mail:* jpalm@cisabroad.com. *World Wide Web:* http://www.cisabroad.com/

IDP EDUCATION AUSTRALIA
UNIVERSITY OF SOUTHERN QUEENSLAND PROGRAM

Hosted by University of Southern Queensland
Academic Focus • Anthropology, Australian studies, business administration/management, communications, computer science, drama/theater, education, engineering, film and media studies, health, international affairs, psychology, teaching, tourism and travel.
Program Information • Students attend classes at University of Southern Queensland.
Sessions • Fall, spring, yearlong.
Eligibility Requirements • Open to freshmen, sophomores, juniors, seniors; good academic standing at home school.
Living Arrangements • Students live in host institution dormitories, locally rented apartments.
Costs (2004) • One term: contact sponsor for cost. Yearlong program: contact sponsor for cost. $100 deposit required.
For More Information • Ms. Deborah Brown, Senior Manager, Study Abroad, IDP Education Australia, 1400 16th Street, NW, Suite 101, Washington, DC 20036-2219; *Phone:* 866-STUDYOZ; *Fax:* 202-332-3297. *E-mail:* studyabroad@washington.idp.com. *World Wide Web:* http://www.idp.com/

STATE UNIVERSITY OF NEW YORK COLLEGE AT BROCKPORT
UNIVERSITY OF SOUTHERN QUEENSLAND PROGRAM

Hosted by University of Southern Queensland
Academic Focus • Full curriculum.
Program Information • Students attend classes at University of Southern Queensland. Field trips to destinations throughout Sydney and environs during orientation.
Sessions • Fall, spring, yearlong.
Eligibility Requirements • Minimum age 18; open to juniors, seniors; 2.5 GPA; 2 letters of recommendation; good academic standing at home school; ability to do upper-division course work in chosen subject.
Living Arrangements • Students live in host institution dormitories, residential colleges, student village. Quarters are shared with

AUSTRALIA
Toowoomba

host institution students. Meals are taken as a group, on one's own, in residences, in central dining facility.

Costs (2003-2004) • One term: $9150 for fall term; $9,250 for spring. Yearlong program: $16,550; includes tuition, housing, excursions, international student ID, student support services, most meals if staying in residential colleges. $350 nonrefundable deposit required. Financial aid available for all students: scholarships, loans, regular financial aid, grants.

For More Information • Dr. John Perry, Director, Office of International Education, State University of New York College at Brockport, 350 New Campus Drive, Brockport, NY 14420; *Phone:* 800-298-SUNY; *Fax:* 585-637-3218. *E-mail:* overseas@brockport.edu. *World Wide Web:* http://www.brockport.edu/studyabroad/

TOWNSVILLE
ARCADIA UNIVERSITY
JAMES COOK UNIVERSITY

Hosted by James Cook University–Cairns Campus, James Cook University–Townsville Campus
Academic Focus • Aboriginal studies, biological/life sciences, business administration/management, engineering, law and legal studies, liberal studies, marine sciences, social sciences.
Program Information • Students attend classes at James Cook University–Cairns Campus, James Cook University–Townsville Campus. Optional travel to destinations arranged by JCU at an extra cost.
Sessions • Fall, spring, yearlong, US academic year.
Eligibility Requirements • Open to sophomores, juniors, seniors; 3.0 GPA; 1 letter of recommendation.
Living Arrangements • Students live in host institution dormitories. Quarters are shared with host institution students. Meals are taken on one's own, in residences.
Costs (2003-2004) • One term: $9990. Yearlong program: $16,590 for Australian academic year; $16,900 for US academic year; includes tuition, insurance, international student ID, student support services, transcript, pre-departure guide. $35 application fee. $500 nonrefundable deposit required. Financial aid available for all students: scholarships, loans.
For More Information • Arcadia University, Center for Education Abroad, 450 South Easton Road, Glenside, PA 19038-3295; *Phone:* 866-927-2234; *Fax:* 215-572-2174. *E-mail:* cea@arcadia.edu. *World Wide Web:* http://www.arcadia.edu/cea/

AUSTRALEARN: NORTH AMERICAN CENTER FOR AUSTRALIAN AND NEW ZEALAND UNIVERSITIES
JAMES COOK UNIVERSITY

Hosted by James Cook University–Cairns Campus, James Cook University–Townsville Campus
Academic Focus • Full curriculum.
Program Information • Students attend classes at James Cook University–Cairns Campus, James Cook University–Townsville Campus. Scheduled travel to a pre-trip excursion to the Great Barrier Reef and an Aboriginal Cultural Park; optional travel to a rainforest, the Outback, Darwin, Brisbane at an extra cost.
Sessions • Fall, spring, yearlong, alternate year.
Eligibility Requirements • Minimum age 18; open to sophomores, juniors, seniors, graduate students; 2.8 GPA; 1 letter of recommendation; good academic standing at home school.
Living Arrangements • Students live in host institution dormitories, locally rented apartments. Quarters are shared with host institution students. Meals are taken as a group, on one's own, in residences, in central dining facility.
Costs (2004) • One term: $10,250. Yearlong program: $19,680; includes tuition, housing, all meals, insurance, excursions, international student ID, student support services. $30 application fee. $300 deposit required. Financial aid available for all students: scholarships, loans.
For More Information • AustraLearn: North American Center for Australian and New Zealand Universities, 12050 North Pecos Street, Suite 320, Westminster, CO 80234; *Phone:* 800-980-0033; *Fax:* 303-446-5955. *E-mail:* studyabroad@australearn.org. *World Wide Web:* http://www.australearn.org/

IDP EDUCATION AUSTRALIA
JAMES COOK UNIVERSITY PROGRAM

Hosted by James Cook University–Townsville Campus
Academic Focus • Full curriculum.
Program Information • Students attend classes at James Cook University–Townsville Campus.
Sessions • Fall, spring, yearlong.
Eligibility Requirements • Open to sophomores, juniors, seniors; 2.8 GPA.
Living Arrangements • Students live in host institution dormitories, locally rented apartments.
Costs (2004) • One term: contact sponsor for cost. Yearlong program: contact sponsor for cost. $100 deposit required.
For More Information • Ms. Deborah Brown, Senior Manager, Study Abroad, IDP Education Australia, 1400 16th Street, NW, Suite 101, Washington, DC 20036-2219; *Phone:* 866-STUDYOZ; *Fax:* 202-332-3297. *E-mail:* studyabroad@washington.idp.com. *World Wide Web:* http://www.idp.com/

INSTITUTE FOR STUDY ABROAD, BUTLER UNIVERSITY
JAMES COOK UNIVERSITY

Hosted by James Cook University–Townsville Campus
Academic Focus • Full curriculum.
Program Information • Students attend classes at James Cook University–Townsville Campus. Scheduled travel to farms; optional travel at an extra cost.
Sessions • Fall, spring, yearlong, US academic year.
Eligibility Requirements • Open to sophomores, juniors, seniors; 2.5 GPA; 1 letter of recommendation; good academic standing at home school; enrollment at an accredited American college or university.
Living Arrangements • Students live in host institution dormitories. Quarters are shared with host institution students. Meals are taken as a group, on one's own, in residences, in central dining facility.
Costs (2003) • One term: $9175. Yearlong program: $15,175; includes tuition, housing, insurance, excursions, international student ID, student support services, cultural and sporting events, pre-departure advising. $40 application fee. $500 nonrefundable deposit required. Financial aid available for all students: scholarships, travel grants.
For More Information • Institute for Study Abroad, Butler University, 1100 West 42nd Street, Suite 305, Indianapolis, IN 46208-3345; *Phone:* 800-858-0229; *Fax:* 317-940-9704. *E-mail:* study-abroad@butler.edu. *World Wide Web:* http://www.ifsa-butler.org/

UNIVERSITY OF MIAMI
JAMES COOK UNIVERSITY, AUSTRALIA

Hosted by James Cook University–Townsville Campus
Academic Focus • Biochemistry, biological/life sciences, chemical sciences, ecology, fisheries studies, marine sciences.
Program Information • Students attend classes at James Cook University–Townsville Campus.
Sessions • Fall, spring, yearlong.
Eligibility Requirements • Minimum age 18; open to sophomores, juniors, seniors; course work in marine biology or science; 3.0 GPA; 2 letters of recommendation; official transcripts.
Living Arrangements • Students live in host institution dormitories. Quarters are shared with host institution students, students from other programs. Meals are taken on one's own, in residences, in central dining facility.
Costs (2003-2004) • One term: $12,919. Yearlong program: $25,838; includes tuition, student support services. $40 application fee. $500 nonrefundable deposit required. Financial aid available for students from sponsoring institution: scholarships, loans.
For More Information • Ms. Glenda Hayley, Assistant Director, University of Miami, International Education and Exchange Programs, 5050 Brunson Drive, Allen Hall 212, PO Box 248005, Coral Gables, FL 33124-1610; *Phone:* 305-284-3434; *Fax:* 305-284-4235. *E-mail:* ieep@miami.edu. *World Wide Web:* http://www.studyabroad.miami.edu/

WAGGA WAGGA

IDP EDUCATION AUSTRALIA
CHARLES STURT UNIVERSITY PROGRAM

Hosted by Charles Sturt University–Wagga Wagga Campus
Academic Focus • Full curriculum.
Program Information • Students attend classes at Charles Sturt University–Wagga Wagga Campus.
Sessions • Fall, spring, yearlong.
Eligibility Requirements • Open to freshmen, sophomores, juniors, seniors; good academic standing at home school.
Living Arrangements • Students live in host institution dormitories, locally rented apartments.
Costs (2004) • One term: contact sponsor for cost. Yearlong program: contact sponsor for cost. $100 deposit required.
For More Information • Ms. Deborah Brown, Senior Manager, Study Abroad, IDP Education Australia, 1400 16th Street, NW, Suite 101, Washington, DC 20036-2219; *Phone:* 866-STUDYOZ; *Fax:* 202-332-3297. *E-mail:* studyabroad@washington.idp.com. *World Wide Web:* http://www.idp.com/

STATE UNIVERSITY OF NEW YORK AT OSWEGO
CHARLES STURT UNIVERSITY

Hosted by Charles Sturt University–Bathurst Campus, Charles Sturt University–Albury Wodonga, Charles Sturt University–Wagga Wagga Campus
Academic Focus • Full curriculum.
Program Information • Students attend classes at Charles Sturt University–Bathurst Campus, Charles Sturt University–Albury Wodonga, Charles Sturt University–Wagga Wagga Campus. Optional travel to Australia, New Zealand, Pacific Islands at an extra cost.
Sessions • Fall, spring, yearlong.
Eligibility Requirements • Open to sophomores, juniors, seniors; 2.5 GPA; 3 letters of recommendation; good academic standing at home school; program study statement.
Living Arrangements • Students live in host institution dormitories, locally rented apartments. Quarters are shared with host institution students. Meals are taken on one's own, in residences, in central dining facility, in restaurants.
Costs (2003-2004) • One term: $5820. Yearlong program: $11,640; includes tuition, insurance, student support services. $250 nonrefundable deposit required. Financial aid available for students: home university financial aid, loan processing and scholarships for Oswego students.
For More Information • Ms. Nefertitti Saheed, Program Specialist, State University of New York at Oswego, 122A Swetman Hall, Oswego, NY 13126; *Phone:* 888-4-OSWEGO; *Fax:* 315-312-2477. *E-mail:* intled@oswego.edu. *World Wide Web:* http://www.oswego.edu/intled/

WOLLONGONG

ALMA COLLEGE
PROGRAM OF STUDIES IN AUSTRALIA

Hosted by University of Wollongong
Academic Focus • Anthropology, Australian studies, business administration/management, English.
Program Information • Students attend classes at University of Wollongong.
Sessions • Fall, spring, yearlong.
Eligibility Requirements • Minimum age 18; open to sophomores, juniors, seniors; 3.0 GPA; 2 letters of recommendation; good academic standing at home school.
Living Arrangements • Students live in host institution dormitories, locally rented apartments. Quarters are shared with host institution students. Meals are taken as a group, on one's own, in residences, in central dining facility.
Costs (2002-2003) • One term: $8500. Yearlong program: $16,550; includes tuition, housing, all meals, student support services. $50 application fee. $200 refundable deposit required. Financial aid available for all students: scholarships.
For More Information • Ms. Julie Elenbaas, Office Coordinator, Alma College, 614 West Superior Street, Alma, MI 48801-1599;

Phone: 989-463-7055; *Fax:* 989-463-7126. *E-mail:* intl_studies@alma.edu. *World Wide Web:* http://international.alma.edu/

ARCADIA UNIVERSITY
UNIVERSITY OF WOLLONGONG

Hosted by University of Wollongong
Academic Focus • Biological/life sciences, engineering, liberal studies, social sciences.
Program Information • Students attend classes at University of Wollongong. Field trips; optional travel at an extra cost.
Sessions • Fall, spring, yearlong, US academic year.
Eligibility Requirements • Open to sophomores, juniors, seniors; 3.0 GPA; 1 letter of recommendation.
Living Arrangements • Students live in host institution dormitories, locally rented apartments. Quarters are shared with host institution students. Meals are taken on one's own, in residences, in central dining facility.
Costs (2003-2004) • One term: $9100. Yearlong program: $15,190 for Australian academic year; $15,390 for US academic year; includes tuition, housing, insurance, international student ID, student support services, transcripts, pre-departure guide. $35 application fee. $500 nonrefundable deposit required. Financial aid available for all students: scholarships, loans.
For More Information • Arcadia University, Center for Education Abroad, 450 South Easton Road, Glenside, PA 19038-3295; *Phone:* 866-927-2234; *Fax:* 215-572-2174. *E-mail:* cea@arcadia.edu. *World Wide Web:* http://www.arcadia.edu/cea/

AUSTRALEARN: NORTH AMERICAN CENTER FOR AUSTRALIAN AND NEW ZEALAND UNIVERSITIES
UNIVERSITY OF WOLLONGONG

Hosted by University of Wollongong
Academic Focus • Full curriculum.
Program Information • Students attend classes at University of Wollongong. Scheduled travel to a pre-trip excursion to the Great Barrier Reef, Aboriginal Cultural Park; optional travel to Sydney, Melbourne, Ayers Rock, Queensland at an extra cost.
Sessions • Fall, spring, yearlong, alternate year.
Eligibility Requirements • Minimum age 18; open to sophomores, juniors, seniors, graduate students; 3.0 GPA; 1 letter of recommendation; good academic standing at home school.
Living Arrangements • Students live in host institution dormitories, locally rented apartments. Quarters are shared with host institution students. Meals are taken on one's own, in residences.
Costs (2004) • One term: $10,765. Yearlong program: $18,975; includes tuition, housing, all meals, insurance, excursions, international student ID, student support services. $30 application fee. $300 deposit required. Financial aid available for all students: scholarships, loans.
For More Information • AustraLearn: North American Center for Australian and New Zealand Universities, 12050 North Pecos Street, Suite 320, Westminster, CO 80234; *Phone:* 800-980-0033; *Fax:* 303-446-5955. *E-mail:* studyabroad@australearn.org. *World Wide Web:* http://www.australearn.org/

CIEE
CIEE STUDY CENTER AT THE UNIVERSITY OF WOLLONGONG, AUSTRALIA

Hosted by University of Wollongong
Academic Focus • Full curriculum.
Program Information • Students attend classes at University of Wollongong. Scheduled travel to Canberra, Sydney, the Blue Mountains, beach campsites; field trips to animal parks, Sydney, mountains, the Snowy Mountain; optional travel to Tasmania, the Great Barrier Reef at an extra cost.
Sessions • Fall, spring, yearlong, alternate year.
Eligibility Requirements • Open to freshmen, sophomores, juniors, seniors; 3.0 GPA; 2 letters of recommendation; good academic standing at home school.
Living Arrangements • Students live in host institution dormitories, locally rented apartments, host institution apartments. Quarters

are shared with host institution students, students from other programs. Meals are taken on one's own, in residences, in central dining facility, in restaurants.

Costs (2004-2005) • One term: $11,500. Yearlong program: $19,900; includes tuition, housing, some meals, insurance, excursions, student support services, pre-departure advising, cultural activities. $30 application fee. $300 deposit required. Financial aid available for all students: scholarships, minority student scholarships, travel grants.

For More Information • Mr. Adam Rubin, Admissions Officer, Asia Pacific, CIEE, 7 Custom House Street, 3rd Floor, Portland, ME 04101; *Phone:* 800-40-STUDY; *Fax:* 207-553-7699. *E-mail:* studyinfo@ciee.org. *World Wide Web:* http://www.ciee.org/isp/

IDP EDUCATION AUSTRALIA
UNIVERSITY OF WOLLONGONG PROGRAM

Hosted by University of Wollongong
Academic Focus • Full curriculum.
Program Information • Students attend classes at University of Wollongong.
Sessions • Fall, spring, yearlong.
Eligibility Requirements • Open to freshmen, sophomores, juniors, seniors; 3.0 GPA; portfolio for some visual/performing arts courses.
Living Arrangements • Students live in host institution dormitories, locally rented apartments.
Costs (2004) • One term: contact sponsor for cost. Yearlong program: contact sponsor for cost. $100 deposit required.
For More Information • Ms. Deborah Brown, Senior Manager, Study Abroad, IDP Education Australia, 1400 16th Street, NW, Suite 101, Washington, DC 20036-2219; *Phone:* 866-STUDYOZ; *Fax:* 202-332-3297. *E-mail:* studyabroad@washington.idp.com. *World Wide Web:* http://www.idp.com/

INSTITUTE FOR STUDY ABROAD, BUTLER UNIVERSITY
UNIVERSITY OF WOLLONGONG

Hosted by University of Wollongong
Academic Focus • Full curriculum.
Program Information • Students attend classes at University of Wollongong. Scheduled travel to farms; field trips; optional travel at an extra cost.
Sessions • Fall, spring, yearlong, US academic year.
Eligibility Requirements • Open to sophomores, juniors, seniors; 3.0 GPA; 1 letter of recommendation; good academic standing at home school.
Living Arrangements • Students live in host institution dormitories. Quarters are shared with host institution students. Meals are taken as a group, in residences, in central dining facility.
Costs (2003) • One term: $9375. Yearlong program: $13,975; includes tuition, housing, insurance, excursions, international student ID, student support services, cultural and sporting events, pre-departure advising. $40 application fee. $500 nonrefundable deposit required. Financial aid available for all students: scholarships, travel grants.
For More Information • Institute for Study Abroad, Butler University, 1100 West 42nd Street, Suite 305, Indianapolis, IN 46208-3345; *Phone:* 800-858-0229; *Fax:* 317-940-9704. *E-mail:* study-abroad@butler.edu. *World Wide Web:* http://www.ifsa-butler.org/

STATE UNIVERSITY OF NEW YORK AT PLATTSBURGH
STUDY IN AUSTRALIA, WOLLONGONG

Hosted by University of Wollongong
Academic Focus • Accounting, Australian studies, biomedical sciences, business administration/management, drama/theater, education, fine/studio arts, journalism, nutrition, philosophy, psychology, sociology.
Program Information • Students attend classes at University of Wollongong.
Sessions • Fall, spring, yearlong.
Eligibility Requirements • Minimum age 18; open to sophomores, juniors, seniors; 2.8 GPA; 3 letters of recommendation; SUNYand UW applications; essay; transcript.

Living Arrangements • Students live in host institution dormitories, locally rented apartments. Quarters are shared with host institution students, students from other programs. Meals are taken on one's own, in residences, in central dining facility, in restaurants.
Costs (2003-2004) • One term: $9670 for New York residents; nonresidents contact sponsor for cost. Yearlong program: $19,340 for New York residents; nonresidents contact sponsor for cost; includes tuition, housing, some meals, insurance, international student ID, student support services, program fees. $20 application fee. $350 nonrefundable deposit required. Financial aid available for students from sponsoring institution: scholarships, loans.
For More Information • Ms. Jo Ann Mackie, Study Abroad Coordinator, State University of New York at Plattsburgh, Study Abroad Office, 101 Broad Street, Plattsburgh, NY 12901; *Phone:* 518-564-2321; *Fax:* 518-564-2326. *E-mail:* international@plattsburgh.edu. *World Wide Web:* http://www.plattsburgh.edu/studyabroad/

UNIVERSITY OF MIAMI
UNIVERSITY OF WOLLONGONG, AUSTRALIA

Hosted by University of Wollongong
Academic Focus • Biological/life sciences, business administration/management, communications, education, engineering, environmental science/studies, history, language studies, mathematics.
Program Information • Students attend classes at University of Wollongong.
Sessions • Fall, spring, yearlong.
Eligibility Requirements • Minimum age 18; open to sophomores, juniors, seniors; 3.0 GPA; 2 letters of recommendation; official transcript.
Living Arrangements • Students live in host institution dormitories, locally rented apartments. Quarters are shared with host institution students, students from other programs. Meals are taken on one's own, in central dining facility.
Costs (2003-2004) • One term: $12,919. Yearlong program: $25,838; includes tuition, student support services. $40 application fee. $500 nonrefundable deposit required. Financial aid available for students from sponsoring institution: scholarships, loans.
For More Information • Ms. Glenda Hayley, Assistant Director, University of Miami, International Education and Exchange Programs, 5050 Brunson Drive, Allen Hall 212, PO Box 248005, Coral Gables, FL 33124-1610; *Phone:* 305-284-3434; *Fax:* 305-284-4235. *E-mail:* ieep@miami.edu. *World Wide Web:* http://www.studyabroad.miami.edu/

THE UNIVERSITY OF NORTH CAROLINA AT CHAPEL HILL
STUDY ABROAD AT UNIVERSITY OF WOLLONGONG

Hosted by University of Wollongong
Academic Focus • Full curriculum.
Program Information • Students attend classes at University of Wollongong.
Sessions • Fall, spring, yearlong, southern hemisphere year.
Eligibility Requirements • Open to sophomores, juniors, seniors, graduate students; 3.0 GPA; 2 letters of recommendation; essay; transcript.
Living Arrangements • Students live in host institution dormitories, locally rented apartments. Quarters are shared with host institution students, students from other programs. Meals are taken on one's own, in residences, in central dining facility.
Costs (2003-2004) • One term: $4535. Yearlong program: $9070; includes tuition, insurance, study abroad fee, room deposit. $100 application fee. $500 nonrefundable deposit required. Financial aid available for students from sponsoring institution: scholarships, loans.
For More Information • Study Abroad Office, The University of North Carolina at Chapel Hill, 201 Porthole Building, CB 3130, Chapel Hill, NC 27599-3130; *Phone:* 919-962-7002; *Fax:* 919-962-2262. *E-mail:* abroad@unc.edu. *World Wide Web:* http://studyabroad.unc.edu/

UNIVERSITY OF WOLLONGONG
STUDY ABROAD PROGRAM

Hosted by University of Wollongong

Academic Focus • Aboriginal studies, Australian studies, biomedical sciences, commerce, communications, comparative literature, earth sciences, economics, education, engineering, geography, geology, health and physical education, history, information science, law and legal studies, liberal studies, marine sciences, nursing, nutrition, physical sciences, physics, science, sociology, visual and performing arts.

Program Information • Students attend classes at University of Wollongong. Field trips to the Wollongong region, the Blue Mountains, the southern coast of New South Wales; optional travel to Queensland, Tasmania, Victoria, Canberra at an extra cost.

Sessions • Fall, spring, yearlong.

Eligibility Requirements • Open to precollege students, freshmen, sophomores, juniors, seniors, graduate students; 3.0 GPA; good academic standing at home school.

Living Arrangements • Students live in host institution dormitories, locally rented apartments, program-owned apartments, host family homes. Quarters are shared with host institution students, students from other programs. Meals are taken as a group, in residences, in central dining facility.

Costs (2002-2003) • One term: A$12,398. Yearlong program: A$25,000; includes tuition, housing, all meals, overseas student health coverage.

For More Information • Study Abroad Coordinator, University of Wollongong, International Office, Northfields Avenue, Wollongong, New South Wales 2522, Australia; *Phone:* +61 2-42-21-3170; *Fax:* +61 4-42-21-3499. *E-mail:* studyabroad@uow.edu.au. *World Wide Web:* http://www.uow.edu.au/. Students may also apply through Arcadia University, Center for Education Abroad, 450 South Easton Road, Glenside, PA 19038-3295; CIEE, 7 Customs House Street, 3rd Floor, Portland, ME 04101.

AUSTRIA

BRAUNAU

WALLA WALLA COLLEGE
ADVENTIST COLLEGES ABROAD

Hosted by Seminar Schloss Bogenhofen

Academic Focus • Full curriculum, German language and literature.

Program Information • Students attend classes at Seminar Schloss Bogenhofen. Scheduled travel to Vienna, the Alps (ski trip), Berlin and other parts of Germany; field trips to Salzburg, Munich, Linz; optional travel at an extra cost.

Sessions • Yearlong.

Eligibility Requirements • Open to freshmen, sophomores, juniors, seniors; 2.5 GPA; 3 letters of recommendation; good academic standing at home school; minimum 3.0 GPA in German; 1 year of college course work in German.

Living Arrangements • Students live in host institution dormitories. Quarters are shared with host institution students, students from other programs. Meals are taken as a group, in central dining facility.

Costs (2002-2003) • Yearlong program: contact sponsor for cost. $100 nonrefundable deposit required. Financial aid available for all students: scholarships, loans.

For More Information • Mr. Jean-Paul Grimaud, Chair of Modern Language Department, Walla Walla College, 204 South College Avenue, College Place, WA 99324; *Phone:* 509-529-7769; *Fax:* 509-527-2253. *E-mail:* grimje@wwc.edu

GRAZ

RIDER UNIVERSITY
STUDY ABROAD IN AUSTRIA

Hosted by Karl Franzens University

Academic Focus • Austrian studies, German language and literature.

Program Information • Students attend classes at Karl Franzens University.

Sessions • Fall, spring, yearlong.

Eligibility Requirements • Open to sophomores, juniors, seniors; 2.5 GPA; 1 letter of recommendation; good academic standing at home school; 1 year of college course work in German.

Living Arrangements • Students live in host institution dormitories, locally rented apartments. Quarters are shared with host institution students, students from other programs. Meals are taken on one's own, in central dining facility, in restaurants.

Costs (2001-2002) • One term: $8995. Yearlong program: $17,990; includes tuition, student support services, administrative fees. $35 application fee. $300 refundable deposit required. Financial aid available for students from sponsoring institution: regular financial aid.

For More Information • Dr. Joseph E. Nadeau, Director, Study Abroad Programs, Rider University, 2083 Lawrenceville Road, Lawrenceville, NJ 08648; *Phone:* 609-896-5314; *Fax:* 609-895-5670. *E-mail:* nadeau@rider.edu. *World Wide Web:* http://www.rider.edu/academic/uwp/index.htm

STATE UNIVERSITY OF NEW YORK AT BINGHAMTON
GRAZ PROGRAM

Hosted by Karl Franzens University

Academic Focus • Austrian studies, full curriculum, German language and literature, German studies, international affairs.

Program Information • Students attend classes at Karl Franzens University. Scheduled travel to Prague, Dresden; field trips to Vienna, Salzburg.

Sessions • Fall, yearlong.

Eligibility Requirements • Open to sophomores, juniors, seniors, graduate students; 3.0 GPA; 3 letters of recommendation; 2 years of college course work in German.

Living Arrangements • Students live in host institution dormitories, locally rented apartments, host family homes. Quarters are shared with host institution students. Meals are taken on one's own, in residences, in central dining facility, in restaurants.

Costs (2003-2004) • One term: $7500 for New York residents; $10,000 for nonresidents. Yearlong program: $13,200 for New York residents; $18,000 for nonresidents; includes tuition, housing, all meals, insurance, excursions, international airfare, books and class materials. $250 nonrefundable deposit required. Financial aid available for students from sponsoring institution: scholarships, loans.

For More Information • Dr. Katharine C. Krebs, Director, State University of New York at Binghamton, Office of International Programs, NARC G-1, Binghamton, NY 13902-6000; *Phone:* 607-777-2336; *Fax:* 607-777-2889. *E-mail:* oip@binghamton.edu. *World Wide Web:* http://oip.binghamton.edu/

INNSBRUCK

UNIVERSITY OF NEW ORLEANS
INNSBRUCK ACADEMIC YEAR ABROAD

Hosted by University of Innsbruck

Academic Focus • Art, German language and literature, history, science.

Program Information • Students attend classes at University of Innsbruck. Field trips to regional sites in Austria, South Tyrol (northern Italy); optional travel to Europe at an extra cost.

Sessions • Fall, spring, yearlong.

Eligibility Requirements • Minimum age 20; open to sophomores, juniors, seniors, adults; 1 letter of recommendation; good academic standing at home school; 1 term course work in German or the equivalent.

Living Arrangements • Students live in host institution dormitories, locally rented apartments. Quarters are shared with host institution students. Meals are taken on one's own, in central dining facility.

Costs (2002-2003) • One term: $7695. Yearlong program: $11,695; includes tuition, housing, some meals, international student ID, student support services, some excursions, some books and class materials, some insurance. $200 refundable deposit required. Financial aid available for all students: scholarships, loans.

For More Information • Ms. Gertraud Griessner, Administrative Assistant, University of New Orleans, PO Box 1338, New Orleans, LA

70148; *Phone:* 504-280-3223; *Fax:* 504-280-7317. *E-mail:* camc@uno. edu. *World Wide Web:* http://inst.uno.edu/

SALZBURG
AMERICAN INSTITUTE FOR FOREIGN STUDY (AIFS)
UNIVERSITY OF SALZBURG

Hosted by University of Salzburg

Academic Focus • Business administration/management, economics, German language and literature, history, literature, music, sociology.

Program Information • Students attend classes at University of Salzburg. Scheduled travel to London; field trips to Vienna, Munich, Prague; optional travel to Alpine skiing at an extra cost.

Sessions • Fall, spring, yearlong.

Eligibility Requirements • Minimum age 17; open to freshmen, sophomores, juniors, seniors; 2.5 GPA; 1 letter of recommendation; good academic standing at home school; no foreign language proficiency required.

Living Arrangements • Students live in host institution dormitories, locally rented apartments, host family homes. Quarters are shared with host institution students, students from other programs. Meals are taken on one's own, in residences, in central dining facility, in restaurants.

Costs (2004-2005) • One term: $10,995. Yearlong program: $20,690; includes tuition, housing, some meals, insurance, student support services, one-way airfare, 2-day London stopover, some excursions. $75 application fee. $350 nonrefundable deposit required. Financial aid available for all students: scholarships.

For More Information • Mr. David Mauro, Admissions Advisor, American Institute For Foreign Study (AIFS), 9 West Broad Street, Stamford, CT 06902-3788; *Phone:* 800-727-2437 Ext. 5163; *Fax:* 203-399-5597. *E-mail:* dmauro@aifs.com. *World Wide Web:* http://www.aifsabroad.com/

BOWLING GREEN STATE UNIVERSITY
ACADEMIC YEAR ABROAD IN AUSTRIA

Hosted by University of Salzburg

Academic Focus • Austrian studies, European studies, German language and literature, German studies, international affairs, music.

Program Information • Students attend classes at University of Salzburg. Scheduled travel to Vienna, Berlin; field trips to a television station, schools, Munich, local and regional museums, Alps.

Sessions • Fall, spring, yearlong.

Eligibility Requirements • Open to sophomores, juniors, seniors, graduate students, adults; 3 letters of recommendation; good academic standing at home school; 2 years of college course work in German.

Living Arrangements • Students live in host institution dormitories, locally rented apartments. Quarters are shared with host institution students. Meals are taken on one's own, in residences, in central dining facility, in restaurants.

Costs (2004-2005) • One term: $5241. Yearlong program: $10,482; includes tuition, housing, all meals, excursions, cultural activities, university facilities. $25 application fee. $200 refundable deposit required. Financial aid available for all students: loans.

For More Information • Ms. Sue Sidor, AYA Assistant, Bowling Green State University, Department of German, Russian, and East Asian Languages, 103 Shatzel Hall, Bowling Green, OH 43403-0219; *Phone:* 419-372-6815; *Fax:* 419-372-2571. *E-mail:* sidors@bgnet.bgsu. edu. *World Wide Web:* http://www.bgsu.edu/

COLLEGE CONSORTIUM FOR INTERNATIONAL STUDIES–MIAMI DADE COLLEGE AND TRUMAN STATE UNIVERSITY
SEMESTER IN AUSTRIA

Hosted by Salzburg College

Academic Focus • Art history, German language and literature, international business, music, music history, photography, social sciences.

Program Information • Students attend classes at Salzburg College. Scheduled travel to Vienna, Germany; field trips to local excursions.

Sessions • Fall, spring, yearlong.

Eligibility Requirements • Minimum age 18; open to freshmen, sophomores, juniors, seniors, adults; 2.7 GPA; 2 letters of recommendation; good academic standing at home school; no foreign language proficiency required.

Living Arrangements • Students live in host family homes. Quarters are shared with host institution students. Meals are taken with host family, in central dining facility.

Costs (2004-2005) • One term: $10,215. Yearlong program: $20,430; includes tuition, housing, all meals, insurance, excursions. $500 nonrefundable deposit required. Financial aid available for students from sponsoring institution: loans.

For More Information • Center for International Education Abroad, College Consortium for International Studies–Miami Dade College and Truman State University, 100 East Normal, Kirksville, MO 63501; *Phone:* 660-785-4076; *Fax:* 660-785-7473. *E-mail:* ciea@truman.edu. *World Wide Web:* http://www.ccisabroad.org/. Students may also apply through Miami Dade College, Miami, FL 33176.

LONGWOOD UNIVERSITY
STUDY ABROAD IN SALZBURG

Hosted by University of Salzburg

Academic Focus • Austrian studies, German language and literature, German studies, international business.

Program Information • Students attend classes at University of Salzburg. Field trips to salt mines, the Danube River, Vienna, Germany.

Sessions • Fall, spring, yearlong.

Eligibility Requirements • Minimum age 18; open to juniors; major in German; 2.5 GPA; good academic standing at home school; fluency in German.

Living Arrangements • Students live in host institution dormitories, locally rented apartments. Quarters are shared with host institution students, students from other programs. Meals are taken on one's own, in residences, in central dining facility.

Costs (2002-2003) • One term: $3200 for Virginia residents. Yearlong program: $4900 for Virginia residents; includes tuition, excursions. $250 nonrefundable deposit required. Financial aid available for students from sponsoring institution: scholarships, loans.

For More Information • Dr. John F. Reynolds, Director, International Affairs Program, Longwood University, International Affairs, 201 High Street, Farmville, VA 23909-1899; *Phone:* 434-395-2172; *Fax:* 434-395-2141. *E-mail:* jreynold@longwood.edu. *World Wide Web:* http://www.longwood.edu/

NORTHERN ILLINOIS UNIVERSITY
EUROPEAN, COMMUNICATION, AND BUSINESS STUDIES

Hosted by Salzburg College

Academic Focus • Art history, communications, European studies, fine/studio arts, German language and literature, international affairs, international business, marketing, music, music performance, photography.

Program Information • Students attend classes at Salzburg College. Scheduled travel; field trips to Salzburg, Vienna, Trier, Cologne, Bonn, Heidelberg, Nuremberg, The Rhine.

Sessions • Fall, spring, yearlong.

Eligibility Requirements • Open to sophomores, juniors, seniors; 2.75 GPA; 2 letters of recommendation; good academic standing at home school; application essay; no foreign language proficiency required.

Living Arrangements • Students live in host family homes. Meals are taken as a group, with host family, in residences, in central dining facility.

Costs (2003-2004) • One term: $8950. Yearlong program: $17,060; includes tuition, housing, all meals, insurance, excursions, student support services, social and cultural activities, internship placement. $45 application fee. $800 refundable deposit required. Financial aid available for students from sponsoring institution: regular financial aid.

For More Information • Ms. Clare Foust, Program Assistant, Northern Illinois University, Study Abroad Office, Williston Hall 417, DeKalb, IL 60115-2854; *Phone:* 815-753-0420; *Fax:* 815-753-0825. *E-mail:* niuabroad@niu.edu. *World Wide Web:* http://www.niu.edu/

niuabroad/. Students may also apply through Salzburg College, Ursulinenplatz 4, 5020 Salzburg, Austria.

NORTHERN ILLINOIS UNIVERSITY
STUDIO ART IN SALZBURG

Hosted by Salzburg College

Academic Focus • Art history, fine/studio arts, photography.

Program Information • Students attend classes at Salzburg College. Scheduled travel to Germany, Vienna; field trips to Salzburg; optional travel to the Czech Republic, Italy, Greece, Europe at an extra cost.

Sessions • Fall, spring, yearlong.

Eligibility Requirements • Open to sophomores, juniors, seniors; course work in photography (1 year); 2.75 GPA; 2 letters of recommendation; essay; portfolio; no foreign language proficiency required.

Living Arrangements • Students live in host family homes. Quarters are shared with host institution students. Meals are taken as a group, with host family, in residences, in central dining facility.

Costs (2003-2004) • One term: $8950. Yearlong program: $17,060; includes tuition, housing, all meals, insurance, excursions, lab equipment, student support services, social and cultural activities. $45 application fee. $800 refundable deposit required. Financial aid available for all students: regular financial aid.

For More Information • Ms. Clare Foust, Program Assistant, Northern Illinois University, Study Abroad Office, Williston Hall 417, DeKalb, IL 60115-2854; *Phone:* 815-753-0420; *Fax:* 815-753-0825. *E-mail:* niuabroad@niu.edu. *World Wide Web:* http://www.niu.edu/niuabroad/. Students may also apply through Salzburg College, Ursulinenplatz 4, 5020 Salzburg, Austria.

SHORTER COLLEGE
SALZBURG COLLEGE

Hosted by Salzburg College

Academic Focus • Full curriculum.

Program Information • Students attend classes at Salzburg College. Scheduled travel to Germany, Vienna; field trips to other locations in Austria; optional travel at an extra cost.

Sessions • Fall, spring.

Eligibility Requirements • Open to sophomores, juniors, seniors; 2.5 GPA; 3 letters of recommendation; good academic standing at home school; no foreign language proficiency required.

Living Arrangements • Students live in host family homes. Quarters are shared with students from other programs. Meals are taken with host family, in residences.

Costs (2002-2003) • One term: $7900; includes tuition, housing, some meals, excursions, student support services. $300 nonrefundable deposit required. Financial aid available for all students: scholarships, work study, loans.

For More Information • Prof. Betty Zane Morris, Director of International Programs and Distinguished Professor of Speech, Shorter College, Box 2040, 315 Shorter Avenue, Rome, GA 30165; *Phone:* 706-233-7270; *Fax:* 706-233-7516. *E-mail:* bmorris@shorter.edu. *World Wide Web:* http://www.shorter.edu.academics.internationalprograms/

UNIVERSITY OF CONNECTICUT
SPRING SEMESTER OR YEAR ABROAD IN AUSTRIA

Hosted by University of Salzburg

Academic Focus • Full curriculum.

Program Information • Students attend classes at University of Salzburg.

Sessions • Spring, yearlong.

Eligibility Requirements • 2.5 GPA; 2 letters of recommendation; good academic standing at home school; 2 years of college course work in German.

Living Arrangements • Meals are taken on one's own.

Costs (2002-2003) • One term: $8200 for consortium members; $8700 for nonmembers. Yearlong program: $10,000 for consortium members; $10,500 for nonmembers; includes tuition, housing, all meals, excursions, books and class materials, international student ID, student support services. $25 application fee. $395 nonrefundable deposit required. Financial aid available for students from sponsoring institution: scholarships, loans.

For More Information • Mr. Gordon Lustila, Acting Director of Study Abroad Programs, University of Connecticut, 843 Bolton Road, Unit 1207, Storrs, CT 06269-1207; *Phone:* 860-486-5022; *Fax:* 860-486-2976. *E-mail:* sabadm03@uconnvm.uconn.edu. *World Wide Web:* http://studyabroad.uconn.edu/

UNIVERSITY OF REDLANDS
SALZBURG SEMESTER

Hosted by University of Redlands–Salzburg

Academic Focus • Art, Austrian studies, European studies, German language and literature, history, music.

Program Information • Students attend classes at University of Redlands–Salzburg. Scheduled travel to Italy, Eastern Europe, Greece; field trips to Vienna; optional travel at an extra cost.

Sessions • Fall, spring.

Eligibility Requirements • Open to juniors, seniors; 3.0 GPA; 2 letters of recommendation; good academic standing at home school; background in German recommended; no foreign language proficiency required.

Living Arrangements • Students live in marketenderschloessl. Quarters are shared with host institution students, students from other programs. Meals are taken as a group, in central dining facility, in restaurants.

Costs (2002-2003) • One term: $11,522 for guest students; includes tuition, housing, all meals, insurance, excursions, student support services. $25 application fee. $300 nonrefundable deposit required. Financial aid available for students from sponsoring institution: scholarships, work study, loans.

For More Information • Mr. Ben Dillow, Dean, Special College Programs, University of Redlands, PO Box 3080, Redlands, CA 92373-0999; *Phone:* 909-335-4044; *Fax:* 909-335-5343. *E-mail:* ben_dillow@redlands.edu. *World Wide Web:* http://www.redlands.edu/x2215.xml

VIENNA

AHA INTERNATIONAL AN ACADEMIC PROGRAM OF THE UNIVERSITY OF OREGON
PROGRAM IN VIENNA, AUSTRIA: MIDWEST CONSORTIUM FOR STUDY ABROAD AND NORTHWEST COUNCIL ON STUDY ABROAD

Hosted by AHA Vienna Center

Academic Focus • Art history, business administration/management, communications, economics, European studies, geography, German language and literature, history, interdisciplinary studies, literature, music, music history, psychology.

Program Information • Students attend classes at AHA Vienna Center. Scheduled travel to Prague, Budapest, Hungary; field trips to local excursions.

Sessions • Fall, spring, winter, yearlong.

Eligibility Requirements • Open to sophomores, juniors, seniors, adults; 2 letters of recommendation; good academic standing at home school; foreign language proficiency requirement varies depending on enrolling university.

Living Arrangements • Students live in host family homes. Quarters are shared with host institution students. Meals are taken on one's own, with host family, in residences.

Costs (2003-2004) • One term: $6460–$6800. Yearlong program: $13,260–$13,600; includes tuition, housing, some meals, insurance, excursions, books and class materials, international student ID, student support services, local transportation pass. $50 application fee. $200 deposit required. Financial aid available for students: scholarships, loans, home institution financial aid.

For More Information • Ms. Gail Lavin, Associate Director for University Programs, AHA International An Academic Program of the University of Oregon, 741 SW Lincoln Street, Portland, OR 97201; *Phone:* 503-295-7730; *Fax:* 503-295-5969. *E-mail:* mail@aha-intl.org. *World Wide Web:* http://www.aha-intl.org/

BENTLEY COLLEGE
STUDY ABROAD PROGRAM IN VIENNA, AUSTRIA

Hosted by Vienna University of Economics and Business Administration

AUSTRIA
Vienna

Academic Focus • Accounting, business administration/management, economics, finance, German language and literature, international affairs, international business, marketing.

Program Information • Students attend classes at Vienna University of Economics and Business Administration. Scheduled travel; field trips; optional travel.

Sessions • Fall, spring, yearlong.

Eligibility Requirements • Open to juniors, seniors; 3.0 GPA; 1 letter of recommendation; good academic standing at home school; essays; no foreign language proficiency required.

Living Arrangements • Students live in host institution dormitories, locally rented apartments. Quarters are shared with host institution students, students from other programs. Meals are taken on one's own, in residences, in central dining facility, in restaurants.

Costs (2002-2003) • One term: $14,600. Yearlong program: $23,480; includes tuition, housing, some meals, excursions, international student ID, student support services. $35 application fee. $500 nonrefundable deposit required. Financial aid available for students from sponsoring institution: scholarships, loans.

For More Information • Ms. Jennifer Aquino, Assistant Director, International Center, Bentley College, 175 Forest Street, Waltham, MA 02452; *Phone:* 781-891-3474; *Fax:* 781-891-2819. *E-mail:* study_abroad@bentley.edu. *World Wide Web:* http://ecampus.bentley.edu/dept/sa/

CENTRAL COLLEGE ABROAD
CENTRAL COLLEGE ABROAD IN VIENNA, AUSTRIA

Hosted by Goethe Institut, University of Vienna

Academic Focus • Aesthetics, art, art history, drama/theater, economics, English literature, German language and literature, history, international affairs, international business, music, music performance, philosophy, political science and government, psychology, religious studies, science, social sciences, sociology.

Program Information • Students attend classes at University of Vienna, Goethe Institut. Field trips to Budapest, Prague, Graz, the Wachau Valley, Melk Monastery, Bratislava.

Sessions • Fall, spring, yearlong.

Eligibility Requirements • Minimum age 18; open to sophomores, juniors, seniors, adults; 2.5 GPA; 2 letters of recommendation; good academic standing at home school; study abroad approval form; transcript; Student Life endorsement; no foreign language proficiency required.

Living Arrangements • Students live in host institution dormitories, locally rented apartments. Quarters are shared with host institution students. Meals are taken on one's own, in residences, in central dining facility, in restaurants.

Costs (2003-2004) • One term: $13,460-$14,840 with Goethe 1-2 month intensive language program; $11,590 without Goethe program. Yearlong program: $22,720-$24,100 with Goethe 1-2 month intensive language program; $20,850 without Goethe program; includes tuition, housing, some meals, excursions, international student ID. $25 application fee. $350 nonrefundable deposit required. Financial aid available for all students: scholarships.

For More Information • Office of International Education, Central College Abroad, 812 University Street, Pella, IA 50219; *Phone:* 800-831-3629; *Fax:* 641-628-5375. *E-mail:* studyabroad@central.edu. *World Wide Web:* http://www.central.edu/abroad/

EUROPEAN HERITAGE INSTITUTE
ACADEMIC YEAR AT THE UNIVERSITY OF VIENNA, AUSTRIA

Hosted by University of Vienna

Academic Focus • German language and literature, German studies.

Program Information • Students attend classes at University of Vienna.

Sessions • Fall, spring, winter, yearlong, trimesters.

Eligibility Requirements • Minimum age 18; open to freshmen, sophomores, juniors, seniors, graduate students, adults; 2.2 GPA; 2 letters of recommendation; no foreign language proficiency required.

Living Arrangements • Students live in locally rented apartments, host family homes. Quarters are shared with students from other programs. Meals are taken on one's own, in central dining facility, in restaurants.

Costs (2004-2005) • One term: $1000 for 9 weeks; $1200 for 13 weeks. Yearlong program: $2400; includes tuition, student support services. $300 refundable deposit required.

For More Information • Dr. Antonio Masullo, Professor, European Heritage Institute, 2708 East Franklin Street, Richmond, VA 23223; *Phone:* 804-643-0661; *Fax:* 804-648-0826. *E-mail:* euritage@i2020.net. *World Wide Web:* http://www.europeabroad.org/

IES, INSTITUTE FOR THE INTERNATIONAL EDUCATION OF STUDENTS
IES–VIENNA

Hosted by University of Music and Performing Arts in Vienna, University of Vienna, Institute for the International Education of Students (IES)–Vienna

Academic Focus • Anthropology, art history, Austrian studies, business administration/management, Central European studies, drama/theater, Eastern European studies, economics, education, European studies, film and media studies, finance, German language and literature, history, international affairs, international business, law and legal studies, literature, music history, music performance, music theory, philosophy, political science and government, psychology, religious studies, science, sociology, women's studies.

Program Information • Students attend classes at University of Music and Performing Arts in Vienna, University of Vienna, Institute for the International Education of Students (IES)–Vienna. Optional travel to Poland, Dresden, Hungary, Czech Republic, Weimar, Wachau, Mauthausen, Austrian Alps, Romania at an extra cost.

Sessions • Fall, spring, yearlong.

Eligibility Requirements • Minimum age 18; open to sophomores, juniors, seniors, graduate students, adults; 3.0 GPA; 1 letter of recommendation; good academic standing at home school; no foreign language proficiency required.

Living Arrangements • Students live in host institution dormitories, locally rented apartments, host family homes. Meals are taken on one's own, in residences, in central dining facility.

Costs (2003-2004) • One term: $11,300. Yearlong program: $20,340; includes tuition, housing, excursions, student support services, resident permit, partial insurance coverage. $50 application fee. $500 nonrefundable deposit required. Financial aid available for all students: scholarships, institutional partner need-based grants.

For More Information • International Education Representative, IES, Institute for the International Education of Students, 33 North LaSalle Street, 15th Floor, Chicago, IL 60602; *Phone:* 800-995-2300; *Fax:* 312-944-1448. *E-mail:* info@iesabroad.org. *World Wide Web:* http://www.IESabroad.org/

NICHOLLS STATE UNIVERSITY
NICHOLLS STATE UNIVERSITY IN VIENNA, AUSTRIA

Hosted by Nicholls State University–Vienna

Academic Focus • Art, German language and literature, history.

Program Information • Students attend classes at Nicholls State University–Vienna. Scheduled travel to the Capital of Styria-Graz, Klosterneuburg, the Wachau region of the Danube Valley, Salzburg, medieval castles; field trips to museums, monuments, the theater; optional travel at an extra cost.

Sessions • Fall, spring, yearlong.

Eligibility Requirements • Minimum age 17; open to freshmen, sophomores, juniors, seniors; no foreign language proficiency required.

Living Arrangements • Students live in host family homes. Quarters are shared with host institution students. Meals are taken with host family, in residences.

Costs (2003-2004) • One term: $4849. Yearlong program: $9697; includes tuition, housing, some meals, insurance, books and class materials, lab equipment, student support services, instructional costs. Financial aid available for all students: loans, all customary sources.

For More Information • Ms. Cynthia Webb, Director of Study Programs Abroad, Nicholls State University, PO Box 2080, Thibodaux, LA 70310; *Phone:* 985-448-4440; *Fax:* 985-449-7028. *E-mail:* spab-caw@nicholls.edu. *World Wide Web:* http://www.nicholls.edu/abroad/

ST. LAWRENCE UNIVERSITY
VIENNA AUSTRIA PROGRAM

Held at Austro American Institute of Education
Academic Focus • Art history, environmental science/studies, European studies, German language and literature, history, music history, psychology.
Program Information • Classes are held on the campus of Austro American Institute of Education. Faculty members are local instructors hired by the sponsor. Scheduled travel to Poland, Germany, the Czech Republic; field trips to sites in and around Vienna.
Sessions • Spring.
Eligibility Requirements • Open to freshmen, sophomores, juniors, seniors; 2.8 GPA; 3 letters of recommendation; 0.5 years of college course work in German.
Living Arrangements • Students live in host family homes. Meals are taken on one's own, with host family, in residences, in restaurants.
Costs (2003-2004) • One term: $17,870; includes tuition, housing, all meals, excursions, student support services. $500 nonrefundable deposit required. Financial aid available for students from sponsoring institution: scholarships, loans.
For More Information • Ms. Sara Hofschulte, Assistant Director, Off-Campus Studies, St. Lawrence University, Center for International and Intercultural Studies, Canton, NY 13617; *Phone:* 315-229-5991; *Fax:* 315-229-5989. *E-mail:* shofschulte@stlawu.edu. *World Wide Web:* http://www.stlawu.edu/ciis/offcampus/

THE UNIVERSITY OF NORTH CAROLINA AT CHAPEL HILL
STUDY ABROAD AT VIENNA UNIVERSITY OF ECONOMICS AND BUSINESS ADMINISTRATION

Hosted by Vienna University of Economics and Business Administration

Academic Focus • Accounting, commerce, economics, finance, German language and literature, history, international affairs, international business, management information systems, marketing, social sciences.
Program Information • Students attend classes at Vienna University of Economics and Business Administration. Optional travel to Europe at an extra cost.
Sessions • Spring, yearlong.
Eligibility Requirements • Open to juniors, seniors, graduate students; 3.0 GPA; 2 letters of recommendation; essay; transcript; 2 years college course work in German or the equivalent.
Living Arrangements • Students live in host institution dormitories, locally rented apartments. Quarters are shared with host institution students. Meals are taken on one's own, in residences.
Costs (2003-2004) • One term: $8170. Yearlong program: $15,900; includes tuition, insurance, study abroad fee. $100 application fee. $500 nonrefundable deposit required. Financial aid available for students from sponsoring institution: scholarships, loans.
For More Information • Study Abroad Office, The University of North Carolina at Chapel Hill, 201 Porthole Building, CB 3130, Chapel Hill, NC 27599-3130; *Phone:* 919-962-7002; *Fax:* 919-962-2262. *E-mail:* abroad@unc.edu. *World Wide Web:* http://studyabroad.unc.edu/

WEBSTER UNIVERSITY
WEBSTER UNIVERSITY IN VIENNA

Hosted by Webster University–Vienna
Academic Focus • Art, communications, history, international business, law and legal studies, peace and conflict studies, political science and government.
Program Information • Students attend classes at Webster University–Vienna. Field trips to biking in Vienna, area museums, Budapest; optional travel to museums, hiking at an extra cost.
Sessions • Fall, spring, yearlong.

AUSTRIA
Vienna

Eligibility Requirements • Minimum age 17; open to sophomores, juniors, seniors, graduate students, adults; 2.5 GPA; 1 letter of recommendation; good academic standing at home school; no foreign language proficiency required.
Living Arrangements • Students live in host institution dormitories. Quarters are shared with host institution students. Meals are taken as a group, on one's own, in residences.
Costs (2003-2004) • One term: $8240. Yearlong program: $15,980; includes tuition, insurance, international student ID, student support services. $30 application fee. $165 refundable deposit required. Financial aid available for students from sponsoring institution: scholarships, loans.
For More Information • Mr. Mark A. Beirn, Coordinator, Office of Study Abroad, Webster University, 470 East Lockwood Avenue, St. Louis, MO 63119; *Phone:* 314-968-6988; *Fax:* 314-968-5938. *E-mail:* worldview@webster.edu. *World Wide Web:* http://www.webster.edu/intl/sa/

AZERBAIJAN
BAKU
ACIE (ACTR/ACCELS)
ACIE–NIS REGIONAL LANGUAGE TRAINING PROGRAM–AZERBAIJAN

Hosted by Baku State University
Academic Focus • Cultural studies, language studies.
Program Information • Students attend classes at Baku State University.
Sessions • Fall, spring, yearlong.
Eligibility Requirements • Minimum age 18; open to sophomores, juniors, seniors, graduate students, adults; 3 letters of recommendation; good academic standing at home school; 1 year of college course work in Russian or Azeri.
Living Arrangements • Students live in host institution dormitories, locally rented apartments, host family homes. Quarters are shared with students from other programs. Meals are taken on one's own, with host family, in residences, in restaurants.
Costs (2002-2003) • One term: contact sponsor for cost. Yearlong program: contact sponsor for cost. $35 application fee. $500 nonrefundable deposit required. Financial aid available for all students: scholarships.
For More Information • Ms. Margaret Stephenson, Russian and Eurasian Program Officer, ACIE (ACTR/ACCELS), 1776 Massachusetts Avenue, NW, Suite 700, Washington, DC 20036; *Phone:* 202-833-7522; *Fax:* 202-833-7523. *E-mail:* outbound@actr.org. *World Wide Web:* http://www.actr.org/

BELARUS
MINSK
ACIE (ACTR/ACCELS)
ACIE–NIS REGIONAL LANGUAGE TRAINING PROGRAM–BELARUS

Academic Focus • Cultural studies, language studies.
Program Information • Faculty members are local instructors hired by the sponsor. Optional travel at an extra cost.
Sessions • Fall, spring, yearlong.
Eligibility Requirements • Minimum age 18; open to sophomores, juniors, seniors, graduate students, adults; 3 letters of recommendation; good academic standing at home school; 1 year of college course work in Russian or Belorussian.
Living Arrangements • Students live in host institution dormitories, host family homes. Quarters are shared with students from other programs. Meals are taken on one's own, with host family, in residences, in central dining facility.

Costs (2002-2003) • One term: contact sponsor for cost. Yearlong program: contact sponsor for cost. $35 application fee. $500 nonrefundable deposit required. Financial aid available for all students: scholarships.
For More Information • Ms. Margaret Stephenson, Russian and Eurasian Program Officer, ACIE (ACTR/ACCELS), 1776 Massachusetts Avenue, NW, Suite 700, Washington, DC 20036; *Phone:* 202-833-7522; *Fax:* 202-833-7523. *E-mail:* outbound@actr.org. *World Wide Web:* http://www.actr.org/

BELGIUM
ANTWERP
INTERSTUDY
UNIVERSITY OF ANTWERP, BELGIUM

Hosted by University of Antwerp
Academic Focus • Accounting, business administration/management, computer science, economics, English, international affairs, marketing, political science and government.
Program Information • Students attend classes at University of Antwerp. Scheduled travel to Bath, Stratford-upon-Avon, Warwick Castle, Oxford, Stonehenge.
Sessions • Fall, spring, yearlong.
Eligibility Requirements • Minimum age 18; open to freshmen, sophomores, juniors, seniors, adults; 3.0 GPA; 2 letters of recommendation; good academic standing at home school; no foreign language proficiency required.
Living Arrangements • Students live in host institution dormitories, locally rented apartments. Quarters are shared with host institution students. Meals are taken on one's own, in residences.
Costs (2003-2004) • One term: $12,350 for fall term; $13,750 for spring. Yearlong program: $22,515; includes tuition, housing, some meals, excursions, international student ID, student support services, Student Union membership, e-mail access, banking facilities, international bank transfers, transcript, cell phone. $35 application fee. $500 nonrefundable deposit required. Financial aid available for all students: scholarships, loans, stipends.
For More Information • InterStudy, Admissions Office, 63 Edward Street, Medford, MA 02155; *Phone:* 800-663-1999; *Fax:* 781-391-7463. *E-mail:* interstudy@interstudy-usa.org. *World Wide Web:* http://www.interstudy.org/. Students may also apply through InterStudy, Admissions Office, 42 Milsom Street, Bath BA1 1DN, England.

JAMES MADISON UNIVERSITY
JMU SEMESTER IN ANTWERP

Hosted by University of Antwerp
Academic Focus • Business administration/management.
Program Information • Students attend classes at University of Antwerp. Scheduled travel to Strasbourg, France, Luxembourg; field trips to Bruges, Ghent, Brussels.
Sessions • Fall.
Eligibility Requirements • Minimum age 18; open to juniors; course work in business; 2.8 GPA; 1 letter of recommendation; good academic standing at home school; no foreign language proficiency required.
Living Arrangements • Students live in host institution dormitories. Quarters are shared with host institution students. Meals are taken as a group, on one's own, in central dining facility, in restaurants.
Costs (2003-2004) • One term: $8597 for Virginia residents; $12,708 for nonresidents; includes tuition, housing, some meals, excursions, books and class materials. $400 nonrefundable deposit required. Financial aid available for students from sponsoring institution: scholarships, work study, loans.
For More Information • Mr. Felix Wang, Director, James Madison University, Office of International Programs, MSC 5731, 1077 South Main Street, Harrisonburg, VA 22807; *Phone:* 540-568-6419; *Fax:* 540-568-3310. *E-mail:* studyabroad@jmu.edu. *World Wide Web:* http://www.jmu.edu/international/

BRUSSELS

AMERICAN UNIVERSITY
SEMESTER IN BRUSSELS: EUROPEAN UNION

Held at Catholic University of Louvain–Brussels

Academic Focus • Economics, European studies, international affairs, political science and government.

Program Information • Classes are held on the campus of Catholic University of Louvain–Brussels. Faculty members are drawn from the sponsor's U.S. staff and local instructors hired by the sponsor. Scheduled travel to Eastern Europe, Russia; field trips to Luxembourg, Antwerp, Bruges.

Sessions • Fall, spring.

Eligibility Requirements • Open to sophomores, juniors, seniors, graduate students; course work in macro and micro economics; 2.75 GPA; 1 letter of recommendation; second semester sophomore status; recommendation of advisor; no foreign language proficiency required.

Living Arrangements • Students live in host family homes. Meals are taken with host family, in residences.

Costs (2002-2003) • One term: $16,434; includes tuition, housing, some meals, excursions, books and class materials, international student ID, student support services. $35 application fee. $300 nonrefundable deposit required. Financial aid available for all students: scholarships, loans.

For More Information • Dr. David C. Brown, Dean, Washington Semester and World Capitals Programs, American University, Tenley Campus–Constitution Building, Washington, DC 20016-8083; *Phone:* 800-424-2600; *Fax:* 202-895-4960. *E-mail:* travel@american.edu. *World Wide Web:* http://www.worldcapitals.american.edu/

AMERICAN UNIVERSITY
SEMESTER IN BRUSSELS: INTERNATIONAL MARKETING

Held at Catholic University of Louvain–Brussels

Academic Focus • Business administration/management, international business, marketing.

Program Information • Classes are held on the campus of Catholic University of Louvain–Brussels. Faculty members are drawn from the sponsor's U.S. staff and local instructors hired by the sponsor. Scheduled travel to Eastern Europe, Russia, Baltic states; field trips to Luxembourg, Bruges, Antwerp.

Sessions • Spring.

Eligibility Requirements • Open to sophomores, juniors, seniors, graduate students; course work in principles of marketing and fundamentals of international business; 2.75 GPA; 1 letter of recommendation; second semester sophomore status; recommendation of advisor; no foreign language proficiency required.

Living Arrangements • Students live in host family homes. Meals are taken with host family, in residences.

Costs (2003) • One term: $16,434; includes tuition, housing, some meals, excursions, books and class materials, international student ID, student support services. $35 application fee. $300 nonrefundable deposit required. Financial aid available for all students: scholarships, loans.

For More Information • Dr. David C. Brown, Dean, Washington Semester and World Capitals Programs, American University, Tenley Campus–Constitution Building, Washington, DC 20016-8083; *Phone:* 800-424-2600; *Fax:* 202-895-4960. *E-mail:* travel@american.edu. *World Wide Web:* http://www.worldcapitals.american.edu/

BENTLEY COLLEGE
BUSINESS PROGRAM ABROAD IN BELGIUM

Hosted by Vesalius College

Academic Focus • Accounting, business administration/management, communications, Dutch, economics, European studies, finance, French language and literature, German language and literature, history, law and legal studies, literature, mathematics, political science and government, science, social sciences.

Program Information • Students attend classes at Vesalius College. Scheduled travel; field trips to Paris, Amsterdam, sites in Brussels; optional travel.

Sessions • Fall, spring.

Eligibility Requirements • Open to juniors, seniors; 3.0 GPA; 1 letter of recommendation; good academic standing at home school; essay; no foreign language proficiency required.

Living Arrangements • Students live in host family homes. Quarters are shared with host institution students, students from other programs. Meals are taken with host family, in residences.

Costs (2002-2003) • One term: $15,600; includes tuition, housing, some meals, excursions, international student ID, student support services. $35 application fee. $500 nonrefundable deposit required. Financial aid available for students from sponsoring institution: scholarships, loans.

For More Information • Mr. Andrew Dusenbery, Education Abroad Advisor, Bentley College, 175 Forest Street, Waltham, MA 02452; *Phone:* 781-891-3474; *Fax:* 781-891-2819. *E-mail:* study_abroad@bentley.edu. *World Wide Web:* http://ecampus.bentley.edu/dept/sa/

BRETHREN COLLEGES ABROAD
BCA PEACE AND JUSTICE PROGRAM IN BRUSSELS, BELGIUM

Hosted by Vesalius College

Academic Focus • Full curriculum.

Program Information • Students attend classes at Vesalius College. Field trips to Brussels and surrounding region; optional travel to Belgium, France, Germany at an extra cost.

Sessions • Spring.

Eligibility Requirements • Minimum age 18; open to juniors, seniors; 2.6 GPA; 3 letters of recommendation; no foreign language proficiency required.

Living Arrangements • Students live in host family homes. Meals are taken with host family, in residences.

Costs (2004) • One term: $11,500; includes tuition, housing, all meals, insurance, excursions, international student ID, student support services. $50 application fee. $100 nonrefundable deposit required.

For More Information • Mr. Jason Sanderson, Program Officer for Belgium, Brethren Colleges Abroad, 50 Alpha Drive, Elizabethtown, PA 17022; *Phone:* 866-222-6188; *Fax:* 717-361-6619. *E-mail:* info@bcanet.org. *World Wide Web:* http://www.bcanet.org/

CIEE
CIEE STUDY CENTER AT VESALIUS COLLEGE AT THE VRIJE UNIVERSITEIT BRUSSELS, BELGIUM

Hosted by Vesalius College

Academic Focus • Art history, economics, European studies, French language and literature, international affairs, liberal studies, political science and government.

Program Information • Students attend classes at Vesalius College. Scheduled travel to Paris, Amsterdam; field trips to Bruges, Ghent, Antwerp, sites of cultural interest in and around Brussels.

Sessions • Fall, spring, yearlong.

Eligibility Requirements • Open to sophomores, juniors, seniors, graduate students, adults; 2.75 GPA; 2 letters of recommendation; no foreign language proficiency required.

Living Arrangements • Students live in locally rented apartments, host family homes. Quarters are shared with host institution students. Meals are taken on one's own, with host family, in residences, in central dining facility, in restaurants.

Costs (2003-2004) • One term: $10,500. Yearlong program: $19,500; includes tuition, housing, all meals, insurance, excursions, student support services, cultural activities, pre-departure advising, optional on-site pick-up. $30 application fee. $300 deposit required. Financial aid available for all students: minority student scholarships, travel grants.

For More Information • Ms. Hannah McChesney, Program Officer, Europe, Middle East, and Africa, CIEE, 7 Custom House Street, 3rd Floor, Portland, ME 04101; *Phone:* 800-40-STUDY; *Fax:* 207-553-7699. *E-mail:* studyinfo@ciee.org. *World Wide Web:* http://www.ciee.org/isp/

LAFAYETTE COLLEGE
FACULTY-LED PROGRAMS, BRUSSELS, BELGIUM

Hosted by Vesalius College

Academic Focus • Full curriculum.

Program Information • Students attend classes at Vesalius College. Scheduled travel; field trips; optional travel at an extra cost.

Sessions • Spring.

Eligibility Requirements • Open to sophomores, juniors, seniors; 2.8 GPA; good academic standing at home school; no foreign language proficiency required.

BELGIUM
Brussels

Living Arrangements • Students live in host family homes. Quarters are shared with host institution students. Meals are taken with host family, in residences.
Costs (2003) • One term: $15,959; includes tuition, housing, some meals, excursions, international airfare. $300 nonrefundable deposit required. Financial aid available for students from sponsoring institution: loans, need-based grants.
For More Information • Mr. Cyrus S. Fleck Jr., Director of Study Abroad, Lafayette College, Provost Office, 219 Markle, Easton, PA 18042; *Phone:* 610-330-5069; *Fax:* 610-330-5068. *E-mail:* fleckc@lafayette.edu. *World Wide Web:* http://www.lafayette.edu/

UNIVERSITY OF ROCHESTER
INTERNSHIPS IN EUROPE–BELGIUM

Hosted by Vesalius College
Academic Focus • Business administration/management, economics, European studies, international affairs, political science and government.
Program Information • Students attend classes at Vesalius College. Scheduled travel to Strasbourg.
Sessions • Fall, spring.
Eligibility Requirements • Open to juniors, seniors; 3.0 GPA; 2 letters of recommendation; good academic standing at home school; fluency in French (for business internships).
Living Arrangements • Students live in locally rented apartments, host family homes. Meals are taken on one's own, in residences, in central dining facility, in restaurants.
Costs (2003) • One term: $10,150; includes tuition, housing, some meals, student support services. $30 application fee. $300 nonrefundable deposit required. Financial aid available for students from sponsoring institution: scholarships, loans.
For More Information • Ms. Jacqueline Levine, Study Abroad Director, University of Rochester, Center for Study Abroad, PO Box 270376, Lattimore 206, Rochester, NY 14627-0376; *Phone:* 585-275-7532; *Fax:* 585-461-5131. *E-mail:* abroad@mail.rochester.edu. *World Wide Web:* http://www.rochester.edu/college/study-abroad/

LEUVEN
THE CATHOLIC UNIVERSITY OF AMERICA
PROGRAM IN EUROPEAN STUDIES

Hosted by Institute for Public Administration
Academic Focus • Economics, history, liberal studies, political science and government.
Program Information • Students attend classes at Institute for Public Administration. Field trips.
Sessions • Fall, spring.
Eligibility Requirements • Open to juniors, adults; 3.0 GPA; no foreign language proficiency required.
Living Arrangements • Students live in a conference center/dormitory.
Costs (2003-2004) • One term: $14,900; includes tuition, housing. $55 application fee. $200 deposit required. Financial aid available for all students: loans.
For More Information • Mr. John Kromkowski, Assistant Dean, School of Arts and Sciences, The Catholic University of America, 303 Marist Hall, C61A, Washington, DC 20064; *Phone:* 202-319-6876; *Fax:* 202-319-6289. *E-mail:* kromkowski@cua.edu. *World Wide Web:* http://www.cua.edu/

BELIZE
CITY TO CITY
BOSTON UNIVERSITY
BELIZE ARCHAEOLOGICAL FIELD SCHOOL

Academic Focus • Archaeology.
Program Information • Faculty members are drawn from the sponsor's U.S. staff. Scheduled travel to Copan, Tikal; field trips to local archaeological sites.

Sessions • Spring.
Eligibility Requirements • Open to freshmen, sophomores, juniors, seniors, graduate students; 3.0 GPA; 2 letters of recommendation; good academic standing at home school; essay; approval of participation; transcript; no foreign language proficiency required.
Living Arrangements • Students live in tents at a research station. Meals are taken as a group, in central dining facility.
Costs (2005) • One term: $19,834; includes tuition, housing, all meals, excursions, international airfare, lab equipment. $50 application fee. $400 nonrefundable deposit required. Financial aid available for all students: scholarships, loans.
For More Information • Division of International Programs, Boston University, 232 Bay State Road, Boston, MA 02215; *Phone:* 617-353-9888; *Fax:* 617-353-5402. *E-mail:* abroad@bu.edu. *World Wide Web:* http://www.bu.edu/abroad/

BELIZE CITY
SCHOOL FOR INTERNATIONAL TRAINING, SIT STUDY ABROAD
BELIZE: NATURAL AND CULTURAL ECOLOGY

Academic Focus • Belizean studies, biological/life sciences, ecology, economics, Latin American studies, marine sciences.
Program Information • Faculty members are drawn from the sponsor's U.S. staff and local instructors hired by the sponsor. Scheduled travel to Guatemala, Turneffe Island, a Mayan village stay, Tikal; field trips to wildlife sanctuaries, cayes, farms, archaelogical sites.
Sessions • Fall, spring.
Eligibility Requirements • Open to sophomores, juniors, seniors; 2.5 GPA; 2 letters of recommendation; good academic standing at home school; no foreign language proficiency required.
Living Arrangements • Students live in host family homes, hotels, campsites, guest houses. Meals are taken as a group, with host family, in residences, in restaurants.
Costs (2003-2004) • One term: $13,200; includes tuition, housing, all meals, insurance, excursions. $50 application fee. $400 nonrefundable deposit required. Financial aid available for all students: scholarships.
For More Information • School for International Training, SIT Study Abroad, Kipling Road, Brattleboro, VT 05302-0676; *Phone:* 888-272-7881; *Fax:* 802-258-3296. *E-mail:* studyabroad@sit.edu. *World Wide Web:* http://www.sit.edu/studyabroad/

STATE UNIVERSITY OF NEW YORK COLLEGE AT CORTLAND
BELIZE DEVELOPMENT INTERNSHIPS

Academic Focus • Anthropology, archaeology, communications, community service, conservation studies, ecology, environmental health, environmental science/studies, finance, health and physical education, international affairs, marketing, nutrition, political science and government, public policy, social services, social work.
Program Information • Faculty members are local instructors hired by the sponsor. Field trips to national parks, Mayan ruins; optional travel to Mexico, the Caribbean, the barrier reef and cayes, Guatemala at an extra cost.
Sessions • Fall, spring.
Eligibility Requirements • Minimum age 19; open to juniors, seniors, graduate students; course work in field related to internship placement; 2.5 GPA; 3 letters of recommendation; good academic standing at home school; strong performance in major; maturity; adaptability; no foreign language proficiency required.
Living Arrangements • Students live in host family homes. Meals are taken with host family, in residences.
Costs (2003-2004) • One term: $6680; includes tuition, housing, all meals, insurance, international airfare, international student ID, student support services, passport fees. $20 application fee. $250 nonrefundable deposit required. Financial aid available for students from sponsoring institution: scholarships, loans.
For More Information • Ms. Liz Kopp, Assistant Director, Office of International Programs, State University of New York College at Cortland, PO Box 2000, Cortland, NY 13045; *Phone:* 607-753-2209; *Fax:* 607-753-5989. *E-mail:* cortlandabroad@cortland.edu. *World Wide Web:* http://www.studyabroad.com/suny/cortland/

BOLIVIA

COCHABAMBA

SCHOOL FOR INTERNATIONAL TRAINING, SIT STUDY ABROAD
BOLIVIA: CULTURE AND DEVELOPMENT

Academic Focus • Anthropology, cultural studies, economics, history, Latin American studies, political science and government, Quechua, Spanish language and literature.

Program Information • Faculty members are drawn from the sponsor's U.S. staff and local instructors hired by the sponsor. Scheduled travel to Sucre, Potosí, La Paz; field trips to Tiwanaku, Santa Cruz, Tarata, Lake Titicaca.

Sessions • Fall, spring.

Eligibility Requirements • Open to sophomores, juniors, seniors; 2.5 GPA; 2 letters of recommendation; good academic standing at home school; 1.5 years of college course work in Spanish.

Living Arrangements • Students live in host family homes, hotels. Meals are taken as a group, on one's own, with host family, in residences, in restaurants.

Costs (2003-2004) • One term: $12,100; includes tuition, housing, all meals, insurance, excursions. $50 application fee. $400 nonrefundable deposit required. Financial aid available for all students: scholarships.

For More Information • School for International Training, SIT Study Abroad, Kipling Road, Brattleboro, VT 05302-0676; *Phone:* 888-272-7881; *Fax:* 802-258-3296. *E-mail:* studyabroad@sit.edu. *World Wide Web:* http://www.sit.edu/studyabroad/

LA PAZ

DUKE UNIVERSITY
DUKE IN THE ANDES, LA PAZ, BOLIVIA

Hosted by Catholic University of Bolivia, University of San Andrés La Paz

Academic Focus • Andean studies, anthropology, Latin American studies, Spanish language and literature.

Program Information • Students attend classes at Catholic University of Bolivia, University of San Andrés La Paz. Scheduled travel to Lake Titicaca, the Amazon basin, Altiplano; field trips to Potosí, Sucre.

Sessions • Fall, spring, yearlong.

Eligibility Requirements • Open to sophomores, juniors; 3.0 GPA; 1 letter of recommendation; good academic standing at home school; 2 years of college course work in Spanish.

Living Arrangements • Students live in host family homes. Meals are taken with host family, in residences.

Costs (2003-2004) • One term: $15,088. Yearlong program: $30,176; includes tuition, housing, all meals, insurance, excursions, student support services. $1000 nonrefundable deposit required. Financial aid available for students from sponsoring institution: scholarships, loans.

For More Information • Dr. Amanda Kelso, Associate Director, Duke University, Office of Study Abroad, 2016 Campus Drive, Box 90057, Durham, NC 27708-0057; *Phone:* 919-684-2174; *Fax:* 919-684-3083. *E-mail:* amanda.kelso@duke.edu. *World Wide Web:* http://www.aas.duke.edu/study_abroad/

SUCRE

ALMA COLLEGE
ALMA IN BOLIVIA

Hosted by Academia Latinoamericana

Academic Focus • Cultural studies, Spanish language and literature.

Program Information • Students attend classes at Academia Latinoamericana. Field trips to Potosí, Caminos, Callejon; optional travel at an extra cost.

Sessions • Fall, spring, winter, yearlong, fall and winter semesters.

Eligibility Requirements • Minimum age 18; open to sophomores, juniors, seniors, graduate students, adults; 2.5 GPA; 2 letters of recommendation; no foreign language proficiency required.

Living Arrangements • Students live in host family homes. Meals are taken with host family, in residences.

Costs (2003-2004) • One term: $6300. Yearlong program: $11,600; includes tuition, housing, some meals, insurance, excursions, books and class materials, international student ID, student support services. $50 application fee. $200 refundable deposit required. Financial aid available for all students: scholarships.

For More Information • Ms. Julie Elenbaas, Office Coordinator, Alma College, 614 West Superior Street, Alma, MI 48801-1599; *Phone:* 989-463-7055; *Fax:* 989-463-7126. *E-mail:* intl_studies@alma.edu. *World Wide Web:* http://international.alma.edu/

BOTSWANA

GABORONE

PITZER COLLEGE
PITZER COLLEGE IN BOTSWANA

Hosted by University of Botswana

Academic Focus • African studies, cultural studies, economics, environmental science/studies, fine/studio arts, history, literature, political science and government, religious studies, Setswana, women's studies.

Program Information • Students attend classes at University of Botswana. Scheduled travel to Victoria Falls, Okavango Delta, Tsodilo Hills; field trips to the Jwaneng Diamond Mine, sites of Gaborone; optional travel to South Africa, Tanzania, Zanzibar, Malawi, Mozambique at an extra cost.

Sessions • Fall, spring, yearlong.

Eligibility Requirements • Open to juniors, seniors; course work in area studies; 2.5 GPA; 2 letters of recommendation; good academic standing at home school; no foreign language proficiency required.

Living Arrangements • Students live in host family homes. Meals are taken on one's own, with host family, in residences.

Costs (2003-2004) • One term: $18,795. Yearlong program: $37,590; includes tuition, housing, all meals, excursions, international airfare, international student ID, student support services, transportation allowance, partial independent study project expenses, evacuation insurance. $25 application fee. $500 nonrefundable deposit required. Financial aid available for students from sponsoring institution: scholarships, loans.

For More Information • Ms. Neva Barker, Director of External Studies Admissions, Pitzer College, 1050 North Mills Avenue, Claremont, CA 91711; *Phone:* 909-621-8104; *Fax:* 909-621-0518. *E-mail:* external_studies@pitzer.edu. *World Wide Web:* http://www.pitzer.edu/external_studies/

SCHOOL FOR INTERNATIONAL TRAINING, SIT STUDY ABROAD
BOTSWANA: ECOLOGY AND CONSERVATION

Academic Focus • African languages and literature, African studies, anthropology, biological/life sciences, conservation studies, ecology, environmental science/studies, history, wildlife studies.

Program Information • Faculty members are drawn from the sponsor's U.S. staff and local instructors hired by the sponsor. Scheduled travel to Okavango Delta, Maun; field trips to research centers, conservation areas, wildlife reserves.

Sessions • Fall, spring.

Eligibility Requirements • Open to sophomores, juniors, seniors; course work in environmental studies, ecology, biology, or related field; 2.5 GPA; 2 letters of recommendation; good academic standing at home school; no foreign language proficiency required.

Living Arrangements • Students live in host family homes, hotels, campsites. Meals are taken as a group, on one's own, with host family, in residences, in restaurants.

Costs (2003-2004) • One term: $11,700; includes tuition, housing, all meals, insurance, excursions. $50 application fee. $400 nonrefundable deposit required. Financial aid available for all students: scholarships.
For More Information • School for International Training, SIT Study Abroad, Kipling Road, Brattleboro, VT 05302-0676; *Phone:* 888-272-7881; *Fax:* 802-258-3296. *E-mail:* studyabroad@sit.edu. *World Wide Web:* http://www.sit.edu/studyabroad/

BRAZIL

CITY TO CITY

ANTIOCH COLLEGE
BRAZILIAN ECOSYSTEMS: THE PROTECTION AND MANAGEMENT OF BIODIVERSITY

Hosted by University of São Paulo, Fundação o Boticário de Proteção à Naturaleza (Curitiba), Words Language Institute (Curitiba), Federal University of Mato Grosso, Salto Morato Natural Reserve (Guaraqueçaba), National Institute of Amazonian Research (INPA) (Manaus), Federal University of Paraná
Academic Focus • Amazonian studies, biological/life sciences, botany, Brazilian studies, conservation studies, ecology, environmental science/studies, natural resources, Portuguese, wildlife studies, zoology.
Program Information • Students attend classes at University of São Paulo (São Paulo), Federal University of Mato Grosso (Cuiabá), Federal University of Paraná (Curitiba), Fundação o Boticário de Proteção à Naturaleza (Curitiba), Words Language Institute (Curitiba), Salto Morato Natural Reserve (Guaraqueçaba), National Institute of Amazonian Research (INPA) (Manaus). Scheduled travel to Pará, Paraná, Amazonas, Santa Catarina, Bahia, Mato Grosso; field trips to Brazilian cities, wetlands, an Amazon old growth rainforest, Atlantic coastal rainforest, extractive reserves, national parks, a hydroelectrical dam.
Sessions • Fall.
Eligibility Requirements • Minimum age 18; open to sophomores, juniors, seniors, graduate students; course work in ecology/conservation biology; 2 letters of recommendation; good academic standing at home school; flexibility; humor; stamina; commitment; no foreign language proficiency required.
Living Arrangements • Students live in host institution dormitories, locally rented apartments, host family homes, hotels. Meals are taken as a group, on one's own, with host family, in central dining facility, in restaurants.
Costs (2003-2004) • One term: $13,055; includes tuition, housing, some meals, excursions, international airfare, books and class materials, international student ID. $35 application fee. $150 nonrefundable deposit required. Financial aid available for students from sponsoring institution: scholarships, loans.
For More Information • Dr. Suzanne Kolb, AEA, Program Director BEP, Antioch College, Antioch Education Abroad, 795 Livermore Street, Yellow Springs, OH 45387-1697; *Phone:* 937-769-1015; *Fax:* 937-769-1019. *E-mail:* suzanne@antioch-college.edu. *World Wide Web:* http://www.antioch-college.edu/aea/

FLORIDA INTERNATIONAL UNIVERSITY
EXCHANGE PROGRAM WITH UNIVERSITY OF SÃO PAULO

Hosted by University of São Paulo
Academic Focus • Full curriculum.
Program Information • Students attend classes at University of São Paulo (São Paulo). Optional travel to anywhere in the country at an extra cost.
Sessions • Fall, spring.
Eligibility Requirements • Open to sophomores, juniors, seniors, graduate students, adults; 3.0 GPA; fluency in Portuguese.
Living Arrangements • Students live in host institution dormitories. Meals are taken on one's own, in central dining facility.

Costs (2002-2003) • One term: $3600 (estimated); includes housing, international airfare, books and class materials, international student ID. $150 application fee. Financial aid available for all students: scholarships.
For More Information • Office of International Studies, Florida International University, University Park Campus–TT100, Miami, FL 33199; *Phone:* 305-348-1913; *Fax:* 305-348-1941. *E-mail:* ois@fiu.edu. *World Wide Web:* http://ois.fiu.edu/

BELEM

SCHOOL FOR INTERNATIONAL TRAINING, SIT STUDY ABROAD
BRAZIL: AMAZON RESOURCE MANAGEMENT AND HUMAN ECOLOGY

Academic Focus • Amazonian studies, biological/life sciences, Brazilian studies, conservation studies, ecology, environmental science/studies, natural resources, Portuguese.
Program Information • Faculty members are drawn from the sponsor's U.S. staff and local instructors hired by the sponsor. Scheduled travel to Manaus, Paragominas, the Mamiraua Sustainable Development Reserve; field trips to Amazon River communities, national forests, research centers.
Sessions • Fall, spring.
Eligibility Requirements • Open to sophomores, juniors, seniors; course work in environmental studies, ecology, biology, or related field; 2.5 GPA; 2 letters of recommendation; good academic standing at home school; background in Portuguese, Spanish or other romance language is strongly recommended.
Living Arrangements • Students live in host family homes, hotels. Meals are taken as a group, on one's own, with host family, in residences, in restaurants.
Costs (2003-2004) • One term: $12,225; includes tuition, housing, all meals, insurance, excursions. $50 application fee. $400 nonrefundable deposit required. Financial aid available for all students: scholarships.
For More Information • School for International Training, SIT Study Abroad, Kipling Road, Brattleboro, VT 05302-0676; *Phone:* 888-272-7881; *Fax:* 802-258-3296. *E-mail:* studyabroad@sit.edu. *World Wide Web:* http://www.sit.edu/studyabroad/

BELO HORIZONTE

MIDDLEBURY COLLEGE SCHOOLS ABROAD
SCHOOL IN LATIN AMERICA–BELO HORIZONTE

Hosted by Federal University of Minas Gerais
Academic Focus • Full curriculum.
Program Information • Students attend classes at Federal University of Minas Gerais. Field trips.
Sessions • Fall, spring, yearlong.
Eligibility Requirements • Open to sophomores, juniors, seniors; 2.7 GPA; 2 letters of recommendation; B average in both Portuguese and major; 2 years of college course work in Portuguese.
Living Arrangements • Students live in host family homes. Meals are taken on one's own, with host family, in residences.
Costs (2004-2005) • One term: $7200. Yearlong program: $14,400; includes tuition, student support services. $50 application fee. $300 nonrefundable deposit required. Financial aid available for students from sponsoring institution: scholarships, loans.
For More Information • Mr. Jamie Northrup, University Relations Coordinator, Middlebury College Schools Abroad, Office of Off-Campus Study, Sunderland Language Center, Middlebury, VT 05753; *Phone:* 802-443-5745; *Fax:* 802-443-3157. *E-mail:* schoolsabroad@middlebury.edu. *World Wide Web:* http://www.middlebury.edu/msa/

CAMPINAS

UNIVERSITY AT ALBANY, STATE UNIVERSITY OF NEW YORK
DIRECT ENROLLMENT AT THE STATE UNIVERSITY OF CAMPINAS

Hosted by State University of Campinas

Academic Focus • Art, computer science, economics, education, engineering, full curriculum, linguistics, literature, philosophy, Portuguese, Portuguese studies, science, social sciences.
Program Information • Students attend classes at State University of Campinas.
Sessions • Fall, spring, yearlong.
Eligibility Requirements • Open to juniors, seniors, graduate students, adults; 2 letters of recommendation; good academic standing at home school; 1 year college course work in Portuguese for fluent speakers of Spanish; 2 years college course work in Portuguese or the equivalent for all others.
Living Arrangements • Students live in locally rented apartments. Meals are taken on one's own.
Costs (2002-2003) • One term: $3713. Yearlong program: $7426; includes housing, all meals, student support services, in-state tuition and fees. $150 nonrefundable deposit required. Financial aid available for students from sponsoring institution: all customary sources.
For More Information • University at Albany, State University of New York, Office of International Education, LI 66, Albany, NY 12222; *Phone:* 518-442-3525; *Fax:* 518-442-3338. *E-mail:* intled@uamail.albany.edu. *World Wide Web:* http://www.albany.edu/intled/

FORTALEZA
SCHOOL FOR INTERNATIONAL TRAINING, SIT STUDY ABROAD
BRAZIL: CULTURE, DEVELOPMENT, AND SOCIAL JUSTICE

Academic Focus • Anthropology, Brazilian studies, cultural studies, economics, political science and government, Portuguese.
Program Information • Faculty members are drawn from the sponsor's U.S. staff and local instructors hired by the sponsor. Scheduled travel to Bahia, Salvador; field trips to Sierra region of Ceará, fishing villages, social service centers.
Sessions • Fall, spring.
Eligibility Requirements • Open to sophomores, juniors, seniors; 2.5 GPA; 2 letters of recommendation; good academic standing at home school; background in Portuguese, Spanish or other romance language is strongly recommended.
Living Arrangements • Students live in host family homes, hotels. Meals are taken as a group, on one's own, with host family, in residences, in restaurants.
Costs (2003-2004) • One term: $12,050; includes tuition, housing, all meals, insurance, excursions. $50 application fee. $400 nonrefundable deposit required. Financial aid available for all students: scholarships.
For More Information • School for International Training, SIT Study Abroad, Kipling Road, Brattleboro, VT 05302-0676; *Phone:* 888-272-7881; *Fax:* 802-258-3296. *E-mail:* studyabroad@sit.edu. *World Wide Web:* http://www.sit.edu/studyabroad/

NITEROI
MIDDLEBURY COLLEGE SCHOOLS ABROAD
SCHOOL IN LATIN AMERICA–NITEROI PROGRAM

Hosted by Fluminense Federal University
Academic Focus • Full curriculum.
Program Information • Students attend classes at Fluminense Federal University. Field trips.
Sessions • Fall, spring, yearlong.
Eligibility Requirements • Open to sophomores, juniors, seniors; 2.7 GPA; 2 letters of recommendation; B average in both Portuguese and major; 2 years of college course work in Portuguese.
Living Arrangements • Students live in host family homes. Meals are taken on one's own, with host family, in residences, in restaurants.
Costs (2004-2005) • One term: $7200. Yearlong program: $14,400; includes tuition, student support services. $50 application fee. $300 nonrefundable deposit required. Financial aid available for students from sponsoring institution: scholarships, loans.
For More Information • Mr. Jamie Northrup, University Relations Coordinator, Middlebury College Schools Abroad, Office of Off-Campus Study, Sunderland Language Center, Middlebury, VT 05753;

Phone: 802-443-5745; *Fax:* 802-443-3157. *E-mail:* schoolsabroad@middlebury.edu. *World Wide Web:* http://www.middlebury.edu/msa/

RIO DE JANEIRO
BROWN UNIVERSITY
BROWN IN BRAZIL

Hosted by Pontifical Catholic University of Rio de Janeiro
Academic Focus • Full curriculum.
Program Information • Students attend classes at Pontifical Catholic University of Rio de Janeiro. Field trips to Ouro Preto, Petropolis, Arraial do Cabo, Ilha Grande.
Sessions • Fall, yearlong.
Eligibility Requirements • Open to sophomores, juniors, seniors; course work in Brazilian history, literature, or social science (1 course); 3.0 GPA; 2 letters of recommendation; 1.5 years of college course work in Portuguese.
Living Arrangements • Students live in locally rented apartments, host family homes. Meals are taken on one's own, with host family, in central dining facility, in restaurants.
Costs (2004-2005) • One term: $15,336. Yearlong program: $30,672; includes tuition, housing, excursions, international student ID, student support services, 1-month language and culture orientation. $250 nonrefundable deposit required. Financial aid available for students from sponsoring institution: scholarships, loans.
For More Information • Ms. Mell Bolen, Director, Brown University, Office of International Programs, Box 1973, Providence, RI 02912-1973; *Phone:* 401-863-3555; *Fax:* 401-863-3311. *E-mail:* oip_office@brown.edu. *World Wide Web:* http://www.brown.edu/OIP/

ST. JOHN'S UNIVERSITY
BRAZIL

Hosted by Pontifical Catholic University of Rio de Janeiro
Academic Focus • Portuguese studies.
Program Information • Students attend classes at Pontifical Catholic University of Rio de Janeiro.
Sessions • Fall, spring, yearlong.
Eligibility Requirements • Minimum age 18; open to sophomores, juniors, seniors; 3.0 GPA; 2 letters of recommendation; interview; 1 year college course work in Portuguese or fluency in Spanish.
Living Arrangements • Students live in host institution dormitories, locally rented apartments, host family homes. Meals are taken on one's own, in restaurants.
Costs (2004-2005) • One term: $9495–$10,120. Yearlong program: contact sponsor for cost; includes tuition, student support services. $30 application fee. $750 nonrefundable deposit required. Financial aid available for students from sponsoring institution: scholarships, work study.
For More Information • Dr. Ruth De Paula, Director, Office of Study Abroad Programs, St. John's University, 8000 Utopia Parkway, Jamaica, NY 11439; *Phone:* 718-990-6105; *Fax:* 718-990-2321. *E-mail:* intled@stjohns.edu. *World Wide Web:* http://www.stjohns.edu/studyabroad/

STATE UNIVERSITY OF NEW YORK AT NEW PALTZ
STUDY ABROAD IN RIO DE JANEIRO, BRAZIL

Hosted by Pontifical Catholic University of Rio de Janeiro
Academic Focus • Full curriculum.
Program Information • Students attend classes at Pontifical Catholic University of Rio de Janeiro.
Sessions • Fall, spring, yearlong.
Eligibility Requirements • Minimum age 18; open to sophomores, juniors, seniors; 2.75 GPA; 2 letters of recommendation; good academic standing at home school; 2 years college course work in Portuguese or average fluency in Spanish.
Living Arrangements • Students live in host family homes. Meals are taken on one's own, in residences.
Costs (2003-2004) • One term: $2799 for New York residents; $5928 for nonresidents. Yearlong program: $5598 for New York

residents; $11,856 for nonresidents; includes tuition, insurance, administrative fee. $25 application fee. $300–$600 nonrefundable deposit required. Financial aid available for students from sponsoring institution: scholarships, loans.

For More Information • Center for International Programs, State University of New York at New Paltz, 75 South Manheim Boulevard, Suite 9, New Paltz, NY 12561; *Phone:* 845-257-3125; *Fax:* 845-257-3129. *E-mail:* international@newpaltz.edu. *World Wide Web:* http://www.newpaltz.edu/studyabroad/

SALVADOR

CIEE
CIEE STUDY CENTER, SALVADOR DE BAHIA, BRAZIL

Hosted by Catholic University of Bahia, Federal University of Bahia
Academic Focus • African studies, anthropology, art, Brazilian studies, drama/theater, history, literature, music, Portuguese.
Program Information • Students attend classes at Federal University of Bahia, Catholic University of Bahia. Field trips to Lençois; optional travel to Fortaleza, Iguazú Falls, Rio de Janeiro, Ouro Preto, the Amazon at an extra cost.
Sessions • Fall, spring, yearlong.
Eligibility Requirements • Minimum age 18; open to sophomores, juniors, seniors, graduate students, adults; 2.75 GPA; 2 letters of recommendation; 1 year college course work in Portugese or 2 years course work in Spanish or the equivalent.
Living Arrangements • Students live in locally rented apartments, host family homes. Meals are taken on one's own, with host family, in residences, in central dining facility.
Costs (2004-2005) • One term: $9000. Yearlong program: $15,250; includes tuition, housing, all meals, insurance, excursions, student support services, computer and library access at host institution, pre-departure advising. $30 application fee. $300 deposit required. Financial aid available for all students: minority student scholarships, travel grants.
For More Information • Ms. Ellen Whitman, Admissions Officer, Spain and Latin America, CIEE, 7 Custom House Street, 3rd Floor, Portland, ME 04101; *Phone:* 800-40-STUDY; *Fax:* 207-553-7699. *E-mail:* studyinfo@ciee.org. *World Wide Web:* http://www.ciee.org/isp/

SÃO PAULO

CIEE
CIEE STUDY CENTER AT THE UNIVERSITY OF SÃO PAULO, BRAZIL

Hosted by University of São Paulo
Academic Focus • African studies, anthropology, art, biological/life sciences, Brazilian studies, business administration/management, communications, economics, film and media studies, history, liberal studies, literature, mathematics, music, philosophy, Portuguese, social sciences.
Program Information • Students attend classes at University of São Paulo. Scheduled travel to Itatiaia National Park, Ouro Preto, Rio de Janeiro; field trips to a Parati colonial town, Ubatuba, museums, a city tour, concerts; optional travel to Iguazú Falls, Bahia, Brasilia at an extra cost.
Sessions • Fall, spring, yearlong.
Eligibility Requirements • Minimum age 18; open to sophomores, juniors, seniors, graduate students, adults; 2.75 GPA; 2 letters of recommendation; good academic standing at home school; 1 year college course work in Portuguese or 2 years in Spanish or the equivalent.
Living Arrangements • Students live in host family homes. Meals are taken on one's own, with host family, in residences.
Costs (2004-2005) • One term: $9300. Yearlong program: $18,500; includes tuition, housing, some meals, insurance, excursions, student support services, pre-departure services, cultural activities. $30 application fee. $300 deposit required. Financial aid available for all students: minority student scholarships, travel grants.
For More Information • Ms. Ellen Whitman, Admissions Officer, Spain and Latin America, CIEE, 7 Custom House Street, 3rd Floor,

Portland, ME 04101; *Phone:* 800-40-STUDY; *Fax:* 207-553-7699. *E-mail:* studyinfo@ciee.org. *World Wide Web:* http://www.ciee.org/isp/

STATE UNIVERSITY OF NEW YORK AT OSWEGO
SÃO PAULO, BRAZIL

Hosted by Pontifical Catholic University of São Paulo
Academic Focus • Brazilian studies, Portuguese.
Program Information • Students attend classes at Pontifical Catholic University of São Paulo. Field trips.
Sessions • Fall, spring, yearlong.
Eligibility Requirements • Open to sophomores, juniors, seniors; 2.5 GPA; 3 letters of recommendation; good academic standing at home school; 1 year of college course work in Portuguese.
Living Arrangements • Students live in locally rented apartments, host family homes. Meals are taken on one's own, with host family, in residences, in restaurants.
Costs (2004) • One term: contact sponsor for cost. Yearlong program: contact sponsor for cost. $250 nonrefundable deposit required. Financial aid available for students: home university financial aid, loan processing and scholarships for Oswego students.
For More Information • Ms. Lizette Alvarado, Program Specialist, State University of New York at Oswego, 122A Swetman Hall, Oswego, NY 13216; *Phone:* 888-4-OSWEGO; *Fax:* 315-312-2477. *E-mail:* intled@oswego.edu. *World Wide Web:* http://www.oswego.edu/intled/

BULGARIA

BLAGOEVGRAD

AMERICAN UNIVERSITY IN BULGARIA
ACADEMIC SEMESTER/ACADEMIC YEAR IN BULGARIA

Hosted by American University in Bulgaria
Academic Focus • American studies, business administration/management, communications, computer science, economics, English, European studies, international affairs, journalism, mathematics, political science and government.
Program Information • Students attend classes at American University in Bulgaria. Field trips; optional travel at an extra cost.
Sessions • Fall, spring, yearlong.
Eligibility Requirements • Open to sophomores, juniors, seniors; 2.75 GPA; 2 letters of recommendation; good academic standing at home school; no foreign language proficiency required.
Living Arrangements • Students live in host institution dormitories. Quarters are shared with host institution students. Meals are taken on one's own, in central dining facility.
Costs (2003-2004) • One term: $7240. Yearlong program: $14,475; includes tuition, housing, all meals, insurance, books and class materials, student support services. $25 application fee. $250 nonrefundable deposit required. Financial aid available for students from sponsoring institution: Salgo-Noren study abroad grants for non-AUBG students.
For More Information • Mr. Benjamin M. Williams, Admissions Office, American University in Bulgaria, 1725 K Street, NW, Suite 411, Washington, DC 20006-1419; *Phone:* 202-955-1400; *Fax:* 202-955-1402. *E-mail:* admissions@aubg.bg. *World Wide Web:* http://www.aubg.bg/. Students may also apply through American University in Bulgaria, Blagoevgrad 2700, Bulgaria.

COLLEGE CONSORTIUM FOR INTERNATIONAL STUDIES–UNIVERSITY OF MAINE
SEMESTER PROGRAM AT THE AMERICAN UNIVERSITY IN BULGARIA

Hosted by American University in Bulgaria
Academic Focus • Full curriculum.

Program Information • Students attend classes at American University in Bulgaria. Field trips to monasteries, museums, archaeological sites; optional travel to Sophia, Turkey, Greece at an extra cost.

Sessions • Fall, spring, yearlong.

Eligibility Requirements • Minimum age 18; open to sophomores, juniors, seniors, adults; 3.0 GPA; 2 letters of recommendation; good academic standing at home school; no foreign language proficiency required.

Living Arrangements • Students live in host institution dormitories. Quarters are shared with host institution students. Meals are taken as a group, in central dining facility.

Costs (2003-2004) • One term: $6520. Yearlong program: $13,040; includes tuition, housing, all meals, books and class materials, student support services, administrative fees. $100 application fee. $300 refundable deposit required. Financial aid available for students from sponsoring institution: scholarships, loans.

For More Information • Ms. Catherine Reader, Study Abroad Advisor, College Consortium for International Studies–University of Maine, Office of International Programs, 5782 Winslow Hall, Room 100, Orono, ME 04469-5782; *Phone:* 207-581-2905; *Fax:* 207-581-2920. *E-mail:* studyabroad@umit.maine.edu. *World Wide Web:* http://www.ccisabroad.org/

STATE UNIVERSITY OF NEW YORK COLLEGE AT FREDONIA
AMERICAN UNIVERSITY IN BULGARIA

Hosted by American University in Bulgaria
Academic Focus • Full curriculum.
Program Information • Students attend classes at American University in Bulgaria. Optional travel to Greece, the Rila Mountains, the Black Sea at an extra cost.
Sessions • Fall, spring, yearlong.
Eligibility Requirements • Open to sophomores, juniors, seniors; 3.0 GPA; 2 letters of recommendation; transcripts; no foreign language proficiency required.
Living Arrangements • Students live in host institution dormitories. Quarters are shared with host institution students, students from other programs. Meals are taken as a group, on one's own, in central dining facility, in restaurants.
Costs (2003-2004) • One term: $7500. Yearlong program: $15,000; includes tuition, housing, all meals, insurance, books and class materials, passport and visa fees, personal transportation. $600 nonrefundable deposit required. Financial aid available for all students: scholarships, loans.
For More Information • Ms. Mary Sasso, Director, International Education, State University of New York College at Fredonia, 8 LoGrasso Hall, Fredonia, NY 14063; *Phone:* 716-673-3451; *Fax:* 716-673-3175. *E-mail:* sasso@fredonia.edu. *World Wide Web:* http://www.fredonia.edu/

VELIKO TURNOVO
COLLEGE CONSORTIUM FOR INTERNATIONAL STUDIES–TRUMAN STATE UNIVERSITY
SEMESTER IN BULGARIA

Hosted by 'St. Cyril and St. Methodius' University of Véliko Turnovo
Academic Focus • Teaching English as a second language.
Program Information • Students attend classes at 'St. Cyril and St. Methodius' University of Véliko Turnovo.
Sessions • Fall, spring, yearlong.
Eligibility Requirements • Minimum age 18; open to freshmen, sophomores, juniors, seniors, graduate students; 3.0 GPA; 2 letters of recommendation; good academic standing at home school; statement of purpose; transcript; no foreign language proficiency required.
Living Arrangements • Students live in host institution dormitories, locally rented apartments. Quarters are shared with students from other programs. Meals are taken on one's own, in residences.
Costs (2004) • One term: $4500. Yearlong program: $9000; includes tuition, housing, all meals, insurance, student support

services. $300 deposit required. Financial aid available for students from sponsoring institution: scholarships, loans.
For More Information • Center for International Education Abroad, College Consortium for International Studies–Truman State University, Truman State University, Kirk Building 114, Kirksville, MO 63501; *Phone:* 660-785-4076; *Fax:* 660-785-7473. *E-mail:* ciea@truman.edu. *World Wide Web:* http://www.ccisabroad.org/

CAMEROON
CITY TO CITY
SCHOOL FOR INTERNATIONAL TRAINING, SIT STUDY ABROAD
CAMEROON: CULTURE AND DEVELOPMENT

Academic Focus • African studies, anthropology, economics, French language and literature, geography, history, political science and government, visual and performing arts.
Program Information • Faculty members are drawn from the sponsor's U.S. staff and local instructors hired by the sponsor. Scheduled travel to Yaounde, Extreme North Province, the Fulani Highlands; field trips to rural areas, coastal area.
Sessions • Fall, spring.
Eligibility Requirements • Open to sophomores, juniors, seniors; 2.5 GPA; 2 letters of recommendation; good academic standing at home school; 1.5 years of college course work in French.
Living Arrangements • Students live in host family homes, hotels, campsites. Meals are taken as a group, on one's own, with host family, in residences, in restaurants.
Costs (2003-2004) • One term: $11,800; includes tuition, housing, all meals, insurance, excursions. $50 application fee. $400 nonrefundable deposit required. Financial aid available for all students: scholarships.
For More Information • ', School for International Training, SIT Study Abroad, Kipling Road, Brattleboro, VT 05302-0676; *Phone:* 888-272-7881; *Fax:* 802-258-3296. *E-mail:* studyabroad@sit.edu. *World Wide Web:* http://www.sit.edu/studyabroad/

YAOUNDÉ
DICKINSON COLLEGE
DICKINSON IN YAOUNDE (CAMEROON)

Hosted by University of Yaoundé I
Academic Focus • English literature, fine/studio arts, history, international affairs, literature, political science and government, religious studies, sociology, women's studies.
Program Information • Students attend classes at University of Yaoundé I. Scheduled travel to northwest and southwest Cameroon; field trips to local sites in Yaoundé; optional travel to north Cameroon at an extra cost.
Sessions • Spring.
Eligibility Requirements • Minimum age 18; open to juniors; 2.8 GPA; 3 letters of recommendation; good academic standing at home school; no foreign language proficiency required.
Living Arrangements • Students live in locally rented apartments. Meals are taken on one's own, in residences.
Costs (2004) • One term: $14,710; includes tuition, housing, all meals, excursions, student support services. $25 application fee. $300 nonrefundable deposit required. Financial aid available for students from sponsoring institution: scholarships, loans.
For More Information • Ms. Karen Peter, Program Manager, Dickinson College, PO Box 1773, Carlisle, PA 17013-2896; *Phone:* 717-245-1341; *Fax:* 717-245-1688. *E-mail:* global@dickinson.edu. *World Wide Web:* http://www.dickinson.edu/global/

CANADA

CITY TO CITY

UNIVERSITY OF CONNECTICUT
NEW ENGLAND/QUÉBEC STUDENT EXCHANGE PROGRAM

Hosted by Laval University, University of Sherbrooke, University of Québec, Ecole Polytechnique, Ecole des Hautes Etudes Commerciales, Bishop's University, Concordia University, McGill University, University of Montreal
Academic Focus • Full curriculum.
Program Information • Students attend classes at Laval University (Québec City), University of Sherbrooke (Sherbrooke), University of Québec (Québec), Ecole Polytechnique (Montreal), Ecole des Hautes Etudes Commerciales (Montreal), Bishop's University (Lennoxville), Concordia University (Montreal), McGill University (Montreal), University of Montreal (Montréal).
Sessions • Fall, spring, yearlong.
Eligibility Requirements • Open to sophomores, juniors, seniors; 2.5 GPA; 2 letters of recommendation; fluency in French (if applicable).
Living Arrangements • Meals are taken on one's own.
Costs (2003-2004) • One term: $2128 for Connecticut residents; $3283 for nonresidents. Yearlong program: $3910 for Connecticut residents; $6220 for nonresidents; includes tuition, fees. $25 application fee. $395 nonrefundable deposit required. Financial aid available for students from sponsoring institution: scholarships.
For More Information • Mr. Gordon Lustila, Acting Director of Study Abroad Programs, University of Connecticut, 843 Bolton Road, Unit 1207, Storrs, CT 06269-1207; *Phone:* 860-486-5022; *Fax:* 860-486-2976. *E-mail:* sabadm03@uconnvm.uconn.edu. *World Wide Web:* http://studyabroad.uconn.edu/

CHICOUTIMI

STATE UNIVERSITY OF NEW YORK AT PLATTSBURGH
STUDY IN CANADA, CHICOUTIMI

Hosted by University of Québec at Chicoutimi
Academic Focus • French language and literature, full curriculum.
Program Information • Students attend classes at University of Québec at Chicoutimi.
Sessions • Fall, spring, yearlong.
Eligibility Requirements • Minimum age 18; open to sophomores, juniors, seniors, adults; 2.5 GPA; 2 letters of recommendation; SUNY application; essay; transcript; no foreign language proficiency requirement for Immersion Program, fluency in French required for Direct Enrollment.
Living Arrangements • Students live in host institution dormitories, locally rented apartments. Quarters are shared with host institution students, students from other programs. Meals are taken on one's own, in central dining facility, in restaurants.
Costs (2003-2004) • One term: $4570. Yearlong program: $9140; includes tuition, housing, all meals, insurance, books and class materials, international student ID, student support services. $20 application fee. $350 nonrefundable deposit required. Financial aid available for students from sponsoring institution: scholarships, loans.
For More Information • Ms. Jo Ann Mackie, Study Abroad Coordinator, State University of New York at Plattsburgh, Study Abroad Office, 101 Broad Street, Plattsburgh, NY 12901; *Phone:* 518-564-2321; *Fax:* 518-564-2326. *E-mail:* international@plattsburgh. edu. *World Wide Web:* http://www.plattsburgh.edu/studyabroad/

MONTRÉAL

STATE UNIVERSITY OF NEW YORK AT PLATTSBURGH
STUDY IN CANADA, MONTREAL (CONCORDIA)

Hosted by Concordia University
Academic Focus • Accounting, anthropology, art, art history, Asian studies, biochemistry, biological/life sciences, Canadian studies, chemical sciences, creative writing, drama/theater, economics, English, English literature, French language and literature, geography, geology, German language and literature, history, international business, Italian language and literature, linguistics, mathematics, music, philosophy, photography, physics, political science and government, psychology, science, sociology, Spanish language and literature, women's studies.
Program Information • Students attend classes at Concordia University.
Sessions • Fall, spring, yearlong.
Eligibility Requirements • Minimum age 18; open to sophomores, juniors, seniors; 3.0 GPA; 2 letters of recommendation; good academic standing at home school; SUNY, Concordia, and Crepuq applications; essay; transcripts; no foreign language proficiency required.
Living Arrangements • Students live in locally rented apartments. Quarters are shared with host institution students, students from other programs. Meals are taken on one's own, in central dining facility, in restaurants.
Costs (2003-2004) • One term: $5470. Yearlong program: $10,940; includes tuition, housing, some meals, insurance, books and class materials, international student ID, student support services, program fee. $20 application fee. $350 nonrefundable deposit required. Financial aid available for students from sponsoring institution: scholarships, loans.
For More Information • Ms. Jo Ann Mackie, Study Abroad Coordinator, State University of New York at Plattsburgh, Study Abroad Office, 101 Broad Street, Plattsburgh, NY 12901; *Phone:* 518-564-2321; *Fax:* 518-564-2326. *E-mail:* international@plattsburgh. edu. *World Wide Web:* http://www.plattsburgh.edu/studyabroad/

STATE UNIVERSITY OF NEW YORK AT PLATTSBURGH
STUDY IN CANADA, MONTREAL (MCGILL)

Hosted by McGill University
Academic Focus • Anthropology, business administration/management, Canadian studies, communications, computer science, economics, environmental science/studies, French Canadian studies, geography, history, language studies, music, political science and government, psychology.
Program Information • Students attend classes at McGill University.
Sessions • Fall, spring, yearlong.
Eligibility Requirements • Minimum age 18; open to sophomores, juniors, seniors; 3.0 GPA; 2 letters of recommendation; SUNY, McGill, and CREPUQ applications; essay; transcript; no foreign language proficiency required.
Living Arrangements • Students live in host institution dormitories, locally rented apartments. Quarters are shared with host institution students, students from other programs. Meals are taken on one's own, in central dining facility, in restaurants.
Costs (2003-2004) • One term: $6400 for New York residents; nonresidents contact sponsor for cost. Yearlong program: $12,800 for New York residents; nonresidents contact sponsor for cost; includes tuition, housing, all meals, insurance, books and class materials, international student ID, student support services, visa and program fees. $20 application fee. $350 nonrefundable deposit required. Financial aid available for students from sponsoring institution: scholarships, loans.
For More Information • Ms. Jo Ann Mackie, Study Abroad Coordinator, State University of New York at Plattsburgh, Study Abroad Office, 101 Broad Street, Plattsburgh, NY 12901; *Phone:* 518-564-2321; *Fax:* 518-564-2326. *E-mail:* international@plattsburgh. edu. *World Wide Web:* http://www.plattsburgh.edu/studyabroad/

NOVA SCOTIA

LOCK HAVEN UNIVERSITY OF PENNSYLVANIA
SEMESTER AT UCCB, NOVA SCOTIA, CANADA

Hosted by University College of Cape Breton
Academic Focus • Full curriculum.
Program Information • Students attend classes at University College of Cape Breton.
Sessions • Fall, spring, yearlong.

Eligibility Requirements • Minimum age 18; open to sophomores, juniors; 2.5 GPA; 3 letters of recommendation; good academic standing at home school; no foreign language proficiency required.
Living Arrangements • Students live in host institution dormitories. Quarters are shared with host institution students. Meals are taken on one's own, in central dining facility.
Costs (2002-2003) • One term: $5450 for Pennsylvania residents; $7360 for nonresidents. Yearlong program: $10,900 for Pennsylvania residents; $14,720 for nonresidents; includes tuition, housing, all meals, fees. $50 application fee. Financial aid available for students from sponsoring institution: scholarships, loans.
For More Information • Dean, Institute for International Studies, Lock Haven University of Pennsylvania, Lock Haven, PA 17745-2390; *Phone:* 570-893-2140; *Fax:* 570-893-2537. *E-mail:* kbrostue@lhup.edu. *World Wide Web:* http://www.lhup.edu/international/goingp/goingplaces_index.htm

OTTAWA

STATE UNIVERSITY OF NEW YORK AT PLATTSBURGH
STUDY IN CANADA, OTTAWA

Hosted by Carleton University
Academic Focus • Anthropology, business administration/management, Canadian studies, communications, Eastern European studies, film and media studies, international affairs, journalism, music, philosophy, political science and government, psychology, Russian studies.
Program Information • Students attend classes at Carleton University.
Sessions • Fall, spring, yearlong.
Eligibility Requirements • Minimum age 18; open to sophomores, juniors, seniors; 3.0 GPA; 3 letters of recommendation; SUNY application; essay; transcript; no foreign language proficiency required.
Living Arrangements • Students live in host institution dormitories, locally rented apartments. Quarters are shared with host institution students, students from other programs. Meals are taken as a group, on one's own, in central dining facility, in restaurants.
Costs (2003-2004) • One term: $5970. Yearlong program: $11,940; includes tuition, housing, some meals, insurance, books and class materials, international student ID, student support services, visa fees. $20 application fee. $350 nonrefundable deposit required. Financial aid available for students from sponsoring institution: scholarships, loans.
For More Information • Ms. Jo Ann Mackie, Study Abroad Coordinator, State University of New York at Plattsburgh, Study Abroad Office, 101 Broad Street, Plattsburgh, NY 12901; *Phone:* 518-564-2321; *Fax:* 518-564-2326. *E-mail:* international@plattsburgh.edu. *World Wide Web:* http://www.plattsburgh.edu/studyabroad/

QUÉBEC

COLLEGE CONSORTIUM FOR INTERNATIONAL STUDIES–BROOKDALE COMMUNITY COLLEGE
SEMESTER FRENCH IMMERSION PROGRAM IN QUÉBEC, CANADA

Hosted by University of Québec at Chicoutimi
Academic Focus • Canadian studies, French language and literature.
Program Information • Students attend classes at University of Québec at Chicoutimi. Scheduled travel to Québec City; field trips to historic sites in Chicoutimi, Musée du Saguenay-Lac Saint Jean, whale watching; optional travel at an extra cost.
Sessions • Fall, spring, winter, yearlong, shorter terms of 7 or 8 weeks also available.
Eligibility Requirements • Minimum age 18; open to freshmen, sophomores, juniors, seniors, graduate students; 2.5 GPA; 3 letters of recommendation; transcript; essay; completion of 15 credits prior to application; no foreign language proficiency required.
Living Arrangements • Students live in host institution dormitories, host family homes. Meals are taken as a group, with host family, in residences, in central dining facility.

Costs (2003-2004) • One term: $2310 for 15 weeks; $1600 for 7 or 8 weeks. Yearlong program: contact sponsor for cost; includes tuition, insurance, student support services, some excursions, fees, e-mail access. $35 application fee. Financial aid available for students from sponsoring institution: scholarships, loans.
For More Information • College Consortium for International Studies–Brookdale Community College, 2000 P Street, NW, Suite 503, Washington, DC 20036; *Phone:* 800-453-6956; *Fax:* 202-223-0999. *E-mail:* info@ccisabroad.org. *World Wide Web:* http://www.ccisabroad.org/. Students may also apply through Brookdale Community College, International Center, 765 Newman Springs Road, Lincroft, NJ 07738-1597.

STATE UNIVERSITY OF NEW YORK AT PLATTSBURGH
STUDY IN CANADA, QUÉBEC CITY

Hosted by Laval University
Academic Focus • French Canadian studies, French language and literature, full curriculum.
Program Information • Students attend classes at Laval University.
Sessions • Fall, spring, yearlong.
Eligibility Requirements • Minimum age 18; open to sophomores, juniors, seniors; 2.5 GPA; 2 letters of recommendation; SUNY application; essay; transcript; no foreign language proficieny requirement for Immersion Program; fluency in French required for Direct Enrollment.
Living Arrangements • Students live in host institution dormitories, locally rented apartments. Quarters are shared with host institution students, students from other programs. Meals are taken on one's own, in residences, in central dining facility, in restaurants.
Costs (2003-2004) • One term: $4570. Yearlong program: $9140; includes tuition, housing, all meals, insurance, program fee. $20 application fee. $350 nonrefundable deposit required. Financial aid available for students from sponsoring institution: scholarships, loans.
For More Information • Ms. Jo Ann Mackie, Study Abroad Coordinator, State University of New York at Plattsburgh, Study Abroad Office, 101 Broad Street, Plattsburgh, NY 12901; *Phone:* 518-564-2321; *Fax:* 518-564-2326. *E-mail:* international@plattsburgh.edu. *World Wide Web:* http://www.plattsburgh.edu/studyabroad/

CHILE
CITY TO CITY

SCHOOL FOR INTERNATIONAL TRAINING, SIT STUDY ABROAD
CHILE: CULTURE, DEVELOPMENT, AND SOCIAL JUSTICE

Academic Focus • Cultural studies, economics, history, Mapuche/Aymara studies, political science and government, sociology, Spanish language and literature.
Program Information • Faculty members are drawn from the sponsor's U.S. staff and local instructors hired by the sponsor. Scheduled travel to Arica, Iquique, Lake Chungará or Temuko, the surrounding region; field trips to Santiago, rural destinations, community organizations.
Sessions • Fall, spring.
Eligibility Requirements • Open to sophomores, juniors, seniors; 2.5 GPA; 2 letters of recommendation; good academic standing at home school; 1.5 years of college course work in Spanish.
Living Arrangements • Students live in host family homes, hotels. Meals are taken as a group, on one's own, with host family, in residences, in restaurants.
Costs (2003-2004) • One term: $12,800; includes tuition, housing, all meals, insurance, excursions. $50 application fee. $400 nonrefundable deposit required. Financial aid available for all students: scholarships.
For More Information • School for International Training, SIT Study Abroad, Kipling Road, Brattleboro, VT 05302-0676; *Phone:* 888-272-7881; *Fax:* 802-258-3296. *E-mail:* studyabroad@sit.edu. *World Wide Web:* http://www.sit.edu/studyabroad/

CONCEPCIÓN

ST. CLOUD STATE UNIVERSITY
SPANISH LANGUAGE AND LATIN AMERICAN STUDIES

Held at University of Concepción
Academic Focus • Latin American studies, Spanish language and literature.
Program Information • Classes are held on the campus of University of Concepción. Faculty members are drawn from the sponsor's U.S. staff and local instructors hired by the sponsor. Scheduled travel to Chile, southern Chile; field trips to Santiago, northern Chile, southern Chile; optional travel at an extra cost.
Sessions • Fall.
Eligibility Requirements • Minimum age 18; open to sophomores, juniors, seniors; 2.5 GPA; 2 letters of recommendation; 1 year of college course work in Spanish.
Living Arrangements • Students live in host family homes. Meals are taken with host family, in residences.
Costs (2003) • One term: $7975 for Minnesota residents; includes tuition, housing, some meals, international airfare, international student ID, some excursions. $75 application fee. Financial aid available for students from sponsoring institution: scholarships, work study, loans.
For More Information • Chunsheng Zhang, Associate Vice President for Academic Affairs/International Studies, St. Cloud State University, Center for International Studies, 720 4th Avenue, South, St. Cloud, MN 56301; *Phone:* 320-308-4287; *Fax:* 320-308-4223. *E-mail:* intstudy@stcloudstate.edu. *World Wide Web:* http://www.stcloudstate.edu/

STATE UNIVERSITY OF NEW YORK AT PLATTSBURGH
LATIN AMERICAN SOUTHERN CONE PROGRAMS, CONCEPCIÓN, WITH MIDDLEBURY COLLEGE

Hosted by University of Concepción
Academic Focus • Full curriculum.
Program Information • Students attend classes at University of Concepción. Field trips to the Lake Region, Bio-Bio River Basin; optional travel to Santiago, the Andes Mountains, Atacama Desert, Patagonia, Chiloe at an extra cost.
Sessions • Fall, spring, yearlong, South American academic year.
Eligibility Requirements • Open to freshmen, sophomores, juniors, seniors, graduate students, adults; 2.5 GPA; 3 letters of recommendation; intermediate-level Spanish.
Living Arrangements • Students live on one's own, with host family, in residences, in restaurants.
Costs (2003-2004) • One term: $7260 for New York residents; $10,235 for nonresidents. Yearlong program: $13,020 for New York residents; $18,970 for nonresidents; includes tuition, housing, all meals, insurance, international airfare, books and class materials, program fee. $20 application fee. $200 nonrefundable deposit required. Financial aid available for all students: scholarships, loans.
For More Information • Ms. Carmen Madariaga Culver, Academic Director, Latin American Southern Cone Programs, State University of New York at Plattsburgh, 101 Broad Street, Plattsburgh, NY 12901-2681; *Phone:* 518-564-2395; *Fax:* 518-564-2300. *E-mail:* socone@plattsburgh.edu. *World Wide Web:* http://www.plattsburgh.edu/studyabroad/

LA SERENA

STATE UNIVERSITY OF NEW YORK AT PLATTSBURGH
LATIN AMERICAN SOUTHERN CONE PROGRAMS–LA SERENA, WITH MIDDLEBURY COLLEGE

Hosted by La Serena University
Academic Focus • Full curriculum.
Program Information • Students attend classes at La Serena University. Field trips to the Lake Region, Atacama Desert, Bio-Bio River Basin; optional travel to Santiago, Patagonia, the Andes Mountains at an extra cost.
Sessions • Fall, spring, yearlong, South American academic year.
Eligibility Requirements • Open to sophomores, juniors, seniors, graduate students, adults; 2.5 GPA; 3 letters of recommendation; intermediate-level Spanish.
Living Arrangements • Students live in host family homes. Meals are taken on one's own, with host family, in residences, in restaurants.
Costs (2003-2004) • One term: $7260 for New York residents; $10,235 for nonresidents. Yearlong program: $13,020 for New York residents; $18,970 for nonresidents; includes tuition, housing, all meals, insurance, international airfare, books and class materials, program fee. $20 application fee. $200 nonrefundable deposit required. Financial aid available for all students: scholarships, loans.
For More Information • Ms. Carmen Madariaga Culver, Academic Director, Latin American Southern Cone Programs, State University of New York at Plattsburgh, 101 Broad Street, Plattsburgh, NY 12901-2681; *Phone:* 518-564-2395; *Fax:* 518-564-2300. *E-mail:* socone@plattsburgh.edu. *World Wide Web:* http://www.plattsburgh.edu/studyabroad/

SANTIAGO

AMERICAN UNIVERSITY
SEMESTER IN SANTIAGO

Held at University of Diego Portales
Academic Focus • History, international affairs, Latin American studies, political science and government, Spanish language and literature.
Program Information • Classes are held on the campus of University of Diego Portales. Faculty members are drawn from the sponsor's U.S. staff and local instructors hired by the sponsor. Scheduled travel to southern Chile, the Andes, the Lake District, north of Chile; field trips to Valparaíso, the coast.
Sessions • Spring.
Eligibility Requirements • Open to sophomores, juniors, seniors, graduate students; 2.75 GPA; 1 letter of recommendation; second semester sophomore status; recommendation of advisor; 2 years of college course work in Spanish.
Living Arrangements • Students live in host family homes. Meals are taken with host family, in residences.
Costs (2003) • One term: $16,934; includes tuition, housing, some meals, excursions, books and class materials, international student ID, student support services. $35 application fee. $300 nonrefundable deposit required. Financial aid available for all students: scholarships, loans.
For More Information • Dr. David C. Brown, Dean, Washington Semester and World Capitals Programs, American University, Tenley Campus–Constitution Building, Washington, DC 20016-8083; *Phone:* 800-424-2600; *Fax:* 202-895-4960. *E-mail:* travel@american.edu. *World Wide Web:* http://www.worldcapitals.american.edu/

CIEE
CIEE STUDY CENTER: SANTIAGO, CHILE

Hosted by University of Santiago de Chile, Catholic University of Chile, University of Chile
Academic Focus • Biological/life sciences, business administration/management, Chilean studies, cultural studies, drama/theater, engineering, history, international business, Latin American studies, literature, political science and government, religious studies, Spanish language and literature, women's studies.
Program Information • Students attend classes at University of Santiago de Chile, Catholic University of Chile, University of Chile. Scheduled travel to La Serena, Mendoza, Puerto Montt, Chiloé Island, Pucon; field trips to Pablo Neruda's house at Isla Negra, ski resorts near Portillos, Valparaíso; optional travel to Temuco, Brazil, Antofagasta, Argentina, Peru, Bolivia, Easter Island at an extra cost.
Sessions • Fall, spring, yearlong.
Eligibility Requirements • Minimum age 18; open to sophomores, juniors, seniors, graduate students, adults; 2.75 GPA; 2 letters of recommendation; 3 years of college course work in Spanish.
Living Arrangements • Students live in locally rented apartments, host family homes. Meals are taken on one's own, with host family, in residences, in central dining facility.
Costs (2004-2005) • One term: $9450. Yearlong program: $18,500; includes tuition, housing, some meals, insurance, excursions, library and computer access at university, pre-departure advising. $30

Chile?

Specialization in Chile ✳ *Personalized Attention* ✳ *Individualized Academic Programs*

Latin American Southern Cone Programs
State University of New York
at Plattsburgh

We offer you choices. Our ten university programs in six Chilean cities allow you to study at a site best suited to your needs. Our internships are available to qualified students as a part of our "cooperative development seminar." Our seven-member staff concentrates on a limited number of students per semester. From inquiry, to application and acceptance, then through planning your individualized academic program, your stay in Chile, and sending out your final academic transcript, we will treat you as an individual.

Programs in six cities:

Santiago	La Serena	Temuco
Valparaíso	Concepción	Valdivia

Collaboration with ten universities:

Universidad de Chile
Pontificia Universidad Católica de Chile
Universidad de Valparaíso
Universidad Católica de Valparaíso
Universidad de Playa Ancha

Universidad de Concepción
Universidad de La Serena
Universidad de la Frontera
Universidad Austral de Chile
Universidad de Adolfo Ibañez

Internships:

Qualified students are placed in sites such as: major communications media, government, business, development and human rights NGOs, political organizations, health care providers, and education at primary and secondary levels. Once accepted to go to Chile, internship opportunities are available by application to the Academic Director who assigns internships on the basis of Spanish oral proficiency, individual background, and approval of home university. These are liberal arts experiences involving cultural immersion while assuming responsibilities in the organization.

Offices and Staff:

The Southern Cone Programs support students in Chile as one "virtual" office. In Plattsburgh, the staff develops each student's individual academic program. In Santiago, the staff implements and assists students in their academic and personal pursuits. We stress self-reliance, personal responsibility and participation as the keys to successful international study. The Southern Cone Programs are selective, and early application is recommended.

PLATTSBURGH OFFICE
William Culver, Director & Distinguished Service Professor
Carmen Madariaga Culver, Academic Director
Pam LeClair, Office Manager
Anna Karlsson, Application Coordinator

SANTIAGO OFFICE
Joseph McSpedon, Academic Representative
Luz Angélica Sandoval, Administrative Representative
María Cristina Cornejo, Office Manager

Latin American Southern Cone Programs
Plattsburgh State University of New York
101 Broad Street
Plattsburgh, New York 12901-2681
Telephone: 518-564-2395 Fax: 518-564-2300
Email: socone@plattsburgh.edu
Web Site: www.plattsburgh.edu/socone

application fee. $300 deposit required. Financial aid available for all students: minority student scholarships, travel grants.

For More Information • Ms. Ellen Whitman, Admissions Officer, Spain and Latin America, CIEE, 7 Custom House Street, 3rd Floor, Portland, ME 04101; *Phone:* 800-40-STUDY; *Fax:* 207-553-7699. *E-mail:* studyinfo@ciee.org. *World Wide Web:* http://www.ciee.org/isp/

IES, INSTITUTE FOR THE INTERNATIONAL EDUCATION OF STUDENTS
IES–SANTIAGO

Hosted by Arturo Prat University, Instituto Tecnológico y de Estudios Superiores de Monterrey–Guaymas Campus, Institute for the International Education of Students (IES)–Santiago, Catholic University of Chile, University of Chile

Academic Focus • Anthropology, art history, economics, environmental science/studies, history, international affairs, international business, Latin American studies, literature, political science and government, sociology, Spanish language and literature.

Program Information • Students attend classes at Catholic University of Chile, University of Chile, Arturo Prat University, Institute for the International Education of Students (IES)–Santiago, Instituto Tecnológico y de Estudios Superiores de Monterrey-Guaymas Campus. Scheduled travel to Atacama Desert, Easter Island; field trips to Valparaíso; optional travel to Easter Island at an extra cost.

Sessions • Fall, spring, yearlong.

Eligibility Requirements • Minimum age 18; open to sophomores, juniors, seniors, graduate students, adults; 3.0 GPA; 1 letter of recommendation; good academic standing at home school; 2 years of college course work in Spanish.

Living Arrangements • Students live in host family homes. Meals are taken with host family, in residences.

Costs (2003-2004) • One term: $8900. Yearlong program: $16,020; includes tuition, housing, some meals, excursions, student support services, partial insurance coverage. $50 application fee. $500 nonrefundable deposit required. Financial aid available for all students: scholarships, institutional partner need-based grants.

For More Information • International Education Representative, IES, Institute for the International Education of Students, 33 North La Salle Street, 15th Floor, Chicago, IL 60602; *Phone:* 800-995-2300; *Fax:* 312-944-1448. *E-mail:* info@iesabroad.org. *World Wide Web:* http://www.IESabroad.org/

INSTITUTE FOR STUDY ABROAD, BUTLER UNIVERSITY
CHILEAN UNIVERSITY PROGRAM, SANTIAGO

Hosted by University of Diego Portales, Catholic University of Chile, University of Chile

Academic Focus • Full curriculum.

Program Information • Students attend classes at University of Diego Portales, Catholic University of Chile, University of Chile. Field trips to Termas de Chillan, hot springs, an Andes ski resort, Pablo Neruda's house at Isla Negra, Valparaiso, La Serena; optional travel to Mendoza, Araucania at an extra cost.

Sessions • Fall, spring, yearlong, US academic year.

Eligibility Requirements • Open to sophomores, juniors, seniors; 3.0 GPA; 1 letter of recommendation; enrollment at an accredited American college or university; Spanish language evaluation; 2 years of college course work in Spanish.

Living Arrangements • Students live in host family homes. Meals are taken with host family.

Costs (2003) • One term: $9150. Yearlong program: $15,580; includes tuition, housing, all meals, excursions, international student ID, student support services, cultural and sporting events, pre-

departure advising. $40 application fee. $500 nonrefundable deposit required. Financial aid available for all students: scholarships, travel grants.

For More Information • Institute for Study Abroad, Butler University, 1100 West 42nd Street, Suite 305, Indianapolis, IN 46208-3345; *Phone:* 800-858-0229; *Fax:* 317-940-9704. *E-mail:* copa@butler.edu. *World Wide Web:* http://www.ifsa-butler.org/

LAKE FOREST COLLEGE
INTERNATIONAL INTERNSHIP/STUDY IN SANTIAGO, CHILE

Hosted by University of Diego Portales
Academic Focus • Business administration/management, economics, international affairs, Spanish language and literature.
Program Information • Students attend classes at University of Diego Portales. Field trips to Viña del Mar, Valparaíso.
Sessions • Fall.
Eligibility Requirements • Open to juniors, seniors; 3.0 GPA; 3 letters of recommendation; good academic standing at home school; Lake Forest College application form; 2.5 years of college course work in Spanish.
Living Arrangements • Students live in host family homes. Meals are taken with host family, in residences, in restaurants.
Costs (2003) • One term: $15,480; includes tuition, housing, all meals, insurance, excursions, student support services. $20 application fee. $500 nonrefundable deposit required. Financial aid available for students from sponsoring institution: scholarships, loans.
For More Information • Mr. George L. Speros, Associate Provost/Dean of Faculty and Director of International Studies, Lake Forest College, Office of the Dean of the Faculty, Lake Forest, IL 60045-2399; *Phone:* 847-735-5020; *Fax:* 847-735-6292. *E-mail:* chile@lfc.edu. *World Wide Web:* http://www.lakeforest.edu/

NIAGARA UNIVERSITY
UNIVERSITY OF SANTO TOMAS–SANTIAGO, CHILE

Hosted by Santo Tomás University
Academic Focus • Full curriculum.
Program Information • Students attend classes at Santo Tomás University. Field trips to Mar del Plata; optional travel to Buenos Aires at an extra cost.
Sessions • Spring.
Eligibility Requirements • Open to juniors, seniors; 2 letters of recommendation; good academic standing at home school; fluency in Spanish.
Living Arrangements • Students live in host family homes. Meals are taken with host family, in residences.
Costs • One term: $12,314; includes tuition, housing, all meals, excursions, international student ID, student support services. Financial aid available for students from sponsoring institution: scholarships, loans, Pell grants and TAP for qualified New York State residents.
For More Information • Ms. Bernadette Brennen, Study Abroad Coordinator, Niagara University, Alumni Hall, Niagara University, NY 14109; *Phone:* 716-286-8360; *Fax:* 716-286-8349. *E-mail:* bmb@niagara.edu. *World Wide Web:* http://www.niagara.edu/sap/

SCHOOL FOR INTERNATIONAL TRAINING, SIT STUDY ABROAD
CHILE: ECONOMIC DEVELOPMENT AND GLOBALIZATION

Academic Focus • Economics, Latin American studies, political science and government, Spanish language and literature.
Program Information • Faculty members are drawn from the sponsor's U.S. staff and local instructors hired by the sponsor. Scheduled travel to Antofagasta, Concepción; field trips to Valparaíso.
Sessions • Fall, spring.
Eligibility Requirements • Open to sophomores, juniors, seniors; course work in economics, political economy and/or development studies; 2.5 GPA; 2 letters of recommendation; good academic standing at home school; 0.5 years of college course work in Spanish.
Living Arrangements • Students live in host family homes, hotels. Meals are taken as a group, on one's own, with host family, in residences, in restaurants.

Costs (2003-2004) • One term: $12,050; includes tuition, housing, all meals, insurance, excursions, lab equipment, international student ID, student support services. $50 application fee. $400 nonrefundable deposit required. Financial aid available for all students: scholarships.
For More Information • School for International Training, SIT Study Abroad, Kipling Road, Brattleboro, VT 05302-0676; *Phone:* 888-272-7881; *Fax:* 802-258-3296. *E-mail:* studyabroad@sit.edu. *World Wide Web:* http://www.sit.edu/studyabroad/

STATE UNIVERSITY OF NEW YORK AT PLATTSBURGH
LATIN AMERICAN SOUTHERN CONE PROGRAMS, SANTIAGO, WITH MIDDLEBURY COLLEGE

Hosted by Catholic University of Chile, University of Chile
Academic Focus • Full curriculum.
Program Information • Students attend classes at Catholic University of Chile, University of Chile. Field trips to Valparaíso, the Andes Mountains; optional travel to the Lake Region of Chile, Patagonia, Chiloe, Atacama Desert at an extra cost.
Sessions • Fall, spring, yearlong, South American academic year.
Eligibility Requirements • Open to freshmen, sophomores, juniors, seniors, graduate students, adults; 2.5 GPA; 3 letters of recommendation; intermediate-level Spanish.
Living Arrangements • Students live in host family homes. Meals are taken on one's own, with host family, in residences, in restaurants.
Costs (2003-2004) • One term: $7260 for New York residents; $10,235 for nonresidents. Yearlong program: $13,020 for New York residents; $18,970 for nonresidents; includes tuition, housing, all meals, insurance, international airfare, books and class materials, program fee. $20 application fee. $200 nonrefundable deposit required. Financial aid available for all students: scholarships, loans.
For More Information • Ms. Carmen Madariaga Culver, Academic Director, Latin American Southern Cone Programs, State University of New York at Plattsburgh, 101 Broad Street, Plattsburgh, NY 12901-2681; *Phone:* 518-564-2395; *Fax:* 518-564-2300. *E-mail:* socone@plattsburgh.edu. *World Wide Web:* http://www.plattsburgh.edu/studyabroad/

TUFTS UNIVERSITY
TUFTS IN CHILE

Hosted by University of Chile
Academic Focus • Full curriculum.
Program Information • Students attend classes at University of Chile. Field trips to the countryside, copper mines, vineyards, nearby tourist attractions; optional travel to Peru, Bolivia at an extra cost.
Sessions • Fall, yearlong.
Eligibility Requirements • Open to juniors, seniors; 3.0 GPA; 2 letters of recommendation; good academic standing at home school; 3 years of college course work in Spanish.
Living Arrangements • Students live in host family homes. Meals are taken with host family, in residences.
Costs (2004-2005) • One term: $19,657. Yearlong program: $39,314; includes tuition, housing, all meals, excursions, international airfare, books and class materials, student support services, cultural activities, extra-curricular activities, laundry service. $40 application fee. $350 nonrefundable deposit required. Financial aid available for students from sponsoring institution: scholarships, loans.
For More Information • Ms. Melanie Armstrong, Program and Marketing Coordinator, Tufts Programs Abroad, Tufts University, Dowling Hall, Medford, MA 02155-7084; *Phone:* 617-627-2000; *Fax:* 617-627-3971. *E-mail:* melanie.armstrong@tufts.edu. *World Wide Web:* http://ase.tufts.edu/studyabroad/

UNIVERSITY OF MIAMI
CATHOLIC UNIVERSITY OF CHILE PROGRAM

Hosted by Catholic University of Chile
Academic Focus • Latin American studies, mathematics, political science and government, social sciences, Spanish language and literature.

CHILE
Santiago

Program Information • Students attend classes at Catholic University of Chile.
Sessions • Fall, spring, yearlong.
Eligibility Requirements • Minimum age 18; open to sophomores, juniors, seniors; 3.0 GPA; 2 letters of recommendation; good academic standing at home school; language evaluation; personal interview; fluency in Spanish.
Living Arrangements • Students live in locally rented apartments, host family homes. Quarters are shared with host institution students. Meals are taken on one's own, with host family, in central dining facility, in restaurants.
Costs (2003-2004) • One term: $12,919. Yearlong program: $25,838; includes tuition, student support services. $40 application fee. $500 nonrefundable deposit required. Financial aid available for students from sponsoring institution: scholarships, loans.
For More Information • Mr. Chris Tingue, Assistant Director, University of Miami, International Education and Exchange Programs, 5050 Brunson Drive, Allen Hall 212, PO Box 248005, Coral Gables, FL 33124-1610; *Phone:* 305-284-3434; *Fax:* 305-284-4235. *E-mail:* ieep@miami.edu. *World Wide Web:* http://www.studyabroad.miami.edu/

UNIVERSITY OF MIAMI
DIEGO PORTALES UNIVERSITY, CHILE

Hosted by University of Diego Portales
Academic Focus • Full curriculum.
Program Information • Students attend classes at University of Diego Portales.
Sessions • Fall, spring, yearlong.
Eligibility Requirements • Minimum age 18; open to sophomores, juniors, seniors; 2.75 GPA; 2 letters of recommendation; good academic standing at home school; 3 years of college course work in Spanish.

Living Arrangements • Students live in host family homes. Quarters are shared with host institution students. Meals are taken on one's own, with host family, in residences, in restaurants.
Costs (2003-2004) • One term: $12,919. Yearlong program: $25,838; includes tuition, student support services. $40 application fee. $500 nonrefundable deposit required. Financial aid available for students from sponsoring institution: scholarships, loans.
For More Information • Mr. Chris Tingue, Assistant Director, University of Miami, International Education and Exchange Programs, 5050 Brunson Drive, Allen Hall 212, PO Box 248005, Coral Gables, FL 33124-1610; *Phone:* 305-284-3434; *Fax:* 305-284-4235. *E-mail:* ieep@miami.edu. *World Wide Web:* http://www.studyabroad.miami.edu/

UNIVERSITY STUDIES ABROAD CONSORTIUM
SPANISH AND LATIN AMERICAN STUDIES: SANTIAGO, CHILE

Hosted by National University Andres Bello Santiago
Academic Focus • Anthropology, art history, dance, economics, history, Latin American studies, political science and government, Spanish language and literature, Spanish studies, women's studies.
Program Information • Students attend classes at National University Andres Bello Santiago. Field trips to Valle del Mar, Isla Negra, Valparaíso, San José, pre-Andean villages, Pomaire, the Acohcagua Region (San Felipe, Rinconada, Putaendo); optional travel to southern Chile, northern Chile at an extra cost.
Sessions • Fall, spring, yearlong.
Eligibility Requirements • Minimum age 18; open to freshmen, sophomores, juniors, seniors, graduate students, adults; 2.5 GPA; no foreign language proficiency required.
Living Arrangements • Students live in host institution dormitories, host family homes. Quarters are shared with host institution

students. Meals are taken on one's own, with host family, in residences, in central dining facility, in restaurants.
Costs (2005-2006) • One term: $4380. Yearlong program: $7480; includes tuition, some meals, insurance, excursions, student support services. $50 application fee. $150 refundable deposit required. Financial aid available for all students: scholarships, work study, loans.
For More Information • University Studies Abroad Consortium, USAC/323, Reno, NV 89557-0093; *Phone:* 775-784-6569; *Fax:* 775-784-6010. *E-mail:* usac@unr.edu. *World Wide Web:* http://usac. unr.edu/

TEMUCO
STATE UNIVERSITY OF NEW YORK AT PLATTSBURGH
LATIN AMERICAN SOUTHERN CONE PROGRAMS–TEMUCO, WITH MIDDLEBURY COLLEGE

Hosted by Frontier University Temuco
Academic Focus • Full curriculum.
Program Information • Students attend classes at Frontier University Temuco. Field trips to the Lake Region, Atacama Desert, Bio-Bio River Basin; optional travel to Santiago, Patagonia, the Andes Mountains at an extra cost.
Sessions • Fall, spring, yearlong, South American academic year.
Eligibility Requirements • Open to sophomores, juniors, seniors, graduate students, adults; 2.5 GPA; 3 letters of recommendation; intermediate-level Spanish.
Living Arrangements • Students live in host family homes. Meals are taken on one's own, with host family, in residences, in restaurants.
Costs (2003-2004) • One term: $7260 for New York residents; $10,235 for nonresidents. Yearlong program: $13,020 for New York residents; $18,970 for nonresidents; includes tuition, housing, all meals, insurance, international airfare, books and class materials, program fee. $20 application fee. $200 nonrefundable deposit required. Financial aid available for all students: scholarships, loans.
For More Information • Ms. Carmen Madariaga Culver, Academic Director, Latin American Southern Cone Programs, State University of New York at Plattsburgh, 101 Broad Street, Plattsburgh, NY 12901-2661; *Phone:* 518-564-2395; *Fax:* 518-564-2300. *E-mail:* socone@plattsburgh.edu. *World Wide Web:* http://www.plattsburgh. edu/studyabroad/

VALDIVIA
AHA INTERNATIONAL AN ACADEMIC PROGRAM OF THE UNIVERSITY OF OREGON
VALDIVIA, CHILE: NORTHWEST COUNCIL ON STUDY ABROAD (NCSA)

Hosted by Austral University of Chile
Academic Focus • Anthropology, Chilean studies, history, interdisciplinary studies, Latin American studies, Mapuche/Aymara studies, social sciences, Spanish language and literature, Spanish studies.
Program Information • Students attend classes at Austral University of Chile. Scheduled travel to Puerto Varas, Frutillar; field trips to Puerto Montt, Pucón, Isla Huapi, a Mapuche village.
Sessions • Fall, spring, yearlong.
Eligibility Requirements • Open to sophomores, juniors, seniors, adults; good academic standing at home school; language proficiency report; 2 letters of recommendation (1 from language professor); 2 years of college course work in Spanish.
Living Arrangements • Students live in host family homes, a boarding house. Quarters are shared with host institution students. Meals are taken on one's own, with host family, in residences.
Costs (2003-2004) • One term: $4940. Yearlong program: $9880; includes tuition, housing, all meals, insurance, excursions, student support services, airport pick-up, most class materials, reception dinner and overnight hotel stay in Valdivia, visa renewal. $50 application fee. $200 refundable deposit required. Financial aid available for students: scholarships, loans.
For More Information • Ms. Carlotta Troy, Associate Director for University Programs, AHA International An Academic Program of the University of Oregon, 741 SW Lincoln Street, Portland, OR 97201;

Phone: 503-295-7730; *Fax:* 503-295-5969. *E-mail:* mail@aha-intl.org. *World Wide Web:* http://www.aha-intl.org/

STATE UNIVERSITY OF NEW YORK AT PLATTSBURGH
LATIN AMERICAN SOUTHERN CONE PROGRAMS–VALDIVIA, WITH MIDDLEBURY COLLEGE

Hosted by Austral University of Chile
Academic Focus • Full curriculum.
Program Information • Students attend classes at Austral University of Chile. Field trips to the Lake Region, Atacama Desert, Bio-Bio River Basin; optional travel to Santiago, Patagonia, the Andes Mountains at an extra cost.
Sessions • Fall, spring, yearlong, South American academic year.
Eligibility Requirements • Open to sophomores, juniors, seniors, graduate students, adults; 2.5 GPA; 3 letters of recommendation; intermediate-level Spanish.
Living Arrangements • Students live in host family homes. Meals are taken on one's own, with host family, in residences, in restaurants.
Costs (2003-2004) • One term: $7260 for New York residents; $10,235 for nonresidents. Yearlong program: $13,020 for New York residents; $18,970 for nonresidents; includes tuition, housing, all meals, international airfare, program fee. $20 application fee. $200 nonrefundable deposit required. Financial aid available for all students: scholarships, loans.
For More Information • Ms. Carmen Madariaga Culver, Academic Director, Latin American Southern Cone Programs, State University of New York at Plattsburgh, 101 Broad Street, Plattsburgh, NY 12901-2661; *Phone:* 518-564-2395; *Fax:* 518-564-2300. *E-mail:* socone@plattsburgh.edu. *World Wide Web:* http://www.plattsburgh. edu/studyabroad/

VALPARAÍSO
CIEE
CIEE STUDY CENTER AT THE CATHOLIC UNIVERSITY OF VALPARAISO, CHILE

Hosted by Catholic University of Valparaíso
Academic Focus • Art, Chilean studies, education, environmental science/studies, geography, literature, music performance, psychology, Spanish language and literature.
Program Information • Students attend classes at Catholic University of Valparaíso. Scheduled travel to La Serena, Mendoza, Puerto Montt, Argentina, Chiloé Island; field trips to Pablo Neruda's house at Isla Negra, ski resorts near Portillos, Santiago; optional travel to Temuco, Anto Fagasta, Peru, Easter Island, Brazil, Bolivia at an extra cost.
Sessions • Fall, spring, yearlong.
Eligibility Requirements • Minimum age 18; open to sophomores, juniors, seniors, graduate students, adults; 2.75 GPA; 2 letters of recommendation; 3 years of college course work in Spanish.
Living Arrangements • Students live in host family homes. Meals are taken on one's own, with host family, in residences, in central dining facility.
Costs (2004-2005) • One term: $8850. Yearlong program: $15,250; includes tuition, housing, insurance, excursions, student support services, computer and library access at host institution, predeparture advising. $30 application fee. $300 deposit required. Financial aid available for all students: minority student scholarships, travel grants.
For More Information • Ms. Ellen Whitman, Admissions Officer, Spain and Latin America, CIEE, 7 Custom House Street, 3rd Floor, Portland, ME 04101; *Phone:* 800-40-STUDY; *Fax:* 207-553-7699. *E-mail:* studyinfo@ciee.org. *World Wide Web:* http://www.ciee.org/ isp/

INSTITUTE FOR STUDY ABROAD, BUTLER UNIVERSITY
CHILEAN UNIVERSITIES PROGRAM, VALPARAÍSO

Hosted by University of Valparaíso, Catholic University of Valparaíso
Academic Focus • Full curriculum.

CHILE
Valparaíso

Program Information • Students attend classes at University of Valparaíso, Catholic University of Valparaíso. Field trips to La Serena, Isla Negra, Santiago.
Sessions • Fall, spring, yearlong, US academic year.
Eligibility Requirements • Open to sophomores, juniors, seniors; 3.0 GPA; 1 letter of recommendation; good academic standing at home school; enrollment at an accredited American college or university; Spanish language evaluation; 2 years of college course work in Spanish.
Living Arrangements • Students live in host family homes. Meals are taken with host family.
Costs (2003) • One term: $8500. Yearlong program: $14,470; includes tuition, housing, all meals, excursions, international student ID, student support services, cultural and sporting events, pre-departure advising. $40 application fee. $500 nonrefundable deposit required. Financial aid available for all students: scholarships, travel grants.
For More Information • Institute for Study Abroad, Butler University, 1100 West 42nd Street, Suite 305, Indianapolis, IN 46208-3345; *Phone:* 800-858-0229; *Fax:* 317-940-9704. *E-mail:* copa@butler.edu. *World Wide Web:* http://www.ifsa-butler.org/

INTERNATIONAL STUDIES ABROAD
VALPARAÍSO, CHILE

Hosted by Catholic University of Valparaíso
Academic Focus • Full curriculum.
Program Information • Students attend classes at Catholic University of Valparaíso. Scheduled travel to Santiago; field trips to Isla Negra, Horcon, La Serena, Santiago, Valle del Elqui; optional travel to Portillo at an extra cost.
Sessions • Fall, spring, yearlong.
Eligibility Requirements • Minimum age 18; open to precollege students, freshmen, sophomores, juniors, seniors, graduate students, adults; 2.75 GPA; 1 letter of recommendation; transcript; 2.5 years of college course work in Spanish.
Living Arrangements • Students live in locally rented apartments, host family homes, hotels. Meals are taken with host family.
Costs (2004-2005) • One term: $7500. Yearlong program: $14,500; includes tuition, housing, all meals, insurance, excursions, student support services, ground transportation, tutoring. $200 nonrefundable deposit required. Financial aid available for all students: scholarships, loans, U.S. federal financial aid via consortium agreement.
For More Information • Ms. Rose Mankins, Chile Site Specialist, International Studies Abroad, 901 West 24th Street, Austin, TX 78705; *Phone:* 800-580-8826; *Fax:* 512-480-8866. *E-mail:* isa@studiesabroad.com. *World Wide Web:* http://www.studiesabroad.com/

STATE UNIVERSITY OF NEW YORK AT PLATTSBURGH
LATIN AMERICAN SOUTHERN CONE PROGRAMS, VALPARAÍSO, WITH MIDDLEBURY COLLEGE

Hosted by Adolfo Ibañez' University, University of Valparaíso, University of Educational Sciences 'Playa Ancha' Valparaíso, Catholic University of Valparaíso
Academic Focus • Full curriculum.
Program Information • Students attend classes at Adolfo Ibañez' University, University of Valparaíso, University of Educational Sciences 'Playa Ancha' Valparaíso, Catholic University of Valparaíso. Field trips to Santiago, the Andes Mountains; optional travel to the Lake Region of Chile, Patagonia, Chiloe, Atacama Desert at an extra cost.
Sessions • Fall, spring, yearlong, South American academic year.
Eligibility Requirements • Minimum age 18; open to sophomores, juniors, seniors, graduate students, adults; 2.5 GPA; 3 letters of recommendation; intermediate-level Spanish.
Living Arrangements • Students live in host family homes. Meals are taken on one's own, with host family, in residences, in restaurants.
Costs (2003-2004) • One term: $7260 for New York residents; $10,235 for nonresidents. Yearlong program: $13,020 for New York residents; $18,970 for nonresidents; includes tuition, housing, all meals, insurance, international airfare, books and class materials,

program fee. $20 application fee. $200 nonrefundable deposit required. Financial aid available for all students: scholarships, loans.
For More Information • Ms. Carmen Madariaga Culver, Academic Director, Latin American Southern Cone Programs, State University of New York at Plattsburgh, 101 Broad Street, Plattsburgh, NY 12901-2681; *Phone:* 518-564-2395; *Fax:* 518-564-2300. *E-mail:* socone@plattsburgh.edu. *World Wide Web:* http://www.plattsburgh.edu/studyabroad/

VIÑA DEL MAR
HARDING UNIVERSITY
HARDING UNIVERSITY IN LATIN AMERICA

Academic Focus • Liberal studies, religious studies, Spanish language and literature.
Program Information • Faculty members are drawn from the sponsor's U.S. staff. Scheduled travel to Portillo, Atacama, Machu Picchu; field trips.
Sessions • Fall.
Eligibility Requirements • Open to sophomores, juniors, seniors; 2.0 GPA; good academic standing at home school; no foreign language proficiency required.
Living Arrangements • Students live in locally rented apartments. Meals are taken as a group.
Costs (2004) • One term: $13,000; includes tuition, housing, all meals, excursions, international airfare, international student ID. $200 application fee. Financial aid available for students from sponsoring institution: scholarships, work study, loans.
For More Information • Dr. Jeffrey T. Hopper, Dean of International Programs, Harding University, 900 East Center Street, Box 10754, Searcy, AR 72149; *Phone:* 501-279-4529; *Fax:* 501-279-4184. *E-mail:* intlprograms@harding.edu

CHINA
CITY TO CITY
STATE UNIVERSITY OF NEW YORK COLLEGE AT BROCKPORT
CHINA: THREE CITIES PROGRAM

Hosted by University of Hong Kong, Beijing University, Shanghai Jiaotong University
Academic Focus • Accounting, art, Asian studies, business administration/management, Chinese language and literature, Chinese studies, cultural studies, economics, finance, history, international affairs, international business, political science and government.
Program Information • Students attend classes at University of Hong Kong (Hong Kong), Beijing University (Beijing), Shanghai Jiaotong University (Shanghai). Field trips to Shanghai, Beijing, Hong Kong.
Sessions • Fall, spring, yearlong.
Eligibility Requirements • Minimum age 18; open to juniors, seniors, graduate students; course work in area of internship, if applicable; 2.75 GPA; 2 letters of recommendation; good academic standing at home school; résumé for internship option; basic knowledge of Chinese recommended.
Living Arrangements • Students live in host institution dormitories, hotels. Quarters are shared with students from other programs. Meals are taken as a group, on one's own, in residences, in restaurants.
Costs (2003-2004) • One term: $13,550. Yearlong program: contact sponsor for cost; includes tuition, housing, some meals, insurance, excursions, international student ID, student support services, program-related travel within China, visa fees, tutoring, group activities, embassy registration. $350 nonrefundable deposit required. Financial aid available for all students: scholarships, loans, regular financial aid, grants.
For More Information • Dr. John Perry, Director, Office of International Education, State University of New York College at Brockport, 350 New Campus Drive, Brockport, NY 14420; *Phone:*

800-298-SUNY; *Fax:* 585-637-3218. *E-mail:* overseas@brockport.edu. *World Wide Web:* http://www.brockport.edu/studyabroad/

BEIJING

AMERICAN UNIVERSITY
SEMESTER IN BEIJING/HONG KONG

Hosted by Beijing University
Academic Focus • Business administration/management, Chinese language and literature, Chinese studies, economics, political science and government.
Program Information • Students attend classes at Beijing University. Scheduled travel to Hong Kong, Guangdong Province, Guilin; field trips to the Great Wall, the Forbidden City.
Sessions • Fall.
Eligibility Requirements • Open to sophomores, juniors, seniors, graduate students; 2.75 GPA; 1 letter of recommendation; second semester sophomore status; recommendation of advisor; no foreign language proficiency required.
Living Arrangements • Students live in host institution dormitories, hotels. Quarters are shared with host institution students. Meals are taken on one's own, in restaurants.
Costs (2001) • One term: $16,084; includes tuition, housing, some meals, insurance, excursions, books and class materials, student support services. $35 application fee. $300 nonrefundable deposit required. Financial aid available for all students: scholarships, loans.
For More Information • Dr. David C. Brown, Dean, Washington Semester and World Capitals Programs, American University, Tenley Campus–Constitution Building, Washington, DC 20016-8083; *Phone:* 800-424-2600; *Fax:* 202-895-4960. *E-mail:* travel@american.edu. *World Wide Web:* http://www.worldcapitals.american.edu/

ASSOCIATED COLLEGES IN CHINA
ASSOCIATED COLLEGES IN CHINA

Held at Capital University of Economics and Business
Academic Focus • Chinese language and literature.
Program Information • Classes are held on the campus of Capital University of Economics and Business. Faculty members are drawn from the sponsor's U.S. staff and local instructors hired by the sponsor. Scheduled travel to Hainan Island, Shanxi Province, Jiangsu Province; field trips to Datong, Suzhou, Shanghai, Xi'an; optional travel to Inner Mongolia, Sichuan, Tibet, Yunnan at an extra cost.
Sessions • Fall, spring, yearlong, both summer and fall terms.
Eligibility Requirements • Minimum age 18; open to sophomores, juniors, seniors, graduate students; course work in Chinese culture; 3.0 GPA; 2 letters of recommendation; good academic standing at home school; 1 year college course work in Chinese for spring term; 2 years for fall term.
Living Arrangements • Students live in host institution dormitories. Quarters are shared with host institution students. Meals are taken on one's own, in restaurants.
Costs (2005-2006) • One term: $9630 ; $14,360 for two terms. Yearlong program: $19,180; includes tuition, housing, excursions, books and class materials, lab equipment, student support services. $40 application fee. $600 nonrefundable deposit required. Financial aid available for all students: scholarships.
For More Information • Ms. Amy James, Program Coordinator, Associated Colleges in China, Hamilton College, 198 College Hill Road, Clinton, NY 13323; *Phone:* 315-859-4326; *Fax:* 315-859-4687. *E-mail:* acchina@hamilton.edu. *World Wide Web:* http://www.hamilton.edu/academics/eal/abroad_link.html

BOSTON UNIVERSITY
BEIJING INTERNSHIP PROGRAM

Hosted by CET Language Training Center, CET Language Training Center, Harbin Institute of Technology
Academic Focus • Chinese language and literature, Chinese studies.
Program Information • Students attend classes at Harbin Institute of Technology, CET Language Training Center, CET Language Training Center. Classes are also held on the campus of Beijing Institute of Education. Scheduled travel to Tianjin, Shanghai, Datong; field trips to historic and cultural sites in Beijing/Harbin.
Sessions • Fall, spring.

Eligibility Requirements • Open to sophomores, juniors, seniors, graduate students, adults; 3.0 GPA; 2 letters of recommendation; good academic standing at home school; essay; transcript; writing sample; interview in Chinese; 2 years of college course work in Chinese.
Living Arrangements • Students live in host institution dormitories. Quarters are shared with host institution students. Meals are taken as a group, on one's own, in central dining facility, in restaurants.
Costs (2004-2005) • One term: $19,834; includes tuition, housing, all meals, insurance, excursions, international airfare, books and class materials, medical evacuation insurance, internship placement, visa fees. $50 application fee. $400 nonrefundable deposit required. Financial aid available for all students: scholarships, loans.
For More Information • Division of International Programs, Boston University, 232 Bay State Road, Boston, MA 02215; *Phone:* 617-353-9888; *Fax:* 617-353-5402. *E-mail:* abroad@bu.edu. *World Wide Web:* http://www.bu.edu/abroad/

CALVIN COLLEGE
SEMESTER IN CHINA

Hosted by Beijing Institute of Technology
Academic Focus • Chinese language and literature, Chinese studies.
Program Information • Students attend classes at Beijing Institute of Technology. Scheduled travel to Xi'an, Shanghai, Kaifeng, Luoyang; field trips to the Great Wall, Ming Tombs, Confucian, Buddhist, and Taoist temples, museums.
Sessions • Fall.
Eligibility Requirements • Open to sophomores, juniors, seniors; 2.5 GPA; 2 letters of recommendation; good academic standing at home school; advisor approval; no foreign language proficiency required.
Living Arrangements • Students live in host institution dormitories. Quarters are shared with host institution students. Meals are taken on one's own, in central dining facility, in restaurants.
Costs (2003-2004) • One term: $11,450; includes tuition, housing, all meals, excursions, international airfare, student support services, immunizations, physical exam. $50 application fee. $400 nonrefundable deposit required. Financial aid available for students from sponsoring institution: scholarships, loans.
For More Information • Dr. Ellen B. Monsma, Director, Calvin College, Office of Off-Campus Programs, 3201 Burton Street, SE, Grand Rapids, MI 49546; *Phone:* 616-526-6551; *Fax:* 616-526-6756. *E-mail:* emonsma@calvin.edu. *World Wide Web:* http://www.calvin.edu/academic/off-campus/

CENTER FOR STUDY ABROAD (CSA)
BEIJING LANGUAGE AND CULTURE UNIVERSITY

Hosted by Beijing Language and Culture University
Academic Focus • Chinese language and literature, Chinese studies.
Program Information • Students attend classes at Beijing Language and Culture University. Optional travel to Beijing tourist attractions, Datong, Tianjin, Chengde at an extra cost.
Sessions • Fall, spring, yearlong.
Eligibility Requirements • Minimum age 17; open to freshmen, sophomores, juniors, seniors, graduate students, adults; good health; no foreign language proficiency required.
Living Arrangements • Students live in host institution dormitories. Quarters are shared with students from other programs. Meals are taken on one's own, in central dining facility.
Costs (2003-2004) • One term: contact sponsor for cost. Yearlong program: contact sponsor for cost. $45 application fee.
For More Information • Ms. Alima K. Virtue, Program Director, Center for Study Abroad (CSA), 325 Washington Avenue South, #93, Kent, WA 98032; *Phone:* 206-726-1498; *Fax:* 253-850-0454. *E-mail:* info@centerforstudyabroad.com. *World Wide Web:* http://www.centerforstudyabroad.com/

CIEE
CIEE STUDY CENTER AT PEKING UNIVERSITY, BEIJING, CHINA

Hosted by Peking University
Academic Focus • Chinese language and literature, Chinese studies, history.

Program Information • Students attend classes at Peking University. Scheduled travel to Xi'an, other cities; field trips to the Great Wall, the Forbidden City, the Summer Palace, Tiananmen Square, Ming Tombs.

Sessions • Fall, spring, yearlong.

Eligibility Requirements • Open to sophomores, juniors, seniors, adults; course work in Asian studies (1 course); 2.75 GPA; 2 letters of recommendation; good academic standing at home school; 1 year of college course work in Chinese.

Living Arrangements • Students live in host institution dormitories. Meals are taken on one's own, in central dining facility, in restaurants.

Costs (2004-2005) • One term: $8250. Yearlong program: $15,800; includes tuition, housing, insurance, excursions, student support services, visa fees, cultural activities, pre-departure advising. $30 application fee. $300 deposit required. Financial aid available for all students: scholarships, minority student scholarships, Department of Education grants, travel grants.

For More Information • Mr. Adam Rubin, Admissions Officer, Asia Pacific, CIEE, 7 Custom House Street, 3rd Floor, Portland, ME 04101; *Phone:* 800-40-STUDY; *Fax:* 207-553-7699. *E-mail:* studyinfo@ciee. org. *World Wide Web:* http://www.ciee.org/isp/

DICKINSON COLLEGE
DICKINSON IN BEIJING (CHINA)

Hosted by Peking University
Academic Focus • Chinese language and literature, Chinese studies.
Program Information • Students attend classes at Peking University. Scheduled travel to other sites in China; field trips to Beijing.

Sessions • Fall, yearlong.

Eligibility Requirements • Minimum age 18; open to juniors, seniors; 2.8 GPA; 3 letters of recommendation; good academic standing at home school; 2 years of college course work in Mandarin Chinese.

Living Arrangements • Students live in host institution dormitories. Quarters are shared with host institution students. Meals are taken on one's own, in central dining facility, in restaurants.

Costs (2003-2004) • One term: $12,010. Yearlong program: $23,900; includes tuition, housing, excursions, transcripts. $25 application fee. $300 nonrefundable deposit required. Financial aid available for students from sponsoring institution: scholarships, loans.

For More Information • Ms. Karen Peter, Program Manager, Dickinson College, PO Box 1773, Carlisle, PA 17013-2896; *Phone:* 717-245-1341; *Fax:* 717-245-1688. *E-mail:* global@dickinson.edu. *World Wide Web:* http://www.dickinson.edu/global/

IES, INSTITUTE FOR THE INTERNATIONAL EDUCATION OF STUDENTS
IES–BEIJING

Hosted by Institute for the International Education of Students (IES)–Beijing, Beijing University of Foreign Studies
Academic Focus • Anthropology, business administration/management, Chinese language and literature, Chinese studies, economics, history, Kazakh, literature, philosophy, political science and government, religious studies, Tibetan.
Program Information • Students attend classes at Beijing University of Foreign Studies, Institute for the International Education of Students (IES)–Beijing. Scheduled travel to the Yunnan Province, Tibet, Xi'an, Shandong Province, Huxian, the Henan province; field trips to Datong, Chengde.

Sessions • Fall, spring, yearlong.

Eligibility Requirements • Minimum age 18; open to sophomores, juniors, seniors, graduate students, adults; 3.0 GPA; 1 letter of recommendation; good academic standing at home school; no foreign language proficiency required.

Living Arrangements • Students live in host institution dormitories, host family homes. Meals are taken on one's own, with host family, in residences, in central dining facility, in restaurants.

Costs (2003-2004) • One term: $9300. Yearlong program: $16,740; includes tuition, housing, excursions, student support services, partial insurance coverage. $50 application fee. $500 nonrefundable deposit required. Financial aid available for all students: scholarships, institutional partner need-based grants.

For More Information • International Education Representative, IES, Institute for the International Education of Students, 33 North LaSalle Street, 15th Floor, Chicago, IL 60602; *Phone:* 800-995-2300; *Fax:* 312-944-1448. *E-mail:* info@iesabroad.org. *World Wide Web:* http://www.IESabroad.org/

LOCK HAVEN UNIVERSITY OF PENNSYLVANIA
SEMESTER IN BEIJING

Hosted by Beijing Institute of Business
Academic Focus • Chinese studies, fine/studio arts.
Program Information • Students attend classes at Beijing Institute of Business.

Sessions • Fall, spring, yearlong.

Eligibility Requirements • Minimum age 18; open to sophomores, juniors, seniors, adults; 2.5 GPA; 3 letters of recommendation; good academic standing at home school; transcript; no foreign language proficiency required.

Living Arrangements • Students live in host institution dormitories, locally rented apartments. Quarters are shared with students from other programs. Meals are taken in central dining facility.

Costs (2002-2003) • One term: $5450 for Pennsylvania residents; $7360 for nonresidents. Yearlong program: $10,900 for Pennsylvania residents; $14,720 for nonresidents; includes tuition, housing, all meals. $50 application fee. Financial aid available for students from sponsoring institution: scholarships, loans.

For More Information • Dean, Institute for International Studies, Lock Haven University of Pennsylvania, Lock Haven, PA 17745-2390; *Phone:* 570-893-2140; *Fax:* 570-893-2537. *E-mail:* intlstudies_webmonitor@lhup.edu. *World Wide Web:* http://www.lhup.edu/international/goingp/goingplaces_index.htm

PITZER COLLEGE
PITZER COLLEGE IN CHINA

Hosted by Beijing University
Academic Focus • Chinese language and literature, Chinese studies, cultural studies, film and media studies, medicine.
Program Information • Students attend classes at Beijing University. Scheduled travel to Wu Taishan, Ping Yao, Nanjing, Shanghai, Suzhou, Huapen; field trips to the Great Wall, the Forbidden City, the Summer Palace, Da Yue Temple; optional travel to Chongqing/Three Gorges, Guilin/Yang Shuo, Hainan Island at an extra cost.

Sessions • Fall, spring, yearlong.

Eligibility Requirements • Open to sophomores, juniors, seniors; course work in area studies; 2.5 GPA; 2 letters of recommendation; good academic standing at home school; previous Chinese study recommended.

Living Arrangements • Students live in host institution dormitories, locally rented apartments, host family homes. Quarters are shared with host institution students. Meals are taken on one's own, with host family, in residences, in central dining facility, in restaurants.

Costs (2003-2004) • One term: $18,795. Yearlong program: $37,590; includes tuition, housing, all meals, excursions, international airfare, books and class materials, international student ID, student support services, evacuation insurance. $25 application fee. $500 nonrefundable deposit required. Financial aid available for students from sponsoring institution: scholarships, loans.

For More Information • Ms. Neva Barker, Director of External Studies Admissions, Pitzer College, 1050 North Mills Avenue, Claremont, CA 91711; *Phone:* 909-621-8104; *Fax:* 909-621-0518. *E-mail:* external_studies@pitzer.edu. *World Wide Web:* http://www.pitzer.edu/external_studies/

SANN RESEARCH INSTITUTE
SEMESTER IN CHINA

Hosted by International College Beijing
Academic Focus • Full curriculum.
Program Information • Students attend classes at International College Beijing. Scheduled travel to Tibet; field trips to the Great Wall, Tiananmen Square, the Forbidden City; optional travel to Thailand, Nepal at an extra cost.

Sessions • Fall, spring.

Eligibility Requirements • Minimum age 18; open to freshmen, sophomores, juniors, seniors; 2.5 GPA; good health; no foreign language proficiency required.
Living Arrangements • Students live in host institution dormitories. Meals are taken as a group, in central dining facility, in restaurants.
Costs (2003-2004) • One term: $7780; includes tuition, housing, all meals, excursions. $475 application fee. $500 refundable deposit required.
For More Information • Narayan Shrestha, President, Sann Research Institute, 948 Pearl Street, Boulder, CO 80302; *Phone:* 303-449-4279; *Fax:* 303-440-7328. *E-mail:* info@sannr.com. *World Wide Web:* http://www.sannr.com/

SKIDMORE COLLEGE
SKIDMORE IN BEIJING

Hosted by Skidmore Program Center, Peking University
Academic Focus • Area studies, art history, Chinese language and literature, Chinese studies, cultural studies, history, interdisciplinary studies, popular culture.
Program Information • Students attend classes at Peking University, Skidmore Program Center. Scheduled travel to outside of Beijing; field trips to outside of Beijing.
Sessions • Fall.
Eligibility Requirements • Course work in Chinese studies (preferred); 3.0 GPA; 2 letters of recommendation; good academic standing at home school; 1 year of college course work in Chinese.
Living Arrangements • Students live in host institution dormitories, host family homes. Quarters are shared with students from other programs. Meals are taken on one's own, in central dining facility.
Costs (2004) • One term: contact sponsor for cost. $25 application fee. $350 nonrefundable deposit required. Financial aid available for students from sponsoring institution: scholarships, loans.
For More Information • Skidmore College, Office of International Programs, 815 North Broadway, Starbuck Center, Saratoga Springs, NY 12866; *Phone:* 518-580 Ext. 5355; *Fax:* 518-580 Ext. 5359. *E-mail:* oip@skidmore.edu. *World Wide Web:* http://www.skidmore.edu/internationalprograms/

STATE UNIVERSITY OF NEW YORK AT BUFFALO
PROGRAM OF CHINESE LANGUAGE AND CULTURE

Hosted by Capital Normal University
Academic Focus • Chinese language and literature, Chinese studies, cultural studies.
Program Information • Students attend classes at Capital Normal University. Field trips to historic points of interest in/around Beijing.
Sessions • Fall, spring, yearlong.
Eligibility Requirements • Minimum age 18; open to sophomores, juniors, seniors, graduate students, adults; 3.0 GPA; 3 letters of recommendation; good academic standing at home school; 1 year college course work in Mandarin Chinese or the equivalent.
Living Arrangements • Students live in host institution dormitories, international residence halls. Quarters are shared with students from other programs. Meals are taken on one's own, in central dining facility.
Costs (2002-2003) • One term: $4500. Yearlong program: $9000; includes tuition, housing, some meals, student support services. $300 nonrefundable deposit required. Financial aid available for all students: scholarships, federal and New York State financial aid.
For More Information • Dr. Sandra J. Flash, Director of Study Abroad Programs, State University of New York at Buffalo, 210 Talbert Hall, Box 601604, Buffalo, NY 14260-1604; *Phone:* 716-645-3912; *Fax:* 716-645-6197. *E-mail:* studyabroad@buffalo.edu. *World Wide Web:* http://www.buffalo.edu/studyabroad/

STATE UNIVERSITY OF NEW YORK AT OSWEGO
CAPITAL NORMAL UNIVERSITY

Hosted by Capital Normal University
Academic Focus • Art, Chinese language and literature, Chinese studies, history.

Program Information • Students attend classes at Capital Normal University. Optional travel to Tiananmen Square, the Forbidden City at an extra cost.
Sessions • Fall, spring, yearlong.
Eligibility Requirements • Open to sophomores, juniors, seniors; 2.5 GPA; 3 letters of recommendation; good academic standing at home school; personal statement; no foreign language proficiency required.
Living Arrangements • Students live in host institution dormitories. Quarters are shared with students from other programs. Meals are taken on one's own, in central dining facility, in restaurants.
Costs (2003-2004) • One term: $4420. Yearlong program: $8840; includes tuition, housing, all meals, insurance, student support services. $250 nonrefundable deposit required. Financial aid available for students: home university financial aid, loan processing and scholarships for Oswego students.
For More Information • Ms. Nefertitti Saheed, Program Specialist, State University of New York at Oswego, 122A Swetman Hall, Oswego, NY 13126; *Phone:* 888-4-OSWEGO; *Fax:* 315-312-2477. *E-mail:* intled@oswego.edu. *World Wide Web:* http://www.oswego.edu/intled/

STATE UNIVERSITY OF NEW YORK COLLEGE AT CORTLAND
BEIJING–CAPITAL NORMAL UNIVERSITY

Hosted by Capital Normal University
Academic Focus • Chinese language and literature, Chinese studies, fine/studio arts, liberal studies, music performance.
Program Information • Students attend classes at Capital Normal University. Field trips to the Great Wall, the Peking Opera, a Peking acrobat show; optional travel to Xi'an, Shanghai at an extra cost.
Sessions • Fall, spring, yearlong.
Eligibility Requirements • Minimum age 18; open to sophomores, juniors, seniors, graduate students; 2.5 GPA; 3 letters of recommendation; good academic standing at home school; 1 year course work in Mandarin Chinese recommended.
Living Arrangements • Students live in host institution dormitories, hotels. Quarters are shared with students from other programs. Meals are taken on one's own, in central dining facility, in restaurants.
Costs (2003-2004) • One term: $8015. Yearlong program: contact sponsor for cost; includes tuition, housing, all meals, excursions, international airfare, books and class materials, international student ID, student support services, passport and visa fees. $20 application fee. $250 nonrefundable deposit required. Financial aid available for students from sponsoring institution: scholarships, loans.
For More Information • Ms. Liz Kopp, Assistant Director, Office of International Programs, State University of New York College at Cortland, PO Box 2000, Cortland, NY 13045; *Phone:* 607-753-2209; *Fax:* 607-753-5989. *E-mail:* cortlandabroad@cortland.edu. *World Wide Web:* http://www.studyabroad.com/suny/cortland/

STATE UNIVERSITY OF NEW YORK COLLEGE AT CORTLAND
BEIJING TEACHERS COLLEGE OF PHYSICAL EDUCATION

Hosted by Beijing Teachers College of Physical Education
Academic Focus • Health and physical education, parks and recreation.
Program Information • Students attend classes at Beijing Teachers College of Physical Education.
Sessions • Fall, spring, yearlong.
Eligibility Requirements • Minimum age 18; open to juniors, seniors, graduate students; 2.5 GPA; 3 letters of recommendation; good academic standing at home school; college major or minor in physical education; 2 years of college course work in Chinese.
Living Arrangements • Students live in host institution dormitories, locally rented apartments. Quarters are shared with host institution students. Meals are taken on one's own, in central dining facility.
Costs (2002-2003) • One term: $4500. Yearlong program: $8500; includes housing, all meals, insurance, international airfare, books and class materials, international student ID, passport and visa fees. $20 application fee. $250 nonrefundable deposit required. Financial aid available for students from sponsoring institution: scholarships, loans.

For More Information • Ms. Liz Kopp, Assistant Director, Office of International Programs, State University of New York College at Cortland, PO Box 2000, Cortland, NY 13045; *Phone:* 607-753-2209; *Fax:* 607-753-5989. *E-mail:* cortlandabroad@cortland.edu. *World Wide Web:* http://www.studyabroad.com/suny/cortland/

UNIVERSITY AT ALBANY, STATE UNIVERSITY OF NEW YORK
LANGUAGE AND CULTURAL STUDIES AT BEIJING NORMAL UNIVERSITY

Hosted by Beijing Normal University
Academic Focus • Chinese language and literature, Chinese studies, liberal studies.
Program Information • Students attend classes at Beijing Normal University.
Sessions • Fall, spring, yearlong.
Eligibility Requirements • Open to sophomores, juniors, seniors, adults; 2 letters of recommendation; good academic standing at home school; 1 year of course work in Mandarin Chinese strongly recommended.
Living Arrangements • Students live in host institution dormitories. Quarters are shared with students from other programs. Meals are taken on one's own, in central dining facility.
Costs (2002-2003) • One term: $4736. Yearlong program: $9472; includes housing, all meals, student support services, in-state tuition and fees. $150 nonrefundable deposit required. Financial aid available for students from sponsoring institution: all customary sources.
For More Information • University at Albany, State University of New York, Office of International Education, LI 66, Albany, NY 12222; *Phone:* 518-442-3525; *Fax:* 518-442-3338. *E-mail:* intled@uamail.albany.edu. *World Wide Web:* http://www.albany.edu/intled/

UNIVERSITY AT ALBANY, STATE UNIVERSITY OF NEW YORK
LANGUAGE AND CULTURAL STUDIES AT PEKING UNIVERSITY

Hosted by Peking University
Academic Focus • Chinese language and literature, Chinese studies, full curriculum, liberal studies.
Program Information • Students attend classes at Peking University.
Sessions • Fall, spring, yearlong.
Eligibility Requirements • Open to sophomores, juniors, seniors, adults; 2 letters of recommendation; good academic standing at home school; 1 year college course work in Mandarin Chinese for language program; fluency in Mandarin Chinese for direct enrollment in host university courses.
Living Arrangements • Students live in host institution dormitories. Quarters are shared with students from other programs. Meals are taken on one's own, in central dining facility.
Costs (2002-2003) • One term: $3013. Yearlong program: $6026; includes housing, all meals, student support services, in-state tuition and fees. $150 nonrefundable deposit required. Financial aid available for students from sponsoring institution: all customary sources.
For More Information • University at Albany, State University of New York, Office of International Education, LI 66, Albany, NY 12222; *Phone:* 518-442-3525; *Fax:* 518-442-3338. *E-mail:* intled@uamail.albany.edu. *World Wide Web:* http://www.albany.edu/intled/

CHANGSHA
LOCK HAVEN UNIVERSITY OF PENNSYLVANIA
SEMESTER IN CHANGSHA

Hosted by Changsha University of Water and Electric Power
Academic Focus • Chinese language and literature, Chinese studies, cultural studies, fine/studio arts, history, social sciences.
Program Information • Students attend classes at Changsha University of Water and Electric Power.
Sessions • Fall, spring, yearlong.

Eligibility Requirements • Minimum age 18; open to freshmen, sophomores, juniors, adults; 2.5 GPA; 3 letters of recommendation; good academic standing at home school; transcript; no foreign language proficiency required.
Living Arrangements • Students live in host institution dormitories, locally rented apartments. Meals are taken in central dining facility.
Costs (2002-2003) • One term: $5450 for Pennsylvania residents; $7360 for nonresidents. Yearlong program: $10,900 for Pennsylvania residents; $14,720 for nonresidents; includes tuition, housing, all meals, fees. $50 application fee. Financial aid available for students from sponsoring institution: scholarships, loans.
For More Information • Dean, Institute for International Studies, Lock Haven University of Pennsylvania, Lock Haven, PA 17745-2390; *Phone:* 570-893-2140; *Fax:* 570-893-2537. *E-mail:* intlstudies_webmonitor@lhup.edu. *World Wide Web:* http://www.lhup.edu/international/goingp/goingplaces_index.htm

CHENGDU
UNIVERSITY STUDIES ABROAD CONSORTIUM
CHINESE STUDIES AND EDUCATION: CHENGDU, CHINA

Hosted by Southwest University for Nationalities
Academic Focus • Art, Asian studies, Chinese language and literature, Chinese studies, culinary arts, cultural studies, economics, education, health and physical education, history, political science and government.
Program Information • Students attend classes at Southwest University for Nationalities. Field trips to Leshan, Emei Shan, a Panda Research Institute, the Sanxigdu Museum, a Chengdu City tour, Baoguang Temple, Dayi, Dujiangyhan, Qiang, the Yellow Dragon River, the Green City Mountain; optional travel to Beijing, Tibet, Shanghai at an extra cost.
Sessions • Fall, spring, yearlong.
Eligibility Requirements • Minimum age 18; open to freshmen, sophomores, juniors, seniors, graduate students, adults; 2.5 GPA; no foreign language proficiency required.
Living Arrangements • Students live in host institution dormitories. Quarters are shared with host institution students. Meals are taken on one's own, in central dining facility, in restaurants.
Costs (2005-2006) • One term: $4260. Yearlong program: $6860; includes tuition, housing, insurance, excursions, student support services. $50 application fee. $150 refundable deposit required. Financial aid available for all students: scholarships, loans.
For More Information • University Studies Abroad Consortium, USAC/323, Reno, NV 89557-0093; *Phone:* 775-784-6569; *Fax:* 775-784-6010. *E-mail:* usac@unr.edu. *World Wide Web:* http://usac.unr.edu/

DALIAN
BRETHREN COLLEGES ABROAD
BCA PROGRAM IN DALIAN, CHINA

Hosted by Dalian University of Foreign Languages
Academic Focus • Accounting, art, Asian studies, Chinese language and literature, Chinese studies, communications, drama/theater, drawing/painting, East Asian studies, Far Eastern languages, film and media studies, fine/studio arts, geography, health and physical education, history, intercultural studies, Japanese, music, music performance, philosophy, political science and government, religious studies, Russian language and literature.
Program Information • Students attend classes at Dalian University of Foreign Languages. Scheduled travel to the Sichuan province, southern China, Beijing; field trips to factories, rural areas, a special economic zone.
Sessions • Fall, yearlong.
Eligibility Requirements • Minimum age 18; open to sophomores, juniors, seniors, graduate students, adults; 2.6 GPA; 3 letters of recommendation; good academic standing at home school; no foreign language proficiency required.
Living Arrangements • Students live in host institution dormitories. Quarters are shared with host institution students. Meals are taken on one's own, in central dining facility, in restaurants.

Costs (2004-2005) • One term: contact sponsor for cost. Yearlong program: contact sponsor for cost. $50 application fee. $100 nonrefundable deposit required.

For More Information • Mr. Thomas V. Millington, Program Officer for China, Brethren Colleges Abroad, 50 Alpha Drive, Elizabethtown, PA 17022-0407; *Phone:* 717-361-6600; *Fax:* 717-361-6619. *E-mail:* info@bcanet.org. *World Wide Web:* http://www.bcanet.org/

HANGZHOU
CENTRAL COLLEGE ABROAD
CENTRAL COLLEGE ABROAD IN HANGZHOU, CHINA

Hosted by Zhejiang University

Academic Focus • Chinese language and literature, drawing/painting, economics, geography, history, political science and government, religious studies.

Program Information • Students attend classes at Zhejiang University. Scheduled travel to Beijing, Shanghai, Suzhou; field trips to Shaoxing; optional travel to University-led excursions at an extra cost.

Sessions • Spring.

Eligibility Requirements • Minimum age 18; open to sophomores, juniors, seniors; 2.5 GPA; 2 letters of recommendation; good academic standing at home school; study abroad approval form; transcript; Student Life endorsement; no foreign language proficiency required.

Living Arrangements • Students live in host institution dormitories. Quarters are shared with host institution students, students from other programs. Meals are taken on one's own, in central dining facility, in restaurants.

Costs (2004) • One term: $9650; includes tuition, housing, all meals, excursions, international student ID, student support services. $25 application fee. $350 nonrefundable deposit required. Financial aid available for all students: scholarships.

For More Information • Office of International Education, Central College Abroad, 812 University Street, Pella, IA 50219; *Phone:* 800-831-3629; *Fax:* 641-628-5375. *E-mail:* studyabroad@central.edu. *World Wide Web:* http://www.central.edu/abroad/

DUKE UNIVERSITY
DUKE STUDY IN CHINA PROGRAM

Hosted by Zhejiang University

Academic Focus • Chinese language and literature, history, literature.

Program Information • Students attend classes at Zhejiang University. Scheduled travel to Xi'an, Changsha, Wuhan; field trips to Ming Tombs, the Great Wall, Chengde, Datong; optional travel to Shanghai, Suzhou at an extra cost.

Sessions • Fall.

Eligibility Requirements • Minimum age 19; open to sophomores, juniors, seniors; 2.7 GPA; 2 letters of recommendation; good academic standing at home school; transcript; 1 year of college course work in Chinese.

Living Arrangements • Students live in host institution dormitories, locally rented apartments. Quarters are shared with host institution students. Meals are taken on one's own, in central dining facility, in restaurants.

Costs (2003) • One term: $14,850; includes tuition, housing, some meals, insurance, excursions, books and class materials, student support services, visa fees. $2000 nonrefundable deposit required. Financial aid available for students from sponsoring institution: loans, grants.

For More Information • Ms. Debbie Hunt, Asian/ Pacific Studies Institute, Duke University, 2111 Campus Drive, Box 90411, Durham, NC 27708-0411; *Phone:* 919-684-2604; *Fax:* 919-684-6247. *E-mail:* ddhunt@duke.edu. *World Wide Web:* http://www.aas.duke.edu/study_abroad/

LONG ISLAND UNIVERSITY
FRIENDS WORLD PROGRAM–CHINA

Hosted by Friends World Program China Center

Academic Focus • Anthropology, Chinese language and literature, Chinese studies, environmental science/studies, interdisciplinary studies, peace and conflict studies, philosophy, religious studies.

Program Information • Students attend classes at Friends World Program China Center. Scheduled travel to Beijing, the Yunnan Province; field trips to Hangzhou sites, Suzhou; optional travel to Korea, Thailand, Mongolia at an extra cost.

Sessions • Fall, spring, yearlong.

Eligibility Requirements • Minimum age 18; open to sophomores, juniors, seniors, adults; good academic standing at home school; interview; essay; no foreign language proficiency required.

Living Arrangements • Students live in host institution dormitories. Quarters are shared with host institution students. Meals are taken as a group, on one's own, in residences, in central dining facility, in restaurants.

Costs (2004-2005) • One term: contact sponsor for cost. Yearlong program: contact sponsor for cost. $30 application fee. $200 deposit required. Financial aid available for students from sponsoring institution: scholarships, loans, need-based grants.

For More Information • Admissions Office, FWP, Long Island University, 239 Montauk Highway, Southampton College, Southampton, NY 11968; *Phone:* 631-287-8474; *Fax:* 631-287-8463. *E-mail:* fw@liu.edu. *World Wide Web:* http://www.southampton.liu.edu/fw/

MIDDLEBURY COLLEGE SCHOOLS ABROAD
SCHOOL IN CHINA–HANGZHOU PROGRAM

Hosted by Zhejiang University of Technology

Academic Focus • Chinese language and literature, Chinese studies.

Program Information • Students attend classes at Zhejiang University of Technology. Field trips.

Sessions • Fall, spring, winter, yearlong.

Eligibility Requirements • Open to sophomores, juniors, seniors; 2.7 GPA; 2 letters of recommendation; B average in both Chinese and major; 2 years of college course work in Chinese.

Living Arrangements • Students live in host institution dormitories. Quarters are shared with host institution students. Meals are taken on one's own.

Costs (2004-2005) • One term: $12,000. Yearlong program: $24,000; includes tuition, housing, excursions, international airfare, books and class materials. $50 application fee. $300 nonrefundable deposit required. Financial aid available for students from sponsoring institution: scholarships, loans.

For More Information • Mr. Jamie Northrup, University Relations Coordinator, Middlebury College Schools Abroad, Office of Off-Campus Study, Sunderland Language Center, Middlebury, VT 05753; *Phone:* 802-443-5745; *Fax:* 802-443-3157. *E-mail:* schoolsabroad@middlebury.edu. *World Wide Web:* http://www.middlebury.edu/msa/

TUFTS UNIVERSITY
TUFTS IN CHINA

Hosted by Zhejiang University

Academic Focus • Chinese language and literature, Chinese studies.

Program Information • Students attend classes at Zhejiang University. Field trips.

Sessions • Fall.

Eligibility Requirements • Open to juniors, seniors; 3.0 GPA; 2 letters of recommendation; good academic standing at home school; 2 years of college course work in Chinese.

Living Arrangements • Students live in host institution dormitories. Quarters are shared with host institution students, students from other programs. Meals are taken as a group, on one's own, in residences, in central dining facility.

Costs (2004) • One term: $19,657; includes tuition, housing, all meals, excursions, international airfare, extra-curricular activities. $40 application fee. $350 nonrefundable deposit required. Financial aid available for students from sponsoring institution: scholarships, loans.

For More Information • Ms. Melanie Armstrong, Program and Marketing Coordinator, Tufts Programs Abroad, Tufts University, Dowling Hall, Medford, MA 02155-7084; *Phone:* 617-627-2000; *Fax:* 617-627-3971. *E-mail:* melanie.armstrong@tufts.edu. *World Wide Web:* http://ase.tufts.edu/studyabroad/

VALPARAISO UNIVERSITY
HANGZHOU PROGRAM

Hosted by Zhejiang University
Academic Focus • Chinese language and literature, Chinese studies, liberal studies.
Program Information • Students attend classes at Zhejiang University. Scheduled travel to Beijing, Xi'an; field trips to Shanghai, Qiantang River; optional travel to Nanjing, Suzhou at an extra cost.
Sessions • Fall.
Eligibility Requirements • Minimum age 19; open to sophomores, juniors, seniors; 3.0 GPA; 2 letters of recommendation; good academic standing at home school; no foreign language proficiency required.
Living Arrangements • Students live in host institution dormitories. Quarters are shared with students from other programs. Meals are taken as a group, in restaurants.
Costs (2003) • One term: $12,859; includes tuition, housing, excursions. $30 application fee. $200 nonrefundable deposit required. Financial aid available for students from sponsoring institution: scholarships, loans.
For More Information • Dr. Hugh McGuigan, Director, International Studies, Valparaiso University, 137 Meier Hall, 1800 Chapel Drive, Valparaiso, IN 46383; *Phone:* 219-464-5333; *Fax:* 219-464-6868. *E-mail:* studyabroad@valpo.edu. *World Wide Web:* http://www.valpo.edu/international/studyabroad.html

ZHEJIANG UNIVERSITY
CHINESE LANGUAGE AND CULTURE

Hosted by Zhejiang University
Academic Focus • Full curriculum.
Program Information • Students attend classes at Zhejiang University. Field trips to Shaoxing, Morgan Hill, the Wuxie Waterfall, Thousand-Isle Lake; optional travel to Beijing, Xi'an, Guilin, the Three Gorges in the Yangtze River, Hainan Island, Yunnan at an extra cost.
Sessions • Fall, spring, yearlong.
Eligibility Requirements • Minimum age 18; open to precollege students, freshmen, sophomores, juniors, seniors, graduate students, adults; no foreign language proficiency required.
Living Arrangements • Students live in host institution dormitories, locally rented apartments, program-owned houses, hotels. Quarters are shared with host institution students. Meals are taken as a group, on one's own, in central dining facility, in restaurants.
Costs (2003-2004) • One term: $1000. Yearlong program: $1800; includes tuition, excursions, international student ID, student support services. $20 application fee. Financial aid available for all students: work study.
For More Information • Ms. Zhou Yan, Student Advisor, Zhejiang University, International College, PO Box W-99, Hangzhou, Zhejiang 310027, China; *Phone:* +86 571-87951-718; *Fax:* +86 571-87951-755. *E-mail:* yzhou@ema.zju.edu.cn. *World Wide Web:* http://www.zju.edu.cn/

ZHEJIANG UNIVERSITY
CHINESE LANGUAGE–BACHELOR DEGREE PROGRAM, MINOR IN INTERNATIONAL TRADE

Hosted by Zhejiang University
Academic Focus • Full curriculum.
Program Information • Students attend classes at Zhejiang University. Field trips; optional travel at an extra cost.
Sessions • Fall, spring, yearlong.
Eligibility Requirements • Minimum age 18; open to precollege students, freshmen; no foreign language proficiency required.
Living Arrangements • Students live in host institution dormitories, locally rented apartments, program-owned houses, hotels. Quarters are shared with host institution students. Meals are taken as a group, on one's own, in central dining facility, in restaurants.
Costs (2003-2004) • One term: $1000. Yearlong program: $2000; includes tuition, international student ID. $20 application fee. Financial aid available for all students: work study.
For More Information • Tang Li, Graduate Student Advisor, Zhejiang University, International College, PO Box W-99, Hangzhou, Zhejiang 310027, China; *Phone:* +86 571-8795-1717; *Fax:* +86 571-8795-1755. *E-mail:* gjxzju@mail.hz.zj.cn. *World Wide Web:* http://www.zju.edu.cn/

HONG KONG
BENTLEY COLLEGE
BUSINESS PROGRAM ABROAD IN HONG KONG

Hosted by University of Hong Kong
Academic Focus • Accounting, business administration/management, computer science, economics, finance, history, law and legal studies, marketing.
Program Information • Students attend classes at University of Hong Kong. Scheduled travel; field trips; optional travel.
Sessions • Fall, spring.
Eligibility Requirements • Open to juniors; 3.0 GPA; 1 letter of recommendation; good academic standing at home school; essay; no foreign language proficiency required.
Living Arrangements • Students live in host institution dormitories. Quarters are shared with host institution students, students from other programs. Meals are taken on one's own.
Costs (2002-2003) • One term: $13,600; includes tuition, housing, international student ID, student support services. $35 application fee. $500 nonrefundable deposit required. Financial aid available for students from sponsoring institution: scholarships, loans.
For More Information • Mr. Andrew Dusenbery, Education Abroad Advisor, Bentley College, 175 Forest Street, Waltham, MA 02452-4705; *Phone:* 781-891-3474; *Fax:* 781-891-2819. *E-mail:* study_abroad@bentley.edu. *World Wide Web:* http://ecampus.bentley.edu/dept/sa/

THE CHINESE UNIVERSITY OF HONG KONG
INTERNATIONAL ASIAN STUDIES PROGRAM

Hosted by The Chinese University of Hong Kong
Academic Focus • Full curriculum.
Program Information • Students attend classes at The Chinese University of Hong Kong. Field trips to business organizations and government entities in Hong Kong and mainland China; optional travel to mainland China, outlying islands of Hong Kong at an extra cost.
Sessions • Fall, spring, yearlong.
Eligibility Requirements • Open to sophomores, juniors, seniors, graduate students, adults; 3.0 GPA; 2 letters of recommendation; statement of purpose; no foreign language proficiency required.
Living Arrangements • Students live in host institution dormitories. Quarters are shared with host institution students. Meals are taken on one's own, in central dining facility.
Costs (2003-2004) • One term: $5433. Yearlong program: $10,866; includes tuition, housing, student support services, basic medical care, language instruction, student union membership, bedding. $52 application fee. $815 nonrefundable deposit required.
For More Information • Shally Fan, Programme Manager, The Chinese University of Hong Kong, Office of Academic Links, Lady Ho Tung Hall, Shatin, N.T., China; *Phone:* +852 2609-7597; *Fax:* +852 2609-5402. *E-mail:* iasp@cuhk.edu.hk. *World Wide Web:* http://www.cuhk.edu.hk/oal/

LINGNAN UNIVERSITY
STUDENT INTERNATIONAL EXCHANGE PROGRAM (SIEP)

Hosted by Lingnan University
Academic Focus • Full curriculum.
Program Information • Students attend classes at Lingnan University.
Sessions • Fall, spring, yearlong.
Eligibility Requirements • Minimum age 18; open to sophomores, juniors, seniors; 3.0 GPA; good academic standing at home school; application; no foreign language proficiency required.
Living Arrangements • Students live in host institution dormitories. Quarters are shared with host institution students. Meals are taken on one's own, in central dining facility, in restaurants.
Costs (2003-2004) • One term: contact sponsor for cost. Yearlong program: contact sponsor for cost.
For More Information • Mrs. Sandy Kwok, Senior International Programmes Officer, Lingnan University, Office of International Programmes, Tuen Mun, New Territories, Hong Kong, China; *Phone:* +852 2616-8970; *Fax:* +852 2465-9660. *E-mail:* exchange@ln.edu.hk. *World Wide Web:* http://www.LN.edu.hk/oip/siep/exchange_index.html

MARIST COLLEGE
HONG KONG PROGRAM

Hosted by The Chinese University of Hong Kong
Academic Focus • Full curriculum.
Program Information • Students attend classes at The Chinese University of Hong Kong.
Sessions • Fall, spring, yearlong.
Eligibility Requirements • Open to sophomores, juniors, seniors; 2.8 GPA; 2 letters of recommendation; good academic standing at home school; no foreign language proficiency required.
Living Arrangements • Students live in host institution dormitories. Quarters are shared with host institution students. Meals are taken on one's own, in residences, in restaurants.
Costs (2003-2004) • One term: $12,500. Yearlong program: $25,000; includes tuition, housing, insurance, student support services. $35 application fee. $300 nonrefundable deposit required. Financial aid available for students from sponsoring institution: scholarships, loans.
For More Information • Mr. Jerald Z. Thornton, Coordinator, Marist College, 3399 North Road, Poughkeepsie, NY 12601; *Phone:* 845-575-3330; *Fax:* 845-575-3294. *E-mail:* jerre.thornton@marist.edu. *World Wide Web:* http://www.marist.edu/international/

STETSON UNIVERSITY
STUDY ABROAD–HONG KONG

Hosted by Hong Kong Baptist University
Academic Focus • Full curriculum.
Program Information • Students attend classes at Hong Kong Baptist University. Field trips to Guangxhue, Macao.
Sessions • Fall, spring, yearlong.
Eligibility Requirements • Minimum age 20; open to sophomores, juniors, seniors; 2.5 GPA; 4 letters of recommendation; good academic standing at home school; completed application; no foreign language proficiency required.

Living Arrangements • Students live in host institution dormitories. Quarters are shared with host institution students. Meals are taken on one's own, in central dining facility.
Costs (2002-2003) • One term: $14,025. Yearlong program: $28,050; includes tuition, housing, all meals, insurance, excursions, international airfare, lab equipment, international student ID, student support services. $50 application fee. $200 nonrefundable deposit required. Financial aid available for students from sponsoring institution: scholarships, loans.
For More Information • Ms. Nancy L. Leonard, Director, Stetson University, Center for International Education, Unit 8412, 421 North Woodland Boulevard, Deland, FL 32723-3757; *Phone:* 386-822-8165; *Fax:* 386-822-8167. *E-mail:* nleonard@stetson.edu. *World Wide Web:* http://www.stetson.edu/international/

SYRACUSE UNIVERSITY
ASIA PROGRAM IN HONG KONG

Hosted by Syracuse University Center–Hong Kong, City University of Hong Kong
Academic Focus • Business administration/management, Chinese language and literature, economics, finance, geography, history, marketing, political science and government.
Program Information • Students attend classes at Syracuse University Center–Hong Kong, City University of Hong Kong. Scheduled travel to Beijing, Shanghai, Guilin.
Sessions • Fall, spring, yearlong.
Eligibility Requirements • Open to freshmen, sophomores, juniors, seniors, graduate students; 2 letters of recommendation; good academic standing at home school; home school approval; essays; no foreign language proficiency required.
Living Arrangements • Students live in host institution dormitories. Quarters are shared with host institution students. Meals are taken as a group, on one's own, in central dining facility, in restaurants.

in 🏴 **HONG KONG**

SYRACUSE
A US News & World Report TOP 5 study abroad program

▶ International Business
▶ East Asian Studies
▶ Arts and Sciences
▶ Intensive internships
▶ Exciting field study
▶ Scholarships and grants
▶ Study in English

SYRACUSE UNIVERSITY ABROAD

http://suabroad.syr.edu   1-800-235-3472

CHINA
Hong Kong

Costs (2004-2005) • One term: $20,130. Yearlong program: $40,260; includes tuition, housing, some meals, excursions, international airfare, international student ID, student support services. $50 application fee. $450 nonrefundable deposit required. Financial aid available for all students: scholarships, work study, loans, tuition differential grants.
For More Information • Mr. James Buschman, Senior Associate Director, Syracuse University, 106 Walnut Place, Syracuse, NY 13244-4170; *Phone:* 800-235-3472; *Fax:* 315-443-4593. *E-mail:* suabroad@syr.edu. *World Wide Web:* http://suabroad.syr.edu/

TUFTS UNIVERSITY
TUFTS IN HONG KONG

Hosted by University of Hong Kong
Academic Focus • Full curriculum.
Program Information • Students attend classes at University of Hong Kong. Field trips.
Sessions • Spring.
Eligibility Requirements • Open to juniors; 3.0 GPA; 2 letters of recommendation; good academic standing at home school; no foreign language proficiency required.
Living Arrangements • Students live in host institution dormitories. Quarters are shared with host institution students. Meals are taken as a group, on one's own, in residences, in central dining facility.
Costs (2004) • One term: $19,657; includes tuition, housing, all meals, excursions, extra-curricular activities. $40 application fee. $350 nonrefundable deposit required. Financial aid available for students from sponsoring institution: scholarships, loans.
For More Information • Ms. Melanie Armstrong, Program and Marketing Coordinator, Tufts Programs Abroad, Tufts University, Dowling Hall, Medford, MA 02155; *Phone:* 617-627-2000; *Fax:* 617-627-3971. *E-mail:* melanie.armstrong@tufts.edu. *World Wide Web:* http://ase.tufts.edu/studyabroad/

UNIVERSITY OF MIAMI
CHINESE UNIVERSITY OF HONG KONG

Hosted by The Chinese University of Hong Kong
Academic Focus • Asian studies, business administration/management, Chinese language and literature, history, information science, religious studies.
Program Information • Students attend classes at The Chinese University of Hong Kong.
Sessions • Fall, spring, yearlong.
Eligibility Requirements • Minimum age 18; open to sophomores, juniors, seniors; 3.0 GPA; 2 letters of recommendation; good academic standing at home school; transcripts; essay; no foreign language proficiency required.
Living Arrangements • Students live in host institution dormitories. Quarters are shared with host institution students, students from other programs. Meals are taken on one's own, in central dining facility.
Costs (2003-2004) • One term: $12,919. Yearlong program: $25,838; includes tuition, student support services. $40 application fee. $500 nonrefundable deposit required. Financial aid available for students from sponsoring institution: scholarships, loans.
For More Information • Ms. Carol Lazzeri, Assistant Director, University of Miami, International Education and Exchange Programs, 5050 Brunson Drive, Allen Hall 212, Box 248005, Coral Gables, FL 33124-1610; *Phone:* 305-284-3434; *Fax:* 305-284-4235. *E-mail:* ieep@miami.edu. *World Wide Web:* http://www.studyabroad.miami.edu/

JINAN
SANTA BARBARA CITY COLLEGE
PACIFIC RIM STUDIES IN CHINA

Held at Shandong Normal University
Academic Focus • History, international affairs, peace and conflict studies, political science and government.
Program Information • Classes are held on the campus of Shandong Normal University. Faculty members are drawn from the sponsor's U.S. staff. Field trips to Beijing.
Sessions • Fall, program runs every other year.

Eligibility Requirements • Minimum age 18; open to juniors, seniors, graduate students, adults; course work in English; 2.0 GPA; 2 letters of recommendation; good academic standing at home school; no foreign language proficiency required.
Living Arrangements • Students live in host institution dormitories, hotels. Quarters are shared with host institution students. Meals are taken on one's own, in central dining facility, in restaurants.
Costs (2004) • One term: $5000 (estimated); includes housing, some meals, excursions, international airfare, international student ID, student support services. $300 refundable deposit required. Financial aid available for all students: scholarships, loans.
For More Information • Ms. Naomi Sullwold, Program Assistant, Santa Barbara City College, 721 Cliff Drive, Santa Barbara, CA 93109; *Phone:* 805-965-0581 Ext. 2494; *Fax:* 805-963-7222. *E-mail:* sullwold@sbcc.edu. *World Wide Web:* http://www.sbcc.edu/studyabroad/

KUNMING
SCHOOL FOR INTERNATIONAL TRAINING, SIT STUDY ABROAD
CHINA: YUNNAN PROVINCE–LANGUAGE AND CULTURES

Academic Focus • Anthropology, Buddhist studies, Chinese language and literature, Chinese studies, East Asian studies, economics, geography, history, liberal studies, political science and government, visual and performing arts.
Program Information • Faculty members are drawn from the sponsor's U.S. staff and local instructors hired by the sponsor. Scheduled travel to Lijiang, Dali, Beijing, Xi'an; field trips to museums, rural villages and farms, places of historic, artistic, or cultural significance.
Sessions • Fall, spring.
Eligibility Requirements • Open to sophomores, juniors, seniors; 2.5 GPA; 2 letters of recommendation; good academic standing at home school; no foreign language proficiency required.
Living Arrangements • Students live in host institution dormitories, host family homes, hotels. Meals are taken as a group, on one's own, with host family, in residences, in central dining facility, in restaurants.
Costs (2003-2004) • One term: $11,750; includes tuition, housing, all meals, insurance, excursions. $50 application fee. $400 nonrefundable deposit required. Financial aid available for all students: scholarships.
For More Information • School for International Training, SIT Study Abroad, Kipling Road, Brattleboro, VT 05302-0676; *Phone:* 888-272-7881; *Fax:* 802-258-3296. *E-mail:* studyabroad@sit.edu. *World Wide Web:* http://www.sit.edu/studyabroad/

NANJING
CIEE
CIEE STUDY CENTER AT NANJING UNIVERSITY, CHINA

Hosted by Nanjing University
Academic Focus • Chinese language and literature, Chinese studies.
Program Information • Students attend classes at Nanjing University. Scheduled travel to the Sichuan Province (1 week); field trips to the Sun Yat-sen Mausoleum, the Nanjing College of Chinese Medicine, cultural performances, the first Ming Emperor's tomb, the Manjing Massacre Memorial.
Sessions • Fall, spring, yearlong.
Eligibility Requirements • Open to sophomores, juniors, seniors, graduate students, adults; course work in Asian studies (1 course); 2.75 GPA; 1 year of college course work in Chinese.
Living Arrangements • Students live in host institution dormitories, host family homes. Quarters are shared with host institution students. Meals are taken on one's own, in central dining facility, in restaurants.
Costs (2004-2005) • One term: $8250. Yearlong program: $15,800; includes tuition, housing, insurance, excursions, student support services, visa fees, pre-departure advising, some meals for homestay students. $30 application fee. $300 deposit required. Financial aid available for all students: scholarships, minority student scholarships, Department of Education grants, travel grants.
For More Information • Mr. Adam Rubin, Admissions Officer, Asia Pacific, CIEE, 7 Custom House Street, 3rd Floor, Portland, ME 04101;

Phone: 800-40-STUDY; *Fax:* 207-553-7699. *E-mail:* studyinfo@ciee.org. *World Wide Web:* http://www.ciee.org/isp/

COLLEGE CONSORTIUM FOR INTERNATIONAL STUDIES–COLLEGE OF STATEN ISLAND/CITY UNIVERSITY OF NEW YORK
CUNY PROGRAM IN NANJING, CHINA

Hosted by Nanjing University

Academic Focus • Chinese language and literature, Chinese studies, cultural studies, geography, history, political science and government.

Program Information • Students attend classes at Nanjing University. Scheduled travel to Beijing, the Great Wall, the Forbidden City, Ming Tombs; field trips to Wuxi, Zhanjiang, Suzhou, Yangzhou; optional travel to Hangzhou, Shanghai at an extra cost.

Sessions • Fall, spring, yearlong.

Eligibility Requirements • Minimum age 18; open to freshmen, sophomores, juniors, seniors, graduate students, adults; 2.5 GPA; 3 letters of recommendation; essay; transcript; no foreign language proficiency required.

Living Arrangements • Students live in host institution dormitories. Quarters are shared with students from other programs. Meals are taken on one's own, in central dining facility, in restaurants.

Costs (2004-2005) • One term: $4370–$5015. Yearlong program: $9385; includes tuition, housing, insurance, excursions, international student ID, student support services, all fees. $265 nonrefundable deposit required. Financial aid available for students from sponsoring institution: scholarships, loans.

For More Information • College Consortium for International Studies, 2000 P Street, NW, Suite 503, Washington, DC 20036; *Phone:* 202-223-0330; *Fax:* 202-223-0999. *E-mail:* info@ccisabroad.org. *World Wide Web:* http://www.ccisabroad.org/. Students may also apply through College of Staten Island, The City University of New York, Center for International Service, Building 2A, Room 206, 2800 Victory Boulevard, Staten Island, NY 10314.

LOCK HAVEN UNIVERSITY OF PENNSYLVANIA
SEMESTER IN NANJING

Hosted by Nanjing University

Academic Focus • Chinese language and literature, Chinese studies, cultural studies, fine/studio arts, history, social sciences.

Program Information • Students attend classes at Nanjing University.

Sessions • Fall, spring, yearlong.

Eligibility Requirements • Minimum age 18; open to sophomores, juniors, seniors, adults; 2.5 GPA; 3 letters of recommendation; good academic standing at home school; transcript; no foreign language proficiency required.

Living Arrangements • Students live in host institution dormitories, locally rented apartments, program-owned apartments. Quarters are shared with students from other programs. Meals are taken in central dining facility.

Costs (2002-2003) • One term: $5450 for Pennsylvania residents; $7360 for nonresidents. Yearlong program: $10,900 for Pennsylvania residents; $14,720 for nonresidents; includes tuition, housing, all meals, fees. $50 application fee. Financial aid available for students from sponsoring institution: scholarships, loans.

For More Information • Dean, Institute for International Studies, Lock Haven University of Pennsylvania, Lock Haven, PA 17745-2390; *Phone:* 570-893-2140; *Fax:* 570-893-2537. *E-mail:* intlstudies_webmonitor@lhup.edu. *World Wide Web:* http://www.lhup.edu/international/goingp/goingplaces_index.htm

WHITWORTH COLLEGE
WHITWORTH/NANJING UNIVERSITY EXCHANGE PROGRAM

Hosted by Nanjing University

Academic Focus • Chinese language and literature, Chinese studies.

Program Information • Students attend classes at Nanjing University. Optional travel at an extra cost.

Sessions • Fall, spring, yearlong.

Eligibility Requirements • Open to sophomores, juniors; 2.5 GPA; 2 letters of recommendation; 2 years of college course work in Chinese.

Living Arrangements • Students live in host institution dormitories, locally rented apartments. Quarters are shared with students from other programs. Meals are taken in central dining facility.

Costs (2003-2004) • One term: $13,034. Yearlong program: $26,068; includes tuition, housing, all meals. Financial aid available for students from sponsoring institution: scholarships, loans.

For More Information • Ms. Sue Jackson, Director, Off-Campus Programs, Whitworth College, Center for International and Multicultural Education, 300 West Hawthorne Road, Spokane, WA 99251-2702; *Phone:* 509-777-4596; *Fax:* 509-777-3723. *E-mail:* sjackson@whitworth.edu. *World Wide Web:* http://www.whitworth.edu/

SHANGHAI

CENTER FOR STUDY ABROAD (CSA)
FUDAN UNIVERSITY

Hosted by Fudan University

Academic Focus • Art, Chinese language and literature, Chinese studies, history, philosophy.

Program Information • Students attend classes at Fudan University. Optional travel to Shanghai tourist sites, Beijing at an extra cost.

Sessions • Fall, spring, yearlong.

Eligibility Requirements • Minimum age 17; open to precollege students, freshmen, sophomores, juniors, seniors, graduate students, adults; no foreign language proficiency required.

Living Arrangements • Students live in host institution dormitories. Quarters are shared with students from other programs. Meals are taken on one's own, in central dining facility.

Costs (2003-2004) • One term: contact sponsor for cost. Yearlong program: contact sponsor for cost. $45 application fee.

For More Information • Ms. Alima K. Virtue, Program Director, Center for Study Abroad (CSA), 325 Washington Avenue South, #93, Kent, WA 98032; *Phone:* 206-726-1498; *Fax:* 253-850-0454. *E-mail:* info@centerforstudyabroad.com. *World Wide Web:* http://www.centerforstudyabroad.com/

CIEE
CIEE STUDY CENTER AT EAST CHINA NORMAL UNIVERSITY, SHANGHAI, CHINA

Hosted by East China Normal University Shanghai

Academic Focus • Chinese language and literature, Chinese studies, economics, international affairs, international business.

Program Information • Students attend classes at East China Normal University Shanghai. Field trips to the Jade Buddha Temple, temples, the countryside, government agencies; optional travel to Yunnan or Sichuan (week-long).

Sessions • Fall, spring, yearlong.

Eligibility Requirements • Open to sophomores, juniors, seniors, graduate students, adults; course work in Asian studies; 2.75 GPA; 1 letter of recommendation; good academic standing at home school; no foreign language proficiency required.

Living Arrangements • Students live in host institution dormitories, locally rented apartments, host family homes. Meals are taken on one's own, with host family, in residences, in restaurants.

Costs (2004-2005) • One term: $9600. Yearlong program: contact sponsor for cost; includes tuition, housing, some meals, insurance, excursions, student support services, visa fees, cultural activities, pre-departure advising. $30 application fee. $300 deposit required. Financial aid available for all students: scholarships, minority student scholarships, Department of Education grant, travel grants.

For More Information • Mr. Adam Rubin, Admissions Officer, Asia Pacific, CIEE, 7 Custom House Street, 3rd Floor, Portland, ME 04101; *Phone:* 800-40-STUDY; *Fax:* 207-553-7699. *E-mail:* studyinfo@ciee.org. *World Wide Web:* http://www.ciee.org/isp/

LEXIA INTERNATIONAL
LEXIA IN SHANGHAI

Hosted by Fudan University

Academic Focus • Anthropology, area studies, art, art history, Asian studies, Buddhist studies, Chinese language and literature, Chinese

CHINA
Shanghai

studies, civilization studies, cultural studies, drawing/painting, economics, environmental science/studies, ethnic studies, film and media studies, fine/studio arts, geography, history, interdisciplinary studies, international affairs, international business, liberal studies, literature, music, music history, music performance, peace and conflict studies, philosophy, political science and government, psychology, religious studies, social sciences, sociology, urban studies.

Program Information • Students attend classes at Fudan University. Scheduled travel to Hong Kong; field trips to the Pudong Economic Zone, Beijing; optional travel to Tibet at an extra cost.
Sessions • Fall, spring, yearlong.
Eligibility Requirements • Minimum age 18; open to sophomores, juniors, seniors, graduate students, adults; 2.5 GPA; 2 letters of recommendation; no foreign language proficiency required.
Living Arrangements • Students live in host institution dormitories. Quarters are shared with host institution students. Meals are taken on one's own, in residences, in central dining facility.
Costs (2003-2004) • One term: $10,950. Yearlong program: $20,550; includes tuition, housing, some meals, insurance, excursions, international student ID, student support services, computer access, transcript. $35 application fee. $300 refundable deposit required. Financial aid available for all students: scholarships, work study.
For More Information • Lexia International, 23 South Main Street, Hanover, NH 03755; *Phone:* 800-775-3942; *Fax:* 603-643-9899. *E-mail:* info@lexiaintl.org. *World Wide Web:* http://www.lexiaintl.org/

ST. OLAF COLLEGE
TERM IN CHINA

Hosted by East China Normal University Shanghai
Academic Focus • Asian studies, Chinese language and literature.
Program Information • Students attend classes at East China Normal University Shanghai. Scheduled travel to Nanjing, Hangzhou, Suzhou; optional travel to Beijing at an extra cost.
Sessions • Fall.
Eligibility Requirements • Open to sophomores, juniors, seniors; 3.0 GPA; 3 letters of recommendation; interview; 2 years of college course work in Chinese.
Living Arrangements • Students live in host institution dormitories, locally rented apartments. Quarters are shared with students from other programs. Meals are taken on one's own in central dining facility, in restaurants.
Costs (2003) • One term: $15,650; includes tuition, housing, some meals, excursions, international airfare, international student ID. $75 application fee. $150 nonrefundable deposit required. Financial aid available for students from sponsoring institution: scholarships, loans.
For More Information • Pin P. Wan, Associate Professor of Chinese, St. Olaf College, Russian/East Asian Languages, Northfield, MN 55057; *Phone:* 507-646-3684; *Fax:* 507-646-3789. *E-mail:* wan@stolaf.edu. *World Wide Web:* http://www.stolaf.edu/services/iso/

UNIVERSITY AT ALBANY, STATE UNIVERSITY OF NEW YORK
LANGUAGE AND CULTURAL STUDIES AT FUDAN UNIVERSITY

Hosted by Fudan University
Academic Focus • Chinese language and literature, Chinese studies, full curriculum, liberal studies.
Program Information • Students attend classes at Fudan University.
Sessions • Fall, spring, yearlong.
Eligibility Requirements • Open to sophomores, juniors, seniors, adults; 2 letters of recommendation; good academic standing at home school; 1 year college course work in Mandarin Chinese for language program; fluency in Mandarin Chinese for direct enrollment in host university courses.
Living Arrangements • Students live in host institution dormitories. Quarters are shared with students from other programs. Meals are taken on one's own, in central dining facility.
Costs (2002-2003) • One term: $3013. Yearlong program: $6026 (cost is higher for non-exchange students); includes housing, all meals, student support services, in-state tuition and fees. $150

nonrefundable deposit required. Financial aid available for students from sponsoring institution: all customary sources.
For More Information • University at Albany, State University of New York, Office of International Education, LI 66, Albany, NY 12222; *Phone:* 518-442-3525; *Fax:* 518-442-3338. *E-mail:* intled@uamail.albany.edu. *World Wide Web:* http://www.albany.edu/intled/

UNIVERSITY OF MASSACHUSETTS AMHERST
CHINESE LANGUAGE PROGRAM AT FUDAN UNIVERSITY

Hosted by Fudan University
Academic Focus • Chinese language and literature.
Program Information • Students attend classes at Fudan University. Scheduled travel to historic and cultural sites of interest in Shanghai; field trips.
Sessions • Fall, spring.
Eligibility Requirements • Open to sophomores, juniors, seniors, graduate students; course work in Asian studies; 2.75 GPA; 2 letters of recommendation; 1 year of college course work in Mandarin Chinese.
Living Arrangements • Students live in host institution dormitories, locally rented apartments. Quarters are shared with students from other programs. Meals are taken on one's own, in central dining facility.
Costs (2003-2004) • One term: $6000; includes tuition, housing, excursions, student support services. $25 application fee. $400 nonrefundable deposit required. Financial aid available for students from sponsoring institution.
For More Information • Ms. Laurel Foster-Moore, Study Abroad Coordinator for Asia, University of Massachusetts Amherst, International Programs, Amherst, MA 01003; *Phone:* 413-545-2710; *Fax:* 413-545-1201. *E-mail:* fostermo@ipo.umass.edu. *World Wide Web:* http://www.umass.edu/ipo/

TAICHUNG
UNIVERSITY OF MASSACHUSETTS AMHERST
UNIVERSITY OF MASSACHUSETTS EXCHANGE WITH TUNGHAI UNIVERSITY

Hosted by Tunghai University
Academic Focus • Chinese language and literature.
Program Information • Students attend classes at Tunghai University.
Sessions • Fall, spring, yearlong.
Eligibility Requirements • Open to freshmen, sophomores, juniors, seniors, adults; 2.75 GPA; 2 letters of recommendation; 1 year of college course work in Chinese.
Living Arrangements • Students live in host institution dormitories, locally rented apartments. Quarters are shared with host institution students. Meals are taken on one's own, in residences, in central dining facility, in restaurants.
Costs (2003-2004) • One term: $7800. Yearlong program: $15,300; includes tuition, housing, excursions, books and class materials. $25 application fee. $400 nonrefundable deposit required. Financial aid available for students from sponsoring institution: scholarships, loans.
For More Information • Ms. Laurel Foster-Moore, Study Abroad Coordinator for Asia, University of Massachusetts Amherst, International Programs, Amherst, MA 01003; *Phone:* 413-545-2710; *Fax:* 413-545-1201. *E-mail:* fostermo@ipo.umass.edu. *World Wide Web:* http://www.umass.edu/ipo/

TAIPEI
CIEE
CIEE STUDY CENTER AT NATIONAL CHENGCHI UNIVERSITY, TAIPEI, TAIWAN

Hosted by National Chengchi University
Academic Focus • Art, art history, Chinese language and literature, Chinese studies, economics, history, political science and government, religious studies, sociology.
Program Information • Students attend classes at National Chengchi University. Scheduled travel to Hualien, Lishan, Taroko

Gorge, Kenting; field trips to the National Palace Museum, Chiang Kai-shek Memorial Hall, Yehliu, Danshui.

Sessions • Fall, spring, yearlong, winter term for full-year students.

Eligibility Requirements • Open to freshmen, sophomores, juniors, seniors, graduate students, adults; course work in Asian studies (1 course); 2.75 GPA; 2 letters of recommendation; good academic standing at home school; no foreign language proficiency required.

Living Arrangements • Students live in host institution dormitories, an international house. Quarters are shared with host institution students. Meals are taken on one's own, in residences, in central dining facility, in restaurants.

Costs (2004-2005) • One term: $8250. Yearlong program: $15,800; includes tuition, housing, insurance, excursions, student support services, visa fees, cultural activities, pre-departure advising. $30 application fee. $300 deposit required. Financial aid available for all students: scholarships, minority student scholarships, Department of Education grants, travel grants.

For More Information • Mr. Adam Rubin, Admissions Officer, Asia Pacific, CIEE, 7 Custom House Street, 3rd Floor, Portland, ME 04101; *Phone:* 800-40-STUDY; *Fax:* 207-553-7699. *E-mail:* studyinfo@ciee.org. *World Wide Web:* http://www.ciee.org/isp/

SOUTHERN METHODIST UNIVERSITY
SMU IN TAIPEI

Hosted by Soochow University

Academic Focus • Art history, Chinese language and literature, Chinese studies, history, political science and government.

Program Information • Students attend classes at Soochow University.

Sessions • Fall, spring, yearlong.

Eligibility Requirements • Open to sophomores, juniors, seniors; 2.7 GPA; 2 letters of recommendation; good academic standing at home school; interview; essay; 1 year of college course work in Chinese.

Living Arrangements • Students live in host institution dormitories. Quarters are shared with host institution students, students from other programs. Meals are taken as a group, in central dining facility.

Costs (2001-2002) • One term: $15,000. Yearlong program: $30,000; includes tuition, housing, some meals, books and class materials, student support services. $40 application fee. $500 nonrefundable deposit required. Financial aid available for students from sponsoring institution: scholarships, loans.

For More Information • Ms. Karen Westergaard, Associate Director, Southern Methodist University, International Office, PO Box 750391, Dallas, TX 75275-0391; *Phone:* 214-768-2338; *Fax:* 214-768-1051. *E-mail:* kwesterg@mail.smu.edu. *World Wide Web:* http://www.smu.edu/studyabroad/

TIANJIN

ST. CLOUD STATE UNIVERSITY
CHINESE CULTURE AND LANGUAGE

Hosted by Tianjin Foreign Studies University

Academic Focus • Chinese language and literature, cultural studies, East Asian studies.

Program Information • Students attend classes at Tianjin Foreign Studies University. Scheduled travel to Beijing, the Great Wall; field trips to local cultural sites; optional travel to Tibet, Mongolia at an extra cost.

Sessions • Spring.

Eligibility Requirements • Minimum age 18; open to freshmen, sophomores, juniors, seniors; 2.25 GPA; 2 letters of recommendation; no foreign language proficiency required.

Living Arrangements • Students live in host institution dormitories, locally rented apartments. Quarters are shared with host institution students. Meals are taken on one's own, in central dining facility.

Costs (2004) • One term: $5700 for Minnesota residents; includes tuition, housing, excursions, international airfare, international student ID. $75 application fee. Financial aid available for students from sponsoring institution: scholarships, work study, loans.

For More Information • Chunsheng Zhang, Associate Vice President for Academic Affairs/International Studies, St. Cloud State University, Center for International Studies, 720 4th Avenue, South, St. Cloud, MN 56301-4498; *Phone:* 320-308-4287; *Fax:* 320-308-4223. *E-mail:* intstudy@stcloudstate.edu. *World Wide Web:* http://www.stcloudstate.edu/

XIAN

UNIVERSITY OF MASSACHUSETTS AMHERST
UNIVERSITY OF MASSACHUSETTS EXCHANGE WITH SHAANXI NORMAL UNIVERSITY

Hosted by Shaanxi Normal University

Academic Focus • Chinese language and literature.

Program Information • Students attend classes at Shaanxi Normal University. Field trips to local museums, historic sites; optional travel.

Sessions • Fall, spring, yearlong.

Eligibility Requirements • Open to sophomores, juniors, seniors, graduate students; 2.75 GPA; 2 letters of recommendation; 2 years of college course work in Mandarin Chinese.

Living Arrangements • Students live in host institution dormitories. Quarters are shared with students from other programs. Meals are taken on one's own, in central dining facility, in restaurants.

Costs (2002-2003) • One term: contact sponsor for cost. Yearlong program: contact sponsor for cost. $25 application fee. $400 nonrefundable deposit required. Financial aid available for students from sponsoring institution: loans.

For More Information • Ms. Laurel Foster-Moore, Study Abroad Coordinator for Asia, University of Massachusetts Amherst, International Programs, Amherst, MA 01003; *Phone:* 413-545-2710; *Fax:* 413-545-1201. *E-mail:* fostermo@ipo.umass.edu. *World Wide Web:* http://www.umass.edu/ipo/

YANJI

SHORTER COLLEGE
YANBIAN UNIVERSITY OF SCIENCE AND TECHNOLOGY

Hosted by Yanbian University

Academic Focus • Full curriculum.

Program Information • Students attend classes at Yanbian University. Optional travel to other locations in China.

Sessions • Fall, spring.

Eligibility Requirements • Open to sophomores, juniors, seniors; 2.5 GPA; 3 letters of recommendation; good academic standing at home school; no foreign language proficiency required.

Living Arrangements • Students live in host institution dormitories. Quarters are shared with host institution students. Meals are taken on one's own, in central dining facility.

Costs (2003-2004) • One term: contact sponsor for cost. $200 refundable deposit required. Financial aid available for students from sponsoring institution: scholarships, work study, loans.

For More Information • Dr. Robert Nash, Dean, School of Religion and International Programs, Shorter College, 315 Shorter Avenue, Rome, GA 30165; *Phone:* 706-233-7257; *Fax:* 706-233-7516. *E-mail:* rnash@shorter.edu. *World Wide Web:* http://www.shorter.edu.academics.internationalprograms/

COSTA RICA

CITY TO CITY

DUKE UNIVERSITY
OTS/DUKE TROPICAL BIOLOGY IN COSTA RICA

Hosted by Organization for Tropical Studies

Academic Focus • Biological/life sciences, ecology, Spanish studies.

Program Information • Students attend classes at Organization for Tropical Studies (). Scheduled travel to Cerro de la Muerte, Palo Verde, La Selva; field trips to Osa Peninsula.

Sessions • Fall, spring.

COSTA RICA
City to City

Eligibility Requirements • Open to freshmen, sophomores, juniors, seniors; course work in biology (1 year); 2 letters of recommendation; good academic standing at home school; 1 year of college course work in Spanish.
Living Arrangements • Students live in host family homes, field stations. Quarters are shared with host institution students. Meals are taken as a group, in central dining facility.
Costs (2003-2004) • One term: $14,900; includes tuition, housing, all meals, excursions, books and class materials, lab equipment, student support services, laundry service. $1000 nonrefundable deposit required. Financial aid available for students from sponsoring institution: scholarships, loans.
For More Information • Mr. Rodney Vargas, Program Officer, Duke University, Organization for Tropical Studies, Box 90633, Durham, NC 27708-0633; *Phone:* 919-684-5774; *Fax:* 919-684-5661. *E-mail:* nao@duke.edu. *World Wide Web:* http://www.aas.duke.edu/study_abroad/

GEORGE MASON UNIVERSITY
COSTA RICA

Hosted by University for Peace (San José)
Academic Focus • Full curriculum.
Program Information • Students attend classes at University for Peace (San José). Scheduled travel; field trips; optional travel at an extra cost.
Sessions • Fall, spring.
Eligibility Requirements • Minimum age 18; open to juniors, seniors, graduate students, adults; 3.0 GPA; good academic standing at home school; no foreign language proficiency required.
Living Arrangements • Meals are taken as a group.
Costs (2003-2004) • One term: contact sponsor for cost. Financial aid available for students from sponsoring institution: scholarships, loans.
For More Information • Program Officer, Center for Abroad Education, George Mason University, 235 Johnson Center, 4400 University Drive, Fairfax, VA 22030; *Phone:* 703-993-2154; *Fax:* 703-993-2153. *E-mail:* cge@gmu.edu. *World Wide Web:* http://www.gmu.edu/departments/cge/

ATENAS
THE SCHOOL FOR FIELD STUDIES
COSTA RICA: SUSTAINABLE DEVELOPMENT STUDIES

Held at Center for Sustainable Development
Academic Focus • Agriculture, biological/life sciences, conservation studies, Costa Rican studies, ecology, economics, environmental science/studies, forestry, Latin American studies, natural resources, Spanish language and literature.
Program Information • Classes are held on the campus of Center for Sustainable Development. Faculty members are drawn from the sponsor's U.S. staff and local instructors hired by the sponsor. Scheduled travel to the Pacific coastal region, Atlantic lowlands, San Gerardo; field trips to Carara Biological Reserve, Poás Volcano, Braulio Carillo National Park, local farms; optional travel to sites in Central America at an extra cost.
Sessions • Fall, spring.
Eligibility Requirements • Minimum age 18; open to freshmen, sophomores, juniors, seniors; course work in biology or ecology, and economics or environmental studies; 2.7 GPA; 2 letters of recommendation; personal statement; 0.5 years of college course work in Spanish.
Living Arrangements • Students live in host institution dormitories. Quarters are shared with host institution students. Meals are taken as a group, in central dining facility.
Costs (2002-2003) • One term: $13,185; includes tuition, housing, all meals, excursions, lab equipment. $45 application fee. $500 nonrefundable deposit required. Financial aid available for all students: scholarships, loans.
For More Information • Admissions Department, The School for Field Studies, 10 Federal Street, Salem, MA 01970-3853; *Phone:* 800-989-4418; *Fax:* 978-741-3551. *E-mail:* admissions@fieldstudies.org. *World Wide Web:* http://www.fieldstudies.org/

HEREDIA
INSTITUTE FOR STUDY ABROAD, BUTLER UNIVERSITY
INTERNATIONAL STUDENT EXCHANGE PROGRAM/INSTITUTE FOR STUDY ABROAD: UNIVERSIDAD NACIONAL, HEREDIA, COSTA RICA

Hosted by National University
Academic Focus • Full curriculum.
Program Information • Students attend classes at National University. Field trips to rainforests, volcanoes, nature preserves.
Sessions • Fall, spring, yearlong.
Eligibility Requirements • Open to sophomores, juniors, seniors; 3.0 GPA; 1 letter of recommendation; good academic standing at home school; Spanish language evaluation; enrollment at an accredited American college or university; 2 years of college course work in Spanish.
Living Arrangements • Students live in host family homes. Meals are taken with host family.
Costs (2002-2003) • One term: $8295. Yearlong program: $14,010; includes tuition, housing, all meals, excursions, international student ID, student support services, cultural and sporting events, predeparture advising. $40 application fee. $500 nonrefundable deposit required. Financial aid available for all students: scholarships, travel grants.
For More Information • Institute for Study Abroad, Butler University, 1100 West 42nd Street, Suite 305, Indianapolis, IN 46208-3345; *Phone:* 800-858-0229; *Fax:* 317-940-9704. *E-mail:* copa@butler.edu. *World Wide Web:* http://www.ifsa-butler.org/. Students may also apply through International Student Exchange Program, (ISEP), 1616 P Street, NW, Suite 150, Washington, DC 20036.

LOCK HAVEN UNIVERSITY OF PENNSYLVANIA
SEMESTER IN COSTA RICA

Hosted by National University
Academic Focus • Economics, environmental science/studies, history, international affairs, Latin American studies, literature, sociology.
Program Information • Students attend classes at National University.
Sessions • Fall, spring, yearlong.
Eligibility Requirements • Minimum age 18; open to sophomores, juniors, seniors, adults; 2.5 GPA; 3 letters of recommendation; good academic standing at home school; fluency in Spanish.
Living Arrangements • Students live in host family homes. Meals are taken with host family, in residences.
Costs (2002-2003) • One term: $5450 for Pennsylvania residents; $7360 for nonresidents. Yearlong program: $10,900 for Pennsylvania residents; $14,720 for nonresidents; includes tuition, housing, all meals, fees. $50 application fee. Financial aid available for students from sponsoring institution: scholarships, loans.
For More Information • Dean, Institute for International Studies, Lock Haven University of Pennsylvania, Lock Haven, PA 17745-2390; *Phone:* 570-893-2140; *Fax:* 570-893-2537. *E-mail:* intlstudies_webmonitor@Ihup.edu. *World Wide Web:* http://www.lhup.edu/international/goingp/goingplaces_index.htm

LONG ISLAND UNIVERSITY
FRIENDS WORLD PROGRAM—LATIN AMERICAN CENTRE, COSTA RICA

Hosted by Friends World Program Latin American Center
Academic Focus • Anthropology, art, education, environmental science/studies, interdisciplinary studies, journalism, Latin American studies, peace and conflict studies, religious studies, sociology, Spanish language and literature, women's studies.
Program Information • Students attend classes at Friends World Program Latin American Center. Scheduled travel to Nicaragua, Guatemala, El Salvador, Honduras, Panama; field trips to a rainforest, international communities, a banana plantation; optional travel to Central America, South America, Mexico, Cuba at an extra cost.
Sessions • Fall, spring, yearlong.

Eligibility Requirements • Minimum age 17; open to sophomores, juniors, seniors, adults; good academic standing at home school; interview; essay; no foreign language proficiency required.
Living Arrangements • Students live in host family homes. Meals are taken as a group, on one's own, with host family, in residences, in restaurants.
Costs (2003-2004) • One term: $14,375 (estimated). Yearlong program: $28,750 (estimated); includes tuition, housing, all meals, excursions, international airfare, books and class materials. $30 application fee. $200 deposit required. Financial aid available for students from sponsoring institution: scholarships, loans, need-based grants.
For More Information • Admissions Office, FWP, Long Island University, 239 Montauk Highway, Southampton College, Southampton, NY 11968; *Phone:* 631-287-8474; *Fax:* 631-287-8463. *E-mail:* fw@liu.edu. *World Wide Web:* http://www.southampton.liu.edu/fw/

UNIVERSITY STUDIES ABROAD CONSORTIUM
SPANISH, ECOLOGY, AND LATIN AMERICAN STUDIES: HEREDIA, COSTA RICA
Hosted by National University
Academic Focus • Art history, biological/life sciences, business administration/management, dance, economics, environmental science/studies, history, Latin American studies, political science and government, Spanish language and literature.
Program Information • Students attend classes at National University. Field trips to Arenal Volcano, Fortuna Waterfall, San José, La Paz Waterfall, Monteverde Cloud Forest, a butterfly farm; optional travel to southern Costa Rica, northern Costa Rica, Nicaragua at an extra cost.
Sessions • Fall, spring, yearlong.
Eligibility Requirements • Minimum age 18; open to freshmen, sophomores, juniors, seniors, graduate students, adults; 2.5 GPA; no foreign language proficiency required.
Living Arrangements • Students live in host family homes. Quarters are shared with host institution students. Meals are taken on one's own, with host family, in residences, in restaurants.
Costs (2005-2006) • One term: $4980. Yearlong program: $8760; includes tuition, some meals, insurance, excursions, student support services. $50 application fee. $150 refundable deposit required. Financial aid available for all students: scholarships, work study, loans.
For More Information • University Studies Abroad Consortium, USAC/323, Reno, NV 89557-0093; *Phone:* 775-784-6569; *Fax:* 775-784-6010. *E-mail:* usac@unr.edu. *World Wide Web:* http://usac.unr.edu/

MONTEVERDE
CIEE
CIEE STUDY CENTER, MONTEVERDE, COSTA RICA
Held at Monteverde Biological Station
Academic Focus • Biological/life sciences, conservation studies, ecology, environmental science/studies, Spanish language and literature.
Program Information • Classes are held on the campus of Monteverde Biological Station. Faculty members are drawn from the sponsor's U.S. staff and local instructors hired by the sponsor. Scheduled travel to Corcovado National Park, Santa Rosa National Park, Tortuguero National Park, La Selva Forest, San José; field trips to San José, Carara National Park, San Gerardo, San Luis; optional travel to Panama.
Sessions • Fall, spring.
Eligibility Requirements • Minimum age 18; open to sophomores, juniors, seniors, graduate students, adults; course work in biological sciences (2 semesters) ecology or environmental science (1 semester); 2.75 GPA; 2 letters of recommendation; proficiency in Spanish recommended.
Living Arrangements • Students live in host family homes, a biological station, hostels, tents. Quarters are shared with host institution students. Meals are taken as a group, in residences, in central dining facility, in restaurants.

Costs (2004-2005) • One term: $9450; includes tuition, housing, all meals, insurance, excursions, books and class materials, lab equipment, student support services, computer and library access at biological station, pre-departure advising, cultural activities, national park entry fees, camping equipment. $30 application fee. $300 deposit required. Financial aid available for all students: minority student scholarships, 1 special program scholarship, travel grants.
For More Information • Ms. Ellen Whitman, Admissions Officer, Spain and Latin America, CIEE, 7 Custom House Street, 3rd Floor, Portland, ME 04101; *Phone:* 800-40-STUDY; *Fax:* 207-553-7699. *E-mail:* studyinfo@ciee.org. *World Wide Web:* http://www.ciee.org/isp/

PUNTARENAS
UNIVERSITY STUDIES ABROAD CONSORTIUM
SPANISH, ECOLOGY, AND LATIN AMERICAN STUDIES: PUNTARENAS, COSTA RICA
Hosted by National University
Academic Focus • Art history, biological/life sciences, business administration/management, dance, economics, environmental science/studies, history, Latin American studies, political science and government, Spanish language and literature.
Program Information • Students attend classes at National University. Field trips to La Paz Waterfall, Monteverde Cloud Forest, a Butterfly Farm, Arenal Volcano, Fortuna Waterfalls; optional travel to southern Costa Rica, northern Costa Rica, Nicaragua at an extra cost.
Sessions • Fall, spring, yearlong.
Eligibility Requirements • Minimum age 18; open to freshmen, sophomores, juniors, seniors, graduate students, adults; 2.5 GPA; no foreign language proficiency required.
Living Arrangements • Students live in locally rented apartments, host family homes. Quarters are shared with host institution students. Meals are taken on one's own, with host family, in residences, in restaurants.
Costs (2005-2006) • One term: $4980. Yearlong program: $8760; includes tuition, some meals, insurance, excursions, student support services. $50 application fee. $150 refundable deposit required. Financial aid available for all students: scholarships, loans.
For More Information • University Studies Abroad Consortium, USAC/323, Reno, NV 89557-0093; *Phone:* 775-784-6569; *Fax:* 775-784-6010. *E-mail:* usac@unr.edu. *World Wide Web:* http://usac.unr.edu/

SAN JOSÉ
ASSOCIATED COLLEGES OF THE MIDWEST
ACM STUDIES IN LATIN AMERICAN CULTURE AND SOCIETY
Academic Focus • Costa Rican studies, Latin American literature, Latin American studies, political science and government, Spanish language and literature.
Program Information • Faculty members are drawn from the sponsor's U.S. staff and local instructors hired by the sponsor. Scheduled travel to rural sites; field trips to beaches, banana plantations, volcanoes.
Sessions • Fall.
Eligibility Requirements • Open to sophomores, juniors, seniors; 2 letters of recommendation; Spanish proficiency reference letter; 2 years of college course work in Spanish.
Living Arrangements • Students live in host family homes. Meals are taken with host family, in residences.
Costs (2004) • One term: contact sponsor for cost. $400 nonrefundable deposit required.
For More Information • Program Associate, ACM Costa Rica Program, Associated Colleges of the Midwest, 205 West Wacker Drive, Suite 1300, Chicago, IL 60606; *Phone:* 312-263-5000; *Fax:* 312-263-5879. *E-mail:* acm@acm.edu. *World Wide Web:* http://www.acm.edu/

COSTA RICA
San José

ASSOCIATED COLLEGES OF THE MIDWEST
ACM TROPICAL FIELD RESEARCH

Academic Focus • Anthropology, archaeology, art, biological/life sciences, chemical sciences, ecology, geology, liberal studies, music, social sciences, Spanish language and literature.

Program Information • Faculty members are drawn from the sponsor's U.S. staff and local instructors hired by the sponsor. Scheduled travel to research sites; field trips to beaches, banana plantations, volcanoes.

Sessions • Spring.

Eligibility Requirements • Open to juniors, seniors; course work in proposed research discipline; 2 letters of recommendation; Spanish proficiency reference letter; 2 years of college course work in Spanish.

Living Arrangements • Students live in host family homes. Meals are taken on one's own, with host family.

Costs (2004) • One term: contact sponsor for cost. $400 nonrefundable deposit required.

For More Information • Program Associate, ACM Costa Rica Program, Associated Colleges of the Midwest, 205 West Wacker Drive, Suite 1300, Chicago, IL 60606; *Phone:* 312-263-5000; *Fax:* 312-263-5879. *E-mail:* acm@acm.edu. *World Wide Web:* http://www.acm.edu/

COLLEGE CONSORTIUM FOR INTERNATIONAL STUDIES–MIAMI DADE COLLEGE AND TRUMAN STATE UNIVERSITY
SEMESTER IN COSTA RICA

Hosted by Veritas University

Academic Focus • Costa Rican studies, ecology, environmental science/studies, international affairs, international business, Latin American literature, marine sciences, social sciences, Spanish language and literature.

Program Information • Students attend classes at Veritas University. Field trips to national parks, San José; optional travel to volcanoes, national parks, the Pacific coast at an extra cost.

Sessions • Fall, spring, yearlong, second spring term with no courses in English.

Eligibility Requirements • Minimum age 18; open to freshmen, sophomores, juniors, seniors, adults; 2.5 GPA; 2 letters of recommendation; good academic standing at home school; no foreign language proficiency required.

Living Arrangements • Students live in locally rented apartments, host family homes. Meals are taken with host family, in residences.

Costs (2004-2005) • One term: $5900 (estimated). Yearlong program: $11,800 (estimated); includes tuition, housing, some meals, insurance, excursions, international student ID, some class materials. $30 application fee. $400 refundable deposit required. Financial aid available for students from sponsoring institution: loans.

For More Information • Mr. Reinaldo Changsut, Director, International Education, College Consortium for International Studies–Miami Dade College and Truman State University, Miami Dade College, 11011 SW 104th Street, Miami, FL 33176-3393; *Phone:* 305-237-2533; *Fax:* 305-237-2949. *E-mail:* reinaldo.changsut@mdc.edu. *World Wide Web:* http://www.ccisabroad.org/. Students may also apply through Truman State University, Center for International Education Abroad, 100 East Normal, Kirksville, MO 63501.

CULTURAL EXPERIENCES ABROAD (CEA)
STUDY SPANISH, ECOLOGY, AND LATIN AMERICAN CULTURE IN SAN JOSÉ

Hosted by Veritas University

Academic Focus • Architecture, art, Costa Rican studies, dance, ecology, economics, environmental science/studies, international business, Latin American literature, Latin American studies, linguistics, photography, Spanish language and literature.

Program Information • Students attend classes at Veritas University. Field trips to Monteverde, Manuel Antonio; optional travel to Panama, Nicaragua at an extra cost.

Sessions • Fall, spring, winter.

Eligibility Requirements • Minimum age 18; open to freshmen, sophomores, juniors, seniors, graduate students, adults; 2.7 GPA; 1 letter of recommendation; good academic standing at home school; previous Spanish study recommended.

Living Arrangements • Students live in locally rented apartments, host family homes. Quarters are shared with students from other programs. Meals are taken on one's own, with host family, in residences.

Costs (2003-2004) • One term: $6395–$6495; includes tuition, housing, some meals, insurance, excursions, books and class materials, lab equipment, student support services, e-mail and Internet access. $50 application fee. $400 nonrefundable deposit required.

For More Information • Cultural Experiences Abroad (CEA), 1400 East Southern Avenue, Suite B-108, Tempe, AZ 85282-8011; *Phone:* 480-557-7900; *Fax:* 480-557-7926. *E-mail:* petersons@gowithcea.com. *World Wide Web:* http://www.gowithcea.com/

EDUCATION ABROAD INC.
TROPICAL FIELD ECOLOGY AND SPANISH

Hosted by University of Costa Rica

Academic Focus • Biological/life sciences, botany, ecology, Spanish language and literature.

Program Information • Students attend classes at University of Costa Rica. Scheduled travel to field stations throughout Costa Rica; field trips to ongoing environment-related projects.

Sessions • Fall, spring.

Eligibility Requirements • Minimum age 18; open to sophomores, juniors, seniors; course work in natural sciences (1 semester); 2.5 GPA; no foreign language proficiency required.

Living Arrangements • Students live in host family homes, hotels, biological field stations. Meals are taken as a group, with host family, in residences, in restaurants.

Costs (2004-2005) • One term: $10,000; includes tuition, housing, all meals, insurance, excursions, books and class materials, lab equipment, international student ID, student support services. $15 application fee. $500 deposit required.

For More Information • Mr. T. Jesse Fox, Director of Education Abroad, Inc., Education Abroad Inc., 17812 S H 16 South, Pipe Creek, TX 78063; *Phone:* 800-321-7625; *Fax:* 800-321-7625. *E-mail:* ucr@educationabroad.com. *World Wide Web:* http://www.educationabroad.com/

INSTITUTE FOR STUDY ABROAD, BUTLER UNIVERSITY
UNIVERSIDAD DE COSTA RICA

Hosted by University of Costa Rica

Academic Focus • Full curriculum.

Program Information • Students attend classes at University of Costa Rica.

Sessions • Fall, spring, yearlong.

Eligibility Requirements • Open to sophomores, juniors, seniors; 3.0 GPA; 1 letter of recommendation; good academic standing at home school; enrollment at an accredited American college or university; Spanish language evaluation; 2 years of college course work in Spanish.

Living Arrangements • Students live in host family homes. Meals are taken with host family.

Costs (2003-2004) • One term: $8295. Yearlong program: $15,750; includes tuition, housing, all meals, excursions, international student ID, student support services, cultural and athletic activities, pre-departure advising. $40 application fee. $500 nonrefundable deposit required. Financial aid available for all students: scholarships, travel grants.

For More Information • Institute for Study Abroad, Butler University, 1100 West 42nd Street, Suite 305, Indianapolis, IN 46208-3345; *Phone:* 800-858-0229; *Fax:* 317-940-9336. *E-mail:* copa@butler.edu. *World Wide Web:* http://www.ifsa-butler.org/

INTERNATIONAL CENTER FOR SUSTAINABLE HUMAN DEVELOPMENT (CIDH)
HUMAN RIGHTS AND JUSTICE IN LATIN AMERICA

Hosted by International Center for Sustainable Human Development (CIDH), Latin University of Costa Rica

Academic Focus • Interdisciplinary studies, Latin American studies, peace and conflict studies, social sciences.

Program Information • Students attend classes at International Center for Sustainable Human Development (CIDH), Latin University of Costa Rica. Scheduled travel to national parks; field trips to rural communities, relevant human rights institutions, sites of cultural and historic interest.

Sessions • Fall, spring.

Eligibility Requirements • Open to sophomores, juniors, seniors; 2.75 GPA; 2 letters of recommendation; good academic standing at home school; college transcripts; 1 year of college course work in Spanish.

Living Arrangements • Students live in host family homes. Meals are taken with host family, in residences.

Costs (2004) • One term: $6975; includes tuition, housing, some meals, excursions, student support services. $200 application fee.

For More Information • Dr. Jorge Nowalski, President and Academic Director, International Center for Sustainable Human Development (CIDH), PO Box 1411-1000, San José 1000, Costa Rica; *Phone:* 506-258-0297; *Fax:* 506-222-3095. *E-mail:* cidhcr@racsa.co. cr. *World Wide Web:* http://www.cidh.ac.cr/

INTERNATIONAL CENTER FOR SUSTAINABLE HUMAN DEVELOPMENT (CIDH)
PEOPLE AND THE ENVIRONMENT IN CENTRAL AMERICA

Hosted by International Center for Sustainable Human Development (CIDH), Latin University of Costa Rica

Academic Focus • Cultural studies, environmental science/studies, interdisciplinary studies, Spanish language and literature.

Program Information • Students attend classes at International Center for Sustainable Human Development (CIDH), Latin University of Costa Rica. Scheduled travel to the Cuerici Biolgical Station, Las Cruces Botanical Gardens, the Marenco Biological Station; field trips to national parks, biological stations, sites of cultural interest.

Sessions • Fall, spring.

Eligibility Requirements • Open to sophomores, juniors, seniors; 2.75 GPA; 2 letters of recommendation; good academic standing at home school; college transcript; 1 year of college course work in Spanish.

Living Arrangements • Students live in host family homes. Meals are taken with host family, in residences.

Costs (2004) • One term: $6975; includes tuition, housing, some meals, excursions, student support services. $200 application fee.

For More Information • Dr. Jorge Nowalski, President and Academic Director, International Center for Sustainable Human Development (CIDH), PO Box 1411-1000, San José 1000, Costa Rica; *Phone:* 506-258-0297; *Fax:* 506-222-3095. *E-mail:* cidhcr@racsa.co. cr. *World Wide Web:* http://www.cidh.ac.cr/

INTERNATIONAL CENTER FOR SUSTAINABLE HUMAN DEVELOPMENT (CIDH)
SUSTAINABLE HUMAN DEVELOPMENT IN LATIN AMERICA

Hosted by International Center for Sustainable Human Development (CIDH), University of Costa Rica

Academic Focus • Interdisciplinary studies, Latin American studies, social sciences, Spanish language and literature.

Program Information • Students attend classes at International Center for Sustainable Human Development (CIDH), University of Costa Rica. Scheduled travel to biological stations; field trips to national parks, sites of cultural or social interest.

Sessions • Fall.

Eligibility Requirements • Open to sophomores, juniors, seniors, graduate students; 2.75 GPA; 2 letters of recommendation; good academic standing at home school; college transcript; 1 year of college course work in Spanish.

COSTA RICA
San José

Living Arrangements • Students live in host family homes. Meals are taken with host family.

Costs (2004) • One term: $6850; includes tuition, housing, some meals, excursions, student support services. $200 application fee.

For More Information • Dr. Jorge Nowalski, President and Academic Director, International Center for Sustainable Human Development (CIDH), PO Box 1411-1000, San José 1000, Costa Rica; *Phone:* 506-258-0297; *Fax:* 506-222-3095. *E-mail:* cidhcr@racsa.co.cr. *World Wide Web:* http://www.cidh.ac.cr/

INTERNATIONAL STUDIES ABROAD
SAN JOSÉ, COSTA RICA–SPANISH LANGUAGE PLUS ELECTIVES IN VARIOUS FIELDS

Hosted by Veritas University

Academic Focus • Business administration/management, ecology, environmental science/studies, Latin American studies, photography, Spanish language and literature.

Program Information • Students attend classes at Veritas University. Scheduled travel to Manuel Antonio National Park, Arenal Volcano; field trips to Monteverde, Manuel Antonio, Arenal Volcano, La Fortuna Waterfall; optional travel at an extra cost.

Sessions • Fall, spring, winter.

Eligibility Requirements • Minimum age 18; open to freshmen, sophomores, juniors, seniors, graduate students, adults; 2.5 GPA; 1 letter of recommendation; no foreign language proficiency required.

Living Arrangements • Students live in locally rented apartments, host family homes, hotels. Quarters are shared with host institution students, students from other programs. Meals are taken with host family, in residences.

Costs (2004-2005) • One term: $6250 for one trimester; $11,500 for two trimesters; includes tuition, housing, all meals, insurance, excursions, student support services, ground transportation. $200 nonrefundable deposit required. Financial aid available for all students: scholarships, loans, U.S. federal financial aid.

For More Information • Ms. Rose Mankins, Costa Rica Site Specialist, International Studies Abroad, 901 West 24th Street, Austin, TX 78705; *Phone:* 800-580-8826; *Fax:* 512-480-8866. *E-mail:* isa@studiesabroad.com. *World Wide Web:* http://www.studiesabroad.com/

INTERNATIONAL STUDIES ABROAD
SAN JOSÉ–SPANISH LANGUAGE COURSES WITH COSTA RICAN STUDENTS

Hosted by Latin American University of Science and Technology

Academic Focus • Accounting, business administration/management, ecology, environmental science/studies, history, Latin American studies, law and legal studies, philosophy, Spanish language and literature.

Program Information • Students attend classes at Latin American University of Science and Technology. Scheduled travel to Manuel Antonio National Park, Arenal Volcano; field trips to Cartago, Irazu Volcano; optional travel at an extra cost.

Sessions • Fall, spring, winter.

Eligibility Requirements • Minimum age 18; open to freshmen, sophomores, juniors, seniors, graduate students, adults; 2.75 GPA; 1 letter of recommendation; 2 years of college course work in Spanish.

Living Arrangements • Students live in locally rented apartments, host family homes, hotels. Quarters are shared with host institution students, students from other programs. Meals are taken with host family, in residences.

Costs (2004-2005) • One term: $6350 for one trimester; $11,700 for two trimesters; includes tuition, housing, all meals, insurance, excursions, student support services, ground transportation. $200 nonrefundable deposit required. Financial aid available for all students: scholarships, loans, U.S. federal financial aid.

For More Information • Ms. Rose Mankins, Costa Rica Site Specialist, International Studies Abroad, 901 West 24th Street, Austin, TX 78705; *Phone:* 800-580-8826; *Fax:* 512-480-8866. *World Wide Web:* http://www.studiesabroad.com/

NICHOLLS STATE UNIVERSITY
STUDY PROGRAM IN COSTA RICA

Hosted by Nicholls State University–San José

Academic Focus • Art, cultural studies, history, Spanish language and literature.

Program Information • Students attend classes at Nicholls State University–San José. Field trips to museums, the theater, markets; optional travel to Manuel Antonio beach, a rainforest, a cloud forest, white water rafting, Arenal Volcano at an extra cost.

Sessions • Fall, spring, yearlong.

Eligibility Requirements • Minimum age 17; open to precollege students, freshmen, sophomores, juniors, seniors, graduate students, adults; no foreign language proficiency required.

Living Arrangements • Students live in host family homes. Quarters are shared with host institution students. Meals are taken with host family, in residences.

Costs (2003-2004) • One term: $4568. Yearlong program: $9135; includes tuition, housing, some meals, insurance, books and class materials, lab equipment, international student ID, airport pick-up, instructional costs. Financial aid available for all students: loans, all customary sources.

For More Information • Ms. Cynthia Webb, Director of Study Programs Abroad, Nicholls State University, PO Box 2080, Thibodaux, LA 70310; *Phone:* 985-448-4440; *Fax:* 985-449-7028. *E-mail:* spab-caw@nicholls.edu. *World Wide Web:* http://www.nicholls.edu/abroad/

ORGANIZATION FOR TROPICAL STUDIES
OTS UNDERGRADUATE SEMESTER ABROAD IN TROPICAL BIOLOGY

Held at Palo Verde Biological Station, Las Cruces Biological Station, La Selva Biological Station

Academic Focus • Biological/life sciences, conservation studies, ecology, environmental science/studies, Spanish language and literature.

Program Information • Classes are held on the campus of Palo Verde Biological Station, La Selva Biological Station, Las Cruces Biological Station. Faculty members are drawn from the sponsor's U.S. staff and local instructors hired by the sponsor. Scheduled travel to native habitats, national parks, agro-ecosystems, biological field stations; field trips to biological reserves.

Sessions • Fall, spring.

Eligibility Requirements • Open to sophomores, juniors, seniors; course work in biology; 2 letters of recommendation; good academic standing at home school; 1 year of college course work in Spanish.

Living Arrangements • Students live in host family homes, biological field stations. Quarters are shared with host institution students. Meals are taken as a group, in central dining facility.

Costs (2003-2004) • One term: $14,317; includes tuition, housing, all meals, excursions, books and class materials, lab equipment. $1000 nonrefundable deposit required. Financial aid available for students: scholarships for students from under-represented groups in the sciences.

For More Information • Mr. Rodney J. Vargas, Undergraduate Program Officer, Organization for Tropical Studies, Box 90630, Durham, NC 27708-0630; *Phone:* 919-684-5774; *Fax:* 919-684-5661. *E-mail:* nao@duke.edu. *World Wide Web:* http://www.ots.duke.edu/

STATE UNIVERSITY OF NEW YORK COLLEGE AT BROCKPORT
COSTA RICA PROGRAM

Hosted by Escuela de Idiomas

Academic Focus • Accounting, anthropology, art history, business administration/management, communications, computer science, criminal justice, ecology, economics, education, finance, health, health and physical education, history, hotel and restaurant management, international affairs, international business, journalism, Latin American studies, nursing, parks and recreation, political science and government, psychology, sociology, Spanish language and literature, Spanish studies, tourism and travel, zoology.

Program Information • Students attend classes at Escuela de Idiomas. Field trips to various sites throughout San José.

Sessions • Fall, spring, yearlong.

Eligibility Requirements • Minimum age 18; open to sophomores, juniors, seniors, graduate students; course work in area of internship, if applicable; 2.5 GPA; 2 letters of recommendation; ability to do upper-division course work; résumé required for internship option; must be at least a second semester sophomore; 1 year college course work in Spanish or the equivalent.

Living Arrangements • Students live in host family homes. Meals are taken with host family, in residences.

Costs (2004-2005) • One term: $6650 for fall; $6900 for spring. Yearlong program: contact sponsor for cost; includes tuition, excursions, international student ID, student support services, airport pick-up upon arrival. $350 nonrefundable deposit required. Financial aid available for all students: scholarships, loans, regular financial aid, grants.

For More Information • Dr. John Perry, Director, Office of International Education, State University of New York College at Brockport, 350 New Campus Drive, Brockport, NY 14420; *Phone:* 800-298-SUNY; *Fax:* 585-637-3218. *E-mail:* overseas@brockport.edu. *World Wide Web:* http://www.brockport.edu/studyabroad/

UNIVERSITY AT ALBANY, STATE UNIVERSITY OF NEW YORK
DIRECT ENROLLMENT AT THE UNIVERSITY OF COSTA RICA

Hosted by University of Costa Rica

Academic Focus • Biological/life sciences, engineering, full curriculum, Latin American studies, liberal studies, linguistics, literature, science, social sciences, Spanish language and literature.

Program Information • Students attend classes at University of Costa Rica.

Sessions • Fall, spring, yearlong.

Eligibility Requirements • Open to juniors, seniors, graduate students, adults; 3.3 GPA; 2 letters of recommendation; good academic standing at home school; advanced college course work in Spanish or the equivalent.

Living Arrangements • Students live in host family homes. Meals are taken with host family, in residences, in central dining facility, in restaurants.

Costs (2002-2003) • One term: $5550. Yearlong program: $11,100; includes housing, all meals, student support services, pre-session and in-state tuition and fees. $150 nonrefundable deposit required. Financial aid available for students from sponsoring institution: all customary sources.

For More Information • University at Albany, State University of New York, Office of International Education, LI 66, Albany, NY 12222; *Phone:* 518-442-3525; *Fax:* 518-442-3338. *E-mail:* intled@uamail.albany.edu. *World Wide Web:* http://www.albany.edu/intled/

UNIVERSITY OF DELAWARE
SPRING SEMESTER IN COSTA RICA

Hosted by University of Costa Rica

Academic Focus • Environmental science/studies, geography, history, intercultural studies, international affairs, political science and government, Spanish language and literature.

Program Information • Students attend classes at University of Costa Rica. Scheduled travel to Manuel Antonio National Park, Cahuita National Park; field trips to the Gold Museum, the National Museum, the National Theater, a coffee plantation, volcanoes Poas and Irazu; optional travel to Latin America at an extra cost.

Sessions • Spring.

Eligibility Requirements • Open to freshmen, sophomores, juniors, seniors, adults; 2.8 GPA; 2 letters of recommendation; 2 years of college course work in Spanish.

Living Arrangements • Students live in host family homes. Meals are taken with host family, in residences.

Costs (2003) • One term: contact sponsor for cost. $200 nonrefundable deposit required. Financial aid available for all students: scholarships.

For More Information • Center for International Studies, University of Delaware, 186 South College Avenue, Newark, DE 19716-1450;

Study Abroad in Costa Rica

Picture yourself...

...studying and making friends with Costa Rican students at the Universidad de Costa Rica, Costa Rica's largest and most prestigious university, in the bustling capital city of San José.

...living for a semester or year in a traveler's paradise, with 400 miles of coastline, 46 national parks, active volcanoes, cloud forests, rain forests and innumerous plant and animal species.

It's closer than you think.

University of Kansas Office of Study Abroad

1410 Jayhawk Blvd., Room 108 ■ Lawrence, KS 66045-7515
785-864-3742 ■ osa@ku.edu ■ www.ku.edu/~osa

COSTA RICA
San José

Phone: 888-831-4685; *Fax:* 302-831-6042. *E-mail:* studyabroad@udel.edu. *World Wide Web:* http://www.udel.edu/studyabroad/

UNIVERSITY OF ILLINOIS AT URBANA-CHAMPAIGN
LANGUAGE AND CULTURE IN COSTA RICA

Hosted by Instituto San Joaquin de Flores
Academic Focus • Area studies, conservation studies, Costa Rican studies, international business, Latin American studies, Spanish language and literature.
Program Information • Students attend classes at Instituto San Joaquin de Flores. Field trips to coffee plantations, the beach, a cloud forest, a rainforest, nature reserves.
Sessions • Fall, spring.
Eligibility Requirements • Open to sophomores, juniors, seniors; 2.5 GPA; 2 letters of recommendation; good academic standing at home school; 2 years of college course work in Spanish.
Living Arrangements • Students live in host family homes. Meals are taken in residences.
Costs (2002-2003) • One term: $6055; includes tuition, housing, all meals, insurance, excursions, student support services. $55 application fee. $500 nonrefundable deposit required. Financial aid available for students from sponsoring institution: scholarships, loans.
For More Information • Ms. Erika Ryser, Assistant Director, University of Illinois at Urbana-Champaign, Study Abroad Office, 910 South Fifth Street, #115, Champaign, IL 61820; *Phone:* 217-333-6322; *Fax:* 217-244-0249. *E-mail:* ryser@uiuc.edu. *World Wide Web:* http://www.ips.uiuc.edu/sao/index.shtml

UNIVERSITY OF KANSAS
STUDY ABROAD IN SAN JOSÉ, COSTA RICA

Hosted by University of Costa Rica
Academic Focus • Full curriculum.
Program Information • Students attend classes at University of Costa Rica. Scheduled travel to Guanacaste, Monteverde; field trips to Cartago, Manuel Antonio.
Sessions • Fall, spring, yearlong.
Eligibility Requirements • Minimum age 18; open to sophomores, juniors, seniors, graduate students; 3.0 GPA; 2 letters of recommendation; good academic standing at home school; essays; language proficiency report; 2.5 years of college course work in Spanish.
Living Arrangements • Students live in host family homes. Meals are taken on one's own, with host family, in residences.
Costs (2003-2004) • One term: $6500. Yearlong program: $11,750; includes tuition, housing, all meals, excursions, student support services, group activities, resident visa, guidebook, emergency medical evacuation and repatriation service. $38 application fee. $300 nonrefundable deposit required. Financial aid available for students from sponsoring institution: scholarships, loans.
For More Information • Ms. Angela Dittrich, Assistant Director, University of Kansas, Office of Study Abroad, Lippincott Hall, 1410 Jayhawk Boulevard, Room 108, Lawrence, KS 66045-7515; *Phone:* 785-864-3742; *Fax:* 785-864-5040. *E-mail:* osa@ku.edu. *World Wide Web:* http://www.ku.edu/~osa/

SAN RAMÓN

ST. CLOUD STATE UNIVERSITY
ENVIRONMENTAL TECHNOLOGY STUDIES AND SPANISH LANGUAGE

Held at University of Costa Rica–San Ramon
Academic Focus • Environmental science/studies, Spanish language and literature.
Program Information • Classes are held on the campus of University of Costa Rica–San Ramon. Faculty members are drawn from the sponsor's U.S. staff and local instructors hired by the sponsor. Scheduled travel to the Pacific coast, the Atlantic coast; field trips to a rainforest, a volcano; optional travel to Panama at an extra cost.
Sessions • Fall, spring.
Eligibility Requirements • Minimum age 18; open to freshmen, sophomores, juniors, seniors; 2.5 GPA; 2 letters of recommendation;

approval by Environmental and Technological Studies Department; no foreign language proficiency required.
Living Arrangements • Students live in host family homes. Meals are taken on one's own, with host family, in residences.
Costs (2003-2004) • One term: $6800 for Minnesota residents; includes tuition, housing, some meals, excursions, international airfare, international student ID. $75 application fee. Financial aid available for students from sponsoring institution: scholarships, work study, loans.
For More Information • Chunsheng Zhang, Associate Vice President for Academic Affairs/International Studies, St. Cloud State University, Center for International Studies, 720 4th Avenue, South, St. Cloud, MN 56301-4498; *Phone:* 320-308-4287; *Fax:* 320-308-4223. *World Wide Web:* http://www.stcloudstate.edu/

CUBA

HAVANA

THE CENTER FOR CROSS CULTURAL STUDY
FALL OR SPRING SEMESTER IN HAVANA, CUBA

Hosted by University of Havana
Academic Focus • Cuban Studies, cultural studies, history, political science and government, sociology, Spanish language and literature.
Program Information • Students attend classes at University of Havana. Field trips to Matanzas Province, Varadero Beach, Ernest Hemingway's home, La Cabaña Fort, Soroa Orchid Nursery, Pinar del Rio.
Sessions • Fall, spring.
Eligibility Requirements • Minimum age 17; open to precollege students, freshmen, sophomores, juniors, seniors, graduate students; 1 letter of recommendation; good academic standing at home school; must be a currently enrolled, degree-seeking student; minimum 3.0 GPA in Spanish; 2 years of college course work in Spanish.
Living Arrangements • Students live in hotels. Quarters are shared with host institution students. Meals are taken as a group, in central dining facility.
Costs (2004-2005) • One term: $9480; includes tuition, housing, some meals, insurance, excursions, books and class materials, student support services, visa fees. $50 application fee. $500 nonrefundable deposit required. Financial aid available for all students: scholarships.
For More Information • Dr. Judith M. Ortiz, Director, U.S., The Center for Cross Cultural Study, Department PY, 446 Main Street, Amherst, MA 01002-2314; *Phone:* 800-377-2621; *Fax:* 413-256-1968. *E-mail:* petersons@cccs.com. *World Wide Web:* http://www.cccs.com/

CIEE
CIEE STUDY CENTER AT THE UNIVERSIDAD DE HABANA, CUBA

Hosted by University of Havana
Academic Focus • Anthropology, art history, biological/life sciences, film and media studies.
Program Information • Students attend classes at University of Havana. Field trips to cultural visits in and around Havana.
Sessions • Fall, spring.
Eligibility Requirements • Minimum age 18; open to freshmen, sophomores, juniors, seniors; 3.2 GPA; phone interview (in English); maximum age of 25; 2.5 years of college course work in Spanish.
Living Arrangements • Students live in host institution dormitories. Quarters are shared with host institution students. Meals are taken on one's own, in restaurants.
Costs (2005-2006) • One term: contact sponsor for cost. $30 application fee. Financial aid available for all students: scholarships, travel grants, minority student scholarships.
For More Information • Ms. Ellen Whitman, Admissions Officer, Spain and Latin America, CIEE, 7 Custom House Street, 3rd Floor, Portland, ME 04101; *Phone:* 800-40-STUDY; *Fax:* 207-553-7699. *E-mail:* ewhitman@ciee.org. *World Wide Web:* http://www.ciee.org/isp/

INSTITUTE FOR STUDY ABROAD, BUTLER UNIVERSITY
UNIVERSIDAD DE LA HABANA

Hosted by University of Havana
Academic Focus • Full curriculum.
Program Information • Students attend classes at University of Havana. Field trips to Varadero, Trinidad, Viñales.
Sessions • Fall, spring.
Eligibility Requirements • Open to juniors, seniors; 3.4 GPA; 1 letter of recommendation; good academic standing at home school; enrollment at an accredited American college or university; Spanish language evaluation; 2.5 years of college course work in Spanish.
Living Arrangements • Students live in locally rented apartments. Meals are taken on one's own, in restaurants.
Costs (2002-2003) • One term: $8975; includes tuition, housing, some meals, insurance, excursions, international student ID, student support services, cultural and sporting events, pre-departure advising. $40 application fee. $500 nonrefundable deposit required. Financial aid available for all students: scholarships.
For More Information • Institute for Study Abroad, Butler University, 1100 West 42nd Street, Suite 305, Indianapolis, IN 46208-3345; *Phone:* 800-858-0229; *Fax:* 317-940-9704. *E-mail:* copa@butler.edu. *World Wide Web:* http://www.ifsa-butler.org/

LEXIA INTERNATIONAL
LEXIA IN HAVANA

Hosted by University of Havana
Academic Focus • Anthropology, area studies, art, art history, business administration/management, civilization studies, comparative history, cultural studies, drawing/painting, environmental science/studies, ethnic studies, film and media studies, fine/studio arts, geography, history, interdisciplinary studies, international affairs, international business, Latin American literature, Latin American studies, liberal studies, literature, music, music history, music performance, philosophy, political science and government, psychology, religious studies, social sciences, sociology, Spanish language and literature, urban studies, visual and performing arts.
Program Information • Students attend classes at University of Havana. Field trips to Pinar del Rio, Guantánamo provinces.
Sessions • Fall, spring, yearlong.
Eligibility Requirements • Minimum age 18; open to sophomores, juniors, seniors, graduate students, adults; 2.5 GPA; 2 letters of recommendation; no foreign language proficiency required.
Living Arrangements • Students live in host institution dormitories, hotels. Quarters are shared with host institution students. Meals are taken on one's own, with host family, in residences.
Costs (2003-2004) • One term: $11,950. Yearlong program: $21,550; includes tuition, housing, all meals, insurance, excursions, international student ID, student support services, transcript. $35 application fee. $300 nonrefundable deposit required. Financial aid available for all students: scholarships, work study.
For More Information • Lexia International, 23 South Main Street, Hanover, NH 03755; *Phone:* 800-775-3942; *Fax:* 603-643-9899. *E-mail:* info@lexiaintl.org. *World Wide Web:* http://www.lexiaintl.org/

SARAH LAWRENCE COLLEGE
SARAH LAWRENCE COLLEGE IN CUBA

Hosted by Facultad Latinoamericana de Ciencias Sociales (FLASCO), Centro de Estudios Demograficos, Centro de Estudios sobre los Estados Unidos, Instituto Superior de Artes, Fundación Del Nuevo Cine Latinos Americanos, University of Havana
Academic Focus • Cuban Studies, film and media studies, fine/studio arts, history, international affairs, Latin American literature, Latin American studies, music, philosophy, psychology, social sciences, sociology, urban studies, women's studies.
Program Information • Students attend classes at University of Havana, Centro de Estudios Demograficos, Centro de Estudios sobre los Estados Unidos, Facultad Latinoamericana de Ciencias Sociales (FLASCO), Fundación Del Nuevo Cine Latinos Americanos, Instituto Superior de Artes. Field trips to Santiago de Cuba.
Sessions • Fall.

Eligibility Requirements • Open to juniors, seniors; 3.5 GPA; 2 letters of recommendation; good academic standing at home school; essay; language recommendation forms; 2 years of college course work in Spanish.
Living Arrangements • Students live in locally rented houses. Meals are taken as a group, on one's own, in residences.
Costs (2003) • One term: $18,060; includes tuition, housing, all meals. $35 application fee. $250 nonrefundable deposit required. Financial aid available for all students: scholarships, loans.
For More Information • Ms. Prema Samuel, Director of International Programs, Sarah Lawrence College, 1 Meadway, Bronxville, NY 10708-5999; *Phone:* 800-873-4752; *Fax:* 914-395-2666. *E-mail:* slcaway@slc.edu. *World Wide Web:* http://www.sarahlawrence.edu/studyabroad/

SCHOOL FOR INTERNATIONAL TRAINING, SIT STUDY ABROAD
CUBA: CULTURE, IDENTITY, AND COMMUNITY

Academic Focus • Cultural studies, Latin American studies, political science and government, sociology, Spanish language and literature.
Program Information • Faculty members are drawn from the sponsor's U.S. staff and local instructors hired by the sponsor. Field trips to agricultural cooperatives, rural communities, work sites, areas of historic and literary significance.
Sessions • Fall, spring.
Eligibility Requirements • Open to sophomores, juniors, seniors; course work in Latin American Studies; 2.5 GPA; 2 letters of recommendation; good academic standing at home school; 2 years of college course work in Spanish.
Living Arrangements • Students live in locally rented apartments. Meals are taken as a group, with host family, in residences, in restaurants.
Costs (2003-2004) • One term: $12,950; includes tuition, housing, all meals, insurance, excursions. $50 application fee. $400 nonrefundable deposit required. Financial aid available for all students: scholarships.
For More Information • School for International Training, SIT Study Abroad, Kipling Road, Brattleboro, VT 05302-0676; *Phone:* 888-272-7881; *Fax:* 802-258-3296. *E-mail:* studyabroad@sit.edu. *World Wide Web:* http://www.sit.edu/studyabroad/

SCHOOL FOR INTERNATIONAL TRAINING, SIT STUDY ABROAD
CUBA: PUBLIC HEALTH AND PUBLIC POLICY

Academic Focus • Public health, public policy.
Program Information • Faculty members are local instructors hired by the sponsor. Scheduled travel; field trips.
Sessions • Fall, spring.
Eligibility Requirements • Open to freshmen, sophomores, juniors; 2.5 GPA; fluency in Spanish.
Living Arrangements • Students live in locally rented apartments.
Costs (2004-2005) • One term: contact sponsor for cost. $50 application fee. $400 nonrefundable deposit required. Financial aid available for all students: scholarships.
For More Information • School for International Training, SIT Study Abroad, Kipling Road, Brattleboro, VT 05302-0676; *Phone:* 888-272-7881; *Fax:* 802-258-3296. *E-mail:* studyabroad@sit.edu. *World Wide Web:* http://www.sit.edu/studyabroad/

STATE UNIVERSITY OF NEW YORK AT OSWEGO
CUBA SEMESTER PROGRAM WITH UNIVERSITY OF HAVANA

Hosted by University of Havana
Academic Focus • Anthropology, Cuban Studies, cultural studies, history, philosophy, political science and government, sociology, Spanish language and literature.
Program Information • Students attend classes at University of Havana. Field trips.
Sessions • Fall, spring.
Eligibility Requirements • Minimum age 18; open to sophomores, juniors, seniors; 3.2 GPA; 3 letters of recommendation; good academic standing at home school; advanced Spanish.

CUBA
Havana

Living Arrangements • Students live in host institution dormitories. Meals are taken as a group, in residences, in central dining facility, in restaurants.
Costs (2003-2004) • One term: $9000 (estimated); includes tuition, housing, all meals, insurance, excursions, international airfare, books and class materials, student support services, spending money. $250 nonrefundable deposit required. Financial aid available for students: home university financial aid and scholarships for Oswego students.
For More Information • Ms. Lizette Alvarado, Program Specialist, State University of New York at Oswego, 122A Swetman Hall, Oswego, NY 13126; *Phone:* 888-4-OSWEGO; *Fax:* 315-312-2477. *E-mail:* intled@oswego.edu. *World Wide Web:* http://www.oswego.edu/intled/

CYPRUS
NICOSIA

COLLEGE CONSORTIUM FOR INTERNATIONAL STUDIES–BROOKDALE COMMUNITY COLLEGE
PROGRAM IN CYPRUS

Hosted by Intercollege–Larnaca, Intercollege–Limassol, Intercollege–Nicosia
Academic Focus • Full curriculum.
Program Information • Students attend classes at Intercollege–Larnaca, Intercollege–Limassol, Intercollege–Nicosia. Optional travel to Israel, Greece, Egypt at an extra cost.
Sessions • Fall, spring, yearlong.
Eligibility Requirements • Minimum age 18; open to freshmen, sophomores, juniors, seniors; 2.5 GPA; 3 letters of recommendation; transcript; application essay; completion of 15 credits prior to application; no foreign language proficiency required.
Living Arrangements • Students live in host institution dormitories, locally rented apartments. Quarters are shared with host institution students. Meals are taken on one's own, in restaurants.
Costs (2004-2005) • One term: $5045. Yearlong program: $10,090; includes tuition, insurance, fees. $35 application fee. Financial aid available for students from sponsoring institution: scholarships, loans.
For More Information • College Consortium for International Studies, 2000 P Street, NW, Suite 503, Washington, DC 20036; *Phone:* 800-453-6956; *Fax:* 202-223-0999. *E-mail:* info@ccisabroad.org. *World Wide Web:* http://www.ccisabroad.org/. Students may also apply through Brookdale Community College, International Center, 765 Newman Springs Road, Lincroft, NJ 07738-1597.

CZECH REPUBLIC
CITY TO CITY

ACIE (ACTR/ACCELS)
ACIE (ACCELS) CZECH LANGUAGE PROGRAMS

Hosted by Masaryk University, Palacky University, CERGE-EI
Academic Focus • Czech.
Program Information • Students attend classes at Masaryk University (Brno), Palacky University (Olomouc), CERGE-EI (Prague).
Sessions • Fall, spring, yearlong.
Eligibility Requirements • Minimum age 18; open to freshmen, sophomores, juniors, seniors, graduate students, adults; 3 letters of recommendation; good academic standing at home school; 1 year of college course work in Czech.

Living Arrangements • Students live in host institution dormitories, locally rented apartments. Quarters are shared with students from other programs. Meals are taken on one's own, in residences, in central dining facility.
Costs (2002-2003) • One term: contact sponsor for cost. Yearlong program: contact sponsor for cost. $35 application fee. $500 nonrefundable deposit required. Financial aid available for all students: scholarships.
For More Information • Nurhan Kocaoglu, Russian and Eurasian Program Manager, ACIE (ACTR/ACCELS), 1776 Massachusetts Avenue, NW, Suite 700, Washington, DC 20036; *Phone:* 202-833-7522; *Fax:* 202-833-7523. *E-mail:* outbound@actr.org. *World Wide Web:* http://www.actr.org/

BRNO

STATE UNIVERSITY OF NEW YORK AT OSWEGO
CENTRAL EUROPEAN STUDIES AT MASARYK UNIVERSITY

Hosted by Masaryk University
Academic Focus • Central European studies, Czech, economics, history, international affairs, political science and government.
Program Information • Students attend classes at Masaryk University. Field trips; optional travel at an extra cost.
Sessions • Fall, spring, yearlong.
Eligibility Requirements • Open to sophomores, juniors, seniors; 2.75 GPA; 3 letters of recommendation; good academic standing at home school; personal statement; no foreign language proficiency required.
Living Arrangements • Students live in host institution dormitories. Quarters are shared with host institution students. Meals are taken on one's own, in central dining facility.
Costs (2003-2004) • One term: $6520. Yearlong program: $13,040; includes tuition, housing, all meals, insurance, student support services. $250 nonrefundable deposit required. Financial aid available for students: home university financial aid, loan processing and scholarships for Oswego students.
For More Information • Mr. Joshua McKeown, Associate Director, State University of New York at Oswego, 122A Swetman Hall, Oswego, NY 13126; *Phone:* 888-4-OSWEGO; *Fax:* 315-312-2477. *E-mail:* intled@oswego.edu. *World Wide Web:* http://www.oswego.edu/intled/

STATE UNIVERSITY OF NEW YORK AT OSWEGO
TESOL TE AT MASARYK UNIVERSITY

Hosted by Masaryk University
Academic Focus • Teaching English as a second language.
Program Information • Students attend classes at Masaryk University. Field trips; optional travel at an extra cost.
Sessions • Fall, spring, yearlong.
Eligibility Requirements • Open to sophomores, juniors, seniors; 2.75 GPA; 3 letters of recommendation; good academic standing at home school; phone interview with Masaryk University representative; background in educational theory; no foreign language proficiency required.
Living Arrangements • Students live in host institution dormitories. Quarters are shared with host institution students. Meals are taken on one's own, in central dining facility.
Costs (2003-2004) • One term: $6520. Yearlong program: $13,040; includes tuition, housing, all meals, insurance, student support services. $250 nonrefundable deposit required. Financial aid available for students: home university financial aid, loan processing and scholarships for Oswego students.
For More Information • Mr. Joshua McKeown, Associate Director, State University of New York at Oswego, 122A Swetman Hall, Oswego, NY 13126; *Phone:* 888-4-OSWEGO; *Fax:* 315-312-2477. *E-mail:* intled@oswego.edu. *World Wide Web:* http://www.oswego.edu/intled/

OLOMOUC

ASSOCIATED COLLEGES OF THE MIDWEST
ACM CENTRAL EUROPEAN STUDIES PROGRAM

Hosted by Palacky University
Academic Focus • Czech, history, literature, political science and government.
Program Information • Students attend classes at Palacky University. Scheduled travel to Bohemia, Slovakia, Krakow; field trips to Prague, Budapest, Vienna.
Sessions • Fall.
Eligibility Requirements • Open to sophomores, juniors, seniors; 3 letters of recommendation; good academic standing at home school; no foreign language proficiency required.
Living Arrangements • Students live in host institution dormitories, host family homes. Quarters are shared with host institution students, students from other programs. Meals are taken on one's own, in residences, in restaurants.
Costs (2004) • One term: contact sponsor for cost. $400 nonrefundable deposit required.
For More Information • Program Associate, Central European Studies Program, Associated Colleges of the Midwest, 205 West Wacker Drive, Suite 1300, Chicago, IL 60606; *Phone:* 312-263-5000; *Fax:* 312-263-5879. *E-mail:* acm@acm.edu. *World Wide Web:* http://www.acm.edu/

ST. CLOUD STATE UNIVERSITY
ART AND MUSIC IN THE CZECH REPUBLIC

Held at Palacky University
Academic Focus • Art, music performance.
Program Information • Classes are held on the campus of Palacky University. Faculty members are drawn from the sponsor's U.S. staff and local instructors hired by the sponsor. Scheduled travel to Europe; field trips to Prague, Berlin, Vienna, Budapest; optional travel to Moscow at an extra cost.
Sessions • Fall.
Eligibility Requirements • Minimum age 18; open to sophomores, juniors, seniors, graduate students; major in art, music; course work in art or music (1 year); 2.5 GPA; 2 letters of recommendation; interview; no foreign language proficiency required.
Living Arrangements • Students live in host institution dormitories. Quarters are shared with host institution students, students from other programs. Meals are taken on one's own, in central dining facility.
Costs (2003) • One term: $7650 for Minnesota residents; includes tuition, housing, excursions, international airfare, international student ID, student support services. $75 application fee. Financial aid available for students from sponsoring institution: scholarships, work study, loans.
For More Information • Chunsheng Zhang, Associate Vice President for Academic Affairs/International Studies, St. Cloud State University, Center for International Studies, 720 4th Avenue, South, St. Cloud, MN 56301-4498; *Phone:* 320-308-4287; *Fax:* 320-308-4223. *E-mail:* intstudy@stcloudstate.edu. *World Wide Web:* http://www.stcloudstate.edu/

UNIVERSITY OF NEBRASKA AT KEARNEY
NEBRASKA SEMESTER ABROAD

Hosted by Palacky University
Academic Focus • Area studies.
Program Information • Students attend classes at Palacky University. Scheduled travel; field trips; optional travel to destinations throughout Europe at an extra cost.
Sessions • Spring.
Eligibility Requirements • Open to juniors, seniors; 2 letters of recommendation; good academic standing at home school; no foreign language proficiency required.
Living Arrangements • Students live in host institution dormitories. Quarters are shared with host institution students. Meals are taken on one's own, in restaurants.
Costs (2003) • One term: $6000; includes tuition, housing, all meals, insurance, excursions, international airfare, books and class materials, student support services. $500 nonrefundable deposit required. Financial aid available for students from sponsoring institution: loans.

For More Information • Ms. Ann Marie Harr, Study Abroad Coordinator, University of Nebraska at Kearney, Welch Hall #104, Kearney, NE 68849; *Phone:* 308-865-8944; *Fax:* 308-865-8947. *E-mail:* harram@unk.edu. *World Wide Web:* http://www.unk.edu/offices/iss/studyabroad.html

PRAGUE

AMERICAN INSTITUTE FOR FOREIGN STUDY (AIFS)
CHARLES UNIVERSITY

Hosted by Charles University
Academic Focus • Art history, Czech, economics, film and media studies, history, literature, music, political science and government, psychology, religious studies, sociology, theater management.
Program Information • Students attend classes at Charles University. Scheduled travel to London; field trips to Vienna.
Sessions • Fall, spring, yearlong.
Eligibility Requirements • Minimum age 17; open to sophomores, juniors, seniors; 2.5 GPA; 1 letter of recommendation; good academic standing at home school; no foreign language proficiency required.
Living Arrangements • Students live in host institution dormitories. Meals are taken on one's own, in central dining facility, in restaurants.
Costs (2004-2005) • One term: $9995. Yearlong program: $18,990; includes tuition, housing, all meals, insurance, excursions, student support services, one-way airfare, 2-day London stopover. $75 application fee. $350 nonrefundable deposit required. Financial aid available for all students: scholarships.
For More Information • Mr. David Mauro, Admissions Advisor, American Institute For Foreign Study (AIFS), 9 West Broad Street, Stamford, CT 06902-3788; *Phone:* 800-727-2437 Ext. 5163; *Fax:* 203-399-5597. *E-mail:* dmauro@aifs.com. *World Wide Web:* http://www.aifsabroad.com/

AMERICAN UNIVERSITY
SEMESTER IN PRAGUE: FILM AND VISUAL MEDIA

Hosted by Academy of Performing Arts–FAMU
Academic Focus • Film and media studies, history, photography.
Program Information • Students attend classes at Academy of Performing Arts–FAMU. Scheduled travel to Italy, Eastern Europe; field trips.
Sessions • Fall, spring.
Eligibility Requirements • Open to sophomores, juniors, seniors, graduate students; course work in basic photography, basic film and visual media production; 2.75 GPA; 1 letter of recommendation; second semester sophomore status; recommendation of advisor; portfolio; no foreign language proficiency required.
Living Arrangements • Students live in host institution dormitories, locally rented apartments. Quarters are shared with host institution students, students from other programs. Meals are taken on one's own, in residences, in central dining facility, in restaurants.
Costs (2002-2003) • One term: $15,734; includes tuition, housing, excursions, books and class materials, student support services. $35 application fee. $300 nonrefundable deposit required. Financial aid available for all students: scholarships, loans.
For More Information • Dr. David C. Brown, Dean, Washington Semester and World Capitals Programs, American University, Tenley Campus–Constitution Building, Washington, DC 20016-8083; *Phone:* 800-424-2600; *Fax:* 202-895-4960. *E-mail:* travel@american.edu. *World Wide Web:* http://www.worldcapitals.american.edu/

AMERICAN UNIVERSITY
SEMESTER IN PRAGUE: HUMANITIES

Hosted by CERGE-EI
Academic Focus • Communications, Czech, economics, history, literature, political science and government.
Program Information • Students attend classes at CERGE-EI. Scheduled travel to Poland, Italy, western Europe; field trips.
Sessions • Fall, spring.

CZECH REPUBLIC
Prague

Eligibility Requirements • Open to sophomores, juniors, seniors, graduate students; 2.75 GPA; 1 letter of recommendation; second semester sophomore status; recommendation of advisor; no foreign language proficiency required.

Living Arrangements • Students live in host institution dormitories, locally rented apartments. Quarters are shared with host institution students, students from other programs. Meals are taken on one's own, in central dining facility, in restaurants.

Costs (2002-2003) • One term: $15,734; includes tuition, housing, excursions, books and class materials, student support services. $35 application fee. $300 nonrefundable deposit required. Financial aid available for all students: scholarships, loans.

For More Information • Dr. David C. Brown, Dean, Washington Semester and World Capitals Programs, American University, Tenley Campus–Constitution Building, Washington, DC 20016-8083; *Phone:* 800-424-2600; *Fax:* 202-895-4960. *E-mail:* travel@american.edu. *World Wide Web:* http://www.worldcapitals.american.edu/

CENTRAL EUROPEAN EDUCATION AND CULTURAL EXCHANGE (CEECE)
PROGRAM IN CZECH REPUBLIC

Hosted by Anglo-American College

Academic Focus • Business administration/management, Central European studies, Czech, Eastern European studies, full curriculum, social sciences.

Program Information • Students attend classes at Anglo-American College. Scheduled travel to southern Bohemia, western Bohemia; field trips to southern Bohemia, western Bohemia; optional travel to Berlin, Vienna, Budapest, Krakow, Munich at an extra cost.

Sessions • Fall, spring, winter, yearlong.

Eligibility Requirements • Minimum age 18; open to freshmen, sophomores, juniors, seniors, graduate students, adults; 2.0 GPA; good academic standing at home school; no foreign language proficiency required.

Living Arrangements • Students live in locally rented apartments. Meals are taken on one's own, in restaurants.

Costs (2004-2005) • One term: $7999. Yearlong program: $13,998; includes tuition, housing, excursions, books and class materials, student support services, local transportation pass, pre-paid cellular phone. $300 refundable deposit required. Financial aid available for all students: home university financial aid.

For More Information • Mr. Eric Molengraf, Executive Director, Central European Education and Cultural Exchange (CEECE), 2956 Florence Drive, Grand Rapids, MI 49418; *Phone:* 800-352-9845. *E-mail:* info@ceece.org. *World Wide Web:* http://www.ceece.org/

CIEE
CIEE STUDY CENTER AT CHARLES UNIVERSITY, PRAGUE, CZECH REPUBLIC

Hosted by Charles University

Academic Focus • Art history, Central European studies, Czech, economics, film and media studies, history, Jewish studies, literature, music history, political science and government, psychology.

Program Information • Students attend classes at Charles University. Scheduled travel to southern Bohemia, Moravia, Plzen; field trips to sites of cultural interest in and around Prague.

Sessions • Fall, spring.

Eligibility Requirements • Open to sophomores, juniors, seniors, graduate students, adults; 2.75 GPA; 2 letters of recommendation; no foreign language proficiency required.

Living Arrangements • Students live in host institution dormitories, locally rented apartments, host family homes. Quarters are shared with host institution students. Meals are taken on one's own, in residences, in central dining facility, in restaurants.

Costs (2003-2004) • One term: $9600; includes tuition, housing, some meals, insurance, excursions, student support services, cultural activities, optional on-site pick-up. $30 application fee. $300 deposit required. Financial aid available for all students: minority student scholarships, non-traditional study scholarships, travel grants.

For More Information • Ms. Hannah McChesney, Admissions Officer, Europe, Middle East, and Africa, CIEE, 7 Custom House Street, 3rd Floor, Portland, ME 04101; *Phone:* 800-40-STUDY; *Fax:* 207-553-7699. *E-mail:* studyinfo@ciee.org. *World Wide Web:* http://www.ciee.org/isp/

COLLEGE CONSORTIUM FOR INTERNATIONAL STUDIES–CENTRAL MICHIGAN UNIVERSITY AND LINCOLN UNIVERSITY
PRAGUE, CZECH REPUBLIC SEMESTER PROGRAM

Hosted by Anglo-americká vysoká Ükola, o.p.s.

Academic Focus • Czech, full curriculum.

Program Information • Students attend classes at Anglo-americká vysoká Ükola, o.p.s..

Sessions • Fall, spring, yearlong.

Eligibility Requirements • Minimum age 18; open to sophomores, juniors, seniors; 2.5 GPA; 2 letters of recommendation; good academic standing at home school; no foreign language proficiency required.

Living Arrangements • Students live in locally rented apartments. Quarters are shared with host institution students. Meals are taken on one's own, in residences, in restaurants.

Costs (2004-2005) • One term: $3600 (estimated). Yearlong program: $6900 (estimated); includes tuition, insurance, international student ID, student support services. $25 application fee. $300 nonrefundable deposit required. Financial aid available for students from sponsoring institution: scholarships, loans, grants.

For More Information • College Consortium for International Studies–Central Michigan University and Lincoln University, Office of International Education, Central Michigan University, Bovee University Center 106, Mt. Pleasant, MI 48859; *Phone:* 989-774-4308; *Fax:* 989-774-3690. *E-mail:* studyabr@cmich.edu. *World Wide Web:* http://www.oie.cmich.edu/. Students may also apply through Lincoln University, Office of International Services, Lincoln Hall, PO Box 179, Lincoln University, PA 19352.

DARTMORE INSTITUTE FOR CENTRAL EUROPEAN STUDIES
ART AND ARCHITECTURE

Hosted by Jagiellonian University, Dartmore Institute for Central European Studies

Academic Focus • Architecture, art history.

Program Information • Students attend classes at Dartmore Institute for Central European Studies, Jagiellonian University. Scheduled travel to Krakow, Berlin, Vienna, Budapest; field trips to Cesky Kramlov, Trebic, Kutna Hora, Terezin; optional travel to Paris, Munich, Amsterdam at an extra cost.

Sessions • Fall, spring.

Eligibility Requirements • Minimum age 18; open to sophomores, juniors, seniors, graduate students, adults; 2.5 GPA; 2 letters of recommendation; good academic standing at home school; essay; no foreign language proficiency required.

Living Arrangements • Students live in locally rented apartments. Quarters are shared with host institution students. Meals are taken on one's own, in residences.

Costs (2003-2004) • One term: €7200; includes tuition, housing, some meals, excursions, books and class materials, student support services. €1500 nonrefundable deposit required. Financial aid available for all students: scholarships.

For More Information • Mr. David Sparandara, Executive Director, Dartmore Institute for Central European Studies, Museum of Modern Art, Dukelskych Hrdinu 47, 170 00 Prague 7, Czech Republic; *Phone:* 516-620-4550. *E-mail:* dsparandara@dartmore.cz. *World Wide Web:* http://www.dartmore.cz/index.html

DARTMORE INSTITUTE FOR CENTRAL EUROPEAN STUDIES
JEWISH STUDIES

Hosted by Dartmore Institute for Central European Studies, Jagiellonian University

Academic Focus • Jewish studies.

Program Information • Students attend classes at Dartmore Institute for Central European Studies, Jagiellonian University. Scheduled travel to Krakow, Berlin, Vienna, Budapest; field trips to

Cesky Kramlov, Trebic, Kutna Hora, Terezin; optional travel to Paris, Munich, Amsterdam at an extra cost.

Sessions • Fall, spring.

Eligibility Requirements • Minimum age 18; open to sophomores, juniors, seniors, graduate students, adults; 2.5 GPA; 2 letters of recommendation; good academic standing at home school; essay; no foreign language proficiency required.

Living Arrangements • Students live in locally rented apartments. Quarters are shared with host institution students. Meals are taken on one's own, in residences.

Costs (2003-2004) • One term: €7800; includes tuition, housing, some meals, excursions, books and class materials, student support services. €1500 nonrefundable deposit required. Financial aid available for all students: scholarships.

For More Information • Mr. David Sparandara, Executive Director, Dartmore Institute for Central European Studies, Museum of Modern Art, Dukelskych Hrdinu 47, 170 00 Prague 7, Czech Republic; *Phone:* 516-620-4550. *E-mail:* dsparandara@dartmore.cz. *World Wide Web:* http://www.dartmore.cz/index.html

DARTMORE INSTITUTE FOR CENTRAL EUROPEAN STUDIES
LIBERAL ARTS STUDY PROGRAM

Hosted by Jagiellonian University, Dartmore Institute for Central European Studies

Academic Focus • Architecture, art history, Central European studies, Jewish studies, liberal studies.

Program Information • Students attend classes at Dartmore Institute for Central European Studies, Jagiellonian University. Scheduled travel to Krakow, Berlin, Vienna, Budapest; field trips to Cesky Kramlov, Trebic, Kutna Hora, Trezin; optional travel to Paris, Munich, Amsterdam at an extra cost.

Sessions • Fall, spring.

Eligibility Requirements • Minimum age 18; open to sophomores, juniors, seniors, graduate students, adults; 2.5 GPA; 2 letters of recommendation; good academic standing at home school; essay; no foreign language proficiency required.

Living Arrangements • Students live in locally rented apartments. Quarters are shared with host institution students. Meals are taken on one's own, in residences.

Costs (2003-2004) • One term: €6850; includes tuition, housing, some meals, excursions, books and class materials, student support services. €1500 nonrefundable deposit required. Financial aid available for all students: scholarships.

For More Information • Mr. David Sparandara, Executive Director, Dartmore Institute for Central European Studies, Museum of Modern Art, Dukelskych Hrdinu 47, 170 00 Prague 7, Czech Republic; *Phone:* 516-620-4550. *E-mail:* dsparandara@dartmore.cz. *World Wide Web:* http://www.dartmore.cz/index.html

THE INTERNATIONAL PARTNERSHIP FOR SERVICE LEARNING
CZECH REPUBLIC SERVICE–LEARNING

Hosted by CERGE-EI

Academic Focus • Art history, Central European studies, community service, Czech, Jewish studies, liberal studies, social sciences.

Program Information • Students attend classes at CERGE-EI. Field trips to sites around Prague, southern Bohemia; optional travel to destinations throughout the Czech Republic, central Europe at an extra cost.

Sessions • Fall, spring, yearlong.

Eligibility Requirements • Minimum age 18; open to freshmen, sophomores, juniors, seniors, graduate students, adults; 2 letters of recommendation; good academic standing at home school; evidence of maturity, responsibility; no foreign language proficiency required.

Living Arrangements • Students live in host family homes. Meals are taken with host family, in residences.

Costs (2003-2004) • One term: $7800–$8100. Yearlong program: $14,900; includes tuition, housing, some meals, excursions. $50 application fee. $250 refundable deposit required. Financial aid available for all students: federal financial aid.

For More Information • Ms. Ilana Golin, Coordinator of Student Programs, The International Partnership for Service Learning, 815 Second Avenue, Suite 315, New York, NY 10017-4594; *Phone:* 212-986-0989; *Fax:* 212-986-5039. *E-mail:* info@ipsl.org. *World Wide Web:* http://www.ipsl.org/

LEXIA INTERNATIONAL
LEXIA IN PRAGUE

Hosted by Charles University

Academic Focus • Anthropology, area studies, art, art history, civilization studies, comparative history, cultural studies, Czech, drawing/painting, Eastern European studies, economics, environmental science/studies, ethnic studies, film and media studies, fine/studio arts, geography, history, interdisciplinary studies, international affairs, international business, liberal studies, literature, music, music history, music performance, peace and conflict studies, philosophy, political science and government, psychology, religious studies, Slavic languages, social sciences, sociology, urban studies.

Program Information • Students attend classes at Charles University. Field trips to Znojmo, Brno, Kutna Hora, Cesky Krumlov.

Sessions • Fall, spring, yearlong.

Eligibility Requirements • Minimum age 18; open to sophomores, juniors, seniors, graduate students, adults; 2.5 GPA; 2 letters of recommendation; no foreign language proficiency required.

Living Arrangements • Students live in host institution dormitories, host family homes. Quarters are shared with students from other programs. Meals are taken on one's own, with host family, in residences, in central dining facility, in restaurants.

Costs (2003-2004) • One term: $9950. Yearlong program: $18,550; includes tuition, housing, some meals, insurance, excursions, international student ID, student support services, computer access, transcript. $35 application fee. $300 refundable deposit required. Financial aid available for all students: scholarships, work study.

For More Information • Lexia International, 23 South Main Street, Hanover, NH 03755; *Phone:* 800-775-3942; *Fax:* 603-643-9899. *E-mail:* info@lexiaintl.org. *World Wide Web:* http://www.lexiaintl.org/

NAROPA UNIVERSITY
STUDY ABROAD–PRAGUE, CZECH REPUBLIC: WRITER AS WITNESS

Academic Focus • Central European studies, comparative literature, creative writing, Czech, Eastern European studies, history, literature.

Program Information • Faculty members are drawn from the sponsor's U.S. staff and local instructors hired by the sponsor. Field trips to Prague, Bohemia; optional travel to Vienna, Budapest at an extra cost.

Sessions • Spring.

Eligibility Requirements • Minimum age 18; open to freshmen, sophomores, juniors, seniors, graduate students, adults; course work in creative writing strongly encouraged; 3.0 GPA; 2 letters of recommendation; good academic standing at home school; must be a serious student with an interest in creative writing; no foreign language proficiency required.

Living Arrangements • Students live in host institution dormitories, locally rented apartments. Meals are taken on one's own, in residences, in restaurants.

Costs (2005) • One term: $13,890; includes tuition, housing, some meals, excursions, student support services, visa fees. $45 application fee. $500 nonrefundable deposit required. Financial aid available for all students: loans, consortium agreement for home institution aid.

For More Information • Ms. Denise Cope, Co-Director, Naropa University, 2130 Arapahoe Avenue, Boulder, CO 80302; *Phone:* 303-245-4707; *Fax:* 303-444-0140. *E-mail:* denise@naropa.edu. *World Wide Web:* http://www.naropa.edu/studyabroad/

NEW YORK UNIVERSITY
NYU IN PRAGUE

Hosted by Charles University, NYU Center

Academic Focus • Art history, Central European studies, communications, Czech, economics, film and media studies, German language and literature, history, international business, Jewish studies, literature, Polish, political science and government, Russian language and literature.

Program Information • Students attend classes at Charles University, NYU Center. Field trips to Bohemia, Czesky Krumlov, Moravia, Karlovy Vary, Kutna Hora.

Sessions • Fall, spring, yearlong.

Eligibility Requirements • Open to sophomores, juniors, seniors; 3.0 GPA; 1 letter of recommendation; good academic standing at home school; transcripts; personal statement; no foreign language proficiency required.

Living Arrangements • Students live in host institution dormitories, locally rented apartments. Meals are taken on one's own, in residences, in restaurants.

Costs (2003-2004) • One term: $14,248. Yearlong program: $28,495; includes tuition, excursions, student support services. $25 application fee. $300 nonrefundable deposit required. Financial aid available for all students: scholarships, loans.

For More Information • Office of Study Abroad Admissions, New York University, 7 East 12th Street, 6th Floor, New York, NY 10003; *Phone:* 212-998-4433; *Fax:* 212-995-4103. *E-mail:* studyabroad@nyu.edu. *World Wide Web:* http://www.nyu.edu/studyabroad/

SCHOOL FOR INTERNATIONAL TRAINING, SIT STUDY ABROAD
CZECH REPUBLIC: ARTS AND SOCIAL CHANGE

Academic Focus • Anthropology, art, Czech, Eastern European studies, European studies, film and media studies, historic preservation, history, photography, political science and government, social sciences, sociology, visual and performing arts.

Program Information • Faculty members are drawn from the sponsor's U.S. staff and local instructors hired by the sponsor. Scheduled travel to Vienna, Austria, Dresden, Germany, Bratislava; field trips to northern Bohemia, Cesky Krumlov, Kutna Hora, museums, the theater, opera concerts.

Sessions • Fall, spring.

Eligibility Requirements • Open to sophomores, juniors, seniors; 2.5 GPA; 2 letters of recommendation; good academic standing at home school; no foreign language proficiency required.

Living Arrangements • Students live in host family homes, hotels. Meals are taken as a group, on one's own, with host family, in residences, in restaurants.

Costs (2003-2004) • One term: $12,325; includes tuition, housing, all meals, insurance, excursions, international student ID. $50 application fee. $400 nonrefundable deposit required. Financial aid available for all students: scholarships.

For More Information • School for International Training, SIT Study Abroad, Kipling Road, Brattleboro, VT 05302-0676; *Phone:* 888-272-7881; *Fax:* 802-258-3296. *E-mail:* studyabroad@sit.edu. *World Wide Web:* http://www.sit.edu/studyabroad/

STATE UNIVERSITY OF NEW YORK AT NEW PALTZ
STUDY ABROAD IN PRAGUE

Hosted by Charles University

Academic Focus • Central European studies, Czech, Eastern European studies.

Program Information • Students attend classes at Charles University. Field trips to sites of local interest in Prague and surrounding areas; optional travel to Bohemia, Moravia at an extra cost.

Sessions • Fall, spring, yearlong.

Eligibility Requirements • Minimum age 18; open to sophomores, juniors, seniors; 2.5 GPA; 2 letters of recommendation; good academic standing at home school; no foreign language proficiency required.

Living Arrangements • Students live in host institution dormitories. Quarters are shared with host institution students. Meals are taken on one's own, in residences, in central dining facility.

Costs (2003-2004) • One term: $3700 for New York residents; $6829 for nonresidents. Yearlong program: $7400 for New York residents; $13,658 for nonresidents; includes tuition, housing, some meals, insurance, excursions, student support services, administrative fee. $25 application fee. $300–$600 nonrefundable deposit required. Financial aid available for students from sponsoring institution: scholarships, loans.
For More Information • Center for International Programs, State University of New York at New Paltz, 75 South Manheim Boulevard, Suite 9, New Paltz, NY 12561; *Phone:* 845-257-3125; *Fax:* 845-257-3129. *E-mail:* international@newpaltz.edu. *World Wide Web:* http://www.newpaltz.edu/studyabroad/

UNIVERSITY STUDIES ABROAD CONSORTIUM
EAST AND CENTRAL EUROPEAN AREA STUDIES: PRAGUE, CZECH REPUBLIC

Hosted by Charles University
Academic Focus • Anthropology, architecture, art, Central European studies, Czech, Eastern European studies, economics, film and media studies, history, Jewish studies, music, political science and government, psychology, sociology, theater management.
Program Information • Students attend classes at Charles University. Field trips to Kutna Hora, Terezin; optional travel to Vienna, Budapest at an extra cost.
Sessions • Fall, spring, yearlong.
Eligibility Requirements • Minimum age 18; open to freshmen, sophomores, juniors, seniors, graduate students, adults; 2.5 GPA; no foreign language proficiency required.
Living Arrangements • Students live in host institution dormitories. Quarters are shared with host institution students. Meals are taken on one's own, in residences, in central dining facility, in restaurants.
Costs (2005-2006) • One term: $5280. Yearlong program: $9980; includes tuition, insurance, excursions, student support services. $50 application fee. $150 refundable deposit required. Financial aid available for all students: scholarships, loans.
For More Information • University Studies Abroad Consortium, USAC/323, Reno, NV 89557-0093; *Phone:* 775-784-6569; *Fax:* 775-784-6010. *E-mail:* usac@unr.edu. *World Wide Web:* http://usac.unr.edu/

DENMARK
CITY TO CITY
UNIVERSITY OF IDAHO
BUSINESS AND DANISH STUDIES PROGRAM

Hosted by University of Southern Denmark, The University of Southern Denmark–Esbjerg Campus (Esbjerg), The University of Southern Denmark–Sonderborg Campus (Sonderborg)
Academic Focus • Area studies, business administration/management, cultural studies, Danish, economics, entrepreneurship, finance, marketing, Scandinavian studies.
Program Information • Students attend classes at University of Southern Denmark (Odense), The University of Southern Denmark–Esbjerg Campus (Esbjerg), The University of Southern Denmark–Sonderborg Campus (Sonderborg). Field trips to company visits, Nordborg on the island of Als; optional travel at an extra cost.
Sessions • Fall, spring, yearlong.
Eligibility Requirements • Open to sophomores, juniors, seniors, graduate students, adults; course work in business (prerequisite course); good academic standing at home school; no foreign language proficiency required.
Living Arrangements • Students live in host institution dormitories, locally rented apartments. Quarters are shared with host institution students, students from other programs. Meals are taken on one's own, in residences, in central dining facility.
Costs (2003-2004) • One term: $2500. Yearlong program: $5000; includes tuition, excursions, student support services. $100

application fee. $200 refundable deposit required. Financial aid available for students from sponsoring institution: scholarships, loans.
For More Information • Ms. Amy Bergmann, Advisor, University of Idaho, Room 209, Morrill Hall, Moscow, ID 83844-3013; *Phone:* 208-885-7870; *Fax:* 208-885-2859. *E-mail:* abroad@uidaho.edu. *World Wide Web:* http://www.ets.uidaho.edu/ipo/abroad/

AALBORG
AALBORG UNIVERSITY
M.SC PROGRAMMES

Hosted by Aalborg University
Academic Focus • Full curriculum.
Program Information • Students attend classes at Aalborg University. Optional travel at an extra cost.
Sessions • Fall, spring.
Eligibility Requirements • Open to graduate students; good academic standing at home school; no foreign language proficiency required.
Living Arrangements • Students live in host institution dormitories, locally rented apartments. Quarters are shared with host institution students, students from other programs. Meals are taken on one's own.
Costs (2003-2004) • One term: contact sponsor for cost. Dkr2000 nonrefundable deposit required. Financial aid available for all students: scholarships.
For More Information • Hanne Hovring Pedersen, Student Coordinator, Aalborg University, E-Study Abroad, FR. Bajers VEJ 7A, 9200 Aaborg 0, Denmark; *Phone:* +45 96-358699; *Fax:* +45 98-153662. *E-mail:* masters@kom.auc.dk. *World Wide Web:* http://www.auc.dk/international/

COPENHAGEN
BENTLEY COLLEGE
STUDY ABROAD PROGRAM IN COPENHAGEN, DENMARK

Hosted by Copenhagen Business School
Academic Focus • Accounting, business administration/management, finance, political science and government.
Program Information • Students attend classes at Copenhagen Business School. Scheduled travel; field trips; optional travel at an extra cost.
Sessions • Fall, spring.
Eligibility Requirements • Open to juniors, seniors; 3.0 GPA; 1 letter of recommendation; good academic standing at home school; essay; no foreign language proficiency required.
Living Arrangements • Students live in host institution dormitories, locally rented apartments. Quarters are shared with host institution students, students from other programs. Meals are taken on one's own, in residences.
Costs (2002-2003) • One term: $15,600; includes tuition, housing, international student ID, student support services. $35 application fee. $500 nonrefundable deposit required. Financial aid available for students from sponsoring institution: scholarships, loans.
For More Information • Ms. Jennifer Aquino, Assistant Director, International Center, Bentley College, 175 Forest Street, Waltham, MA 02452; *Phone:* 781-891-3474; *Fax:* 781-891-2819. *E-mail:* study_abroad@bentley.edu. *World Wide Web:* http://ecampus.bentley.edu/dept/sa/

DIS, DENMARK'S INTERNATIONAL STUDY PROGRAM
DIS PROGRAM

Hosted by DIS, Denmark's International Study Program
Academic Focus • Full curriculum.
Program Information • Students attend classes at DIS, Denmark's International Study Program. Scheduled travel to Sweden, Belgium, Finland, Germany, Czech Republic, Netherlands, Russia, Norway, Poland, Luxembourg; field trips to Denmark, Sweden; optional travel to Russia at an extra cost.
Sessions • Fall, spring, yearlong.

DENMARK
Copenhagen

Eligibility Requirements • Open to sophomores, juniors, seniors, graduate students; 3.0 GPA; good academic standing at home school; college major requirement dependent on intended course of study; no foreign language proficiency required.
Living Arrangements • Students live in locally rented apartments, host family homes, a Danish Higher Education "Kollegium". Quarters are shared with host institution students. Meals are taken on one's own, with host family, in residences.
Costs (2004-2005) • One term: $12,500. Yearlong program: $22,500; includes tuition, housing, all meals, insurance, excursions, books and class materials, lab equipment, student support services, local commuting. $500 nonrefundable deposit required. Financial aid available for all students: scholarships, work study.
For More Information • Mr. Brad Stepan, DIS Field Director, DIS, Denmark's International Study Program, North American Office, 94 Blegen Hall, University of Minnesota, 269 19th Avenue South, Minneapolis, MN 55455; *Phone:* 800-247-3477; *Fax:* 612-626-8009. *E-mail:* dis@umn.edu. *World Wide Web:* http://www.disp.dk/. Students may also apply through DIS Denmark's International Study Program, Vestergade 7, DK 1456, Copenhagen K, Denmark.

UNIVERSITY OF MIAMI
UNIVERSITY OF COPENHAGEN

Hosted by University of Copenhagen
Academic Focus • Liberal studies, religious studies, science, social sciences.
Program Information • Students attend classes at University of Copenhagen.
Sessions • Fall, spring, yearlong.
Eligibility Requirements • Minimum age 18; open to sophomores, juniors, seniors; 3.0 GPA; 2 letters of recommendation; good academic standing at home school; no foreign language proficiency required.
Living Arrangements • Students live in host institution dormitories, locally rented apartments. Quarters are shared with host institution students, students from other programs. Meals are taken on one's own, in residences, in central dining facility, in restaurants.
Costs (2003-2004) • One term: $12,919. Yearlong program: $25,838; includes tuition, student support services. $40 application fee. $500 nonrefundable deposit required. Financial aid available for students from sponsoring institution: scholarships, loans.
For More Information • Ms. Diane Mahin, Study Abroad Advisor, University of Miami, International Education and Exchange Program, 5050 Brunson Drive, Allen Hall 212, PO Box 248005, Coral Gables, FL 33124-1610; *Phone:* 305-284-3434; *Fax:* 305-284-4235. *E-mail:* ieep@miami.edu. *World Wide Web:* http://www.studyabroad.miami.edu/

THE UNIVERSITY OF NORTH CAROLINA AT CHAPEL HILL
STUDY ABROAD IN COPENHAGEN

Hosted by DIS, Denmark's International Study Program
Academic Focus • Art, biological/life sciences, environmental science/studies, international business, premedical studies, social sciences.
Program Information • Students attend classes at DIS, Denmark's International Study Program. Scheduled travel to western Denmark; field trips to museums, a ballet, Danish Parliament; optional travel to Moscow, St. Petersburg, Berlin at an extra cost.
Sessions • Fall, spring, yearlong.
Eligibility Requirements • Open to juniors, seniors; 3.0 GPA; 3 letters of recommendation; good academic standing at home school; essay; transcript; no foreign language proficiency required.
Living Arrangements • Students live in host institution dormitories, host family homes. Quarters are shared with host institution students. Meals are taken on one's own, with host family, in residences.
Costs (2003-2004) • One term: $12,579. Yearlong program: $22,689; includes tuition, housing, some meals, insurance, excursions, study abroad fee, damage deposit, library deposit. $100 application fee. $500 nonrefundable deposit required. Financial aid available for students from sponsoring institution: scholarships, loans.
For More Information • Study Abroad Office, The University of North Carolina at Chapel Hill, 201 Porthole Building, CB 3130, Chapel Hill, NC 27599-3130; *Phone:* 919-962-7002; *Fax:* 919-962-2262. *E-mail:* abroad@unc.edu. *World Wide Web:* http://studyabroad.unc.edu/

UNIVERSITY STUDIES ABROAD CONSORTIUM
INTERNATIONAL BUSINESS AND ECONOMIC STUDIES: COPENHAGEN, DENMARK

Hosted by Copenhagen Business School
Academic Focus • Accounting, business administration/management, Danish, economics, finance, human resources, international business, labor and industrial relations, management information systems, marketing.
Program Information • Students attend classes at Copenhagen Business School.
Sessions • Fall, spring, yearlong.
Eligibility Requirements • Minimum age 18; open to sophomores, juniors, seniors, graduate students, adults; 2.5 GPA; no foreign language proficiency required.
Living Arrangements • Students live in host institution dormitories, locally rented apartments. Quarters are shared with host institution students, students from other programs. Meals are taken on one's own, in residences, in central dining facility, in restaurants.
Costs (2005-2006) • One term: $4880. Yearlong program: $9480; includes tuition, insurance, student support services, Danish language "crash" course. $50 application fee. $150 refundable deposit required. Financial aid available for all students: scholarships, loans.
For More Information • University Studies Abroad Consortium, USAC/323, Reno, NV 89557-0093; *Phone:* 775-784-6569; *Fax:* 775-784-6010. *E-mail:* usac@unr.edu. *World Wide Web:* http://usac.unr.edu/

ODENSE
UNIVERSITY OF MIAMI
UNIVERSITY OF SOUTHERN DENMARK

Hosted by University of Southern Denmark
Academic Focus • Business administration/management, environmental science/studies, international affairs, Scandinavian studies.
Program Information • Students attend classes at University of Southern Denmark.
Sessions • Fall, spring, yearlong.
Eligibility Requirements • Minimum age 18; open to sophomores, juniors, seniors; 3.0 GPA; 2 letters of recommendation; good academic standing at home school; no foreign language proficiency required.
Living Arrangements • Students live in host institution dormitories, locally rented apartments. Quarters are shared with host institution students, students from other programs. Meals are taken on one's own, in residences, in central dining facility, in restaurants.
Costs (2003-2004) • One term: $12,919. Yearlong program: $25,838; includes tuition, student support services. $40 application fee. $500 nonrefundable deposit required. Financial aid available for students from sponsoring institution: scholarships, loans.
For More Information • Ms. Diane Mahin, Study Abroad Advisor, University of Miami, International Education and Exchange Programs, 5050 Brunson Drive, Allen Hall 212, PO Box 248005, Coral Gables, FL 33124-1610; *Phone:* 305-284-3434; *Fax:* 305-284-4235. *E-mail:* ieep@miami.edu. *World Wide Web:* http://www.studyabroad.miami.edu/

DOMINICAN REPUBLIC
SANTIAGO
CIC STUDY ABROAD PROGRAMS
CIC LATIN AMERICAN HEALTH, NUTRITION, AND ENVIRONMENTAL ISSUES IN THE DOMINICAN REPUBLIC (FALL)

Hosted by Catholic University 'Madre y Maestra,' El Campus de Santiago de los Caballeros

Academic Focus • Environmental health, health-care management, nutrition, public health, social sciences, Spanish language and literature.

Program Information • Students attend classes at Catholic University 'Madre y Maestra,' El Campus de Santiago de los Caballeros. Field trips to Puerto Plata, Jarabaloa, Salcedo, rural towns/bateys, clinics and NGOs.

Sessions • Fall.

Eligibility Requirements • Open to freshmen, sophomores, juniors, seniors, graduate students, adults; 2.5 GPA; 1 letter of recommendation; good academic standing at home school; language evaluation reference; 3 years of college course work in Spanish.

Living Arrangements • Students live in host family homes. Meals are taken with host family, in residences.

Costs (2004) • One term: $6234 for consortium members; $7751 for all others; includes tuition, housing, all meals, excursions, international student ID, student support services. $35 application fee. $200 refundable deposit required. Financial aid available for students from sponsoring institution: scholarships, loans.

For More Information • Ms. Autumn Tallman, CIC Program Coordinator, CIC Study Abroad Programs, 120 International Center, Office for Study Abroad, The University of Iowa, Iowa City, IA 52242; *Phone:* 319-335-0353; *Fax:* 319-335-2021. *E-mail:* cic-abroad@uiowa.edu. *World Wide Web:* http://www.uiowa.edu/~viabroad/

CIEE
CIEE STUDY CENTER AT PONTIFICIA UNIVERSIDAD CATÓLICA MADRE Y MAESTRA, SANTIAGO, DOMINICAN REPUBLIC

Hosted by Catholic University 'Madre y Maestra'

Academic Focus • Community service, economics, history, Latin American literature, Latin American studies, liberal studies, social services, social work, sociology, Spanish language and literature, teaching English as a second language, women's studies.

Program Information • Students attend classes at Catholic University 'Madre y Maestra'. Scheduled travel to Santo Domingo, Samaná, La Romana, Altos de Chavon, Higuey; field trips to Rio San Juan, Jarabacoa, La Vega Vieja, Bateyes; optional travel to Puerto Rico at an extra cost.

Sessions • Fall, spring, yearlong.

Eligibility Requirements • Minimum age 18; open to sophomores, juniors, seniors; 2.75 GPA; 2 letters of recommendation; good academic standing at home school; nomination from home school; personal statement; 2 years of college course work in Spanish.

Living Arrangements • Students live with host family, in residences.

Costs (2004-2005) • One term: $7900. Yearlong program: $13,250; includes tuition, housing, all meals, insurance, excursions, student support services, computer and library access at host institutions, pre-departure advising, cultural activities. $30 application fee. $300 deposit required. Financial aid available for all students: minority student scholarships, travel grants, U.S. Department of Education aid.

For More Information • Ms. Ellen Whitman, Admissions Officer, Spain and Latin America, CIEE, 7 Custom House Street, 3rd Floor, Portland, ME 04101; *Phone:* 800-40-STUDY; *Fax:* 207-553-7699. *E-mail:* studyinfo@ciee.org. *World Wide Web:* http://www.ciee.org/isp/

INTERNATIONAL STUDIES ABROAD
SPANISH LANGUAGE AND CULTURE

Held at Catholic University 'Madre y Maestra,' El Campus de Santiago de los Caballeros

Academic Focus • Civilization studies, liberal studies, Spanish language and literature, Spanish studies.

Program Information • Classes are held on the campus of Catholic University 'Madre y Maestra,' El Campus de Santiago de los Caballeros. Faculty members are local instructors hired by the sponsor. Field trips to Jarabaloa, Santo Domingo, Puerto Plata, Samaná Bay; optional travel at an extra cost.

Sessions • Fall, spring, yearlong.

Eligibility Requirements • Minimum age 18; open to freshmen, sophomores, juniors, seniors, graduate students, adults; 2.5 GPA; 1 letter of recommendation; good academic standing at home school; transcript; 2 years of college course work in Spanish.

Living Arrangements • Students live in locally rented apartments, host family homes. Quarters are shared with host institution students, students from other programs. Meals are taken with host family, in residences.

Costs (2004-2005) • One term: $6900. Yearlong program: $12,900; includes tuition, housing, all meals, insurance, excursions, student support services, excursion transportation, Internet access, tutoring. $200 deposit required. Financial aid available for all students: scholarships, work study, U.S. federal financial aid.

For More Information • Dominican Republic Site Specialist, International Studies Abroad, 901 West 24th Street, Austin, TX 78705; *Phone:* 800-580-8826; *Fax:* 512-480-8866. *E-mail:* isa@studiesabroad.com. *World Wide Web:* http://www.studiesabroad.com/

SANTO DOMINGO
CIEE
CIEE STUDY CENTER IN SANTO DOMINGO, DOMINICAN REPUBLIC

Hosted by Facultad Latinoamericana de Ciencias Sociales (FLACSO)

Academic Focus • Anthropology, community service, history, Latin American literature, Latin American studies, philosophy, political science and government, psychology, religious studies, social sciences, sociology, Spanish language and literature.

Program Information • Students attend classes at Facultad Latinoamericana de Ciencias Sociales (FLACSO). Scheduled travel to the Samaná peninsula, Santiago, Moca; field trips to Higuey, La Romana, city tours, concerts, Altos de Chavón; optional travel to Haiti, Puerto Rico at an extra cost.

Sessions • Fall, spring, yearlong.

Eligibility Requirements • Minimum age 18; open to sophomores, juniors, seniors, graduate students, adults; 2.75 GPA; 2 letters of recommendation; 2.5 years of college course work in Spanish.

Living Arrangements • Students live in host family homes. Meals are taken on one's own, with host family, in residences, in restaurants.

Costs (2004-2005) • One term: $7900. Yearlong program: $13,250; includes tuition, housing, some meals, insurance, excursions, student support services, pre-departure advising, cultural activities, internship placement. $30 application fee. $300 deposit required. Financial aid available for all students: minority student scholarships, travel grants.

For More Information • Ms. Ellen Whitman, Admissions Officer, Spain and Latin America, CIEE, 7 Custom House Street, 3rd Floor, Portland, ME 04101; *Phone:* 800-40-STUDY; *Fax:* 207-553-7699. *E-mail:* studyinfo@ciee.org. *World Wide Web:* http://www.ciee.org/isp/

COLLEGE CONSORTIUM FOR INTERNATIONAL STUDIES–BROOME COMMUNITY COLLEGE, STATE UNIVERSITY OF NEW YORK
PROGRAM IN THE DOMINICAN REPUBLIC

Hosted by Catholic University 'Madre y Maestra'

Academic Focus • Community service, international affairs, Latin American studies, Spanish language and literature.

Program Information • Students attend classes at Catholic University 'Madre y Maestra'. Field trips to La Romana, Santiago.

Sessions • Fall, spring, yearlong.

Eligibility Requirements • Minimum age 17; open to freshmen, sophomores, juniors, seniors, adults; 2.5 GPA; 3 letters of recommendation; good academic standing at home school; no foreign language proficiency required.

Living Arrangements • Students live in host family homes. Quarters are shared with students from other programs. Meals are taken with host family, in residences.

Costs (2004-2005) • One term: $5545 for New York residents; $5670 for nonresidents. Yearlong program: $11,090 for New York residents; $11,340 for nonresidents; includes tuition, housing, some meals, insurance, excursions, student support services. $200 nonrefundable deposit required. Financial aid available for all students: all customary sources.

DOMINICAN REPUBLIC
Santo Domingo

For More Information • College Consortium for International Studies, 2000 P Street, NW, Suite 503, Washington, DC 20036; *Phone:* 800-453-6956; *Fax:* 202-223-0999. *E-mail:* info@ccisabroad. org. *World Wide Web:* http://www.ccisabroad.org/. Students may also apply through Broome Community College, State University of New York, PO Box 1017, Binghamton, NY 13902.

GOSHEN COLLEGE
DOMINICAN REPUBLIC STUDY SERVICE TERM

Held at Entrena
Academic Focus • Cultural studies, liberal studies, social sciences, Spanish language and literature.
Program Information • Classes are held on the campus of Entrena. Faculty members are drawn from the sponsor's U.S. staff and local instructors hired by the sponsor. Scheduled travel to Haitian border area; field trips to a colonial city, botanical gardens, the sugar cane industry.
Sessions • Fall, spring, winter.
Eligibility Requirements • Open to sophomores, juniors, seniors; 2.0 GPA; 2 letters of recommendation; good academic standing at home school; 1 year of college course work in Spanish.
Living Arrangements • Students live in host family homes. Meals are taken with host family, in residences.
Costs (2003-2004) • One term: $11,225; includes tuition, housing, all meals, excursions, international airfare, student support services. $300 nonrefundable deposit required. Financial aid available for students from sponsoring institution: scholarships, loans.
For More Information • Dr. Thomas J. Meyers, Director of International Education, Goshen College, 1700 South Main, Goshen, IN 46526; *Phone:* 574-535-7346; *Fax:* 574-535-7319. *E-mail:* tomjm@goshen.edu. *World Wide Web:* http://www.goshen.edu/sst/

UNIVERSITY AT ALBANY, STATE UNIVERSITY OF NEW YORK
LANGUAGE AND CULTURAL STUDIES IN ENGLISH AT THE PUCMM

Hosted by Catholic University 'Madre y Maestra'
Academic Focus • African-American studies, cultural studies, full curriculum, Spanish language and literature.
Program Information • Students attend classes at Catholic University 'Madre y Maestra'. Field trips to cultural sites related to course syllabus.
Sessions • Fall, spring, yearlong.
Eligibility Requirements • Open to sophomores, juniors, seniors; 2 letters of recommendation; good academic standing at home school; fluency in Spanish required for direct enrollment students; no foreign language proficiency requirement for regular program students.
Living Arrangements • Students live in host family homes. Meals are taken with host family, in residences, in restaurants.
Costs (2002-2003) • One term: $5988. Yearlong program: $11,976; includes housing, all meals, excursions, student support services, in-state tuition and fees. $150 nonrefundable deposit required. Financial aid available for students from sponsoring institution: all customary sources.
For More Information • University at Albany, State University of New York, Office of International Education, LI 66, Albany, NY 12222; *Phone:* 518-442-3525; *Fax:* 518-442-3337. *E-mail:* intled@ uamail.albany.edu. *World Wide Web:* http://www.albany.edu/intled/

ECUADOR
CUENCA
ROUND RIVER CONSERVATION STUDIES
ECUADOR: ECUADOREAN CLOUD FOREST CONSERVATION PROJECT

Academic Focus • Biological/life sciences, conservation studies, ecology, wildlife studies.

Program Information • Faculty members are drawn from the sponsor's U.S. staff and local instructors hired by the sponsor. Scheduled travel to the Andes Mountains (backpacking); field trips to neighboring rural communities; optional travel to Quito, coastal Ecuador.
Sessions • Fall, spring.
Eligibility Requirements • Minimum age 18; open to freshmen, sophomores, juniors, seniors; 3.0 GPA; 2 letters of recommendation; good academic standing at home school; no foreign language proficiency required.
Living Arrangements • Students live in program-owned houses, remote field camps, a house in Cuenca, traditional rural housing. Meals are taken as a group, in central dining facility.
Costs (2003) • One term: $11,500; includes tuition, housing, all meals, excursions, lab equipment, student support services. $50 application fee. $1000 nonrefundable deposit required. Financial aid available for all students: scholarships.
For More Information • Mr. Doug Milek, Student Programs Director, Round River Conservation Studies, 404 North 300 West, #102, Salt Lake City, UT 84103; *Phone:* 801-694-3321. *E-mail:* dougmilek@roundriver.org. *World Wide Web:* http://www.roundriver. org/

GALAPAGOS ISLANDS
COLLEGE CONSORTIUM FOR INTERNATIONAL STUDIES–COLLEGE OF STATEN ISLAND/CUNY AND BROOKDALE COMMUNITY COLLEGE
PROGRAM IN GALAPAGOS ISLANDS, ECUADOR–GALAPAGOS ACADEMIC INSTITUTE FOR THE ARTS AND SCIENCES (GAIAS)

Hosted by Galapagos Academic Institute for the Arts and Sciences (GAIAS)
Academic Focus • Biological/life sciences, botany, ecology, Ecuadorian studies, environmental science/studies, Galapagos area studies, marine sciences, oceanography, zoology.
Program Information • Students attend classes at Galapagos Academic Institute for the Arts and Sciences (GAIAS). Classes are also held on the campus of Universidad San Francisco de Quito. Scheduled travel to Quito; field trips to Quito, Mitad del Mundo, Cotopaxi, Otavalo, Isla de la Plata.
Sessions • Fall, spring.
Eligibility Requirements • Minimum age 18; open to sophomores, juniors, seniors; course work in 1 biology and 1 ecology course; 3.0 GPA; 3 letters of recommendation; transcript; essay; no foreign language proficiency required.
Living Arrangements • Students live in host institution dormitories, host family homes. Quarters are shared with host institution students, students from other programs. Meals are taken as a group, on one's own, with host family, in residences, in central dining facility.
Costs (2004-2005) • One term: $10,550; includes tuition, housing, all meals, insurance, excursions, lab equipment, student support services, airfare between Quito and Galapagos, e-mail access, airport transfers, national park fees. Financial aid available for students from sponsoring institution: scholarships, loans.
For More Information • College Consortium for International Studies–College of Staten Island/CUNY and Brookdale Community College, 2000 P Street, NW, Suite 503, Washington, DC 20036; *Phone:* 800-453-6956; *Fax:* 202-223-0999. *E-mail:* info@ccisabroad. org. *World Wide Web:* http://www.ccisabroad.org/. Students may also apply through College of Staten Island, The City University of New York, Center for International Service, Building 2A, Room 206, 2800 Victory Boulevard, Staten Island, NY 10314.

GUAYAQUIL
COLLEGE CONSORTIUM FOR INTERNATIONAL STUDIES–COLLEGE OF STATEN ISLAND/CUNY AND BROOKDALE COMMUNITY COLLEGE
PROGRAM IN GUAYAQUIL, ECUADOR

Hosted by Catholic University of Santiago of Guayaquil

Academic Focus • Ecuadorian studies, Latin American studies, Spanish language and literature.
Program Information • Students attend classes at Catholic University of Santiago of Guayaquil. Field trips to Manabi, Quito, Cerro Blanco, Otavalo; optional travel to Salinas, Baños, Cuenca, the jungle, Galápagos at an extra cost.
Sessions • Fall, winter.
Eligibility Requirements • Minimum age 18; open to freshmen, sophomores, juniors, seniors, graduate students, adults; 2.5 GPA; 3 letters of recommendation; essay; transcript; no foreign language proficiency required.
Living Arrangements • Students live in host family homes. Meals are taken with host family, in residences.
Costs (2004-2005) • One term: $3952 for fall; $2097 for winter; includes tuition, housing, some meals, insurance, excursions, student support services, fees, airport pick-up. Financial aid available for students from sponsoring institution: scholarships, loans.
For More Information • College Consortium for International Studies, 2000 P Street, NW, Suite 503, Washington, DC 20036; *Phone:* 800-453-6956; *Fax:* 202-223-0999. *E-mail:* info@ccisabroad. org. *World Wide Web:* http://www.ccisabroad.org/. Students may also apply through College of Staten Island, The City University of New York, Center for International Service, Building 2A, Room 206, 2800 Victory Boulevard, Staten Island, NY 10314; Brookdale Community College, International Center, 765 Newman Springs Road, Lincroft, NJ 07738-1597.

THE INTERNATIONAL PARTNERSHIP FOR SERVICE LEARNING
ECUADOR SERVICE–LEARNING (GUAYAQUIL)

Hosted by 'Espiritu Santo' University Guayaquil
Academic Focus • Community service, education, international affairs, Latin American studies, liberal studies, social sciences, Spanish language and literature.
Program Information • Students attend classes at 'Espiritu Santo' University Guayaquil. Field trips to Quito, Cuenca; optional travel to the Galapagos Islands, the Amazon at an extra cost.
Sessions • Fall, spring, yearlong.
Eligibility Requirements • Minimum age 18; open to freshmen, sophomores, juniors, seniors, graduate students, adults; 2 letters of recommendation; good academic standing at home school; evidence of maturity, responsibility; 1 year of college course work in Spanish.
Living Arrangements • Students live in host family homes. Meals are taken with host family, in residences.
Costs (2003-2004) • One term: $8750. Yearlong program: $16,900; includes tuition, housing, some meals, student support services, service placement and supervision. $50 application fee. $250 refundable deposit required. Financial aid available for all students: federal financial aid.
For More Information • Ms. Ilana Golin, Coordinator of Student Programs, The International Partnership for Service Learning, 815 Second Avenue, Suite 315, New York, NY 10017-4594; *Phone:* 212-986-0989; *Fax:* 212-986-5039. *E-mail:* info@ipsl.org. *World Wide Web:* http://www.ipsl.org/

STATE UNIVERSITY OF NEW YORK AT NEW PALTZ
INTENSIVE SPANISH LANGUAGE–LATIN AMERICAN STUDIES PROGRAM

Hosted by 'Espiritu Santo' University Guayaquil
Academic Focus • Education, Latin American studies, social services, Spanish language and literature.
Program Information • Students attend classes at 'Espiritu Santo' University Guayaquil. Field trips to coastal Ecuador (beach, parks), local attractions, Cuenca, Quito; optional travel to Indian markets of the highlands, adventure travel destinations, the Galapagos Islands, the Amazon rainforest at an extra cost.
Sessions • Fall, spring, yearlong.
Eligibility Requirements • Minimum age 18; open to sophomores, juniors, seniors; 2.5 GPA; 2 letters of recommendation; good academic standing at home school; 1 year of college course work in Spanish.
Living Arrangements • Students live in host family homes. Quarters are shared with host institution students. Meals are taken with host family, in residences.

Costs (2003-2004) • One term: $5139 for New York residents; $8269 for nonresidents. Yearlong program: $10,278 for New York residents; $16,538 for nonresidents; includes tuition, housing, all meals, insurance, excursions, administrative fees. $25 application fee. $300–$600 nonrefundable deposit required. Financial aid available for students from sponsoring institution: scholarships, loans.
For More Information • Center for International Programs, State University of New York at New Paltz, 75 South Manheim Boulevard, Suite 9, New Paltz, NY 12561; *Phone:* 845-257-3125; *Fax:* 845-257-3129. *E-mail:* international@newpaltz.edu. *World Wide Web:* http://www.newpaltz.edu/studyabroad/

QUITO
ALMA COLLEGE
PROGRAM OF STUDIES IN QUITO, ECUADOR

Hosted by Academia Latinoamericana
Academic Focus • Cultural studies, Spanish language and literature.
Program Information • Students attend classes at Academia Latinoamericana. Field trips to the "Middle of the World" (Equator monument), folk ballet; optional travel to a cloud forest, the Galapagos Islands at an extra cost.
Sessions • Fall, spring, winter, yearlong, fall and winter semesters.
Eligibility Requirements • Minimum age 18; open to sophomores, juniors, seniors; 2.5 GPA; 2 letters of recommendation; good academic standing at home school; no foreign language proficiency required.
Living Arrangements • Students live in host family homes. Quarters are shared with students from other programs. Meals are taken with host family.
Costs (2003-2004) • One term: $6300. Yearlong program: $11,600; includes tuition, housing, some meals, insurance, excursions, books and class materials, international student ID, student support services. $50 application fee. $200 refundable deposit required. Financial aid available for all students: scholarships.
For More Information • Ms. Julie Elenbaas, Office Coordinator, Alma College, 614 West Superior Street, Alma, MI 48801-1599; *Phone:* 989-463-7055; *Fax:* 989-463-7126. *E-mail:* intl_studies@alma. edu. *World Wide Web:* http://international.alma.edu/

BELOIT COLLEGE
ECUADOR PROGRAM

Hosted by Pontifical Catholic University of Ecuador Quito
Academic Focus • Ecuadorian studies, science, social sciences, Spanish language and literature.
Program Information • Students attend classes at Pontifical Catholic University of Ecuador Quito. Scheduled travel to the Galapagos Islands, the Amazon basin; field trips to Otavalo; optional travel at an extra cost.
Sessions • Fall, spring, yearlong.
Eligibility Requirements • Open to sophomores, juniors, seniors; course work in Latin American studies; 4 letters of recommendation; 2 years of college course work in Spanish.
Living Arrangements • Students live in host family homes. Meals are taken with host family, in residences.
Costs (2002-2003) • One term: $14,232. Yearlong program: contact sponsor for cost; includes tuition, housing, all meals, excursions. $100 nonrefundable deposit required. Financial aid available for all students: loans.
For More Information • Office of International Education, Beloit College, 700 College Street, Beloit, WI 53511; *Phone:* 608-363-2269; *Fax:* 608-363-2689. *E-mail:* oie@beloit.edu. *World Wide Web:* http://www.beloit.edu/~oie/

BOSTON UNIVERSITY
ECUADOR TROPICAL ECOLOGY PROGRAM

Hosted by Universidad San Francisco de Quito
Academic Focus • Biological/life sciences, ecology, environmental science/studies, Spanish language and literature.
Program Information • Students attend classes at Universidad San Francisco de Quito. Classes are also held on the campus of Tiputini

ECUADOR
Quito

Biodiversity Station. Scheduled travel to a rainforest, the Andes Mountains, the Galapagos Islands; field trips to a cloud forest, Otavalo.

Sessions • Fall, spring.

Eligibility Requirements • Open to sophomores, juniors, seniors, graduate students, adults; course work in introductory biology, ecology; 3.0 GPA; 2 letters of recommendation; good academic standing at home school; essay; approval of participation; transcript; 1 year of college course work in Spanish.

Living Arrangements • Students live in host family homes, the Tiputini Biodiversity Station. Quarters are shared with host institution students. Meals are taken as a group, in residences, in central dining facility.

Costs (2004-2005) • One term: $19,834; includes tuition, housing, all meals, excursions, international airfare, books and class materials, medical evacuation insurance. $50 application fee. $400 nonrefundable deposit required. Financial aid available for all students: scholarships, loans.

For More Information • Division of International Programs, Boston University, 232 Bay State Road, Boston, MA 02215; *Phone:* 617-353-9888; *Fax:* 617-353-5402. *E-mail:* abroad@bu.edu. *World Wide Web:* http://www.bu.edu/abroad/. Students may also apply through Boston University Center for Ecology and Conservation Biology, 5 Cummington Street, Boston, MA 02215.

BOSTON UNIVERSITY
QUITO LANGUAGE AND LIBERAL ARTS PROGRAM

Hosted by Universidad San Francisco de Quito

Academic Focus • Full curriculum.

Program Information • Students attend classes at Universidad San Francisco de Quito. Scheduled travel to the rainforest of Ecuador, the Galapagos Islands; field trips to the "Middle of the World" (Equator monument), Otavalo.

Sessions • Fall, spring, yearlong.

Eligibility Requirements • Open to sophomores, juniors, seniors; 3.0 GPA; 2 letters of recommendation; good academic standing at home school; essay; writing sample in Spanish; approval of participation; transcript; 2 years of college course work in Spanish.

Living Arrangements • Students live in host family homes. Meals are taken with host family, in residences.

Costs (2004-2005) • One term: $19,834. Yearlong program: $39,668; includes tuition, housing, all meals, insurance, excursions, international airfare, books and class materials, medical evacuation insurance, limited reimbursement for cultural activities. $50 application fee. $400 nonrefundable deposit required. Financial aid available for all students: scholarships, loans.

For More Information • Division of International Programs, Boston University, 232 Bay State Road, Boston, MA 02215; *Phone:* 617-353-9888; *Fax:* 617-353-5402. *E-mail:* abroad@bu.edu. *World Wide Web:* http://www.bu.edu/abroad/

BRETHREN COLLEGES ABROAD
BCA PROGRAM IN QUITO, ECUADOR

Hosted by Universidad San Francisco de Quito

Academic Focus • Full curriculum.

Program Information • Students attend classes at Universidad San Francisco de Quito. Scheduled travel to the Galapagos Islands, Amazon headwaters; field trips to Otavalo, a rainforest; optional travel to Inca ruins at an extra cost.

Sessions • Fall, spring, yearlong.

Eligibility Requirements • Minimum age 18; open to sophomores, juniors, seniors, graduate students; 2.6 GPA; 3 letters of recommendation; good academic standing at home school; 1 year of college course work in Spanish.

Living Arrangements • Students live in host family homes. Meals are taken on one's own, with host family, in residences.

Costs (2003-2004) • One term: $11,500. Yearlong program: $19,900; includes tuition, housing, all meals, insurance, excursions, international student ID, student support services. $50 application fee. $100 nonrefundable deposit required.

For More Information • Mr. Thomas V. Millington, Program Officer for Ecuador, Brethren Colleges Abroad, 50 Alpha Drive, Elizabethtown, PA 17022-0407; *Phone:* 717-361-6600; *Fax:* 717-361-6619. *E-mail:* info@bcanet.org. *World Wide Web:* http://www.bcanet.org/

COLLEGE CONSORTIUM FOR INTERNATIONAL STUDIES–COLLEGE OF STATEN ISLAND/CUNY AND BROOKDALE COMMUNITY COLLEGE
PROGRAM IN QUITO, ECUADOR

Hosted by Universidad San Francisco de Quito

Academic Focus • Andean studies, anthropology, archaeology, art history, biological/life sciences, civilization studies, ecology, Ecuadorian studies, environmental science/studies, geology, history, international affairs, Latin American studies, political science and government, Quechua, sociology, Spanish language and literature.

Program Information • Students attend classes at Universidad San Francisco de Quito. Scheduled travel to the jungle and the coast; field trips to Yanahurco, Otavalo; optional travel to Baños, Esmeraldas, the Galapagos Islands at an extra cost.

Sessions • Fall, spring, yearlong.

Eligibility Requirements • Minimum age 18; open to freshmen, sophomores, juniors, seniors, graduate students, adults; 2.5 GPA; 3 letters of recommendation; essay; transcript; student visa; 2 years of college course work in Spanish.

Living Arrangements • Students live in host family homes. Meals are taken with host family, in residences.

Costs (2004-2005) • One term: $7335. Yearlong program: $13,350; includes tuition, housing, some meals, insurance, excursions, student support services, fees, airport pick-up. Financial aid available for students from sponsoring institution: scholarships, loans.

For More Information • College Consortium for International Studies, 2000 P Street, NW, Suite 503, Washington, DC 20036; *Phone:* 800-453-6956; *Fax:* 202-223-0999. *E-mail:* info@ccisabroad. org. *World Wide Web:* http://www.ccisabroad.org/. Students may also apply through College of Staten Island, The City University of New York, Center for International Service, Building 2A, Room 206, 2800 Victory Boulevard, Staten Island, NY 10314; Brookdale Community College, International Center, 765 Newman Springs Road, Lincroft, NJ 07738-1597.

FLORIDA INTERNATIONAL UNIVERSITY
EXCHANGE PROGRAM–UNIVERSITY SAN FRANCISCO DE QUITO

Hosted by Universidad San Francisco de Quito

Academic Focus • Full curriculum.

Program Information • Students attend classes at Universidad San Francisco de Quito.

Sessions • Fall, spring.

Eligibility Requirements • Open to sophomores, juniors, seniors, graduate students, adults; 3.0 GPA; fluency in Spanish.

Living Arrangements • Students live in host family homes. Quarters are shared with host institution students. Meals are taken on one's own, in residences.

Costs (2003-2004) • One term: $5000; includes housing, all meals, insurance, international airfare, books and class materials, international student ID. $150 application fee. Financial aid available for all students: scholarships, loans.

For More Information • Office of International Studies, Florida International University, University Park Campus–TT100, Miami, FL 33199; *Phone:* 305-348-1913; *Fax:* 305-348-1941. *E-mail:* ois@fiu. edu. *World Wide Web:* http://ois.fiu.edu/

HIGHER EDUCATION CONSORTIUM FOR URBAN AFFAIRS (HECUA)
COMMUNITY INTERNSHIPS IN LATIN AMERICA

Held at Instituto de Estudios Ecuatorianos

Academic Focus • Community service, Ecuadorian studies, interdisciplinary studies, Latin American studies, peace and conflict studies, social sciences, social services, sociology, women's studies.

Program Information • Classes are held on the campus of Instituto de Estudios Ecuatorianos. Faculty members are local instructors hired by the sponsor. Field trips to community programs in other areas of Ecuador.

Sessions • Fall.

Eligibility Requirements • Open to sophomores, juniors, seniors, graduate students, adults; 2.5 GPA; 2 letters of recommendation; good academic standing at home school; 2 years of college course work in Spanish.

Living Arrangements • Students live in host family homes. Meals are taken with host family, in residences.

Costs (2003) • One term: $11,000; includes tuition, housing, all meals, insurance, excursions, student support services, internship placement and supervision. $75 application fee. $400 nonrefundable deposit required. Financial aid available for all students: scholarships.

For More Information • Mr. Michael Eaton, Director of Admissions and Student Services, Higher Education Consortium for Urban Affairs (HECUA), 2233 University Avenue West, Suite 210, St. Paul, MN 55114-1629; *Phone:* 800-554-1089; *Fax:* 651-659-9421. *E-mail:* info@hecua.org. *World Wide Web:* http://www.hecua.org/

THE INTERNATIONAL PARTNERSHIP FOR SERVICE LEARNING
ECUADOR SERVICE–LEARNING (QUITO)

Hosted by Universidad San Francisco de Quito

Academic Focus • Andean studies, ethnic studies, history, Spanish language and literature.

Program Information • Students attend classes at Universidad San Francisco de Quito. Scheduled travel to the Amazon; field trips to a farm outside of Quito, Andes villages; optional travel to volcano climbs and hikes at an extra cost.

Sessions • Fall, spring, yearlong.

Eligibility Requirements • Minimum age 18; open to freshmen, sophomores, juniors, seniors, graduate students, adults; 2 letters of recommendation; good academic standing at home school; evidence of maturity, responsibility; 2 years of college course work in Spanish.

Living Arrangements • Students live in host family homes. Meals are taken with host family, in residences.

Costs (2003-2004) • One term: $9400. Yearlong program: $18,000; includes tuition, housing, all meals, excursions, student support services. $50 application fee. $250 refundable deposit required. Financial aid available for all students: loans, federal financial aid.

For More Information • Ms. Ilana Golin, Coordinator of Student Programs, The International Partnership for Service Learning, 815 Second Avenue, Suite 315, New York, NY 10017-4594; *Phone:* 212-986-0989; *Fax:* 212-986-5039. *E-mail:* info@ipsl.org. *World Wide Web:* http://www.ipsl.org/

NICHOLLS STATE UNIVERSITY
STUDY PROGRAM IN ECUADOR

Hosted by Nicholls State University–Quito

Academic Focus • Art, cultural studies, history, Spanish language and literature.

Program Information • Students attend classes at Nicholls State University–Quito. Field trips to museums, the theater, a Mérida marketplace, a cathedral, a state building, city hall; optional travel to volcanoes, the Galapagos Islands, the Amazon region, Cuenca at an extra cost.

Sessions • Fall, spring, yearlong.

Eligibility Requirements • Minimum age 17; open to precollege students, freshmen, sophomores, juniors, seniors, graduate students, adults; no foreign language proficiency required.

Living Arrangements • Students live in host family homes. Quarters are shared with host institution students. Meals are taken with host family, in residences.

Costs (2003-2004) • One term: $4676. Yearlong program: $9351; includes tuition, housing, all meals, insurance, books and class materials, lab equipment, airport pick-up, instructional costs. Financial aid available for all students: loans, all customary sources.

For More Information • Ms. Cynthia Webb, Director of Study Programs Abroad, Nicholls State University, PO Box 2080, Thibodaux, LA 70310; *Phone:* 985-448-4440; *Fax:* 985-449-7028. *E-mail:* spab-caw@nicholls.edu. *World Wide Web:* http://www.nicholls.edu/abroad/

PITZER COLLEGE
PITZER COLLEGE IN ECUADOR

Hosted by Universidad San Francisco de Quito

Academic Focus • Full curriculum.

Program Information • Students attend classes at Universidad San Francisco de Quito. Scheduled travel to the Galapagos Islands, Cuenca, the Amazon jungle, Latacunga-Riobamba; field trips to a local non-governmental organization, homes for abandoned children, museums; optional travel to Peru, other colonial cities in Ecuador, Chimborazo Mountain at an extra cost.

Sessions • Fall, spring, yearlong.

Eligibility Requirements • Open to sophomores, juniors, seniors; course work in area studies; 2.5 GPA; 2 letters of recommendation; good academic standing at home school; 2 years of college course work in Spanish.

Living Arrangements • Students live in host family homes. Meals are taken with host family, in residences.

Costs (2003-2004) • One term: $18,795. Yearlong program: $37,590; includes tuition, housing, all meals, excursions, international airfare, international student ID, student support services. $25 application fee. $500 nonrefundable deposit required. Financial aid available for students from sponsoring institution: scholarships, loans.

For More Information • Ms. Neva Barker, Director of External Studies Admissions, Pitzer College, 1050 North Mills Avenue, Claremont, CA 91711; *Phone:* 909-621-8104; *Fax:* 909-621-0518. *E-mail:* external_studies@pitzer.edu. *World Wide Web:* http://www.pitzer.edu/external_studies/

SCHOOL FOR INTERNATIONAL TRAINING, SIT STUDY ABROAD
ECUADOR: COMPARATIVE ECOLOGY AND CONSERVATION

Academic Focus • Amazonian studies, anthropology, biological/life sciences, cultural studies, ecology, environmental science/studies, Galapagos area studies, Spanish language and literature.

Program Information • Faculty members are drawn from the sponsor's U.S. staff and local instructors hired by the sponsor. Scheduled travel to the Galapagos Islands, the Amazon rainforest, a paramo region of the Andes, the Highland Andes; field trips to rural areas, environmental reserves, coastal area, national parks.

Sessions • Fall, spring.

Eligibility Requirements • Open to sophomores, juniors, seniors; course work in environmental studies, ecology, biology or related field; 2.5 GPA; 2 letters of recommendation; good academic standing at home school; 2 years of college course work in Spanish.

Living Arrangements • Students live in host family homes, hotels. Meals are taken as a group, with host family, in residences, in restaurants.

Costs (2003-2004) • One term: $13,050; includes tuition, housing, all meals, insurance, excursions. $50 application fee. $400 nonrefundable deposit required. Financial aid available for all students: scholarships.

For More Information • School for International Training, SIT Study Abroad, Kipling Road, Brattleboro, VT 05302-0676; *Phone:* 888-272-7881; *Fax:* 802-258-3296. *E-mail:* studyabroad@sit.edu. *World Wide Web:* http://www.sit.edu/studyabroad/

SCHOOL FOR INTERNATIONAL TRAINING, SIT STUDY ABROAD
ECUADOR: CULTURE AND DEVELOPMENT

Academic Focus • Anthropology, cultural studies, economics, Ecuadorian studies, history, political science and government, Spanish language and literature.

Program Information • Faculty members are drawn from the sponsor's U.S. staff and local instructors hired by the sponsor. Scheduled travel to an Andean cloud forest, Sierra and rainforest villages, Guayaquil and coastal Ecuador; field trips to community organizations, human rights groups, indigenous centers.

Sessions • Fall, spring.

Eligibility Requirements • Open to sophomores, juniors, seniors; 2.5 GPA; 2 letters of recommendation; good academic standing at home school; 1.5 years of college course work in Spanish.

Living Arrangements • Students live in host family homes, hotels. Meals are taken as a group, on one's own, with host family, in residences, in restaurants.

Costs (2003-2004) • One term: $12,400; includes tuition, housing, all meals, insurance, excursions. $50 application fee. $400 nonrefundable deposit required. Financial aid available for all students: scholarships.

For More Information • School for International Training, SIT Study Abroad, Kipling Road, Brattleboro, VT 05302-0676; *Phone:* 888-272-7881; *Fax:* 802-258-3296. *E-mail:* studyabroad@sit.edu. *World Wide Web:* http://www.sit.edu/studyabroad/

ECUADOR
Quito

UNIVERSITY OF IDAHO
SPANISH AND LATIN AMERICAN STUDIES WITH SERVICE LEARNING

Hosted by Pontifical Catholic University of Ecuador Quito
Academic Focus • Ecuadorian studies, full curriculum, Spanish language and literature.
Program Information • Students attend classes at Pontifical Catholic University of Ecuador Quito. Scheduled travel to the Amazon; field trips to Valle de los Chillos, Otavalo, Cotacachi, Lake Cuicocha; optional travel to the Galapagos Islands at an extra cost.
Sessions • Fall, spring, yearlong, fall semester extends into Feb and spring semester extends into Jul for direct enrollment students.
Eligibility Requirements • Open to freshmen, sophomores, juniors, seniors, graduate students, adults; good academic standing at home school; 2.5 years course work in Spanish for direct enrollment; no foreign language proficiency requirement for intensive language program.
Living Arrangements • Students live in host family homes. Meals are taken with host family, in residences.
Costs (2003-2004) • One term: $6000. Yearlong program: $11,500; includes tuition, all meals, excursions, international student ID, student support services, housing for intensive course students. $100 application fee. $200 refundable deposit required. Financial aid available for students from sponsoring institution: scholarships, loans.
For More Information • Ms. Amy Bergmann, Advisor, University of Idaho, Room 209, Morrill Hall, Moscow, ID 83844-3013; *Phone:* 208-885-7870; *Fax:* 208-885-2859. *E-mail:* abroad@uidaho.edu. *World Wide Web:* http://www.ets.uidaho.edu/ipo/abroad/

UNIVERSITY OF ILLINOIS AT URBANA-CHAMPAIGN
ECUADORIAN UNIVERSITY PROGRAM

Hosted by Universidad San Francisco de Quito
Academic Focus • Full curriculum.
Program Information • Students attend classes at Universidad San Francisco de Quito. Scheduled travel to a rainforest, the beach; field trips to Otavalo, hot springs; optional travel to the Galapagos Islands at an extra cost.
Sessions • Fall, spring, yearlong.
Eligibility Requirements • Open to sophomores, juniors, seniors; 2.5 GPA; 2 letters of recommendation; good academic standing at home school; 2 years of college course work in Spanish.
Living Arrangements • Students live in host family homes. Meals are taken on one's own, with host family, in residences, in restaurants.
Costs (2002-2003) • One term: $7100. Yearlong program: $13,700; includes tuition, housing, some meals, insurance, excursions, student support services. $55 application fee. $500 nonrefundable deposit required. Financial aid available for students from sponsoring institution: scholarships, loans.
For More Information • Ms. Erika Ryser, Assistant Director, University of Illinois at Urbana-Champaign, Study Abroad Office, 910 South Fifth Street, #115, Champaign, IL 61820; *Phone:* 217-333-6322; *Fax:* 217-244-0249. *E-mail:* ryser@uiuc.edu. *World Wide Web:* http://www.ips.uiuc.edu/sao/index.shtml

UNIVERSITY OF MINNESOTA
MINNESOTA STUDIES IN INTERNATIONAL DEVELOPMENT (MSID), ECUADOR

Hosted by Fundación Cimas del Ecuador
Academic Focus • Agriculture, Andean studies, anthropology, community service, conservation studies, economics, Ecuadorian studies, education, environmental health, environmental science/studies, international affairs, Latin American studies, natural resources, nutrition, public policy, social sciences, social services, Spanish language and literature, urban/regional planning, wildlife studies, women's studies.
Program Information • Students attend classes at Fundación Cimas del Ecuador. Field trips to development projects, a rainforest; optional travel to sites in Ecuador at an extra cost.
Sessions • Fall, spring, yearlong.
Eligibility Requirements • Minimum age 19; open to juniors, seniors, graduate students, adults; course work in development

studies, social sciences, area studies; 2.5 GPA; 2 letters of recommendation; 2 years of college course work in Spanish.
Living Arrangements • Students live in host family homes. Meals are taken with host family, in residences.
Costs (2004-2005) • One term: contact sponsor for cost. Yearlong program: contact sponsor for cost. $50 application fee. $400 nonrefundable deposit required. Financial aid available for students from sponsoring institution: scholarships, loans.
For More Information • University of Minnesota, Learning Abroad Center, 230 Heller Hall, 271 19th Avenue South, Minneapolis, MN 55455; *Phone:* 612-626-9000; *Fax:* 612-626-8009. *E-mail:* umabroad@umn.edu. *World Wide Web:* http://www.umabroad.umn.edu/

UNIVERSITY OF NORTH CAROLINA AT WILMINGTON
NORTH CAROLINA SEMESTER IN QUITO, ECUADOR

Hosted by Universidad San Francisco de Quito
Academic Focus • Full curriculum.
Program Information • Students attend classes at Universidad San Francisco de Quito. Field trips to an Otavalo Indian Market, attractions around Quito, the "Middle of the World" (Equator monument); optional travel to the Galapagos Islands, the Tiputini Biodiversity Station at an extra cost.
Sessions • Fall, spring, yearlong.
Eligibility Requirements • Minimum age 18; open to sophomores, juniors, seniors, adults; 2.5 GPA; 2 letters of recommendation; good academic standing at home school; 2 years of college course work in Spanish.
Living Arrangements • Students live in host family homes. Meals are taken with host family, in residences.
Costs (2002-2003) • One term: $6210. Yearlong program: $12,420; includes tuition, housing, all meals, insurance, student support services, laundry service. $200 nonrefundable deposit required. Financial aid available for students from sponsoring institution: scholarships, loans.
For More Information • Ms. Elizabeth A. Adams, Education Abroad Coordinator, Office of International Programs, University of North Carolina at Wilmington, 601 South College Road, Wilmington, NC 28403; *Phone:* 910-962-3685; *Fax:* 910-962-4053. *E-mail:* adamse@uncw.edu. *World Wide Web:* http://www.uncw.edu/intprogs/

EGYPT
CAIRO
AMERICAN UNIVERSITY IN CAIRO
INTENSIVE ARABIC PROGRAM

Hosted by American University in Cairo
Academic Focus • Arabic, Fusha.
Program Information • Students attend classes at American University in Cairo. Scheduled travel to Sinai, desert/oasis villages; field trips to local museums, St. Catherine Monastery; optional travel to upper Egypt, Alexandria at an extra cost.
Sessions • Fall, spring, yearlong.
Eligibility Requirements • Open to freshmen, sophomores, juniors, seniors, graduate students, adults; 1 letter of recommendation; no foreign language proficiency required.
Living Arrangements • Students live in host institution dormitories, locally rented apartments. Quarters are shared with host institution students, students from other programs. Meals are taken on one's own, in central dining facility, in restaurants.
Costs (2003-2004) • One term: $6335. Yearlong program: $12,590; includes tuition, insurance, excursions, books and class materials, student support services, visa and other fees, spending money. $100 nonrefundable deposit required. Financial aid available for students: loans (for full-year students only).
For More Information • Mrs. Mary W. Davidson, Senior Student Affairs Officer, American University in Cairo, 420 Fifth Avenue, 3rd Floor, New York, NY 10018-2729; *Phone:* 212-730-8800; *Fax:* 212-730-1600. *E-mail:* mdavidson@aucnyo.edu. *World Wide Web:* http://www.aucegypt.edu/catalog03/undergrad/studabroad/

studabroad.html. Students may also apply through Arabic Language Institute, PO Box 2511, Cairo 11511, Egypt.

MORE ABOUT THE PROGRAM

The Arabic Language Institute at the American University in Cairo offers full-time contemporary Arabic language training in Egyptian Colloquial and Modern Standard Arabic for students, businesspeople, diplomats, and scholars at the elementary, intermediate, and advanced levels. The academic-year program leads to a certificate in Arabic language proficiency; students may also enroll for 1 semester of language training. The program requires a minimum of 20 contact hours per week, with equal time spent on assignments outside of class. Course-related travel around Egypt enhances the language instruction.

AMERICAN UNIVERSITY IN CAIRO
STUDY ABROAD PROGRAMS

Hosted by American University in Cairo
Academic Focus • Full curriculum.
Program Information • Students attend classes at American University in Cairo. Scheduled travel to Abu Simbel, Aswan, Luxor, El-Menia, Hurghada; field trips to the Giza Plateau, Memphis, local tours; optional travel at an extra cost.
Sessions • Fall, spring, winter, yearlong.
Eligibility Requirements • Open to sophomores, juniors, graduate students; 2.0 GPA; 2 letters of recommendation; good academic standing at home school; no foreign language proficiency required.
Living Arrangements • Students live in host institution dormitories, locally rented apartments. Quarters are shared with students from other programs. Meals are taken on one's own, in residences, in central dining facility, in restaurants.
Costs (2003-2004) • One term: $6200. Yearlong program: $12,400; includes tuition, student support services.
For More Information • Mrs. Mary W. Davidson, Senior Student Affairs Officer, American University in Cairo, 420 Fifth Avenue, 3rd Floor, New York, NY 10018-2729; *Phone:* 212-730-8800 Ext. 223; *Fax:* 212-730-1600. *E-mail:* mdavidson@aucnyo.edu. *World Wide Web:* http://www.aucegypt.edu/catalog03/undergrad/studabroad/studabroad.html

MORE ABOUT THE PROGRAM

The American University in Cairo (AUC) offers students an exceptional opportunity to learn about Egyptian, Arab, and Middle Eastern societies at an American-style liberal arts university in downtown Cairo. Courses are taught in English. The Study Abroad Program enrolls about 200 international students who study full-time alongside their Egyptian peers for 1 or 2 semesters. Three-week winter sessions are available. Popular academic areas are anthropology, Arabic language and literature, Egyptology, environmental sciences, Islamic studies, ancient to modern Middle Eastern history, and sociology. AUC is accredited by the Middle States Association of Colleges and Schools and has professional accreditation from the Accreditation Board for Engineering and Technology, Inc. (ABET) and the Computing Sciences Accreditation Board (CSAB). A dormitory and support services that are similar to U.S. colleges are available. Campus social activities and regional travel opportunities abound.

Preprogram orientation is required; it is included in program cost and held at program site.

STATE UNIVERSITY OF NEW YORK COLLEGE AT CORTLAND
AMERICAN UNIVERSITY CAIRO

Hosted by American University in Cairo
Academic Focus • Full curriculum.
Program Information • Students attend classes at American University in Cairo. Field trips to Red Sea, Alexandria; optional travel to Luxor, Aswan, Red Sea, Mount Sinai, Petra, Istanbul, Jerusalem at an extra cost.

Sessions • Fall, spring, yearlong.
Eligibility Requirements • Minimum age 19; open to sophomores, juniors, seniors; 2.5 GPA; 2 letters of recommendation; good academic standing at home school; no foreign language proficiency required.
Living Arrangements • Students live in host institution dormitories, locally rented apartments. Meals are taken on one's own, in central dining facility, in restaurants.
Costs (2003-2004) • One term: $7000. Yearlong program: $14,000; includes housing, all meals, insurance, excursions, books and class materials, student support services. $20 application fee. $200 nonrefundable deposit required. Financial aid available for students from sponsoring institution: scholarships, loans.
For More Information • Ms. Liz Kopp, Assistant Director, Office of International Programs, State University of New York College at Cortland, PO Box 2000, Cortland, NY 13045; *Phone:* 607-753-2209; *Fax:* 607-753-5989. *E-mail:* cortlandabroad@cortland.edu. *World Wide Web:* http://www.studyabroad.com/suny/cortland/

EL SALVADOR

SAN SALVADOR

AUGSBURG COLLEGE
SUSTAINABLE DEVELOPMENT AND SOCIAL CHANGE IN CENTRAL AMERICA

Hosted by Center for Global Education
Academic Focus • Economics, history, interdisciplinary studies, Latin American studies, peace and conflict studies, religious studies, Spanish language and literature.
Program Information • Students attend classes at Center for Global Education. Scheduled travel to Guatemala, El Salvador, Nicaragua; field trips; optional travel at an extra cost.
Sessions • Fall, spring.
Eligibility Requirements • Open to sophomores, juniors, seniors; course work in economics (1 course); 2.5 GPA; 2 letters of recommendation; good academic standing at home school; 0.5 years of college course work in Spanish.
Living Arrangements • Students live in program-owned houses, host family homes, hotels, guest houses. Quarters are shared with host institution students. Meals are taken as a group, with host family, in central dining facility, in restaurants.
Costs (2004-2005) • One term: sliding fee scale for consortium partners; $13,400 for transfers; includes tuition, housing, all meals, insurance, excursions, international student ID, some books and class materials. $50 application fee. $500 nonrefundable deposit required. Financial aid available for students from sponsoring institution: scholarships, loans.
For More Information • Ms. Margaret Anderson, Coordinator, Semester Programs Abroad, Augsburg College, 2211 Riverside Avenue, Minneapolis, MN 55454; *Phone:* 800-299-8889; *Fax:* 612-330-1695. *E-mail:* globaled@augsburg.edu. *World Wide Web:* http://www.augsburg.edu/global/

ENGLAND

See also Ireland, Northern Ireland, Scotland, and Wales.

CITY TO CITY
FLORIDA INTERNATIONAL UNIVERSITY
EXCHANGE PROGRAM–UNIVERSITY OF HULL

Hosted by University of Hull
Academic Focus • Full curriculum.
Program Information • Students attend classes at University of Hull (Hull).

Sessions • Fall, spring.
Eligibility Requirements • Open to sophomores, juniors, seniors, graduate students, adults; 3.0 GPA.
Living Arrangements • Students live in host institution dormitories. Quarters are shared with students from other programs. Meals are taken on one's own, in central dining facility.
Costs (2003-2004) • One term: $5000; includes housing, all meals, insurance, international airfare, books and class materials, international student ID. $150 application fee. Financial aid available for all students: scholarships, loans.
For More Information • Office of International Studies, Florida International University, University Park Campus–TT100, Miami, FL 33199; *Phone:* 305-348-1913; *Fax:* 305-348-1941. *E-mail:* ois@fiu. edu. *World Wide Web:* http://ois.fiu.edu/

ALNWICK
ST. CLOUD STATE UNIVERSITY
ALNWICK CASTLE PROGRAM

Held at Alnwick Castle
Academic Focus • Art, biological/life sciences, business administration/management, communications, history, marketing, photography, social sciences.
Program Information • Classes are held on the campus of Alnwick Castle. Faculty members are drawn from the sponsor's U.S. staff and local instructors hired by the sponsor. Scheduled travel to London; field trips to local historic/cultural sites, Edinburgh; optional travel to Africa, Europe at an extra cost.
Sessions • Fall, spring.
Eligibility Requirements • Minimum age 18; open to freshmen, sophomores, juniors, seniors; 2.25 GPA; 2 letters of recommendation.
Living Arrangements • Students live in a modernized 12th-century castle. Meals are taken as a group, in central dining facility.
Costs (2003-2004) • One term: $6475 for Minnesota residents; includes tuition, housing, some meals, excursions, international airfare, international student ID, student support services. $75 application fee. Financial aid available for students from sponsoring institution: scholarships, work study, loans.
For More Information • Chunsheng Zhang, Associate Vice President for Academic Affairs/International Studies, St. Cloud State University, Center for International Studies, 720 4th Avenue, South, St. Cloud, MN 56301-4498; *Phone:* 320-308-4287; *Fax:* 320-308-4223. *E-mail:* intstudy@stcloudstate.edu. *World Wide Web:* http://www. stcloudstate.edu/

BATH
BATH SPA UNIVERSITY COLLEGE
STUDY ABROAD PROGRAM IN BATH

Hosted by Bath Spa University College
Academic Focus • Art, ceramics and pottery, creative writing, cultural studies, dance, design and applied arts, drama/theater, education, English, environmental science/studies, fashion design, fine/studio arts, food science, geography, graphic design/illustration, health-care management, history, Irish studies, music, music performance, psychology, religious studies, sociology, textiles, tourism and travel, visual and performing arts.
Program Information • Students attend classes at Bath Spa University College. Field trips to London, Cardiff, Glastonbury, Stonehenge, Oxford, Cambridge; optional travel to Dublin, Paris.
Sessions • Fall, spring, yearlong.
Eligibility Requirements • Minimum age 18; open to sophomores, juniors, adults; 2.7 GPA; 2 letters of recommendation.
Living Arrangements • Students live in host institution dormitories, host family homes. Quarters are shared with host institution students, students from other programs. Meals are taken as a group, on one's own, with host family, in residences, in central dining facility.
Costs (2003-2004) • One term: £6630. Yearlong program: £13,260; includes tuition, housing, books and class materials, local transportation. Financial aid available for students from sponsoring institution.
For More Information • Ms. Doris Bechstein, Head, International Recruitment, Bath Spa University College, Newton Park, Bath BA2

9BN, England; *Phone:* +44 122-5876110; *Fax:* +44 122-5875-501. *E-mail:* d.bechstein@bathspa.ac.uk. *World Wide Web:* http://www. bathspa.ac.uk/

UNIVERSITY OF BATH
STUDY ABROAD PROGRAMME

Hosted by University of Bath
Academic Focus • Biological/life sciences, business administration/management, chemical sciences, computer science, economics, engineering, mathematics, physics, psychology, social sciences.
Program Information • Students attend classes at University of Bath. Field trips to Oxford, Windsor, Stonehenge, Bristol.
Sessions • Fall, spring, yearlong.
Eligibility Requirements • Open to juniors, seniors; 3.0 GPA; 1 letter of recommendation.
Living Arrangements • Students live in host institution dormitories. Quarters are shared with host institution students. Meals are taken as a group, on one's own, in residences, in central dining facility.
Costs (2003-2004) • One term: £3950–£5050. Yearlong program: £7900–£10,100; includes tuition.
For More Information • Ms. Sarah Crampin, Study Abroad Administrator, University of Bath, Claverton Down, Bath BA2 7AY, England; *Phone:* +44 122-386766; *Fax:* +44 122-366366. *E-mail:* student-exchange@bath.ac.uk. *World Wide Web:* http://www.bath. ac.uk/study-abroad/

BIRMINGHAM
ARCADIA UNIVERSITY
UNIVERSITY OF BIRMINGHAM

Hosted by University of Birmingham
Academic Focus • African studies, biological/life sciences, business administration/management, classics and classical languages, drama/theater, Eastern European studies, health and physical education, language studies, liberal studies, social sciences.
Program Information • Students attend classes at University of Birmingham.
Sessions • Fall, spring, yearlong, fall semester.
Eligibility Requirements • Open to juniors, seniors; 3.0 GPA; 1 letter of recommendation.
Living Arrangements • Students live in host institution dormitories. Quarters are shared with host institution students, students from other programs. Meals are taken on one's own, in residences.
Costs (2003-2004) • One term: $11,350–$12,450. Yearlong program: $20,750; includes tuition, housing, insurance, international student ID, student support services, pre-departure guide, transcripts. $35 application fee. $500 nonrefundable deposit required. Financial aid available for all students: scholarships, loans.
For More Information • Arcadia University, Center for Education Abroad, 450 South Easton Road, Glenside, PA 19038-3295; *Phone:* 866-927-2234; *Fax:* 215-572-2174. *E-mail:* cea@arcadia.edu. *World Wide Web:* http://www.arcadia.edu/cea/

INTERSTUDY
UNIVERSITY OF CENTRAL ENGLAND IN BIRMINGHAM

Hosted by University of Central England in Birmingham
Academic Focus • Art history, business administration/management, communications, computer science, design and applied arts, economics, education, engineering, English, film and media studies, fine/studio arts, history, journalism, music, political science and government, psychology, sociology.
Program Information • Students attend classes at University of Central England in Birmingham. Scheduled travel to Bath, Stratford-upon-Avon, Warwick Castle, Oxford, Stonehenge.
Sessions • Fall, spring, yearlong.
Eligibility Requirements • Minimum age 18; open to freshmen, sophomores, juniors, seniors, adults; 2.5 GPA; 2 letters of recommendation; good academic standing at home school.
Living Arrangements • Students live in host institution dormitories. Quarters are shared with host institution students. Meals are taken on one's own, in residences.
Costs (2003-2004) • One term: $11,215 for fall term; $12,650 for spring. Yearlong program: $20,975; includes tuition, housing, some

meals, excursions, international student ID, student support services, Student Union membership, e-mail access, banking facilities, international bank transfers, transcript, cell phone. $35 application fee. $500 nonrefundable deposit required. Financial aid available for all students: scholarships, loans, stipends.

For More Information • InterStudy, Admissions Office, 63 Edward Street, Medford, MA 02155; *Phone:* 800-663-1999; *Fax:* 781-391-7463. *E-mail:* interstudy@interstudy-usa.org. *World Wide Web:* http://www.interstudy.org/

UNIVERSITY OF CENTRAL ENGLAND IN BIRMINGHAM
STUDY ABROAD IN CENTRAL ENGLAND

Hosted by University of Central England in Birmingham
Academic Focus • Accounting, architecture, art history, business administration/management, communications, computer science, criminal justice, design and applied arts, engineering, English, environmental science/studies, fashion design, film and media studies, finance, fine/studio arts, human resources, law and legal studies, management information systems, marketing, music, political science and government, sociology, urban/regional planning.
Program Information • Students attend classes at University of Central England in Birmingham. Optional travel to London, Stratford-upon-Avon, Scotland, Ireland, Paris, Amsterdam.
Sessions • Fall, spring, yearlong.
Eligibility Requirements • Minimum age 18; open to sophomores, juniors, seniors, adults; 2.8 GPA; 1 letter of recommendation; good academic standing at home school; prerequisite courses for some academic programs.
Living Arrangements • Students live in host institution dormitories, locally rented apartments, program-owned apartments, host family homes. Quarters are shared with host institution students. Meals are taken on one's own, in residences, in central dining facility.
Costs (2003-2004) • One term: £5500–£6500 (estimated). Yearlong program: £11,500 (estimated); includes tuition, housing, student support services, course handouts and materials for art and design courses, information technology facilities. Financial aid available for students from sponsoring institution: loans, access funds, hardship loans.
For More Information • Mrs. Frances Thomas, Head of Admissions Support, University of Central England in Birmingham, Academic Registry, Perry Barr, Birmingham B42 2SU, England; *Phone:* +44 121-331-6650; *Fax:* +44 121-331-6706. *E-mail:* fran.thomas@uce.ac.uk. *World Wide Web:* http://www.uce.ac.uk/

UNIVERSITY OF MINNESOTA, DULUTH
STUDY IN ENGLAND

Held at University of Birmingham–Selly Oak Campus
Academic Focus • Art, history, liberal studies, sociology.
Program Information • Classes are held on the campus of University of Birmingham–Selly Oak Campus. Faculty members are drawn from the sponsor's U.S. staff and local instructors hired by the sponsor. Scheduled travel to the Lake District, London, Edinburgh, Wales; field trips to Oxford, Warwick.
Sessions • Yearlong.
Eligibility Requirements • Minimum age 18; open to sophomores, juniors, seniors; 2.4 GPA.
Living Arrangements • Students live in host institution dormitories. Quarters are shared with host institution students. Meals are taken as a group, in central dining facility.
Costs (2003-2004) • Yearlong program: $14,450; includes tuition, housing, all meals, insurance, excursions, international airfare, books and class materials, lab equipment, international student ID, student guild card, administrative costs, local bus pass. $100 application fee. $850 nonrefundable deposit required. Financial aid available for students from sponsoring institution: scholarships, work study, loans, grants.
For More Information • Ms. Deborah V. Good, Program Associate, University of Minnesota, Duluth, International Education Office, 110 Cina, Duluth, MN 55812; *Phone:* 218-726-8764; *Fax:* 218-726-6386. *E-mail:* dgood@d.umn.edu. *World Wide Web:* http://www.d.umn.edu/ieo/

BRIGHTON
ARCADIA UNIVERSITY
UNIVERSITY OF SUSSEX

Hosted by University of Sussex
Academic Focus • African studies, American studies, art history, business administration/management, film and media studies, history, international affairs, law and legal studies, premedical studies, science, women's studies.
Program Information • Students attend classes at University of Sussex.
Sessions • Fall, spring, yearlong, pre-session.
Eligibility Requirements • Open to sophomores, juniors, seniors; 3.0 GPA; 1 letter of recommendation.
Living Arrangements • Students live in host institution dormitories, host family homes. Quarters are shared with host institution students, students from other programs. Meals are taken on one's own, in residences.
Costs (2003-2004) • One term: $9650 for fall term; $12,990 for two spring terms ($1590 for pre-session). Yearlong program: $19,250; includes tuition, housing, insurance, international student ID, student support services, pre-departure guide, transcripts. $35 application fee. $500 nonrefundable deposit required. Financial aid available for all students: scholarships, loans.
For More Information • Arcadia University, Center for Education Abroad, 450 South Easton Road, Glenside, PA 19038-3295; *Phone:* 866-927-2234; *Fax:* 215-572-2174. *E-mail:* cea@arcadia.edu. *World Wide Web:* http://www.arcadia.edu/cea/

INSTITUTE FOR STUDY ABROAD, BUTLER UNIVERSITY
UNIVERSITY OF SUSSEX

Hosted by University of Sussex
Academic Focus • Full curriculum.
Program Information • Students attend classes at University of Sussex. Field trips to London.
Sessions • Fall, spring, yearlong, early start session.
Eligibility Requirements • Open to juniors, seniors; 3.0 GPA; 1 letter of recommendation; good academic standing at home school; enrollment at an accredited American college or university.
Living Arrangements • Students live in host institution dormitories, locally rented apartments. Quarters are shared with host institution students. Meals are taken on one's own, in residences, in central dining facility.
Costs (2002-2003) • One term: $8775 for fall ($10,375 with early start session); $11,675 for spring. Yearlong program: $16,775 ($18,375 with early start session); includes tuition, housing, excursions, international student ID, student support services, family visit, cultural and sporting events, pre-departure advising. $40 application fee. $500 nonrefundable deposit required. Financial aid available for all students: scholarships, travel grants.
For More Information • Institute for Study Abroad, Butler University, 1100 West 42nd Street, Suite 305, Indianapolis, IN 46208-3345; *Phone:* 800-858-0229; *Fax:* 317-940-9704. *E-mail:* study-abroad@butler.edu. *World Wide Web:* http://www.ifsa-butler.org/

RUTGERS, THE STATE UNIVERSITY OF NEW JERSEY
STUDY ABROAD IN BRITAIN: BRIGHTON, UNIVERSITY OF SUSSEX

Hosted by University of Sussex
Academic Focus • Full curriculum.
Program Information • Students attend classes at University of Sussex. Field trips to London, Stonehenge, Oxford.
Sessions • Fall, spring, yearlong.
Eligibility Requirements • Open to sophomores, juniors, seniors; 3.0 GPA; 2 letters of recommendation; good academic standing at home school; official transcript from each tertiary school attended.
Living Arrangements • Students live in host institution dormitories. Quarters are shared with host institution students. Meals are taken on one's own, in residences, in central dining facility.
Costs (2003-2004) • One term: $9940–$12,848 for New Jersey residents; $12,590–$15,498 for nonresidents. Yearlong program:

ENGLAND
Brighton

$17,965 for New Jersey residents; $23,265 for nonresidents; includes tuition, insurance, excursions, student support services. $20 application fee. $750 nonrefundable deposit required. Financial aid available for students from sponsoring institution: scholarships, loans.

For More Information • Ms. Karin Bonello, Regional Coordinator, Rutgers, The State University of New Jersey, 102 College Avenue, New Brunswick, NJ 08901-8543; *Phone:* 732-932-7787; *Fax:* 732-932-8659. *E-mail:* ru_abroad@email.rutgers.edu. *World Wide Web:* http://studyabroad.rutgers.edu/

UNIVERSITY OF MIAMI
UNIVERSITY OF BRIGHTON

Hosted by University of Brighton
Academic Focus • Business administration/management.
Program Information • Students attend classes at University of Brighton.
Sessions • Spring, yearlong.
Eligibility Requirements • Minimum age 18; open to sophomores, juniors, seniors; major in business; 2 letters of recommendation; good academic standing at home school.
Living Arrangements • Students live in host institution dormitories. Quarters are shared with host institution students, students from other programs. Meals are taken on one's own, in central dining facility.
Costs (2003-2004) • One term: $12,919. Yearlong program: $25,838; includes tuition, student support services. $40 application fee. $500 nonrefundable deposit required. Financial aid available for students from sponsoring institution: scholarships, loans.
For More Information • Ms. Elyse Resnick, Assistant Director, University of Miami, International Education and Exchange Programs, 5050 Brunson Drive, Allen Hall 212, PO Box 248005, Coral Gables, FL 33124-1610; *Phone:* 305-284-3434; *Fax:* 305-284-4235. *E-mail:* ieep@miami.edu. *World Wide Web:* http://www.studyabroad.miami.edu/

UNIVERSITY OF MIAMI
UNIVERSITY OF SUSSEX

Hosted by University of Sussex
Academic Focus • Biological/life sciences, international affairs, social sciences.
Program Information • Students attend classes at University of Sussex.
Sessions • Fall, spring, yearlong.
Eligibility Requirements • Minimum age 18; open to sophomores, juniors, seniors; 3.0 GPA; 2 letters of recommendation; official transcripts; essay.
Living Arrangements • Students live in host institution dormitories. Quarters are shared with host institution students. Meals are taken on one's own, in residences, in central dining facility, in restaurants.
Costs (2003-2004) • One term: $12,919. Yearlong program: $25,838; includes tuition, student support services. $40 application fee. $500 nonrefundable deposit required. Financial aid available for students from sponsoring institution: loans.
For More Information • Ms. Elyse Resnick, Assistant Director, University of Miami, International Education and Exchange Programs, 5050 Brunson Drive, Allen Hall 212, PO Box 248005, Coral Gables, FL 33124-1610; *Phone:* 305-284-3434; *Fax:* 305-284-4235. *E-mail:* ieep@miami.edu. *World Wide Web:* http://www.studyabroad.miami.edu/

THE UNIVERSITY OF NORTH CAROLINA AT CHAPEL HILL
STUDY ABROAD AT THE UNIVERSITY OF SUSSEX

Hosted by University of Sussex
Academic Focus • Full curriculum.
Program Information • Students attend classes at University of Sussex.
Sessions • Fall, spring, yearlong.
Eligibility Requirements • Open to sophomores, juniors, seniors, graduate students, adults; 3.0 GPA; 2 letters of recommendation; good academic standing at home school; transcripts; essays.

Living Arrangements • Students live in host institution dormitories, locally rented apartments. Quarters are shared with host institution students. Meals are taken on one's own, in residences, in central dining facility, in restaurants.
Costs (2003-2004) • One term: $9789. Yearlong program: $17,250; includes tuition, housing, insurance, study abroad fee. $100 application fee. $500 nonrefundable deposit required. Financial aid available for students from sponsoring institution: scholarships, loans.
For More Information • Study Abroad Office, The University of North Carolina at Chapel Hill, 201 Porthole Building, CB 3130, Chapel Hill, NC 27599-3130; *Phone:* 919-962-7002; *Fax:* 919-962-2262. *E-mail:* abroad@unc.edu. *World Wide Web:* http://studyabroad.unc.edu/

UNIVERSITY OF SUSSEX
STUDY ABROAD AT THE UNIVERSITY OF SUSSEX

Hosted by University of Sussex
Academic Focus • Full curriculum.
Program Information • Students attend classes at University of Sussex. Field trips to course-related destinations.
Sessions • Fall, spring, yearlong, Sussex in September.
Eligibility Requirements • Minimum age 18; open to sophomores, juniors, seniors, adults; 3.0 GPA; 1 letter of recommendation; good academic standing at home school.
Living Arrangements • Students live in host institution dormitories, locally rented apartments, program-owned apartments, program-owned houses, host family homes. Quarters are shared with host institution students, students from other programs. Meals are taken as a group, on one's own, in residences, in central dining facility, in restaurants.
Costs (2003-2004) • One term: £3116 for fall term; £4674 for spring. Yearlong program: £7790; includes tuition, lab equipment, student support services, computing and library facilities.
For More Information • Ms. Emily Sinclair, International Programmes Officer, University of Sussex, International and Study Abroad Office, Mantell Building, Falmer, Brighton BN1 9QN, England; *Phone:* +44 1273-678422; *Fax:* +44 1273-678640. *E-mail:* international@sussex.ac.uk. *World Wide Web:* http://www.sussex.ac.uk/Units/publications/sabroad2000/

UNIVERSITY STUDIES ABROAD CONSORTIUM
FULL CURRICULUM STUDIES: BRIGHTON, ENGLAND

Hosted by University of Brighton
Academic Focus • Full curriculum.
Program Information • Students attend classes at University of Brighton. Optional travel to Paris, Oxford, Stratford-upon-Avon, London, East Sussex, Dublin, Bath, Stonehenge at an extra cost.
Sessions • Fall, spring, yearlong.
Eligibility Requirements • Minimum age 18; open to freshmen, sophomores, juniors, seniors, graduate students, adults; 2.75 GPA.
Living Arrangements • Students live in host institution dormitories. Quarters are shared with host institution students. Meals are taken on one's own, in residences, in central dining facility.
Costs (2005-2006) • One term: $4880. Yearlong program: $9480; includes tuition, insurance, student support services. $50 application fee. $150 refundable deposit required. Financial aid available for all students: scholarships, loans.
For More Information • University Studies Abroad Consortium, USAC/323, Reno, NV 89557-0093; *Phone:* 775-784-6569; *Fax:* 775-784-6010. *E-mail:* usac@unr.edu. *World Wide Web:* http://usac.unr.edu/

BRISTOL
INSTITUTE FOR STUDY ABROAD, BUTLER UNIVERSITY
UNIVERSITY OF BRISTOL

Hosted by University of Bristol
Academic Focus • Full curriculum.
Program Information • Students attend classes at University of Bristol. Field trips to London, Wales, the Lake District.

Sessions • Fall, spring, yearlong.

Eligibility Requirements • Open to sophomores, juniors, seniors; 3.2 GPA; 1 letter of recommendation; good academic standing at home school; enrollment at an accredited American college or university; minimum 3.5 GPA for science courses, minimum 3.2 GPA for all others.

Living Arrangements • Students live in host institution dormitories, locally rented apartments, university student houses. Quarters are shared with host institution students, students from other programs. Meals are taken on one's own, in residences, in central dining facility, in restaurants.

Costs (2002-2003) • One term: $11,475. Yearlong program: $18,875; includes tuition, housing, excursions, international student ID, student support services, family visit, cultural and sporting events, pre-departure advising. $40 application fee. $500 nonrefundable deposit required. Financial aid available for all students: scholarships, travel grants.

For More Information • Institute for Study Abroad, Butler University, 1100 West 42nd Street, Suite 305, Indianapolis, IN 46208-3345; *Phone:* 800-858-0229; *Fax:* 317-940-9704. *E-mail:* study-abroad@butler.edu. *World Wide Web:* http://www.ifsa-butler.org/

RUTGERS, THE STATE UNIVERSITY OF NEW JERSEY
STUDY ABROAD IN BRITAIN: BRISTOL

Hosted by University of Bristol
Academic Focus • Full curriculum.
Program Information • Students attend classes at University of Bristol. Field trips to London, Stonehenge, Oxford.
Sessions • Spring, yearlong.
Eligibility Requirements • Open to sophomores, juniors, seniors; 3.0 GPA; 2 letters of recommendation; good academic standing at home school.
Living Arrangements • Students live in host institution dormitories. Quarters are shared with host institution students. Meals are taken on one's own, in residences.
Costs (2003-2004) • One term: $10,770 for New Jersey residents; $13,420 for nonresidents. Yearlong program: $19,014 for New Jersey residents; $24,314 for nonresidents; includes tuition, insurance, excursions, student support services. $20 application fee. $750 nonrefundable deposit required. Financial aid available for students from sponsoring institution: scholarships, loans.
For More Information • Ms. Karin Bonello, Regional Coordinator, Rutgers, The State University of New Jersey, 102 College Avenue, New Brunswick, NJ 08901-8543; *Phone:* 732-932-7787; *Fax:* 732-932-8659. *E-mail:* ru_abroad@email.rutgers.edu. *World Wide Web:* http://studyabroad.rutgers.edu/

UNIVERSITY OF BRISTOL
STABEL–STUDY ABROAD WITH ENGLISH LANGUAGE

Hosted by University of Bristol
Academic Focus • Engineering, law and legal studies, liberal studies, science, social sciences.
Program Information • Students attend classes at University of Bristol. Optional travel to Europe, Britain at an extra cost.
Sessions • Fall, yearlong.
Eligibility Requirements • Open to sophomores, juniors, graduate students, adults; 3.2 GPA; 2 letters of recommendation; good academic standing at home school.
Living Arrangements • Students live in host institution dormitories, locally rented apartments, host family homes. Quarters are shared with host institution students. Meals are taken as a group, in residences.
Costs (2002-2003) • One term: contact sponsor for cost. Yearlong program: contact sponsor for cost.
For More Information • Ms. Wendy Davies, Programme Coordinator, University of Bristol, University Union, Queen's Road, Study Abroad Programme, International Centre, Bristol BS8 1LN, England; *Phone:* +44 117-923-9159; *Fax:* +44 117-923-9085. *E-mail:* jya@bristol.ac.uk. *World Wide Web:* http://www.bris.ac.uk/IC/JYA/

UNIVERSITY OF BRISTOL
STUDY ABROAD PROGRAMME

Hosted by University of Bristol
Academic Focus • Engineering, law and legal studies, liberal studies, science, social sciences.
Program Information • Students attend classes at University of Bristol. Optional travel to Europe, the former Soviet Union, Britain at an extra cost.
Sessions • Spring, yearlong.
Eligibility Requirements • Open to sophomores, juniors, graduate students, adults; 3.2 GPA; 2 letters of recommendation; good academic standing at home school.
Living Arrangements • Students live in host institution dormitories, locally rented apartments. Quarters are shared with host institution students. Meals are taken as a group, in residences.
Costs (2002-2003) • One term: £3875. Yearlong program: £7750; includes tuition, student support services.
For More Information • Ms. Wendy Davies, Programme Coordinator, University of Bristol, University Union, Queen's Road, Study Abroad Programme, International Centre, Bristol BS8 1LN, England; *Phone:* +44 117-923-9159; *Fax:* +44 117-923-9085. *E-mail:* jya@bris.ac.uk. *World Wide Web:* http://www.bris.ac.uk/IC/JYA/. Students may also apply through Butler University, Institute for Study Abroad, 1100 West 42nd Street, Suite 305, Indianapolis, IN 46208-3345.

UNIVERSITY STUDIES ABROAD CONSORTIUM
FULL CURRICULUM STUDIES: BRISTOL, ENGLAND

Hosted by University of Bristol
Academic Focus • Full curriculum.
Program Information • Students attend classes at University of Bristol.
Sessions • Fall, spring, yearlong.
Eligibility Requirements • Minimum age 18; open to freshmen, sophomores, juniors, seniors, graduate students, adults; 3.2 GPA.
Living Arrangements • Students live in host institution dormitories. Quarters are shared with host institution students. Meals are taken on one's own, in residences, in central dining facility.
Costs (2005-2006) • One term: $6280. Yearlong program: $12,280; includes tuition, insurance, student support services. $50 application fee. $150 refundable deposit required. Financial aid available for all students: scholarships, loans.
For More Information • University Studies Abroad Consortium, USAC/323, Reno, NV 89557-0093; *Phone:* 775-784-6569; *Fax:* 775-784-6010. *E-mail:* usac@unr.edu. *World Wide Web:* http://usac.unr.edu/

BUCKINGHAM
UNIVERSITY OF BUCKINGHAM
VISITING STUDENTS PROGRAMME

Hosted by University of Buckingham
Academic Focus • Accounting, art history, business administration/management, computer science, economics, English literature, finance, historic preservation, history, hotel and restaurant management, information science, language studies, law and legal studies, political science and government, psychology.
Program Information • Students attend classes at University of Buckingham.
Sessions • Fall, spring, yearlong.
Eligibility Requirements • Minimum age 18; open to freshmen, sophomores, juniors, seniors, adults; 2.5 GPA; 1 letter of recommendation.
Living Arrangements • Students live in host institution dormitories, locally rented apartments. Quarters are shared with host institution students. Meals are taken as a group, in residences, in central dining facility.
Costs (2000-2001) • One term: £2625. Yearlong program: £10,500; includes tuition. £1000 refundable deposit required.
For More Information • Mr. Michael J. McCrostie, Director, Visiting Students Program, University of Buckingham, Hunter Street, Buckingham MK18 1EG, England; *Phone:* +44 1280-814080; *Fax:* +44 1280-822245. *E-mail:* mjm@buck.ac.uk. *World Wide Web:* http://www.buckingham.ac.uk/

CAMBRIDGE

INSTITUTE FOR STUDY ABROAD, BUTLER UNIVERSITY
CAMBRIDGE UNIVERSITY PROGRAMS

Hosted by University of Cambridge
Academic Focus • Art history, economics, engineering, English, history, philosophy, political science and government, science.
Program Information • Students attend classes at University of Cambridge. Field trips to London.
Sessions • Spring, yearlong.
Eligibility Requirements • Open to juniors, seniors; 3.7 GPA; 2 letters of recommendation; good academic standing at home school; writing sample; résumé; enrollment in accredited American college or university.
Living Arrangements • Students live in host institution dormitories, locally rented apartments. Quarters are shared with host institution students. Meals are taken on one's own, in residences, in central dining facility.
Costs (2002-2003) • One term: $19,575. Yearlong program: $23,000–$24,000 (cost varies by college); includes tuition, housing, excursions, international student ID, student support services, family visit, cultural and sporting events, pre-departure advising. $40 application fee. $500 nonrefundable deposit required. Financial aid available for all students: scholarships, travel grants.
For More Information • Institute for Study Abroad, Butler University, 1100 West 42nd Street, Suite 305, Indianapolis, IN 46208-3345; *Phone:* 800-858-0229; *Fax:* 317-940-9704. *E-mail:* study-abroad@butler.edu. *World Wide Web:* http://www.ifsa-butler.org/

STATE UNIVERSITY OF NEW YORK COLLEGE AT BROCKPORT
UNIVERSITY OF CAMBRIDGE PROGRAM

Hosted by University of Cambridge–Robinson College
Academic Focus • Anthropology, area studies, art history, classics and classical languages, economics, English literature, European studies, geography, history, international affairs, linguistics, mathematics, music, music history, music theory, philosophy, political science and government, psychology, religious studies, statistics.
Program Information • Students attend classes at University of Cambridge–Robinson College. Field trips to the London weekend program.
Sessions • Yearlong, two-term spring.
Eligibility Requirements • Minimum age 18; open to juniors, seniors, graduate students; 3.6 GPA; 2 letters of recommendation; good academic standing at home school; ability to do upper-division course work in chosen "supervision".
Living Arrangements • Students live in locally rented apartments. Meals are taken on one's own, in residences, in central dining facility.
Costs (2003-2004) • One term: $16,600 for two-term spring. Yearlong program: $27,000; includes tuition, housing, excursions, international student ID, student support services, membership in Cambridge Union, JCR membership at Robinson College. $350 nonrefundable deposit required. Financial aid available for all students: scholarships, loans, regular financial aid, grants.
For More Information • Dr. John Perry, Director, Office of International Education, State University of New York College at Brockport, 350 New Campus Drive, Brockport, NY 14420; *Phone:* 800-298-SUNY; *Fax:* 585-637-3218. *E-mail:* overseas@brockport.edu. *World Wide Web:* http://www.brockport.edu/studyabroad/

VALPARAISO UNIVERSITY
CAMBRIDGE PROGRAM

Hosted by Valparaiso University–Cambridge Study Center
Academic Focus • Art history, British studies, computer science, geography, history.
Program Information • Students attend classes at Valparaiso University–Cambridge Study Center. Field trips to the Lake District, southwest England; optional travel to Edinburgh at an extra cost.
Sessions • Fall, spring.

Eligibility Requirements • Minimum age 19; open to sophomores, juniors, seniors; 3.0 GPA; 2 letters of recommendation; good academic standing at home school.
Living Arrangements • Students live in host institution dormitories. Meals are taken on one's own, in residences.
Costs (2003-2004) • One term: $12,859; includes tuition, housing, excursions. $30 application fee. $200 nonrefundable deposit required. Financial aid available for students from sponsoring institution: scholarships, loans.
For More Information • Mr. Holly Singh, Assistant Director, International Studies, Valparaiso University, 137 Meier Hall, 1800 Chapel Drive, Valparaiso, IN 46383; *Phone:* 219-464-5333; *Fax:* 219-464-6868. *E-mail:* studyabroad@valpo.edu. *World Wide Web:* http://www.valpo.edu/international/studyabroad.html

CANTERBURY

INSTITUTE FOR STUDY ABROAD, BUTLER UNIVERSITY
UNIVERSITY OF KENT

Hosted by University of Kent
Academic Focus • Full curriculum.
Program Information • Students attend classes at University of Kent. Field trips to London.
Sessions • Fall, spring, yearlong.
Eligibility Requirements • Open to juniors, seniors; 3.0 GPA; 1 letter of recommendation; good academic standing at home school; enrollment at an accredited American college or university.
Living Arrangements • Students live in host institution dormitories, locally rented apartments. Quarters are shared with host institution students. Meals are taken on one's own, in residences, in central dining facility.
Costs (2002-2003) • One term: $9875 for fall term; $12,675 for spring. Yearlong program: $18,975; includes tuition, housing, excursions, international student ID, student support services, family visit, cultural and sporting events, pre-departure advising. $40 application fee. $500 nonrefundable deposit required. Financial aid available for all students: scholarships, travel grants.
For More Information • Institute for Study Abroad, Butler University, 1100 West 42nd Street, Suite 305, Indianapolis, IN 46208-3345; *Phone:* 800-858-0229; *Fax:* 317-940-9704. *E-mail:* study-abroad@butler.edu. *World Wide Web:* http://www.ifsa-butler.org/

ST. LOUIS COMMUNITY COLLEGE AT MERAMEC
CANTERBURY SEMESTER STUDY PROGRAM

Hosted by Canterbury Christ Church College
Academic Focus • American studies, art, English literature, history.
Program Information • Students attend classes at Canterbury Christ Church College. Field trips to London, Bath, Stonehenge; optional travel to Paris, Edinburgh at an extra cost.
Sessions • Fall, spring.
Eligibility Requirements • Open to freshmen, sophomores, juniors, seniors, graduate students, adults; 2.5 GPA; 2 letters of recommendation; minimum 12 college credit hours completed; essay; completion of Composition I with a grade of C or higher.
Living Arrangements • Students live in host family homes. Meals are taken with host family, in residences.
Costs (2003-2004) • One term: $5380; includes tuition, housing, some meals, excursions, books and class materials, student support services. $200 refundable deposit required. Financial aid available for students from sponsoring institution: loans.
For More Information • Ms. Sonia Ahuja, Study Abroad Coordinator, St. Louis Community College at Meramec, 300 South Broadway, St. Louis, MO 63102; *Phone:* 314-539-5350; *Fax:* 314-539-5489. *E-mail:* sahuja@stlcc.edu. *World Wide Web:* http://www.shcc.edu/oie/. Students may also apply through Canterbury Christ Church University College, North Holmes Road, Canterbury, Kent CT1 1QU, England.

UNIVERSITY OF KENT
JUNIOR YEAR ABROAD IN CANTERBURY

Hosted by University of Kent
Academic Focus • Accounting, actuarial science, American studies, anthropology, archaeology, art history, biological/life sciences, biomedical sciences, business administration/management, comparative literature, computer science, creative writing, cultural studies, drama/theater, economics, electrical engineering, English literature, environmental science/studies, European studies, French language and literature, German language and literature, history, human resources, international affairs, law and legal studies, marketing, mathematics, philosophy, physics, political science and government, psychology, public policy, religious studies, social sciences, sociology, Spanish language and literature, statistics, urban studies, visual and performing arts.
Program Information • Students attend classes at University of Kent. Field trips to Canterbury (town and cathedral), Leeds Castle, Kent.
Sessions • Fall, spring, yearlong, Trinity term.
Eligibility Requirements • Minimum age 18; open to sophomores, juniors, seniors, graduate students; 3.0 GPA; 2 letters of recommendation; personal statement.
Living Arrangements • Students live in program-owned houses, single study college bedrooms. Quarters are shared with host institution students, students from other programs. Meals are taken as a group, in residences, in central dining facility.
Costs (2004-2005) • One term: £3300-£4280. Yearlong program: £8250-£10,700; includes tuition.
For More Information • Ms. Hazel Lander, Support Officer, Junior Year Abroad, University of Kent, International Office, Canterbury, Kent CT2 7NZ, England; *Phone:* +44 1227-827994; *Fax:* +44 1227-823247. *E-mail:* h.lander@kent.ac.uk. *World Wide Web:* http://www.kent.ac.uk/

CHELTENHAM
BRETHREN COLLEGES ABROAD
BCA PROGRAM IN CHELTENHAM, ENGLAND

Hosted by University of Gloucestershire
Academic Focus • Full curriculum.
Program Information • Students attend classes at University of Gloucestershire. Field trips to Cotswolds, Gloucester Cathedral, Stonehenge, Avebury.
Sessions • Fall, spring, yearlong.
Eligibility Requirements • Minimum age 18; open to sophomores, juniors, seniors; 2.6 GPA; 3 letters of recommendation; good academic standing at home school.
Living Arrangements • Students live in host institution dormitories. Meals are taken on one's own, in central dining facility, in restaurants.
Costs (2003-2004) • One term: $11,500. Yearlong program: $19,900; includes tuition, housing, all meals, insurance, excursions, international student ID, student support services. $50 application fee. $100 nonrefundable deposit required.
For More Information • Ms. Natalya Latysheva-Derova, Program Officer for England, Brethren Colleges Abroad, 50 Alpha Drive, Elizabethtown, PA 17022; *Phone:* 866-222-6188; *Fax:* 717-361-6619. *E-mail:* info@bcanet.org. *World Wide Web:* http://www.bcanet.org/

CHESTER
STATE UNIVERSITY OF NEW YORK AT PLATTSBURGH
STUDY IN ENGLAND, CHESTER

Hosted by University College Chester

ENGLAND
Chester

Academic Focus • Art, biological/life sciences, communications, computer science, drama/theater, education, English literature, geography, health and physical education, history, music, psychology.
Program Information • Students attend classes at University College Chester.
Sessions • Fall, spring, yearlong.
Eligibility Requirements • Minimum age 18; open to sophomores, juniors, seniors; 2.7 GPA; 2 letters of recommendation; SUNY and Chester applications; essay; transcript.
Living Arrangements • Students live in host institution dormitories, locally rented apartments. Quarters are shared with host institution students, students from other programs. Meals are taken on one's own, in residences, in central dining facility, in restaurants.
Costs (2003-2004) • One term: $6100 for New York residents; nonresidents contact sponsor for cost. Yearlong program: $12,200 for New York residents; nonresidents contact sponsor for cost; includes tuition, housing, all meals, insurance, books and class materials, international student ID, student support services, program fee. $20 application fee. $350 nonrefundable deposit required. Financial aid available for students from sponsoring institution: scholarships, loans.
For More Information • Ms. Jo Ann Mackie, Study Abroad Coordinator, State University of New York at Plattsburgh, Study Abroad Office, 101 Broad Street, Plattsburgh, NY 12901; *Phone:* 518-564-2321; *Fax:* 518-564-2326. *E-mail:* international@plattsburgh.edu. *World Wide Web:* http://www.plattsburgh.edu/studyabroad/

COLCHESTER
ARCADIA UNIVERSITY
UNIVERSITY OF ESSEX

Hosted by University of Essex
Academic Focus • Area studies, biological/life sciences, computer science, engineering, English, history, liberal studies, social sciences.
Program Information • Students attend classes at University of Essex.
Sessions • Fall, spring, yearlong.
Eligibility Requirements • Open to sophomores, juniors, seniors; 3.0 GPA; 1 letter of recommendation.
Living Arrangements • Students live in host institution dormitories. Quarters are shared with host institution students, students from other programs. Meals are taken on one's own, in residences.
Costs (2003-2004) • One term: $9350–$12,850. Yearlong program: $19,790; includes tuition, housing, insurance, international student ID, student support services, pre-departure guide, transcripts. $35 application fee. $500 nonrefundable deposit required. Financial aid available for all students: scholarships, loans.
For More Information • Arcadia University, Center for Education Abroad, 450 South Easton Road, Glenside, PA 19038-3295; *Phone:* 866-927-2234; *Fax:* 215-572-2174. *E-mail:* cea@arcadia.edu. *World Wide Web:* http://www.arcadia.edu/cea/

CENTRAL COLLEGE ABROAD
CENTRAL COLLEGE ABROAD AT THE UNIVERSITY OF ESSEX

Hosted by University of Essex
Academic Focus • Accounting, art history, biochemistry, biological/life sciences, computer science, drama/theater, health and physical education, literature, social sciences.
Program Information • Students attend classes at University of Essex. Optional travel to sites arranged through the Students' Union at an extra cost.
Sessions • Fall, spring, yearlong.
Eligibility Requirements • Minimum age 18; open to sophomores, juniors, seniors; 2.8 GPA; 2 letters of recommendation; study abroad approval form; transcript; Student Life endorsement.
Living Arrangements • Students live in host institution dormitories. Quarters are shared with host institution students. Meals are taken on one's own, in residences.
Costs (2002-2003) • One term: $8600 for fall term; $13,100 for spring. Yearlong program: $21,825; includes tuition, housing, international student ID, student support services. $25 application fee. $350 nonrefundable deposit required. Financial aid available for all students: scholarships.

For More Information • Office of International Education, Central College Abroad, 812 University Street, Pella, IA 50219; *Phone:* 800-831-3629; *Fax:* 641-628-5375. *E-mail:* studyabroad@central.edu. *World Wide Web:* http://www.central.edu/abroad/

INSTITUTE FOR STUDY ABROAD, BUTLER UNIVERSITY
UNIVERSITY OF ESSEX

Hosted by University of Essex
Academic Focus • Full curriculum.
Program Information • Students attend classes at University of Essex. Field trips to London.
Sessions • Fall, spring, yearlong.
Eligibility Requirements • Open to juniors, seniors; 3.0 GPA; 1 letter of recommendation; good academic standing at home school; enrollment at an accredited American college or university.
Living Arrangements • Students live in host institution dormitories, locally rented apartments. Quarters are shared with host institution students. Meals are taken on one's own, in residences, in central dining facility.
Costs (2002-2003) • One term: $8975 for fall term; $11,775 for spring. Yearlong program: $17,575; includes tuition, housing, excursions, international student ID, student support services, family visit, cultural and sporting events, pre-departure advising. $40 application fee. $500 nonrefundable deposit required. Financial aid available for all students: scholarships, travel grants.
For More Information • Institute for Study Abroad, Butler University, 1100 West 42nd Street, Suite 305, Indianapolis, IN 46208-3345; *Phone:* 800-858-0229; *Fax:* 317-940-9704. *E-mail:* study-abroad@butler.edu. *World Wide Web:* http://www.ifsa-butler.org/

INTERSTUDY
UNIVERSITY OF ESSEX

Hosted by University of Essex
Academic Focus • Accounting, art history, biological/life sciences, business administration/management, computer science, economics, English, finance, French language and literature, German language and literature, history, law and legal studies, linguistics, literature, management information systems, mathematics, philosophy, physics, political science and government, psychology, sociology, theater management.
Program Information • Students attend classes at University of Essex. Scheduled travel to Bath, Stratford-upon-Avon, Warwick Castle, Oxford, Stonehenge.
Sessions • Fall, spring, yearlong.
Eligibility Requirements • Minimum age 18; open to freshmen, sophomores, juniors, seniors, adults; 3.0 GPA; 2 letters of recommendation; good academic standing at home school.
Living Arrangements • Students live in host institution dormitories. Quarters are shared with host institution students. Meals are taken on one's own, in residences.
Costs (2003-2004) • One term: $10,150 for fall term; $13,475 for spring. Yearlong program: $20,625; includes tuition, housing, some meals, excursions, international student ID, student support services, Student Union membership, e-mail access, banking facilities, international bank transfers, transcript, cell phone. $35 application fee. $500 nonrefundable deposit required. Financial aid available for all students: scholarships, loans, stipends.
For More Information • InterStudy, Admissions Office, 63 Edward Street, Medford, MA 02155; *Phone:* 800-663-1999; *Fax:* 781-391-7463. *E-mail:* interstudy@interstudy-usa.org. *World Wide Web:* http://www.interstudy.org/

UNIVERSITY OF CONNECTICUT
ESSEX YEAR OR TERM IN SOCIAL SCIENCES, LIBERAL ARTS, ENGINEERING, COMPUTER SCIENCE

Hosted by University of Essex
Academic Focus • Computer science, economics, electrical engineering, history, liberal studies, literature, philosophy.
Program Information • Students attend classes at University of Essex.
Sessions • Fall, spring, yearlong.

Eligibility Requirements • Open to sophomores, juniors, seniors; 2.7 GPA; 2 letters of recommendation; engineering courses have prerequisites.

Living Arrangements • Students live in host institution dormitories, locally rented apartments. Quarters are shared with host institution students. Meals are taken on one's own, in residences.

Costs (2003-2004) • One term: $5528 for fall term; $8050 for spring. Yearlong program: $13,500; includes tuition, housing, fees, one-way airfare. $25 application fee. $350 nonrefundable deposit required. Financial aid available for students from sponsoring institution: scholarships, loans.

For More Information • Mr. Gordon Lustila, Acting Director of Study Abroad Programs, University of Connecticut, 843 Bolton Road, Unit 1207, Storrs, CT 06269-1207; *Phone:* 860-486-5022; *Fax:* 860-486-2976. *E-mail:* sabadm03@uconnvm.uconn.edu. *World Wide Web:* http://studyabroad.uconn.edu/

UNIVERSITY OF ESSEX
INTERNATIONAL PROGRAMMES

Hosted by University of Essex
Academic Focus • Full curriculum.
Program Information • Students attend classes at University of Essex. Scheduled travel to Florence, the European Commission headquarters; field trips to London, Cambridge, Norwich; optional travel to Britain, continental Europe at an extra cost.
Sessions • Fall, spring, yearlong.
Eligibility Requirements • Minimum age 18; open to freshmen, sophomores, juniors, seniors, adults; 2.8 GPA; 2 letters of recommendation; current transcript.
Living Arrangements • Students live in host institution dormitories, program-owned apartments. Quarters are shared with host institution students, students from other programs. Meals are taken on one's own, in residences, in central dining facility.

Costs (2004-2005) • One term: $9636 for fall term; $17,184 for spring/summer term. Yearlong program: $26,567; includes tuition, housing, all meals, books and class materials, estimated personal expenses.

For More Information • Ms. Linda K. Gossett, Coordinator of International Programmes, University of Essex, Wivenhoe Park, Colchester, Essex CO4 3SQ, England; *Phone:* +44 120-687-2988; *Fax:* +44 120-687-2808. *E-mail:* intprogs@essex.ac.uk. *World Wide Web:* http://www2.essex.ac.uk/international/. Students may also apply through Arcadia University, Center for Education Abroad, 450 South Easton Road, Glenside, PA 19038-3295; Butler University, Institute for Study Abroad, 1100 West 42nd Street, Suite 305, Indianapolis, IN 46208-3345; InterStudy, Admissions Office, 42 Milsom Street, Bath BA1 1DN, England; Central College Abroad, Office of International Education, 812 University Street, Pella, IA 50219.

UNIVERSITY OF MIAMI
UNIVERSITY OF ESSEX, ENGLAND

Hosted by University of Essex
Academic Focus • Art history, business administration/management, economics, engineering, European studies, history, international affairs, language studies, literature, philosophy, political science and government, psychology, sociology.
Program Information • Students attend classes at University of Essex.
Sessions • Fall, spring, yearlong.
Eligibility Requirements • Minimum age 18; open to freshmen, sophomores, juniors, seniors; 3.0 GPA; 2 letters of recommendation; good academic standing at home school; official transcripts; essay; no foreign language proficiency required.

Living Arrangements • Students live in host institution dormitories. Quarters are shared with host institution students. Meals are taken on one's own, in residences, in central dining facility, in restaurants.
Costs (2003-2004) • One term: $12,919. Yearlong program: $25,838; includes tuition, student support services. $40 application fee. $500 nonrefundable deposit required. Financial aid available for students from sponsoring institution: scholarships, loans.
For More Information • Ms. Elyse Resnick, Assistant Director, University of Miami, International Education and Exchange Programs, 5050 Brunson Drive, Allen Hall 212, PO Box 248005, Coral Gables, FL 33124-1610; *Phone:* 305-284-3434; *Fax:* 305-284-4235. *E-mail:* ieep@miami.edu. *World Wide Web:* http://www.studyabroad.miami.edu/

COVENTRY

INSTITUTE FOR STUDY ABROAD, BUTLER UNIVERSITY
UNIVERSITY OF WARWICK

Hosted by University of Warwick
Academic Focus • Full curriculum.
Program Information • Students attend classes at University of Warwick. Field trips to London.
Sessions • Fall, spring, yearlong.
Eligibility Requirements • Open to juniors, seniors; 3.0 GPA; 2 letters of recommendation; good academic standing at home school; enrollment at an accredited American college or university.
Living Arrangements • Students live in host institution dormitories, locally rented apartments. Quarters are shared with host institution students. Meals are taken on one's own, in residences, in central dining facility.
Costs (2002-2003) • One term: $9575 for fall term; $13,375 for spring. Yearlong program: $19,375; includes tuition, housing, excursions, international student ID, student support services, cultural and sporting events, pre-departure advising, family visit. $40 application fee. $500 nonrefundable deposit required. Financial aid available for all students: scholarships, travel grants.
For More Information • Institute for Study Abroad, Butler University, 1100 West 42nd Street, Suite 305, Indianapolis, IN 46208-3345; *Phone:* 800-858-0229; *Fax:* 317-940-9704. *E-mail:* study-abroad@butler.edu. *World Wide Web:* http://www.ifsa-butler.org/

INTERSTUDY
UNIVERSITY OF WARWICK

Hosted by University of Warwick
Academic Focus • American studies, ancient history, art history, biological/life sciences, business administration/management, chemical sciences, classics and classical languages, computer science, drama/theater, ecology, economics, education, engineering, English, environmental science/studies, film and media studies, history, law and legal studies, mathematics, philosophy, political science and government, psychology, science, sociology.
Program Information • Students attend classes at University of Warwick. Scheduled travel to Bath, Stratford-upon-Avon, Warwick Castle, Oxford, Stonehenge.
Sessions • Fall, spring, yearlong.
Eligibility Requirements • Minimum age 18; open to freshmen, sophomores, juniors, seniors, adults; 3.0 GPA; 2 letters of recommendation; good academic standing at home school.
Living Arrangements • Students live in host institution dormitories. Quarters are shared with host institution students. Meals are taken as a group, on one's own, in residences.
Costs (2003-2004) • One term: $11,450 for fall term; $13,550 for spring. Yearlong program: $22,425; includes tuition, housing, some meals, excursions, international student ID, student support services, Student Union membership, e-mail access, banking facilities, international bank transfers, transcript, cell phone. $35 application fee. $500 nonrefundable deposit required. Financial aid available for all students: scholarships, loans, stipends.
For More Information • InterStudy, Admissions Office, 63 Edward Street, Medford, MA 02155; *Phone:* 800-663-1999; *Fax:* 781-391-7463. *E-mail:* interstudy@interstudy-usa.org. *World Wide Web:* http://www.interstudy.org/

STATE UNIVERSITY OF NEW YORK COLLEGE AT BROCKPORT
UNIVERSITY OF WARWICK PROGRAM

Hosted by University of Warwick
Academic Focus • Full curriculum.
Program Information • Students attend classes at University of Warwick. Field trips to the London weekend program.
Sessions • Fall, yearlong, spring and summer terms.
Eligibility Requirements • Minimum age 18; open to juniors, seniors; 3.0 GPA; 2 letters of recommendation; good academic standing at home school; ability to do upper-division course work in chosen subjects.
Living Arrangements • Students live in host institution dormitories. Quarters are shared with host institution students. Meals are taken on one's own, in residences.
Costs (2003-2004) • One term: $10,825 for fall term; $13,725 for spring and summer terms. Yearlong program: $21,950; includes tuition, housing, excursions, international student ID, student support services. $350 nonrefundable deposit required. Financial aid available for all students: scholarships, loans, regular financial aid, grants.
For More Information • Dr. John Perry, Director, Office of International Education, State University of New York College at Brockport, 350 New Campus Drive, Brockport, NY 14420; *Phone:* 800-298-SUNY; *Fax:* 585-637-3218. *E-mail:* overseas@brockport.edu. *World Wide Web:* http://www.brockport.edu/studyabroad/

UNIVERSITY OF WARWICK
ACADEMIC YEAR/SEMESTER ABROAD

Hosted by University of Warwick
Academic Focus • Full curriculum.
Program Information • Students attend classes at University of Warwick. Field trips to Oxford, Cambridge, London, Bath.
Sessions • Fall, spring, yearlong.
Eligibility Requirements • Minimum age 18; open to sophomores, juniors; 3.0 GPA; 2 letters of recommendation; good academic standing at home school.
Living Arrangements • Students live in host institution dormitories. Quarters are shared with host institution students. Meals are taken on one's own, in residences, in central dining facility.
Costs (2003-2004) • One term: £2650 for fall term; £5300 for spring/summer term. Yearlong program: £7950; includes tuition, fees. Financial aid available for all students: on-campus employment.
For More Information • Ms. Caroline Pack, Deputy Director, International Office, University of Warwick, Senate House, Coventry CV4 7AL, England; *Phone:* +44 24-765-23705; *Fax:* +44 24-765-24337. *E-mail:* c.m.pack@warwick.ac.uk. *World Wide Web:* http://www.warwick.ac.uk/. Students may also apply through InterStudy, Admissions Office, 42 Milsom Street, Bath BA1 1DN, England; Butler University, Institute for Study Abroad, 1100 West 42nd Street, Suite 305, Indianapolis, IN 46208-3345; InterStudy USA, 63 Edward Street, Medford, MA 02155.

EASTBOURNE

STATE UNIVERSITY OF NEW YORK COLLEGE AT BROCKPORT
UNIVERSITY OF BRIGHTON, CHELSEA PROGRAM

Hosted by University of Brighton
Academic Focus • Full curriculum.
Program Information • Students attend classes at University of Brighton. Field trips to the London Weekend Program.
Sessions • Spring.
Eligibility Requirements • Minimum age 18; open to juniors, seniors; course work in physical education, sports science, dance or leisure management; 2.5 GPA; 2 letters of recommendation; ability to do upper-division course work in chosen subject.
Living Arrangements • Students live in host institution dormitories, host family homes. Quarters are shared with host institution students. Meals are taken on one's own, with host family, in residences.
Costs (2003-2004) • One term: $13,200; includes tuition, housing, some meals, excursions, international student ID, student support

services. $350 nonrefundable deposit required. Financial aid available for all students: scholarships, loans, regular financial aid, grants.

For More Information • Dr. John Perry, Director, Office of International Education, State University of New York College at Brockport, 350 New Campus Drive, Brockport, NY 14420; *Phone:* 800-298-SUNY; *Fax:* 585-637-3218. *E-mail:* overseas@brockport.edu. *World Wide Web:* http://www.brockport.edu/studyabroad/

UNIVERSITY OF IDAHO
PHYSICAL EDUCATION, SPORTS SCIENCE, DANCE, AND LEISURE STUDIES PROGRAM

Hosted by University of Brighton
Academic Focus • Dance, health and physical education, sports management.
Program Information • Students attend classes at University of Brighton.
Sessions • Fall, spring, winter, yearlong.
Eligibility Requirements • Open to freshmen, sophomores, juniors, seniors, graduate students; major in sports science, physical education, leisure studies, dance; good academic standing at home school; minimum 2.8 GPA overall and minimum 3.0 GPA in major.
Living Arrangements • Students live in host institution dormitories, program-owned apartments. Quarters are shared with host institution students, students from other programs. Meals are taken on one's own, in residences.
Costs (2003-2004) • One term: $2500. Yearlong program: $5000; includes tuition, student support services. $100 application fee. $200 refundable deposit required. Financial aid available for students from sponsoring institution: scholarships, loans.
For More Information • Ms. Amy S. Bergmann, Advisor, University of Idaho, Room 209, Morrill Hall, Moscow, ID 83844-3013; *Phone:* 208-885-4075; *Fax:* 208-885-2859. *E-mail:* abroad@uidaho.edu. *World Wide Web:* http://www.ets.uidaho.edu/ipo/abroad/

EXETER
RUTGERS, THE STATE UNIVERSITY OF NEW JERSEY
STUDY ABROAD IN BRITAIN: EXETER

Hosted by University of Exeter
Academic Focus • Full curriculum.
Program Information • Students attend classes at University of Exeter. Field trips to London, Stonehenge, Oxford.
Sessions • Fall, spring, yearlong.
Eligibility Requirements • Open to juniors, seniors; 3.0 GPA; 2 letters of recommendation; good academic standing at home school.
Living Arrangements • Students live in host institution dormitories. Quarters are shared with host institution students. Meals are taken on one's own, in residences, in central dining facility.
Costs (2003-2004) • One term: $9950–$13,656 for New Jersey residents; $12,600–$16,306 for nonresidents. Yearlong program: $18,190 for New Jersey residents; $23,490 for nonresidents; includes tuition, insurance, excursions, student support services. $20 application fee. $750 nonrefundable deposit required. Financial aid available for students from sponsoring institution: scholarships, loans.
For More Information • Ms. Karin Bonello, Regional Coordinator, Rutgers, The State University of New Jersey, 102 College Avenue, New Brunswick, NJ 08901-8543; *Phone:* 732-932-7787; *Fax:* 732-932-8659. *E-mail:* ru_abroad@email.rutgers.edu. *World Wide Web:* http://studyabroad.rutgers.edu/

GRANTHAM
UNIVERSITY OF EVANSVILLE
HARLAXTON COLLEGE

Hosted by University of Evansville–Harlaxton College
Academic Focus • Art, art history, biological/life sciences, British studies, business administration/management, computer science, creative writing, English literature, history, management information

systems, marketing, mathematics, music, nursing, philosophy, political science and government, psychology, religious studies, social sciences.
Program Information • Students attend classes at University of Evansville–Harlaxton College. Field trips to Lincoln, London, Belvoir Castle; optional travel to Italy, Ireland, Paris, North Wales, Oxford, Bath, Stonehenge, the Lake District, Edinburgh at an extra cost.
Sessions • Fall, spring.
Eligibility Requirements • Minimum age 19; open to sophomores, juniors, seniors; 2.5 GPA; 1 letter of recommendation; good academic standing at home school; approval of advisor.
Living Arrangements • Students live in a Victorian manor house and carriage house. Quarters are shared with host institution students, students from other programs. Meals are taken as a group, in central dining facility.
Costs (2003-2004) • One term: $12,920; includes tuition, housing, all meals, excursions, London arrival transport, local shuttle. $100 nonrefundable deposit required. Financial aid available for students from sponsoring institution: scholarships, work study, loans.
For More Information • Mr. Earl Kirk, Harlaxton Coordinator, University of Evansville, 1800 Lincoln Avenue, Evansville, IN 47722; *Phone:* 812-488-1040; *Fax:* 812-475-6389. *E-mail:* ek43@evansville.edu. *World Wide Web:* http://www.ueharlax.ac.uk/

HIGH WYCOMBE
UNIVERSITY OF MIAMI
BUCKINGHAM CHILTERNS UNIVERSITY COLLEGE, ENGLAND

Hosted by Buckinghamshire Chilterns University College
Academic Focus • Business administration/management, music.
Program Information • Students attend classes at Buckinghamshire Chilterns University College. Field trips to London.
Sessions • Fall, spring, yearlong.
Eligibility Requirements • Minimum age 18; open to sophomores, juniors, seniors, graduate students; major in music industry management; 2 letters of recommendation; good academic standing at home school; essay; transcript; no foreign language proficiency required.
Living Arrangements • Students live in host institution dormitories. Quarters are shared with host institution students. Meals are taken on one's own, in residences.
Costs (2003-2004) • One term: $12,919. Yearlong program: $25,838; includes tuition, student support services. $40 application fee. $500 nonrefundable deposit required. Financial aid available for students from sponsoring institution: scholarships, loans.
For More Information • Ms. Elyse Resnick, Assistant Director, University of Miami, International Education and Exchange Programs, 5050 Brunson Drive, Allen Hall 212, PO Box 248005, Coral Gables, FL 33124-1610; *Phone:* 305-284-3434; *Fax:* 305-284-4235. *E-mail:* ieep@miami.edu. *World Wide Web:* http://www.studyabroad.miami.edu/

HULL
UNIVERSITY AT ALBANY, STATE UNIVERSITY OF NEW YORK
DIRECT ENROLLMENT AT THE UNIVERSITY OF HULL

Hosted by University of Hull
Academic Focus • Full curriculum.
Program Information • Students attend classes at University of Hull. Optional travel to England, Scotland, Wales at an extra cost.
Sessions • Fall, spring, yearlong.
Eligibility Requirements • Open to sophomores, juniors, seniors; 3.0 GPA; 2 letters of recommendation; good academic standing at home school.
Living Arrangements • Students live in host institution dormitories, program-owned apartments. Quarters are shared with host institution students. Meals are taken on one's own, in residences, in central dining facility.
Costs (2002-2003) • One term: $6513. Yearlong program: $13,026; includes housing, all meals, student support services, in-state tuition and fees. $150 nonrefundable deposit required. Financial aid available for students from sponsoring institution: all customary sources.

For More Information • University at Albany, State University of New York, Office of International Education, LI 66, Albany, NY 12222; *Phone:* 518-442-3525; *Fax:* 518-442-3338. *E-mail:* intled@uamail.albany.edu. *World Wide Web:* http://www.albany.edu/intled/

UNIVERSITY OF HULL
STUDY ABROAD PROGRAMME

Hosted by University of Hull, Scarborough, University of Hull
Academic Focus • Full curriculum.
Program Information • Students attend classes at University of Hull, University of Hull, Scarborough.
Sessions • Fall, spring, yearlong.
Eligibility Requirements • Minimum age 18; open to sophomores, juniors; 3.0 GPA; 1 letter of recommendation; good academic standing at home school.
Living Arrangements • Students live in host institution dormitories, program-owned apartments, program-owned houses, student housing. Quarters are shared with host institution students, students from other programs. Meals are taken on one's own, in residences.
Costs (2003-2004) • One term: £3075. Yearlong program: £6150; includes tuition. Financial aid available for all students: loans.
For More Information • Mr. James Richardson, Director Director, University of Hull, Cottingham Road, Hull HU6 7RX, England; *Phone:* +44 1482-466-904; *Fax:* +44 1482-466-554. *E-mail:* j.a.richardson@hull.ac.uk. *World Wide Web:* http://www.hull.ac.uk/

KINGSTON UPON THAMES
KINGSTON UNIVERSITY
AMERICAN VISITING STUDENT PROGRAMME

Hosted by Kingston University
Academic Focus • Architecture, art history, biological/life sciences, biomedical sciences, business administration/management, chemical sciences, computer science, drama/theater, earth sciences, economics, engineering, English literature, geography, geology, history, information science, language studies, mathematics, music, pharmacology, physical sciences, political science and government, psychology, sociology, statistics.
Program Information • Students attend classes at Kingston University. Field trips to Oxford, Stonehenge, Bath, a heater trip to London; optional travel to Paris, Edinburgh, Amsterdam, Dublin at an extra cost.
Sessions • Fall, spring, yearlong.
Eligibility Requirements • Minimum age 18; open to freshmen, sophomores, juniors, seniors; 2.75 GPA; 1 letter of recommendation; good academic standing at home school.
Living Arrangements • Students live in host institution dormitories, host family homes. Quarters are shared with host institution students. Meals are taken on one's own, in central dining facility, in restaurants.
Costs (2003-2004) • One term: £4100. Yearlong program: £8500; includes tuition, housing. Financial aid available for all students: loans, home institution aid.
For More Information • Ms. Alison Morris, Study Abroad Manager, Kingston University, Millennium House, 21 Eden Street, Kingston upon Thames KT1 18L, England; *Phone:* +44 208-547-7784; *Fax:* +44 208-547-7789. *E-mail:* avsp-info@kingston.ac.uk. *World Wide Web:* http://www.kingston.ac.uk/avsp/

LANCASTER
ARCADIA UNIVERSITY
LANCASTER UNIVERSITY

Hosted by Lancaster University
Academic Focus • Biological/life sciences, business administration/management, chemical sciences, engineering, liberal studies, religious studies, social sciences.
Program Information • Students attend classes at Lancaster University.
Sessions • Fall, spring, yearlong, two-term fall/spring program; fall pre-session.
Eligibility Requirements • Open to precollege students, sophomores, juniors, seniors; 3.0 GPA; 1 letter of recommendation.

Living Arrangements • Students live in host institution dormitories, host family homes. Quarters are shared with host institution students, students from other programs. Meals are taken on one's own, in residences.
Costs (2003-2004) • One term: $9550–$12,090 ($1870 for pre-session). Yearlong program: $17,690; includes tuition, housing, insurance, international student ID, student support services, pre-departure guide, transcripts. $35 application fee. $500 nonrefundable deposit required. Financial aid available for all students: scholarships, loans.
For More Information • Arcadia University, Center for Education Abroad, 450 South Easton Road, Glenside, PA 19038-3295; *Phone:* 866-927-2234; *Fax:* 215-572-2174. *E-mail:* cea@arcadia.edu. *World Wide Web:* http://www.arcadia.edu/cea/

INSTITUTE FOR STUDY ABROAD, BUTLER UNIVERSITY
LANCASTER UNIVERSITY

Hosted by Lancaster University
Academic Focus • Full curriculum.
Program Information • Students attend classes at Lancaster University. Field trips to London.
Sessions • Fall, spring, yearlong, early start fall pre-session.
Eligibility Requirements • Open to sophomores, juniors, seniors; 2.8 GPA; 1 letter of recommendation; good academic standing at home school; enrollment at an accredited American college or university.
Living Arrangements • Students live in host institution dormitories. Quarters are shared with host institution students, students from other programs. Meals are taken on one's own, in residences, in central dining facility, in restaurants.
Costs (2002-2003) • One term: $9175 for fall term ($11,075 with early start session); $11,575 for spring. Yearlong program: $16,375 ($19,975 with early start session); includes tuition, housing, excursions, international student ID, student support services, family visit, cultural and sporting events, pre-departure advising. $40 application fee. $500 nonrefundable deposit required. Financial aid available for all students: scholarships, travel grants.
For More Information • Institute for Study Abroad, Butler University, 1100 West 42nd Street, Suite 305, Indianapolis, IN 46208-3345; *Phone:* 800-858-0229; *Fax:* 317-940-9704. *E-mail:* study-abroad@butler.edu. *World Wide Web:* http://www.ifsa-butler.org/

INTERSTUDY
LANCASTER UNIVERSITY

Hosted by Lancaster University
Academic Focus • Accounting, American studies, biochemistry, chemical sciences, computer science, creative writing, design and applied arts, drama/theater, economics, education, engineering, English, environmental science/studies, finance, international affairs, law and legal studies, linguistics, marketing, mathematics, philosophy, political science and government, psychology, religious studies, science, social sciences, women's studies.
Program Information • Students attend classes at Lancaster University. Field trips to Stratford-upon-Avon, Bath, Oxford, Stonehenge.
Sessions • Fall, spring, yearlong, early start British history and culture session.
Eligibility Requirements • Minimum age 18; open to freshmen, sophomores, juniors, seniors, adults; 3.0 GPA; 2 letters of recommendation; good academic standing at home school.
Living Arrangements • Students live in host institution dormitories. Quarters are shared with host institution students. Meals are taken as a group, on one's own, in residences.
Costs (2003-2004) • One term: $9915 for fall term; $12,815 for spring term; $500 for pre-session. Yearlong program: $18,425; includes tuition, housing, some meals, excursions, international student ID, student support services, Student Union membership, e-mail access, banking facilities, international bank transfers, transcript, cell phone. $35 application fee. $500 nonrefundable deposit required. Financial aid available for all students: scholarships, loans, stipends.

For More Information • InterStudy, Admissions Office, 63 Edward Street, Medford, MA 02155; *Phone:* 800-663-1999; *Fax:* 781-391-7463. *E-mail:* interstudy@interstudy-usa.org. *World Wide Web:* http://www.interstudy.org/

LANCASTER UNIVERSITY
LANCASTER UNIVERSITY STUDY ABROAD PROGRAM

Hosted by Lancaster University

Academic Focus • Biological/life sciences, business administration/management, communications, computer science, creative writing, criminal justice, drama/theater, earth sciences, economics, education, engineering, English, environmental science/studies, finance, geography, history, international affairs, international business, law and legal studies, liberal studies, mathematics, peace and conflict studies, physical sciences, premedical studies, psychology, public policy, religious studies, social sciences, social work, sociology, visual and performing arts, women's studies.

Program Information • Students attend classes at Lancaster University. Field trips to the Lake District.

Sessions • Fall, spring, yearlong, 3 pre-sessional programs available: "This Scepter'd Isle, Aspects of British History & Culture," "Changing Places: Lancaster & The Lake District," and "World About Us: Explorations in History, Principles & Applications of Science".

Eligibility Requirements • Minimum age 18; open to sophomores, juniors, seniors, graduate students; 2 letters of recommendation; good academic standing at home school; academic transcript; B-level work or better in subjects relevant to study abroad.

Living Arrangements • Students live in host institution dormitories. Quarters are shared with host institution students. Meals are taken on one's own, in residences.

Costs (2005-2006) • One term: $9000 for fall term; $13,500 for two spring terms (estimated). Yearlong program: $21,000 for 3 terms (estimated); includes tuition, housing, all meals, lab equipment, student support services, many campus activities, special lectures, Thanksgiving dinner, some class materials. Financial aid available for students: scholarship for minority students.

For More Information • Ms. Jane Atkinson, Director, Study Abroad Program, Lancaster University, University House, Lancaster LA1 4YW, England; *Phone:* +44 1524-592035; *Fax:* +44 1524-593907. *E-mail:* nao@lancaster.ac.uk. *World Wide Web:* http://www.lancs.ac.uk/users/international/overseas/indx.htm. Students may also apply through Arcadia University, Center for Education Abroad, 450 South Easton Road, Glenside, PA 19038-3295; Butler University, Institute for Study Abroad, 1100 West 42nd Street, Suite 305, Indianapolis, IN 46208-3345; InterStudy USA, 63 Edward Street, Medford, MA 02155; Marymount College, Office of Study Abroad, 100 Marymount Avenue, Tarrytown, NY 10591-3796.

MORE ABOUT THE PROGRAM

Lancaster, ranked among the top U.K. universities for teaching and research, is an ideal choice for study abroad, with its flexible curriculum and long experience educating North Americans, including science, premedical, engineering, and business students. Situated on a beautiful, self-contained, fully accessible campus that offers sports, cultural activities, and recreational activities, the University is friendly and manageable. Its spectacular northern location near the Lake District, the Yorkshire Dales, and Scotland is ideal for outdoor pursuits and convenient to all of Britain. A diverse student body includes students from racial and ethnic minority groups and those with disabilities. Study-abroad students are completely integrated into the University's academic and social life. On-campus housing with British students is guaranteed. Comprehensive orientation and support services are provided through full-time study-abroad staff at Lancaster, who also provide experienced help, materials, and alumni contacts to interested students, advisers, and parents. Graduate programs are available in all departments.

LYCOMING COLLEGE
STUDY ABROAD AT LANCASTER UNIVERSITY, ENGLAND

Hosted by Lancaster University
Academic Focus • Full curriculum.

Program Information • Students attend classes at Lancaster University. Scheduled travel; field trips; optional travel at an extra cost.

Sessions • Fall, spring, winter, pre-sessional program.

Eligibility Requirements • Open to sophomores, juniors, seniors; 2.5 GPA; 1 letter of recommendation; good academic standing at home school.

Living Arrangements • Students live in host institution dormitories, host family homes. Quarters are shared with host institution students, students from other programs. Meals are taken as a group, on one's own, with host family, in residences, in central dining facility, in restaurants.

Costs (2002-2003) • One term: contact sponsor for cost. $300 refundable deposit required. Financial aid available for students from sponsoring institution: scholarships, loans.

For More Information • Dr. Barbara Buedel, Coordinator of Study Abroad Program, Lycoming College, Campus Box 2, 700 College Place, Williamsport, PA 17701-5192; *Phone:* 570-321-4210; *Fax:* 570-321-4389. *E-mail:* buedel@lycoming.edu. *World Wide Web:* http://www.lycoming.edu/

STATE UNIVERSITY OF NEW YORK COLLEGE AT CORTLAND
SAINT MARTIN'S COLLEGE

Hosted by Saint Martin's College
Academic Focus • Full curriculum.

Program Information • Students attend classes at Saint Martin's College. Scheduled travel to Yorkshire, the Lake District, London, Carlisle, York; optional travel to Spain, Holland, Ireland, Scotland, West Indies at an extra cost.

Sessions • Fall, spring, yearlong.

Eligibility Requirements • Minimum age 18; open to sophomores, juniors, seniors; 2.5 GPA; 3 letters of recommendation; good academic standing at home school.

Living Arrangements • Students live in host institution dormitories, locally rented apartments. Quarters are shared with host institution students. Meals are taken on one's own, in residences.

Costs (2003-2004) • One term: $4900. Yearlong program: contact sponsor for cost; includes tuition, housing, all meals, international airfare, books and class materials, international student ID, student support services, train transportation from Manchester to Lancaster, passport fees. $20 application fee. $250 nonrefundable deposit required. Financial aid available for students from sponsoring institution: scholarships, loans.

For More Information • Dr. John Ogden, Director, Office of International Programs, State University of New York College at Cortland, PO Box 2000, Cortland, NY 13045; *Phone:* 607-753-2209; *Fax:* 607-753-5989. *E-mail:* cortlandabroad@cortland.edu. *World Wide Web:* http://www.studyabroad.com/suny/cortland/

UNIVERSITY OF IDAHO
ENGLAND STUDIES PROGRAM

Hosted by Lancaster University
Academic Focus • Full curriculum.

Program Information • Students attend classes at Lancaster University.

Sessions • Fall, spring, winter, yearlong.

Eligibility Requirements • Open to freshmen, sophomores, juniors, seniors, graduate students, adults; 2.75 GPA; good academic standing at home school.

Living Arrangements • Students live in host institution dormitories, locally rented apartments. Quarters are shared with host institution students, students from other programs. Meals are taken on one's own, in residences, in central dining facility.

Costs (2003-2004) • One term: $5100 ; $7500 for two terms. Yearlong program: $12,000 for 3 terms; includes tuition, student support services. $100 application fee. $200 refundable deposit required. Financial aid available for students from sponsoring institution: scholarships, loans.

For More Information • Ms. Amy S. Bergmann, Advisor, University of Idaho, Room 209, Morrill Hall, Moscow, ID 83844-3013; *Phone:* 208-885-4075; *Fax:* 208-885-2859. *E-mail:* abroad@uidaho.edu. *World Wide Web:* http://www.ets.uidaho.edu/ipo/abroad/

UNIVERSITY OF MIAMI
LANCASTER UNIVERSITY

Hosted by Lancaster University

Academic Focus • Art, business administration/management, communications, science.

Program Information • Students attend classes at Lancaster University.

Sessions • Fall, spring, yearlong.

Eligibility Requirements • Minimum age 18; open to sophomores, juniors; 3.0 GPA; 2 letters of recommendation; official transcripts; essay.

Living Arrangements • Students live in host institution dormitories. Quarters are shared with host institution students. Meals are taken on one's own, in residences, in central dining facility, in restaurants.

Costs (2003-2004) • One term: $12,919. Yearlong program: $25,838; includes tuition, student support services. $40 application fee. $500 nonrefundable deposit required. Financial aid available for students from sponsoring institution: loans.

For More Information • Ms. Elyse Resnick, Assistant Director, University of Miami, International Education and Exchange Programs, 5050 Brunson Drive, Allen Hall 212, PO Box 248005, Coral Gables, FL 33124-1610; *Phone:* 305-284-3434; *Fax:* 305-284-4235. *E-mail:* ieep@miami.edu. *World Wide Web:* http://www.studyabroad.miami.edu/

LEEDS
THE CATHOLIC UNIVERSITY OF AMERICA
PROGRAM IN BRITISH POLITICS AND SOCIETY

Hosted by University of Leeds

Academic Focus • British studies, political science and government.

Program Information • Students attend classes at University of Leeds.

Sessions • Spring.

Eligibility Requirements • Open to sophomores, juniors; 3.0 GPA; good academic standing at home school.

Living Arrangements • Students live in locally rented apartments. Meals are taken in residences.

Costs (2004) • One term: $14,600; includes tuition, housing. $200 deposit required. Financial aid available for all students: scholarships.

For More Information • Mr. John Kromkowski, Assistant Dean, School of Arts and Sciences, The Catholic University of America, 303 Marist Hall, Washington, DC 20064; *Phone:* 202-319-6876; *Fax:* 202-319-6289. *E-mail:* kromkowski@cua.edu. *World Wide Web:* http://www.cua.edu/

INSTITUTE FOR STUDY ABROAD, BUTLER UNIVERSITY
UNIVERSITY OF LEEDS

Hosted by University of Leeds

Academic Focus • Full curriculum.

Program Information • Students attend classes at University of Leeds. Field trips to London.

Sessions • Fall, spring, yearlong.

Eligibility Requirements • Open to sophomores, juniors, seniors; 3.0 GPA; 2 letters of recommendation; good academic standing at home school; enrollment at an accredited American college or university; writing sample.

Living Arrangements • Students live in host institution dormitories, locally rented apartments. Quarters are shared with host institution students. Meals are taken as a group, on one's own, in residences, in central dining facility.

Costs (2002-2003) • One term: $10,375. Yearlong program: $16,675; includes tuition, housing, excursions, international student ID, student support services, family visit, cultural and sporting events, pre-departure advising. $40 application fee. $500 nonrefundable deposit required. Financial aid available for all students: scholarships, travel grants.

For More Information • Institute for Study Abroad, Butler University, 1100 West 42nd Street, Suite 305, Indianapolis, IN 46208-3345; *Phone:* 800-858-0229; *Fax:* 317-940-9704. *E-mail:* study-abroad@butler.edu. *World Wide Web:* http://www.ifsa-butler.org/

MARIST COLLEGE
BRITISH INTERNSHIP PROGRAM

Hosted by Trinity and All Saints University College

Academic Focus • Business administration/management, communications, English literature, psychology, Romance languages, social sciences.

Program Information • Students attend classes at Trinity and All Saints University College. Field trips to Leeds environs.

Sessions • Fall, spring, yearlong.

Eligibility Requirements • Open to sophomores, juniors, seniors; 2.8 GPA; 2 letters of recommendation; good academic standing at home school.

Living Arrangements • Students live in host institution dormitories. Quarters are shared with host institution students. Meals are taken on one's own, in central dining facility.

Costs (2003-2004) • One term: $12,500. Yearlong program: $25,000; includes tuition, housing, all meals, insurance, excursions, student support services, internship. $35 application fee. $300 nonrefundable deposit required. Financial aid available for students from sponsoring institution: scholarships, loans.

For More Information • Ms. Carol Toufali, Coordinator, Marist Abroad Program, Marist College, 3399 North Road, Poughkeepsie, NY 12601-1387; *Phone:* 845-575-3330; *Fax:* 845-575-3294. *E-mail:* international@marist.edu. *World Wide Web:* http://www.marist.edu/international/

NORTH AMERICAN INSTITUTE FOR STUDY ABROAD
STUDY IN ENGLAND

Hosted by University of Leeds

Academic Focus • Full curriculum.

Program Information • Students attend classes at University of Leeds.

Sessions • Fall, spring, yearlong.

Eligibility Requirements • Minimum age 18; open to sophomores, juniors, seniors; 3.0 GPA; 2 letters of recommendation; good academic standing at home school.

Living Arrangements • Students live in host institution dormitories, locally rented apartments. Quarters are shared with host institution students, students from other programs. Meals are taken as a group, on one's own, in residences, in central dining facility, in restaurants.

Costs (2001-2002) • One term: $9750. Yearlong program: $18,000; includes tuition, housing, insurance, international student ID, student support services, transcripts. $50 application fee. $500 nonrefundable deposit required. Financial aid available for all students: scholarships.

For More Information • Dr. Michael Currid, Director, North American Institute for Study Abroad, 129 Mill Street, Danville, PA 17821; *Phone:* 570-275-5099; *Fax:* 570-275-1644. *E-mail:* naisa@naisa.com. *World Wide Web:* http://www.naisa.com/

STATE UNIVERSITY OF NEW YORK AT PLATTSBURGH
STUDY IN ENGLAND, LEEDS

Hosted by Trinity and All Saints University College

Academic Focus • Accounting, American studies, business administration/management, computer science, education, English, French language and literature, health and physical education, history, marketing, mathematics, psychology, religious studies, Spanish language and literature.

Program Information • Students attend classes at Trinity and All Saints University College.

Sessions • Fall, spring, yearlong.

Eligibility Requirements • Minimum age 18; open to sophomores, juniors, seniors; 2.8 GPA; 2 letters of recommendation; good academic standing at home school; SUNY and TAS applications; essay; transcripts.

Living Arrangements • Students live in host institution dormitories, locally rented apartments. Quarters are shared with host

institution students, students from other programs. Meals are taken on one's own, in residences, in central dining facility, in restaurants.
Costs (2003-2004) • One term: $6250 for New York residents; nonresidents contact sponsor for cost. Yearlong program: $12,500 for New York residents; nonresidents contact sponsor for cost; includes tuition, housing, some meals, insurance, books and class materials, international student ID, student support services. $20 application fee. $350 nonrefundable deposit required. Financial aid available for students from sponsoring institution: scholarships, loans.
For More Information • Ms. Jo Ann Mackie, Study Abroad Coordinator, State University of New York at Plattsburgh, Study Abroad Office, 101 Broad Street, Plattsburgh, NY 12901; *Phone:* 518-564-2321; *Fax:* 518-564-2326. *E-mail:* international@plattsburgh. edu. *World Wide Web:* http://www.plattsburgh.edu/studyabroad/

STATE UNIVERSITY OF NEW YORK COLLEGE AT BROCKPORT
UNIVERSITY OF LEEDS PROGRAM

Hosted by University of Leeds
Academic Focus • Full curriculum.
Program Information • Students attend classes at University of Leeds. Field trips to the London weekend program.
Sessions • Fall, spring, yearlong.
Eligibility Requirements • Minimum age 18; open to juniors, seniors; 3.0 GPA; 2 letters of recommendation; good academic standing at home school; ability to do upper-division course work in chosen subject.
Living Arrangements • Students live in host institution dormitories. Quarters are shared with host institution students. Meals are taken on one's own, in residences.
Costs (2003-2004) • One term: $10,325 for fall term; $10,500 for spring. Yearlong program: $19,475; includes tuition, housing, excursions, international student ID, student support services. $350 nonrefundable deposit required. Financial aid available for all students: scholarships, loans, regular financial aid, grants.
For More Information • Dr. John Perry, Director, Office of International Education, State University of New York College at Brockport, 350 New Campus Drive, Brockport, NY 14420; *Phone:* 800-298-SUNY; *Fax:* 585-637-3218. *E-mail:* overseas@brockport.edu. *World Wide Web:* http://www.brockport.edu/studyabroad/

UNIVERSITY OF LEEDS
JYA AT THE UNIVERSITY OF LEEDS

Hosted by University of Leeds
Academic Focus • Full curriculum.
Program Information • Students attend classes at University of Leeds.
Sessions • Fall, spring, yearlong.
Eligibility Requirements • Open to juniors; 3.0 GPA; 2 letters of recommendation; good academic standing at home school; academic transcript.
Living Arrangements • Students live in host institution dormitories, locally rented apartments. Quarters are shared with host institution students. Meals are taken on one's own, in residences.
Costs (2004-2005) • One term: £3600. Yearlong program: £6900; includes tuition, lab equipment, student support services.
For More Information • Ms. Naomi French, Study Abroad Adviser, University of Leeds, Study Abroad Office, Leeds LS2 9JT, England; *Phone:* +44 113-343-1734; *Fax:* +44 113-343-4968. *E-mail:* n.r.french@ adm.leeds.ac.uk. *World Wide Web:* http://www.leeds.ac.uk/ studyabroad/

LEICESTER

ST. JOHN'S UNIVERSITY
ENGLAND

Hosted by University of Leicester
Academic Focus • Criminal justice, sports management.
Program Information • Students attend classes at University of Leicester. Scheduled travel to Rome; field trips to other areas of England, other European countries; optional travel to Rome.
Sessions • Spring.

Eligibility Requirements • Minimum age 18; open to freshmen, sophomores, juniors, seniors, graduate students; 2.75 GPA; 2 letters of recommendation; good academic standing at home school; interview.
Living Arrangements • Students live in program-owned apartments. Quarters are shared with host institution students, students from other programs. Meals are taken on one's own, in residences, in central dining facility.
Costs (2004) • One term: $15,972–$16,698; includes tuition, housing, some meals, international airfare, student support services. $30 application fee. $750 nonrefundable deposit required. Financial aid available for students from sponsoring institution: scholarships, loans.
For More Information • Dr. Ruth De Paula, Director, Office of Study Abroad Programs, St. John's University, 8000 Utopia Parkway, Jamaica, NY 11439; *Phone:* 718-990-6105; *Fax:* 718-990-2321. *E-mail:* intled@stjohns.edu. *World Wide Web:* http://www.stjohns. edu/studyabroad/

UNIVERSITY OF LEICESTER
STUDY ABROAD AT UNIVERSITY OF LEICESTER

Hosted by University of Leicester
Academic Focus • Full curriculum.
Program Information • Students attend classes at University of Leicester. Scheduled travel to London (for fall), Rome (for spring); field trips to London, Stratford, Warwick, Cambridge (for fall), Rome (for spring).
Sessions • Fall, spring, yearlong.
Eligibility Requirements • Open to juniors, seniors; 3.0 GPA.
Living Arrangements • Students live in host institution dormitories, program-owned apartments. Quarters are shared with host institution students. Meals are taken as a group, on one's own, in residences, in central dining facility.
Costs (2003-2004) • One term: £4605. Yearlong program: contact sponsor for cost; includes tuition, housing, some meals, excursions, student support services.
For More Information • Mr. Paul Beavitt, Study Abroad Coordinator, University of Leicester, International Office, University Road, Leicester LE1 7RH, England; *Phone:* +44 116-252-2600; *Fax:* +44 116-252-5127. *E-mail:* studyabroad@le.ac.uk. *World Wide Web:* http://www.le.ac.uk/international/sa/

UNIVERSITY OF MIAMI
UNIVERSITY OF LEICESTER

Hosted by University of Leicester
Academic Focus • Full curriculum.
Program Information • Students attend classes at University of Leicester. Optional travel to Greece or Italy at an extra cost.
Sessions • Fall, spring, yearlong.
Eligibility Requirements • Minimum age 18; open to sophomores, juniors, seniors; 3.0 GPA; 2 letters of recommendation.
Living Arrangements • Students live in host institution dormitories. Quarters are shared with host institution students, students from other programs. Meals are taken on one's own, in residences, in central dining facility.
Costs (2003-2004) • One term: $12,919. Yearlong program: $25,838; includes tuition, student support services. $40 application fee. $500 nonrefundable deposit required. Financial aid available for students from sponsoring institution: scholarships, loans.
For More Information • Ms. Elyse Resnick, Assistant Director, University of Miami, International Education and Exchange Programs, 5050 Brunson Drive, Allen Hall 212, PO Box 248005, Coral Gables, FL 33124-1610; *Phone:* 305-284-3434; *Fax:* 305-284-4235. *E-mail:* ieep@miami.edu. *World Wide Web:* http://www.studyabroad. miami.edu/

LIVERPOOL

LOCK HAVEN UNIVERSITY OF PENNSYLVANIA
SEMESTER IN LIVERPOOL

Hosted by Liverpool Hope University College
Academic Focus • Full curriculum.

ENGLAND
Liverpool

Program Information • Students attend classes at Liverpool Hope University College.
Sessions • Fall, spring, yearlong.
Eligibility Requirements • Minimum age 18; open to sophomores, juniors, seniors, adults; 2.5 GPA; 3 letters of recommendation; transcript.
Living Arrangements • Students live in host institution dormitories, locally rented apartments. Quarters are shared with host institution students, students from other programs. Meals are taken in central dining facility.
Costs (2003-2004) • One term: $5600 for Pennsylvania residents; $7500 for nonresidents. Yearlong program: $10,900 for Pennsylvania residents; $14,720 for nonresidents; includes tuition, housing, all meals, fees. $50 application fee. Financial aid available for students from sponsoring institution: scholarships, loans.
For More Information • Dean, Institute for International Studies, Lock Haven University of Pennsylvania, Lock Haven, PA 17745-2390; *Phone:* 570-893-2140; *Fax:* 570-893-2537. *E-mail:* intlstudies_webmonitor@lhup.edu. *World Wide Web:* http://www.lhup.edu/international/goingp/goingplaces_index.htm

STATE UNIVERSITY OF NEW YORK AT PLATTSBURGH
STUDY IN ENGLAND, LIVERPOOL

Hosted by Liverpool Hope University College
Academic Focus • American studies, art, biological/life sciences, business administration/management, computer science, drama/theater, education, English, environmental science/studies, European studies, French language and literature, geography, health and physical education, health-care management, history, information science, mathematics, music, psychology, religious studies, science, sociology, women's studies.
Program Information • Students attend classes at Liverpool Hope University College.
Sessions • Fall, spring, yearlong.
Eligibility Requirements • Minimum age 18; open to sophomores, juniors, seniors; 2.8 GPA; 2 letters of recommendation; good academic standing at home school; SUNY and Liverpool applications; essay; transcripts; no foreign language proficiency required.
Living Arrangements • Students live in host institution dormitories, locally rented apartments. Quarters are shared with host institution students, students from other programs. Meals are taken on one's own, in residences, in central dining facility, in restaurants.
Costs (2003-2004) • One term: $6058. Yearlong program: $12,116; includes tuition, housing, all meals, insurance, books and class materials, international student ID, student support services. $20 application fee. $350 nonrefundable deposit required. Financial aid available for students from sponsoring institution: scholarships, loans.
For More Information • Ms. Jo Ann Mackie, Study Abroad Coordinator, State University of New York at Plattsburgh, Study Abroad Office, 101 Broad Street, Plattsburgh, NY 12901; *Phone:* 518-564-2321; *Fax:* 518-564-2326. *E-mail:* international@plattsburgh.edu. *World Wide Web:* http://www.plattsburgh.edu/studyabroad/

UNIVERSITY OF LIVERPOOL
UNIVERSITY OF LIVERPOOL STUDY ABROAD PROGRAMME

Hosted by University of Liverpool
Academic Focus • Full curriculum.
Program Information • Students attend classes at University of Liverpool.
Sessions • Fall, spring, yearlong.
Eligibility Requirements • Minimum age 17; open to sophomores, juniors, seniors; 3.0 GPA; good academic standing at home school.
Living Arrangements • Students live in host institution dormitories, locally rented apartments, program-owned apartments. Quarters are shared with host institution students, students from other programs. Meals are taken as a group, on one's own, in residences, in central dining facility.
Costs (2003-2004) • One term: £3750. Yearlong program: £7500; includes tuition.
For More Information • Mr. Jason Thomas, International Officer, University of Liverpool, International Recruitment and Relations Office, 6 Abercromby Square, Liverpool L69 7WY, England; *Phone:*

+44 151-794-6730; *Fax:* +44 151-794-6733. *E-mail:* irro@liv.ac.uk. *World Wide Web:* http://www.liv.ac.uk/international/exchange/

LONDON
AHA INTERNATIONAL AN ACADEMIC PROGRAM OF THE UNIVERSITY OF OREGON
LONDON, ENGLAND: NORTHWEST COUNCIL ON STUDY ABROAD

Hosted by AHA London Centre
Academic Focus • Art history, drama/theater, English literature, history, political science and government, sociology.
Program Information • Students attend classes at AHA London Centre. Field trips to Hampton Court, Bath, Stonehenge, Stratford-upon-Avon, Canterbury.
Sessions • Fall, spring, winter, yearlong.
Eligibility Requirements • Open to sophomores, juniors, seniors; 2.5 GPA; 2 letters of recommendation; good academic standing at home school.
Living Arrangements • Students live in host family homes. Quarters are shared with host institution students. Meals are taken with host family.
Costs (2003-2004) • One term: $7820. Yearlong program: $23,460; includes tuition, housing, some meals, insurance, excursions, books and class materials, international student ID, student support services, London Tube Pass, theatre tickets, museum admissions. $50 application fee. $200 refundable deposit required. Financial aid available for all students: scholarships, loans, grants.
For More Information • Ms. Amy Hunter, Associate Director for University Programs Abroad, AHA International An Academic Program of the University of Oregon, 741 SW Lincoln Street, Portland, OR 97201; *Phone:* 503-295-7730; *Fax:* 503-295-5969. *E-mail:* mail@aha-intl.org. *World Wide Web:* http://www.aha-intl.org/

ALMA COLLEGE
PROGRAM OF STUDIES IN LONDON, ENGLAND (WESTMINSTER)

Hosted by University of Westminster
Academic Focus • Anthropology, business administration/management, communications, cultural studies.
Program Information • Students attend classes at University of Westminster.
Sessions • Fall, spring, yearlong.
Eligibility Requirements • Minimum age 18; open to sophomores, juniors, seniors; 3.0 GPA; 2 letters of recommendation; good academic standing at home school.
Living Arrangements • Students live in host institution dormitories, locally rented apartments, host family homes. Quarters are shared with host institution students, students from other programs. Meals are taken on one's own, in residences.
Costs (2002-2003) • One term: $9500. Yearlong program: $17,990; includes tuition, housing, some meals, insurance, international student ID, student support services, Metro pass. $50 application fee. $200 refundable deposit required. Financial aid available for all students: scholarships.
For More Information • Ms. Julie Elenbaas, Office Coordinator, Alma College, 614 West Superior Street, Alma, MI 48801-1599; *Phone:* 989-463-7055; *Fax:* 989-463-7126. *E-mail:* intl_studies@alma.edu. *World Wide Web:* http://international.alma.edu/

AMERICAN INSTITUTE FOR FOREIGN STUDY (AIFS)
RICHMOND INTERNATIONAL INTERNSHIP PROGRAM

Hosted by Richmond–The American International University in London
Academic Focus • Business administration/management, communications, drama/theater, economics, fine/studio arts, political science and government, social sciences.
Program Information • Students attend classes at Richmond–The American International University in London.
Sessions • Fall, spring.

Eligibility Requirements • Minimum age 17; open to juniors, seniors, graduate students; 2.5 GPA; good academic standing at home school; 2 letters of recommendation (1 academic, 1 from employer).

Living Arrangements • Students live in host institution dormitories. Quarters are shared with host institution students. Meals are taken on one's own.

Costs (2004-2005) • One term: $10,995; includes tuition, housing, insurance, student support services, one-way airfare. $75 application fee. $350 nonrefundable deposit required. Financial aid available for all students: scholarships.

For More Information • Mr. David Mauro, Admissions Advisor, American Institute For Foreign Study (AIFS), 9 West Broad Street, Stamford, CT 06902-3788; *Phone:* 800-727-2437 Ext. 5163; *Fax:* 203-399-5597. *E-mail:* dmauro@aifs.com. *World Wide Web:* http://www.aifsabroad.com/

AMERICAN INSTITUTE FOR FOREIGN STUDY (AIFS)
RICHMOND, THE AMERICAN INTERNATIONAL UNIVERSITY IN LONDON

Hosted by Richmond–The American International University in London

Academic Focus • Full curriculum.

Program Information • Students attend classes at Richmond–The American International University in London. Field trips to Windsor Castle, Hampton Court, Greenwich; optional travel to Bath, Stratford-upon-Avon at an extra cost.

Sessions • Fall, spring, yearlong.

Eligibility Requirements • Minimum age 17; open to freshmen, sophomores, juniors, seniors; 2.5 GPA; 1 letter of recommendation; good academic standing at home school.

Living Arrangements • Students live in host institution dormitories, host family homes. Quarters are shared with host institution students. Meals are taken as a group, on one's own, in central dining facility.

Costs (2004-2005) • One term: $12,495. Yearlong program: $24,490; includes tuition, housing, some meals, insurance, excursions, student support services, one-way airfare. $75 application fee. $350 nonrefundable deposit required. Financial aid available for all students: scholarships.

For More Information • Mr. David Mauro, Admissions Advisor, American Institute For Foreign Study (AIFS), 9 West Broad Street, Stamford, CT 06902-3788; *Phone:* 800-727-2437 Ext. 5163; *Fax:* 203-399-5597. *E-mail:* dmauro@aifs.com. *World Wide Web:* http://www.aifsabroad.com/

AMERICAN INTERCONTINENTAL UNIVERSITY
LONDON STUDY ABROAD AND INTERNSHIP PROGRAM

Hosted by American InterContinental University–London

Academic Focus • Advertising and public relations, art, British studies, business administration/management, commercial art, communications, design and applied arts, fashion design, fashion merchandising, film and media studies, fine/studio arts, graphic design/illustration, intercultural studies, interior design, international business, liberal studies, management information systems, marketing, photography, textiles.

Program Information • Students attend classes at American InterContinental University–London. Field trips to other areas of the United Kingdom, Europe; optional travel to Paris, Prague, Mumbai, Barcelona, Rome, Bruges, Wales, Ireland, Hong Kong at an extra cost.

Sessions • Fall, spring, winter.

Eligibility Requirements • Open to freshmen, sophomores, juniors, seniors, graduate students, adults; 2.0 GPA; good academic standing at home school; approval of advisor, dean/department chair, and study abroad office; college transcripts.

Living Arrangements • Students live in locally rented apartments. Quarters are shared with host institution students. Meals are taken on one's own, in residences, in central dining facility, in restaurants.

Costs (2004) • One term: $6500–$9000; includes tuition, housing, student support services. $150 refundable deposit required. Financial aid available for all students: scholarships, loans.

For More Information • American InterContinental University, Study Abroad Programs, 3150 West Higgins Road, Suite 105, Hoffman Estates, IL 60195; *Phone:* 800-255-6839; *Fax:* 847-885-8422. *E-mail:* studyabroad@aiuniv.edu. *World Wide Web:* http://www.studyabroad.aiuniv.edu/

AMERICAN UNIVERSITY
SEMESTER IN LONDON

Held at Centers for Academic Programs Abroad (CAPA)

Academic Focus • British studies, communications, drama/theater, European studies, history, international affairs, political science and government.

Program Information • Classes are held on the campus of Centers for Academic Programs Abroad (CAPA). Faculty members are drawn from the sponsor's U.S. staff and local instructors hired by the sponsor. Scheduled travel to Ireland; field trips to Bath, Stratford-upon-Avon, Stonehenge.

Sessions • Fall, spring.

Eligibility Requirements • Open to sophomores, juniors, seniors, graduate students; 2.75 GPA; 2 letters of recommendation; second semester sophomore status; recommendation of advisor.

Living Arrangements • Students live in host institution dormitories. Meals are taken on one's own, in residences.

Costs (2001-2002) • One term: $16,734; includes tuition, housing, student support services. $35 application fee. $300 nonrefundable deposit required. Financial aid available for all students: scholarships, loans.

For More Information • Dr. David C. Brown, Dean, Washington Semester and World Capitals Programs, American University, Tenley Campus–Constitution Building, Washington, DC 20016-8083; *Phone:* 800-424-2600; *Fax:* 202-895-4960. *E-mail:* travel@american.edu. *World Wide Web:* http://www.worldcapitals.american.edu/

ARCADIA UNIVERSITY
CITY UNIVERSITY

Hosted by City University

Academic Focus • Business administration/management, economics, engineering, mathematics, philosophy, psychology, social sciences.

Program Information • Students attend classes at City University.

Sessions • Fall, spring, yearlong.

Eligibility Requirements • Open to sophomores, juniors, seniors; 3.0 GPA; 1 letter of recommendation; statistics background for psychology courses.

Living Arrangements • Students live in host institution dormitories, program-owned apartments, program-owned houses. Quarters are shared with host institution students, students from other programs. Meals are taken on one's own, in residences.

Costs (2003-2004) • One term: $10,590 for fall term; $13,290 for spring. Yearlong program: $20,390; includes tuition, housing, insurance, international student ID, student support services, pre-departure guide, transcripts. $35 application fee. $500 nonrefundable deposit required. Financial aid available for all students: scholarships, loans.

For More Information • Arcadia University, Center for Education Abroad, 450 South Easton Road, Glenside, PA 19038-3295; *Phone:* 866-927-2234; *Fax:* 215-572-2174. *E-mail:* cea@arcadia.edu. *World Wide Web:* http://www.arcadia.edu/cea/

ARCADIA UNIVERSITY
GOLDSMITHS COLLEGE

Hosted by Goldsmiths College, University of London

Academic Focus • Full curriculum.

Program Information • Students attend classes at Goldsmiths College, University of London. Field trips to Bath, Oxford, Stratford-upon-Avon, Leeds Castle, Canterbury; optional travel to Wales at an extra cost.

Sessions • Fall, spring, yearlong.

Eligibility Requirements • Open to sophomores, juniors, seniors; 3.0 GPA; 1 letter of recommendation.

Living Arrangements • Students live in host institution dormitories. Quarters are shared with host institution students, students from other programs. Meals are taken on one's own, in residences.

Costs (2003-2004) • One term: $10,990–$14,390. Yearlong program: $21,890; includes tuition, housing, insurance, international student ID, student support services, pre-departure guide, transcripts. $35 application fee. $500 nonrefundable deposit required. Financial aid available for all students: scholarships, loans.

For More Information • Arcadia University, Center for Education Abroad, 450 South Easton Road, Glenside, PA 19038-3295; *Phone:* 866-927-2234; *Fax:* 215-572-2174. *E-mail:* cea@arcadia.edu. *World Wide Web:* http://www.arcadia.edu/cea/

ARCADIA UNIVERSITY
KING'S COLLEGE, LONDON

Hosted by King's College London, University of London

Academic Focus • Full curriculum.

Program Information • Students attend classes at King's College London, University of London. Field trips to Bath, Oxford, Leeds Castle, Canterbury, Stratford-upon-Avon; optional travel to Wales at an extra cost.

Sessions • Fall, spring, yearlong.

Eligibility Requirements • Open to juniors, seniors; course work in subject(s) to be studied at King's; 3.3 GPA; 1 letter of recommendation.

Living Arrangements • Students live in host institution dormitories, locally rented apartments, program-owned apartments, program-owned houses. Quarters are shared with host institution students, students from other programs. Meals are taken on one's own, in residences.

Costs (2003-2004) • One term: $12,150–$15,290 for fall semester; $13,990 for spring. Yearlong program: $23,490; includes tuition, housing, insurance, international student ID, student support services, pre-departure guide, transcripts. $35 application fee. $500 nonrefundable deposit required. Financial aid available for all students: scholarships, loans.

For More Information • Arcadia University, Center for Education Abroad, 450 South Easton Road, Glenside, PA 19038-3295; *Phone:* 866-927-2234; *Fax:* 215-572-2174. *E-mail:* cea@arcadia.edu. *World Wide Web:* http://www.arcadia.edu/cea/

ARCADIA UNIVERSITY
LONDON INTERNSHIP

Hosted by City University

Academic Focus • Business administration/management, communications, public policy, social sciences.

Program Information • Students attend classes at City University.

Sessions • Fall, spring.

Eligibility Requirements • Open to juniors, seniors; 3.3 GPA; 2 letters of recommendation; minimum 3.0 GPA in background courses for internship.

Living Arrangements • Students live in program-owned apartments, program-owned houses. Quarters are shared with students from other programs. Meals are taken on one's own, in residences.

Costs (2003-2004) • One term: $10,690–$11,190; includes tuition, housing, insurance, international student ID, student support services, pre-departure guide, transcripts. $35 application fee. $500 nonrefundable deposit required. Financial aid available for all students: scholarships, loans.

For More Information • Arcadia University, Center for Education Abroad, 450 South Easton Road, Glenside, PA 19038-3295; *Phone:* 866-927-2234; *Fax:* 215-572-2174. *E-mail:* cea@arcadia.edu. *World Wide Web:* http://www.arcadia.edu/cea/

ARCADIA UNIVERSITY
LONDON SEMESTER

Hosted by City University

Academic Focus • Accounting, business administration/ management, computer science, drama/theater, fine/studio arts, liberal studies, mathematics, social sciences.
Program Information • Students attend classes at City University.
Sessions • Fall, spring, yearlong.
Eligibility Requirements • Open to juniors, seniors; 3.0 GPA; 1 letter of recommendation.
Living Arrangements • Students live in program-owned apartments, program-owned houses, host family homes. Quarters are shared with students from other programs. Meals are taken on one's own, in residences.
Costs (2003-2004) • One term: $10,690–$11,190. Yearlong program: $17,990; includes tuition, housing, insurance, international student ID, student support services, pre-departure guide, transcripts. $35 application fee. $500 nonrefundable deposit required. Financial aid available for all students: scholarships, loans.
For More Information • Arcadia University, Center for Education Abroad, 450 South Easton Road, Glenside, PA 19038-3295; *Phone:* 866-927-2234; *Fax:* 215-572-2174. *E-mail:* cea@arcadia.edu. *World Wide Web:* http://www.arcadia.edu/cea/

ARCADIA UNIVERSITY
MIDDLESEX UNIVERSITY

Hosted by Middlesex University
Academic Focus • American studies, business administration/ management, computer science, language studies, liberal studies, music, performing arts, religious studies, social sciences.
Program Information • Students attend classes at Middlesex University.
Sessions • Fall, spring, yearlong.
Eligibility Requirements • Open to sophomores, juniors, seniors; 3.0 GPA; 1 letter of recommendation.
Living Arrangements • Students live in host institution dormitories, program-owned apartments. Quarters are shared with host institution students, students from other programs. Meals are taken on one's own, in residences.
Costs (2003-2004) • One term: $11,590. Yearlong program: $19,290; includes tuition, housing, insurance, international student ID, student support services, pre-departure guide, transcripts. $35 application fee. $500 nonrefundable deposit required. Financial aid available for all students: scholarships, loans.
For More Information • Arcadia University, Center for Education Abroad, 450 South Easton Road, Glenside, PA 19038-3295; *Phone:* 866-927-2234; *Fax:* 215-572-2174. *E-mail:* cea@arcadia.edu. *World Wide Web:* http://www.arcadia.edu/cea/

ARCADIA UNIVERSITY
QUEEN MARY, UNIVERSITY OF LONDON

Hosted by Queen Mary, University of London
Academic Focus • Full curriculum.
Program Information • Students attend classes at Queen Mary, University of London. Field trips to Bath, Oxford, Leeds Castle, Canterbury, Stratford-upon-Avon; optional travel to Wales at an extra cost.
Sessions • Fall, spring, yearlong.
Eligibility Requirements • Open to sophomores, juniors, seniors; 3.0 GPA; 1 letter of recommendation.
Living Arrangements • Students live in host institution dormitories, locally rented apartments, program-owned apartments, program-owned houses. Quarters are shared with host institution students, students from other programs. Meals are taken on one's own, in residences.
Costs (2003-2004) • One term: $12,690–$13,590. Yearlong program: $22,390; includes tuition, housing, insurance, international student ID, student support services, pre-departure guide, transcripts. $35 application fee. $500 nonrefundable deposit required. Financial aid available for all students: scholarships, loans.
For More Information • Arcadia University, Center for Education Abroad, 450 South Easton Road, Glenside, PA 19038-3295; *Phone:* 866-927-2234; *Fax:* 215-572-2174. *E-mail:* cea@arcadia.edu. *World Wide Web:* http://www.arcadia.edu/cea/

ARCADIA UNIVERSITY
ROYAL HOLLOWAY

Hosted by Royal Holloway–University of London
Academic Focus • Full curriculum.
Program Information • Students attend classes at Royal Holloway– University of London. Field trips to Bath, Oxford, Leeds Castle, Canterbury, Stratford-upon-Avon; optional travel to Wales at an extra cost.
Sessions • Fall, spring, yearlong.
Eligibility Requirements • Open to juniors, seniors; 3.3 GPA; 2 letters of recommendation.
Living Arrangements • Students live in host institution dormitories. Quarters are shared with host institution students, students from other programs. Meals are taken as a group, on one's own, in residences, in central dining facility.
Costs (2003-2004) • One term: $11,790–$12,990. Yearlong program: $21,990; includes tuition, housing, insurance, international student ID, student support services, pre-departure guide, transcripts. $35 application fee. $500 nonrefundable deposit required. Financial aid available for all students: scholarships, loans.
For More Information • Arcadia University, Center for Education Abroad, 450 South Easton Road, Glenside, PA 19038-3295; *Phone:* 866-927-2234; *Fax:* 215-572-2174. *E-mail:* cea@arcadia.edu. *World Wide Web:* http://www.arcadia.edu/cea/

ARCADIA UNIVERSITY
SCHOOL OF ORIENTAL AND AFRICAN STUDIES

Hosted by School of Oriental and African Studies–University of London
Academic Focus • African languages and literature, African studies, anthropology, archaeology, art history, Asian languages, Asian studies, Chinese language and literature, economics, history, Japanese, language studies, linguistics, Middle Eastern languages, Middle Eastern studies, music, political science and government, religious studies.
Program Information • Students attend classes at School of Oriental and African Studies–University of London. Field trips to Bath, Oxford, Leeds Castle, Canterbury, Stratford-upon-Avon; optional travel to Wales at an extra cost.
Sessions • Fall, spring, yearlong.
Eligibility Requirements • Open to juniors, seniors; course work in African studies, Asian studies, or related field; 3.0 GPA; 2 letters of recommendation.
Living Arrangements • Students live in host institution dormitories, locally rented apartments, program-owned apartments, program-owned houses. Quarters are shared with students from other programs. Meals are taken on one's own, in residences.
Costs (2003-2004) • One term: $13,550–$15,990. Yearlong program: $24,790; includes tuition, housing, insurance, international student ID, student support services, pre-departure guide, transcripts. $35 application fee. $500 nonrefundable deposit required. Financial aid available for all students: scholarships, loans.
For More Information • Arcadia University, Center for Education Abroad, 450 South Easton Road, Glenside, PA 19038-3295; *Phone:* 866-927-2234; *Fax:* 215-572-2174. *E-mail:* cea@arcadia.edu. *World Wide Web:* http://www.arcadia.edu/cea/

ARCADIA UNIVERSITY
UNIVERSITY COLLEGE LONDON

Hosted by University College London
Academic Focus • Full curriculum.
Program Information • Students attend classes at University College London. Field trips to Bath, Oxford, Leeds Castle, Canterbury, Stratford-upon-Avon; optional travel to Wales at an extra cost.
Sessions • Fall, spring, yearlong.
Eligibility Requirements • Open to juniors, seniors; 3.0 GPA; 2 letters of recommendation; slide portfolio for Slade independent studio program.
Living Arrangements • Students live in host institution dormitories, locally rented apartments, program-owned apartments. Quarters are shared with host institution students, students from other programs. Meals are taken on one's own, in residences.
Costs (2003-2004) • One term: $13,790–$15,390. Yearlong program: $23,890; includes tuition, housing, insurance, excursions,

international student ID, student support services, pre-departure guide, transcripts. $35 application fee. $500 nonrefundable deposit required. Financial aid available for all students: scholarships, loans.
For More Information • Arcadia University, Center for Education Abroad, 450 South Easton Road, Glenside, PA 19038-3295; *Phone:* 866-927-2234; *Fax:* 215-572-2174. *E-mail:* cea@arcadia.edu. *World Wide Web:* http://www.arcadia.edu/cea/

ARCADIA UNIVERSITY
UNIVERSITY OF GREENWICH

Hosted by University of Greenwich
Academic Focus • Full curriculum.
Program Information • Students attend classes at University of Greenwich.
Sessions • Fall, spring, yearlong.
Eligibility Requirements • Open to freshmen, sophomores, juniors, seniors; 3.0 GPA; 1 letter of recommendation.
Living Arrangements • Students live in host institution dormitories. Quarters are shared with host institution students, students from other programs. Meals are taken on one's own, in residences, in restaurants.
Costs (2003-2004) • One term: contact sponsor for cost. Yearlong program: contact sponsor for cost. $500 nonrefundable deposit required. Financial aid available for all students: scholarships, loans.
For More Information • Arcadia University, Center for Education Abroad, 450 South Easton Road, Glenside, PA 19038-3295; *Phone:* 866-927-2234; *Fax:* 215-572-2174. *E-mail:* cea@arcadia.edu. *World Wide Web:* http://www.arcadia.edu/cea/

ARCADIA UNIVERSITY
UNIVERSITY OF WESTMINSTER

Hosted by University of Westminster
Academic Focus • Business administration/management, communications, criminal justice, economics, English, finance, geography, history, human resources, psychology, sociology.
Program Information • Students attend classes at University of Westminster.
Sessions • Fall, spring, yearlong.
Eligibility Requirements • Open to sophomores, juniors, seniors; 3.0 GPA; 1 letter of recommendation.
Living Arrangements • Students live in host institution dormitories, locally rented apartments. Quarters are shared with host institution students, students from other programs. Meals are taken on one's own, in residences.
Costs (2003-2004) • One term: $11,650. Yearlong program: $19,890; includes tuition, housing, insurance, international student ID, student support services, pre-departure guide, transcripts. $35 application fee. $500 nonrefundable deposit required. Financial aid available for all students: scholarships, loans.
For More Information • Arcadia University, Center for Education Abroad, 450 South Easton Road, Glenside, PA 19038-3295; *Phone:* 866-927-2234; *Fax:* 215-572-2174. *E-mail:* cea@arcadia.edu. *World Wide Web:* http://www.arcadia.edu/cea/

BENTLEY COLLEGE
STUDY ABROAD PROGRAM IN LONDON, ENGLAND

Hosted by European Business School London
Academic Focus • Accounting, business administration/management, economics, finance, information science, international affairs, law and legal studies, marketing.
Program Information • Students attend classes at European Business School London. Scheduled travel; field trips to Suffolk Village, Stonehenge, Bath; optional travel to Stonehenge, Bath, Paris, Dublin at an extra cost.
Sessions • Fall, spring, yearlong.
Eligibility Requirements • Open to juniors, seniors; 3.0 GPA; 1 letter of recommendation; good academic standing at home school; essays.
Living Arrangements • Students live in host institution dormitories, locally rented apartments. Quarters are shared with host institution students, students from other programs. Meals are taken in central dining facility.
Costs (2002-2003) • One term: $18,600. Yearlong program: $25,080; includes tuition, housing, all meals, international student

ID, student support services. $35 application fee. $500 nonrefundable deposit required. Financial aid available for students from sponsoring institution: scholarships, loans.
For More Information • Mr. Andrew Dusenbery, Education Abroad Advisor, Bentley College, 175 Forest Street, Waltham, MA 02452; *Phone:* 781-891-3474; *Fax:* 781-891-2819. *E-mail:* study_abroad@bentley.edu. *World Wide Web:* http://ecampus.bentley.edu/dept/sa/

BOSTON UNIVERSITY
LONDON INTERNSHIP PROGRAM

Academic Focus • Advertising and public relations, art history, business administration/management, commerce, communications, drama/theater, economics, education, film and media studies, international affairs, journalism, law and legal studies, liberal studies, political science and government, psychology, social sciences.
Program Information • Faculty members are local instructors hired by the sponsor. Field trips to the House of Commons, art museums, theaters; optional travel to Oxford, Wales, Stonehenge at an extra cost.
Sessions • Fall, spring.
Eligibility Requirements • Open to sophomores, juniors, seniors, adults; 3.0 GPA; 2 letters of recommendation; good academic standing at home school; essay; approval of participation; transcript.
Living Arrangements • Students live in locally rented apartments, program-owned apartments. Meals are taken on one's own, in residences, in restaurants.
Costs (2004-2005) • One term: $12,100; includes tuition, housing, internship placement. $50 application fee. $400 nonrefundable deposit required. Financial aid available for all students: scholarships, loans, resident assistant and office assistant positions.
For More Information • Division of International Programs, Boston University, 232 Bay State Road, Boston, MA 02215; *Phone:* 617-353-9888; *Fax:* 617-353-5402. *E-mail:* abroad@bu.edu. *World Wide Web:* http://www.bu.edu/abroad/

BOSTON UNIVERSITY
LONDON MUSIC PROGRAM WITH THE ROYAL COLLEGE OF MUSIC

Hosted by Royal College of Music
Academic Focus • Liberal studies, music, music performance.
Program Information • Students attend classes at Royal College of Music.
Sessions • Fall.
Eligibility Requirements • Open to juniors; 3.0 GPA; 1 letter of recommendation; good academic standing at home school; essay; approval of participation.
Living Arrangements • Students live in locally rented apartments, program-owned apartments. Quarters are shared with host institution students. Meals are taken on one's own, in restaurants.
Costs (2004) • One term: $18,084; includes tuition, housing, excursions, international airfare, telecommunication fee. $50 application fee. $400 nonrefundable deposit required. Financial aid available for all students: scholarships, loans.
For More Information • Division of International Programs, Boston University, 232 Bay State Road, Boston, MA 02215; *Phone:* 617-353-9888; *Fax:* 617-353-5402. *E-mail:* abroad@bu.edu. *World Wide Web:* http://www.bu.edu/abroad/

BRITISH AMERICAN COLLEGE LONDON
STUDY ABROAD AT THE BRITISH AMERICAN COLLEGE LONDON

Hosted by British American College London
Academic Focus • Business administration/management, communications, international affairs, psychology, social sciences.
Program Information • Students attend classes at British American College London. Field trips to theaters, museums, locations throughout the United Kingdom, European cities; optional travel to the United Kingdom, Europe at an extra cost.
Sessions • Fall, spring, yearlong.
Eligibility Requirements • Minimum age 18; open to freshmen, sophomores, juniors, seniors, adults; 2.5 GPA; 2 letters of recommendation.
Living Arrangements • Students live in host institution dormitories, locally rented apartments, host family homes. Quarters are

shared with host institution students, students from other programs. Meals are taken as a group, in central dining facility.

Costs (2003-2004) • One term: £4600. Yearlong program: £9200; includes tuition. £300 nonrefundable deposit required. Financial aid available for all students: scholarships, work study, loans.

For More Information • Ms. Erin McGuigan, Senior International Officer, British American College London, Inner Circle, Regents Park, London NW1 4NS, England; *Phone:* +44 (0)20-7487-7452; *Fax:* +44 (0)20-7487-7425. *E-mail:* bacl@regents.ac.uk. *World Wide Web:* http://www.bacl.ac.uk/

CALVIN COLLEGE
SEMESTER IN BRITAIN

Hosted by Middlesex University, Oak Hill College

Academic Focus • Biblical studies, British studies, English literature, ethics, history, sociology.

Program Information • Students attend classes at Middlesex University, Oak Hill College. Scheduled travel to Stratford-upon-Avon, Bath, Stonehenge, Salisbury; field trips to theatres and museums in London, the Philharmonic, Parliament.

Sessions • Spring.

Eligibility Requirements • Open to sophomores, juniors, seniors; 2.5 GPA; 2 letters of recommendation; good academic standing at home school; interview with program director; advisor approval; no foreign language proficiency required.

Living Arrangements • Students live in host institution dormitories. Quarters are shared with host institution students. Meals are taken on one's own, in central dining facility.

Costs (2004) • One term: $12,500; includes tuition, housing, some meals, excursions, international airfare, student support services. $50 application fee. $400 nonrefundable deposit required. Financial aid available for students from sponsoring institution: scholarships, loans.

For More Information • Dr. Ellen B. Monsma, Director, Calvin College, Office of Off-Campus Programs, 3201 Burton Street, SE, Grand Rapids, MI 49546; *Phone:* 616-526-6551; *Fax:* 616-526-6756. *E-mail:* emonsma@calvin.edu. *World Wide Web:* http://www.calvin.edu/academic/off-campus/

CAMBERWELL COLLEGE OF ARTS
SEMESTER STUDY ABROAD

Hosted by Camberwell College of Arts

Academic Focus • Art conservation studies, ceramics and pottery, design and applied arts, drawing/painting, fine/studio arts, graphic design/illustration, photography.

Program Information • Students attend classes at Camberwell College of Arts.

Sessions • Fall, spring, yearlong.

Eligibility Requirements • Minimum age 19; open to sophomores, juniors, seniors, graduate students, adults; major in art, design, or a conservation-related subject; 3.0 GPA; 1 letter of recommendation; portfolio of work; transcript; completed application form.

Living Arrangements • Students live in host institution dormitories. Quarters are shared with host institution students. Meals are taken on one's own, in residences.

Costs (2003-2004) • One term: £3000. Yearlong program: £9000; includes tuition, student support services. £250 nonrefundable deposit required.

For More Information • Ms. Kate Ibbotson, Marketing and Semester Study Abroad, Camberwell College of Arts, Camberwell Study Abroad Office, The London Institute, Millbank, London SW1P 4RJ, England; *Phone:* +44 (0)-207514 8514; *Fax:* +44 (0)-207514 6315. *E-mail:* k.ibbotson@dali.linst.ac.uk. *World Wide Web:* http://www.camb.linst.ac.uk/studyabroad/

CENTER FOR INTERNATIONAL STUDIES
UNIVERSITY OF SURREY ROEHAMPTON

Hosted by University of Surrey Roehampton

Academic Focus • Full curriculum.

Program Information • Students attend classes at University of Surrey Roehampton. Field trips to London; optional travel to Stonehenge, Cambridge, Oxford, Bath, Europe at an extra cost.

Sessions • Fall, spring, yearlong.

Eligibility Requirements • Minimum age 18; open to sophomores, juniors, seniors, graduate students, adults; 2.75 GPA; 1 letter of recommendation; good academic standing at home school; personal essay.

Living Arrangements • Students live in host institution dormitories, program-owned apartments. Quarters are shared with host institution students. Meals are taken on one's own, in residences, in central dining facility, in restaurants.

Costs (2003-2004) • One term: $9500. Yearlong program: $17,600; includes tuition, housing, some meals, international student ID, student support services, airport reception. $50 application fee. $500 nonrefundable deposit required. Financial aid available for all students: scholarships.

For More Information • Mr. Jeff Palm, Program Director, Center for International Studies, 17 New South Street, #105, Northampton, MA 01060; *Phone:* 413-582-0407; *Fax:* 413-582-0327. *E-mail:* jpalm@cisabroad.com. *World Wide Web:* http://www.cisabroad.com/

CENTRAL COLLEGE ABROAD
CENTRAL COLLEGE ABROAD IN LONDON, ENGLAND

Hosted by Birkbeck College, University of London, City Lit, Morley College, University of North London

Academic Focus • Art history, business administration/management, communications, computer science, drama/theater, education, engineering, English, environmental science/studies, health-care management, international affairs, international business, law and legal studies, liberal studies, literature, mathematics, music, philosophy, political science and government, psychology, science, social sciences.

Program Information • Students attend classes at Birkbeck College, University of London, University of North London, City Lit, Morley College. Scheduled travel to Stratford-upon-Avon, the Cotswolds, Liverpool, Leeds and the Yorkshire Dales; field trips to Stonehenge, Bath, Warwick Castle, Greenwich, a walking tour of London, a panoramic tour of London.

Sessions • Fall, spring, yearlong.

Eligibility Requirements • Minimum age 18; open to sophomores, juniors, seniors, adults; 2.5 GPA; 2 letters of recommendation; good academic standing at home school; study abroad approval form; transcript; Student Life endorsement.

Living Arrangements • Students live in a residence in the heart of London. Quarters are shared with host institution students. Meals are taken on one's own, in residences, in central dining facility, in restaurants.

Costs (2003-2004) • One term: $12,825. Yearlong program: $25,650; includes tuition, housing, some meals, excursions, international student ID, student support services, two-zone tube pass for London subway system. $25 application fee. $350 nonrefundable deposit required. Financial aid available for all students: scholarships.

For More Information • Office of International Education, Central College Abroad, 812 University Street, Pella, IA 50219; *Phone:* 800-831-3629; *Fax:* 641-628-5375. *E-mail:* studyabroad@central.edu. *World Wide Web:* http://www.central.edu/abroad/

CENTRAL SAINT MARTINS COLLEGE OF ART AND DESIGN
SEMESTER STUDY ABROAD PROGRAM

Hosted by Central Saint Martins College of Art and Design

Academic Focus • Art, ceramics and pottery, commercial art, costume design, crafts, design and applied arts, drama/theater, drawing/painting, fashion design, fine/studio arts, performing arts, textiles, visual and performing arts.

Program Information • Students attend classes at Central Saint Martins College of Art and Design. Optional travel to Milan, Paris, Tokyo, destinations within the United Kingdom at an extra cost.

Sessions • Fall, spring, yearlong, spring/summer term.

Eligibility Requirements • Minimum age 18; open to sophomores, juniors, seniors, graduate students; major in art, design; 3.0 GPA; 2 letters of recommendation; good academic standing at home school; slide portfolio.

Living Arrangements • Students live in host institution dormitories, locally rented apartments. Quarters are shared with host

institution students. Meals are taken on one's own, in residences, in central dining facility, in restaurants.

Costs (2003-2004) • One term: £3150. Yearlong program: £9450; includes tuition, lab equipment, student support services. £250 nonrefundable deposit required.

For More Information • Ms. Naomi Davies, Study Abroad Administrator, Central Saint Martins College of Art and Design, Developments at Central Saint Martins, Southampton Row, London WCIB 4AP, England; *Phone:* +44 20-7514 7015; *Fax:* +44 20-7514 7016. *E-mail:* shortcourse@csm.linst.ac.uk. *World Wide Web:* http://www.csm.linst.ac.uk/

CHELSEA COLLEGE OF ART AND DESIGN
SEMESTER STUDY ABROAD

Hosted by Chelsea College of Art and Design

Academic Focus • Design and applied arts, drawing/painting, fine/studio arts, graphic design/illustration, interior design, textiles.

Program Information • Students attend classes at Chelsea College of Art and Design.

Sessions • Fall, spring, yearlong, fall and spring.

Eligibility Requirements • Minimum age 19; open to sophomores, juniors, seniors, graduate students, adults; major in art/design-related field; 3.0 GPA; 1 letter of recommendation; portfolio; transcript; completed application.

Living Arrangements • Students live in host institution dormitories, locally rented apartments. Quarters are shared with host institution students. Meals are taken on one's own, in residences.

Costs (2004-2005) • One term: £3100 ; £6200 for two terms. Yearlong program: £9300; includes tuition, student support services. £250 nonrefundable deposit required.

For More Information • Ms. Kate Ibbotson, Marketing and Semester Study Abroad, Chelsea College of Art and Design, Camberwell and Chelsea Study Abroad Office, The London Institute, Millbank, London SW1P 4RJ, England; *Phone:* +44 020-7514 8514; *Fax:* +44 020-7514 6315. *E-mail:* k.ibbotson@arts.ac.uk. *World Wide Web:* http://www.chelsea.linst.ac.uk/studyabroad/

CIEE
CIEE STUDY CENTER AT UNIVERSITY OF WESTMINISTER, LONDON, ENGLAND–LONDON UNIVERSITIES PROGRAM

Hosted by University of Westminster, Goldsmiths College, University of London

Academic Focus • Full curriculum.

Program Information • Students attend classes at University of Westminster, Goldsmiths College, University of London. Scheduled travel to Paris, Dublin, Wales; field trips to sites around London.

Sessions • Fall, spring, yearlong.

Eligibility Requirements • Open to sophomores, juniors, seniors; 3.0 GPA; 2 letters of recommendation.

Living Arrangements • Students live in host institution dormitories. Quarters are shared with host institution students, students from other programs. Meals are taken on one's own, in central dining facility, in restaurants.

Costs (2003-2004) • One term: $10,500 for Goldsmiths; $11,250 for Westminster. Yearlong program: $19,500; includes tuition, housing, insurance, excursions, student support services, pre-departure advising, host institution student card, cultural activities, optional on-site pick-up. $30 application fee. $300 deposit required. Financial aid available for all students: minority student scholarships, travel grants.

For More Information • Ms. Hannah McChesney, Admissions Officer, Europe, Middle East, and Africa, CIEE, 7 Custom House Street, 3rd Floor, Portland, ME 04101; *Phone:* 800-40-STUDY; *Fax:* 207-553-7699. *E-mail:* studyinfo@ciee.org. *World Wide Web:* http://www.ciee.org/isp/

COLBY COLLEGE, BATES COLLEGE AND BOWDOIN COLLEGE
CBB LONDON CENTRE

Hosted by University of East London

Academic Focus • Biomedical sciences, English, history, performing arts, political science and government, psychology.

Program Information • Students attend classes at University of East London. Scheduled travel to Edinburgh, Cork, Paris, Brussels, Amsterdam; field trips to Cambridge, Hampton Court, Stratford, Oxford.

Sessions • Fall, spring.

Eligibility Requirements • Open to juniors; 2.7 GPA; 1 letter of recommendation; good academic standing at home school.

Living Arrangements • Students live in locally rented apartments. Meals are taken on one's own, in residences.

Costs (2002-2003) • One term: $17,900; includes tuition, housing, all meals, insurance, excursions, international airfare, books and class materials, lab equipment, international student ID, student support services. $500 nonrefundable deposit required. Financial aid available for students from sponsoring institution: scholarships, loans.

For More Information • Ms. Claire Allum, CBB Coordinator, Colby College, Bates College and Bowdoin College, CBB Off-Campus Study, Bowdoin College, 4850 College Station, Brunswick, ME 04011-8439; *Phone:* 207-725-3899; *Fax:* 207-275-3988. *E-mail:* cbbawau@bowdoin.edu

COLLEGE CONSORTIUM FOR INTERNATIONAL STUDIES–SUNY ROCKLAND COMMUNITY COLLEGE AND MONTANA STATE UNIVERSITY
CCIS PROGRAM AT KINGSTON UNIVERSITY, LONDON, ENGLAND

Hosted by Kingston University

Academic Focus • Art, British studies, business administration/management, computer science, design and applied arts, drama/theater, engineering, English literature, geography, information science, music, philosophy, science, social sciences, women's studies.

Program Information • Students attend classes at Kingston University. Field trips to Stonehenge, Hampton Court Palace, Kew Gardens, the Globe Theatre, the Museum of London.

Sessions • Fall, spring, yearlong.

Eligibility Requirements • Minimum age 18; open to freshmen, sophomores, juniors, seniors; 2.5 GPA; 2 letters of recommendation; good academic standing at home school.

Living Arrangements • Students live in host institution dormitories, host family homes. Quarters are shared with host institution students. Meals are taken on one's own, in residences, in restaurants.

Costs (2004-2005) • One term: $4560 for fall term; $5590 for spring. Yearlong program: $10,150; includes tuition, some meals, insurance, international student ID, student support services, transportation from airport. $400 nonrefundable deposit required. Financial aid available for students from sponsoring institution: scholarships, loans.

For More Information • Ms. Melissa Gluckmann, Coordinator of Study Abroad, College Consortium for International Studies–SUNY Rockland Community College and Montana State University, 145 College Road, Suffern, NY 10901; *Phone:* 845-574-4205; *Fax:* 845-574-4423. *E-mail:* study-abroad@sunyrockland.edu. *World Wide Web:* http://www.ccisabroad.org/. Students may also apply through Montana State University, Office of International Programs, 400 Culbertson Hall, Bozeman, MT 59717.

COLLEGE CONSORTIUM FOR INTERNATIONAL STUDIES–SUNY ROCKLAND COMMUNITY COLLEGE AND MONTANA STATE UNIVERSITY
CCIS PROGRAM AT THAMES VALLEY UNIVERSITY, LONDON

Hosted by Thames Valley University

Academic Focus • Accounting, advertising and public relations, business administration/management, criminal justice, culinary arts, film and media studies, hospitality services, human resources, information science, journalism, marketing, music, music performance, photography, psychology, tourism and travel.

Program Information • Students attend classes at Thames Valley University. Field trips to Stonehenge, Salisbury, Windsor Castle, Hampton Court, Oxford, Blenheim Palace, Canterbury, Dover Castle; optional travel to Scotland, Paris, Amsterdam, a European tour at an extra cost.

Sessions • Fall, spring, yearlong.
Eligibility Requirements • Minimum age 18; open to freshmen, sophomores, juniors, seniors; 2.5 GPA; 3 letters of recommendation; good academic standing at home school.
Living Arrangements • Students live in host family homes. Quarters are shared with host institution students. Meals are taken on one's own, with host family, in residences, in restaurants.
Costs (2004-2005) • One term: $6795 for fall term; $7795 for spring. Yearlong program: $14,590; includes tuition, housing, some meals, insurance, excursions, books and class materials, international student ID, transportation from airport. $400 nonrefundable deposit required. Financial aid available for all students: scholarships, loans, federal and state grants.
For More Information • Ms. Melissa Gluckmann, Coordinator of Study Abroad, College Consortium for International Studies, 145 College Road, Suffern, NY 10901; *Phone:* 845-574-4205; *Fax:* 845-574-4423. *E-mail:* study-abroad@sunyrockland.edu. *World Wide Web:* http://www.ccisabroad.org/. Students may also apply through Montana State University, Office of International Programs, 400 Culbertson Hall, Bozeman, MT 59717.

CULTURAL EXPERIENCES ABROAD (CEA)
STUDY ARTS AND SCIENCES IN LONDON

Hosted by London Metropolitan University
Academic Focus • Full curriculum.
Program Information • Students attend classes at London Metropolitan University. Field trips to Oxford, Stratford-upon-Avon, Stonehenge, Bath, Brighton, Brugge; optional travel to Edinburgh, Amsterdam, Dublin, Swansea, Paris at an extra cost.
Sessions • Fall, spring, yearlong.
Eligibility Requirements • Minimum age 18; open to sophomores, juniors, seniors; 2.7 GPA; 1 letter of recommendation.
Living Arrangements • Students live in locally rented apartments. Quarters are shared with host institution students. Meals are taken on one's own, in residences, in central dining facility, in restaurants.
Costs (2003-2004) • One term: $10,995–$11,495. Yearlong program: $21,095; includes tuition, housing, insurance, excursions, student support services, University ID, airport pick-up, travelcard, social and immersion activities. $50 application fee. $400 nonrefundable deposit required.
For More Information • Cultural Experiences Abroad (CEA), 1400 East Southern Avenue, Suite B-108, Tempe, AZ 85282-8011; *Phone:* 480-557-7900; *Fax:* 480-557-7926. *E-mail:* petersons@gowithcea. com. *World Wide Web:* http://www.gowithcea.com/

CULTURAL EXPERIENCES ABROAD (CEA)
STUDY LIBERAL ARTS AND BUSINESS IN LONDON

Hosted by Middlesex University
Academic Focus • Full curriculum.
Program Information • Students attend classes at Middlesex University. Field trips to Bath, Stonehenge, Brugge, Cambridge, Brighton, Stratford-upon-Avon.
Sessions • Fall, spring, yearlong.
Eligibility Requirements • Minimum age 18; open to sophomores, juniors, seniors; 2.7 GPA.
Living Arrangements • Students live in host institution dormitories. Quarters are shared with host institution students. Meals are taken on one's own, in residences, in central dining facility, in restaurants.
Costs (2003-2004) • One term: contact sponsor for cost. Yearlong program: contact sponsor for cost. $50 application fee. $400 nonrefundable deposit required.
For More Information • Cultural Experiences Abroad (CEA), 1400 East Southern Avenue, Suite B-108, Tempe, AZ 85282-8011; *Phone:* 480-557-7900; *Fax:* 480-557-7926. *E-mail:* petersons@gowithcea. com. *World Wide Web:* http://www.gowithcea.com/

CULTURAL EXPERIENCES ABROAD (CEA)
STUDY LIBERAL ARTS, BUSINESS, AND SCIENCE IN LONDON

Hosted by University of Westminster
Academic Focus • Full curriculum.
Program Information • Students attend classes at University of Westminster. Field trips to Oxford, Stratford-upon-Avon, Stonehenge,

Bath, Brighton, Canterbury, Brugge; optional travel to Edinburgh, Amsterdam, Dublin, Swansea, Paris at an extra cost.
Sessions • Fall, spring, yearlong.
Eligibility Requirements • Minimum age 18; open to sophomores, juniors, seniors; 3.0 GPA; 2 letters of recommendation; good academic standing at home school.
Living Arrangements • Students live in locally rented apartments. Quarters are shared with host institution students. Meals are taken on one's own, in residences, in central dining facility, in restaurants.
Costs (2003-2004) • One term: $11,995–$12,593. Yearlong program: $22,995; includes tuition, housing, insurance, excursions, student support services, University ID, airport pick-up, travelcard, social and immersion activities. $50 application fee. $400 nonrefundable deposit required.
For More Information • Cultural Experiences Abroad (CEA), 1400 East Southern Avenue, Suite B-108, Tempe, AZ 85282-8011; *Phone:* 480-557-7900; *Fax:* 480-557-7926. *E-mail:* petersons@gowithcea. com. *World Wide Web:* http://www.gowithcea.com/

DOMINICAN UNIVERSITY
FALL SEMESTER IN LONDON PROGRAM

Academic Focus • Art, business administration/management, chemical sciences, communications, drama/theater, English, fashion design, finance, history, international business, liberal studies, literature, political science and government, science, social sciences, sociology.
Program Information • Faculty members are local instructors hired by the sponsor. Scheduled travel to York, the Lake District, Edinburgh, Oxford; field trips to Stratford-upon-Avon, Bath, Canterbury, Cambridge.
Sessions • Fall.
Eligibility Requirements • Open to juniors, seniors; 2.9 GPA; 3 letters of recommendation; good academic standing at home school; medical report.
Living Arrangements • Students live in host institution dormitories. Quarters are shared with students from other programs. Meals are taken on one's own, in residences, in restaurants.
Costs (2003) • One term: $12,725; includes tuition, housing, excursions, student support services. $25 application fee. $400 refundable deposit required. Financial aid available for students from sponsoring institution: scholarships, loans.
For More Information • Ms. Pat Klbecka, Adjunct Director, Study Abroad, Dominican University, 7900 West Division Street, River Forest, IL 60305-1066; *Phone:* 708-524-6814; *Fax:* 708-366-5360. *E-mail:* intstudy@dom.edu. *World Wide Web:* http://www.dom.edu/academics/studyabroad.asp?nav_id=3229&snav_id=2014

DREW UNIVERSITY
LONDON SEMESTER

Academic Focus • British studies, drama/theater, history, literature, political science and government.
Program Information • Faculty members are drawn from the sponsor's U.S. staff and local instructors hired by the sponsor. Field trips to Stratford-upon-Avon, Oxford, Stonehenge, Cambridge; optional travel to Wales, Ireland, Scotland at an extra cost.
Sessions • Fall.
Eligibility Requirements • Open to sophomores, juniors, seniors; 2.7 GPA; 1 letter of recommendation; good academic standing at home school; personal statement.
Living Arrangements • Students live in locally rented apartments. Meals are taken on one's own, in residences.
Costs (2003) • One term: $17,775; includes tuition, housing, all meals, insurance, excursions, student support services, health service, Underground pass, library memberships, cultural events. $25 application fee. $300 nonrefundable deposit required. Financial aid available for all students: scholarships.
For More Information • Mr. Carlo Colecchia, Director, Drew University, International and Off-Campus Programs, 36 Madison Avenue, Madison, NJ 07940; *Phone:* 973-408-3438; *Fax:* 973-408-3768. *E-mail:* intlprog@drew.edu. *World Wide Web:* http://www.depts.drew.edu/offcamp/

DREXEL UNIVERSITY
DREXEL IN LONDON: BUSINESS AND ADMINISTRATION

Academic Focus • Business administration/management, finance, international business, marketing.

Program Information • Faculty members are drawn from the sponsor's U.S. staff and local instructors hired by the sponsor. Field trips to museums, financial institutions, a football game, the theatre; optional travel to Scotland, Dublin, Wales, Oxford, Bath at an extra cost.

Sessions • Fall, spring, winter, internships available after 3 or 6 months of study.

Eligibility Requirements • Open to sophomores, juniors, seniors; 2.5 GPA; 2 letters of recommendation; good academic standing at home school; essay; résumé if interested in internship program; approval of home institution.

Living Arrangements • Students live in host institution dormitories, program-owned apartments. Quarters are shared with students from other programs. Meals are taken on one's own, in residences, in restaurants.

Costs (2003-2004) • One term: $9750 ($13,750 for 6 month study/internship program); includes tuition, housing, student support services. $35 application fee. $300 nonrefundable deposit required. Financial aid available for all students: grants.

For More Information • Ms. Daniela Ascarelli, Study Abroad Director, Drexel University, 3141 Chestnut Street, 2-230, Philadelphia, PA 19104; *Phone:* 215-895-1704; *Fax:* 215-895-6184. *E-mail:* studyabroad@drexel.edu. *World Wide Web:* http://www.drexel.edu/Studyabroad/

DREXEL UNIVERSITY
DREXEL IN LONDON: DESIGN AND MERCHANDISING

Academic Focus • Design and applied arts, fashion merchandising, interior design, marketing.

Program Information • Faculty members are drawn from the sponsor's U.S. staff and local instructors hired by the sponsor. Field trips to fashion shows, design museums, the theatre, merchandise marketing firms; optional travel to Dublin, Bath, Oxford, Wales, Edinburgh at an extra cost.

Sessions • Fall, spring, winter, internships available after 3 or 6 months of study.

Eligibility Requirements • Open to sophomores, juniors, seniors; 2.5 GPA; 2 letters of recommendation; good academic standing at home school; essay; résumé if interested in internship program; approval of home institution.

Living Arrangements • Students live in host institution dormitories, program-owned apartments. Quarters are shared with students from other programs. Meals are taken on one's own, in residences, in restaurants.

Costs (2003-2004) • One term: $9750 ($13,750 for 6 month study/internship program); includes tuition, housing, student support services. $35 application fee. $300 nonrefundable deposit required. Financial aid available for all students: grants.

For More Information • Ms. Daniela Ascarelli, Study Abroad Director, Drexel University, 3141 Chestnut Street, 2-230, Philadelphia, PA 19104; *Phone:* 215-895-1704; *Fax:* 215-895-6184. *E-mail:* studyabroad@drexel.edu. *World Wide Web:* http://www.drexel.edu/Studyabroad/

DREXEL UNIVERSITY
DREXEL IN LONDON: HOTEL AND RESTAURANT MANAGEMENT, CULINARY ARTS

Academic Focus • Business administration/management, culinary arts, hotel and restaurant management, marketing.

Program Information • Faculty members are drawn from the sponsor's U.S. staff and local instructors hired by the sponsor. Field trips to vineyards, a Michelin one-star restaurant, a brewery, Vinopolis; optional travel to Bath, Dublin, Oxford, Wales, Edinburgh at an extra cost.

Sessions • Fall, spring, winter, internships available after 3 or 6 months of study.

Eligibility Requirements • Open to sophomores, juniors, seniors; 2.5 GPA; 2 letters of recommendation; good academic standing at home school; essay; résumé if interested in internship program; approval of home institution.

Living Arrangements • Students live in host institution dormitories, program-owned apartments. Quarters are shared with students from other programs. Meals are taken on one's own, in residences, in restaurants.

Costs (2003-2004) • One term: $9750 ($13,750 for 6 month study/internship program); includes tuition, housing, student support services. $35 application fee. $300 nonrefundable deposit required. Financial aid available for all students: grants.

For More Information • Ms. Daniela Ascarelli, Study Abroad Director, Drexel University, 3141 Chestnut Street, 2-230, Philadelphia, PA 19104; *Phone:* 215-895-1704; *Fax:* 215-895-6184. *E-mail:* studyabroad@drexel.edu. *World Wide Web:* http://www.drexel.edu/Studyabroad/

DREXEL UNIVERSITY
DREXEL IN LONDON: INTERNATIONAL BUSINESS

Academic Focus • Business administration/management, finance, international business, marketing.

Program Information • Faculty members are drawn from the sponsor's U.S. staff and local instructors hired by the sponsor. Field trips to museums, financial institutions, football games, the theatre; optional travel to Bath, Oxford, Cambridge, Stonehenge at an extra cost.

Sessions • Fall, spring, winter, internships available after 3 or 6 months of study.

Eligibility Requirements • Open to sophomores, juniors, seniors; 2 letters of recommendation; good academic standing at home school; essay; résumé if interested in internship programs; approval of home institution.

Living Arrangements • Students live in host institution dormitories, locally rented apartments. Quarters are shared with students from other programs. Meals are taken on one's own, in residences, in restaurants.

Costs (2002-2003) • One term: $8850 ($12,950 for 6 month study/internship program); includes tuition, housing, student support services. $35 application fee. $300 nonrefundable deposit required. Financial aid available for all students: grants.

For More Information • Ms. Daniela Ascarelli, Study Abroad Director, Drexel University, 3141 Chestnut Street, 2-230, Philadelphia, PA 19104; *Phone:* 215-895-1704; *Fax:* 215-895-6184. *E-mail:* studyabroad@drexel.edu. *World Wide Web:* http://www.drexel.edu/Studyabroad/

ECKERD COLLEGE
ECKERD IN LONDON

Held at Eckerd College–London

Academic Focus • Art history, drama/theater, economics, history, literature, political science and government.

Program Information • Classes are held on the campus of Eckerd College–London. Faculty members are drawn from the sponsor's U.S. staff and local instructors hired by the sponsor. Field trips to Stratford-upon-Avon, Cambridge; optional travel to Europe, Ireland, Scotland at an extra cost.

Sessions • Fall, spring.

Eligibility Requirements • Open to sophomores, juniors, seniors; 2.8 GPA; good academic standing at home school.

Living Arrangements • Students live in the Eckerd London Study Centre. Quarters are shared with host institution students. Meals are taken as a group, on one's own, in central dining facility, in restaurants.

Costs (2003-2004) • One term: $15,116; includes tuition, housing, some meals, international student ID. Financial aid available for students from sponsoring institution: scholarships, work study, loans.

For More Information • Ms. Diane Ferris, Director, Eckerd College, International Education, 4200 54th Avenue, South, St. Petersburg, FL 33711; *Phone:* 727-864-8381; *Fax:* 727-864-7995. *E-mail:* ferrisdl@eckerd.edu. *World Wide Web:* http://www.eckerd.edu/

EUROPEAN BUSINESS SCHOOL LONDON
EUROPEAN BUSINESS SCHOOL LONDON

Hosted by European Business School London

Academic Focus • Business administration/management, international business.

Program Information • Students attend classes at European Business School London. Field trips to the Bank of England, the British museum; optional travel to Wales, Scotland, Europe, Ireland, skiing trips at an extra cost.
Sessions • Fall, spring, yearlong, 2-week non-credit terms offering prerequisite courses available May–August.
Eligibility Requirements • Minimum age 18; open to freshmen, sophomores, juniors, seniors, graduate students, adults; 2 letters of recommendation; good academic standing at home school.
Living Arrangements • Students live in host institution dormitories, locally rented apartments, host family homes. Quarters are shared with host institution students, students from other programs. Meals are taken as a group, in residences, in central dining facility.
Costs (2002-2003) • One term: £5175. Yearlong program: £10,350; includes tuition, student support services. £300 nonrefundable deposit required. Financial aid available for all students: scholarships, work study.
For More Information • Ms. Rachel L. Waites, Senior Admissions and Business Development Officer, European Business School London, Regents Park, London NW1 4NS, England; *Phone:* +44 20-7487-7454; *Fax:* +44 20-7487-7465. *E-mail:* ebs@regents.ac.uk. *World Wide Web:* http://www.regents.ac.uk/

FLORIDA STATE UNIVERSITY
ENGLAND: LONDON PROGRAM

Hosted by Florida State University–London Study Center
Academic Focus • Anthropology, art history, drama/theater, economics, English, history, information science, liberal studies, mathematics, music, political science and government, psychology, teaching.
Program Information • Students attend classes at Florida State University–London Study Center. Scheduled travel to Paris; field trips to Oxford, Stonehenge, Salisbury, Bath, Blenheim, Cambridge, Canterbury, Stratford-upon-Avon.
Sessions • Fall, spring, yearlong, application deadlines differ for internship applicants.
Eligibility Requirements • Open to freshmen, sophomores, juniors, seniors; 2.5 GPA; good academic standing at home school.
Living Arrangements • Students live in program-owned apartments. Quarters are shared with host institution students. Meals are taken on one's own, in residences, in restaurants.
Costs (2002-2003) • One term: $8500. Yearlong program: $17,000; includes tuition, housing, insurance, excursions, international student ID, student support services, program T-shirt or cap. $50 application fee. $500 nonrefundable deposit required. Financial aid available for students from sponsoring institution: scholarships, work study, loans.
For More Information • International Programs, Florida State University, A5500 University Center, Tallahassee, FL 32306-2420; *Phone:* 850-644-3272; *Fax:* 850-644-8817. *E-mail:* intprog@www.fsu.edu. *World Wide Web:* http://www.international.fsu.edu/

FOUNDATION FOR INTERNATIONAL EDUCATION
LONDON INTERNSHIP PROGRAM

Hosted by Foundation for International Education
Academic Focus • British studies, design and applied arts, English literature, history, intercultural studies, international business, marketing, political science and government.
Program Information • Students attend classes at Foundation for International Education. Field trips to Oxford, Cambridge, Bath; optional travel to Prague, Paris, Wales, Scotland.
Sessions • Fall, spring.
Eligibility Requirements • Minimum age 18; open to sophomores, juniors, seniors; 2.75 GPA; advisor's approval.
Living Arrangements • Students live in host institution dormitories, program-owned apartments. Quarters are shared with students from other programs. Meals are taken on one's own, in residences, in restaurants.
Costs (2004-2005) • One term: $9815 ($10,190 with optional transcript fee); includes tuition, housing, insurance, excursions, student support services, membership of Imperial College Student Union, travel pass, co- and extra-curricular program, internship placement. $500 deposit required.

For More Information • Ms. Erika Richards, Director of Program Development, Foundation for International Education, PMB 326, 5 Bessom Street, Marblehead, MA 01945; *Phone:* 781-631-6153. *E-mail:* studyabroad@fie.co.uk. *World Wide Web:* http://www.fie.org.uk/

FOUNDATION FOR INTERNATIONAL EDUCATION
LONDON STUDY PROGRAM

Hosted by Foundation for International Education
Academic Focus • British studies, design and applied arts, English literature, history, intercultural studies, international business, marketing, political science and government.
Program Information • Students attend classes at Foundation for International Education. Field trips to Oxford, Cambridge, Bath; optional travel to Prague, Paris, Wales, Scotland at an extra cost.
Sessions • Fall, spring.
Eligibility Requirements • Minimum age 18; open to sophomores, juniors, seniors; 2.75 GPA; advisor's approval.
Living Arrangements • Students live in host institution dormitories, program-owned apartments. Quarters are shared with students from other programs. Meals are taken on one's own, in residences, in restaurants.
Costs (2004-2005) • One term: $9815 ($10,190 with optional transcript fee); includes tuition, housing, insurance, excursions, student support services, membership of Imperial College Student Union, travel pass, co- and extra-curricular program. $500 deposit required.
For More Information • Ms. Erika Richards, Director of Program Development, Foundation for International Education, PMB 326, 5 Bessom Street, Marblehead, MA 01945; *Phone:* 781-631-6153. *E-mail:* studyabroad@fie.co.uk. *World Wide Web:* http://www.fie.org.uk/

GOLDSMITHS COLLEGE, UNIVERSITY OF LONDON
STUDY IN LONDON

Hosted by Goldsmiths College, University of London
Academic Focus • Anthropology, art, art administration, communications, computer science, drama/theater, education, English, history, mathematics, music, psychology, social sciences, Spanish studies.
Program Information • Students attend classes at Goldsmiths College, University of London. Field trips to the theatre.
Sessions • Fall, spring, yearlong, spring/summer.
Eligibility Requirements • Minimum age 18; open to freshmen, sophomores, juniors, seniors, graduate students; 2.8 GPA; 1 letter of recommendation; minimum 3.0 GPA in major.
Living Arrangements • Students live in host institution dormitories, locally rented apartments. Quarters are shared with host institution students. Meals are taken in residences, in central dining facility.
Costs (2003-2004) • One term: $9431 for fall and spring terms; $6591–$8652 for spring/summer term. Yearlong program: $22,000; includes tuition, housing, books and class materials, student support services, local travel, food shopping allowance.
For More Information • Ms. Jill Thorn, Assistant Registrar, Goldsmiths College, University of London, International Office, New Cross, London SE 14 6NW, England; *Phone:* +44 207-919-7700; *Fax:* +44 207-919-7704. *E-mail:* j.thorn@gold.ac.uk. *World Wide Web:* http://www.goldsmiths/study-options/study-in-london/. Students may also apply through InterStudy, Admissions Office, 42 Milsom Street, Bath BA1 1DN, England; Arcadia University, Center for Education Abroad, 450 South Easton Road, Glenside, PA 19038-3295.

HARDING UNIVERSITY
HARDING UNIVERSITY IN LONDON, ENGLAND

Academic Focus • English literature, liberal studies, religious studies.
Program Information • Faculty members are drawn from the sponsor's U.S. staff. Scheduled travel to England, Scotland, Ireland; field trips to Stonehenge, sites close to London; optional travel to western Europe at an extra cost.
Sessions • Fall.

Eligibility Requirements • Open to sophomores, juniors, seniors; 2.0 GPA; 2 letters of recommendation; good academic standing at home school.

Living Arrangements • Students live in locally rented apartments. Meals are taken as a group, in central dining facility.

Costs (2003) • One term: $13,000; includes tuition, housing, some meals, excursions, international airfare, international student ID. $200 application fee. Financial aid available for students from sponsoring institution: scholarships, work study, loans.

For More Information • Dr. Jeffrey T. Hopper, Dean of International Programs, Harding University, 900 East Center Street, Box 10754, Searcy, AR 72149; *Phone:* 501-279-4529; *Fax:* 501-279-4184. *E-mail:* intlprograms@harding.edu

HOLLINS UNIVERSITY
HOLLINS ABROAD LONDON

Hosted by City University, London Metropolitan University

Academic Focus • Architecture, art history, drama/theater, English, full curriculum, history, political science and government.

Program Information • Students attend classes at City University, London Metropolitan University. Classes are also held on the campus of College Hall, University of London. Scheduled travel to Bath, York, Edinburgh; field trips to sites in London, Stratford-upon-Avon, Westminster Abbey, Houses of Parliament, the National Gallery, the Tate Museum, other museums; optional travel to Amsterdam, Venice, Barcelona, Rome, Prague at an extra cost.

Sessions • Fall, spring.

Eligibility Requirements • Minimum age 18; open to sophomores, juniors, seniors; 2.5 GPA; 2 letters of recommendation; good academic standing at home school; approval from home institution.

Living Arrangements • Students live in host institution dormitories, locally rented apartments, host family homes. Quarters are shared with host institution students, students from other programs. Meals are taken on one's own, with host family, in residences, in central dining facility, in restaurants.

Costs (2004) • One term: $13,995; includes tuition, housing, all meals, excursions, international student ID, student support services, local transportation (Tube and bus pass), some books and class materials. $25 application fee. $200 nonrefundable deposit required. Financial aid available for students from sponsoring institution: scholarships, loans.

For More Information • Ms. Lorraine Fleck, Director of International Programs, Hollins University, PO Box 9597, Roanoke, VA 24020; *Phone:* 800-511-6612; *Fax:* 540-362-6693. *E-mail:* abroad@hollins.edu. *World Wide Web:* http://www.hollins.edu/

HURON UNIVERSITY USA IN LONDON
STUDY ABROAD PROGRAM

Hosted by Huron University USA in London

Academic Focus • Full curriculum.

Program Information • Students attend classes at Huron University USA in London. Field trips to museums, galleries, places of interest throughout Great Britain, the theatre; optional travel to Scotland, Ireland, France, Spain, Italy, Tenerife at an extra cost.

Sessions • Fall, spring, yearlong.

Eligibility Requirements • Minimum age 17; open to freshmen, sophomores, juniors, seniors, graduate students, adults; 2 letters of recommendation; good academic standing at home school; official transcript.

Living Arrangements • Students live in host institution dormitories. Quarters are shared with host institution students, students from other programs. Meals are taken as a group, in residences, in restaurants.

Costs (2003-2004) • One term: $8995. Yearlong program: $17,990; includes tuition, housing, international student ID, student support services. $60 application fee. $1300 deposit required. Financial aid available for all students: loans.

For More Information • Mr. Jack Ricard, U.S. Director of Admissions, Huron University USA in London, 10 South Windjammer, Naperville, IL 60564; *Phone:* 630-983-6902; *Fax:* 630-983-6998. *E-mail:* usa@huron.ac.uk. *World Wide Web:* http://www.huron.ac.uk/. Students may also apply through Huron University USA in London, 58 Princes Gate, Exhibition Road, London SW7 2PG, England.

IES, INSTITUTE FOR THE INTERNATIONAL EDUCATION OF STUDENTS
IES–LONDON

Hosted by Regents Business School London, University of Oxford–Harris Manchester College, Institute for the International Education of Students (IES)–London, London Academy of Music and Dramatic Art, Slade School of Fine Art, University of London–The Courtauld Institute of Art, School of Oriental and African Studies–University of London, Queen Mary, University of London, City University

Academic Focus • Full curriculum.

Program Information • Students attend classes at Regents Business School London, University of Oxford–Harris Manchester College, London Academy of Music and Dramatic Art, Slade School of Fine Art, University of London–The Courtauld Institute of Art, School of Oriental and African Studies–University of London, Queen Mary, University of London, City University, Institute for the International Education of Students (IES)–London. Field trips to museums; optional travel to the Lake District, Wales, Northern Ireland, Canterbury, York, Scottish Highlands, Edinburgh, Cornwall, Bath, Oxford at an extra cost.

Sessions • Fall, spring, yearlong, full-integration year.

Eligibility Requirements • Minimum age 18; open to sophomores, juniors, seniors, graduate students, adults; 3.0 GPA; 1 letter of recommendation; good academic standing at home school.

Living Arrangements • Students live in host family homes, the IES London Student Residence Hall. Quarters are shared with host institution students. Meals are taken on one's own, with host family, in residences, in restaurants.

Costs (2003-2004) • One term: $12,300. Yearlong program: $22,140; includes tuition, housing, excursions, student support services, partial insurance coverage. $50 application fee. $500 nonrefundable deposit required. Financial aid available for all students: scholarships, institutional partner need-based grants.

For More Information • International Education Representative, IES, Institute for the International Education of Students, 33 North LaSalle Street, 15th Floor, Chicago, IL 60602; *Phone:* 800-995-2300; *Fax:* 312-944-1448. *E-mail:* info@iesabroad.org. *World Wide Web:* http://www.IESabroad.org/

INSTITUTE FOR STUDY ABROAD, BUTLER UNIVERSITY
CITY UNIVERSITY

Hosted by City University

Academic Focus • Full curriculum.

Program Information • Students attend classes at City University. Field trips to Stratford-upon-Avon, Bath, Brighton, the Lake District, Wales.

Sessions • Fall, spring, yearlong.

Eligibility Requirements • Open to juniors, seniors; 3.0 GPA; 1 letter of recommendation; good academic standing at home school; enrollment at an accredited American college or university.

Living Arrangements • Students live in host institution dormitories, locally rented apartments, program-owned houses. Quarters are shared with host institution students. Meals are taken on one's own, in residences, in central dining facility.

Costs (2002-2003) • One term: $9475 for fall term; $11,975 for spring. Yearlong program: $17,675; includes tuition, housing, excursions, international student ID, student support services, family visit, cultural and sporting events, pre-departure advising. $40 application fee. $500 nonrefundable deposit required. Financial aid available for all students: scholarships, travel grants.

For More Information • Institute for Study Abroad, Butler University, 1100 West 42nd Street, Suite 305, Indianapolis, IN 46208-3345; *Phone:* 800-858-0229; *Fax:* 317-940-9704. *E-mail:* study-abroad@butler.edu. *World Wide Web:* http://www.ifsa-butler.org/

INSTITUTE FOR STUDY ABROAD, BUTLER UNIVERSITY
KING'S COLLEGE LONDON, UNIVERSITY OF LONDON

Hosted by King's College London, University of London

Academic Focus • Full curriculum.

Program Information • Students attend classes at King's College London, University of London. Field trips to Stratford-upon-Avon, Ely, Bath, Brighton; optional travel to the Lake District (adventure weekend) at an extra cost.

Sessions • Fall, spring, yearlong.

Eligibility Requirements • Open to juniors, seniors; 3.0 GPA; 2 letters of recommendation; good academic standing at home school; enrollment at an accredited American college or university (some majors require additional materials and higher minimum GPA).

Living Arrangements • Students live in host institution dormitories, locally rented apartments, program-owned houses. Quarters are shared with host institution students. Meals are taken on one's own, in residences, in central dining facility.

Costs (2002-2003) • One term: $11,575. Yearlong program: $21,575; includes tuition, housing, excursions, international student ID, student support services, family visit, cultural and sporting events, pre-departure advising. $40 application fee. $500 nonrefundable deposit required. Financial aid available for all students: scholarships, travel grants.

For More Information • Institute for Study Abroad, Butler University, 1100 West 42nd Street, Suite 305, Indianapolis, IN 46208-3345; *Phone:* 800-858-0229; *Fax:* 317-940-9704. *E-mail:* study-abroad@butler.edu. *World Wide Web:* http://www.ifsa-butler.org/

INSTITUTE FOR STUDY ABROAD, BUTLER UNIVERSITY
LABAN

Hosted by Laban Centre London
Academic Focus • Dance.
Program Information • Students attend classes at Laban Centre London. Field trips to Stratford-upon-Avon, Bath, Brighton, Wales, the Lake District.

Sessions • Fall, yearlong.

Eligibility Requirements • Open to juniors, seniors; major in dance; course work in dance; 3.0 GPA; 2 letters of recommendation; good academic standing at home school; enrollment at an accredited American college or university.

Living Arrangements • Students live in program-owned apartments, program-owned houses. Quarters are shared with students from other programs. Meals are taken on one's own, in residences.

Costs (2002-2003) • One term: $11,875. Yearlong program: $23,975; includes tuition, housing, excursions, international student ID, student support services, family visit, cultural and sporting events, pre-departure advising. $40 application fee. $500 nonrefundable deposit required. Financial aid available for all students: scholarships, travel grants.

For More Information • Institute for Study Abroad, Butler University, 1100 West 42nd Street, Suite 305, Indianapolis, IN 46208-3345; *Phone:* 800-858-0229; *Fax:* 317-940-9704. *E-mail:* study-abroad@butler.edu. *World Wide Web:* http://www.ifsa-butler.org/

INSTITUTE FOR STUDY ABROAD, BUTLER UNIVERSITY
LONDON SEMESTER AT BIRKBECK, UNIVERSITY OF LONDON

Hosted by Birkbeck College, University of London
Academic Focus • Full curriculum.
Program Information • Students attend classes at Birkbeck College, University of London. Field trips to Stratford-upon-Avon, Ely, Bath, Brighton, the Lake district, Wales.

Sessions • Fall, spring.

Eligibility Requirements • Open to juniors, seniors; 3.0 GPA; 1 letter of recommendation; good academic standing at home school; enrollment at an accredited American college or university.

Living Arrangements • Students live in program-owned apartments, program-owned houses. Quarters are shared with students from other programs. Meals are taken on one's own, in residences.

Costs (2002-2003) • One term: $10,775; includes tuition, housing, excursions, international student ID, student support services, family visit, cultural and sporting events, pre-departure advising. $40 application fee. $500 nonrefundable deposit required. Financial aid available for all students: scholarships, travel grants.

For More Information • Institute for Study Abroad, Butler University, 1100 West 42nd Street, Suite 305, Indianapolis, IN

46208-3345; *Phone:* 800-858-0229; *Fax:* 317-940-9704. *E-mail:* study-abroad@butler.edu. *World Wide Web:* http://www.ifsa-butler.org/

INSTITUTE FOR STUDY ABROAD, BUTLER UNIVERSITY
MIDDLESEX UNIVERSITY

Hosted by Middlesex University
Academic Focus • Full curriculum.
Program Information • Students attend classes at Middlesex University. Field trips to Stratford-upon-Avon, Bath, Brighton; optional travel to the Lake District (adventure weekend) at an extra cost.

Sessions • Fall, spring, yearlong.

Eligibility Requirements • Open to juniors, seniors; 2.8 GPA; 1 letter of recommendation; good academic standing at home school; enrollment at an accredited American college or university.

Living Arrangements • Students live in host institution dormitories, locally rented apartments, program-owned apartments, program-owned houses. Quarters are shared with host institution students, students from other programs. Meals are taken on one's own, in residences.

Costs (2002-2003) • One term: $10,875. Yearlong program: $18,275; includes tuition, housing, excursions, international student ID, student support services, family visit, cultural and sporting events, pre-departure advising. $40 application fee. $500 nonrefundable deposit required. Financial aid available for all students: scholarships, travel grants.

For More Information • Institute for Study Abroad, Butler University, 1100 West 42nd Street, Suite 305, Indianapolis, IN 46208-3345; *Phone:* 800-858-0229; *Fax:* 317-940-9704. *E-mail:* study-abroad@butler.edu. *World Wide Web:* http://www.ifsa-butler.org/

INSTITUTE FOR STUDY ABROAD, BUTLER UNIVERSITY
QUEEN MARY, UNIVERSITY OF LONDON

Hosted by Queen Mary, University of London
Academic Focus • Full curriculum.
Program Information • Students attend classes at Queen Mary, University of London. Field trips to Stratford-upon-Avon, Ely, Bath, Brighton, the Lake district, Wales.

Sessions • Fall, spring, yearlong.

Eligibility Requirements • Open to juniors, seniors; 3.0 GPA; 1 letter of recommendation; enrollment at an accredited American college or university.

Living Arrangements • Students live in host institution dormitories, locally rented apartments. Quarters are shared with host institution students, students from other programs. Meals are taken on one's own, in residences.

Costs (2002-2003) • One term: $11,775 for fall term; $12,575 for spring. Yearlong program: $20,575; includes tuition, housing, excursions, international student ID, student support services, family visit, cultural and sporting events, pre-departure advising. $40 application fee. $500 nonrefundable deposit required. Financial aid available for all students: scholarships, travel grants.

For More Information • Institute for Study Abroad, Butler University, 1100 West 42nd Street, Suite 305, Indianapolis, IN 46208-3345; *Phone:* 800-858-0229; *Fax:* 317-940-9704. *E-mail:* study-abroad@butler.edu. *World Wide Web:* http://www.ifsa-butler.org/

INSTITUTE FOR STUDY ABROAD, BUTLER UNIVERSITY
SLADE SCHOOL OF FINE ART

Hosted by Slade School of Fine Art
Academic Focus • Drawing/painting.
Program Information • Students attend classes at Slade School of Fine Art. Field trips to Stratford-upon-Avon, Bath, Ely, Brighton, Wales.

Sessions • Fall, spring, yearlong.

ENGLAND
London

Eligibility Requirements • Open to juniors, seniors; major in studio art; 3.0 GPA; 2 letters of recommendation; good academic standing at home school; enrollment at an accredited American college or university; portfolio.

Living Arrangements • Students live in host institution dormitories, locally rented apartments, program-owned apartments, program-owned houses. Quarters are shared with host institution students, students from other programs. Meals are taken on one's own, in residences, in central dining facility.

Costs (2002–2003) • One term: $13,675 for fall term; $16,175 for spring. Yearlong program: $25,275; includes tuition, housing, excursions, international student ID, student support services, family visit, cultural and sporting events, pre-departure advising. $40 application fee. $500 nonrefundable deposit required. Financial aid available for all students: scholarships, travel grants.

For More Information • Institute for Study Abroad, Butler University, 1100 West 42nd Street, Suite 305, Indianapolis, IN 46208-3345; *Phone:* 800-858-0229; *Fax:* 317-940-9704. *E-mail:* study-abroad@butler.edu. *World Wide Web:* http://www.ifsa-butler.org/

INSTITUTE FOR STUDY ABROAD, BUTLER UNIVERSITY
SOAS, UNIVERSITY OF LONDON

Hosted by School of Oriental and African Studies–University of London

Academic Focus • Full curriculum.

Program Information • Students attend classes at School of Oriental and African Studies–University of London. Field trips to Stratford-upon-Avon, Ely, Bath, Brighton.

Sessions • Fall, spring, yearlong.

Eligibility Requirements • Open to juniors, seniors; 3.0 GPA; 2 letters of recommendation; good academic standing at home school; enrollment at an accredited American college or university.

Living Arrangements • Students live in host institution dormitories, locally rented apartments. Quarters are shared with host institution students. Meals are taken on one's own, in central dining facility.

Costs (2002–2003) • One term: $12,675 for fall term; $14,475 for spring. Yearlong program: $22,475; includes tuition, housing, excursions, international student ID, student support services, family visit, cultural and sporting events, pre-departure advising. $40 application fee. $500 nonrefundable deposit required. Financial aid available for all students: scholarships, travel grants.

For More Information • Institute for Study Abroad, Butler University, 1100 West 42nd Street, Suite 305, Indianapolis, IN 46208-3345; *Phone:* 800-858-0229; *Fax:* 317-940-9704. *E-mail:* study-abroad@butler.edu. *World Wide Web:* http://www.ifsa-butler.org/

INSTITUTE FOR STUDY ABROAD, BUTLER UNIVERSITY
UNIVERSITY COLLEGE LONDON, UNIVERSITY OF LONDON

Hosted by University College London

Academic Focus • Full curriculum.

Program Information • Students attend classes at University College London. Field trips to Stratford-upon-Avon, Ely, Bath, Brighton, Wales.

Sessions • Fall, spring, yearlong.

Eligibility Requirements • Open to juniors, seniors; 3.0 GPA; 2 letters of recommendation; good academic standing at home school; enrollment at an accredited American college or university.

Living Arrangements • Students live in host institution dormitories, locally rented apartments, program-owned apartments, program-owned houses. Quarters are shared with host institution students, students from other programs. Meals are taken on one's own, in residences, in central dining facility.

Costs (2002–2003) • One term: $12,275 for fall term; $13,975 for spring. Yearlong program: $21,275; includes tuition, housing, excursions, international student ID, student support services, family visit, cultural and sporting events, pre-departure advising. $40 application fee. $500 nonrefundable deposit required. Financial aid available for all students: scholarships, travel grants.

For More Information • Institute for Study Abroad, Butler University, 1100 West 42nd Street, Suite 305, Indianapolis, IN 46208-3345; *Phone:* 800-858-0229; *Fax:* 317-940-9704. *E-mail:* study-abroad@butler.edu. *World Wide Web:* http://www.ifsa-butler.org/

INSTITUTE FOR STUDY ABROAD, BUTLER UNIVERSITY
UNIVERSITY OF WESTMINSTER

Hosted by University of Westminster

Academic Focus • Full curriculum.

Program Information • Students attend classes at University of Westminster. Field trips to Stratford-upon-Avon, Bath, Brighton, the Lake District, Wales.

Sessions • Fall, spring, yearlong.

Eligibility Requirements • Open to juniors, seniors; 3.0 GPA; 1 letter of recommendation; good academic standing at home school; enrollment at an accredited American college or university.

Living Arrangements • Students live in host institution dormitories. Quarters are shared with host institution students. Meals are taken on one's own, in residences.

Costs (2002–2003) • One term: $11,975. Yearlong program: $19,475; includes tuition, housing, excursions, international student ID, student support services, family visit, cultural and sporting events, pre-departure advising. $40 application fee. $500 nonrefundable deposit required. Financial aid available for all students: scholarships, travel grants.

For More Information • Institute for Study Abroad, Butler University, 1100 West 42nd Street, Suite 305, Indianapolis, IN 46208-3345; *Phone:* 800-858-0229; *Fax:* 317-940-9704. *E-mail:* study-abroad@butler.edu. *World Wide Web:* http://www.ifsa-butler.org/

THE INTERNATIONAL PARTNERSHIP FOR SERVICE LEARNING
ENGLAND SERVICE–LEARNING

Hosted by University of Surrey Roehampton

Academic Focus • British studies, community service, education, English literature, European studies, international affairs, liberal studies, social sciences.

Program Information • Students attend classes at University of Surrey Roehampton. Field trips to Parliament, the East End of London, Greenwich, the Royal Observatory; optional travel to Oxford, Scotland, France at an extra cost.

Sessions • Fall, spring, yearlong.

Eligibility Requirements • Minimum age 18; open to freshmen, sophomores, juniors, seniors, graduate students, adults; 2 letters of recommendation; good academic standing at home school; evidence of maturity, responsibility.

Living Arrangements • Students live in host institution dormitories. Quarters are shared with host institution students, students from other programs. Meals are taken on one's own, in residences.

Costs (2003–2004) • One term: $9600–$9900. Yearlong program: $18,900; includes tuition, housing, some meals, student support services, service placement and supervision. $50 application fee. $250 refundable deposit required. Financial aid available for all students: federal financial aid.

For More Information • Ms. Ilana Golin, Coordinator of Student Programs, The International Partnership for Service Learning, 815 Second Avenue, Suite 315, New York, NY 10017-4594; *Phone:* 212-986-0989; *Fax:* 212-986-5039. *E-mail:* info@ipsl.org. *World Wide Web:* http://www.ipsl.org/

INTERSTUDY
GOLDSMITHS COLLEGE, UNIVERSITY OF LONDON

Hosted by Goldsmiths College, University of London

Academic Focus • Anthropology, archaeology, art, art history, communications, computer science, creative writing, design and applied arts, drama/theater, education, English, film and media studies, fine/studio arts, French language and literature, German language and literature, history, mathematics, music, political science and government, Portuguese, psychology, social sciences, Spanish language and literature, statistics.

Program Information • Students attend classes at Goldsmiths College, University of London. Scheduled travel to Bath, Stratford-upon-Avon, Warwick Castle, Oxford, Stonehenge.

Sessions • Fall, spring, yearlong, extended full-year and spring terms.

Eligibility Requirements • Minimum age 18; open to freshmen, sophomores, juniors, seniors, adults; 3.0 GPA; 2 letters of recommendation; good academic standing at home school.

Living Arrangements • Students live in host institution dormitories. Quarters are shared with host institution students. Meals are taken on one's own, in residences.

Costs (2003-2004) • One term: $12,215. Yearlong program: $20,975; includes tuition, housing, some meals, excursions, international student ID, student support services, Student Union membership, e-mail access, banking facilities, international bank transfers, transcript, cell phone. $35 application fee. $500 nonrefundable deposit required. Financial aid available for all students: scholarships, loans, stipends.

For More Information • InterStudy, Admissions Office, 63 Edward Street, Medford, MA 02155; *Phone:* 800-663-1999; *Fax:* 781-391-7463. *E-mail:* interstudy@interstudy-usa.org. *World Wide Web:* http://www.interstudy.org/

INTERSTUDY
KING'S COLLEGE, UNIVERSITY OF LONDON

Hosted by King's College London, University of London

Academic Focus • Anatomy, Arabic, biochemistry, biological/life sciences, chemical sciences, classics and classical languages, computer science, electrical engineering, English, environmental science/studies, French language and literature, geography, German language and literature, Greek, history, Italian language and literature, mathematics, mechanical engineering, music, nursing, nutrition, philosophy, physics, Portuguese, religious studies, Spanish language and literature.

Program Information • Students attend classes at King's College London, University of London. Scheduled travel to Bath, Stratford-upon-Avon, Warwick Castle, Oxford, Stonehenge.

Sessions • Fall, spring, yearlong.

Eligibility Requirements • Minimum age 18; open to freshmen, sophomores, juniors, seniors, adults; 3.3 GPA; 2 letters of recommendation; good academic standing at home school.

Living Arrangements • Students live in host institution dormitories. Quarters are shared with host institution students. Meals are taken on one's own, in residences.

Costs (2003-2004) • One term: $13,350 for fall term; $14,375 for spring. Yearlong program: $23,375; includes tuition, housing, some meals, excursions, books and class materials, international student ID, student support services, Student Union membership, e-mail access, banking facilities, international bank transfers, transcript, cell phone. $35 application fee. $500 nonrefundable deposit required. Financial aid available for all students: scholarships, loans, stipends.

For More Information • InterStudy, Admissions Office, 63 Edward Street, Medford, MA 02155; *Phone:* 800-663-1999; *Fax:* 781-391-7463. *E-mail:* interstudy@interstudy-usa.org. *World Wide Web:* http://www.interstudy.org/

INTERSTUDY
QUEEN MARY AND WESTFIELD COLLEGE, UNIVERSITY OF LONDON

Hosted by Queen Mary, University of London

Academic Focus • Biological/life sciences, business administration/management, chemical sciences, computer science, drama/theater, economics, electrical engineering, engineering, English, environmental science/studies, French language and literature, geography, German language and literature, history, law and legal studies, linguistics, mathematics, physics, political science and government, Russian language and literature.

Program Information • Students attend classes at Queen Mary, University of London. Scheduled travel to Bath, Stratford-upon-Avon, Warwick Castle, Oxford, Stonehenge.

Sessions • Fall, spring, yearlong.

Eligibility Requirements • Minimum age 18; open to freshmen, sophomores, juniors, seniors, adults; 3.0 GPA; 2 letters of recommendation; good academic standing at home school.

Living Arrangements • Students live in host institution dormitories. Quarters are shared with host institution students. Meals are taken on one's own, in residences.

Costs (2003-2004) • One term: $12,350 for fall term; $13,350 for spring. Yearlong program: $22,450; includes tuition, housing, some meals, excursions, international student ID, student support services, Student Union membership, e-mail access, banking facilities, international bank transfers, transcript, cell phone. $35 application fee. $500 nonrefundable deposit required. Financial aid available for all students: scholarships, loans, stipends.

For More Information • InterStudy, Admissions Office, 63 Edward Street, Medford, MA 02155; *Phone:* 800-663-1999; *Fax:* 781-391-7463. *E-mail:* interstudy@interstudy-usa.org. *World Wide Web:* http://www.interstudy.org/

INTERSTUDY
THE UNIVERSITY OF WESTMINSTER

Hosted by University of Westminster

Academic Focus • Architecture, biochemistry, business administration/management, computer science, design and applied arts, economics, English, environmental science/studies, film and media studies, finance, health-care management, history, human resources, law and legal studies, linguistics, management information systems, marketing, political science and government, psychology, science, social sciences, tourism and travel.

Program Information • Students attend classes at University of Westminster. Scheduled travel to Bath, Stratford-upon-Avon, Warwick Castle, Oxford, Stonehenge.

Sessions • Fall, spring, yearlong.

Eligibility Requirements • Minimum age 18; open to freshmen, sophomores, juniors, seniors, adults; 3.0 GPA; 2 letters of recommendation; good academic standing at home school.

Living Arrangements • Students live in host institution dormitories. Quarters are shared with host institution students. Meals are taken on one's own, in residences.

Costs (2003-2004) • One term: $11,975 for fall term; $13,315 for spring. Yearlong program: $21,550; includes tuition, housing, some meals, excursions, lab equipment, international student ID, student support services, Student Union membership, e-mail access, banking facilities, international bank transfers, transcript, cell phone. $35 application fee. $500 nonrefundable deposit required. Financial aid available for all students: scholarships, loans, stipends.

For More Information • InterStudy, Admissions Office, 63 Edward Street, Medford, MA 02155; *Phone:* 800-663-1999; *Fax:* 781-391-7463. *E-mail:* interstudy@interstudy-usa.org. *World Wide Web:* http://www.interstudy.org/

ITHACA COLLEGE
ITHACA COLLEGE LONDON CENTER

Hosted by Ithaca College–London Center

Academic Focus • Art history, British studies, Celtic studies, communications, drama/theater, English literature, film and media studies, history, interdisciplinary studies, international affairs, international business, Irish literature, literature, music, political science and government, psychology, sociology.

Program Information • Students attend classes at Ithaca College–London Center. Scheduled travel to Dublin, Edinburgh; field trips to Stratford-upon-Avon, Bath; optional travel to Edinburgh, Dublin, Paris at an extra cost.

Sessions • Fall, spring, yearlong.

Eligibility Requirements • Open to sophomores, juniors, seniors; 2.5 GPA; 2 letters of recommendation; good academic standing at home school; judicial review.

Living Arrangements • Students live in locally rented apartments, host family homes. Quarters are shared with host institution students, students from other programs. Meals are taken on one's own, in residences, in restaurants.

Costs (2002-2003) • One term: $17,000. Yearlong program: $34,000; includes tuition, housing, all meals, insurance, international airfare, books and class materials, student support services. $50 application fee. $500 nonrefundable deposit required. Financial aid available for all students: scholarships, work study, loans.

For More Information • Ms. Rachel Cullenen, Associate Director for Study Abroad, Ithaca College, Office of International Programs, 214 Muller Faculty Center, Ithaca, NY 14850-7150; *Phone:* 607-274-3306; *Fax:* 607-274-1515. *E-mail:* rcullenen@ithaca.edu. *World Wide Web:* http://www.ithaca.edu/oip/. Students may also

ENGLAND
London

apply through Ithaca College London Center, 35 Harrington Gardens, London SW74JU, England.

JAMES MADISON UNIVERSITY
SEMESTER IN LONDON

Hosted by James Madison University–London
Academic Focus • Architecture, art history, drama/theater, English, history, literature, music, political science and government.
Program Information • Students attend classes at James Madison University–London. Scheduled travel to Stratford-upon-Avon, Bath, Wales; field trips to Cambridge, Oxford.
Sessions • Fall, spring.
Eligibility Requirements • Minimum age 18; open to sophomores, juniors, seniors; 2.8 GPA; 1 letter of recommendation; good academic standing at home school.
Living Arrangements • Students live in the Madison House. Quarters are shared with host institution students. Meals are taken as a group, on one's own, in central dining facility, in restaurants.
Costs (2003-2004) • One term: $8322 for Virginia residents; $12,433 for nonresidents; includes tuition, housing, some meals, excursions, books and class materials. $400 nonrefundable deposit required. Financial aid available for students from sponsoring institution: scholarships, work study, loans.
For More Information • Mr. Felix Wang, Director, James Madison University, Office of International Programs, MSC 5731, 1077 South Main Street, Harrisonburg, VA 22807; *Phone:* 540-568-6419; *Fax:* 540-568-3310. *E-mail:* studyabroad@jmu.edu. *World Wide Web:* http://www.jmu.edu/international/

LEXIA INTERNATIONAL
LEXIA IN LONDON

Hosted by Foundation for International Education
Academic Focus • Ancient history, anthropology, area studies, art, art conservation studies, art history, British studies, civilization studies, classics and classical languages, comparative history, cultural studies, drawing/painting, economics, environmental science/studies, ethnic studies, European studies, film and media studies, fine/studio arts, geography, history, interdisciplinary studies, international affairs, international business, liberal studies, literature, music, music history, music performance, philosophy, political science and government, psychology, religious studies, social sciences, urban studies, visual and performing arts.
Program Information • Students attend classes at Foundation for International Education. Field trips to Bath, Stonehenge, Oxford, Cambridge.
Sessions • Fall, spring, yearlong.
Eligibility Requirements • Minimum age 18; open to sophomores, juniors, seniors, graduate students, adults; 2.5 GPA; 2 letters of recommendation.
Living Arrangements • Students live in locally rented apartments. Quarters are shared with host institution students. Meals are taken on one's own, with host family, in residences.
Costs (2003-2004) • One term: $11,950. Yearlong program: $21,550; includes tuition, housing, insurance, excursions, international student ID, student support services, transcript, computer access. $35 application fee. $300 refundable deposit required. Financial aid available for all students: scholarships, work study.
For More Information • Lexia International, 23 South Main Street, Hanover, NH 03755; *Phone:* 800-775-3942; *Fax:* 603-643-9899. *E-mail:* info@lexiaintl.org. *World Wide Web:* http://www.lexiaintl.org/

LONDON COLLEGE OF FASHION
STUDY ABROAD SEMESTER PROGRAM

Hosted by London College of Fashion
Academic Focus • Costume design, design and applied arts, fashion design, fashion merchandising.
Program Information • Students attend classes at London College of Fashion. Field trips to museums, fashion-related visits, art galleries, fashion shows; optional travel to Paris at an extra cost.
Sessions • Fall, spring.
Eligibility Requirements • Open to freshmen, sophomores, juniors, seniors, graduate students, adults; major in fashion design, merchandising, or a related field; 2.8 GPA; 2 letters of recommendation; good academic standing at home school; application essay and/or examples of work.
Living Arrangements • Students live in host institution dormitories, locally rented apartments. Quarters are shared with host institution students, students from other programs. Meals are taken on one's own, in residences.
Costs (2004-2005) • One term: £3500 for design, merchandising, or theater programs; £4100 for make-up program; includes tuition, excursions, lab equipment, student support services, membership in International Student House. £300 nonrefundable deposit required.
For More Information • Ms. Basia Szkutnicka, Director of Study Abroad, London College of Fashion, 20 John Princes Street, London W1M 0BJ, England; *Phone:* +44 207-514-7540; *Fax:* +44 207-514-7490. *E-mail:* studyabroad@lcf.linst.ac.uk. *World Wide Web:* http://www.fashion.arts.ac.uk/

LONG ISLAND UNIVERSITY
FRIENDS WORLD PROGRAM—EUROPEAN CENTER-LONDON

Hosted by Friends World Program European Center
Academic Focus • Anthropology, art, communications, creative writing, environmental science/studies, European studies, fine/studio arts, French language and literature, Gaelic, German language and literature, interdisciplinary studies, international affairs, Italian language and literature, peace and conflict studies, political science and government, Russian language and literature.
Program Information • Students attend classes at Friends World Program European Center. Scheduled travel to Eastern Europe, Ireland, southern Europe; field trips to Parliament, historic sites, museums, theatre performances; optional travel to Europe, other parts of the United Kingdom at an extra cost.
Sessions • Fall, spring, yearlong.
Eligibility Requirements • Minimum age 18; open to freshmen, sophomores, juniors, seniors, adults; good academic standing at home school; interview; essay.
Living Arrangements • Students live in host institution dormitories, locally rented apartments, host family homes. Quarters are shared with host institution students. Meals are taken as a group, on one's own, with host family, in residences, in restaurants.
Costs (2003-2004) • One term: $15,625 (estimated). Yearlong program: $31,250 (estimated); includes tuition, housing, all meals, excursions, international airfare, books and class materials. $30 application fee. $200 deposit required. Financial aid available for students from sponsoring institution: scholarships, loans, need-based grants.
For More Information • Admissions Office, FWP, Long Island University, 239 Montauk Highway, Southampton College, Southampton, NY 11968; *Phone:* 631-287-8474; *Fax:* 631-287-8463. *E-mail:* fw@liu.edu. *World Wide Web:* http://www.southampton.liu.edu/fw/

LYCOMING COLLEGE
STUDY ABROAD AT REGENT'S COLLEGE

Hosted by Regent's College
Academic Focus • Full curriculum.
Program Information • Students attend classes at Regent's College. Optional travel.
Sessions • Fall, spring.
Eligibility Requirements • Open to sophomores, juniors, seniors; 2.5 GPA; 1 letter of recommendation.
Living Arrangements • Students live in host institution dormitories, locally rented apartments. Quarters are shared with host institution students. Meals are taken on one's own, in residences, in restaurants.
Costs (2002-2003) • One term: $9940; includes tuition, housing, some meals, books and class materials. $300 deposit required.
For More Information • Dr. Barbara Buedel, Coordinator of Study Abroad Program, Lycoming College, Campus Box 2, 700 College Place, Williamsport, PA 17701; *Phone:* 570-321-4210; *Fax:* 570-321-4389. *E-mail:* buedel@lycoming.edu. *World Wide Web:* http://www.lycoming.edu/

MARIST COLLEGE
LONDON FASHION PROGRAM

Hosted by London College of Fashion

Academic Focus • Costume design, fashion design, fashion merchandising.

Program Information • Students attend classes at London College of Fashion. Scheduled travel to Paris; field trips to London museums and art galleries.

Sessions • Fall, spring, yearlong.

Eligibility Requirements • Open to sophomores, juniors, seniors; 2.8 GPA; 2 letters of recommendation; good academic standing at home school.

Living Arrangements • Students live in locally rented apartments. Quarters are shared with host institution students, students from other programs. Meals are taken on one's own, in residences, in central dining facility, in restaurants.

Costs (2003-2004) • One term: $12,500. Yearlong program: $25,000; includes tuition, housing, insurance, excursions, student support services, London airport pick-up. $35 application fee. $300 nonrefundable deposit required. Financial aid available for students from sponsoring institution: scholarships, loans.

For More Information • Ms. Carol Toufali, Coordinator, Marist Abroad Program, Marist College, 3399 North Road, Poughkeepsie, NY 12601-1387; *Phone:* 845-575-3330; *Fax:* 845-575-3294. *E-mail:* international@marist.edu. *World Wide Web:* http://www.marist.edu/international/

MARQUETTE UNIVERSITY
MARQUETTE AT CITY UNIVERSITY–LONDON

Hosted by City University

Academic Focus • Full curriculum.

Program Information • Students attend classes at City University. Field trips to sites throughout England; optional travel to University-sponsored student activities at an extra cost.

Sessions • Fall, spring, yearlong.

Eligibility Requirements • Open to sophomores, juniors, seniors, graduate students; 3.0 GPA; good academic standing at home school.

Living Arrangements • Students live in host institution dormitories, locally rented apartments. Quarters are shared with host institution students, students from other programs. Meals are taken on one's own, in residences, in restaurants.

Costs (2003-2004) • One term: £4200. Yearlong program: £8400; includes tuition, excursions, lab equipment, student support services. £600 refundable deposit required. Financial aid available for students from sponsoring institution: scholarships, work study, loans.

For More Information • Dr. Jamshid Hosseini, Director, International Business Studies, Marquette University, College of Business Administration, 606 North 13th Street, David Straz, Jr. Building, Milwaukee, WI 53233; *Phone:* 414-288-7534; *Fax:* 414-288-7440. *E-mail:* jamshid.hosseini@marquette.edu. *World Wide Web:* http://www.marquette.edu/studyabroad/

MARYMOUNT UNIVERSITY
GRADUATE MBA LONDON PROGRAM

Hosted by London Metropolitan University

Academic Focus • Business administration/management, human resources, international business, management information systems.

Program Information • Students attend classes at London Metropolitan University. Field trips.

Sessions • Fall, spring.

Eligibility Requirements • Open to graduate students; 3.0 GPA; 2 letters of recommendation; must be an MBA student.

Living Arrangements • Students live in locally rented apartments. Quarters are shared with host institution students. Meals are taken on one's own.

Costs (2002-2003) • One term: $8487; includes tuition, housing, insurance, excursions, student support services, local transportation in London, computer and e-mail access. $25 application fee. $250 nonrefundable deposit required. Financial aid available for students from sponsoring institution: scholarships, loans.

For More Information • Dr. Linda Goff, Director, Study Abroad, Marymount University, 2807 North Glebe Road, Arlington, VA 22207; *Phone:* 703-284-1677; *Fax:* 703-284-1553. *E-mail:* mulondon@marymount.edu. *World Wide Web:* http://mu.marymount.edu/academic/studyabroad/index.html

MARYMOUNT UNIVERSITY
LONDON PROGRAM

Held at Marymount London Center

Academic Focus • Art history, British studies, drama/theater, history, international affairs, sociology.

Program Information • Classes are held on the campus of Marymount London Center. Faculty members are local instructors hired by the sponsor. Field trips to Bath, Stonehenge, Salisbury, Wells, Stratford-upon-Avon, Oxford, Blenheim, Warwick.

Sessions • Fall, spring.

Eligibility Requirements • Open to juniors, seniors; 2.75 GPA; 2 letters of recommendation; good academic standing at home school.

Living Arrangements • Students live in locally rented apartments. Quarters are shared with host institution students. Meals are taken on one's own, in residences, in restaurants.

Costs (2003-2004) • One term: $12,545; includes tuition, housing, insurance, excursions, student support services, local transportation, computer and e-mail access. $25 application fee. $250 nonrefundable deposit required. Financial aid available for students from sponsoring institution: scholarships, loans.

For More Information • Dr. Linda Goff, Director, London Program, Marymount University, 2807 North Glebe Road, Arlington, VA 22207; *Phone:* 703-284-1677; *Fax:* 703-284-1553. *E-mail:* mulondon@marymount.edu. *World Wide Web:* http://mu.marymount.edu/academic/studyabroad/index.html

MICHIGAN STATE UNIVERSITY
COMBINED ARTS AND HUMANITIES/SOCIAL SCIENCE IN THE U.K.

Hosted by Birkbeck College, University of London

Academic Focus • British studies, comparative literature, creative writing, English literature, social sciences.

Program Information • Students attend classes at Birkbeck College, University of London. Scheduled travel to Edinburgh, Scotland; field trips to York, the Lake District, Cambridge, Oxford, Canterbury.

Sessions • Spring.

Eligibility Requirements • Minimum age 18; open to freshmen, sophomores, juniors, seniors; 2.0 GPA; good academic standing at home school; approval of faculty director.

Living Arrangements • Students live in locally rented apartments. Quarters are shared with host institution students. Meals are taken on one's own, in restaurants.

Costs (2003) • One term: $3800 (estimated); includes housing, some meals, insurance, excursions, student support services. $100 application fee. $200 nonrefundable deposit required. Financial aid available for students from sponsoring institution: scholarships, loans.

For More Information • Ms. Sherry Martinez-Bonilla, Office Assistant, Michigan State University, Office of Study Abroad, 109 International Center, East Lansing, MI 48824-1035; *Phone:* 517-353-8920; *Fax:* 517-432-2082. *E-mail:* marti269@msu.edu. *World Wide Web:* http://studyabroad.msu.edu/

MIDDLESEX UNIVERSITY
STUDY IN LONDON

Hosted by Middlesex University

Academic Focus • Full curriculum.

Program Information • Students attend classes at Middlesex University.

Sessions • Fall, spring, yearlong.

Eligibility Requirements • Minimum age 17; open to freshmen, sophomores, juniors, seniors; 2.7 GPA; transcript.

Living Arrangements • Students live in host institution dormitories. Meals are taken on one's own, in residences, in central dining facility.

Costs (2003-2004) • One term: £3850. Yearlong program: £7700; includes tuition, student support services. Financial aid available for all students: loans.

For More Information • Ms. Angelika Nielsen, Study Abroad Officer, Middlesex University, Trent Park, Bramley Road, London N14 4YZ, England; *Phone:* +44 20-8411-6760; *Fax:* +44 20-8411-4758. *E-mail:* a.nielsen@mdx.ac.uk. *World Wide Web:* http://www.mdx.ac.uk/worldwide/northamerica/index.htm. Students may also apply through Arcadia University, Center for Education Abroad, 450 South Easton Road, Glenside, PA 19038-3295; State University of New York at Brockport, Office of International Education, 350 New Campus Drive, Brockport, NY 14420; Butler University, Institute for Study Abroad, 1100 West 42nd Street, Suite 305, Indianapolis, IN 46208-3345.

NEW YORK UNIVERSITY
ADVANCED PLAYWRITING

Hosted by Writer's Guild of Great Britain

Academic Focus • British studies, creative writing, drama/theater, English literature, visual and performing arts.

Program Information • Students attend classes at Writer's Guild of Great Britain. Classes are also held on the campus of Institute of Contemporary Arts. Field trips to Stratford-upon-Avon, theater visits.

Sessions • Fall, spring.

Eligibility Requirements • Minimum age 18; open to sophomores, juniors, seniors, graduate students, adults; 2 letters of recommendation; good academic standing at home school; previous experience/course work in playwriting; interview.

Living Arrangements • Students live in host institution dormitories, locally rented apartments. Meals are taken on one's own, in residences, in restaurants.

Costs (2002-2003) • One term: $20,636–$22,156; includes tuition, housing, excursions, lab equipment, student support services, registration fees. $35 application fee. $350 nonrefundable deposit required. Financial aid available for students from sponsoring institution: scholarships, loans.

For More Information • Ms. Peggy Sotirhos, Associate Director of Special Programs Recruitment, New York University, 721 Broadway, 12th Floor, New York, NY 10003; *Phone:* 212-998-1500; *Fax:* 212-995-4610. *E-mail:* tisch.special.info@nyu.edu. *World Wide Web:* http://www.nyu.edu/studyabroad/

NEW YORK UNIVERSITY
ADVANCED SCREENWRITING

Hosted by Writer's Guild of Great Britain

Academic Focus • British studies, visual and performing arts.

Program Information • Students attend classes at Writer's Guild of Great Britain. Classes are also held on the campus of Institute of Contemporary Arts. Field trips to Stratford-upon-Avon.

Sessions • Spring.

Eligibility Requirements • Minimum age 18; open to sophomores, juniors, seniors, graduate students, adults; 1 letter of recommendation; good academic standing at home school; previous experience/course work in screenwriting or writing sample and permission of instructor; interview.

Living Arrangements • Students live in host institution dormitories, locally rented apartments. Meals are taken on one's own, in residences, in restaurants.

Costs (2001) • One term: $20,636–$22,156; includes tuition, housing, excursions, student support services, registration fees. $35 application fee. $350 nonrefundable deposit required. Financial aid available for students from sponsoring institution: scholarships, loans.

For More Information • Ms. Peggy Sotirhos, Associate Director of Special Programs Recruitment, New York University, 721 Broadway, 12th Floor, New York, NY 10003; *Phone:* 212-998-1500; *Fax:* 212-995-4610. *E-mail:* tisch.special.info@nyu.edu. *World Wide Web:* http://www.nyu.edu/studyabroad/

NEW YORK UNIVERSITY
BBC TELEVISION PRODUCTION

Hosted by BBC

Academic Focus • British studies, communications, English literature, film and media studies, journalism, telecommunications, visual and performing arts.

Program Information • Students attend classes at BBC. Classes are also held on the campus of Institute of Contemporary Arts. Field trips to Stratford-upon-Avon, theater excursions, museums, galleries.

Sessions • Fall, spring, yearlong.

Eligibility Requirements • Minimum age 18; open to sophomores, juniors, seniors, graduate students, adults; course work in filmmaking and TV/video production; 2 letters of recommendation; good academic standing at home school; filmmaking and video production experience and/or training or permission of instructor; interview.

Living Arrangements • Students live in host institution dormitories, locally rented apartments. Quarters are shared with host institution students, students from other programs. Meals are taken on one's own, in residences, in restaurants.

Costs (2002-2003) • One term: $20,100–$21,635. Yearlong program: $21,705–$39,810; includes tuition, housing, excursions, lab equipment, student support services, registration fees. $35 application fee. $350 nonrefundable deposit required. Financial aid available for students from sponsoring institution: scholarships, loans.

For More Information • Ms. Peggy Sotirhos, Associate Director of Special Programs Recruitment, New York University, 721 Broadway, 12th Floor, New York, NY 10003; *Phone:* 212-998-1500; *Fax:* 212-995-4610. *E-mail:* tisch.special.info@nyu.edu. *World Wide Web:* http://www.nyu.edu/studyabroad/

NEW YORK UNIVERSITY
MUSICAL THEATRE PERFORMANCE

Hosted by Institute of Contemporary Arts, Trinity College of Music

Academic Focus • British studies, dance, drama/theater, music, visual and performing arts.

Program Information • Students attend classes at Institute of Contemporary Arts, Trinity College of Music. Field trips to theater excursions, Stratford-upon-Avon, museums.

Sessions • Spring.

Eligibility Requirements • Minimum age 18; open to sophomores, juniors, seniors, adults; course work in acting/performance; good academic standing at home school.

Living Arrangements • Students live in host institution dormitories, locally rented apartments. Quarters are shared with host institution students, students from other programs. Meals are taken on one's own, in residences, in restaurants.

Costs (2003) • One term: $20,636–$22,156; includes tuition, housing, excursions, lab equipment, student support services, registration fees. $35 application fee. $350 nonrefundable deposit required. Financial aid available for students from sponsoring institution: scholarships, loans.

For More Information • Ms. Peggy Sotirhos, Associate Director of Special Programs Recruitment, New York University, 721 Broadway, 12th Floor, New York, NY 10003; *Phone:* 212-998-1500; *Fax:* 212-995-4610. *E-mail:* tisch.special.info@nyu.edu. *World Wide Web:* http://www.nyu.edu/studyabroad/

NEW YORK UNIVERSITY
NYU IN LONDON

Hosted by NYU Center

Academic Focus • Art history, biological/life sciences, business administration/management, communications, economics, film and media studies, history, international business, literature, philosophy, physics, political science and government, psychology.

Program Information • Students attend classes at NYU Center. Field trips to London sites, Oxford, Canterbury, Greenwich, North Wales, Liverpool, Stratford-upon-Avon.

Sessions • Fall, spring, yearlong.

Eligibility Requirements • Open to sophomores, juniors, seniors; 3.0 GPA; 1 letter of recommendation; good academic standing at home school; transcripts; personal statement.

Living Arrangements • Students live in host institution dormitories, locally rented apartments. Quarters are shared with host institution students. Meals are taken on one's own, in residences, in restaurants.

Costs (2003-2004) • One term: $14,248. Yearlong program: $28,495; includes tuition, excursions, student support services. $25 application fee. $300 nonrefundable deposit required. Financial aid available for all students: scholarships, loans.

For More Information • Office of Study Abroad Admissions, New York University, 7 East 12th Street, 6th Floor, New York, NY 10003; *Phone:* 212-998-4433; *Fax:* 212-995-4103. *E-mail:* studyabroad@nyu.edu. *World Wide Web:* http://www.nyu.edu/studyabroad/

NEW YORK UNIVERSITY
SHAKESPEARE IN PERFORMANCE WITH RADA

Hosted by Royal Academy of Dramatic Art
Academic Focus • British studies, creative writing, drama/theater, film and media studies, performing arts, visual and performing arts.
Program Information • Students attend classes at Royal Academy of Dramatic Art. Classes are also held on the campus of Institute of Contemporary Arts. Field trips to Stratford-upon-Avon, theatre excursions, museums.
Sessions • Fall, spring.
Eligibility Requirements • Minimum age 18; open to sophomores, juniors, seniors, graduate students, adults; course work in acting; 2 letters of recommendation; good academic standing at home school; prior acting training and/or experience; audition; interview.
Living Arrangements • Students live in host institution dormitories, locally rented apartments. Quarters are shared with host institution students. Meals are taken on one's own, in residences, in restaurants.
Costs (2002-2003) • One term: $20,636–$22,156; includes tuition, housing, excursions, lab equipment, student support services, registration fees. $35 application fee. $350 nonrefundable deposit required. Financial aid available for students from sponsoring institution: scholarships, loans.
For More Information • Ms. Peggy Sotirhos, Associate Director of Special Programs Recruitment, New York University, 721 Broadway, 12th Floor, New York, NY 10003; *Phone:* 212-998-1500; *Fax:*

212-995-4610. *E-mail:* tisch.special.info@nyu.edu. *World Wide Web:* http://www.nyu.edu/studyabroad/

NEW YORK UNIVERSITY
TOPICS IN BRITISH LITERARY, VISUAL AND PERFORMING ARTS

Held at Institute of Contemporary Arts
Academic Focus • Art history, British studies, creative writing, drama/theater, English literature, film and media studies, interdisciplinary studies, performing arts.
Program Information • Classes are held on the campus of Institute of Contemporary Arts. Faculty members are local instructors hired by the sponsor. Field trips to theater excursions, museums, galleries, historic landmarks, Stratford-upon-Avon, Scotland, Ireland.
Sessions • Fall, spring.
Eligibility Requirements • Minimum age 18; open to freshmen, sophomores, juniors, seniors, graduate students, adults; 2.5 GPA; 2 letters of recommendation; good academic standing at home school; interview.
Living Arrangements • Students live in host institution dormitories, locally rented apartments. Quarters are shared with host institution students, students from other programs. Meals are taken on one's own, in residences, in restaurants.
Costs (2002-2003) • One term: $20,636–$22,156; includes tuition, housing, excursions, student support services, registration fees. $35 application fee. $350 nonrefundable deposit required. Financial aid available for students from sponsoring institution: scholarships, loans.
For More Information • Ms. Peggy Sotirhos, Associate Director of Special Programs Recruitment, New York University, 721 Broadway, 12th Floor, New York, NY 10003; *Phone:* 212-998-1500; *Fax:* 212-995-4610. *E-mail:* tisch.special.info@nyu.edu. *World Wide Web:* http://www.nyu.edu/studyabroad/

ENGLAND
London

NORTHERN ILLINOIS UNIVERSITY
ACADEMIC INTERNSHIPS IN LONDON, ENGLAND

Hosted by University of London–London School of Economics and Political Science, Birkbeck College, University of London
Academic Focus • Art history, drama/theater, education, history, literature, music history, political science and government, social services, urban/regional planning.
Program Information • Students attend classes at University of London–London School of Economics and Political Science, Birkbeck College, University of London. Optional travel at an extra cost.
Sessions • Fall, spring.
Eligibility Requirements • Open to juniors, seniors; 3.0 GPA; 2 letters of recommendation; good academic standing at home school; essay; résumé.
Living Arrangements • Students live in locally rented apartments, host family homes. Quarters are shared with students from other programs. Meals are taken on one's own, with host family, in residences.
Costs (2003-2004) • One term: $8525; includes tuition, housing, some meals, insurance, international student ID, internship placement. $45 application fee. $800 refundable deposit required. Financial aid available for students from sponsoring institution: regular financial aid.
For More Information • Ms. Clare Foust, Program Assistant, Northern Illinois University, Study Abroad Office, Williston Hall 417, DeKalb, IL 60115-2854; *Phone:* 815-753-0420; *Fax:* 815-753-0825. *E-mail:* niuabroad@niu.edu. *World Wide Web:* http://www.niu.edu/niuabroad/

ROGER WILLIAMS UNIVERSITY
SEMESTER ABROAD STUDIES IN LONDON

Academic Focus • British studies, drama/theater.

Program Information • Faculty members are drawn from the sponsor's U.S. staff and local instructors hired by the sponsor. Scheduled travel to Stratford-upon-Avon, Bath, York, a tour of Britain; field trips to Windsor, Greenwich, Hampton Court, St. Albans (Shaw's House); optional travel to Paris, Amsterdam at an extra cost.
Sessions • Fall.
Eligibility Requirements • Minimum age 18; open to sophomores, juniors, seniors; 2.5 GPA; 2 letters of recommendation; good judicial standing.
Living Arrangements • Students live in program-owned apartments. Meals are taken on one's own, in residences.
Costs (2003-2004) • One term: $15,473; includes tuition, housing, all meals, insurance, excursions, international airfare, books and class materials, travel pass, admission to over 60 plays, operas, and concerts. $650 nonrefundable deposit required. Financial aid available for students from sponsoring institution: scholarships, loans, governmental financial aid.
For More Information • Ms. Gina M. Lopardo, Coordinator of Study Abroad Programs, Roger Williams University, One Old Ferry Road, Bristol, RI 02809-2921; *Phone:* 401-254-3040; *Fax:* 401-253-7768. *E-mail:* glopardo@rwu.edu. *World Wide Web:* http://www.rwu.edu/academics/special+programs/study+abroad/

RUTGERS, THE STATE UNIVERSITY OF NEW JERSEY
CONSERVATORY THEATRE TRAINING PROGRAM IN LONDON

Held at London Academy of Theatre
Academic Focus • Design and applied arts.
Program Information • Classes are held on the campus of London Academy of Theatre. Faculty members are drawn from the sponsor's U.S. staff and local instructors hired by the sponsor. Scheduled travel to local theatres and shows.

Why is this globe upside down?

?right to left read Why

Why drive on the
right-hand side of the road?

It's all a matter of perspective.

Studying abroad changes your perspective and gives you new insight into how the world looks to different people and cultures.

See for yourself in one of our 40 programs worldwide. Enjoy your crossing...

732.932.7787
RU_Abroad@email.rutgers.edu
http://studyabroad.rutgers.edu

Rutgers
Study Abroad

Sessions • Fall, spring.

Eligibility Requirements • Open to sophomores, juniors, seniors; major in theatre design, stage management; 3.0 GPA; 1 letter of recommendation; good academic standing at home school; audition.

Living Arrangements • Students live in locally rented apartments. Quarters are shared with host institution students. Meals are taken on one's own, in residences, in restaurants.

Costs (2003-2004) • One term: $15,635 for New Jersey residents; $18,285 for nonresidents; includes tuition, housing, insurance, excursions, student support services. $20 application fee. $750 nonrefundable deposit required. Financial aid available for all students: scholarships, loans.

For More Information • Ms. Karin Bonello, Regional Coordinator, Rutgers, The State University of New Jersey, 102 College Avenue, New Brunswick, NJ 08901-8543; *Phone:* 732-932-7787; *Fax:* 732-932-8659. *E-mail:* ru_abroad@email.rutgers.edu. *World Wide Web:* http://studyabroad.rutgers.edu/

RUTGERS, THE STATE UNIVERSITY OF NEW JERSEY
STUDY ABROAD IN BRITAIN: LONDON, CITY UNIVERSITY

Hosted by City University

Academic Focus • Full curriculum.

Program Information • Students attend classes at City University. Field trips to Stonehenge, Oxford.

Sessions • Fall, spring, yearlong.

Eligibility Requirements • Open to juniors, seniors; 3.0 GPA; 2 letters of recommendation; good academic standing at home school.

Living Arrangements • Students live in host institution dormitories. Quarters are shared with host institution students. Meals are taken on one's own, in residences, in central dining facility.

Costs (2003-2004) • One term: $11,889–$12,830 for New Jersey residents; $14,539–$15,480 for nonresidents. Yearlong program: $18,637 for New Jersey residents; $23,937 for nonresidents; includes tuition, insurance, excursions. $20 application fee. $750 nonrefundable deposit required. Financial aid available for students from sponsoring institution: scholarships, loans.

For More Information • Ms. Karin Bonello, Regional Coordinator, Rutgers, The State University of New Jersey, 102 College Avenue, New Brunswick, NJ 08901-8543; *Phone:* 732-932-7787; *Fax:* 732-932-8659. *E-mail:* ru_abroad@email.rutgers.edu. *World Wide Web:* http://studyabroad.rutgers.edu/

RUTGERS, THE STATE UNIVERSITY OF NEW JERSEY
STUDY ABROAD IN BRITAIN: LONDON, UNIVERSITY COLLEGE

Hosted by University College London

Academic Focus • Full curriculum.

Program Information • Students attend classes at University College London. Field trips to Stonehenge, Oxford.

Sessions • Fall, spring, yearlong.

Eligibility Requirements • Open to juniors, seniors; 3.2 GPA; 2 letters of recommendation; good academic standing at home school; official transcript from each tertiary school attended.

Living Arrangements • Students live in host institution dormitories. Quarters are shared with host institution students. Meals are taken on one's own, in residences, in central dining facility.

Costs (2003-2004) • One term: $15,076–$16,032 for New Jersey residents; $17,726–$18,682 for nonresidents. Yearlong program: $23,138 for New Jersey residents; $28,438 for nonresidents; includes tuition, insurance, excursions, student support services. $20 application fee. $750 nonrefundable deposit required. Financial aid available for students from sponsoring institution: scholarships, loans.

For More Information • Ms. Karin Bonello, Regional Coordinator, Rutgers, The State University of New Jersey, 102 College Avenue, New Brunswick, NJ 08901-8543; *Phone:* 732-932-7787; *Fax:* 732-932-8659. *E-mail:* ru_abroad@email.rutgers.edu. *World Wide Web:* http://studyabroad.rutgers.edu/

ST. LAWRENCE UNIVERSITY
LONDON SEMESTER PROGRAM

Held at University of Westminster

Academic Focus • Art history, drama/theater, economics, history, literature, political science and government, sociology.

Program Information • Classes are held on the campus of University of Westminster. Faculty members are drawn from the sponsor's U.S. staff and local instructors hired by the sponsor. Scheduled travel to Stratford-upon-Avon, Edinburgh; field trips to Canterbury, Bath, Salisbury, Stonehenge.

Sessions • Fall, spring.

Eligibility Requirements • Open to sophomores, juniors, seniors; course work in theater arts, art history, literature, European studies, British studies; 2.8 GPA; 2 letters of recommendation.

Living Arrangements • Students live in host family homes. Meals are taken on one's own, with host family.

Costs (2003-2004) • One term: $17,870; includes tuition, housing, all meals, excursions, theater performances 2-3 times a week. $500 nonrefundable deposit required. Financial aid available for students from sponsoring institution: scholarships, loans.

For More Information • Ms. Sara Hofschulte, Assistant Director, Off-Campus Programs, St. Lawrence University, Center for International and Intercultural Studies, Canton, NY 13617; *Phone:* 315-229-5991; *Fax:* 315-229-5989. *E-mail:* shofschulte@stlawu.edu. *World Wide Web:* http://www.stlawu.edu/ciis/offcampus/

SARAH LAWRENCE COLLEGE
LONDON THEATRE PROGRAM

Hosted by British American Drama Academy

Academic Focus • Drama/theater.

Program Information • Students attend classes at British American Drama Academy. Field trips to Stratford-upon-Avon, London theaters, Bath.

Sessions • Fall, spring, yearlong.

Eligibility Requirements • Open to sophomores, juniors, seniors; course work in theater arts/drama; 2 letters of recommendation; good academic standing at home school; brief video audition or on-campus audition (Bronxville).

Living Arrangements • Students live in locally rented apartments. Quarters are shared with host institution students. Meals are taken on one's own, in residences.

Costs (2003-2004) • One term: $18,460. Yearlong program: $36,920; includes tuition, housing, excursions, books and class materials, student support services, weekly trips to the London theater and master classes. $35 application fee. $250 nonrefundable deposit required. Financial aid available for all students: scholarships, loans.

For More Information • Ms. Prema Samuel, Director of International Programs, Sarah Lawrence College, 1 Meadway, Bronxville, NY 10708-5999; *Phone:* 800-873-4752; *Fax:* 914-395-2666. *E-mail:* slcaway@slc.edu. *World Wide Web:* http://www.sarahlawrence.edu/studyabroad/

MORE ABOUT THE PROGRAM

The London Theatre Program, cosponsored with the British American Drama Academy (BADA), takes students to the heart of London's theater district for immersion in professional acting training, master classes with celebrated dramatic artists, and numerous trips to the theater.

Scene study from classical and modern works makes up the core of the program. BADA's distinguished faculty members also teach courses in voice, movement, stage fighting, theater history, and dramatic criticism. In keeping with the Sarah Lawrence commitment to personalized instruction, the program includes individual or small-group acting tutorials. Each semester culminates in a fully staged production. Merit grants are available. Sarah Lawrence also sponsors programs in Paris, Florence, Cuba, and at Oxford.

SCHILLER INTERNATIONAL UNIVERSITY
STUDY ABROAD PROGRAM, UNDERGRADUATE AND GRADUATE PROGRAM

Hosted by Schiller International University

Academic Focus • Art, business administration/management, computer science, drama/theater, economics, English, English literature, European studies, finance, full curriculum, history, hotel and restaurant management, interdisciplinary studies, international affairs, international business, management information systems, marketing, mathematics, political science and government, premedical studies, psychology, tourism and travel.

Program Information • Students attend classes at Schiller International University. Field trips to Wales, Oxford, Cambridge, Paris; optional travel to the Netherlands, France, Spain, Switzerland, Germany, Italy at an extra cost.

Sessions • Fall, spring, yearlong.

Eligibility Requirements • Minimum age 17; open to freshmen, sophomores, juniors, seniors, graduate students; 2.0 GPA.

Living Arrangements • Students live in host institution dormitories, locally rented apartments, host family homes, hotels. Quarters are shared with host institution students, students from other programs. Meals are taken as a group, on one's own, with host family, in residences, in central dining facility, in restaurants.

Costs (2003-2004) • One term: $6890. Yearlong program: $13,685; includes tuition, housing, all meals, lab equipment, student support services, activity fee, liability deposit. $35 application fee. $300 nonrefundable deposit required. Financial aid available for all students: scholarships, loans, federal grants, Exchange Student Scholarship Award, graduate assistantship award.

For More Information • Ms. Kamala Dontamsetti, Admissions Office, Florida Campus, Schiller International University, 453 Edgewater Drive, Dunedin, FL 34698; *Phone:* 727-736-5082 Ext. 240; *Fax:* 727-734-0359. *E-mail:* admissions@schiller.edu. *World Wide Web:* http://www.schiller.edu/. Students may also apply through Schiller International University, Royal Waterloo House, 51-55 Waterloo Road, London SE1 8TX, England.

SHORTER COLLEGE
STUDY ABROAD AT REGENT'S COLLEGE, LONDON, ENGLAND

Hosted by Regent's College
Academic Focus • Full curriculum.

Program Information • Students attend classes at Regent's College. Field trips to London, Stratford-upon-Avon, York; optional travel to Europe at an extra cost.

Sessions • Fall, spring.

Eligibility Requirements • Open to sophomores, juniors; 3.0 GPA; 2 letters of recommendation; good academic standing at home school.

Living Arrangements • Students live in host institution dormitories. Quarters are shared with students from other programs. Meals are taken as a group, in central dining facility.

Costs (2002-2003) • One term: $9540 (estimated); includes tuition, housing, all meals, student support services. $1500 refundable deposit required. Financial aid available for students from sponsoring institution: scholarships, work study, loans.

For More Information • Prof. Betty Zane Morris, Director of International Programs, Shorter College, Box 2040, 315 Shorter Avenue, Rome, GA 30165; *Phone:* 706-233-7270; *Fax:* 706-233-7516. *E-mail:* bmorris@shorter.edu. *World Wide Web:* http://www.shorter.edu.academics.internationalprograms/

SKIDMORE COLLEGE
SHAKESPEARE PROGRAMME

Hosted by British American Drama Academy (BADA)
Academic Focus • Creative writing, drama/theater, English literature, performing arts, theater management.

Program Information • Students attend classes at British American Drama Academy (BADA). Scheduled travel to Stratford-upon-Avon; field trips to weekly theater visits.

Sessions • Fall.

Eligibility Requirements • Minimum age 18; open to sophomores, juniors, seniors; course work in theater, English; 3.0 GPA; 2 letters of recommendation; good academic standing at home school; minimum 3.2 GPA in major; résumé for acting students.

Living Arrangements • Students live in locally rented apartments. Meals are taken on one's own, in residences.

Costs (2002) • One term: $18,178; includes tuition, housing, all meals, insurance, excursions, books and class materials, international student ID, student support services. $50 application fee. $500 nonrefundable deposit required. Financial aid available for

students from sponsoring institution: scholarships, BADA offers financial aid to other participants.

For More Information • Ms. Barbara Opitz, Associate Director, Shakespeare Programme, Skidmore College, 815 North Broadway, Saratoga Springs, NY 12866; *Phone:* 518-580-5720; *Fax:* 518-580-5749. *E-mail:* bopitz@skidmore.edu. *World Wide Web:* http://www.skidmore.edu/internationalprograms/

SOUTHWEST MISSOURI STATE UNIVERSITY
LONDON PROGRAM

Held at Imperial College
Academic Focus • British studies, business administration/management, comparative history, English literature, journalism, music history, photography, political science and government, psychology, social sciences, visual and performing arts.

Program Information • Classes are held on the campus of Imperial College. Faculty members are drawn from the sponsor's U.S. staff and local instructors hired by the sponsor. Field trips to London environs, Bath, Dover, Stonehenge, Stratford-upon-Avon; optional travel to Paris, Amsterdam, Wales at an extra cost.

Sessions • Fall, spring.

Eligibility Requirements • Open to sophomores, juniors, seniors; 2.5 GPA; good academic standing at home school.

Living Arrangements • Students live in locally rented apartments. Quarters are shared with host institution students. Meals are taken on one's own, in residences, in central dining facility, in restaurants.

Costs (2003-2004) • One term: $11,050 (estimated); includes tuition, housing, some meals, excursions, international airfare, international student ID. $395 application fee. Financial aid available for students from sponsoring institution: scholarships, loans.

For More Information • Dr. Curtis P. Lawrence, Dean, University College, Southwest Missouri State University, 901 South National Avenue, Springfield, MO 65804; *Phone:* 417-836-6370; *Fax:* 417-836-6372. *E-mail:* cpl142F@smsu.edu. *World Wide Web:* http://www.smsu.edu/studyaway/. Students may also apply through University of Missouri–St. Louis, Center for International Studies, 8001 Natural Bridge Road, St. Louis, MO 63121-4499.

STATE UNIVERSITY OF NEW YORK AT BINGHAMTON
LONDON SEMESTER

Held at Florida State University–London Study Center
Academic Focus • Art history, drama/theater, English literature, history, political science and government.

Program Information • Classes are held on the campus of Florida State University–London Study Center. Faculty members are drawn from the sponsor's U.S. staff and local instructors hired by the sponsor. Scheduled travel to the Lake District, western England; field trips to Stratford-upon-Avon, Stonehenge, Oxford.

Sessions • Fall, spring.

Eligibility Requirements • Open to sophomores, juniors, seniors; 2.5 GPA; 3 letters of recommendation; good academic standing at home school.

Living Arrangements • Students live in locally rented apartments. Quarters are shared with host institution students. Meals are taken on one's own, in residences, in restaurants.

Costs (2003-2004) • One term: $9500 for New York residents; $12,000 for nonresidents; includes tuition, housing, all meals, insurance, excursions, international airfare, books and class materials, international student ID, student support services. $250 nonrefundable deposit required. Financial aid available for students from sponsoring institution: scholarships, loans.

For More Information • Dr. Bernard Rosenthal, London Program Director, State University of New York at Binghamton, Department of English, General Literature, and Rhetoric, Binghamton, NY 13902-6000; *Phone:* 607-777-2087; *Fax:* 607-777-2408. *E-mail:* oip@binghamton.edu. *World Wide Web:* http://oip.binghamton.edu/

STATE UNIVERSITY OF NEW YORK AT NEW PALTZ
STUDY ABROAD IN LONDON, ENGLAND AT MIDDLESEX UNIVERSITY

Hosted by Middlesex University
Academic Focus • Full curriculum.

ENGLAND
London

Program Information • Students attend classes at Middlesex University. Optional travel to Paris, Amsterdam, Ireland, sites throughout the United Kingdom at an extra cost.

Sessions • Fall, spring, yearlong.

Eligibility Requirements • Minimum age 18; open to sophomores, juniors, seniors; 2.5 GPA; 2 letters of recommendation; good academic standing at home school.

Living Arrangements • Students live in host institution dormitories. Quarters are shared with host institution students, students from other programs. Meals are taken on one's own, in residences, in restaurants.

Costs (2003-2004) • One term: $7823 for New York residents; $8128 for nonresidents. Yearlong program: $15,600 for New York residents; $16,257 for nonresidents; includes tuition, housing, insurance, student support services, administrative fee. $25 application fee. $300–$600 nonrefundable deposit required. Financial aid available for students from sponsoring institution: scholarships, loans.

For More Information • Center for International Programs, State University of New York at New Paltz, 75 South Manheim Boulevard, Suite 9, New Paltz, NY 12561; *Phone:* 845-257-3125; *Fax:* 845-257-3129. *E-mail:* international@newpaltz.edu. *World Wide Web:* http://www.newpaltz.edu/studyabroad/

STATE UNIVERSITY OF NEW YORK AT NEW PALTZ
STUDY ABROAD: KINGSTON UNIVERSITY

Hosted by Kingston University

Academic Focus • Full curriculum.

Program Information • Students attend classes at Kingston University. Field trips to Oxford, Bath, Stonehenge; optional travel to Paris, Amsterdam, Edinburgh, Dublin at an extra cost.

Sessions • Fall, spring, yearlong.

Eligibility Requirements • Minimum age 18; open to sophomores, juniors, seniors; 2.5 GPA; 2 letters of recommendation; good academic standing at home school.

Living Arrangements • Students live in locally rented apartments, host family homes. Quarters are shared with host institution students, students from other programs. Meals are taken on one's own, in residences, in restaurants.

Costs (2003-2004) • One term: $4423 for New York residents; $5928 for nonresidents. Yearlong program: $8846 for New York residents; $11,857 for nonresidents; includes tuition, all meals, insurance, excursions, administrative fee. $25 application fee. $300–$600 nonrefundable deposit required. Financial aid available for students from sponsoring institution: scholarships, loans.

For More Information • Center for International Programs, State University of New York at New Paltz, 75 South Manheim Boulevard, Suite 9, New Paltz, NY 12561; *Phone:* 845-257-3125; *Fax:* 845-257-3129. *E-mail:* international@newpaltz.edu. *World Wide Web:* http://www.newpaltz.edu/studyabroad/

STATE UNIVERSITY OF NEW YORK AT OSWEGO
CAPA LONDON CENTER

Hosted by Centre for Academic Programmes Abroad

Academic Focus • Art, business administration/management, communications, European studies, liberal studies, literature, psychology, theater management.

Program Information • Students attend classes at Centre for Academic Programmes Abroad. Field trips to Kent, Stratford-upon-Avon, Stonehenge; optional travel to Paris, Scotland, Wales at an extra cost.

Sessions • Fall, spring, yearlong.

Eligibility Requirements • Open to sophomores, juniors, seniors; 2.5 GPA; 3 letters of recommendation; good academic standing at home school; personal statement.

Living Arrangements • Students live in residence halls in London. Quarters are shared with host institution students. Meals are taken on one's own, in residences, in restaurants.

Costs (2003-2004) • One term: $8000 (estimated). Yearlong program: $16,000 (estimated); includes tuition, housing, insurance, excursions, student support services, food stipend, Tube pass, cultural events. $250 nonrefundable deposit required. Financial aid

available for students: home university financial aid, loan processing and scholarships for Oswego students.

For More Information • Ms. Mary Kerr, Program Specialist, State University of New York at Oswego, 122A Swetman Hall, Oswego, NY 13126; *Phone:* 888-4-OSWEGO; *Fax:* 315-312-2477. *E-mail:* intled@oswego.edu. *World Wide Web:* http://www.oswego.edu/intled/

STATE UNIVERSITY OF NEW YORK AT OSWEGO
OSWEGO LONDON CENTRE AT HURON UNIVERSITY

Hosted by Huron University USA in London

Academic Focus • Art, business administration/management, commerce; communications, finance, international business, marketing.

Program Information • Students attend classes at Huron University USA in London. Field trips; optional travel to different areas of continental Europe at an extra cost.

Sessions • Fall, spring, yearlong.

Eligibility Requirements • Open to sophomores, juniors, seniors; 2.5 GPA; 3 letters of recommendation; good academic standing at home school; personal statement.

Living Arrangements • Students live in host institution dormitories. Quarters are shared with host institution students. Meals are taken on one's own, in residences, in restaurants.

Costs (2003-2004) • One term: $8770. Yearlong program: $17,540; includes tuition, housing, insurance, excursions, student support services, Tube pass, airport pick-up, cultural events. $250 nonrefundable deposit required. Financial aid available for students: home university financial aid, loan processing and scholarships for Oswego students.

For More Information • Ms. Mary Kerr, Program Specialist, State University of New York at Oswego, 122A Swetman Hall, Oswego, NY 13126; *Phone:* 888-4-OSWEGO; *Fax:* 315-312-2477. *E-mail:* intled@oswego.edu. *World Wide Web:* http://www.oswego.edu/intled/

STATE UNIVERSITY OF NEW YORK COLLEGE AT BROCKPORT
BRUNEL UNIVERSITY PROGRAM

Hosted by Brunel University

Academic Focus • Full curriculum.

Program Information • Students attend classes at Brunel University. Scheduled travel to Paris; field trips to the London Extras program, Wales, Bath.

Sessions • Fall, yearlong.

Eligibility Requirements • Minimum age 18; open to juniors, seniors; 2.5 GPA; 2 letters of recommendation; ability to do upper-division coursework in chosen subject.

Living Arrangements • Students live in host institution dormitories. Quarters are shared with host institution students. Meals are taken on one's own, in residences.

Costs (2003-2004) • One term: $9250. Yearlong program: $17,625; includes tuition, housing, excursions, international student ID, student support services. $350 nonrefundable deposit required. Financial aid available for all students: scholarships, loans, federal financial aid, grants.

For More Information • Dr. John Perry, Director, Office of International Education, State University of New York College at Brockport, 350 New Campus Drive, Brockport, NY 14420; *Phone:* 800-298-SUNY; *Fax:* 585-637-3218. *E-mail:* overseas@brockport.edu. *World Wide Web:* http://www.brockport.edu/studyabroad/

STATE UNIVERSITY OF NEW YORK COLLEGE AT BROCKPORT
CITY UNIVERSITY PROGRAM

Hosted by City University

Academic Focus • Full curriculum.

Program Information • Students attend classes at City University. Field trips to the London Extras Program, Wales.

Sessions • Fall, spring, yearlong.

Eligibility Requirements • Minimum age 18; open to juniors, seniors; 3.0 GPA; 2 letters of recommendation; good academic standing at home school; ability to do upper-division course work in chosen subject.

Living Arrangements • Students live in host institution dormitories. Quarters are shared with host institution students. Meals are taken on one's own, in residences.

Costs (2003-2004) • One term: $9250 for fall term; $11,450 for spring. Yearlong program: $18,875; includes tuition, housing, excursions, international student ID, student support services. $350 nonrefundable deposit required. Financial aid available for all students: scholarships, loans, regular financial aid, grants.

For More Information • Dr. John J. Perry, Director, Office of International Education, State University of New York College at Brockport, 350 New Campus Drive, Brockport, NY 14420; *Phone:* 800-298-SUNY; *Fax:* 585-637-3218. *E-mail:* overseas@brockport.edu. *World Wide Web:* http://www.brockport.edu/studyabroad/

STATE UNIVERSITY OF NEW YORK COLLEGE AT BROCKPORT
KING'S COLLEGE LONDON PROGRAM

Hosted by King's College London, University of London
Academic Focus • Full curriculum.
Program Information • Students attend classes at King's College London, University of London. Field trips to the London Extras Program, Wales.
Sessions • Fall, spring, yearlong.
Eligibility Requirements • Minimum age 18; open to juniors, seniors; 3.25 GPA; 2 letters of recommendation; good academic standing at home school; demonstrated ability to do upper-division work in subject chosen.
Living Arrangements • Students live in host institution dormitories. Quarters are shared with host institution students. Meals are taken on one's own, in residences.
Costs (2003-2004) • One term: $12,535 for fall term; $13,535 for spring. Yearlong program: $23,720; includes tuition, housing, excursions, international student ID, student support services. $350 nonrefundable deposit required. Financial aid available for all students: scholarships, loans, regular financial aid, grants.
For More Information • Dr. John Perry, Director, Office of International Education, State University of New York College at Brockport, 350 New Campus Drive, Brockport, NY 14420; *Phone:* 800-298-SUNY; *Fax:* 585-637-3218. *E-mail:* overseas@brockport.edu. *World Wide Web:* http://www.brockport.edu/studyabroad/

STATE UNIVERSITY OF NEW YORK COLLEGE AT BROCKPORT
LONDON INTERNSHIP PROGRAM

Academic Focus • Accounting, advertising and public relations, art administration, business administration/management, chemical sciences, communications, criminal justice, ecology, film and media studies, health and physical education, history, international business, journalism, law and legal studies, marketing, nursing, parks and recreation, political science and government, radio, social work.
Program Information • Faculty members are local instructors hired by the sponsor. Field trips to the London Extras Program, Wales, Paris.
Sessions • Fall, spring.
Eligibility Requirements • Minimum age 18; open to juniors, seniors, graduate students; course work in area of internship; 2.5 GPA; 2 letters of recommendation; résumé.
Living Arrangements • Students live in locally rented apartments, hotels. Meals are taken on one's own, in residences.
Costs (2004-2005) • One term: $6850 for fall; $7850 for spring; includes tuition, excursions, international student ID, student support services, internship placement. $350 nonrefundable deposit required. Financial aid available for all students: scholarships, loans, regular financial aid, grants.
For More Information • Dr. John Perry, Director, Office of International Education, State University of New York College at Brockport, 350 New Campus Drive, Brockport, NY 14420; *Phone:* 800-298-SUNY; *Fax:* 585-637-3218. *E-mail:* overseas@brockport.edu. *World Wide Web:* http://www.brockport.edu/studyabroad/

STATE UNIVERSITY OF NEW YORK COLLEGE AT BROCKPORT
MIDDLESEX UNIVERSITY PROGRAM

Hosted by Middlesex University
Academic Focus • Full curriculum.
Program Information • Students attend classes at Middlesex University. Scheduled travel to Wales, Bath; field trips to the London extras program sites.
Sessions • Fall, spring, yearlong.
Eligibility Requirements • Minimum age 18; open to sophomores, juniors, seniors; course work in area of internship, if applicable; 2.5 GPA; 2 letters of recommendation; ability to do upper-division course work in chosen subject; must be at least a second-semester sophomore; résumé required for part-time internship option.
Living Arrangements • Students live in host institution dormitories. Quarters are shared with host institution students. Meals are taken on one's own, in residences.
Costs (2003-2004) • One term: $10,325 for fall; $10,525 for spring. Yearlong program: $19,500; includes tuition, housing, excursions, international student ID, student support services. $350 nonrefundable deposit required. Financial aid available for all students: scholarships, loans, regular financial aid, grants.
For More Information • Dr. John Perry, Director, Office of International Education, State University of New York College at Brockport, 350 New Campus Drive, Brockport, NY 14420; *Phone:* 800-298-SUNY; *Fax:* 585-637-3218. *E-mail:* overseas@brockport.edu. *World Wide Web:* http://www.brockport.edu/studyabroad/

STATE UNIVERSITY OF NEW YORK COLLEGE AT BROCKPORT
QUEEN MARY COLLEGE PROGRAM

Hosted by Queen Mary, University of London
Academic Focus • Full curriculum.
Program Information • Students attend classes at Queen Mary, University of London. Field trips to the London Extras Program, Wales, Bath.
Sessions • Fall, spring, yearlong.
Eligibility Requirements • Minimum age 18; open to juniors, seniors; 2.5 GPA; 2 letters of recommendation; good academic standing at home school; demonstrated ability to do upper-division work in the subjects chosen.
Living Arrangements • Students live in host institution dormitories. Quarters are shared with host institution students. Meals are taken on one's own, in residences.
Costs (2003-2004) • One term: $12,025 for fall term; $13,025 for spring. Yearlong program: $22,950; includes tuition, housing, excursions, international student ID, student support services, airport pick-up upon arrival. $350 nonrefundable deposit required. Financial aid available for all students: scholarships, loans, regular financial aid, grants.
For More Information • Dr. John Perry, Director, Office of International Education, State University of New York College at Brockport, 350 New Campus Drive, Brockport, NY 14420; *Phone:* 800-298-SUNY; *Fax:* 585-637-3218. *E-mail:* overseas@brockport.edu. *World Wide Web:* http://www.brockport.edu/studyabroad/

STATE UNIVERSITY OF NEW YORK COLLEGE AT BROCKPORT
UNIVERSITY COLLEGE LONDON PROGRAM

Hosted by University College London
Academic Focus • Full curriculum.
Program Information • Students attend classes at University College London. Field trips to the London Extras Program, Wales, Bath.
Sessions • Fall, yearlong, spring and summer terms.
Eligibility Requirements • Minimum age 18; open to juniors, seniors; course work in English, history; if applicable to track chosen; 2 letters of recommendation; good academic standing at home school; demonstrated ability to do upper-division work in subject chosen; minimum 3.5 GPA for some courses.
Living Arrangements • Students live in host institution dormitories. Quarters are shared with host institution students. Meals are taken on one's own, in residences.

Costs (2003-2004) • One term: $12,735 for fall term; $14,100 for two-term spring. Yearlong program: $24,010; includes tuition, housing, excursions, international student ID, student support services. $350 nonrefundable deposit required. Financial aid available for all students: scholarships, loans, regular financial aid, grants.

For More Information • Dr. John Perry, Director, Office of International Education, State University of New York College at Brockport, 350 New Campus Drive, Brockport, NY 14420; *Phone:* 800-298-SUNY; *Fax:* 585-637-3218. *E-mail:* overseas@brockport.edu. *World Wide Web:* http://www.brockport.edu/studyabroad/

STATE UNIVERSITY OF NEW YORK COLLEGE AT BROCKPORT
UNIVERSITY OF SURREY, ROEHAMPTON PROGRAM

Hosted by University of Surrey Roehampton
Academic Focus • Full curriculum.
Program Information • Students attend classes at University of Surrey Roehampton. Field trips to the London Extras Program: Wales, Bath.
Sessions • Fall, spring, yearlong.
Eligibility Requirements • Minimum age 18; open to juniors, seniors; course work in area of internship, if applicable; 2.85 GPA; 2 letters of recommendation; ability to do upper division course work in chosen subject; résumé for internship option.
Living Arrangements • Students live in host institution dormitories. Quarters are shared with host institution students. Meals are taken on one's own, in residences.
Costs (2004-2005) • One term: $10,650 for fall; $13,000 for spring. Yearlong program: contact sponsor for cost; includes tuition, housing, excursions, international student ID, student support services. $350 nonrefundable deposit required. Financial aid available for all students: scholarships, loans, regular financial aid, grants.
For More Information • Dr. John Perry, Director, Office of International Education, State University of New York College at Brockport, 350 New Campus Drive, Brockport, NY 14420; *Phone:* 800-298-SUNY; *Fax:* 585-637-3218. *E-mail:* overseas@brockport.edu. *World Wide Web:* http://www.brockport.edu/studyabroad/

STATE UNIVERSITY OF NEW YORK COLLEGE AT BROCKPORT
UNIVERSITY OF WESTMINSTER PROGRAM

Hosted by University of Westminster
Academic Focus • Full curriculum.
Program Information • Students attend classes at University of Westminster. Field trips to the London Extras Program, Wales, Bath.
Sessions • Fall, spring, yearlong.
Eligibility Requirements • Minimum age 18; open to juniors, seniors; course work in area of internship, if applicable; 3.0 GPA; 2 letters of recommendation; good academic standing at home school; demonstrated ability to do upper-division work in subject chosen; résumé required for part-time internship option.
Living Arrangements • Students live in host institution dormitories. Quarters are shared with host institution students. Meals are taken on one's own, in residences.
Costs (2003-2004) • One term: $10,425 for fall term; $10,725 for spring. Yearlong program: $19,300; includes tuition, housing, excursions, international student ID, student support services, some meals on field trip to Wales. $350 nonrefundable deposit required. Financial aid available for all students: scholarships, loans, regular financial aid, grants.
For More Information • Dr. John Perry, Director, Office of International Education, State University of New York College at Brockport, 350 New Campus Drive, Brockport, NY 14420; *Phone:* 800-298-SUNY; *Fax:* 585-637-3218. *E-mail:* overseas@brockport.edu. *World Wide Web:* http://www.brockport.edu/studyabroad/

SYRACUSE UNIVERSITY
BUSINESS ADMINISTRATION IN LONDON

Hosted by Syracuse University–London
Academic Focus • Accounting, business administration/management, finance, labor and industrial relations, marketing.

Program Information • Students attend classes at Syracuse University–London. Field trips to Stratford-upon-Avon, Greenwich, Windsor, Stonehenge; optional travel to Paris, Amsterdam at an extra cost.
Sessions • Fall, spring, yearlong.
Eligibility Requirements • Open to sophomores, juniors, seniors; 1 letter of recommendation; good academic standing at home school; approval of Syracuse School of Management.
Living Arrangements • Students live in locally rented apartments. Quarters are shared with host institution students. Meals are taken on one's own, in residences.
Costs (2004-2005) • One term: $18,650. Yearlong program: $37,300; includes tuition, housing, insurance, excursions, international student ID, student support services, one-way international airfare. $50 application fee. $450 nonrefundable deposit required. Financial aid available for all students: scholarships, work study, loans, tuition differential grants.
For More Information • Mr. James Buschman, Senior Associate Director, Syracuse University, 106 Walnut Place, Syracuse, NY 13244-4170; *Phone:* 315-443-3471; *Fax:* 315-443-4593. *E-mail:* suabroad@syr.edu. *World Wide Web:* http://suabroad.syr.edu/

SYRACUSE UNIVERSITY
ENGINEERING YEAR IN LONDON

Hosted by Syracuse University–London, University College London, City University
Academic Focus • Computer science, electrical engineering, engineering, industrial management, mathematics.
Program Information • Students attend classes at Syracuse University–London, University College London, City University.
Sessions • Yearlong.
Eligibility Requirements • Open to juniors; major in engineering; 3.0 GPA; 1 letter of recommendation; good academic standing at home school; home school approval.
Living Arrangements • Students live in locally rented apartments. Meals are taken on one's own, in residences.
Costs (2004-2005) • Yearlong program: $25,720; includes tuition, international student ID. $50 application fee. $450 nonrefundable deposit required. Financial aid available for all students: scholarships, loans.
For More Information • Mr. James Buschman, Senior Associate Director, Syracuse University, 106 Walnut Place, Syracuse, NY 13244-4170; *Phone:* 315-443-3471; *Fax:* 315-443-4593. *E-mail:* suabroad@syr.edu. *World Wide Web:* http://suabroad.syr.edu/

SYRACUSE UNIVERSITY
LONDON COMMUNICATIONS PROGRAM

Hosted by Syracuse University–London
Academic Focus • Advertising and public relations, communications, journalism, telecommunications.
Program Information • Students attend classes at Syracuse University–London. Field trips to Stratford-upon-Avon, Greenwich, Windsor, Stonehenge; optional travel to Paris, Amsterdam at an extra cost.
Sessions • Fall, spring, yearlong.
Eligibility Requirements • Open to sophomores, juniors, seniors; 1 letter of recommendation; good academic standing at home school; home school approval; essays.
Living Arrangements • Students live in locally rented apartments. Quarters are shared with host institution students. Meals are taken on one's own, in residences.
Costs (2004-2005) • One term: $18,650. Yearlong program: $37,300; includes tuition, housing, excursions, international student ID, student support services, one-way international airfare. $50 application fee. $450 nonrefundable deposit required. Financial aid available for all students: scholarships, work study, loans, tuition differential grants.
For More Information • Mr. James Buschman, Senior Associate Director, Syracuse University, 106 Walnut Place, Syracuse, NY 13244-4170; *Phone:* 315-443-3471; *Fax:* 315-443-4593. *E-mail:* suabroad@syr.edu. *World Wide Web:* http://suabroad.syr.edu/

SYRACUSE UNIVERSITY
LONDON DRAMA PROGRAM

Hosted by Syracuse University–London

Academic Focus • Drama/theater, music performance, performing arts, theater management, visual and performing arts.

Program Information • Students attend classes at Syracuse University–London. Field trips to Stratford-upon-Avon, Greenwich, Windsor, Stonehenge; optional travel to Paris, Amsterdam at an extra cost.

Sessions • Fall, spring, yearlong.

Eligibility Requirements • Open to sophomores, juniors, seniors; 2 letters of recommendation; good academic standing at home school; approval by College of Visual and Performing Arts.

Living Arrangements • Students live in locally rented apartments. Meals are taken on one's own, in residences.

Costs (2004-2005) • One term: $18,650. Yearlong program: $37,300; includes tuition, housing, excursions, international student ID, student support services, one-way international airfare. $50 application fee. $450 nonrefundable deposit required. Financial aid available for all students: scholarships, work study, loans, tuition differential grants.

For More Information • Mr. James Buschman, Senior Associate Director, Syracuse University, 106 Walnut Place, Syracuse, NY 13244-4170; *Phone:* 315-443-3471; *Fax:* 315-443-4593. *E-mail:* suabroad@syr.edu. *World Wide Web:* http://suabroad.syr.edu/

SYRACUSE UNIVERSITY
LONDON PROGRAM

Hosted by Syracuse University–London, City University

Academic Focus • Advertising and public relations, business administration/management, communications, creative writing, drama/theater, economics, engineering, English literature, fashion design, fine/studio arts, history, marketing, political science and government, psychology, public policy, women's studies.

Program Information • Students attend classes at Syracuse University–London, City University. Field trips to Stratford-upon-Avon, Windsor, Greewich, Stonehenge, Scotland, northern England; optional travel to Paris, Amsterdam at an extra cost.

Sessions • Fall, spring, yearlong.

Eligibility Requirements • Open to freshmen, sophomores, juniors, seniors, graduate students; 2 letters of recommendation; good academic standing at home school; maturity; essay.

Living Arrangements • Students live in locally rented apartments. Quarters are shared with host institution students. Meals are taken on one's own, in residences.

Costs (2004-2005) • One term: $18,650. Yearlong program: $37,300; includes tuition, housing, excursions, lab equipment, international student ID, student support services, one-way international airfare. $50 application fee. $450 nonrefundable deposit required. Financial aid available for all students: scholarships, work study, loans, tuition differential grants.

For More Information • Mr. James Buschman, Senior Associate Director, Syracuse University, 106 Walnut Place, Syracuse, NY 13244-4170; *Phone:* 800-235-3472; *Fax:* 315-443-4593. *E-mail:* suabroad@syr.edu. *World Wide Web:* http://suabroad.syr.edu/

TEMPLE UNIVERSITY
TEMPLE UNIVERSITY LONDON

Hosted by Temple University London

Academic Focus • Communications, film and media studies, history, journalism, performing arts, political science and government, telecommunications.

Program Information • Students attend classes at Temple University London. Field trips to Stonehenge, the Globe Theatre.

Sessions • Fall.

Eligibility Requirements • Open to juniors, seniors, graduate students; 1 letter of recommendation; good academic standing at home school; official transcripts.

ENGLAND
London

Living Arrangements • Students live in host institution dormitories. Quarters are shared with host institution students. Meals are taken on one's own, in central dining facility.
Costs (2002) • One term: $14,300; includes tuition, housing, all meals, international airfare, books and class materials. $20 application fee. $100 refundable deposit required. Financial aid available for students from sponsoring institution: scholarships, loans.
For More Information • Ms. Debbie Marshall, Administrative Coordinator, Temple University, Office of Dean, School of Communications and Theater, Philadelphia, PA 19122; *Phone:* 215-204-1961. *E-mail:* deborah.marshall@temple.edu. *World Wide Web:* http://www.temple.edu/studyabroad/

TUFTS UNIVERSITY
TUFTS IN LONDON

Hosted by School of Oriental and African Studies–University of London, University College London
Academic Focus • Full curriculum.
Program Information • Students attend classes at School of Oriental and African Studies–University of London, University College London. Field trips to Stratford-upon-Avon, Edinburgh, Oxford, Cambridge; optional travel to Brussels, Bruges, Paris, Amsterdam at an extra cost.
Sessions • Yearlong.
Eligibility Requirements • Open to sophomores, juniors, seniors; 3.3 GPA; 2 letters of recommendation; good academic standing at home school; minimum 3.3 GPA in major if overall GPA is less than 3.3.
Living Arrangements • Students live in host institution dormitories. Quarters are shared with host institution students. Meals are taken on one's own, in residences.
Costs (2004-2005) • Yearlong program: $39,314; includes tuition, housing, all meals, excursions, student support services, cost-of-living allowance, monthly transportation pass, subsidized cultural activities. $40 application fee. $350 nonrefundable deposit required. Financial aid available for students from sponsoring institution: scholarships, loans.
For More Information • Ms. Melanie Armstrong, Program and Marketing Coordinator, Tufts Programs Abroad, Tufts University, Dowling Hall, Medford, MA 02155-7084; *Phone:* 617-627-2000; *Fax:* 617-627-3971. *E-mail:* melanie.armstrong@tufts.edu. *World Wide Web:* http://ase.tufts.edu/studyabroad/

UNIVERSITY OF CONNECTICUT
LONDON PROGRAM

Hosted by City University
Academic Focus • Art history, English, science, social sciences.
Program Information • Students attend classes at City University. Classes are also held on the campus of Globe Theatre. Scheduled travel to the Lake District, Bath, Stratford-upon-Avon; field trips to Bath, Stonehenge, Stratford-upon-Avon.
Sessions • Fall, spring, yearlong.
Eligibility Requirements • Open to sophomores, juniors, seniors, graduate students; 2.5 GPA; 2 letters of recommendation; good academic standing at home school.
Living Arrangements • Students live in locally rented apartments. Quarters are shared with host institution students, students from other programs. Meals are taken on one's own, in residences, in restaurants.
Costs (2003-2004) • One term: $12,205 for Connecticut residents; $13,520 for nonresidents. Yearlong program: $22,625 for Connecticut residents; $25,255 for nonresidents; includes tuition, housing, all meals, excursions, international student ID, fees, one-way airfare. $25 application fee. $350 nonrefundable deposit required. Financial aid available for students from sponsoring institution: scholarships, loans.
For More Information • Mr. Gordon Lustila, Acting Director of Study Abroad Programs, University of Connecticut, 843 Bolton Road, Unit 1207, Storrs, CT 06269-1207; *Phone:* 860-486-5022; *Fax:* 860-486-2976. *E-mail:* sabadm03@uconnvm.uconn.edu. *World Wide Web:* http://studyabroad.uconn.edu/

UNIVERSITY OF DELAWARE
SPRING AND FALL SEMESTER IN LONDON

Hosted by University of Delaware London Centre
Academic Focus • Art history, economics, English, history, music, political science and government, sociology.
Program Information • Students attend classes at University of Delaware London Centre. Field trips to local and regional cultural sites; optional travel to Europe at an extra cost.
Sessions • Fall, spring.
Eligibility Requirements • Open to freshmen, sophomores, juniors, seniors, adults; 2.0 GPA; 2 letters of recommendation.
Living Arrangements • Students live in locally rented apartments. Quarters are shared with host institution students. Meals are taken on one's own, in residences.
Costs (2002-2003) • One term: contact sponsor for cost. $200 nonrefundable deposit required. Financial aid available for all students: scholarships.
For More Information • Center for International Studies, University of Delaware, 186 South College Avenue, Newark, DE 19716-1450; *Phone:* 888-831-4685; *Fax:* 302-831-6042. *E-mail:* studyabroad@udel.edu. *World Wide Web:* http://www.udel.edu/studyabroad/

UNIVERSITY OF LONDON–LONDON SCHOOL OF ECONOMICS AND POLITICAL SCIENCE
THE GENERAL COURSE

Hosted by University of London–London School of Economics and Political Science
Academic Focus • Full curriculum.
Program Information • Students attend classes at University of London–London School of Economics and Political Science.
Sessions • Yearlong.
Eligibility Requirements • Open to juniors, seniors, graduate students, adults; 3.3 GPA; 2 letters of recommendation; good academic background in chosen course of study.
Living Arrangements • Students live in host institution dormitories, locally rented apartments, program-owned apartments, program-owned houses, host family homes, host institution apartments. Quarters are shared with host institution students, students from other programs. Meals are taken on one's own, in residences, in central dining facility.
Costs (2003-2004) • Yearlong program: £20,639; includes tuition, housing, all meals, insurance, books and class materials, student support services, local transportation, heating, some entertainment.
For More Information • Mr. Will Breare-Hall, Student Recruitment Officer, University of London–London School of Economics and Political Science, Houghton Street, London WC2A 2AE, England; *Phone:* +44 207-955-7928; *Fax:* +44 207-955-7421. *E-mail:* w.s.breare-hall@lse.ac.uk. *World Wide Web:* http://www.lse.ac.uk/general-course/

UNIVERSITY OF MARYLAND, COLLEGE PARK
MARYLAND IN LONDON

Hosted by London Metropolitan University
Academic Focus • Art history, British studies, business administration/management, computer science, criminal justice, drama/theater, economics, English, full curriculum, history, nutrition, political science and government, psychology, sociology.
Program Information • Students attend classes at London Metropolitan University. Field trips to theaters, Parliament.
Sessions • Fall, spring, yearlong.
Eligibility Requirements • Open to sophomores, juniors, seniors; 2.75 GPA; 1 letter of recommendation; demonstration of writing ability.
Living Arrangements • Students live in host institution dormitories, locally rented apartments. Quarters are shared with host institution students. Meals are taken on one's own, in residences, in restaurants.
Costs (2002-2003) • One term: $5595. Yearlong program: $11,190; includes tuition, excursions, student support services, academic and personal advising, faculty director. $50 application fee. $500 nonrefundable deposit required. Financial aid available for students from sponsoring institution: scholarships.

For More Information • Dr. Michael Ulrich, International Studies Coordinator, University of Maryland, College Park, Study Abroad Office, 3125 Mitchell Building, College Park, MD 20742-5215; *Phone:* 301-314-7746; *Fax:* 301-314-9347. *E-mail:* studyabr@deans. umd.edu. *World Wide Web:* http://www.umd.edu/studyabroad/

UNIVERSITY OF MIAMI
QUEEN MARY, UNIVERSITY OF LONDON, ENGLAND

Hosted by Queen Mary, University of London
Academic Focus • Economics, English, European studies, geography, history, international affairs, language studies, physics, political science and government, science, social sciences.
Program Information • Students attend classes at Queen Mary, University of London.
Sessions • Fall, spring, yearlong.
Eligibility Requirements • Minimum age 18; open to sophomores, juniors, seniors; 3.0 GPA; 2 letters of recommendation; official transcripts; essay.
Living Arrangements • Students live in host institution dormitories. Quarters are shared with host institution students. Meals are taken on one's own, in residences, in central dining facility.
Costs (2003-2004) • One term: $12,919. Yearlong program: $25,838; includes tuition, student support services. $40 application fee. $500 nonrefundable deposit required. Financial aid available for students from sponsoring institution: scholarships, loans.
For More Information • Ms. Elyse Resnick, Assistant Director, University of Miami, International Education and Exchange Programs, 5050 Brunson Drive, Allen Hall 212, PO Box 248005, Coral Gables, FL 33124-1610; *Phone:* 305-284-3434; *Fax:* 305-284-4235. *E-mail:* ieep@miami. edu. *World Wide Web:* http://www.studyabroad.miami.edu/

UNIVERSITY OF MIAMI
UNIVERSITY OF WESTMINSTER

Hosted by University of Westminster
Academic Focus • English literature, psychology, Romance languages, social sciences.
Program Information • Students attend classes at University of Westminster.
Sessions • Fall, spring, yearlong.
Eligibility Requirements • Minimum age 18; open to sophomores, juniors, seniors; 3.0 GPA; 2 letters of recommendation; good academic standing at home school; official transcript; essay.
Living Arrangements • Students live in host institution dormitories, locally rented apartments. Quarters are shared with host institution students, students from other programs. Meals are taken on one's own, in residences, in restaurants.
Costs (2003-2004) • One term: $12,919. Yearlong program: contact sponsor for cost; includes tuition, student support services. $40 application fee. $500 nonrefundable deposit required. Financial aid available for students from sponsoring institution: scholarships, loans.
For More Information • Ms. Carol Lazzeri, Assistant Director, University of Miami, International Education and Exchange Programs, 5050 Brunson Drive, Allen Hall 212, PO Box 248005, Coral Gables, FL 33124-1610; *Phone:* 305-284-3434; *Fax:* 305-284-4235. *E-mail:* ieep@miami. edu. *World Wide Web:* http://www.studyabroad.miami.edu/

UNIVERSITY OF MINNESOTA
STUDY AND INTERNSHIPS IN LONDON

Hosted by Centre for Academic Programmes Abroad
Academic Focus • Art, cultural studies, drama/theater, economics, English literature, film and media studies, finance, history, international affairs, international business, marketing, political science and government, radio, women's studies.
Program Information • Students attend classes at Centre for Academic Programmes Abroad. Field trips to local areas of interest, Bath, Stonehenge; optional travel at an extra cost.
Sessions • Fall, spring.
Eligibility Requirements • Minimum age 18; open to freshmen, sophomores, juniors, seniors, graduate students, adults; 2.5 GPA; good academic standing at home school; 1 letter of recommendation for regular session, 2 for internship.

Living Arrangements • Students live in locally rented apartments. Quarters are shared with host institution students, students from other programs. Meals are taken on one's own, in residences, in restaurants.
Costs (2004-2005) • One term: contact sponsor for cost. $50 application fee. $400 nonrefundable deposit required. Financial aid available for students from sponsoring institution: scholarships, loans.
For More Information • University of Minnesota, Learning Abroad Center, 230 Heller Hall, 271 19th Avenue South, Minneapolis, MN 55455; *Phone:* 888-700-UOFM; *Fax:* 612-626-8009. *E-mail:* umabroad@ umn.edu. *World Wide Web:* http://www.umabroad.umn.edu/

UNIVERSITY OF NEW HAMPSHIRE
LONDON PROGRAM

Hosted by Regent's College
Academic Focus • Art, British studies, business administration/ management, communications, computer science, drama/theater, English, history, music, political science and government, social sciences.
Program Information • Students attend classes at Regent's College. Field trips to Cambridge, Ely Cathedral, Avebury Stone Ring, Bath, Stratford-upon-Avon, Warwick Castle, Canterbury, Dover Castle; optional travel to Scotland, Ireland, Wales at an extra cost.
Sessions • Fall, spring, yearlong.
Eligibility Requirements • Open to sophomores, juniors, seniors; 2.5 GPA; 3 letters of recommendation; must be a New Hampshire student or resident.
Living Arrangements • Students live in host institution dormitories, locally rented apartments. Quarters are shared with host institution students, students from other programs. Meals are taken on one's own, in central dining facility.
Costs (2004-2005) • One term: $10,780. Yearlong program: $21,560; includes tuition, housing, all meals, student support services. $20 application fee. $2000 nonrefundable deposit required. Financial aid available for students from sponsoring institution: scholarships, loans.
For More Information • Coordinator, UNH London Program, University of New Hampshire, Hamilton Smith Hall, 95 Main Street, Durham, NH 03824-3574; *Phone:* 603-862-3962; *Fax:* 603-862-3962. *E-mail:* london.program@unh.edu. *World Wide Web:* http://www. unh.edu/

UNIVERSITY OF PITTSBURGH
PITT IN LONDON

Held at Centre for Academic Programmes Abroad
Academic Focus • Art history, British studies, business administration/management, drama/theater, English literature, history, political science and government.
Program Information • Classes are held on the campus of Centre for Academic Programmes Abroad. Faculty members are drawn from the sponsor's U.S. staff and local instructors hired by the sponsor. Field trips to Bath, Stonehenge; optional travel to Paris, Wales at an extra cost.
Sessions • Fall, spring.
Eligibility Requirements • Open to sophomores, juniors, seniors; 2.75 GPA; 1 letter of recommendation.
Living Arrangements • Students live in program-owned apartments, host family homes. Quarters are shared with students from other programs. Meals are taken on one's own, with host family, in residences, in restaurants.
Costs (2002-2003) • One term: $7750 for University of Pittsburgh students; $8050 for non-University of Pittsburgh students; includes tuition, housing, all meals, insurance, student support services, London Tube pass, Imperial College Student Union membership, library membership, social events. $50 application fee. $250 nonrefundable deposit required. Financial aid available for students from sponsoring institution: scholarships, loans.
For More Information • Ms. Erin Sunday, Study Abroad Advisor, University of Pittsburgh, Study Abroad Office, 802 William Pitt Union, Pittsburgh, PA 15260; *Phone:* 412-383-7489; *Fax:* 412-383-7166. *E-mail:* sunday@ucis.pitt.edu. *World Wide Web:* http://www. pitt.edu/~abroad/

ENGLAND
London

UNIVERSITY OF ROCHESTER
INTERNSHIPS IN EUROPE–ENGLAND

Held at University of London–London School of Economics and Political Science, Birkbeck College, University of London
Academic Focus • Advertising and public relations, art administration, art history, biomedical sciences, business administration/management, drama/theater, health-care management, history, international affairs, law and legal studies, marketing, political science and government, psychology, public policy.
Program Information • Classes are held on the campus of University of London–London School of Economics and Political Science, Birkbeck College, University of London. Faculty members are local instructors hired by the sponsor. Field trips to London.
Sessions • Fall, spring.
Eligibility Requirements • Open to juniors, seniors; 3.0 GPA; 2 letters of recommendation; good academic standing at home school.
Living Arrangements • Students live in locally rented apartments, host family homes. Meals are taken on one's own, in residences.
Costs (2003) • One term: $10,750; includes tuition, housing, student support services, some meals if homestay option chosen. $30 application fee. $300 nonrefundable deposit required. Financial aid available for students from sponsoring institution: scholarships, loans.
For More Information • Ms. Jacqueline Levine, Study Abroad Director, University of Rochester, Center for Study Abroad, PO Box 270376, Lattimore 206, Rochester, NY 14627-0376; *Phone:* 585-275-7532; *Fax:* 585-461-5131. *E-mail:* abroad@mail.rochester.edu. *World Wide Web:* http://www.rochester.edu/college/study-abroad/

UNIVERSITY OF TULSA
AUTUMN SEMESTER IN LONDON–LAW

Held at Florida State Center
Academic Focus • Law and legal studies.
Program Information • Classes are held on the campus of Florida State Center. Faculty members are drawn from the sponsor's U.S. staff and local instructors hired by the sponsor. Field trips to Bath, Stonehenge, Windsor castle, Oxford; optional travel at an extra cost.
Sessions • Fall.
Eligibility Requirements • Open to graduate students; course work in law; 1 letter of recommendation; good academic standing at home school; must be second year law student.
Living Arrangements • Students live in locally rented apartments. Meals are taken on one's own, in residences, in restaurants.
Costs (2002) • One term: $9200; includes tuition, some meals. $200 nonrefundable deposit required. Financial aid available for students from sponsoring institution: loans.
For More Information • Ms. Linda Lacey, Executive Director, CILC, University of Tulsa, 3120 East 4th Place, Tulsa, OK 74104; *Phone:* 918-631-2451; *Fax:* 918-631-2194. *E-mail:* linda-lacey@utulsa.edu. *World Wide Web:* http://www.utulsa.edu/studyabroad/

UNIVERSITY OF WESTMINSTER
GRADUATE STUDY ABROAD

Hosted by University of Westminster
Academic Focus • Full curriculum.
Program Information • Students attend classes at University of Westminster. Field trips to sites within London; optional travel to European cities, other cities in the United Kingdom at an extra cost.
Sessions • Fall, spring.
Eligibility Requirements • Minimum age 22; open to graduate students; 3.0 GPA; 1 letter of recommendation; good academic standing at home school; must be a graduate student in a chosen area of study and/or have professional experience.
Living Arrangements • Students live in host institution dormitories, locally rented apartments, host family homes. Quarters are shared with host institution students, students from other programs. Meals are taken as a group, on one's own, with host family, in residences, in restaurants.
Costs (2004-2005) • One term: £3500–£4500; includes tuition, student societies, some social activities, membership in some student organizations. £500 nonrefundable deposit required.
For More Information • Ms. Jane Wallis, Head of Study Abroad and Exhanges, University of Westminster, 16 Little Titchfield Street, London W1W 7UW, England; *Phone:* +44 207-911-5815; *Fax:* +44 207-911-5132. *E-mail:* jwallis@wmin.ac.uk. *World Wide Web:* http://www.wmin.ac.uk/international/

UNIVERSITY OF WESTMINSTER
UNDERGRADUATE STUDY ABROAD

Hosted by University of Westminster
Academic Focus • Full curriculum.
Program Information • Students attend classes at University of Westminster. Optional travel to European cities, other parts of the United Kingdom, cultural attractions in London at an extra cost.
Sessions • Fall, spring, yearlong.
Eligibility Requirements • Minimum age 18; open to sophomores, juniors, seniors, graduate students; 2.8 GPA; 1 letter of recommendation; good academic standing at home school; minimum 3.0 GPA for communications, design, and media students.
Living Arrangements • Students live in host institution dormitories, locally rented apartments, program-owned houses, host family homes. Quarters are shared with host institution students. Meals are taken as a group, on one's own, in residences, in restaurants.
Costs (2004-2005) • One term: £3940. Yearlong program: £7380; includes tuition, lab equipment, student support services, membership in all student societies, use of some university facilities, some social activities. £500 nonrefundable deposit required.
For More Information • Ms. Jane Wallis, Head of Study Abroad and Exchanges, University of Westminster, 16 Little Titchfield Street, London W1W 7UW, England; *Phone:* +44 207-911-5815; *Fax:* +44 207-911-5132. *E-mail:* study-abroad@westminster.ac.uk. *World Wide Web:* http://www.wmin.ac.uk/international/. Students may also apply through InterStudy USA, 63 Edward Street, Medford, MA 02155; State University of New York at Brockport, Office of International Education, 350 New Campus Drive, Brockport, NY 14420; Butler University, Institute for Study Abroad, 1100 West 42nd Street, Suite 305, Indianapolis, IN 46208-3345; Marymount College, Office of Study Abroad, 100 Marymount Avenue, Tarrytown, NY 10591-3796; Arcadia University, Center for Education Abroad, 450 South Easton Road, Glenside, PA 19038-3295.

UNIVERSITY OF WISCONSIN–PLATTEVILLE
LONDON STUDY CENTER

Hosted by Saint Mary's College
Academic Focus • Communications, drama/theater, education, English literature, environmental science/studies, geography, health and physical education, history, international business, Irish studies, philosophy, psychology, religious studies, sociology, women's studies.
Program Information • Students attend classes at Saint Mary's College. Field trips to the Houses of Parliament, Victoria and Albert Museum, Windsor Castle, Hampton Court, the Imperial War Museum; optional travel to Scotland, Paris, Amsterdam, a European tour at an extra cost.
Sessions • Fall, spring, yearlong.
Eligibility Requirements • Minimum age 18; open to freshmen, sophomores, juniors, seniors; 2.5 GPA; 2 letters of recommendation; good academic standing at home school.
Living Arrangements • Students live in host family homes. Meals are taken as a group, on one's own, with host family, in residences, in central dining facility, in restaurants.
Costs (2004-2005) • One term: $7100 for Wisconsin and Minnesota residents; $7700 nonresidents. Yearlong program: $14,200 for Wisconsin and Minnesota residents; $15,400 for nonresidents; includes tuition, housing, some meals, insurance, excursions, international student ID, student support services. $25 application fee. $400 nonrefundable deposit required. Financial aid available for all students: loans, federal and state grants, scholarships for Platteville students.
For More Information • Ms. Donna Anderson, Director, University of Wisconsin–Platteville, Institute for Study Abroad Programs, 111 Royce Hall, University Plaza, Platteville, WI 53818-3099; *Phone:* 800-342-1725; *Fax:* 608-342-1736. *E-mail:* studyabroad@uwplatt.edu. *World Wide Web:* http://www.uwplatt.edu/~studyabroad/

UNIVERSITY OF WISCONSIN–STEVENS POINT
SEMESTER IN LONDON, ENGLAND

Held at International Student House
Academic Focus • Anthropology, art history, drama/theater, English, geography, history, women's studies.

Program Information • Classes are held on the campus of International Student House. Faculty members are drawn from the sponsor's U.S. staff and local instructors hired by the sponsor. Scheduled travel to Germany, France, locations in England, Switzerland, Italy, Austria; field trips to Stratford-upon-Avon, the Lake District, Cambridge; optional travel to Scotland, Wales, Ireland at an extra cost.

Sessions • Fall, spring.

Eligibility Requirements • Minimum age 18; open to freshmen, sophomores, juniors, seniors, adults; 2.25 GPA; 3 letters of recommendation; good academic standing at home school.

Living Arrangements • Students live in program-arranged housing. Quarters are shared with students from other programs. Meals are taken in central dining facility, in restaurants.

Costs (2003-2004) • One term: $7100 for Wisconsin residents; $12,300 for nonresidents (estimated); includes tuition, housing, some meals, excursions, international airfare, books and class materials, international student ID, student support services. $15 application fee. $150 nonrefundable deposit required. Financial aid available for all students: scholarships, work study, loans.

For More Information • Mr. Mark Koepke, Associate Director, University of Wisconsin–Stevens Point, International Programs Office, Stevens Point, WI 54481; *Phone:* 715-346-2717; *Fax:* 715-346-3591. *E-mail:* intlprog@uwsp.edu. *World Wide Web:* http://www.uwsp.edu/studyabroad/

WEBSTER UNIVERSITY

WEBSTER UNIVERSITY AT REGENT'S COLLEGE IN LONDON

Hosted by Regent's College

Academic Focus • Business administration/management, communications, comparative literature, computer science, economics, history, international affairs, journalism, literature, psychology.

Program Information • Students attend classes at Regent's College. Field trips to Stonehenge, Stratford-upon-Avon, Bath; optional travel to Bath, Cambridge, London theatres, pony trekking in Wales, Leeds at an extra cost.

Sessions • Fall, spring, yearlong.

Eligibility Requirements • Open to sophomores, juniors, seniors, graduate students, adults; 2.5 GPA; 1 letter of recommendation; good academic standing at home school; no foreign language proficiency required.

Living Arrangements • Students live in host institution dormitories. Quarters are shared with host institution students, students from other programs. Meals are taken on one's own, in residences, in central dining facility.

Costs (2003-2004) • One term: $12,190. Yearlong program: $23,880; includes tuition, housing, all meals, insurance, international student ID, student support services. $30 application fee. $165 refundable deposit required. Financial aid available for students from sponsoring institution: scholarships, loans.

For More Information • Mr. Mark A. Beirn, Coordinator, Office of Study Abroad, Webster University, 470 East Lockwood Avenue, St. Louis, MO 63119; *Phone:* 314-968-6988; *Fax:* 314-968-5938. *E-mail:* worldview@webster.edu. *World Wide Web:* http://www.webster.edu/intl/sa/

MANCHESTER

ARCADIA UNIVERSITY

UNIVERSITY OF MANCHESTER

Hosted by University of Manchester

Academic Focus • Biblical studies, biological/life sciences, classics and classical languages, engineering, liberal studies, public policy, social sciences.

ENGLAND
Manchester

Program Information • Students attend classes at University of Manchester.

Sessions • Spring, yearlong.

Eligibility Requirements • Open to juniors, seniors; 3.0 GPA; 2 letters of recommendation.

Living Arrangements • Students live in host institution dormitories, locally rented apartments. Quarters are shared with host institution students. Meals are taken on one's own, in residences, in central dining facility.

Costs (2003-2004) • One term: $11,490. Yearlong program: $19,750; includes tuition, housing, insurance, international student ID, student support services, pre-departure guide, transcripts. $35 application fee. $500 nonrefundable deposit required. Financial aid available for all students: scholarships, loans.

For More Information • Arcadia University, Center for Education Abroad, 450 South Easton Road, Glenside, PA 19038-3295; *Phone:* 866-927-2234; *Fax:* 215-572-2174. *E-mail:* cea@arcadia.edu. *World Wide Web:* http://www.arcadia.edu/cea/

RUTGERS, THE STATE UNIVERSITY OF NEW JERSEY
STUDY ABROAD IN BRITAIN: MANCHESTER

Hosted by University of Manchester

Academic Focus • Full curriculum.

Program Information • Students attend classes at University of Manchester. Field trips to London, Stonehenge, Oxford.

Sessions • Spring, yearlong.

Eligibility Requirements • Open to sophomores, juniors, seniors; 3.0 GPA; 2 letters of recommendation; good academic standing at home school; official transcript from each tertiary school attended.

Living Arrangements • Students live in host institution dormitories. Quarters are shared with host institution students. Meals are taken on one's own, in residences, in central dining facility.

Costs (2003-2004) • One term: $10,922 for New Jersey residents; $13,572 for nonresidents. Yearlong program: $19,391 for New Jersey residents; $24,691 for nonresidents; includes tuition, insurance, excursions, student support services. $20 application fee. $750 nonrefundable deposit required. Financial aid available for students from sponsoring institution: scholarships, loans.

For More Information • Ms. Karin Bonello, Regional Coordinator, Rutgers, The State University of New Jersey, 102 College Avenue, New Brunswick, NJ 08901-8543; *Phone:* 732-932-7787; *Fax:* 732-932-8659. *E-mail:* ru_abroad@email.rutgers.edu. *World Wide Web:* http://studyabroad.rutgers.edu/

STATE UNIVERSITY OF NEW YORK COLLEGE AT BUFFALO
MANCHESTER EXCHANGE/STUDY ABROAD

Hosted by Manchester Metropolitan University

Academic Focus • Full curriculum.

Program Information • Students attend classes at Manchester Metropolitan University.

Sessions • Fall, spring, yearlong.

Eligibility Requirements • Open to sophomores, juniors, seniors, graduate students; 2.5 GPA; 2 letters of recommendation.

Living Arrangements • Students live in host institution dormitories, locally rented apartments. Quarters are shared with host institution students, students from other programs. Meals are taken on one's own, in residences, in central dining facility.

Costs (2003-2004) • One term: $6866–$8066 for New York residents; $10,896-$11,316 for nonresidents (undergraduate). Yearlong program: $13,047–$15,447 for New York residents; $21,107-$21,947 for nonresidents (undergraduate); includes tuition, housing, all meals, insurance, international airfare, books and class materials, administrative, college, and passport fees. $10 application fee. $200

nonrefundable deposit required. Financial aid available for students from sponsoring institution: scholarships, loans.

For More Information • Dr. Lee Ann Grace, Director, International Education, State University of New York College at Buffalo, 1300 Elmwood Avenue, Buffalo, NY 14222-1095; *Phone:* 716-878-4620; *Fax:* 716-878-3054. *E-mail:* intleduc@buffalostate.edu. *World Wide Web:* http://www.buffalostate.edu/intnated/

UNIVERSITY OF MANCHESTER
STUDY ABROAD PROGRAMME

Hosted by Manchester Metropolitan University, University of Manchester Institute of Science and Technology UMIST, University of Manchester

Academic Focus • Full curriculum.

Program Information • Students attend classes at Manchester Metropolitan University, University of Manchester Institute of Science and Technology UMIST, University of Manchester. Optional travel to Dublin, Amsterdam, Paris at an extra cost.

Sessions • Fall, spring, yearlong.

Eligibility Requirements • Minimum age 19; open to sophomores, juniors, seniors, graduate students; 3.0 GPA; 2 letters of recommendation; good academic standing at home school; transcript.

Living Arrangements • Students live in host institution dormitories, locally rented apartments, program-owned apartments. Quarters are shared with host institution students. Meals are taken as a group, on one's own, in residences, in central dining facility.

Costs (2003-2004) • One term: £8960 (estimated). Yearlong program: £17,920 (estimated); includes tuition, housing, all meals, lab equipment. £150 refundable deposit required.

For More Information • Mrs. Sarah Bloor, Coordinator, University of Manchester, Study Abroad Unit, International Office, Beyer Building, Manchester M13 9PL, England; *Phone:* +44 161-275-8021; *Fax:* +44 161-275-3052. *E-mail:* evsu@man.ac.uk. *World Wide Web:* http://www.man.ac.uk/. Students may also apply through Arcadia University, Center for Education Abroad, 450 South Easton Road, Glenside, PA 19038-3295.

THE UNIVERSITY OF NORTH CAROLINA AT CHAPEL HILL
STUDY ABROAD AT THE UNIVERSITY OF MANCHESTER

Hosted by University of Manchester

Academic Focus • Full curriculum.

Program Information • Students attend classes at University of Manchester.

Sessions • Spring, yearlong.

Eligibility Requirements • Open to sophomores, juniors, seniors, graduate students, adults; 3.0 GPA; 2 letters of recommendation; good academic standing at home school; essay; transcript.

Living Arrangements • Students live in host institution dormitories, locally rented apartments. Quarters are shared with host institution students. Meals are taken as a group, on one's own, in residences.

Costs (2003-2004) • One term: $5200. Yearlong program: $9362; includes tuition, insurance, study abroad fee. $100 application fee. $500 nonrefundable deposit required. Financial aid available for students from sponsoring institution: scholarships, loans.

For More Information • Study Abroad Office, The University of North Carolina at Chapel Hill, 201 Porthole Building, CB 3130, Chapel Hill, NC 27599-3130; *Phone:* 919-962-7002; *Fax:* 919-962-2262. *E-mail:* abroad@unc.edu. *World Wide Web:* http://studyabroad.unc.edu/

NORWICH
COOPERATIVE CENTER FOR STUDY ABROAD
SEMESTER IN ENGLAND

Hosted by University of East Anglia

Academic Focus • Full curriculum.

Program Information • Students attend classes at University of East Anglia.

Sessions • Fall, spring.

Eligibility Requirements • Open to sophomores, juniors, seniors; 3.0 GPA; 1 letter of recommendation; 500 word essay describing reasons for wanting to participate.

Living Arrangements • Students live in host institution dormitories. Quarters are shared with students from other programs. Meals are taken on one's own, in central dining facility, in restaurants.

Costs (2005) • One term: $8995 for fall term; $9495 for spring; includes tuition, housing, insurance, international student ID. $200 nonrefundable deposit required. Financial aid available for students from sponsoring institution: scholarships, loans.

For More Information • Dr. Michael A. Klembara, Executive Director, Cooperative Center for Study Abroad, Northern Kentucky University, Nunn Drive, BEP 301, Highland Heights, KY 41099; *Phone:* 800-319-6015; *Fax:* 859-572-6650. *E-mail:* ccsa@nku.edu. *World Wide Web:* http://www.ccsa.cc/

DICKINSON COLLEGE
DICKINSON HUMANITIES PROGRAM NORWICH (ENGLAND)

Hosted by University of East Anglia

Academic Focus • American studies, economics, English literature, history, liberal studies, music, political science and government, visual and performing arts.

Program Information • Students attend classes at University of East Anglia. Scheduled travel to London; field trips to sites in and around London, sites throughout East Anglia; optional travel at an extra cost.

Sessions • Yearlong.

Eligibility Requirements • Minimum age 18; open to juniors, seniors; 3.0 GPA; 3 letters of recommendation; good academic standing at home school.

Living Arrangements • Students live in host institution dormitories. Quarters are shared with host institution students. Meals are taken on one's own, in residences, in central dining facility.

Costs (2003-2004) • Yearlong program: $35,590; includes tuition, housing, all meals, excursions. $25 application fee. $300 nonrefundable deposit required. Financial aid available for students from sponsoring institution: scholarships, loans.

For More Information • Ms. Karen Peter, Program Manager, Dickinson College, PO Box 1773, Carlisle, PA 17013-2896; *Phone:* 717-245-1341; *Fax:* 717-245-1688. *E-mail:* global@dickinson.edu. *World Wide Web:* http://www.dickinson.edu/global/

DICKINSON COLLEGE
DICKINSON SCIENCE PROGRAM IN NORWICH (ENGLAND)

Hosted by University of East Anglia

Academic Focus • Biological/life sciences, chemical sciences, computer science, environmental science/studies, geology, mathematics, physics.

Program Information • Students attend classes at University of East Anglia. Scheduled travel to London; field trips to sites in and around London, sites throughout East Anglia, Ireland.

Sessions • Fall, spring, yearlong.

Eligibility Requirements • Minimum age 18; open to juniors, seniors; 3.0 GPA; 3 letters of recommendation; good academic standing at home school.

Living Arrangements • Students live in host institution dormitories. Quarters are shared with host institution students. Meals are taken on one's own, in residences, in central dining facility.

Costs (2003-2004) • One term: $17,795. Yearlong program: $35,590; includes tuition, housing, all meals, excursions. $25 application fee. $300 nonrefundable deposit required. Financial aid available for students from sponsoring institution: scholarships, loans.

For More Information • Ms. Karen Peter, Program Manager, Dickinson College, PO Box 1773, Carlisle, PA 17013-2896; *Phone:* 717-245-1341; *Fax:* 717-245-1688. *E-mail:* global@dickinson.edu. *World Wide Web:* http://www.dickinson.edu/global/

INSTITUTE FOR STUDY ABROAD, BUTLER UNIVERSITY
UNIVERSITY OF EAST ANGLIA

Hosted by University of East Anglia

Academic Focus • Full curriculum.

Program Information • Students attend classes at University of East Anglia. Field trips to London.

ENGLAND
Norwich

Sessions • Fall, spring, yearlong.
Eligibility Requirements • Open to juniors, seniors; 2.8 GPA; 1 letter of recommendation; good academic standing at home school; enrollment at an accredited American college or university.
Living Arrangements • Students live in host institution dormitories, locally rented apartments. Quarters are shared with host institution students. Meals are taken on one's own, in residences, in central dining facility.
Costs (2002-2003) • One term: $10,675. Yearlong program: $18,275; includes tuition, housing, excursions, international student ID, student support services, family visit, cultural and sporting events, pre-departure advising. $40 application fee. $500 nonrefundable deposit required. Financial aid available for all students: scholarships, travel grants.
For More Information • Institute for Study Abroad, Butler University, 1100 West 42nd Street, Suite 305, Indianapolis, IN 46208-3345; *Phone:* 800-858-0229; *Fax:* 317-940-9704. *E-mail:* study-abroad@butler.edu. *World Wide Web:* http://www.ifsa-butler.org/

RUTGERS, THE STATE UNIVERSITY OF NEW JERSEY
STUDY ABROAD IN BRITAIN (AT U.E.A.)

Hosted by University of East Anglia
Academic Focus • Full curriculum.
Program Information • Students attend classes at University of East Anglia.
Sessions • Fall, spring, yearlong.
Eligibility Requirements • Open to sophomores, juniors, seniors; 3.0 GPA; 2 letters of recommendation; good academic standing at home school; no foreign language proficiency required.
Living Arrangements • Students live in host institution dormitories. Quarters are shared with students from other programs. Meals are taken on one's own, in residences, in central dining facility.
Costs (2003-2004) • One term: $10,915 for New Jersey residents; $13,565 for nonresidents. Yearlong program: $20,614 for New Jersey residents; $25,914 for nonresidents; includes tuition, insurance, student support services. $20 application fee. $750 nonrefundable deposit required. Financial aid available for students from sponsoring institution: scholarships, loans.
For More Information • Ms. Karin Bonello, Regional Coordinator, Rutgers, The State University of New Jersey, 102 College Avenue, New Brunswick, NJ 08901-8543; *Phone:* 732-932-7787; *Fax:* 732-932-8659. *E-mail:* ru_abroad@email.rutgers.edu. *World Wide Web:* http://studyabroad.rutgers.edu/

STATE UNIVERSITY OF NEW YORK AT PLATTSBURGH
STUDY IN ENGLAND, NORWICH

Hosted by University of East Anglia
Academic Focus • American studies, art history, biological/life sciences, business administration/management, chemical sciences, computer science, creative writing, economics, education, English literature, environmental science/studies, film and media studies, French studies, history, information science, international affairs, language studies, mathematics, music, philosophy, physics, social sciences, social work.
Program Information • Students attend classes at University of East Anglia.
Sessions • Fall, spring, yearlong.
Eligibility Requirements • Minimum age 18; open to sophomores, juniors, seniors; 2.8 GPA; 2 letters of recommendation; SUNY and UEA applications; essay; transcript.
Living Arrangements • Students live in host institution dormitories, locally rented apartments. Quarters are shared with host institution students, students from other programs. Meals are taken on one's own, in residences, in central dining facility, in restaurants.
Costs (2003-2004) • One term: $6134. Yearlong program: $12,268; includes tuition, housing, some meals, insurance, books and class materials, international student ID, student support services, program fee. $20 application fee. $350 nonrefundable deposit required. Financial aid available for students from sponsoring institution: scholarships, loans.
For More Information • Ms. Jo Ann Mackie, Study Abroad Coordinator, State University of New York at Plattsburgh, Study Abroad Office, 101 Broad Street, Plattsburgh, NY 12901; *Phone:* 518-564-2321; *Fax:* 518-564-2326. *E-mail:* international@plattsburgh.edu. *World Wide Web:* http://www.plattsburgh.edu/studyabroad/

UNIVERSITY OF EAST ANGLIA
JUNIOR YEAR OR SEMESTER ABROAD

Hosted by University of East Anglia
Academic Focus • American studies, art history, biological/life sciences, chemical sciences, creative writing, drama/theater, English literature, environmental science/studies, film and media studies, history, language studies, mathematics, social sciences.
Program Information • Students attend classes at University of East Anglia. Optional travel to Venice, Valencia at an extra cost.
Sessions • Fall, spring, yearlong.
Eligibility Requirements • Minimum age 17; open to sophomores, juniors, seniors; 3.0 GPA.
Living Arrangements • Students live in host institution dormitories. Quarters are shared with host institution students. Meals are taken in residences, in central dining facility.
Costs (2003-2004) • One term: $8795 for fall term; $10,303 for spring (estimated). Yearlong program: $19,099 (estimated); includes tuition, housing. Financial aid available for all students: scholarships.
For More Information • Mr. Mike Roberts, International Officer, University of East Anglia, Norwich, Norfolk NR4 7TJ, England; *Phone:* +44 160-345-6161; *Fax:* +44 160-345-8596. *E-mail:* m.roberts@uea.ac.uk. *World Wide Web:* http://www.uea.ac.uk/international/. Students may also apply through Dickinson College, PO Box 1773, Carlisle, PA 17013-2896; Butler University, Institute for Study Abroad, 1100 West 42nd Street, Suite 305, Indianapolis, IN 46208-3345; Arcadia University, Center for Education Abroad, 450 South Easton Road, Glenside, PA 19038-3295.

UNIVERSITY OF MIAMI
UNIVERSITY OF EAST ANGLIA, ENGLAND

Hosted by University of East Anglia
Academic Focus • Biological/life sciences, comparative literature, creative writing, English literature, environmental science/studies, science.
Program Information • Students attend classes at University of East Anglia. Field trips to research-based field trips for some science classes.
Sessions • Fall, spring, yearlong.
Eligibility Requirements • Minimum age 18; open to sophomores, juniors; 3.0 GPA; 2 letters of recommendation; official transcripts; essay.
Living Arrangements • Students live in host institution dormitories. Quarters are shared with host institution students. Meals are taken on one's own, in residences, in central dining facility, in restaurants.
Costs (2003-2004) • One term: $12,919. Yearlong program: $25,838; includes tuition. $40 application fee. $500 nonrefundable deposit required. Financial aid available for students from sponsoring institution: scholarships, loans.
For More Information • Ms. Elyse Resnick, Assistant Director, University of Miami, International Education and Exchange Programs, 5050 Brunson Drive, Allen Hall 212, PO Box 248005, Coral Gables, FL 33124-1610; *Phone:* 305-284-3434; *Fax:* 305-284-4235. *E-mail:* ieep@miami.edu. *World Wide Web:* http://www.studyabroad.miami.edu/

NOTTINGHAM
ARCADIA UNIVERSITY
UNIVERSITY OF NOTTINGHAM

Hosted by University of Nottingham
Academic Focus • American studies, architecture, art history, classics and classical languages, engineering, English, history, language studies, liberal studies, science.
Program Information • Students attend classes at University of Nottingham.
Sessions • Fall, spring, yearlong, fall semester.
Eligibility Requirements • Open to precollege students, sophomores, juniors, seniors; 3.0 GPA; 1 letter of recommendation.

Living Arrangements • Students live in host institution dormitories, locally rented apartments, host family homes. Quarters are shared with host institution students, students from other programs. Meals are taken on one's own, in residences.
Costs (2003-2004) • One term: $9150–$10,790. Yearlong program: $18,290; includes tuition, housing, insurance, international student ID, student support services, pre-departure guide, transcripts. $35 application fee. $500 nonrefundable deposit required. Financial aid available for all students: scholarships, loans.
For More Information • Arcadia University, Center for Education Abroad, 450 South Easton Road, Glenside, PA 19038-3295; *Phone:* 866-927-2234; *Fax:* 215-572-2174. *E-mail:* cea@arcadia.edu. *World Wide Web:* http://www.arcadia.edu/cea/

INSTITUTE FOR STUDY ABROAD, BUTLER UNIVERSITY
UNIVERSITY OF NOTTINGHAM

Hosted by University of Nottingham
Academic Focus • Full curriculum.
Program Information • Students attend classes at University of Nottingham. Field trips to London.
Sessions • Fall, spring, yearlong, fall semester for sciences, architecture, and engineering.
Eligibility Requirements • Open to juniors, seniors; 3.0 GPA; 1 letter of recommendation; good academic standing at home school; enrollment at an accredited American college or university.
Living Arrangements • Students live in host institution dormitories, locally rented apartments. Quarters are shared with host institution students, students from other programs. Meals are taken on one's own, in residences, in central dining facility, in restaurants.
Costs (2002-2003) • One term: $9975. Yearlong program: $16,475; includes tuition, housing, excursions, international student ID, student support services, family visit, cultural and sporting events, pre-departure advising. $40 application fee. $500 nonrefundable deposit required. Financial aid available for all students: scholarships, travel grants.
For More Information • Institute for Study Abroad, Butler University, 1100 West 42nd Street, Suite 305, Indianapolis, IN 46208-3345; *Phone:* 800-858-0229; *Fax:* 317-940-9704. *E-mail:* study-abroad@butler.edu. *World Wide Web:* http://www.ifsa-butler.org/

STETSON UNIVERSITY
STUDY ABROAD–NOTTINGHAM

Hosted by Nottingham Trent University
Academic Focus • Biological/life sciences, business administration/management, education, liberal studies, social sciences.
Program Information • Students attend classes at Nottingham Trent University. Field trips to Wales, Scotland, London, Stonehenge; optional travel to Amsterdam, Paris at an extra cost.
Sessions • Fall, spring, yearlong.
Eligibility Requirements • Minimum age 20; open to sophomores, juniors, seniors; 2.8 GPA; 4 letters of recommendation; good academic standing at home school; completed application.
Living Arrangements • Students live in host institution dormitories. Meals are taken on one's own, in central dining facility.
Costs (2002-2003) • One term: $14,025. Yearlong program: $28,050; includes tuition, housing, all meals, insurance, excursions, international airfare, lab equipment, international student ID, student support services. $50 application fee. $200 nonrefundable deposit required. Financial aid available for students from sponsoring institution: scholarships, loans.
For More Information • Ms. Nancy L. Leonard, Director, Stetson University, Center for International Education, Unit 8412, 421 North Woodland Boulevard, Deland, FL 32723-3757; *Phone:* 386-822-8165; *Fax:* 386-822-8167. *E-mail:* nleonard@stetson.edu. *World Wide Web:* http://www.stetson.edu/international/

UNIVERSITY AT ALBANY, STATE UNIVERSITY OF NEW YORK
DIRECT ENROLLMENT AT THE UNIVERSITY OF NOTTINGHAM

Hosted by University of Nottingham
Academic Focus • Full curriculum.

Program Information • Students attend classes at University of Nottingham.
Sessions • Fall, spring, yearlong.
Eligibility Requirements • Open to sophomores, juniors, seniors; 3.0 GPA; 2 letters of recommendation; good academic standing at home school; no foreign language proficiency required.
Living Arrangements • Students live in host institution dormitories, program-owned apartments. Quarters are shared with host institution students, students from other programs. Meals are taken on one's own, in residences, in central dining facility.
Costs (2002-2003) • One term: $6513. Yearlong program: $13,026; includes housing, all meals, student support services, in-state tuition and fees. $150 nonrefundable deposit required. Financial aid available for students from sponsoring institution: all customary sources.
For More Information • University at Albany, State University of New York, Office of International Education, LI 66, Albany, NY 12222; *Phone:* 518-442-3525; *Fax:* 518-442-3338. *E-mail:* intled@uamail.albany.edu. *World Wide Web:* http://www.albany.edu/intled/

UNIVERSITY OF NOTTINGHAM
STUDY ABROAD

Hosted by University of Nottingham
Academic Focus • Full curriculum.
Program Information • Students attend classes at University of Nottingham.
Sessions • Spring, yearlong, extended fall term.
Eligibility Requirements • Minimum age 17; open to freshmen, sophomores, juniors, seniors, graduate students; 3.0 GPA; 1 letter of recommendation.
Living Arrangements • Students live in host institution dormitories, host institution apartments. Quarters are shared with host institution students, students from other programs. Meals are taken as a group, in residences, in central dining facility.
Costs (2003-2004) • One term: £3190. Yearlong program: £6380; includes tuition, student support services.
For More Information • Ms. Eleanor Feather, Study Abroad Coordinator, International Office, University of Nottingham, University Park, Nottingham NG7 2RD, England; *Phone:* +44 115-951-4379; *Fax:* +44 115-951-5155. *E-mail:* eleanor.feather@nottingham.ac.uk. *World Wide Web:* http://www.nottingham.ac.uk/international/. Students may also apply through Butler University, Institute for Study Abroad, 1100 West 42nd Street, Suite 305, Indianapolis, IN 46208-3345; Arcadia University, Center for Education Abroad, 450 South Easton Road, Glenside, PA 19038-3295.

ORMSKIRK

COLLEGE CONSORTIUM FOR INTERNATIONAL STUDIES–SUNY ROCKLAND COMMUNITY COLLEGE AND TRUMAN STATE UNIVERSITY
CCIS PROGRAM AT EDGE HILL COLLEGE, LANCASHIRE, ENGLAND

Hosted by Edge Hill University College
Academic Focus • Biological/life sciences, business administration/management, communications, criminal justice, drama/theater, European studies, liberal studies, mathematics, science, social sciences, teaching.
Program Information • Students attend classes at Edge Hill University College.
Sessions • Fall, spring, yearlong.
Eligibility Requirements • Minimum age 18; open to freshmen, sophomores, juniors, seniors, adults; 2.5 GPA; 2 letters of recommendation; good academic standing at home school.
Living Arrangements • Students live in host institution dormitories. Quarters are shared with host institution students. Meals are taken on one's own, in central dining facility.
Costs (2004-2005) • One term: $6495 for fall term; $6495 for spring. Yearlong program: $12,990; includes tuition, housing, some meals, international student ID, student support services. $400 nonrefundable deposit required. Financial aid available for students from sponsoring institution: scholarships, loans.

For More Information • Ms. Melissa Gluckmann, Coordinator of Study Abroad, College Consortium for International Studies, 145 College Road, Suffern, NY 10901; *Phone:* 845-574-4205; *Fax:* 845-574-4423. *E-mail:* study-abroad@sunyrockland.edu. *World Wide Web:* http://www.ccisabroad.org/

OXFORD

ARCADIA UNIVERSITY
OXFORD UNIVERSITY, VISITING STUDENT PROGRAM

Hosted by University of Oxford Saint Hilda's College, University of Oxford–Lady Margaret Hall, University of Oxford–Saint Edmund Hall, University of Oxford–Saint Anne's College
Academic Focus • Full curriculum.
Program Information • Students attend classes at University of Oxford Saint Hilda's College, University of Oxford–Lady Margaret Hall, University of Oxford–Saint Edmund Hall, University of Oxford–Saint Anne's College. Field trips to Bath, Stratford-upon-Avon, Leeds Castle, Canterbury; optional travel to Wales at an extra cost.
Sessions • Fall, spring, yearlong.
Eligibility Requirements • Open to juniors, seniors; 3.6 GPA; 2 letters of recommendation; 2 graded writing samples from field of major.
Living Arrangements • Students live in host institution dormitories. Quarters are shared with host institution students. Meals are taken as a group, on one's own, in residences, in central dining facility.
Costs (2003-2004) • One term: $13,390 for fall term; $20,990–$21,990 for two spring terms. Yearlong program: $29,950–$31,090; includes tuition, housing, insurance, international student ID, student support services, pre-departure guide, transcripts. $35 application fee. $500 nonrefundable deposit required. Financial aid available for all students: scholarships, loans.
For More Information • Arcadia University, Center for Education Abroad, 450 South Easton Road, Glenside, PA 19038-3295; *Phone:* 866-927-2234; *Fax:* 215-572-2174. *E-mail:* cea@arcadia.edu. *World Wide Web:* http://www.arcadia.edu/cea/

BOSTON UNIVERSITY
OXFORD HONORS STUDIES PROGRAM

Hosted by University of Oxford–Saint Anne's College
Academic Focus • History, literature, political science and government.
Program Information • Students attend classes at University of Oxford–Saint Anne's College. Field trips to Blenheim Palace, Stratford-upon-Avon, Parliament.
Sessions • Fall, spring, yearlong.
Eligibility Requirements • Open to sophomores, juniors, seniors; course work in literature, political science, history; 2 letters of recommendation; good academic standing at home school; essay; transcript; approval of participation; minimum 3.0 GPA overall and minimum 3.30 GPA in major.
Living Arrangements • Students live in host institution dormitories. Quarters are shared with host institution students. Meals are taken on one's own, in central dining facility, in restaurants.
Costs (2004-2005) • One term: $19,834. Yearlong program: $39,668; includes tuition, housing, all meals, excursions, international airfare, fees, membership to the Oxford Union, use of Bodleian Library. $50 application fee. $400 nonrefundable deposit required. Financial aid available for all students: scholarships, loans.
For More Information • Division of International Programs, Boston University, 232 Bay State Road, Boston, MA 02215; *Phone:* 617-353-9888; *Fax:* 617-353-5402. *E-mail:* abroad@bu.edu. *World Wide Web:* http://www.bu.edu/abroad/

INSTITUTE FOR STUDY ABROAD, BUTLER UNIVERSITY
OXFORD UNIVERSITY PROGRAMS

Hosted by University of Oxford
Academic Focus • Art history, classics and classical languages, computer science, economics, engineering, English, geography, history, philosophy, political science and government, psychology, religious studies, science, sociology.
Program Information • Students attend classes at University of Oxford. Field trips to London.
Sessions • Fall, spring, yearlong.
Eligibility Requirements • Open to juniors, seniors; 3.4 GPA; 2 letters of recommendation; good academic standing at home school; enrollment at an accredited American college or university; 2 writing samples.
Living Arrangements • Students live in host institution dormitories, locally rented apartments. Quarters are shared with host institution students. Meals are taken as a group, on one's own, in residences, in central dining facility.
Costs (2002-2003) • One term: $12,000–$14,000. Yearlong program: $26,000–$30,000; includes tuition, housing, some meals, excursions, international student ID, student support services, family visit, cultural and sporting events, pre-departure advising. $40 application fee. $500 nonrefundable deposit required. Financial aid available for all students: scholarships, travel grants.
For More Information • Institute for Study Abroad, Butler University, 1100 West 42nd Street, Suite 305, Indianapolis, IN 46208-3345; *Phone:* 800-858-0229; *Fax:* 317-940-9704. *E-mail:* study-abroad@butler.edu. *World Wide Web:* http://www.ifsa-butler.org/

LYCOMING COLLEGE
STUDY ABROAD AT OXFORD BROOKES UNIVERSITY

Hosted by Oxford Brookes University
Academic Focus • Full curriculum.
Program Information • Students attend classes at Oxford Brookes University. Scheduled travel; field trips; optional travel at an extra cost.
Sessions • Fall, spring, winter.
Eligibility Requirements • Open to sophomores, juniors, seniors; 2.5 GPA; good academic standing at home school.
Living Arrangements • Students live in host institution dormitories, host family homes. Quarters are shared with host institution students. Meals are taken as a group, on one's own.
Costs (2002-2003) • One term: contact sponsor for cost. $300 refundable deposit required.
For More Information • Dr. Barbara Buedel, Coordinator of Study Abroad Program, Lycoming College, Campus Box 2, 700 College Place, Williamsport, PA 17701-5192; *Phone:* 570-321-4210; *Fax:* 570-321-4389. *E-mail:* buedel@lycoming.edu. *World Wide Web:* http://www.lycoming.edu/

MANHATTANVILLE COLLEGE
ST. CLARE'S COLLEGE LIBERAL ARTS PROGRAM AT OXFORD

Hosted by Saint Clare's, Oxford
Academic Focus • Art history, drama/theater, English literature, fine/studio arts, history, philosophy, social sciences.
Program Information • Students attend classes at Saint Clare's, Oxford. Scheduled travel to Amsterdam, Paris; field trips to London, the English countryside; optional travel to Europe, Ireland, Belgium at an extra cost.
Sessions • Fall, spring, yearlong.
Eligibility Requirements • Minimum age 19; open to sophomores, juniors; course work in Europe/Britain; 3.0 GPA; 3 letters of recommendation; good academic standing at home school.
Living Arrangements • Students live in host institution dormitories, program-owned houses, host family homes. Quarters are shared with students from other programs. Meals are taken on one's own, with host family, in residences, in restaurants.
Costs (2004-2005) • One term: $9050. Yearlong program: $18,100; includes tuition, excursions. $80 application fee. $320 nonrefundable deposit required. Financial aid available for students from sponsoring institution: scholarships, loans.
For More Information • Mr. Andrew Bodenrader, Director of Study Abroad Program, Manhattanville College, 2900 Purchase Street, Purchase, NY 10577; *Phone:* 914-798-2755; *Fax:* 914-323-5338. *E-mail:* bodenradera@mville.edu. *World Wide Web:* http://www.mville.edu/

MARQUETTE UNIVERSITY
MARQUETTE AT ST. CLARE'S OXFORD, ENGLAND

Hosted by Saint Clare's, Oxford

Academic Focus • Art history, communications, drama/theater, economics, English literature, ethics, European studies, fine/studio arts, history, language studies, literature, marketing, mathematics, philosophy, political science and government, religious studies, social sciences.

Program Information • Students attend classes at Saint Clare's, Oxford. Field trips to Salisbury, Stonehenge, Bath, London, Stratford-upon-Avon, Cambridge; optional travel to Amsterdam, Nirobi, Kenya at an extra cost.

Sessions • Fall, spring, yearlong.

Eligibility Requirements • Open to sophomores, juniors, seniors; 2.75 GPA; 1 letter of recommendation; good academic standing at home school.

Living Arrangements • Students live in host institution dormitories, locally rented apartments, program-owned apartments, program-owned houses. Quarters are shared with host institution students. Meals are taken as a group, on one's own, in residences, in restaurants.

Costs (2004-2005) • One term: $10,575. Yearlong program: $21,150; includes tuition, excursions, books and class materials, lab equipment, student support services. $80 application fee. $320 refundable deposit required. Financial aid available for students from sponsoring institution: scholarships, loans.

For More Information • Dr. Jamshid Hosseini, Director of International Business Studies, Marquette University, College of Business Administration, 606 North 13th Street, David Strat, Jr. Building, Milwaukee, WI 53233; *Phone:* 414-288-7534; *Fax:* 414-288-7440. *E-mail:* jamshid.hosseini@marquette.edu. *World Wide Web:* http://www.marquette.edu/studyabroad/

MINNESOTA STATE UNIVERSITY MOORHEAD
EUROSPRING

Held at Wycliffe Hall

Academic Focus • Liberal studies.

Program Information • Classes are held on the campus of Wycliffe Hall. Faculty members are drawn from the sponsor's U.S. staff and local instructors hired by the sponsor. Scheduled travel to Paris, Florence, Rome, Venice, Italy, Amsterdam, Germany, Austria; field trips to Stonehenge, Bath, Portsmouth, Blenheim, Warwick Castle, Salisbury Cathedral; optional travel to Scotland, Ireland at an extra cost.

Sessions • Spring.

Eligibility Requirements • Open to sophomores, juniors, seniors; 2.25 GPA.

Living Arrangements • Students live in host institution dormitories, hotels. Quarters are shared with host institution students. Meals are taken as a group, in central dining facility, in restaurants.

Costs (2004) • One term: $6350; includes tuition, housing, some meals, excursions, international airfare, international student ID, activities, entrance fees, gratuities. $50 application fee. $1000 refundable deposit required. Financial aid available for all students: loans.

For More Information • Ms. Jill I. Holsen, Director, International Programs, Minnesota State University Moorhead, 1104 7th Avenue South, Moorhead, MN 56563; *Phone:* 218-477-2956; *Fax:* 218-477-5928. *E-mail:* holsenj@mnstate.edu. *World Wide Web:* http://www.mnstate.edu/intl/

OXFORD BROOKES UNIVERSITY
INTERNATIONAL STUDY ABROAD PROGRAMME

Hosted by Oxford Brookes University

Academic Focus • Full curriculum.

Program Information • Students attend classes at Oxford Brookes University. Optional travel to Scotland, Ireland, France at an extra cost.

Sessions • Fall, spring, winter, yearlong.

Eligibility Requirements • Minimum age 18; open to juniors, seniors, graduate students; 3.0 GPA; 1 letter of recommendation; good academic standing at home school.

Living Arrangements • Students live in host institution dormitories. Quarters are shared with host institution students. Meals are taken as a group, in residences.

Costs (2001-2002) • One term: £2870–£3220. Yearlong program: contact sponsor for cost; includes tuition, housing, some meals, student support services.

For More Information • Ms. Hilary Churchley, Student Liaison, Oxford Brookes University, Headington, Oxford OX3 OBP, England; *Phone:* +44 1865-484301; *Fax:* +44 1865-483616. *E-mail:* hachurchley@brookes.ac.uk. *World Wide Web:* http://www.brookes.ac.uk/

ST. CLOUD STATE UNIVERSITY
OXFORD

Held at Center for Medieval and Renaissance Studies

Academic Focus • Ancient history, archaeology, history, social sciences.

Program Information • Classes are held on the campus of Center for Medieval and Renaissance Studies. Faculty members are local instructors hired by the sponsor. Optional travel to Europe at an extra cost.

Sessions • Fall, spring.

Eligibility Requirements • Minimum age 18; open to freshmen, sophomores, juniors, seniors; 3.0 GPA; must be accepted into the St. Cloud State University honors program.

Living Arrangements • Students live in host institution dormitories, locally rented apartments. Quarters are shared with students from other programs. Meals are taken on one's own, in residences.

Costs (2003-2004) • One term: $9000 for Minnesota residents; includes tuition, housing. $75 application fee. Financial aid available for students from sponsoring institution: scholarships, loans.

For More Information • Chunsheng Zhang, Associate Vice President for Academic Affairs/International Studies, St. Cloud State University, Center for International Studies, 720 4th Avenue, South, St. Cloud, MN 56301-4498; *Phone:* 320-308-4287; *Fax:* 320-308-4223. *E-mail:* intstudy@stcloudstate.edu. *World Wide Web:* http://www.stcloudstate.edu/

SARAH LAWRENCE COLLEGE
SARAH LAWRENCE COLLEGE, PROGRAM AFFILIATED WITH WADHAM COLLEGE OF THE UNIVERSITY OF OXFORD

Hosted by University of Oxford

Academic Focus • Anthropology, art history, Biblical studies, classics and classical languages, comparative literature, economics, history, international affairs, law and legal studies, liberal studies, literature, music history, music theory, philosophy, political science and government, religious studies, social sciences.

Program Information • Students attend classes at University of Oxford. Field trips to London, Stratford-upon-Avon.

Sessions • Yearlong.

Eligibility Requirements • Open to juniors, seniors; 3.5 GPA; 2 letters of recommendation; good academic standing at home school; essay.

Living Arrangements • Meals are taken on one's own, in residences.

Costs (2003-2004) • Yearlong program: $37,314; includes tuition, housing, excursions, student support services, university lecture pass, access to university libraries. $35 application fee. $250 nonrefundable deposit required. Financial aid available for all students: scholarships, loans.

For More Information • Ms. Prema Samuel, Director of International Programs, Sarah Lawrence College, 1 Meadway, Bronxville, NY 10708-5999; *Phone:* 800-873-4752; *Fax:* 914-395-2666. *E-mail:* slcaway@slc.edu. *World Wide Web:* http://www.sarahlawrence.edu/studyabroad/

MORE ABOUT THE PROGRAM

Students in the Sarah Lawrence College at Oxford program have been granted Visiting Student status, a special designation available only to a select few American programs. This status allows American graduates the most extensive range of privileges available at Oxford.

Students work with Oxford scholars in weekly private tutorials, which are the heart of the academic program. No other

ENGLAND
Oxford

U.S.-sponsored program offers undergraduates the full range of tutors and disciplines of Oxford's colleges. The program is hosted by Wadham College, which gives participants access to its junior common room, student government, dining hall, social events, and all Oxford libraries and athletic teams. Participants also have voting rights in the student union. Merit grants are available.

Sarah Lawrence also sponsors programs in Cuba, Paris, and Florence and a London Theatre program.

STATE UNIVERSITY OF NEW YORK COLLEGE AT BROCKPORT
OXFORD BROOKES UNIVERSITY

Hosted by Oxford Brookes University
Academic Focus • Full curriculum.
Program Information • Students attend classes at Oxford Brookes University. Field trips to the London weekend program.
Sessions • Fall, spring, yearlong, 2 term spring.
Eligibility Requirements • Minimum age 18; open to juniors, seniors; 3.0 GPA; 2 letters of recommendation; good academic standing at home school; ability to do upper-division course work in chosen subject.
Living Arrangements • Students live in host institution dormitories. Quarters are shared with host institution students. Meals are taken on one's own, in residences.
Costs (2003-2004) • One term: $9550 for fall; $10,025 for single-term spring; $13,575 for two-term spring. Yearlong program: $17,750; includes tuition, housing, excursions, international student ID, student support services. $350 nonrefundable deposit required. Financial aid available for all students: scholarships, loans, regular financial aid, grants.

For More Information • Dr. John J. Perry, Director, Office of International Education, State University of New York College at Brockport, 350 New Campus Drive, Brockport, NY 14420; *Phone:* 800-298-SUNY; *Fax:* 585-637-3218. *E-mail:* overseas@brockport.edu. *World Wide Web:* http://www.brockport.edu/studyabroad/

STATE UNIVERSITY OF NEW YORK COLLEGE AT BROCKPORT
UNIVERSITY OF OXFORD PROGRAM

Hosted by University of Oxford
Academic Focus • Architecture, art history, economics, English, geography, history, international affairs, language studies, linguistics, literature, mathematics, music history, philosophy, physical sciences, political science and government, psychology, religious studies, sociology, women's studies.
Program Information • Students attend classes at University of Oxford. Field trips to the London weekend program, Oxford and the surrounding area.
Sessions • Fall, spring, yearlong, two-term spring.
Eligibility Requirements • Minimum age 18; open to juniors, seniors, graduate students; course work in area of tutorial; 3.0 GPA; 2 letters of recommendation; good academic standing at home school; ability to do upper-division research in chosen tutorial subjects.
Living Arrangements • Students live in locally rented apartments. Meals are taken on one's own, in residences.
Costs (2003-2004) • One term: $11,100 for fall term; $12,075 for spring. Yearlong program: $26,750 for full year; $16,075 with two-term spring; includes tuition, housing, excursions, international student ID, student support services, college memberships, Oxford Union membership, computer access. $350 nonrefundable deposit required. Financial aid available for all students: scholarships, loans, regular financial aid, grants.

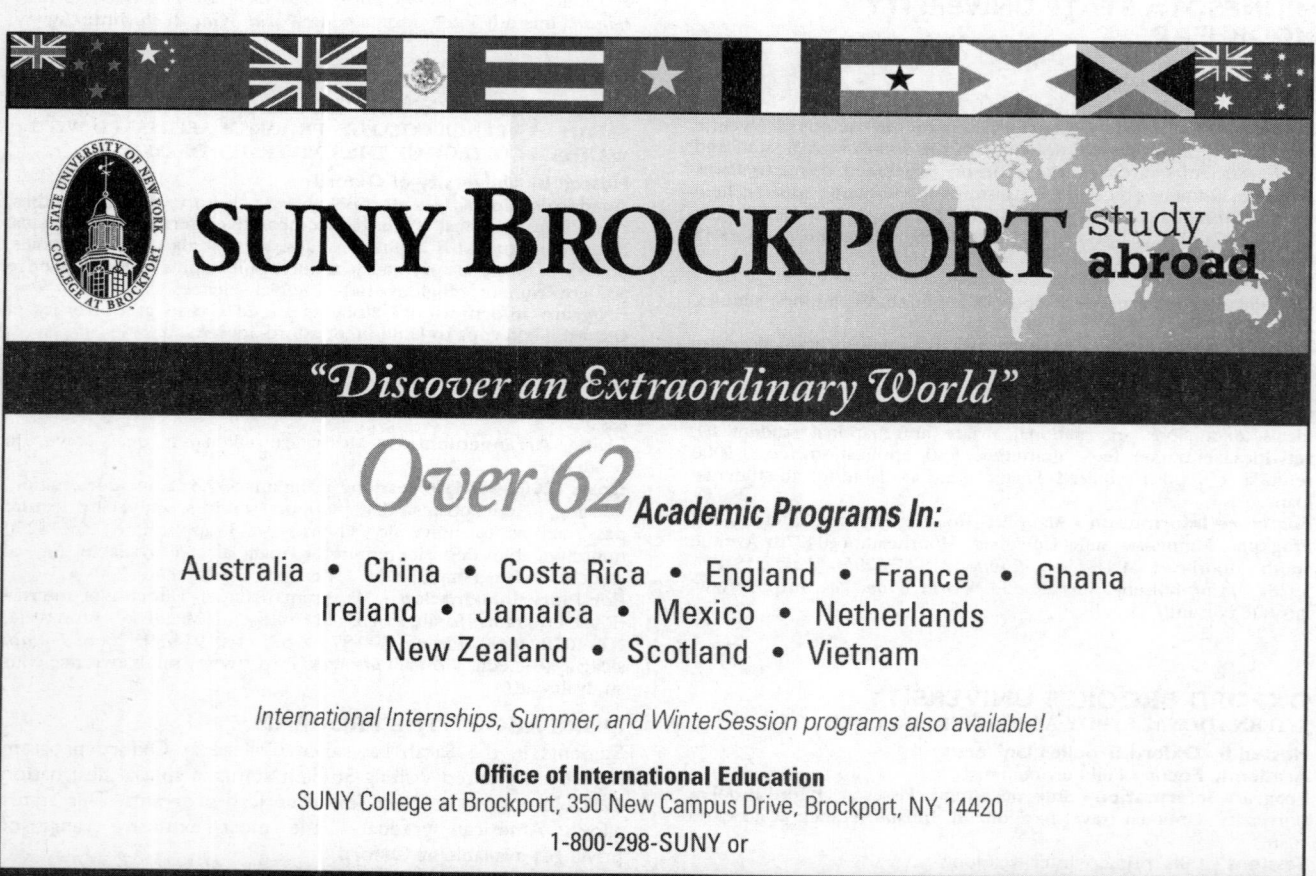

For More Information • Dr. John Perry, Director, Office of International Education, State University of New York College at Brockport, 350 New Campus Drive, Brockport, NY 14420; *Phone:* 800-298-SUNY; *Fax:* 585-637-3218. *E-mail:* overseas@brockport.edu. *World Wide Web:* http://www.brockport.edu/studyabroad/

MORE ABOUT THE PROGRAM

Oxford, Matthew Arnold's "city of dreaming spires," continues to inspire students from throughout the world. The Brockport Oxford Program enables qualified students to experience the life of an Oxford undergraduate for 1 term, 2 terms, or a full academic year. Instruction is in one-on-one tutorials conducted by Oxford University tutors. Participants are enrolled in the Junior Common Room of one of Oxford's 43 colleges and have membership in the Oxford Union Society and access to the Bodleian Library. Housing is with some Oxford University undergraduates in nearby off-campus accommodations. A full program of excursions, field trips, and social events is included.

UNIVERSITY OF GEORGIA
UNIVERSITY OF GEORGIA AT OXFORD

Held at University of Oxford–Keble College
Academic Focus • English literature, history, language studies, liberal studies, political science and government.
Program Information • Classes are held on the campus of University of Oxford–Keble College. Faculty members are drawn from the sponsor's U.S. staff and local instructors hired by the sponsor. Field trips to Bath, Lake District, London, Tintern Abbey, Stourhead Gardens, Stonehenge.
Sessions • Fall, spring.
Eligibility Requirements • Minimum age 18; open to freshmen, sophomores, juniors, seniors, graduate students; 3.0 GPA; good academic standing at home school.
Living Arrangements • Students live in program-owned houses. Quarters are shared with students from other programs. Meals are taken as a group, in central dining facility.
Costs (2003-2004) • One term: $7575; includes tuition, housing, all meals, insurance, student support services. $300 refundable deposit required. Financial aid available for students from sponsoring institution: scholarships, loans.
For More Information • Ms. Margaret F. Perry, Assistant Director, University of Georgia, Park Hall 326A, Athens, GA 30602; *Phone:* 706-542-2244; *Fax:* 706-583-0604. *E-mail:* mfperry@uga.edu. *World Wide Web:* http://www.uga.edu/oie/studyabroad.htm

WASHINGTON INTERNATIONAL STUDIES COUNCIL
WISC OXFORD COLLEGES PROGRAM (VISITING STUDENTS AND ASSOCIATE STUDENTS)

Held at University of Oxford–Magdalen College, University of Oxford–Trinity College, University of Oxford–New College
Academic Focus • Full curriculum.
Program Information • Classes are held on the campus of University of Oxford–Magdalen College, University of Oxford–Trinity College, University of Oxford–New College. Faculty members are local instructors hired by the sponsor. Field trips to Cambridge, Bath, Stratford-upon-Avon, London, Warwick, Stonehenge; optional travel to Paris, Dublin, Amsterdam, Vienna at an extra cost.
Sessions • Fall, spring, winter, yearlong.
Eligibility Requirements • Minimum age 17; open to juniors, seniors, graduate students, adults; 3.5 GPA; 2 letters of recommendation; good academic standing at home school; minimum 3.2 GPA for Trinity College; essay for New College and Magdalen College.
Living Arrangements • Students live in host institution dormitories, locally rented apartments, program-owned apartments, program-owned houses. Quarters are shared with host institution students. Meals are taken as a group, on one's own, in residences, in central dining facility.
Costs (2003-2004) • One term: $12,560. Yearlong program: $34,500 (Visiting Student prices are slightly higher); includes tuition, housing, insurance, excursions, books and class materials, international student ID, student support services, Oxford Union Society

membership, library fees. $300 refundable deposit required. Financial aid available for all students: scholarships, work study.
For More Information • Ms. Stacey Bustillos, Associate Director, Washington International Studies Council, 214 Massachusetts Avenue, NE, Suite 370, Washington, DC 20002; *Phone:* 800-323-WISC; *Fax:* 202-547-1470. *E-mail:* wisc@erols.com. *World Wide Web:* http://www.wiscabroad.com/. Students may also apply through WISC, 21-27 George Street Chester House, Oxford OX1 4DN, England.

PRESTON
STATE UNIVERSITY OF NEW YORK AT PLATTSBURGH
STUDY IN ENGLAND, PRESTON

Hosted by University of Central Lancashire
Academic Focus • Accounting, art, business administration/management, communications, design and applied arts, economics, geography, information science, interdisciplinary studies, journalism, management information systems, music, science.
Program Information • Students attend classes at University of Central Lancashire.
Sessions • Fall, spring, yearlong.
Eligibility Requirements • Minimum age 18; open to sophomores, juniors, seniors; 2.8 GPA; 2 letters of recommendation; good academic standing at home school; SUNY application; essay; transcripts.
Living Arrangements • Students live in host institution dormitories, locally rented apartments. Quarters are shared with host institution students, students from other programs. Meals are taken on one's own, in residences, in central dining facility, in restaurants.
Costs (2003-2004) • One term: $6058 for New York residents; nonresidents contact sponsor for cost. Yearlong program: $12,116 for New York residents; nonresidents contact sponsor for cost; includes tuition, housing, all meals, insurance, books and class materials, international student ID, student support services. $20 application fee. $350 nonrefundable deposit required. Financial aid available for students from sponsoring institution: scholarships, loans.
For More Information • Ms. Jo Ann Mackie, Study Abroad Coordinator, State University of New York at Plattsburgh, Study Abroad Office, 101 Broad Street, Plattsburgh, NY 12901; *Phone:* 518-564-2321; *Fax:* 518-564-2326. *E-mail:* international@plattsburgh.edu. *World Wide Web:* http://www.plattsburgh.edu/studyabroad/

READING
ARCADIA UNIVERSITY
UNIVERSITY OF READING

Hosted by University of Reading
Academic Focus • Full curriculum.
Program Information • Students attend classes at University of Reading.
Sessions • Fall, spring, yearlong.
Eligibility Requirements • Open to juniors, seniors; 3.0 GPA; 1 letter of recommendation.
Living Arrangements • Students live in host institution dormitories, locally rented apartments, host family homes. Quarters are shared with host institution students, students from other programs. Meals are taken on one's own, in central dining facility.
Costs (2002-2003) • One term: $9290 for fall term; $13,750 for two spring terms. Yearlong program: $18,990; includes tuition, housing, insurance, international student ID, student support services, pre-departure guide, transcript. $35 application fee. $500 nonrefundable deposit required. Financial aid available for all students: scholarships, loans.
For More Information • Arcadia University, Center for Education Abroad, 450 South Easton Road, Glenside, PA 19038-3295; *Phone:* 866-927-2234; *Fax:* 215-572-2174. *E-mail:* cea@arcadia.edu. *World Wide Web:* http://www.arcadia.edu/cea/

INTERNATIONAL STUDIES ABROAD
READING, ENGLAND–SEMESTER/YEAR AT THE UNIVERSITY OF READING

Hosted by University of Reading
Academic Focus • Full curriculum.
Program Information • Students attend classes at University of Reading. Optional travel to Oxford, Stratford-upon-Avon, Stonehenge, Salisbury, Brighton, Bath at an extra cost.
Sessions • Fall, yearlong, fall and winter quarters.
Eligibility Requirements • Minimum age 18; open to freshmen, sophomores, juniors, seniors; 2.5 GPA; 1 letter of recommendation; good academic standing at home school; transcript.
Living Arrangements • Students live in host institution dormitories. Meals are taken as a group, on one's own, in central dining facility, in restaurants.
Costs (2004-2005) • One term: $9000 for fall term; $16,800 for fall and winter. Yearlong program: $20,990; includes tuition, housing, some meals, insurance, student support services. $200 deposit required. Financial aid available for all students: loans, U.S. federal financial aid.
For More Information • England Site Specialist, International Studies Abroad, 901 West 24th Street, Austin, TX 78705; *Phone:* 800-580-8826; *Fax:* 512-480-8866. *E-mail:* isa@studiesabroad.com. *World Wide Web:* http://www.studiesabroad.com/

RANDOLPH-MACON WOMAN'S COLLEGE
JUNIOR YEAR ABROAD AT THE UNIVERSITY OF READING, ENGLAND

Hosted by University of Reading
Academic Focus • Archaeology, art, art history, classics and classical languages, communications, creative writing, economics, English, English literature, fine/studio arts, international affairs, liberal studies, mathematics, music, nutrition, philosophy, political science and government, premedical studies, psychology, science, social sciences.
Program Information • Students attend classes at University of Reading. Scheduled travel to Bath, the Lake District, Worcester, Hereford; field trips to London, Stratford-upon-Avon, Woburn Abbey, Hampton Court Palace; optional travel to France, Italy, Spain, Greece, Ireland, Scotland at an extra cost.
Sessions • Yearlong.
Eligibility Requirements • Open to juniors; 2.7 GPA; 3 letters of recommendation; good academic standing at home school; minimum 58 semester hours of college credit.
Living Arrangements • Students live in program-owned houses. Meals are taken as a group, in central dining facility.
Costs (2003-2004) • Yearlong program: $28,976; includes tuition, housing, all meals, excursions, international airfare, books and class materials. $25 application fee. $300 refundable deposit required. Financial aid available for all students: scholarships, loans.
For More Information • Dr. Paul L. Irwin, Coordinator, University of Reading Program, Randolph-Macon Woman's College, Lynchburg, VA 24503-1526; *Phone:* 434-947-8549; *Fax:* 434-947-8138. *E-mail:* pirwin@rmwc.edu. *World Wide Web:* http://www.rmwc.edu/ureading/

RUTGERS, THE STATE UNIVERSITY OF NEW JERSEY
STUDY ABROAD IN BRITAIN: READING

Hosted by University of Reading
Academic Focus • Full curriculum.
Program Information • Students attend classes at University of Reading. Field trips to London, Stonehenge, Oxford.
Sessions • Fall, spring, yearlong.
Eligibility Requirements • Open to sophomores, juniors, seniors; 3.0 GPA; 2 letters of recommendation; good academic standing at home school.
Living Arrangements • Students live in host institution dormitories. Quarters are shared with host institution students. Meals are taken on one's own, in residences, in central dining facility.
Costs (2003-2004) • One term: $10,051–$13,936 for New Jersey residents; $12,701–$16,586 for nonresidents. Yearlong program: $18,394 for New Jersey residents; $23,694 for nonresidents; includes tuition, insurance, excursions, student support services.

$20 application fee. $750 nonrefundable deposit required. Financial aid available for students from sponsoring institution: scholarships, loans.
For More Information • Ms. Karin Bonello, Regional Coordinator, Rutgers, The State University of New Jersey, 102 College Avenue, New Brunswick, NJ 08901-8543; *Phone:* 732-932-7787; *Fax:* 732-932-8659. *E-mail:* ru_abroad@email.rutgers.edu. *World Wide Web:* http://studyabroad.rutgers.edu/

UNIVERSITY STUDIES ABROAD CONSORTIUM
FULL CURRICULUM STUDIES: READING, ENGLAND

Hosted by University of Reading
Academic Focus • Full curriculum.
Program Information • Students attend classes at University of Reading.
Sessions • Fall, spring, yearlong.
Eligibility Requirements • Minimum age 18; open to freshmen, sophomores, juniors, seniors, graduate students, adults; 3.0 GPA.
Living Arrangements • Students live in host institution dormitories. Quarters are shared with host institution students. Meals are taken on one's own, in residences, in central dining facility.
Costs (2005-2006) • One term: $5980. Yearlong program: $11,680; includes tuition, insurance, student support services. $50 application fee. $150 refundable deposit required. Financial aid available for all students: scholarships, loans.
For More Information • University Studies Abroad Consortium, USAC/323, Reno, NV 89557-0093; *Phone:* 775-784-6569; *Fax:* 775-784-6010. *E-mail:* usac@unr.edu. *World Wide Web:* http://usac.unr.edu/

SHEFFIELD
UNIVERSITY OF SHEFFIELD
STUDY ABROAD PROGRAMME

Hosted by University of Sheffield
Academic Focus • American studies, anthropology, archaeology, architecture, Biblical studies, biochemistry, biological/life sciences, biomedical sciences, botany, business administration/management, Chinese language and literature, Chinese studies, commerce, comparative literature, computer science, criminal justice, Czech, Dutch, earth sciences, East Asian studies, economics, electrical engineering, engineering, English, English literature, environmental science/studies, finance, French language and literature, French studies, geography, German language and literature, German studies, history, information science, international business, Japanese, Japanese studies, journalism, Korean, Korean Studies, law and legal studies, linguistics, literature, management information systems, marketing, mathematics, music, music theory, philosophy, physics, Polish, political science and government, Portuguese, psychology, Russian language and literature, Russian studies, science, social sciences, sociology, Spanish language and literature, Spanish studies, speech pathology, statistics, urban studies, urban/regional planning, zoology.
Program Information • Students attend classes at University of Sheffield.
Sessions • Fall, spring, yearlong.
Eligibility Requirements • Minimum age 18; open to sophomores, juniors, seniors, adults; 3.0 GPA; 2 letters of recommendation; good academic standing at home school; personal statement.
Living Arrangements • Students live in host institution dormitories, locally rented apartments. Quarters are shared with host institution students. Meals are taken as a group, on one's own, in residences, in restaurants.
Costs (2004-2005) • One term: $10,565. Yearlong program: $19,768; includes tuition, housing, all meals, books and class materials, international student ID, student support services.
For More Information • Ms. Angela Bingley, Associate Director, University of Sheffield, International Office, 8 Palmerston Road, Sheffield S10 2TE, England; *Phone:* +44 114-222-1255; *Fax:* +44 114-272-9145. *E-mail:* international@sheffield.ac.uk. *World Wide Web:* http://www.shef.ac.uk/international/sa/sain.htm

SUNDERLAND

CENTER FOR INTERNATIONAL STUDIES
UNIVERSITY OF SUNDERLAND

Hosted by University of Sunderland
Academic Focus • Full curriculum.
Program Information • Students attend classes at University of Sunderland. Field trips to a Sunderland City tour; optional travel to London, Edinburgh at an extra cost.
Sessions • Fall, spring, yearlong.
Eligibility Requirements • Minimum age 18; open to sophomores, juniors, seniors, graduate students, adults; 2.7 GPA; 1 letter of recommendation; good academic standing at home school; personal essay.
Living Arrangements • Students live in program-owned apartments. Quarters are shared with host institution students. Meals are taken on one's own, in residences, in central dining facility, in restaurants.
Costs (2003-2004) • One term: $8250. Yearlong program: $14,600; includes tuition, housing, international student ID, student support services, airport reception. $50 application fee. $500 nonrefundable deposit required. Financial aid available for all students: scholarships.
For More Information • Mr. Jeff Palm, Program Director, Center for International Studies, 17 New South Street, #105, Northampton, MA 01060; *Phone:* 413-582-0407; *Fax:* 413-582-0327. *E-mail:* jpalm@cisabroad.com. *World Wide Web:* http://www.cisabroad.com/

WROXTON

FAIRFIELD UNIVERSITY
WROXTON COLLEGE PROGRAM

Hosted by Fairleigh Dickinson University–Wroxton College
Academic Focus • Art history, drama/theater, economics, English literature, history, international affairs, international business, political science and government.
Program Information • Students attend classes at Fairleigh Dickinson University–Wroxton College. Scheduled travel to Edinburgh, Brussels; field trips to London, Bath, Oxford, historic sites; optional travel at an extra cost.
Sessions • Fall, spring, yearlong.
Eligibility Requirements • Minimum age 19; open to sophomores, juniors, seniors, graduate students, adults; 2.5 GPA; 2 letters of recommendation; good academic standing at home school; must be at least a second semester sophomore.
Living Arrangements • Students live in a 16th century abbey. Quarters are shared with host institution students. Meals are taken as a group, in central dining facility.
Costs • One term: $13,600. Yearlong program: $23,800; includes tuition, housing, all meals, excursions, books and class materials, student support services, theatrical performances, special trips and activities, maid service, bedding. $25 application fee. $1000 refundable deposit required.
For More Information • Christine Bowers, Study Abroad Coordinator, Fairfield University, Dolan House, Fairfield, CT 06430; *Phone:* 203-254-4220; *Fax:* 203-254-4106. *E-mail:* cbbowers@fair1.fairfield.edu. *World Wide Web:* http://www.fairfield.edu/sce/studyabroad/

FAIRLEIGH DICKINSON UNIVERSITY
WROXTON COLLEGE, ENGLAND

Hosted by Fairleigh Dickinson University–Wroxton College
Academic Focus • Drama/theater, economics, education, English literature, fine/studio arts, history, political science and government, sociology.
Program Information • Students attend classes at Fairleigh Dickinson University–Wroxton College. Scheduled travel to Edinburgh; field trips to Stratford-upon-Avon, London, Bath, Cambridge; optional travel to Brussels, Paris at an extra cost.
Sessions • Fall, spring, yearlong.
Eligibility Requirements • Open to sophomores, juniors, seniors, graduate students, adults; 2.75 GPA; 3 letters of recommendation; short essay.

Living Arrangements • Students live in private rooms in Wroxton Abbey. Quarters are shared with host institution students. Meals are taken as a group, in central dining facility.
Costs (2002-2003) • One term: $12,933. Yearlong program: $25,866; includes tuition, housing, all meals, excursions, books and class materials, lab equipment, housekeeping service, fees. $40 application fee. $100 nonrefundable deposit required. Financial aid available for students from sponsoring institution: scholarships, loans.
For More Information • Mr. Brian Swanzey, Director of Wroxton College, Fairleigh Dickinson University, 285 Madison Avenue, M-MSO-03, Madison, NJ 07940; *Phone:* 973-443-8086; *Fax:* 973-443-8989. *E-mail:* brian_swanzey@fdu.edu. *World Wide Web:* http://www.fdu.edu/wroxton/

YORK

ARCADIA UNIVERSITY
UNIVERSITY OF YORK

Hosted by University of York
Academic Focus • Archaeology, business administration/management, education, engineering, English, environmental science/studies, history, liberal studies, science, social sciences, women's studies.
Program Information • Students attend classes at University of York.
Sessions • Fall, spring, yearlong.
Eligibility Requirements • Open to juniors, seniors; 3.0 GPA; 1 letter of recommendation; graded writing sample for English courses.
Living Arrangements • Students live in host institution dormitories, locally rented apartments, host family homes. Quarters are shared with host institution students, students from other programs. Meals are taken on one's own, in residences.
Costs (2003-2004) • One term: $8690 for fall term; $13690 for two spring terms. Yearlong program: $19,090; includes tuition, housing, insurance, international student ID, student support services, pre-departure guide, transcripts. $35 application fee. $500 nonrefundable deposit required. Financial aid available for all students: scholarships, loans.
For More Information • Arcadia University, Center for Education Abroad, 450 South Easton Road, Glenside, PA 19038-3295; *Phone:* 866-927-2234; *Fax:* 215-572-2174. *E-mail:* cea@arcadia.edu. *World Wide Web:* http://www.arcadia.edu/cea/

INSTITUTE FOR STUDY ABROAD, BUTLER UNIVERSITY
UNIVERSITY OF YORK

Hosted by University of York
Academic Focus • Full curriculum.
Program Information • Students attend classes at University of York. Field trips to London.
Sessions • Fall, spring, yearlong.
Eligibility Requirements • Open to juniors, seniors; 3.0 GPA; 1 letter of recommendation; good academic standing at home school; enrollment at an accredited American college or university.
Living Arrangements • Students live in host institution dormitories, locally rented apartments. Quarters are shared with host institution students. Meals are taken on one's own, in residences, in central dining facility.
Costs (2002-2003) • One term: $8275 for fall term; $12,275 for spring. Yearlong program: $16,975; includes tuition, housing, excursions, international student ID, student support services, family visit, cultural and sporting events, pre-departure advising. $40 application fee. $500 nonrefundable deposit required. Financial aid available for all students: scholarships, travel grants.
For More Information • Institute for Study Abroad, Butler University, 1100 West 42nd Street, Suite 305, Indianapolis, IN 46208-3345; *Phone:* 800-858-0229; *Fax:* 317-940-9704. *E-mail:* study-abroad@butler.edu. *World Wide Web:* http://www.ifsa-butler.org/

INTERSTUDY
UNIVERSITY COLLEGE OF RIPON AND YORK SAINT JOHN

Hosted by University College of Ripon and York Saint John
Academic Focus • American studies, art history, business administration/management, dance, design and applied arts, drama/theater, education, English, film and media studies, fine/studio arts, history, linguistics, literature, psychology, religious studies, social sciences, social work, sports management, women's studies.
Program Information • Students attend classes at University College of Ripon and York Saint John. Scheduled travel to Bath, Stratford-upon-Avon, Warwick Castle, Oxford, Stonehenge.
Sessions • Fall, spring, yearlong.
Eligibility Requirements • Minimum age 18; open to freshmen, sophomores, juniors, seniors, adults; 2.8 GPA; 2 letters of recommendation; good academic standing at home school.
Living Arrangements • Students live in host institution dormitories, locally rented apartments. Quarters are shared with host institution students. Meals are taken as a group, on one's own, in residences, in central dining facility.
Costs (2003-2004) • One term: $11,415 for fall term; $12,975 for spring. Yearlong program: $20,625; includes tuition, housing, some meals, excursions, international student ID, student support services, Student Union membership, e-mail access, banking facilities, international bank transfers facility, transcript, cell phone. $35 application fee. $500 nonrefundable deposit required. Financial aid available for all students: scholarships, loans, stipends.
For More Information • InterStudy, Admissions Office, 63 Edward Street, Medford, MA 02155; *Phone:* 800-663-1999; *Fax:* 781-391-7463. *E-mail:* interstudy@interstudy-usa.org. *World Wide Web:* http://www.interstudy.org/

RUTGERS, THE STATE UNIVERSITY OF NEW JERSEY
STUDY ABROAD IN BRITAIN: YORK, UNIVERSITY OF YORK

Hosted by University of York
Academic Focus • Full curriculum.
Program Information • Students attend classes at University of York. Field trips to London, Stonehenge, Oxford.
Sessions • Fall, spring, yearlong.
Eligibility Requirements • Open to juniors, seniors; 3.0 GPA; 2 letters of recommendation; good academic standing at home school.
Living Arrangements • Students live in host institution dormitories. Quarters are shared with host institution students, students from other programs. Meals are taken on one's own, in residences, in central dining facility.
Costs (2003-2004) • One term: $11,790–$15,066 for New Jersey residents; $14,440–$17,716 for nonresidents. Yearlong program: $19,952 for New Jersey residents; $25,252 for nonresidents; includes tuition, insurance, excursions, student support services. $20 application fee. $750 nonrefundable deposit required. Financial aid available for students from sponsoring institution: scholarships, loans.
For More Information • Ms. Karin Bonello, Regional Coordinator, Rutgers, The State University of New Jersey, 102 College Avenue, New Brunswick, NJ 08901-8543; *Phone:* 732-932-7787; *Fax:* 732-932-8659. *E-mail:* ru_abroad@email.rutgers.edu. *World Wide Web:* http://studyabroad.rutgers.edu/

UNIVERSITY OF YORK
VISITING STUDENT PROGRAMME

Hosted by University of York
Academic Focus • Full curriculum.
Program Information • Students attend classes at University of York. Optional travel to destinations within the United Kingdom at an extra cost.
Sessions • Fall, spring, yearlong.
Eligibility Requirements • Open to sophomores, juniors; 3.0 GPA; 1 letter of recommendation; good academic standing at home school; sample essay for admission to English literature courses.
Living Arrangements • Students live in host institution dormitories, locally rented apartments. Quarters are shared with host institution students. Meals are taken as a group, on one's own, in residences.

Costs (2003-2004) • One term: £2614 ; £5228 for two terms. Yearlong program: £7842; includes tuition, student support services, access to library and computing facilities including e-mail.
For More Information • Mr. Simon Willis, Director, International Office, University of York, Heslington, York YO1 5DD, England; *Phone:* +44 190-443-3532; *Fax:* +44 190-434-4268. *E-mail:* international@york.ac.uk. *World Wide Web:* http://www.york.ac.uk/admin/intnat/. Students may also apply through Butler University, Institute for Study Abroad, 1100 West 42nd Street, Suite 305, Indianapolis, IN 46208-3345; Arcadia University, Center for Education Abroad, 450 South Easton Road, Glenside, PA 19038-3295.

ESTONIA
TARTU
UNIVERSITY OF TARTU
PROMETHEUS PROGRAM ON TRANSITION STUDIES

Hosted by University of Tartu
Academic Focus • Eastern European studies, economics, international affairs, political science and government, Russian studies.
Program Information • Students attend classes at University of Tartu. Scheduled travel to St. Petersburg, Novgorod; field trips to Riga; optional travel to Baltic states, Scandinavia at an extra cost.
Sessions • Spring.
Eligibility Requirements • Minimum age 17; open to sophomores, juniors, seniors; 2.5 GPA; good academic standing at home school; no foreign language proficiency required.
Living Arrangements • Students live in host institution dormitories, locally rented apartments. Meals are taken on one's own, in residences; in restaurants.
Costs (2004) • One term: $3000; includes tuition, excursions, student support services.
For More Information • Ms. Piret Ehin, Vice Director, University of Tartu, Lossi 3-310, Tartu 51003, Estonia; *Phone:* +372 737-6378; *Fax:* +372 744-1290. *E-mail:* piret.ehin@ec.ut.ee. *World Wide Web:* http://ec.ut.ee/transition/

ETHIOPIA
ADDIS ABABA
BROWN UNIVERSITY
BROWN IN ETHIOPIA

Hosted by Addis Ababa University
Academic Focus • African languages and literature, African studies, biological/life sciences, drama/theater, social sciences.
Program Information • Students attend classes at Addis Ababa University. Field trips to Addis Ababa, the Lake Region of Ethiopia.
Sessions • Fall, yearlong.
Eligibility Requirements • Open to juniors, seniors; 3.0 GPA; 2 letters of recommendation; good academic standing at home school; demonstrated academic interest in Africa; no foreign language proficiency required.
Living Arrangements • Students live in host institution dormitories, locally rented apartments. Quarters are shared with host institution students, students from other programs. Meals are taken on one's own, in residences.
Costs (2004-2005) • One term: $15,336. Yearlong program: $30,672; includes tuition, housing, some meals, excursions, international student ID, special Amharic language course. $250 nonrefundable deposit required. Financial aid available for students from sponsoring institution: scholarships, loans.
For More Information • Ms. Mell Bolen, Director, Brown University, Office of International Programs, Box 1973, Providence, RI 02912-1973; *Phone:* 401-863-3555; *Fax:* 401-863-3311. *E-mail:* oip_office@brown.edu. *World Wide Web:* http://www.brown.edu/OIP/

FIJI

SUVA

SCHOOL FOR INTERNATIONAL TRAINING, SIT STUDY ABROAD
FIJI: CULTURAL HISTORY AND GEOGRAPHY

Academic Focus • Ecology, ethnic studies, geography, Pacific studies.
Program Information • Faculty members are local instructors hired by the sponsor. Scheduled travel to rural Fiji (2 weeks); field trips to the Great Astrolabe Reef, the Rewa River Watershed.
Sessions • Fall, spring.
Eligibility Requirements • Open to sophomores, juniors, seniors; 2.5 GPA; 2 letters of recommendation; no foreign language proficiency required.
Living Arrangements • Students live in host family homes. Meals are taken with host family, in residences.
Costs (2004-2005) • One term: contact sponsor for cost. $50 application fee. $400 nonrefundable deposit required. Financial aid available for all students: scholarships.
For More Information • School for International Training, SIT Study Abroad, Kipling Road, Brattleboro, VT 05302-0676; *Phone:* 888-272-7881; *Fax:* 802-258-3296. *E-mail:* studyabroad@sit.edu. *World Wide Web:* http://www.sit.edu/studyabroad/

FINLAND

CITY TO CITY

LOCK HAVEN UNIVERSITY OF PENNSYLVANIA
SEMESTER IN FINLAND

Hosted by Central Ostrobothnia Polytechnic, Ylivieska Institute of Technology
Academic Focus • Economics, international affairs, international business, management information systems, marketing.
Program Information • Students attend classes at Central Ostrobothnia Polytechnic (Kokkola), Ylivieska Institute of Technology (Ylivieska).
Sessions • Fall, spring, yearlong.
Eligibility Requirements • Minimum age 18; open to sophomores, juniors, seniors, adults; 2.5 GPA; 3 letters of recommendation; good academic standing at home school; transcript; no foreign language proficiency required.
Living Arrangements • Students live in locally rented apartments. Quarters are shared with host institution students, students from other programs. Meals are taken on one's own.
Costs (2002-2003) • One term: $3850 for Pennsylvania residents; $6125 for nonresidents. Yearlong program: $7680 for Pennsylvania residents; $12,250 for nonresidents; includes tuition, housing, fees. $50 application fee. Financial aid available for students from sponsoring institution: scholarships.
For More Information • Dean, Institute for International Studies, Lock Haven University of Pennsylvania, Lock Haven, PA 17745-2390; *Phone:* 570-893-2140; *Fax:* 570-893-2537. *E-mail:* intlstudies_webmonitor@lhup.edu. *World Wide Web:* http://www.lhup.edu/international/goingp/goingplaces_index.htm

HELSINKI

HELSINKI UNIVERSITY OF TECHNOLOGY
INFOCOM MANAGEMENT PROGRAM

Hosted by Helsinki University of Technology
Academic Focus • Business administration/management, entrepreneurship, management information systems.

Program Information • Students attend classes at Helsinki University of Technology. Field trips to Tallinn, St. Petersburg, major cities in Finland; optional travel to St. Petersburg, Moscow.
Sessions • Yearlong.
Eligibility Requirements • Minimum age 20; open to graduate students, adults; major in engineering, information technology, business management; no foreign language proficiency required.
Living Arrangements • Students live in host institution dormitories. Quarters are shared with host institution students, students from other programs. Meals are taken on one's own.
Costs (2003-2004) • Yearlong program: €5000; includes tuition, some meals, excursions, student support services, some books and class materials. Financial aid available for all students: scholarships.
For More Information • Ms. Valoria Baryshnikova, Program Coordinator, Helsinki University of Technology, Institute of Industrial Management, Infocom Management Program, Otakaari 4, 02150 Espoo, Finland; *Phone:* +358 451-3395; *Fax:* +358 451-3095. *E-mail:* infocom.management@hut.fi. *World Wide Web:* http://www.hut.fi/

HELSINKI UNIVERSITY OF TECHNOLOGY
INTERNATIONAL BUSINESS LINKAGE PROGRAM

Hosted by Helsinki University of Technology
Academic Focus • Business administration/management, entrepreneurship, international business, marketing.
Program Information • Students attend classes at Helsinki University of Technology. Field trips to Stockholm, Tallinn, St. Petersburg, major cities in Finland; optional travel to St. Petersburg.
Sessions • Yearlong.
Eligibility Requirements • Minimum age 20; open to graduate students, adults; major in engineering, economics, business management; no foreign language proficiency required.
Living Arrangements • Students live in host institution dormitories. Quarters are shared with host institution students, students from other programs. Meals are taken on one's own, in residences, in restaurants.
Costs (2003-2004) • Yearlong program: €5000; includes tuition, some meals, excursions, student support services, most recreation fees, some books and class materials. Financial aid available for all students: scholarships.
For More Information • Ms. Valoria Baryshnikova, Program Coordinator, Helsinki University of Technology, Institute of Industrial Management, International Business Linkage Program, Office U502, Otakaari 4, 02150 Espoo, Finland; *Phone:* +358 451-3395; *Fax:* +358 451-3095. *E-mail:* business.linkage@hut.fi. *World Wide Web:* http://www.hut.fi/

JOENSUU

UNIVERSITY OF JOENSUU
AN INTERNATIONAL MASTER'S DEGREE PROGRAM IN HUMAN GEOGRAPHY–NORTHERN AND EASTERN EUROPE IN A GLOBAL CONTEXT

Hosted by University of Joensuu
Academic Focus • Cultural studies, Eastern European studies, economics, environmental science/studies, geography.
Program Information • Students attend classes at University of Joensuu. Field trips to St. Petersburg, Petrozavodsk, Tartu; optional travel to St. Petersburg, Petrozavodsk, Tartu at an extra cost.
Sessions • Fall, spring, yearlong.
Eligibility Requirements • Open to juniors, seniors, graduate students, adults; course work in geography or a related field; no foreign language proficiency required.
Living Arrangements • Students live in locally rented apartments, a private student hostel. Meals are taken on one's own, in central dining facility.
Costs (2003-2004) • One term: contact sponsor for cost. Yearlong program: contact sponsor for cost.
For More Information • Ms. Paivi Haltilahti, International Studies Coordinator, University of Joensuu, International Student Services, PO Box 111, FIN-80101 Joensuu, Finland; *Phone:* +358 13-251-4301; *Fax:* +358 13-251-2010. *E-mail:* intnl@joensuu.fi. *World Wide Web:* http://www.joensuu.fi/englishindex.html. Students may also apply through International Student Exchange Program, (ISEP), 1616 P Street, NW, Suite 150, Washington, DC 20036.

UNIVERSITY OF JOENSUU
INTERNATIONAL STUDY PROGRAM IN EDUCATIONAL SCIENCES

Hosted by University of Joensuu
Academic Focus • Education, teaching.
Program Information • Students attend classes at University of Joensuu. Optional travel to St. Petersburg, Petrozavodsk, Tartu at an extra cost.
Sessions • Fall, spring, yearlong.
Eligibility Requirements • Open to sophomores, juniors, seniors, graduate students, adults; no foreign language proficiency required.
Living Arrangements • Students live in locally rented apartments, a private student hostel. Meals are taken on one's own, in central dining facility.
Costs (2003-2004) • One term: contact sponsor for cost. Yearlong program: contact sponsor for cost.
For More Information • Ms. Paivi Haltilahti, International Studies Coordinator, University of Joensuu, International Student Services, University of Joensuu, PO Box 111, FIN-80101 Joensuu, Finland; *Phone:* +358 13-251-4301; *Fax:* +358 13-251-2010. *E-mail:* intnl@joensuu.fi. *World Wide Web:* http://www.joensuu.fi/englishindex.html. Students may also apply through International Student Exchange Program, (ISEP), 1616 P Street, NW, Suite 150, Washington, DC 20036.

UNIVERSITY OF JOENSUU
INTERNATIONAL STUDY PROGRAM IN ENVIRONMENTAL SCIENCE AND FORESTRY

Hosted by University of Joensuu
Academic Focus • Botany, conservation studies, ecology, environmental science/studies, forestry, natural resources, zoology.
Program Information • Students attend classes at University of Joensuu. Optional travel to the Finnish Lapland, St. Petersburg, Petrozavodsk, Tartu at an extra cost.
Sessions • Fall, spring, yearlong.
Eligibility Requirements • Open to juniors, seniors, graduate students, adults; course work in environmental science/biology/forestry or a related field; no foreign language proficiency required.
Living Arrangements • Students live in locally rented apartments, a private student hostel. Meals are taken on one's own, in central dining facility.
Costs (2003-2004) • One term: $1750. Yearlong program: $3500; includes tuition, lab equipment, student support services.
For More Information • Ms. Paivi Haltilahti, International Studies Coordinator, University of Joensuu, International Student Services, PO Box 111, FIN-80101 Joensuu, Finland; *Phone:* +358 13-251-4301; *Fax:* +358 13-251 2010. *E-mail:* intnl@joensuu.fi. *World Wide Web:* http://www.joensuu.fi/englishindex.html. Students may also apply through International Student Exchange Program, (ISEP), 1616 P Street, NW, Suite 150, Washington, DC 20036.

UNIVERSITY OF JOENSUU
INTERNATIONAL STUDY PROGRAM IN SOCIAL SCIENCES

Hosted by University of Joensuu
Academic Focus • Business administration/management, economics, law and legal studies, psychology, public policy, social sciences, sociology.
Program Information • Students attend classes at University of Joensuu. Optional travel to St. Petersburg, Petrozavodsk, Tartu at an extra cost.
Sessions • Fall, spring, yearlong.
Eligibility Requirements • Open to sophomores, juniors, seniors, graduate students, adults; no foreign language proficiency required.
Living Arrangements • Students live in locally rented apartments, a private student hostel. Meals are taken on one's own, in central dining facility.
Costs (2003-2004) • One term: $1750. Yearlong program: $3500; includes tuition, lab equipment, student support services.
For More Information • Ms. Paivi Haltilahti, International Studies Coordinator, University of Joensuu, International Student Services, PO Box 111, FIN-80101 Joensuu, Finland; *Phone:* +358 13-251-4301; *Fax:* +358 13-251-2010. *E-mail:* intnl@joensuu.fi. *World Wide Web:* http://www.joensuu.fi/englishindex.html. Students may also apply through International Student Exchange Program, (ISEP), 1616 P Street, NW, Suite 150, Washington, DC 20036.

UNIVERSITY OF JOENSUU
INTERNATIONAL STUDY PROGRAM ON KARELIA, RUSSIA AND THE BALTIC AREA

Hosted by University of Joensuu
Academic Focus • Area studies, cultural studies, economics, geography, history, interdisciplinary studies, Russian studies, social sciences.
Program Information • Students attend classes at University of Joensuu. Field trips to Petrozavodsk, Russian Karelia, Tartu, Estonia, St. Petersburg; optional travel to Petrozavodsk, Russian Karelia, Tartu, St. Petersburg at an extra cost.
Sessions • Fall, spring, yearlong, session includes an optional sub-program in Russian studies.
Eligibility Requirements • Open to sophomores, juniors, seniors, graduate students, adults; 1 year college course work in Russian for optional Russian Studies sub-program.
Living Arrangements • Students live in locally rented apartments, a private student hostel. Meals are taken on one's own, in central dining facility.
Costs (2003-2004) • One term: $1750. Yearlong program: $3500; includes tuition, lab equipment, student support services.
For More Information • Ms. Paivi Haltilahti, International Studies Coordinator, University of Joensuu, International Student Services, PO Box 111, FIN-80101 Joensuu, Finland; *Phone:* +358 13-251-4301; *Fax:* +358 13-251 2010. *E-mail:* intnl@joensuu.fi. *World Wide Web:* http://www.joensuu.fi/englishindex.html. Students may also apply through International Student Exchange Program, (ISEP), 1616 P Street, NW, Suite 150, Washington, DC 20036.

UNIVERSITY OF JOENSUU
ISLAM AND THE WEST: AN INTERNATIONAL MASTER'S DEGREE PROGRAM IN CULTURAL DIVERSITY

Hosted by University of Joensuu
Academic Focus • Cultural studies, ethics, history, Islamic studies, peace and conflict studies, religious studies, sociology.
Program Information • Students attend classes at University of Joensuu. Optional travel to St. Petersburg, Petrozavodsk, Tartu at an extra cost.
Sessions • Fall, spring, yearlong.
Eligibility Requirements • Open to juniors, seniors, graduate students, adults; course work in humanities, social sciences, educational sciences, or theology; no foreign language proficiency required.
Living Arrangements • Students live in locally rented apartments, a private student hostel. Meals are taken on one's own, in central dining facility.
Costs (2003-2004) • One term: contact sponsor for cost. Yearlong program: contact sponsor for cost.
For More Information • Ms. Paivi Haltilahti, International Studies Coordinator, University of Joensuu, International Student Services, PO Box 111, FIN-80101 Joensuu, Finland; *Phone:* +358 13-251-4301; *Fax:* +358 13-251-2010. *E-mail:* intnl@joensuu.fi. *World Wide Web:* http://www.joensuu.fi/englishindex.html. Students may also apply through International Student Exchange Program, (ISEP), 1616 P Street, NW, Suite 150, Washington, DC 20036.

MIKKELI
UNIVERSITY OF IDAHO
SEMESTER IN FINLAND

Hosted by Mikkeli Polytechnic, Mikkeli Polytechnic, Mikkeli Polytechnic
Academic Focus • Costume design, forestry, information science, international business, marketing, nursing, telecommunications.
Program Information • Students attend classes at Mikkeli Polytechnic, Mikkeli Polytechnic, Mikkeli Polytechnic. Field trips to local cultural sites, lakes, national parks; optional travel at an extra cost.
Sessions • Fall, spring, yearlong.
Eligibility Requirements • Open to sophomores, juniors, seniors, graduate students; good academic standing at home school; no foreign language proficiency required.

Living Arrangements • Students live in host institution dormitories, locally rented apartments, program-owned apartments. Quarters are shared with host institution students. Meals are taken on one's own, in residences.

Costs (2003-2004) • One term: $2500. Yearlong program: $5000; includes tuition, excursions, student support services. $100 application fee. $200 refundable deposit required. Financial aid available for students from sponsoring institution: scholarships, loans, grants.

For More Information • Ms. Amy Bergmann, Advisor, University of Idaho, 209 Morrill Hall, Moscow, ID 83844-3013; *Phone:* 208-885-7870; *Fax:* 208-885-2859. *E-mail:* abroad@uidaho.edu. *World Wide Web:* http://www.ets.uidaho.edu/ipo/abroad/

OULU

UNIVERSITY AT ALBANY, STATE UNIVERSITY OF NEW YORK
DIRECT ENROLLMENT AT THE UNIVERSITY OF OULU

Hosted by University of Oulu
Academic Focus • Anthropology, architecture, Asian studies, ecology, Scandinavian studies.
Program Information • Students attend classes at University of Oulu. Field trips to the Arctic Circle, Bay of Finland, Helsinki.
Sessions • Fall, spring, yearlong.
Eligibility Requirements • Minimum age 18; open to sophomores, juniors, seniors, adults; 3.0 GPA; 2 letters of recommendation; good academic standing at home school; no foreign language proficiency required.
Living Arrangements • Students live in host institution dormitories. Quarters are shared with host institution students. Meals are taken on one's own, in residences, in central dining facility, in restaurants.
Costs (2002-2003) • One term: $5328. Yearlong program: $11,655; includes housing, all meals, student support services, in-state tuition and fees. $150 nonrefundable deposit required. Financial aid available for students from sponsoring institution: all customary sources.
For More Information • University at Albany, State University of New York, Office of International Education, LI 66, Albany, NY 12222; *Phone:* 518-442-3525; *Fax:* 518-442-3338. *E-mail:* intled@uamail.albany.edu. *World Wide Web:* http://www.albany.edu/intled/

UNIVERSITY OF OULU
NORTHERN CULTURES AND SOCIETIES

Hosted by University of Oulu
Academic Focus • Anthropology, archaeology, art history, cultural studies, history, literature.
Program Information • Students attend classes at University of Oulu. Scheduled travel to sites in Lapland, sites in northern Norway, Aland Islands; field trips to prehistoric sites in Northern Finland.
Sessions • Spring.
Eligibility Requirements • Open to juniors, seniors, graduate students, adults; major in anthropology, archaeology, humanities, liberal arts; good academic standing at home school; no foreign language proficiency required.
Living Arrangements • Students live in host institution dormitories. Quarters are shared with students from other programs. Meals are taken on one's own, in central dining facility.
Costs (2004) • One term: €2600; includes tuition, excursions.
For More Information • Ms. Riitta Kataja, Coordinator of International Programmes, University of Oulu, Office of International Relations, PO Box 8000, FIN-90014, Finland; *Phone:* +358 8-553-4050; *Fax:* +358 8-553-4040. *E-mail:* riitta.kataja@oulu.fi. *World Wide Web:* http://www.oulu.fi/intl/

UNIVERSITY OF OULU
NORTHERN NATURE AND ENVIRONMENT STUDIES

Hosted by University of Oulu
Academic Focus • Biological/life sciences, botany, geography, zoology.

Program Information • Students attend classes at University of Oulu. Scheduled travel to research stations; field trips to research stations.
Sessions • Fall, spring, yearlong.
Eligibility Requirements • Open to juniors, seniors, graduate students, adults; major in biological sciences; 2 letters of recommendation; no foreign language proficiency required.
Living Arrangements • Students live in host institution dormitories. Quarters are shared with students from other programs. Meals are taken on one's own, in residences, in central dining facility.
Costs (2002-2003) • One term: €2600. Yearlong program: €5200; includes tuition.
For More Information • Anja Malaska, Deputy Director, University of Oulu, PO Box 8100, FIN-90014, Finland; *Phone:* +358 8-553-4042; *Fax:* +358 8-553-4041. *E-mail:* international.office@oulu.fi. *World Wide Web:* http://www.oulu.fi/intl/. Students may also apply through University of Oulu, Department of Biology, PO Box 3000 FIN-90014, Finland.

UNIVERSITY OF OULU
SCANDINAVIAN STUDIES

Hosted by University of Oulu
Academic Focus • Art, biological/life sciences, cultural studies, film and media studies, geography, history, literature, music history, social sciences.
Program Information • Students attend classes at University of Oulu. Scheduled travel to Helsinki, Oulanka Biological Research Station, Stockholm, Lapland, Tallinn, Estonia; field trips to architectural sites, art galleries, a local newspaper, local schools, churches.
Sessions • Fall.
Eligibility Requirements • Open to sophomores, juniors, seniors, graduate students, adults; major in liberal arts, humanities; 2 letters of recommendation; no foreign language proficiency required.
Living Arrangements • Students live in host institution dormitories. Quarters are shared with students from other programs. Meals are taken on one's own, in residences, in central dining facility.
Costs (2003) • One term: €2600; includes tuition, excursions.
For More Information • Ms. Sanna Waris, Coordinator of International Programs, University of Oulu, Office of International Relations, PO Box 8000, FIN-90014, Finland; *Phone:* +358 8-553-4023; *Fax:* +358 8-553-4040. *E-mail:* sanna.waris@oulu.fi. *World Wide Web:* http://www.oulu.fi/intl/. Students may also apply through University of North Carolina at Greensboro, International Programs Center, 127 McIver Street, PO Box 26170, Greensboro, NC 27402-6170.

FRANCE
CITY TO CITY
NICHOLLS STATE UNIVERSITY
STUDY PROGRAM IN PARIS AND NICE, FRANCE

Hosted by Nicholls State University–Nice, Nicholls State University–Paris
Academic Focus • Art, cultural studies, French language and literature, history.
Program Information • Students attend classes at Nicholls State University–Nice (Nice), Nicholls State University–Paris (Paris). Field trips to museums, markets, monuments, the theater; optional travel to Monaco, museums, markets, Saint Tropez, monuments, the theater.
Sessions • Fall, spring, yearlong.
Eligibility Requirements • Minimum age 17; open to precollege students, freshmen, sophomores, juniors, seniors, graduate students, adults; no foreign language proficiency required.
Living Arrangements • Students live in host family homes. Quarters are shared with host institution students. Meals are taken with host family, in residences.
Costs (2003-2004) • One term: $5801. Yearlong program: $11,601; includes tuition, housing, some meals, insurance, books and class

materials, lab equipment, international student ID, instructional costs. Financial aid available for all students: loans, all customary sources.
For More Information • Ms. Cynthia Webb, Director of Study Programs Abroad, Nicholls State University, PO Box 2080, Thibodaux, LA 70310; *Phone:* 985-448-4440; *Fax:* 985-449-7028. *E-mail:* spab-caw@nicholls.edu. *World Wide Web:* http://www.nicholls.edu/abroad/

UNIVERSITY OF SOUTHERN MISSISSIPPI
THE ABBEY OF PONTLEVOY

Hosted by European American Center for International Education (Pontlevoy)
Academic Focus • Art history, French language and literature, history, interdisciplinary studies, liberal studies, social sciences.
Program Information • Students attend classes at European American Center for International Education (Pontlevoy). Scheduled travel to Paris; field trips to sites associated with courses.
Sessions • Fall, spring.
Eligibility Requirements • Minimum age 18; open to freshmen, sophomores, juniors; 2.0 GPA; good academic standing at home school; must be a second semester freshman; no foreign language proficiency required.
Living Arrangements • Students live in host institution dormitories. Quarters are shared with host institution students. Meals are taken as a group, on one's own, in residences, in restaurants.
Costs (2003-2004) • One term: $11,500–$14,500; includes tuition, housing, some meals, excursions, international airfare, student support services. $200 nonrefundable deposit required. Financial aid available for students from sponsoring institution: scholarships, loans.
For More Information • Ms. Melissa Ravencraft, Coordinator, University of Southern Mississippi, Box 10047, Hattiesburg, MS 39406; *Phone:* 601-266-5009; *Fax:* 601-266-5699. *E-mail:* melissa.ravencraft@usm.edu. *World Wide Web:* http://www.cice.usm.edu/

WHITWORTH COLLEGE
FRENCH STUDY PROGRAM

Academic Focus • Art, French language and literature, history.
Program Information • Faculty members are drawn from the sponsor's U.S. staff.
Sessions • Spring, program runs every 3 years.
Eligibility Requirements • Open to sophomores, juniors, seniors, adults; 2.5 GPA; 2 letters of recommendation; 1 year of college course work in French.
Living Arrangements • Students live in host family homes, hotels, bed-and-breakfast facilities. Meals are taken as a group, in residences, in restaurants.
Costs (2003-2004) • One term: $16,000; includes tuition, housing, all meals, excursions, international airfare. $500 nonrefundable deposit required. Financial aid available for students from sponsoring institution: scholarships, loans.
For More Information • Ms. Sue Jackson, Director, Off-Campus Programs, Whitworth College, Center for International and Multicultural Education, 300 West Hawthorne Road, Spokane, WA 99251-2702; *Phone:* 509-777-4596; *Fax:* 509-777-3723. *E-mail:* sjackson@whitworth.edu. *World Wide Web:* http://www.whitworth.edu/

AIX-EN-PROVENCE
AMERICAN UNIVERSITY CENTER OF PROVENCE

AIX-EN-PROVENCE PROGRAM

Hosted by Institute of Political Studies, Ecole de Beaux-Arts, University of Provence (Aix Marseilles I), American University Center of Provence

Academic Focus • Architecture, art, communications, drama/theater, European studies, film and media studies, fine/studio arts, French language and literature, intercultural studies, literature.

Program Information • Students attend classes at Institute of Political Studies, University of Provence (Aix Marseilles I), American University Center of Provence, Ecole de Beaux-Arts. Field trips to regional monuments, museums, Haute Provence, Arles/Avignon.

Sessions • Fall, spring, yearlong.

Eligibility Requirements • Open to sophomores, juniors, seniors, graduate students, adults; 3.0 GPA; 2 letters of recommendation; good academic standing at home school; 2 years of college course work in French.

Living Arrangements • Students live in host family homes. Meals are taken with host family.

Costs (2004-2005) • One term: $12,000. Yearlong program: $22,900; includes tuition, housing, some meals, excursions, books and class materials, student support services. $30 application fee. $500 nonrefundable deposit required.

For More Information • Ms. Lilli Engle, Director, American University Center of Provence, 19, cours des Arts-et-Métiers, 13100 Aix-en-Provence, France; *Phone:* +33-442-38-42-38; *Fax:* +33-442-38-95-66. *E-mail:* info@aucp.org. *World Wide Web:* http://www.aucp.org/. Students may also apply through Marist College, Office of International Education, 3399 North Road, Poughkeepsie, NY 12601-1387.

MORE ABOUT THE PROGRAM

Nationally acclaimed, challenging, and comprehensive, the American University Center of Provence (AUCP) in Aix motivates learning both inside and outside the classroom. The advanced-level, all-French academic program emphasizes cross-cultural communication, French and European studies, literature, and the arts. Pertinent course offerings, taught in French by French university faculty members, combine with the personalized experiential learning components of the celebrated French Practicum core program, which include individual placement in a carefully selected French host family, community service, personal-interest extracurricular activities, and a French-language exchange partner.

Seeking more than a tourist experience abroad, AUCP students participate fully in the local life of Aix-Provence, a vibrant university town well-known for its stately beauty, brilliant sunshine, and elegant *art de vivre*.

Documented by the highest-level independent testing, the progress in both language acquisition and cross-cultural competence achieved by AUCP students is a reference in the field and a testimony to their commitment to true cultural exchange. There are fall, spring, and full-year enrollment options.

COLLEGE CONSORTIUM FOR INTERNATIONAL STUDIES–MIAMI DADE COLLEGE AND TRUMAN STATE UNIVERSITY
SEMESTER/YEAR IN FRANCE (AIX-EN-PROVENCE)

Hosted by Institute for American Universities (IAU)–Aix-en-Provence

Academic Focus • Archaeology, art history, education, fine/studio arts, French language and literature, geography, history, international affairs, international business, law and legal studies, psychology.

Program Information • Students attend classes at Institute for American Universities (IAU)–Aix-en-Provence. Field trips to Paris, Provence, the Riviera, Geneva.

Sessions • Fall, spring, yearlong.

Eligibility Requirements • Minimum age 18; open to freshmen, sophomores, juniors, seniors, adults; 2.5 GPA; 2 letters of recommendation; good academic standing at home school; statement of purpose; no foreign language proficiency required.

Living Arrangements • Students live in host family homes. Quarters are shared with students from other programs. Meals are taken with host family.

Costs (2004-2005) • One term: $11,435 for non-CCIS members; members contact sponsor for cost. Yearlong program: $22,780 for non-CCIS members; members contact sponsor for cost; includes tuition, housing, some meals, insurance, excursions, books and class materials, international student ID, student support services. $30 application fee. $400 refundable deposit required. Financial aid available for students from sponsoring institution: grants.

For More Information • Mr. Reinaldo Changsut, Director, International Education, College Consortium for International Studies, Miami Dade College, 11011 SW 104th Street, Miami, FL 33176-3393; *Phone:* 305-237-2533; *Fax:* 305-237-2949. *E-mail:* reinaldo.changsut@mdc.edu. *World Wide Web:* http://www.ccisabroad.org/. Students may also apply through Truman State University, Center for International Education Abroad, 100 East Normal, Kirksville, MO 63501.

COLLEGE CONSORTIUM FOR INTERNATIONAL STUDIES–MIAMI DADE COLLEGE AND TRUMAN STATE UNIVERSITY
STUDIO ART IN PROVENCE

Hosted by Institute for American Universities (IAU)–Marchutz School of Painting and Drawing

Academic Focus • Art history, drawing/painting, fine/studio arts.

Program Information • Students attend classes at Institute for American Universities (IAU)–Marchutz School of Painting and Drawing. Scheduled travel to Italy; field trips to Venice (during spring term only).

Sessions • Fall, spring, yearlong.

Eligibility Requirements • Minimum age 18; open to freshmen, sophomores, juniors, seniors, adults; 2.5 GPA; no foreign language proficiency required.

Living Arrangements • Students live in locally rented apartments, host family homes. Quarters are shared with students from other programs. Meals are taken with host family, in residences.

Costs (2004-2005) • One term: $11,595 for non-CCIS members; members contact sponsor for cost. Yearlong program: $23,190 for non-CCIS members; members contact sponsor for cost; includes tuition, housing, some meals, insurance, excursions, books and class materials, student support services, art supplies. $30 application fee. $400 refundable deposit required. Financial aid available for students from sponsoring institution: scholarships, loans, grants.

For More Information • Mr. Reinaldo Changsut, Director, International Education, College Consortium for International Studies, Miami Dade College, 11011 SW 104th Street, Miami, FL 33176-3393; *Phone:* 305-237-2533; *Fax:* 305-237-2949. *E-mail:* reinaldo.changsut@mdc.edu. *World Wide Web:* http://www.ccisabroad.org/. Students may also apply through Truman State University, Center for International Education Abroad, 100 East Normal, Kirksville, MO 63501.

CULTURAL EXPERIENCES ABROAD (CEA)
STUDY FRENCH LANGUAGE AND CULTURE IN AIX-EN-PROVENCE

Hosted by University of Law, Economics and Science (Aix-Marseilles III)

Academic Focus • Art history, communications, comparative history, economics, French language and literature, French studies, history, political science and government, sociology.

Program Information • Students attend classes at University of Law, Economics and Science (Aix-Marseilles III). Field trips to Nice, Cassis, Montpellier.

Sessions • Fall, spring, yearlong.

Eligibility Requirements • Minimum age 18; open to freshmen, sophomores, juniors, seniors, graduate students, adults; 2.5 GPA; 1 letter of recommendation; good academic standing at home school; previous French study recommended.

Living Arrangements • Students live in locally rented apartments, host family homes. Quarters are shared with host institution students, students from other programs. Meals are taken on one's own, with host family, in residences, in restaurants.

FRANCE
Aix-en-Provence

Costs (2003-2004) • One term: $8595–$8795. Yearlong program: $14,995; includes tuition, housing, some meals, insurance, excursions, books and class materials, student support services. $50 application fee. $400 nonrefundable deposit required.
For More Information • Cultural Experiences Abroad (CEA), 1400 East Southern Avenue, Suite B-108, Tempe, AZ 85282-8011; *Phone:* 480-557-7900; *Fax:* 480-557-7926. *E-mail:* petersons@gowithcea.com. *World Wide Web:* http://www.gowithcea.com/

ECKERD COLLEGE
SEMESTER/YEAR ABROAD: AIX-EN-PROVENCE

Held at Institute for American Universities (IAU)–Aix-en-Provence
Academic Focus • Art, art history, economics, French language and literature, history, international business, political science and government, social sciences.
Program Information • Classes are held on the campus of Institute for American Universities (IAU)–Aix-en-Provence. Faculty members are local instructors hired by the sponsor. Field trips to Avignon, Arles, Marseille; optional travel to Monaco, Nice, ski resorts in the French Alps, Cannes at an extra cost.
Sessions • Fall, spring, yearlong.
Eligibility Requirements • Open to sophomores, juniors, seniors; 3.0 GPA; 2 letters of recommendation; good academic standing at home school; no foreign language proficiency required.
Living Arrangements • Students live in locally rented apartments, host family homes. Quarters are shared with students from other programs. Meals are taken with host family, in residences.
Costs (2003-2004) • One term: $10,730. Yearlong program: $21,460; includes tuition, housing, some meals, international student ID. $50 application fee. $200 nonrefundable deposit required. Financial aid available for all students: scholarships, loans.
For More Information • Ms. Diane Ferris, Director, Eckerd College, International Education, 4200 54th Avenue, South, St. Petersburg, FL 33711; *Phone:* 727-864-8381; *Fax:* 727-864-7995. *E-mail:* ferrisdl@eckerd.edu. *World Wide Web:* http://www.eckerd.edu/

ECKERD COLLEGE
SEMESTER/YEAR ABROAD: MARCHUTZ

Held at Institute for American Universities (IAU)–Marchutz School of Painting and Drawing, Institute for American Universities (IAU)–Aix-en-Provence
Academic Focus • Art, art history, fine/studio arts, French language and literature, international business.
Program Information • Classes are held on the campus of Institute for American Universities (IAU)–Marchutz School of Painting and Drawing, Institute for American Universities (IAU)–Aix-en-Provence. Faculty members are local instructors hired by the sponsor. Field trips to Avignon, Arles, Aix-en-Provence, Marseille; optional travel to Monaco, Cannes, Nice at an extra cost.
Sessions • Fall, spring, yearlong.
Eligibility Requirements • Open to sophomores, juniors, seniors, adults; 3.0 GPA; 2 letters of recommendation; no foreign language proficiency required.
Living Arrangements • Students live in locally rented apartments, host family homes. Quarters are shared with students from other programs. Meals are taken with host family, in residences.
Costs (2003-2004) • One term: $11,140 for fall term; $11,640 for spring. Yearlong program: $22,780; includes tuition, housing, some meals, international student ID. $50 application fee. $200 nonrefundable deposit required. Financial aid available for all students: scholarships, loans.
For More Information • Ms. Diane Ferris, Director, Eckerd College, International Education, 4200 54th Avenue, South, St. Petersburg, FL 33711; *Phone:* 727-864-8381; *Fax:* 727-864-7995. *E-mail:* ferrisdl@eckerd.edu. *World Wide Web:* http://www.eckerd.edu/

FRENCH-AMERICAN EXCHANGE
SEMESTER/ACADEMIC YEAR ABROAD IN AIX-EN-PROVENCE

Hosted by University of Law, Economics and Science (Aix-Marseilles III)

Academic Focus • Art history, civilization studies, drama/theater, European studies, film and media studies, French language and literature, French studies, history, linguistics, music, political science and government.
Program Information • Students attend classes at University of Law, Economics and Science (Aix-Marseilles III). Field trips to the French Riviera, villages of Provence, walking tours; optional travel to Europe, Paris at an extra cost.
Sessions • Fall, spring, yearlong.
Eligibility Requirements • Minimum age 19; open to sophomores, juniors, seniors, graduate students, adults; 2.5 GPA; 1 letter of recommendation; good academic standing at home school; essay; 1 year college course work in French (high school French is an added plus).
Living Arrangements • Students live in locally rented apartments, host family homes. Meals are taken on one's own, with host family, in residences, in restaurants.
Costs (2003-2004) • One term: $6575. Yearlong program: $13,150; includes tuition, housing, all meals, books and class materials, lab equipment, student support services. $50 application fee. $500 refundable deposit required.
For More Information • Mr. James Pondolfino, Executive Director, French-American Exchange, 3213 Duke Street, #620, Alexandria, VA 22314; *Phone:* 800-995-5087; *Fax:* 703-823-4447. *E-mail:* info@frenchamericanexchange.com. *World Wide Web:* http://www.frenchamericanexchange.com/

INSTITUTE FOR AMERICAN UNIVERSITIES (IAU)
CENTER FOR ART AND CULTURE

Hosted by Maryland Institute, College of Art (MICA), Institute for American Universities (IAU)–Aix-en-Provence
Academic Focus • Art, drawing/painting, fine/studio arts.
Program Information • Students attend classes at Institute for American Universities (IAU)–Aix-en-Provence, Maryland Institute, College of Art (MICA). Scheduled travel to Paris; field trips to Arles, St. Remy, Lubéron Valley; optional travel to Côte d'Azur at an extra cost.
Sessions • Fall, spring, yearlong.
Eligibility Requirements • Minimum age 18; open to juniors, seniors, graduate students; major in studio art; 3.0 GPA; 1 letter of recommendation; good academic standing at home school; portfolio; no foreign language proficiency required.
Living Arrangements • Students live in locally rented apartments, host family homes. Quarters are shared with host institution students, students from other programs. Meals are taken on one's own, with host family.
Costs (2004-2005) • One term: $8990. Yearlong program: $17,980; includes tuition, insurance, excursions, books and class materials, student support services, activity fee. $30 application fee. $500 nonrefundable deposit required. Financial aid available for all students: scholarships.
For More Information • Mr. Kurt Schick, Director of Enrollment Management, Institute for American Universities (IAU), I.A.U. U.S. Office, 1830 Sherman Avenue at University Place, Evanston, IL 60204; *Phone:* 800-221-2051; *Fax:* 847-864-6897. *E-mail:* usa@iaufrance.org. *World Wide Web:* http://www.iaufrance.org/. Students may also apply through Institute for American Universities, 27 place de l'Université, 13625 Aix-en-Provence Cedex, France; Maryland Institute College of Art, 1300 Mount Royal Avenue, Baltimore, MD 21217.

INSTITUTE FOR AMERICAN UNIVERSITIES (IAU)
LE CENTRE D'AIX

Hosted by Institute for American Universities (IAU)–Aix-en-Provence
Academic Focus • Archaeology, art history, fine/studio arts, French language and literature, international affairs, international business, literature, political science and government, social sciences.
Program Information • Students attend classes at Institute for American Universities (IAU)–Aix-en-Provence. Scheduled travel to Paris, Geneva; field trips to Avignon, Arles, Lubéron Valley, Marseille; optional travel to Nice, Côte d'Azur, the French Alps at an extra cost.

Sessions • Fall, spring, yearlong.

Eligibility Requirements • Minimum age 18; open to sophomores, juniors, seniors, graduate students, adults; 2.75 GPA; good academic standing at home school; no foreign language proficiency required.

Living Arrangements • Students live in locally rented apartments, host family homes. Quarters are shared with host institution students, students from other programs. Meals are taken with host family.

Costs (2004-2005) • One term: $11,350. Yearlong program: $22,700; includes tuition, housing, some meals, insurance, excursions, books and class materials, international student ID, student support services, damage deposit, student activity fee. $30 application fee. $500 nonrefundable deposit required. Financial aid available for all students: scholarships.

For More Information • Mr. Kurt Schick, Director of Enrollment Management, Institute for American Universities (IAU), I.A.U. U.S. Office, 1830 Sherman Avenue at University Place, Evanston, IL 60204; *Phone:* 800-221-2051; *Fax:* 847-864-6897. *E-mail:* usa@ iaufrance.org. *World Wide Web:* http://www.iaufrance.org/. Students may also apply through College Consortium for International Studies, c/o Miami Dade Community College, Department of Foreign Languages, South Campus, 11011 SW 104th Street, Miami, FL 33176; Northern Illinois University, Study Abroad Office, Williston Hall 417, De Kalb, IL 60115-2854; Eckerd College, International Education and Off-Campus Programs, 4200 54th Avenue South, St. Petersburg, FL 33711.

INSTITUTE FOR AMERICAN UNIVERSITIES (IAU)
INSTITUTE FOR AMERICAN UNIVERSITIES

Hosted by Institute for American Universities (IAU)–Aix-en-Provence

Academic Focus • Archaeology, art history, fine/studio arts, French language and literature, international affairs, international business, literature, political science and government, social sciences.

Program Information • Students attend classes at Institute for American Universities (IAU)–Aix-en-Provence. Classes are also held on the campus of University of Provence, Aix-Marseilles. Scheduled travel to Paris, Venice.

Sessions • Fall, spring, yearlong.

Eligibility Requirements • Minimum age 18; open to sophomores, juniors, seniors, graduate students, adults; 2.75 GPA; 1 letter of recommendation; good academic standing at home school; no foreign language proficiency required.

Living Arrangements • Students live in locally rented apartments, host family homes. Quarters are shared with host institution students, students from other programs. Meals are taken with host family.

Costs (2004-2005) • One term: contact sponsor for cost. Yearlong program: contact sponsor for cost. $30 application fee. $500 nonrefundable deposit required. Financial aid available for all students: scholarships.

For More Information • Mr. Kurt Schick, Director of Enrollment Management, Institute for American Universities (IAU), I.A.U. U.S. Office, 1830 Sherman Avenue at University Place, Evanston, IL 60204; *Phone:* 800-221-2051; *Fax:* 847-864-6897. *E-mail:* usa@ iaufrance.org. *World Wide Web:* http://www.iaufrance.org/. Students may also apply through College Consortium for International Studies, c/o Miami Dade Community College, Department of Foreign Languages, South Campus, 11011 SW 104th Street, Miami, FL 33176; Northern Illinois University, Study Abroad Office, Williston Hall 417, De Kalb, IL 60115-2854; Eckerd College, International Education and Off-Campus Programs, 4200 54th Avenue South, St. Petersburg, FL 33711.

INSTITUTE FOR AMERICAN UNIVERSITIES (IAU)
MARCHUTZ SCHOOL OF PAINTING AND DRAWING

Hosted by Institute for American Universities (IAU)–Marchutz School of Painting and Drawing
Academic Focus • Aesthetics, art history, drawing/painting.
Program Information • Students attend classes at Institute for American Universities (IAU)–Marchutz School of Painting and Drawing. Scheduled travel to Paris, Venice; field trips to Arles, St. Remy, Vaucluse, Aix countryside; optional travel to Nice, the French Alps at an extra cost.
Sessions • Fall, spring, yearlong.
Eligibility Requirements • Minimum age 18; open to freshmen, sophomores, juniors, seniors, graduate students, adults; 2.75 GPA; 1 letter of recommendation; interest in and commitment to art or art history; no foreign language proficiency required.
Living Arrangements • Students live in locally rented apartments, host family homes. Quarters are shared with host institution students, students from other programs. Meals are taken with host family.
Costs (2004-2005) • One term: $12,260. Yearlong program: $24,520; includes tuition, housing, some meals, insurance, excursions, books and class materials, international student ID, student support services, damage deposit, student activity fee. $30 application fee. $500 nonrefundable deposit required. Financial aid available for all students: scholarships.
For More Information • Mr. Kurt Schick, Director of Enrollment Management, Institute for American Universities (IAU), I.A.U. U.S. Office, 1830 Sherman Avenue at University Place, Evanston, IL 60204; *Phone:* 800-221-2051; *Fax:* 847-864-6897. *E-mail:* usa@iaufrance.org. *World Wide Web:* http://www.iaufrance.org/. Students may also apply through College Consortium for International Studies, c/o Miami Dade Community College, Department of Foreign Languages, South Campus, 11011 SW 104th Street, Miami, FL 33176; Northern Illinois University, Study Abroad Office, Williston Hall 417, De Kalb, IL 60115-2854; Eckerd College, International Education and Off-Campus Programs, 4200 54th Avenue South, St. Petersburg, FL 33711.

NORTHERN ILLINOIS UNIVERSITY
FRENCH STUDIES AT LE CENTRE D'AIX

Hosted by Institute for American Universities (IAU)–Aix-en-Provence
Academic Focus • Art history, business administration/management, economics, fine/studio arts, French language and literature, geography, history, philosophy, political science and government, psychology.
Program Information • Students attend classes at Institute for American Universities (IAU)–Aix-en-Provence. Field trips to southern France; optional travel to Vienna, Paris, Venice, Switzerland at an extra cost.
Sessions • Fall, spring, yearlong.
Eligibility Requirements • Open to sophomores, juniors, seniors; 2.75 GPA; 2 letters of recommendation; good academic standing at home school; application essay; no foreign language proficiency required.
Living Arrangements • Students live in host family homes. Quarters are shared with host institution students. Meals are taken with host family, in residences.
Costs (2003-2004) • One term: $10,875. Yearlong program: $21,750; includes tuition, some meals, insurance, books and class materials, student support services, advisory services, activity fee, computer lab access. $45 application fee. $800 refundable deposit required. Financial aid available for students from sponsoring institution: regular financial aid.
For More Information • Ms. Clare Foust, Program Assistant, Northern Illinois University, Study Abroad Office, Williston Hall 417, DeKalb, IL 60115-2854; *Phone:* 815-753-0420; *Fax:* 815-753-0825. *E-mail:* niuabroad@niu.edu. *World Wide Web:* http://www.niu.edu/niuabroad/

NORTHERN ILLINOIS UNIVERSITY
PAINTING AND DRAWING

Hosted by Institute for American Universities (IAU)–Marchutz School of Painting and Drawing
Academic Focus • Art, drawing/painting.
Program Information • Students attend classes at Institute for American Universities (IAU)–Marchutz School of Painting and Drawing. Optional travel to Venice, Paris at an extra cost.
Sessions • Fall, spring, yearlong.
Eligibility Requirements • Open to juniors, seniors; major in art; course work in art; 2.75 GPA; 2 letters of recommendation; good academic standing at home school; essay; portfolio; no foreign language proficiency required.
Living Arrangements • Students live in host family homes. Quarters are shared with host institution students. Meals are taken on one's own, with host family.
Costs (2003-2004) • One term: $11,400. Yearlong program: $22,800; includes tuition, housing, some meals, insurance, excursions, books and class materials, student support services, cultural activities. $45 application fee. $800 refundable deposit required. Financial aid available for students from sponsoring institution: loans.
For More Information • Ms. Clare Foust, Program Assistant, Northern Illinois University, Study Abroad Office, Williston Hall 417, DeKalb, IL 60115-2854; *Phone:* 815-753-0420; *Fax:* 815-753-0825. *E-mail:* niuabroad@niu.edu. *World Wide Web:* http://www.niu.edu/niuabroad/

UNIVERSITY OF MICHIGAN
UNIVERSITY OF MICHIGAN/UNIVERSITY OF WISCONSIN/INDIANA UNIVERSITY JUNIOR YEAR IN AIX-EN-PROVENCE, FRANCE

Hosted by University of Provence, Aix-Marseilles
Academic Focus • Economics, liberal studies, political science and government.
Program Information • Students attend classes at University of Provence, Aix-Marseilles. Field trips to Arles, Nîmes, Cassis, Lubéron, Côte d'Azur, Marseilles.
Sessions • Winter, yearlong.
Eligibility Requirements • Open to juniors, seniors; 2.5 GPA; 3 letters of recommendation; examination of abilities in French; personal interview; 2.5 years of college course work in French.
Living Arrangements • Students live in host institution dormitories, locally rented apartments, host family homes. Meals are taken as a group, on one's own, with host family, in residences.
Costs (2002-2003) • One term: contact sponsor for cost. Yearlong program: contact sponsor for cost. $50 application fee. $250 nonrefundable deposit required. Financial aid available for students from sponsoring institution: scholarships, loans, application fee waiver.
For More Information • University of Michigan, Office of International Programs, G-513 Michigan Union, 530 South State Street, Ann Arbor, MI 48109-1349; *Phone:* 734-764-4311; *Fax:* 734-764-3229. *E-mail:* oip@umich.edu. *World Wide Web:* http://www.umich.edu/~iinet/oip/

VANDERBILT UNIVERSITY
VANDERBILT IN FRANCE

Hosted by Vanderbilt in France Center
Academic Focus • Art history, French language and literature, French studies, history, political science and government.
Program Information • Students attend classes at Vanderbilt in France Center. Field trips to Mont-Saint-Michel, Arles, Cassis.
Sessions • Fall, spring, yearlong.
Eligibility Requirements • Open to sophomores, juniors, seniors; 2.7 GPA; 1 letter of recommendation; good academic standing at home school; personal essay; 2 years of college course work in French.
Living Arrangements • Students live in host family homes. Meals are taken on one's own, with host family, in residences, in restaurants.
Costs (2003-2004) • One term: $16,360. Yearlong program: $32,720; includes tuition, housing, some meals, excursions. $200 nonrefundable deposit required. Financial aid available for students from sponsoring institution: scholarships, loans.
For More Information • Mr. Gary Johnston, Director of Study Abroad Programs, Vanderbilt University, Study Abroad Office, Box 1573, Station B, Nashville, TN 37235-1573; *Phone:* 615-343-3139;

Fax: 615-343-5774. E-mail: gary.w.johnston@vanderbilt.edu. *World Wide Web:* http://www.vanderbilt.edu/studyabroad/

WHITWORTH COLLEGE
WHITWORTH/UNIVERSITY OF PROVENCE EXCHANGE PROGRAM

Hosted by University of Provence, Aix-Marseilles
Academic Focus • French language and literature.
Program Information • Students attend classes at University of Provence, Aix-Marseilles. Optional travel at an extra cost.
Sessions • Fall, yearlong.
Eligibility Requirements • Open to sophomores, juniors, seniors; major in French; 2.5 GPA; 2 letters of recommendation; 2 years of college course work in French.
Living Arrangements • Students live in host institution dormitories, locally rented apartments. Quarters are shared with host institution students. Meals are taken in central dining facility.
Costs (2003-2004) • One term: $11,684. Yearlong program: $23,368; includes tuition, housing. Financial aid available for students from sponsoring institution: scholarships, loans.
For More Information • Ms. Sue Jackson, Director, Off-Campus Programs, Whitworth College, Center for International and Multicultural Education, 300 West Hawthorne Road, Spokane, WA 99251-2702; *Phone:* 509-777-4596; *Fax:* 509-777-3723. *E-mail:* sjackson@whitworth.edu. *World Wide Web:* http://www.whitworth.edu/

AMIENS

UNIVERSITY OF TULSA
UNIVERSITY OF TULSA IN AMIENS

Hosted by Ecole Supérieure de Commerce d'Amiens Picarde, University of Picardie Jules Verne Amiens
Academic Focus • French language and literature, international business.
Program Information • Students attend classes at Ecole Supérieure de Commerce d'Amiens Picarde, University of Picardie Jules Verne Amiens. Scheduled travel to Bretagne; field trips to Paris; optional travel at an extra cost.
Sessions • Spring.
Eligibility Requirements • Open to sophomores, juniors, seniors; 2.5 GPA; good academic standing at home school; 1.5 years of college course work in French, with demonstrated fluency.
Living Arrangements • Students live in program-owned apartments, host family homes. Quarters are shared with host institution students. Meals are taken on one's own, with host family, in residences, in central dining facility.
Costs (2003) • One term: $10,516; includes tuition, housing, all meals, excursions. $200 deposit required. Financial aid available for students from sponsoring institution: loans.
For More Information • Ms. Missy Burchette, Assistant to the Director, University of Tulsa, Study Abroad Office, 600 South College Avenue, Tulsa, OK 74104; *Phone:* 918-631-3229; *Fax:* 918-631-2158. *E-mail:* studyabroad@utulsa.edu. *World Wide Web:* http://www.utulsa.edu/studyabroad/

ANGERS

AHA INTERNATIONAL AN ACADEMIC PROGRAM OF THE UNIVERSITY OF OREGON
ANGERS, FRANCE: NORTHWEST COUNCIL ON STUDY ABROAD (NCSA)

Hosted by Catholic University of the West, Angers
Academic Focus • Art history, French language and literature, French studies, history, political science and government, translation.
Program Information • Students attend classes at Catholic University of the West, Angers. Field trips to châteaux of the Loire, Mont-Saint-Michel, Saint-Malo, Normandy.
Sessions • Fall, spring, yearlong, fall semester.

Eligibility Requirements • Open to sophomores, juniors, seniors, adults; 2 letters of recommendation; good academic standing at home school; 1 term college course work in French or the equivalent.
Living Arrangements • Students live in host family homes. Quarters are shared with host institution students, students from other programs. Meals are taken on one's own, with host family, in central dining facility, in restaurants.
Costs (2003-2004) • One term: $6840–$8735 for fall term; $9090 for spring. Yearlong program: $17,240; includes tuition, housing, all meals, insurance, excursions, books and class materials, student support services. $50 application fee. $200 refundable deposit required.
For More Information • Ms. Marcy Supnet, Associate Director for University Programs, AHA International An Academic Program of the University of Oregon, 741 SW Lincoln Street, Portland, OR 97201; *Phone:* 503-295-7730; *Fax:* 503-295-5969. *E-mail:* mail@aha-intl.org. *World Wide Web:* http://www.aha-intl.org/

NIAGARA UNIVERSITY
THE UNIVERSITE CATHOLIQUE DE L'OUEST

Hosted by Catholic University of the West, Angers
Academic Focus • French language and literature.
Program Information • Students attend classes at Catholic University of the West, Angers. Field trips to castles in the Loire Valley, Futuroscope in Poitou; optional travel to student-arranged sites at an extra cost.
Sessions • Fall, spring.
Eligibility Requirements • Open to juniors, seniors; 2.5 GPA; 2 letters of recommendation; good academic standing at home school; 2 years of college course work in French.
Living Arrangements • Students live in host family homes. Meals are taken on one's own, with host family, in residences, in restaurants.
Costs (2003-2004) • One term: $8479; includes tuition, excursions, international student ID, student support services. Financial aid available for students from sponsoring institution: Pell grants and TAP for qualified New York State residents.
For More Information • Dr. Henrik Borgstrom, Assistant Professor of Foreign Languages, Niagara University, St. Vincents Hall, 4th Floor, Niagara University, NY 14109; *Phone:* 716-286-8214; *Fax:* 716-286-8349. *E-mail:* hcb@niagara.edu. *World Wide Web:* http://www.niagara.edu/sap/

TRUMAN STATE UNIVERSITY
BUSINESS PROGRAM IN FRANCE–ESSCA, ANGERS

Hosted by Ecole Supérieure des Sciences Commerciales d'Angers ESSCA
Academic Focus • Business administration/management, commerce, finance, international business, marketing.
Program Information • Students attend classes at Ecole Supérieure des Sciences Commerciales d'Angers ESSCA.
Sessions • Fall, spring.
Eligibility Requirements • Minimum age 18; open to sophomores, juniors, seniors; course work in business; 3.0 GPA; 3 letters of recommendation; good academic standing at home school; no foreign language proficiency required.
Living Arrangements • Students live in host institution dormitories, locally rented apartments, host family homes. Quarters are shared with host institution students, students from other programs. Meals are taken on one's own, in residences, in central dining facility.
Costs (2003-2004) • One term: $3900; includes tuition, insurance. $200 nonrefundable deposit required. Financial aid available for students from sponsoring institution: scholarships, loans.
For More Information • Truman State University, Center for International Education Abroad, Kirk Building, 120, Kirksville, MO 63501; *Phone:* 660-785-4076; *Fax:* 660-785-7473. *E-mail:* ciea@truman.edu. *World Wide Web:* http://www2.truman.edu/ciea/

TRUMAN STATE UNIVERSITY
INTENSIVE FRENCH IN ANGERS

Hosted by Catholic University of the West, Angers
Academic Focus • French language and literature.

FRANCE
Angers

Program Information • Students attend classes at Catholic University of the West, Angers. Field trips to Loire Valley castles, prehistoric sites, a light and sound show.
Sessions • Fall, spring.
Eligibility Requirements • Minimum age 18; open to freshmen, sophomores, juniors, seniors, graduate students, adults; 2.5 GPA; 3 letters of recommendation; good academic standing at home school; no foreign language proficiency required.
Living Arrangements • Students live in host institution dormitories, host family homes. Quarters are shared with students from other programs. Meals are taken on one's own, in residences, in central dining facility.
Costs (2003) • One term: $4500; includes tuition, housing, all meals, insurance, excursions, books and class materials. $200 nonrefundable deposit required. Financial aid available for students from sponsoring institution: scholarships, loans.
For More Information • Truman State University, Center for International Education Abroad, Kirk Building, 120, Kirksville, MO 63501; *Phone:* 660-785-4076; *Fax:* 660-785-7473. *E-mail:* ciea@truman. edu. *World Wide Web:* http://www2.truman.edu/ciea/

TRUMAN STATE UNIVERSITY
TRUMAN STATE IN FRANCE

Hosted by Catholic University of the West, Angers
Academic Focus • Art history, French studies, religious studies, translation.
Program Information • Students attend classes at Catholic University of the West, Angers. Optional travel to the Loire Valley, the Atlantic coast, Mont-Saint-Michael, Saint-Malo, Angers, Anjou, Saumur, troglodyte caves, Abbey of Fontevraud at an extra cost.
Sessions • Fall, spring, yearlong.
Eligibility Requirements • Open to freshmen, sophomores, juniors, seniors; 3.0 GPA; 3 years college course work in French for advanced program; no foreign language proficiency requirement for elementary level.
Living Arrangements • Students live in host family homes. Meals are taken on one's own, in central dining facility.
Costs (2003-2004) • One term: $4000 for fall term; $2420 for spring. Yearlong program: $6120; includes tuition, insurance, room and board (fall term only). $200 nonrefundable deposit required. Financial aid available for students from sponsoring institution: scholarships, loans.
For More Information • Truman State University, Center for International Education Abroad, Kirk Building, 120, Kirksville, MO 63501; *Phone:* 660-785-4076; *Fax:* 660-785-7473. *E-mail:* ciea@truman. edu. *World Wide Web:* http://www2.truman.edu/ciea/

ANNECY

COLLEGE CONSORTIUM FOR INTERNATIONAL STUDIES–MIAMI DADE COLLEGE AND TRUMAN STATE UNIVERSITY
SEMESTER IN FRANCE

Hosted by Institut Français des Alpes
Academic Focus • French language and literature, French studies.
Program Information • Students attend classes at Institut Français des Alpes. Optional travel at an extra cost.
Sessions • Fall, spring, yearlong.
Eligibility Requirements • Minimum age 18; open to freshmen, sophomores, juniors, seniors, adults; 2.5 GPA; 2 letters of recommendation; good academic standing at home school; no foreign language proficiency required.
Living Arrangements • Students live in host institution dormitories, locally rented apartments, host family homes. Quarters are shared with host institution students. Meals are taken on one's own, with host family.
Costs (2004-2005) • One term: $2950 for CCIS members; $3150 for nonmembers. Yearlong program: $5900 for CCIS members; $6100 for nonmembers; includes tuition, insurance, books and class materials, student support services, housing deposit. $30 application fee. $400 refundable deposit required. Financial aid available for students from sponsoring institution: scholarships, loans.
For More Information • Mr. Reinaldo Changsut, Director, International Education, College Consortium for International Studies–Miami Dade College and Truman State University, Miami

Dade College, 11011 SW 104th Street, Miami, FL 33176-3393; *Phone:* 305-237-2533; *Fax:* 305-237-2949. *E-mail:* reinaldo.changsut@mdc. edu. *World Wide Web:* http://www.ccisabroad.org/. Students may also apply through Truman State University, Center for International Education Abroad, 100 East Normal, Kirksville, MO 63501.

AVIGNON
COLLEGE CONSORTIUM FOR INTERNATIONAL STUDIES–MIAMI DADE COLLEGE AND TRUMAN STATE UNIVERSITY
SEMESTER/YEAR IN FRANCE (AVIGNON)

Hosted by Institute for American Universities (IAU)–Avignon
Academic Focus • Art history, French language and literature, French studies, international affairs, international business.
Program Information • Students attend classes at Institute for American Universities (IAU)–Avignon. Field trips to the Provence area.
Sessions • Fall, spring, yearlong.
Eligibility Requirements • Minimum age 18; open to freshmen, sophomores, juniors, seniors, adults; 2.5 GPA; 2 letters of recommendation; good academic standing at home school; statement of purpose in French; 2 years of college course work in French.
Living Arrangements • Students live in host family homes. Quarters are shared with host institution students. Meals are taken with host family, in residences.
Costs (2004-2005) • One term: $11,435 for non-CCIS members; members contact sponsor for cost. Yearlong program: $22,870 for non-CCIS members; members contact sponsor for cost; includes tuition, housing, some meals, insurance, excursions, books and class materials, international student ID. $30 application fee. $400 refundable deposit required. Financial aid available for students from sponsoring institution: grants.
For More Information • Mr. Reinaldo Changsut, Director, International Education, College Consortium for International Studies, Miami Dade College, 11011 SW 104th Street, Miami, FL 33176-3393; *Phone:* 305-237-2533; *Fax:* 305-237-2949. *E-mail:* reinaldo.chanqsut@mdc.edu. *World Wide Web:* http://www. ccisabroad.org/. Students may also apply through Truman State University, Center for International Education Abroad, 100 East Normal, Kirksville, MO 63501.

ECKERD COLLEGE
SEMESTER/YEAR ABROAD: AVIGNON

Held at Institute for American Universities (IAU)–Avignon
Academic Focus • Art history, French language and literature, history, liberal studies, philosophy.
Program Information • Classes are held on the campus of Institute for American Universities (IAU)–Avignon. Faculty members are local instructors hired by the sponsor. Field trips to Aix-en-Provence, Marseille, Arles; optional travel to Monaco, Nice, ski resorts in the French Alps, Cannes at an extra cost.
Sessions • Fall, spring, yearlong.
Eligibility Requirements • Open to sophomores, juniors, seniors; 3.0 GPA; good academic standing at home school; no foreign language proficiency required.
Living Arrangements • Students live in locally rented apartments, host family homes. Quarters are shared with students from other programs. Meals are taken with host family, in residences.
Costs (2003-2004) • One term: $10,730. Yearlong program: $21,460; includes tuition, housing, some meals, international student ID. $50 application fee. $200 nonrefundable deposit required. Financial aid available for all students: scholarships, loans.
For More Information • Ms. Diane Ferris, Director, Eckerd College, International Education, 4200 54th Avenue, South, St. Petersburg, FL 33711; *Phone:* 727-864-8381; *Fax:* 727-864-7995. *E-mail:* ferrisdl@ eckerd.edu. *World Wide Web:* http://www.eckerd.edu/

INSTITUTE FOR AMERICAN UNIVERSITIES (IAU)
LE CENTRE D'AVIGNON

Hosted by Institute for American Universities (IAU)–Avignon

Academic Focus • Archaeology, art history, French language and literature, international affairs, liberal studies, political science and government, social sciences, visual and performing arts.

Program Information • Students attend classes at Institute for American Universities (IAU)–Avignon. Field trips to Arles, the Riviera, Paris, Marseille.

Sessions • Fall, spring, yearlong.

Eligibility Requirements • Minimum age 18; open to juniors, seniors, graduate students, adults; 3.0 GPA; 2 letters of recommendation; good academic standing at home school; 2 years of college course work in French.

Living Arrangements • Students live in host family homes. Meals are taken with host family.

Costs (2004-2005) • One term: $11,350. Yearlong program: $22,700; includes tuition, housing, some meals, insurance, excursions, books and class materials, international student ID, student support services, damage deposit, activity deposit. $30 application fee. $500 nonrefundable deposit required. Financial aid available for all students: scholarships.

For More Information • Mr. Kurt Schick, Director of Enrollment Management, Institute for American Universities (IAU), I.A.U. U.S. Office, 1830 Sherman Avenue at University Place, Evanston, IL 60204; *Phone:* 800-221-2051; *Fax:* 847-864-6897. *E-mail:* usa@iaufrance.org. *World Wide Web:* http://www.iaufrance.org/. Students may also apply through College Consortium for International Studies, c/o Miami Dade Community College, Department of Foreign Languages, South Campus, 11011 SW 104th Street, Miami, FL 33176; Northern Illinois University, Study Abroad Office, Williston Hall 417, De Kalb, IL 60115-2854; Eckerd College, International Education and Off-Campus Programs, 4200 54th Avenue South, St. Petersburg, FL 33711.

NORTHERN ILLINOIS UNIVERSITY
FRENCH STUDIES AT THE CENTRE D'AVIGNON

Hosted by Institute for American Universities (IAU)–Avignon

Academic Focus • Art history, French language and literature, history.

Program Information • Students attend classes at Institute for American Universities (IAU)–Avignon. Field trips to southern France; optional travel to Venice, Switzerland, Vienna at an extra cost.

Sessions • Fall, spring, yearlong.

Eligibility Requirements • Open to sophomores, juniors, seniors; 2.75 GPA; 2 letters of recommendation; essay in French; minimum 3.0 GPA in French; 2.5 years of college course work in French.

Living Arrangements • Students live in host family homes. Quarters are shared with host institution students. Meals are taken with host family, in residences.

Costs (2003-2004) • One term: $10,875. Yearlong program: $21,750; includes tuition, housing, some meals, insurance, excursions, books and class materials, advisory services and computer room. $45 application fee. $800 refundable deposit required. Financial aid available for students from sponsoring institution: regular financial aid.

For More Information • Ms. Clare Foust, Program Assistant, Northern Illinois University, Study Abroad Office, Williston Hall 417, DeKalb, IL 60115-2854; *Phone:* 815-753-0420; *Fax:* 815-753-0825. *E-mail:* niuabroad@niu.edu. *World Wide Web:* http://www.niu.edu/niuabroad/

STETSON UNIVERSITY
STUDY ABROAD–AVIGNON

Hosted by University of Avignon

Academic Focus • French language and literature.

Program Information • Students attend classes at University of Avignon. Field trips to Paris, Aix-en-Provence.

Sessions • Fall, spring, yearlong.

Eligibility Requirements • Minimum age 20; open to sophomores, juniors, seniors; 3.0 GPA; 3 letters of recommendation; good academic standing at home school; minimum 3.0 GPA in French; completed application; 1 year of college course work in French.

Living Arrangements • Students live in host family homes. Meals are taken on one's own, in residences.

Costs (2002-2003) • One term: $14,025. Yearlong program: $28,050; includes tuition, housing, all meals, insurance, excursions, international airfare, international student ID, student support

services. $50 application fee. $200 nonrefundable deposit required. Financial aid available for students from sponsoring institution: scholarships, loans.

For More Information • Ms. Nancy L. Leonard, Director, Stetson University, Center for International Education, Unit 8412, 421 North Woodland Boulevard, Deland, FL 32723-3757; *Phone:* 386-822-8165; *Fax:* 386-822-8167. *E-mail:* nleonard@stetson.edu. *World Wide Web:* http://www.stetson.edu/international/

BESANÇON
KNOX COLLEGE
BESANÇON PROGRAM

Hosted by Centre de Linguistique Appliquée, University of Franche Comté Besançon

Academic Focus • African studies, fine/studio arts, French language and literature, French studies, history, international affairs, liberal studies, music performance, political science and government, science, social sciences.

Program Information • Students attend classes at Centre de Linguistique Appliquée, University of Franche Comté Besançon. Scheduled travel to Paris, the Loire Valley; field trips to Salins-les-Bains, Arc-et-Senans, Arbois; optional travel to north Africa, Greece, England, Spain at an extra cost.

Sessions • Fall, spring, winter, yearlong.

Eligibility Requirements • Minimum age 19; open to juniors, seniors; 2.0 GPA; 4 letters of recommendation; good academic standing at home school; 2 years of college course work in French.

Living Arrangements • Students live in host institution dormitories, locally rented apartments, host family homes. Quarters are shared with host institution students. Meals are taken with host family, in central dining facility.

Costs (2004-2005) • One term: $10,282 for single term; $20,564 for two-term session. Yearlong program: $30,566; includes tuition, housing, all meals, insurance, excursions, student support services, transportation to and from arrival/departure site and in Besançon. $650 nonrefundable deposit required. Financial aid available for all students: scholarships, loans.

For More Information • Ms. Karen Hawkinson, Campus Director, Program in Besançon, Knox College, Box 225, Galesburg, IL 61401; *Phone:* 309-341-7331; *Fax:* 309-341-7824. *E-mail:* besancon@knox.edu. *World Wide Web:* http://www.knox.edu/offcampus/. Students may also apply through Knox College Program, 1 rue des Vieilles Perrières, Batiment B, 25000 Besançon, France.

RIDER UNIVERSITY
STUDY ABROAD IN FRANCE

Hosted by University of Franche Comté Besançon

Academic Focus • French language and literature, French studies.

Program Information • Students attend classes at University of Franche Comté Besançon.

Sessions • Fall, spring, yearlong.

Eligibility Requirements • Open to sophomores, juniors, seniors; 2.5 GPA; 1 letter of recommendation; good academic standing at home school; 2 years college course work in French or completion of sponsor's Intensive French program.

Living Arrangements • Students live in host institution dormitories, locally rented apartments. Quarters are shared with host institution students, students from other programs. Meals are taken on one's own, in central dining facility, in restaurants.

Costs (2001-2002) • One term: $8995. Yearlong program: $17,990; includes tuition, student support services, administrative fees. $35 application fee. $300 refundable deposit required. Financial aid available for students from sponsoring institution: regular financial aid.

For More Information • Dr. Joseph E. Nadeau, Director of Study Abroad, Rider University, 2083 Lawrenceville Road, Lawrenceville, NJ 08648; *Phone:* 609-896-5314; *Fax:* 609-895-5670. *E-mail:* nadeau@rider.edu. *World Wide Web:* http://www.rider.edu/academic/uwp/index.htm

STATE UNIVERSITY OF NEW YORK AT NEW PALTZ

STUDY ABROAD IN BESANÇON, FRANCE

Hosted by University of Franche Comté Besançon
Academic Focus • French language and literature, French studies.
Program Information • Students attend classes at University of Franche Comté Besançon. Scheduled travel to Paris; field trips to southern France.
Sessions • Fall, spring, yearlong.
Eligibility Requirements • Minimum age 18; open to sophomores, juniors, seniors; 2.5 GPA; 2 letters of recommendation; good academic standing at home school; 2 years of college course work in French.
Living Arrangements • Students live in host institution dormitories. Quarters are shared with host institution students, students from other programs. Meals are taken on one's own, in central dining facility.
Costs (2003-2004) • One term: $6300 for New York residents; $9428 for nonresidents. Yearlong program: $12,600 for New York residents; $18,858 for nonresidents; includes tuition, housing, all meals, insurance, excursions, books and class materials, student support services, administrative fee. $25 application fee. $300–$600 nonrefundable deposit required. Financial aid available for students from sponsoring institution: scholarships, loans.
For More Information • Center for International Programs, State University of New York at New Paltz, 75 South Manheim Boulevard, Suite 9, New Paltz, NY 12561; *Phone:* 845-257-3125; *Fax:* 845-257-3129. *E-mail:* international@newpaltz.edu. *World Wide Web:* http://www.newpaltz.edu/studyabroad/

UNIVERSITY OF KANSAS

STUDY ABROAD IN BESANÇON, FRANCE

Hosted by University of Franche Comté Besançon
Academic Focus • Full curriculum.

Program Information • Students attend classes at University of Franche Comté Besançon. Field trips to Dijon, the Jura Mountains; optional travel to Prague, Italy, Provence at an extra cost.
Sessions • Yearlong.
Eligibility Requirements • Minimum age 18; open to sophomores, juniors, seniors, graduate students; 2 letters of recommendation; good academic standing at home school; minimum 2.75 GPA overall; minimum 3.0 GPA in French; 3 years of college course work in French.
Living Arrangements • Students live in host institution dormitories, locally rented apartments, host family homes. Quarters are shared with host institution students. Meals are taken on one's own, in residences, in central dining facility.
Costs (2003-2004) • Yearlong program: $14,500; includes tuition, housing, all meals, student support services, stipend for meals and monthly bus pass, limited excursions and social activities, medical evacuation and repatriation insurance. $38 application fee. $300 nonrefundable deposit required. Financial aid available for students from sponsoring institution: scholarships, loans.
For More Information • Mr. Beau Pritchett, Program Coordinator, Study Abroad in Besançon, France, University of Kansas, Office of Study Abroad, 1410 Jayhawk Boulevard, Room 108, Lippincott Hall, Lawrence, KS 66045-7515; *Phone:* 785-864-3742; *Fax:* 785-864-5040. *E-mail:* osa@ku.edu. *World Wide Web:* http://www.ku.edu/~osa/

CAEN

UNIVERSITY OF WISCONSIN–STEVENS POINT

SEMESTER IN FRANCE

Hosted by University of Caen
Academic Focus • Art history, cultural studies, economics, film and media studies, French language and literature, history.

Program Information • Students attend classes at University of Caen. Scheduled travel to Paris; field trips to Mont-Saint-Michel, the Loire Valley; optional travel to France, Italy, Germany, Belgium at an extra cost.

Sessions • Spring.

Eligibility Requirements • Minimum age 18; open to freshmen, sophomores, juniors, seniors, adults; 2.5 GPA; 3 letters of recommendation; good academic standing at home school; 2 years of college course work in French.

Living Arrangements • Students live in host family homes. Quarters are shared with students from other programs. Meals are taken with host family, in residences, in central dining facility.

Costs (2003-2004) • One term: $5000 for Wisconsin residents; $10,500 for nonresidents (estimated); includes tuition, housing, all meals, excursions, international airfare, books and class materials, student support services. $15 application fee. $150 nonrefundable deposit required. Financial aid available for all students: scholarships, work study, loans.

For More Information • Mr. Mark Koepke, Associate Director, University of Wisconsin–Stevens Point, International Programs Office, Stevens Point, WI 54481; *Phone:* 715-346-2717; *Fax:* 715-346-3591. *E-mail:* intlprog@uwsp.edu. *World Wide Web:* http://www.uwsp.edu/studyabroad/

CANNES

AMERICAN INSTITUTE FOR FOREIGN STUDY (AIFS)
COLLÈGE INTERNATIONAL DE CANNES

Hosted by Collège International de Cannes

Academic Focus • Art history, business administration/management, drama/theater, French language and literature, history, literature, political science and government, sociology.

Program Information • Students attend classes at Collège International de Cannes. Scheduled travel to London; field trips to Paris, Provence.

Sessions • Fall, spring.

Eligibility Requirements • Minimum age 17; open to freshmen, sophomores, juniors, seniors; 2.5 GPA; 1 letter of recommendation; good academic standing at home school; no foreign language proficiency required.

Living Arrangements • Students live in host institution dormitories. Quarters are shared with host institution students. Meals are taken as a group, on one's own, in central dining facility.

Costs (2004-2005) • One term: $12,995; includes tuition, housing, some meals, insurance, excursions, student support services, one-way international airfare, 2-day London stopover. $75 application fee. $350 nonrefundable deposit required. Financial aid available for all students: scholarships.

For More Information • Mr. David Mauro, Admissions Advisor, American Institute For Foreign Study (AIFS), 9 West Broad Street, Stamford, CT 06902-3788; *Phone:* 800-727-2437 Ext. 5163; *Fax:* 203-399-5597. *E-mail:* dmauro@aifs.com. *World Wide Web:* http://www.aifsabroad.com/

CENTER FOR STUDY ABROAD (CSA)
FRENCH LANGUAGE AND CULTURE, CANNES–COLLÈGE INTERNATIONAL DE CANNES

Hosted by Collège International de Cannes

Academic Focus • French language and literature, French studies.

Program Information • Students attend classes at Collège International de Cannes. Field trips to Paris, Nice; optional travel at an extra cost.

Sessions • Fall, spring, winter.

Eligibility Requirements • Minimum age 18; open to precollege students, freshmen, sophomores, juniors, seniors, graduate students, adults; students aged 15-17 may attend with parental permission; no foreign language proficiency required.

Living Arrangements • Students live in host institution dormitories, host family homes. Quarters are shared with host institution students. Meals are taken on one's own, with host family, in residences, in central dining facility.

Costs (2003-2004) • One term: contact sponsor for cost. $45 application fee.

For More Information • Ms. Alima K. Virtue, Program Director, Center for Study Abroad (CSA), 325 Washington Avenue South, #93, Kent, WA 98032; *Phone:* 206-726-1498; *Fax:* 253-850-0454. *E-mail:* info@centerforstudyabroad.com. *World Wide Web:* http://www.centerforstudyabroad.com/

CHAMBÉRY
COLLEGE CONSORTIUM FOR INTERNATIONAL STUDIES–MIAMI DADE COLLEGE AND TRUMAN STATE UNIVERSITY
SEMESTER IN FRANCE

Hosted by Institut Français des Alpes

Academic Focus • French language and literature, French studies, international affairs, international business.

Program Information • Students attend classes at Institut Français des Alpes. Optional travel at an extra cost.

Sessions • Fall, spring, yearlong.

Eligibility Requirements • Minimum age 18; open to freshmen, sophomores, juniors, seniors, adults; 2.5 GPA; 2 letters of recommendation; good academic standing at home school; no foreign language proficiency required.

Living Arrangements • Students live in host institution dormitories, locally rented apartments, host family homes. Quarters are shared with host institution students. Meals are taken on one's own, with host family.

Costs (2004-2005) • One term: $2950 (estimated). Yearlong program: $5900 (estimated); includes tuition, some meals, books and class materials, housing deposit. $30 application fee. $400 refundable deposit required. Financial aid available for students from sponsoring institution: scholarships, loans.

For More Information • Mr. Reinaldo Changsut, Director, International Education, College Consortium for International Studies–Miami Dade College and Truman State University, Miami Dade College, 11011 SW 104th Street, Miami, FL 33176-3393; *Phone:* 305-237-2533; *Fax:* 305-237-2949. *E-mail:* reinaldo.changsut@mdc.edu. *World Wide Web:* http://www.ccisabroad.org/. Students may also apply through Truman State University, Center for International Education Abroad, 100 East Normal, Kirksville, MO 63501.

UNIVERSITY OF IDAHO
FRENCH BUSINESS PROGRAM

Hosted by Ecole Supérieure de Commerce de Chambery

Academic Focus • Accounting, business administration/management, commerce, finance, international business, management information systems, marketing.

Program Information • Students attend classes at Ecole Supérieure de Commerce de Chambery. Field trips to regional/local business and companies, Chamonix, Mt. Blanc; optional travel to Geneva, World Trade Organization at an extra cost.

Sessions • Fall, spring, yearlong.

Eligibility Requirements • Open to sophomores, juniors, seniors, graduate students, adults; course work in business or economics; good academic standing at home school; 2 years of college course work in French.

Living Arrangements • Students live in host institution dormitories, locally rented apartments. Quarters are shared with host institution students, students from other programs. Meals are taken on one's own, in residences, in central dining facility.

Costs (2003-2004) • One term: $2500. Yearlong program: $5000; includes tuition, excursions, student support services. $100 application fee. $200 refundable deposit required. Financial aid available for students from sponsoring institution: scholarships, loans.

For More Information • Ms. Amy Bergmann, Advisor, University of Idaho, Room 209, Morrill Hall, Moscow, ID 83844-3013; *Phone:* 208-885-7870; *Fax:* 208-885-2859. *E-mail:* abroad@uidaho.edu. *World Wide Web:* http://www.ets.uidaho.edu/ipo/abroad/

CHOLET

TRUMAN STATE UNIVERSITY
BUSINESS PROGRAM IN FRANCE

Hosted by ESIAME

Academic Focus • Accounting, business administration/management, commerce, finance, international business, marketing.
Program Information • Students attend classes at ESIAME. Optional travel to the Loire Valley, the Atlantic coast at an extra cost.
Sessions • Fall, spring, yearlong.
Eligibility Requirements • Open to sophomores, juniors, seniors, graduate students; course work in business; 3.0 GPA; fluency in French.
Living Arrangements • Students live in locally rented apartments, host family homes. Meals are taken on one's own, in central dining facility.
Costs (2003-2004) • One term: $2300 for Missouri residents; $4200 for nonresidents. Yearlong program: $4600 for Missouri residents; $8400 for nonresidents; includes tuition, insurance. $200 nonrefundable deposit required. Financial aid available for students from sponsoring institution: scholarships, loans.
For More Information • Truman State University, Center for International Education Abroad, Kirk Building, 120, Kirksville, MO 63501; *Phone:* 660-785-4076; *Fax:* 660-785-7473. *E-mail:* ciea@truman.edu. *World Wide Web:* http://www2.truman.edu/ciea/

CLERMONT-FERRAND

KALAMAZOO COLLEGE
BUSINESS AND CULTURE STUDIES IN FRANCE

Hosted by Ecole Supérieure de Commerce de Clermont Ferrand

Academic Focus • Business administration/management, French language and literature, French studies, marketing.
Program Information • Students attend classes at Ecole Supérieure de Commerce de Clermont Ferrand. Field trips to Perpignan, Auvergne; optional travel at an extra cost.
Sessions • Fall, yearlong.
Eligibility Requirements • Open to juniors; course work in business/marketing; 2.75 GPA; 2 letters of recommendation; essay; student must be a degree-seeking student at an accredited American college or university; 2 years of college course work in French.
Living Arrangements • Students live in host family homes. Meals are taken with host family, in residences.
Costs (2003-2004) • One term: $19,592. Yearlong program: $29,388; includes tuition, housing, all meals, excursions, international airfare. $50 application fee. $300 nonrefundable deposit required. Financial aid available for students from sponsoring institution: scholarships, loans.
For More Information • Dr. Joseph L. Brockington, Director, Center for International Programs, Kalamazoo College, 1200 Academy Street, Kalamazoo, MI 49006; *Phone:* 269-337-7133; *Fax:* 269-337-7400. *E-mail:* cip@kzoo.edu. *World Wide Web:* http://www.kzoo.edu/cip/

COLLONGES-SOUS-SALEVE

WALLA WALLA COLLEGE
ADVENTIST COLLEGES ABROAD

Hosted by Saleve Adventist University

Academic Focus • French language and literature, full curriculum.
Program Information • Students attend classes at Saleve Adventist University. Scheduled travel to Paris, Côte d'Azur; optional travel at an extra cost.
Sessions • Yearlong.
Eligibility Requirements • Open to freshmen, sophomores, juniors, seniors; 2.5 GPA; 3 letters of recommendation; good academic standing at home school; minimum 3.0 GPA in French; 1 year of college course work in French.
Living Arrangements • Students live in host institution dormitories. Quarters are shared with host institution students, students from other programs. Meals are taken as a group, in central dining facility.

Costs (2002-2003) • Yearlong program: contact sponsor for cost. $100 nonrefundable deposit required. Financial aid available for all students: scholarships, loans.
For More Information • Mr. Jean-Paul Grimaud, Chair of Modern Language Department, Walla Walla College, 204 South College Avenue, College Place, WA 99324; *Phone:* 509-529-7769; *Fax:* 509-527-2253. *E-mail:* grimje@wwc.edu

DIJON

CENTER FOR STUDY ABROAD (CSA)
UNIVERSITY OF BURGUNDY (DIJON)

Hosted by University of Burgundy Dijon

Academic Focus • Art history, drama/theater, French language and literature, French studies, history, music, philosophy.
Program Information • Students attend classes at University of Burgundy Dijon. Optional travel at an extra cost.
Sessions • Fall, winter, yearlong.
Eligibility Requirements • Minimum age 18; open to precollege students, freshmen, sophomores, juniors, seniors, graduate students, adults; students under 17 may apply with parental permission; placement test to determine French ability.
Living Arrangements • Students live in host institution dormitories. Quarters are shared with students from other programs. Meals are taken on one's own, in central dining facility.
Costs (2003-2004) • One term: contact sponsor for cost. Yearlong program: contact sponsor for cost. $45 application fee.
For More Information • Ms. Alima K. Virtue, Program Director, Center for Study Abroad (CSA), 325 Washington Avenue South, #93, Kent, WA 98032; *Phone:* 206-726-1498; *Fax:* 253-850-0454. *E-mail:* info@centerforstudyabroad.com. *World Wide Web:* http://www.centerforstudyabroad.com/

COLBY COLLEGE
COLBY IN DIJON

Hosted by University of Burgundy Dijon

Academic Focus • French language and literature, French studies.
Program Information • Students attend classes at University of Burgundy Dijon. Scheduled travel to south of France, Annecy, Paris; field trips to Cluny, Vézelay, Châteauneuf, Le Creusot.
Sessions • Fall.
Eligibility Requirements • Open to freshmen, sophomores, juniors; 2.7 GPA; 2 letters of recommendation; good academic standing at home school; 2 years college course work in French or the equivalent.
Living Arrangements • Students live in host family homes. Meals are taken with host family, in residences.
Costs (2002-2003) • One term: $17,900; includes tuition, housing, all meals, insurance, excursions, international airfare, student support services. $500 nonrefundable deposit required. Financial aid available for students from sponsoring institution: scholarships, loans.
For More Information • Ms. Martha J. Denney, Director, Off-Campus Study, Colby College, Waterville, ME 04901; *Phone:* 207-872-3648; *Fax:* 207-872-3061. *E-mail:* mjdenney@colby.edu. *World Wide Web:* http://www.colby.edu/off-campus/

CULTURAL EXPERIENCES ABROAD (CEA)
STUDY FRENCH LANGUAGE AND CULTURE IN DIJON

Hosted by University of Burgundy Dijon

Academic Focus • Art history, drama/theater, economics, French language and literature, French studies, international affairs, international business, music history, philosophy, political science and government, popular culture, translation.
Program Information • Students attend classes at University of Burgundy Dijon. Field trips to Burgundy region, Beaune, wine tasting in vineyards, Paris; optional travel to the Alps, Provence, Switzerland at an extra cost.
Sessions • Fall, spring, yearlong, fall quarter.
Eligibility Requirements • Minimum age 18; open to freshmen, sophomores, juniors, seniors, graduate students, adults; 2.5 GPA; 1 letter of recommendation; good academic standing at home school; previous French study recommended.

Living Arrangements • Students live in host institution dormitories, host family homes. Quarters are shared with students from other programs. Meals are taken on one's own, with host family, in residences, in central dining facility, in restaurants.
Costs (2003-2004) • One term: $7095–$7995. Yearlong program: $13,995; includes tuition, housing, some meals, insurance, excursions, books and class materials, lab equipment, student support services. $50 application fee. $400 nonrefundable deposit required.
For More Information • Cultural Experiences Abroad (CEA), 1400 East Southern Avenue, Suite B-108, Tempe, AZ 85282-8011; *Phone:* 480-557-7900; *Fax:* 480-557-7926. *E-mail:* petersons@gowithcea.com. *World Wide Web:* http://www.gowithcea.com/

IES, INSTITUTE FOR THE INTERNATIONAL EDUCATION OF STUDENTS
IES–DIJON

Hosted by Institute for the International Education of Students (IES)–Dijon, Ecole Supérieure de Commerce de Dijon
Academic Focus • Accounting, area studies, business administration/management, computer science, economics, European studies, finance, French language and literature, French studies, history, human resources, international affairs, international business, marketing, political science and government.
Program Information • Students attend classes at Ecole Supérieure de Commerce de Dijon, Institute for the International Education of Students (IES)–Dijon. Scheduled travel to Brussels, Strasbourg; field trips to Burgundy, Fontenay, Vézelay, Autun, Beaune; optional travel at an extra cost.
Sessions • Fall, spring, yearlong.
Eligibility Requirements • Minimum age 18; open to sophomores, juniors, seniors, graduate students, adults; course work in basic micro and macro economics; 3.0 GPA; 1 letter of recommendation; good academic standing at home school; college major or minor in business, economics, or international relations; 1 year of college course work in French.
Living Arrangements • Students live in host institution dormitories, host family homes. Meals are taken with host family, in residences.
Costs (2003-2004) • One term: $10,300. Yearlong program: $18,540; includes tuition, housing, some meals, excursions, student support services, partial insurance coverage. $50 application fee. $500 nonrefundable deposit required. Financial aid available for all students: scholarships, institutional partner need-based grants.
For More Information • International Education Representative, IES, Institute for the International Education of Students, 33 North LaSalle Street, 15th Floor, Chicago, IL 60602; *Phone:* 800-995-2300; *Fax:* 312-944-1448. *E-mail:* info@iesabroad.org. *World Wide Web:* http://www.IESabroad.org/

OTTERBEIN COLLEGE
DIJON PROGRAM

Hosted by University of Burgundy Dijon
Academic Focus • Civilization studies, French language and literature, history, literature, philosophy.
Program Information • Students attend classes at University of Burgundy Dijon. Field trips to Paris, Burgundy region; optional travel to western Europe, France at an extra cost.
Sessions • Fall, spring, yearlong.
Eligibility Requirements • Open to freshmen, sophomores, juniors, adults; good academic standing at home school; minimum 3.0 GPA in French; 2 years of college course work in French.
Living Arrangements • Students live in host institution dormitories, locally rented apartments, host family homes. Quarters are shared with students from other programs. Meals are taken on one's own, in restaurants.
Costs (2003-2004) • One term: $4788. Yearlong program: $14,364; includes tuition, housing, insurance, excursions. Financial aid available for students from sponsoring institution: scholarships, loans.
For More Information • Dr. Levilson Reis, Coordinator, Dijon Program, Otterbein College, Foreign Language Department, Westerville, OH 43081-2006; *Phone:* 614-823-1112; *Fax:* 614-823-1315. *E-mail:* lreis@otterbein.edu. *World Wide Web:* http://www.otterbein.edu/

DUNKIRK
STATE UNIVERSITY OF NEW YORK COLLEGE AT FREDONIA
UNIVERSITY DU LITTORAL

Hosted by University of the Littoral Côte d'Opale
Academic Focus • Business administration/management, communications, economics, engineering, environmental science/studies, French language and literature, geography, history, mathematics.
Program Information • Students attend classes at University of the Littoral Côte d'Opale. Field trips to Lille, Belgium; optional travel to Nice, Paris, Belgium, London at an extra cost.
Sessions • Fall, spring, yearlong.
Eligibility Requirements • Open to juniors, seniors, graduate students, adults; 3.0 GPA; 2 letters of recommendation; transcript; fluency in French.
Living Arrangements • Students live in host institution dormitories, locally rented apartments, host family homes. Quarters are shared with host institution students, students from other programs. Meals are taken on one's own, in central dining facility, in restaurants.
Costs (2003-2004) • One term: $7500. Yearlong program: $15,000; includes tuition, housing, some meals, insurance, books and class materials, student support services, passport and visa fees, personal expenses. $600 nonrefundable deposit required. Financial aid available for all students: loans.
For More Information • Ms. Mary Sasso, Director, International Education, State University of New York College at Fredonia, 8 LoGrasso Hall, Fredonia, NY 14063; *Phone:* 716-673-3451; *Fax:* 716-673-3175. *E-mail:* sasso@fredonia.edu. *World Wide Web:* http://www.fredonia.edu/

GRENOBLE
ACADEMIC PROGRAMS INTERNATIONAL (API)
(API)–GRENOBLE, FRANCE

Hosted by University Stendhal Grenoble III
Academic Focus • Art history, civilization studies, comparative history, French language and literature, French studies, history, political science and government.
Program Information • Students attend classes at University Stendhal Grenoble III. Scheduled travel to Paris, Versailles; field trips to Chamonix, Chartreuse, Lyon, Chambery, Strasbourg, Geneva, Aix-en-Provence, Burgundy, Strasbourg.
Sessions • Fall, spring, yearlong, fall B; spring B; spring B1; year B; year B1.
Eligibility Requirements • Minimum age 18; open to freshmen, sophomores, juniors, seniors, graduate students, adults; 2.75 GPA; 1 letter of recommendation; good academic standing at home school; official transcript from home university; no foreign language proficiency required.
Living Arrangements • Students live in host institution dormitories, host family homes. Quarters are shared with host institution students. Meals are taken on one's own, with host family, in residences, in central dining facility.
Costs (2004-2005) • One term: $8500–$9500. Yearlong program: $16,500–$17,900; includes tuition, housing, some meals, insurance, excursions, student support services, airport pick-up, ground transportation, monthly transit pass. $150 nonrefundable deposit required. Financial aid available for all students: scholarships.
For More Information • Ms. Jennifer C. Allen, Director, Academic Programs International (API), 107 East Hopkins, San Marcos, TX 78666; *Phone:* 800-844-4124; *Fax:* 512-392-8420. *E-mail:* api@academicintl.com. *World Wide Web:* http://www.academicintl.com/

AMERICAN INSTITUTE FOR FOREIGN STUDY (AIFS)
UNIVERSITY OF GRENOBLE

Hosted by University Stendhal Grenoble III
Academic Focus • Art history, economics, French language and literature, history, literature, political science and government.

Program Information • Students attend classes at University Stendhal Grenoble III. Scheduled travel to London; field trips to Paris, Burgundy, Provence.
Sessions • Fall, spring, yearlong.
Eligibility Requirements • Minimum age 17; open to freshmen, sophomores, juniors, seniors; 2.5 GPA; 1 letter of recommendation; good academic standing at home school; 1 year of college course work in French.
Living Arrangements • Students live in host family homes. Meals are taken on one's own, with host family, in residences, in central dining facility.
Costs (2004-2005) • One term: $12,995. Yearlong program: $24,490; includes tuition, housing, all meals, insurance, excursions, student support services, one-way airfare, 2-day London stopover. $75 application fee. $350 nonrefundable deposit required. Financial aid available for all students: scholarships.
For More Information • Mr. David Mauro, Admissions Advisor, American Institute For Foreign Study (AIFS), 9 West Broad Street, Stamford, CT 06902-3788; *Phone:* 800-727-2437 Ext. 5163; *Fax:* 203-399-5597. *E-mail:* dmauro@aifs.com. *World Wide Web:* http://www.aifsabroad.com/

BOSTON UNIVERSITY
GRENOBLE LANGUAGE AND LIBERAL ARTS PROGRAM

Hosted by Centre Universitaire d'Etudes Francaises CUEF, University of Grenoble
Academic Focus • Civilization studies, French language and literature, French studies, liberal studies, social sciences.
Program Information • Students attend classes at Centre Universitaire d'Etudes Francaises CUEF, University of Grenoble. Scheduled travel to Paris, Colmar, Strasbourg, Avignon, Dijon; field trips to Arles, Chartreuse, Vienne.
Sessions • Fall, spring, yearlong.
Eligibility Requirements • Open to sophomores, juniors, seniors, graduate students, adults; 2 letters of recommendation; good academic standing at home school; essay; writing sample in French; approval of participation; transcript; minimum 3.0 GPA in major; 1 year of college course work in French.
Living Arrangements • Students live in host family homes. Meals are taken on one's own, with host family, in residences.
Costs (2004-2005) • One term: $19,834. Yearlong program: $39,668; includes tuition, housing, all meals, excursions, international airfare. $50 application fee. $400 nonrefundable deposit required. Financial aid available for all students: scholarships, loans.
For More Information • Division of International Programs, Boston University, 232 Bay State Road, Boston, MA 02215; *Phone:* 617-353-9888; *Fax:* 617-353-5402. *E-mail:* abroad@bu.edu. *World Wide Web:* http://www.bu.edu/abroad/

CALVIN COLLEGE
SEMESTER IN FRANCE

Hosted by University of Grenoble
Academic Focus • French language and literature, French studies.
Program Information • Students attend classes at University of Grenoble. Scheduled travel to Paris; field trips to the Alps, Lyon, Geneva, Avignon; optional travel at an extra cost.
Sessions • Spring, program runs every other year.
Eligibility Requirements • Open to sophomores, juniors, seniors; 2.5 GPA; 2 letters of recommendation; good academic standing at home school; interview with program director; advisor approval; 2 years college course work for advanced students; no foreign language proficiency requirement for beginning students.
Living Arrangements • Students live in host family homes. Meals are taken with host family, in residences, in restaurants.
Costs (2004-2005) • One term: $13,150 (estimated); includes tuition, housing, all meals, excursions, international airfare, student support services. $50 application fee. $400 nonrefundable deposit required. Financial aid available for students from sponsoring institution: scholarships, loans.
For More Information • Dr. Ellen B. Monsma, Director, Calvin College, Office of Off-Campus Programs, 3201 Burton Street, SE, Grand Rapids, MI 49546; *Phone:* 616-526-6551; *Fax:* 616-526-6756. *E-mail:* emonsma@calvin.edu. *World Wide Web:* http://www.calvin.edu/academic/off-campus/

CULTURAL EXPERIENCES ABROAD (CEA)
STUDY FRENCH LANGUAGE AND CULTURE IN GRENOBLE

Hosted by University of Grenoble
Academic Focus • Art history, communications, culinary arts, economics, French language and literature, French studies, history, international affairs, international business, philosophy, political science and government, translation.
Program Information • Students attend classes at University of Grenoble. Field trips to Avignon, Chartreuse, Geneva, Lyon, skiing in French Alps, Chamonix, Nice, Cannes; optional travel to Switzerland, the Alps at an extra cost.
Sessions • Fall, spring, yearlong, fall quarter; fall II semester.
Eligibility Requirements • Minimum age 18; open to freshmen, sophomores, juniors, seniors, graduate students, adults; 2.5 GPA; 1 letter of recommendation; good academic standing at home school; previous French study recommended.
Living Arrangements • Students live in host institution dormitories, locally rented apartments, host family homes. Quarters are shared with host institution students, students from other programs. Meals are taken on one's own, with host family, in residences, in restaurants.
Costs (2003-2004) • One term: $7595–$8995. Yearlong program: $13,595; includes tuition, housing, some meals, insurance, excursions, books and class materials, lab equipment, student support services. $50 application fee. $400 nonrefundable deposit required.
For More Information • Cultural Experiences Abroad (CEA), 1400 East Southern Avenue, Suite B-108, Tempe, AZ 85282-8011; *Phone:* 480-557-7900; *Fax:* 480-557-7926. *E-mail:* petersons@gowithcea.com. *World Wide Web:* http://www.gowithcea.com/

GRENOBLE GRADUATE SCHOOL OF BUSINESS
BACHELOR IN INTERNATIONAL BUSINESS

Hosted by Grenoble Graduate School of Business
Academic Focus • Accounting, commerce, finance, French language and literature, international affairs, international business, law and legal studies, management information systems, marketing.
Program Information • Students attend classes at Grenoble Graduate School of Business. Optional travel to other European cities at an extra cost.
Sessions • Yearlong, alternate year.
Eligibility Requirements • Open to seniors; 2 letters of recommendation; no foreign language proficiency required.
Living Arrangements • Students live in locally rented apartments. Quarters are shared with host institution students, students from other programs. Meals are taken on one's own, in residences, in central dining facility, in restaurants.
Costs (2002-2003) • Yearlong program: €10,900; includes tuition. €500 nonrefundable deposit required. Financial aid available for all students: scholarships.
For More Information • Ms. Claudia Fackler-Hopf, BIB Programme Administrator, Grenoble Graduate School of Business, 12, rue Pierre Semard, BP 127, 38003 Grenoble Cedex 01, France; *Phone:* +33 476-706432; *Fax:* +33 476-706099. *E-mail:* claudia.fackler-hopf@ggsb.com. *World Wide Web:* http://www.ggsb.com/

GRENOBLE GRADUATE SCHOOL OF BUSINESS
CERTIFICATE IN INTERNATIONAL BUSINESS

Hosted by Grenoble Graduate School of Business
Academic Focus • Accounting, commerce, finance, French language and literature, international affairs, international business, law and legal studies, management information systems, marketing.
Program Information • Students attend classes at Grenoble Graduate School of Business. Optional travel to other European cities at an extra cost.
Sessions • Fall, spring.
Eligibility Requirements • Open to juniors, seniors, adults; 2 letters of recommendation; no foreign language proficiency required.
Living Arrangements • Students live in locally rented apartments. Quarters are shared with host institution students, students from other programs. Meals are taken on one's own, in residences, in central dining facility, in restaurants.

Costs (2002-2003) • One term: €5600; includes tuition. €500 nonrefundable deposit required. Financial aid available for all students: scholarships.

For More Information • Ms. Julie Scrimgeour, CIB Programme Administrator, Grenoble Graduate School of Business, 12, rue Pierre Semard, BP 127, 38003 Grenoble Cedex 01, France; *Phone:* +33 476-70-64-32; *Fax:* +33 476-70-60-99. *E-mail:* julie.scrimgeour@ggsb.com. *World Wide Web:* http://www.ggsb.com/

LYCOMING COLLEGE
STUDY ABROAD IN FRANCE

Hosted by University of Grenoble
Academic Focus • French language and literature, French studies.
Program Information • Students attend classes at University of Grenoble. Scheduled travel; field trips; optional travel at an extra cost.
Sessions • Fall, spring.
Eligibility Requirements • Open to sophomores, juniors, seniors; 2.5 GPA; 1 letter of recommendation; good academic standing at home school; college major or minor in French; 2 years of college course work in French.
Living Arrangements • Students live in host institution dormitories, host family homes. Quarters are shared with host institution students, students from other programs. Meals are taken on one's own, with host family, in residences, in restaurants.
Costs (2002-2003) • One term: contact sponsor for cost. $300 refundable deposit required.
For More Information • Dr. Garett Heysel, Coordinator of Study Abroad Program, Lycoming College, Campus Box 2, 700 College Place, Williamsport, PA 17701-5192; *Phone:* 570-321-4211; *Fax:* 570-321-4389. *E-mail:* heysel@lycoming.edu. *World Wide Web:* http://www.lycoming.edu/

SWARTHMORE COLLEGE
PROGRAM IN GRENOBLE, FRANCE

Hosted by University Pierre Mandés France Grenoble II, Centre Universitaire d'Etudes Francaises CUEF, University Stendhal Grenoble III
Academic Focus • Art, art history, economics, French language and literature, French studies, history, political science and government, psychology, sociology.
Program Information • Students attend classes at University Pierre Mandés France Grenoble II, Centre Universitaire d'Etudes Francaises CUEF, University Stendhal Grenoble III. Scheduled travel to south of France, Paris, Venice, the Loire Valley, Burgundy, Alsace, Bordeaux, Toulouse; field trips to Savoie, south of France, Paris, Burgundy; optional travel to central Europe, Eastern Europe, French provinces, Italy, Switzerland, Spain at an extra cost.
Sessions • Fall, spring, yearlong.
Eligibility Requirements • Open to sophomores, juniors, seniors; 3 letters of recommendation; good academic standing at home school; 1.5 years of college course work in French.
Living Arrangements • Students live in host family homes. Meals are taken on one's own, with host family, in residences, in central dining facility, in restaurants.
Costs (2003-2004) • One term: $18,707. Yearlong program: $37,414; includes tuition, housing, all meals, insurance, excursions, books and class materials, entertainment allowance, local transportation. $30 application fee. $250 nonrefundable deposit required. Financial aid available for students from sponsoring institution: scholarships, loans.
For More Information • Ms. Eleonore Baginski, Administrative Coordinator, Swarthmore College, Department of Modern Languages and Literatures, 500 College Avenue, Swarthmore, PA 19081; *Phone:* 610-328-8143; *Fax:* 610-328-7769. *E-mail:* ebagins1@swarthmore.edu. *World Wide Web:* http://www.swarthmore.edu/Humanities/clicnet/grenoble.program.html

UNIVERSITY OF CONNECTICUT
INTERNATIONAL BUSINESS IN GRENOBLE, FRANCE

Hosted by Ecole Supérieure de Commerce de Grenoble ESC
Academic Focus • Business administration/management, civilization studies, economics, French language and literature, international business, marketing, sociology.

Program Information • Students attend classes at Ecole Supérieure de Commerce de Grenoble ESC. Field trips to ITO Geneva, local company visits.
Sessions • Spring.
Eligibility Requirements • Open to juniors, seniors; course work in economics (micro and macro), marketing (if applicable); 2.7 GPA; 2 letters of recommendation; no foreign language proficiency required.
Living Arrangements • Students live in host institution dormitories. Quarters are shared with host institution students. Meals are taken on one's own, in residences, in central dining facility, in restaurants.
Costs (2002-2003) • One term: $9200 for Connecticut residents; $10,250 for nonresidents; includes tuition, housing, all meals, excursions, one-way airfare. $25 application fee. $350 nonrefundable deposit required. Financial aid available for students from sponsoring institution: scholarships, loans.
For More Information • Mr. Gordon Lustila, Acting Director of Study Abroad Programs, University of Connecticut, 843 Bolton Road, Unit 1207, Storrs, CT 06269-1207; *Phone:* 860-486-5022; *Fax:* 860-486-2976. *E-mail:* sabadm03@uconnvm.uconn.edu. *World Wide Web:* http://studyabroad.uconn.edu/

LA ROCHELLE
STATE UNIVERSITY OF NEW YORK COLLEGE AT CORTLAND
UNIVERSITY OF LA ROCHELLE, LA ROCHELLE, FRANCE

Hosted by University of La Rochelle
Academic Focus • French language and literature.
Program Information • Students attend classes at University of La Rochelle.
Sessions • Fall, spring, yearlong.
Eligibility Requirements • Minimum age 18; open to sophomores, juniors, seniors; 2.5 GPA; 3 letters of recommendation; good academic standing at home school; 3 years of college course work in French.
Living Arrangements • Students live in host institution dormitories, locally rented apartments, host family homes. Quarters are shared with host institution students. Meals are taken on one's own, in central dining facility.
Costs (2003-2004) • One term: $9335. Yearlong program: contact sponsor for cost; includes tuition, housing, all meals, insurance, excursions, international airfare, books and class materials, international student ID, student support services, passport and visa fees, residence card. $20 application fee. $250 nonrefundable deposit required. Financial aid available for students from sponsoring institution: scholarships, loans.
For More Information • Dr. John Ogden, Director, State University of New York College at Cortland, Office of International Programs, PO Box 2000, Cortland, NY 13045; *Phone:* 607-753-2209; *Fax:* 607-753-5989. *E-mail:* cortlandabroad@cortland.edu. *World Wide Web:* http://www.studyabroad.com/suny/cortland/

LYON
BROWN UNIVERSITY
BROWN IN FRANCE

Hosted by University of Lyon
Academic Focus • Full curriculum.
Program Information • Students attend classes at University of Lyon. Field trips to Paris, the Loire Valley.
Sessions • Fall, spring, yearlong.
Eligibility Requirements • Open to sophomores, juniors, seniors; 3.0 GPA; 2 letters of recommendation; good academic standing at home school; 3 years of college course work in French.
Living Arrangements • Meals are taken on one's own.
Costs (2004-2005) • One term: $15,336. Yearlong program: $30,672; includes tuition, excursions, international student ID, student support services, language and orientation program (with housing). $250 nonrefundable deposit required. Financial aid available for students from sponsoring institution: scholarships, loans.

For More Information • Ms. Mell Bolen, Director, Brown University, Office of International Programs, Box 1973, Providence, RI 02912-1973; *Phone:* 401-863-3555; *Fax:* 401-863-3311. *E-mail:* oip_office@brown.edu. *World Wide Web:* http://www.brown.edu/OIP/

MARSEILLES

AMERICAN UNIVERSITY CENTER OF PROVENCE
MARSEILLES PROGRAM

Hosted by University of Provence (Aix Marseilles I), Arabic Language Institute in Fez, American University Center of Provence
Academic Focus • Anthropology, communications, French language and literature, intercultural studies, international affairs, peace and conflict studies, religious studies.
Program Information • Students attend classes at University of Provence (Aix Marseilles I), American University Center of Provence, Arabic Language Institute in Fez. Scheduled travel to Fez (study tour); field trips to regional monuments, museums.
Sessions • Spring.
Eligibility Requirements • Open to juniors, seniors, graduate students, adults; 3.0 GPA; 2 letters of recommendation; good academic standing at home school; 2 years of college course work in French.
Living Arrangements • Students live in host family homes. Meals are taken with host family.
Costs (2004-2005) • One term: $13,400; includes tuition, housing, some meals, excursions, books and class materials, student support services, round-trip flight Marseille/Casablanca and ground transportation in Morocco. $30 application fee. $500 nonrefundable deposit required.
For More Information • Ms. Lilli Engle, Director, American University Center of Provence, Head Admissions Office, 19, cours des Arts-Et-Metiers, 13100 Aix-en-Provence; *Phone:* +33 442-38-42-38; *Fax:* +33 442-38-95-66. *E-mail:* info.marseille@aucp.org. *World Wide Web:* http://www.aucp.org/. Students may also apply through Marist College, Office of International Education, 3399 North Road, Poughkeepsie, NY 12601-1387.

MORE ABOUT THE PROGRAM
Providing a timely, specific, academic focus, this advanced-level French immersion program draws creatively on the exceptional resources of Marseille, France's gateway to the Mediterranean and bridge to the immense cultural, religious, and political heritage of North Africa and the Middle East. Offering courses such as Understanding Islam, Middle Eastern Political Developments, Immigrant Identities in Contemporary France, and French and North African Cultural Patterns, the program highlights an intensive week of on-site study in Fez, Morocco, with housing in French-speaking Moroccan families.

New to study abroad and unspoiled by globalization, Marseille, with its cultural and religious pluralism, inspires true international education in reaching across cultures for greater knowledge and understanding. This spring-only program complements the highly regarded liberal arts program in Aix-en-Provence and, likewise, combines challenging academics ensured by a French university faculty and enhanced by the celebrated French Practicum cultural integration components: individual homestay placement, community service, club memberships, and language exchange partners.

CENTER FOR STUDY ABROAD (CSA)
UNIVERSITY OF AIX-MARSEILLES III

Hosted by University of Law, Economics and Science (Aix-Marseilles III)
Academic Focus • French language and literature, French studies.
Program Information • Students attend classes at University of Law, Economics and Science (Aix-Marseilles III). Optional travel.
Sessions • Fall, spring, yearlong.

Eligibility Requirements • Minimum age 18; open to precollege students, freshmen, sophomores, juniors, seniors, graduate students, adults; no foreign language proficiency required.
Living Arrangements • Quarters are shared with students from other programs. Meals are taken on one's own, in residences, in central dining facility, in restaurants.
Costs (2003-2004) • One term: contact sponsor for cost. Yearlong program: contact sponsor for cost. $45 application fee.
For More Information • Ms. Alima K. Virtue, Program Director, Center for Study Abroad (CSA), 325 Washington Avenue South, #93, Kent, WA 98032; *Phone:* 206-726-1498; *Fax:* 253-850-0454. *E-mail:* info@centerforstudyabroad.com. *World Wide Web:* http://www.centerforstudyabroad.com/

MONTPELLIER

FRENCH-AMERICAN EXCHANGE
SEMESTER/ACADEMIC YEAR ABROAD IN MONTPELLIER

Hosted by University Paul Valéry (Montpellier III)
Academic Focus • Art history, civilization studies, drama/theater, film and media studies, French language and literature, French studies, linguistics, political science and government, translation.
Program Information • Students attend classes at University Paul Valéry (Montpellier III). Field trips to Nîmes, Avignon, Camargue, Aigue-Morte, Carcassone; optional travel to Europe, Paris at an extra cost.
Sessions • Fall, spring, yearlong.
Eligibility Requirements • Minimum age 19; open to sophomores, juniors, seniors, graduate students, adults; 2.5 GPA; 1 letter of recommendation; good academic standing at home school; essay; 1 year college course work in French (high school French is an added plus).
Living Arrangements • Students live in locally rented apartments, host family homes. Meals are taken on one's own, with host family, in residences, in central dining facility, in restaurants.
Costs (2003-2004) • One term: $7115. Yearlong program: $14,230; includes tuition, housing, all meals, books and class materials, lab equipment, student support services. $50 application fee. $500 refundable deposit required.
For More Information • Mr. James Pondolfino, Executive Director, French-American Exchange, 3213 Duke Street, #620, Alexandria, VA 22314; *Phone:* 800-995-5087; *Fax:* 703-823-4447. *E-mail:* info@frenchamericanexchange.com. *World Wide Web:* http://www.frenchamericanexchange.com/

THE INTERNATIONAL PARTNERSHIP FOR SERVICE LEARNING
FRANCE SERVICE–LEARNING

Hosted by University of Montpellier
Academic Focus • Community service, French language and literature, French studies, international affairs, liberal studies, social sciences.
Program Information • Students attend classes at University of Montpellier. Field trips to southern France; optional travel at an extra cost.
Sessions • Fall, spring, yearlong.
Eligibility Requirements • Minimum age 18; open to freshmen, sophomores, juniors, seniors, graduate students, adults; 2 letters of recommendation; good academic standing at home school; evidence of maturity, responsibility; 2 years of college course work in French.
Living Arrangements • Students live in host family homes. Meals are taken with host family, in residences.
Costs (2003-2004) • One term: $10,600. Yearlong program: $20,800; includes tuition, housing, some meals, student support services, community service placement. $50 application fee. $250 refundable deposit required. Financial aid available for all students: federal financial aid.
For More Information • Ms. Ilana Golin, Coordinator of Student Programs, The International Partnership for Service Learning, 815 Second Avenue, Suite 315, New York, NY 10017-4594; *Phone:* 212-986-0989; *Fax:* 212-986-5039. *E-mail:* info@ipsl.org. *World Wide Web:* http://www.ipsl.org/

NORTHERN ARIZONA UNIVERSITY
STUDY ABROAD IN FRANCE

Hosted by University Paul Valéry (Montpellier III)
Academic Focus • French studies, liberal studies.
Program Information • Students attend classes at University Paul Valéry (Montpellier III). Field trips to the Cevennes Mountains, Sete, Pont du Gard, Roquefort, wineries, Camargue, Carcassonne.
Sessions • Yearlong.
Eligibility Requirements • Minimum age 18; open to sophomores, juniors, seniors, graduate students, adults; 2.5 GPA; 2 letters of recommendation; good academic standing at home school; 2 years of college course work in French.
Living Arrangements • Students live in host institution dormitories, locally rented apartments, host family homes. Meals are taken on one's own, with host family, in residences, in central dining facility, in restaurants.
Costs (2003-2004) • Yearlong program: $5000 for Arizona residents; $13,544 for nonresidents; includes tuition, excursions, international student ID, student support services, intensive 5-week French course, fees. $100 application fee. Financial aid available for all students: scholarships, loans.
For More Information • International Office, Northern Arizona University, PO Box 5598, Flagstaff, AZ 86011-5598; *Phone:* 928-523-2409; *Fax:* 928-523-9489. *E-mail:* international.office@nau.edu. *World Wide Web:* http://internationaloffice.nau.edu/

UNIVERSITY AT ALBANY, STATE UNIVERSITY OF NEW YORK
LANGUAGE AND BUSINESS STUDIES IN ENGLISH AT THE UNIVERSITY OF MONTPELLIER

Hosted by University of Montpellier
Academic Focus • Business administration/management, French language and literature.
Program Information • Students attend classes at University of Montpellier. Field trips.
Sessions • Fall, spring, yearlong, 3 month fall program.
Eligibility Requirements • Open to sophomores, juniors, seniors; 2 letters of recommendation; good academic standing at home school; college course work in business and French recommended; no foreign language proficiency required.
Living Arrangements • Students live in host family homes. Meals are taken with host family, in residences, in restaurants.
Costs (2002-2003) • One term: $7108-$7358 for 3 months; $11,009-$11,643 for 5 months. Yearlong program: $18,117-$19,001 (cost is lower for students accepted for exchange program); includes housing, all meals, excursions, student support services, in-state tuition and fees. $150 nonrefundable deposit required. Financial aid available for students from sponsoring institution: all customary sources.
For More Information • University at Albany, State University of New York, Office of International Education, LI 66, Albany, NY 12222; *Phone:* 518-442-3525; *Fax:* 518-442-3338. *E-mail:* intled@uamail.albany.edu. *World Wide Web:* http://www.albany.edu/intled/

UNIVERSITY AT ALBANY, STATE UNIVERSITY OF NEW YORK
LANGUAGE AND BUSINESS STUDIES IN FRENCH AT THE UNIVERSITY OF MONTPELLIER

Hosted by University of Montpellier
Academic Focus • Business administration/management, French language and literature.
Program Information • Students attend classes at University of Montpellier. Field trips.
Sessions • Fall, spring, yearlong, 3 month fall program.
Eligibility Requirements • Open to juniors, seniors, graduate students; course work in business administration or courses in advanced French; 2 letters of recommendation; good academic standing at home school; fluency in French.
Living Arrangements • Students live in host family homes. Meals are taken with host family, in residences, in restaurants.
Costs (2002-2003) • One term: $7358 for 3 months; $11,643 for 5 months. Yearlong program: $19,001 (cost is for students accepted for exchange program); includes housing, all meals, excursions, student support services, in-state tuition and fees. $150 nonrefund-

able deposit required. Financial aid available for students from sponsoring institution: all customary sources.
For More Information • University at Albany, State University of New York, Office of International Education, LI 66, Albany, NY 12222; *Phone:* 518-442-3525; *Fax:* 518-442-3338. *E-mail:* intled@uamail.albany.edu. *World Wide Web:* http://www.albany.edu/intled/

UNIVERSITY OF MINNESOTA
STUDY ABROAD IN MONTPELLIER

Hosted by University Paul Valéry (Montpellier III)
Academic Focus • Art history, economics, French language and literature, French studies, geography, history, international affairs, language studies, literature, science.
Program Information • Students attend classes at University Paul Valéry (Montpellier III). Field trips to the Provence area; optional travel to other areas of France and Europe at an extra cost.
Sessions • Fall, spring, yearlong.
Eligibility Requirements • Minimum age 18; open to freshmen, sophomores, juniors, seniors, graduate students, adults; 2.5 GPA; 1 letter of recommendation; good academic standing at home school; B average in French; 1 year of college course work in French.
Living Arrangements • Students live in host institution dormitories, locally rented apartments, host family homes. Quarters are shared with host institution students. Meals are taken on one's own, with host family, in residences, in restaurants.
Costs (2004-2005) • One term: contact sponsor for cost. Yearlong program: contact sponsor for cost. $50 application fee. $400 nonrefundable deposit required. Financial aid available for students from sponsoring institution: scholarships, loans.
For More Information • University of Minnesota, Learning Abroad Center, 230 Heller Hall, 271 19th Avenue South, Minneapolis, MN 55455; *Phone:* 888-700-UOFM; *Fax:* 612-626-8009. *E-mail:* umabroad@umn.edu. *World Wide Web:* http://www.umabroad.umn.edu/

NANCY

BRETHREN COLLEGES ABROAD
BCA PROGRAM IN NANCY, FRANCE

Hosted by Institut Commercial de Nancy
Academic Focus • International business.
Program Information • Students attend classes at Institut Commercial de Nancy. Scheduled travel to Paris, the Loire Valley; field trips to Strasbourg, Metz.
Sessions • Fall, spring, yearlong, early fall option.
Eligibility Requirements • Minimum age 18; open to sophomores, juniors, seniors, graduate students; 2.6 GPA; 3 letters of recommendation; 1 year of college course work in French.
Living Arrangements • Students live in host institution dormitories, host family homes. Quarters are shared with host institution students. Meals are taken on one's own, with host family, in residences, in restaurants.
Costs (2003-2004) • One term: $11,500. Yearlong program: $19,900; includes tuition, housing, all meals, insurance, excursions, international student ID, student support services. $50 application fee. $100 nonrefundable deposit required.
For More Information • Mr. Jason Sanderson, Program Officer for France, Brethren Colleges Abroad, 50 Alpha Drive, Elizabethtown, PA 17022; *Phone:* 866-222-6188; *Fax:* 717-361-6619. *E-mail:* info@bcanet.org. *World Wide Web:* http://www.bcanet.org/

NANTES

IES, INSTITUTE FOR THE INTERNATIONAL EDUCATION OF STUDENTS
IES–NANTES

Hosted by Conservatoire National de Region, Audencia, Ecole des Beaux Arts, Institute for the International Education of Students (IES)–Nantes, University of Nantes
Academic Focus • Art, art history, business administration/management, computer science, drama/theater, economics, education, engineering, European studies, French language and literature,

history, international affairs, mathematics, music, physics, political science and government, psychology, science, social work, sociology.

Program Information • Students attend classes at University of Nantes, Audencia, Conservatoire National de Region, Ecole des Beaux Arts, Institute for the International Education of Students (IES)–Nantes. Field trips to the Loire Valley, Mont-Saint-Michel, Muscadet vineyard, Saint-Malo; optional travel to Provence, Bordeaux, Normandy, Brittany at an extra cost.

Sessions • Fall, spring, yearlong.

Eligibility Requirements • Minimum age 18; open to sophomores, juniors, seniors, graduate students, adults; 3.0 GPA; 1 letter of recommendation; good academic standing at home school; 2 years of college course work in French.

Living Arrangements • Students live in host family homes. Meals are taken with host family, in residences, in central dining facility.

Costs (2003-2004) • One term: $9900. Yearlong program: $17,820; includes tuition, housing, some meals, excursions, student support services, partial insurance coverage. $50 application fee. $500 nonrefundable deposit required. Financial aid available for all students: scholarships, institutional partner need-based grants.

For More Information • International Education Representative, IES, Institute for the International Education of Students, 33 North LaSalle Street, 15th Floor, Chicago, IL 60602; *Phone:* 800-995-2300; *Fax:* 312-944-1448. *E-mail:* info@iesabroad.org. *World Wide Web:* http://www.IESabroad.org/

NICE

COLLEGE CONSORTIUM FOR INTERNATIONAL STUDIES–MIAMI DADE COLLEGE AND TRUMAN STATE UNIVERSITY
BUSINESS PROGRAM IN NICE, FRANCE

Hosted by Institut de Préparation á l'Administration et á la Gestion (IPAG)

Academic Focus • Business administration/management, finance, French language and literature, marketing.

Program Information • Students attend classes at Institut de Préparation á l'Administration et á la Gestion (IPAG).

Sessions • Fall, spring, yearlong.

Eligibility Requirements • Open to freshmen, sophomores, juniors, seniors, graduate students; course work in business; 3.0 GPA; 3 letters of recommendation; transcript; statement of purpose; no foreign language proficiency required.

Living Arrangements • Students live in locally rented apartments, host family homes. Quarters are shared with host institution students, students from other programs. Meals are taken on one's own, with host family.

Costs (2004-2005) • One term: $3390 for Missouri residents; $5440 for nonresidents. Yearlong program: $6780 for Missouri residents; $10,880 for nonresidents; includes tuition, insurance, fees. $300 nonrefundable deposit required. Financial aid available for students from sponsoring institution: scholarships, loans.

For More Information • Center for International Education Abroad, College Consortium for International Studies, Kirk Building 120, Kirksville, MO 63501; *Phone:* 660-785-4076; *Fax:* 660-785-7473. *E-mail:* ciea@truman.edu. *World Wide Web:* http://www.ccisabroad.org/. Students may also apply through Miami Dade College, Miami, FL 33176.

FRENCH-AMERICAN EXCHANGE
TRIMESTER/ACADEMIC YEAR ABROAD IN NICE

Hosted by Ecole France Langue

Academic Focus • Civilization studies, French language and literature, French studies, linguistics, political science and government.

Program Information • Students attend classes at Ecole France Langue. Field trips to the French Riviera, museums, Old Town, Eze Village, St. Paul-de-Vence; optional travel to Europe, Paris at an extra cost.

Sessions • Fall, spring, winter, yearlong.

Eligibility Requirements • Minimum age 19; open to sophomores, juniors, seniors, graduate students, adults; 2.5 GPA; 1 letter of

recommendation; good academic standing at home school; essay; 1 year college course work in French (high school French is an added plus).

Living Arrangements • Students live in locally rented apartments, host family homes. Meals are taken on one's own, with host family, in residences, in restaurants.

Costs (2003-2004) • One term: $6515. Yearlong program: $19,545; includes tuition, housing, all meals, lab equipment, student support services. $50 application fee. $500 refundable deposit required.

For More Information • Mr. James Pondolfino, Executive Director, French-American Exchange, 3213 Duke Street, #620, Alexandria, VA 22314; *Phone:* 800-995-5087; *Fax:* 703-823-4447. *E-mail:* info@frenchamericanexchange.com. *World Wide Web:* http://www.frenchamericanexchange.com/

NICHOLLS STATE UNIVERSITY
STUDY PROGRAM IN NICE, FRANCE

Hosted by Nicholls State University–Nice

Academic Focus • Art, cultural studies, French language and literature, history.

Program Information • Students attend classes at Nicholls State University–Nice. Field trips to museums, monuments, markets, the theater; optional travel to Monaco, Saint Tropez, sporting events.

Sessions • Fall, spring, yearlong.

Eligibility Requirements • Minimum age 17; open to precollege students, freshmen, sophomores, juniors, seniors, graduate students, adults; no foreign language proficiency required.

Living Arrangements • Students live in host family homes. Quarters are shared with host institution students. Meals are taken with host family, in residences.

Costs (2003-2004) • One term: $6137. Yearlong program: $12,275; includes tuition, housing, some meals, insurance, books and class materials, lab equipment, international student ID, instructional costs. Financial aid available for all students: loans, all customary sources.

For More Information • Ms. Cynthia Webb, Director of Study Programs Abroad, Nicholls State University, PO Box 2080, Thibodaux, LA 70310; *Phone:* 985-448-4440; *Fax:* 985-449-7028. *E-mail:* spab-caw@nicholls.edu. *World Wide Web:* http://www.nicholls.edu/abroad/

STATE UNIVERSITY OF NEW YORK AT OSWEGO
BUSINESS IN THE SOUTH OF FRANCE

Hosted by Institut de Préparation á l'Administration et á la Gestion (IPAG)

Academic Focus • Business administration/management, economics, finance, French language and literature, international business, marketing.

Program Information • Students attend classes at Institut de Préparation á l'Administration et á la Gestion (IPAG).

Sessions • Fall, spring, yearlong.

Eligibility Requirements • Open to sophomores, juniors, seniors; 2.5 GPA; 3 letters of recommendation; good academic standing at home school; personal statement; no foreign language proficiency required.

Living Arrangements • Students live in locally rented apartments. Meals are taken on one's own, in residences, in restaurants.

Costs (2003-2004) • One term: $2320. Yearlong program: $4640; includes tuition, insurance, student support services. $250 nonrefundable deposit required. Financial aid available for students: home university financial aid, loan processing and scholarships for Oswego students.

For More Information • Mr. Joshua McKeown, Associate Director, State University of New York at Oswego, 122A Swetman Hall, Oswego, NY 13126; *Phone:* 888-4-OSWEGO; *Fax:* 315-312-2477. *E-mail:* intled@oswego.edu. *World Wide Web:* http://www.oswego.edu/intled/

UNIVERSITY OF MARYLAND, COLLEGE PARK
MARYLAND IN NICE

Hosted by University of Nice–Sophia Antipolis

Academic Focus • French language and literature, French studies, geography, history, literature.

Program Information • Students attend classes at University of Nice–Sophia Antipolis. Field trips to Menton, St. Paul de Vence, Saint Tropez, Cannes, Paris, Avignon.
Sessions • Spring, yearlong.
Eligibility Requirements • Open to sophomores, juniors, seniors; 2.5 GPA; 1 letter of recommendation; good academic standing at home school; minimum 3.0 GPA in French courses; 2 years of college course work in French.
Living Arrangements • Students live in host institution dormitories, locally rented apartments, host family homes. Quarters are shared with host institution students, students from other programs. Meals are taken on one's own, with host family, in residences, in central dining facility, in restaurants.
Costs (2003-2004) • One term: $3785. Yearlong program: $6995; includes tuition, excursions, student support services, personal and academic advisement. $50 application fee. $500 nonrefundable deposit required. Financial aid available for students from sponsoring institution: scholarships.
For More Information • Ms. Samantha Brandauer, Study Abroad Advisor, University of Maryland, College Park, Study Abroad Office, 3125 Mitchell Building, College Park, MD 20742-5215; *Phone:* 301-314-7746; *Fax:* 301-314-9347. *E-mail:* studyabr@deans.umd.edu. *World Wide Web:* http://www.umd.edu/studyabroad/

ORLÉANS
UNIVERSITY OF MIAMI
UNIVERSITY OF ORLÉANS, FRANCE

Hosted by University of Orléans
Academic Focus • Business administration/management, economics, engineering, geography, history, literature, science.
Program Information • Students attend classes at University of Orléans.
Sessions • Fall, spring, yearlong.

Eligibility Requirements • Minimum age 18; open to sophomores, juniors, seniors, adults; 3.0 GPA; 2 letters of recommendation; essay; official transcript; language evaluation form; 3 years college course work in French or near fluency.
Living Arrangements • Students live in host institution dormitories, host family homes. Quarters are shared with host institution students. Meals are taken on one's own, in central dining facility, in restaurants.
Costs (2003-2004) • One term: $12,919. Yearlong program: $25,838; includes tuition, student support services. $40 application fee. $500 nonrefundable deposit required. Financial aid available for students from sponsoring institution: scholarships, loans.
For More Information • Ms. Diane Mahin, Study Abroad Advisor, University of Miami, International Education and Exchange Programs, 5050 Brunson Drive, Allen Hall 212, PO Box 248005, Coral Gables, FL 33124-1610; *Phone:* 305-284-3434; *Fax:* 305-284-4235. *E-mail:* ieep@miami.edu. *World Wide Web:* http://www.studyabroad.miami.edu/

PARIS
ACADEMIC YEAR ABROAD
ACADEMIC YEAR ABROAD: PARIS CONSORTIUM

Hosted by Institut Catholique, University Paris-Sorbonne (Paris IV)
Academic Focus • Full curriculum.
Program Information • Students attend classes at University Paris-Sorbonne (Paris IV), Institut Catholique. Field trips to Mont-Saint-Michel, Normandy, the Loire Valley.
Sessions • Fall, spring, yearlong.
Eligibility Requirements • Open to juniors, seniors, graduate students; 3.0 GPA; 3 letters of recommendation; good academic

standing at home school; language evaluation; letter of recommendation; statement of purpose in French; 2 years of college course work in French.

Living Arrangements • Students live in host institution dormitories, locally rented apartments, host family homes. Meals are taken with host family, in residences.

Costs (2004-2005) • One term: $11,100. Yearlong program: $19,200; includes tuition, housing, insurance, excursions, international student ID, student support services, cultural activities, tutoring, most meals. $30 application fee. $500 refundable deposit required. Financial aid available for all students: scholarships, loans, consortium agreement for financial aid.

For More Information • Dr. Anthony M. Cinquemani, Director, Academic Year Abroad, PO Box 67, Red Hook, NY 12571; *Phone:* 845-758-9655; *Fax:* 845-758-1588. *E-mail:* aya@ayabroad.com. *World Wide Web:* http://www.ayabroad.com/. Students may also apply through Academic Year Abroad, Reid Hall, 4 Rue de Chevreuse, Paris 75006, France.

ACCENT INTERNATIONAL CONSORTIUM FOR ACADEMIC PROGRAMS ABROAD
INTERNATIONAL BUSINESS: A EUROPEAN PERSPECTIVE, SEMESTER IN PARIS WITH UNIVERSITY OF COLORADO AT DENVER

Hosted by Académie Commerciale Internationale

Academic Focus • Business administration/management, international business, law and legal studies, marketing, political science and government.

Program Information • Students attend classes at Académie Commerciale Internationale. Scheduled travel to Normandy, Brittany; field trips to Chartres, Versailles.

Sessions • Spring.

Eligibility Requirements • Minimum age 18; open to juniors, seniors, adults; major in business; course work in marketing, business law; 2.5 GPA; 1 letter of recommendation; official transcript; no foreign language proficiency required.

Living Arrangements • Students live in host institution dormitories, host family homes. Quarters are shared with students from other programs. Meals are taken on one's own, in residences, in restaurants.

Costs (2004) • One term: $7400; includes tuition, housing, excursions, books and class materials, international student ID, student support services, extra-curricular activities, Paris transit pass. $250 nonrefundable deposit required.

For More Information • ACCENT International Consortium for Academic Programs Abroad, 870 Market Street, Suite 1026, San Francisco, CA 94102; *Phone:* 800-869-9291; *Fax:* 415-835-3749. *E-mail:* info@accentintl.com. *World Wide Web:* http://www.accentintl.com/. Students may also apply through University of Colorado at Denver, Office of International Education, Campus Box 185, PO Box 173364, Denver, CO 80217-3364.

ACCENT INTERNATIONAL CONSORTIUM FOR ACADEMIC PROGRAMS ABROAD
SEMESTER IN PARIS WITH CITY COLLEGE OF SAN FRANCISCO

Hosted by University Paris-Sorbonne (Paris IV)

Academic Focus • Art history, French language and literature, French studies, liberal studies.

Program Information • Students attend classes at University Paris-Sorbonne (Paris IV). Scheduled travel to Brittany, Normandy; field trips to Fontainebleau, Vaux-le-Vicomte, Chartres, Versailles.

Sessions • Fall, spring, yearlong.

Eligibility Requirements • Minimum age 18; open to freshmen, sophomores, juniors, seniors, adults; no foreign language proficiency required.

Living Arrangements • Students live in host institution dormitories, host family homes. Quarters are shared with host institution students, students from other programs. Meals are taken on one's own, in residences, in restaurants.

Costs (2003-2004) • One term: $6100 for fall term; $6700 for spring. Yearlong program: $12,800 (estimated); includes housing, some meals, excursions, books and class materials, international student ID, student support services, extra-curricular activities, Paris transit pass. $250 nonrefundable deposit required.

For More Information • ACCENT International Consortium for Academic Programs Abroad, 870 Market Street, Suite 1026, San Francisco, CA 94102; *Phone:* 800-869-9291; *Fax:* 415-835-3749. *E-mail:* info@accentintl.com. *World Wide Web:* http://www.accentintl.com/. Students may also apply through City College of San Francisco, Study Abroad Office, Box A-71, 50 Phelan Avenue, San Francisco, CA 94112.

ACCENT INTERNATIONAL CONSORTIUM FOR ACADEMIC PROGRAMS ABROAD
SEMESTER IN PARIS WITH UNIVERSITY OF COLORADO AT DENVER

Hosted by University Paris-Sorbonne (Paris IV)

Academic Focus • Art history, French language and literature, French studies, liberal studies.

Program Information • Students attend classes at University Paris-Sorbonne (Paris IV). Scheduled travel to Brittany, Normandy; field trips to Fontainebleau, Vaux-le-Vicomte, Chartres, Versailles.

Sessions • Fall, spring, yearlong.

Eligibility Requirements • Minimum age 18; open to sophomores, juniors, seniors, adults; 2.5 GPA; 1 letter of recommendation; transcript; 2 years of college course work in French.

Living Arrangements • Students live in host institution dormitories, host family homes. Quarters are shared with host institution students, students from other programs. Meals are taken on one's own, in residences, in restaurants.

Costs (2003-2004) • One term: $7950 for fall term; $8050 for spring. Yearlong program: $16,000 (estimated); includes tuition, housing, excursions, books and class materials, international student ID, student support services, extra-curricular activities, Paris Metro pass. $250 nonrefundable deposit required.

For More Information • ACCENT International Consortium for Academic Programs Abroad, 870 Market Street, Suite 1026, San Francisco, CA 94102; *Phone:* 800-869-9291; *Fax:* 415-835-3749. *E-mail:* info@accentintl.com. *World Wide Web:* http://www.accentintl.com/. Students may also apply through University of Colorado at Denver, Office of International Education, Campus Box 185, PO Box 173364, Denver, CO 80217-3364.

ALMA COLLEGE
PROGRAM OF STUDIES IN FRANCE

Hosted by Alliance Française

Academic Focus • Art history, drama/theater, French language and literature, history, political science and government.

Program Information • Students attend classes at Alliance Française. Field trips to Giverny, the Loire Valley, Reims, Mont-Saint-Michel.

Sessions • Fall, winter, yearlong.

Eligibility Requirements • Minimum age 18; open to freshmen, sophomores, juniors, seniors, adults; 2.5 GPA; 2 letters of recommendation; good academic standing at home school; no foreign language proficiency required.

Living Arrangements • Students live in locally rented apartments, host family homes. Quarters are shared with host institution students. Meals are taken with host family, in residences.

Costs (2002-2003) • One term: $9950. Yearlong program: $21,110; includes tuition, housing, some meals, insurance, excursions, international student ID, student support services, Metro pass, e-mail access. $50 application fee. $200 refundable deposit required. Financial aid available for all students: scholarships.

For More Information • Ms. Julie Elenbaas, Office Coordinator, Alma College, 614 West Superior Street, Alma, MI 48801-1599; *Phone:* 989-463-7055; *Fax:* 989-463-7126. *E-mail:* intl_studies@alma.edu. *World Wide Web:* http://international.alma.edu/

AMERICAN INSTITUTE FOR FOREIGN STUDY (AIFS)
UNIVERSITY OF PARIS IV (SORBONNE)

Hosted by Esmod International, Goethe-Institut, Académie de Port Royal, University of London–British Institute in Paris, The American University of Paris, University Paris-Sorbonne (Paris IV)

Academic Focus • Art history, business administration/management, French language and literature, history, literature, philosophy, political science and government.
Program Information • Students attend classes at University of London–British Institute in Paris, The American University of Paris, University Paris-Sorbonne (Paris IV), Académie de Port Royal, Esmod International, Goethe-Institut. Scheduled travel to London; field trips to Normandy, Mont-Saint-Michel, the Loire Valley; optional travel at an extra cost.
Sessions • Fall, spring, yearlong, fall quarter.
Eligibility Requirements • Minimum age 17; open to freshmen, sophomores, juniors, seniors; 2.5 GPA; 1 letter of recommendation; good academic standing at home school; no foreign language proficiency required.
Living Arrangements • Students live in host institution dormitories, host family homes. Meals are taken on one's own, in restaurants.
Costs (2004-2005) • One term: $12,995. Yearlong program: $24,490; includes tuition, housing, some meals, insurance, excursions, student support services, one-way airfare, 2-day London stopover. $75 application fee. $350 nonrefundable deposit required. Financial aid available for all students: scholarships.
For More Information • Mr. David Mauro, Admissions Advisor, American Institute For Foreign Study (AIFS), 9 West Broad Street, Stamford, CT 06902-3788; *Phone:* 800-727-2437 Ext. 5163; *Fax:* 203-399-5597. *E-mail:* dmauro@aifs.com. *World Wide Web:* http://www.aifsabroad.com/

AMERICAN UNIVERSITY
SEMESTER IN PARIS: FRENCH LANGUAGE IMMERSION
Hosted by University Paris-Sorbonne (Paris IV)
Academic Focus • Art history, French language and literature, French studies, history.
Program Information • Students attend classes at University Paris-Sorbonne (Paris IV). Classes are also held on the campus of ACCENT Paris Center. Field trips to Normandy, Burgundy.
Sessions • Spring.
Eligibility Requirements • Open to sophomores, juniors, seniors, graduate students; 2.75 GPA; 1 letter of recommendation; second semester sophomore status; recommendation of advisor; no foreign language proficiency required.
Living Arrangements • Students live in host family homes. Meals are taken with host family, in residences.
Costs (2003) • One term: $17,684; includes tuition, housing, some meals, excursions, international student ID, student support services. $35 application fee. $300 nonrefundable deposit required. Financial aid available for all students: scholarships.
For More Information • Dr. David C. Brown, Dean, Washington Semester and World Capitals Programs, American University, Tenley Campus–Constitution Building, Washington, DC 20016-8083; *Phone:* 800-424-2600; *Fax:* 202-895-4960. *E-mail:* travel@american.edu. *World Wide Web:* http://www.worldcapitals.american.edu/

THE AMERICAN UNIVERSITY OF PARIS
STUDY IN FRANCE
Hosted by The American University of Paris
Academic Focus • Art history, communications, comparative literature, computer science, economics, European studies, film and media studies, finance, French studies, history, international affairs, international business, philosophy, political science and government, social sciences.
Program Information • Students attend classes at The American University of Paris. Scheduled travel to European cities, London, Brussels, Rome, Geneva, Berlin; field trips to Paris museums, Loire Valley châteaux, Normandy, Mont-Saint-Michel, international organizations; optional travel to Russia, Turkey, the Alps, Morocco at an extra cost.
Sessions • Fall, spring, yearlong.
Eligibility Requirements • Open to freshmen, sophomores, juniors, seniors; 2 letters of recommendation; good academic standing at home school; transcripts; essay; no foreign language proficiency required.
Living Arrangements • Students live in locally rented apartments, host family homes. Quarters are shared with host institution

students, students from other programs. Meals are taken on one's own, with host family, in restaurants.
Costs (2003-2004) • One term: $15,886. Yearlong program: $31,748; includes tuition, housing, some meals, insurance, books and class materials, international student ID, student support services. $55 application fee. $350 nonrefundable deposit required. Financial aid available for all students: scholarships, work study, loans, grants.
For More Information • United States Office, The American University of Paris, 950 South Cherry Street, Suite 210, Denver, CO 80246; *Phone:* 303-757-6333; *Fax:* 303-757-6444. *E-mail:* usoffice@aup.edu. *World Wide Web:* http://www.aup.edu/

BENTLEY COLLEGE
STUDY ABROAD PROGRAM IN PARIS, FRANCE
Hosted by American Business School
Academic Focus • Accounting, business administration/management, economics, finance, French language and literature, law and legal studies, marketing, mathematics, political science and government, sociology.
Program Information • Students attend classes at American Business School. Scheduled travel; field trips to local museums, cultural sites; optional travel to a pring ski trip at an extra cost.
Sessions • Fall, spring, yearlong.
Eligibility Requirements • Open to sophomores, juniors, seniors; 3.0 GPA; 1 letter of recommendation; good academic standing at home school; essays; no foreign language proficiency required.
Living Arrangements • Students live in locally rented apartments. Quarters are shared with host institution students, students from other programs. Meals are taken on one's own, in residences, in restaurants.
Costs (2002-2003) • One term: $16,600. Yearlong program: $26,080; includes tuition, housing, excursions, international student ID, student support services. $35 application fee. $500 nonrefundable deposit required. Financial aid available for students from sponsoring institution: scholarships, loans.
For More Information • Ms. Jennifer Aquino, Assistant Director, International Center, Bentley College, 175 Forest Street, Waltham, MA 02452; *Phone:* 781-891-3474; *Fax:* 781-891-2819. *E-mail:* study_abroad@bentley.edu. *World Wide Web:* http://ecampus.bentley.edu/dept/sa/

BOSTON UNIVERSITY
PARIS INTERNSHIP PROGRAM
Held at Boston University Paris Center
Academic Focus • Art history, economics, French language and literature, French studies, political science and government.
Program Information • Classes are held on the campus of Boston University Paris Center. Faculty members are local instructors hired by the sponsor. Field trips to theatre productions, film showings, political institutions; optional travel to Rennes at an extra cost.
Sessions • Fall, spring, yearlong.
Eligibility Requirements • Open to freshmen, sophomores, juniors, seniors, graduate students, adults; 2 letters of recommendation; good academic standing at home school; essay; writing sample in French; approval of participation; transcript; minimum 3.0 GPA in major; 2 years of college course work in French.
Living Arrangements • Students live in host institution dormitories, host family homes. Quarters are shared with students from other programs. Meals are taken on one's own, with host family, in residences, in central dining facility, in restaurants.
Costs (2004-2005) • One term: $12,100. Yearlong program: $24,200; includes tuition, housing, internship placement. $50 application fee. $400 nonrefundable deposit required. Financial aid available for all students: scholarships, loans.
For More Information • Division of International Programs, Boston University, 232 Bay State Road, Boston, MA 02215; *Phone:* 617-353-9888; *Fax:* 617-353-5402. *E-mail:* abroad@bu.edu. *World Wide Web:* http://www.bu.edu/abroad/

BROWN UNIVERSITY
BROWN IN FRANCE
Hosted by University of Vincennes at Saint Denis Paris VIII, University Pierre and Marie Curie Paris VI, University

THE AMERICAN UNIVERSITY OF PARIS

Are you adventurous enough to try it?

It's like no other **American university.**

It's like no other university *anywhere.*

If you're ready for an unparalleled education— in a peerless city, and within a world-spanning group of students and professors— you might be ready for AUP.

U.S. Office
950 South Cherry Street
Suite 210
Denver, Colorado 80246
Tel. (303) 757-6333

http://adventurous.aup.edu

Paris-Sorbonne (Paris IV), University of the New Sorbonne Paris III, Institute of Political Studies Paris 'SciencesPo', University of Paris I Panthéon Sorbonne

Academic Focus • Full curriculum.

Program Information • Students attend classes at University of Vincennes at Saint Denis Paris VIII, University Pierre and Marie Curie Paris VI, University Paris-Sorbonne (Paris IV), University of the New Sorbonne Paris III, Institute of Political Studies Paris 'SciencesPo', University of Paris I Panthéon Sorbonne. Field trips to Paris, the Loire Valley.

Sessions • Fall, spring, yearlong.

Eligibility Requirements • Open to sophomores, juniors, seniors; 3.0 GPA; 2 letters of recommendation; good academic standing at home school; 3 years of college course work in French.

Living Arrangements • Meals are taken on one's own.

Costs (2004-2005) • One term: $15,336. Yearlong program: $30,672; includes tuition, excursions, international student ID, student support services, language and orientation program (with housing). $250 nonrefundable deposit required. Financial aid available for students from sponsoring institution: scholarships, loans.

For More Information • Ms. Mell Bolen, Director, Brown University, Office of International Programs, Box 1973, Providence, RI 02912-1973; *Phone:* 401-863-3555; *Fax:* 401-863-3311. *E-mail:* oip_office@brown.edu. *World Wide Web:* http://www.brown.edu/OIP/

CENTER FOR STUDY ABROAD (CSA)
INTENSIVE FRENCH LANGUAGE AND CULTURE, PARIS– UNIVERSITY OF PARIS-SORBONNE

Hosted by University Paris-Sorbonne (Paris IV)

Academic Focus • Art history, French language and literature, French studies, geography.

Program Information • Students attend classes at University Paris-Sorbonne (Paris IV). Optional travel at an extra cost.

Sessions • Fall, spring, yearlong.

Eligibility Requirements • Minimum age 18; open to precollege students, freshmen, sophomores, juniors, seniors, graduate students, adults; no foreign language proficiency required.

Living Arrangements • Quarters are shared with students from other programs. Meals are taken on one's own, in residences, in central dining facility, in restaurants.

Costs (2003-2004) • One term: $1995. Yearlong program: $3795; includes tuition, insurance, international student ID, registration fees. $45 application fee.

For More Information • Ms. Alima K. Virtue, Program Director, Center for Study Abroad (CSA), 325 Washington Avenue South, #93, Kent, WA 98032; *Phone:* 206-726-1498; *Fax:* 253-850-0454. *E-mail:* info@centerforstudyabroad.com. *World Wide Web:* http://www.centerforstudyabroad.com/

CENTER FOR UNIVERSITY PROGRAMS ABROAD (CUPA)
CUPA–CENTER FOR UNIVERSITY PROGRAMS ABROAD

Hosted by Catholic University of Paris, University Pierre and Marie Curie Paris VI, University of the New Sorbonne Paris III, University of Vincennes at Saint Denis Paris VIII, University of Paris X Nanterre, Institute of Political Studies Paris 'SciencesPo', University Paris-Sorbonne (Paris IV)

Academic Focus • Full curriculum.

Program Information • Students attend classes at Catholic University of Paris, University Pierre and Marie Curie Paris VI, University of the New Sorbonne Paris III, University of Vincennes at Saint Denis Paris VIII, University of Paris X Nanterre, Institute of Political Studies Paris 'SciencesPo', University Paris-Sorbonne (Paris IV). Field trips to the Loire Valley, Normandy, Bourgogne, Rouen, Arles, Giverny, Caen, Reims.

Sessions • Fall, spring, yearlong.

Eligibility Requirements • Open to juniors, seniors; 3.0 GPA; 3 letters of recommendation; approval of home institution; advanced French.

Living Arrangements • Students live in locally rented apartments, host family homes. Meals are taken with host family, in residences.

Costs (2004-2005) • One term: $18,600. Yearlong program: $29,600; includes tuition, housing, some meals, excursions, international student ID, student support services, museum visits, theater tickets. $30 application fee. $500 nonrefundable deposit required. Financial aid available for all students: CUPA Merit Award.

For More Information • Dr. Mary S. Cattani, Director, CUPA-USA, Center for University Programs Abroad (CUPA), PO Box 9611, North Amherst, MA 01059; *Phone:* 413-549-6960; *Fax:* 413-549-5868. *E-mail:* cupausa@aol.com. *World Wide Web:* http://www.cupa-paris.org/

MORE ABOUT THE PROGRAM
The Center for University Programs Abroad (CUPA) has made it possible for American college students to pursue individualized programs of study in Paris for more than 40 years, offering access to and immersion in most of the branches of the University of Paris, a number of Grandes Ecoles, and numerous institutes. The program appeals to highly motivated students with proficient French who wish to study a broad range of subjects in the humanities, social sciences, and the fine and performing arts. CUPA maintains its commitment to academic excellence, recommending the best and most interesting courses, providing high-quality academic support, and fostering reciprocal cooperation between American and French universities while keeping home campus requirements and standards in mind. CUPA provides social and cultural opportunities for its students and offers, but does not require, a homestay with a carefully selected family. CUPA is small and selective, encouraging students to embark on an exciting academic adventure in what remains one of the world's last great romantic cities.

CENTRAL COLLEGE ABROAD
CENTRAL COLLEGE ABROAD IN PARIS, FRANCE

Hosted by Catholic University of Paris, Alliance Francaise de Nice, Chamber of Commerce and Industry, University Paris-Sorbonne (Paris IV)

Academic Focus • Art history, drama/theater, economics, French language and literature, French studies, history, international business, philosophy, political science and government, sociology.

Program Information • Students attend classes at Catholic University of Paris, University Paris-Sorbonne (Paris IV), Alliance Francaise de Nice, Chamber of Commerce and Industry. Field trips to the cathedral at Reims, Giverny, châteaux of the Loire, the cathedral at Chartres, Vaux-le-Vicomte, Fontainebleau, Normandy.

Sessions • Fall, spring, yearlong, shorter fall semester.

Eligibility Requirements • Minimum age 18; open to sophomores, juniors, seniors; 2.5 GPA; 2 letters of recommendation; good academic standing at home school; study abroad approval form; transcript; Student Life endorsement; no foreign language proficiency required.

Living Arrangements • Students live in host institution dormitories, host family homes. Quarters are shared with students from other programs. Meals are taken on one's own, in residences, in central dining facility, in restaurants.

Costs (2003-2004) • One term: $12,150 for regular semester; $11,500 for shorter option. Yearlong program: $22,190; includes tuition, housing, some meals, excursions, international student ID. $25 application fee. $500 nonrefundable deposit required. Financial aid available for all students: scholarships.

For More Information • Office of International Education, Central College Abroad, 812 University Street, Pella, IA 50219; *Phone:* 800-831-3629; *Fax:* 641-628-5375. *E-mail:* studyabroad@central.edu. *World Wide Web:* http://www.central.edu/abroad/

CIEE
CIEE STUDY CENTER AT THE PARIS CENTER FOR CRITICAL STUDIES, FRANCE–CONTEMPORARY FRENCH STUDIES PROGRAM

Hosted by Paris Center for Critical Studies

Academic Focus • French language and literature, French studies.

Program Information • Students attend classes at Paris Center for Critical Studies. Field trips to sites of cultural interest in and around Paris, Chartres, Giverny.

Sessions • Fall, spring, yearlong.

Eligibility Requirements • Open to sophomores, juniors, seniors, graduate students; 2.75 GPA; 2 letters of recommendation; 1 year of college course work in French.

Living Arrangements • Students live in locally rented apartments, host family homes. Meals are taken on one's own, with host family, in residences, in restaurants.

Costs (2003-2004) • One term: $10,250. Yearlong program: $13,250; includes tuition, housing, insurance, excursions, student support services, temporary housing at beginning of program, monthly transportation pass, cultural activities, pre-departure activity, optional on-site pick-up. $30 application fee. $300 deposit required. Financial aid available for all students: minority student scholarships, travel grants.

For More Information • Ms. Hannah McChesney, Admissions Officer, Europe, Middle East, and Africa, CIEE, 7 Custom House Street, 3rd Floor, Portland, ME 04101; *Phone:* 800-40-STUDY; *Fax:* 207-553-7699. *E-mail:* studyinfo@ciee.org. *World Wide Web:* http://www.ciee.org/isp/

CIEE
CIEE STUDY CENTER AT THE PARIS CENTER FOR CRITICAL STUDIES, FRANCE–CRITICAL STUDIES PROGRAM

Hosted by Paris Center for Critical Studies, University of the New Sorbonne Paris III

Academic Focus • Art history, comparative literature, drama/theater, film and media studies, French language and literature, French studies, literature, philosophy.

Program Information • Students attend classes at University of the New Sorbonne Paris III, Paris Center for Critical Studies. Field trips to Chartres, Vaux-le-Vicomte, Giverny.

Sessions • Fall, spring, yearlong.

Eligibility Requirements • Open to sophomores, juniors, seniors, graduate students, adults; 3.0 GPA; 2 letters of recommendation; 2.5 years of college course work in French.

Living Arrangements • Students live in locally rented apartments. Meals are taken on one's own, in residences, in restaurants.

Costs (2003-2004) • One term: $7900. Yearlong program: $13,250; includes tuition, insurance, excursions, student support services, housing at start of program, monthly transportation pass, Vidéothèque de Paris subscription, cultural activities, pre-departure advising, student card. $30 application fee. $300 deposit required. Financial aid available for all students: minority student scholarships, travel grants.

For More Information • Ms. Hannah McChesney, Program Officer, Europe, Middle East, and Africa, CIEE, 7 Custom House Street, 3rd Floor, Portland, ME 04101; *Phone:* 800-40-STUDY; *Fax:* 207-553-7699. *E-mail:* studyinfo@ciee.org. *World Wide Web:* http://www.ciee.org/isp/

CITY COLLEGE OF SAN FRANCISCO
SEMESTER IN PARIS

Hosted by University Paris-Sorbonne (Paris IV)

Academic Focus • Art history, language studies, liberal studies.

Program Information • Students attend classes at University Paris-Sorbonne (Paris IV). Scheduled travel to Normandy, Brittany; field trips to Chartres, Fontainebleau, Vaux-le-Vicomte, Versailles.

Sessions • Fall, spring, yearlong.

Eligibility Requirements • Minimum age 18; open to freshmen, sophomores, juniors, seniors, adults; 2.0 GPA; no foreign language proficiency required.

Living Arrangements • Students live in locally rented apartments, host family homes. Quarters are shared with host institution students, students from other programs. Meals are taken on one's own, with host family, in residences, in restaurants.

Costs (2004-2005) • One term: $6300–$7000 for fall; $6800–$7500 for spring. Yearlong program: $13,100; includes tuition, housing, some meals, insurance, excursions, international student ID, student support services. $250 nonrefundable deposit required. Financial aid available for students from sponsoring institution: scholarships, loans.

For More Information • Ms. Jill Heffron, Study Abroad Coordinator, City College of San Francisco, 50 Phelan Avenue, Box C212, San Francisco, CA 94112; *Phone:* 415-239-3778; *Fax:* 415-239-3804. *E-mail:* studyabroad@ccsf.edu. *World Wide Web:* http://www.ccsf.

edu/studyabroad/. Students may also apply through ACCENT, 870 Market Street, Suite 1026, San Francisco, CA 94102.

COLUMBIA UNIVERSITY
COLUMBIA UNIVERSITY PROGRAMS IN PARIS AT REID HALL

Hosted by University Paris-Sorbonne (Paris IV), Reid Hall, Institute of Political Studies Paris 'SciencesPo', University Denis Diderot (Paris VII)

Academic Focus • Art history, comparative literature, film and media studies, French language and literature, French studies, history, philosophy, political science and government, women's studies.

Program Information • Students attend classes at University Paris-Sorbonne (Paris IV), Reid Hall, Institute of Political Studies Paris 'SciencesPo', University Denis Diderot (Paris VII). Scheduled travel to Besançon, Valence, Marseille, Avignon; field trips to Burgundy, Normandy, Champagne, Ecouen, Ile-de-France; optional travel to sites in France and other countries at an extra cost.

Sessions • Fall, spring, yearlong.

Eligibility Requirements • Open to sophomores, juniors, seniors; 3.0 GPA; 2 letters of recommendation; good academic standing at home school; B average in French; 2 years of college course work in French.

Living Arrangements • Students live in host institution dormitories, locally rented apartments, host family homes. Meals are taken on one's own, with host family, in residences, in restaurants.

Costs (2003-2004) • One term: $12,800. Yearlong program: $25,600; includes tuition, student support services, computer laboratory access. $35 application fee. $500 nonrefundable deposit required.

For More Information • Information Center, 303 Lewisohn, Columbia University, 2970 Broadway, MC 4110, New York, NY 10027-6902; *Phone:* 212-854-9699; *Fax:* 212-854-5841. *E-mail:* reidhall@columbia.edu. *World Wide Web:* http://www.ce.columbia.edu/op/

CULTURAL EXPERIENCES ABROAD (CEA)
STUDY FRENCH LANGUAGE AND CULTURE IN PARIS

Hosted by University Paris-Sorbonne (Paris IV)

Academic Focus • Art history, communications, comparative history, economics, French language and literature, French studies, history, philosophy, political science and government, sociology.

Program Information • Students attend classes at University Paris-Sorbonne (Paris IV). Field trips to Chartres, Versailles, Giverny, Reims, Lyon, Beaujolais, Dijon, Fontainebleau; optional travel to Normandy, the Alps, Bordeaux, Provence at an extra cost.

Sessions • Fall, spring, yearlong, fall II.

Eligibility Requirements • Minimum age 18; open to freshmen, sophomores, juniors, seniors, graduate students, adults; 2.5 GPA; 1 letter of recommendation; good academic standing at home school; previous French study recommended.

Living Arrangements • Students live in host institution dormitories, locally rented apartments, program-owned apartments, host family homes. Quarters are shared with host institution students, students from other programs. Meals are taken on one's own, in residences, in restaurants.

Costs (2003-2004) • One term: $9695–$10,995. Yearlong program: $17,995; includes tuition, housing, some meals, insurance, excursions, books and class materials, lab equipment, student support services. $50 application fee. $400 nonrefundable deposit required.

For More Information • Cultural Experiences Abroad (CEA), 1400 East Southern Avenue, Suite B-108, Tempe, AZ 85282-8011; *Phone:* 480-557-7900; *Fax:* 480-557-7926. *E-mail:* petersons@gowithcea.com. *World Wide Web:* http://www.gowithcea.com/

EDUCO
EMORY, DUKE, AND CORNELL IN PARIS

Hosted by Institute of Political Studies Paris 'SciencesPo', University of Paris I Panthéon Sorbonne, University Denis Diderot (Paris VII)

Academic Focus • Full curriculum.

Program Information • Students attend classes at Institute of Political Studies Paris 'SciencesPo', University of Paris I Panthéon

Sorbonne, University Denis Diderot (Paris VII). Field trips to various locations in Paris, Burgundy, the Loire Valley.

Sessions • Fall, spring, yearlong.

Eligibility Requirements • Open to sophomores, juniors, seniors; 3.0 GPA; 2 letters of recommendation; good academic standing at home school; interview; 2 years of college course work in French.

Living Arrangements • Students live in host institution dormitories, locally rented apartments, host family homes. Meals are taken on one's own, with host family, in residences.

Costs (2002-2003) • One term: contact sponsor for cost. Yearlong program: contact sponsor for cost. $300 nonrefundable deposit required. Financial aid available for students from sponsoring institution: scholarships, work study, loans.

For More Information • Ms. Tami Scheibach, Study Abroad Advisor, EDUCO, Center for International Programs Abroad, 1385 Oxford Road, Atlanta, GA 30322; *Phone:* 404-727-2240; *Fax:* 404-727-6724. *E-mail:* cipa@emory.edu. *World Wide Web:* http://www.emory.edu/CIPA/

EUROPEAN HERITAGE INSTITUTE
ACADEMIC YEAR IN PARIS AT LA SORBONNE–FRANCE

Hosted by University Paris-Sorbonne (Paris IV)

Academic Focus • Civilization studies, French language and literature, French studies, history.

Program Information • Students attend classes at University Paris-Sorbonne (Paris IV). Field trips to Mont-Saint-Michel, Avignon.

Sessions • Fall, spring, winter, yearlong, alternate year.

Eligibility Requirements • Minimum age 18; open to freshmen, sophomores, juniors, seniors, graduate students, adults; 2.2 GPA; 2 letters of recommendation; no foreign language proficiency required.

Living Arrangements • Students live in host institution dormitories, locally rented apartments. Quarters are shared with host institution students, students from other programs. Meals are taken on one's own, in residences, in restaurants.

Costs (2004-2005) • One term: $2200–$3550. Yearlong program: $4400–$7000; includes tuition, student support services, administrative fees. $300 refundable deposit required.

For More Information • Dr. Antonio Masullo, Professor, European Heritage Institute, 2708 East Franklin Street, Richmond, VA 23223; *Phone:* 804-643-0661; *Fax:* 804-648-0826. *E-mail:* euritage@i2020.net. *World Wide Web:* http://www.europeabroad.org/

EUROPEAN HERITAGE INSTITUTE
ART, FASHION, AND INTERIOR DESIGN IN PARIS

Hosted by Paris American Academy

Academic Focus • Art, costume design, design and applied arts, drawing/painting, fashion design, fine/studio arts, French language and literature, interior design, textiles.

Program Information • Students attend classes at Paris American Academy. Field trips to Versailles, Giverny; optional travel to the Loire Valley, Mont-Saint-Michel, Normandy, southern France at an extra cost.

Sessions • Fall, spring, yearlong.

Eligibility Requirements • Minimum age 18; open to freshmen, sophomores, juniors, seniors, graduate students, adults; 2.2 GPA; 2 letters of recommendation; no foreign language proficiency required.

Living Arrangements • Students live in locally rented apartments, host family homes. Quarters are shared with host institution students, students from other programs. Meals are taken on one's own, in residences, in restaurants.

Costs (2004-2005) • One term: $5700 (estimated). Yearlong program: $10,400 (estimated); includes tuition, excursions, lab equipment, student support services. $300 refundable deposit required.

FRANCE
Paris

For More Information • Dr. Antonio Masullo, Professor, European Heritage Institute, 2708 East Franklin Street, Richmond, VA 23223; *Phone:* 804-643-0661; *Fax:* 804-648-0826. *E-mail:* euritage@i2020. net. *World Wide Web:* http://www.europeabroad.org/

FLORIDA INTERNATIONAL UNIVERSITY
MICEFA UNIVERSITY CONSORTIUM

Hosted by Mission Interuniversitaire de Coordination des Echanges Franco-Americains
Academic Focus • Full curriculum.
Program Information • Students attend classes at Mission Interuniversitaire de Coordination des Echanges Franco-Americains.
Sessions • Fall, spring.
Eligibility Requirements • Open to sophomores, juniors, seniors, graduate students, adults; 3.0 GPA; fluency in French.
Living Arrangements • Students live in locally rented apartments. Quarters are shared with host institution students. Meals are taken on one's own, in central dining facility.
Costs (2004) • One term: $6000; includes housing, some meals, international airfare, books and class materials, lab equipment, international student ID. $150 application fee. Financial aid available for all students: scholarships, loans.
For More Information • Office of International Studies, Florida International University, University Park Campus–TT100, Miami, FL 33199; *Phone:* 305-348-1913; *Fax:* 305-348-1941. *E-mail:* ois@fiu. edu. *World Wide Web:* http://ois.fiu.edu/

FRENCH-AMERICAN EXCHANGE
TRIMESTER/ACADEMIC YEAR ABROAD IN PARIS

Hosted by Ecole France Langue
Academic Focus • Art history, civilization studies, French language and literature, French studies, linguistics, political science and government.
Program Information • Students attend classes at Ecole France Langue. Field trips to museums, monuments, Versailles, Paris, Fontainebleau, Chartres, Vaux-le-Vicomte; optional travel to Europe at an extra cost.
Sessions • Fall, spring, winter, yearlong.
Eligibility Requirements • Minimum age 19; open to sophomores, juniors, seniors, graduate students, adults; 2.5 GPA; 1 letter of recommendation; good academic standing at home school; essay; 1 year college course work in French (high school French is an added plus).
Living Arrangements • Students live in locally rented apartments, host family homes. Meals are taken on one's own, with host family, in residences, in restaurants.
Costs (2003-2004) • One term: $6223. Yearlong program: $18,669; includes tuition, housing, all meals, lab equipment, student support services. $50 application fee. $500 refundable deposit required.
For More Information • Mr. James Pondolfino, Executive Director, French-American Exchange, 3213 Duke Street, #620, Alexandria, VA 22314; *Phone:* 800-995-5087; *Fax:* 703-823-4447. *E-mail:* info@frenchamericanexchange.com. *World Wide Web:* http://www.frenchamericanexchange.com/

GEORGE MASON UNIVERSITY
PARIS, FRANCE

Hosted by ACCENT Paris Center
Academic Focus • French language and literature, French studies, history.
Program Information • Students attend classes at ACCENT Paris Center. Field trips to Fontainebleau, Vaux-le-Vicomte, Chartres, Brittany, Normandy; optional travel at an extra cost.
Sessions • Fall.
Eligibility Requirements • Minimum age 18; open to sophomores, juniors, seniors, adults; 2.5 GPA; good academic standing at home school; 1 year of college course work in French.
Living Arrangements • Students live in host institution dormitories. Quarters are shared with host institution students.
Costs (2004) • One term: contact sponsor for cost. $75 application fee. Financial aid available for students from sponsoring institution: scholarships, loans.
For More Information • Program Officer, Center for Global Education, George Mason University, 235 Johnson Center, 4400

University Drive, Fairfax, VA 22030; *Phone:* 703-993-2154; *Fax:* 703-993-2153. *E-mail:* cge@gmu.edu. *World Wide Web:* http://www.gmu.edu/departments/cge/

HAMILTON COLLEGE
JUNIOR YEAR IN FRANCE

Hosted by Catholic University of Paris, Ecole du Louvre, Institute of Political Studies Paris 'SciencesPo', University of the New Sorbonne Paris III
Academic Focus • Art history, comparative literature, dance, drama/theater, economics, fine/studio arts, French language and literature, history, photography, political science and government.
Program Information • Students attend classes at Catholic University of Paris, Ecole du Louvre, Institute of Political Studies Paris 'SciencesPo', University of the New Sorbonne Paris III. Scheduled travel to Biarritz; field trips to Basque country, Burgundy, Mont-Saint-Michel, the Loire Valley.
Sessions • Yearlong.
Eligibility Requirements • Open to juniors; 3.0 GPA; good academic standing at home school; 2 years of college course work in French.
Living Arrangements • Students live in host family homes. Quarters are shared with host institution students. Meals are taken with host family, in residences.
Costs (2003-2004) • Yearlong program: $32,000; includes tuition, housing, some meals, excursions, international airfare, reimbursement for theater and museum fees related to courses. $25 application fee. $600 deposit required. Financial aid available for all students: scholarships.
For More Information • Ms. Gena Hasburgh, Coordinator, Hamilton College Programs Abroad, Hamilton College, 198 College Hill Road, Clinton, NY 13323; *Phone:* 315-859-4201; *Fax:* 315-859-4969. *E-mail:* ghasburgh@hamilton.edu. *World Wide Web:* http://www.hamilton.edu/academics/programs_abroad/

MORE ABOUT THE PROGRAM
The Hamilton College Junior Year in France program begins with a 3-week orientation in the seaside resort of Biarritz, followed by a full academic year in Paris. Students choose the Hamilton College program because of its extensive course offerings at a variety of Paris institutions, its small groups, and the individualized attention and thorough orientation they receive in Biarritz. Care is taken to avoid hidden costs and maintain academic standards. Hamilton has offered the program for more than 40 years. The College's liberal arts philosophy frames the program's goals, emphasizing proficiency in French and meaningful intercultural exchange. Homestay with carefully selected families provides an unforgettable personal link with the people of France.

First-year students are encouraged to request information on the program to begin planning their junior year abroad. Motivated students in good academic standing who have completed their sophomore year and the equivalent of 4 semesters of French at the college level are encouraged to apply.

The 2004–05 Director-in-Residence is Roberta Krueger.

HOLLINS UNIVERSITY
HOLLINS ABROAD PARIS

Held at Reid Hall
Academic Focus • Architecture, art history, drama/theater, economics, French language and literature, history, music history, political science and government.
Program Information • Classes are held on the campus of Reid Hall. Faculty members are local instructors hired by the sponsor. Scheduled travel to southern France, Normandy; field trips to Chartres, Giverny, Versailles, the Loire Valley, Burgundy; optional travel to the Loire Valley, Burgundy.
Sessions • Fall, spring, yearlong, calendar year.

Eligibility Requirements • Minimum age 18; open to sophomores, juniors, seniors; 2.5 GPA; 1 letter of recommendation; good academic standing at home school; evaluation of language level; approval from home institution; 2 years of college course work in French.

Living Arrangements • Students live in host family homes. Quarters are shared with host institution students. Meals are taken on one's own, with host family, in residences, in restaurants.

Costs (2004) • One term: $13,995. Yearlong program: $27,990; includes tuition, housing, all meals, excursions, international student ID, student support services, Paris Metro and bus passes, some books and class materials. $25 application fee. $200 nonrefundable deposit required. Financial aid available for students from sponsoring institution: scholarships, loans.

For More Information • Ms. Lorraine Fleck, Director of International Programs, Hollins University, PO Box 9597, Roanoke, VA 24020; *Phone:* 800-511-6612; *Fax:* 540-362-6693. *E-mail:* abroad@hollins.edu. *World Wide Web:* http://www.hollins.edu/

IES, INSTITUTE FOR THE INTERNATIONAL EDUCATION OF STUDENTS
IES–PARIS

Hosted by Ecole de Psychologues Practiciens, European Business School, Institute for the International Education of Students (IES)–Paris, University of Vincennes at Saint Denis Paris VIII, Ecole Normale de Musique de Paris/Alfred Cortot, Atelier Nicolas Poussin, University Paris-Sorbonne (Paris IV), Catholic University of Paris

Academic Focus • African studies, archaeology, art, art history, drama/theater, economics, education, film and media studies, French language and literature, history, international affairs, international business, music, philosophy, political science and government, religious studies, sociology, women's studies.

Program Information • Students attend classes at University of Vincennes at Saint Denis Paris VIII, Atelier Nicolas Poussin, University Paris-Sorbonne (Paris IV), Catholic University of Paris, Ecole de Psychologues Practiciens, Ecole Normale de Musique de Paris/Alfred Cortot, European Business School, Institute for the International Education of Students (IES)–Paris. Field trips to châteaux of the Loire Valley, Vaux-le-Vicomte, Fontainebleau; optional travel to sites within France, Spain, Marseille at an extra cost.

Sessions • Fall, spring, yearlong.

Eligibility Requirements • Minimum age 18; open to sophomores, juniors, seniors, graduate students, adults; 3.0 GPA; 1 letter of recommendation; good academic standing at home school; 2 years of college course work in French.

Living Arrangements • Students live in host family homes. Meals are taken with host family, in residences, in central dining facility.

Costs (2003-2004) • One term: $10,950. Yearlong program: $19,710; includes tuition, housing, some meals, excursions, student support services, partial insurance coverage. $50 application fee. $500 nonrefundable deposit required. Financial aid available for all students: scholarships, institutional partner need-based grants.

For More Information • International Education Representative, IES, Institute for the International Education of Students, 33 North LaSalle Street, 15th Floor, Chicago, IL 60602; *Phone:* 800-995-2300; *Fax:* 312-944-1448. *E-mail:* info@iesabroad.org. *World Wide Web:* http://www.IESabroad.org/

INTERNATIONAL STUDIES ABROAD
PARIS, FRANCE–COURSE WITH FRENCH STUDENTS

Hosted by Catholic University of Paris

Academic Focus • French language and literature, history, liberal studies, philosophy.

Program Information • Students attend classes at Catholic University of Paris. Field trips to Chartres, Mont-Saint-Michel, Normandy, château country, Versailles; optional travel to Nice at an extra cost.

Sessions • Fall, winter, yearlong, fall 4.

Eligibility Requirements • Minimum age 18; open to freshmen, sophomores, juniors, seniors, graduate students, adults; 2.5 GPA; 1 letter of recommendation; good academic standing at home school; transcript; 2 years of college course work in French.

Living Arrangements • Students live in locally rented apartments, host family homes. Quarters are shared with host institution students. Meals are taken with host family, in residences.

Costs (2004-2005) • One term: $9350–$10,350. Yearlong program: $17,500; includes tuition, housing, some meals, insurance, excursions, student support services, excursion transportation, laundry service. $200 deposit required. Financial aid available for all students: scholarships, work study, U.S. federal financial aid.

For More Information • France Site Specialist, International Studies Abroad, 901 West 24th Street, Austin, TX 78705; *Phone:* 800-580-8826; *Fax:* 512-480-8866. *E-mail:* isa@studiesabroad.com. *World Wide Web:* http://www.studiesabroad.com/

INTERNATIONAL STUDIES ABROAD
PARIS, FRANCE–LANGUAGE AND CULTURE

Hosted by Catholic University of Paris

Academic Focus • Civilization studies, communications, cultural studies, film and media studies, French language and literature, history.

Program Information • Students attend classes at Catholic University of Paris. Field trips to Versailles, Normandy, Chartres, the Loire Valley, Château country, Mont-Saint-Michel; optional travel to Nice at an extra cost.

Sessions • Fall, spring, yearlong, fall II.

Eligibility Requirements • Minimum age 18; open to precollege students, freshmen, sophomores, juniors, seniors, adults; 2.5 GPA; 1 letter of recommendation; good academic standing at home school; transcript; minimum 2.5 GPA or 2 letters of recommendation; 1 year college course work in French for upper-division courses.

Living Arrangements • Students live in host institution dormitories, locally rented apartments, host family homes. Quarters are shared with host institution students, students from other programs. Meals are taken with host family, in residences.

Costs (2004-2005) • One term: $9350–$10,350. Yearlong program: $17,500; includes tuition, housing, some meals, insurance, excursions, student support services, tutorials, ground transportation, laundry service (for students with host families only), Internet access. $200 deposit required. Financial aid available for all students: scholarships, loans, U.S. federal financial aid.

For More Information • France Site Specialist, International Studies Abroad, 901 West 24th Street, Austin, TX 78705; *Phone:* 800-580-8826; *Fax:* 512-480-8866. *E-mail:* isa@studiesabroad.com. *World Wide Web:* http://www.studiesabroad.com/

LAKE FOREST COLLEGE
INTERNATIONAL INTERNSHIP/STUDY IN PARIS

Academic Focus • Business administration/management, education, French language and literature, international affairs, political science and government.

Program Information • Faculty members are drawn from the sponsor's U.S. staff and local instructors hired by the sponsor. Field trips to the Loire Valley, Normandy.

Sessions • Fall.

Eligibility Requirements • Open to juniors, seniors; 2.75 GPA; 3 letters of recommendation; good academic standing at home school; Lake Forest College application form; 2.5 years of college course work in French.

Living Arrangements • Students live in host family homes. Meals are taken with host family, in residences, in restaurants.

Costs (2003) • One term: $15,948; includes tuition, housing, some meals, insurance, excursions, books and class materials, student support services. $20 application fee. $500 nonrefundable deposit required. Financial aid available for students from sponsoring institution: scholarships, loans.

For More Information • Ms. Cynthia T. Hahn, Professor of French and Associate Dean of Faculty, Lake Forest College, Paris Internship Program, Office of the Dean of the Faculty, Lake Forest, IL 60045-2399; *Phone:* 847-735-5024; *Fax:* 847-735-6292. *E-mail:* hahn@lfc.edu. *World Wide Web:* http://www.lakeforest.edu/

LEXIA INTERNATIONAL
LEXIA IN PARIS

Hosted by University Paris-Sorbonne (Paris IV)

FRANCE
Paris

Academic Focus • Ancient history, anthropology, area studies, art, art conservation studies, art history, civilization studies, classics and classical languages, comparative history, cultural studies, drawing/painting, economics, environmental science/studies, ethnic studies, European studies, film and media studies, fine/studio arts, French language and literature, French studies, geography, history, interdisciplinary studies, international affairs, international business, liberal studies, literature, music, music history, music performance, philosophy, political science and government, psychology, religious studies, social sciences, urban studies, visual and performing arts.
Program Information • Students attend classes at University Paris-Sorbonne (Paris IV). Field trips to sites in and around Paris, Normandy, Brittany.
Sessions • Fall, spring, yearlong.
Eligibility Requirements • Minimum age 18; open to sophomores, juniors, seniors, graduate students, adults; 2.5 GPA; 2 letters of recommendation; no foreign language proficiency required.
Living Arrangements • Students live in host family homes. Meals are taken on one's own, with host family, in residences.
Costs (2003-2004) • One term: $11,950. Yearlong program: $21,550; includes tuition, housing, insurance, excursions, international student ID, student support services, transcript, computer access. $35 application fee. $300 refundable deposit required. Financial aid available for all students: scholarships, work study.
For More Information • Lexia International, 23 South Main Street, Hanover, NH 03755; *Phone:* 800-775-3942; *Fax:* 603-643-9899. *E-mail:* info@lexiaintl.org. *World Wide Web:* http://www.lexiaintl.org/

MIDDLEBURY COLLEGE SCHOOLS ABROAD
SCHOOL IN FRANCE–PARIS PROGRAM

Hosted by University Paris-Sorbonne (Paris IV), Catholic University of Paris, University of the New Sorbonne Paris III, Institute of Political Studies Paris 'SciencesPo'
Academic Focus • American studies, art history, economics, film and media studies, French language and literature, history, international affairs, liberal studies, music, political science and government.
Program Information • Students attend classes at University Paris-Sorbonne (Paris IV), Catholic University of Paris, University of the New Sorbonne Paris III, Institute of Political Studies Paris 'SciencesPo'. Classes are also held on the campus of Le Centre Madeleine. Field trips to Mont-Saint-Michel, Burgundy, Giverny, châteaux of the Loire, Toulouse.
Sessions • Fall, spring, yearlong.
Eligibility Requirements • Open to sophomores, juniors, seniors, graduate students; 2.7 GPA; 2 letters of recommendation; B average in both French and major; 2.5 years college course work in French, including at least 1 content course.
Living Arrangements • Students live in host institution dormitories, locally rented apartments, host family homes. Meals are taken on one's own, with host family, in residences, in restaurants.
Costs (2004-2005) • One term: $7200. Yearlong program: $14,400; includes tuition, excursions, student support services. $50 application fee. $300 nonrefundable deposit required. Financial aid available for students from sponsoring institution: scholarships, loans.
For More Information • Mr. Jamie Northrup, University Relations Coordinator, Middlebury College Schools Abroad, Office of Off-Campus Study, Sunderland Language Center, Middlebury, VT 05753; *Phone:* 802-443-5745; *Fax:* 802-443-3157. *E-mail:* schoolsabroad@middlebury.edu. *World Wide Web:* http://www.middlebury.edu/msa/

NEW YORK UNIVERSITY
NYU IN PARIS

Hosted by Catholic University of Paris, Spéos "Paris Photographic Institute", NYU Center, University of Paris I Panthéon Sorbonne, University Denis Diderot (Paris VII), Institute of Political Studies Paris 'SciencesPo'
Academic Focus • Art history, film and media studies, French language and literature, French studies, history, international affairs, political science and government, women's studies.
Program Information • Students attend classes at Catholic University of Paris, Spéos "Paris Photographic Institute", University

of Paris I Panthéon Sorbonne, University Denis Diderot (Paris VII), Institute of Political Studies Paris 'SciencesPo', NYU Center. Field trips to historic sites, cultural festivals, Normandy, Giverny, Versailles.
Sessions • Fall, spring, yearlong.
Eligibility Requirements • Open to sophomores, juniors, seniors; 3.0 GPA; 1 letter of recommendation; good academic standing at home school; transcript; personal statement; foreign language requirement dependent on track chosen.
Living Arrangements • Students live in locally rented apartments, host family homes. Quarters are shared with host institution students. Meals are taken on one's own, with host family, in residences, in restaurants.
Costs (2003-2004) • One term: $14,248. Yearlong program: $28,495; includes tuition, excursions, student support services. $25 application fee. $300 nonrefundable deposit required. Financial aid available for all students: scholarships, loans.
For More Information • Office of Study Abroad Admissions, New York University, 7 East 12th Street, 6th Floor, New York, NY 10003; *Phone:* 212-998-4433; *Fax:* 212-995-4103. *E-mail:* studyabroad@nyu.edu. *World Wide Web:* http://www.nyu.edu/studyabroad/

NICHOLLS STATE UNIVERSITY
STUDY PROGRAM IN PARIS, FRANCE

Hosted by Nicholls State University–Paris
Academic Focus • Art, cultural studies, French language and literature, history.
Program Information • Students attend classes at Nicholls State University–Paris. Field trips to museums, monuments, markets, the theater; optional travel to Monaco, museums, Saint Tropez, Versailles at an extra cost.
Sessions • Fall, spring, yearlong.
Eligibility Requirements • Minimum age 17; open to precollege students, freshmen, sophomores, juniors, seniors, graduate students, adults; no foreign language proficiency required.
Living Arrangements • Students live in host family homes. Quarters are shared with host institution students. Meals are taken with host family, in residences.
Costs (2003-2004) • One term: $6632. Yearlong program: $13,265; includes tuition, housing, some meals, insurance, books and class materials, lab equipment, international student ID, instructional costs. Financial aid available for all students: loans, all customary sources.
For More Information • Ms. Cynthia Webb, Director of Study Programs Abroad, Nicholls State University, PO Box 2080, Thibodaux, LA 70310; *Phone:* 985-448-4440; *Fax:* 985-449-7028. *E-mail:* spab-caw@nicholls.edu. *World Wide Web:* http://www.nicholls.edu/abroad/

PARSONS SCHOOL OF DESIGN
PARSONS PARIS

Hosted by Parsons School of Design–Paris
Academic Focus • Commercial art, design and applied arts, fashion design, fine/studio arts, graphic design/illustration, marketing, photography.
Program Information • Students attend classes at Parsons School of Design–Paris. Field trips to various destinations in Europe/Africa; optional travel to Europe, Africa, the Mediterranean Sea at an extra cost.
Sessions • Fall, spring, yearlong.
Eligibility Requirements • Open to freshmen, sophomores, juniors, seniors, adults; 2.0 GPA; good academic standing at home school; portfolio; no foreign language proficiency required.
Living Arrangements • Students live in locally rented apartments. Quarters are shared with host institution students. Meals are taken on one's own, in residences, in restaurants.
Costs (2003-2004) • One term: €8925. Yearlong program: €17,850; includes tuition, student support services. €50 application fee. €400 nonrefundable deposit required. Financial aid available for students from sponsoring institution: scholarships, work study, loans.
For More Information • Ms. Sara Krauskopf, Admissions Officer, Parsons School of Design, 14 Rue Letellier, 75015 Paris, France; *Phone:* +33-45-77-39-66; *Fax:* +33-45-77-44-12. *E-mail:* parsonsparis@compuserve.com. *World Wide Web:* http://www.parsons-paris.com/

RIDER UNIVERSITY
BUSINESS STUDY IN FRANCE

Hosted by American Business School

Academic Focus • Business administration/management, international business.

Program Information • Students attend classes at American Business School.

Sessions • Fall, spring, yearlong.

Eligibility Requirements • Open to sophomores, juniors, seniors; major in business; 2.5 GPA; 1 letter of recommendation; good academic standing at home school; no foreign language proficiency required.

Living Arrangements • Students live in locally rented apartments. Quarters are shared with host institution students. Meals are taken on one's own, in residences, in restaurants.

Costs (2001-2002) • One term: $8995. Yearlong program: $17,990; includes tuition, student support services, administrative fees. $35 application fee. $300 refundable deposit required. Financial aid available for students from sponsoring institution: regular financial aid.

For More Information • Dr. Joseph E. Nadeau, Director of Study Abroad, Rider University, 2083 Lawrenceville Road, Lawrenceville, NJ 08648; *Phone:* 609-896-5314; *Fax:* 609-895-5670. *E-mail:* nadeau@rider.edu. *World Wide Web:* http://www.rider.edu/academic/uwp/index.htm

ST. JOHN'S UNIVERSITY
FRANCE SEMESTER PROGRAM

Hosted by University of Paris Dauphine (Paris IX)

Academic Focus • Art, French language and literature, history, international business, marketing, political science and government.

Program Information • Students attend classes at University of Paris Dauphine (Paris IX).

Sessions • Fall, spring.

Eligibility Requirements • Open to freshmen, sophomores, juniors, seniors; 2.75 GPA; 2 letters of recommendation; good academic standing at home school; interview; proficiency in French required for internship.

Living Arrangements • Students live in locally rented apartments. Meals are taken on one's own, in restaurants.

Costs (2003-2004) • One term: $15,972–$16,698; includes tuition, housing, some meals, international airfare, student support services, transportation to and from Paris airport. $30 application fee. $750 nonrefundable deposit required. Financial aid available for students from sponsoring institution: scholarships, loans.

For More Information • Dr. Ruth De Paula, Director, Office of Study Abroad Programs, St. John's University, 8000 Utopia Parkway, Jamaica, NY 11439; *Phone:* 718-990-6105; *Fax:* 718-990-2321. *E-mail:* intled@stjohns.edu. *World Wide Web:* http://www.stjohns.edu/studyabroad/

SARAH LAWRENCE COLLEGE
SARAH LAWRENCE COLLEGE IN PARIS

Hosted by University of Paris VII–Jussieu Campus, University of Paris X Nanterre, Catholic University of Paris, University Paris-Sorbonne (Paris IV), Ecole du Louvre, Institute of Political Studies Paris 'SciencesPo'

Academic Focus • Art history, dance, drama/theater, European studies, French language and literature, French studies, history, literature, music, philosophy, photography, political science and government, translation, visual and performing arts.

Program Information • Students attend classes at University of Paris VII–Jussieu Campus, University of Paris X Nanterre, Catholic University of Paris, University Paris-Sorbonne (Paris IV), Ecole du Louvre, Institute of Political Studies Paris 'SciencesPo'. Classes are also held on the campus of Reid Hall. Field trips to Chartres Cathedral, Vaux-le-Vicomte, Normandy, Val de Loire, Provence.

Sessions • Fall, spring, yearlong.

Eligibility Requirements • Open to sophomores, juniors, seniors; 3.0 GPA; 2 letters of recommendation; good academic standing at home school; essay; recommendation evaluating language proficiency; 2 years of college course work in French.

Living Arrangements • Students live in host institution dormitories, locally rented apartments, host family homes. Meals are taken on one's own, with host family, in residences, in central dining facility.

Costs (2003-2004) • One term: $15,060. Yearlong program: $30,120; includes tuition, insurance, excursions, student support services, University of Paris student card, library passes, Pompidou Center pass. $35 application fee. $250 nonrefundable deposit required. Financial aid available for all students: scholarships, loans.

For More Information • Ms. Prema Samuel, Director of International Programs, Sarah Lawrence College, 1 Meadway, Bronxville, NY 10708-5999; *Phone:* 800-873-4752; *Fax:* 914-395-2666. *E-mail:* slcaway@slc.edu. *World Wide Web:* http://www.sarahlawrence.edu/studyabroad/

MORE ABOUT THE PROGRAM
Sarah Lawrence College in Paris offers total immersion in the city's academic and cultural life through individually designed programs and enrollment in the leading French institutions of higher learning. The program gives American students access to courses usually open only to French students.

Most students enroll in classes at the University of Paris IV (Sorbonne), VII (Jussieu), and X (Nanterre); the Institut Catholique; the École du Louvre; or the Institut d'Études Politiques. They may also elect to study the visual and performing arts in artists' ateliers and in specialized schools of the arts.

The program is open to qualified students who have completed intermediate college French. All courses—seminars and lectures—are supplemented with tutorials in which students have weekly or biweekly meetings with their French professors, a distinguishing feature of the Sarah Lawrence program. Merit grants are available. Sarah Lawrence also sponsors programs at Oxford and in Cuba and Florence as well as a London theater program.

SCHILLER INTERNATIONAL UNIVERSITY
STUDY ABROAD, UNDERGRADUATE AND GRADUATE PROGRAMS

Hosted by Schiller International University

Academic Focus • French language and literature, interdisciplinary studies, international affairs, international business, marketing, physical sciences, political science and government.

Program Information • Students attend classes at Schiller International University. Scheduled travel to Ibiza, Barcelona, the Alps (ski trips), Russia, Bordeaux, Chartres, Reims; field trips to the waterworks in Paris, art museums, places of historic interest; optional travel to Switzerland, England, Spain, Germany at an extra cost.

Sessions • Fall, spring, yearlong.

Eligibility Requirements • Minimum age 17; open to freshmen, sophomores, juniors, seniors, graduate students; 2.0 GPA; no foreign language proficiency required.

Living Arrangements • Students live in locally rented apartments, host family homes, hotels. Quarters are shared with host institution students, students from other programs. Meals are taken on one's own, with host family, in residences, in restaurants.

Costs (2003-2004) • One term: €7500. Yearlong program: €14,850; includes tuition, lab equipment, student support services, activities fee, liability deposit. €500 nonrefundable deposit required. Financial aid available for all students: scholarships, loans, federal grants, graduate assistantship, Exchange Student Scholarship.

For More Information • Ms. Kamala Dontamsetti, Admissions Office, Florida Campus, Schiller International University, 453 Edgewater Drive, Dunedin, FL 34698; *Phone:* 727-735-5082 Ext. 240; *Fax:* 727-734-0359. *E-mail:* admissions@schiller.edu. *World Wide Web:* http://www.schiller.edu/

SKIDMORE COLLEGE
SKIDMORE IN PARIS

Hosted by Skidmore Program Center, University of Paris

FRANCE
Paris

Academic Focus • Art, art history, business administration/management, dance, drama/theater, economics, English literature, fine/studio arts, French language and literature, French studies, history, marketing, music, political science and government, psychology, sociology.

Program Information • Students attend classes at University of Paris, Skidmore Program Center. Scheduled travel to the Midi, Normandy; field trips to Mont-Saint-Michel, the Loire Valley, Chartres, Giverny; optional travel to the Alps, the Rhone Valley, Côte d'Azur, Morocco at an extra cost.

Sessions • Fall, spring, yearlong.

Eligibility Requirements • Open to juniors; 3.0 GPA; 2 letters of recommendation; good academic standing at home school; 2 years college course work in French or the equivalent.

Living Arrangements • Students live in host family homes. Meals are taken with host family, in residences.

Costs (2003-2004) • One term: contact sponsor for cost. Yearlong program: contact sponsor for cost. $25 application fee. $350 nonrefundable deposit required. Financial aid available for students from sponsoring institution: scholarships, loans.

For More Information • Office of International Programs, Skidmore College, 815 North Broadway, Starbuck Center, Saratoga Springs, NY 12866; *Phone:* 518-580-5555; *Fax:* 518-580-5359. *E-mail:* oip@skidmore.edu. *World Wide Web:* http://www.skidmore.edu/internationalprograms/

SMITH COLLEGE
JUNIOR YEAR IN PARIS

Hosted by Smith College Center, Institute of Political Studies Paris 'SciencesPo', University Paris-Sorbonne (Paris IV)

Academic Focus • Art history, comparative literature, economics, fine/studio arts, French language and literature, French studies, history, music, philosophy, political science and government, psychology, religious studies, visual and performing arts.

Program Information • Students attend classes at Institute of Political Studies Paris 'SciencesPo', University Paris-Sorbonne (Paris IV), Smith College Center. Scheduled travel to Aix-en-Provence; field trips to Arles/Avignon, Côte d'Azur, Normandy, the Loire Valley, Burgundy, Chartres.

Sessions • Yearlong.

Eligibility Requirements • Open to juniors, seniors; 3.0 GPA; 3 letters of recommendation; good academic standing at home school; fluency in French.

Living Arrangements • Students live in host family homes. Quarters are shared with host institution students. Meals are taken with host family, in residences.

Costs (2004-2005) • Yearlong program: $39,814; includes tuition, housing, all meals, insurance, excursions, student support services, museum tickets for art history classes. $35 application fee. $300 refundable deposit required. Financial aid available for students from sponsoring institution: scholarships, loans.

For More Information • Office for International Study, Smith College, College Hall 24, Northampton, MA 01063; *Phone:* 413-585-4905; *Fax:* 413-585-4906. *E-mail:* studyabroad@smith.edu. *World Wide Web:* http://www.smith.edu/studyabroad/

SOUTHERN METHODIST UNIVERSITY
SMU IN PARIS

Held at Reid Hall

Academic Focus • Art history, business administration/management, communications, comparative literature, fine/studio arts, French language and literature, history, music history, political science and government.

Program Information • Classes are held on the campus of Reid Hall. Faculty members are local instructors hired by the sponsor. Scheduled travel to Normandy, southern France, Brittany; field trips.

Sessions • Fall, spring, yearlong.

Eligibility Requirements • Open to sophomores, juniors, seniors; 2.7 GPA; 2 letters of recommendation; good academic standing at home school; essay; personal interview; no foreign language proficiency required.

Living Arrangements • Students live in host family homes. Quarters are shared with host institution students. Meals are taken on one's own, with host family, in residences.

Costs (2002-2003) • One term: $15,744. Yearlong program: $29,488; includes tuition, housing, some meals, excursions, student support services, fees, lodging and meals on excursions. $40 application fee. $500 nonrefundable deposit required. Financial aid available for students from sponsoring institution: scholarships, work study, loans.

For More Information • Ms. Karen Westergaard, Associate Director, Southern Methodist University, International Office, PO Box 750391, Dallas, TX 75275-0391; *Phone:* 214-768-2338; *Fax:* 214-768-1051. *E-mail:* intlpro@mail.smu.edu. *World Wide Web:* http://www.smu.edu/studyabroad/

STATE UNIVERSITY OF NEW YORK AT OSWEGO
MICEFA

Hosted by University of Paris

Academic Focus • Full curriculum.

Program Information • Students attend classes at University of Paris.

Sessions • Fall, spring, yearlong.

Eligibility Requirements • Open to sophomores, juniors, seniors, graduate students; 2.5 GPA; 3 letters of recommendation; good academic standing at home school; language proficiency form; personal study statement; 2 years of college course work in French.

Living Arrangements • Students live in host institution dormitories, locally rented apartments. Quarters are shared with host institution students, students from other programs. Meals are taken on one's own, in central dining facility, in restaurants.

Costs (2003-2004) • One term: $2320. Yearlong program: $4640; includes tuition, insurance, student support services. $250 nonrefundable deposit required. Financial aid available for students: home university financial aid, loan processing and scholarships for Oswego students.

For More Information • Mr. Joshua McKeown, Associate Director, State University of New York at Oswego, 122A Swetman Hall, Oswego, NY 13126; *Phone:* 888-4-OSWEGO; *Fax:* 315-312-2477. *E-mail:* intled@oswego.edu. *World Wide Web:* http://www.oswego.edu/intled/

STATE UNIVERSITY OF NEW YORK AT OSWEGO
SUNY AT THE SORBONNE

Hosted by University Paris-Sorbonne (Paris IV)

Academic Focus • Art, art history, drama/theater, European studies, French language and literature, French studies, history, international business, music.

Program Information • Students attend classes at University Paris-Sorbonne (Paris IV). Field trips to Normandy, the Loire Valley, site visits in Paris.

Sessions • Fall, spring, yearlong.

Eligibility Requirements • Open to sophomores, juniors, seniors; 2.5 GPA; 3 letters of recommendation; good academic standing at home school; language proficiency form; personal study statement; 1 year of college course work in French.

Living Arrangements • Students live in host institution dormitories, locally rented apartments, host family homes, foyers. Quarters are shared with host institution students, students from other programs. Meals are taken on one's own, with host family, in residences, in central dining facility, in restaurants.

Costs (2003-2004) • One term: $4820. Yearlong program: $9640; includes tuition, insurance, excursions, student support services. $250 nonrefundable deposit required. Financial aid available for students: home university financial aid, loan processing and scholarships for Oswego students.

For More Information • Mr. Joshua McKeown, Associate Director, State University of New York at Oswego, 122A Swetman Hall, Oswego, NY 13126; *Phone:* 888-4-OSWEGO; *Fax:* 315-312-2477. *E-mail:* intled@oswego.edu. *World Wide Web:* http://www.oswego.edu/intled/. Students may also apply through State University of New York at Binghamton, Office of International Programs, PO Box 6000, Binghamton, NY 13902-6000.

STATE UNIVERSITY OF NEW YORK COLLEGE AT BROCKPORT
PARIS PROGRAM

Held at Reid Hall

Academic Focus • Art history, European studies, French language and literature, French studies, history, international affairs, literature, political science and government, sociology.

Program Information • Classes are held on the campus of Reid Hall. Faculty members are local instructors hired by the sponsor. Scheduled travel to Normandy, Montpellier; field trips to the Loire Valley, Brittany; optional travel to Chamonix ski resort at an extra cost.

Sessions • Fall, spring, yearlong.

Eligibility Requirements • Minimum age 18; open to sophomores, juniors, seniors; 2.5 GPA; 2 letters of recommendation; must be at least a second semester sophomore; basic knowledge of French recommended.

Living Arrangements • Students live in locally rented apartments, host family homes. Meals are taken on one's own, with host family, in residences.

Costs (2004-2005) • One term: $11,850 for fall; $12,850 for spring. Yearlong program: contact sponsor for cost; includes tuition, housing, some meals, excursions, international student ID, student support services. $350 nonrefundable deposit required. Financial aid available for all students: scholarships, loans, regular financial aid, grants.

For More Information • Dr. John Perry, Director, Office of International Education, State University of New York College at Brockport, 350 New Campus Drive, Brockport, NY 14420; *Phone:* 800-298-SUNY; *Fax:* 585-637-3218. *E-mail:* overseas@brockport.edu. *World Wide Web:* http://www.brockport.edu/studyabroad/

STONY BROOK UNIVERSITY
STONY BROOK ABROAD: PARIS

Hosted by University Denis Diderot (Paris VII), University Paris-Sorbonne (Paris IV), University of Paris X Nanterre

Academic Focus • Area studies, art history, comparative literature, drama/theater, economics, French language and literature, history, linguistics, music theory, philosophy, political science and government.

Program Information • Students attend classes at University Denis Diderot (Paris VII), University Paris-Sorbonne (Paris IV), University of Paris X Nanterre. Field trips to châteaux of the Loire, Burgundy, Strasbourg, Normandy; optional travel to England, Italy, Spain, Portugal, north Africa at an extra cost.

Sessions • Spring, yearlong.

Eligibility Requirements • Open to sophomores, juniors, seniors, graduate students, adults; 2.75 GPA; 3 letters of recommendation; personal statement of purpose; 2 years of college course work in French.

Living Arrangements • Students live in host institution dormitories, locally rented apartments, host family homes. Quarters are shared with host institution students, students from other programs. Meals are taken on one's own, with host family, in residences, in central dining facility, in restaurants.

Costs (2002-2003) • One term: $7500. Yearlong program: $13,000; includes housing, all meals, insurance, excursions, international airfare, books and class materials, cultural events and activities, tutorials for academic assistance, in-state tuition. $200 nonrefundable deposit required. Financial aid available for students from sponsoring institution: scholarships, loans.

For More Information • Ms. Gretchen Gosnell, Study Abroad Advisor, Stony Brook University, Study Abroad Office, Melville Library, Room E5340, Stony Brook, NY 11794-3397; *Phone:*

631-632-7030; *Fax:* 631-632-6544. *E-mail:* studyabroad@sunysb.edu. *World Wide Web:* http://www.sunysb.edu/studyabroad/

SWEET BRIAR COLLEGE
JUNIOR YEAR IN FRANCE

Hosted by University of Paris Dauphine (Paris IX), Catholic University of Paris, University Denis Diderot (Paris VII), University Paris-Sorbonne (Paris IV), University of the New Sorbonne Paris III

Academic Focus • Art history, business administration/management, economics, European studies, fine/studio arts, French language and literature, history, international affairs, literature, performing arts, philosophy, political science and government, psychology, science.

Program Information • Students attend classes at University of Paris Dauphine (Paris IX), Catholic University of Paris, University Denis Diderot (Paris VII), University Paris-Sorbonne (Paris IV), University of the New Sorbonne Paris III. Field trips to the Loire Valley, Mont-Saint-Michel, Giverny, Vaux-le-Vicomte, Burgundy; optional travel to Europe, Egypt, Morocco at an extra cost.

Sessions • Fall, spring, yearlong.

Eligibility Requirements • Open to juniors; 3.0 GPA; 1 letter of recommendation; good academic standing at home school; 2 years of college course work in French.

Living Arrangements • Students live in host institution dormitories, locally rented apartments, host family homes. Meals are taken with host family, in residences.

Costs (2004-2005) • One term: $15,500. Yearlong program: $26,250; includes tuition, housing, some meals, insurance, excursions, international airfare, student support services, baggage handling, theatre and museum costs related to courses. $50 application fee. $500 nonrefundable deposit required. Financial aid available for all students: scholarships, loans.

For More Information • Dr. Margaret Scouten, Director, Junior Year in France, Sweet Briar College, Sweet Briar, VA 24595; *Phone:* 434-381-6109; *Fax:* 434-381-6283. *E-mail:* jyf@sbc.edu

TUFTS UNIVERSITY
TUFTS IN PARIS

Hosted by Goethe-Institut, Centro Linguistico Italiano Dante Alighieri, University Paris-Sorbonne (Paris IV), Catholic University of Paris, Ecole du Louvre, Institute of Political Studies Paris 'SciencesPo', University New Sorbonne Paris III

Academic Focus • Art, art history, drama/theater, economics, education, English literature, French language and literature, German language and literature, history, international affairs, Italian language and literature, music, political science and government, psychology, sociology, Spanish language and literature.

Program Information • Students attend classes at University Paris-Sorbonne (Paris IV), Catholic University of Paris, Ecole du Louvre, Institute of Political Studies Paris 'SciencesPo', University New Sorbonne Paris III, Centro Linguistico Italiano Dante Alighieri, Goethe-Institut. Scheduled travel to Talloires; field trips to Mont-Saint-Michel, the Loire Valley.

Sessions • Spring, yearlong.

Eligibility Requirements • Open to sophomores, juniors, seniors; 3.0 GPA; 2 letters of recommendation; good academic standing at home school; 3 years of college course work in French.

Living Arrangements • Students live in host family homes. Meals are taken with host family, in residences.

Costs (2004-2005) • One term: $19,657. Yearlong program: $39,314; includes tuition, housing, all meals, excursions, student support services, reimbursement for cultural activities and public transportation. $40 application fee. $350 nonrefundable deposit required. Financial aid available for students from sponsoring institution: scholarships, work study, loans.

For More Information • Ms. Melanie Armstrong, Program and Marketing Coordinator, Tufts Programs Abroad, Tufts University, Dowling Hall, Medford, MA 02155-7084; *Phone:* 617-627-2000; *Fax:* 617-627-3971. *E-mail:* melanie.armstrong@tufts.edu. *World Wide Web:* http://ase.tufts.edu/studyabroad/

UNIVERSITY OF CONNECTICUT
STUDY ABROAD PROGRAM IN PARIS

Hosted by University of Paris Valde Marne Paris XII, University of Paris X Nanterre, University of Vincennes at Saint Denis Paris VIII, University of the New Sorbonne Paris III, University Paris-Sorbonne (Paris IV)

Academic Focus • Civilization studies, French language and literature, history, social sciences.

Program Information • Students attend classes at University of Paris Valde Marne Paris XII, University of Paris X Nanterre, University of Vincennes at Saint Denis Paris VIII, University of the New Sorbonne Paris III, University Paris-Sorbonne (Paris IV). Scheduled travel to the Loire Valley, southern France; field trips to Mont-Saint-Michel, Normandy; optional travel to Morocco, Senegal, London, Italy at an extra cost.

Sessions • Fall, spring, yearlong.

Eligibility Requirements • Open to sophomores, juniors, seniors; 2.5 GPA; 2 letters of recommendation; 2 years of college course work in French.

Living Arrangements • Students live in host institution dormitories, locally rented apartments. Quarters are shared with host institution students. Meals are taken on one's own, in residences.

Costs (2003-2004) • One term: $8999 for fall term, $9950 for spring for Connecticut residents; $10,315 for fall term, $11,065 for spring for nonresidents. Yearlong program: $18,950 for Connecticut residents; $21,555 for nonresidents; includes tuition, housing, some meals, insurance, excursions, international student ID, one-way airfare. $25 application fee. $350 nonrefundable deposit required. Financial aid available for students from sponsoring institution: scholarships, loans.

For More Information • Ms. Eliane Dalmoulin, Professor, University of Connecticut, Department of Modern and Classical Languages, 337 Mansfield Road, Unit 57, Storrs, CT 06269-1057; *Phone:* 860-486-3313; *Fax:* 860-486-4392. *E-mail:* eliane.dalmoulin@uconn.edu. *World Wide Web:* http://studyabroad.uconn.edu/

UNIVERSITY OF DELAWARE
FALL SEMESTER IN PARIS, FRANCE

Held at Reid Hall

Academic Focus • Art history, French language and literature, French studies, history, political science and government.

Program Information • Classes are held on the campus of Reid Hall. Faculty members are local instructors hired by the sponsor. Scheduled travel to Normandy, Brittany; field trips to Versailles, the Loire Valley; optional travel to Europe at an extra cost.

Sessions • Fall.

Eligibility Requirements • Open to freshmen, sophomores, juniors, seniors, adults; 2.8 GPA; 2 letters of recommendation; 2 courses beyond intermediate French.

Living Arrangements • Students live in host family homes. Meals are taken on one's own, with host family, in residences, in restaurants.

Costs (2003) • One term: contact sponsor for cost. $200 nonrefundable deposit required. Financial aid available for all students: scholarships.

For More Information • Center for International Studies, University of Delaware, 186 South College Avenue, Newark, DE 19716-1450; *Phone:* 888-831-4685; *Fax:* 302-831-6042. *E-mail:* studyabroad@udel.edu. *World Wide Web:* http://www.udel.edu/studyabroad/

UNIVERSITY OF DELAWARE
SPRING SEMESTER IN PARIS

Held at Reid Hall

Academic Focus • Art history, French language and literature, French studies, history, political science and government.

Program Information • Classes are held on the campus of Reid Hall. Faculty members are local instructors hired by the sponsor. Field trips to Musée d'Orsay, the Louvre, museums; optional travel to Europe at an extra cost.

Sessions • Spring.

Eligibility Requirements • Open to freshmen, sophomores, juniors, seniors, adults; 2.0 GPA; 2 letters of recommendation; no foreign language proficiency required.

Living Arrangements • Students live in host family homes. Meals are taken on one's own, with host family, in residences.

Costs (2003) • One term: contact sponsor for cost. $200 nonrefundable deposit required. Financial aid available for all students: scholarships.

For More Information • Center for International Studies, University of Delaware, 186 South College Avenue, Newark, DE 19716-1450; *Phone:* 888-831-4685; *Fax:* 302-831-6042. *E-mail:* studyabroad@udel. edu. *World Wide Web:* http://www.udel.edu/studyabroad/

UNIVERSITY OF NORTH CAROLINA AT WILMINGTON
NORTH CAROLINA SEMESTER IN PARIS

Hosted by University Paris-Sorbonne (Paris IV)

Academic Focus • Art history, film and media studies, French language and literature, political science and government.

Program Information • Students attend classes at University Paris-Sorbonne (Paris IV). Field trips to the Loire Valley, Fontainebleau, Versailles, attractions in and around Paris; optional travel to other European sites at an extra cost.

Sessions • Fall, spring, yearlong.

Eligibility Requirements • Minimum age 19; open to sophomores, juniors, seniors, graduate students, adults; 2.75 GPA; 2 letters of recommendation; good academic standing at home school; 1.5 years of college course work in French.

Living Arrangements • Students live in host family homes. Meals are taken with host family, in residences.

Costs (2002-2003) • One term: $7900. Yearlong program: $15,800; includes tuition, housing, some meals, insurance, excursions, international student ID, student support services. $200 nonrefundable deposit required. Financial aid available for students from sponsoring institution: scholarships, loans.

For More Information • Mr. James McNab, Assistant Provost for International Programs, University of North Carolina at Wilmington, 601 South College Road, Wilmington, NC 28403; *Phone:* 910-962-3685; *Fax:* 910-962-4053. *E-mail:* mcnabj@uncw.edu. *World Wide Web:* http://www.uncw.edu/intprogs/

UNIVERSITY OF ROCHESTER
INTERNSHIPS IN EUROPE–FRANCE

Held at Le Forum

Academic Focus • Art history, business administration/management, film and media studies, political science and government, social sciences, urban/regional planning.

Program Information • Classes are held on the campus of Le Forum. Faculty members are local instructors hired by the sponsor.

Sessions • Fall.

Eligibility Requirements • Open to juniors, seniors; 3.0 GPA; 2 letters of recommendation; good academic standing at home school; 2 years of college course work in French.

Living Arrangements • Students live in host family homes. Meals are taken with host family, in residences.

Costs (2003) • One term: $9350; includes tuition, housing, some meals, student support services. $30 application fee. $300 nonrefundable deposit required. Financial aid available for students from sponsoring institution: scholarships, loans.

For More Information • Ms. Jacqueline Levine, Study Abroad Director, University of Rochester, Center for Study Abroad, PO Box 270376, Lattimore 206, Rochester, NY 14627-0376; *Phone:* 585-275-7532; *Fax:* 585-461-5131. *E-mail:* abroad@mail.rochester.edu. *World Wide Web:* http://www.rochester.edu/college/study-abroad/

UNIVERSITY OF SOUTHERN MISSISSIPPI
UNIVERSITY OF SOUTHERN MISSISSIPPI–ECOLE SUPÉRIEURE DU COMMERCE EXTÉRIEUR EXCHANGE

Hosted by Ecole Supérieure du Commerce Extérieur

Academic Focus • Business administration/management, French language and literature, international affairs, marketing.

Program Information • Students attend classes at Ecole Supérieure du Commerce Extérieur.

Sessions • Spring, yearlong.

Eligibility Requirements • Minimum age 18; open to seniors; 2.0 GPA; 2 letters of recommendation; good academic standing at home school; interviews; 2.5 years of college course work in French.

Living Arrangements • Students live in program-owned apartments. Quarters are shared with host institution students, students

from other programs. Meals are taken on one's own, in residences, in central dining facility, in restaurants.

Costs (2003-2004) • One term: $2100 for Mississippi residents; $4358 for nonresidents. Yearlong program: $3950 for Mississippi residents; $8466 for nonresidents; includes tuition, student support services. $250 nonrefundable deposit required. Financial aid available for students from sponsoring institution: scholarships, loans.

For More Information • Ms. Holly Buckner, International Programs Coordinator, University of Southern Mississippi, Box 10047, Hattiesburg, MS 39406-0047; *Phone:* 601-266-5624; *Fax:* 601-266-5699. *E-mail:* holly.buckner@usm.edu. *World Wide Web:* http://www.cice.usm.edu/

VASSAR COLLEGE AND WESLEYAN UNIVERSITY
VASSAR–WESLEYAN PROGRAM IN PARIS

Hosted by Institute of Political Studies Paris 'SciencesPo', University Paris-Sorbonne (Paris IV), University of Paris Valde Marne Paris XII, University Denis Diderot (Paris VII)

Academic Focus • Art history, biological/life sciences, drama/theater, film and media studies, French language and literature, French studies, history, political science and government, psychology, sociology.

Program Information • Students attend classes at Institute of Political Studies Paris 'SciencesPo', University Paris-Sorbonne (Paris IV), University of Paris Valde Marne Paris XII, University Denis Diderot (Paris VII). Classes are also held on the campus of Reid Hall. Scheduled travel to Alsace, the Loire Valley, Burgundy, Mont-Saint-Michel; field trips to Chartres, Giverny, Rouen, Vaux-le-Vicomte.

Sessions • Fall, spring, yearlong.

Eligibility Requirements • Open to sophomores, juniors, seniors; 3.0 GPA; 1 letter of recommendation; good academic standing at home school; B average in French; 2.5 years college course work in French or the equivalent.

Living Arrangements • Students live in host family homes. Quarters are shared with host institution students. Meals are taken on one's own, with host family, in residences.

Costs (2002-2003) • One term: $19,150. Yearlong program: $38,300; includes tuition, housing, all meals, excursions, international airfare, books and class materials, student support services, program fee, spending money. $25 application fee. $200 nonrefundable deposit required. Financial aid available for students from sponsoring institution: scholarships, loans.

For More Information • Ms. Gail Winter, Assistant Director, Vassar College and Wesleyan University, Office of International Studies, Wesleyan University, Middletown, CT 06459-0400; *Phone:* 860-685-2550; *Fax:* 860-685-2551. *E-mail:* gwinter@wesleyan.edu. *World Wide Web:* http://www.wesleyan.edu/ois/

WELLS COLLEGE
PROGRAM FOR THE ARTS IN PARIS

Hosted by PERL, University of Paris X Nanterre

Academic Focus • Art history, ceramics and pottery, comparative literature, dance, drama/theater, fine/studio arts, French language and literature, French studies, history, music, performing arts, photography.

Program Information • Students attend classes at University of Paris X Nanterre, PERL. Field trips to the Loire Valley, Chartres, Vézelay, Rouen, Normandy, Giverny.

Sessions • Fall, spring, yearlong.

Eligibility Requirements • Minimum age 18; open to precollege students, freshmen, sophomores, juniors, seniors, graduate students, adults; course work in art, art history; 2.5 GPA; 2 letters of recommendation; good academic standing at home school; transcript; previous study in French recommended.

Living Arrangements • Students live in host institution dormitories, host family homes. Quarters are shared with students from other programs. Meals are taken as a group, on one's own, with host family, in residences, in central dining facility.

Costs (2004-2005) • One term: $11,300. Yearlong program: $22,000; includes tuition, housing, some meals, excursions, international airfare, international student ID, student support services, transportation in Paris, museum pass, some books and class materials, programmed cultural events, limited insurance coverage.

$55 application fee. $750 refundable deposit required. Financial aid available for students from sponsoring institution: scholarships, loans.

For More Information • Dr. Lydie J. Haenlin, Program Director, Wells College, Cleveland Hall, Aurora, NY 13026; *Phone:* 315-364-3308; *Fax:* 315-364-3257. *E-mail:* paris@wells.edu. *World Wide Web:* http://www.wells.edu/academic/ac2d.htm

PAU

UNIVERSITY STUDIES ABROAD CONSORTIUM

FRENCH STUDIES: PAU, FRANCE

Hosted by University of Pau

Academic Focus • Art history, culinary arts, cultural studies, French language and literature, French studies, history, political science and government, sociology.

Program Information • Students attend classes at University of Pau. Field trips to Toulouse, Carcassonne, Bordeaux, Basque country, the Pyrenees Mountains, St. Bertrand de Comminges; optional travel to Paris at an extra cost.

Sessions • Fall, spring, yearlong.

Eligibility Requirements • Minimum age 18; open to freshmen, sophomores, juniors, seniors, graduate students, adults; 2.5 GPA; no foreign language proficiency required.

Living Arrangements • Students live in host institution dormitories, host family homes. Quarters are shared with host institution students. Meals are taken on one's own, with host family, in residences, in central dining facility.

Costs (2005-2006) • One term: $4980. Yearlong program: $9680; includes tuition, some meals, insurance, excursions, student support services. $50 application fee. $150 refundable deposit required. Financial aid available for all students: scholarships, loans.

For More Information • University Studies Abroad Consortium, USAC/323, Reno, NV 89557-0093; *Phone:* 775-784-6569; *Fax:* 775-784-6010. *E-mail:* usac@unr.edu. *World Wide Web:* http://usac.unr.edu/

POITIERS

MIDDLEBURY COLLEGE SCHOOLS ABROAD

SCHOOL IN FRANCE–POITIERS

Hosted by University of Poitiers

Academic Focus • Full curriculum.

Program Information • Students attend classes at University of Poitiers.

Sessions • Fall, spring, yearlong.

Eligibility Requirements • Open to sophomores, juniors, seniors; 2.7 GPA; 2 letters of recommendation; B average in both French and major; 2.5 years college course work in French, including at least 1 content course.

Living Arrangements • Students live in locally rented apartments, host family homes. Meals are taken on one's own, with host family, in residences.

Costs (2004-2005) • One term: $7200. Yearlong program: $14,400; includes tuition, student support services. $50 application fee. $300 nonrefundable deposit required. Financial aid available for students from sponsoring institution: scholarships, loans.

For More Information • Mr. Jamie Northrup, University Relations Coordinator, Middlebury College Schools Abroad, Office of Off-Campus Study, Sunderland Language Center, Middlebury, VT 05753; *Phone:* 802-443-5745; *Fax:* 802-443-3157. *E-mail:* schoolsabroad@middlebury.edu. *World Wide Web:* http://www.middlebury.edu/msa/

RENNES

BELOIT COLLEGE
FRANCE PROGRAM

Hosted by University of Rennes II–Haute-Bretangne

Academic Focus • European studies, French language and literature, history, international affairs.

Program Information • Students attend classes at University of Rennes II–Haute-Bretangne. Scheduled travel to castles of the Loire Valley, Paris, Geneva, Strasbourg; field trips to museums, architectural sites; optional travel to other parts of France, Europe at an extra cost.

Sessions • Spring.

Eligibility Requirements • Open to sophomores, juniors, seniors; 2.5 GPA; 4 letters of recommendation; 2 or more related courses in economics, history, art history, or political science strongly recommended; 3 years of college course work in French.

Living Arrangements • Students live in host family homes. Meals are taken on one's own, with host family, in residences, in central dining facility.

Costs (2003) • One term: $14,232; includes tuition, housing, all meals, excursions. $100 nonrefundable deposit required. Financial aid available for all students: loans.

For More Information • Office of International Education, Beloit College, 700 College Street, Beloit, WI 53511; *Phone:* 608-363-2269; *Fax:* 608-363-2689. *E-mail:* oie@beloit.edu. *World Wide Web:* http://www.beloit.edu/~oie/

CIEE
CIEE STUDY CENTER AT THE UNIVERSITY OF HAUTE-BRETAGNE, RENNES, FRANCE

Hosted by University of Rennes II–Haute-Bretangne

Academic Focus • Art history, economics, French language and literature, French studies, history, literature, political science and government, teaching English as a second language.

Program Information • Students attend classes at University of Rennes II–Haute-Bretangne. Field trips to Saint Malo, Carnac, Normandy, including Mont-Saint-Michel, the Loire Valley.

Sessions • Fall, spring, yearlong.

Eligibility Requirements • Open to sophomores, juniors, seniors, graduate students, adults; 2 letters of recommendation; minimum 2.75 GPA overall; minimum 3.0 GPA in French; 2 years of college course work in French.

Living Arrangements • Students live in host institution dormitories, host family homes. Quarters are shared with host institution students. Meals are taken on one's own, with host family, in residences, in central dining facility.

Costs (2003-2004) • One term: $9450. Yearlong program: $15,250; includes tuition, housing, all meals, insurance, excursions, student support services. $30 application fee. $300 deposit required. Financial aid available for all students: minority student scholarships, travel grants.

For More Information • Ms. Hannah McChesney, Admissions Officer, Europe, Middle East, and Africa, CIEE, 7 Custom House Street, 3rd Floor, Portland, ME 04101; *Phone:* 800-40-STUDY; *Fax:* 207-553-7699. *E-mail:* studyinfo@ciee.org. *World Wide Web:* http://www.ciee.org/isp/

ROUEN

ST. LAWRENCE UNIVERSITY
FRANCE PROGRAM

Held at University of Rouen–Haute Normandie

Academic Focus • African studies, art history, economics, French language and literature, French studies, political science and government, sociology.

Program Information • Classes are held on the campus of University of Rouen–Haute Normandie. Faculty members are drawn from the sponsor's U.S. staff and local instructors hired by the sponsor. Scheduled travel to Québec, Canada, Mont-Saint-Michel, southern France, Paris, Senegal (spring only); field trips to Versailles, Chartres, Étretat, Vaux-le-Vicomte.

Sessions • Fall, spring, yearlong.

Eligibility Requirements • Open to freshmen, sophomores, juniors, seniors; 2.8 GPA; 3 letters of recommendation; 3 years college course work in French for fall and year-long sessions; 1 semester college course work in French for spring.

Living Arrangements • Students live in host family homes. Meals are taken with host family.

Costs (2003-2004) • One term: $17,870. Yearlong program: $35,740; includes tuition, housing, some meals, excursions, books and class materials. $500 nonrefundable deposit required. Financial aid available for students from sponsoring institution: scholarships, loans.

For More Information • Ms. Sara Hofschulte, Assistant Director, Off-Campus Programs, St. Lawrence University, Center for International and Intercultural Studies, Canton, NY 13617; *Phone:* 315-229-5991; *Fax:* 315-229-5989. *E-mail:* shofschulte@stlawu.edu. *World Wide Web:* http://www.stlawu.edu/ciis/offcampus/

STRASBOURG

BRETHREN COLLEGES ABROAD
BCA PROGRAM IN STRASBOURG, FRANCE

Hosted by University of Strasbourg

Academic Focus • Full curriculum.

Program Information • Students attend classes at University of Strasbourg. Scheduled travel to Paris; field trips to Nancy, Colmar, Vosges.

Sessions • Fall, spring, yearlong.

Eligibility Requirements • Minimum age 18; open to sophomores, juniors, seniors, graduate students, adults; 2.6 GPA; 3 letters of recommendation; good academic standing at home school; 2 years of college course work in French.

Living Arrangements • Students live in host institution dormitories, locally rented apartments, host family homes. Quarters are shared with host institution students, students from other programs. Meals are taken on one's own, with host family, in residences, in restaurants.

Costs (2003-2004) • One term: $11,500. Yearlong program: $19,900; includes tuition, housing, all meals, insurance, excursions, international student ID, student support services. $50 application fee. $100 nonrefundable deposit required.

For More Information • Mr. Jason Sanderson, Program Officer for France, Brethren Colleges Abroad, 50 Alpha Drive, Elizabethtown, PA 17022; *Phone:* 866-222-6188; *Fax:* 717-361-6619. *E-mail:* info@bcanet.org. *World Wide Web:* http://www.bcanet.org/

SAINT JOSEPH'S UNIVERSITY
SPRING SEMESTER IN STRASBOURG

Held at University of Strasbourg

Academic Focus • Economics, French language and literature, French studies, religious studies.

Program Information • Classes are held on the campus of University of Strasbourg. Faculty members are drawn from the sponsor's U.S. staff and local instructors hired by the sponsor. Scheduled travel.

Sessions • Spring.

Eligibility Requirements • Minimum age 18; open to sophomores, juniors, seniors; 3.0 GPA; 2 letters of recommendation; 2 years of college course work in French.

Living Arrangements • Students live in host institution dormitories, host family homes. Quarters are shared with host institution students. Meals are taken on one's own, with host family, in central dining facility, in restaurants.

Costs (2004) • One term: contact sponsor for cost. $150 nonrefundable deposit required. Financial aid available for students from sponsoring institution: scholarships, loans.

For More Information • Ms. Susan Plummer, Assistant Director, Saint Joseph's University, 5600 City Avenue, Philadelphia, PA 19131; *Phone:* 610-660-1835; *Fax:* 610-660-1697. *E-mail:* cip@sju.edu. *World Wide Web:* http://www.sju.edu/cip/

SYRACUSE UNIVERSITY
EUROPEAN PROGRAM IN STRASBOURG

Hosted by Marc Bloch University (Strasboug II), Syracuse University–Strasbourg, Robert Schuman University Strasbourg

FRANCE
Strasbourg

Academic Focus • Economics, fine/studio arts, French language and literature, German language and literature, history, international affairs, music, political science and government.

Program Information • Students attend classes at Marc Bloch University (Strasboug II), Syracuse University–Strasbourg, Robert Schuman University Strasbourg. Scheduled travel to Brussels, Prague, Venice, Vienna; field trips to Alsace, Heidelberg, Paris, Geneva, Amsterdam; optional travel to Paris, Geneva, Amsterdam at an extra cost.

Sessions • Fall, spring, yearlong.

Eligibility Requirements • Open to freshmen, sophomores, juniors, seniors; 2 letters of recommendation; good academic standing at home school; essays; no foreign language proficiency required.

Living Arrangements • Students live in host family homes. Meals are taken with host family, in residences.

Costs (2004-2005) • One term: $19,430. Yearlong program: $38,860; includes tuition, housing, some meals, excursions, lab equipment, international student ID, student support services, traveling seminar and one-way airfare. $50 application fee. $450 nonrefundable deposit required. Financial aid available for all students: scholarships, work study, loans, tuition differential grants.

For More Information • Mr. James Buschman, Senior Associate Director, Syracuse University, 106 Walnut Place, Syracuse, NY 13244-4170; *Phone:* 800-235-3472; *Fax:* 315-443-4593. *E-mail:* suabroad@syr.edu. *World Wide Web:* http://suabroad.syr.edu/

Program Information • Students attend classes at Syracuse University–Strasbourg, Robert Schuman University Strasbourg. Scheduled travel to Vienna, Prague, Budapest, Dresden; field trips to Alsace, Heidelberg, Paris; optional travel to Brussels, Geneva at an extra cost.

Sessions • Fall, spring, yearlong.

Eligibility Requirements • Open to sophomores, juniors, seniors; 2 letters of recommendation; good academic standing at home school; essays; home school approval; no foreign language proficiency required.

Living Arrangements • Students live in host family homes. Meals are taken with host family, in residences.

Costs (2004-2005) • One term: $19,430. Yearlong program: $38,860; includes tuition, housing, some meals, excursions, books and class materials, international student ID, student support services, traveling seminar and one-way international airfare. $50 application fee. $450 nonrefundable deposit required. Financial aid available for all students: scholarships, work study, loans, tuition differential grants.

For More Information • Mr. James Buschman, Senior Associate Director, Syracuse University, 106 Walnut Place, Syracuse, NY 13244-4170; *Phone:* 315-443-3471; *Fax:* 315-443-4593. *E-mail:* suabroad@syr.edu. *World Wide Web:* http://suabroad.syr.edu/

SYRACUSE UNIVERSITY
INTERNATIONAL RELATIONS PROGRAM IN STRASBOURG

Hosted by Syracuse University–Strasbourg, Robert Schuman University Strasbourg

Academic Focus • Economics, French language and literature, German language and literature, history, political science and government.

UNIVERSITY OF IDAHO
FRENCH STUDIES PROGRAM

Hosted by Institut International d'Etudes Francaises IIEF

Academic Focus • French language and literature.

Program Information • Students attend classes at Institut International d'Etudes Francaises IIEF. Field trips to local attractions.

Sessions • Fall, spring, yearlong.

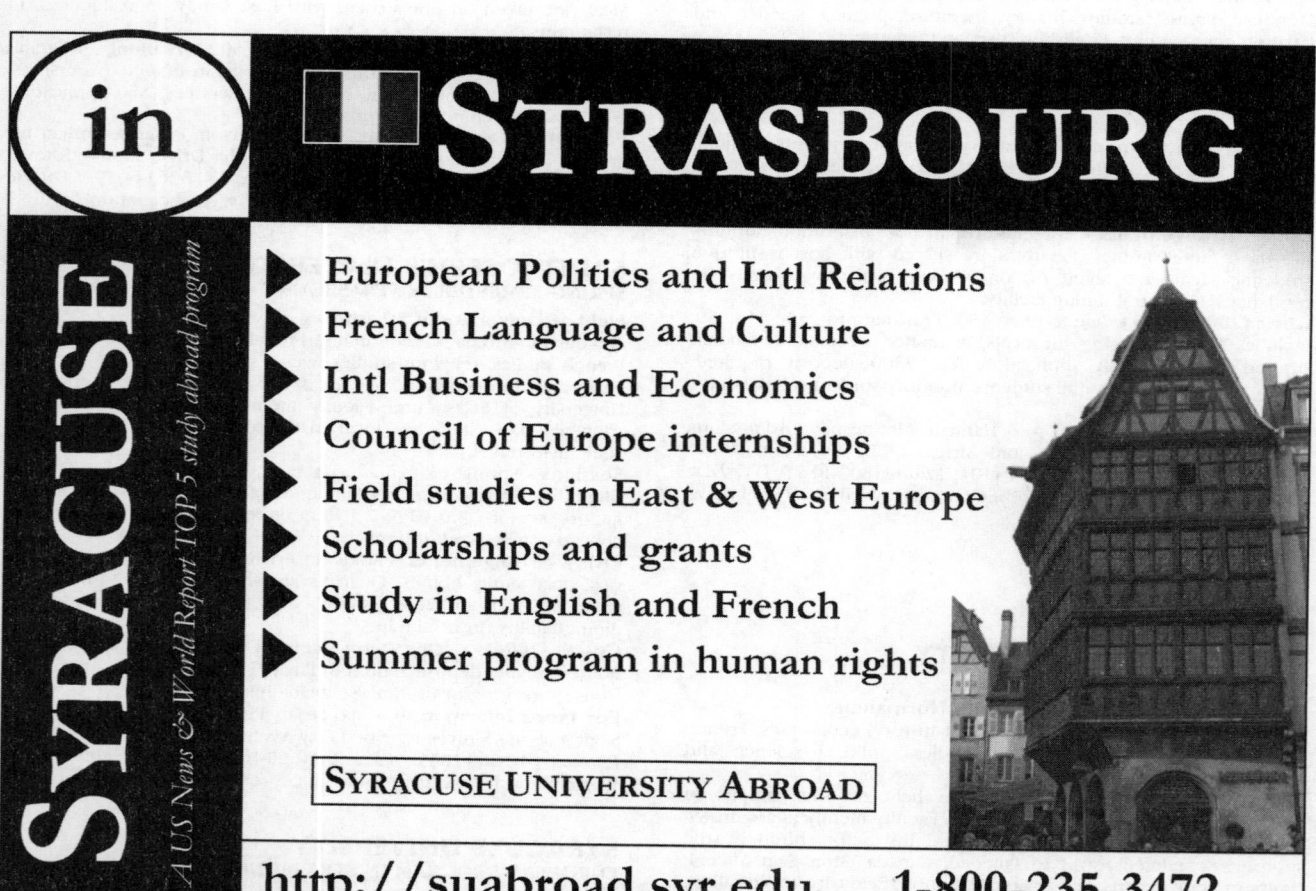

Eligibility Requirements • Open to freshmen, sophomores, juniors, seniors, graduate students, adults; good academic standing at home school; no foreign language proficiency required.
Living Arrangements • Students live in locally rented apartments, program-owned apartments. Quarters are shared with host institution students, students from other programs. Meals are taken on one's own, in residences.
Costs (2003-2004) • One term: $2500. Yearlong program: $5000; includes tuition, student support services. $100 application fee. $200 refundable deposit required. Financial aid available for students from sponsoring institution: scholarships, loans.
For More Information • Ms. Amy S. Bergmann, Advisor, University of Idaho, Room 209, Morrill Hall, Moscow, ID 83844-3013; *Phone:* 208-885-7870; *Fax:* 208-885-2859. *E-mail:* abroad@uidaho.edu. *World Wide Web:* http://www.ets.uidaho.edu/ipo/abroad/

TOULOUSE

DICKINSON COLLEGE
DICKINSON STUDY CENTER IN TOULOUSE (FRANCE)

Hosted by Dickinson Study Center, University of Social Sciences Toulouse I, University of Toulouse–Le Mirail Toulouse
Academic Focus • Art history, French studies, international affairs, liberal studies, political science and government.
Program Information • Students attend classes at Dickinson Study Center, University of Social Sciences Toulouse I, University of Toulouse–Le Mirail Toulouse. Scheduled travel to Paris; field trips to Albi, Carcassonne; optional travel to Provence, the Loire Valley.
Sessions • Fall, spring, yearlong.
Eligibility Requirements • Minimum age 18; open to juniors; course work in French literature; 2.8 GPA; 3 letters of recommendation; good academic standing at home school; 3 years of college course work in French.
Living Arrangements • Students live in host family homes. Meals are taken on one's own, with host family, in residences, in central dining facility.
Costs (2003-2004) • One term: $17,795. Yearlong program: $35,590; includes tuition, housing, all meals, excursions. $25 application fee. $300 nonrefundable deposit required. Financial aid available for students from sponsoring institution: scholarships, work study, loans.
For More Information • Ms. Karen Peter, Program Manager, Dickinson College, PO Box 1773, Carlisle, PA 17013-2896; *Phone:* 717-245-1341; *Fax:* 717-245-1688. *E-mail:* global@dickinson.edu. *World Wide Web:* http://www.dickinson.edu/global/

ST. CLOUD STATE UNIVERSITY
FRENCH LANGUAGE AND CULTURE

Held at University of Social Sciences Toulouse I
Academic Focus • French language and literature, French studies.
Program Information • Classes are held on the campus of University of Social Sciences Toulouse I. Faculty members are drawn from the sponsor's U.S. staff and local instructors hired by the sponsor. Field trips to local cultural centers; optional travel to Paris, southern France at an extra cost.
Sessions • Spring.
Eligibility Requirements • Minimum age 18; open to freshmen, sophomores, juniors, seniors; major in French; 3.0 GPA; 2 letters of recommendation; fluency in French.
Living Arrangements • Students live in host institution dormitories, host family homes. Quarters are shared with students from other programs. Meals are taken on one's own, with host family, in central dining facility, in restaurants.
Costs (2004) • One term: $7750 for Minnesota residents ($8750 for homestay with meals); includes tuition, housing, excursions, international airfare, international student ID. $75 application fee. Financial aid available for students from sponsoring institution: scholarships, work study, loans.
For More Information • Chunsheng Zhang, Associate Vice President for Academic Affairs/International Studies, St. Cloud State University, Center for International Studies, 720 4th Avenue, South, St. Cloud, MN 56301-4498; *Phone:* 320-308-4287; *Fax:* 320-308-4223. *E-mail:* intstudy@stcloudstate.edu. *World Wide Web:* http://www.stcloudstate.edu/

SCHOOL FOR INTERNATIONAL TRAINING, SIT STUDY ABROAD
FRANCE: CULTURE AND SOCIETY

Academic Focus • Economics, French language and literature, French studies, geography, history, political science and government, visual and performing arts.
Program Information • Faculty members are drawn from the sponsor's U.S. staff and local instructors hired by the sponsor. Scheduled travel to Paris, St. Martin de Canigou, the Pyrenees Mountains; field trips to the countryside, monasteries, Roman ruins, prehistoric caves.
Sessions • Fall, spring.
Eligibility Requirements • Open to sophomores, juniors, seniors; 2.5 GPA; 2 letters of recommendation; good academic standing at home school; 2 years of college course work in French.
Living Arrangements • Students live in host family homes, hotels. Meals are taken as a group, on one's own, with host family, in residences, in restaurants.
Costs (2003-2004) • One term: $12,700; includes tuition, housing, all meals, insurance, excursions. $50 application fee. $400 nonrefundable deposit required. Financial aid available for all students: scholarships.
For More Information • School for International Training, SIT Study Abroad, Kipling Road, Brattleboro, VT 05302-0676; *Phone:* 888-272-7881; *Fax:* 802-258-3296. *E-mail:* studyabroad@sit.edu. *World Wide Web:* http://www.sit.edu/studyabroad/

SCHOOL FOR INTERNATIONAL TRAINING, SIT STUDY ABROAD
FRANCE: INTENSIVE LANGUAGE AND CULTURE

Academic Focus • Economics, French language and literature, French studies, geography, history, political science and government, visual and performing arts.
Program Information • Faculty members are drawn from the sponsor's U.S. staff and local instructors hired by the sponsor. Scheduled travel to Paris, Provence, Ariege region; field trips to village sites, Roman ruins, Augustins Art Museum, prehistoric caves.
Sessions • Fall, spring.
Eligibility Requirements • Open to sophomores, juniors, seniors; 2.5 GPA; 2 letters of recommendation; good academic standing at home school; no foreign language proficiency required.
Living Arrangements • Students live in host family homes, hotels. Meals are taken as a group, on one's own, with host family, in residences, in restaurants.
Costs (2003-2004) • One term: $12,700; includes tuition, housing, all meals, insurance, excursions, international student ID. $50 application fee. $400 nonrefundable deposit required. Financial aid available for all students: scholarships.
For More Information • School for International Training, SIT Study Abroad, Kipling Road, Brattleboro, VT 05302-0676; *Phone:* 888-272-7881; *Fax:* 802-258-3296. *E-mail:* studyabroad@sit.edu. *World Wide Web:* http://www.sit.edu/studyabroad/

TOURS

BOWLING GREEN STATE UNIVERSITY
ACADEMIC YEAR/SEMESTER IN FRANCE

Hosted by Institut d'Etudes Françaises de Touraine, Alliance Française
Academic Focus • French language and literature.
Program Information • Students attend classes at Institut d'Etudes Françaises de Touraine, Alliance Française. Scheduled travel to Dordogne, Normandie, Mont-Saint-Michel, La Rochelle, Strasbourg; field trips to various châteaux of the Loire, Chartres.
Sessions • Fall, spring, yearlong, option without Paris.
Eligibility Requirements • Minimum age 17; open to precollege students, freshmen, sophomores, juniors, seniors; 2.5 GPA; 1 letter of recommendation; good academic standing at home school; essay; no foreign language proficiency required.
Living Arrangements • Students live in host family homes. Meals are taken with host family.
Costs (2004-2005) • One term: $8404 for Ohio residents; $12,058 for nonresidents. Yearlong program: $15,848 for Ohio residents; $23,156 for nonresidents; includes tuition, housing, all meals,

excursions, books and class materials, student support services, local transportation, airport pick-up, 2-week optional Paris module. $25 application fee. Financial aid available for students from sponsoring institution: scholarships, loans, travel grants from Center for International Programs.

For More Information • Ms. Heather Gabel, Director, AYA France/Burkina Faso, Bowling Green State University, Department of Romance Languages, Bowling Green, OH 43403; *Phone:* 419-372-7146; *Fax:* 419-372-7332. *E-mail:* ayafran@bgnet.bgsu.edu. *World Wide Web:* http://www.bgsu.edu/

DAVIDSON COLLEGE
DAVIDSON IN TOURS, FRANCE

Hosted by Alliance Française, Institut de Touraine, University of Tours
Academic Focus • Art history, French language and literature, liberal studies, social sciences.
Program Information • Students attend classes at Alliance Française, Institut de Touraine, University of Tours. Scheduled travel to southern France; field trips to Loire Valley castles, Brittany, Normandy.
Sessions • Fall, spring, yearlong.
Eligibility Requirements • Open to sophomores, juniors; 2.75 GPA; 2 letters of recommendation; good academic standing at home school; 2 years college course work in French or the equivalent.
Living Arrangements • Students live in host family homes. Quarters are shared with students from other programs. Meals are taken with host family, in residences.
Costs (2003-2004) • One term: $16,650. Yearlong program: $33,300; includes tuition, housing, all meals, excursions, international airfare, international student ID, student support services, September intensive language course in Paris (including room and board), cultural activities. $500 nonrefundable deposit required. Financial aid available for students from sponsoring institution: scholarships, work study, loans.
For More Information • Ms. Carolyn Ortmayer, Study Abroad Coordinator, Davidson College, Box 7155, Davidson, NC 28035-7155; *Phone:* 704-894-2250; *Fax:* 704-894-2120. *E-mail:* abroad@davidson.edu. *World Wide Web:* http://www.davidson.edu/international/

FRENCH-AMERICAN EXCHANGE
TRIMESTER/ACADEMIC YEAR ABROAD IN TOURS

Hosted by Institut d'Etudes Françaises de Touraine
Academic Focus • Art history, civilization studies, European studies, French language and literature, French studies, linguistics, political science and government, translation.
Program Information • Students attend classes at Institut d'Etudes Françaises de Touraine. Field trips to the Loire River Valley, châteaux and vineyards; optional travel to Europe, Paris at an extra cost.
Sessions • Fall, spring, winter, yearlong.
Eligibility Requirements • Minimum age 19; open to sophomores, juniors, seniors, graduate students, adults; 2.5 GPA; 1 letter of recommendation; good academic standing at home school; essay; 1 year college course work in French (high school French is an added plus).
Living Arrangements • Students live in locally rented apartments, host family homes. Meals are taken on one's own, with host family, in residences, in central dining facility, in restaurants.
Costs (2003-2004) • One term: $5810. Yearlong program: $17,430; includes tuition, housing, all meals, books and class materials, lab equipment, student support services. $50 application fee. $500 refundable deposit required.
For More Information • Mr. James Pondolfino, Executive Director, French-American Exchange, 3213 Duke Street, #620, Alexandria, VA 22314; *Phone:* 800-995-5087; *Fax:* 703-823-4447. *E-mail:* info@frenchamericanexchange.com. *World Wide Web:* http://www.frenchamericanexchange.com/

RUTGERS, THE STATE UNIVERSITY OF NEW JERSEY
STUDY ABROAD IN FRANCE

Hosted by University François Rabelais of Tours
Academic Focus • Full curriculum.
Program Information • Students attend classes at University François Rabelais of Tours. Scheduled travel to Dordogne, Chartres; field trips to châteaux, national museums; optional travel to Mont-Saint-Michel, film festivals at an extra cost.
Sessions • Spring, yearlong.
Eligibility Requirements • Open to sophomores, juniors, seniors; 2.5 GPA; 2 letters of recommendation; 2 years of college course work in French.
Living Arrangements • Students live in host institution dormitories, locally rented apartments. Quarters are shared with host institution students. Meals are taken on one's own, in residences, in central dining facility.
Costs (2003-2004) • One term: $9488 for New Jersey residents; $12,138 for nonresidents. Yearlong program: $17,240 for New Jersey residents; $22,540 for nonresidents; includes tuition, housing, insurance, excursions, student support services. $20 application fee. $750 nonrefundable deposit required. Financial aid available for students from sponsoring institution: scholarships, loans.
For More Information • Ms. Karin Bonello, Regional Coordinator, Rutgers, The State University of New Jersey, 102 College Avenue, New Brunswick, NJ 08901-8543; *Phone:* 732-932-7787; *Fax:* 732-932-8659. *E-mail:* ru_abroad@email.rutgers.edu. *World Wide Web:* http://studyabroad.rutgers.edu/

STATE UNIVERSITY OF NEW YORK COLLEGE AT BROCKPORT
FRENCH LANGUAGE IMMERSION PROGRAM

Hosted by Institut d'Etudes Françaises de Touraine
Academic Focus • Art history, cultural studies, French language and literature, French studies, history, international affairs, linguistics, literature, political science and government.
Program Information • Students attend classes at Institut d'Etudes Françaises de Touraine. Field trips to Azay le Rideau, Paris, Normandy, Versailles.
Sessions • Fall, spring, winter, yearlong.
Eligibility Requirements • Minimum age 18; open to juniors, seniors; 2.5 GPA; 2 letters of recommendation; ability to do upper-division course work; 1 year college course work in French or the equivalent.
Living Arrangements • Students live in host family homes. Meals are taken with host family, in residences.
Costs (2004-2005) • One term: $8750. Yearlong program: contact sponsor for cost; includes tuition, housing, some meals, excursions, international student ID, student support services. $350 nonrefundable deposit required. Financial aid available for all students: scholarships, loans, regular financial aid, grants.
For More Information • Dr. John Perry, Director, Office of International Education, State University of New York College at Brockport, 350 New Campus Drive, Brockport, NY 14420; *Phone:* 800-298-SUNY; *Fax:* 585-637-3218. *E-mail:* overseas@brockport.edu. *World Wide Web:* http://www.brockport.edu/studyabroad/

GEORGIA
TBILISI
ACIE (ACTR/ACCELS)
ACIE–NIS REGIONAL LANGUAGE TRAINING PROGRAM–GEORGIA

Hosted by Tbilisi State University
Academic Focus • Cultural studies, language studies, Russian language and literature.
Program Information • Students attend classes at Tbilisi State University.
Sessions • Fall, spring, yearlong.

Eligibility Requirements • Minimum age 18; open to sophomores, juniors, seniors, graduate students, adults; 3 letters of recommendation; good academic standing at home school; 1 year of college course work in Russian or Georgian.

Living Arrangements • Students live in host institution dormitories, host family homes. Quarters are shared with students from other programs. Meals are taken on one's own, with host family, in residences, in restaurants.

Costs (2002-2003) • One term: contact sponsor for cost. Yearlong program: contact sponsor for cost. $35 application fee. $500 nonrefundable deposit required. Financial aid available for all students: scholarships.

For More Information • Ms. Margaret Stephenson, Russian and Eurasian Program Officer, ACIE (ACTR/ACCELS), 1776 Massachusetts Avenue, NW, Suite 700, Washington, DC 20036; *Phone:* 202-833-7522; *Fax:* 202-833-7523. *E-mail:* outbound@actr.org. *World Wide Web:* http://www.actr.org/

GERMANY

CITY TO CITY

NORTHERN ILLINOIS UNIVERSITY
ACADEMIC INTERNSHIPS IN BONN/COLOGNE, GERMANY

Academic Focus • Social services.

Program Information • Faculty members are local instructors hired by the sponsor. Optional travel at an extra cost.

Sessions • Fall, spring.

Eligibility Requirements • Open to juniors, seniors; 3.0 GPA; 2 letters of recommendation; good academic standing at home school; application essay; résumé; 3 years of college course work in German.

Living Arrangements • Students live in host family homes. Quarters are shared with students from other programs. Meals are taken on one's own, with host family, in residences.

Costs (2003-2004) • One term: $8325; includes tuition, housing, some meals, insurance, international student ID, internship placement. $45 application fee. $800 refundable deposit required. Financial aid available for all students: regular financial aid.

For More Information • Ms. Clare Foust, Program Assistant, Northern Illinois University, Study Abroad Office, Williston Hall 417, DeKalb, IL 60115-2854; *Phone:* 815-753-0420; *Fax:* 815-753-0825. *E-mail:* niuabroad@niu.edu. *World Wide Web:* http://www.niu.edu/niuabroad/

UNIVERSITY OF CONNECTICUT
BADEN-WÜRTTEMBERG EXCHANGE PROGRAM

Hosted by University of Ulm, University of Karlsruhe, University of Mannheim, University of Stuttgart, University of Konstanz, University of Tübingen, Universität Freiburg, University of Hohenheim, Universität Heidelberg

Academic Focus • Business administration/management, computer science, economics, German language and literature, liberal studies, mathematics, philosophy, science, social sciences.

Program Information • Students attend classes at University of Ulm (Ulm), University of Karlsruhe (Karlsruhe), University of Mannheim (Mannheim), University of Stuttgart (Stuttgart), University of Konstanz (Konstanz), University of Tübingen (Tübingen), Universität Freiburg (Freiburg), University of Hohenheim (Hohenheim), Universität Heidelberg (Heidelberg).

Sessions • Fall, spring, yearlong.

Eligibility Requirements • Open to juniors, seniors; 2.7 GPA; 2 letters of recommendation; good academic standing at home school; 2 years of college course work in German.

Living Arrangements • Students live in host institution dormitories, locally rented apartments. Quarters are shared with host institution students, students from other programs. Meals are taken on one's own, in residences, in restaurants.

Costs (2003-2004) • One term: $2368 for Connecticut residents; $3683 for nonresidents. Yearlong program: $4385 for Connecticut residents; $7015 for nonresidents; includes tuition, insurance,

international student ID, fees. $25 application fee. $350 nonrefundable deposit required. Financial aid available for all students: scholarships, loans, stipends.

For More Information • Mr. Gordon Lustila, Acting Director of Study Abroad Programs, University of Connecticut, 843 Bolton Road, Unit 1207, Storrs, CT 06269-1207; *Phone:* 860-486-5022; *Fax:* 860-486-2976. *E-mail:* sabadm03@uconnvm.uconn.edu. *World Wide Web:* http://studyabroad.uconn.edu/

UNIVERSITY OF ROCHESTER
INTERNSHIPS IN EUROPE–GERMANY

Academic Focus • Advertising and public relations, art administration, business administration/management, computer science, drama/theater, history, journalism, law and legal studies, political science and government, psychology, social sciences.

Program Information • Faculty members are local instructors hired by the sponsor. Scheduled travel to Berlin; field trips to Cologne, Bonn (introductory tour), Berlin; optional travel to Heidelberg, Koblenz, Limburg an der Lahn at an extra cost.

Sessions • Fall, spring.

Eligibility Requirements • Open to juniors, seniors; 3.0 GPA; 2 letters of recommendation; good academic standing at home school; 2 years of college course work in German.

Living Arrangements • Students live in locally rented apartments, host family homes. Meals are taken on one's own, with host family, in residences, in restaurants.

Costs (2003) • One term: $9700; includes tuition, housing, some meals, student support services. $30 application fee. $300 nonrefundable deposit required. Financial aid available for students from sponsoring institution: scholarships, loans.

For More Information • Ms. Jacqueline Levine, Study Abroad Director, University of Rochester, Center for Study Abroad, PO Box 270376, Lattimore 206, Rochester, NY 14627-0376; *Phone:* 585-275-7532; *Fax:* 585-461-5131. *E-mail:* abroad@mail.rochester.edu. *World Wide Web:* http://www.rochester.edu/college/study-abroad/

BAYREUTH

UNIVERSITY OF DELAWARE
SPRING SEMESTER IN BAYREUTH, GERMANY

Hosted by University of Bayreuth

Academic Focus • Art history, German language and literature, German studies, history, political science and government.

Program Information • Students attend classes at University of Bayreuth. Scheduled travel to Berlin, Rhineland, Vienna; field trips to Nuremberg, Bamberg; optional travel to Europe at an extra cost.

Sessions • Spring.

Eligibility Requirements • Open to freshmen, sophomores, juniors, seniors, adults; 2.8 GPA; 2 letters of recommendation; 2 college courses beyond intermediate German.

Living Arrangements • Students live in host institution dormitories. Quarters are shared with host institution students. Meals are taken on one's own, in residences, in central dining facility, in restaurants.

Costs (2003) • One term: contact sponsor for cost. $200 nonrefundable deposit required. Financial aid available for all students: scholarships.

For More Information • Center for International Studies, University of Delaware, 186 South College Avenue, Newark, DE 19716-1450; *Phone:* 888-831-4685; *Fax:* 302-831-6042. *E-mail:* studyabroad@udel.edu. *World Wide Web:* http://www.udel.edu/studyabroad/

BERLIN

AMERICAN UNIVERSITY
SEMESTER IN BERLIN

Hosted by Free University of Berlin

Academic Focus • German language and literature, history, international affairs, political science and government.

Program Information • Students attend classes at Free University of Berlin. Scheduled travel to Bonn, Prague, Vienna; field trips to Frankfurt, Potsdam, Quedlinburg, Auschwitz-Birkeneau, Buchenwald.

Sessions • Fall.

GERMANY
Berlin

Eligibility Requirements • Open to sophomores, juniors, seniors, graduate students; 2.75 GPA; 1 letter of recommendation; second semester sophomore status; recommendation of advisor; no foreign language proficiency required.

Living Arrangements • Students live in host institution dormitories, locally rented apartments, host family homes. Quarters are shared with host institution students, students from other programs. Meals are taken as a group, on one's own, with host family, in residences, in central dining facility, in restaurants.

Costs (2002) • One term: $16,309–$16,534; includes tuition, housing, some meals, excursions, books and class materials, international student ID, student support services. $35 application fee. $300 nonrefundable deposit required. Financial aid available for all students: scholarships, loans.

For More Information • Dr. David C. Brown, Dean, Washington Semester and World Capitals Programs, American University, Tenley Campus–Constitution Building, Washington, DC 20016-8083; *Phone:* 800-424-2600; *Fax:* 202-895-4960. *E-mail:* travel@american.edu. *World Wide Web:* http://www.worldcapitals.american.edu/

BROWN UNIVERSITY
BROWN IN GERMANY

Hosted by Humboldt University of Berlin
Academic Focus • Full curriculum.
Program Information • Students attend classes at Humboldt University of Berlin. Field trips to sites around Berlin.
Sessions • Spring, yearlong.
Eligibility Requirements • Open to sophomores, juniors, seniors; 3.0 GPA; 2 letters of recommendation; good academic standing at home school; 2.5 years of college course work in German.
Living Arrangements • Students live in host institution dormitories, locally rented apartments. Quarters are shared with host institution students. Meals are taken on one's own, in residences.
Costs (2004-2005) • One term: $15,336. Yearlong program: $30,672; includes tuition, housing, insurance, international student ID, registration fees, 1-month language and orientation program. $250 nonrefundable deposit required. Financial aid available for students from sponsoring institution: scholarships, loans.
For More Information • Ms. Mell Bolen, Director, Brown University, Office of International Programs, Box 1973, Providence, RI 02912-1973; *Phone:* 401-863-3555; *Fax:* 401-863-3311. *E-mail:* oip_office@brown.edu. *World Wide Web:* http://www.brown.edu/OIP/

COLUMBIA UNIVERSITY
BERLIN CONSORTIUM FOR GERMAN STUDIES

Hosted by Free University of Berlin
Academic Focus • Full curriculum, German language and literature, German studies.
Program Information • Students attend classes at Free University of Berlin. Scheduled travel to Cologne; field trips to Weimar, Bonn; optional travel to sites around Germany.
Sessions • Fall, spring, yearlong.
Eligibility Requirements • Open to sophomores, juniors, seniors; 3.0 GPA; 2 letters of recommendation; good academic standing at home school; B average in German; 2 years of college course work in German.
Living Arrangements • Students live in host institution dormitories, locally rented apartments, host family homes, university-owned apartments. Quarters are shared with host institution students. Meals are taken on one's own, with host family, in residences, in central dining facility, in restaurants.
Costs (2003-2004) • One term: $12,800. Yearlong program: $25,600; includes tuition, housing, excursions, student support services, computer laboratory, e-mail access. $35 application fee. $500 nonrefundable deposit required.
For More Information • Information Center, 203 Lewisohn, Columbia University, 2970 Broadway, MC 4110, New York, NY 10027-6902; *Phone:* 212-854-9699; *Fax:* 212-854-5841. *E-mail:* berlin@columbia.edu. *World Wide Web:* http://www.ce.columbia.edu/op/

DUKE UNIVERSITY
DUKE IN BERLIN

Hosted by Technical University of Berlin, Free University of Berlin
Academic Focus • Economics, environmental science/studies, German language and literature, history, literature, political science and government.
Program Information • Students attend classes at Technical University of Berlin, Free University of Berlin. Classes are also held on the campus of Humboldt University of Berlin. Scheduled travel to Dresden, Jena, Prague, Thuringia, Brussels; optional travel to other areas of Europe at an extra cost.
Sessions • Fall, spring, yearlong.
Eligibility Requirements • Minimum age 19; open to sophomores, juniors, seniors; 3.0 GPA; no foreign language proficiency required.
Living Arrangements • Students live in host family homes. Meals are taken on one's own, with host family, in residences, in central dining facility.
Costs (2003-2004) • One term: $15,500. Yearlong program: $31,000; includes tuition, housing, some meals, insurance, excursions, books and class materials, international student ID, student support services. $2000 nonrefundable deposit required. Financial aid available for students from sponsoring institution: scholarships, loans, institutional grants.
For More Information • Mr. Stephen Lemoine, Associate Director, Duke University, Office of Study Abroad, 2016 Campus Drive, Box 90057, Durham, NC 27708-0057; *Phone:* 919-684-2174; *Fax:* 919-684-3083. *E-mail:* slemoine@asdean.duke.edu. *World Wide Web:* http://www.aas.duke.edu/study_abroad/

IES, INSTITUTE FOR THE INTERNATIONAL EDUCATION OF STUDENTS
IES–BERLIN

Hosted by Institute for the International Education of Students (IES)–Berlin, Humboldt University of Berlin
Academic Focus • Full curriculum.
Program Information • Students attend classes at Humboldt University of Berlin, Institute for the International Education of Students (IES)–Berlin. Field trips to Dresden, Hamburg, Gorlitz; optional travel to Eastern European capitals, the Baltic Hanse cities at an extra cost.
Sessions • Fall, spring, yearlong.
Eligibility Requirements • Minimum age 18; open to sophomores, juniors, seniors; 3.0 GPA; 1 letter of recommendation; good academic standing at home school; 2 years of college course work in German.
Living Arrangements • Students live in locally rented apartments, host family homes. Meals are taken on one's own, in residences, in central dining facility.
Costs (2003-2004) • One term: $10,400. Yearlong program: $18,720; includes tuition, housing, excursions, student support services, resident permit, partial insurance coverage. $50 application fee. $500 nonrefundable deposit required. Financial aid available for all students: scholarships, institutional partner need-based grants.
For More Information • International Education Representative, IES, Institute for the International Education of Students, 33 North LaSalle Street, 15th Floor, Chicago, IL 60602; *Phone:* 800-995-2300; *Fax:* 312-944-1448. *E-mail:* info@iesabroad.org. *World Wide Web:* http://www.IESabroad.org/

LEXIA INTERNATIONAL
LEXIA IN BERLIN

Hosted by Die Neue Schule
Academic Focus • Anthropology, area studies, art, art history, civilization studies, comparative history, cultural studies, drawing/painting, Eastern European studies, economics, environmental science/studies, ethnic studies, film and media studies, fine/studio arts, geography, German language and literature, German studies, history, interdisciplinary studies, international affairs, international business, liberal studies, literature, music, music history, music performance, peace and conflict studies, philosophy, political science and government, psychology, religious studies, social sciences, sociology, urban studies, visual and performing arts.
Program Information • Students attend classes at Die Neue Schule. Field trips to Potsdam, Weimar, Poland, Dresden.

Sessions • Fall, spring, yearlong.
Eligibility Requirements • Minimum age 18; open to sophomores, juniors, seniors, graduate students, adults; 2.5 GPA; 2 letters of recommendation; no foreign language proficiency required.
Living Arrangements • Students live in locally rented apartments, host family homes. Quarters are shared with host institution students. Meals are taken on one's own, with host family, in residences, in restaurants.
Costs (2003-2004) • One term: $11,950. Yearlong program: $21,550; includes tuition, housing, insurance, excursions, international student ID, student support services, transcript. $35 application fee. $300 refundable deposit required. Financial aid available for all students: scholarships, work study.
For More Information • Lexia International, 23 South Main Street, Hanover, NH 03755; *Phone:* 800-775-3942; *Fax:* 603-643-9899. *E-mail:* info@lexiaintl.org. *World Wide Web:* http://www.lexiaintl.org/

LOYOLA UNIVERSITY NEW ORLEANS
LOYOLA IN BERLIN

Held at Free University of Berlin
Academic Focus • German language and literature, German studies, history, international affairs, psychology.
Program Information • Classes are held on the campus of Free University of Berlin. Faculty members are local instructors hired by the sponsor. Scheduled travel to Krakow, Auschwitz, Prague, Vienna; field trips to Munich, Dresden, Weimar, Buchenwald.
Sessions • Fall.
Eligibility Requirements • Minimum age 18; open to freshmen, sophomores, juniors, seniors; 2.0 GPA; good academic standing at home school; no foreign language proficiency required.
Living Arrangements • Students live in locally rented apartments, host family homes. Meals are taken on one's own, with host family, in residences.
Costs (2002) • One term: $12,850; includes tuition, housing, some meals, excursions, books and class materials, student support services, cultural events. $100 application fee. Financial aid available for students from sponsoring institution: scholarships, loans.
For More Information • Mr. Robert Dewell, Professor of German, Loyola University New Orleans, 6363 Saint Charles Avenue, New Orleans, LA 70118; *Phone:* 504-865-2689; *Fax:* 504-865-2348. *E-mail:* dewell@loyno.edu. *World Wide Web:* http://www.loyno.edu/cie/

MIDDLEBURY COLLEGE SCHOOLS ABROAD
SCHOOL IN GERMANY–BERLIN PROGRAM

Hosted by Free University of Berlin
Academic Focus • Full curriculum.
Program Information • Students attend classes at Free University of Berlin.
Sessions • Fall, spring, yearlong.
Eligibility Requirements • Open to juniors, seniors; 2.7 GPA; 2 letters of recommendation; B average in both German and major; 3 years college course work in German, including at least 2 content courses at the 300-level.
Living Arrangements • Students live in host institution dormitories, locally rented apartments. Quarters are shared with host institution students. Meals are taken on one's own, in residences, in central dining facility.
Costs (2004-2005) • One term: $7200. Yearlong program: $14,400; includes tuition, student support services. $50 application fee. $300 nonrefundable deposit required. Financial aid available for students from sponsoring institution: scholarships, loans.
For More Information • Mr. Jamie Northrup, University Relations Coordinator, Middlebury College Schools Abroad, Office of Off-Campus Study, Sunderland Language Center, Middlebury, VT 05753; *Phone:* 802-443-5745; *Fax:* 802-443-3157. *E-mail:* schoolsabroad@middlebury.edu. *World Wide Web:* http://www.middlebury.edu/msa/

SCHOOL FOR INTERNATIONAL TRAINING, SIT STUDY ABROAD
CENTRAL EUROPE: NATIONALISM, ETHNICITY, AND CULTURE

Academic Focus • Anthropology, Central European studies, ethnic studies, European studies, German language and literature, German studies, history, international affairs, peace and conflict studies, political science and government, refugee studies, social sciences.
Program Information • Faculty members are drawn from the sponsor's U.S. staff and local instructors hired by the sponsor. Scheduled travel to Krakow/Auschwitz, Vienna, Belgrade and/or other parts of former Yugoslavia; field trips to the old Jewish quarter, Buchenwald concentration camp, museums.
Sessions • Fall, spring.
Eligibility Requirements • Open to sophomores, juniors, seniors; 2.5 GPA; 2 letters of recommendation; good academic standing at home school; no foreign language proficiency required.
Living Arrangements • Students live in host family homes, hotels. Meals are taken as a group, on one's own, with host family, in residences, in restaurants.
Costs (2003-2004) • One term: $13,050; includes tuition, housing, all meals, insurance, excursions, international student ID. $50 application fee. $400 nonrefundable deposit required. Financial aid available for all students: scholarships.
For More Information • School for International Training, SIT Study Abroad, Kipling Road, Brattleboro, VT 05302-0676; *Phone:* 888-272-7881; *Fax:* 802-258-3296. *E-mail:* studyabroad@sit.edu. *World Wide Web:* http://www.sit.edu/studyabroad/

UNIVERSITY OF IDAHO
SEMESTER IN BERLIN

Hosted by Fachhochschule für Technik und Wirtschaft Berlin
Academic Focus • Business administration/management, German studies, information science, marketing, telecommunications.
Program Information • Students attend classes at Fachhochschule für Technik und Wirtschaft Berlin. Optional travel at an extra cost.
Sessions • Fall, spring, yearlong.
Eligibility Requirements • Open to juniors, seniors, graduate students, adults; course work in business or information technology; good academic standing at home school; no foreign language proficiency required.
Living Arrangements • Students live in host institution dormitories, locally rented apartments. Quarters are shared with host institution students, students from other programs. Meals are taken on one's own, in residences, in central dining facility.
Costs (2003-2004) • One term: $2500. Yearlong program: $5000; includes tuition, student support services. $100 application fee. $200 refundable deposit required. Financial aid available for students from sponsoring institution: scholarships, loans.
For More Information • Ms. Amy Bergmann, Advisor, University of Idaho, Room 209, Morrill Hall, Moscow, ID 83844-3013; *Phone:* 208-885-7870; *Fax:* 208-885-2859. *E-mail:* abroad@uidaho.edu. *World Wide Web:* http://www.ets.uidaho.edu/ipo/abroad/

BONN
RIPON COLLEGE
INTERNATIONAL STUDY PROGRAM AT BONN

Hosted by University of Bonn
Academic Focus • Full curriculum.
Program Information • Students attend classes at University of Bonn. Scheduled travel to Berlin; field trips to Cologne, Trier; optional travel to Berlin (week-long trip).
Sessions • Fall, spring, yearlong.
Eligibility Requirements • Minimum age 19; open to sophomores, juniors, seniors; 3.0 GPA; 2 letters of recommendation; 2 years of college course work in German.
Living Arrangements • Students live in host institution dormitories, locally rented apartments. Quarters are shared with host institution students. Meals are taken on one's own, in residences, in central dining facility, in restaurants.
Costs (2003-2004) • One term: $9000. Yearlong program: $17,500; includes tuition, housing, all meals, insurance, excursions, international airfare, books and class materials, lab equipment, theater tickets, local transportation and rail discount card, supplemental allowance. $55 application fee. $500 nonrefundable deposit required. Financial aid available for students from sponsoring institution: scholarships, loans.
For More Information • Ms. Lorna Sopcak, Director, Ripon College, International Study Program, PO Box 248, 300 Seward Street, Ripon, WI 54971-0248; *Phone:* 920-748-8127; *Fax:* 920-748-

7243. *E-mail:* sopcakl@ripon.edu. *World Wide Web:* http://www.ripon.edu/academics/german/bonn/index.html

UNIVERSITY OF SOUTHERN MISSISSIPPI
UNIVERSITY OF BONN EXCHANGE YEAR ABROAD

Hosted by University of Bonn
Academic Focus • Full curriculum.
Program Information • Students attend classes at University of Bonn. Field trips; optional travel at an extra cost.
Sessions • Yearlong.
Eligibility Requirements • Minimum age 18; open to seniors; 2.0 GPA; 2 letters of recommendation; good academic standing at home school; interview; 2 years of college course work in German.
Living Arrangements • Students live in host institution dormitories, locally rented apartments. Quarters are shared with host institution students. Meals are taken on one's own, in residences.
Costs (2003-2004) • Yearlong program: $3950 for Mississippi residents; $8466 for nonresidents; includes tuition, student support services. $250 nonrefundable deposit required. Financial aid available for students from sponsoring institution: scholarships, loans.
For More Information • Ms. Holly Buckner, International Programs Coordinator, University of Southern Mississippi, Box 10047, Hattiesburg, MS 39406-0047; *Phone:* 601-266-5624; *Fax:* 601-266-5699. *E-mail:* holly.buckner@usm.edu. *World Wide Web:* http://www.cice.usm.edu/

BREMEN
DICKINSON COLLEGE
DICKINSON IN BREMEN (GERMANY)

Hosted by University of Bremen
Academic Focus • Full curriculum.
Program Information • Students attend classes at University of Bremen. Scheduled travel to Berlin, the Rhine Valley; field trips to Bremen, Bremerhaven; optional travel to Vienna, Prague at an extra cost.
Sessions • Spring, yearlong.
Eligibility Requirements • Minimum age 18; open to juniors; 2.8 GPA; 3 letters of recommendation; good academic standing at home school; fluency in German.
Living Arrangements • Students live in host institution dormitories, locally rented apartments, host family homes. Quarters are shared with host institution students. Meals are taken on one's own, with host family, in residences, in central dining facility.
Costs (2003-2004) • One term: $17,795. Yearlong program: $35,590; includes tuition, housing, all meals, insurance, excursions. $25 application fee. $300 nonrefundable deposit required. Financial aid available for students from sponsoring institution: scholarships, loans.
For More Information • Ms. Karen Peter, Program Manager, Dickinson College, PO Box 1773, Carlisle, PA 17013-2896; *Phone:* 717-245-1341; *Fax:* 717-245-1688. *E-mail:* global@dickinson.edu. *World Wide Web:* http://www.dickinson.edu/global/

COLOGNE
AHA INTERNATIONAL AN ACADEMIC PROGRAM OF THE UNIVERSITY OF OREGON
PROGRAM IN COLOGNE, GERMANY

Hosted by AHA Cologne, Carl Duisberg Center
Academic Focus • Business administration/management, economics, German language and literature, history, international business.
Program Information • Students attend classes at AHA Cologne, Carl Duisberg Center. Field trips to Brussels, Belgium, Maastricht, the Netherlands.
Sessions • Spring, winter.
Eligibility Requirements • Open to sophomores, juniors, seniors; 2 letters of recommendation; good academic standing at home school; foreign language proficiency requirement varies depending on enrolling university.

Living Arrangements • Students live in host family homes. Quarters are shared with host institution students. Meals are taken with host family.
Costs (2003-2004) • One term: $7985; includes tuition, housing, some meals, insurance, excursions, books and class materials, international student ID, student support services, local transportation pass. $50 application fee. $200 deposit required.
For More Information • Ms. Gail Lavin, Associate Director for University Programs, AHA International An Academic Program of the University of Oregon, 741 SW Lincoln Street, Portland, OR 97201; *Phone:* 503-295-7730; *Fax:* 503-295-5969. *E-mail:* mail@aha-intl.org. *World Wide Web:* http://www.aha-intl.org/

STATE UNIVERSITY OF NEW YORK COLLEGE AT CORTLAND
GERMAN SPORT UNIVERSITY OF COLOGNE–COLOGNE, GERMANY

Hosted by German Sport University of Cologne
Academic Focus • Health and physical education, sports management.
Program Information • Students attend classes at German Sport University of Cologne. Scheduled travel to Berlin; field trips to local and regional institutions and exhibits; optional travel to continental European cities at an extra cost.
Sessions • Spring.
Eligibility Requirements • Minimum age 19; open to sophomores, juniors, seniors; major in physical education, sports management, coaching, rehabilitation; 2.5 GPA; 2 letters of recommendation; good academic standing at home school; 1 year of college course work in German.
Living Arrangements • Students live in host institution dormitories. Quarters are shared with students from other programs. Meals are taken on one's own, in central dining facility.
Costs (2004) • One term: $4800; includes tuition, housing, all meals, insurance, excursions, international airfare, books and class materials, international student ID, student support services, residence permit. $20 application fee. $250 nonrefundable deposit required. Financial aid available for students from sponsoring institution: scholarships, loans.
For More Information • Ms. Liz Kopp, Assistant Director, Office of International Programs, State University of New York College at Cortland, PO Box 2000, Cortland, NY 13045; *Phone:* 607-753-2209; *Fax:* 607-753-5989. *E-mail:* cortlandabroad@cortland.edu. *World Wide Web:* http://www.studyabroad.com/suny/cortland/

DEGGENDORF
FACHHOCHSCHULE DEGGENDORF–UNIVERSITY OF APPLIED SCIENCES
INTERNATIONAL MANAGEMENT

Hosted by Fachhochschule Deggendorf–University of Applied Sciences
Academic Focus • International business.
Program Information • Students attend classes at Fachhochschule Deggendorf-University of Applied Sciences. Field trips to business sites.
Sessions • Spring, winter, yearlong.
Eligibility Requirements • Minimum age 18; open to freshmen, sophomores, juniors; course work in math, computing; basic knowledge of German.
Living Arrangements • Students live in locally rented apartments, host family homes. Quarters are shared with host institution students, students from other programs. Meals are taken on one's own, in central dining facility.
Costs (2003) • One term: contact sponsor for cost. Yearlong program: €5500 for 10 months; includes housing, insurance, books and class materials, lab equipment, student support services.
For More Information • Dr. Elise von Randow, Akademisches Auslandsamt/International Office, Fachhochschule Deggendorf-University of Applied Sciences, Postfach 1320, D-94453 Deggendorf, Germany; *Phone:* +49 99-1-3615-202; *Fax:* +49 99-1-3615-299. *E-mail:* evr@fh-deggendorf.de. *World Wide Web:* http://www.fh-deggendorf.de/

DRESDEN

BOSTON UNIVERSITY
DRESDEN ENGINEERING AND SCIENCE PROGRAM

Hosted by Technical University of Dresden
Academic Focus • Biological/life sciences, engineering, German language and literature, history, physics.
Program Information • Students attend classes at Technical University of Dresden. Scheduled travel to the Czech Republic; field trips to museums, companies, research institutions; optional travel at an extra cost.
Sessions • Fall, spring.
Eligibility Requirements • Open to sophomores; major in engineering; course work in mathematics, physics, engineering; 3.0 GPA; 2 letters of recommendation; good academic standing at home school; essay; approval of participation; transcript; no foreign language proficiency required.
Living Arrangements • Students live in host institution dormitories. Quarters are shared with host institution students. Meals are taken on one's own, in residences, in central dining facility.
Costs (2004-2005) • One term: $19,834; includes tuition, housing, all meals, excursions, international airfare, some books and class materials. $50 application fee. $400 nonrefundable deposit required. Financial aid available for all students: scholarships, loans.
For More Information • Division of International Programs, Boston University, 232 Bay State Road, Boston, MA 02215; *Phone:* 617-353-9888; *Fax:* 617-353-5402. *E-mail:* abroad@bu.edu. *World Wide Web:* http://www.bu.edu/abroad/

BOSTON UNIVERSITY
DRESDEN INTERNSHIP PROGRAM

Hosted by Technical University of Dresden
Academic Focus • Full curriculum.
Program Information • Students attend classes at Technical University of Dresden. Scheduled travel to Moritzburg, Meissen, Fortress of Koeningstein, Prague, Berlin; field trips.
Sessions • Fall, spring, yearlong.
Eligibility Requirements • Open to juniors, seniors; 3.0 GPA; 2 letters of recommendation; good academic standing at home school; advisor approval; transcript; essay; writing sample in German; 2 years of college course work in German.
Living Arrangements • Students live in host institution dormitories. Quarters are shared with host institution students. Meals are taken on one's own, in residences, in central dining facility.
Costs (2004-2005) • One term: $19,834. Yearlong program: contact sponsor for cost; includes tuition, housing, all meals, excursions, international airfare, books and class materials. $50 application fee. $400 deposit required. Financial aid available for all students: scholarships, loans.
For More Information • Division of International Programs, Boston University, 232 Bay State Road, Boston, MA 02215; *Phone:* 617-353-9888; *Fax:* 617-353-5402. *E-mail:* abroad@bu.edu. *World Wide Web:* http://www.bu.edu/abroad/

BOSTON UNIVERSITY
DRESDEN MUSIC STUDIES PROGRAM

Hosted by Hochschule für Musik 'Carl Maria von Weber'
Academic Focus • German language and literature, music, music history, music performance, music theory.
Program Information • Students attend classes at Hochschule für Musik 'Carl Maria von Weber'. Scheduled travel to the Czech Republic; field trips; optional travel at an extra cost.
Sessions • Fall, spring.
Eligibility Requirements • Open to sophomores, juniors, seniors; 3.0 GPA; 2 letters of recommendation; good academic standing at home school; essay; approval of participation; transcript; 2 years of college course work in German.
Living Arrangements • Students live in host institution dormitories. Quarters are shared with host institution students. Meals are taken on one's own, in residences, in central dining facility.
Costs (2004-2005) • One term: $19,834; includes tuition, housing, all meals, excursions, international airfare, books and class materials. $50 application fee. $400 nonrefundable deposit required. Financial aid available for all students: scholarships, loans.
For More Information • Division of International Programs, Boston University, 232 Bay State Road, Boston, MA 02215; *Phone:* 617-353-9888; *Fax:* 617-353-5402. *E-mail:* abroad@bu.edu. *World Wide Web:* http://www.bu.edu/abroad/

BOSTON UNIVERSITY
DRESDEN UNIVERSITY STUDIES PROGRAM

Hosted by Technical University of Dresden
Academic Focus • Full curriculum.
Program Information • Students attend classes at Technical University of Dresden. Scheduled travel to the Czech Republic; field trips; optional travel at an extra cost.
Sessions • Fall, spring, yearlong.
Eligibility Requirements • Open to sophomores, juniors, seniors; 3.0 GPA; 2 letters of recommendation; good academic standing at home school; essay; writing sample in German; approval of participation; transcript; 1 year of college course work in German.
Living Arrangements • Students live in host institution dormitories. Quarters are shared with host institution students. Meals are taken on one's own, in residences, in central dining facility, in restaurants.
Costs (2004-2005) • One term: $19,834. Yearlong program: $39,668; includes tuition, housing, all meals, excursions, international airfare, books and class materials. $50 application fee. $400 nonrefundable deposit required. Financial aid available for all students: scholarships, loans.
For More Information • Division of International Programs, Boston University, 232 Bay State Road, Boston, MA 02215; *Phone:* 617-353-9888; *Fax:* 617-353-5402. *E-mail:* abroad@bu.edu. *World Wide Web:* http://www.bu.edu/abroad/

FLENSBURG

UNIVERSITY OF MIAMI
FLENSBURG UNIVERSITÄT

Hosted by University of Flensburg
Academic Focus • Full curriculum.
Program Information • Students attend classes at University of Flensburg.
Sessions • Fall, spring, yearlong.
Eligibility Requirements • Minimum age 18; open to sophomores, juniors, seniors; 2 letters of recommendation; good academic standing at home school; 3 years course work in German or near-native proficiency.
Living Arrangements • Students live in host institution dormitories. Quarters are shared with host institution students. Meals are taken on one's own, in central dining facility.
Costs (2003-2004) • One term: $12,919. Yearlong program: $25,838; includes tuition, student support services. $40 application fee. $500 nonrefundable deposit required. Financial aid available for students from sponsoring institution: scholarships, loans.
For More Information • Ms. Elyse Resnick, Assistant Director, University of Miami, International Education and Exchange Programs, 5050 Brunson Drive, Allen Hall 212, PO Box 248005, Coral Gables, FL 33124-1610; *Phone:* 305-284-3434; *Fax:* 305-284-4235. *E-mail:* ieep@miami.edu. *World Wide Web:* http://www.studyabroad.miami.edu/

FREIBURG

ACADIA UNIVERSITY, TRENT UNIVERSITY, BROOK UNIVERSITY AND UNIVERSITY OF BRITISH COLUMBIA
CANADIAN YEAR IN FREIBURG

Held at Universität Freiburg
Academic Focus • German language and literature.
Program Information • Classes are held on the campus of Universität Freiburg. Faculty members are drawn from the sponsor's U.S. staff. Field trips.
Sessions • Yearlong.
Eligibility Requirements • Minimum age 18; open to sophomores; 3.0 GPA; good academic standing at home school; 2 years of college course work in German.

GERMANY
Freiburg

Living Arrangements • Students live in host institution dormitories. Meals are taken on one's own.
Costs (2000-2001) • Yearlong program: Can$1100; includes insurance, excursions. Can$350 application fee. Can$300 refundable deposit required. Financial aid available for students from sponsoring institution: scholarships.
For More Information • Prof. Arndt Krüger, Professor, Acadia University, Trent University, Brook University and University of British Columbia, Peterborough, Ontario K9J 7B8, Canada; *Phone:* 705-748-1394; *Fax:* 705-748-1630. *E-mail:* akruger@trentu.ca

IES, INSTITUTE FOR THE INTERNATIONAL EDUCATION OF STUDENTS
IES–FREIBURG, EUROPEAN UNION

Hosted by Institute for the International Education of Students (IES)–Freiburg
Academic Focus • Economics, European studies, German language and literature, international affairs, international business, political science and government.
Program Information • Students attend classes at Institute for the International Education of Students (IES)–Freiburg. Scheduled travel to Strasbourg, Geneva, Paris, Brussels, Frankfurt, Luxembourg, Eastern Europe; field trips to the Black Forest, Alsace, Vosges.
Sessions • Fall, spring.
Eligibility Requirements • Minimum age 18; open to sophomores, juniors, seniors, graduate students, adults; course work in economics/finance; modern European history, international relations; 3.0 GPA; 1 letter of recommendation; good academic standing at home school; no foreign language proficiency required.
Living Arrangements • Students live in host institution dormitories. Quarters are shared with host institution students. Meals are taken on one's own, in residences, in central dining facility, in restaurants.
Costs (2003-2004) • One term: $10,200; includes tuition, housing, excursions, student support services, partial insurance coverage. $50 application fee. $500 nonrefundable deposit required. Financial aid available for all students: scholarships, institutional partner need-based grants.
For More Information • International Education Representative, IES, Institute for the International Education of Students, 33 North LaSalle Street, 15th Floor, Chicago, IL 60602; *Phone:* 800-995-2300; *Fax:* 312-944-1448. *E-mail:* info@iesabroad.org. *World Wide Web:* http://www.IESabroad.org/

IES, INSTITUTE FOR THE INTERNATIONAL EDUCATION OF STUDENTS
IES–FREIBURG, GERMAN PROGRAM

Hosted by University of Education of Frieburg, Institute for the International Education of Students (IES)–Freiburg, Albert Ludwig University of Freiburg im Breisgau
Academic Focus • Full curriculum.
Program Information • Students attend classes at University of Education of Frieburg, Albert Ludwigs University of Freiburg im Breisgau, Institute for the International Education of Students (IES)–Freiburg. Field trips to Alsace, the Vosges region, the Black Forest, Basel; optional travel to Berlin, East Germany, Bonn, Cologne at an extra cost.
Sessions • Fall, spring, yearlong.
Eligibility Requirements • Minimum age 18; open to sophomores, juniors, seniors, graduate students, adults; 3.0 GPA; 1 letter of recommendation; good academic standing at home school; 2 years of college course work in German.
Living Arrangements • Students live in host institution dormitories. Quarters are shared with host institution students. Meals are taken on one's own, in residences, in central dining facility, in restaurants.
Costs (2003-2004) • One term: $9700. Yearlong program: $17,460; includes tuition, housing, excursions, student support services, resident permit, partial insurance coverage. $50 application fee. $500 nonrefundable deposit required. Financial aid available for all students: scholarships, institutional partner need-based grants.
For More Information • International Education Representative, IES, Institute for the International Education of Students, 33 North

LaSalle Street, 15th Floor, Chicago, IL 60602; *Phone:* 800-995-2300; *Fax:* 312-944-1448. *E-mail:* info@iesabroad.org. *World Wide Web:* http://www.IESabroad.org/

NICHOLLS STATE UNIVERSITY
NICHOLLS STATE IN GERMANY

Hosted by Nicholls State University–Freiburg
Academic Focus • Art, German language and literature, history.
Program Information • Students attend classes at Nicholls State University–Freiburg. Field trips to Basel, Strasbourg, Colmar, Black Forest Lakes; optional travel to Berlin at an extra cost.
Sessions • Fall, spring, yearlong.
Eligibility Requirements • Minimum age 17; open to sophomores, juniors, seniors, graduate students; no foreign language proficiency required.
Living Arrangements • Students live in host family homes. Quarters are shared with host institution students. Meals are taken with host family, in residences.
Costs (2003) • One term: $3958. Yearlong program: $7915; includes tuition, housing, some meals, insurance, books and class materials, lab equipment, student support services, instructional costs. Financial aid available for all students: loans, all customary sources.
For More Information • Ms. Cynthia Webb, Director of Study Programs Abroad, Nicholls State University, PO Box 2080, Thibodaux, LA 70310; *Phone:* 985-448-4440; *Fax:* 985-449-7028. *E-mail:* spab-caw@nicholls.edu. *World Wide Web:* http://www.nicholls.edu/abroad/

STETSON UNIVERSITY
STUDY ABROAD–FREIBURG

Hosted by College of Education of Freiburg
Academic Focus • Full curriculum.
Program Information • Students attend classes at College of Education of Freiburg. Field trips to Munich, the Black Forest.
Sessions • Fall, spring, yearlong.
Eligibility Requirements • Minimum age 20; open to sophomores, juniors, seniors; 3.0 GPA; 3 letters of recommendation; good academic standing at home school; completed application; 2 years of college course work in German.
Living Arrangements • Students live in host institution dormitories, locally rented apartments. Quarters are shared with host institution students. Meals are taken on one's own, in residences, in central dining facility.
Costs (2002-2003) • One term: $14,025. Yearlong program: $28,050; includes tuition, housing, all meals, insurance, excursions, international airfare, international student ID, student support services. $50 application fee. $200 nonrefundable deposit required. Financial aid available for students from sponsoring institution: scholarships, loans.
For More Information • Ms. Nancy L. Leonard, Director, Stetson University, Center for International Education, Unit 8412, 421 North Woodland Boulevard, Deland, FL 32723-3757; *Phone:* 386-822-8165; *Fax:* 386-822-8167. *E-mail:* nleonard@stetson.edu. *World Wide Web:* http://www.stetson.edu/international/

UNIVERSITY OF WISCONSIN–MADISON
ACADEMIC YEAR IN FREIBURG, GERMANY

Hosted by Albert Ludwigs University of Freiburg im Breisgau
Academic Focus • Biological/life sciences, German language and literature, liberal studies, social sciences.
Program Information • Students attend classes at Albert Ludwigs University of Freiburg im Breisgau. Field trips to Schauinsland, Alsace.
Sessions • Yearlong.
Eligibility Requirements • Open to juniors, seniors; 2.5 GPA; 2 letters of recommendation; good academic standing at home school; minimum 3.0 GPA in German; 2 years of college course work in German.
Living Arrangements • Students live in host institution dormitories. Quarters are shared with host institution students, students from other programs. Meals are taken on one's own, in residences, in central dining facility.

Costs (2003-2004) • Yearlong program: $16,800 for Wisconsin residents; $21,500 for nonresidents; includes tuition, housing, all meals, insurance, excursions, international airfare, books and class materials, student support services, housing fees. $100 nonrefundable deposit required. Financial aid available for students from sponsoring institution: scholarships, loans.

For More Information • Peer Advisor, University of Wisconsin–Madison, Office of International Studies and Programs, 261 Bascom Hall, 500 Lincoln Drive, Madison, WI 53706; *Phone:* 608-265-6329; *Fax:* 608-262-6998. *E-mail:* peeradvisor@bascom.wisc.edu. *World Wide Web:* http://www.studyabroad.wisc.edu/. Students may also apply through Michigan State University, Office of International Educational Exchange/Overseas Study, 109 International Center, East Lansing, MI 48824-1035; University of Iowa, Office of Study Abroad, 28 International Center, Iowa City, IA 52242; University of Michigan, Office of International Programs, G-513 Michigan Union, 530 South State Street, Ann Arbor, MI 48109-1349.

HAMBURG

SMITH COLLEGE
JUNIOR YEAR IN HAMBURG

Hosted by Smith College Center, University of Hamburg

Academic Focus • Art history, biological/life sciences, economics, education, German language and literature, German studies, history, linguistics, mathematics, physical sciences, political science and government, social sciences, women's studies.

Program Information • Students attend classes at Smith College Center, University of Hamburg. Scheduled travel to Berlin, Munich, Dresden; field trips to North Sea, Lübeck, new German states.

Sessions • Yearlong.

Eligibility Requirements • Open to juniors, seniors; 3.0 GPA; 3 letters of recommendation; good academic standing at home school; 2 years of college course work in German.

Living Arrangements • Students live in host institution dormitories, locally rented apartments. Quarters are shared with host institution students. Meals are taken on one's own, in residences, in central dining facility.

Costs (2004-2005) • Yearlong program: $39,814; includes tuition, housing, all meals, insurance, excursions, lab equipment, local public transportation subsidy. $35 application fee. $300 refundable deposit required. Financial aid available for students from sponsoring institution: scholarships, loans.

For More Information • Office for International Study, Smith College, College Hall 24, Northampton, MA 01063; *Phone:* 413-585-4905; *Fax:* 413-585-4906. *E-mail:* studyabroad@smith.edu. *World Wide Web:* http://www.smith.edu/studyabroad/

HEIDELBERG

COLLEGE CONSORTIUM FOR INTERNATIONAL STUDIES–OCEAN COUNTY COLLEGE AND ST. AMBROSE UNIVERSITY
BUSINESS/LIBERAL ARTS IN GERMANY

Hosted by Schiller International University

Academic Focus • Accounting, economics, finance, German language and literature, German studies, history, international affairs, international business, liberal studies, marketing.

Program Information • Students attend classes at Schiller International University. Field trips to Munich, Frankfurt, Rothenburg, Bamberg; optional travel to other countries in Europe at an extra cost.

Sessions • Fall, spring, yearlong.

Eligibility Requirements • Minimum age 18; open to freshmen, sophomores, juniors, seniors, graduate students, adults; 2.5 GPA; 2 letters of recommendation; no foreign language proficiency required.

Living Arrangements • Students live in host institution dormitories, locally rented apartments, host family homes. Quarters are shared with host institution students, students from other programs. Meals are taken on one's own, with host family, in residences, in central dining facility, in restaurants.

Costs (2003-2004) • One term: $6990. Yearlong program: $13,980; includes tuition, insurance, cultural activity fee, CCIS fee, adminis-

trative fee, some support services. $80 application fee. $200 nonrefundable deposit required. Financial aid available for students from sponsoring institution: scholarships, loans, federal financial aid.

For More Information • College Consortium for International Studies, 2000 P Street, NW, Suite 503, Washington, DC 20036; *Phone:* 800-453-6956; *Fax:* 202-223-0999. *E-mail:* info@ccisabroad. org. *World Wide Web:* http://www.ccisabroad.org/. Students may also apply through Ocean County College, International Education, PO Box 2001, Toms River, NJ 08754-2001; St. Ambrose University, Study Abroad Office, 518 West Locust, Davenport, IA 52803.

HEIDELBERG COLLEGE
THE AMERICAN JUNIOR YEAR AT HEIDELBERG UNIVERSITY PROGRAM

Hosted by Heidelberg University–American Junior Year Center

Academic Focus • Full curriculum.

Program Information • Students attend classes at Heidelberg University–American Junior Year Center. Scheduled travel to Berlin, Weimer, Dresden, southern Germany (the Alps); field trips to the Black Forest, the European Parliament, the Romantic Road (Wertheim, Creglingen and Rotheuburgobder Taubis).

Sessions • Fall, spring, yearlong, full fall/winter semester.

Eligibility Requirements • Open to sophomores, juniors, seniors; 3.0 GPA; 2 letters of recommendation; sophomore participants must have strong SAT/ACT scores; 2 years of college course work in German.

Living Arrangements • Students live in host institution dormitories, locally rented apartments. Quarters are shared with host institution students. Meals are taken on one's own, in residences, in central dining facility.

Costs (2003-2004) • One term: $7275 for fall term; $7450 for spring; $7750 for fall/winter. Yearlong program: $15,200; includes tuition, housing, insurance, student support services, program-sponsored excursions. $20 application fee. $100 nonrefundable deposit required. Financial aid available for students from sponsoring institution: loans.

For More Information • Ms. Mary Nepper, Secretary of International and Multicultural Programs, Heidelberg College, 310 East Market Street, Tiffin, OH 44883; *Phone:* 419-448-2207; *Fax:* 419-448-2209. *E-mail:* ajy@heidelberg.edu. *World Wide Web:* http://www.heidelberg.edu/offices/global-ed/study-abroad/ajy/

SCHILLER INTERNATIONAL UNIVERSITY
STUDY ABROAD UNDERGRADUATE AND GRADUATE PROGRAMS

Hosted by Schiller International University

Academic Focus • Business administration/management, computer science, economics, English, full curriculum, German language and literature, interdisciplinary studies, international affairs, international business, management information systems, marketing, political science and government, psychology.

Program Information • Students attend classes at Schiller International University. Field trips to Strasbourg, Frankfurt, Baden-Baden, Cologne; optional travel to north Africa, France, Eastern Europe, England at an extra cost.

Sessions • Fall, spring, yearlong.

Eligibility Requirements • Minimum age 17; open to freshmen, sophomores, juniors, seniors, graduate students; 2.0 GPA; no foreign language proficiency required.

Living Arrangements • Students live in host institution dormitories, locally rented apartments, host family homes. Quarters are shared with host institution students, students from other programs. Meals are taken as a group, on one's own, with host family, in residences, in central dining facility, in restaurants.

Costs (2003-2004) • One term: €8000. Yearlong program: €15,850; includes tuition, housing, lab equipment, student support services, activities fee, liability deposit. €500 nonrefundable deposit required. Financial aid available for all students: scholarships, loans, federal grants, Exchange Student Scholar Award, graduate assistantships.

For More Information • Ms. Kamala Dontamsetti, Admissions Office, Florida Campus, Schiller International University, 453

Edgewater Drive, Dunedin, FL 34698; *Phone:* 727-736-5082 Ext. 240; *Fax:* 727-734-0359. *E-mail:* admissions@schiller.edu. *World Wide Web:* http://www.schiller.edu/

SCRIPPS COLLEGE
SCRIPPS COLLEGE IN GERMANY

Hosted by Rupert Charles University of Heidelberg
Academic Focus • German language and literature, literature, social sciences.
Program Information • Students attend classes at Rupert Charles University of Heidelberg. Field trips to Odenwald, Bergstrasse, Alsace; optional travel to Berlin, Prague at an extra cost.
Sessions • Spring, yearlong.
Eligibility Requirements • Open to juniors, seniors; 2.85 GPA; 2 letters of recommendation; good academic standing at home school; 2 years of college course work in German.
Living Arrangements • Students live in host institution dormitories. Quarters are shared with host institution students. Meals are taken on one's own, in residences, in central dining facility, in restaurants.
Costs (2003-2004) • One term: $17,882. Yearlong program: $35,764; includes tuition, housing, all meals, insurance, excursions, international airfare, international student ID, student support services, local transportation pass, bahncard (train discount card), field trip allowance, university excursion subsidy. $350 nonrefundable deposit required. Financial aid available for students from sponsoring institution: scholarships, loans, institutional grants.
For More Information • Ms. Valerie M. Eastman, Director, Off-Campus Study, Scripps College, 1030 Columbia Avenue, Claremont, CA 91711; *Phone:* 909-621-8306; *Fax:* 909-621-8983. *E-mail:* valerie_eastman@scrippscollege.edu. *World Wide Web:* http://scrippscollege.edu/academics/off-campusstudy/

INGOLSTADT

ST. CLOUD STATE UNIVERSITY
GERMAN STUDIES—BUSINESS

Hosted by Fachhochschule Ingolstadt
Academic Focus • German studies, international business.
Program Information • Students attend classes at Fachhochschule Ingolstadt. Scheduled travel to Europe; field trips to Berlin; optional travel at an extra cost.
Sessions • Fall, spring.
Eligibility Requirements • Minimum age 18; open to sophomores, juniors, seniors; major in business, engineering; 2.65 GPA; 2 letters of recommendation; approval from the College of Business; no foreign language proficiency required.
Living Arrangements • Students live in a villa. Meals are taken on one's own, in residences.
Costs (2003-2004) • One term: $6975 for fall term, $7900 for spring for Minnesota residents; includes tuition, housing, excursions, international airfare, international student ID. $75 application fee. Financial aid available for students from sponsoring institution: scholarships, work study, loans.
For More Information • Chunsheng Zhang, Associate Vice President for Academic Affairs/International Studies, St. Cloud State University, Center for International Studies, 720 4th Avenue, South, St. Cloud, MN 56301; *Phone:* 320-308-4287; *Fax:* 320-308-4223. *E-mail:* intstudy@stcloudstate.edu. *World Wide Web:* http://www.stcloudstate.edu/

ST. CLOUD STATE UNIVERSITY
GERMAN STUDIES—LANGUAGE

Academic Focus • German language and literature, German studies.
Program Information • Faculty members are drawn from the sponsor's U.S. staff and local instructors hired by the sponsor. Scheduled travel to Europe; field trips to Berlin; optional travel at an extra cost.
Sessions • Spring.
Eligibility Requirements • Minimum age 18; open to freshmen, sophomores, juniors, seniors; 2.5 GPA; 2 letters of recommendation; 1 year of college course work in German.
Living Arrangements • Students live in host family homes. Meals are taken with host family, in residences.

Costs (2004) • One term: $7950 for Minnesota residents; includes tuition, housing, some meals, excursions, international airfare, international student ID. $75 application fee. Financial aid available for students from sponsoring institution: scholarships, work study, loans.
For More Information • Chunsheng Zhang, Associate Vice President for Academic Affairs/International Studies, St. Cloud State University, Center for International Studies, 720 4th Avenue, South, St. Cloud, MN 56301; *Phone:* 320-308-4287; *Fax:* 320-308-4223. *E-mail:* intstudy@stcloudstate.edu. *World Wide Web:* http://www.stcloudstate.edu/

JENA

NORTHERN ARIZONA UNIVERSITY
STUDY ABROAD IN GERMANY

Hosted by Friedrich Schiller University of Jena
Academic Focus • Full curriculum.
Program Information • Students attend classes at Friedrich Schiller University of Jena. Optional travel at an extra cost.
Sessions • Spring, yearlong.
Eligibility Requirements • Open to sophomores, juniors, seniors; 2.5 GPA; 2 letters of recommendation; good academic standing at home school; 2 years of college course work in German.
Living Arrangements • Students live in host institution dormitories, locally rented apartments. Quarters are shared with host institution students. Meals are taken on one's own, in residences, in central dining facility.
Costs (2003-2004) • One term: $1754 for Arizona residents; $6008 for nonresidents. Yearlong program: $3508 for Arizona residents; $12,016 for nonresidents; includes tuition, international student ID, student support services, fees. $150 application fee. Financial aid available for all students: scholarships, loans, federal grants.
For More Information • International Office, Northern Arizona University, PO Box 5598, Flagstaff, AZ 86011-5598; *Phone:* 928-523-2409; *Fax:* 928-523-9489. *E-mail:* international.office@nau.edu. *World Wide Web:* http://internationaloffice.nau.edu/

KASSEL

ALMA COLLEGE
PROGRAM OF STUDIES IN GERMANY

Hosted by Europa Kolleg
Academic Focus • German language and literature, German studies.
Program Information • Students attend classes at Europa Kolleg. Field trips to Weimar, Buchenwald, Marburg, Fulda, Eisenach, Wartburg.
Sessions • Fall, spring, winter, yearlong, fall and winter semesters.
Eligibility Requirements • Minimum age 18; open to precollege students, sophomores, juniors, seniors, adults; 2.5 GPA; 2 letters of recommendation; good academic standing at home school; no foreign language proficiency required.
Living Arrangements • Students live in host family homes. Quarters are shared with host institution students, students from other programs. Meals are taken on one's own, with host family, in residences.
Costs (2002-2003) • One term: $7250. Yearlong program: $14,100; includes tuition, housing, some meals, insurance, excursions, books and class materials, student support services. $50 application fee. $200 nonrefundable deposit required. Financial aid available for all students: scholarships.
For More Information • Ms. Julie Elenbaas, Office Coordinator, Alma College, 614 West Superior Street, Alma, MI 48801-1599; *Phone:* 989-463-7055; *Fax:* 989-463-7126. *E-mail:* intl_studies@alma.edu. *World Wide Web:* http://international.alma.edu/

KONSTANZ

NORTHERN ARIZONA UNIVERSITY
STUDY ABROAD IN GERMANY

Hosted by University of Konstanz
Academic Focus • Full curriculum, German language and literature, German studies.

Program Information • Students attend classes at University of Konstanz. Optional travel at an extra cost.

Sessions • Spring, yearlong.

Eligibility Requirements • Minimum age 18; open to sophomores, juniors, seniors; 2.5 GPA; 2 letters of recommendation; good academic standing at home school; 1 year of college course work in German.

Living Arrangements • Students live in host institution dormitories, locally rented apartments. Quarters are shared with host institution students. Meals are taken on one's own, in residences, in central dining facility.

Costs (2003–2004) • One term: $1754 for Arizona residents; $6008 for nonresidents. Yearlong program: $3508 for Arizona residents; $12,016 for nonresidents; includes tuition, international student ID, student support services, fees. $150 application fee. Financial aid available for all students: scholarships, loans, grants, some German government aid.

For More Information • International Office, Northern Arizona University, PO Box 5598, Flagstaff, AZ 86011-5598; *Phone:* 928-523-2409; *Fax:* 928-523-9489. *E-mail:* international.office@nau. edu. *World Wide Web:* http://internationaloffice.nau.edu/

RUTGERS, THE STATE UNIVERSITY OF NEW JERSEY
STUDY ABROAD IN GERMANY

Hosted by University of Konstanz

Academic Focus • Full curriculum.

Program Information • Students attend classes at University of Konstanz. Scheduled travel to Rome; field trips to Munich, Nuremberg; optional travel to Berlin, Freiburg, Strasbourg, Zurich at an extra cost.

Sessions • Spring, yearlong.

Eligibility Requirements • Open to sophomores, juniors, seniors; 2.5 GPA; 2 letters of recommendation; 2 years of college course work in German.

Living Arrangements • Students live in host institution dormitories. Quarters are shared with host institution students. Meals are taken on one's own, in residences, in central dining facility, in restaurants.

Costs (2003–2004) • One term: $8343 for New Jersey residents; $10,993 for nonresidents. Yearlong program: $15,332 for New Jersey residents; $20,632 for nonresidents; includes tuition, housing, insurance, excursions, student support services. $20 application fee. $750 nonrefundable deposit required. Financial aid available for students from sponsoring institution: scholarships, loans.

For More Information • Ms. Karin Bonello, Regional Coordinator, Rutgers, The State University of New Jersey, 102 College Avenue, New Brunswick, NJ 08901-8543; *Phone:* 732-932-7787; *Fax:* 732-932-8659. *E-mail:* ru_abroad@email.rutgers.edu. *World Wide Web:* http://studyabroad.rutgers.edu/

LEIPZIG
STATE UNIVERSITY OF NEW YORK AT BINGHAMTON
UNIVERSITY OF LEIPZIG EXCHANGE

Hosted by University of Leipzig

Academic Focus • Biological/life sciences, business administration/management, full curriculum, history, journalism, literature, philosophy, physical sciences, political science and government, psychology, sociology.

Program Information • Students attend classes at University of Leipzig.

Sessions • Fall, spring, yearlong.

Eligibility Requirements • Open to sophomores, juniors, seniors, graduate students; 3.0 GPA; 3 letters of recommendation; 3 years of college course work in German.

Living Arrangements • Students live in host institution dormitories, locally rented apartments. Quarters are shared with host institution students. Meals are taken on one's own, in residences, in central dining facility, in restaurants.

Costs (2003–2004) • One term: $7600 for New York residents; $10,000 for nonresidents. Yearlong program: $13,000 for New York residents; $18,000 for nonresidents; includes tuition, housing, all meals, insurance, international airfare, books and class materials.

$250 nonrefundable deposit required. Financial aid available for students from sponsoring institution: scholarships, loans.

For More Information • Dr. Rosemarie Morewedge, Leipzig Program Director, State University of New York at Binghamton, Department of German, Russian, and East Asian Languages, Binghamton, NY 13902-6000; *Phone:* 607-777-2656; *Fax:* 607-777-2642. *E-mail:* rmorewed@binghamton.edu. *World Wide Web:* http://oip.binghamton.edu/

UNIVERSITY OF MIAMI
UNIVERSITY OF LEIPZIG

Hosted by University of Leipzig

Academic Focus • Full curriculum.

Program Information • Students attend classes at University of Leipzig.

Sessions • Fall, spring, yearlong.

Eligibility Requirements • Minimum age 18; open to sophomores, juniors, seniors; 3.0 GPA; 2 letters of recommendation; good academic standing at home school; essay; official transcript; 3 years of college course work in German.

Living Arrangements • Students live in host institution dormitories. Quarters are shared with host institution students, students from other programs. Meals are taken on one's own, in residences, in central dining facility.

Costs (2003–2004) • One term: $12,919. Yearlong program: $25,838; includes tuition, student support services. $40 application fee. $500 nonrefundable deposit required. Financial aid available for students from sponsoring institution: scholarships, loans.

For More Information • Ms. Carol Lazzeri, Assistant Director, University of Miami, International Education and Exchange Programs, 5050 Brunson Drive, Allen Hall 212, PO Box 248005, Coral Gables, FL 33124-1610; *Phone:* 305-284-3434; *Fax:* 305-284-4235. *E-mail:* ieep@miami.edu. *World Wide Web:* http://www.studyabroad. miami.edu/

LÜNEBURG
UNIVERSITY STUDIES ABROAD CONSORTIUM
GERMAN STUDIES: LÜNEBURG, GERMANY

Hosted by University of Lüneburg

Academic Focus • Art history, cultural studies, economics, German language and literature, German studies, political science and government.

Program Information • Students attend classes at University of Lüneburg. Field trips to Hamburg, Lübeck, Bremen, Travemünde, Wolfsburg, Celle, Kloster Lüne; optional travel to Berlin at an extra cost.

Sessions • Fall, spring, yearlong.

Eligibility Requirements • Minimum age 18; open to freshmen, sophomores, juniors, seniors, graduate students, adults; 2.5 GPA; no foreign language proficiency required.

Living Arrangements • Students live in host institution dormitories, locally rented apartments, host family homes. Quarters are shared with host institution students. Meals are taken on one's own, with host family, in residences, in central dining facility, in restaurants.

Costs (2005–2006) • One term: $4380. Yearlong program: $7480; includes tuition, some meals, insurance, excursions, student support services. $50 application fee. $150 refundable deposit required. Financial aid available for all students: scholarships, work study, loans.

For More Information • University Studies Abroad Consortium, USAC/323, Reno, NV 89557-0093; *Phone:* 775-784-6569; *Fax:* 775-784-6010. *E-mail:* usac@unr.edu. *World Wide Web:* http://usac. unr.edu/

MAGDEBURG
UNIVERSITY OF WISCONSIN–STEVENS POINT
SEMESTER IN GERMANY: MAGDEBURG

Hosted by Otto von Guerick University of Magdeburg

Academic Focus • Cultural studies, German language and literature.

GERMANY
Magdeburg

Program Information • Students attend classes at Otto von Guerick University of Magdeburg. Scheduled travel to Berlin; field trips to Harz Mountains, Eisenach, Wittenberg, Potsdam; optional travel to Italy, Switzerland, Denmark, the Czech Republic at an extra cost.

Sessions • Spring.

Eligibility Requirements • Minimum age 18; open to sophomores, juniors, seniors; 2.5 GPA; 3 letters of recommendation; good academic standing at home school; 2 years of college course work in German.

Living Arrangements • Students live in host institution dormitories, host family homes. Quarters are shared with host institution students. Meals are taken as a group, on one's own, with host family, in residences, in central dining facility, in restaurants.

Costs (2003-2004) • One term: $5000 for Wisconsin residents; $10,500 for nonresidents (estimated); includes tuition, housing, all meals, excursions, international airfare, books and class materials, international student ID. $15 application fee. $150 nonrefundable deposit required. Financial aid available for all students: scholarships, work study, loans.

For More Information • Mr. Mark Koepke, Associate Director, University of Wisconsin–Stevens Point, International Programs Office, Stevens Point, WI 54481; *Phone:* 715-346-2717; *Fax:* 715-346-3591. *E-mail:* intlprog@uwsp.edu. *World Wide Web:* http://www.uwsp.edu/studyabroad/

MAINZ
MIDDLEBURY COLLEGE SCHOOLS ABROAD
SCHOOL IN GERMANY–MAINZ PROGRAM

Hosted by Johannes Gutenberg University of Mainz
Academic Focus • Full curriculum.
Program Information • Students attend classes at Johannes Gutenberg University of Mainz. Field trips to the Rhine River, the Rhine-Palatinate region, the Nahe River, Nuremberg, Weimer; optional travel to Berlin at an extra cost.

Sessions • Fall, spring, yearlong.

Eligibility Requirements • Open to juniors, seniors, graduate students; 2.7 GPA; 2 letters of recommendation; B average in both German and major; 3 years college course work in German, including at least 2 content courses at the 300-level.

Living Arrangements • Students live in host institution dormitories, locally rented apartments. Quarters are shared with host institution students. Meals are taken on one's own, in residences, in central dining facility.

Costs (2004-2005) • One term: $7200. Yearlong program: $14,400; includes tuition, excursions, student support services. $50 application fee. $300 nonrefundable deposit required. Financial aid available for students from sponsoring institution: scholarships, loans.

For More Information • Mr. Jamie Northrup, University Relations Coordinator, Middlebury College Schools Abroad, Office of Off-Campus Study, Sunderland Language Center, Middlebury, VT 05753; *Phone:* 802-443-5745; *Fax:* 802-443-3157. *E-mail:* schoolsabroad@middlebury.edu. *World Wide Web:* http://www.middlebury.edu/msa/

MARBURG
BRETHREN COLLEGES ABROAD
BCA PROGRAM IN MARBURG, GERMANY

Hosted by Philipps University of Marburg
Academic Focus • Full curriculum.
Program Information • Students attend classes at Philipps University of Marburg. Field trips to Frankfurt, Mainz, Rothenburg.
Sessions • Fall, spring, yearlong.
Eligibility Requirements • Minimum age 18; open to juniors, seniors, graduate students, adults; 2.6 GPA; 3 letters of recommendation; 2 years of college course work in German.
Living Arrangements • Students live in host institution dormitories, locally rented apartments. Quarters are shared with host institution students. Meals are taken on one's own, in residences, in central dining facility, in restaurants.
Costs (2003-2004) • One term: $11,500. Yearlong program: $19,900; includes tuition, housing, all meals, insurance, excursions,

international student ID, student support services. $50 application fee. $100 nonrefundable deposit required.
For More Information • Mr. Jason Sanderson, Program Officer for Germany, Brethren Colleges Abroad, 50 Alpha Drive, Elizabethtown, PA 17022; *Phone:* 866-222-6188; *Fax:* 717-361-6619. *E-mail:* info@bcanet.org. *World Wide Web:* http://www.bcanet.org/

MUNICH
UNIVERSITY OF WISCONSIN–STEVENS POINT
SEMESTER IN GERMANY: MUNICH

Held at Ludwig Maximillians University of Munich
Academic Focus • Art history, cultural studies, German language and literature, history, political science and government.
Program Information • Classes are held on the campus of Ludwig Maximillians University of Munich. Faculty members are drawn from the sponsor's U.S. staff and local instructors hired by the sponsor. Scheduled travel to Prague, Berlin, Vienna, Dresden; field trips to Salzburg, Dachau, Füssen; optional travel to Italy, Switzerland at an extra cost.

Sessions • Fall.

Eligibility Requirements • Minimum age 18; open to sophomores, juniors, seniors; 2.25 GPA; 3 letters of recommendation; good academic standing at home school; no foreign language proficiency required.

Living Arrangements • Students live in host family homes, hotels. Quarters are shared with students from other programs. Meals are taken on one's own, in residences, in restaurants.

Costs (2003-2004) • One term: $6400 for Wisconsin residents; $12,000 for nonresidents (estimated); includes tuition, housing, all meals, excursions, international airfare, books and class materials, student support services. $15 application fee. $150 nonrefundable deposit required. Financial aid available for all students: scholarships, work study, loans.

For More Information • Mr. Mark Koepke, Associate Director, University of Wisconsin–Stevens Point, International Programs Office, Stevens Point, WI 54481; *Phone:* 715-346-2717; *Fax:* 715-346-3591. *E-mail:* intlprog@uwsp.edu. *World Wide Web:* http://www.uwsp.edu/studyabroad/

WAYNE STATE UNIVERSITY
JUNIOR YEAR IN MUNICH

Hosted by Ludwig Maximillians University of Munich
Academic Focus • Full curriculum.
Program Information • Students attend classes at Ludwig Maximillians University of Munich. Field trips to the Alps, Nuremberg, Augsburg, Neuschwanstein; optional travel to a seminar at Humboldt University Berlin at an extra cost.
Sessions • Fall, spring, yearlong.
Eligibility Requirements • Open to juniors, seniors, graduate students; 3.0 GPA; 1 letter of recommendation; 2 years of college course work in German.
Living Arrangements • Students live in host institution dormitories. Quarters are shared with host institution students. Meals are taken on one's own, in residences, in central dining facility, in restaurants.
Costs (2003-2004) • One term: $8600. Yearlong program: $16,800; includes tuition, housing, insurance, excursions, student support services, tutorials, WSU transcript, residency permit, extra-curricular activities, Internet access. $20 application fee. $300 nonrefundable deposit required. Financial aid available for all students: scholarships.
For More Information • Ms. Louise Speed, Assistant to the Director, Wayne State University, Junior Year in Munich, 471 Manoogian Hall, Detroit, MI 48202; *Phone:* 313-577-4605; *Fax:* 313-577-3266. *E-mail:* jym@wayne.edu. *World Wide Web:* http://www.worldbridge.wayne.edu/

WHITWORTH COLLEGE
ACADEMY OF MUSIC IN MUNICH

Hosted by Academy of Music
Academic Focus • Music, music education.

Program Information • Students attend classes at Academy of Music. Optional travel at an extra cost.
Sessions • Yearlong.
Eligibility Requirements • Open to sophomores, juniors, seniors; major in music; 2.5 GPA; 2 letters of recommendation; 2 years of college course work in German.
Living Arrangements • Students live in host institution dormitories. Quarters are shared with host institution students. Meals are taken on one's own, in residences, in central dining facility, in restaurants.
Costs (2003-2004) • Yearlong program: $19,810; includes tuition, private lessons. Financial aid available for students from sponsoring institution: scholarships, loans.
For More Information • Ms. Sue Jackson, Director, Off-Campus Programs, Whitworth College, Center for International and Multicultural Education, 300 West Hawthorne Road, Spokane, WA 99251-2702; *Phone:* 509-777-4596; *Fax:* 509-777-3723. *E-mail:* sjackson@whitworth.edu. *World Wide Web:* http://www.whitworth.edu/

OSNABRÜCK

STATE UNIVERSITY OF NEW YORK AT OSWEGO
UNIVERSITY OF OSNABRÜCK

Hosted by University of Osnabrück
Academic Focus • Business administration/management, computer science, education, English literature, German language and literature, German studies, management information systems, social sciences.
Program Information • Students attend classes at University of Osnabrück.
Sessions • Fall, spring, yearlong.
Eligibility Requirements • Open to sophomores, juniors, seniors; 2.5 GPA; 3 letters of recommendation; good academic standing at home school; language proficiency form; personal study statement; 1 year of college course work in German.
Living Arrangements • Students live in host institution dormitories, locally rented apartments. Quarters are shared with host institution students. Meals are taken on one's own, in central dining facility, in restaurants.
Costs (2003-2004) • One term: $2320. Yearlong program: $4640; includes tuition, insurance, student support services. $250 nonrefundable deposit required. Financial aid available for students: home university financial aid, loan processing and scholarships for Oswego students.
For More Information • Mr. Joshua McKeown, Associate Director, State University of New York at Oswego, 122A Swetman Hall, Oswego, NY 13126; *Phone:* 888-4-OSWEGO; *Fax:* 315-312-2477. *E-mail:* intled@oswego.edu. *World Wide Web:* http://www.oswego.edu/intled/

PADERBORN

LOCK HAVEN UNIVERSITY OF PENNSYLVANIA
SEMESTER IN GERMANY

Hosted by University of Paderborn
Academic Focus • Business administration/management, German language and literature.
Program Information • Students attend classes at University of Paderborn.
Sessions • Fall, spring.
Eligibility Requirements • Minimum age 18; open to sophomores, juniors, seniors, adults; 2.5 GPA; 3 letters of recommendation; good academic standing at home school; no foreign language proficiency required.
Living Arrangements • Quarters are shared with host institution students, students from other programs. Meals are taken on one's own.
Costs (2002-2003) • One term: $2750 for Pennsylvania residents; $4650 for nonresidents; includes tuition, fees. $50 application fee. Financial aid available for students from sponsoring institution: scholarships, loans.

For More Information • Dean, Institute for International Studies, Lock Haven University of Pennsylvania, Lock Haven, PA 17745-2390; *Phone:* 570-893-2140; *Fax:* 570-893-2537. *E-mail:* intlstudies_webmonitor@lhup.edu. *World Wide Web:* http://www.lhup.edu/international/goingp/goingplaces_index.htm

REGENSBURG

KENTUCKY INSTITUTE FOR INTERNATIONAL STUDIES
SEMESTER PROGRAM IN REGENSBURG, GERMANY

Hosted by University of Regensburg
Academic Focus • German language and literature, German studies.
Program Information • Students attend classes at University of Regensburg. Field trips to surrounding points of interest; optional travel to other areas of Germany, surrounding European countries at an extra cost.
Sessions • Fall.
Eligibility Requirements • Minimum age 18; open to sophomores, juniors, seniors, graduate students; 2.5 GPA; 2 letters of recommendation; minimum 3.0 GPA in German; 2 years of college course work in German.
Living Arrangements • Students live in host family homes. Meals are taken with host family, in residences.
Costs (2003) • One term: $5450; includes housing, some meals, excursions, international airfare, international student ID, instructional costs. $150 application fee. Financial aid available for all students: scholarships.
For More Information • Ms. Nancy Martin, Coordinator, Kentucky Institute for International Studies, Murray State University, PO Box 9, Murray, KY 42071-0009; *Phone:* 270-762-3091; *Fax:* 270-762-3434. *E-mail:* kiismsu@murraystate.edu. *World Wide Web:* http://www.kiis.org/

MURRAY STATE UNIVERSITY
SEMESTER IN REGENSBURG

Hosted by University of Regensburg
Academic Focus • Finance, German language and literature, German studies, history, international business.
Program Information • Students attend classes at University of Regensburg. Scheduled travel to Berlin (typically); field trips to Prague, local sites, Munich; optional travel to Salzburg, Paris, Vienna, Venice at an extra cost.
Sessions • Fall.
Eligibility Requirements • Open to sophomores, juniors, seniors; 2.5 GPA; 1 letter of recommendation; good academic standing at home school; transcript; no foreign language proficiency required.
Living Arrangements • Students live in host institution dormitories, locally rented apartments. Quarters are shared with host institution students, students from other programs. Meals are taken on one's own, in residences, in central dining facility.
Costs (2004) • One term: $6500 for Kentucky residents; $8500 for nonresidents (estimated); includes tuition, housing, some meals, excursions, international airfare, books and class materials, international student ID, Eurail pass. $50 application fee. $400 nonrefundable deposit required. Financial aid available for students from sponsoring institution: scholarships, loans.
For More Information • Dr. Fred Miller, Director of Regensburg Programs, Murray State University, Department of Management and Marketing, Murray, KY 42071-0009; *Phone:* 270-762-6206; *Fax:* 270-762-3740. *E-mail:* fred.miller@murraystate.edu. *World Wide Web:* http://web2.murraystate.edu/fred.miller/sir/

UNIVERSITY OF COLORADO AT BOULDER
REGENSBURG PROGRAM

Hosted by University of Regensburg
Academic Focus • Biological/life sciences, business administration/management, economics, German language and literature, international affairs, liberal studies, political science and government, social sciences.

GERMANY
Regensburg

Program Information • Students attend classes at University of Regensburg. Scheduled travel to Berlin; field trips to Dresden, Austria; optional travel to Germany and neighboring countries at an extra cost.

Sessions • Yearlong.

Eligibility Requirements • Open to sophomores, juniors, seniors, adults; 2.7 GPA; 2 letters of recommendation; 2 years of college course work in German.

Living Arrangements • Students live in host institution dormitories. Quarters are shared with host institution students. Meals are taken on one's own, in residences, in central dining facility, in restaurants.

Costs (2003-2004) • Yearlong program: $22,276; includes tuition, housing, all meals, insurance, excursions, international airfare, books and class materials, student support services. $400 nonrefundable deposit required. Financial aid available for students from sponsoring institution: scholarships, loans.

For More Information • University of Colorado at Boulder, Office of International Education, UCB 123, Boulder, CO 80309-0123; *Phone:* 303-492-7741; *Fax:* 303-492-5185. *E-mail:* studyabr@colorado.edu. *World Wide Web:* http://www.colorado.edu/OIE/

UNIVERSITY OF CONNECTICUT
REGENSBURG EXCHANGE: BUSINESS, COMPUTER SCIENCE, AND ENGINEERING WORK/STUDY ABROAD PROGRAM

Hosted by Fachhochschule Regensburg

Academic Focus • Business administration/management, computer science, engineering, German language and literature.

Program Information • Students attend classes at Fachhochschule Regensburg.

Sessions • Fall, yearlong.

Eligibility Requirements • Major in business, engineering, computer science; 2.7 GPA; 2 letters of recommendation; good academic standing at home school; 2 years of college course work in German.

Living Arrangements • Students live in host institution dormitories, locally rented apartments. Quarters are shared with host institution students. Meals are taken on one's own, in residences, in restaurants.

Costs (2003-2004) • One term: $2370 for Connecticut residents; $3690 for nonresidents. Yearlong program: $4385 for Connecticut residents; $7015 for nonresidents (estimated); includes tuition, international student ID, fees. $25 application fee. $395 nonrefundable deposit required. Financial aid available for students from sponsoring institution: scholarships, loans.

For More Information • Mr. Gordon Lustila, Acting Director of Study Abroad Programs, University of Connecticut, 843 Bolton Road, Unit 1207, Storrs, CT 06269-1207; *Phone:* 860-486-5022; *Fax:* 860-486-2976. *E-mail:* sabadm03@uconnvm.uconn.edu. *World Wide Web:* http://studyabroad.uconn.edu/

VANDERBILT UNIVERSITY
VANDERBILT IN GERMANY

Hosted by University of Regensburg

Academic Focus • Full curriculum.

Program Information • Students attend classes at University of Regensburg. Field trips to Berlin, Vienna, Munich.

Sessions • Fall, spring, yearlong.

Eligibility Requirements • Open to juniors; 2.7 GPA; 1 letter of recommendation; good academic standing at home school; personal essay; 2 years college course work in German (1.5 years with special permission).

Living Arrangements • Students live in host institution dormitories. Quarters are shared with host institution students. Meals are taken on one's own, in residences, in central dining facility, in restaurants.

Costs (2003-2004) • One term: $16,360. Yearlong program: $32,720; includes tuition, housing, insurance, excursions, student support services. $200 nonrefundable deposit required. Financial aid available for students from sponsoring institution: scholarships, loans.

For More Information • Mr. Gary Johnston, Director of Study Abroad Programs, Vanderbilt University, Study Abroad Office, Box 1573, Station B, Nashville, TN 37235-1573; *Phone:* 615-343-3139; *Fax:* 615-343-5774. *E-mail:* gary.w.johnston@vanderbilt.edu. *World Wide Web:* http://www.vanderbilt.edu/studyabroad/

WESLEYAN UNIVERSITY
WESLEYAN PROGRAM IN GERMANY

Hosted by University of Regensburg

Academic Focus • Anthropology, art history, German studies, history, music, philosophy, political science and government, psychology, sociology.

Program Information • Students attend classes at University of Regensburg. Scheduled travel to Berlin; field trips to Munich, Nuremberg, Prague, Vienna; optional travel to Prague, Vienna at an extra cost.

Sessions • Spring.

Eligibility Requirements • Open to sophomores, juniors; 3.0 GPA; good academic standing at home school; B average in German; 1.5 years college course work in German or the equivalent.

Living Arrangements • Students live in host institution dormitories. Quarters are shared with host institution students, students from other programs. Meals are taken on one's own, in residences, in central dining facility.

Costs (2003) • One term: $18,850; includes tuition, housing, all meals, insurance, excursions, international airfare, books and class materials, student support services. $25 application fee. $200 nonrefundable deposit required. Financial aid available for students from sponsoring institution: scholarships, work study, loans.

For More Information • Ms. Gail Winter, Assistant Director, Wesleyan University, Office of International Studies, Wesleyan University, Middletown, CT 06459-0400; *Phone:* 860-685-2550; *Fax:* 860-685-2551. *E-mail:* gwinter@wesleyan.edu. *World Wide Web:* http://www.wesleyan.edu/ois/

REUTLINGEN
VALPARAISO UNIVERSITY
REUTLINGEN SEMESTER

Hosted by Fachhochschule Reutlingen

Academic Focus • Art history, business administration/management, economics, German language and literature, German studies, international business.

Program Information • Students attend classes at Fachhochschule Reutlingen. Scheduled travel to Berlin, Prague, Leipzig; field trips to Munich, Ulm; optional travel to Paris at an extra cost.

Sessions • Fall, spring.

Eligibility Requirements • Minimum age 19; open to sophomores, juniors, seniors; 3.0 GPA; 2 letters of recommendation; good academic standing at home school; no foreign language proficiency required.

Living Arrangements • Students live in host institution dormitories. Quarters are shared with host institution students, students from other programs. Meals are taken on one's own, in residences, in central dining facility.

Costs (2003-2004) • One term: $12,859; includes tuition, housing, some meals, excursions, books and class materials. $30 application fee. $200 nonrefundable deposit required. Financial aid available for students from sponsoring institution: scholarships, loans.

For More Information • Dr. Hugh McGuigan, Director, International Studies, Valparaiso University, 137 Meier Hall, 1800 Chapel Drive, Valparaiso, IN 46383; *Phone:* 219-464-5333; *Fax:* 219-464-6868. *E-mail:* studyabroad@valpo.edu. *World Wide Web:* http://www.valpo.edu/international/studyabroad.html

SIEGEN
UNIVERSITY OF TULSA
GERMAN IMMERSION PROGRAM IN SIEGEN

Hosted by University of Siegen

Academic Focus • Full curriculum.

Program Information • Students attend classes at University of Siegen. Field trips to Berlin, Cologne; optional travel to independent travel destinations at an extra cost.

Sessions • Spring.

Eligibility Requirements • Minimum age 18; open to sophomores, juniors, seniors; 2.5 GPA; 1 letter of recommendation; good academic standing at home school; 1.5 years of college course work in German.

Living Arrangements • Students live in host family homes. Meals are taken with host family, in residences.

Costs (2003) • One term: $10,516; includes tuition, housing, some meals, excursions. $200 deposit required. Financial aid available for students from sponsoring institution: loans.

For More Information • Ms. Missy Burchette, Assistant to the Director, University of Tulsa, Study Abroad Office, 600 South College Avenue, Tulsa, OK 74104; *Phone:* 918-631-3229; *Fax:* 918-631-2158. *E-mail:* studyabroad@utulsa.edu. *World Wide Web:* http://www.utulsa.edu/studyabroad/

STUTTGART

MARIST COLLEGE
GERMAN INTERNSHIP PROGRAM

Hosted by VWA-Studienakademie (University of Cooperative Education)

Academic Focus • Business administration/management.

Program Information • Students attend classes at VWA-Studienakademie (University of Cooperative Education).

Sessions • 3-6 month paid internship anytime during year.

Eligibility Requirements • Open to sophomores, juniors, seniors; 2.8 GPA; 2 letters of recommendation; good academic standing at home school; 1 year of college course work in German.

Living Arrangements • Students live in locally rented apartments. Meals are taken on one's own, in residences, in restaurants.

Costs (2003-2004) • One term: $12,500; includes tuition, insurance, student support services. $35 application fee. $300 nonrefundable deposit required. Financial aid available for students from sponsoring institution: scholarships, loans.

For More Information • Mr. Jerald Z. Thornton, Coordinator, Marist College, 3399 North Road, Poughkeepsie, NY 12601; *Phone:* 845-575-3330; *Fax:* 845-575-3294. *E-mail:* jerre.thornton@marist.edu. *World Wide Web:* http://www.marist.edu/international/

TÜBINGEN

ANTIOCH COLLEGE
ANTIOCH IN TÜBINGEN

Hosted by University Conference and Study Center, Goethe-Institut, Eberhard Karls University of Tübingen

Academic Focus • Anthropology, business administration/management, comparative literature, economics, full curriculum, German language and literature, history, language studies, law and legal studies, medicine, music, philosophy, physical sciences, religious studies, social sciences.

Program Information • Students attend classes at Eberhard Karls University of Tübingen, Goethe-Institut, University Conference and Study Center. Scheduled travel to Blaubeuren; field trips to nearby cultural sites (while enrolled in Goethe Institutes); optional travel to Germany, Europe at an extra cost.

Sessions • Fall, spring, yearlong.

Eligibility Requirements • Minimum age 18; open to sophomores, juniors, seniors; 2 letters of recommendation; good academic standing at home school; 2 years of college course work German is highly recommended.

Living Arrangements • Students live in host institution dormitories. Quarters are shared with host institution students. Meals are taken on one's own, in residences, in central dining facility, in restaurants.

Costs (2003-2004) • One term: $13,645. Yearlong program: $23,575; includes tuition, housing, all meals, insurance, international student ID, student support services, in-country language study. $35 application fee. $150 nonrefundable deposit required. Financial aid available for students from sponsoring institution: scholarships, loans.

For More Information • Dr. Dale Gardner, Assistant Director, Antioch College, Antioch Education Abroad, 795 Livermore Street, Yellow Springs, OH 45387; *Phone:* 937-769-1015; *Fax:* 937-769-1019. *E-mail:* aea@antioch-college.edu. *World Wide Web:* http://www.antioch-college.edu/aea/

BROWN UNIVERSITY
BROWN IN GERMANY

Hosted by Eberhard Karls University of Tübingen

Academic Focus • Full curriculum.

Program Information • Students attend classes at Eberhard Karls University of Tübingen. Field trips to Berlin.

Sessions • Spring, yearlong.

Eligibility Requirements • Open to sophomores, juniors, seniors; 3.0 GPA; 2 letters of recommendation; good academic standing at home school; 2.5 years of college course work in German.

Living Arrangements • Students live in host institution dormitories. Quarters are shared with host institution students. Meals are taken on one's own, in central dining facility.

Costs (2004-2005) • One term: $15,336. Yearlong program: $30,672; includes tuition, housing, excursions, international student ID, registration fees, language program. $250 nonrefundable deposit required. Financial aid available for students from sponsoring institution: scholarships, loans.

For More Information • Ms. Mell Bolen, Director, Brown University, Office of International Programs, Box 1973, Providence, RI 02912-1973; *Phone:* 401-863-3555; *Fax:* 401-863-3311. *E-mail:* oip_office@brown.edu. *World Wide Web:* http://www.brown.edu/OIP/

NORTHERN ARIZONA UNIVERSITY
GERMAN INTENSIVE LANGUAGE PROGRAM

Hosted by University of Tübingen

Academic Focus • German language and literature.

Program Information • Students attend classes at University of Tübingen. Scheduled travel to a 5-day retreat in Blaubeuren; field trips to various cities in Baden-Wurttemberg and the Bodensee; optional travel at an extra cost.

Sessions • Spring.

Eligibility Requirements • Minimum age 18; open to sophomores, juniors, seniors, graduate students; 2.5 GPA; 2 letters of recommendation; good academic standing at home school; 0.5 years of college course work in German.

Living Arrangements • Students live in host institution dormitories. Quarters are shared with host institution students, students from other programs. Meals are taken on one's own, in residences, in central dining facility.

Costs (2003-2004) • One term: $3400 for Arizona residents; $7300 for nonresidents; includes tuition, housing, insurance, excursions, books and class materials, international student ID, student support services. $150 application fee. Financial aid available for all students: scholarships, loans, Pell grants, Supplemental Educational Opportunity Grant (SEOG).

For More Information • International Office, Northern Arizona University, PO Box 5598, Flagstaff, AZ 86011-5598; *Phone:* 928-523-2409; *Fax:* 928-523-9489. *E-mail:* international.office@nau.edu. *World Wide Web:* http://internationaloffice.nau.edu/

STONY BROOK UNIVERSITY
STONY BROOK ABROAD: TÜBINGEN, GERMANY

Hosted by Eberhard Karls University of Tübingen

Academic Focus • Full curriculum.

Program Information • Students attend classes at Eberhard Karls University of Tübingen. Optional travel to western Europe at an extra cost.

Sessions • Fall, spring, yearlong.

Eligibility Requirements • Open to freshmen, sophomores, juniors, seniors, graduate students; 2.5 GPA; 3 letters of recommendation; good academic standing at home school; statement of purpose; 2 years of college course work in German.

Living Arrangements • Students live in host institution dormitories, locally rented apartments. Quarters are shared with host institution students, students from other programs. Meals are taken on one's own, in central dining facility, in restaurants.

Costs (2002-2003) • One term: contact sponsor for cost. Yearlong program: contact sponsor for cost. $200 nonrefundable deposit required. Financial aid available for students from sponsoring institution: loans, German stipends and grants.

For More Information • Ms. Gretchen Gosnell, Study Abroad Advisor, Stony Brook University, Study Abroad Office, Melville Library, Room E5340, Stony Brook, NY 11794-3397; *Phone:*

GERMANY
Tübingen

631-632-7030; *Fax:* 631-632-6544. *E-mail:* studyabroad@sunysb.edu. *World Wide Web:* http://www.sunysb.edu/studyabroad/

TUFTS UNIVERSITY
TUFTS IN TÜBINGEN

Hosted by Eberhard Karls University of Tübingen
Academic Focus • Full curriculum.
Program Information • Students attend classes at Eberhard Karls University of Tübingen. Scheduled travel to Jena, Weimar, Berlin, Potsdam; field trips.
Sessions • Spring, yearlong.
Eligibility Requirements • Open to sophomores, juniors, seniors; 3.0 GPA; 2 letters of recommendation; good academic standing at home school; 2 years of college course work in German.
Living Arrangements • Students live in host institution dormitories. Quarters are shared with host institution students. Meals are taken on one's own, in residences, in central dining facility.
Costs (2004-2005) • One term: $19,657. Yearlong program: $39,314; includes tuition, housing, all meals, insurance, excursions, monthly transportation pass, cultural activities. $40 application fee. $350 nonrefundable deposit required. Financial aid available for students from sponsoring institution: scholarships, work study, loans.
For More Information • Ms. Melanie Armstrong, Program and Marketing Coordinator, Tufts Programs Abroad, Tufts University, Dowling Hall, Medford, MA 02155-7084; *Phone:* 617-627-2000; *Fax:* 617-627-3971. *E-mail:* melanie.armstrong@tufts.edu. *World Wide Web:* http://ase.tufts.edu/studyabroad/

UNIVERSITY OF MIAMI
UNIVERSITY OF TÜBINGEN, GERMANY

Hosted by Eberhard Karls University of Tübingen
Academic Focus • Biological/life sciences, German language and literature, history, literature, philosophy, political science and government, Slavic languages.
Program Information • Students attend classes at Eberhard Karls University of Tübingen.
Sessions • Fall, spring, yearlong.
Eligibility Requirements • Minimum age 18; open to sophomores, juniors, seniors, adults; 3.0 GPA; 2 letters of recommendation; good academic standing at home school; essay; 3 years college course work in German or near fluency.
Living Arrangements • Students live in host institution dormitories, locally rented apartments. Quarters are shared with host institution students, students from other programs. Meals are taken as a group, on one's own, in central dining facility.
Costs (2003-2004) • One term: $12,919. Yearlong program: $25,838; includes tuition. $40 application fee. $500 nonrefundable deposit required. Financial aid available for students from sponsoring institution: scholarships, loans.
For More Information • Ms. Elyse Resnick, Assistant Director, University of Miami, International Education and Exchange Programs, 5050 Brunson Drive, Allen Hall 212, PO Box 248005, Coral Gables, FL 33124-1610; *Phone:* 305-284-3434; *Fax:* 305-284-4235. *E-mail:* ieep@miami.edu. *World Wide Web:* http://www.studyabroad.miami.edu/

THE UNIVERSITY OF NORTH CAROLINA AT CHAPEL HILL
EXCHANGE PROGRAM AT EBERHARD-KARLS-UNIVERSITAET

Hosted by Eberhard Karls University of Tübingen
Academic Focus • Full curriculum.
Program Information • Students attend classes at Eberhard Karls University of Tübingen. Field trips to local attractions.
Sessions • Yearlong.
Eligibility Requirements • Open to sophomores, juniors, seniors, graduate students, adults; 2.75 GPA; 2 letters of recommendation; essay; transcript; 2 years of college course work in German.
Living Arrangements • Students live in host institution dormitories, locally rented apartments. Quarters are shared with host institution students. Meals are taken on one's own, in central dining facility, in restaurants.

Costs (2003-2004) • Yearlong program: $15,640; includes tuition, study abroad fee. $100 application fee. $500 nonrefundable deposit required. Financial aid available for students from sponsoring institution: scholarships, loans.
For More Information • Study Abroad Office, The University of North Carolina at Chapel Hill, 201 Porthole Building, CB 3130, Chapel Hill, NC 27599-3130; *Phone:* 919-962-7002; *Fax:* 919-962-2262. *E-mail:* abroad@unc.edu. *World Wide Web:* http://studyabroad.unc.edu/

WIESBADEN
TRUMAN STATE UNIVERSITY
BUSINESS PROGRAM IN GERMANY

Hosted by Fachhochschule Wiesbaden
Academic Focus • Accounting, business administration/management, finance, international business, marketing.
Program Information • Students attend classes at Fachhochschule Wiesbaden.
Sessions • Fall, spring, yearlong.
Eligibility Requirements • Open to sophomores, juniors, seniors, graduate students, adults; course work in business; 3.0 GPA; fluency in German.
Living Arrangements • Students live in locally rented apartments. Quarters are shared with host institution students, students from other programs. Meals are taken on one's own, in residences.
Costs (2003-2004) • One term: $2500 for Missouri residents; $4500 for nonresidents. Yearlong program: $5000 for Missouri residents; $9000 for nonresidents; includes tuition. $200 nonrefundable deposit required. Financial aid available for students from sponsoring institution: scholarships, loans.
For More Information • Truman State University, Center for International Education Abroad, Kirk Building, 120, Kirksville, MO 63501; *Phone:* 660-785-4076; *Fax:* 660-785-7473. *E-mail:* ciea@truman.edu. *World Wide Web:* http://www2.truman.edu/ciea/

UNIVERSITY OF MIAMI
FACHHOCHSCHULE WIESBADEN

Hosted by Fachhochschule Wiesbaden
Academic Focus • Communications, international business.
Program Information • Students attend classes at Fachhochschule Wiesbaden.
Sessions • Fall, spring, yearlong.
Eligibility Requirements • Minimum age 18; open to sophomores, juniors, seniors; 2 letters of recommendation; good academic standing at home school; 3 years college course work in German or near fluency.
Living Arrangements • Quarters are shared with host institution students. Meals are taken on one's own, in central dining facility, in restaurants.
Costs (2003-2004) • One term: $12,919. Yearlong program: $25,838; includes tuition, student support services. $40 application fee. $500 nonrefundable deposit required. Financial aid available for students from sponsoring institution: scholarships, loans.
For More Information • Ms. Elyse Resnick, Assistant Director, University of Miami, International Education and Exchange Programs, 5050 Brunson Drive, Allen Hall 212, PO Box 248005, Coral Gables, FL 33124-1610; *Phone:* 305-284-3434; *Fax:* 305-284-4235. *E-mail:* ieep@miami.edu. *World Wide Web:* http://www.studyabroad.miami.edu/

WITTENBERG
UNIVERSITY OF WISCONSIN–EAU CLAIRE
INSTITUTE FOR GERMAN LANGUAGE AND CULTURE

Hosted by Martin Luther University of Halle Wittenberg
Academic Focus • German language and literature, German studies.
Program Information • Students attend classes at Martin Luther University of Halle Wittenberg. Field trips to Berlin, Leipzig, Halle, Weimar.
Sessions • Spring.

Eligibility Requirements • Open to sophomores, juniors, seniors; 2.8 GPA; good academic standing at home school; 1.5 years of college course work in German.

Living Arrangements • Students live in host family homes. Meals are taken with host family, in residences.

Costs (2002-2003) • One term: $3765 for Wisconsin residents; $4665 for nonresidents (estimated); includes tuition, housing, some meals, insurance, excursions, books and class materials, student support services. $30 application fee. $150 nonrefundable deposit required. Financial aid available for all students: scholarships, loans.

For More Information • Ms. Cheryl Lochner-Wright, Study Abroad Coordinator, University of Wisconsin–Eau Claire, Center for International Education, 111 Schofield Hall, Eau Claire, WI 54702-4004; *Phone:* 715-836-4411; *Fax:* 715-836-4948. *E-mail:* studyabroad@uwec.edu. *World Wide Web:* http://www.uwec.edu/Cie/

WUPPERTAL

BETHEL COLLEGE
BETHEL/WUPPERTAL EXCHANGE PROGRAM

Hosted by University of Wuppertal

Academic Focus • Full curriculum.

Program Information • Students attend classes at University of Wuppertal. Optional travel at an extra cost.

Sessions • Yearlong.

Eligibility Requirements • Open to juniors, seniors; 2.5 GPA; good academic standing at home school; 2 years of college course work in German.

Living Arrangements • Students live in host institution dormitories. Quarters are shared with host institution students. Meals are taken on one's own, in residences.

Costs (2003-2004) • Yearlong program: $16,525; includes tuition, housing, all meals. Financial aid available for students from sponsoring institution: scholarships, loans, monthly stipend from German university for living expenses.

For More Information • Mr. Merle Schlabaugh, Study Abroad Advisor, Bethel College, 300 East 27th Street, North Newton, KS 67117; *Phone:* 316-284-5336; *Fax:* 316-284-5286. *E-mail:* mschlab@bethelks.edu

WÜRZBURG

DAVIDSON COLLEGE
DAVIDSON JUNIOR YEAR IN WÜRZBURG, GERMANY

Hosted by Bayerische Julius Maximilians University of Würzburg

Academic Focus • Full curriculum.

Program Information • Students attend classes at Bayerische Julius Maximilians University of Würzburg. Scheduled travel to Berlin, Prague, Vienna, Budapest; field trips to Munich, Coburg, Bamberg, Frankfurt; optional travel to sites in Germany.

Sessions • Yearlong.

Eligibility Requirements • Open to juniors; 2.75 GPA; 2 letters of recommendation; good academic standing at home school; 2 years college course work in German or the equivalent.

Living Arrangements • Students live in host institution dormitories, host family homes. Quarters are shared with host institution students. Meals are taken on one's own, in residences, in central dining facility, in restaurants.

Costs (2003-2004) • Yearlong program: $29,000; includes tuition, housing, insurance, excursions, international airfare, international student ID, student support services, September homestay, intensive language course, cultural activities. $500 nonrefundable deposit required. Financial aid available for students from sponsoring institution: scholarships, work study, loans.

For More Information • Ms. Carolyn Ortmayer, Study Abroad Coordinator, Davidson College, Box 7155, Davidson, NC 28035-7155; *Phone:* 704-894-2250; *Fax:* 704-894-2120. *E-mail:* abroad@davidson.edu. *World Wide Web:* http://www.davidson.edu/international/

UNIVERSITY AT ALBANY, STATE UNIVERSITY OF NEW YORK
DIRECT ENROLLMENT AT THE UNIVERSITY OF WÜRZBURG

Hosted by University of Würzburg

Academic Focus • Full curriculum.

Program Information • Students attend classes at University of Würzburg. Field trips to the local area, the Main River; optional travel to other cities in Germany, holiday home stays at an extra cost.

Sessions • Fall, spring, yearlong.

Eligibility Requirements • Open to sophomores, juniors, seniors, graduate students, adults; 2.7 GPA; 2 letters of recommendation; good academic standing at home school; 2 years college course work in German, ability to undertake course work taught in German.

Living Arrangements • Students live in host institution dormitories. Quarters are shared with host institution students, students from other programs. Meals are taken on one's own, in residences, in central dining facility, in restaurants.

Costs (2002-2003) • One term: $4613. Yearlong program: $9225; includes housing, all meals, excursions, student support services, in-state tuition and fees. $150 nonrefundable deposit required. Financial aid available for students from sponsoring institution: scholarships, work study, all customary sources.

For More Information • University at Albany, State University of New York, Office of International Education, LI 66, Albany, NY 12222; *Phone:* 518-442-3525; *Fax:* 518-442-3338. *E-mail:* intled@uamail.albany.edu. *World Wide Web:* http://www.albany.edu/intled/

ZITTAU

NORTHERN ARIZONA UNIVERSITY
STUDY ABROAD IN GERMANY

Hosted by Hochschule fur Technik Wirtschaft und Sozialwesen Zittau Gorlitz

Academic Focus • Business administration/management, engineering, German language and literature, information science, social work.

Program Information • Students attend classes at Hochschule fur Technik Wirtschaft und Sozialwesen Zittau Gorlitz. Optional travel at an extra cost.

Sessions • Yearlong.

Eligibility Requirements • Minimum age 18; open to sophomores, juniors, seniors; 2.5 GPA; 2 letters of recommendation; good academic standing at home school; 1 year of college course work in German.

Living Arrangements • Students live in host institution dormitories, locally rented apartments. Quarters are shared with host institution students, students from other programs. Meals are taken on one's own, in residences, in central dining facility.

Costs (2003-2004) • Yearlong program: $3508 for Arizona residents; $12,016 for nonresidents; includes tuition, international student ID, student support services, fees. $150 application fee. Financial aid available for all students: scholarships, loans, grants, some German government aid.

For More Information • International Office, Northern Arizona University, PO Box 5598, Flagstaff, AZ 86011-5598; *Phone:* 928-523-2409; *Fax:* 928-523-9489. *E-mail:* international.office@nau.edu. *World Wide Web:* http://internationaloffice.nau.edu/

GHANA

CITY TO CITY

SCHOOL FOR INTERNATIONAL TRAINING, SIT STUDY ABROAD
GHANA: ARTS AND CULTURE

Academic Focus • African studies, anthropology, history, language studies, sociology, visual and performing arts.

Program Information • Faculty members are drawn from the sponsor's U.S. staff and local instructors hired by the sponsor.

GHANA
City to City

Scheduled travel to Tamale, Ashanti region; field trips to artist workshops, rural areas, national parks, slave castles.
Sessions • Fall, spring.
Eligibility Requirements • Open to sophomores, juniors, seniors; 2.5 GPA; 2 letters of recommendation; good academic standing at home school; no foreign language proficiency required.
Living Arrangements • Students live in host family homes, hotels. Meals are taken as a group, on one's own, with host family, in residences, in restaurants.
Costs (2003-2004) • One term: $11,650; includes tuition, housing, all meals, insurance, excursions. $50 application fee. $400 nonrefundable deposit required. Financial aid available for all students: scholarships.
For More Information • School for International Training, SIT Study Abroad, Kipling Road, Brattleboro, VT 05302-0676; *Phone:* 888-272-7881; *Fax:* 802-258-3296. *E-mail:* studyabroad@sit.edu. *World Wide Web:* http://www.sit.edu/studyabroad/

ACCRA
CALVIN COLLEGE
STUDY IN GHANA PROGRAM

Hosted by University of Ghana
Academic Focus • African languages and literature, African studies, civilization studies, political science and government.
Program Information • Students attend classes at University of Ghana. Scheduled travel to northern Ghana (7 days); field trips to museums in Accra, botanical gardens, Gold Coast.
Sessions • Fall.
Eligibility Requirements • Open to sophomores, juniors, seniors; 2.5 GPA; 2 letters of recommendation; good academic standing at home school; interview with program director; no foreign language proficiency required.
Living Arrangements • Students live in host institution dormitories. Quarters are shared with host institution students. Meals are taken on one's own, in central dining facility, in restaurants.
Costs (2003) • One term: $11,750; includes tuition, housing, all meals, excursions, international airfare, student support services, immunizations. $50 application fee. $400 nonrefundable deposit required. Financial aid available for students from sponsoring institution: scholarships, loans.
For More Information • Dr. Ellen B. Monsma, Director, Calvin College, Office of Off-Campus Programs, 3201 Burton Street, SE, Grand Rapids, MI 49546; *Phone:* 616-526-6551; *Fax:* 616-526-6756. *E-mail:* emonsma@calvin.edu. *World Wide Web:* http://www.calvin.edu/academic/off-campus/

CIEE
CIEE STUDY CENTER AT THE UNIVERSITY OF GHANA, ACCRA

Hosted by University of Ghana
Academic Focus • Full curriculum.
Program Information • Students attend classes at University of Ghana. Scheduled travel to Togo; field trips to Elmira Castle, Kumasi, Mole Game Reserve, Aburi Botanical Garden.
Sessions • Fall, spring, yearlong.
Eligibility Requirements • Open to juniors, seniors, graduate students, adults; course work in African studies (recommended); 3.0 GPA; 2 letters of recommendation; no foreign language proficiency required.
Living Arrangements • Students live in host institution dormitories, locally rented apartments. Quarters are shared with host institution students, students from other programs. Meals are taken on one's own, in central dining facility, in restaurants.
Costs (2003-2004) • One term: $8500. Yearlong program: $15,520; includes tuition, housing, insurance, excursions, student support services, visa fees, pre-departure advising, cultural activities, optional on-site pick-up. $30 application fee. $300 deposit required. Financial aid available for all students: minority student scholarships, non-traditional study scholarships, travel grants.
For More Information • Ms. Hannah McChesney, Admissions Officer, Europe, Middle East, and Africa, CIEE, 7 Custom House Street, 3rd Floor, Portland, ME 04101; *Phone:* 800-40-STUDY; *Fax:* 207-553-7699. *E-mail:* studyinfo@ciee.org. *World Wide Web:* http://www.ciee.org/isp/

NORTH CAROLINA STATE UNIVERSITY
STUDY ABROAD PROGRAM IN GHANA

Hosted by University of Ghana
Academic Focus • Full curriculum.
Program Information • Students attend classes at University of Ghana. Scheduled travel to Ho, the Yolta region; field trips to El Mina, Kakum National Forest; optional travel to Kumasi at an extra cost.
Sessions • Fall, spring, yearlong.
Eligibility Requirements • Minimum age 18; open to sophomores, juniors, seniors, graduate students; 2.75 GPA; 2 letters of recommendation; good academic standing at home school; essay; no foreign language proficiency required.
Living Arrangements • Students live in host institution dormitories. Quarters are shared with host institution students, students from other programs. Meals are taken on one's own, in residences, in central dining facility, in restaurants.
Costs (2003-2004) • One term: $4950. Yearlong program: $8950; includes tuition, housing, insurance, excursions, international student ID, student support services. $200 nonrefundable deposit required. Financial aid available for students from sponsoring institution: scholarships, loans.
For More Information • Ms. Ingrid Schmidt, Director of Study Abroad, North Carolina State University, 2118 Pullen Hall, Box 7344, Raleigh, NC 27695-7344; *Phone:* 919-515-2087; *Fax:* 919-515-6021. *E-mail:* study_abroad@ncsu.edu. *World Wide Web:* http://www.ncsu.edu/studyabroad/

STATE UNIVERSITY OF NEW YORK COLLEGE AT BROCKPORT
UNIVERSITY OF GHANA PROGRAM

Hosted by University of Ghana
Academic Focus • Full curriculum.
Program Information • Students attend classes at University of Ghana. Field trips to Kumasi, Elmina, Volta Lake, Cape Coast, homestay weekend.
Sessions • Fall, spring, yearlong.
Eligibility Requirements • Minimum age 18; open to juniors, seniors; 3.0 GPA; 2 letters of recommendation; good academic standing at home school; ability to do upper-division course work in chosen subject; no foreign language proficiency required.
Living Arrangements • Students live in host institution dormitories. Quarters are shared with host institution students. Meals are taken on one's own, in central dining facility.
Costs (2004-2005) • One term: $7850 for fall; $8350 for spring. Yearlong program: contact sponsor for cost; includes tuition, housing, excursions, international student ID, student support services. $350 nonrefundable deposit required. Financial aid available for all students: scholarships, loans, regular financial aid, grants.
For More Information • Dr. John Perry, Director, Office of International Education, State University of New York College at Brockport, 350 New Campus Drive, Brockport, NY 14420; *Phone:* 800-298-SUNY; *Fax:* 585-637-3218. *E-mail:* overseas@brockport.edu. *World Wide Web:* http://www.brockport.edu/studyabroad/

UNIVERSITY OF MINNESOTA
MINNESOTA STUDIES IN INTERNATIONAL DEVELOPMENT (MSID) GHANA

Hosted by Student Youth Travel Organization
Academic Focus • African studies, agriculture, anthropology, community service, conservation studies, economics, education, environmental health, environmental science/studies, forestry, health and physical education, international affairs, natural resources, nutrition, public policy, refugee studies, social services, sociology, Swahili, urban/regional planning, wildlife studies, women's studies.
Program Information • Students attend classes at Student Youth Travel Organization. Field trips to development projects; optional travel to sites in Ghana at an extra cost.
Sessions • Fall, spring, yearlong.
Eligibility Requirements • Minimum age 19; open to juniors, seniors, graduate students, adults; course work in development studies, area studies, social sciences; 2.5 GPA; 1 letter of recommendation; no foreign language proficiency required.

Living Arrangements • Students live in host family homes. Meals are taken with host family, in residences.

Costs (2004-2005) • One term: contact sponsor for cost. Yearlong program: contact sponsor for cost. $50 application fee. $400 nonrefundable deposit required. Financial aid available for students from sponsoring institution: scholarships, loans.

For More Information • University of Minnesota, Learning Abroad Center, 230 Heller Hall, 271 19th Avenue South, Minneapolis, MN 55455; *Phone:* 612-626-9000; *Fax:* 612-626-8009. *E-mail:* umabroad@ umn.edu. *World Wide Web:* http://www.umabroad.umn.edu/

UNIVERSITY STUDIES ABROAD CONSORTIUM
FULL CURRICULUM AND AFRICAN STUDIES: ACCRA, GHANA

Hosted by University of Ghana

Academic Focus • African studies, full curriculum.

Program Information • Students attend classes at University of Ghana. Field trips to Cape Coast, Accra; optional travel to Kumasi, Damongo, Larabanga, Ahwiaa, Ntonso at an extra cost.

Sessions • Fall, spring, yearlong.

Eligibility Requirements • Minimum age 18; open to freshmen, sophomores, juniors, seniors, graduate students, adults; 3.0 GPA; no foreign language proficiency required.

Living Arrangements • Students live in host institution dormitories. Quarters are shared with host institution students. Meals are taken as a group, on one's own, in residences.

Costs (2005-2006) • One term: $6880. Yearlong program: $13,480; includes tuition, housing, insurance, excursions, student support services. $50 application fee. $150 refundable deposit required. Financial aid available for all students: scholarships, loans.

For More Information • University Studies Abroad Consortium, USAC/323, Reno, NV 89557-0093; *Phone:* 775-784-6569; *Fax:* 775-784-6010. *E-mail:* usac@unr.edu. *World Wide Web:* http://usac. unr.edu/

CAPE COAST

NORTH CAROLINA STATE UNIVERSITY
STUDY ABROAD PROGRAM IN GHANA

Hosted by University of Cape Coast

Academic Focus • Full curriculum.

Program Information • Students attend classes at University of Cape Coast. Field trips to Kumasi; optional travel at an extra cost.

Sessions • Fall, spring, yearlong.

Eligibility Requirements • Minimum age 18; open to sophomores, juniors, seniors, graduate students; 2.75 GPA; 2 letters of recommendation; good academic standing at home school; essay; no foreign language proficiency required.

Living Arrangements • Students live in host institution dormitories. Quarters are shared with host institution students, students from other programs. Meals are taken on one's own, in central dining facility, in restaurants.

Costs (2003-2004) • One term: $4950. Yearlong program: $8950; includes tuition, housing, insurance, excursions, international student ID, student support services. $200 nonrefundable deposit required. Financial aid available for students from sponsoring institution: scholarships, loans.

For More Information • Ms. Ingrid Schmidt, Director of Study Abroad, North Carolina State University, 2118 Pullen Hall, Box 7344, Raleigh, NC 27695-7344; *Phone:* 919-515-2087; *Fax:* 919-515-6021. *E-mail:* study_abroad@ncsu.edu. *World Wide Web:* http://www.ncsu. edu/studyabroad/

SCHOOL FOR INTERNATIONAL TRAINING, SIT STUDY ABROAD
GHANA: AFRICAN DIASPORA STUDIES

Academic Focus • African studies, anthropology, economics, geography, history, intercultural studies, language studies, sociology.

Program Information • Faculty members are drawn from the sponsor's U.S. staff and local instructors hired by the sponsor. Scheduled travel to Accra, Benin; field trips to rural areas, historic sites, slave castles.

Sessions • Fall, spring.

Eligibility Requirements • Open to sophomores, juniors, seniors; 2.5 GPA; 2 letters of recommendation; good academic standing at home school; no foreign language proficiency required.

Living Arrangements • Students live in host family homes, hotels. Meals are taken as a group, on one's own, with host family, in residences, in restaurants.

Costs (2003-2004) • One term: $11,650; includes tuition, housing, all meals, insurance, excursions. $50 application fee. $400 nonrefundable deposit required. Financial aid available for all students: scholarships.

For More Information • School for International Training, SIT Study Abroad, Kipling Road, Brattleboro, VT 05302-0676; *Phone:* 888-272-7881; *Fax:* 802-258-3296. *E-mail:* studyabroad@sit.edu. *World Wide Web:* http://www.sit.edu/studyabroad/

KUMASI

NORTH CAROLINA STATE UNIVERSITY
STUDY ABROAD PROGRAM IN GHANA

Hosted by 'Kwame Nkrumah' University of Science and Technology

Academic Focus • Full curriculum.

Program Information • Students attend classes at 'Kwame Nkrumah' University of Science and Technology. Field trips to El Mina, Kakum National Forest, craft villages; optional travel to Kumasi at an extra cost.

Sessions • Fall, spring, yearlong.

Eligibility Requirements • Minimum age 18; open to sophomores, juniors, seniors, graduate students; 2.75 GPA; 2 letters of recommendation; good academic standing at home school; essay; no foreign language proficiency required.

Living Arrangements • Students live in host institution dormitories. Quarters are shared with host institution students, students from other programs. Meals are taken on one's own, in residences, in central dining facility, in restaurants.

Costs (2003-2004) • One term: $4950. Yearlong program: $8950; includes tuition, housing, insurance, excursions, international student ID, student support services. $200 nonrefundable deposit required. Financial aid available for students from sponsoring institution: scholarships, loans.

For More Information • Ms. Ingrid Schmidt, Director of Study Abroad, North Carolina State University, 2118 Pullen Hall, Box 7344, Raleigh, NC 27695-7344; *Phone:* 919-515-2087; *Fax:* 919-515-6021. *E-mail:* study_abroad@ncsu.edu. *World Wide Web:* http://www.ncsu. edu/studyabroad/

GREECE

ATHENS

AHA INTERNATIONAL AN ACADEMIC PROGRAM OF THE UNIVERSITY OF OREGON
ATHENS, GREECE: NORTHWEST COUNCIL ON STUDY ABROAD

Hosted by Athens Centre

Academic Focus • Ancient history, archaeology, art, art history, costume design, drama/theater, English, Greek, Greek studies, history, literature, visual and performing arts.

Program Information • Students attend classes at Athens Centre. Scheduled travel to Crete, Spetses, Aegina; field trips to Delphi, Peloponnese.

Sessions • Fall, spring.

Eligibility Requirements • Open to sophomores, juniors, seniors; 2.5 GPA; 2 letters of recommendation; good academic standing at home school; no foreign language proficiency required.

Living Arrangements • Students live in locally rented apartments, hotels. Quarters are shared with host institution students. Meals are taken on one's own, in residences, in restaurants.

Costs (2003-2004) • One term: $6690; includes tuition, housing, insurance, excursions, books and class materials, international

GREECE
Athens

student ID, student support services. $50 application fee. $200 refundable deposit required. Financial aid available for all students: scholarships, loans, grants.
For More Information • Ms. Amy Hunter, Associate Director for University Programs, AHA International An Academic Program of the University of Oregon, 741 SW Lincoln Street, Portland, OR 97201; *Phone:* 503-295-7730; *Fax:* 503-295-5969. *E-mail:* mail@aha-intl.org. *World Wide Web:* http://www.aha-intl.org/

ARCADIA UNIVERSITY
ARCADIA CENTER FOR MEDITERRANEAN AND BALKAN STUDIES AND RESEARCH

Hosted by Arcadia Center for Mediterranean and Balkan Studies and Research
Academic Focus • Archaeology, art, Byzantine studies, classics and classical languages, Greek, Greek studies.
Program Information • Students attend classes at Arcadia Center for Mediterranean and Balkan Studies and Research. Scheduled travel to Crete, Thessaloniki; field trips to museums, ruins, archaeological sites; optional travel to Delphi, islands.
Sessions • Fall, spring, yearlong.
Eligibility Requirements • Open to sophomores, juniors, seniors; 3.0 GPA; 1 letter of recommendation; previous study in chosen field; no foreign language proficiency required.
Living Arrangements • Students live in locally rented apartments. Quarters are shared with host institution students. Meals are taken on one's own, in residences, in restaurants.
Costs (2003-2004) • One term: $9990. Yearlong program: $17,490; includes tuition, housing, insurance, excursions, international student ID, student support services, field study expenses, transcripts, pre-departure guide. $35 application fee. $500 nonrefundable deposit required. Financial aid available for all students: scholarships, loans.
For More Information • Arcadia University, Center for Education Abroad, 450 South Easton Road, Glenside, PA 19038-3295; *Phone:* 866-927-2234; *Fax:* 215-572-2174. *E-mail:* cea@arcadia.edu. *World Wide Web:* http://www.arcadia.edu/cea/

BRETHREN COLLEGES ABROAD
BCA PROGRAM IN ATHENS, GREECE

Hosted by University of LaVerne Athens Campus
Academic Focus • Full curriculum.
Program Information • Students attend classes at University of LaVerne Athens Campus. Scheduled travel to Greek Islands, rural Greece; field trips to Delphi, Mycenae, Meteora, Corinth; optional travel to Mount Parnassus, Greek Islands at an extra cost.
Sessions • Fall, spring, yearlong.
Eligibility Requirements • Minimum age 18; open to sophomores, juniors, seniors, graduate students, adults; 2.6 GPA; 3 letters of recommendation; good academic standing at home school; no foreign language proficiency required.
Living Arrangements • Students live in program-owned apartments. Quarters are shared with host institution students. Meals are taken on one's own, in residences, in restaurants.
Costs (2003-2004) • One term: $11,500. Yearlong program: $19,900; includes tuition, housing, all meals, insurance, excursions, international student ID, student support services. $50 application fee. $100 nonrefundable deposit required.
For More Information • Mr. Jason Sanderson, Program Officer for Greece, Brethren Colleges Abroad, 50 Alpha Drive, Elizabethtown, PA 17022; *Phone:* 866-222-6188; *Fax:* 717-361-6619. *E-mail:* info@bcanet.org. *World Wide Web:* http://www.bcanet.org/

COLLEGE YEAR IN ATHENS
COLLEGE YEAR IN ATHENS

Hosted by College Year in Athens
Academic Focus • Anthropology, archaeology, art history, Byzantine studies, classics and classical languages, Greek, Greek studies, history, literature, Mediterranean studies, philosophy, political science and government, religious studies.
Program Information • Students attend classes at College Year in Athens. Scheduled travel to Peloponnese, Crete, northern Greece; field trips to Attica, Delphi; optional travel to Egypt, Tunisia, Turkey, Santorini at an extra cost.

Sessions • Fall, spring, yearlong.
Eligibility Requirements • Minimum age 18; open to freshmen, sophomores, juniors, seniors, graduate students, adults; 2 letters of recommendation; good academic standing at home school; no foreign language proficiency required.
Living Arrangements • Students live in program-owned apartments, hotels. Meals are taken as a group, in central dining facility.
Costs (2003-2004) • One term: $11,100. Yearlong program: $20,300; includes tuition, housing, some meals, insurance, excursions, books and class materials, student support services. $35 application fee. $600 deposit required. Financial aid available for all students: scholarships.
For More Information • College Year in Athens, PO Box 390890, Department E, Cambridge, MA 02139-0010; *Phone:* 617-868-8200; *Fax:* 617-868-8207. *E-mail:* info@cyathens.org. *World Wide Web:* http://www.cyathens.org/

HARDING UNIVERSITY
HARDING UNIVERSITY IN ATHENS, GREECE

Hosted by Harding University
Academic Focus • Greek, liberal studies, religious studies.
Program Information • Students attend classes at Harding University. Scheduled travel to Turkey, Egypt, Greek Isles; field trips to Corinth, Athens, Aegina, Delphi; optional travel to western Europe at an extra cost.
Sessions • Fall, spring.
Eligibility Requirements • Open to sophomores, juniors, seniors; 2.0 GPA; good academic standing at home school; no foreign language proficiency required.
Living Arrangements • Students live in hotels, a program-owned hotel. Quarters are shared with host institution students. Meals are taken as a group, in central dining facility.
Costs (2003-2004) • One term: $13,000; includes tuition, housing, some meals, excursions, international airfare, international student ID. $200 application fee. Financial aid available for students from sponsoring institution: scholarships, work study, loans.
For More Information • Dr. Jeffrey T. Hopper, Dean of International Programs, Harding University, 900 East Center Street, Box 10754, Searcy, AR 72149; *Phone:* 501-279-4529; *Fax:* 501-279-4184. *E-mail:* intlprograms@harding.edu

LAFAYETTE COLLEGE
FACULTY-LED PROGRAMS, ATHENS, GREECE

Hosted by College Year in Athens
Academic Focus • Full curriculum.
Program Information • Students attend classes at College Year in Athens. Scheduled travel; field trips; optional travel at an extra cost.
Sessions • Fall.
Eligibility Requirements • Open to sophomores, juniors, seniors; 2.8 GPA; good academic standing at home school; no foreign language proficiency required.
Living Arrangements • Students live in host institution dormitories. Quarters are shared with host institution students. Meals are taken on one's own, in central dining facility, in restaurants.
Costs (2002) • One term: $15,959; includes tuition, housing, some meals, excursions, international airfare. $300 nonrefundable deposit required. Financial aid available for students from sponsoring institution: loans, need-based grants.
For More Information • Mr. Cyrus S. Fleck Jr., Director of Study Abroad, Lafayette College, Provost Office, 219 Markle, Easton, PA 18042; *Phone:* 610-330-5069; *Fax:* 610-330-5068. *E-mail:* fleckc@lafayette.edu. *World Wide Web:* http://www.lafayette.edu/

UNIVERSITY OF INDIANAPOLIS–ATHENS CAMPUS
ODYSSEY IN ATHENS

Hosted by University of Indianapolis–Athens Campus
Academic Focus • Anthropology, business administration/management, economics, Greek, Greek studies, history, international affairs, journalism, political science and government, psychology.

Program Information • Students attend classes at University of Indianapolis–Athens Campus. Field trips to Delphi, Mycenae, Epidauros, the Saronic Gulf islands, Olympia; optional travel at an extra cost.
Sessions • Fall, spring, yearlong.
Eligibility Requirements • Minimum age 17; open to freshmen, sophomores, juniors, seniors, graduate students; good academic standing at home school; potential to benefit from experience; no foreign language proficiency required.
Living Arrangements • Students live in locally rented apartments. Quarters are shared with host institution students. Meals are taken on one's own, in residences, in restaurants.
Costs (2002-2003) • One term: $7600. Yearlong program: $14,330; includes tuition, housing, excursions, student support services, transcripts, fees. $50 application fee. $750 nonrefundable deposit required. Financial aid available for all students: limited scholarships.
For More Information • Ms. Barbara Tsairis, U.S. Director, University of Indianapolis–Athens Campus, PO Box 5666, Portsmouth, NH 03802-5666; *Phone:* 603-431-4999; *Fax:* 603-431-4999. *E-mail:* odyssey@star.net. *World Wide Web:* http://www.star.net/People/~odyssey/. Students may also apply through Odyssey in Athens, 29 Voulis Street, 10557 Athens, Greece.

UNIVERSITY OF LAVERNE
UNIVERSITY OF LAVERNE, ATHENS

Hosted by University of LaVerne Athens Campus
Academic Focus • Accounting, art, biological/life sciences, business administration/management, computer science, education, English, history, international business, marketing, mathematics, philosophy, political science and government, psychology, sociology.
Program Information • Students attend classes at University of LaVerne Athens Campus. Scheduled travel to Crete, Cairo, Istanbul;

field trips to Olympia, Delphi, Corinth, Meteora; optional travel to Lebanon, Cyprus, Israel, Turkey at an extra cost.
Sessions • Fall, spring, winter, yearlong.
Eligibility Requirements • Minimum age 18; open to freshmen, sophomores, juniors, seniors, graduate students, adults; 2.3 GPA; 3 letters of recommendation; good academic standing at home school; no foreign language proficiency required.
Living Arrangements • Students live in host institution dormitories, locally rented apartments. Quarters are shared with host institution students. Meals are taken as a group, in restaurants.
Costs (2003-2004) • One term: $14,260. Yearlong program: $28,520; includes tuition, housing, all meals, insurance, excursions, student support services. $50 application fee. $100 nonrefundable deposit required. Financial aid available for students from sponsoring institution: scholarships, loans.
For More Information • Dr. Rahavia Yakovee, Director of Admissions, Greece, University of LaVerne, PO Box 51105, Kifissia, Athens 145 10, Greece; *Phone:* +301 620-6188; *Fax:* +301 620-5929. *E-mail:* ryako@laverne.edu.gr. *World Wide Web:* http://www.ulv.edu/studyabroad/. Students may also apply through Brethren Colleges Abroad, PO Box 407, Elizabethtown, PA 17022.

KOLIMBARI
ITHAKA CULTURAL STUDY PROGRAM IN GREECE
CULTURAL STUDY SEMESTER IN GREECE

Hosted by ITHAKA Cultural Study Program in Greece
Academic Focus • Anthropology, archaeology, classics and classical languages, creative writing, Greek, Greek studies, history, literature.

GREECE
Kolimbari

Program Information • Students attend classes at ITHAKA Cultural Study Program in Greece. Scheduled travel to locations around Crete, museums, Knossos; field trips to villages, archaeological sites, churches, Samarian Gorge.
Sessions • Fall, spring.
Eligibility Requirements • Minimum age 16; open to precollege students, freshmen, sophomores, juniors; 2 letters of recommendation; no foreign language proficiency required.
Living Arrangements • Students live in a program-rented house. Quarters are shared with host institution students. Meals are taken as a group, in residences, in central dining facility.
Costs (2003-2004) • One term: $14,500 for fall term; contact sponsor for spring cost; includes tuition, housing, all meals, excursions. $50 application fee. $2000 nonrefundable deposit required. Financial aid available for all students: scholarships.
For More Information • Ms. Catherine K. Hunter, U.S. Director, ITHAKA Cultural Study Program in Greece, 5500 Prytania Street, #102, New Orleans, LA 70115; *Phone:* 504-269-2303; *Fax:* 504-269-2301. *E-mail:* ithakagr@msn.com. *World Wide Web:* http://www.ithaka.org/. Students may also apply through ITHAKA, Cultural Study Programs in Greece, ELTA Kolimbari, Crete 73006, Greece.

PAROS
HELLENIC INTERNATIONAL STUDIES IN THE ARTS
HELLENIC INTERNATIONAL STUDIES IN THE ARTS

Hosted by Hellenic International Studies in the Arts
Academic Focus • Art, art history, comparative literature, creative writing, drawing/painting, film and media studies, fine/studio arts, philosophy, photography.
Program Information • Students attend classes at Hellenic International Studies in the Arts. Field trips to Greek Islands, historic sites, museums; optional travel to Turkey at an extra cost.
Sessions • Fall, spring.
Eligibility Requirements • Minimum age 18; open to freshmen, sophomores, juniors, seniors, graduate students, adults; good academic standing at home school; seriousness of purpose; real desire to experience something new; no foreign language proficiency required.
Living Arrangements • Students live in locally rented apartments. Meals are taken on one's own, in residences.
Costs (2004) • One term: $7500; includes tuition, housing, excursions, books and class materials, lab equipment. $500 deposit required. Financial aid available for all students: scholarships, work study, early payment plan.
For More Information • Dr. Dion Nittis, Director, Hellenic International Studies in the Arts, Box 11, Paroikin, Paros, Cyclades 84400, Greece; *Phone:* +30 694-608-7430. *E-mail:* hisa@otcnet.gr. *World Wide Web:* http://www.hellenicinternational.org/

THESSALONIKI
COLLEGE CONSORTIUM FOR INTERNATIONAL STUDIES–COLLEGE OF STATEN ISLAND/CITY UNIVERSITY OF NEW YORK
PROGRAM IN THESSALONIKI, GREECE

Hosted by American University of Thessaloniki
Academic Focus • Accounting, anthropology, business administration/management, civilization studies, economics, English literature, European studies, finance, Greek, Greek studies, history, international business, marketing, philosophy, political science and government, psychology, sociology.
Program Information • Students attend classes at American University of Thessaloniki. Field trips to Athens, Vergina, Dion, Meteora, Mount Athos, Mount Olympus.
Sessions • Fall, spring, yearlong.
Eligibility Requirements • Minimum age 18; open to freshmen, sophomores, juniors, seniors; 2.5 GPA; 3 letters of recommendation; essay; transcript; no foreign language proficiency required.

Living Arrangements • Students live in host institution dormitories, locally rented apartments, program-owned apartments. Quarters are shared with host institution students. Meals are taken on one's own, in residences.
Costs (2004-2005) • One term: $7230 for CCIS members and CUNY students; $7480 for all others. Yearlong program: $14,460 for CCIS members and CUNY students; $14,960 for all others; includes tuition, housing, insurance, excursions, student support services, fees, airport pick-up. $265 nonrefundable deposit required. Financial aid available for students from sponsoring institution: scholarships, loans.
For More Information • College Consortium for International Studies, 2000 P Street, NW, Suite 503, Washington, DC 20036; *Phone:* 800-453-6956; *Fax:* 202-223-0999. *E-mail:* info@ccisabroad. org. *World Wide Web:* http://www.ccisabroad.org/. Students may also apply through College of Staten Island, The City University of New York, Center for International Service, Building 2A, Room 206, 2800 Victory Boulevard, Staten Island, NY 10314.

UNIVERSITY OF CONNECTICUT
STUDY ABROAD PROGRAM IN THESSALONIKI, GREECE

Hosted by Aristotle University of Thessaloniki
Academic Focus • Ancient history, archaeology, Greek, Greek studies, history, philosophy.
Program Information • Students attend classes at Aristotle University of Thessaloniki. Field trips to museums, monuments, historic and archaeological sites; optional travel to Greek Islands, Athens, continental Europe at an extra cost.
Sessions • Fall, spring, yearlong.
Eligibility Requirements • Open to sophomores, juniors, seniors; 2.5 GPA; good academic standing at home school; interest in Hellenic studies, archaeology, ancient/modern Greece; some Greek recommended.
Living Arrangements • Students live in locally rented apartments, host family homes. Quarters are shared with host institution students. Meals are taken on one's own, with host family, in restaurants.
Costs (2002-2003) • One term: $5500. Yearlong program: $11,000; includes tuition, housing, all meals, international student ID. $25 application fee. $350 nonrefundable deposit required. Financial aid available for students from sponsoring institution.
For More Information • Mr. Gordon Lustila, Acting Director of Study Abroad Programs, University of Connecticut, 843 Bolton Road, Unit 1207, Storrs, CT 06269-1207; *Phone:* 860-486-5022; *Fax:* 860-486-2976. *E-mail:* sabadm03@uconnvm.uconn.edu. *World Wide Web:* http://studyabroad.uconn.edu/

GUATEMALA
GUATEMALA CITY
HIGHER EDUCATION CONSORTIUM FOR URBAN AFFAIRS (HECUA)
ENVIRONMENT, ECONOMY, AND COMMUNITY IN LATIN AMERICA

Held at University of the Valley of Guatemala
Academic Focus • Anthropology, economics, environmental science/studies, ethics, interdisciplinary studies, Latin American studies, liberal studies, Mayan studies, social sciences, Spanish language and literature.
Program Information • Classes are held on the campus of University of the Valley of Guatemala. Faculty members are local instructors hired by the sponsor. Scheduled travel to Lake Atitlán area in Guatemala, Tikal, Havana; field trips to a marketplace in Guatemala, urban and rural settings in Guatemala and Cuba.
Sessions • Spring.
Eligibility Requirements • Open to sophomores, juniors, seniors, graduate students, adults; 2.5 GPA; 2 letters of recommendation; good academic standing at home school; 2 years of college course work in Spanish.

Living Arrangements • Students live in host family homes, hotels. Meals are taken with host family, in residences.
Costs (2004) • One term: $11,000; includes tuition, housing, all meals, insurance, excursions, student support services. $75 application fee. $400 nonrefundable deposit required. Financial aid available for all students: scholarships.
For More Information • Mr. Michael Eaton, Director of Admissions and Student Services, Higher Education Consortium for Urban Affairs (HECUA), 2233 University Avenue West, Suite 210, St. Paul, MN 55114-1629; *Phone:* 800-554-1089; *Fax:* 651-659-9421. *E-mail:* info@hecua.org. *World Wide Web:* http://www.hecua.org/

HIGHER EDUCATION CONSORTIUM FOR URBAN AFFAIRS (HECUA)
GUATEMALA: POLITICS, DEVELOPMENT, AND THE CITY

Held at University of the Valley of Guatemala
Academic Focus • Anthropology, economics, interdisciplinary studies, international affairs, Latin American studies, political science and government, social sciences, sociology, Spanish language and literature, urban studies, urban/regional planning.
Program Information • Classes are held on the campus of University of the Valley of Guatemala. Faculty members are local instructors hired by the sponsor. Scheduled travel to Guatemala City, Lake Atitlan area, Havana; field trips to a marketplace in Guatemala, urban and rural settings in Guatemala and Cuba.
Sessions • Fall.
Eligibility Requirements • Open to sophomores, juniors, seniors, graduate students, adults; 2.5 GPA; 1 letter of recommendation; good academic standing at home school; 2 years of college course work in Spanish.
Living Arrangements • Students live in host family homes, hotels. Meals are taken with host family, in residences.
Costs (2003) • One term: $11,000; includes tuition, housing, all meals, insurance, excursions, student support services. $75 application fee. $400 nonrefundable deposit required. Financial aid available for all students: scholarships.
For More Information • Mr. Michael Eaton, Director of Admissions and Student Services, Higher Education Consortium for Urban Affairs (HECUA), 2233 University Avenue West, Suite 210, St. Paul, MN 55114-1629; *Phone:* 800-554-1089; *Fax:* 651-659-9421. *E-mail:* info@hecua.org. *World Wide Web:* http://www.hecua.org/

QUETZALTENGO
AUGSBURG COLLEGE
SUSTAINABLE DEVELOPMENT AND SOCIAL CHANGE IN CENTRAL AMERICA

Hosted by Proyecto Linguistico School, Center for Global Education
Academic Focus • Economics, history, interdisciplinary studies, Latin American studies, peace and conflict studies, religious studies, Spanish language and literature.
Program Information • Students attend classes at Center for Global Education, Proyecto Linguistico School. Scheduled travel to Guatemala, El Salvador, Nicaragua; field trips; optional travel at an extra cost.
Sessions • Fall, spring.
Eligibility Requirements • Open to sophomores, juniors, seniors; course work in economics (1 course); 2.5 GPA; 2 letters of recommendation; good academic standing at home school; 0.5 years of college course work in Spanish.
Living Arrangements • Students live in program-owned houses, host family homes, hotels, guest houses. Quarters are shared with host institution students. Meals are taken as a group, with host family, in central dining facility, in restaurants.
Costs (2004-2005) • One term: sliding fee scale for consortium partners; $13,400 for transfers; includes tuition, housing, all meals, insurance, excursions, international student ID, some books and class materials. $50 application fee. $500 nonrefundable deposit required. Financial aid available for students from sponsoring institution: scholarships, loans.
For More Information • Ms. Margaret Anderson, Coordinator, Semester Programs Abroad, Augsburg College, 2211 Riverside

Avenue, Minneapolis, MN 55454; *Phone:* 800-299-8889; *Fax:* 612-330-1695. *E-mail:* globaled@augsburg.edu. *World Wide Web:* http://www.augsburg.edu/global/

HONDURAS
TEGUCIGALPA
CALVIN COLLEGE
SPANISH STUDIES IN HONDURAS

Hosted by National Pedagogical University 'Francisco Morazán'
Academic Focus • Economics, Latin American literature, Latin American studies, linguistics, Spanish language and literature.
Program Information • Students attend classes at National Pedagogical University 'Francisco Morazán'. Scheduled travel to Copan, Nicaragua, a rainforest, Guatemala; field trips to barrios, museums, plantations, government agencies.
Sessions • Fall.
Eligibility Requirements • Open to sophomores, juniors, seniors; 2.5 GPA; 2 letters of recommendation; good academic standing at home school; interview with program director; advisor approval; 2 years of college course work in Spanish.
Living Arrangements • Students live in host family homes. Meals are taken with host family, in residences.
Costs (2003) • One term: $11,325; includes tuition, housing, all meals, excursions, international airfare, student support services, immunizations. $50 application fee. $400 nonrefundable deposit required. Financial aid available for students from sponsoring institution: scholarships, loans.
For More Information • Dr. Ellen B. Monsma, Director, Calvin College, Office of Off-Campus Programs, 3201 Burton Street, SE, Grand Rapids, MI 49546; *Phone:* 616-526-6551; *Fax:* 616-526-6756. *E-mail:* emonsma@calvin.edu. *World Wide Web:* http://www.calvin.edu/academic/off-campus/

HUNGARY
CITY TO CITY
ACIE (ACTR/ACCELS)
ACIE (ACCELS) HUNGARIAN LANGUAGE PROGRAM

Hosted by Debrecen Summer School (Debrecen), Eötvös Loránd University Budapest (ELTE)
Academic Focus • Area studies, Hungarian.
Program Information • Students attend classes at Eötvös Loránd University Budapest (ELTE) (Budapest), Debrecen Summer School (Debrecen).
Sessions • Fall, spring, yearlong.
Eligibility Requirements • Minimum age 18; open to freshmen, sophomores, juniors, seniors, graduate students, adults; 3 letters of recommendation; good academic standing at home school; 1 year of college course work in Hungarian.
Living Arrangements • Students live in host institution dormitories, locally rented apartments. Quarters are shared with students from other programs. Meals are taken on one's own, in residences, in central dining facility.
Costs (2002-2003) • One term: contact sponsor for cost. Yearlong program: contact sponsor for cost. $35 application fee. $500 nonrefundable deposit required. Financial aid available for all students: scholarships.
For More Information • Nurhan Kocaoglu, Russian and Eurasian Program Manager, ACIE (ACTR/ACCELS), 1776 Massachusetts Avenue, NW, Suite 700, Washington, DC 20036; *Phone:* 202-833-7522; *Fax:* 202-833-7523. *E-mail:* outbound@actr.org. *World Wide Web:* http://www.actr.org/

BUDAPEST

ACADEMIC PROGRAMS INTERNATIONAL (API)

(API)–BUDAPEST, HUNGARY

Hosted by Budapest University of Economic Sciences and Public Administration
Academic Focus • Accounting, business administration/ management, computer science, economics, European studies, history, Hungarian, Hungarian studies, international business, law and legal studies, marketing, mathematics, political science and government, sociology.
Program Information • Students attend classes at Budapest University of Economic Sciences and Public Administration. Scheduled travel to Krakow; field trips to Esztergom, Sopron, Szentandre, Visigrad, Krakow.
Sessions • Fall, spring, yearlong.
Eligibility Requirements • Minimum age 18; open to freshmen, sophomores, juniors, seniors, graduate students, adults; 2.75 GPA; 1 letter of recommendation; good academic standing at home school; official transcript from home university; no foreign language proficiency required.
Living Arrangements • Students live in host institution dormitories, locally rented apartments. Quarters are shared with host institution students. Meals are taken on one's own, in residences, in restaurants.
Costs (2004-2005) • One term: $8600–$8800. Yearlong program: $16,800; includes tuition, housing, insurance, excursions, student support services, airport pick-up, ground transportation. $150 nonrefundable deposit required. Financial aid available for all students: scholarships.
For More Information • Ms. Jennifer C. Allen, Director, Academic Programs International (API), 107 East Hopkins, San Marcos, TX 78666; *Phone:* 800-844-4124; *Fax:* 512-392-8420. *E-mail:* api@academicintl.com. *World Wide Web:* http://www.academicintl.com/

BENTLEY COLLEGE

STUDY ABROAD PROGRAM, BUDAPEST HUNGARY

Hosted by Budapest University of Economic Sciences and Public Administration
Academic Focus • Business administration/management, economics, finance, Hungarian, international affairs, international business, marketing, political science and government, sociology.
Program Information • Students attend classes at Budapest University of Economic Sciences and Public Administration. Scheduled travel; field trips; optional travel at an extra cost.
Sessions • Fall, spring, yearlong.
Eligibility Requirements • Open to sophomores, juniors, seniors; 3.0 GPA; 1 letter of recommendation; good academic standing at home school; essays; no foreign language proficiency required.
Living Arrangements • Students live in host institution dormitories, locally rented apartments. Quarters are shared with students from other programs. Meals are taken on one's own, in residences, in central dining facility, in restaurants.
Costs (2002-2003) • One term: $13,600. Yearlong program: $21,880; includes tuition, housing, excursions, international student ID, student support services. $35 application fee. $500 nonrefundable deposit required. Financial aid available for students from sponsoring institution: scholarships, loans.
For More Information • Ms. Jennifer Aquino, Assistant Director, International Center, Bentley College, 175 Forest Street, Waltham, MA 02452; *Phone:* 781-891-3474; *Fax:* 781-891-2819. *E-mail:* study_abroad@bentley.edu. *World Wide Web:* http://ecampus.bentley.edu/dept/sa/

CALVIN COLLEGE

SEMESTER IN HUNGARY

Hosted by Technical University of Budapest, Budapest University of Economic Sciences and Public Administration, 'Károli Gáspár' University of the Hungarian Reformed Church
Academic Focus • Full curriculum, Hungarian studies.
Program Information • Students attend classes at Technical University of Budapest, Budapest University of Economic Sciences and Public Administration, 'Károli Gáspár' University of the Hungarian Reformed Church. Scheduled travel to Krakow, Prague, Vienna; field trips to Parliament, museums; optional travel to the Ukraine, Slovakia at an extra cost.
Sessions • Fall.
Eligibility Requirements • Open to sophomores, juniors, seniors; 2.5 GPA; 2 letters of recommendation; good academic standing at home school; interviews with program director; advisor approval; no foreign language proficiency required.
Living Arrangements • Students live in host institution dormitories. Quarters are shared with host institution students. Meals are taken on one's own, in restaurants.
Costs (2003-2004) • One term: $11,450; includes tuition, housing, all meals, excursions, international airfare, student support services, immunizations. $50 application fee. $400 nonrefundable deposit required. Financial aid available for students from sponsoring institution: scholarships, loans.
For More Information • Dr. Ellen B. Monsma, Director, Calvin College, Office of Off-Campus Programs, 3201 Burton Street, SE, Grand Rapids, MI 49546; *Phone:* 616-526-6551; *Fax:* 616-526-6756. *E-mail:* emonsma@calvin.edu. *World Wide Web:* http://www.calvin.edu/academic/off-campus/

CIEE

CIEE STUDY CENTER AT THE BUDAPEST UNIVERSITY OF ECONOMIC SCIENCES AND PUBLIC ADMINISTRATION, HUNGARY

Hosted by Budapest University of Economic Sciences and Public Administration
Academic Focus • Art history, Central European studies, economics, ethnic studies, history, Hungarian, international affairs, political science and government.
Program Information • Students attend classes at Budapest University of Economic Sciences and Public Administration. Scheduled travel to Transylvania; field trips to southern Hungary, Danube Bend, western Hungary, sites of cultural interest in and around Budapest.
Sessions • Fall, spring, yearlong.
Eligibility Requirements • Open to sophomores, juniors, seniors, adults; 2.75 GPA; 2 letters of recommendation; no foreign language proficiency required.
Living Arrangements • Students live in locally rented apartments, host family homes. Quarters are shared with host institution students. Meals are taken on one's own, in residences, in restaurants.
Costs (2003-2004) • One term: $8500. Yearlong program: $15,800; includes tuition, housing, insurance, excursions, student support services, visa fees, cultural activities, pre-departure advising, optional on-site pick-up. $30 application fee. $300 deposit required. Financial aid available for all students: minority student scholarships, non-traditional study scholarships, travel grants.
For More Information • Ms. Hannah McChesney, Admissions Officer, Europe, Middle East, and Africa, CIEE, 7 Custom House Street, 3rd Floor, Portland, ME 04101; *Phone:* 800-40-STUDY; *Fax:* 207-553-7699. *E-mail:* studyinfo@ciee.org. *World Wide Web:* http://www.ciee.org/isp/

LEXIA INTERNATIONAL

LEXIA IN BUDAPEST

Hosted by Pázmány Péter Catholic University, Eötvös Collegium Budapest
Academic Focus • Anthropology, area studies, art, art history, Central European studies, civilization studies, comparative history, cultural studies, drawing/painting, Eastern European studies, economics, environmental science/studies, ethnic studies, European studies, film and media studies, fine/studio arts, geography, history, Hungarian, Hungarian studies, interdisciplinary studies, international affairs, international business, liberal studies, literature, music, music history, music performance, peace and conflict studies, philosophy, political science and government, psychology, religious studies, Slavic languages, social sciences, sociology, urban studies.
Program Information • Students attend classes at Pázmány Péter Catholic University, Eötvös Collegium Budapest. Field trips to Szeged, Transylvania, Eger.
Sessions • Fall, spring, yearlong.
Eligibility Requirements • Minimum age 18; open to sophomores, juniors, seniors, graduate students, adults; 2.5 GPA; 2 letters of recommendation; no foreign language proficiency required.

Living Arrangements • Students live in host institution dormitories, locally rented apartments. Quarters are shared with host institution students. Meals are taken on one's own, in residences, in central dining facility, in restaurants.

Costs (2003-2004) • One term: $9950. Yearlong program: $18,550; includes tuition, housing, some meals, insurance, excursions, student support services, computer access, transcript. $35 application fee. $300 refundable deposit required. Financial aid available for all students: scholarships, work study.

For More Information • Lexia International, 23 South Main Street, Hanover, NH 03755; *Phone:* 800-775-3942; *Fax:* 603-643-9899. *E-mail:* info@lexiaintl.org. *World Wide Web:* http://www.lexiaintl.org/

STATE UNIVERSITY OF NEW YORK AT OSWEGO
BUDAPEST UNIVERSITY OF ECONOMIC SCIENCES AND PUBLIC ADMINISTRATION

Hosted by Budapest University of Economic Sciences and Public Administration
Academic Focus • Business administration/management, economics, finance, history, Hungarian, Hungarian studies, international affairs, international business, marketing, political science and government.
Program Information • Students attend classes at Budapest University of Economic Sciences and Public Administration. Field trips to Lake Balaton.
Sessions • Fall, spring, yearlong.
Eligibility Requirements • Open to sophomores, juniors, seniors; 2.5 GPA; 3 letters of recommendation; good academic standing at home school; personal statement; no foreign language proficiency required.
Living Arrangements • Students live in locally rented apartments. Meals are taken on one's own, in central dining facility, in restaurants.
Costs (2003-2004) • One term: $2320. Yearlong program: $4640; includes tuition, insurance, excursions, student support services. $250 nonrefundable deposit required. Financial aid available for students: home university financial aid, loan processing and scholarships for Oswego students.
For More Information • Mr. Joshua McKeown, Associate Director, State University of New York at Oswego, 122A Swetman Hall, Oswego, NY 13126; *Phone:* 888-4-OSWEGO; *Fax:* 315-312-2477. *E-mail:* intled@oswego.edu. *World Wide Web:* http://www.oswego.edu/intled/

UNIVERSITY OF SAN FRANCISCO
USF IN BUDAPEST

Hosted by Pázmány Péter Catholic University
Academic Focus • Full curriculum.
Program Information • Students attend classes at Pázmány Péter Catholic University. Field trips to Budapest, nearby cities; optional travel to Vienna, Prague, Bratislava at an extra cost.
Sessions • Fall, spring, yearlong.
Eligibility Requirements • Minimum age 18; open to sophomores, juniors, seniors; 2.5 GPA; 1 letter of recommendation; good academic standing at home school; statement of purpose; no foreign language proficiency required.
Living Arrangements • Students live in locally rented apartments. Quarters are shared with host institution students. Meals are taken on one's own, in residences.
Costs (2002-2003) • One term: $13,690. Yearlong program: $27,380; includes tuition, housing, student support services. $200 nonrefundable deposit required. Financial aid available for students from sponsoring institution: scholarships, work study, loans.
For More Information • Ms. Sharon Li, Program Coordinator, University of San Francisco, 2130 Fulton Street, San Francisco, CA 94117-1080; *Phone:* 415-422-2335; *Fax:* 415-422-6212. *E-mail:* lis@usfca.edu. *World Wide Web:* http://artsci.usfca.edu/academics/internationalprograms.html

KECSKEMÉT
COLLEGE CONSORTIUM FOR INTERNATIONAL STUDIES–CAPITAL UNIVERSITY
MUSIC IN HUNGARY

Hosted by Zoltan Kodaly Pedagogical Institute
Academic Focus • Music, music education, music performance, music theory.
Program Information • Students attend classes at Zoltan Kodaly Pedagogical Institute. Field trips to Budapest, Opusztaszer, Szeged, Tihany; optional travel to Budapest, Vienna at an extra cost.
Sessions • Fall.
Eligibility Requirements • Open to juniors, seniors, adults; major in music; 3.0 GPA; 2 letters of recommendation; satisfactory aural skills assessment; audition tape; no foreign language proficiency required.
Living Arrangements • Students live in host institution dormitories. Quarters are shared with host institution students, students from other programs. Meals are taken on one's own, in residences.
Costs (2004) • One term: $8100; includes tuition, housing, insurance, excursions, student support services. $1200 nonrefundable deposit required. Financial aid available for students from sponsoring institution: scholarships, loans, state and federal grants.
For More Information • College Consortium for International Studies, 2000 P Street, NW, Suite 503, Washington, DC 20036; *Phone:* 800-453-6956; *Fax:* 202-223-0999. *E-mail:* info@ccisabroad.org. *World Wide Web:* http://www.ccisabroad.org/. Students may also apply through Capital University, Office of International Education, 2199 East Main Street, Columbus, OH 43209.

PÉCS
STATE UNIVERSITY OF NEW YORK AT OSWEGO
THE UNIVERSITY OF PÉCS

Hosted by University Pécs
Academic Focus • Business administration/management, economics, history, Hungarian, Hungarian studies, political science and government, psychology, sociology, teaching.
Program Information • Students attend classes at University Pécs.
Sessions • Fall, spring, yearlong.
Eligibility Requirements • Open to sophomores, juniors, seniors; 2.5 GPA; 3 letters of recommendation; good academic standing at home school; personal statement; no foreign language proficiency required.
Living Arrangements • Students live in host institution dormitories, locally rented apartments. Quarters are shared with host institution students, students from other programs. Meals are taken on one's own, in central dining facility, in restaurants.
Costs (2003-2004) • One term: $2720. Yearlong program: $5440; includes tuition, insurance, student support services. $250 nonrefundable deposit required. Financial aid available for students: home university financial aid, loan processing and scholarships for Oswego students.
For More Information • Mr. Joshua McKeown, Associate Director, State University of New York at Oswego, 122A Swetman Hall, Oswego, NY 13126; *Phone:* 888-4-OSWEGO; *Fax:* 315-312-2477. *E-mail:* intled@oswego.edu. *World Wide Web:* http://www.oswego.edu/intled/

SZEGED
UNIVERSITY OF WISCONSIN–STEVENS POINT
SEMESTER IN HUNGARY

Hosted by Attila József University Szeged
Academic Focus • Film and media studies, geography, history, Hungarian, Hungarian studies, international affairs, political science and government, social sciences.
Program Information • Students attend classes at Attila József University Szeged. Field trips to Budapest; optional travel to Germany, Austria, Poland, Slovakia at an extra cost.
Sessions • Spring.

Eligibility Requirements • Minimum age 18; open to sophomores, juniors, seniors, adults; 2.25 GPA; good academic standing at home school; no foreign language proficiency required.

Living Arrangements • Students live in host institution dormitories, locally rented apartments, host family homes, hotels. Quarters are shared with host institution students, students from other programs. Meals are taken on one's own, with host family, in residences, in restaurants.

Costs (2003-2004) • One term: $3900 for Wisconsin residents; $9000 for nonresidents; includes tuition, housing, all meals, excursions, books and class materials, international student ID, student support services. $15 application fee. $150 nonrefundable deposit required. Financial aid available for all students: work study, loans.

For More Information • Mr. Mark Koepke, Associate Director, University of Wisconsin–Stevens Point, International Programs, 108 Collins, Stevens Ponit, WI 54481; *Phone:* 715-346-2717; *Fax:* 715-346-3591. *E-mail:* intlprog@uwsp.edu. *World Wide Web:* http://www.uwsp.edu/studyabroad/

SZOMBATHELY
BRETHREN COLLEGES ABROAD
BCA PEACE AND JUSTICE PROGRAM IN SZOMBATHELY, HUNGARY

Hosted by Berzsenyi Daniel College

Academic Focus • International affairs, political science and government.

Program Information • Students attend classes at Berzsenyi Daniel College. Field trips to Budapest, the Transdanubia Region.

Sessions • Spring.

Eligibility Requirements • Minimum age 18; open to juniors, seniors; 2.6 GPA; 3 letters of recommendation; no foreign language proficiency required.

Living Arrangements • Students live in locally rented apartments. Meals are taken on one's own, in residences.

Costs (2004) • One term: $11,500; includes tuition, housing, all meals, insurance, excursions, international student ID, student support services. $50 application fee. $100 nonrefundable deposit required.

For More Information • Mr. Jason Sanderson, Program Officer for Hungary, Brethren Colleges Abroad, 50 Alpha Drive, Elizabethtown, PA 17022; *Phone:* 866-222-6188; *Fax:* 717-361-6619. *E-mail:* info@bcanet.org. *World Wide Web:* http://www.bcanet.org/

INDIA
CITY TO CITY
UNIVERSITY OF WISCONSIN–MADISON
COLLEGE YEAR IN INDIA

Academic Focus • Fine/studio arts, Hindi, liberal studies, performing arts, religious studies, social sciences, Tamil, Telugu, Urdu.

Program Information • Faculty members are drawn from the sponsor's U.S. staff and local instructors hired by the sponsor. Scheduled travel to Godavari River, Manali, villages, temples; field trips to cultural sites.

Sessions • Yearlong, pre-departure language program also available.

Eligibility Requirements • Open to juniors, seniors; 2.5 GPA; good academic standing at home school; no foreign language proficiency required.

Living Arrangements • Students live in locally rented apartments, program-owned houses, host family homes. Meals are taken as a group, in central dining facility.

Costs (2002-2003) • Yearlong program: $24,400; includes tuition, housing, some meals, insurance, excursions, international airfare, books and class materials, personal spending, inoculations, pre-departure expenses. $100 nonrefundable deposit required. Financial aid available for all students: scholarships, loans.

For More Information • Peer Advisor, University of Wisconsin–Madison, Office of International Studies and Programs, 261 Bascom Hall, 500 Lincoln Drive, Madison, WI 53706; *Phone:* 608-265-6329; *Fax:* 608-262-6998. *E-mail:* peeradvisor@bascom.wisc.edu. *World Wide Web:* http://www.studyabroad.wisc.edu/

AUROVILLE
LIVING ROUTES–STUDY ABROAD IN ECOVILLAGES
LIVING ROUTES–INDIA: SUSTAINABILITY IN PRACTICE AT AUROVILLE

Hosted by Auroville International Community

Academic Focus • Agriculture, community service, conservation studies, ecology, environmental health, environmental science/studies, ethics, interdisciplinary studies, peace and conflict studies, urban/regional planning.

Program Information • Students attend classes at Auroville International Community. Scheduled travel to Madurai, a tiger reserve, a rainforest, Hampi, Mitraniketan-Gandhian community in Kerala, Fireflies, Palani Hills; field trips to Pondicherry, Gingee, village homestays.

Sessions • Fall, spring.

Eligibility Requirements • Minimum age 18; open to precollege students, freshmen, sophomores, juniors, seniors, graduate students, adults; 2.5 GPA; 2 letters of recommendation; good academic standing at home school; no foreign language proficiency required.

Living Arrangements • Students live in host institution dormitories, host family homes. Quarters are shared with host institution students. Meals are taken as a group, in central dining facility.

Costs (2003-2004) • One term: $10,750; includes tuition, housing, all meals, excursions, student support services. $50 application fee. $800 nonrefundable deposit required. Financial aid available for all students: scholarships.

For More Information • Dr. Daniel Greenberg, Director, Living Routes–Study Abroad in Ecovillages, 79 South Pleasant Street, Suite 302, Amherst, MA 01002; *Phone:* 888-515-7333; *Fax:* 413-259-1256. *E-mail:* programs@livingroutes.org. *World Wide Web:* http://www.LivingRoutes.org/

BANGALORE
CONCORDIA COLLEGE AND GUSTAVUS ADOLPHUS COLLEGE
SOCIAL JUSTICE, PEACE, AND DEVELOPMENT: A SEMESTER IN INDIA

Academic Focus • Economics, environmental science/studies, peace and conflict studies, urban studies, women's studies.

Program Information • Faculty members are drawn from the sponsor's U.S. staff and local instructors hired by the sponsor. Scheduled travel to Bombay (Mumbai); field trips to Calcutta, southern India, Waynad, Bagayam; optional travel to Nepal, Calcutta at an extra cost.

Sessions • Fall.

Eligibility Requirements • Open to sophomores, juniors, seniors; 2.75 GPA; good academic standing at home school; no foreign language proficiency required.

Living Arrangements • Students live in host institution dormitories, locally rented apartments, host family homes, hostels, a YWCA. Quarters are shared with students from other programs. Meals are taken as a group, in central dining facility.

Costs (2002) • One term: $12,550; includes tuition, housing, some meals, insurance, excursions, international airfare, international student ID, student support services. $50 application fee. $300 refundable deposit required. Financial aid available for all students: scholarships, loans.

For More Information • Dr. John Y. Cha, Director of International Education, Concordia College and Gustavus Adolphus College, 800 West College Avenue, St. Peter, MN 56082; *Phone:* 507-933-7545; *Fax:* 507-933-7900. *E-mail:* jcha@gac.edu. *World Wide Web:* http://www.gac.edu/Academics/ied/inted.html. Students may also apply through Concordia College, 901 8th Street South, Moorhead, MN 56562.

LONG ISLAND UNIVERSITY
FRIENDS WORLD PROGRAM–SOUTH ASIAN CENTRE (INDIA)

Hosted by Friends World Program
Academic Focus • Anthropology, crafts, dance, Hindi, Indian studies, interdisciplinary studies, music, peace and conflict studies, religious studies, women's studies.
Program Information • Students attend classes at Friends World Program. Scheduled travel to New Delhi, Madras, Bombay, Nepal; field trips to a Tibetan refugee camp, a yoga retreat, temples, a meditation camp, local sites; optional travel to Thailand, other parts of India, Tibet (when permitted) at an extra cost.
Sessions • Fall, spring, yearlong.
Eligibility Requirements • Minimum age 18; open to sophomores, juniors, seniors, adults; good academic standing at home school; interview; essay; no foreign language proficiency required.
Living Arrangements • Students live in locally rented apartments. Quarters are shared with host institution students. Meals are taken as a group, on one's own, in residences, in central dining facility, in restaurants.
Costs (2003-2004) • One term: $14,575 (estimated). Yearlong program: $29,150 (estimated); includes tuition, housing, all meals, excursions, international airfare, books and class materials. $30 application fee. $200 deposit required. Financial aid available for students from sponsoring institution: scholarships, loans, need-based grants.
For More Information • Admissions Office, FWP, Long Island University, 239 Montauk Highway, Southampton, NY 11968; *Phone:* 631-287-8474; *Fax:* 631-287-8463. *E-mail:* fw@liu.edu. *World Wide Web:* http://www.southampton.liu.edu/fw/

SCHOOL FOR INTERNATIONAL TRAINING, SIT STUDY ABROAD
INDIA: CULTURE AND DEVELOPMENT

Academic Focus • Anthropology, economics, geography, history, Indian studies, Kannada, liberal studies, political science and government, religious studies, visual and performing arts.
Program Information • Faculty members are drawn from the sponsor's U.S. staff and local instructors hired by the sponsor. Scheduled travel to Mysore, Kerala; field trips to rural areas near Mysore, development project sites, cultural and historic sites.
Sessions • Fall, spring.
Eligibility Requirements • Open to sophomores, juniors, seniors; 2.5 GPA; 2 letters of recommendation; good academic standing at home school; no foreign language proficiency required.
Living Arrangements • Students live in host institution dormitories, host family homes, hotels. Meals are taken as a group, on one's own, with host family, in residences, in central dining facility, in restaurants.
Costs (2003-2004) • One term: $12,400; includes tuition, housing, all meals, insurance, excursions. $50 application fee. $400 nonrefundable deposit required. Financial aid available for all students: scholarships.
For More Information • School for International Training, SIT Study Abroad, Kipling Road, Brattleboro, VT 05302-0676; *Phone:* 888-272-7881; *Fax:* 802-258-3296. *E-mail:* studyabroad@sit.edu. *World Wide Web:* http://www.sit.edu/studyabroad/

BODH GAYA
ANTIOCH COLLEGE
BUDDHIST STUDIES IN INDIA

Held at Burmese Monastery
Academic Focus • Ancient history, anthropology, Buddhist studies, Hindi, Indian studies, philosophy, religious studies, Tibetan.
Program Information • Classes are held on the campus of Burmese Monastery. Faculty members are drawn from the sponsor's U.S. staff and local instructors hired by the sponsor. Field trips to Varanasi, Rajgir; optional travel to other areas of India, Nepal.
Sessions • Fall.
Eligibility Requirements • Minimum age 18; open to sophomores, juniors, seniors, adults; 2 letters of recommendation; good academic standing at home school; maturity, sensitivity; no foreign language proficiency required.

Living Arrangements • Students live in the guest house of a Burmese Monastery. Meals are taken as a group.
Costs (2003-2004) • One term: $14,285; includes tuition, housing, all meals, international student ID, airfare from London. $35 application fee. $150 nonrefundable deposit required. Financial aid available for students from sponsoring institution: scholarships, loans.
For More Information • Prof. C. Robert Pryor, Director, Buddhist Studies Program, Antioch College, Antioch Education Abroad, 795 Livermore Street, Yellow Springs, OH 45387-1697; *Phone:* 800-874-7986; *Fax:* 937-769-1019. *E-mail:* aea@antioch-college.edu. *World Wide Web:* http://www.antioch-college.edu/aea/

CALCUTTA
THE INTERNATIONAL PARTNERSHIP FOR SERVICE LEARNING
INDIA SERVICE–LEARNING

Hosted by Indian Institute for Social Welfare and Business Management
Academic Focus • Community service, history, Indian studies, international affairs, social sciences.
Program Information • Students attend classes at Indian Institute for Social Welfare and Business Management. Classes are also held on the campus of Partnership for Service–Learning Center. Scheduled travel to Delhi, Agra, the Taj Mahal, Konarak; field trips to Calcutta and surrounding villages, archaeological sites; optional travel to sites in India at an extra cost.
Sessions • Fall, spring, winter.
Eligibility Requirements • Minimum age 18; open to freshmen, sophomores, juniors, seniors, graduate students, adults; 2 letters of recommendation; good academic standing at home school; evidence of maturity, responsibility; no foreign language proficiency required.
Living Arrangements • Students live in host family homes. Meals are taken with host family, in residences.
Costs (2003-2004) • One term: $10,400; includes tuition, housing, some meals, excursions, international airfare, books and class materials, student support services, service placement and supervision. $50 application fee. $250 refundable deposit required. Financial aid available for all students: federal financial aid.
For More Information • Ms. Ilana Golin, Coordinator of Student Programs, The International Partnership for Service Learning, 815 Second Avenue, Suite 315, New York, NY 10017-4594; *Phone:* 212-986-0989; *Fax:* 212-986-5039. *E-mail:* info@ipsl.org. *World Wide Web:* http://www.ipsl.org/

COCHIN
SAINT MARY'S COLLEGE
SEMESTER AROUND THE WORLD PROGRAM

Hosted by Sacred Hearts College
Academic Focus • Anthropology, art, drama/theater, economics, fine/studio arts, history, literature, music, philosophy, political science and government, religious studies, sociology, visual and performing arts.
Program Information • Students attend classes at Sacred Hearts College. Scheduled travel to Xi'an, Beijing, Tokyo, Hong Kong, Singapore, Kuala Lampur, Ho Chi Minh City, Bangkok, New Delhi, Bombay, Madras, Jaipur; field trips to local factories, schools, tourist sites, art galleries, government offices, churches, temples; optional travel to Eastern and Western European countries.
Sessions • Fall, program runs every other year.
Eligibility Requirements • Open to sophomores, juniors, seniors; 3.0 GPA; 3 letters of recommendation; good academic standing at home school; no foreign language proficiency required.
Living Arrangements • Students live in hotels, host family homes for weekend stays. Meals are taken as a group, in central dining facility.
Costs (2001) • One term: $17,500; includes tuition, housing, all meals, excursions, around-the-world air ticket. $25 application fee. $1000 nonrefundable deposit required. Financial aid available for students from sponsoring institution: scholarships, loans.

For More Information • Dr. Cyriac K. Pullapilly, Director, Saint Mary's College, Department of History, Notre Dame, IN 46556; *Phone:* 574-284-4468; *Fax:* 574-273-5973. *E-mail:* crosscult@aol.com

DELHI

BROWN UNIVERSITY
BROWN IN INDIA

Hosted by Lady Shri Ram College for Women, Saint Stephen's College
Academic Focus • Full curriculum.
Program Information • Students attend classes at Saint Stephen's College, Lady Shri Ram College for Women. Field trips to sites around Delhi area.
Sessions • Fall, yearlong.
Eligibility Requirements • Open to juniors, seniors; 3.0 GPA; 2 letters of recommendation; good academic standing at home school; interest in and previous study related to Southern Asian studies; no foreign language proficiency required.
Living Arrangements • Students live in host institution dormitories, locally rented apartments, guest houses. Quarters are shared with host institution students, students from other programs. Meals are taken on one's own, in residences.
Costs (2004-2005) • One term: $15,336. Yearlong program: $30,672; includes tuition, housing, international student ID, student support services, Hindi language course. $250 nonrefundable deposit required. Financial aid available for students from sponsoring institution: scholarships, loans.
For More Information • Ms. Mell Bolen, Director, Brown University, Office of International Programs, Box 1973, Providence, RI 02912-1973; *Phone:* 401-863-3555; *Fax:* 401-863-3311. *E-mail:* oip_office@brown.edu. *World Wide Web:* http://www.brown.edu/OIP/

MICHIGAN STATE UNIVERSITY
MULTIDISCIPLINARY STUDIES IN NEW DELHI

Academic Focus • Community service, Indian studies, social sciences, social work.
Program Information • Faculty members are drawn from the sponsor's U.S. staff and local instructors hired by the sponsor. Field trips to the Taj Mahal, Jaipur, Red Fort.
Sessions • Spring.
Eligibility Requirements • Minimum age 18; open to juniors, seniors, graduate students; 2.5 GPA; good academic standing at home school; faculty approval; no foreign language proficiency required.
Living Arrangements • Students live in host institution dormitories, locally rented apartments, host family homes. Meals are taken on one's own, with host family, in residences, in central dining facility, in restaurants.
Costs (2003) • One term: $2300 (estimated); includes housing, insurance, excursions, student support services. $100 application fee. $200 nonrefundable deposit required. Financial aid available for students from sponsoring institution: scholarships, loans.
For More Information • Ms. Sherry Martinez-Bonilla, Office Assistant, Michigan State University, Office of Study Abroad, 109 International Center, East Lansing, MI 48824-1035; *Phone:* 517-353-8920; *Fax:* 517-432-2082. *E-mail:* marti269@msu.edu. *World Wide Web:* http://studyabroad.msu.edu/

RUTGERS, THE STATE UNIVERSITY OF NEW JERSEY
STUDY ABROAD IN INDIA

Hosted by Saint Stephen's College
Academic Focus • Full curriculum.
Program Information • Students attend classes at Saint Stephen's College. Scheduled travel to Kerala, Madras; field trips to Agra.
Sessions • Fall, yearlong.
Eligibility Requirements • Open to sophomores, juniors, seniors; 2.5 GPA; 2 letters of recommendation; good academic standing at home school; no foreign language proficiency required.
Living Arrangements • Students live in program-owned apartments. Meals are taken on one's own, in residences.

Costs (2003-2004) • One term: $8675 for New Jersey residents; $11,325 for nonresidents. Yearlong program: $15,529 for New Jersey residents; $20,829 for nonresidents; includes tuition, housing, insurance, excursions, student support services. $20 application fee. $750 nonrefundable deposit required. Financial aid available for all students: scholarships, loans.
For More Information • Ms. Karin Bonello, Regional Coordinator, Rutgers, The State University of New Jersey, 102 College Avenue, New Brunswick, NJ 08901-8543; *Phone:* 732-932-7787; *Fax:* 732-932-8659. *E-mail:* ru_abroad@email.rutgers.edu. *World Wide Web:* http://studyabroad.rutgers.edu/

DHARAMSALA

EMORY UNIVERSITY
TIBETAN STUDIES PROGRAM IN DHARAMSALA, INDIA

Hosted by Institute of Buddhist Dialectics
Academic Focus • Civilization studies, philosophy, Tibetan.
Program Information • Students attend classes at Institute of Buddhist Dialectics. Field trips to Delhi; optional travel to various sites throughout India.
Sessions • Spring.
Eligibility Requirements • Minimum age 18; open to sophomores, juniors, seniors; 3.0 GPA; 2 letters of recommendation; good academic standing at home school; at least 3 semesters of college-level work; no foreign language proficiency required.
Living Arrangements • Students live in a guest house. Quarters are shared with host institution students. Meals are taken as a group, in central dining facility.
Costs (2004) • One term: $17,300–$17,800; includes tuition, housing, all meals, insurance, international airfare, student support services. $300 nonrefundable deposit required. Financial aid available for students from sponsoring institution: scholarships, loans.
For More Information • Ms. Kristi Hubbard, Study Abroad Advisor, Emory University, Center for International Programs Abroad, 1385 Oxford Road, Atlanta, GA 30322; *Phone:* 404-727-2240; *Fax:* 404-727-6724. *E-mail:* khubba2@emory.edu

GANGTOK

NAROPA UNIVERSITY
STUDY ABROAD–SIKKIM, NORTH INDIA

Academic Focus • Anthropology, Asian studies, Buddhist studies, intercultural studies, language studies, Nepali, Nepali studies, religious studies, Tibetan.
Program Information • Faculty members are drawn from the sponsor's U.S. staff and local instructors hired by the sponsor. Scheduled travel to western Sikkim, Darjeeling; field trips to western Sikkim, Darjeeling, Kalimpong; optional travel to northern India, Nepal, Tibet at an extra cost.
Sessions • Fall, spring.
Eligibility Requirements • Minimum age 18; open to precollege students, freshmen, sophomores, juniors, seniors, graduate students, adults; 3.0 GPA; 2 letters of recommendation; good academic standing at home school; must be a serious student/adult with commitment to rigorous study; no foreign language proficiency required.
Living Arrangements • Students live in hotels, a guest house. Meals are taken as a group, in central dining facility.
Costs (2004-2005) • One term: $11,500; includes tuition, housing, some meals, excursions, student support services, visa fees. $45 application fee. $500 refundable deposit required. Financial aid available for all students: consortium agreement for home institution aid.
For More Information • Mr. Peter S. Volz, Co-Director, Office of International Education, Naropa University, 2130 Arapahoe Avenue, Boulder, CO 80302; *Phone:* 303-546-3594; *Fax:* 303-444-0410. *E-mail:* peter@naropa.edu. *World Wide Web:* http://www.naropa.edu/studyabroad/

HYDERABAD

CIEE
CIEE STUDY CENTER AT THE UNIVERSITY OF HYDERABAD, INDIA

Hosted by University of Hyderabad

Academic Focus • Anthropology, art history, business administration/management, dance, economics, film and media studies, fine/studio arts, geography, Hindi, history, Indian studies, philosophy, political science and government, psychology, religious studies, Telugu, Urdu, visual and performing arts.

Program Information • Students attend classes at University of Hyderabad. Scheduled travel to sites around India; field trips to sites around India.

Sessions • Fall, spring, yearlong.

Eligibility Requirements • Open to sophomores, juniors, seniors, graduate students, adults; 3.0 GPA; 2 letters of recommendation; good academic standing at home school; no foreign language proficiency required.

Living Arrangements • Students live in an international student guest house. Quarters are shared with students from other programs. Meals are taken on one's own, in residences, in central dining facility, in restaurants.

Costs (2004-2005) • One term: $8700. Yearlong program: $15,800; includes tuition, housing, all meals, insurance, excursions, student support services, pre-departure advising, cultural activities, train fare from Delhi to Hyderabad. $30 application fee. $300 deposit required. Financial aid available for all students: scholarships, minority student scholarships, travel grants.

For More Information • Mr. Adam Rubin, Admissions Officer, Asia Pacific, CIEE, 7 Custom House Street, 3rd Floor, Portland, ME 04101; *Phone:* 800-40-STUDY; *Fax:* 207-553-7699. *E-mail:* studyinfo@ciee.org. *World Wide Web:* http://www.ciee.org/isp/

JAIPUR

SCHOOL FOR INTERNATIONAL TRAINING, SIT STUDY ABROAD
INDIA: ARTS AND CULTURE

Academic Focus • Anthropology, crafts, economics, geography, Hindi, history, Indian studies, political science and government, religious studies, textiles, visual and performing arts.

Program Information • Faculty members are drawn from the sponsor's U.S. staff and local instructors hired by the sponsor. Scheduled travel to Jodhpur, Udaipur, Fatehpur Sikri; field trips to arts performances, historic and religious sites, museums.

Sessions • Fall, spring.

Eligibility Requirements • Open to sophomores, juniors, seniors; 2.5 GPA; 2 letters of recommendation; good academic standing at home school; no foreign language proficiency required.

Living Arrangements • Students live in host family homes, hotels. Meals are taken as a group, on one's own, with host family, in residences, in central dining facility, in restaurants.

Costs (2003-2004) • One term: $11,800; includes tuition, housing, all meals, insurance, excursions. $50 application fee. $400 nonrefundable deposit required. Financial aid available for all students: scholarships.

For More Information • School for International Training, SIT Study Abroad, Kipling Road, Brattleboro, VT 05302-0676; *Phone:* 888-272-7881; *Fax:* 802-258-3296. *E-mail:* studyabroad@sit.edu. *World Wide Web:* http://www.sit.edu/studyabroad/

UNIVERSITY OF MINNESOTA
MINNESOTA STUDIES IN INTERNATIONAL DEVELOPMENT (MSID), INDIA

Hosted by Institute for Rajasthan Studies

Academic Focus • Agriculture, anthropology, Asian studies, community service, conservation studies, economics, education, environmental health, environmental science/studies, forestry, Hindi, Indian studies, international affairs, natural resources, nutrition, social sciences, social services, urban/regional planning, wildlife studies, women's studies.

Program Information • Students attend classes at Institute for Rajasthan Studies. Field trips to development projects; optional travel to sites in India at an extra cost.

Sessions • Fall, spring, yearlong.

Eligibility Requirements • Minimum age 19; open to juniors, seniors, graduate students, adults; course work in development studies, area studies, social sciences; 2.5 GPA; 1 letter of recommendation; no foreign language proficiency required.

Living Arrangements • Students live in host family homes. Meals are taken with host family, in residences.

Costs (2004-2005) • One term: contact sponsor for cost. Yearlong program: contact sponsor for cost. $50 application fee. $400 nonrefundable deposit required. Financial aid available for students from sponsoring institution: scholarships, loans.

For More Information • University of Minnesota, Learning Abroad Center, 230 Heller Hall, 271 19th Avenue South, Minneapolis, MN 55455; *Phone:* 612-626-9000; *Fax:* 612-626-8009. *E-mail:* umabroad@umn.edu. *World Wide Web:* http://www.umabroad.umn.edu/

MADRAS

DAVIDSON COLLEGE
FALL SEMESTER IN INDIA AND NEPAL PROGRAM

Hosted by Madras Christian College

Academic Focus • Asian studies, history, public health, religious studies, sociology.

Program Information • Students attend classes at Madras Christian College. Scheduled travel to Bangalore, Calcutta, Madurai, Varanasi, Jaipar, Delhi, Lucknow, Cochin, Munnar, Nepal (two weeks); field trips to Mahabalipuram, Pondicherry.

Sessions • Fall, program runs every even-numbered year.

Eligibility Requirements • Minimum age 19; open to sophomores, juniors, seniors; course work in South Asian studies; 2.7 GPA; 2 letters of recommendation; good academic standing at home school; no foreign language proficiency required.

Living Arrangements • Students live in host family homes, a host institution guest house. Meals are taken as a group, in central dining facility.

Costs (2002) • One term: $16,000; includes tuition, housing, all meals, excursions, international airfare, international student ID, student support services. $500 nonrefundable deposit required. Financial aid available for students from sponsoring institution: scholarships, loans.

For More Information • Ms. Carolyn Ortmayer, Study Abroad Coordinator, Davidson College, Box 7155, Davidson, NC 28035-7155; *Phone:* 704-894-2250; *Fax:* 704-894-2120. *E-mail:* abroad@davidson.edu. *World Wide Web:* http://www.davidson.edu/international/

MYSORE

NAROPA UNIVERSITY
STUDY ABROAD–SOUTH INDIA

Held at University of Mysore

Academic Focus • Anthropology, community service, Indian studies, intercultural studies, native languages, philosophy, religious studies.

Program Information • Classes are held on the campus of University of Mysore. Faculty members are drawn from the sponsor's U.S. staff and local instructors hired by the sponsor. Scheduled travel to a 10-day pilgrimage through Tamil Nadu; field trips to Chamundi Hill, Bylakuppe Buddhist temple, Chidambaram, Tirumvannamalai.

Sessions • Fall.

Eligibility Requirements • Minimum age 18; open to sophomores, juniors, seniors, graduate students, adults; 3.0 GPA; 2 letters of recommendation; good academic standing at home school; must be a serious, mature student or adult with commitment to rigorous study; no foreign language proficiency required.

Living Arrangements • Students live in locally rented apartments. Quarters are shared with host institution students. Meals are taken as a group, in central dining facility.

Costs (2005) • One term: $12,500; includes tuition, housing, all meals, excursions, student support services. $45 application fee. $500 refundable deposit required. Financial aid available for all students: loans, consortium agreement for home institution aid.

INDIA
Mysore

For More Information • Mr. Peter S. Volz, Co-Director, Office of International Education, Naropa University, 2130 Arapahoe Avenue, Boulder, CO 80302; *Phone:* 303-546-3594; *Fax:* 303-444-0410. *E-mail:* peter@naropa.edu. *World Wide Web:* http://www.naropa.edu/studyabroad/

UNIVERSITY OF IOWA
SEMESTER IN SOUTH INDIA

Academic Focus • Hindi, Indian studies, Kannada, Sanskrit, social sciences, women's studies.
Program Information • Faculty members are local instructors hired by the sponsor. Scheduled travel to important historical and cultural sites such as Vijayanagara; field trips to an organic farm, a women's organization; optional travel to northern India, regional travel at an extra cost.
Sessions • Fall.
Eligibility Requirements • Open to sophomores, juniors, seniors; 2 letters of recommendation; good academic standing at home school; no foreign language proficiency required.
Living Arrangements • Students live in host institution dormitories. Meals are taken on one's own, in restaurants.
Costs (2003-2004) • One term: $4825 for University of Iowa resident students; $5757 for University of Iowa nonresident students; $6257 for all others; includes tuition, housing, all meals, insurance, excursions, student support services. $35 application fee. $200 deposit required. Financial aid available for students from sponsoring institution: scholarships, loans.
For More Information • Mr. Philip Carls, Assistant Director, University of Iowa, Office for Study Abroad, 120 International Center, Iowa City, IA 52242; *Phone:* 319-335-0353; *Fax:* 319-335-2021. *E-mail:* philip-carls@uiowa.edu

PUNE
ASSOCIATED COLLEGES OF THE MIDWEST
ACM INDIA STUDIES PROGRAM

Hosted by Tilak Maharashtra Vidyapeeth
Academic Focus • Anthropology, fine/studio arts, history, Indian studies, literature, Marathi, music, philosophy, political science and government, religious studies, sociology.
Program Information • Students attend classes at Tilak Maharashtra Vidyapeeth. Scheduled travel to Ellora, Ajanta; field trips to Mahabaleshwar, Pandharpur; optional travel to other areas in India, Gujarat, Goa, Sri Lanka at an extra cost.
Sessions • Fall.
Eligibility Requirements • Open to sophomores, juniors, seniors; 3 letters of recommendation; good academic standing at home school; no foreign language proficiency required.
Living Arrangements • Students live in host family homes, hotels. Meals are taken with host family, in residences.
Costs (2004) • One term: contact sponsor for cost. $400 nonrefundable deposit required.
For More Information • Ms. Whitney Kidd, Program Associate, ACM India Studies Program, Associated Colleges of the Midwest, 205 West Wacker Drive, Suite 1300, Chicago, IL 60606; *Phone:* 312-263-5000; *Fax:* 312-263-5879. *E-mail:* acm@acm.edu. *World Wide Web:* http://www.acm.edu/

INDONESIA
UBUD
NAROPA UNIVERSITY
STUDY ABROAD–BALI: ARTS AND SPIRITUALITY

Held at Munut Guest House
Academic Focus • Anthropology, fine/studio arts, Indonesian, intercultural studies, language studies, music.
Program Information • Classes are held on the campus of Munut Guest House. Faculty members are drawn from the sponsor's U.S. staff and local instructors hired by the sponsor. Scheduled travel to a Marga village stay; field trips to local temples and villages; optional travel to Java, Bali at an extra cost.
Sessions • Spring.
Eligibility Requirements • Minimum age 18; open to precollege students, freshmen, sophomores, juniors, seniors, graduate students, adults; 3.0 GPA; 2 letters of recommendation; must be serious student with commitment to experiential-based education; no foreign language proficiency required.
Living Arrangements • Students live in host family homes, a guest house. Quarters are shared with host institution students. Meals are taken as a group, on one's own, with host family, in central dining facility, in restaurants.
Costs (2005) • One term: $12,190; includes tuition, housing, some meals, excursions, student support services, visa fees. $45 application fee. $500 refundable deposit required. Financial aid available for all students: loans, consortium agreement for home institution aid.
For More Information • Mr. Peter S. Volz, Co-Director, Study Abroad Programs, Naropa University, 2130 Arapahoe Avenue, Boulder, CO 80302; *Phone:* 303-546-3594; *Fax:* 303-444-0410. *E-mail:* denise@naropa.edu. *World Wide Web:* http://www.naropa.edu/studyabroad/

SCHOOL FOR INTERNATIONAL TRAINING, SIT STUDY ABROAD
INDONESIA: BALI–ARTS AND CULTURE

Academic Focus • Anthropology, art, dance, economics, geography, history, Indonesian, liberal studies, political science and government, religious studies, visual and performing arts.
Program Information • Faculty members are drawn from the sponsor's U.S. staff and local instructors hired by the sponsor. Scheduled travel to northern Bali coast, rural Bali, Java; field trips to temple festivals, religious and historic sites, artistic communities.
Sessions • Fall, spring.
Eligibility Requirements • Open to sophomores, juniors, seniors; 2.5 GPA; 2 letters of recommendation; good academic standing at home school; no foreign language proficiency required.
Living Arrangements • Students live in host family homes, hotels. Meals are taken as a group, on one's own, with host family, in residences, in central dining facility, in restaurants.
Costs (2003-2004) • One term: $11,900; includes tuition, housing, all meals, insurance, excursions. $50 application fee. $400 nonrefundable deposit required. Financial aid available for all students: scholarships.
For More Information • School for International Training, SIT Study Abroad, Kipling Road, Brattleboro, VT 05302-0676; *Phone:* 888-272-7881; *Fax:* 802-258-3296. *E-mail:* studyabroad@sit.edu. *World Wide Web:* http://www.sit.edu/studyabroad/

IRELAND

See also England, Northern Ireland, Scotland, and Wales.

CITY TO CITY
RUTGERS, THE STATE UNIVERSITY OF NEW JERSEY
STUDY ABROAD IN IRELAND

Hosted by University College Cork–National University of Ireland, Cork, University College Dublin–National University of Ireland, Dublin
Academic Focus • Full curriculum.
Program Information • Students attend classes at University College Cork–National University of Ireland, Cork (Cork), University College Dublin–National University of Ireland, Dublin (Dublin).
Sessions • Fall, spring, yearlong.

Eligibility Requirements • Open to sophomores, juniors, seniors; 3.0 GPA; 2 letters of recommendation; good academic standing at home school.

Living Arrangements • Students live in host institution dormitories, locally rented apartments. Quarters are shared with host institution students, students from other programs. Meals are taken on one's own, in residences.

Costs (2003-2004) • One term: $11,388 for New Jersey residents; $14,038 for nonresidents. Yearlong program: $20,956 for New Jersey residents; $26,256 for nonresidents; includes tuition, housing, insurance, student support services. $20 application fee. $750 nonrefundable deposit required. Financial aid available for students from sponsoring institution: scholarships, loans.

For More Information • Ms. Karin Bonello, Regional Coordinator, Rutgers, The State University of New Jersey, 102 College Avenue, New Brunswick, NJ 08901-8543; *Phone:* 732-932-7787; *Fax:* 732-932-8659. *E-mail:* ru_abroad@email.rutgers.edu. *World Wide Web:* http://studyabroad.rutgers.edu/

SCHOOL FOR INTERNATIONAL TRAINING, SIT STUDY ABROAD
IRELAND: PEACE AND CONFLICT STUDIES

Academic Focus • Economics, history, Irish studies, peace and conflict studies, political science and government, social sciences, sociology, visual and performing arts.

Program Information • Faculty members are drawn from the sponsor's U.S. staff and local instructors hired by the sponsor. Scheduled travel to County Wicklow, Derry, Belfast, Aran Islands; field trips to the Northern Ireland parliament, community centers, the Aran Islands, Corrymeela Peace and Reconciliation Center.

Sessions • Fall, spring.

Eligibility Requirements • Open to sophomores, juniors, seniors; 2.5 GPA; 2 letters of recommendation; good academic standing at home school.

Living Arrangements • Students live in host family homes, hotels. Meals are taken as a group, on one's own, with host family, in residences, in restaurants.

Costs (2003-2004) • One term: $13,150; includes tuition, housing, all meals, excursions, international student ID. $50 application fee. $400 nonrefundable deposit required. Financial aid available for all students: scholarships.

For More Information • School for International Training, SIT Study Abroad, Kipling Road, Brattleboro, VT 05302-0676; *Phone:* 888-272-7881; *Fax:* 802-258-3296. *E-mail:* studyabroad@sit.edu. *World Wide Web:* http://www.sit.edu/studyabroad/

BALLYVAUGHAN
ARCADIA UNIVERSITY
BURREN COLLEGE OF ART

Hosted by Burren College of Art

Academic Focus • Art history, creative writing, drawing/painting, fine/studio arts, Irish studies, photography.

Program Information • Students attend classes at Burren College of Art. Field trips to Paris, Amsterdam.

Sessions • Fall, spring, yearlong.

Eligibility Requirements • Open to sophomores, juniors, seniors; major in art/fine arts; 3.0 GPA; 1 letter of recommendation; 10-12 slides of recent work; 3 semester transcript.

Living Arrangements • Students live in locally rented apartments, program-owned houses. Quarters are shared with host institution students. Meals are taken as a group, on one's own, in residences, in restaurants.

Costs (2003-2004) • One term: $11,990. Yearlong program: $20,190; includes tuition, housing, insurance, international student ID, student support services, pre-departure guide, transcripts. $35 application fee. $500 nonrefundable deposit required. Financial aid available for all students: scholarships, loans.

For More Information • Arcadia University, Center for Education Abroad, 450 South Easton Road, Glenside, PA 19038-3295; *Phone:* 866-927-2234; *Fax:* 215-572-2174. *E-mail:* cea@arcadia.edu. *World Wide Web:* http://www.arcadia.edu/cea/

INSTITUTE FOR STUDY ABROAD, BUTLER UNIVERSITY
BURREN COLLEGE OF ART

Hosted by Burren College of Art

Academic Focus • Art, drawing/painting, fine/studio arts, photography.

Program Information • Students attend classes at Burren College of Art. Field trips to Northern Ireland, Delphi or Killarney; optional travel to London/Dublin, Dublin/Paris at an extra cost.

Sessions • Fall, spring, yearlong.

Eligibility Requirements • Open to sophomores, juniors, seniors; 3.0 GPA; 2 letters of recommendation; good academic standing at home school; portfolio; enrollment at an accredited American college or university.

Living Arrangements • Students live in locally rented apartments. Quarters are shared with host institution students. Meals are taken on one's own, in residences, in central dining facility.

Costs (2002-2003) • One term: $11,375. Yearlong program: $19,275; includes tuition, housing, excursions, international student ID, student support services, family visit, cultural and sporting events, pre-departure advising. $40 application fee. $500 nonrefundable deposit required. Financial aid available for all students: scholarships, travel grants.

For More Information • Institute for Study Abroad, Butler University, 1100 West 42nd Street, Suite 305, Indianapolis, IN 46208-3345; *Phone:* 800-858-0229; *Fax:* 317-940-9704. *E-mail:* study-abroad@butler.edu. *World Wide Web:* http://www.ifsa-butler.org/

NORTH AMERICAN INSTITUTE FOR STUDY ABROAD
STUDY AT THE BURREN

Hosted by Burren College of Art

Academic Focus • Art, commercial art, drawing/painting.

Program Information • Students attend classes at Burren College of Art. Optional travel at an extra cost.

Sessions • Fall, spring, yearlong.

Eligibility Requirements • Minimum age 18; open to sophomores, juniors, seniors; 3.0 GPA; good academic standing at home school.

Living Arrangements • Students live in host institution dormitories, locally rented apartments, host family homes. Quarters are shared with host institution students. Meals are taken on one's own, in residences, in central dining facility, in restaurants.

Costs (2001-2002) • One term: $7900. Yearlong program: $15,000; includes tuition, housing, international student ID, student support services, transcripts. $50 application fee. $500 nonrefundable deposit required. Financial aid available for all students: scholarships.

For More Information • Dr. Michael Currid, Director, North American Institute for Study Abroad, 129 Mill Street, Danville, PA 17821; *Phone:* 570-275-5099; *Fax:* 570-275-1644. *E-mail:* naisa@naisa.com. *World Wide Web:* http://www.naisa.com/

CORK
ARCADIA UNIVERSITY
UNIVERSITY COLLEGE, CORK

Hosted by University College Cork–National University of Ireland, Cork

Academic Focus • Archaeology, Celtic studies, classics and classical languages, economics, English, European studies, history, Irish studies, language studies, science, social sciences.

Program Information • Students attend classes at University College Cork–National University of Ireland, Cork. Scheduled travel to sites within Ireland.

Sessions • Fall, spring, yearlong, early start pre-session.

Eligibility Requirements • Open to sophomores, juniors, seniors; 3.0 GPA; 1 letter of recommendation.

Living Arrangements • Students live in locally rented apartments, program-owned apartments, host family homes. Quarters are shared with host institution students, students from other programs. Meals are taken on one's own, in residences, in restaurants.

Costs (2003-2004) • One term: $9950. Yearlong program: $16,390 ($17,080 with Early Start session); includes tuition, housing, insurance, international student ID, student support services, pre-departure guide, transcripts. $35 application fee. $500 nonrefundable deposit required. Financial aid available for all students: scholarships, loans.

For More Information • Arcadia University, Center for Education Abroad, 450 South Easton Road, Glenside, PA 19038-3295; *Phone:* 866-927-2234; *Fax:* 215-572-2174. *E-mail:* cea@arcadia.edu. *World Wide Web:* http://www.arcadia.edu/cea/

COLBY COLLEGE
COLBY IN CORK

Hosted by University College Cork–National University of Ireland, Cork

Academic Focus • Art, biological/life sciences, English, history, international affairs, Irish studies.

Program Information • Students attend classes at University College Cork-National University of Ireland, Cork. Scheduled travel to Dingle Peninsula, Aran Islands; field trips to Blarney Castle, Kinsale, Dublin.

Sessions • Fall, spring, yearlong.

Eligibility Requirements • Open to juniors; 3.0 GPA; 2 letters of recommendation; good academic standing at home school.

Living Arrangements • Students live in host institution dormitories, locally rented apartments. Quarters are shared with host institution students. Meals are taken on one's own, in residences, in restaurants.

Costs (2002-2003) • One term: $17,900. Yearlong program: $35,800; includes tuition, housing, all meals, insurance, excursions, international airfare, student support services. $500 nonrefundable deposit required. Financial aid available for students from sponsoring institution: scholarships.

For More Information • Ms. Martha J. Denney, Director, Off-Campus Study, Colby College, Waterville, ME 04901; *Phone:* 207-872-3648; *Fax:* 207-872-3061. *E-mail:* mjdenney@colby.edu. *World Wide Web:* http://www.colby.edu/off-campus/

CULTURAL EXPERIENCES ABROAD (CEA)
STUDY LIBERAL ARTS AND SCIENCES IN CORK

Hosted by University College Cork–National University of Ireland, Cork

Academic Focus • Full curriculum.

Program Information • Students attend classes at University College Cork–National University of Ireland, Cork. Field trips to Dingle Peninsula, Blarney Castle, Kilkenny, Skellig Islands, Cobh; optional travel to London, Paris, Amsterdam, Rome, Barcelona at an extra cost.

Sessions • Fall, spring, yearlong, early start program.

Eligibility Requirements • Minimum age 18; open to sophomores, juniors, seniors; 3.0 GPA; 1 letter of recommendation.

Living Arrangements • Students live in locally rented apartments. Quarters are shared with host institution students. Meals are taken on one's own, in residences, in central dining facility, in restaurants.

Costs (2003-2004) • One term: $9795–$12,395. Yearlong program: $19,295–$23,295; includes tuition, housing, insurance, excursions, student support services, University ID, airport reception, social activities. $50 application fee. $400 nonrefundable deposit required.

For More Information • Cultural Experiences Abroad (CEA), 1400 East Southern Avenue, Suite B-108, Tempe, AZ 85282-8011; *Phone:* 480-557-7900; *Fax:* 480-557-7926. *E-mail:* petersons@gowithcea.com. *World Wide Web:* http://www.gowithcea.com/

GEORGE MASON UNIVERSITY
CORK, IRELAND

Hosted by University College Cork–National University of Ireland, Cork

Academic Focus • Full curriculum.

Program Information • Students attend classes at University College Cork–National University of Ireland, Cork. Scheduled travel; field trips; optional travel at an extra cost.

Sessions • Fall, spring.

Eligibility Requirements • Minimum age 18; open to sophomores, juniors, seniors, adults; 2.8 GPA; good academic standing at home school.

Living Arrangements • Students live in host institution dormitories. Quarters are shared with host institution students.

Costs (2003-2004) • One term: contact sponsor for cost. $75 application fee. Financial aid available for students from sponsoring institution: scholarships, loans.

For More Information • Program Officer, Center for Global Education, George Mason University, 235 Johnson Center, 4400 University Drive, Fairfax, VA 22030; *Phone:* 703-993-2154; *Fax:* 703-993-2153. *E-mail:* cge@gmu.edu. *World Wide Web:* http://www.gmu.edu/departments/cge/

INSTITUTE FOR STUDY ABROAD, BUTLER UNIVERSITY
UNIVERSITY COLLEGE CORK

Hosted by University College Cork–National University of Ireland, Cork

Academic Focus • Full curriculum.

Program Information • Students attend classes at University College Cork–National University of Ireland, Cork. Field trips to Delphi, Killarney, Northern Ireland.

Sessions • Fall, spring, yearlong, early start fall semester.

Eligibility Requirements • Open to sophomores, juniors, seniors; 3.0 GPA; 1 letter of recommendation; good academic standing at home school; enrollment at an accredited American college or university.

Living Arrangements • Students live in host institution dormitories, locally rented apartments. Quarters are shared with host institution students, students from other programs. Meals are taken on one's own, in residences, in central dining facility, in restaurants.

Costs (2002-2003) • One term: $8775 ($9275 for early start fall semester). Yearlong program: $14,875 with early start fall semester; $14,275 for regular start; includes tuition, housing, excursions, international student ID, student support services, family visit, cultural and sporting events, pre-departure advising. $40 application fee. $500 nonrefundable deposit required. Financial aid available for all students: scholarships, travel grants.

For More Information • Institute for Study Abroad, Butler University, 1100 West 42nd Street, Suite 305, Indianapolis, IN 46208-3345; *Phone:* 800-858-0229; *Fax:* 317-940-9704. *E-mail:* study-abroad@butler.edu. *World Wide Web:* http://www.ifsa-butler.org/

INTERSTUDY
UNIVERSITY COLLEGE, CORK, REPUBLIC OF IRELAND

Hosted by University College Cork–National University of Ireland, Cork

Academic Focus • Archaeology, Celtic studies, computer science, economics, English, European studies, French language and literature, geography, Greek, history, Irish studies, Italian language and literature, mathematics, music, philosophy, psychology, social sciences, sociology, Spanish language and literature.

Program Information • Students attend classes at University College Cork–National University of Ireland, Cork. Scheduled travel to Bath, Stratford-upon-Avon, Warwick Castle, Oxford, Stonehenge.

Sessions • Fall, spring, yearlong, pre-session courses: "The Archaeology of Prehistoric and Historic Ireland," "History and Modern Ireland," "Irish Ecosystems," "Literature in Ireland."

Eligibility Requirements • Minimum age 18; open to freshmen, sophomores, juniors, seniors, adults; 3.0 GPA; 2 letters of recommendation; good academic standing at home school.

Living Arrangements • Students live in host institution dormitories, locally rented apartments. Quarters are shared with host institution students. Meals are taken on one's own, in residences.

Costs (2003-2004) • One term: $10,325 for fall term; $11,350 for spring term; $500 for pre-session. Yearlong program: $18,995; includes tuition, housing, some meals, excursions, international student ID, student support services, Student Union membership, e-mail access, banking facilities, international bank transfers, transcript, cell phone. $35 application fee. $500 nonrefundable deposit required. Financial aid available for all students: scholarships, loans, stipends.

For More Information • InterStudy, Admissions Office, 63 Edward Street, Medford, MA 02155; *Phone:* 800-663-1999; *Fax:* 781-391-7463. *E-mail:* interstudy@interstudy-usa.org. *World Wide Web:* http://www.interstudy.org/

NORTH AMERICAN INSTITUTE FOR STUDY ABROAD
STUDY IN IRELAND

Hosted by University College Cork–National University of Ireland, Cork
Academic Focus • Full curriculum.
Program Information • Students attend classes at University College Cork-National University of Ireland, Cork.
Sessions • Fall, spring, yearlong.
Eligibility Requirements • Minimum age 18; open to sophomores, juniors, seniors; 3.0 GPA; 2 letters of recommendation; good academic standing at home school.
Living Arrangements • Students live in host institution dormitories, host family homes. Quarters are shared with host institution students. Meals are taken on one's own, in residences, in central dining facility, in restaurants.
Costs (2003-2004) • One term: $9000. Yearlong program: $17,000; includes tuition, housing, international student ID, student support services, transcripts. $50 application fee. $500 nonrefundable deposit required. Financial aid available for all students: scholarships.
For More Information • Dr. Michael Currid, Director, North American Institute for Study Abroad, 129 Mill Street, Danville, PA 17821; *Phone:* 570-275-5099; *Fax:* 570-275-1644. *E-mail:* naisa@naisa. com. *World Wide Web:* http://www.naisa.com/

UNIVERSITY COLLEGE CORK–NATIONAL UNIVERSITY OF IRELAND, CORK
CERTIFICATE IN IRISH STUDIES

Hosted by University College Cork–National University of Ireland, Cork
Academic Focus • Celtic studies, Irish studies.
Program Information • Students attend classes at University College Cork–National University of Ireland, Cork.
Sessions • Yearlong.
Eligibility Requirements • Minimum age 17; open to sophomores, juniors, seniors, graduate students; 3.0 GPA.
Living Arrangements • Students live in locally rented apartments, program-owned apartments. Quarters are shared with host institution students, students from other programs. Meals are taken as a group, on one's own, in residences, in central dining facility.
Costs (2003-2004) • Yearlong program: €20,500 (estimated); includes tuition, housing, all meals, excursions, international airfare, books and class materials, local transportation, laundry service, social functions.
For More Information • Ms. Marita Foster, Educational Advisor, University College Cork–National University of Ireland, Cork, International Education Office, Cork, Ireland; *Phone:* +353 21-4902022; *Fax:* +353 21-4903118. *E-mail:* isoffice@ucc.ie. *World Wide Web:* http://www.ucc.ie/services/iso/. Students may also apply through Arcadia University, Center for Education Abroad, 450 South Easton Road, Glenside, PA 19038-3295; Butler University, Institute for Study Abroad, 1100 West 42nd Street, Suite 305, Indianapolis, IN 46208-3345; CEA, Cultural Experiences Abroad, 1400 East Southern Avenue, Suite B-108, Tempe, AZ 85282-8011; InterStudy, Admissions Office, 42 Milsom Street, Bath BA1 1DN, England; University Studies Abroad Consortium, University of Nevada, Reno/323, Reno, NV 89557.

UNIVERSITY COLLEGE CORK–NATIONAL UNIVERSITY OF IRELAND, CORK
CERTIFICATE IN POLITICAL ISSUES IN IRELAND TODAY

Hosted by University College Cork–National University of Ireland, Cork
Academic Focus • European studies, peace and conflict studies, political science and government.
Program Information • Students attend classes at University College Cork–National University of Ireland, Cork. Scheduled travel to Belfast; field trips to Dublin, local destinations in Cork.
Sessions • Spring.
Eligibility Requirements • Minimum age 17; open to sophomores, juniors, seniors; 3.0 GPA.
Living Arrangements • Students live in locally rented apartments, program-owned apartments. Quarters are shared with host institu-

tion students, students from other programs. Meals are taken as a group, on one's own, in residences, in central dining facility.
Costs (2003-2004) • One term: €11,000 (estimated); includes tuition, housing, all meals, excursions, international airfare, books and class materials.
For More Information • Ms. Marita Foster, Educational Advisor, University College Cork–National University of Ireland, Cork, International Education Office, Cork, Ireland; *Phone:* +353 21-4902022; *Fax:* +353 21-4903118. *E-mail:* isoffice@ucc.ie. *World Wide Web:* http://www.ucc.ie/services/iso/. Students may also apply through CEA, Cultural Experiences Abroad, 1400 East Southern Avenue, Suite B-108, Tempe, AZ 85282-8011; University Studies Abroad Consortium, University of Nevada, Reno/323, Reno, NV 89557; Arcadia University, Center for Education Abroad, 450 South Easton Road, Glenside, PA 19038-3295; InterStudy, Admissions Office, 42 Milsom Street, Bath BA1 1DN, England; Butler University, Institute for Study Abroad, 1100 West 42nd Street, Suite 305, Indianapolis, IN 46208-3345.

UNIVERSITY COLLEGE CORK–NATIONAL UNIVERSITY OF IRELAND, CORK
EARLY START SEMESTER PROGRAM/AUTUMN SEMESTER/SPRING SEMESTER

Hosted by University College Cork–National University of Ireland, Cork
Academic Focus • Archaeology, biological/life sciences, botany, business administration/management, Celtic studies, civilization studies, ecology, English, English literature, European studies, Gaelic, history, Irish literature, Irish studies, marketing, music, music performance, philosophy, zoology.
Program Information • Students attend classes at University College Cork–National University of Ireland, Cork. Field trips to Dublin, Kerry, Clare, Cork, Belfast.
Sessions • Fall, spring, early start semester.
Eligibility Requirements • Minimum age 17; open to sophomores, juniors, seniors; 3.0 GPA.
Living Arrangements • Students live in locally rented apartments, program-owned apartments. Quarters are shared with host institution students, students from other programs. Meals are taken as a group, on one's own, in residences, in central dining facility.
Costs (2003-2004) • One term: €10,500 for fall and spring semesters; €11,500 for early start session (estimated); includes tuition, housing, all meals, excursions, international airfare, books and class materials, local transportation, laundry service, social functions.
For More Information • Ms. Marita Foster, Educational Advisor, University College Cork–National University of Ireland, Cork, International Education Office, Cork, Ireland; *Phone:* +353 21-4902022; *Fax:* +353 21-4903118. *E-mail:* isoffice@ucc.ie. *World Wide Web:* http://www.ucc.ie/services/iso/. Students may also apply through Arcadia University, Center for Education Abroad, 450 South Easton Road, Glenside, PA 19038-3295; Butler University, Institute for Study Abroad, 1100 West 42nd Street, Suite 305, Indianapolis, IN 46208-3345; InterStudy, Admissions Office, 42 Milsom Street, Bath BA1 1DN, England; CEA, Cultural Experiences Abroad, 1400 East Southern Avenue, Suite B-108, Tempe, AZ 85282-8011; University Studies Abroad Consortium, University of Nevada, Reno/323, Reno, NV 89557.

UNIVERSITY COLLEGE CORK–NATIONAL UNIVERSITY OF IRELAND, CORK
VISITING STUDENT PROGRAM IN BUSINESS

Hosted by University College Cork–National University of Ireland, Cork
Academic Focus • Accounting, business administration/management, commerce, economics, finance, management information systems, public administration.
Program Information • Students attend classes at University College Cork–National University of Ireland, Cork.
Sessions • Yearlong.
Eligibility Requirements • Minimum age 18; open to sophomores, juniors, seniors; 3.0 GPA.
Living Arrangements • Students live in locally rented apartments, program-owned apartments. Quarters are shared with host institu-

tion students, students from other programs. Meals are taken as a group, on one's own, in residences, in central dining facility.

Costs (2003–2004) • Yearlong program: €20,500 (estimated); includes tuition, housing, all meals, excursions, international airfare, books and class materials, local transportation, laundry service, social functions.

For More Information • Ms. Marita Foster, Educational Advisor, University College Cork–National University of Ireland, Cork, International Education Office, Cork, Ireland; *Phone:* +353 21-4902022; *Fax:* +353 21-4903118. *E-mail:* isoffice@ucc.ie. *World Wide Web:* http://www.ucc.ie/services/iso/. Students may also apply through CEA, Cultural Experiences Abroad, 1400 East Southern Avenue, Suite B-108, Tempe, AZ 85282-8011; University Studies Abroad Consortium, University of Nevada, Reno/323, Reno, NV 89557; Arcadia University, Center for Education Abroad, 450 South Easton Road, Glenside, PA 19038-3295; InterStudy, Admissions Office, 42 Milsom Street, Bath BA1 1DN, England; Butler University, Institute for Study Abroad, 1100 West 42nd Street, Suite 305, Indianapolis, IN 46208-3345.

UNIVERSITY COLLEGE CORK–NATIONAL UNIVERSITY OF IRELAND, CORK
VISITING STUDENT PROGRAM IN FOOD SCIENCE AND TECHNOLOGY

Hosted by University College Cork–National University of Ireland, Cork

Academic Focus • Agriculture, biochemistry, biological/life sciences, chemical sciences, food science, nutrition, physics.

Program Information • Students attend classes at University College Cork–National University of Ireland, Cork.

Sessions • Yearlong.

Eligibility Requirements • Minimum age 17; open to sophomores, juniors, seniors; course work in food science/technology; 3.0 GPA.

Living Arrangements • Students live in locally rented apartments, program-owned apartments. Quarters are shared with host institution students, students from other programs. Meals are taken as a group, on one's own, in residences, in central dining facility.

Costs (2003–2004) • Yearlong program: €24,420; includes tuition, housing, all meals, excursions, international airfare, books and class materials, lab equipment, local transportation, laundry service, social functions.

For More Information • Ms. Marita Foster, Educational Advisor, University College Cork–National University of Ireland, Cork, International Education Office, Cork, Ireland; *Phone:* +353 21-4902022; *Fax:* +353 21-4903118. *E-mail:* isoffice@ucc.ie. *World Wide Web:* http://www.ucc.ie/services/iso/. Students may also apply through Butler University, Institute for Study Abroad, 1100 West 42nd Street, Suite 305, Indianapolis, IN 46208-3345; InterStudy, Admissions Office, 42 Milsom Street, Bath BA1 1DN, England; CEA, Cultural Experiences Abroad, 1400 East Southern Avenue, Suite B-108, Tempe, AZ 85282-8011; Arcadia University, Center for Education Abroad, 450 South Easton Road, Glenside, PA 19038-3295; University Studies Abroad Consortium, University of Nevada, Reno/323, Reno, NV 89557.

UNIVERSITY COLLEGE CORK–NATIONAL UNIVERSITY OF IRELAND, CORK
VISITING STUDENT PROGRAM IN LIBERAL ARTS

Hosted by University College Cork–National University of Ireland, Cork

Academic Focus • Archaeology, art history, Celtic studies, computer science, economics, education, English, European studies, French language and literature, Gaelic, geography, German language and literature, Greek, history, interdisciplinary studies, Irish literature, Irish studies, Italian language and literature, literature, mathematics, music performance, philosophy, psychology, social sciences, social services, social work, Spanish language and literature.

Program Information • Students attend classes at University College Cork–National University of Ireland, Cork.

Sessions • Yearlong.

Eligibility Requirements • Minimum age 17; open to sophomores, juniors, seniors; 3.0 GPA.

Living Arrangements • Students live in locally rented apartments, program-owned apartments. Quarters are shared with host institu-

tion students, students from other programs. Meals are taken as a group, on one's own, in residences, in central dining facility.

Costs (2003–2004) • Yearlong program: €20,500 (estimated); includes tuition, housing, all meals, excursions, international airfare, books and class materials, local transportation, laundry service, social functions.

For More Information • Ms. Marita Foster, Educational Advisor, University College Cork–National University of Ireland, Cork, International Education Office, Cork, Ireland; *Phone:* +353 21-4902022; *Fax:* +353 21-4903118. *E-mail:* isoffice@ucc.ie. *World Wide Web:* http://www.ucc.ie/services/iso/. Students may also apply through Butler University, Institute for Study Abroad, 1100 West 42nd Street, Suite 305, Indianapolis, IN 46208-3345; InterStudy, Admissions Office, 42 Milsom Street, Bath BA1 1DN, England; Arcadia University, Center for Education Abroad, 450 South Easton Road, Glenside, PA 19038-3295; CEA, Cultural Experiences Abroad, 1400 East Southern Avenue, Suite B-108, Tempe, AZ 85282-8011; University Studies Abroad Consortium, University of Nevada, Reno/323, Reno, NV 89557.

UNIVERSITY COLLEGE CORK–NATIONAL UNIVERSITY OF IRELAND, CORK
VISITING STUDENT PROGRAM IN SCIENCE

Hosted by University College Cork–National University of Ireland, Cork

Academic Focus • Anatomy, archaeology, biochemistry, biological/life sciences, biomedical sciences, botany, chemical sciences, computer science, ecology, economics, environmental science/studies, geography, geology, mathematics, nutrition, pharmacology, physics, psychology, statistics, zoology.

Program Information • Students attend classes at University College Cork–National University of Ireland, Cork.

Sessions • Yearlong.

Eligibility Requirements • Minimum age 17; open to sophomores, juniors, seniors; course work in science subjects; 3.0 GPA.

Living Arrangements • Students live in locally rented apartments, program-owned apartments. Quarters are shared with host institution students, students from other programs. Meals are taken as a group, on one's own, in residences, in central dining facility.

Costs (2003–2004) • Yearlong program: €24,420; includes tuition, housing, all meals, excursions, international airfare, books and class materials, lab equipment, local transportation, laundry service, social functions.

For More Information • Ms. Marita Foster, Educational Advisor, University College Cork–National University of Ireland, Cork, International Education Office, Cork, Ireland; *Phone:* +353 21-4902022; *Fax:* +353 21-4903118. *E-mail:* isoffice@ucc.ie. *World Wide Web:* http://www.ucc.ie/services/iso/. Students may also apply through Butler University, Institute for Study Abroad, 1100 West 42nd Street, Suite 305, Indianapolis, IN 46208-3345; InterStudy, Admissions Office, 42 Milsom Street, Bath BA1 1DN, England; CEA, Cultural Experiences Abroad, 1400 East Southern Avenue, Suite B-108, Tempe, AZ 85282-8011; University Studies Abroad Consortium, University of Nevada, Reno/323, Reno, NV 89557; Arcadia University, Center for Education Abroad, 450 South Easton Road, Glenside, PA 19038-3295.

UNIVERSITY STUDIES ABROAD CONSORTIUM
FULL CURRICULUM STUDIES IN CORK, IRELAND

Hosted by University College Cork–National University of Ireland, Cork

Academic Focus • Full curriculum.

Program Information • Students attend classes at University College Cork–National University of Ireland, Cork.

Sessions • Fall, spring, yearlong, early start session.

Eligibility Requirements • Minimum age 18; open to freshmen, sophomores, juniors, seniors, graduate students, adults; 3.0 GPA.

Living Arrangements • Students live in locally rented apartments, host family homes. Quarters are shared with host institution students. Meals are taken on one's own, with host family, in residences, in central dining facility, in restaurants.

Costs (2005–2006) • One term: $6680 for regular session; $7450 for early session. Yearlong program: $12,980 for regular session; $13,780 for early session; includes tuition, insurance, student

support services. $50 application fee. $150 refundable deposit required. Financial aid available for all students: scholarships, loans.
For More Information • University Studies Abroad Consortium, USAC/323, Reno, NV 89557-0093; *Phone:* 775-784-6569; *Fax:* 775-784-6010. *E-mail:* usac@unr.edu. *World Wide Web:* http://usac.unr.edu/

DUBLIN
AMERICAN COLLEGE DUBLIN
AMERICAN COLLEGE DUBLIN STUDY ABROAD PROGRAM

Hosted by American College Dublin
Academic Focus • Art history, French language and literature, German language and literature, history, hospitality services, hotel and restaurant management, human resources, international business, Irish literature, Irish studies, marketing, mathematics, political science and government, psychology, sociology, Spanish language and literature, tourism and travel.
Program Information • Students attend classes at American College Dublin. Scheduled travel to Italy, Ireland; field trips to sites on the Irish History Seminar; optional travel to Italy (International art and humanities tour) at an extra cost.
Sessions • Fall, spring, yearlong.
Eligibility Requirements • Minimum age 18; open to freshmen, sophomores, juniors, seniors; 2.5 GPA; good academic standing at home school; must be at least a second semester freshman; no foreign language proficiency required.
Living Arrangements • Students live in host institution dormitories. Quarters are shared with host institution students. Meals are taken as a group, in central dining facility.
Costs (2003-2004) • One term: $9150–$10,500 with optional study tour. Yearlong program: $20,050 with optional study tour; includes tuition, housing, some meals, student support services. $35 application fee. $500 nonrefundable deposit required.

For More Information • Ms. Jan Glitz, Director, American College Dublin Study Abroad Program, American College Dublin, 103 Second Street, Lewes, DE 19958; *Phone:* 302-645-0547; *Fax:* 302-422-6370. *E-mail:* acdinfo@att.net. *World Wide Web:* http://www.acdireland.edu/

ARCADIA UNIVERSITY
DUBLIN PARLIAMENTARY INTERNSHIP

Held at Institute of Public Administration
Academic Focus • Cultural studies, history, literature, political science and government.
Program Information • Classes are held on the campus of Institute of Public Administration. Faculty members are local instructors hired by the sponsor. Scheduled travel to sites within Ireland.
Sessions • Fall, spring.
Eligibility Requirements • Open to sophomores, juniors, seniors, graduate students; 3.0 GPA; 1 letter of recommendation; previous internship experience; current résumé.
Living Arrangements • Students live in locally rented apartments, host family homes. Quarters are shared with students from other programs. Meals are taken on one's own, in residences, in restaurants.
Costs (2003-2004) • One term: $9990; includes tuition, housing, insurance, excursions, international student ID, student support services, pre-departure guide, transcripts. $35 application fee. $500 nonrefundable deposit required. Financial aid available for all students: scholarships, loans.
For More Information • Arcadia University, Center for Education Abroad, 450 South Easton Road, Glenside, PA 19038-3295; *Phone:* 866-927-2234; *Fax:* 215-572-2174. *E-mail:* cea@arcadia.edu. *World Wide Web:* http://www.arcadia.edu/cea/

ARCADIA UNIVERSITY
TRINITY COLLEGE, DUBLIN

Hosted by University of Dublin–Trinity College
Academic Focus • Art history, classics and classical languages, engineering, English, Gaelic, history, language studies, literature, science, social sciences.
Program Information • Students attend classes at University of Dublin–Trinity College. Scheduled travel to sites within Ireland.
Sessions • Yearlong.
Eligibility Requirements • Open to juniors; 3.3 GPA; 1 letter of recommendation; minimum 3.7 GPA in English and history.
Living Arrangements • Students live in locally rented apartments, program-owned apartments, host family homes. Quarters are shared with students from other programs. Meals are taken on one's own, in residences.
Costs (2003-2004) • Yearlong program: $20,990; includes tuition, housing, insurance, excursions, international student ID, student support services, pre-departure guide, transcripts. $35 application fee. $500 nonrefundable deposit required. Financial aid available for all students: scholarships, loans.
For More Information • Arcadia University, Center for Education Abroad, 450 South Easton Road, Glenside, PA 19038-3295; *Phone:* 866-927-2234; *Fax:* 215-572-2174. *E-mail:* cea@arcadia.edu. *World Wide Web:* http://www.arcadia.edu/cea/

ARCADIA UNIVERSITY
UNIVERSITY COLLEGE, DUBLIN

Hosted by University College Dublin–National University of Ireland, Dublin
Academic Focus • Classics and classical languages, economics, English, history, literature, mathematics, political science and government, social sciences, sociology.
Program Information • Students attend classes at University College Dublin–National University of Ireland, Dublin. Scheduled travel to sites within Ireland.
Sessions • Fall, spring, yearlong.
Eligibility Requirements • Open to juniors, seniors; 3.0 GPA; 1 letter of recommendation.
Living Arrangements • Students live in locally rented apartments, program-owned apartments, host family homes. Quarters are shared with host institution students, students from other programs. Meals are taken on one's own, in residences.
Costs (2003-2004) • One term: $10,390. Yearlong program: $16,690; includes tuition, housing, insurance, international student ID, student support services, pre-departure guide, transcripts. $35 application fee. $500 nonrefundable deposit required. Financial aid available for all students: scholarships, loans.
For More Information • Arcadia University, Center for Education Abroad, 450 South Easton Road, Glenside, PA 19038-3295; *Phone:* 866-927-2234; *Fax:* 215-572-2174. *E-mail:* cea@arcadia.edu. *World Wide Web:* http://www.arcadia.edu/cea/

BENTLEY COLLEGE
BUSINESS PROGRAM ABROAD IN IRELAND

Hosted by University College Dublin–National University of Ireland, Dublin
Academic Focus • Accounting, business administration/management, computer science, economics, finance, Irish studies, marketing.
Program Information • Students attend classes at University College Dublin–National University of Ireland, Dublin. Scheduled travel; field trips to Dublin, Belfast; optional travel at an extra cost.
Sessions • Fall, spring.
Eligibility Requirements • Open to juniors, seniors; 3.0 GPA; 1 letter of recommendation; good academic standing at home school; essay.
Living Arrangements • Students live in host institution dormitories, locally rented apartments. Quarters are shared with students from other programs. Meals are taken on one's own, in residences.
Costs (2002-2003) • One term: $16,600; includes tuition, housing, excursions, international student ID, student support services. $35 application fee. $500 nonrefundable deposit required. Financial aid available for students from sponsoring institution: scholarships, loans.

For More Information • Mr. Andrew Dusenbery, Education Abroad Advisor, Bentley College, 175 Forest Street, Waltham, MA 02452-4705; *Phone:* 781-891-3474; *Fax:* 781-891-2819. *E-mail:* study_abroad@bentley.edu. *World Wide Web:* http://ecampus.bentley.edu/dept/sa/

BOSTON UNIVERSITY
DUBLIN INTERNSHIP PROGRAM

Held at Dublin City University
Academic Focus • Communications, economics, Irish literature, Irish studies, political science and government, sociology, visual and performing arts.
Program Information • Classes are held on the campus of Dublin City University. Faculty members are local instructors hired by the sponsor. Field trips.
Sessions • Fall, spring.
Eligibility Requirements • Open to sophomores, juniors, seniors, graduate students, adults; 2 letters of recommendation; good academic standing at home school; essay; approval of participation; transcript; minimum 3.0 GPA in major.
Living Arrangements • Students live in program-owned apartments, host family homes. Meals are taken on one's own, with host family, in residences, in restaurants.
Costs (2004-2005) • One term: $12,100; includes tuition, housing, some meals, internship placement. $50 application fee. $400 nonrefundable deposit required. Financial aid available for all students: scholarships, work study, loans.
For More Information • Division of International Programs, Boston University, 232 Bay State Road, Boston, MA 02215; *Phone:* 617-353-9888; *Fax:* 617-353-5402. *E-mail:* abroad@bu.edu. *World Wide Web:* http://www.bu.edu/abroad/

THE CATHOLIC UNIVERSITY OF AMERICA
PROGRAM IN IRISH SOCIETY AND POLITICS

Held at Institute of Public Administration
Academic Focus • Economics, history, liberal studies, political science and government.
Program Information • Classes are held on the campus of Institute of Public Administration. Faculty members are local instructors hired by the sponsor. Field trips to Belfast; optional travel to Belfast at an extra cost.
Sessions • Fall, spring.
Eligibility Requirements • Open to sophomores, juniors, adults; 3.0 GPA.
Living Arrangements • Students live in host family homes. Meals are taken with host family.
Costs (2003-2004) • One term: $13,800; includes tuition, housing, excursions. $55 application fee. $200 nonrefundable deposit required. Financial aid available for all students: scholarships, loans.
For More Information • Mr. John Kromkowski, Assistant Dean, School of Arts and Sciences, The Catholic University of America, 303 Marist Hall, Washington, DC 20064; *Phone:* 202-319-6876; *Fax:* 202-319-6289. *E-mail:* kromkowski@cua.edu. *World Wide Web:* http://www.cua.edu/

CIEE
CIEE STUDY CENTER AT DBS SCHOOL OF ARTS, DUBLIN, IRELAND

Hosted by DBS School of Arts
Academic Focus • Full curriculum.
Program Information • Students attend classes at DBS School of Arts. Scheduled travel to sites around Dublin and Ireland; field trips to sites around Dublin and Ireland.
Sessions • Fall, spring, yearlong.
Eligibility Requirements • Open to sophomores, juniors, seniors; 2.75 GPA; 2 letters of recommendation.
Living Arrangements • Students live in host family homes. Meals are taken with host family, in residences.
Costs (2003-2004) • One term: $9450. Yearlong program: $17,500; includes tuition, housing, all meals, insurance, excursions. $30 application fee. $300 deposit required. Financial aid available for all students: minority student scholarships, travel grants.
For More Information • Ms. Hannah McChesney, Admissions Officer, Europe, Middle East, and Africa, CIEE, 7 Custom House

Street, 3rd Floor, Portland, ME 04101; *Phone:* 800-40-STUDY; *Fax:* 207-553-7699. *E-mail:* studyinfo@ciee.org. *World Wide Web:* http://www.ciee.org/isp/

IES, INSTITUTE FOR THE INTERNATIONAL EDUCATION OF STUDENTS

IES–DUBLIN

Hosted by The Gaiety School of Acting, European Business School, St. Patrick's College, Institute for the International Education of Students (IES)–Dublin, University of Dublin–Trinity College, University College Dublin–National University of Ireland, Dublin

Academic Focus • Anthropology, biological/life sciences, botany, business administration/management, drama/theater, economics, European studies, film and media studies, history, Irish literature, mathematics, physics, political science and government, sociology, women's studies.

Program Information • Students attend classes at The Gaiety School of Acting, St. Patrick's College, University of Dublin-Trinity College, University College Dublin–National University of Ireland, Dublin, European Business School, Institute for the International Education of Students (IES)–Dublin. Scheduled travel; field trips to Glendalough, Bray; optional travel to Northern Ireland at an extra cost.

Sessions • Fall, spring, yearlong.

Eligibility Requirements • Minimum age 18; open to sophomores, juniors, seniors, graduate students, adults; 3.0 GPA; 1 letter of recommendation; good academic standing at home school.

Living Arrangements • Students live in locally rented apartments. Quarters are shared with host institution students. Meals are taken on one's own, in residences, in restaurants.

Costs (2003-2004) • One term: $11,250. Yearlong program: $20,250; includes tuition, housing, excursions, student support services, partial insurance coverage. $50 application fee. $500 nonrefundable deposit required. Financial aid available for all students: scholarships, institutional partner need-based grants.

For More Information • International Education Representative, IES, Institute for the International Education of Students, 33 North LaSalle Street, 15th Floor, Chicago, IL 60602; *Phone:* 800-995-2300; *Fax:* 312-944-1448. *E-mail:* info@iesabroad.org. *World Wide Web:* http://www.IESabroad.org/

INSTITUTE FOR STUDY ABROAD, BUTLER UNIVERSITY

TRINITY COLLEGE, DUBLIN

Hosted by University of Dublin–Trinity College

Academic Focus • Full curriculum.

Program Information • Students attend classes at University of Dublin–Trinity College. Field trips to Delphi, Killarney, Northern Ireland.

Sessions • Yearlong.

Eligibility Requirements • Open to juniors, seniors; 3.0 GPA; 1 letter of recommendation; good academic standing at home school; enrollment at an accredited American college or university.

Living Arrangements • Students live in program-owned apartments, program-owned houses. Quarters are shared with host institution students. Meals are taken on one's own, in residences, in central dining facility, in restaurants.

Costs (2002-2003) • Yearlong program: $18,575; includes tuition, housing, excursions, international student ID, student support services, family visit, cultural and sporting events, pre-departure advising. $40 application fee. $500 nonrefundable deposit required. Financial aid available for all students: scholarships, travel grants.

For More Information • Institute for Study Abroad, Butler University, 1100 West 42nd Street, Suite 305, Indianapolis, IN 46208-3345; *Phone:* 800-858-0229; *Fax:* 317-940-9704. *E-mail:* study-abroad@butler.edu. *World Wide Web:* http://www.ifsa-butler.org/

INSTITUTE FOR STUDY ABROAD, BUTLER UNIVERSITY

UNIVERSITY COLLEGE DUBLIN

Hosted by University College Dublin–National University of Ireland, Dublin

Academic Focus • Full curriculum.

Program Information • Students attend classes at University College Dublin–National University of Ireland, Dublin. Field trips to Delphi, Killarney, Northern Ireland.

Sessions • Fall, spring, yearlong.

Eligibility Requirements • Open to juniors, seniors; 3.0 GPA; 1 letter of recommendation; good academic standing at home school; enrollment at an accredited American college or university.

Living Arrangements • Students live in host institution dormitories, locally rented apartments, program-owned houses. Quarters are shared with host institution students, students from other programs. Meals are taken on one's own, in residences, in central dining facility, in restaurants.

Costs (2002-2003) • One term: $9275 for arts; $10,575 for sciences; $9975 for commerce and agriculture. Yearlong program: $14,575 for arts; $16,975 for sciences; $16,975 for commerce and agriculture; includes tuition, housing, excursions, international student ID, student support services, family visit, cultural and sporting events, pre-departure advising. $40 application fee. $500 nonrefundable deposit required. Financial aid available for all students: scholarships, travel grants.

For More Information • Institute for Study Abroad, Butler University, 1100 West 42nd Street, Suite 305, Indianapolis, IN 46208-3345; *Phone:* 800-858-0229; *Fax:* 317-940-9704. *E-mail:* study-abroad@butler.edu. *World Wide Web:* http://www.ifsa-butler.org/

INTERSTUDY

TRINITY COLLEGE, DUBLIN

Hosted by University of Dublin–Trinity College

Academic Focus • Art history, biochemistry, biological/life sciences, botany, classics and classical languages, computer science, drama/theater, economics, engineering, English, European studies, geography, history, law and legal studies, mathematics, music, political science and government, psychology, religious studies, social sciences, sociology.

Program Information • Students attend classes at University of Dublin–Trinity College. Scheduled travel to Bath, Stratford-upon-Avon, Oxford, Warwick Castle, Stonehenge.

Sessions • Yearlong.

Eligibility Requirements • Minimum age 18; open to freshmen, sophomores, juniors, seniors, adults; 3.3 GPA; 2 letters of recommendation; good academic standing at home school.

Living Arrangements • Students live in host institution dormitories, locally rented apartments. Quarters are shared with host institution students. Meals are taken on one's own, in residences.

Costs (2003-2004) • Yearlong program: $20,995; includes tuition, housing, some meals, excursions, international student ID, student support services, Student Union membership, e-mail access, banking facilities, international bank transfers, transcript, cell phones. $35 application fee. $500 nonrefundable deposit required. Financial aid available for all students: scholarships, loans, stipends.

For More Information • InterStudy, Admissions Office, 63 Edward Street, Medford, MA 02155; *Phone:* 800-663-1999; *Fax:* 781-391-7463. *E-mail:* interstudy@interstudy-usa.org. *World Wide Web:* http://www.interstudy.org/

INTERSTUDY

UNIVERSITY COLLEGE, DUBLIN, REPUBLIC OF IRELAND

Hosted by University College Dublin–National University of Ireland, Dublin

Academic Focus • Archaeology, art history, classics and classical languages, economics, English, French language and literature, geography, German language and literature, history, Irish studies, Italian language and literature, linguistics, mathematics, music, philosophy, physics, political science and government, Portuguese, psychology, social work, Spanish language and literature, statistics.

Program Information • Students attend classes at University College Dublin–National University of Ireland, Dublin. Scheduled travel to Bath, Stratford-upon-Avon, Warwick Castle, Oxford, Stonehenge.
Sessions • Fall, spring, yearlong.
Eligibility Requirements • Minimum age 18; open to freshmen, sophomores, juniors, seniors, adults; 3.0 GPA; 2 letters of recommendation; good academic standing at home school.
Living Arrangements • Students live in host institution dormitories, locally rented apartments. Quarters are shared with host institution students. Meals are taken as a group, on one's own, in residences.
Costs (2003-2004) • One term: $11,175 for fall term; $11,915 for spring. Yearlong program: $20,850; includes tuition, housing, some meals, excursions, international student ID, student support services, Student Union membership, e-mail access, banking facilities, international bank transfers, transcript, cell phone. $35 application fee. $500 nonrefundable deposit required. Financial aid available for all students: scholarships, loans, stipends.
For More Information • InterStudy, Admissions Office, 63 Edward Street, Medford, MA 02155; *Phone:* 800-663-1999; *Fax:* 781-391-7463. *E-mail:* interstudy@interstudy-usa.org. *World Wide Web:* http://www.interstudy.org/

LYNN UNIVERSITY
ACADEMIC ADVENTURE ABROAD–IRELAND

Hosted by American College Dublin
Academic Focus • Accounting, anthropology, art history, business administration/management, communications, economics, English, English literature, finance, French language and literature, German language and literature, history, hospitality services, hotel and restaurant management, human resources, international affairs, international business, Irish literature, Irish studies, literature, marketing, mathematics, psychology, sociology, Spanish language and literature, statistics, tourism and travel.
Program Information • Students attend classes at American College Dublin. Optional travel to Italy (10-day International art and humanities tour), Ireland (10-day tour) at an extra cost.
Sessions • Fall, spring, yearlong.
Eligibility Requirements • Open to freshmen, sophomores, juniors, seniors, graduate students, adults; 2.0 GPA; good academic standing at home school.
Living Arrangements • Students live in host institution dormitories. Quarters are shared with host institution students. Meals are taken as a group, on one's own, in central dining facility.
Costs (2004-2005) • One term: $13,025 (estimated). Yearlong program: contact sponsor for cost; includes tuition, housing, some meals, insurance, student support services. $35 application fee. $500 nonrefundable deposit required. Financial aid available for students from sponsoring institution: scholarships, loans, consortium agreements for all non-Lynn University students.
For More Information • Study Abroad Advisor, Ireland Programs, Lynn University, 3601 North Military Trail, Boca Raton, FL 33431-5598; *Phone:* 800-453-8306; *Fax:* 561-237-7095. *E-mail:* studyabroad@lynn.edu. *World Wide Web:* http://www.lynn.edu/studyabroad/

MARIST COLLEGE
IRISH INTERNSHIP PROGRAM

Hosted by DBS School of Arts
Academic Focus • Business administration/management, communications, Irish studies, psychology, social sciences.
Program Information • Students attend classes at DBS School of Arts. Scheduled travel to Galway, Aran Islands, Cork, Limerick, Belfast; field trips to Dublin and environs.
Sessions • Fall, spring, yearlong.
Eligibility Requirements • Open to sophomores, juniors; 2.8 GPA; 2 letters of recommendation; good academic standing at home school.
Living Arrangements • Students live in host family homes. Meals are taken with host family.
Costs (2003-2004) • One term: $12,500. Yearlong program: $25,000; includes tuition, housing, some meals, insurance, excursions, student support services, internship. $35 application fee. $300

nonrefundable deposit required. Financial aid available for students from sponsoring institution: scholarships, loans.
For More Information • Ms. Carol Toufali, Coordinator, Marist Abroad Program, Marist College, 3399 North Road, Poughkeepsie, NY 12601-1387; *Phone:* 845-575-3330; *Fax:* 845-575-3294. *E-mail:* international@marist.edu. *World Wide Web:* http://www.marist.edu/international/

MICHIGAN STATE UNIVERSITY
ENGLISH LITERATURE IN DUBLIN

Held at Irish Writers Centre
Academic Focus • Creative writing, drama/theater, English literature, film and media studies, Irish literature.
Program Information • Classes are held on the campus of Irish Writers Centre. Faculty members are drawn from the sponsor's U.S. staff and local instructors hired by the sponsor. Field trips to the International Dublin Film Festival, Yeats County, the Cúirt Literature Festival, Galway.
Sessions • Spring.
Eligibility Requirements • Minimum age 18; open to freshmen, sophomores, juniors, seniors, graduate students; 2.0 GPA; 2 letters of recommendation; good academic standing at home school; approval of faculty director.
Living Arrangements • Students live in locally rented apartments. Quarters are shared with host institution students. Meals are taken on one's own, in residences, in restaurants.
Costs (2003) • One term: $3100 (estimated); includes housing, insurance, excursions, student support services. $100 application fee. $200 nonrefundable deposit required. Financial aid available for students from sponsoring institution: scholarships, loans.
For More Information • Ms. Sherry Martinez-Bonilla, Office Assistant, Michigan State University, Office of Study Abroad, 109 International Center, East Lansing, MI 48824-1035; *Phone:* 517-353-8920; *Fax:* 517-432-2082. *E-mail:* marti269@msu.edu. *World Wide Web:* http://studyabroad.msu.edu/

NEW YORK UNIVERSITY
FILM PRODUCTION: MAKING THE DOCUMENTARY AND MUSIC VIDEO PRODUCTION

Held at Irish Film Centre
Academic Focus • Creative writing, film and media studies, Irish studies, journalism, telecommunications.
Program Information • Classes are held on the campus of Irish Film Centre. Faculty members are drawn from the sponsor's U.S. staff and local instructors hired by the sponsor. Field trips to Dublin and environs, theater visits, museums, Galway.
Sessions • Fall, spring.
Eligibility Requirements • Minimum age 18; open to freshmen, sophomores, juniors, seniors, graduate students, adults; course work in filmmaking and video production; 2 letters of recommendation; good academic standing at home school; interview.
Living Arrangements • Students live in host institution dormitories, locally rented apartments. Meals are taken on one's own, in residences, in restaurants.
Costs (2002-2003) • One term: $20,261–$21,611; includes tuition, housing, excursions, student support services, registration fees. $35 application fee. $350 nonrefundable deposit required. Financial aid available for students from sponsoring institution: scholarships, loans.
For More Information • Ms. Peggy Sotirhos, Associate Director of Special Programs Recruitment, New York University, 721 Broadway, 12th Floor, New York, NY 10003; *Phone:* 212-998-1500; *Fax:* 212-995-4610. *E-mail:* tisch.special.info@nyu.edu. *World Wide Web:* http://www.nyu.edu/studyabroad/

NEW YORK UNIVERSITY
PERFORMANCE WORKSHOP: IRISH PLAYWRIGHTS

Hosted by Abbey Theatre
Academic Focus • Creative writing, cultural studies, drama/theater, Irish studies, performing arts, visual and performing arts.
Program Information • Students attend classes at Abbey Theatre. Classes are also held on the campus of Irish Film Centre. Field trips to Dublin and environs, theater visits, museums, Galway.
Sessions • Fall, spring.

Eligibility Requirements • Minimum age 18; open to freshmen, sophomores, juniors, seniors, graduate students, adults; ? letters of recommendation; good academic standing at home school; audition; interview; acting training and/or experience.

Living Arrangements • Students live in locally rented apartments. Meals are taken on one's own, in restaurants.

Costs (2002-2003) • One term: $20,261–$21,611; includes tuition, housing, excursions, student support services, registration fees. $35 application fee. $350 nonrefundable deposit required. Financial aid available for students from sponsoring institution: scholarships, loans.

For More Information • Ms. Peggy Sotirhos, Associate Director of Special Programs Recruitment, New York University, 721 Broadway, 12th Floor, New York, NY 10003; *Phone:* 212-998-1500; *Fax:* 212-995-4610. *E-mail:* tisch.special.info@nyu.edu. *World Wide Web:* http://www.nyu.edu/studyabroad/

NEW YORK UNIVERSITY
SCREENWRITING

Hosted by Gate Theatre

Academic Focus • Cinematography, creative writing, film and media studies, Irish studies, journalism, telecommunications.

Program Information • Students attend classes at Gate Theatre. Classes are also held on the campus of Irish Film Centre. Field trips to Dublin and environs, theater visits, museums, Galway.

Sessions • Fall, spring.

Eligibility Requirements • Minimum age 18; open to sophomores, juniors, seniors, adults; course work in dramatic writing; 2 letters of recommendation; good academic standing at home school; interview; writing sample required for some students.

Living Arrangements • Students live in locally rented apartments. Meals are taken on one's own, in residences, in restaurants.

Costs (2002-2003) • One term: $20,261–$21,611; includes tuition, housing, insurance, excursions, lab equipment, student support services, registration fees. $35 application fee. $350 nonrefundable deposit required. Financial aid available for students from sponsoring institution: scholarships, loans.

For More Information • Ms. Peggy Sotirhos, Associate Director of Special Programs Recruitment, New York University, 721 Broadway, 12th Floor, New York, NY 10003; *Phone:* 212-998-1500; *Fax:* 212-995-4610. *E-mail:* tisch.special.info@nyu.edu. *World Wide Web:* http://www.nyu.edu/studyabroad/

NEW YORK UNIVERSITY
TOPICS IN IRISH LITERARY, VISUAL AND PERFORMING ARTS

Held at Irish Film Centre

Academic Focus • Art, art history, creative writing, cultural studies, drama/theater, film and media studies, interdisciplinary studies, Irish literature, Irish studies, performing arts, visual and performing arts.

Program Information • Classes are held on the campus of Irish Film Centre. Faculty members are drawn from the sponsor's U.S. staff and local instructors hired by the sponsor. Field trips to Dublin and environs, theater visits, museums, Galway.

Sessions • Fall, spring.

Eligibility Requirements • Minimum age 18; open to freshmen, sophomores, juniors, seniors, graduate students, adults; 2 letters of recommendation; good academic standing at home school; interview.

Living Arrangements • Students live in locally rented apartments. Meals are taken on one's own, in residences, in restaurants.

Costs (2002-2003) • One term: $20,636–$22,156; includes tuition, housing, excursions, student support services, registration fees. $35 application fee. $350 nonrefundable deposit required. Financial aid available for students from sponsoring institution: scholarships, loans.

For More Information • Ms. Peggy Sotirhos, Associate Director of Special Programs Recruitment, New York University, 721 Broadway, 12th Floor, New York, NY 10003; *Phone:* 212-998-1500; *Fax:* 212-995-4610. *E-mail:* tisch.special.info@nyu.edu. *World Wide Web:* http://www.nyu.edu/studyabroad/

NORTH AMERICAN INSTITUTE FOR STUDY ABROAD
STUDY IN DUBLIN

Hosted by Dublin Institute of Technology

Academic Focus • Full curriculum.

Program Information • Students attend classes at Dublin Institute of Technology.

Sessions • Fall, spring, yearlong.

Eligibility Requirements • Minimum age 18; open to sophomores, juniors, seniors; 3.0 GPA.

Living Arrangements • Students live in host institution dormitories, locally rented apartments, host family homes. Quarters are shared with host institution students. Meals are taken on one's own, in residences, in central dining facility, in restaurants.

Costs (2001-2002) • One term: $8000. Yearlong program: $15,500; includes tuition, housing, international student ID, student support services, transcripts. $50 application fee. $500 nonrefundable deposit required. Financial aid available for all students: scholarships.

For More Information • Dr. Michael Currid, Director, North American Institute for Study Abroad, 129 Mill Street, Danville, PA 17821; *Phone:* 570-275-5099; *Fax:* 570-275-1644. *E-mail:* naisa@naisa.com. *World Wide Web:* http://www.naisa.com/

NORTH AMERICAN INSTITUTE FOR STUDY ABROAD
STUDY IN DUBLIN

Hosted by American College Dublin

Academic Focus • Full curriculum.

Program Information • Students attend classes at American College Dublin.

Sessions • Fall, spring, yearlong.

Eligibility Requirements • Minimum age 18; open to sophomores, juniors, seniors; 2.5 GPA; good academic standing at home school.

Living Arrangements • Students live in host institution dormitories, locally rented apartments, host family homes. Quarters are shared with host institution students. Meals are taken on one's own, in residences, in central dining facility, in restaurants.

Costs (2003-2004) • One term: $8500. Yearlong program: $16,000; includes tuition, housing, international student ID, student support services, transcripts. $50 application fee. $500 deposit required. Financial aid available for all students: scholarships.

For More Information • Dr. Michael Currid, Director, North American Institute for Study Abroad, 129 Mill Street, Danville, PA 17821; *Phone:* 570-275-5099; *Fax:* 570-275-1644. *E-mail:* naisa@naisa.com. *World Wide Web:* http://www.naisa.com/

NORTH AMERICAN INSTITUTE FOR STUDY ABROAD
STUDY IN DUBLIN, IRELAND

Hosted by Institute of Public Administration

Academic Focus • Full curriculum.

Program Information • Students attend classes at Institute of Public Administration. Optional travel at an extra cost.

Sessions • Fall, spring, yearlong.

Eligibility Requirements • Minimum age 18; open to sophomores, juniors, seniors; 3.0 GPA; good academic standing at home school.

Living Arrangements • Students live in host institution dormitories, locally rented apartments, host family homes. Quarters are shared with host institution students. Meals are taken on one's own, in residences, in central dining facility, in restaurants.

Costs (2003-2004) • One term: $8900. Yearlong program: $17,000; includes tuition, housing, insurance, international student ID, student support services, transcripts. $50 application fee. $500 nonrefundable deposit required. Financial aid available for all students: scholarships.

For More Information • Dr. Michael Currid, Director, North American Institute for Study Abroad, 129 Mill Street, Danville, PA 17821; *Phone:* 570-275-5099; *Fax:* 570-275-1644. *E-mail:* naisa@naisa.com. *World Wide Web:* http://www.naisa.com/

IRELAND
Dublin

NORTH AMERICAN INSTITUTE FOR STUDY ABROAD
STUDY IN IRELAND

Hosted by University of Dublin–Trinity College
Academic Focus • Full curriculum.
Program Information • Students attend classes at University of Dublin–Trinity College. Optional travel at an extra cost.
Sessions • Yearlong.
Eligibility Requirements • Minimum age 18; open to juniors, seniors; 3.0 GPA; 2 letters of recommendation; good academic standing at home school.
Living Arrangements • Students live in host institution dormitories, locally rented apartments, host family homes. Quarters are shared with host institution students. Meals are taken on one's own, with host family, in residences, in central dining facility, in restaurants.
Costs (2003-2004) • Yearlong program: $15,500; includes tuition, housing, international student ID, student support services, transcripts. $50 application fee. $500 nonrefundable deposit required. Financial aid available for all students: scholarships.
For More Information • Dr. Michael Currid, Director, North American Institute for Study Abroad, 129 Mill Street, Danville, PA 17821; *Phone:* 570-275-5099; *Fax:* 570-275-1644. *E-mail:* naisa@naisa. com. *World Wide Web:* http://www.naisa.com/

NORTH AMERICAN INSTITUTE FOR STUDY ABROAD
STUDY IN IRELAND

Hosted by University College Dublin–National University of Ireland, Dublin
Academic Focus • Full curriculum.
Program Information • Students attend classes at University College Dublin–National University of Ireland, Dublin. Optional travel at an extra cost.
Sessions • Fall, spring, yearlong.
Eligibility Requirements • Minimum age 18; open to juniors, seniors; 3.0 GPA; 2 letters of recommendation; good academic standing at home school.
Living Arrangements • Students live in host institution dormitories, locally rented apartments, host family homes. Quarters are shared with host institution students. Meals are taken on one's own, in residences, in central dining facility, in restaurants.
Costs (2003-2004) • One term: $8500. Yearlong program: $14,750; includes tuition, housing, insurance, international student ID, student support services, transcripts. $50 application fee. $500 nonrefundable deposit required. Financial aid available for all students: scholarships.
For More Information • Dr. Michael Currid, Director, North American Institute for Study Abroad, 129 Mill Street, Danville, PA 17821; *Phone:* 570-275-5099; *Fax:* 570-275-1644. *E-mail:* naisa@naisa. com. *World Wide Web:* http://www.naisa.com/

NORTH AMERICAN INSTITUTE FOR STUDY ABROAD
STUDY IN IRELAND

Hosted by Dublin City University
Academic Focus • Full curriculum.
Program Information • Students attend classes at Dublin City University. Optional travel at an extra cost.
Sessions • Fall, spring, yearlong.
Eligibility Requirements • Minimum age 18; open to sophomores, juniors, seniors; 3.0 GPA; 2 letters of recommendation; good academic standing at home school.
Living Arrangements • Students live in locally rented apartments, host family homes. Quarters are shared with host institution students. Meals are taken on one's own, with host family, in residences, in central dining facility, in restaurants.
Costs (2003-2004) • One term: $9000. Yearlong program: $17,000; includes tuition, housing, insurance, international student ID, student support services, transcripts. $50 application fee. $500 nonrefundable deposit required. Financial aid available for all students: scholarships.
For More Information • Dr. Michael Currid, Director, North American Institute for Study Abroad, 129 Mill Street, Danville, PA

17821; *Phone:* 570-275-5099; *Fax:* 570-275-1644. *E-mail:* naisa@naisa. com. *World Wide Web:* http://www.naisa.com/

NORTH AMERICAN INSTITUTE FOR STUDY ABROAD
STUDY IN IRELAND/STUDENT TEACHING IN IRELAND

Hosted by Marino Institute of Education
Academic Focus • Full curriculum.
Program Information • Students attend classes at Marino Institute of Education. Optional travel at an extra cost.
Sessions • Fall, spring, yearlong.
Eligibility Requirements • Minimum age 18; open to sophomores, juniors, seniors; 2.75 GPA; 2 letters of recommendation; good academic standing at home school.
Living Arrangements • Students live in host institution dormitories, locally rented apartments, host family homes. Quarters are shared with host institution students. Meals are taken on one's own, with host family, in central dining facility, in restaurants.
Costs (2003-2004) • One term: $6500 for regular term; $2500 for student teaching term. Yearlong program: $14,000; includes tuition, housing, insurance, international student ID, student support services, transcripts, Dublin arrival and departure ground transport. $50 application fee. $500 nonrefundable deposit required. Financial aid available for all students: scholarships.
For More Information • Dr. Michael Currid, Director, North American Institute for Study Abroad, 129 Mill Street, Danville, PA 17821; *Phone:* 570-275-5099; *Fax:* 570-275-1644. *E-mail:* naisa@naisa. com. *World Wide Web:* http://www.naisa.com/

ST. JOHN'S UNIVERSITY
STUDY ABROAD IRELAND–DUBLIN

Hosted by University College Dublin–National University of Ireland, Dublin
Academic Focus • Arabic, archaeology, art history, Celtic studies, civilization studies, economics, French language and literature, Gaelic, geography, German language and literature, Greek, Hebrew, history, Italian language and literature, mathematics, philosophy, political science and government, sociology, Spanish language and literature, statistics, Welsh.
Program Information • Students attend classes at University College Dublin–National University of Ireland, Dublin.
Sessions • Yearlong, single semesters also available.
Eligibility Requirements • Minimum age 18; open to sophomores, juniors, seniors; 3.3 GPA; 2 letters of recommendation; good academic standing at home school; interview.
Living Arrangements • Students live in host institution dormitories, program-owned apartments. Quarters are shared with host institution students, students from other programs. Meals are taken on one's own, in residences.
Costs (2004) • One term: contact sponsor for cost. Yearlong program: $21,979–$25,728; includes tuition, student support services, administrative fees. $30 application fee. $750 nonrefundable deposit required. Financial aid available for students from sponsoring institution: scholarships, loans.
For More Information • Dr. Ruth DePaula, Director, Office of Study Abroad Programs, St. John's University, 8000 Utopia Parkway, Jamaica, NY 11439; *Phone:* 718-990-6105; *Fax:* 718-990-2321. *E-mail:* intled@stjohns.edu. *World Wide Web:* http://www.stjohns. edu/studyabroad/

ST. JOHN'S UNIVERSITY
STUDY ABROAD IRELAND–DUBLIN

Hosted by University of Dublin–Trinity College
Academic Focus • Arabic, archaeology, art history, Celtic studies, civilization studies, economics, French language and literature, Gaelic, geography, German language and literature, Greek, Hebrew, history, Italian language and literature, mathematics, philosophy, political science and government, sociology, Spanish language and literature, statistics, Welsh.
Program Information • Students attend classes at University of Dublin–Trinity College.
Sessions • Fall term.

Eligibility Requirements • Minimum age 18; open to sophomores, juniors, seniors; 3.3 GPA; 2 letters of recommendation; good academic standing at home school; interview.

Living Arrangements • Students live in host institution dormitories, program-owned apartments. Quarters are shared with host institution students, students from other programs. Meals are taken on one's own, in residences.

Costs (2004) • One term: contact sponsor for cost. $30 application fee. $750 nonrefundable deposit required. Financial aid available for students from sponsoring institution: scholarships, loans.

For More Information • Dr. Ruth De Paula, Director, Office of Study Abroad Programs, St. John's University, 8000 Utopia Parkway, Jamaica, NY 11439; *Phone:* 718-990-6105; *Fax:* 718-990-2321. *E-mail:* intled@stjohns.edu. *World Wide Web:* http://www.stjohns.edu/studyabroad/

STATE UNIVERSITY OF NEW YORK AT OSWEGO
UNIVERSITY COLLEGE DUBLIN

Hosted by University College Dublin–National University of Ireland, Dublin

Academic Focus • Accounting, art history, business administration/management, Celtic studies, commerce, economics, finance, geography, history, human resources, management information systems, marketing, philosophy, sociology.

Program Information • Students attend classes at University College Dublin–National University of Ireland, Dublin.

Sessions • Fall, spring, yearlong.

Eligibility Requirements • Open to sophomores, juniors, seniors; 3.0 GPA; 3 letters of recommendation; good academic standing at home school; personal statement.

Living Arrangements • Students live in host institution dormitories, locally rented apartments. Quarters are shared with host institution students. Meals are taken on one's own, in residences, in restaurants.

Costs (2003-2004) • One term: $5920–$7320. Yearlong program: $11,840–$14,640; includes tuition, insurance, student support services. $250 nonrefundable deposit required. Financial aid available for students: home university financial aid, loan processing and scholarships for Oswego students.

For More Information • Ms. Mary Kerr, Program Specialist, State University of New York at Oswego, 122A Swetman Hall, Oswego, NY 13126; *Phone:* 888-4-OSWEGO; *Fax:* 315-312-2477. *E-mail:* intled@oswego.edu. *World Wide Web:* http://www.oswego.edu/intled/

STATE UNIVERSITY OF NEW YORK COLLEGE AT CORTLAND
CORTLAND/DUBLIN INTERNSHIPS

Held at Dublin Internships

Academic Focus • Full curriculum.

Program Information • Classes are held on the campus of Dublin Internships.

Sessions • Fall, spring.

Eligibility Requirements • Minimum age 19; open to sophomores, juniors, seniors; course work in field related to internship placement; 2.5 GPA; 2 letters of recommendation; good academic standing at home school.

Living Arrangements • Students live in locally rented apartments, host family homes. Meals are taken on one's own, with host family, in residences, in restaurants.

Costs (2003-2004) • One term: $5000; includes housing, all meals, insurance, international airfare, student support services, passport fees, bus pass. $20 application fee. $200 nonrefundable deposit required. Financial aid available for students from sponsoring institution: scholarships, loans.

For More Information • Ms. Liz Kopp, Assistant Director, Office of International Programs, State University of New York College at Cortland, PO Box 2000, Cortland, NY 13045; *Phone:* 607-753-2209; *Fax:* 607-753-5989. *E-mail:* cortlandabroad@cortland.edu. *World Wide Web:* http://www.studyabroad.com/suny/cortland/

GALWAY
ACADEMIC PROGRAMS INTERNATIONAL (API)
(API)–GALWAY, IRELAND

Hosted by National University of Ireland, Galway

Academic Focus • Full curriculum.

Program Information • Students attend classes at National University of Ireland, Galway. Scheduled travel to Dublin, other European cities; field trips to Cliffs of Moher, Cork, Blarney Castle, Bunratty Castle and Folk Park, Connemara.

Sessions • Fall, spring, yearlong.

Eligibility Requirements • Minimum age 18; open to juniors, seniors; 3.0 GPA; 1 letter of recommendation; good academic standing at home school; official transcript from home university; no foreign language proficiency required.

Living Arrangements • Students live in host institution dormitories, locally rented apartments. Quarters are shared with host institution students. Meals are taken on one's own, in residences, in restaurants.

Costs (2004-2005) • One term: $10,800–$10,900. Yearlong program: $21,500; includes tuition, housing, insurance, excursions, student support services, ground transportation, airport pick-up. $150 nonrefundable deposit required. Financial aid available for all students: scholarships.

For More Information • Ms. Jennifer C. Allen, Director, Academic Programs International (API), 107 East Hopkins, San Marcos, TX 78666; *Phone:* 800-844-4124; *Fax:* 512-392-8420. *E-mail:* api@academicintl.com. *World Wide Web:* http://www.academicintl.com/

ARCADIA UNIVERSITY
NATIONAL UNIVERSITY OF IRELAND, GALWAY

Hosted by National University of Ireland, Galway

Academic Focus • Business administration/management, classics and classical languages, economics, English, labor and industrial relations, law and legal studies, liberal studies, political science and government, science.

Program Information • Students attend classes at National University of Ireland, Galway. Scheduled travel to sites within Ireland.

Sessions • Fall, spring, yearlong.

Eligibility Requirements • Open to sophomores, juniors, seniors; 3.0 GPA; 1 letter of recommendation.

Living Arrangements • Students live in program-owned apartments, host family homes. Quarters are shared with host institution students, students from other programs. Meals are taken on one's own, in residences.

Costs (2003-2004) • One term: $10,690. Yearlong program: $17,890; includes tuition, housing, insurance, international student ID, student support services, pre-departure guide, transcripts. $35 application fee. $500 nonrefundable deposit required. Financial aid available for all students: scholarships, loans.

For More Information • Arcadia University, Center for Education Abroad, 450 South Easton Road, Glenside, PA 19038-3295; *Phone:* 866-927-2234; *Fax:* 215-572-2174. *E-mail:* cea@arcadia.edu. *World Wide Web:* http://www.arcadia.edu/cea/

BRETHREN COLLEGES ABROAD
BCA PEACE AND JUSTICE PROGRAM IN GALWAY, IRELAND

Hosted by National University of Ireland, Galway

Academic Focus • Full curriculum, peace and conflict studies.

Program Information • Students attend classes at National University of Ireland, Galway. Field trips.

Sessions • Spring.

Eligibility Requirements • Minimum age 18; open to sophomores, juniors, seniors; 3.0 GPA; 3 letters of recommendation; good academic standing at home school.

Living Arrangements • Students live in host institution dormitories. Meals are taken on one's own, in residences.

Costs (2003-2004) • One term: $11,500; includes tuition, housing, all meals, insurance, excursions, international student ID, student support services. $50 application fee. $100 nonrefundable deposit required.

For More Information • Ms. Natalya Latysheva-Derova, Program Officer, Brethren Colleges Abroad, 50 Alpha Drive, Elizabethtown,

PA 17022; *Phone:* 866-222-6188; *Fax:* 717-361-6619. *E-mail:* info@bcanet.org. *World Wide Web:* http://www.bcanet.org/

COLLEGE CONSORTIUM FOR INTERNATIONAL STUDIES–ST. BONAVENTURE UNIVERSITY AND TRUMAN STATE UNIVERSITY
IRELAND PROGRAM–GALWAY

Hosted by National University of Ireland, Galway
Academic Focus • Full curriculum.
Program Information • Students attend classes at National University of Ireland, Galway.
Sessions • Fall, spring, yearlong.
Eligibility Requirements • Minimum age 18; open to sophomores, juniors, seniors; 3.0 GPA; 3 letters of recommendation; essay.
Living Arrangements • Students live in host institution dormitories, locally rented apartments, host family homes. Quarters are shared with host institution students, students from other programs. Meals are taken as a group, on one's own, with host family, in residences.
Costs (2004-2005) • One term: $6367. Yearlong program: $12,734; includes tuition, insurance, instructional and administrative fees. $30 application fee. $300 nonrefundable deposit required. Financial aid available for students from sponsoring institution: scholarships, loans.
For More Information • Center for International Education Abroad, College Consortium for International Studies–St. Bonaventure University and Truman State University, Truman State University, Kirk Building 114, Kirksville, MO 63501; *Phone:* 660-785-4076; *Fax:* 660-785-7473. *E-mail:* ciea@truman.edu. *World Wide Web:* http://www.ccisabroad.org/. Students may also apply through St. Bonaventure University, St. Bonaventure, NY 14778.

FAIRFIELD UNIVERSITY
FAIRFIELD UNIVERSITY GALWAY CAMPUS

Hosted by National University of Ireland, Galway
Academic Focus • Full curriculum.
Program Information • Students attend classes at National University of Ireland, Galway. Optional travel at an extra cost.
Sessions • Fall, spring, yearlong.
Eligibility Requirements • Minimum age 18; open to juniors, seniors; 3.0 GPA; 2 letters of recommendation; good academic standing at home school; transcript.
Living Arrangements • Students live in locally rented apartments. Quarters are shared with host institution students, students from other programs. Meals are taken on one's own, in residences.
Costs (2003-2004) • One term: $12,825. Yearlong program: $25,650; includes tuition, insurance, excursions, international student ID, student support services, activities, airport pick-up. $50 application fee. $1000 refundable deposit required. Financial aid available for students from sponsoring institution.
For More Information • Office of International Education, Fairfield University, Dolan Office, 1073 North Benson Road, Fairfield, CT 06824; *Phone:* 203-254-4332; *Fax:* 203-254-4261. *E-mail:* studyabroadoffice@mail.fairfield.edu. *World Wide Web:* http://www.fairfield.edu/sce/studyabroad/

INSTITUTE FOR STUDY ABROAD, BUTLER UNIVERSITY
NATIONAL UNIVERSITY OF IRELAND, GALWAY

Hosted by National University of Ireland, Galway
Academic Focus • Full curriculum.
Program Information • Students attend classes at National University of Ireland, Galway. Field trips to Delphi, Killarney, Northern Ireland.
Sessions • Fall, spring, yearlong.
Eligibility Requirements • Open to sophomores, juniors, seniors; 3.0 GPA; 1 letter of recommendation; good academic standing at home school; enrollment at an accredited American college or university.
Living Arrangements • Students live in locally rented apartments. Quarters are shared with host institution students. Meals are taken on one's own, in residences, in restaurants.

Costs (2002-2003) • One term: $9275. Yearlong program: $15,275; includes tuition, housing, excursions, international student ID, student support services, family visit, cultural and sporting events, pre-departure advising. $40 application fee. $500 nonrefundable deposit required. Financial aid available for all students: scholarships, travel grants.
For More Information • Institute for Study Abroad, Butler University, 1100 West 42nd Street, Suite 305, Indianapolis, IN 46208-3345; *Phone:* 800-858-0229; *Fax:* 317-940-9704. *E-mail:* study-abroad@butler.edu. *World Wide Web:* http://www.ifsa-butler.org/

INTERSTUDY
NATIONAL UNIVERSITY OF IRELAND, UNIVERSITY COLLEGE, GALWAY, REPUBLIC OF IRELAND

Hosted by National University of Ireland, Galway
Academic Focus • Accounting, anatomy, archaeology, biochemistry, botany, chemical sciences, classics and classical languages, computer science, economics, engineering, English, geography, history, Irish studies, law and legal studies, management information systems, marketing, mathematics, philosophy, physics, political science and government, psychology, sociology, zoology.
Program Information • Students attend classes at National University of Ireland, Galway. Scheduled travel to Bath, Stratford-upon-Avon, Warwick Castle, Oxford, Stonehenge.
Sessions • Fall, spring, yearlong.
Eligibility Requirements • Minimum age 18; open to freshmen, sophomores, juniors, seniors, adults; 3.0 GPA; 2 letters of recommendation; good academic standing at home school.
Living Arrangements • Students live in host institution dormitories, locally rented apartments. Quarters are shared with host institution students. Meals are taken on one's own, in residences.
Costs (2003-2004) • One term: $10,415 for fall term; $11,450 for spring. Yearlong program: $19,150; includes tuition, housing, some meals, excursions, international student ID, student support services, Student Union membership, e-mail access, banking facilities, international bank transfers, transcript, cell phone. $35 application fee. $500 nonrefundable deposit required. Financial aid available for all students: scholarships, loans, stipends.
For More Information • InterStudy, Admissions Office, 63 Edward Street, Medford, MA 02155; *Phone:* 800-663-1999; *Fax:* 781-391-7463. *E-mail:* interstudy@interstudy-usa.org. *World Wide Web:* http://www.interstudy.org/

NORTH AMERICAN INSTITUTE FOR STUDY ABROAD
STUDY IN IRELAND

Hosted by National University of Ireland, Galway
Academic Focus • Full curriculum.
Program Information • Students attend classes at National University of Ireland, Galway.
Sessions • Fall, spring, yearlong.
Eligibility Requirements • Minimum age 18; open to sophomores, juniors, seniors; 3.0 GPA; 2 letters of recommendation; good academic standing at home school.
Living Arrangements • Students live in host institution dormitories, locally rented apartments, host family homes. Quarters are shared with host institution students. Meals are taken on one's own, with host family, in residences, in central dining facility, in restaurants.
Costs (2003-2004) • One term: $7750. Yearlong program: $14,000; includes tuition, housing, international student ID, student support services, transcripts. $50 application fee. $500 nonrefundable deposit required. Financial aid available for all students: scholarships.
For More Information • Dr. Michael Currid, Director, North American Institute for Study Abroad, 129 Mill Street, Danville, PA 17821; *Phone:* 570-275-5099; *Fax:* 570-275-1644. *E-mail:* naisa@naisa.com. *World Wide Web:* http://www.naisa.com/

ST. JOHN'S UNIVERSITY
STUDY ABROAD IRELAND–GALWAY

Hosted by National University of Ireland, Galway
Academic Focus • Full curriculum.

Program Information • Students attend classes at National University of Ireland, Galway.

Sessions • Fall, spring, yearlong.

Eligibility Requirements • Minimum age 18; open to sophomores, juniors; 3.0 GPA; 2 letters of recommendation; good academic standing at home school; interview.

Living Arrangements • Students live in host institution dormitories, locally rented apartments, host family homes. Quarters are shared with host institution students. Meals are taken on one's own, in residences.

Costs (2004-2005) • One term: $11,513–$13,476. Yearlong program: contact sponsor for cost; includes tuition, student support services, administrative fee. $30 application fee. $750 nonrefundable deposit required. Financial aid available for students from sponsoring institution: scholarships, loans.

For More Information • Dr. Ruth De Paula, Director, Office of Study Abroad Programs, St. John's University, 8000 Utopia Parkway, Jamaica, NY 11439; *Phone:* 718-990-6105; *Fax:* 718-990-2321. *E-mail:* intled@stjohns.edu. *World Wide Web:* http://www.stjohns.edu/studyabroad/

UNIVERSITY AT ALBANY, STATE UNIVERSITY OF NEW YORK
DIRECT ENROLLMENT AT UNIVERSITY COLLEGE GALWAY

Hosted by National University of Ireland, Galway

Academic Focus • Full curriculum.

Program Information • Students attend classes at National University of Ireland, Galway.

Sessions • Fall, spring, yearlong.

Eligibility Requirements • Open to juniors, seniors; 3.0 GPA; 2 letters of recommendation.

Living Arrangements • Students live in host institution dormitories. Quarters are shared with host institution students, students from other programs. Meals are taken on one's own, in residences, in restaurants.

Costs (2002-2003) • One term: $9470. Yearlong program: $18,940; includes housing, all meals, student support services, in-state tuition and fees. $150 nonrefundable deposit required. Financial aid available for students from sponsoring institution: all customary sources.

For More Information • University at Albany, State University of New York, Office of International Education, LI 66, Albany, NY 12222; *Phone:* 518-442-3525; *Fax:* 518-442-3338. *E-mail:* intled@uamail.albany.edu. *World Wide Web:* http://www.albany.edu/intled/

LETTERKENNY

BRETHREN COLLEGES ABROAD
BCA PROGRAM IN LETTERKENNY, IRELAND

Hosted by Letterkenny Institute of Technology

Academic Focus • Full curriculum.

Program Information • Students attend classes at Letterkenny Institute of Technology. Field trips to Galway, Dublin.

Sessions • Fall, yearlong.

Eligibility Requirements • Minimum age 18; open to sophomores, juniors, seniors; 2.6 GPA; 3 letters of recommendation; good academic standing at home school.

Living Arrangements • Students live in locally rented apartments. Meals are taken on one's own, in residences, in restaurants.

Costs (2003-2004) • One term: $11,500. Yearlong program: $19,900; includes tuition, housing, all meals, insurance, excursions, international student ID, student support services. $50 application fee. $100 nonrefundable deposit required.

For More Information • Ms. Natalya Latysheva-Derova, Program Officer, Brethren Colleges Abroad, 50 Alpha Drive, Elizabethtown, PA 17022; *Phone:* 866-222-6188; *Fax:* 717-361-6619. *E-mail:* info@bcanet.org. *World Wide Web:* http://www.bcanet.org/

LIMERICK

ACADEMIC PROGRAMS INTERNATIONAL (API)
(API)–LIMERICK, IRELAND

Hosted by University of Limerick

Academic Focus • Full curriculum.

Program Information • Students attend classes at University of Limerick. Scheduled travel to Dublin, other European cities; field trips to Cliffs of Moher, Cork, Blarney Castle, Bunratty Castle and Folk Park, Connemara.

Sessions • Fall, spring, yearlong, fall B.

Eligibility Requirements • Minimum age 18; open to freshmen, sophomores, juniors, seniors, graduate students, adults; 2.9 GPA; 1 letter of recommendation; good academic standing at home school; official transcript from home university.

Living Arrangements • Students live in host institution dormitories, locally rented apartments. Quarters are shared with host institution students. Meals are taken on one's own, in residences, in restaurants.

Costs (2004-2005) • One term: $10,800–$11,400. Yearlong program: $22,100; includes tuition, housing, insurance, excursions, student support services, ground transportation, airport pick-up. $150 nonrefundable deposit required. Financial aid available for all students: scholarships.

For More Information • Ms. Jennifer C. Allen, Director, Academic Programs International (API), 107 East Hopkins, San Marcos, TX 78666; *Phone:* 800-844-4124; *Fax:* 512-392-8420. *E-mail:* api@academicintl.com. *World Wide Web:* http://www.academicintl.com/

AMERICAN INSTITUTE FOR FOREIGN STUDY (AIFS)
UNIVERSITY OF LIMERICK

Hosted by University of Limerick

Academic Focus • Business administration/management, engineering, equine science, health and physical education, Irish studies, public administration, science.

Program Information • Students attend classes at University of Limerick. Scheduled travel to London; field trips to the west of Ireland, Dublin.

Sessions • Fall, spring, yearlong.

Eligibility Requirements • Minimum age 17; open to freshmen, sophomores, juniors, seniors; 2.5 GPA; 1 letter of recommendation; good academic standing at home school.

Living Arrangements • Students live in program-owned houses. Quarters are shared with students from other programs. Meals are taken on one's own, in residences, in central dining facility, in restaurants.

Costs (2004-2005) • One term: $11,995. Yearlong program: $22,890; includes tuition, housing, all meals, insurance, excursions, student support services, one-way airfare, 2-day London stopover. $75 application fee. $350 nonrefundable deposit required. Financial aid available for all students: scholarships.

For More Information • Mr. David Mauro, Admissions Advisor, American Institute For Foreign Study (AIFS), 9 West Broad Street, Stamford, CT 06902-3788; *Phone:* 800-737-2437 Ext. 5163; *Fax:* 203-399-5597. *E-mail:* dmauro@aifs.com. *World Wide Web:* http://www.aifsabroad.com/

ARCADIA UNIVERSITY
UNIVERSITY OF LIMERICK

Hosted by University of Limerick

Academic Focus • Business administration/management, computer science, engineering, Irish studies, liberal studies, political science and government, sociology, women's studies.

Program Information • Students attend classes at University of Limerick. Scheduled travel to sites within Ireland, Dublin.

Sessions • Fall, spring, yearlong, fall semester.

Eligibility Requirements • Open to sophomores, juniors, seniors; 2.9 GPA; 1 letter of recommendation.

Living Arrangements • Students live in locally rented apartments, program-owned apartments, host family homes. Quarters are shared with host institution students, students from other programs. Meals are taken on one's own, in residences.

Costs (2003-2004) • One term: $9690. Yearlong program: $16,190; includes tuition, housing, insurance, international student ID, student support services, pre-departure guide, transcripts. $35 application fee. $500 nonrefundable deposit required. Financial aid available for all students: scholarships, loans.

For More Information • Arcadia University, Center for Education Abroad, 450 South Easton Road, Glenside, PA 19038-3295; *Phone:*

866-927-2234; *Fax:* 215-572-2174. *E-mail:* cea@arcadia.edu. *World Wide Web:* http://www.arcadia.edu/cea/

CENTER FOR INTERNATIONAL STUDIES
UNIVERSITY OF LIMERICK

Hosted by University of Limerick
Academic Focus • Full curriculum.
Program Information • Students attend classes at University of Limerick. Scheduled travel to Dublin; field trips to Limerick; optional travel at an extra cost.
Sessions • Fall, spring, yearlong.
Eligibility Requirements • Minimum age 18; open to sophomores, juniors, seniors, graduate students, adults; 2.9 GPA; 1 letter of recommendation; good academic standing at home school; personal essay.
Living Arrangements • Students live in program-owned apartments. Quarters are shared with host institution students. Meals are taken on one's own, in residences, in restaurants.
Costs (2003-2004) • One term: $9300. Yearlong program: $17,300; includes tuition, housing, excursions, international student ID, student support services, airport reception. $50 application fee. $500 nonrefundable deposit required. Financial aid available for all students: scholarships.
For More Information • Mr. Jeff Palm, Program Director, Center for International Studies, 17 New South Street, #105, Northampton, MA 01060; *Phone:* 413-582-0407; *Fax:* 413-582-0337. *E-mail:* jpalm@cisabroad.com. *World Wide Web:* http://www.cisabroad.com/

COLLEGE CONSORTIUM FOR INTERNATIONAL STUDIES–ST. BONAVENTURE UNIVERSITY AND TRUMAN STATE UNIVERSITY
IRELAND PROGRAM–LIMERICK

Hosted by University of Limerick
Academic Focus • Full curriculum.
Program Information • Students attend classes at University of Limerick. Field trips to Aran Islands, Clare, Limerick, Dublin, Kilfinane; optional travel to England, France at an extra cost.
Sessions • Fall, spring, yearlong.
Eligibility Requirements • Minimum age 18; open to freshmen, sophomores, juniors, seniors; 2.9 GPA; 3 letters of recommendation; good academic standing at home school; essay.
Living Arrangements • Students live in host institution dormitories. Quarters are shared with host institution students, students from other programs. Meals are taken as a group, on one's own, in residences.
Costs (2004-2005) • One term: $5900. Yearlong program: $11,800; includes tuition, insurance, excursions, student support services. $30 application fee. $300 nonrefundable deposit required. Financial aid available for students from sponsoring institution: scholarships, loans.
For More Information • Center for International Education Abroad, College Consortium for International Studies–St. Bonaventure University and Truman State University, Truman State University, Kirk Building 114, Kirksville, MO 63501; *Phone:* 660-785-4076; *Fax:* 660-785-7473. *E-mail:* ciea@truman.edu. *World Wide Web:* http://www.ccisabroad.org/. Students may also apply through St. Bonaventure University, St. Bonaventure, NY 14778.

INSTITUTE FOR STUDY ABROAD, BUTLER UNIVERSITY
UNIVERSITY OF LIMERICK

Hosted by University of Limerick
Academic Focus • Full curriculum.
Program Information • Students attend classes at University of Limerick. Field trips to Delphi, Killarney, Northern Ireland.
Sessions • Fall, spring, yearlong.
Eligibility Requirements • Open to juniors, seniors; 2.8 GPA; 1 letter of recommendation; good academic standing at home school; enrollment at an accredited American college or university.
Living Arrangements • Students live in host institution dormitories, locally rented apartments. Quarters are shared with host institution students, students from other programs. Meals are taken on one's own, in residences, in central dining facility, in restaurants.
Costs (2002-2003) • One term: $8475. Yearlong program: $13,575; includes tuition, housing, excursions, international student ID, student support services, family visit, cultural and sporting events, pre-departure advising. $40 application fee. $500 nonrefundable deposit required. Financial aid available for all students: scholarships, travel grants.
For More Information • Institute for Study Abroad, Butler University, 1100 West 42nd Street, Suite 305, Indianapolis, IN 46208-3345; *Phone:* 800-858-0229; *Fax:* 317-940-9704. *E-mail:* study-abroad@butler.edu. *World Wide Web:* http://www.ifsa-butler.org/

INTERSTUDY
UNIVERSITY OF LIMERICK

Hosted by University of Limerick
Academic Focus • Accounting, biochemistry, chemical sciences, economics, education, engineering, English, history, Irish studies, Japanese studies, law and legal studies, linguistics, marketing, physics, political science and government, psychology, science.
Program Information • Students attend classes at University of Limerick. Scheduled travel to Bath, Stratford-upon-Avon, Warwick Castle, Oxford, Stonehenge.
Sessions • Fall, spring, yearlong.
Eligibility Requirements • Minimum age 18; open to freshmen, sophomores, juniors, seniors, adults; 3.0 GPA; 2 letters of recommendation; good academic standing at home school.
Living Arrangements • Students live in host institution dormitories. Quarters are shared with host institution students. Meals are taken on one's own, in residences.
Costs (2003-2004) • One term: $10,325 for fall term; $11,350 for spring. Yearlong program: $18,995; includes tuition, housing, some meals, excursions, international student ID, student support services, Student Union membership, e-mail access, banking facilities, international bank transfers, transcript, cell phone. $35 application fee. $500 nonrefundable deposit required. Financial aid available for all students: scholarships, loans, stipends.
For More Information • InterStudy, Admissions Office, 63 Edward Street, Medford, MA 02155; *Phone:* 800-663-1999; *Fax:* 781-391-7463. *E-mail:* interstudy@interstudy-usa.org. *World Wide Web:* http://www.interstudy.org/

MARYMOUNT UNIVERSITY
IRELAND PROGRAM

Hosted by University of Limerick
Academic Focus • Full curriculum.
Program Information • Students attend classes at University of Limerick. Field trips to Dublin.
Sessions • Fall, spring.
Eligibility Requirements • Open to juniors, seniors; 2.9 GPA; 2 letters of recommendation; good academic standing at home school.
Living Arrangements • Students live in host institution dormitories. Quarters are shared with host institution students. Meals are taken on one's own, in residences.
Costs (2003-2004) • One term: $10,280; includes tuition, housing, insurance, student support services. $25 application fee. $250 nonrefundable deposit required. Financial aid available for students from sponsoring institution: scholarships, loans.
For More Information • Dr. Linda Goff, Director, Study Abroad, Marymount University, 2807 North Glebe Road, Arlington, VA 22207; *Phone:* 703-284-1677; *Fax:* 703-284-1553. *E-mail:* mulondon@marymount.edu. *World Wide Web:* http://mu.marymount.edu/academic/studyabroad/index.html

NORTH AMERICAN INSTITUTE FOR STUDY ABROAD
STUDY IN IRELAND

Hosted by University of Limerick
Academic Focus • Full curriculum.
Program Information • Students attend classes at University of Limerick. Optional travel at an extra cost.
Sessions • Fall, spring, yearlong.

Eligibility Requirements • Minimum age 18; open to sophomores, juniors, seniors; 3.0 GPA; 2 letters of recommendation; good academic standing at home school.

Living Arrangements • Students live in host institution dormitories, locally rented apartments, host family homes. Quarters are shared with host institution students. Meals are taken on one's own, with host family, in residences, in central dining facility, in restaurants.

Costs (2003-2004) • One term: $7500 for fall term; $7500 for spring. Yearlong program: $13,750; includes tuition, housing, international student ID, student support services, transcripts. $50 application fee. $500 nonrefundable deposit required. Financial aid available for all students: scholarships.

For More Information • Dr. Michael Currid, Director, North American Institute for Study Abroad, 129 Mill Street, Danville, PA 17821; *Phone:* 570-275-5099; *Fax:* 570-275-1644. *E-mail:* naisa@naisa. com. *World Wide Web:* http://www.naisa.com/

NORTH AMERICAN INSTITUTE FOR STUDY ABROAD
STUDY IN IRELAND/STUDENT TEACHING IN IRELAND

Hosted by Mary Immaculate College
Academic Focus • Full curriculum.
Program Information • Students attend classes at Mary Immaculate College. Optional travel at an extra cost.
Sessions • Fall, spring, yearlong.
Eligibility Requirements • Minimum age 18; open to sophomores, juniors, seniors; 3.0 GPA; 2 letters of recommendation; good academic standing at home school.
Living Arrangements • Students live in host institution dormitories, locally rented apartments, host family homes. Quarters are shared with host institution students. Meals are taken on one's own, with host family, in residences, in central dining facility, in restaurants.
Costs (2003-2004) • One term: $6500 for regular term; $2500 for student teaching term. Yearlong program: $13,750; includes tuition, housing, insurance, international student ID, student support services, transcripts. $50 application fee. $500 nonrefundable deposit required. Financial aid available for all students: scholarships.
For More Information • Dr. Michael Currid, Director, North American Institute for Study Abroad, 129 Mill Street, Danville, PA 17821; *Phone:* 570-275-5099; *Fax:* 570-275-1644. *E-mail:* naisa@naisa. com. *World Wide Web:* http://www.naisa.com/

STATE UNIVERSITY OF NEW YORK AT NEW PALTZ
STUDY ABROAD IN LIMERICK, IRELAND

Hosted by University of Limerick
Academic Focus • Full curriculum.
Program Information • Students attend classes at University of Limerick. Field trips to Dublin, sites throughout western Ireland.
Sessions • Fall, spring, yearlong.
Eligibility Requirements • Minimum age 18; open to sophomores, juniors, seniors; 2.9 GPA; 2 letters of recommendation; good academic standing at home school.
Living Arrangements • Students live in host institution dormitories. Quarters are shared with host institution students. Meals are taken on one's own, in residences, in restaurants.
Costs (2003-2004) • One term: $6500 for New York residents; $6654 for nonresidents. Yearlong program: $13,000 for New York residents; $13,308 for nonresidents; includes tuition, insurance, excursions, student support services, administrative fee. $25 application fee. $300–$600 nonrefundable deposit required. Financial aid available for students from sponsoring institution: scholarships, loans.
For More Information • Center for International Programs, State University of New York at New Paltz, 75 South Manheim Boulevard, Suite 9, New Paltz, NY 12561; *Phone:* 845-257-3125; *Fax:* 845-257-3129. *E-mail:* international@newpaltz.edu. *World Wide Web:* http://www.newpaltz.edu/studyabroad/

LOUISBURGH
COLLEGE OF ST. SCHOLASTICA
STUDY ABROAD–IRELAND

Academic Focus • Communications, history, international business, liberal studies, music, religious studies.
Program Information • Faculty members are drawn from the sponsor's U.S. staff and local instructors hired by the sponsor. Scheduled travel to cities in Ireland, scenic areas; field trips to historic sites, environmental areas, cultural events; optional travel to Britain, Europe at an extra cost.
Sessions • Spring.
Eligibility Requirements • Minimum age 18; open to freshmen, sophomores, juniors, seniors; 2.5 GPA; 2 letters of recommendation.
Living Arrangements • Students live in locally rented cottages. Meals are taken as a group, on one's own, in residences.
Costs (2004) • One term: $14,160; includes tuition, housing, some meals, insurance, excursions, books and class materials. $100 deposit required. Financial aid available for all students: scholarships, loans, need-based state and federal grants.
For More Information • Sr. Mary Odile Cahoon, Senior Vice President, College of St. Scholastica, 1200 Kenwood Avenue, Duluth, MN 55811; *Phone:* 218-723-6032; *Fax:* 218-723-6278. *E-mail:* mcahoon@css.edu. *World Wide Web:* http://www.css.edu: 80/study_abroad/study.html

MAYNOOTH
COLLEGE CONSORTIUM FOR INTERNATIONAL STUDIES–ST. BONAVENTURE UNIVERSITY AND TRUMAN STATE UNIVERSITY
IRELAND PROGRAM–MAYNOOTH

Hosted by National University of Ireland–Maynooth
Academic Focus • Anthropology, classics and classical languages, drama/theater, geography, history, liberal studies, literature, philosophy, religious studies, science, sociology.
Program Information • Students attend classes at National University of Ireland–Maynooth. Field trips to Aran Islands, Northern Ireland, Newgrange.
Sessions • Fall, spring, yearlong.
Eligibility Requirements • Minimum age 18; open to freshmen, sophomores, juniors, seniors, adults; 2.9 GPA; 3 letters of recommendation; good academic standing at home school; essay.
Living Arrangements • Students live in host institution dormitories, host family homes. Quarters are shared with host institution students, students from other programs. Meals are taken as a group, on one's own, with host family, in residences.
Costs (2004-2005) • One term: $6682. Yearlong program: $13,364; includes tuition, insurance, excursions, student support services, cultural events. $30 application fee. $300 nonrefundable deposit required. Financial aid available for students from sponsoring institution: scholarships, loans.
For More Information • Center for International Education Abroad, College Consortium for International Studies–St. Bonaventure University and Truman State University, Truman State University, Kirk Building 114, Kirksville, MO 63501; *Phone:* 660-785-4076; *Fax:* 660-785-7473. *E-mail:* ciea@truman.edu. *World Wide Web:* http:// www.ccisabroad.org/. Students may also apply through St. Bonaventure University, St. Bonaventure, NY 14778.

INSTITUTE FOR STUDY ABROAD, BUTLER UNIVERSITY
NATIONAL UNIVERSITY OF IRELAND, MAYNOOTH

Hosted by National University of Ireland–Maynooth
Academic Focus • Full curriculum.
Program Information • Students attend classes at National University of Ireland-Maynooth. Field trips to Killarney, Delphi, Northern Ireland.
Sessions • Fall, spring, yearlong.
Eligibility Requirements • Open to sophomores, juniors, seniors; 2.8 GPA; 1 letter of recommendation; good academic standing at home school; enrollment at an accredited American college or university.

IRELAND
Maynooth

Living Arrangements • Students live in locally rented apartments. Quarters are shared with host institution students. Meals are taken on one's own, in residences.
Costs (2002-2003) • One term: $8675. Yearlong program: $13,875; includes tuition, housing, excursions, international student ID, student support services, family visit, cultural and sporting events, pre-departure advising. $40 application fee. $500 nonrefundable deposit required. Financial aid available for all students: scholarships, travel grants.
For More Information • Institute for Study Abroad, Butler University, 1100 West 42nd Street, Suite 305, Indianapolis, IN 46208-3345; *Phone:* 800-858-0229; *Fax:* 317-940-9704. *E-mail:* study-abroad@butler.edu. *World Wide Web:* http://www.ifsa-butler.org/

NORTH AMERICAN INSTITUTE FOR STUDY ABROAD
STUDY IN IRELAND

Hosted by National University of Ireland–Maynooth
Academic Focus • Full curriculum.
Program Information • Students attend classes at National University of Ireland-Maynooth. Optional travel at an extra cost.
Sessions • Fall, spring, yearlong.
Eligibility Requirements • Minimum age 18; open to sophomores, juniors, seniors; 3.0 GPA; 2 letters of recommendation; good academic standing at home school.
Living Arrangements • Students live in host institution dormitories, locally rented apartments, host family homes. Quarters are shared with host institution students. Meals are taken on one's own, in residences, in central dining facility, in restaurants.
Costs (2003-2004) • One term: $6950. Yearlong program: $13,750; includes tuition, housing, insurance, international student ID, student support services, transcripts. $50 application fee. $500 nonrefundable deposit required. Financial aid available for all students: scholarships.
For More Information • Dr. Michael Currid, Director, North American Institute for Study Abroad, 129 Mill Street, Danville, PA 17821; *Phone:* 570-275-5099; *Fax:* 570-275-1644. *E-mail:* naisa@naisa.com. *World Wide Web:* http://www.naisa.com/

ST. JOHN'S UNIVERSITY
STUDY ABROAD IRELAND–MAYNOOTH

Hosted by National University of Ireland–Maynooth
Academic Focus • Full curriculum.
Program Information • Students attend classes at National University of Ireland-Maynooth.
Sessions • Fall, spring, yearlong.
Eligibility Requirements • Minimum age 18; open to sophomores, juniors, seniors; 3.0 GPA; 2 letters of recommendation; good academic standing at home school; interview.
Living Arrangements • Students live in host institution dormitories, locally rented apartments, program-owned apartments, program-owned houses, host family homes, hostels. Quarters are shared with host institution students, students from other programs. Meals are taken on one's own, in residences, in central dining facility.
Costs (2003-2004) • One term: contact sponsor for cost. Yearlong program: $20,933–$24,550; includes tuition, student support services, administrative fees. $30 application fee. $750 nonrefundable deposit required. Financial aid available for students from sponsoring institution: scholarships, loans.
For More Information • Dr. Ruth De Paula, Director, Office of Study Abroad Programs, St. John's University, 8000 Utopia Parkway, Jamaica, NY 11439; *Phone:* 718-990-6105; *Fax:* 718-990-2321. *E-mail:* intled@stjohns.edu. *World Wide Web:* http://www.stjohns.edu/studyabroad/

STATE UNIVERSITY OF NEW YORK COLLEGE AT BROCKPORT
NATIONAL UNIVERSITY OF IRELAND, MAYNOOTH PROGRAM

Hosted by National University of Ireland–Maynooth
Academic Focus • Full curriculum.
Program Information • Students attend classes at National University of Ireland-Maynooth.
Sessions • Fall, spring, yearlong.

Eligibility Requirements • Minimum age 18; open to juniors, seniors; 3.0 GPA; 2 letters of recommendation; good academic standing at home school; demonstrated ability to do upper-division work in the subjects chosen.
Living Arrangements • Students live in host institution dormitories. Quarters are shared with host institution students. Meals are taken on one's own, in residences.
Costs (2004-2005) • One term: $9100. Yearlong program: contact sponsor for cost; includes tuition, excursions, international student ID, student support services. $350 nonrefundable deposit required. Financial aid available for all students: scholarships, loans, regular financial aid, grants.
For More Information • Dr. John Perry, Director, Office of International Education, State University of New York College at Brockport, 350 New Campus Drive, Brockport, NY 14420; *Phone:* 800-298-SUNY; *Fax:* 585-637-3218. *E-mail:* overseas@brockport.edu. *World Wide Web:* http://www.brockport.edu/studyabroad/

MORE ABOUT THE PROGRAM
National University of Ireland (NUI), Maynooth, traces its roots to the foundation of St. Patrick's College in 1795. In 1910, Maynooth became a recognized college of the National University of Ireland for the purpose of awarding degrees in art, science, Celtic studies, and philosophy. Then in 1997, NUI, Maynooth, was established with full university status as the National University of Ireland, Maynooth, and now has in excess of 5,000 students from all over Ireland and overseas. Located about 15 miles west of Dublin, the town of Maynooth comprises a large student population and offers a full range of shopping and restaurant facilities. Through SUNY Brockport, participants have the opportunity to directly enroll in the courses offered at NUI, Maynooth, while living on campus in one of the University's residential facilities.

TRALEE
IRISH COLLEGE FOR THE HUMANITIES
IRISH COLLEGE FOR THE HUMANITIES

Hosted by Irish College for the Humanities
Academic Focus • Art history, fine/studio arts, history, Irish literature, Irish studies, literature, social sciences.
Program Information • Students attend classes at Irish College for the Humanities. Field trips to Dingle Peninsula, the Hunt Museum, the Crawford Art Gallery, the Ring of Kerry; optional travel to Dublin, Donegal, Galway, London at an extra cost.
Sessions • Fall, spring, winter, yearlong.
Eligibility Requirements • Minimum age 18; open to freshmen, sophomores, juniors, seniors, adults; 2 letters of recommendation; good academic standing at home school.
Living Arrangements • Students live in host family homes, study bedrooms at the college. Quarters are shared with host institution students. Meals are taken as a group, in central dining facility.
Costs (2003-2004) • One term: $11,000. Yearlong program: $22,000; includes tuition, housing, some meals, at least one field trip for on-site teaching per week, Distinguished Guest lecture program, evening social events. $50 application fee. $1500 refundable deposit required. Financial aid available for all students: scholarships.
For More Information • Ms. Kathryn Kissane, Administrator, Irish College for the Humanities, Kilteely House, Ballyard, Tralee, County Kerry, Ireland; *Phone:* +353 66-7120540; *Fax:* +353 66-7120540. *E-mail:* ichkerry@iol.ie. *World Wide Web:* http://www.iol.ie/~ichkerry/

ISRAEL
BEER SHEVA
BEN-GURION UNIVERSITY OF THE NEGEV
FRESHMAN YEAR PROGRAM

Hosted by Ben-Gurion University of the Negev

Academic Focus • Anthropology, archaeology, art, biological/life sciences, community service, comparative literature, ecology, environmental science/studies, geography, Hebrew, history, Israeli studies, Jewish studies, literature, Middle Eastern studies, peace and conflict studies, philosophy, political science and government, premedical studies, psychology, religious studies, social sciences, sociology, women's studies.
Program Information • Students attend classes at Ben-Gurion University of the Negev. Scheduled travel to Jerusalem, Eilat, Galilee, the Judean Desert; field trips to kibbutzim, Massada, Tel Aviv, the Dead Sea, museums, archaeological sites, Bedouin villages; optional travel to Jordan, Egypt, Sinai, Turkey, Russia at an extra cost.
Sessions • Fall, spring, yearlong.
Eligibility Requirements • Minimum age 17; open to freshmen; 2.5 GPA; 3 letters of recommendation; good academic standing at home school; transcripts; test scores; physician's report; personal statement; no foreign language proficiency required.
Living Arrangements • Students live in host institution dormitories, host family homes. Quarters are shared with host institution students. Meals are taken on one's own, in residences, in central dining facility, in restaurants.
Costs (2004-2005) • One term: $7810. Yearlong program: $11,415; includes tuition, housing, insurance, excursions, lab equipment, student support services, intensive Hebrew course, student activity fee (sports center and Israeli student union memberships). $55 application fee. $250 nonrefundable deposit required. Financial aid available for all students: scholarships, fellowships, need-based aid.
For More Information • Ms. Rebecca Weinstein, Director, Office of Student Services, Ben-Gurion University of the Negev, 1430 Broadway, 8th Floor, New York, NY 10018; *Phone:* 800-962-2248; *Fax:* 212-302-6443. *E-mail:* osp@aabgu.org. *World Wide Web:* http://www.bgu-osp.org/

BEN-GURION UNIVERSITY OF THE NEGEV
MASTER OF ARTS PROGRAM IN MIDDLE EAST STUDIES (MAPMES)

Hosted by Ben-Gurion University of the Negev
Academic Focus • Arabic, Egyptian studies, Hebrew, Islamic studies, Israeli studies, Middle Eastern studies, peace and conflict studies, Turkish studies.
Program Information • Students attend classes at Ben-Gurion University of the Negev.
Sessions • Yearlong.
Eligibility Requirements • Open to graduate students; 3.0 GPA; 2 letters of recommendation; good academic standing at home school; medical report; writing sample; personal essay; transcripts; no foreign language proficiency required.
Living Arrangements • Students live in host institution dormitories, locally rented apartments. Quarters are shared with host institution students. Meals are taken on one's own, in residences.
Costs (2004-2005) • Yearlong program: $12,370; includes tuition, housing, insurance, excursions, intensive language course. $55 application fee. $250 nonrefundable deposit required. Financial aid available for all students: scholarships, loans.
For More Information • Dr. Sam Kaplan, Director, MAPMES, Ben-Gurion University of the Negev, Room 204, Building 72, Beer Sheva 84105, Israel; *Phone:* +972 8-646-1455; *Fax:* +972 8-647-2952. *E-mail:* skaplan@bgumail.bgu.ac.il. *World Wide Web:* http://www.bgu-osp.org/

BEN-GURION UNIVERSITY OF THE NEGEV
OVERSEAS STUDENT PROGRAM

Hosted by Ben-Gurion University of the Negev
Academic Focus • Agriculture, anthropology, archaeology, art, art history, biological/life sciences, biomedical sciences, community service, comparative literature, creative writing, drama/theater, drawing/painting, earth sciences, ecology, education, engineering, environmental science/studies, ethics, geography, Hebrew, history, Islamic studies, Israeli studies, Jewish studies, literature, Middle Eastern studies, peace and conflict studies, philosophy, photography, political science and government, premedical studies, psychology, religious studies, social sciences, sociology, teaching, teaching English as a second language, women's studies.
Program Information • Students attend classes at Ben-Gurion University of the Negev. Scheduled travel to Jerusalem, Eilat, Galilee,

the Judean Desert; field trips to kibbutzim, Negon, Tel Aviv, museums, Jerusalem, archaeological sites, Bedouin villages; optional travel to Jordan, Egypt, Turkey, Russia at an extra cost.
Sessions • Fall, spring, yearlong.
Eligibility Requirements • Minimum age 18; open to freshmen, sophomores, juniors, seniors, graduate students, adults; 2.5 GPA; 3 letters of recommendation; good academic standing at home school; transcript; physician's report; personal statement; no foreign language proficiency required.
Living Arrangements • Students live in host institution dormitories, locally rented apartments, host family homes. Quarters are shared with host institution students. Meals are taken on one's own, in residences, in central dining facility, in restaurants.
Costs (2004-2005) • One term: $7810. Yearlong program: $11,415; includes tuition, housing, insurance, excursions, lab equipment, student support services, intensive Hebrew course, student activity fee (sports center and student union memberships). $55 application fee. $250 nonrefundable deposit required. Financial aid available for all students: scholarships, fellowships, need-based aid.
For More Information • Ms. Rebecca Weinstein, Director, Office of Student Services, Ben-Gurion University of the Negev, 1430 Broadway, 8th Floor, New York, NY 10018; *Phone:* 800-962-2248; *Fax:* 212-302-6443. *E-mail:* osp@aabgu.org. *World Wide Web:* http://www.bgu-osp.org/. Students may also apply through The Partnership for Service-Learning, 815 Second Avenue, Suite 315, New York, NY 10017.

THE INTERNATIONAL PARTNERSHIP FOR SERVICE LEARNING
ISRAEL SERVICE–LEARNING

Hosted by Ben-Gurion University of the Negev
Academic Focus • Area studies, community service, Hebrew, social sciences.
Program Information • Students attend classes at Ben-Gurion University of the Negev. Optional travel to an archaeological dig, kibbutz, Egypt/Jordan at an extra cost.
Sessions • Fall, spring, yearlong.
Eligibility Requirements • Minimum age 18; open to freshmen, sophomores, juniors, seniors, graduate students, adults; 2 letters of recommendation; good academic standing at home school; evidence of maturity, responsibility; no foreign language proficiency required.
Living Arrangements • Students live in host institution dormitories. Quarters are shared with host institution students. Meals are taken on one's own, in residences, in central dining facility.
Costs (2003-2004) • One term: $9400. Yearlong program: $17,900; includes tuition, housing. $50 application fee. $250 refundable deposit required. Financial aid available for all students: scholarships, federal financial aid.
For More Information • Ms. Ilana Golin, Coordinator of Student Programs, The International Partnership for Service Learning, 815 Second Avenue, Suite 315, New York, NY 10017-4594; *Phone:* 212-986-0989; *Fax:* 212-986-5039. *E-mail:* info@ipsl.org. *World Wide Web:* http://www.ipsl.org/

UNIVERSITY STUDIES ABROAD CONSORTIUM
ISRAELI AND GENERAL STUDIES: BEER SHEVA, ISRAEL

Hosted by Ben-Gurion University of the Negev
Academic Focus • Anthropology, archaeology, art, environmental science/studies, Hebrew, history, Israeli studies, Jewish studies, philosophy, political science and government, religious studies, sociology.
Program Information • Students attend classes at Ben-Gurion University of the Negev. Field trips to Golan, Galilee, Jerusalem, the Judean Desert, Masada; optional travel to a kibbutz, an archaeological dig, Israel army non-combat experience, Jordan, Egypt at an extra cost.
Sessions • Fall, spring, yearlong.
Eligibility Requirements • Minimum age 18; open to sophomores, juniors, seniors, graduate students, adults; 2.5 GPA; no foreign language proficiency required.
Living Arrangements • Students live in host institution dormitories. Quarters are shared with host institution students. Meals are taken as a group, on one's own, in central dining facility.

ISRAEL
Beer Sheva

Costs (2005-2006) • One term: contact sponsor for cost. Yearlong program: contact sponsor for cost. $50 application fee. $150 refundable deposit required. Financial aid available for all students: scholarships, loans.
For More Information • University Studies Abroad Consortium, USAC/323, Reno, NV 89557-0093; *Phone:* 775-784-6569; *Fax:* 775-784-6010. *E-mail:* usac@unr.edu. *World Wide Web:* http://usac.unr.edu/

HAIFA
BOSTON UNIVERSITY
HAIFA LANGUAGE AND LIBERAL ARTS PROGRAM

Hosted by University of Haifa
Academic Focus • Full curriculum.
Program Information • Students attend classes at University of Haifa. Scheduled travel to Jerusalem; field trips to Tel Aviv, Druze village, Tel Gezer.
Sessions • Fall, spring, yearlong.
Eligibility Requirements • Open to sophomores, juniors, seniors, adults; 3.0 GPA; 2 letters of recommendation; good academic standing at home school; essay; approval of participation; transcript; 1-2 semesters course work in Hebrew recommended.
Living Arrangements • Students live in host institution dormitories, locally rented apartments. Quarters are shared with host institution students, students from other programs. Meals are taken on one's own, in residences, in central dining facility.
Costs (2004-2005) • One term: $18,084. Yearlong program: $36,168; includes tuition, housing, excursions, international airfare. $50 application fee. $400 nonrefundable deposit required. Financial aid available for all students: scholarships, loans.
For More Information • Division of International Programs, Boston University, 232 Bay State Road, Boston, MA 02215; *Phone:* 617-353-9888; *Fax:* 617-353-5402. *E-mail:* abroad@bu.edu. *World Wide Web:* http://www.bu.edu/abroad/

UNIVERSITY OF HAIFA
OVERSEAS STUDENT STUDIES PROGRAM

Hosted by University of Haifa
Academic Focus • Arabic, archaeology, communications, English literature, Hebrew, history, Israeli studies, Jewish studies, liberal studies, Middle Eastern studies, political science and government, psychology, sociology.
Program Information • Students attend classes at University of Haifa. Scheduled travel to various sites in Israel; field trips to various sites in Israel.
Sessions • Fall, spring, yearlong.
Eligibility Requirements • Minimum age 19; open to sophomores, juniors, seniors, graduate students, adults; 2.8 GPA; 2 letters of recommendation; good academic standing at home school; no foreign language proficiency required.
Living Arrangements • Students live in host institution dormitories. Quarters are shared with host institution students. Meals are taken on one's own, in residences.
Costs (2003-2004) • One term: $6310. Yearlong program: $10,700; includes tuition, housing, excursions. $50 application fee. $500 refundable deposit required. Financial aid available for all students: scholarships, federal loans for U.S. students.
For More Information • Ms. Lisa Berman, Admissions Coordinator, University of Haifa, Department of Overseas Studies, Haifa 31905, Israel; *Phone:* 972-4-824-0766; *Fax:* 972-4-884-0391. *E-mail:* info@mail.uhaifa.org. *World Wide Web:* http://www.uhaifa.org/

JERUSALEM
HEBREW UNIVERSITY OF JERUSALEM
MASTER OF ARTS, GRADUATE AND UNDERGRADUATE PROGRAMS, ROTHBERG INTERNATIONAL SCHOOL

Hosted by Hebrew University of Jerusalem
Academic Focus • Full curriculum.

Program Information • Students attend classes at Hebrew University of Jerusalem. Scheduled travel to Negev, Galilee, Golan Heights, the Dead Sea; field trips to historic, religious, and cultural sites in the vicinity of Jerusalem.
Sessions • Fall, spring, yearlong.
Eligibility Requirements • Open to freshmen, sophomores, juniors, seniors, graduate students, adults; 3.0 GPA; 2 letters of recommendation; good academic standing at home school; current transcripts; relevant standardized exam scores; medical forms; foreign language proficiency requirement varies depending on course of study.
Living Arrangements • Students live in host institution dormitories, locally rented apartments. Quarters are shared with host institution students, students from other programs. Meals are taken on one's own, in residences, in central dining facility, in restaurants.
Costs (2003-2004) • One term: $11,000 for fall semester; $10,500 for spring. Yearlong program: $18,500; includes tuition, housing, all meals, insurance, excursions, international airfare, books and class materials, lab equipment, student support services, activity fee, personal expenses. $55 application fee. Financial aid available for all students: scholarships, loans, need and merit-based aid.
For More Information • Ms. Elisabeth Covitt, Office of Academic Affairs, Hebrew University of Jerusalem, One Battery Park Plaza, 25th Floor, New York, NY 10004; *Phone:* 800-404-8622; *Fax:* 212-809-4183. *E-mail:* hebrewu@hebrewu.com. *World Wide Web:* http://overseas.huji.ac.il/

JERUSALEM UNIVERSITY COLLEGE
MASTER OF ARTS, GRADUATE AND UNDERGRADUATE STUDY ABROAD

Hosted by Jerusalem University College
Academic Focus • Ancient history, Arabic, archaeology, Biblical studies, Egyptian studies, geography, Hebrew, history, Islamic studies, Jewish studies, linguistics, Middle Eastern studies.
Program Information • Students attend classes at Jerusalem University College. Scheduled travel to Galilee, Jordan, Egypt, Sinai, Turkey, Greece; field trips to Caesarea, Jezreel Valley, Sharon Plain, Jerusalem, Bethlehem; optional travel to Turkey, Egypt at an extra cost.
Sessions • Fall, spring.
Eligibility Requirements • Minimum age 18; open to sophomores, juniors, seniors, graduate students, adults; 2.5 GPA; 3 letters of recommendation; good academic standing at home school; minimum 3.0 GPA for graduate students; good physical condition; no foreign language proficiency required.
Living Arrangements • Students live in host institution dormitories, locally rented apartments. Quarters are shared with host institution students. Meals are taken as a group, in central dining facility.
Costs (2003-2004) • One term: $9235; includes tuition, housing, all meals, student support services, required field trips. $50 application fee. $100 refundable deposit required. Financial aid available for all students: scholarships, work study.
For More Information • Ms. Amelia Nakai, Program Coordinator, Jerusalem University College, 4249 East State Street, Suite 203, Rockford, IL 61108; *Phone:* 815-229-5900; *Fax:* 815-229-5901. *E-mail:* admissions@juc.edu. *World Wide Web:* http://www.juc.edu/

TEL AVIV
TEL AVIV UNIVERSITY
LOWY SCHOOL FOR OVERSEAS STUDENTS/SEMESTER OR YEAR ABROAD

Hosted by Tel Aviv University
Academic Focus • Archaeology, art history, biological/life sciences, business administration/management, communications, comparative literature, creative writing, geology, Hebrew, international affairs, international business, Israeli studies, Jewish studies, Middle Eastern studies, political science and government.
Program Information • Students attend classes at Tel Aviv University. Field trips to Jerusalem, Negev, Galilee, Ein Gedi.
Sessions • Fall, spring, yearlong.
Eligibility Requirements • Open to freshmen, sophomores, juniors, seniors, graduate students; 3.0 GPA; 2 letters of recommendation; good academic standing at home school; medical forms; transcripts; personal essay; no foreign language proficiency required.

Living Arrangements • Students live in host institution dormitories. Quarters are shared with host institution students. Meals are taken on one's own, in residences, in restaurants.

Costs (2002-2003) • One term: $12,000. Yearlong program: $18,000; includes tuition, housing, all meals, insurance, excursions, international airfare, books and class materials, student support services. $60 application fee. Financial aid available for all students: loans, need-based institutional aid, essay scholarships.

For More Information • Mr. Ami Dviri, Director, Tel Aviv University, Lowy School for Overseas Students, 39 Broadway, 15th Floor, New York, NY 10006; *Phone:* 800-665-9828 Ext. 11; *Fax:* 212-742-9031. *E-mail:* quest@telavivuniv.org. *World Wide Web:* http://www.telavivuniv.org/

TEL AVIV UNIVERSITY
MA JEWISH STUDIES

Hosted by Tel Aviv University
Academic Focus • Full curriculum.
Program Information • Students attend classes at Tel Aviv University. Field trips to Israel.
Sessions • Yearlong.
Eligibility Requirements • Open to graduate students; 3.0 GPA; 2 letters of recommendation; no foreign language proficiency required.
Living Arrangements • Students live in host institution dormitories, locally rented apartments. Meals are taken on one's own, in residences, in restaurants.
Costs (2004-2005) • Yearlong program: $21,440; includes tuition, housing, all meals, insurance, excursions, international airfare, books and class materials, student support services. $60 application fee. $300 nonrefundable deposit required. Financial aid available for all students: scholarships.
For More Information • Mr. Ami Dviri, Director, Tel Aviv University, 39 Broadway, 15th Floor, New York, NY 10006; *Phone:* 800-665-9828; *Fax:* 212-742-9031. *E-mail:* quest@telavivuniv.org. *World Wide Web:* http://www.telavivuniv.org/

TEL AVIV UNIVERSITY
MA PROGRAM IN MIDDLE EASTERN HISTORY

Hosted by Tel Aviv University
Academic Focus • Arabic, archaeology, Hebrew, international affairs, Islamic studies, Israeli studies, Jewish studies, Middle Eastern studies, political science and government.
Program Information • Students attend classes at Tel Aviv University. Field trips to Jerusalem, Negev, Galilee, Eln Gedi.
Sessions • Fall, spring, yearlong.
Eligibility Requirements • Open to graduate students; major in Middle Eastern Studies or a related field; 3.0 GPA; 2 letters of recommendation; medical forms; transcripts; no foreign language proficiency required.
Living Arrangements • Students live in host institution dormitories. Quarters are shared with host institution students. Meals are taken on one's own, in residences, in restaurants.
Costs (2003-2004) • One term: contact sponsor for cost. Yearlong program: $18,000; includes tuition, housing, insurance, excursions, international airfare, books and class materials, student support services. $60 application fee. Financial aid available for all students: loans, need and merit-based scholarships, external aid.
For More Information • Mr. Ami Dviri, Director, Tel Aviv University, Lowy School for Overseas Students, 39 Broadway, 15th Floor, New York, NY 10006; *Phone:* 800-665-9828; *Fax:* 212-742-9031. *E-mail:* quest@telavivuniv.org. *World Wide Web:* http://www.telavivuniv.org/

ITALY

AREZZO
UNIVERSITY OF ROCHESTER
ROCHESTER IN AREZZO, ITALY
Held at The University of Siena, British Institute

Academic Focus • Art history, history, Italian language and literature, Italian studies.
Program Information • Classes are held on the campus of British Institute, The University of Siena. Faculty members are drawn from the sponsor's U.S. staff and local instructors hired by the sponsor. Scheduled travel to Venice, Ravenna; field trips to Florence, Siena, Pisa, Rome.
Sessions • Spring.
Eligibility Requirements • Open to sophomores, juniors, seniors; 3.0 GPA; 1 letter of recommendation; good academic standing at home school; no foreign language proficiency required.
Living Arrangements • Students live in host institution dormitories, host family homes. Meals are taken as a group, with host family, in residences, in central dining facility.
Costs (2002-2003) • One term: $15,900; includes tuition, housing, some meals, excursions, student support services. $20 application fee. $300 nonrefundable deposit required. Financial aid available for students from sponsoring institution: scholarships, loans.
For More Information • Ms. Donatella Stocchi-Perucchio, Associate Professor, University of Rochester, Department of Modern Languages and Cultures, PO Box 270082, Rochester, NY 14627-0082; *Phone:* 585-275-4251; *Fax:* 585-273-1097. *E-mail:* dstocchi@mail.rochester.edu. *World Wide Web:* http://www.rochester.edu/college/study-abroad/

BOLOGNA
BROWN UNIVERSITY
BROWN IN BOLOGNA

Hosted by University of Bologna
Academic Focus • Full curriculum.
Program Information • Students attend classes at University of Bologna. Field trips to Ferrara, Ravenna, Modena.
Sessions • Fall, spring, yearlong.
Eligibility Requirements • Open to sophomores, juniors, seniors; 3.0 GPA; 2 letters of recommendation; good academic standing at home school; essay; 1 year college course work in Italian for full year session; .5 years for single semester.
Living Arrangements • Students live in program-owned apartments. Meals are taken on one's own, in residences, in central dining facility, in restaurants.
Costs (2003-2004) • One term: $14,600. Yearlong program: $29,200; includes tuition, housing, excursions, international student ID, student support services, 10-week language and orientation program. $250 nonrefundable deposit required. Financial aid available for students from sponsoring institution: scholarships, loans.
For More Information • Ms. Mell Bolen, Director, Brown University, Office of International Programs, Box 1973, Providence, RI 02912-1973; *Phone:* 401-863-3555; *Fax:* 401-863-3311. *E-mail:* oip_office@brown.edu. *World Wide Web:* http://www.brown.edu/OIP/

DICKINSON COLLEGE
K. ROBERT NILSSON CENTER FOR EUROPEAN STUDIES IN BOLOGNA (ITALY)

Hosted by University of Bologna, Johns Hopkins University–Bologna Center Paul H. Nitze School of Advanced International Studies, K. Robert Nilsson Center for European Studies
Academic Focus • Art history, economics, European studies, history, international affairs, Italian language and literature, Italian studies, political science and government.
Program Information • Students attend classes at University of Bologna, Johns Hopkins University–Bologna Center Paul H. Nitze School of Advanced International Studies, K. Robert Nilsson Center for European Studies. Scheduled travel to southern Italy, Pompeii; field trips to cultural sites of Bologna and surrounding area; optional travel.
Sessions • Yearlong.
Eligibility Requirements • Minimum age 18; open to juniors, seniors; 2.8 GPA; 3 letters of recommendation; good academic standing at home school; no foreign language proficiency required.
Living Arrangements • Students live in locally rented apartments. Meals are taken on one's own, with host family, in residences, in restaurants.

ITALY
Bologna

Costs (2003-2004) • Yearlong program: $35,590; includes tuition, housing, all meals, insurance, excursions, student support services. $25 application fee. $300 nonrefundable deposit required. Financial aid available for students from sponsoring institution: scholarships, work study, loans.
For More Information • Ms. Karen Peter, Program Manager, Dickinson College, PO Box 1773, Carlisle, PA 17013-2896; *Phone:* 717-245-1341; *Fax:* 717-245-1688. *E-mail:* global@dickinson.edu. *World Wide Web:* http://www.dickinson.edu/global/

INDIANA UNIVERSITY
BOLOGNA CONSORTIAL STUDIES PROGRAM

Hosted by University of Bologna
Academic Focus • Full curriculum.
Program Information • Students attend classes at University of Bologna. Field trips to Siena, San Gimignano, Dozza, Ravenna.
Sessions • Spring, yearlong.
Eligibility Requirements • Open to juniors, seniors; 3.0 GPA; 2 letters of recommendation; good academic standing at home school; 2 years of college course work in Italian.
Living Arrangements • Students live in locally rented apartments. Quarters are shared with host institution students. Meals are taken on one's own, in residences.
Costs (2004-2005) • One term: $11,500. Yearlong program: $18,900; includes tuition, insurance, excursions, student support services. $500 nonrefundable deposit required. Financial aid available for students from sponsoring institution: scholarships, work study, loans.
For More Information • Indiana University, Office of Overseas Study, Franklin Hall 303, Bloomington, IN 47405; *Phone:* 812-855-9304; *Fax:* 812-855-6452. *E-mail:* overseas@indiana.edu. *World Wide Web:* http://www.indiana.edu/~overseas/bcsp.html

VASSAR COLLEGE, WESLEYAN UNIVERSITY AND WELLESLEY COLLEGE
E.C.C.O. PROGRAM IN BOLOGNA (EASTERN COLLEGE CONSORTIUM)

Hosted by University of Bologna
Academic Focus • Art history, drama/theater, film and media studies, history, Italian language and literature, Italian studies, political science and government, psychology, sociology, theater management.
Program Information • Students attend classes at University of Bologna. Classes are also held on the campus of Eastern College Consortium (E.C.C.O.). Scheduled travel to Sicily; field trips to various regions/cities.
Sessions • Fall, spring, yearlong.
Eligibility Requirements • Open to sophomores, juniors, seniors; 3.0 GPA; 2 letters of recommendation (1 language, 1 non-language); 1 year college course work in Italian or the equivalent.
Living Arrangements • Students live in host institution dormitories. Quarters are shared with host institution students. Meals are taken on one's own, in residences, in central dining facility, in restaurants.
Costs (2002-2003) • One term: $18,300 for fall term; $17,300 for spring. Yearlong program: $35,600; includes tuition, housing, all meals, excursions, international airfare, books and class materials, student support services. $25 application fee. $200 nonrefundable deposit required. Financial aid available for students from sponsoring institution: scholarships, loans.
For More Information • Ms. Gail Winter, Assistant Director, Vassar College, Wesleyan University and Wellesley College, Office of International Studies, Wesleyan University, Middletown, CT 06459; *Phone:* 860-685-2550; *Fax:* 860-685-2551. *E-mail:* gwinter@wesleyan.edu. *World Wide Web:* http://www.wesleyan.edu/ois/

CASSINO
LOCK HAVEN UNIVERSITY OF PENNSYLVANIA
SEMESTER IN ITALY

Hosted by University of Cassino
Academic Focus • Italian studies.

Program Information • Students attend classes at University of Cassino.
Sessions • Fall, spring, yearlong.
Eligibility Requirements • Minimum age 18; open to sophomores, juniors, seniors, adults; 2.5 GPA; 3 letters of recommendation; good academic standing at home school; no foreign language proficiency required.
Living Arrangements • Students live in host institution dormitories, locally rented apartments. Quarters are shared with host institution students. Meals are taken on one's own, in central dining facility.
Costs (2002-2003) • One term: $5450 for Pennsylvania residents; $7360 for nonresidents. Yearlong program: $10,900 for Pennsylvania residents; $14,720 for nonresidents; includes tuition, housing, all meals, fees. $50 application fee. Financial aid available for students from sponsoring institution: scholarships, loans.
For More Information • Dean, Institute for International Studies, Lock Haven University of Pennsylvania, Lock Haven, PA 17745-2390; *Phone:* 570-893-2140; *Fax:* 570-893-2537. *E-mail:* intlstudies_webmonitor@lhup.edu. *World Wide Web:* http://www.lhup.edu/international/goingp/goingplaces_index.htm

CORCIANO
AMERICAN UNIVERSITY
ART IN ITALY

Academic Focus • Art, art history, commercial art, drawing/painting, fine/studio arts, Italian language and literature.
Program Information • Faculty members are drawn from the sponsor's U.S. staff and local instructors hired by the sponsor. Field trips to Florence, Siena, Rome; optional travel to Italian cities at an extra cost.
Sessions • Fall.
Eligibility Requirements • Open to sophomores, juniors, seniors, graduate students; 2.75 GPA; 1 letter of recommendation; second semester sophomore status; recommendation of advisor; no foreign language proficiency required.
Living Arrangements • Students live in locally rented apartments. Meals are taken on one's own, in residences, in restaurants.
Costs (2001) • One term: $14,234; includes tuition, excursions, student support services. $35 application fee. $400 nonrefundable deposit required. Financial aid available for students: member-school scholarships.
For More Information • Dr. David C. Brown, Dean, Washington Semester and World Capitals Programs, American University, Tenley Campus–Constitution Building, Washington, DC 20016-8083; *Phone:* 800-424-2600; *Fax:* 202-895-4960. *E-mail:* travel@american.edu. *World Wide Web:* http://www.worldcapitals.american.edu/

CORTONA
UNIVERSITY OF GEORGIA
STUDY ABROAD PROGRAM–CORTONA, ITALY

Hosted by Lamar Dodd School of Art, University of Georgia
Academic Focus • Architecture, art, art history, ceramics and pottery, creative writing, drawing/painting, fine/studio arts, Italian language and literature, Italian studies, photography.
Program Information • Students attend classes at Lamar Dodd School of Art, University of Georgia. Scheduled travel to Rome, Naples, Venice; field trips to Florence, Siena, Ravenna, Bologna.
Sessions • Fall, spring.
Eligibility Requirements • Minimum age 18; open to juniors, seniors, graduate students, adults; 2.5 GPA; 2 letters of recommendation; good academic standing at home school; no foreign language proficiency required.
Living Arrangements • Students live in host institution dormitories, hotels. Quarters are shared with students from other programs. Meals are taken as a group, in central dining facility.
Costs (2005) • One term: $9145; includes tuition, housing, some meals, insurance, excursions, international student ID. $50 application fee. Financial aid available for all students: work study.
For More Information • Ms. Mary Van Nus, Administrative Secretary, University of Georgia, 257 West Broad Street, Studio #2, Studies Abroad Program–Cortona, Italy, Athens, GA 30602; *Phone:*

706-425-2900; *Fax:* 706-425-2903. *E-mail:* cortona@uga.edu. *World Wide Web:* http://www.uga.edu/oie/studyabroad.htm

FERRARA

CIEE

CIEE STUDY CENTER AT THE UNIVERSITY OF FERRARA, ITALY

Hosted by University of Ferrara
Academic Focus • Art history, history, Italian language and literature, Italian studies.
Program Information • Students attend classes at University of Ferrara. Field trips to Venice, Florence, Bologna.
Sessions • Fall, spring.
Eligibility Requirements • Open to sophomores, juniors, seniors; 2.75 GPA; 2 letters of recommendation; no foreign language proficiency required.
Living Arrangements • Students live in locally rented apartments. Quarters are shared with host institution students. Meals are taken on one's own, in central dining facility, in restaurants.
Costs (2003-2004) • One term: $9000; includes tuition, housing, insurance, excursions, student support services, pre-departure advising, cultural activities, optional on-site pick-up. $30 application fee. $300 deposit required. Financial aid available for all students: minority student scholarships, travel grants.
For More Information • Ms. Hannah McChesney, Admissions Officer, Europe, Middle East, and Africa, CIEE, 7 Custom House Street, 3rd Floor, Portland, ME 04101; *Phone:* 800-40-STUDY; *Fax:* 207-553-7699. *E-mail:* studyinfo@ciee.org. *World Wide Web:* http://www.ciee.org/isp/

MIDDLEBURY COLLEGE SCHOOLS ABROAD
SCHOOL IN ITALY–FERRARA PROGRAM

Hosted by University of Ferrara
Academic Focus • Full curriculum.
Program Information • Students attend classes at University of Ferrara.
Sessions • Fall, spring, yearlong.
Eligibility Requirements • Open to juniors, seniors; 2.7 GPA; 2 letters of recommendation; B average in both Italian and major; 2.5 years college course work in Italian, including at least 1 content course.
Living Arrangements • Students live in host institution dormitories, locally rented apartments. Quarters are shared with host institution students. Meals are taken on one's own, in central dining facility, in restaurants.
Costs (2004-2005) • One term: $7200. Yearlong program: $14,400; includes tuition, student support services. $50 application fee. $300 nonrefundable deposit required. Financial aid available for students from sponsoring institution: scholarships, loans.
For More Information • Mr. Jamie Northrup, University Relations Coordinator, Middlebury College Schools Abroad, Office of Off-Campus Study, Sunderland Language Center, Middlebury, VT 05753; *Phone:* 802-443-5745; *Fax:* 802-443-3157. *E-mail:* schoolsabroad@middlebury.edu. *World Wide Web:* http://www.middlebury.edu/msa/

FLORENCE

ACADEMIC PROGRAMS INTERNATIONAL (API)
(API) AT APICIUS, THE CULINARY INSTITUTE OF FLORENCE

Hosted by Apicius, The Culinary Institute of Florence

Academic Focus • Culinary arts, food service, hospitality services, hotel and restaurant management, Italian language and literature.

Program Information • Students attend classes at Apicius, The Culinary Institute of Florence. Scheduled travel to Rome, Venice; field trips to Cinque Terre, Perugia, Lucca, Versilia, Lake Garda, Velana.

Sessions • Fall, spring, yearlong.

Eligibility Requirements • Minimum age 18; open to freshmen, sophomores, juniors, seniors, graduate students, adults; 2.75 GPA; good academic standing at home school; official transcript from home university; no foreign language proficiency required.

Living Arrangements • Students live in locally rented apartments. Quarters are shared with host institution students. Meals are taken on one's own, in residences, in restaurants.

Costs (2005-2006) • One term: $12,900–$13,000. Yearlong program: $24,900; includes tuition, housing, insurance, excursions, student support services, airport reception. $150 nonrefundable deposit required. Financial aid available for all students: scholarships.

For More Information • Ms. Jennifer C. Allen, Director, Academic Programs International (API), 107 East Hopkins, San Marcos, TX 78666; *Phone:* 800-844-4124; *Fax:* 512-392-8420. *E-mail:* api@academicintl.com. *World Wide Web:* http://www.academicintl.com/

ACADEMIC PROGRAMS INTERNATIONAL (API)
(API)–LORENZO DE MEDICI IN FLORENCE, ITALY

Hosted by Lorenzo de Medici School

Academic Focus • Full curriculum.

Program Information • Students attend classes at Lorenzo de Medici School. Scheduled travel to Rome, Venice; field trips to Cinque Terre, Perugia, Lucca, Vesilia, Lake Gasda, Verona.

Sessions • Fall, spring, yearlong.

Eligibility Requirements • Minimum age 18; open to freshmen, sophomores, juniors, seniors, adults; 2.75 GPA; 1 letter of recommendation; good academic standing at home school; official transcript from home university; no foreign language proficiency required.

Living Arrangements • Students live in locally rented apartments. Quarters are shared with host institution students, students from other programs. Meals are taken on one's own, in residences, in restaurants.

Costs (2005-2006) • One term: $12,500–$12,600. Yearlong program: $24,200; includes tuition, housing, insurance, excursions, student support services, airport reception. $150 nonrefundable deposit required. Financial aid available for all students: scholarships.

For More Information • Ms. Jennifer C. Allen, Director, Academic Programs International (API), 107 East Hopkins, San Marcos, TX 78666; *Phone:* 800-844-4124; *Fax:* 512-392-8420. *E-mail:* api@academicintl.com. *World Wide Web:* http://www.academicintl.com/

ACCADEMIA RIACI
MASTER PROGRAM IN FLORENCE, ITALY

Hosted by Accademia Riaci

Academic Focus • Art, art conservation studies, ceramics and pottery, crafts, drawing/painting, fashion design, fine/studio arts, graphic design/illustration, interior design, leather working, translation.

Program Information • Students attend classes at Accademia Riaci. Optional travel to Rome, Venice, a winery, the Mediterranean Sea, a farm visit at an extra cost.

Sessions • Yearlong.

Eligibility Requirements • Open to graduate students, adults; course work in a related field; 3.0 GPA; 2 letters of recommendation;

good academic standing at home school; portfolio with 12 works; transcript; no foreign language proficiency required.

Living Arrangements • Students live in locally rented apartments, host family homes, hotels. Quarters are shared with host institution students, students from other programs. Meals are taken on one's own, in residences, in central dining facility, in restaurants.

Costs (2005) • Yearlong program: €12,000 for European Union students; €14,000 for non-European Union students; includes tuition, lab equipment, international student ID, student support services, enrollment fee. Financial aid available for all students: scholarships.

For More Information • Ms. Yoshiko Kasazaki, Secretary, Accademia Riaci, Via de'Conti 4, 50123 Florence, Italy; *Phone:* +39 055-289831; *Fax:* +39 055-212791. *E-mail:* accademiariaci@ accademiariaci.info. *World Wide Web:* http://www.accademiariaci. info/

ACCADEMIA RIACI
ONE-YEAR/ONE-SEMESTER PROGRAM IN FLORENCE

Hosted by Accademia Riaci

Academic Focus • Art, art conservation studies, ceramics and pottery, crafts, drawing/painting, fashion design, fine/studio arts, graphic design/illustration, interior design, leather working.

Program Information • Students attend classes at Accademia Riaci. Optional travel to Rome, Venice, a winery, the Mediterranean Sea, a farm visit.

Sessions • Fall, spring, yearlong, alternate fall, spring, and year terms.

Eligibility Requirements • Minimum age 18; open to freshmen, sophomores, juniors, seniors, graduate students, adults; 2.7 GPA; 2 letters of recommendation; portfolio (if available); transcript; no foreign language proficiency required.

Living Arrangements • Students live in locally rented apartments, host family homes, hotels. Quarters are shared with host institution

students, students from other programs. Meals are taken on one's own, in residences, in central dining facility, in restaurants.

Costs (2005) • One term: €7200 for European Union students; €8200 for non-European Union students. Yearlong program: €12,000 for European Union students; €14,000 for non-European Union students; includes tuition, lab equipment, international student ID, student support services, enrollment fee. Financial aid available for all students: scholarships.

For More Information • Ms. Yoshiko Kasazaki, Secretary, Accademia Riaci, Via de'Conti 4, 50123 Florence, Italy; *Phone:* +39 055-289831; *Fax:* +39 055-212791. *E-mail:* accademiariaci@ accademiariaci.info. *World Wide Web:* http://www.accademiariaci. info/

ACCENT INTERNATIONAL CONSORTIUM FOR ACADEMIC PROGRAMS ABROAD
SEMESTER IN FLORENCE WITH CITY COLLEGE OF SAN FRANCISCO

Hosted by Scuola Leonardo daVinci, Florence

Academic Focus • Art history, history, Italian language and literature, Italian studies, liberal studies.

Program Information • Students attend classes at Scuola Leonardo daVinci, Florence. Scheduled travel to Venice, Rome; field trips to Siena, Pisa, San Gimignano, Lucca, Assisi.

Sessions • Fall, spring, yearlong.

Eligibility Requirements • Minimum age 18; open to freshmen, sophomores, juniors, seniors, adults; no foreign language proficiency required.

Living Arrangements • Students live in locally rented apartments. Quarters are shared with host institution students, students from other programs. Meals are taken on one's own, in residences, in restaurants.

Costs (2003-2004) • One term: $5150. Yearlong program: $10,300 (estimated); includes housing, excursions, international student ID, student support services, extra-curricular activities. $250 nonrefundable deposit required.

For More Information • ACCENT International Consortium for Academic Programs Abroad, 870 Market Street, Suite 1026, San Francisco, CA 94102; *Phone:* 800-869-9291; *Fax:* 415-835-3749. *E-mail:* info@accentintl.com. *World Wide Web:* http://www.accentintl.com/. Students may also apply through City College of San Francisco, Study Abroad Office, Box A-71, 50 Phelan Avenue, San Francisco, CA 94112.

ACCENT INTERNATIONAL CONSORTIUM FOR ACADEMIC PROGRAMS ABROAD
SEMESTER IN FLORENCE WITH UNIVERSITY OF COLORADO AT DENVER

Hosted by Scuola Leonardo daVinci, Florence
Academic Focus • Art history, history, Italian language and literature, Italian studies, liberal studies.
Program Information • Students attend classes at Scuola Leonardo daVinci, Florence. Scheduled travel to Rome or Venice; field trips to Siena, San Gimignano, Pisa, Lucca, Assisi.
Sessions • Fall, spring, yearlong.
Eligibility Requirements • Minimum age 18; open to freshmen, sophomores, juniors, seniors, adults; 2.5 GPA; 1 letter of recommendation; transcript; 0.5 years of college course work in Italian.
Living Arrangements • Students live in locally rented apartments. Quarters are shared with host institution students, students from other programs. Meals are taken on one's own, in residences, in restaurants.
Costs (2003-2004) • One term: $6600. Yearlong program: $13,200 (estimated); includes tuition, housing, excursions, international student ID, student support services, extra-curricular activities. $250 nonrefundable deposit required.
For More Information • ACCENT International Consortium for Academic Programs Abroad, 870 Market Street, Suite 1026, San Francisco, CA 94102; *Phone:* 800-869-9291; *Fax:* 415-835-3749. *E-mail:* info@accentintl.com. *World Wide Web:* http://www.accentintl.com/. Students may also apply through University of Colorado at Denver, Office of International Education, Campus Box 185, PO Box 173364, Denver, CO 80217-3364.

AMERICAN INSTITUTE FOR FOREIGN STUDY (AIFS)
RICHMOND IN FLORENCE

Hosted by Richmond in Florence
Academic Focus • Art history, economics, fine/studio arts, history, Italian language and literature, literature, music, photography, political science and government.
Program Information • Students attend classes at Richmond in Florence. Scheduled travel to London; field trips to Rome, Venice, Ravenna.
Sessions • Fall, spring, yearlong.
Eligibility Requirements • Minimum age 17; open to sophomores, juniors, seniors; 2.5 GPA; 1 letter of recommendation; good academic standing at home school; no foreign language proficiency required.
Living Arrangements • Students live in program-owned apartments, host family homes. Meals are taken on one's own, in restaurants.
Costs (2004-2005) • One term: $12,995. Yearlong program: $23,790; includes tuition, housing, some meals, insurance, excursions, student support services, one-way airfare, 2-day London stop-over. $75 application fee. $350 nonrefundable deposit required. Financial aid available for all students: scholarships.
For More Information • Mr. David Mauro, Admissions Advisor, American Institute For Foreign Study (AIFS), 9 West Broad Street, Stamford, CT 06902-3788; *Phone:* 800-727-2437 Ext. 5163; *Fax:* 203-399-5597. *E-mail:* dmauro@aifs.com. *World Wide Web:* http://www.aifsabroad.com/

ARCADIA UNIVERSITY
ACCADEMIA ITALIANA, FLORENCE

Hosted by Accademia Italiana
Academic Focus • Fashion design, interior design, textiles.
Program Information • Students attend classes at Accademia Italiana. Field trips; optional travel at an extra cost.
Sessions • Fall, spring, yearlong.
Eligibility Requirements • Open to sophomores, juniors, seniors; 3.0 GPA; 1 letter of recommendation; slide portfolio of recent work for upper-division courses; no foreign language proficiency required.
Living Arrangements • Students live in locally rented apartments. Quarters are shared with host institution students. Meals are taken on one's own, in residences.
Costs (2003-2004) • One term: $9990. Yearlong program: $17,350; includes tuition, housing, insurance, international student ID, student support services, pre-departure guide, transcript. $35 application fee. $500 nonrefundable deposit required. Financial aid available for all students: scholarships, loans.
For More Information • Arcadia University, Center for Education Abroad, 450 South Easton Road, Glenside, PA 19038-3295; *Phone:* 866-927-2234; *Fax:* 215-572-2174. *E-mail:* cea@arcadia.edu. *World Wide Web:* http://www.arcadia.edu/cea/

ART UNDER ONE ROOF
ART UNDER ONE ROOF

Hosted by Art Under One Roof
Academic Focus • Art history, ceramics and pottery, commercial art, drawing/painting, fine/studio arts, interior design, Italian language and literature, photography.
Program Information • Students attend classes at Art Under One Roof. Field trips to Rome, Venice, Siena, Lucca; optional travel at an extra cost.
Sessions • Fall, spring, yearlong.
Eligibility Requirements • Minimum age 18; open to freshmen, sophomores, juniors, seniors, adults; 2.5 GPA; good academic standing at home school; photos/slides for non-beginners; no foreign language proficiency required.
Living Arrangements • Students live in locally rented apartments, host family homes. Quarters are shared with host institution students, students from other programs. Meals are taken on one's own, with host family.
Costs (2003-2004) • One term: €3500. Yearlong program: €6000; includes tuition, lab equipment. €50 application fee. €1200 nonrefundable deposit required.
For More Information • Mrs. Kirste Milligan, School Secretary, Art Under One Roof, Vua dei Pandolfini 46R, 50122 Florence, Italy; *Phone:* +39 055-247-8867; *Fax:* +39 055-247-8867. *E-mail:* arte1@arteurope.it. *World Wide Web:* http://www.arteuropa.org/

ASSOCIATED COLLEGES OF THE MIDWEST
ACM FLORENCE PROGRAM

Held at Linguaviva Italian School
Academic Focus • Architecture, art history, fine/studio arts, history, Italian language and literature, Renaissance studies.
Program Information • Classes are held on the campus of Linguaviva Italian School. Faculty members are drawn from the sponsor's U.S. staff and local instructors hired by the sponsor. Scheduled travel to Rome, Venice; field trips to Pisa, Siena; optional travel to Europe, Italy at an extra cost.
Sessions • Fall.
Eligibility Requirements • Open to sophomores, juniors, seniors; 3 letters of recommendation; good academic standing at home school; no foreign language proficiency required.
Living Arrangements • Students live in host family homes. Meals are taken with host family, in residences.
Costs (2003) • One term: contact sponsor for cost. $400 nonrefundable deposit required.
For More Information • Program Associate, ACM Florence Program, Associated Colleges of the Midwest, 205 West Wacker Drive, Suite 1300, Chicago, IL 60606; *Phone:* 312-263-5000; *Fax:* 312-263-5879. *E-mail:* acm@acm.edu. *World Wide Web:* http://www.acm.edu/

BENTLEY COLLEGE
BUSINESS PROGRAM ABROAD IN ITALY

Hosted by Lorenzo de Medici School
Academic Focus • Art history, business administration/management, Italian language and literature, Italian studies, literature, marketing, political science and government.
Program Information • Students attend classes at Lorenzo de Medici School. Scheduled travel; field trips to Venice, Rome, small Italian towns; optional travel to Venice, Verona at an extra cost.
Sessions • Fall, spring.
Eligibility Requirements • Open to sophomores, juniors, seniors; 3.0 GPA; 1 letter of recommendation; good academic standing at home school; essay; no foreign language proficiency required.
Living Arrangements • Students live in hotels. Quarters are shared with students from other programs. Meals are taken on one's own, in central dining facility.
Costs (2002-2003) • One term: $15,600; includes tuition, housing, some meals, excursions, international student ID, student support services. $35 application fee. $500 nonrefundable deposit required. Financial aid available for students from sponsoring institution: scholarships, loans.
For More Information • Mr. Andrew Dusenbery, Education Abroad Advisor, Bentley College, 175 Forest Street, Waltham, MA 02452; *Phone:* 781-891-3474; *Fax:* 781-891-2819. *E-mail:* study_abroad@bentley.edu. *World Wide Web:* http://ecampus.bentley.edu/dept/sa/

CITY COLLEGE OF SAN FRANCISCO
SEMESTER IN FLORENCE

Hosted by Scuola Leonardo daVinci, Florence
Academic Focus • Art history, language studies, liberal studies.
Program Information • Students attend classes at Scuola Leonardo daVinci, Florence. Field trips to Rome, San Gimignano, Arezzo, Siena.
Sessions • Fall, spring, yearlong.
Eligibility Requirements • Minimum age 18; open to freshmen, sophomores, juniors, seniors, graduate students, adults; 2.0 GPA; good academic standing at home school; no foreign language proficiency required.
Living Arrangements • Students live in locally rented apartments. Quarters are shared with host institution students, students from other programs. Meals are taken on one's own, in residences, in restaurants.
Costs (2004-2005) • One term: $5300–$5800. Yearlong program: $10,600; includes tuition, housing, insurance, excursions, international student ID, student support services. $250 nonrefundable deposit required. Financial aid available for students from sponsoring institution: scholarships, loans.
For More Information • Ms. Jill Heffron, Study Abroad Coordinator, City College of San Francisco, 50 Phelan Avenue, Box C212, San Francisco, CA 94112; *Phone:* 415-239-3778; *Fax:* 415-239-3804. *E-mail:* studyabroad@ccsf.edu. *World Wide Web:* http://www.ccsf.edu/studyabroad/. Students may also apply through ACCENT, 870 Market Street, Suite 1026, San Francisco, CA 94102.

COLLEGE CONSORTIUM FOR INTERNATIONAL STUDIES–COLLEGE OF STATEN ISLAND/CITY UNIVERSITY OF NEW YORK
PROGRAM IN FLORENCE, ITALY: LIBERAL ARTS AND STUDIO ART

Hosted by Lorenzo de' Medici–The Art Institute of Florence
Academic Focus • Art conservation studies, art history, communications, drawing/painting, film and media studies, fine/studio arts, history, international affairs, Italian language and literature, Italian studies, literature, photography, political science and government.
Program Information • Students attend classes at Lorenzo de' Medici–The Art Institute of Florence. Field trips to Florence and environs; optional travel to Rome, Verona, Lake Garda, Venice, Umbria, the Adriatic Riviera, Assisi, Orvieto, Tivoli, Villa Adriana, Portofino and Cinque Terre at an extra cost.
Sessions • Fall, spring, yearlong.
Eligibility Requirements • Minimum age 18; open to freshmen, sophomores, juniors, seniors, adults; 2.5 GPA; 3 letters of recommendation; essay; transcript; no foreign language proficiency required.
Living Arrangements • Students live in locally rented apartments, hotels. Quarters are shared with students from other programs. Meals are taken on one's own, in residences, in restaurants.
Costs (2004-2005) • One term: $6255 for New York residents and CCIS member students; all others contact the College of Staten Island for cost. Yearlong program: $10,975 for New York residents and CCIS member students; all others contact the College of Staten Island for cost; includes tuition, insurance, excursions, student support services, fees. $265 nonrefundable deposit required. Financial aid available for students from sponsoring institution: loans, grants.
For More Information • College Consortium for International Studies, 2000 P Street, NW, Suite 503, Washington, DC 20036; *Phone:* 800-453-6956; *Fax:* 202-223-0999. *E-mail:* info@ccisabroad.org. *World Wide Web:* http://www.ccisabroad.org/. Students may also apply through College of Staten Island, The City University of New York, Center for International Service, Building 2A, Room 206, 2800 Victory Boulevard, Staten Island, NY 10314.

COLLEGE CONSORTIUM FOR INTERNATIONAL STUDIES–COLLEGE OF STATEN ISLAND/CITY UNIVERSITY OF NEW YORK
PROGRAM IN FLORENCE, ITALY: SUPER-INTENSIVE ITALIAN

Hosted by Lorenzo de' Medici–The Art Institute of Florence
Academic Focus • Italian language and literature.
Program Information • Students attend classes at Lorenzo de' Medici–The Art Institute of Florence. Field trips to Florence and environs; optional travel to Verona, Lake Garda, Venice, Rome, Umbria, the Adriatic Riviera, Assisi, Orvieto, Tivoli, Villa Adriana, Portofino, Cinque Terre at an extra cost.
Sessions • Fall, spring, yearlong.
Eligibility Requirements • Minimum age 18; open to freshmen, sophomores, juniors, seniors, adults; 2.5 GPA; 3 letters of recommendation; essay; transcript; no foreign language proficiency required.
Living Arrangements • Students live in locally rented apartments, hotels. Quarters are shared with students from other programs. Meals are taken on one's own, in residences, in restaurants.
Costs (2004-2005) • One term: $4005 for New York residents and CCIS member students; all others contact the College of Staten Island for cost. Yearlong program: $7475 for New York residents and CCIS member students; all others contact the College of Staten Island for cost; includes tuition, insurance, excursions, student support services, fees. $265 nonrefundable deposit required. Financial aid available for students from sponsoring institution: loans, grants.
For More Information • College Consortium for International Studies, 2000 P Street, NW, Suite 503, Washington, DC 20036; *Phone:* 800-453-6956; *Fax:* 202-223-0999. *E-mail:* info@ccisabroad.org. *World Wide Web:* http://www.ccisabroad.org/. Students may also apply through College of Staten Island, The City University of New York, Center for International Service, Building 2A, Room 206, 2800 Victory Boulevard, Staten Island, NY 10314.

CULTURAL EXPERIENCES ABROAD (CEA)
STUDY FINE AND LIBERAL ARTS IN FLORENCE

Hosted by Palazzo Rucellai, The Institute for Fine and Liberal Arts
Academic Focus • Architecture, art history, fine/studio arts, history, Italian language and literature, music, political science and government.
Program Information • Students attend classes at Palazzo Rucellai, The Institute for Fine and Liberal Arts. Field trips to Venice, Rome, Chianti, Verona, Assisi, Pompeii; optional travel to France, Switzerland, Sicily.
Sessions • Fall, spring, yearlong.
Eligibility Requirements • Minimum age 18; open to sophomores, juniors, seniors; 2.7 GPA; 1 letter of recommendation; good academic standing at home school; no foreign language proficiency required.

ITALY
Florence

Living Arrangements • Students live in locally rented apartments. Meals are taken on one's own, in residences, in restaurants.
Costs (2003-2004) • One term: $11,975. Yearlong program: $23,795; includes tuition, housing, excursions, student support services, ID card, e-mail access, social activities. $50 application fee. $400 nonrefundable deposit required.
For More Information • Cultural Experiences Abroad (CEA), 1400 East Southern Avenue, Suite B-108, Tempe, AZ 85282-8011; *Phone:* 480-557-7900; *Fax:* 480-557-7926. *E-mail:* petersons@gowithcea. com. *World Wide Web:* http://www.gowithcea.com/

CULTURAL EXPERIENCES ABROAD (CEA)
STUDY STUDIO ART, ITALIAN LANGUAGE, AND CULTURE IN FLORENCE

Hosted by Santa Reparata International School of Art
Academic Focus • Art history, drawing/painting, fashion design, fine/studio arts, Italian language and literature, Italian studies, photography, textiles.
Program Information • Students attend classes at Santa Reparata International School of Art. Field trips to Venice, Rome, Chianti, Verona, Assisi, Pompeii, Siena.
Sessions • Fall, spring, yearlong.
Eligibility Requirements • Minimum age 18; open to freshmen, sophomores, juniors, seniors; 2.5 GPA; 1 letter of recommendation; good academic standing at home school; no foreign language proficiency required.
Living Arrangements • Students live in locally rented apartments. Meals are taken on one's own, in residences, in restaurants.
Costs (2003-2004) • One term: $10,995-$11,295. Yearlong program: $20,995; includes tuition, housing, excursions, student support services. $50 application fee. $400 nonrefundable deposit required.
For More Information • Cultural Experiences Abroad (CEA), 1400 East Southern Avenue, Suite B-108, Tempe, AZ 85282-8011; *Phone:* 480-557-7900; *Fax:* 480-557-7926. *E-mail:* petersons@gowithcea. com. *World Wide Web:* http://www.gowithcea.com/

DRAKE UNIVERSITY
INSTITUTE OF ITALIAN STUDIES–FLORENCE

Hosted by Lorenzo de' Medici–The Art Institute of Florence, Lorenzo de Medici School, Institute of Italian Studies–Florence
Academic Focus • Architecture, art, art history, communications, culinary arts, film and media studies, international business, Italian language and literature, Italian studies, liberal studies.
Program Information • Students attend classes at Lorenzo de' Medici–The Art Institute of Florence, Lorenzo de Medici School, Institute of Italian Studies–Florence. Scheduled travel to Florence, Rome; field trips to Pompeii, Venice, Siena; optional travel to Rome, Venice at an extra cost.
Sessions • Fall, spring, winter, yearlong.
Eligibility Requirements • Minimum age 19; open to sophomores, juniors, seniors, graduate students, adults; course work in liberal arts, studio art, international business, journalism; 2.75 GPA; 0.5 years of college course work in Italian.
Living Arrangements • Students live in host institution dormitories, locally rented apartments, host family homes. Quarters are shared with host institution students. Meals are taken on one's own, in residences, in central dining facility, in restaurants.
Costs (2003-2004) • One term: $6300. Yearlong program: $11,900; includes tuition. $35 application fee. $500 refundable deposit required.
For More Information • Mr. Rick Soria, Director, Drake University, PO Box 27077, West Des Moines, IA 50265; *Phone:* 800-443-7253 Ext. 3984; *Fax:* 515-225-0196. *E-mail:* drakeiis@drake.edu. *World Wide Web:* http://www.mac.drake.edu/iis/

EUROPEAN HERITAGE INSTITUTE
ACADEMIC YEAR IN FLORENCE, ITALY

Hosted by Lorenzo de' Medici–The Art Institute of Florence
Academic Focus • Full curriculum.
Program Information • Students attend classes at Lorenzo de' Medici–The Art Institute of Florence. Field trips to Rome, Pompeii, Venice, Tuscany; optional travel to Venice, Rome, southern Italy at an extra cost.

Sessions • Fall, spring, yearlong.
Eligibility Requirements • Minimum age 18; open to freshmen, sophomores, juniors, seniors, graduate students, adults; 2.2 GPA; 2 letters of recommendation; no foreign language proficiency required.
Living Arrangements • Students live in host institution dormitories, locally rented apartments, host family homes. Quarters are shared with host institution students, students from other programs. Meals are taken on one's own, in residences, in restaurants.
Costs (2004-2005) • One term: $3200-$5800. Yearlong program: $6400-$11,600; includes tuition, student support services, administrative fees, some excursions. $300 refundable deposit required.
For More Information • Dr. Antonio Masullo, Professor, European Heritage Institute, 2708 East Franklin Street, Richmond, VA 23223; *Phone:* 804-643-0661; *Fax:* 804-648-0826. *World Wide Web:* http://www.europeabroad.org/

EUROPEAN HERITAGE INSTITUTE
MUSIC AND ART IN FLORENCE

Hosted by Istituto Europeo
Academic Focus • Art, art history, civilization studies, drawing/painting, fine/studio arts, history, Italian language and literature, Italian studies, music, music history, music performance, photography, visual and performing arts.
Program Information • Students attend classes at Istituto Europeo. Field trips to Verona, areas around Florence; optional travel to Venice, Rome at an extra cost.
Sessions • Fall, spring, yearlong.
Eligibility Requirements • Minimum age 18; open to freshmen, sophomores, juniors, seniors, graduate students, adults; 2.25 GPA; 2 letters of recommendation; good academic standing at home school; no foreign language proficiency required.
Living Arrangements • Students live in locally rented apartments, host family homes. Quarters are shared with host institution students, students from other programs. Meals are taken on one's own, with host family, in residences, in restaurants.
Costs (2004-2005) • One term: $3700-$4850 (estimated). Yearlong program: $7400-$9700 (estimated); includes tuition, excursions, student support services. $300 refundable deposit required.
For More Information • Dr. Antonio Masullo, Professor, European Heritage Institute, 2708 East Franklin Street, Richmond, VA 23223; *Phone:* 804-643-0661; *Fax:* 804-648-2826. *E-mail:* euritage@i2020. net. *World Wide Web:* http://www.europeabroad.org/

FAIRFIELD UNIVERSITY
FAIRFIELD UNIVERSITY LAUREA PROGRAM IN FLORENCE

Hosted by Lorenzo de' Medici–The Art Institute of Florence
Academic Focus • Full curriculum.
Program Information • Students attend classes at Lorenzo de' Medici–The Art Institute of Florence. Field trips to Medici country villas, museums, cultural events; optional travel to Venice, Rome at an extra cost.
Sessions • Fall, spring, winter, yearlong.
Eligibility Requirements • Minimum age 18; open to sophomores, juniors, seniors, adults; 2.8 GPA; 2 letters of recommendation; good academic standing at home school; good social standing; no foreign language proficiency required.
Living Arrangements • Students live in locally rented apartments. Quarters are shared with host institution students. Meals are taken on one's own, in residences.
Costs (2003-2004) • One term: $14,100. Yearlong program: $28,200; includes tuition, housing, some meals, insurance, international student ID, student support services, regular group activities. $50 application fee. $1000 refundable deposit required. Financial aid available for students from sponsoring institution.
For More Information • Office of International Education, Fairfield University, Dolan House, 1073 North Benson Road, Fairfield, CT 06824; *Phone:* 203-254-4332; *Fax:* 203-254-4261. *E-mail:* studyabroadoffice@mail.fairfield.edu. *World Wide Web:* http://www. fairfield.edu/sce/studyabroad/

Fairfield University Laurea Program in

FLORENCE

Benvenuti! – WELCOME! Begin your Italian experience at Fairfield

University's Florence campus, where, since 1994, thousands of students have enjoyed an outstanding semester or year experience. The Laurea program offers a comprehensive package through our host school, the Lorenzo de'Medici Institute.

- Up to 18 Fairfield credits each semester.

- **Special Scholars Program** available for qualified students.

- A wide variety of disciplines. All courses are taught in English (except Italian language) by a talented international faculty.

- Advisement and individual attention for all health, housing, and academic concerns; 24-hour emergency coverage provided.

- Housing in shared apartments, located in the city's historic center, within walking distance to school.

- Short-term programs available during summer and January intersession.

**FAIRFIELD UNIVERSITY LAUREA PROGRAM
DOLAN HOUSE/FAIRFIELD UNIVERSITY**
Fairfield, CT 06824-5195
Phone: (888) 254-1566 (toll-free) or (203) 254-4332
Fax: (203) 254-4261
E-mail: studyabroadoffice@mail.fairfield.edu

UNIVERSITY COLLEGE AT

Jesuit. Personal. Powerful.

www.fairfield.edu/sce/studyabroad

ITALY
Florence

FASHION INSTITUTE OF TECHNOLOGY
FIT INTERNATIONAL FASHION DESIGN PROGRAM IN NEW YORK AND FLORENCE

Hosted by Polimoda

Academic Focus • Art history, costume design, fashion design, Italian language and literature.

Program Information • Students attend classes at Polimoda. Scheduled travel to Paris; field trips to Milan.

Sessions • Yearlong.

Eligibility Requirements • Open to freshmen, sophomores, juniors; major in fashion design; 3.0 GPA; 4 letters of recommendation; 0.5 years of college course work in Italian.

Living Arrangements • Students live in locally rented apartments. Quarters are shared with host institution students. Meals are taken on one's own, in residences.

Costs (2002-2003) • Yearlong program: $18,225–$20,000 (estimated); includes tuition, housing, insurance, excursions, international airfare, books and class materials, student support services. $120 application fee. Financial aid available for students from sponsoring institution: scholarships, loans.

For More Information • Ms. Georgianna Appignani, Director, Office of International Programs, Fashion Institute of Technology, 7th Avenue at 27th Street, New York, NY 10001-5992; *Phone:* 212-217-7601; *Fax:* 212-217-7010. *E-mail:* fitintlpgms@fitnyc.edu. *World Wide Web:* http://www.fitnyc.edu/

FASHION INSTITUTE OF TECHNOLOGY
FIT INTERNATIONAL FASHION MERCHANDISING MANAGEMENT PROGRAM IN NEW YORK AND FLORENCE

Hosted by Polimoda

Academic Focus • Art history, fashion merchandising, Italian language and literature, photography.

Program Information • Students attend classes at Polimoda. Field trips to Paris, Milan.

Sessions • Yearlong.

Eligibility Requirements • Open to juniors; major in fashion merchandising management; 3.0 GPA; 4 letters of recommendation; no foreign language proficiency required.

Living Arrangements • Students live in locally rented apartments. Quarters are shared with host institution students. Meals are taken on one's own, in residences.

Costs (2002-2003) • Yearlong program: $18,225–$20,000 (estimated); includes tuition, housing, insurance, international airfare, books and class materials, student support services. $120 application fee. Financial aid available for students from sponsoring institution: scholarships, loans.

For More Information • Ms. Carole De Santis, Student Services Coordinator, Fashion Institute of Technology, 7th Avenue at 27th Street, Room A605, New York, NY 10001-5992; *Phone:* 212-217-7601; *Fax:* 212-217-7010. *E-mail:* carole_desantis@fitnyc.edu. *World Wide Web:* http://www.fitnyc.edu/

FLORIDA STATE UNIVERSITY
ITALY: FLORENCE PROGRAM

Hosted by Florida State University–Florence Study Center

Academic Focus • Art history, creative writing, drawing/painting, history, Italian language and literature, literature, photography, political science and government.

Program Information • Students attend classes at Florida State University–Florence Study Center. Scheduled travel to Rome, Venice; field trips to Fiesole, Siena, San Gimignano, Pisa; optional travel to Austria, France, Germany at an extra cost.

Sessions • Fall, spring, yearlong.

Eligibility Requirements • Open to freshmen, sophomores, juniors, seniors; 2.5 GPA; good academic standing at home school; previous Italian study recommended.

Living Arrangements • Students live in locally rented apartments, hotels. Quarters are shared with host institution students. Meals are taken on one's own, in restaurants.

Costs (2002-2003) • One term: $9800. Yearlong program: $19,600; includes tuition, housing, some meals, insurance, excursions, international student ID, student support services, program T-shirt or cap. $50 application fee. $500 nonrefundable deposit required. Financial aid available for students from sponsoring institution: scholarships, work study, loans.

For More Information • International Programs, Florida State University, A5500 University Center, Tallahassee, FL 32306-2420; *Phone:* 850-644-3272; *Fax:* 850-644-8817. *E-mail:* intprog@www.fsu.edu. *World Wide Web:* http://www.international.fsu.edu/

GEORGE MASON UNIVERSITY
FLORENCE, ITALY

Hosted by Scuola Leonardo daVinci, Florence

Academic Focus • History, Italian language and literature, Italian studies.

Program Information • Students attend classes at Scuola Leonardo daVinci, Florence. Field trips to Venice; optional travel at an extra cost.

Sessions • Spring.

Eligibility Requirements • Minimum age 18; open to freshmen, sophomores, juniors, seniors, adults; 2.5 GPA; good academic standing at home school; no foreign language proficiency required.

Living Arrangements • Students live in locally rented apartments. Quarters are shared with host institution students. Meals are taken on one's own.

Costs (2004) • One term: contact sponsor for cost. $75 application fee. Financial aid available for students from sponsoring institution: scholarships, loans.

For More Information • Program Officer, Center for Global Education, George Mason University, 235 Johnson Center, 4400 University Drive, Fairfax, VA 22030; *Phone:* 703-993-2154; *Fax:* 703-993-2153. *E-mail:* cge@gmu.edu. *World Wide Web:* http://www.gmu.edu/departments/cge/

GONZAGA UNIVERSITY
GONZAGA-IN-FLORENCE

Hosted by Gonzaga in Florence

Academic Focus • Art, art history, economics, English literature, finance, history, Italian language and literature, law and legal studies, management information systems, marketing, music, philosophy, political science and government, religious studies, sociology.

Program Information • Students attend classes at Gonzaga in Florence. Scheduled travel to Germany, Austria, Turkey; optional travel to Greece, Switzerland, Italy, Turkey, the Netherlands, France, Prague at an extra cost.

Sessions • Yearlong.

Eligibility Requirements • Open to juniors, adults; 3.0 GPA; 2 letters of recommendation; Dean of Students' approval; no foreign language proficiency required.

Living Arrangements • Students live in hotels. Quarters are shared with host institution students. Meals are taken as a group, in residences.

Costs (2003-2004) • Yearlong program: $30,210; includes tuition, housing, some meals, international student ID, student support services, travel tours. $50 application fee. $500 refundable deposit required. Financial aid available for all students: scholarships, loans, federal financial aid.

For More Information • Ms. Wanda Reynolds, Studies Abroad Director, Gonzaga University, East 502 Boone Avenue, Spokane, WA 99258; *Phone:* 800-440-5391; *Fax:* 509-323-5987. *E-mail:* reynolds@gu.gonzaga.edu. *World Wide Web:* http://www.gonzaga.edu/studyabroad/

HARDING UNIVERSITY
HARDING UNIVERSITY IN FLORENCE, ITALY

Hosted by Harding University in Florence

Academic Focus • Italian language and literature, liberal studies, religious studies.

Program Information • Students attend classes at Harding University in Florence. Scheduled travel to Sicily; field trips to Rome, Tuscany, Pisa, Siena, Lucca, San Gimignano; optional travel to western Europe.

Sessions • Fall, spring.

Eligibility Requirements • Open to sophomores, juniors, seniors; 2.0 GPA; good academic standing at home school; no foreign language proficiency required.

Living Arrangements • Students live in a program-owned villa. Meals are taken as a group, in central dining facility.

Costs (2003-2004) • One term: $13,000; includes tuition, housing, all meals, international airfare, books and class materials. $200 application fee. Financial aid available for students from sponsoring institution: scholarships, work study, loans.
For More Information • Dr. Jeffrey T. Hopper, Dean of International Programs, Harding University, 900 East Center Street, Box 10754, Searcy, AR 72149; *Phone:* 501-279-4529; *Fax:* 501-279-4184. *E-mail:* intlprograms@harding.edu

JAMES MADISON UNIVERSITY
SEMESTER IN FLORENCE
Hosted by James Madison University–Florence
Academic Focus • Art history, film and media studies, Italian language and literature, Italian studies, literature, music, political science and government.
Program Information • Students attend classes at James Madison University–Florence. Classes are also held on the campus of British Institute of Florence. Scheduled travel to Rome; field trips to Milan, Venice, Ravenna, Siena.
Sessions • Fall, spring.
Eligibility Requirements • Minimum age 18; open to freshmen, sophomores, juniors, seniors; 2.8 GPA; 1 letter of recommendation; good academic standing at home school; no foreign language proficiency required.
Living Arrangements • Students live in host family homes. Quarters are shared with host institution students. Meals are taken on one's own, with host family, in residences, in restaurants.
Costs (2003-2004) • One term: $7772 for Virginia residents; $11,883 for nonresidents; includes tuition, housing, some meals, excursions, books and class materials, lab equipment. $400 nonrefundable deposit required. Financial aid available for students from sponsoring institution: scholarships, work study, loans.
For More Information • Mr. Felix Wang, Director, James Madison University, Office of International Programs, MSC 5731, 1077 South Main Street, Harrisonburg, VA 22807; *Phone:* 540-568-6419; *Fax:* 540-568-3310. *E-mail:* studyabroad@jmu.edu. *World Wide Web:* http://www.jmu.edu/international/

MARIST COLLEGE
ITALIAN INTERNSHIP, LANGUAGE AND CULTURE PROGRAM
Hosted by Lorenzo de Medici School
Academic Focus • Art history, fine/studio arts, Italian language and literature, liberal studies, photography, social sciences.
Program Information • Students attend classes at Lorenzo de Medici School. Scheduled travel to Rome, Venice, Padova, Verona, Mantova, Adriatic Riviera, Umbria; field trips to Florence environs, Rome, Venice, Padova, Verona, Umbria.
Sessions • Fall, spring, yearlong.
Eligibility Requirements • Open to sophomores, juniors, seniors; 2.8 GPA; 2 letters of recommendation; good academic standing at home school; previous Italian study preferred.
Living Arrangements • Students live in locally rented apartments. Quarters are shared with host institution students. Meals are taken on one's own.
Costs (2003-2004) • One term: $12,500. Yearlong program: $25,000; includes tuition, housing, insurance, excursions, student support services. $35 application fee. $300 nonrefundable deposit required. Financial aid available for students from sponsoring institution: scholarships, loans.
For More Information • Ms. Carol Toufali, Coordinator, Marist Abroad Program, Marist College, 3399 North Road, Poughkeepsie, NY 12601-1387; *Phone:* 845-575-3330; *Fax:* 845-575-3294. *E-mail:* international@marist.edu. *World Wide Web:* http://www.marist.edu/international/

MARYWOOD UNIVERSITY
MARYWOOD/SACI ART STUDY ABROAD PROGRAM
Hosted by Studio Art Centers International
Academic Focus • Art history, design and applied arts, fine/studio arts, Italian language and literature.
Program Information • Students attend classes at Studio Art Centers International. Field trips to Siena, Rome, Venice, Padua, Lucca, Arezzo, Pisa, Ravenna.
Sessions • Fall, spring.

Eligibility Requirements • Open to sophomores, juniors, seniors, graduate students, adults; course work in studio or applied arts, art history; 2.75 GPA; 2 letters of recommendation; good academic standing at home school; no foreign language proficiency required.
Living Arrangements • Students live in program-owned apartments. Quarters are shared with host institution students, students from other programs. Meals are taken on one's own, in residences, in restaurants.
Costs (2002-2003) • One term: $11,600; includes tuition, housing, excursions, international student ID, student support services. $300 refundable deposit required. Financial aid available for students from sponsoring institution: scholarships, loans.
For More Information • Mr. Steven Alexander, Associate Professor of Art, Marywood University, 2300 Adams Avenue, Scranton, PA 18509; *Phone:* 570-348-6211; *Fax:* 570-961-4769. *E-mail:* salexander@es.marywood.edu

MIDDLEBURY COLLEGE SCHOOLS ABROAD
SCHOOL IN ITALY–FLORENCE PROGRAM
Hosted by Middlebury School at the Sede, University of Florence
Academic Focus • Art history, cultural studies, film and media studies, history, Italian language and literature.
Program Information • Students attend classes at University of Florence, Middlebury School at the Sede. Field trips to Milan, Siena, Assisi.
Sessions • Fall, spring, yearlong.
Eligibility Requirements • Open to juniors, seniors, graduate students; 2.7 GPA; 2 letters of recommendation; B average in both Italian and major; 2.5 years college course work in Italian, including at least 1 content course.
Living Arrangements • Students live in locally rented apartments, host family homes. Meals are taken on one's own, in residences, in restaurants.
Costs (2004-2005) • One term: $7200. Yearlong program: $14,400; includes tuition, excursions, student support services. $50 application fee. $300 nonrefundable deposit required. Financial aid available for students from sponsoring institution: scholarships, loans.
For More Information • Mr. Jamie Northrup, University Relations Coordinator, Middlebury College Schools Abroad, Office of Off-Campus Study, Sunderland Language Center, Middlebury, VT 05753; *Phone:* 802-443-5745; *Fax:* 802-443-3157. *E-mail:* schoolsabroad@middlebury.edu. *World Wide Web:* http://www.middlebury.edu/msa/

NEW YORK UNIVERSITY
NYU IN FLORENCE
Hosted by University of Florence, NYU Center
Academic Focus • Accounting, art history, drawing/painting, earth sciences, economics, film and media studies, fine/studio arts, history, Italian language and literature, Italian studies, literature, political science and government, psychology, Renaissance studies, sociology, statistics, urban studies, women's studies.
Program Information • Students attend classes at University of Florence, NYU Center. Field trips to Fiesole, Siena, Rome.
Sessions • Fall, spring, yearlong.
Eligibility Requirements • Open to sophomores, juniors, seniors; 3.0 GPA; 1 letter of recommendation; good academic standing at home school; transcripts; personal statement; no foreign language proficiency required.
Living Arrangements • Students live in host institution dormitories, locally rented apartments, host family homes. Quarters are shared with host institution students. Meals are taken on one's own, in residences, in restaurants.
Costs (2003-2004) • One term: $14,248. Yearlong program: $28,495; includes tuition, excursions, student support services. $25 application fee. $300 nonrefundable deposit required. Financial aid available for all students: scholarships, loans.
For More Information • Office of Study Abroad Admissions, New York University, 7 East 12th Street, 6th Floor, New York, NY 10003; *Phone:* 212-998-4433; *Fax:* 212-995-4103. *E-mail:* studyabroad@nyu.edu. *World Wide Web:* http://www.nyu.edu/studyabroad/

NICHOLLS STATE UNIVERSITY
STUDY PROGRAM IN ITALY

Hosted by Nicholls State University–Florence
Academic Focus • Art, cultural studies, history, Italian language and literature.
Program Information • Students attend classes at Nicholls State University–Florence. Field trips to museums, the theater, markets; optional travel to sports events, festivals at an extra cost.
Sessions • Fall, spring, yearlong.
Eligibility Requirements • Minimum age 17; open to precollege students, freshmen, sophomores, juniors, seniors, graduate students, adults; no foreign language proficiency required.
Living Arrangements • Students live in host family homes. Quarters are shared with host institution students. Meals are taken with host family, in residences.
Costs (2003-2004) • One term: $5630. Yearlong program: $11,259; includes tuition, housing, all meals, insurance, books and class materials, lab equipment, student support services, instructional costs. Financial aid available for all students: loans, all customary sources.
For More Information • Ms. Cynthia Webb, Director of Study Programs Abroad, Nicholls State University, PO Box 2080, Thibodaux, LA 70310; *Phone:* 985-448-4440; *Fax:* 985-449-7028. *E-mail:* spab-caw@nicholls.edu. *World Wide Web:* http://www.nicholls.edu/abroad/

ROGER WILLIAMS UNIVERSITY
SEMESTER ABROAD STUDIES IN FLORENCE

Hosted by Institute of Fine and Liberal Arts at Palazzo Rucellai
Academic Focus • Architecture, art history, history, Italian studies, political science and government, visual and performing arts.
Program Information • Students attend classes at Institute of Fine and Liberal Arts at Palazzo Rucellai. Field trips to Siena, Lucca, San Gimignano, Pisa; optional travel to Rome, Venice, Amalfi Coast at an extra cost.
Sessions • Fall, spring.
Eligibility Requirements • Minimum age 18; open to juniors, seniors; 2.5 GPA; 2 letters of recommendation; good judicial standing; no foreign language proficiency required.
Living Arrangements • Students live in program-owned apartments. Meals are taken on one's own, in residences.
Costs (2003-2004) • One term: $16,148 ($17,576 for architecture); includes tuition, housing, some meals, excursions, international airfare, student support services. $650 nonrefundable deposit required. Financial aid available for students from sponsoring institution: scholarships, loans, governmental financial aid.
For More Information • Ms. Gina M. Lopardo, Coordinator of Study Abroad Programs, Roger Williams University, One Old Ferry Road, Bristol, RI 02809-2921; *Phone:* 401-254-3040; *Fax:* 401-253-7768. *E-mail:* glopardo@rwu.edu. *World Wide Web:* http://www.rwu.edu/academics/special+programs/study+abroad/

RUTGERS, THE STATE UNIVERSITY OF NEW JERSEY
STUDY ABROAD IN FLORENCE

Hosted by Linguaviva Italian School
Academic Focus • Art history, Italian studies, liberal studies, social sciences.
Program Information • Students attend classes at Linguaviva Italian School. Scheduled travel to Rome, Sicily; field trips to Bologna, Pisa.
Sessions • Fall, spring.
Eligibility Requirements • Open to sophomores, juniors, seniors; 2.5 GPA; 2 letters of recommendation; good academic standing at home school; no foreign language proficiency required.
Living Arrangements • Students live in locally rented apartments, host family homes. Quarters are shared with host institution students. Meals are taken on one's own, with host family, in residences.
Costs (2003-2004) • One term: $7234 for New Jersey residents; $9884 for nonresidents; includes tuition, insurance, excursions, student support services. $20 application fee. $750 nonrefundable deposit required. Financial aid available for students from sponsoring institution: scholarships, loans.
For More Information • Ms. Karin Bonello, Regional Coordinator, Rutgers, The State University of New Jersey, 102 College Avenue, New Brunswick, NJ 08901-8543; *Phone:* 732-932-7787; *Fax:* 732-932-8659. *E-mail:* ru_abroad@email.rutgers.edu. *World Wide Web:* http://studyabroad.rutgers.edu/

RUTGERS, THE STATE UNIVERSITY OF NEW JERSEY
STUDY ABROAD IN ITALY

Hosted by University of Florence
Academic Focus • Full curriculum.
Program Information • Students attend classes at University of Florence. Scheduled travel to Sicily, Venice; field trips to Pisa, Siena.
Sessions • Yearlong.
Eligibility Requirements • Open to juniors, seniors; 2.5 GPA; 2 letters of recommendation; good academic standing at home school; 2 years of college course work in Italian.
Living Arrangements • Students live in locally rented apartments, host family homes. Quarters are shared with host institution students. Meals are taken on one's own, with host family, in residences.
Costs (2003-2004) • Yearlong program: $13,653 for New Jersey residents; $18,953 for nonresidents; includes tuition, insurance, excursions, student support services. $20 application fee. $750 nonrefundable deposit required. Financial aid available for students from sponsoring institution: scholarships, loans.
For More Information • Ms. Karin Bonello, Regional Coordinator, Rutgers, The State University of New Jersey, 102 College Avenue, New Brunswick, NJ 08901-8543; *Phone:* 732-932-7787; *Fax:* 732-932-8659. *E-mail:* ru_abroad@email.rutgers.edu. *World Wide Web:* http://studyabroad.rutgers.edu/

SANTA BARBARA CITY COLLEGE
SEMESTER PROGRAM IN FLORENCE, ITALY

Hosted by Scuola Leonardo daVinci, Florence
Academic Focus • Art history, creative writing, history, Italian language and literature, literature.
Program Information • Students attend classes at Scuola Leonardo daVinci, Florence. Scheduled travel to Rome, Venice; field trips to Siena, San Gimignano, Ravenna, Pisa, Lucca.
Sessions • Spring.
Eligibility Requirements • Minimum age 18; open to freshmen, sophomores, juniors, seniors, graduate students, adults; course work in English; 2.0 GPA; good academic standing at home school; no foreign language proficiency required.
Living Arrangements • Students live in locally rented apartments. Quarters are shared with host institution students. Meals are taken on one's own, in residences.
Costs (2004-2005) • One term: $6000 (estimated); includes housing, excursions, international student ID, student support services. $300 nonrefundable deposit required. Financial aid available for all students: scholarships, loans.
For More Information • Ms. Naomi Sullwold, Program Assistant, Santa Barbara City College, 721 Cliff Drive, Santa Barbara, CA 93109; *Phone:* 805-965-0581 Ext. 2494; *Fax:* 805-963-7222. *E-mail:* sullwold@sbcc.edu. *World Wide Web:* http://www.sbcc.edu/studyabroad/

SANTA BARBARA CITY COLLEGE
SEMESTER PROGRAM IN FLORENCE, ITALY

Hosted by Scuola Leonardo daVinci, Florence
Academic Focus • Art history, communications, creative writing, Italian language and literature.
Program Information • Students attend classes at Scuola Leonardo daVinci, Florence. Scheduled travel to Rome, Venice; field trips to Siena, San Gimignano, Ravenna, Pisa, Lucca.
Sessions • Spring.
Eligibility Requirements • Minimum age 18; open to freshmen, sophomores, juniors, seniors, graduate students, adults; course work in English; 2.0 GPA; good academic standing at home school; no foreign language proficiency required.
Living Arrangements • Students live in locally rented apartments. Quarters are shared with host institution students. Meals are taken on one's own, in residences.

Costs (2003) • One term: $5050; includes housing, insurance, excursions, international student ID, student support services. $250 nonrefundable deposit required. Financial aid available for all students: scholarships, loans.

For More Information • Ms. Naomi Sullwold, Program Assistant, Santa Barbara City College, 721 Cliff Drive, Santa Barbara, CA 93109; *Phone:* 805-965-0581 Ext. 2494; *Fax:* 805-963-7222. *E-mail:* sullwold@sbcc.edu. *World Wide Web:* http://www.sbcc.edu/studyabroad/

SARAH LAWRENCE COLLEGE
SARAH LAWRENCE COLLEGE IN FLORENCE

Hosted by Studio Il Bisonte, Scuola di Musica di Fiesole, University of Florence

Academic Focus • Art conservation studies, art history, film and media studies, fine/studio arts, history, Italian language and literature, literature, music, photography.

Program Information • Students attend classes at Scuola di Musica di Fiesole, University of Florence, Studio Il Bisonte. Field trips to Venice, Rome, Urbino, Cannes.

Sessions • Spring, yearlong.

Eligibility Requirements • Open to juniors, seniors; 3.0 GPA; 2 letters of recommendation; good academic standing at home school; essay; 1 year of college course work in Italian (for spring term).

Living Arrangements • Students live in host family homes. Meals are taken on one's own, with host family.

Costs (2003-2004) • One term: $21,136. Yearlong program: $39,896; includes tuition, housing, some meals, excursions, books and class materials, student support services, lectures, library fees, concert, movie and theater tickets. $35 application fee. $250 nonrefundable deposit required. Financial aid available for all students: scholarships, loans.

For More Information • Ms. Prema Samuel, Director of International Programs, Sarah Lawrence College, 1 Meadway, Bronxville, NY 10708-5999; *Phone:* 800-873-4752; *Fax:* 914-395-2666. *E-mail:* slcaway@slc.edu. *World Wide Web:* http://www.sarahlawrence.edu/studyabroad/

MORE ABOUT THE PROGRAM

Sarah Lawrence College in Florence offers an individually designed program of study, with emphasis in the humanities, music, and the visual arts. This program is open to students who are seeking to study Italian for the first time as well as those who are at the intermediate or advanced level.

Students may also enroll at the University of Florence or at the local conservatories for music. Those with an interest in fine arts study with Florentine artists in their studios.

Intensive language study is complemented by course work in art history, literature, history, Italian cinema, and art restoration. Individual tutorials supplement each course.

Trips and extracurricular activities are plentiful, including a "language partner" program with Italian students. Merit grants are available.

Sarah Lawrence also sponsors programs in Cuba, Paris, and Oxford as well as a London Theatre Program.

SMITH COLLEGE
JUNIOR YEAR IN FLORENCE

Hosted by Smith College Center, University of Florence

Academic Focus • Art history, communications, drama/theater, economics, fine/studio arts, history, Italian language and literature, music, political science and government, psychology, religious studies.

Program Information • Students attend classes at Smith College Center, University of Florence. Scheduled travel to Amalfi Coast, Bay of Naples; field trips to Venice, Ravenna, Umbrian towns, Tuscan towns.

Sessions • Yearlong.

Eligibility Requirements • Open to juniors, seniors, graduate students; 3.0 GPA; 3 letters of recommendation; good academic standing at home school; 2 years of college course work in Italian.

Living Arrangements • Students live in host family homes. Quarters are shared with host institution students, students from other programs. Meals are taken on one's own, with host family, in residences.

Costs (2004-2005) • Yearlong program: $39,814; includes tuition, housing, all meals, insurance, excursions, museum tickets for art history classes, laundry service. $35 application fee. $300 refundable deposit required. Financial aid available for students from sponsoring institution: scholarships, loans.

For More Information • Office for International Study, Smith College, College Hall 24, Northampton, MA 01063; *Phone:* 413-585-4905; *Fax:* 413-585-4906. *E-mail:* studyabroad@smith.edu. *World Wide Web:* http://www.smith.edu/studyabroad/

STUDIO ART CENTERS INTERNATIONAL (SACI)
ARCHITECTURE PROGRAM

Hosted by Studio Art Centers International

Academic Focus • Architecture, art history, historic preservation, interior design, photography.

Program Information • Students attend classes at Studio Art Centers International. Scheduled travel to Carrara, Milan, Naples, Rome, Venice; field trips to Siena, Pisa, Lucca, Ravenna, Assisi, Urbano, Arezzo, Bologna.

Sessions • Fall, spring, yearlong.

Eligibility Requirements • Minimum age 18; open to freshmen, sophomores, juniors, seniors, graduate students; 2.7 GPA; 2 letters of recommendation; statement of intent; official transcript; no foreign language proficiency required.

Living Arrangements • Students live in locally rented apartments. Quarters are shared with host institution students. Meals are taken on one's own, in residences.

Costs (2004-2005) • One term: $8775. Yearlong program: $17,550; includes tuition. $50 application fee. Financial aid available for all students: scholarships.

For More Information • Mr. Karl Baisch, Program Specialist, Studio Art Centers International (SACI), Institute of International Education, 809 United Nations Plaza, New York, NY 10017; *Phone:* 212-984-5548; *Fax:* 212-984-5325. *E-mail:* kbaisch@iie.org. *World Wide Web:* http://www.saci-florence.org/

STUDIO ART CENTERS INTERNATIONAL (SACI)
ART CONSERVATION

Hosted by Studio Art Centers International

Academic Focus • Archaeology, art conservation studies, art history, historic preservation.

Program Information • Students attend classes at Studio Art Centers International. Scheduled travel to Carra, Milan, Naples, Rome, Venice; field trips to Siena, Pisa, Bologna, Ravenna, Lucca, Assisi, Urbana, Elba.

Sessions • Fall, spring, yearlong.

Eligibility Requirements • Minimum age 18; open to freshmen, sophomores, juniors, seniors; 2.7 GPA; 2 letters of recommendation; statement of intent; official transcript; no foreign language proficiency required.

Living Arrangements • Students live in locally rented apartments. Quarters are shared with host institution students. Meals are taken on one's own, in residences.

Costs (2004-2005) • One term: $8775. Yearlong program: $17,550; includes tuition. $50 application fee. Financial aid available for all students: scholarships.

For More Information • Mr. Karl Baisch, Program Specialist, Studio Art Centers International (SACI), Institute of International Education, 809 United Nations Plaza, New York, NY 10017; *Phone:* 212-984-5548; *Fax:* 212-984-5325. *E-mail:* kbaisch@iie.org. *World Wide Web:* http://www.saci-florence.org/

STUDIO ART CENTERS INTERNATIONAL (SACI)
YEAR/SEMESTER ABROAD

Hosted by Studio Art Centers International

Academic Focus • Archaeology, architecture, art conservation studies, art history, ceramics and pottery, crafts, creative writing, design and applied arts, drawing/painting, film and media studies, fine/studio arts, graphic design/illustration, historic preservation, interior design, Italian language and literature, Italian studies, photography, visual and performing arts.

Program Information • Students attend classes at Studio Art Centers International. Scheduled travel to Carrara, Milan, Naples, Rome, Venice; field trips to Siena, Pisa, Arezzo, Bologna, Ravenna, Lucca, San Gimignano, Assisi, Urbano; optional travel to Pompeii, Amsterdam, Paris, London at an extra cost.

Sessions • Fall, spring, yearlong.

Eligibility Requirements • Minimum age 18; open to precollege students, freshmen, sophomores, juniors, seniors, graduate students, adults; 2.7 GPA; 2 letters of recommendation; statement of intent; official transcript; no foreign language proficiency required.

Living Arrangements • Students live in locally rented apartments. Quarters are shared with host institution students. Meals are taken on one's own, in residences.

Costs (2004-2005) • One term: $8775. Yearlong program: $17,550; includes tuition. $50 application fee. Financial aid available for all students: scholarships.

For More Information • Studio Art Centers International (SACI), Institute of International Education, 809 United Nations Plaza, New York, NY 10017; *Phone:* 212-984-5548; *Fax:* 212-984-5325. *E-mail:* saci@iie.org. *World Wide Web:* http://www.saci-florence.org/

STUDY ABROAD ITALY
LORENZO DE' MEDICI–THE ART INSTITUTE OF FLORENCE

Hosted by Lorenzo de' Medici–The Art Institute of Florence

Academic Focus • Full curriculum.

Program Information • Students attend classes at Lorenzo de' Medici–The Art Institute of Florence. Scheduled travel to Rome, Siena, Venice, Pompeii.

Sessions • Fall, spring, yearlong, intersession.

Eligibility Requirements • Minimum age 18; open to freshmen, sophomores, juniors, seniors, graduate students, adults; 2.5 GPA; no foreign language proficiency required.

Living Arrangements • Students live in locally rented apartments, host family homes. Quarters are shared with host institution students. Meals are taken on one's own, in residences, in restaurants.

Costs (2003-2004) • One term: $9000. Yearlong program: $18,000; includes tuition, housing, all meals, excursions, books and class materials, student support services, emergency medical and repatriation insurance. $50 application fee. $1600–$2750 refundable deposit required. Financial aid available for all students: scholarships, loans.

For More Information • Ms. Susan Mall, Admissions Officer, Study Abroad Italy, 7151 Wilton Avenue, Suite 202, Sebastopol, CA 95472; *Phone:* 707-824-8965; *Fax:* 707-824-0198. *E-mail:* smd@studyabroad-italy.com. *World Wide Web:* http://www.studyabroad-italy.com/

SYRACUSE UNIVERSITY
FLORENCE ARCHITECTURE PROGRAM

Hosted by Syracuse University Center–Florence

Academic Focus • Architecture, art history, fine/studio arts, Italian language and literature.

Program Information • Students attend classes at Syracuse University Center–Florence. Field trips to Rome, Siena, Venice, Assisi; optional travel to Verona, Mantua, Pompeii at an extra cost.

Sessions • Fall, spring, yearlong.

Eligibility Requirements • Open to juniors, seniors; course work in architecture; 2 letters of recommendation; good academic standing at home school; essays; no foreign language proficiency required.

Living Arrangements • Students live in locally rented apartments, host family homes. Meals are taken with host family, in residences.

Costs (2004-2005) • One term: $19,430. Yearlong program: $38,860; includes tuition, housing, some meals, excursions, lab

equipment, international student ID, student support services, one-way international airfare. $50 application fee. $450 nonrefundable deposit required. Financial aid available for all students: scholarships, work study, loans, tuition differential grants.

For More Information • Mr. James Buschman, Senior Associate Director, Syracuse University, 106 Walnut Place, Syracuse, NY 13244-4170; *Phone:* 315-443-3471; *Fax:* 315-443-4593. *E-mail:* suabroad@syr.edu. *World Wide Web:* http://suabroad.syr.edu/

SYRACUSE UNIVERSITY
FLORENCE ART PROGRAM

Hosted by Syracuse University Center–Florence, University of Florence

Academic Focus • Art, art history, drawing/painting, Italian language and literature, literature.

Program Information • Students attend classes at Syracuse University Center-Florence, University of Florence. Field trips to Rome, Siena, Venice, Assisi; optional travel to Verona, Mantua, Pompeii at an extra cost.

Sessions • Fall, spring, yearlong.

Eligibility Requirements • Open to freshmen, sophomores, juniors, seniors; 2 letters of recommendation; good academic standing at home school; approval of School of Visual/Performing Arts; slide portfolio; no foreign language proficiency required.

Living Arrangements • Students live in locally rented apartments, host family homes. Meals are taken with host family, in residences.

Costs (2004-2005) • One term: $19,430. Yearlong program: $38,860; includes tuition, housing, some meals, excursions, student support services, monthly bus pass, one-way international airfare. $50 application fee. $450 nonrefundable deposit required. Financial aid available for all students: scholarships, work study, loans, tuition differential grants.

For More Information • Mr. James Buschman, Senior Associate Director, Syracuse University, 106 Walnut Place, Syracuse, NY

13244-4170; *Phone:* 315-443-3471; *Fax:* 315-443-4593. *E-mail:* suabroad@syr.edu. *World Wide Web:* http://suabroad.syr.edu/

SYRACUSE UNIVERSITY
FLORENCE PROGRAM

Hosted by Syracuse University Center–Florence, University of Florence

Academic Focus • Architecture, art, art history, business administration/management, drawing/painting, fine/studio arts, history, Italian language and literature, literature, political science and government, women's studies.

Program Information • Students attend classes at Syracuse University Center-Florence, University of Florence. Field trips to Rome, Venice, Siena, Assisi; optional travel to Verona, Pompeii, Mantua at an extra cost.

Sessions • Fall, spring, yearlong.

Eligibility Requirements • Open to freshmen, sophomores, juniors, seniors, graduate students; 2 letters of recommendation; good academic standing at home school; essays; no foreign language proficiency required.

Living Arrangements • Students live in locally rented apartments, host family homes. Meals are taken with host family, in residences.

Costs (2004-2005) • One term: $19,430. Yearlong program: $38,860; includes tuition, housing, some meals, excursions, lab equipment, international student ID, student support services, monthly bus pass, one-way international airfare. $50 application fee. $450 nonrefundable deposit required. Financial aid available for all students: scholarships, work study, loans, tuition differential grants.

For More Information • Mr. James Buschman, Senior Associate Director, Syracuse University, 106 Walnut Place, Syracuse, NY 13244-4170; *Phone:* 800-235-3472; *Fax:* 315-443-4593. *E-mail:* suabroad@syr.edu. *World Wide Web:* http://suabroad.syr.edu/

SYRACUSE UNIVERSITY
PRE-ARCHITECTURE PROGRAM

Hosted by Syracuse University Center–Florence
Academic Focus • Architecture.
Program Information • Students attend classes at Syracuse University Center–Florence. Field trips to Rome, Siena, Venice, Assisi; optional travel to Verona, Mantua, Pompeii at an extra cost.
Sessions • Fall, spring, yearlong.
Eligibility Requirements • Open to sophomores, juniors, seniors, graduate students; 2 letters of recommendation; good academic standing at home school; essays; no foreign language proficiency required.
Living Arrangements • Students live in locally rented apartments, host family homes. Meals are taken with host family, in residences.
Costs (2004-2005) • One term: $19,430. Yearlong program: $38,860; includes tuition, housing, some meals, lab equipment, student support services, bus passes, one-way international airfare. $50 application fee. $450 nonrefundable deposit required. Financial aid available for all students: scholarships, work study, loans, tuition differential grants.
For More Information • Mr. James Buschman, Senior Associate Director, Syracuse University, 106 Walnut Place, Syracuse, NY 13244-4170; *Phone:* 800-235-3472; *Fax:* 315-443-4593. *E-mail:* suabroad@syr.edu. *World Wide Web:* http://suabroad.syr.edu/

UNIVERSITY OF CONNECTICUT
FLORENCE STUDY PROGRAM–SEMESTER OR YEAR

Hosted by University of Florence
Academic Focus • Full curriculum.
Program Information • Students attend classes at University of Florence. Classes are also held on the campus of University of Connecticut Florence Center. Scheduled travel to Venice, Naples; field trips to Siena, San Gimignano.
Sessions • Fall, spring, yearlong.
Eligibility Requirements • Open to sophomores, juniors, seniors; 2.5 GPA; 2 letters of recommendation; good academic standing at home school; 1 year college course work in Italian for spring session; no foreign language proficiency requirement for full semester.
Living Arrangements • Students live in locally rented apartments. Quarters are shared with host institution students. Meals are taken on one's own, in residences, in restaurants.
Costs (2003-2004) • One term: $9940. Yearlong program: $19,700; includes tuition, housing, all meals, insurance, excursions, fees, one-way airfare. $25 application fee. $350 nonrefundable deposit required. Financial aid available for students from sponsoring institution: scholarships, loans.
For More Information • Mr. Gordon Lustila, Acting Director of Study Abroad Programs, University of Connecticut, 843 Bolton Road, Unit 1207, Storrs, CT 06269-1207; *Phone:* 860-486-5022; *Fax:* 860-486-2976. *E-mail:* sabadm03@uconnvm.uconn.edu. *World Wide Web:* http://studyabroad.uconn.edu/

UNIVERSITY OF MICHIGAN
UNIVERSITY OF MICHIGAN/UNIVERSITY OF WISCONSIN/ DUKE UNIVERSITY ACADEMIC YEAR PROGRAM IN FLORENCE, ITALY

Held at Villa Corsi Salviati
Academic Focus • Art history, film and media studies, fine/studio arts, Italian language and literature, Italian studies, social sciences.
Program Information • Classes are held on the campus of Villa Corsi Salviati. Faculty members are drawn from the sponsor's U.S. staff and local instructors hired by the sponsor. Field trips to Rome, Assisi, Siena.
Sessions • Fall, winter.
Eligibility Requirements • Open to sophomores, juniors, seniors; 3.0 GPA; 2 letters of recommendation; good academic standing at home school; official transcripts from all colleges attended; no foreign language proficiency required.
Living Arrangements • Students live in Villa Corsi Salviati, Sesto Fiorentino. Quarters are shared with host institution students. Meals are taken as a group, in central dining facility.
Costs (2002-2003) • One term: contact sponsor for cost. $50 application fee. $250 nonrefundable deposit required. Financial aid available for students from sponsoring institution: scholarships, work study, loans, application fee waiver.
For More Information • University of Michigan, Office of International Programs, G-513 Michigan Union, 530 South State Street, Ann Arbor, MI 48109-1349; *Phone:* 734-764-4311; *Fax:* 734-764-3229. *E-mail:* oip@umich.edu. *World Wide Web:* http://www.umich.edu/~iinet/oip/

UNIVERSITY OF MINNESOTA
STUDY ABROAD IN FLORENCE

Held at Centers for Academic Programs Abroad (CAPA)
Academic Focus • Art, art history, international business, Italian language and literature, Italian studies, political science and government.
Program Information • Classes are held on the campus of Centers for Academic Programs Abroad (CAPA). Faculty members are local instructors hired by the sponsor. Field trips to Siena, San Gimignano; optional travel to other cities in Italy as well as neighboring countries at an extra cost.
Sessions • Fall, spring, yearlong.
Eligibility Requirements • Minimum age 18; open to freshmen, sophomores, juniors, seniors; 2.5 GPA; good academic standing at home school; no foreign language proficiency required.
Living Arrangements • Students live in locally rented apartments. Quarters are shared with host institution students. Meals are taken on one's own, in residences.
Costs (2005) • One term: $8200 for University of Minnesota students; $8300 for non-University of Minnesota students. Yearlong program: contact sponsor for cost; includes tuition, housing, insurance, student support services, some books and class materials. $50 application fee. $400 nonrefundable deposit required. Financial aid available for students from sponsoring institution: scholarships.
For More Information • University of Minnesota, Learning Abroad Center, 230 Heller Hall, 271 19th Avenue South, Minneapolis, MN 55455; *Phone:* 612-626-9000; *Fax:* 612-626-8009. *E-mail:* umabroad@umn.edu. *World Wide Web:* http://www.umabroad.umn.edu/

THE UNIVERSITY OF NORTH CAROLINA AT CHAPEL HILL
STUDY ABROAD AT THE LORENZO DE' MEDICI INSTITUTE

Hosted by Lorenzo de' Medici–The Art Institute of Florence
Academic Focus • European studies, international affairs, Italian language and literature, Italian studies, social sciences.
Program Information • Students attend classes at Lorenzo de' Medici–The Art Institute of Florence. Field trips to Rome, Venice, Tuscan villages.
Sessions • Fall, spring, yearlong.
Eligibility Requirements • Open to sophomores, juniors, seniors, graduate students, adults; 2.7 GPA; 2 letters of recommendation; good academic standing at home school; essay; transcript; no foreign language proficiency required.
Living Arrangements • Students live in locally rented apartments, host family homes. Quarters are shared with host institution students. Meals are taken on one's own, with host family, in residences, in restaurants.
Costs (2003-2004) • One term: $9593. Yearlong program: $18,706; includes tuition, housing, insurance, excursions, study abroad fee. $100 application fee. $500 nonrefundable deposit required. Financial aid available for students from sponsoring institution: scholarships, loans.
For More Information • Study Abroad Office, The University of North Carolina at Chapel Hill, 201 Porthole Building, CB 3130, Chapel Hill, NC 27599-3130; *Phone:* 919-962-7002; *Fax:* 919-962-2262. *E-mail:* abroad@unc.edu. *World Wide Web:* http://studyabroad.unc.edu/

WALLA WALLA COLLEGE
ADVENTIST COLLEGES ABROAD

Hosted by Instituto Avventista Villa Aurora
Academic Focus • Full curriculum, Italian language and literature.
Program Information • Students attend classes at Instituto Avventista Villa Aurora. Scheduled travel to Siena, Chianti, Rome, Venice; optional travel at an extra cost.
Sessions • Yearlong.

Eligibility Requirements • Open to freshmen, sophomores, juniors, seniors; 2.5 GPA; 3 letters of recommendation; good academic standing at home school; minimum 3.0 GPA in Italian; 1 year of college course work in Italian.

Living Arrangements • Students live in host institution dormitories. Quarters are shared with host institution students, students from other programs. Meals are taken as a group, in central dining facility.

Costs (2002-2003) • Yearlong program: contact sponsor for cost. $100 nonrefundable deposit required. Financial aid available for all students: scholarships, loans.

For More Information • Mr. Jean-Paul Grimaud, Chair of Modern Language Department, Walla Walla College, 204 South College Avenue, College Place, WA 99324; *Phone:* 509-529-7769; *Fax:* 509-527-2253. *E-mail:* grimje@wwc.edu

WASHINGTON UNIVERSITY SCHOOL OF ART
ART HISTORY PROGRAM IN FLORENCE

Hosted by Washington University Art Center

Academic Focus • Art conservation studies, art history, Italian language and literature, Italian studies.

Program Information • Students attend classes at Washington University Art Center. Scheduled travel to Siena, Rome, Venice; field trips to Siena, Rome, Venice; optional travel to Pompeii.

Sessions • Fall.

Eligibility Requirements • Minimum age 18; open to sophomores, juniors, seniors; major in art history (or minor in art history); course work in introductory course in western art; 3.0 GPA; 2 letters of recommendation; good academic standing at home school; 0.5 years of college course work in Italian.

Living Arrangements • Students live in locally rented apartments, host family homes. Quarters are shared with host institution students. Meals are taken on one's own, in residences, in restaurants.

Costs (2005) • One term: $22,500; includes tuition, excursions, lab equipment, student support services. $225 application fee. $275 nonrefundable deposit required. Financial aid available for students from sponsoring institution: scholarships, loans.

For More Information • Ms. Belinda Lee, Assistant Dean of Undergraduate Programs and Advising, Washington University School of Art, Campus Box 1031, One Brookings Drive, St. Louis, MO 63130-4899; *Phone:* 314-935-4643; *Fax:* 314-935-4862. *E-mail:* bslee@art.wustl.edu. *World Wide Web:* http://www.artsci.wustl.edu/~overseas/program_descrips/florence.html

WELLS COLLEGE
FLORENCE PROGRAM

Hosted by Lorenzo de' Medici–The Art Institute of Florence

Academic Focus • Architecture, art conservation studies, art history, ceramics and pottery, civilization studies, classics and classical languages, communications, crafts, culinary arts, fashion design, film and media studies, fine/studio arts, interior design, international affairs, international business, Italian language and literature, liberal studies, performing arts, political science and government, social sciences, women's studies.

Program Information • Students attend classes at Lorenzo de' Medici–The Art Institute of Florence. Scheduled travel to Rome; field trips to Pompeii, Rome, Sorrento, Amalfi, San Gimignano, Assisi, Siena; optional travel to Venice, San Marino, Ravenna at an extra cost.

Sessions • Fall, spring, yearlong.

Eligibility Requirements • Minimum age 18; open to precollege students, freshmen, sophomores, juniors, seniors, adults; 2.7 GPA; 2 letters of recommendation; good academic standing at home school; transcript; no foreign language proficiency required.

Living Arrangements • Students live in locally rented apartments, host family homes. Quarters are shared with host institution students. Meals are taken as a group, on one's own, with host family.

Costs (2004-2005) • One term: $14,990. Yearlong program: contact sponsor for cost; includes tuition, housing, some meals, excursions, international airfare, student support services, cultural and social activities. $50 application fee. $1000 deposit required. Financial aid available for students from sponsoring institution: scholarships, loans.

For More Information • Dr. Giorgio Renzi, Director, Florence Program, Wells College, 52 Rose Terrace, Chatham, NJ 07928; *Phone:* 973-665-0089; *Fax:* 973-665-1258. *E-mail:* florence-program@wells.edu. *World Wide Web:* http://www.wells.edu/academic/ac2d.htm

L'AQUILA
UNIVERSITY OF MIAMI
UNIVERSITY OF L'AQUILA, ITALY

Hosted by University of L'Aquila
Academic Focus • Art history, economics, history, Italian language and literature, literature.
Program Information • Students attend classes at University of L'Aquila.
Sessions • Fall, spring, yearlong.
Eligibility Requirements • Minimum age 18; open to sophomores, juniors, seniors; 2 letters of recommendation; good academic standing at home school; essay; 3 years college course work in Italian or near fluency.
Living Arrangements • Quarters are shared with host institution students, students from other programs. Meals are taken on one's own, in residences, in restaurants.
Costs (2003-2004) • One term: $12,919. Yearlong program: $25,838; includes tuition, student support services. $40 application fee. $500 nonrefundable deposit required. Financial aid available for students from sponsoring institution: scholarships, loans.

For More Information • Ms. Elyse Resnick, Assistant Director, University of Miami, International Education and Exchange Programs, 5050 Brunson Drive, Allen Hall 212, PO Box 248005, Coral Gables, FL 33124-1610; *Phone:* 305-284-3434; *Fax:* 305-284-4235. *E-mail:* ieep@miami.edu. *World Wide Web:* http://www.studyabroad.miami.edu/

MACERATA
AHA INTERNATIONAL AN ACADEMIC PROGRAM OF THE UNIVERSITY OF OREGON
PROGRAM IN MACERATA, ITALY: MIDWEST CONSORTIUM FOR STUDY ABROAD AND NORTHWEST COUNCIL ON STUDY ABROAD

Hosted by AHA Macerata Center, University of Macerata
Academic Focus • Art history, communications, economics, English, film and media studies, fine/studio arts, history, Italian language and literature, Italian studies, literature, telecommunications.
Program Information • Students attend classes at University of Macerata, AHA Macerata Center. Scheduled travel to Rome, Florence; field trips to Ancona, Assisi, Urbino, Loreto.
Sessions • Fall, winter, yearlong.
Eligibility Requirements • Open to sophomores, juniors, seniors, adults; 2 letters of recommendation; good academic standing at home school; foreign language proficiency requirement varies depending on enrolling university.
Living Arrangements • Students live in locally rented apartments, host family homes. Quarters are shared with host institution students. Meals are taken on one's own, in residences, in central dining facility, in restaurants.
Costs (2003-2004) • One term: $6930 for fall term; $7275 for winter. Yearlong program: $14,205; includes tuition, housing,

insurance, excursions, books and class materials, international student ID, student support services, local transportation pass. $50 application fee. $200 refundable deposit required. Financial aid available for students: scholarships, loans, home institution financial aid.

For More Information • Ms. Gail Lavin, Associate Director for University Programs, AHA International An Academic Program of the University of Oregon, 741 SW Lincoln Street, Portland, OR 97201; *Phone:* 503-295-7730; *Fax:* 503-295-5969. *E-mail:* mail@aha-intl.org. *World Wide Web:* http://www.aha-intl.org/

MESSINA

STONY BROOK UNIVERSITY
UNIVERSITY OF MESSINA, SICILY EXCHANGE

Hosted by University of Messina
Academic Focus • Full curriculum.
Program Information • Students attend classes at University of Messina.
Sessions • Fall, spring, yearlong.
Eligibility Requirements • Open to juniors, seniors, graduate students; 2.5 GPA; 3 letters of recommendation; good academic standing at home school; essay; 2 years of college course work in Italian.
Living Arrangements • Students live in host institution dormitories. Meals are taken on one's own, in residences.
Costs (2002-2003) • One term: $4500–$5000. Yearlong program: $9000–$11,000; includes tuition, housing, some meals. $200 nonrefundable deposit required. Financial aid available for students from sponsoring institution: loans.
For More Information • Mr. Alfredo Varela, Assistant Dean, Stony Brook University, Study Abroad Office, Melville Library, Room E5340, Stony Brook, NY 11794-3397; *Phone:* 631-632-7030; *Fax:* 631-632-6544. *E-mail:* studyabroad@sunysb.edu. *World Wide Web:* http://www.sunysb.edu/studyabroad/

MILAN

IES, INSTITUTE FOR THE INTERNATIONAL EDUCATION OF STUDENTS
IES–MILAN, ADVANCED ITALIAN PROGRAM

Hosted by Academia Internazionale della Musica, Institute for the International Education of Students (IES)–Milan, Conservatorio G. Verdi, Scuola Musicale di Milano, Scuola Politecnica di Design, University of Commerce "Luigi Bocconi" Milan, Catholic University of the Sacred Heart Milan, Libera Università di Lingue e Comunicazione IULM
Academic Focus • Architecture, art, art history, business administration/management, cinematography, communications, computer science, design and applied arts, drama/theater, economics, European studies, fashion merchandising, finance, international affairs, Italian language and literature, Italian studies, marketing, music, political science and government, social sciences.
Program Information • Students attend classes at University of Commerce "Luigi Bocconi" Milan, Catholic University of the Sacred Heart Milan, Libera Università di Lingue e Comunicazione IULM, Academia Internazionale della Musica, Conservatorio G. Verdi, Institute for the International Education of Students (IES)–Milan, Scuola Musicale di Milano, Scuola Politecnica di Design. Field trips to Lago Maggiore, Dolomites, Tuscany, Bormio, the Abbeys of Lombardy, the Italian Riviera, the Italian Alps.
Sessions • Fall, spring, yearlong.
Eligibility Requirements • Minimum age 18; open to sophomores, juniors, seniors, graduate students, adults; 3.0 GPA; 1 letter of recommendation; good academic standing at home school; 2 years of college course work in Italian.
Living Arrangements • Students live in locally rented apartments. Quarters are shared with host institution students. Meals are taken on one's own, in residences, in restaurants.
Costs (2003-2004) • One term: $11,440. Yearlong program: $20,592; includes tuition, housing, excursions, student support services, partial insurance coverage. $50 application fee. $500 nonrefundable deposit required. Financial aid available for all students: scholarships, institutional partner need-based grants.

For More Information • International Education Representative, IES, Institute for the International Education of Students, 33 North LaSalle Street, 15th Floor, Chicago, IL 60602; *Phone:* 800-995-2300; *Fax:* 312-944-1448. *E-mail:* info@iesabroad.org. *World Wide Web:* http://www.IESabroad.org/

IES, INSTITUTE FOR THE INTERNATIONAL EDUCATION OF STUDENTS
IES–MILAN, BEGINNING AND INTERMEDIATE ITALIAN PROGRAM

Hosted by Institute for the International Education of Students (IES)–Milan
Academic Focus • Art history, design and applied arts, film and media studies, history, Italian language and literature, music, music history, music performance, political science and government, psychology.
Program Information • Students attend classes at Institute for the International Education of Students (IES)–Milan. Field trips to Lago, Dolomites, Tuscany, Abbeys of Lombardy, the Italian Alps, the Italian Riviera, Lago Maggiore.
Sessions • Fall, spring, yearlong.
Eligibility Requirements • Minimum age 18; open to sophomores, juniors, seniors, graduate students, adults; 3.0 GPA; 1 letter of recommendation; good academic standing at home school; no foreign language proficiency required.
Living Arrangements • Students live in locally rented apartments. Quarters are shared with host institution students. Meals are taken on one's own, in residences, in restaurants.
Costs (2003-2004) • One term: $11,440. Yearlong program: $20,592; includes tuition, housing, excursions, student support services, partial insurance coverage. $50 application fee. $500 nonrefundable deposit required. Financial aid available for all students: scholarships, institutional partner need-based grants.
For More Information • International Education Representative, IES, Institute for the International Education of Students, 33 North LaSalle Street, 15th Floor, Chicago, IL 60602; *Phone:* 800-995-2300; *Fax:* 312-944-1448. *E-mail:* info@iesabroad.org. *World Wide Web:* http://www.IESabroad.org/

NUOVO ACCADEMIA DI BELLE ARTI
SEMESTER STUDY ABROAD

Hosted by Nuovo Accademia di Belle Arti
Academic Focus • Design and applied arts, fashion design, fine/studio arts, interior design.
Program Information • Students attend classes at Nuovo Accademia di Belle Arti. Scheduled travel to Venice, Rome, Florence; field trips to Venice, Rome, Florence; optional travel to sites all over Italy at an extra cost.
Sessions • Fall, spring, yearlong.
Eligibility Requirements • Minimum age 18; open to freshmen, sophomores, juniors, seniors, graduate students, adults; 2.0 GPA; 1 letter of recommendation; good academic standing at home school; basic knowledge of Italian recommended.
Living Arrangements • Students live in locally rented apartments, hotels. Quarters are shared with host institution students. Meals are taken on one's own, in residences, in restaurants.
Costs (2003) • One term: €3900. Yearlong program: €5900; includes tuition, lab equipment, student support services. €1500 nonrefundable deposit required.
For More Information • Ms. Adrian Kiger, International Relations, Nuovo Accademia di Belle Arti, Via Darwin 20, 20143 Milan, Italy; *Phone:* +39 333-200 8099; *Fax:* +39 03-6684413. *E-mail:* int.info@naba.it. *World Wide Web:* http://www.naba.it/

PADUA

BOSTON UNIVERSITY
PADOVA LANGUAGE AND LIBERAL ARTS PROGRAM

Hosted by University of Padua
Academic Focus • Art history, Italian language and literature, Italian studies, liberal studies, social sciences.

Program Information • Students attend classes at University of Padua. Scheduled travel to various destinations; field trips to Venice, Verona, Vicenza, Treviso.
Sessions • Fall, spring, yearlong.
Eligibility Requirements • Open to sophomores, juniors, seniors, adults; 3.0 GPA; 2 letters of recommendation; good academic standing at home school; essay; writing sample in Italian; approval of participation; transcript; 1 year of college course work in Italian.
Living Arrangements • Students live in host institution dormitories, host family homes. Meals are taken on one's own, with host family, in residences, in central dining facility.
Costs (2004-2005) • One term: $19,834. Yearlong program: $39,668; includes tuition, housing, all meals, excursions, international airfare. $50 application fee. $400 nonrefundable deposit required. Financial aid available for all students: scholarships, loans.
For More Information • Division of International Programs, Boston University, 232 Bay State Road, Boston, MA 02215; *Phone:* 617-353-9888; *Fax:* 617-353-5402. *E-mail:* abroad@bu.edu. *World Wide Web:* http://www.bu.edu/abroad/

PARMA

PITZER COLLEGE
PITZER COLLEGE IN ITALY

Hosted by University of Modena, University of Parma
Academic Focus • Art history, fine/studio arts, history, Italian language and literature, Italian studies, political science and government, sociology.
Program Information • Students attend classes at University of Modena, University of Parma. Scheduled travel to Rome, Naples, Pompeii; field trips to Parma or Modena, Florence, Venice.
Sessions • Fall, spring, yearlong.
Eligibility Requirements • Open to juniors, seniors; course work in area studies; 2.5 GPA; 2 letters of recommendation; good academic standing at home school; previous Italian study recommended.
Living Arrangements • Students live in host family homes. Meals are taken with host family, in residences.
Costs (2003-2004) • One term: $18,795. Yearlong program: $37,590; includes tuition, housing, all meals, excursions, international airfare, books and class materials, international student ID, student support services. $25 application fee. $500 nonrefundable deposit required. Financial aid available for students from sponsoring institution: scholarships, loans.
For More Information • Ms. Neva Barker, Director of External Studies Admissions, Pitzer College, 1050 North Mills Avenue, Claremont, CA 91711; *Phone:* 909-621-8104; *Fax:* 909-621-0518. *E-mail:* external_studies@pitzer.edu. *World Wide Web:* http://www.pitzer.edu/external_studies/

PERUGIA

ARCADIA UNIVERSITY
UMBRA INSTITUTE, PERUGIA

Hosted by The Umbra Institute
Academic Focus • Liberal studies.
Program Information • Students attend classes at The Umbra Institute. Field trips; optional travel at an extra cost.
Sessions • Fall, spring, yearlong.
Eligibility Requirements • Open to sophomores, juniors, seniors; 3.0 GPA; 1 letter of recommendation; no foreign language proficiency required.
Living Arrangements • Students live in locally rented apartments. Quarters are shared with host institution students. Meals are taken on one's own, in residences.
Costs (2003-2004) • One term: $10,290. Yearlong program: $18,450; includes tuition, housing, insurance, international student ID, student support services, pre-departure guide, transcript. $35 application fee. $500 nonrefundable deposit required. Financial aid available for all students: scholarships, loans.
For More Information • Arcadia University, Center for Education Abroad, 450 South Easton Road, Glenside, PA 19038-3295; *Phone:* 866-927-2234; *Fax:* 215-572-2174. *E-mail:* cea@arcadia.edu. *World Wide Web:* http://www.arcadia.edu/cea/

EUROPEAN HERITAGE INSTITUTE
ACADEMIC YEAR IN PERUGIA

Hosted by University for Foreigners Perugia
Academic Focus • Civilization studies, commerce, history, Italian language and literature, Italian studies.
Program Information • Students attend classes at University for Foreigners Perugia. Field trips to Umbria, Tuscany, southern Italy; optional travel to Venice, southern Italy, Rome at an extra cost.
Sessions • Fall, spring, winter, yearlong.
Eligibility Requirements • Minimum age 18; open to freshmen, sophomores, juniors, seniors, graduate students, adults; 2.5 GPA; 2 letters of recommendation; no foreign language proficiency required.
Living Arrangements • Students live in locally rented apartments, host family homes. Quarters are shared with host institution students. Meals are taken on one's own, in central dining facility.
Costs (2004-2005) • One term: $2000 for 3 months; $3050 for 6 months. Yearlong program: $4050 for academic year; $5000 for full year; includes tuition, insurance, student support services, 1-month standard housing. $300 refundable deposit required.
For More Information • Dr. Antonio Masullo, Professor, European Heritage Institute, 2708 East Franklin Street, Richmond, VA 23223; *Phone:* 804-643-0661; *Fax:* 804-648-0826. *E-mail:* euritage@i2020.net. *World Wide Web:* http://www.europeabroad.org/

ROME

ACADEMIC PROGRAMS INTERNATIONAL (API)
(API)–JOHN CABOT UNIVERSITY IN ROME, ITALY

Hosted by John Cabot University
Academic Focus • Full curriculum.
Program Information • Students attend classes at John Cabot University. Scheduled travel to Florence; field trips to Tivoli, Capri, Perugia, Cortona, Ponza, Naples, Sorrento, Pompeii, Amalfi Coast.
Sessions • Fall, spring, yearlong.
Eligibility Requirements • Minimum age 18; open to freshmen, sophomores, juniors, seniors, graduate students, adults; 2.75 GPA; 1 letter of recommendation; good academic standing at home school; official transcript from home university; no foreign language proficiency required.
Living Arrangements • Students live in locally rented apartments. Quarters are shared with host institution students, students from other programs. Meals are taken on one's own, in residences.
Costs (2005-2006) • One term: $13,900–$13,950. Yearlong program: $26,900; includes tuition, housing, insurance, excursions, student support services, ground transportation, language course, airport pick-up. $150 nonrefundable deposit required. Financial aid available for all students: scholarships.
For More Information • Ms. Jennifer C. Allen, Director, Academic Programs International (API), 107 East Hopkins, San Marcos, TX 78666; *Phone:* 800-844-4124; *Fax:* 512-392-8420. *E-mail:* api@academicintl.com. *World Wide Web:* http://www.academicintl.com/

AMERICAN INSTITUTE FOR FOREIGN STUDY (AIFS)
RICHMOND IN ROME

Hosted by Richmond Study Center
Academic Focus • Art history, economics, history, Italian language and literature, literature, political science and government.
Program Information • Students attend classes at Richmond Study Center. Scheduled travel to London; field trips to Naples, Pompeii, Venice, Ravenna.
Sessions • Fall, spring, yearlong.
Eligibility Requirements • Minimum age 17; open to sophomores, juniors, seniors; 2.5 GPA; 1 letter of recommendation; good academic standing at home school; no foreign language proficiency required.
Living Arrangements • Students live in locally rented apartments, host family homes. Quarters are shared with host institution students. Meals are taken on one's own, in restaurants.
Costs (2004-2005) • One term: $12,995. Yearlong program: $23,790; includes tuition, housing, some meals, insurance, excursions, student support services, one-way airfare, 2-day London

stopover. $75 application fee. $350 nonrefundable deposit required. Financial aid available for all students: scholarships.

For More Information • Mr. David Mauro, Admissions Advisor, American Institute For Foreign Study (AIFS), 9 West Broad Street, Stamford, CT 06902-3788; *Phone:* 800-727-2437 Ext. 5163; *Fax:* 203-399-5597. *E-mail:* dmauro@aifs.com. *World Wide Web:* http://www.aifsabroad.com/

AMERICAN UNIVERSITY
SEMESTER IN ROME

Hosted by John Cabot University

Academic Focus • Architecture, art, drama/theater, film and media studies, history, Italian language and literature, literature, music, political science and government, sociology.

Program Information • Students attend classes at John Cabot University. Scheduled travel; optional travel at an extra cost.

Sessions • Fall, spring, yearlong.

Eligibility Requirements • Open to sophomores, juniors, seniors, graduate students; 2.75 GPA; 1 letter of recommendation; second semester sophomore status; recommendation of advisor; no foreign language proficiency required.

Living Arrangements • Students live in locally rented apartments. Quarters are shared with students from other programs. Meals are taken on one's own, in residences, in restaurants.

Costs (2002-2003) • One term: $16,459. Yearlong program: $32,918; includes tuition, housing, student support services. $35 application fee. $300 nonrefundable deposit required. Financial aid available for all students: scholarships, loans.

For More Information • Dr. David C. Brown, Dean, Washington Semester and World Capitals Programs, American University, Tenley Campus–Constitution Building, Washington, DC 20016-8083; *Phone:* 800-424-2600; *Fax:* 202-895-4960. *E-mail:* travel@american.edu. *World Wide Web:* http://www.worldcapitals.american.edu/

THE AMERICAN UNIVERSITY OF ROME
STUDY ABROAD AT THE AMERICAN UNIVERSITY OF ROME

Hosted by The American University of Rome

Academic Focus • Full curriculum.

Program Information • Students attend classes at The American University of Rome. Scheduled travel to Siena, Bologna, Ravenna, Ferrara; field trips to Venice, Pompeii, Florence.

Sessions • Fall, spring, yearlong.

Eligibility Requirements • Open to freshmen, sophomores, juniors, seniors, adults; 2.5 GPA; 1 letter of recommendation; good academic standing at home school; personal statement; no foreign language proficiency required.

Living Arrangements • Students live in locally rented apartments. Quarters are shared with host institution students, students from other programs. Meals are taken on one's own, in restaurants.

Costs (2002-2003) • One term: $10,815 (estimated). Yearlong program: $20,000 (estimated); includes tuition, housing, all meals, excursions, books and class materials, activity fee, registration fee, local transportation. $55 application fee. $350 nonrefundable deposit required. Financial aid available for all students: loans.

For More Information • Ms. Mara Nisdeo, Assistant Director of Admissions, The American University of Rome, Via Pietro Roselli, 4, 00153 Rome, Italy; *Phone:* +39 06-58330919; *Fax:* +39 06-58330992. *E-mail:* admissions@aur.edu. *World Wide Web:* http://www.aur.edu/

ARCADIA UNIVERSITY
ROME

Academic Focus • Business administration/management, fine/studio arts, history, political science and government.

Program Information • Faculty members are local instructors hired by the sponsor.

Sessions • Fall, spring, yearlong.

Eligibility Requirements • Open to sophomores, juniors, seniors; 3.0 GPA; 1 letter of recommendation; no foreign language proficiency required.

Living Arrangements • Students live in locally rented apartments. Quarters are shared with students from other programs. Meals are taken on one's own, in residences, in restaurants.

Costs (2003-2004) • One term: $10,300. Yearlong program: $18,500; includes tuition, housing, insurance, excursions, interna-

tional student ID, student support services, field study expenses, transcripts, pre-departure guide. $35 application fee. $500 nonrefundable deposit required. Financial aid available for all students: scholarships, loans.

For More Information • Arcadia University, Center for Education Abroad, 450 South Easton Road, Glenside, PA 19038; *Phone:* 866-927-2234; *Fax:* 215-572-2174. *E-mail:* cea@arcadia.edu. *World Wide Web:* http://www.arcadia.edu/cea/

COLLEGE CONSORTIUM FOR INTERNATIONAL STUDIES–COLLEGE OF STATEN ISLAND/CITY UNIVERSITY OF NEW YORK
PROGRAM IN ROME, ITALY

Hosted by The American University of Rome

Academic Focus • Accounting, architecture, art history, business administration/management, communications, drama/theater, economics, European studies, film and media studies, finance, history, international affairs, international business, Italian language and literature, Italian studies, marketing, political science and government.

Program Information • Students attend classes at The American University of Rome. Scheduled travel to Pompeii, Paestum, Tuscany, Umbria, Capri, Naples; field trips to sites in Rome and environs; optional travel to Florence, Venice at an extra cost.

Sessions • Fall, spring, yearlong.

Eligibility Requirements • Minimum age 18; open to freshmen, sophomores, juniors, seniors; 2.5 GPA; 3 letters of recommendation; essay; transcript; no foreign language proficiency required.

Living Arrangements • Students live in locally rented apartments. Quarters are shared with host institution students, students from other programs. Meals are taken on one's own, in residences, in restaurants.

Costs (2004-2005) • One term: $6760. Yearlong program: $13,412; includes tuition, insurance, student support services, fees, one field trip. $265 nonrefundable deposit required. Financial aid available for students from sponsoring institution: loans, grants.

For More Information • College Consortium for International Studies, 2000 P Street, NW, Suite 503, Washington, DC 20036; *Phone:* 800-453-6956; *Fax:* 202-223-0999. *E-mail:* info@ccisabroad.org. *World Wide Web:* http://www.ccisabroad.org/. Students may also apply through College of Staten Island, The City University of New York, Center for International Service, Building 2A, Room 206, 2800 Victory Boulevard, Staten Island, NY 10314.

CORNELL UNIVERSITY
CORNELL IN ROME

Hosted by Cornell University–Rome

Academic Focus • Architecture, art, art history, drawing/painting, fine/studio arts, Italian language and literature, liberal studies, urban studies, urban/regional planning.

Program Information • Students attend classes at Cornell University–Rome. Scheduled travel to Tuscany, Sicily, Florence, Venice, northern Italy; field trips to Tarquinia, Cerveteri, Ostia Antica, Hadrian's Villa, Palestrina, Caprarola, Napoli, Pompeii.

Sessions • Fall, spring, yearlong.

Eligibility Requirements • Open to juniors, seniors, graduate students; major in architecture (5 year program); course work in studio work (3 years) for architecture studio program; 2.8 GPA; 2 letters of recommendation; good academic standing at home school; non-Cornell fine arts/architecture students must submit a portfolio; at least 1 semester of Italian is strongly encouraged.

Living Arrangements • Students live in locally rented apartments. Quarters are shared with host institution students. Meals are taken on one's own, in residences, in restaurants.

Costs (2004-2005) • One term: $25,700 (estimated). Yearlong program: $51,400; includes tuition, housing, all meals, insurance, excursions, international airfare, books and class materials, lab equipment, student support services, transportation in Italy, personal expenses, studio supplies. $300 nonrefundable deposit required. Financial aid available for students from sponsoring institution: scholarships, work study, loans.

For More Information • Ms. Margherita Fabrizio, Coordinator, Cornell University, 149 East Sibley Hall, Ithaca, NY 14853-7601;

Phone: 607-255-6807; *Fax:* 607-255-8476. *E-mail:* romeprogram@cornell.edu. *World Wide Web:* http://www.cuabroad.cornell.edu/

DRAKE UNIVERSITY
INSTITUTE OF ITALIAN STUDIES–ROME

Hosted by Institute of Italian Studies–Rome, The American University of Rome

Academic Focus • International affairs, international business, Italian language and literature, Italian studies, liberal studies, music.

Program Information • Students attend classes at Institute of Italian Studies–Rome, The American University of Rome. Optional travel to Naples, Florence, Venice at an extra cost.

Sessions • Fall, spring, yearlong.

Eligibility Requirements • Minimum age 19; open to sophomores, juniors, seniors; course work in liberal arts, business administration/management, journalism; 2.5 GPA; no foreign language proficiency required.

Living Arrangements • Students live in host institution dormitories, locally rented apartments, host family homes. Quarters are shared with host institution students, students from other programs. Meals are taken on one's own, in residences, in restaurants.

Costs (2003-2004) • One term: $6300. Yearlong program: $11,900; includes tuition. $35 application fee. $500 refundable deposit required.

For More Information • Mr. Rich Soria, Director, Drake University, PO Box 27077, West Des Moines, IA 50265; *Phone:* 800-443-7253 Ext. 3984; *Fax:* 515-225-0196. *E-mail:* drakeiis@drake.edu. *World Wide Web:* http://www.mac.drake.edu/iis/

DUKE UNIVERSITY
INTERCOLLEGIATE CENTER FOR CLASSICAL STUDIES IN ROME (ICCS)

Held at Intercollegiate Center for Classical Studies

Academic Focus • Art history, classics and classical languages, Italian language and literature.

Program Information • Classes are held on the campus of Intercollegiate Center for Classical Studies. Faculty members are drawn from the sponsor's U.S. staff and local instructors hired by the sponsor. Scheduled travel to Campania, Sicily; optional travel to other parts of Italy, France, Greece at an extra cost.

Sessions • Fall, spring.

Eligibility Requirements • Open to sophomores, juniors, seniors; major in classics, art, archaeology; course work in Roman history; 3.0 GPA; 2 letters of recommendation; no foreign language proficiency required.

Living Arrangements • Students live in a program building. Meals are taken as a group, in central dining facility.

Costs (2003-2004) • One term: $14,238 for consortium members; $14,538 for nonmembers; includes tuition, housing, some meals, excursions. $250 nonrefundable deposit required. Financial aid available for all students: scholarships.

For More Information • Mr. Kurt Olausen, Assistant Director, Duke University, Office of Study Abroad, 2016 Campus Drive, Box 90057, Durham, NC 27708-0057; *Phone:* 919-684-2174; *Fax:* 919-684-3083. *E-mail:* kolausen@asdean.duke.edu. *World Wide Web:* http://www.aas.duke.edu/study_abroad/

IES, INSTITUTE FOR THE INTERNATIONAL EDUCATION OF STUDENTS
IES–ROME

Hosted by University of Rome, Rome University of Fine Arts (RUFA), Free International University of Social Studies 'Guido Carli', Institute for the International Education of Students (IES)–Rome

Academic Focus • Art history, business administration/management, communications, economics, fine/studio arts, history, international affairs, Italian language and literature, Italian studies, political science and government, psychology, religious studies, sociology.

Program Information • Students attend classes at Free International University of Social Studies 'Guido Carli', Institute for the International Education of Students (IES)–Rome, Rome University of Fine Arts (RUFA), University of Rome. Scheduled travel to Sicily, Venice, Florence, Ravenna, Pompeii; field trips.

Sessions • Fall, spring, yearlong.

Eligibility Requirements • Minimum age 18; open to sophomores, juniors, seniors, graduate students, adults; 3.0 GPA; 1 letter of recommendation; good academic standing at home school; no foreign language proficiency required.

Living Arrangements • Students live in locally rented apartments, host family homes. Meals are taken with host family, in residences.

Costs (2003-2004) • One term: $11,440. Yearlong program: $20,592; includes tuition, housing, some meals, excursions, student support services, partial insurance coverage. $50 application fee. $500 nonrefundable deposit required. Financial aid available for all students: scholarships, institutional partner need-based grants.

For More Information • International Education Representative, IES, Institute for the International Education of Students, 33 North LaSalle Street 15th Floor, Chicago, IL 60602; *Phone:* 800-995-2300; *Fax:* 312-944-1448. *E-mail:* info@iesabroad.org. *World Wide Web:* http://www.IESabroad.org/

LEXIA INTERNATIONAL
LEXIA IN ROME

Hosted by Instituto Italiano

Academic Focus • Ancient history, anthropology, area studies, art, art conservation studies, art history, civilization studies, classics and classical languages, comparative history, cultural studies, drawing/painting, economics, environmental science/studies, ethnic studies, European studies, film and media studies, fine/studio arts, history, hospitality services, interdisciplinary studies, international affairs, international business, Italian language and literature, Italian studies, liberal studies, literature, music, music history, music performance, philosophy, political science and government, psychology, religious studies, social sciences, urban studies, visual and performing arts.

Program Information • Students attend classes at Instituto Italiano. Field trips to Florence, Venice, Sorrento, southern Italy.

Sessions • Fall, spring, yearlong.

Eligibility Requirements • Minimum age 18; open to sophomores, juniors, seniors, graduate students, adults; 2.5 GPA; 2 letters of recommendation; no foreign language proficiency required.

Living Arrangements • Students live in locally rented apartments, host family homes. Quarters are shared with host institution students. Meals are taken on one's own, with host family, in residences.

Costs (2003-2004) • One term: $11,950. Yearlong program: $21,550; includes tuition, housing, insurance, excursions, international student ID, student support services, transcript, computer access. $35 application fee. $300 refundable deposit required. Financial aid available for all students: scholarships, work study.

For More Information • Lexia International, 23 South Main Street, Hanover, NH 03755; *Phone:* 800-775-3942; *Fax:* 603-643-9899. *E-mail:* info@lexiaintl.org. *World Wide Web:* http://www.lexiaintl.org/

LOYOLA UNIVERSITY CHICAGO
ROME CENTER

Hosted by Loyola University Chicago's Rome Center

Academic Focus • Art history, civilization studies, classics and classical languages, economics, European studies, fine/studio arts, history, international affairs, Italian language and literature, Italian studies, Mediterranean studies, music, philosophy, political science and government, religious studies, Renaissance studies.

Program Information • Students attend classes at Loyola University Chicago's Rome Center. Scheduled travel to Dubrovnik, Korcula, Romania, Tunisia, Urbino, Ravenna, San Marino, Verona, Sicily, Berlin, Barcelona, Krakow, Auschwitz; field trips to Sorrento, Herculaneum, Capri, Florence, Pompeii; optional travel to Greece, Turkey, Morocco, Egypt, Spain at an extra cost.

Sessions • Fall, spring, yearlong.

Eligibility Requirements • Open to sophomores, juniors, seniors; 2.75 GPA; 2 letters of recommendation; good academic standing at home school; good disciplinary standing; no foreign language proficiency required.

Living Arrangements • Students live in host institution dormitories. Quarters are shared with host institution students. Meals are taken as a group, in central dining facility.

Costs (2003-2004) • One term: $14,801. Yearlong program: $29,602; includes tuition, housing, all meals, insurance, student support services. $30 application fee. $200 nonrefundable deposit required. Financial aid available for all students: scholarships, travelling fellowships.

For More Information • Ms. Paula Vecchione DeVoto, Director, Rome Center's Chicago Office, Loyola University Chicago, 6525 North Sheridan Road, Chicago, IL 60626-5385; *Phone:* 800-344-ROMA; *Fax:* 773-508-8797. *E-mail:* romeinfo@luc.edu. *World Wide Web:* http://www.luc.edu/romecenter/

NIAGARA UNIVERSITY
ST. JOHN'S CAMPUS IN ROME, ITALY

Hosted by Saint John's University Rome Campus
Academic Focus • Full curriculum.
Program Information • Students attend classes at Saint John's University Rome Campus. Scheduled travel to 9-day study tour in Brussels, Strasbourg, and Luxembourg.
Sessions • Fall, spring.
Eligibility Requirements • Minimum age 20; open to sophomores, juniors, seniors; 2.5 GPA; 2 letters of recommendation; good academic standing at home school; good conduct record; no foreign language proficiency required.
Living Arrangements • Students live in program-owned apartments. Quarters are shared with host institution students. Meals are taken as a group, on one's own.
Costs (2002-2003) • One term: $11,749; includes tuition, housing, some meals, excursions, international student ID, student support services. Financial aid available for students from sponsoring institution: scholarships, Kakos Alumni Scholarship, TAP and Pell grants available for qualified students.
For More Information • Dr. Daniel Pinti, Associate Professor of English, Niagara University, Dunleavy Hall, Room 363, Niagara University, NY 14109; *Phone:* 716-286-8629; *Fax:* 716-286-8308. *E-mail:* dpinti@niagara.edu. *World Wide Web:* http://www.niagara.edu/sap/

PRATT INSTITUTE
SPRING SEMESTER, ROME PROGRAM IN ARCHITECTURE

Held at Pratt Studios
Academic Focus • Architecture, art, art history, drawing/painting, history, Italian language and literature, Italian studies.
Program Information • Classes are held on the campus of Pratt Studios. Faculty members are drawn from the sponsor's U.S. staff and local instructors hired by the sponsor. Field trips to architectural sites, Veneto, Tuscany, Napoli, Puglia; optional travel at an extra cost.
Sessions • Spring.
Eligibility Requirements • Open to juniors, seniors, graduate students; major in architecture; course work in art, architecture or culture of Italy (2 courses); 3.0 GPA; 1 letter of recommendation; portfolio examples; statement of interest; 0.5 years of college course work in Italian.
Living Arrangements • Students live in locally rented apartments. Quarters are shared with host institution students. Meals are taken as a group, on one's own, in residences, in central dining facility, in restaurants.
Costs (2003) • One term: contact sponsor for cost. Financial aid available for students from sponsoring institution: work study, loans.
For More Information • Mr. Frederick Biehle, Director, Rome Program, Pratt Institute, 200 Willoughby Avenue, Brooklyn, NY 11205; *Phone:* 718-399-4307; *Fax:* 212-227-0334. *E-mail:* fbiehle@pratt.edu. *World Wide Web:* http://www.pratt.edu/abroad/

ST. JOHN'S UNIVERSITY
ITALY SEMESTER PROGRAM

Hosted by Saint John's University Rome Campus
Academic Focus • Art history, communications, drawing/painting, history, international business, Italian language and literature, philosophy, political science and government.
Program Information • Students attend classes at Saint John's University Rome Campus. Scheduled travel to Brussels, Luxembourg, Strasbourg; field trips; optional travel to Brussels, Luxembourg, Strasbourg.
Sessions • Fall, spring, yearlong.

Eligibility Requirements • Minimum age 18; open to sophomores, juniors, seniors, graduate students, adults; 2.75 GPA; 2 letters of recommendation; good academic standing at home school; interview; no foreign language proficiency required.
Living Arrangements • Students live in locally rented apartments. Quarters are shared with host institution students. Meals are taken as a group, on one's own, in residences, in restaurants.
Costs (2003-2004) • One term: $17,569-$18,367. Yearlong program: $36,735; includes tuition, housing, some meals, international airfare, student support services, survival Italian class. $30 application fee. $750 nonrefundable deposit required. Financial aid available for students from sponsoring institution: scholarships, loans.
For More Information • Dr. Ruth De Paula, Director, Office of Study Abroad Programs, St. John's University, 8000 Utopia Parkway, Jamaica, NY 11439; *Phone:* 718-990-6105; *Fax:* 718-990-2321. *E-mail:* intled@stjohns.edu. *World Wide Web:* http://www.stjohns.edu/studyabroad/

SAINT MARY'S COLLEGE
ROME PROGRAM

Hosted by Saint Mary's College in Rome
Academic Focus • Art history, business administration/management, history, international business, Italian language and literature, literature, marketing, philosophy, religious studies.
Program Information • Students attend classes at Saint Mary's College in Rome. Scheduled travel to Naples, Pompeii, Ferrara, Paestum, Capri, Ravenna; field trips to Palestrina, Ostia Antica, Cerveteri, Tarquinia, Siena; optional travel to Austria, Florence at an extra cost.
Sessions • Fall, spring, yearlong.
Eligibility Requirements • Minimum age 18; open to sophomores, juniors, seniors; 2.5 GPA; 4 letters of recommendation; good academic standing at home school; no foreign language proficiency required.
Living Arrangements • Students live in hotels. Meals are taken as a group, on one's own, in residences, in restaurants.
Costs (2003-2004) • One term: $16,625. Yearlong program: $33,270; includes tuition, housing, some meals, insurance, excursions. $25 application fee. $2000 nonrefundable deposit required. Financial aid available for students from sponsoring institution: scholarships, work study, loans.
For More Information • Dr. Peter Checca, Counselor of the Rome Program, Saint Mary's College, 145A Regina Hall, Notre Dame, IN 46556; *Phone:* 574-284-4586; *Fax:* 574-284-4716. *E-mail:* pchecca@saintmarys.edu

STONY BROOK UNIVERSITY
ROME ACADEMIC YEAR PROGRAM

Hosted by University of Rome 'La Sapienza'
Academic Focus • Area studies, art history, economics, Italian language and literature, liberal studies, psychology, social sciences.
Program Information • Students attend classes at University of Rome 'La Sapienza'. Field trips to Venice, Siena; optional travel to Florence, Paris, Sicily at an extra cost.
Sessions • Fall, spring, yearlong.
Eligibility Requirements • Open to sophomores, juniors, seniors, graduate students; 2.5 GPA; 3 letters of recommendation; good academic standing at home school; statement of purpose; enrollment at an accredited college or university; 2 years of college course work in Italian.
Living Arrangements • Students live in locally rented apartments. Quarters are shared with host institution students. Meals are taken on one's own, in residences, in central dining facility, in restaurants.
Costs (2000-2001) • One term: $7750. Yearlong program: $18,500; includes tuition, housing, insurance, excursions, international airfare, books and class materials, tutorials. $200 nonrefundable deposit required. Financial aid available for students from sponsoring institution: scholarships, loans.
For More Information • Ms. Gretchen Gosnell, Study Abroad Advisor, Stony Brook University, Study Abroad Office, Melville Library, Room E5340, Stony Brook, NY 11794-3397; *Phone:* 631-632-7030; *Fax:* 631-632-6544. *E-mail:* studyabroad@sunysb.edu. *World Wide Web:* http://www.sunysb.edu/studyabroad/

The international experience you just can't get from a book.

study abroad

There's no better way to experience the world's many diverse and exciting cultures than by spending a summer, a semester or a year abroad. Through St. John's University Study Abroad programs, you gain invaluable international skills and experience – skills and experience you will use for the rest of your life – while earning credits toward your bachelor's degree.

The academic curriculum in Italy is supplemented by visits to social and political European Union institutions in Brussels, Luxembourg and Strasbourg, as well as by lectures with outstanding representatives of the cultural world. Rome's museums, libraries, archaeological and artistic treasures are the core of the liberal arts and business curriculum.

Semester programs are offered in Australia, Barbados, Brazil, Chile, England, France, The Gambia, Greece, Ireland, Italy, Jamaica, Japan, Sweden and Trinidad and Tobago. We offer short-term programs (summer and winter intersession) in Argentina, Brazil, France, the Galapagos Islands, The Gambia, Greece, Italy, Spain and Vietnam.

This unique curriculum prepares you to accept the challenges as a career professional in a world that is rapidly becoming internationalized politically, economically, and culturally.

For information please contact:
Office of Study Abroad Programs
Tel: (718) 990-6105
Fax: (718) 990-2321
E-mail: intled@stjohns.edu
Website: www.stjohns.edu/studyabroad

- *Argentina*
- *Australia*
- *Barbados*
- *Brazil*
- *Chile*
- *England*
- *France*
- *The Galapagos Islands*
- *The Gambia*
- *Greece*
- *Ireland*
- *Italy*
- *Jamaica*
- *Japan*
- *Spain*
- *Sweden*
- *Trinidad and Tobago*
- *Vietnam*

STUDY ABROAD ITALY
JOHN CABOT UNIVERSITY

Hosted by John Cabot University
Academic Focus • Art history, business administration/management, classics and classical languages, communications, computer science, creative writing, economics, English, English literature, film and media studies, history, Italian language and literature, mathematics, Mediterranean studies, philosophy, political science and government, psychology, religious studies, science, theater management.
Program Information • Students attend classes at John Cabot University. Field trips to Florence, Pompeii, Naples; optional travel to Florence, Pompeii, Naples, Venice, Amalfi Coast, Capri at an extra cost.
Sessions • Fall, spring, yearlong.
Eligibility Requirements • Minimum age 18; open to freshmen, sophomores, juniors, seniors, graduate students, adults; 2.75 GPA; no foreign language proficiency required.
Living Arrangements • Students live in locally rented apartments. Quarters are shared with host institution students. Meals are taken on one's own, in residences, in restaurants.
Costs (2003-2004) • One term: $10,925. Yearlong program: $21,850; includes tuition, housing, insurance, excursions, student support services, computer lab fee, bus and metro passes, airport transfer, food coupons, cell phone. $50 application fee. $1350 nonrefundable deposit required. Financial aid available for students from sponsoring institution: scholarships, work study, loans, federal financial aid, veterans' benefits.
For More Information • Mr. Rod Harris, Admissions Officer, Study Abroad Italy, 7151 Wilton Avenue, Suite 202, Sebastopol, CA 95472; *Phone:* 707-824-8965; *Fax:* 707-824-0198. *E-mail:* rsh@studyabroad-italy.com. *World Wide Web:* http://www.studyabroad-italy.com/

TEMPLE UNIVERSITY
TEMPLE UNIVERSITY ROME

Hosted by Temple University Rome
Academic Focus • Architecture, art history, finance, fine/studio arts, history, international business, Italian language and literature, liberal studies, marketing.
Program Information • Students attend classes at Temple University Rome. Scheduled travel to Venice; field trips to Florence, Pompeii, Naples.
Sessions • Fall, spring, yearlong.
Eligibility Requirements • Minimum age 19; open to juniors, seniors; 2.75 GPA; 2 letters of recommendation; good academic standing at home school; official transcripts; no foreign language proficiency required.
Living Arrangements • Students live in locally rented apartments. Quarters are shared with host institution students. Meals are taken on one's own, in residences.
Costs (2003-2004) • One term: $6700–$9100. Yearlong program: $13,400–$18,200; includes tuition, housing, activity fee. $30 application fee. $150 refundable deposit required. Financial aid available for students from sponsoring institution: scholarships, work study, loans.
For More Information • Ms. Erin Joslyn, Study Abroad Coordinator, Temple University, International Programs, 200 Tuttleman Learning Center, 1809 North 13th Street, Philadelphia, PA 19122; *Phone:* 215-204-0720; *Fax:* 215-204-0729. *E-mail:* study.abroad@temple.edu. *World Wide Web:* http://www.temple.edu/studyabroad/

TRINITY COLLEGE
TRINITY COLLEGE–ROME CAMPUS

Hosted by Trinity College–Rome Campus
Academic Focus • Art history, classics and classical languages, economics, history, Italian language and literature, political science and government.
Program Information • Students attend classes at Trinity College–Rome Campus. Scheduled travel to Florence, Naples, Pompeii, Venice, Herculaneum, Capri; field trips to the city.
Sessions • Fall, spring.
Eligibility Requirements • Minimum age 18; open to sophomores, juniors, seniors; 3.0 GPA; 1 letter of recommendation; good academic standing at home school; no foreign language proficiency required.

Living Arrangements • Students live in hotels, a renovated convent. Quarters are shared with host institution students. Meals are taken as a group, in central dining facility.
Costs (2002-2003) • One term: $16,540; includes tuition, housing, some meals, insurance, excursions, student support services, local bus pass. $30 application fee. $500 nonrefundable deposit required. Financial aid available for students from sponsoring institution: scholarships, work study, loans.
For More Information • Ms. Jane Decatur, Assistant Director of International Programs, Trinity College, 300 Summit Street, Hartford, CT 06106-3100; *Phone:* 860-297-2364; *Fax:* 860-297-5218. *E-mail:* jane.decatur@trincoll.edu. *World Wide Web:* http://www.trincoll.edu/depts/rome/

UNIVERSITY OF WISCONSIN–PLATTEVILLE
ROME STUDY CENTER

Hosted by The American University of Rome
Academic Focus • Advertising and public relations, art history, communications, economics, film and media studies, history, international business, Italian language and literature, Italian studies, political science and government.
Program Information • Students attend classes at The American University of Rome. Optional travel to Pompeii, Venice, Bologna, Ferrara, Ravenna at an extra cost.
Sessions • Fall, spring, yearlong.
Eligibility Requirements • Minimum age 18; open to sophomores, juniors, seniors; 2.5 GPA; 2 letters of recommendation; good academic standing at home school; no foreign language proficiency required.
Living Arrangements • Students live in locally rented apartments. Quarters are shared with host institution students. Meals are taken on one's own, in residences.
Costs (2004-2005) • One term: $7100 for Wisconsin and Minnesota residents; $7400 for nonresidents. Yearlong program: $14,200 for Wisconsin and Minnesota residents; $14,800 for nonresidents; includes tuition, insurance, international student ID, student support services. $25 application fee. $400 nonrefundable deposit required. Financial aid available for all students: loans, federal and state grants, scholarships for Platteville students.
For More Information • Ms. Donna Anderson, Director, University of Wisconsin–Platteville, Institute for Study Abroad Programs, 111 Royce Hall, 1 University Plaza, Platteville, WI 53818-3099; *Phone:* 800-342-1725; *Fax:* 608-342-1736. *E-mail:* studyabroad@uwplatt.edu. *World Wide Web:* http://www.uwplatt.edu/~studyabroad/

UNIVERSITY SYSTEM OF MARYLAND
PROGRAM IN ROME

Hosted by The American University of Rome
Academic Focus • Full curriculum.
Program Information • Students attend classes at The American University of Rome. Field trips to Venice, Ravenna, Pompeii; optional travel to other sites in Italy at an extra cost.
Sessions • Fall, spring, yearlong.
Eligibility Requirements • Minimum age 18; open to sophomores, juniors, seniors; 2.8 GPA; 2 letters of recommendation; good academic standing at home school; most recent official transcript; no foreign language proficiency required.
Living Arrangements • Students live in locally rented apartments, a residence. Quarters are shared with students from other programs. Meals are taken on one's own, in restaurants.
Costs (2003-2004) • One term: $6360. Yearlong program: $12,720; includes tuition, student support services, partial excursion cost. $50 application fee. $250 nonrefundable deposit required. Financial aid available for students from sponsoring institution: scholarships, loans.
For More Information • Ms. Sara Dumont, Director, University System of Maryland, Study Abroad Office, Towson University, 8000 York Road, Towson, MD 21252; *Phone:* 410-704-2451; *Fax:* 410-704-4703. *E-mail:* sdumont@towson.edu. *World Wide Web:* http://www.towson.edu/studyabroad/

SIENA

AHA INTERNATIONAL AN ACADEMIC PROGRAM OF THE UNIVERSITY OF OREGON
PROGRAM IN SIENA, ITALY: NORTHWEST COUNCIL ON STUDY ABROAD

Hosted by AHA Siena Center, University for Foreigners Siena
Academic Focus • Art history, classics and classical languages, communications, economics, English, history, Italian language and literature, literature, political science and government, sociology.
Program Information • Students attend classes at University for Foreigners Siena, AHA Siena Center. Scheduled travel to Rome, Venice; field trips to San Gimignano, Florence, Pisa, Assisi.
Sessions • Fall, spring, winter, yearlong, fall intensive language session.
Eligibility Requirements • Open to sophomores, juniors, seniors, adults; 2 letters of recommendation; good academic standing at home school; foreign language proficiency requirement varies depending on enrolling university.
Living Arrangements • Students live in locally rented apartments, host family homes. Quarters are shared with host institution students, students from other programs. Meals are taken on one's own, in residences, in central dining facility, in restaurants.
Costs (2003-2004) • One term: $6130 ($1660 for fall intensive session). Yearlong program: $20,050; includes tuition, housing, insurance, excursions, books and class materials, international student ID, student support services, local transportation pass. $50 application fee. $200 refundable deposit required. Financial aid available for students: scholarships, loans, home institution financial aid.
For More Information • Ms. Gail Lavin, Associate Director for University Programs, AHA International An Academic Program of the University of Oregon, 741 SW Lincoln Street, Portland, OR 97201; *Phone:* 503-295-7730; *Fax:* 503-295-5969. *E-mail:* mail@aha-intl.org. *World Wide Web:* http://www.aha-intl.org/

STATE UNIVERSITY OF NEW YORK COLLEGE AT BUFFALO
PROGRAM IN SIENA

Held at Art Institute
Academic Focus • Art history, fine/studio arts, Italian language and literature, Italian studies.
Program Information • Classes are held on the campus of Art Institute. Faculty members are drawn from the sponsor's U.S. staff and local instructors hired by the sponsor. Scheduled travel to Rome, Naples, Pompeii; field trips to Florence, Assisi, San Gimignano, Orvieto.
Sessions • Fall, spring, yearlong.
Eligibility Requirements • Open to sophomores, juniors, seniors, adults; 2.5 GPA; 2 letters of recommendation; 0.5 years of college course work in Italian.
Living Arrangements • Students live in host family homes. Meals are taken with host family, in residences.
Costs (2003-2004) • One term: $9119. Yearlong program: $17,233; includes tuition, housing, all meals, insurance, excursions, international airfare, books and class materials, student support services, studio, passport, and visa fees. $10 application fee. $200 nonrefundable deposit required. Financial aid available for students from sponsoring institution: loans, 1 scholarship available to all students.
For More Information • Dr. Lee Ann Grace, Director, International Education, State University of New York College at Buffalo, 1300 Elmwood Avenue, Buffalo, NY 14222-1095; *Phone:* 716-878-4620; *Fax:* 716-878-3054. *E-mail:* intleduc@buffalostate.edu. *World Wide Web:* http://www.buffalostate.edu/intnated/

STATE UNIVERSITY OF NEW YORK COLLEGE AT BUFFALO
SIENA EXCHANGE

Hosted by University of Siena
Academic Focus • Archaeology, art history, communications, history, Italian language and literature, linguistics, philosophy.
Program Information • Students attend classes at University of Siena. Optional travel to San Gimignano, Orvieto, Rome, Assisi at an extra cost.

Sessions • Fall, spring, yearlong.
Eligibility Requirements • Open to juniors, seniors, graduate students; 3.0 GPA; 2 letters of recommendation; interview in Italian; 2 years of college course work in Italian.
Living Arrangements • Students live in host institution dormitories. Quarters are shared with host institution students. Meals are taken on one's own, in central dining facility.
Costs (2003-2004) • One term: $7290 for New York residents; $11,740 for nonresidents (undergraduate). Yearlong program: $13,575 for New York residents; $22,475 for nonresidents (undergraduate); includes tuition, housing, all meals, insurance, international airfare, books and class materials, administrative, passport, and college fees. $10 application fee. $200 nonrefundable deposit required. Financial aid available for students from sponsoring institution: scholarships, loans.
For More Information • Dr. Lee Ann Grace, Director, International Education, State University of New York College at Buffalo, 1300 Elmwood Avenue, Buffalo, NY 14222-1095; *Phone:* 716-878-4620; *Fax:* 716-878-3054. *E-mail:* intleduc@buffalostate.edu. *World Wide Web:* http://www.buffalostate.edu/intnated/

UNIVERSITY OF DELAWARE
SPRING SEMESTER IN SIENA, ITALY

Hosted by University for Foreigners Siena
Academic Focus • Art history, history, Italian language and literature, Italian studies, political science and government.
Program Information • Students attend classes at University for Foreigners Siena. Scheduled travel to Rome, Venice; field trips to Florence, Assisi; optional travel to Europe at an extra cost.
Sessions • Spring.
Eligibility Requirements • Open to freshmen, sophomores, juniors, seniors, adults; 2.8 GPA; 2 letters of recommendation; 0.5 years of college course work in Italian.
Living Arrangements • Students live in host family homes. Meals are taken with host family, in residences.
Costs (2003) • One term: contact sponsor for cost. $200 nonrefundable deposit required. Financial aid available for all students: scholarships.
For More Information • Center for International Studies, University of Delaware, 186 South College Avenue, Newark, DE 19716-1450; *Phone:* 888-831-4685; *Fax:* 302-831-6042. *E-mail:* studyabroad@udel.edu. *World Wide Web:* http://www.udel.edu/studyabroad/

SIRACUSA

ACADEMIC PROGRAMS INTERNATIONAL (API)
(API)–SICILY, ITALY

Hosted by Mediterranean Center for Arts and Sciences
Academic Focus • Full curriculum.
Program Information • Students attend classes at Mediterranean Center for Arts and Sciences. Scheduled travel to Rome; field trips to Palermo, Etna, Catania, Malta, Aeolian Islands, Agrigonto, Taormina.
Sessions • Fall, spring, yearlong.
Eligibility Requirements • Minimum age 18; open to freshmen, sophomores, juniors, seniors, adults; 2.75 GPA; 1 letter of recommendation; good academic standing at home school; official transcript from home university; no foreign language proficiency required.
Living Arrangements • Students live in locally rented apartments, host family homes. Quarters are shared with students from other programs. Meals are taken on one's own, with host family, in residences, in restaurants.
Costs (2005-2006) • One term: $12,200–$12,350. Yearlong program: $23,600; includes tuition, housing, insurance, excursions, student support services, airport reception. $150 nonrefundable deposit required. Financial aid available for all students: scholarships.
For More Information • Ms. Jennifer C. Allen, Director, Academic Programs International (API), 107 East Hopkins, San Marcos, TX 78666; *Phone:* 800-844-4124; *Fax:* 512-392-8420. *E-mail:* api@academicintl.com. *World Wide Web:* http://www.academicintl.com/

STUDY ABROAD ITALY
THE MEDITERRANEAN CENTER FOR ARTS AND SCIENCES

Hosted by The Mediterranean Center for Arts and Sciences
Academic Focus • Full curriculum.
Program Information • Students attend classes at The Mediterranean Center for Arts and Sciences. Field trips to Malta, the Aeolian Islands, Etna, Palermo, Agrigento; optional travel to Cyprus, Greece, Tunisia, a Rome tour (5 days) at an extra cost.
Sessions • Fall, spring, yearlong.
Eligibility Requirements • Minimum age 18; open to freshmen, sophomores, juniors, seniors, graduate students, adults; 2.5 GPA; no foreign language proficiency required.
Living Arrangements • Students live in locally rented apartments. Quarters are shared with host institution students. Meals are taken on one's own, in residences, in restaurants.
Costs (2003-2004) • One term: $8250–$11,400. Yearlong program: $16,500–$22,800; includes tuition, housing, some meals, excursions, international student ID, student support services, emergency medical and repatriation insurance. $50 application fee. $500 nonrefundable deposit required. Financial aid available for all students: scholarships, loans.
For More Information • Ms. Chelsea Brand, Admissions Officer, Study Abroad Italy, 7151 Wilton Avenue, Suite 202, Sebastopol, CA 95472; *Phone:* 707-824-8965; *Fax:* 707-824-0198. *E-mail:* cab@studyabroad-italy.com. *World Wide Web:* http://www.studyabroad-italy.com/

TURIN

UNIVERSITY STUDIES ABROAD CONSORTIUM
INTERNATIONAL BUSINESS, ART AND ARCHITECTURE, AND ITALIAN STUDIES: TURIN, ITALY

Hosted by University of Turin
Academic Focus • Anthropology, architecture, art history, business administration/management, culinary arts, cultural studies, design and applied arts, economics, finance, international business, Italian language and literature, Italian studies, marketing, political science and government.
Program Information • Students attend classes at University of Turin. Field trips; optional travel to Tuscany, Veneto at an extra cost.
Sessions • Fall, spring, yearlong.
Eligibility Requirements • Minimum age 18; open to freshmen, sophomores, juniors, seniors, graduate students, adults; 2.5 GPA; no foreign language proficiency required.
Living Arrangements • Students live in locally rented apartments. Quarters are shared with host institution students. Meals are taken on one's own, with host family, in residences, in central dining facility, in restaurants.
Costs (2005-2006) • One term: $4980. Yearlong program: $9480; includes tuition, some meals, insurance, excursions, student support services. $50 application fee. $150 refundable deposit required. Financial aid available for all students: scholarships, loans.
For More Information • University Studies Abroad Consortium, USAC/323, Reno, NV 89557-0093; *Phone:* 775-784-6569; *Fax:* 775-784-6010. *E-mail:* usac@unr.edu. *World Wide Web:* http://usac.unr.edu/

URBINO

SOUTHERN CONNECTICUT STATE UNIVERSITY
SOUTHERN CONNECTICUT STATE UNIVERSITY IN URBINO, ITALY

Hosted by University of Urbino
Academic Focus • Art, art history, Italian language and literature.
Program Information • Students attend classes at University of Urbino. Scheduled travel to Venice, Florence, Rome; field trips to Ravenna, Assisi, Gubbio, San Marino; optional travel at an extra cost.
Sessions • Fall, yearlong.
Eligibility Requirements • Minimum age 18; open to precollege students, freshmen, sophomores, juniors, seniors; major in humanities, arts; course work in history, art; 2.5 GPA; 1 letter of recommendation; 1 year of college course work in Italian.
Living Arrangements • Students live in host institution dormitories, locally rented apartments. Quarters are shared with host institution students, students from other programs. Meals are taken as a group, in central dining facility.
Costs (2003-2004) • One term: $5000. Yearlong program: $10,000; includes housing, all meals. $150 application fee. $500 deposit required. Financial aid available for all students: federal and state loans.
For More Information • Dr. Michael Vena, Professor of Foreign Language, Southern Connecticut State University, 501 Crescent Street, New Haven, CT 06515; *Phone:* 203-392-6766; *Fax:* 203-392-6136.

STATE UNIVERSITY OF NEW YORK AT NEW PALTZ
STUDY ABROAD IN URBINO, ITALY

Hosted by University of Urbino
Academic Focus • Economics, education, Italian language and literature, Italian studies, liberal studies, philosophy, political science and government, social sciences.
Program Information • Students attend classes at University of Urbino. Scheduled travel to Rome; field trips to Florence, Venice, Gubbio, Assisi.
Sessions • Fall, spring, yearlong.
Eligibility Requirements • Minimum age 18; open to juniors, seniors; 2.5 GPA; 2 letters of recommendation; good academic standing at home school; 2 years of college course work in Italian.
Living Arrangements • Students live in host institution dormitories. Quarters are shared with host institution students, students from other programs. Meals are taken on one's own, in central dining facility.
Costs (2003-2004) • One term: $5699 for New York residents; $8829 for nonresidents. Yearlong program: $11,398 for New York residents; $17,658 for nonresidents; includes tuition, housing, all meals, insurance, excursions, books and class materials, administrative fee. $25 application fee. $300–$600 nonrefundable deposit required. Financial aid available for students from sponsoring institution: scholarships, loans.
For More Information • Center for International Programs, State University of New York at New Paltz, 75 South Manheim Boulevard, Suite 9, New Paltz, NY 12561; *Phone:* 845-257-3125; *Fax:* 845-257-3129. *E-mail:* international@newpaltz.edu. *World Wide Web:* http://www.newpaltz.edu/studyabroad/

VENICE

BOSTON UNIVERSITY
VENICE STUDIO ARTS PROGRAM

Hosted by Scuola Internazionale di Grafica
Academic Focus • Art history, design and applied arts, drawing/painting, Italian language and literature.
Program Information • Students attend classes at Scuola Internazionale di Grafica. Field trips to local museums.
Sessions • Spring.
Eligibility Requirements • Open to sophomores, juniors, seniors; major in graphic design, painting; 3.0 GPA; 2 letters of recommendation; good academic standing at home school; essay; transcript; 20 slides of work; approval of participation; 0.5 years of college course work in Italian.
Living Arrangements • Students live in program-owned apartments. Quarters are shared with host institution students. Meals are taken as a group, on one's own, in residences, in restaurants.
Costs (2005) • One term: $19,854; includes tuition, housing, all meals, excursions, international airfare, some art supplies. $50 application fee. $400 nonrefundable deposit required. Financial aid available for all students: scholarships, loans.
For More Information • Division of International Programs, Boston University, 232 Bay State Road, Boston, MA 02215; *Phone:* 617-353-9888; *Fax:* 617-353-5402. *E-mail:* abroad@bu.edu. *World Wide Web:* http://www.bu.edu/abroad/

COLLEGE CONSORTIUM FOR INTERNATIONAL STUDIES–COLLEGE OF STATEN ISLAND/CITY UNIVERSITY OF NEW YORK
PROGRAM IN VENICE, ITALY: LIBERAL ARTS AND STUDIO ART

Hosted by Lorenzo de' Medici School in affiliation with The Venice Institute

Academic Focus • Art, art history, environmental science/studies, film and media studies, history, Italian language and literature, Italian studies, Jewish studies, literature, music history, religious studies.

Program Information • Students attend classes at Lorenzo de' Medici School in affiliation with The Venice Institute. Field trips to Venice and environs; optional travel to Padua, Ferrara, Verona, Palladio's villas at an extra cost.

Sessions • Fall, spring, yearlong.

Eligibility Requirements • Minimum age 18; open to freshmen, sophomores, juniors, seniors; 2.5 GPA; 3 letters of recommendation; essay; transcript; no foreign language proficiency required.

Living Arrangements • Students live in locally rented apartments. Quarters are shared with host institution students, students from other programs. Meals are taken on one's own, in residences, in restaurants.

Costs (2004-2005) • One term: $6255 for New York residents and CCIS member students; all others contact the College of Staten Island for cost. Yearlong program: $10,975 for New York residents and CCIS member students; all others contact the College of Staten Island for cost; includes tuition, insurance, excursions, student support services, fees. $265 nonrefundable deposit required. Financial aid available for students from sponsoring institution: loans, grants.

For More Information • College Consortium for International Studies–College of Staten Island/City University of New York, 2000 P Street, NW, Suite 503, Washington, DC 20036; *Phone:* 800-453-6956; *Fax:* 202-223-0999. *E-mail:* info@ccisabroad.org. *World Wide Web:* http://www.ccisabroad.org/. Students may also apply through College of Staten Island, The City University of New York, Center for International Service, Building 2A, Room 206, 2800 Victory Boulevard, Staten Island, NY 10314.

COLLEGE CONSORTIUM FOR INTERNATIONAL STUDIES–COLLEGE OF STATEN ISLAND/CITY UNIVERSITY OF NEW YORK
PROGRAM IN VENICE, ITALY: SUPER-INTENSIVE ITALIAN

Hosted by Lorenzo de' Medici School in affiliation with The Venice Institute

Academic Focus • Italian language and literature.

Program Information • Students attend classes at Lorenzo de' Medici School in affiliation with The Venice Institute. Field trips to Venice and environs; optional travel to Padua, Ferrara, Verona, Palladio's villas at an extra cost.

Sessions • Fall, spring, yearlong.

Eligibility Requirements • Minimum age 18; open to freshmen, sophomores, juniors, seniors; 2.5 GPA; 3 letters of recommendation; essay; transcript; no foreign language proficiency required.

Living Arrangements • Students live in locally rented apartments. Quarters are shared with host institution students, students from other programs. Meals are taken on one's own, in residences, in restaurants.

Costs (2004-2005) • One term: $4005 for New York residents and CCIS member students; all others contact the College of Staten Island for cost. Yearlong program: $7475 for New York residents and CCIS member students; all others contact the College of Staten Island for cost; includes tuition, insurance, excursions, student support services, fees. $265 nonrefundable deposit required. Financial aid available for students from sponsoring institution: loans, grants.

For More Information • College Consortium for International Studies–College of Staten Island/City University of New York, 2000 P Street, NW, Suite 503, Washington, DC 20036; *Phone:* 800-453-6956; *Fax:* 202-223-0999. *E-mail:* info@ccisabroad.org. *World Wide Web:* http://www.ccisabroad.org/. Students may also apply through College of Staten Island, The City University of New York, Center for International Service, Building 2A, Room 206, 2800 Victory Boulevard, Staten Island, NY 10314.

DUKE UNIVERSITY
DUKE IN VENICE

Hosted by Venice International University

Academic Focus • Anthropology, art history, economics, history, Italian language and literature, Italian studies, literature, political science and government, religious studies.

Program Information • Students attend classes at Venice International University. Field trips; optional travel to Europe at an extra cost.

Sessions • Fall, spring, yearlong.

Eligibility Requirements • Open to sophomores, juniors, seniors; 3.0 GPA; 1 letter of recommendation; good academic standing at home school; no foreign language proficiency required.

Living Arrangements • Students live in host institution dormitories. Quarters are shared with host institution students. Meals are taken as a group, on one's own, in central dining facility, in restaurants.

Costs (2003-2004) • One term: $15,438. Yearlong program: $30,875; includes tuition, housing, some meals, insurance, excursions, student support services, transcript fee. $1000 nonrefundable deposit required. Financial aid available for students from sponsoring institution: scholarships, loans.

For More Information • Mr. Kurt Olausen, Assistant Director, Duke University, Office of Study Abroad, 2016 Campus Drive, Box 90057, Durham, NC 27708-0057; *Phone:* 919-684-2174; *Fax:* 919-684-3083. *E-mail:* kolausen@asdean.duke.edu. *World Wide Web:* http://www.aas.duke.edu/study_abroad/

EUROPEAN HERITAGE INSTITUTE
ACADEMIC YEAR IN VENICE

Hosted by The Venice Institute, Lorenzo de' Medici–The Art Institute of Florence

Academic Focus • Art, art history, drawing/painting, history, Italian language and literature, Italian studies, literature, performing arts, sociology.

Program Information • Students attend classes at Lorenzo de' Medici–The Art Institute of Florence, The Venice Institute. Field trips to cultural sites throughout Venice.

Sessions • Fall, spring, yearlong.

Eligibility Requirements • Minimum age 18; open to freshmen, sophomores, juniors, seniors, graduate students, adults; 2.2 GPA; 2 letters of recommendation; no foreign language proficiency required.

Living Arrangements • Students live in locally rented apartments, host family homes. Quarters are shared with host institution students, students from other programs. Meals are taken on one's own, with host family.

Costs (2004-2005) • One term: $3100-$4200. Yearlong program: $6200-$8400; includes tuition, student support services. $300 refundable deposit required.

For More Information • Dr. Antonio Masullo, Professor, European Heritage Institute, 2708 East Franklin Street, Richmond, VA 23223; *Phone:* 804-643-0661; *Fax:* 804-648-0826. *E-mail:* euritage@i2020.net. *World Wide Web:* http://www.europeabroad.org/

LEXIA INTERNATIONAL
LEXIA IN VENICE

Hosted by The Venice Institute

Academic Focus • Ancient history, anthropology, area studies, art, art conservation studies, art history, civilization studies, classics and classical languages, comparative history, cultural studies, drawing/painting, economics, environmental science/studies, ethnic studies, European studies, film and media studies, fine/studio arts, geography, history, interdisciplinary studies, international affairs, international business, Italian language and literature, Italian studies, liberal studies, literature, music, music history, music performance, philosophy, political science and government, psychology, religious studies, social sciences, urban studies, visual and performing arts.

Program Information • Students attend classes at The Venice Institute. Field trips to a Palladian Villa tour, Florence, Verona, Urbino, Padova, Rome.

Sessions • Fall, spring, yearlong.
Eligibility Requirements • Minimum age 18; open to sophomores, juniors, seniors, graduate students, adults; 2.5 GPA; 2 letters of recommendation; no foreign language proficiency required.
Living Arrangements • Students live in locally rented apartments, host family homes. Quarters are shared with host institution students. Meals are taken on one's own, with host family, in residences, in central dining facility, in restaurants.
Costs (2003-2004) • One term: $11,950. Yearlong program: $21,550; includes tuition, housing, insurance, excursions, student support services, computer access, transcript. $35 application fee. $300 refundable deposit required. Financial aid available for all students: scholarships, work study.
For More Information • Lexia International, 23 South Main Street, Hanover, NH 03755; *Phone:* 800-775-3942; *Fax:* 603-643-9899. *E-mail:* info@lexiaintl.org. *World Wide Web:* http://www.lexiaintl.org/

JAMAICA
KINGSTON
THE INTERNATIONAL PARTNERSHIP FOR SERVICE LEARNING
JAMAICA SERVICE–LEARNING

Hosted by University of Technology
Academic Focus • Community service, education, intercultural studies, international affairs, liberal studies, social sciences.
Program Information • Students attend classes at University of Technology. Field trips; optional travel at an extra cost.
Sessions • Fall, spring, yearlong.
Eligibility Requirements • Minimum age 18; open to freshmen, sophomores, juniors, seniors, graduate students, adults; 2 letters of recommendation; good academic standing at home school; evidence of maturity, responsibility; no foreign language proficiency required.
Living Arrangements • Students live in host family homes. Meals are taken with host family, in residences.
Costs (2003-2004) • One term: $8600. Yearlong program: $16,000; includes tuition, housing, some meals, excursions, student support services, community service placement. $50 application fee. $250 refundable deposit required. Financial aid available for all students: federal financial aid.
For More Information • Ms. Ilana Golin, Coordinator of Student Programs, The International Partnership for Service Learning, 815 Second Avenue, Suite 315, New York, NY 10017-4594; *Phone:* 212-986-0989; *Fax:* 212-986-5039. *E-mail:* info@ipsl.org. *World Wide Web:* http://www.ipsl.org/

SCHOOL FOR INTERNATIONAL TRAINING, SIT STUDY ABROAD
JAMAICA: GENDER AND DEVELOPMENT

Academic Focus • Cultural studies, history, political science and government, social sciences, women's studies.
Program Information • Faculty members are drawn from the sponsor's U.S. staff and local instructors hired by the sponsor. Scheduled travel to Portland, St. Mary and Hanover, Montego Bay, Negril, St. Elizabeth; field trips to women's projects, cultural institutions, service agencies.
Sessions • Fall, spring.
Eligibility Requirements • Open to sophomores, juniors, seniors; 2.5 GPA; 2 letters of recommendation; good academic standing at home school.
Living Arrangements • Students live in host family homes, hotels. Meals are taken as a group, on one's own, with host family, in residences, in restaurants.
Costs (2003-2004) • One term: $12,850; includes tuition, housing, all meals, insurance, excursions, international student ID. $50 application fee. $400 nonrefundable deposit required. Financial aid available for all students: scholarships.
For More Information • School for International Training, SIT Study Abroad, Kipling Road, Brattleboro, VT 05302-0676; *Phone:*

888-272-7881; *Fax:* 802-258-3296. *E-mail:* studyabroad@sit.edu. *World Wide Web:* http://www.sit.edu/studyabroad/

STATE UNIVERSITY OF NEW YORK COLLEGE AT BROCKPORT
JAMAICA PERFORMING ARTS PROGRAM

Hosted by Edna Manley College of Visual and Performing Arts
Academic Focus • Area studies, art, communications, dance, drama/theater, drawing/painting, education, fine/studio arts, language studies, music, performing arts, visual and performing arts.
Program Information • Students attend classes at Edna Manley College of Visual and Performing Arts.
Sessions • Fall, spring, yearlong.
Eligibility Requirements • Minimum age 18; open to juniors, seniors; course work in art, fine arts, dance, theater arts, or music; 2.75 GPA; 2 letters of recommendation; portfolio (for some).
Living Arrangements • Students live in host institution dormitories. Quarters are shared with host institution students. Meals are taken on one's own, in residences.
Costs (2003-2004) • One term: $7350. Yearlong program: $12,350; includes tuition, housing, international student ID, student support services. $350 nonrefundable deposit required. Financial aid available for all students: scholarships, loans, regular financial aid, grants.
For More Information • Dr. John Perry, Director, Office of International Education, State University of New York College at Brockport, 350 New Campus Drive, Brockport, NY 14420; *Phone:* 800-298-SUNY; *Fax:* 585-637-3218. *E-mail:* overseas@brockport.edu. *World Wide Web:* http://www.brockport.edu/studyabroad/

JAPAN
CITY TO CITY
FLORIDA INTERNATIONAL UNIVERSITY
EXCHANGE PROGRAM–KANSAI GAIDAI INTERNATIONAL UNIVERSITY

Hosted by Kansai Gaidai University
Academic Focus • Full curriculum.
Program Information • Students attend classes at Kansai Gaidai University (Hirakata). Optional travel.
Sessions • Fall, spring.
Eligibility Requirements • Open to sophomores, juniors, seniors, graduate students, adults; 3.0 GPA; no foreign language proficiency required.
Living Arrangements • Students live in host institution dormitories, host family homes. Quarters are shared with students from other programs. Meals are taken on one's own, in residences, in central dining facility.
Costs (2003-2004) • One term: $6000; includes housing, all meals, excursions, international airfare, books and class materials, international student ID, student support services. $150 application fee. Financial aid available for all students: scholarships, loans.
For More Information • Office of International Studies, Florida International University, University Park Campus–TT100, Miami, FL 33199; *Phone:* 305-348-1913; *Fax:* 305-348-1941. *E-mail:* ois@fiu.edu. *World Wide Web:* http://ois.fiu.edu/

AKITA
ST. CLOUD STATE UNIVERSITY
JAPAN

Hosted by Akita University
Academic Focus • East Asian studies, Japanese studies.
Program Information • Students attend classes at Akita University. Optional travel at an extra cost.
Sessions • Yearlong.

Eligibility Requirements • Minimum age 18; open to juniors, seniors; 3.0 GPA; 2 letters of recommendation; good academic standing at home school; fluency in Japanese.

Living Arrangements • Students live in host institution dormitories, locally rented apartments. Quarters are shared with host institution students. Meals are taken on one's own.

Costs (2003-2004) • Yearlong program: Full scholarship given if student is accepted into the program; includes tuition, housing, all meals, international airfare, books and class materials, student support services, stipend. $75 application fee. Financial aid available for students from sponsoring institution: scholarships.

For More Information • Chunsheng Zhang, Associate Vice President for Academic Affairs/International Studies, St. Cloud State University, Center for International Studies, 720 4th Avenue, South, St. Cloud, MN 56301-4498; *Phone:* 320-308-4287; *Fax:* 320-308-4223. *E-mail:* intstudy@stcloudstate.edu. *World Wide Web:* http://www. stcloudstate.edu/

CHIBA

FLORIDA INTERNATIONAL UNIVERSITY
KANDA UNIVERSITY, JAPAN

Hosted by Kanda University of International Studies

Academic Focus • Japanese, Japanese studies.

Program Information • Students attend classes at Kanda University of International Studies.

Sessions • Fall, spring.

Eligibility Requirements • Open to sophomores, juniors, seniors, graduate students; 3.0 GPA; 2 years of college course work in Japanese.

Living Arrangements • Students live in host family homes.

Costs (2004) • One term: $6000; includes housing, all meals, international airfare, books and class materials, student support services. $150 application fee. Financial aid available for students from sponsoring institution: scholarships, loans.

For More Information • Office of International Studies, Florida International University, University Park Campus-TT100, Miami, FL 33199; *Phone:* 305-348-1913; *Fax:* 305-348-1941. *E-mail:* ois@fiu. edu. *World Wide Web:* http://ois.fiu.edu/

HIKONE

JAPAN CENTER FOR MICHIGAN UNIVERSITIES
ENVIRONMENTAL SCIENCES IN JAPAN

Hosted by Shiga Prefectural University, Shiga University, Japan Center for Michigan Universities

Academic Focus • Environmental science/studies, Japanese, natural resources.

Program Information • Students attend classes at Shiga Prefectural University, Shiga University, Japan Center for Michigan Universities. Scheduled travel to Osaka, Nara; field trips to Lake Biwa, Kusatsu, Otsu; optional travel to various sites in Japan, Kyoto, environmental sites, various sites along Lake Biwa at an extra cost.

Sessions • Spring.

Eligibility Requirements • Minimum age 18; open to sophomores, juniors, seniors, graduate students, adults; 2.5 GPA; 2 letters of recommendation; good academic standing at home school; no foreign language proficiency required.

Living Arrangements • Students live in program-owned apartments, host family homes. Quarters are shared with host institution students. Meals are taken on one's own, with host family, in residences.

Costs (2004) • One term: $9200; includes tuition, housing, some meals, insurance, excursions, books and class materials, lab equipment, international student ID, student support services, internship. $100 nonrefundable deposit required. Financial aid available for all students: scholarships, loans, grants.

For More Information • Ms. Mandy Brookins, Program Coordinator, Japan Center for Michigan Universities, 110 International Center, East Lansing, MI 48824; *Phone:* 517-355-4654; *Fax:* 517-353-8727. *E-mail:* jcmu@msu.edu. *World Wide Web:* http://www. isp.msu.edu/JCMU/. Students may also apply through Japan Center

for Michigan Universities, 1435-86 Ajiroguchi, Matsubara-cho, Hikone-Shi, Shiga 522-0002, Japan.

HIRAKATA

SHORTER COLLEGE
KANSAI GAIDAI UNIVERSITY, OSAKA, JAPAN

Hosted by Kansai Gaidai University

Academic Focus • Full curriculum.

Program Information • Students attend classes at Kansai Gaidai University.

Sessions • Fall, spring.

Eligibility Requirements • Open to sophomores, juniors, seniors; 2.5 GPA; 2 letters of recommendation; good academic standing at home school; personal essay; no foreign language proficiency required.

Living Arrangements • Students live in host institution dormitories. Quarters are shared with host institution students.

Costs (2003-2004) • One term: $10,000 (estimated). Financial aid available for students from sponsoring institution: scholarships, work study, loans.

For More Information • Dr. Robert Nash, Dean, School of Religion and International Programs, Shorter College, 315 Shorter Avenue, Rome, GA 30165; *Phone:* 706-233-7257; *Fax:* 703-233-7516. *E-mail:* rnash@shorter.edu. *World Wide Web:* http://www.shorter.edu. academics.internationalprograms/

UNIVERSITY AT ALBANY, STATE UNIVERSITY OF NEW YORK
LANGUAGE AND CULTURAL STUDIES IN ENGLISH AT KANSAI GAIDAI UNIVERSITY

Hosted by Kansai Gaidai University

Academic Focus • Asian studies, business administration/management, Japanese, Japanese studies.

Program Information • Students attend classes at Kansai Gaidai University.

Sessions • Fall, spring, yearlong.

Eligibility Requirements • Open to sophomores, juniors, seniors, adults; 3.0 GPA; 2 letters of recommendation; good academic standing at home school; college course work in East Asian studies recommended; no foreign language proficiency required.

Living Arrangements • Students live in host institution dormitories, host family homes. Quarters are shared with students from other programs. Meals are taken on one's own, with host family, in residences, in central dining facility, in restaurants.

Costs (2002-2003) • One term: $6539. Yearlong program: $13,078; includes housing, all meals, student support services, in-state tuition and fees. $150 nonrefundable deposit required. Financial aid available for all students: AIEJ scholarships (all customary sources also available for Albany students).

For More Information • University at Albany, State University of New York, Office of International Education, LI 66, Albany, NY 12222; *Phone:* 518-442-3525; *Fax:* 518-442-3338. *E-mail:* intled@ uamail.albany.edu. *World Wide Web:* http://www.albany.edu/intled/

UNIVERSITY OF MIAMI
STUDY ABROAD AT KANSAI GAIDAI UNIVERSITY, JAPAN

Hosted by Kansai Gaidai University

Academic Focus • Cultural studies, fine/studio arts, international business, Japanese, Japanese studies, marketing, religious studies, social sciences.

Program Information • Students attend classes at Kansai Gaidai University.

Sessions • Fall, spring, yearlong.

Eligibility Requirements • Minimum age 18; open to sophomores, juniors, seniors; 2.75 GPA; 2 letters of recommendation; official transcript; no foreign language proficiency required.

Living Arrangements • Students live in host institution dormitories, host family homes. Quarters are shared with students from other programs. Meals are taken as a group, on one's own.

Costs (2003-2004) • One term: $12,919. Yearlong program: $25,838; includes tuition, student support services. $40 application fee. $500 nonrefundable deposit required. Financial aid available for students from sponsoring institution: scholarships, loans.

For More Information • Ms. Glenda Hayley, Assistant Director, University of Miami, International Education and Exchange Programs, 5050 Brunson Drive, Allen Hall 212, PO Box 248005, Coral Gables, FL 33124-1610; *Phone:* 305-284-3434; *Fax:* 305-284-4235. *E-mail:* ieep@miami.edu. *World Wide Web:* http://www.studyabroad.miami.edu/

HIROSHIMA

UNIVERSITY STUDIES ABROAD CONSORTIUM
FULL CURRICULUM STUDIES: HIROSHIMA, JAPAN

Hosted by Hiroshima University
Academic Focus • Full curriculum.
Program Information • Students attend classes at Hiroshima University. Field trips to Miyajima Island, rice harvesting sites, local festivities, a Zen Buddhist Temple.
Sessions • Fall, spring, yearlong.
Eligibility Requirements • Minimum age 18; open to freshmen, sophomores, juniors, seniors, graduate students, adults; 2.8 GPA; no foreign language proficiency required.
Living Arrangements • Students live in host institution dormitories. Quarters are shared with host institution students. Meals are taken on one's own, in residences.
Costs (2005-2006) • One term: $4980. Yearlong program: $9680; includes tuition, insurance, student support services. $50 application fee. $150 refundable deposit required. Financial aid available for all students: scholarships, loans.
For More Information • University Studies Abroad Consortium, USAC/323, Reno, NV 89557-0093; *Phone:* 775-784-6569; *Fax:* 775-784-6010. *E-mail:* usac@unr.edu. *World Wide Web:* http://usac.unr.edu/

KANAZAWA

TUFTS UNIVERSITY
TUFTS IN JAPAN

Hosted by Kanazawa University
Academic Focus • Biological/life sciences, chemical sciences, engineering, Japanese, Japanese studies, mathematics, physics.
Program Information • Students attend classes at Kanazawa University. Field trips.
Sessions • Spring, yearlong.
Eligibility Requirements • Open to juniors; 3.0 GPA; 2 letters of recommendation; good academic standing at home school; 1 year of college course work in Japanese.
Living Arrangements • Students live in host institution dormitories. Quarters are shared with host institution students. Meals are taken on one's own, in central dining facility.
Costs (2004-2005) • One term: $19,657. Yearlong program: $39,314; includes tuition, housing, all meals, excursions, student support services. $40 application fee. $350 nonrefundable deposit required. Financial aid available for students from sponsoring institution: scholarships, loans.
For More Information • Ms. Melanie Armstrong, Program and Marketing Coordinator, Tufts Programs Abroad, Tufts University, Dowling Hall, Medford, MA 02155-7084; *Phone:* 617-627-2000; *Fax:* 617-627-3971. *E-mail:* melanie.armstrong@tufts.edu. *World Wide Web:* http://ase.tufts.edu/studyabroad/

KASUGAI

IES, INSTITUTE FOR THE INTERNATIONAL EDUCATION OF STUDENTS
IES–KASUGAI

Hosted by Chubu University
Academic Focus • Business administration/management, chemical sciences, engineering, information science, international affairs, international business, Japanese, Japanese studies, mathematics, physical sciences.

Program Information • Students attend classes at Chubu University. Scheduled travel to Kyoto; field trips to Nagoya, Toyota, Tokyo, Nara, Osaka, Mt. Fuji.
Sessions • Fall, spring, yearlong.
Eligibility Requirements • Minimum age 18; open to sophomores, juniors, seniors, graduate students, adults; course work in engineering, physical sciences, business, international studies; 3.0 GPA; 1 letter of recommendation; good academic standing at home school; 1 term college course work in Japanese.
Living Arrangements • Students live in host institution dormitories. Quarters are shared with host institution students, students from other programs. Meals are taken on one's own, in central dining facility.
Costs (2003-2004) • One term: $11,700. Yearlong program: $21,060; includes tuition, housing, some meals, excursions, lab equipment, student support services, partial insurance coverage. $50 application fee. $500 nonrefundable deposit required. Financial aid available for all students: scholarships, institutional partner need-based grants.
For More Information • International Education Representative, IES, Institute for the International Education of Students, 33 North LaSalle Street, 15th Floor, Chicago, IL 60602; *Phone:* 800-995-2300; *Fax:* 312-944-1448. *E-mail:* info@iesabroad.org. *World Wide Web:* http://www.IESabroad.org/

KAWAGOE

TOKYO INTERNATIONAL UNIVERSITY
JAPAN STUDIES PROGRAM

Hosted by Tokyo International University
Academic Focus • Japanese, Japanese studies.
Program Information • Students attend classes at Tokyo International University. Field trips to elementary schools, festivals, museums, historic sights, Kabuki, local craftsmen; optional travel to Kansai (Kyoto, Hiroshima) at an extra cost.
Sessions • Fall, spring.
Eligibility Requirements • Minimum age 18; open to freshmen, sophomores, juniors, seniors; 2.5 GPA; 2 letters of recommendation; good academic standing at home school; enrollment at a college or university; no foreign language proficiency required.
Living Arrangements • Students live in host family homes. Meals are taken with host family, in residences.
Costs (2003-2004) • One term: ¥760,000; includes tuition, housing, some meals, excursions, books and class materials, lab equipment, student support services, language texts. ¥80,000 nonrefundable deposit required.
For More Information • Mr. Lorenzo Lambertino, Coordinator, Japan Studies Program, Tokyo International University, International Exchange Center, 1-13-1 Matobakita, Kawagoe, Saitama, 350-1197, Japan; *Phone:* +81 49-232-1111; *Fax:* +81 49-234-3824. *E-mail:* llambert@tic.ac.jp. *World Wide Web:* http://www.tiu.ac.jp/jsp/

KYOTO

ANTIOCH COLLEGE
BUDDHIST STUDIES IN JAPAN

Hosted by Koyasan University, Saikyoji Temple, Kojirin Temple
Academic Focus • East Asian studies, Japanese, Japanese studies, philosophy, religious studies.
Program Information • Students attend classes at Koyasan University, Kojirin Temple, Saikyoji Temple. Scheduled travel to monasteries, temples, Nara, Shikoku, Tokyo, Kyushu; field trips to Kyoto and environs, Hiroshima, Nara, Shikoku; optional travel to sites determined by independent research topics at an extra cost.
Sessions • Fall.
Eligibility Requirements • Minimum age 19; open to sophomores, juniors, seniors, graduate students, adults; 2 letters of recommendation; good academic standing at home school; maturity, sensitivity; no foreign language proficiency required.
Living Arrangements • Students live in a hostel, monastery guest houses, temples. Meals are taken as a group, in residences, in central dining facility.
Costs (2003-2004) • One term: $14,660; includes tuition, housing, all meals, insurance, excursions, international airfare, international

JAPAN
Kyoto

student ID, student support services, most class materials. $35 application fee. $150 nonrefundable deposit required. Financial aid available for students from sponsoring institution: scholarships, loans, Japan-affiliated organizations offer assistance.

For More Information • Dr. Lea Millay, Director, Buddhist Studies Japan, Antioch College, Antioch Education Abroad, 795 Livermore Street, Yellow Springs, OH 45387-1697; *Phone:* 937-769-1015; *Fax:* 937-769-1019. *E-mail:* aea@antioch-college.edu. *World Wide Web:* http://www.antioch-college.edu/aea/

ASSOCIATED KYOTO PROGRAM
ASSOCIATED KYOTO PROGRAM

Held at Doshisha University

Academic Focus • Asian studies, Japanese, Japanese studies, literature.

Program Information • Classes are held on the campus of Doshisha University. Faculty members are drawn from the sponsor's U.S. staff and local instructors hired by the sponsor. Field trips to Izumo, Ise shrine, Koya-san, Hiroshima.

Sessions • Yearlong.

Eligibility Requirements • Open to juniors; course work in Japanese area studies; 3.0 GPA; 3 letters of recommendation; good academic standing at home school; 1 year of college course work in Japanese.

Living Arrangements • Students live in host family homes. Meals are taken with host family, in residences.

Costs (2002-2003) • Yearlong program: contact sponsor for cost. $10 application fee. $500 refundable deposit required. Financial aid available for all students: scholarships, student research grants.

For More Information • Ms. Ashley Davis, Program Administrator, Associated Kyoto Program, Smith College, Northampton, MA 01063; *Phone:* 800-940-7070; *Fax:* 413-585-4627. *E-mail:* akp@smith.edu. *World Wide Web:* http://www.associatedkyotoprogram.org/

KYOTO CENTER FOR JAPANESE STUDIES
KYOTO CENTER FOR JAPANESE STUDIES

Hosted by Stanford Japan Center

Academic Focus • Japanese, Japanese studies.

Program Information • Students attend classes at Stanford Japan Center. Scheduled travel to class-related destinations; field trips to museums, temples, shrines, theatres.

Sessions • Fall, spring, yearlong.

Eligibility Requirements • Open to sophomores, juniors, seniors; 2 letters of recommendation; good academic standing at home school; 2 years of college course work in Japanese.

Living Arrangements • Students live in locally rented apartments, program-owned apartments, host family homes. Meals are taken as a group, on one's own, with host family, in residences, in restaurants.

Costs (2003-2004) • One term: $19,000. Yearlong program: $37,000; includes tuition, housing, all meals, some activities. $500 nonrefundable deposit required. Financial aid available for all students: scholarships, home institution aid for consortium students.

For More Information • Ms. Trudi Reinhardt, KCJS Manager, Kyoto Center for Japanese Studies, KCJS c/o Stanford Overseas Studies, First Floor, Sweet Hall, 590 Escondido Mall, Stanford, CA 94035; *Phone:* 650-725-0233; *Fax:* 650-725-7355. *E-mail:* kcjs@osp.stanford.edu. *World Wide Web:* http://kcjs.stanford.edu/

LONG ISLAND UNIVERSITY
FRIENDS WORLD PROGRAM–EAST ASIAN CENTER-JAPAN

Hosted by Friends World Program East Asian Centre

Academic Focus • Anthropology, communications, cultural studies, East Asian studies, interdisciplinary studies, Japanese, peace and conflict studies, religious studies, teaching English as a second language.

Program Information • Students attend classes at Friends World Program East Asian Centre. Scheduled travel to many locations throughout East Asia; field trips to Hiroshima, local historic sites, temples; optional travel to Korea, Indonesia, Thailand at an extra cost.

Sessions • Fall, spring, yearlong.

Eligibility Requirements • Minimum age 18; open to sophomores, juniors, seniors, adults; good academic standing at home school; interview; essay; no foreign language proficiency required.

Living Arrangements • Students live in host institution dormitories, locally rented apartments. Quarters are shared with host institution students, students from other programs. Meals are taken as a group, on one's own, in residences, in restaurants.

Costs (2003-2004) • One term: $15,775 (estimated). Yearlong program: $31,550 (estimated); includes tuition, housing, all meals, excursions, international airfare, books and class materials. $30 application fee. $200 deposit required. Financial aid available for students from sponsoring institution: scholarships, loans, need-based aid.

For More Information • Admissions Office, FWP, Long Island University, 239 Montauk Highway, Southampton, NY 11968; *Phone:* 631-287-8474; *Fax:* 631-287-8463. *E-mail:* fw@liu.edu. *World Wide Web:* http://www.southampton.liu.edu/fw/

RUTGERS, THE STATE UNIVERSITY OF NEW JERSEY
STUDY ABROAD IN JAPAN

Hosted by Ritsumeikan University

Academic Focus • Japanese, Japanese studies.

Program Information • Students attend classes at Ritsumeikan University.

Sessions • Yearlong.

Eligibility Requirements • Open to sophomores, juniors, seniors; 3.0 GPA; 2 letters of recommendation; good academic standing at home school; 2 years of college course work in Japanese.

Living Arrangements • Students live in host institution dormitories. Quarters are shared with students from other programs. Meals are taken on one's own, in residences, in central dining facility.

Costs (2003-2004) • Yearlong program: $14,746 for New Jersey residents; $20,046 for nonresidents; includes tuition, insurance, student support services. $20 application fee. $750 nonrefundable deposit required. Financial aid available for students from sponsoring institution: scholarships, loans.

For More Information • Ms. Karin Bonello, Regional Coordinator, Rutgers, The State University of New Jersey, 102 College Avenue, New Brunswick, NJ 08901-8543; *Phone:* 732-932-7787; *Fax:* 732-932-8659. *E-mail:* ru_abroad@email.rutgers.edu. *World Wide Web:* http://studyabroad.rutgers.edu/

MORIOKA
EARLHAM COLLEGE
STUDIES IN CROSS-CULTURAL EDUCATION: JAPAN

Held at Iwate Medical University

Academic Focus • Education, Japanese, Japanese studies.

Program Information • Classes are held on the campus of Iwate Medical University. Faculty members are drawn from the sponsor's U.S. staff and local instructors hired by the sponsor. Scheduled travel to Tokyo; field trips to local points of interest, businesses, festivals, historic sites; optional travel to Hokkaido, local points of interest in Iwate at an extra cost.

Sessions • Fall.

Eligibility Requirements • Minimum age 18; open to sophomores, juniors, seniors; 2 letters of recommendation; good academic standing at home school; 1 year of college course work in Japanese.

Living Arrangements • Students live in host family homes. Meals are taken with host family, in residences.

Costs (2003) • One term: $14,988; includes tuition, housing, all meals, excursions, international student ID. $350 nonrefundable deposit required. Financial aid available for students from sponsoring institution: scholarships, loans.

For More Information • Ms. Amanda Shaw, Program Associate, Earlham College, Drawer 13, 801 National Road West, Richmond, IN 47374; *Phone:* 765-983-1224; *Fax:* 765-983-1798. *E-mail:* japanstu@earlham.edu. *World Wide Web:* http://www.earlham.edu/~ipo/offcampus.html

NAGASAKI
STATE UNIVERSITY OF NEW YORK AT NEW PALTZ
STUDY ABROAD IN NAGASAKI, JAPAN

Hosted by Nagasaki College of Foreign Languages

Academic Focus • Art history, Japanese, Japanese studies.

Program Information • Students attend classes at Nagasaki College of Foreign Languages. Field trips to topic-related sites in Nagasaki.

Sessions • Fall, spring, yearlong.

Eligibility Requirements • Minimum age 18; open to sophomores, juniors, seniors; 2.5 GPA; 2 letters of recommendation; good academic standing at home school; no foreign language proficiency required.

Living Arrangements • Students live in host family homes. Meals are taken with host family, in residences.

Costs (2004-2005) • One term: contact sponsor for cost. Yearlong program: contact sponsor for cost. $25 application fee. $300–$600 nonrefundable deposit required. Financial aid available for students from sponsoring institution: scholarships, loans.

For More Information • Center for International Programs, State University of New York at New Paltz, 75 South Manheim Boulevard, Suite 9, New Paltz, NY 12561; *Phone:* 845-257-3125; *Fax:* 845-257-3129. *E-mail:* international@newpaltz.edu. *World Wide Web:* http://www.newpaltz.edu/studyabroad/

UNIVERSITY OF IDAHO
JAPANESE LANGUAGE AND CULTURE PROGRAM

Hosted by Nagasaki University of Foreign Studies

Academic Focus • Business administration/management, education, fine/studio arts, history, Japanese, literature.

Program Information • Students attend classes at Nagasaki University of Foreign Studies. Field trips to local attractions.

Sessions • Fall, spring, yearlong, Japanese academic year.

Eligibility Requirements • Open to sophomores, juniors, seniors, graduate students; 2.5 GPA; good academic standing at home school; no foreign language proficiency required.

Living Arrangements • Students live in host family homes. Quarters are shared with host institution students, students from other programs. Meals are taken with host family, in residences.

Costs (2003-2004) • One term: $2500. Yearlong program: $5000; includes tuition, student support services. $100 application fee. $200 refundable deposit required. Financial aid available for students from sponsoring institution: scholarships, loans.

For More Information • Ms. Amy S. Bergmann, Advisor, University of Idaho, Room 209, Morrill Hall, Moscow, ID 83844-3013; *Phone:* 208-885-4075; *Fax:* 208-885-2859. *E-mail:* abroad@uidaho.edu. *World Wide Web:* http://www.ets.uidaho.edu/ipo/abroad/

UNIVERSITY OF WISCONSIN–PLATTEVILLE
NAGASAKI STUDY CENTER

Hosted by Nagasaki College of Foreign Languages

Academic Focus • Business administration/management, education, history, Japanese, Japanese studies, sociology.

Program Information • Students attend classes at Nagasaki College of Foreign Languages. Field trips to Unzen National Park.

Sessions • Fall, spring, yearlong.

Eligibility Requirements • Minimum age 18; open to sophomores, juniors, seniors; 2.5 GPA; 2 letters of recommendation; good academic standing at home school; no foreign language proficiency required.

Living Arrangements • Students live in host family homes. Meals are taken as a group, with host family, in residences, in central dining facility.

Costs (2004-2005) • One term: $5995 for Wisconsin and Minnesota residents; $6595 for nonresidents. Yearlong program: $11,990 for Wisconsin and Minnesota residents; $13,190 for nonresidents; includes tuition, housing, some meals, insurance, excursions, international student ID, student support services. $25 application fee. $400 nonrefundable deposit required. Financial aid available for all students: loans, federal and state grants, scholarships for Platteville students.

For More Information • Ms. Donna Anderson, Director, University of Wisconsin–Platteville, Institute for Study Abroad Programs, 111 Royce Hall, 1 University, Platteville, WI 53818-3099; *Phone:* 800-342-1725; *Fax:* 608-342-1736. *E-mail:* studyabroad@uwplatt.edu. *World Wide Web:* http://www.uwplatt.edu/~studyabroad/

NAGOYA
DICKINSON COLLEGE
DICKINSON IN NAGOYA (JAPAN)

Hosted by Nanzan University

Academic Focus • Japanese, Japanese studies.

Program Information • Students attend classes at Nanzan University. Field trips to Nagoya sites.

Sessions • Fall, spring, yearlong.

Eligibility Requirements • Minimum age 18; open to juniors; 3.0 GPA; 3 letters of recommendation; good academic standing at home school; 2 years college course work in Japanese or the equivalent.

Living Arrangements • Students live in host institution dormitories, host family homes. Meals are taken with host family, in residences.

Costs (2003-2004) • One term: $17,795. Yearlong program: $35,590; includes tuition, housing, all meals, excursions. $25 application fee. $300 nonrefundable deposit required. Financial aid available for students from sponsoring institution: scholarships, loans.

For More Information • Ms. Karen Peter, Program Manager, Dickinson College, PO Box 1773, Carlisle, PA 17013-2896; *Phone:* 717-245-1341; *Fax:* 717-245-1688. *E-mail:* global@dickinson.edu. *World Wide Web:* http://www.dickinson.edu/global/

IES, INSTITUTE FOR THE INTERNATIONAL EDUCATION OF STUDENTS
IES–NAGOYA

Hosted by New England College

Academic Focus • Anthropology, business administration/management, economics, fine/studio arts, history, Japanese, Japanese studies, literature, political science and government, religious studies, sociology.

Program Information • Students attend classes at New England College. Scheduled travel to Kanazawa; field trips to Kyoto, Nara, Tokyo, Okinawa, Osaka, Hiroshima, Kurashiki; optional travel at an extra cost.

Sessions • Fall, spring, yearlong.

Eligibility Requirements • Minimum age 18; open to sophomores, juniors, seniors, graduate students, adults; 3.0 GPA; 1 letter of recommendation; good academic standing at home school; some knowledge of Japanese (for semester applicants).

Living Arrangements • Students live in host institution dormitories, host family homes. Meals are taken with host family, in residences, in central dining facility.

Costs (2003-2004) • One term: $11,950. Yearlong program: $21,510; includes tuition, housing, some meals, excursions, student support services, partial insurance coverage. $50 application fee. $500 nonrefundable deposit required. Financial aid available for all students: scholarships, institutional partner need-based grants.

For More Information • International Education Representative, IES, Institute for the International Education of Students, 33 North LaSalle Street, 15th Floor, Chicago, IL 60602; *Phone:* 800-995-2300; *Fax:* 312-944-1448. *E-mail:* info@iesabroad.org. *World Wide Web:* http://www.IESabroad.org/

UNIVERSITY OF MASSACHUSETTS AMHERST
UNIVERSITY OF MASSACHUSETTS AMHERST EXCHANGE WITH NANZAN UNIVERSITY

Hosted by Nanzan University

Academic Focus • Art, economics, Japanese, Japanese studies, liberal studies, social sciences.

Program Information • Students attend classes at Nanzan University.

Sessions • Fall, spring, yearlong.

Eligibility Requirements • Open to sophomores, juniors; 1 year of college course work in Japanese.

Living Arrangements • Students live in host family homes. Meals are taken with host family, in restaurants.

Costs (2002-2003) • One term: contact sponsor for cost. Yearlong program: contact sponsor for cost. $25 application fee. $400 nonrefundable deposit required. Financial aid available for students from sponsoring institution: scholarships, loans.

For More Information • Ms. Laurel Foster-Moore, Study Abroad Coordinator for Asia, University of Massachusetts Amherst, International Programs, Amherst, MA 01003; *Phone:* 413-545-2710; *Fax:* 413-545-1201. *E-mail:* abroad@ipo.umass.edu. *World Wide Web:* http://www.umass.edu/ipo/

NISHINOMIYA

SOUTHERN METHODIST UNIVERSITY
SMU IN JAPAN

Hosted by Kwansei Gakuin University

Academic Focus • Economics, history, international business, Japanese, political science and government, religious studies, sociology.

Program Information • Students attend classes at Kwansei Gakuin University.

Sessions • Yearlong.

Eligibility Requirements • Open to sophomores, juniors, seniors; 2.7 GPA; 2 letters of recommendation; good academic standing at home school; interview; essay; 2 years of college course work in Japanese.

Living Arrangements • Students live in host institution dormitories, host family homes. Quarters are shared with students from other programs. Meals are taken with host family, in residences.

Costs (2002-2003) • Yearlong program: $33,251; includes tuition, housing, some meals, books and class materials, student support services, estimated personal expenses. $40 application fee. $500 nonrefundable deposit required. Financial aid available for students from sponsoring institution: scholarships, loans.

For More Information • Ms. Karen Westergaard, Associate Director, Southern Methodist University, International Office, PO Box 750391, Dallas, TX 75275-0391; *Phone:* 214-768-2338; *Fax:* 214-768-1051. *E-mail:* intlpro@mail.smu.edu. *World Wide Web:* http://www.smu.edu/studyabroad/

UNIVERSITY OF MASSACHUSETTS AMHERST
UNIVERSITY OF MASSACHUSETTS AMHERST EXCHANGE WITH KWANSEI GAKUIN

Hosted by Kwansei Gakuin University

Academic Focus • Japanese, Japanese studies, liberal studies, social sciences.

Program Information • Students attend classes at Kwansei Gakuin University.

Sessions • Fall, spring, yearlong.

Eligibility Requirements • Open to juniors, seniors; 2 years of college course work in Japanese.

Living Arrangements • Students live in host family homes. Meals are taken with host family.

Costs (2002-2003) • One term: contact sponsor for cost. Yearlong program: contact sponsor for cost. $25 application fee. $400 nonrefundable deposit required. Financial aid available for students from sponsoring institution: scholarships, loans.

For More Information • Ms. Laurel Foster-Moore, Study Abroad Coordinator for Asia, University of Massachusetts Amherst, International Programs, Amherst, MA 01003; *Phone:* 413-545-2710; *Fax:* 413-545-1201. *E-mail:* abroad@ipo.umass.edu. *World Wide Web:* http://www.umass.edu/ipo/

OITA

RITSUMEIKAN ASIA PACIFIC UNIVERSITY
GRADUATE PROGRAM

Hosted by Ritsumeikan Asia Pacific University

Academic Focus • Asian studies, business administration/management, international affairs.

Program Information • Students attend classes at Ritsumeikan Asia Pacific University. Optional travel to Tokyo, Seoul at an extra cost.

Sessions • Fall, spring, yearlong, full year.

Eligibility Requirements • Open to graduate students, adults; 2 letters of recommendation; good academic standing at home school; GMAT for the MBA Program; no foreign language proficiency required.

Living Arrangements • Students live in host institution dormitories, locally rented apartments. Quarters are shared with host institution students. Meals are taken on one's own, in residences.

Costs (2005-2006) • One term: $5910-$7600. Yearlong program: $11,820-$15,200 (estimated); includes tuition. $50 application fee. Financial aid available for all students: scholarships, tuition reductions.

For More Information • Ms. Aoi Goto, Associate Manager, Admissions Office, Ritsumeikan Asia Pacific University, 1-1 Jumonjibaru, Beppu, Oita 874-8577, Japan; *Phone:* +81 977-78-1119; *Fax:* +81 977-78-1121. *E-mail:* apugrad@apu.ac.jp. *World Wide Web:* http://www.apu.ac.jp/

RITSUMEIKAN ASIA PACIFIC UNIVERSITY
UNDERGRADUATE PROGRAM

Hosted by Ritsumeikan Asia Pacific University

Academic Focus • Accounting, Asian languages, Asian studies, business administration/management, environmental science/studies, finance, human resources, international affairs, Japanese, Japanese studies, journalism, marketing, social sciences, tourism and travel.

Program Information • Students attend classes at Ritsumeikan Asia Pacific University.

Sessions • Fall, spring, yearlong, full year.

Eligibility Requirements • Open to freshmen, sophomores, juniors, seniors, graduate students, adults; 1 letter of recommendation; good academic standing at home school; no foreign language proficiency required.

Living Arrangements • Students live in host institution dormitories. Quarters are shared with host institution students. Meals are taken on one's own, in residences.

Costs (2005-2006) • One term: $5830 (estimated). Yearlong program: $11,000 (estimated); includes tuition. $50 application fee. Financial aid available for all students: scholarships, tuition reductions.

For More Information • Mr. Jeremy Breadon, Associate Manager, Admissions Office, Ritsumeikan Asia Pacific University, 1-1 Jumonjibaru, Beppu, Oita 874-8577, Japan; *Phone:* +81 977-78-1119; *Fax:* +81 977-78-1121. *E-mail:* welcome@apu.ac.jp. *World Wide Web:* http://www.apu.ac.jp/

OSAKA

WEBSTER UNIVERSITY
WEBSTER UNIVERSITY–KANSAI UNIVERSITY EXCHANGE

Hosted by Kansai University

Academic Focus • Japanese, Japanese studies.

Program Information • Students attend classes at Kansai University. Optional travel at an extra cost.

Sessions • Yearlong.

Eligibility Requirements • Open to sophomores, juniors, seniors; 2.5 GPA; 1 letter of recommendation; good academic standing at home school; 1 year of college course work in Japanese.

Living Arrangements • Students live in host institution dormitories. Quarters are shared with host institution students. Meals are taken on one's own, in central dining facility.

Costs (2003-2004) • Yearlong program: $15,980; includes tuition, insurance, international student ID, student support services. $30 application fee. $165 refundable deposit required. Financial aid available for students from sponsoring institution.

For More Information • Mr. Mark A. Beirn, Coordinator, Webster University, Office of Study Abroad, 470 East Lockwood Avenue, St. Louis, MO 63119; *Phone:* 314-968-6988; *Fax:* 314-968-5938. *E-mail:* worldview@webster.edu. *World Wide Web:* http://www.webster.edu/intl/sa/

SAPPORO

BRETHREN COLLEGES ABROAD
BCA PROGRAM IN SAPPORO, JAPAN

Hosted by Hokusei Gakuen University

Academic Focus • Art history, business administration/management, economics, history, intercultural studies, Japanese, Japanese studies, sociology.

Program Information • Students attend classes at Hokusei Gakuen University. Scheduled travel to Kyoto, Tokyo, Nara, Hiroshima; field trips to national parks, natural mineral baths.

Sessions • Fall, spring, yearlong.

Eligibility Requirements • Minimum age 18; open to sophomores, juniors, seniors, graduate students, adults; 2.6 GPA; 3 letters of recommendation; good academic standing at home school; no foreign language proficiency required.

Living Arrangements • Students live in host family homes. Meals are taken on one's own, with host family, in residences, in central dining facility, in restaurants.

Costs (2003–2004) • One term: $11,500. Yearlong program: $19,900; includes tuition, housing, all meals, insurance, excursions, international student ID, student support services. $50 application fee. $100 nonrefundable deposit required. Financial aid available for all students: scholarships.

For More Information • Mr. Jason Sanderson, Program Officer for Japan, Brethren Colleges Abroad, 50 Alpha Drive, Elizabethtown, PA 17022-0407; *Phone:* 866-222-6188; *Fax:* 717-361-6619. *E-mail:* info@bcanet.org. *World Wide Web:* http://www.bcanet.org/

TOKYO

CIEE
CIEE STUDY CENTER AT SOPHIA UNIVERSITY, TOKYO, JAPAN

Hosted by Sophia University Tokyo

Academic Focus • Anthropology, art history, business administration/management, comparative history, comparative literature, economics, international affairs, international business, Japanese, Japanese studies, literature, political science and government, religious studies, sociology.

Program Information • Students attend classes at Sophia University Tokyo. Field trips to National Diet, Kabuki, major corporations, Nikko, Sumo practice.

Sessions • Fall, spring, yearlong, spring term with language pre-session.

Eligibility Requirements • Open to sophomores, juniors, seniors, graduate students, adults; 3.0 GPA; 2 letters of recommendation; good academic standing at home school; no foreign language proficiency required.

Living Arrangements • Students live in host family homes. Meals are taken on one's own, with host family, in residences, in restaurants.

Costs (2004) • One term: $15,800 ($18,300 with pre-session). Yearlong program: $28,000; includes tuition, housing, all meals, insurance, excursions, student support services, local commuter pass for Tokyo, pre-departure advising, visa assistance. $30 application fee. $300 deposit required. Financial aid available for all students: scholarships, minority student scholarships, travel grants.

For More Information • Mr. Adam Rubin, Admissions Officer, Asia Pacific, CIEE, 7 Custom House Street, 3rd Floor, Portland, ME 04101; *Phone:* 800-40-STUDY; *Fax:* 207-553-7699. *E-mail:* studyinfo@ciee.org. *World Wide Web:* http://www.ciee.org/isp/

EARLHAM COLLEGE
JAPAN STUDY

Hosted by Waseda University

Academic Focus • Economics, international affairs, Japanese, Japanese studies, social sciences.

Program Information • Students attend classes at Waseda University. Scheduled travel to Daito-cho (Shimane), Daito-shi (Osaka), Nagano; field trips to museums, cultural centers; optional travel to Kyoto, Nara, southeast Asia, Kyushu, Hokkaido at an extra cost.

Sessions • Spring, yearlong, spring term with language intensive option.

Eligibility Requirements • Minimum age 18; open to sophomores, juniors, seniors; 3.0 GPA; 3 letters of recommendation; 0.5 years of college course work in Japanese.

Living Arrangements • Students live in host family homes. Meals are taken on one's own, with host family, in residences.

Costs (2003–2004) • One term: contact sponsor for cost. Yearlong program: $30,440; includes tuition, housing, some meals, excursions, student support services, daily commute costs. $500 nonrefundable deposit required.

For More Information • Ms. Amanda Shaw, Program Associate, Japan Study, Earlham College, Drawer 13, 801 National Road West, Richmond, IN 47374; *Phone:* 765-983-1224; *Fax:* 765-983-1798. *E-mail:* japanstu@earlham.edu. *World Wide Web:* http://www.earlham.edu/~ipo/offcampus.html

IES, INSTITUTE FOR THE INTERNATIONAL EDUCATION OF STUDENTS
IES–TOKYO

Hosted by Institute for the International Education of Students (IES)–Tokyo, Kanda University for International Studies

Academic Focus • Anthropology, architecture, art, economics, history, international business, Japanese, Japanese studies, marketing, political science and government, sociology, urban studies.

Program Information • Students attend classes at Institute for the International Education of Students (IES)–Tokyo, Kanda University for International Studies. Scheduled travel to Kyoto, northern Japan, South Korea; field trips to Kamakura, Nikko, a rural village; optional travel to South Korea at an extra cost.

Sessions • Fall, spring, yearlong.

Eligibility Requirements • Minimum age 18; open to sophomores, juniors, seniors, graduate students, adults; 3.0 GPA; 1 letter of recommendation; good academic standing at home school; no foreign language proficiency required.

Living Arrangements • Students live in host institution dormitories, host family homes. Quarters are shared with host institution students. Meals are taken on one's own, with host family, in residences, in central dining facility.

Costs (2003–2004) • One term: $12,900. Yearlong program: $23,220; includes tuition, housing, some meals, excursions, student support services, partial insurance coverage. $50 application fee. $500 nonrefundable deposit required. Financial aid available for all students: scholarships, institutional partner need-based grants.

For More Information • International Education Representative, IES, Institute for the International Education of Students, 33 North LaSalle Street, 15th Floor, Chicago, IL 60602; *Phone:* 800-995-2300; *Fax:* 312-944-1448. *E-mail:* info@iesabroad.org. *World Wide Web:* http://www.IESabroad.org/

KCP INTERNATIONAL LANGUAGE INSTITUTE
KCP INTERNATIONAL LANGUAGE INSTITUTE

Hosted by KCP International Language Institute

Academic Focus • Japanese, Japanese studies.

Program Information • Students attend classes at KCP International Language Institute. Scheduled travel to Kamakura, Hakone; field trips to a Sumo beya, museums, temples.

Sessions • Fall, spring, winter, yearlong, fall extended.

Eligibility Requirements • Minimum age 18; open to freshmen, sophomores, juniors, seniors, graduate students, adults; 2.5 GPA; 1 letter of recommendation; no foreign language proficiency required.

Living Arrangements • Students live in host institution dormitories, locally rented apartments, host family homes, hotels. Quarters are shared with host institution students, students from other programs. Meals are taken as a group, on one's own, with host family, in residences.

Costs (2003–2004) • One term: $1800–$5500 depending on session and housing option selected. Yearlong program: contact sponsor for cost; includes tuition, housing, some meals, insurance, excursions, books and class materials, student support services. $350 application fee. Financial aid available for students: scholarships and loans for U.S. citizens.

For More Information • Mr. Mike Anderson, Director, KCP International Language Institute, PO Box 28028, Bellingham, WA 98228-0028; *Phone:* 360-441-1800; *Fax:* 360-647-0736. *E-mail:* mike@kcp-usa.com. *World Wide Web:* http://www.Lincoln-japan.com/

JAPAN
Tokyo

LAKELAND COLLEGE
STUDY ABROAD AT LAKELAND COLLEGE JAPAN

Hosted by Lakeland College Japan
Academic Focus • Full curriculum.
Program Information • Students attend classes at Lakeland College Japan.
Sessions • Fall, spring, winter.
Eligibility Requirements • Open to freshmen, sophomores, juniors, seniors, adults; minimum 2.0 GPA required, but minimum 2.5 GPA preferred (based on a minimum of 12 credits); high school transcript for adult students; no foreign language proficiency required.
Living Arrangements • Students live in host institution dormitories, host family homes. Meals are taken with host family, in residences.
Costs (2004-2005) • One term: $11,300; includes tuition, housing, some meals, insurance, books and class materials, student support services, train pass. $20 application fee. $500 nonrefundable deposit required. Financial aid available for all students: scholarships, loans.
For More Information • Ms. Rebecca Boyko, Assistant to the Vice President of International Programs, Lakeland College, PO Box 359, Sheboygan, WI 53082-0359; *Phone:* 888-525-3638; *Fax:* 920-565-1206. *E-mail:* studyabroad@lakeland.edu. *World Wide Web:* http://www.lakeland.edu/studyabroad/studyabroad_home.asp

LINCOLN UNIVERSITY
KCP INTERNATIONAL LANGUAGE INSTITUTE

Hosted by KCP International Language Institute
Academic Focus • Japanese, Japanese studies.
Program Information • Students attend classes at KCP International Language Institute. Field trips to Kamakura, the Edo-Tokyo Museum, Nikko, Asakusa Temple, the Imperial Palace, NHK Broadcasting Company, a Sumo beya, Kabuki and Bunraku theaters; optional travel at an extra cost.

Sessions • Fall, spring, winter, yearlong, spring and fall extended terms.
Eligibility Requirements • Minimum age 18; open to freshmen, sophomores, juniors, seniors, graduate students, adults; 2.7 GPA; 1 letter of recommendation; good academic standing at home school; completion of 20 college semester hours; 0.5 years of college course work in Japanese.
Living Arrangements • Students live in host institution dormitories, host family homes. Quarters are shared with host institution students, students from other programs. Meals are taken on one's own, with host family, in residences, in central dining facility.
Costs (2005-2006) • One term: $5820–$6020 for regular term; $11,640-$12,040 for extended term. Yearlong program: $17,460–$18,060; includes tuition, housing, insurance, excursions, books and class materials, fees. $350 application fee. Financial aid available for students from sponsoring institution: scholarships, loans, grants.
For More Information • Ms. Constance Lundy, Director of International Services, Lincoln University, PO Box 179, MSC 50, Lincoln University, PA 19352; *Phone:* 610-932-1286; *Fax:* 610-998-6022. *E-mail:* paletsa2001@yahoo.com. *World Wide Web:* http://www.kcpinternational.com/. Students may also apply through KCP International USA, PO Box 28028, Bellingham, WA 98228-0028.

ST. JOHN'S UNIVERSITY
STUDY ABROAD JAPAN PROGRAM

Hosted by Sophia University Tokyo
Academic Focus • Anthropology, art history, business administration/management, French language and literature, geography, German language and literature, Japanese, Japanese studies, mathematics, philosophy, political science and government, psychology, religious studies, social sciences, sociology.
Program Information • Students attend classes at Sophia University Tokyo.

LAKELAND
COLLEGE

Invites you to spend a semester in Tokyo at

Lakeland College Japan

- Classes are taught in English

- Earn credit toward your degree

- Highly supportive faculty and staff

- Live with a Japanese family or in an international residence hall

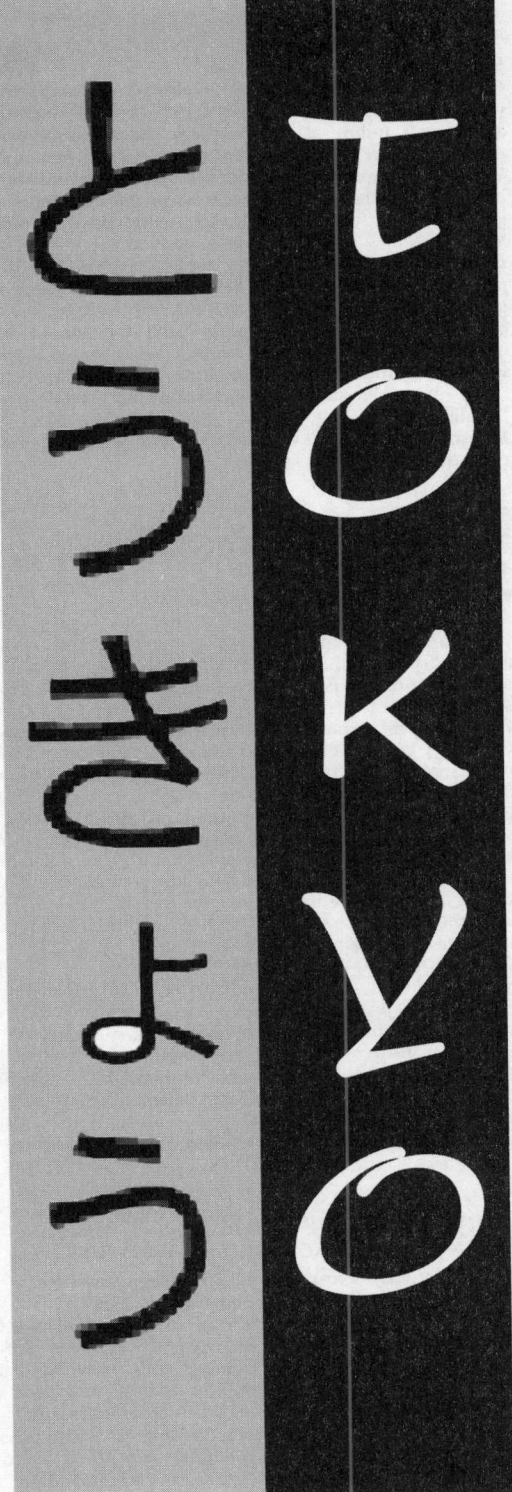

For information or an application contact
888-525-3638 (toll free)
www.lakeland.edu/studyabroad/studyabroad_home.asp
studyabroad@lakeland.edu

JAPAN
Tokyo

Sessions • Fall, spring, yearlong.
Eligibility Requirements • Minimum age 18; open to sophomores, juniors, seniors; 3.0 GPA; 2 letters of recommendation; good academic standing at home school; interview; 1 year of college course work in Japanese.
Living Arrangements • Students live in host institution dormitories, program-owned apartments, host family homes. Quarters are shared with host institution students, students from other programs. Meals are taken on one's own, in residences.
Costs (2003-2004) • One term: $19,819–$20,763. Yearlong program: $40,656–$42,592; includes tuition, housing, some meals, student support services. $30 application fee. $750 nonrefundable deposit required. Financial aid available for students from sponsoring institution: scholarships, loans.
For More Information • Dr. Ruth De Paula, Director, Office of Study Abroad Programs, St. John's University, 8000 Utopia Parkway, Jamaica, NY 11439; *Phone:* 718-990-6105; *Fax:* 718-990-2321. *E-mail:* intled@stjohns.edu. *World Wide Web:* http://www.stjohns.edu/studyabroad/

TEMPLE UNIVERSITY
TEMPLE UNIVERSITY JAPAN

Hosted by Temple University Japan
Academic Focus • American studies, art history, Asian studies, Chinese language and literature, communications, economics, film and media studies, geography, history, Japanese, political science and government, psychology, religious studies, sociology, urban studies.
Program Information • Students attend classes at Temple University Japan. Field trips to a Japanese high school and traditional castle in Odawara; optional travel to Kyoto, Nikko at an extra cost.
Sessions • Fall, spring, yearlong.
Eligibility Requirements • Minimum age 19; open to juniors, seniors; 2.5 GPA; 2 letters of recommendation; good academic standing at home school; intent to enroll as a full-time student; official transcripts; no foreign language proficiency required.
Living Arrangements • Students live in program-owned apartments. Quarters are shared with host institution students. Meals are taken on one's own, in residences.
Costs (2003-2004) • One term: $9300. Yearlong program: $18,600; includes tuition, housing, activity fee. $30 application fee. $150 refundable deposit required. Financial aid available for students from sponsoring institution: scholarships, work study, loans.
For More Information • Ms. Erin Joslyn, Study Abroad Coordinator, Temple University, International Programs, 200 Tuttleman Learning Center, 1809 North 13th Street, Philadelphia, PA 19122; *Phone:* 215-204-0720; *Fax:* 215-204-0729. *E-mail:* study.abroad@temple.edu. *World Wide Web:* http://www.temple.edu/studyabroad/

UNIVERSITY OF IDAHO
KCP INTERNATIONAL LANGUAGE INSTITUTE

Hosted by KCP International Language Institute
Academic Focus • Japanese, Japanese studies.
Program Information • Students attend classes at KCP International Language Institute. Field trips to Kamakura, the Edo-Tokyo Museum, Nikko, Asakusa Temple, the Imperial Palace, NHK Broadcasting Company, a Sumo beya, Kabuki and Bunrako theaters; optional travel to other parts of Japan at an extra cost.
Sessions • Fall, spring, winter, extended terms also possible.
Eligibility Requirements • Minimum age 18; open to freshmen, sophomores, juniors, seniors, graduate students, adults; 2.5 GPA; 1 letter of recommendation; good academic standing at home school; completion of 30 quarter (20 semester) hours; no foreign language proficiency required.
Living Arrangements • Students live in host institution dormitories, host family homes. Quarters are shared with host institution students, students from other programs. Meals are taken on one's own, with host family, in residences, in central dining facility.
Costs (2003-2004) • One term: $5725–$5925; includes tuition, housing, some meals, insurance, excursions, books and class materials, student support services, local transportation pass, airport pick-up. $150 application fee. $200 nonrefundable deposit required. Financial aid available for students from sponsoring institution: scholarships, loans.

For More Information • Ms. Amy Bergmann, Advisor, University of Idaho, Room 209, Morrill Hall, Moscow, ID 83844-3013; *Phone:* 208-885-7870; *Fax:* 208-885-2859. *E-mail:* abroad@uidaho.edu. *World Wide Web:* http://www.ets.uidaho.edu/ipo/abroad/

UNIVERSITY OF MASSACHUSETTS AMHERST
UNIVERSITY OF MASSACHUSETTS AMHERST EXCHANGE WITH INTERNATIONAL CHRISTIAN UNIVERSITY

Hosted by International Christian University
Academic Focus • Art, Japanese, Japanese studies, liberal studies, social sciences.
Program Information • Students attend classes at International Christian University. Optional travel to Hokkaido at an extra cost.
Sessions • Yearlong.
Eligibility Requirements • Open to juniors, seniors, graduate students; 1 year of college course work in Japanese.
Living Arrangements • Students live in host institution dormitories, locally rented apartments, host family homes. Quarters are shared with host institution students. Meals are taken on one's own, with host family, in residences, in central dining facility.
Costs (2002-2003) • Yearlong program: contact sponsor for cost. $25 application fee. $400 nonrefundable deposit required. Financial aid available for students from sponsoring institution: scholarships, loans.
For More Information • Ms. Laurel Foster-Moore, Study Abroad Coordinator for Asia, University of Massachusetts Amherst, International Programs, Amherst, MA 01003; *Phone:* 413-545-2710; *Fax:* 413-545-1201. *E-mail:* abroad@ipo.umass.edu. *World Wide Web:* http://www.umass.edu/ipo/

UNIVERSITY OF MIAMI
SOPHIA UNIVERSITY

Hosted by Sophia University Tokyo
Academic Focus • Anthropology, art history, East Asian studies, economics, history, international business, Japanese, Japanese studies, linguistics, literature, philosophy, political science and government, religious studies, sociology.
Program Information • Students attend classes at Sophia University Tokyo.
Sessions • Fall, spring, yearlong.
Eligibility Requirements • Minimum age 18; open to sophomores, juniors, seniors; 3.0 GPA; 2 letters of recommendation; official transcript; 1 year of college course work in Japanese.
Living Arrangements • Students live in host institution dormitories, locally rented apartments, host family homes. Quarters are shared with host institution students, students from other programs. Meals are taken on one's own, with host family, in residences, in central dining facility, in restaurants.
Costs (2003-2004) • One term: $12,919. Yearlong program: $25,838; includes tuition, student support services. $40 application fee. $500 nonrefundable deposit required. Financial aid available for students from sponsoring institution: scholarships, loans.
For More Information • Ms. Glenda Hayley, Assistant Director, University of Miami, International Education and Exchange Programs, 5050 Brunson Drive, Allen Hall 212, PO Box 248005, Coral Gables, FL 33124-1610; *Phone:* 305-284-3434; *Fax:* 305-284-4235. *E-mail:* ieep@miami.edu. *World Wide Web:* http://www.studyabroad.miami.edu/

WASEDA UNIVERSITY
INTERNATIONAL DIVISION PROGRAM

Hosted by Waseda University
Academic Focus • Anthropology, architecture, art, Asian studies, communications, economics, environmental science/studies, history, international affairs, international business, Japanese, Japanese studies, literature, performing arts, political science and government, religious studies, social sciences.
Program Information • Students attend classes at Waseda University. Field trips to Sumo wrestling, Kabuki, suburban Tokyo; optional travel to Kyushu, Kyoto, Nara, Nagano, Okinawa, Hiroshima at an extra cost.
Sessions • Fall, spring, yearlong, autumn term.

Eligibility Requirements • Open to sophomores, juniors, seniors; 3.0 GPA; 2 letters of recommendation; good academic standing at home school; 0.5 years of college course work in Japanese.

Living Arrangements • Students live in host institution dormitories, locally rented apartments, host family homes. Quarters are shared with host institution students, students from other programs. Meals are taken on one's own, with host family, in residences, in restaurants.

Costs (2003-2004) • One term: ¥486,100 for fall term; 364,500 for spring term; 364,500 for autumn term. Yearlong program: ¥850,600; includes tuition, books and class materials, lab equipment, student support services. ¥17,500 application fee. ¥60,000 nonrefundable deposit required. Financial aid available for all students: scholarships.

For More Information • Chie Akaishi, International Program Coordinator, Waseda University, Center for International Education, #404 1-7-14 Nishi-Waseda, Shinjuku-ku, Tokyo 169-0051, Japan; *Phone:* +81 3-3207-1454; *Fax:* +81 3-3202-8638. *E-mail:* cie@list. waseda.jp. *World Wide Web:* http://www.waseda.ac.jp/cie/international/IDP.html. Students may also apply through California State University International Programs, 400 Golden Shore, Suite 300, Long Beach, CA 90802; Oregon University System, International Programs in Japan, Oregon State University, 444 Shell Hall, Corvallis, OR 97331; University of Southern California, CALPUC Year-in-Japan Program, Los Angeles, CA 90041; GLCA/ACM Japan Study, Earlham College, Drawer 202, 801 National Road West, Richmond, IN 47374.

WESTERN WASHINGTON UNIVERSITY
KCP INTERNATIONAL LANGUAGE INSTITUTE

Hosted by KCP International Language Institute
Academic Focus • Japanese, Japanese studies.
Program Information • Students attend classes at KCP International Language Institute. Field trips to Kamakura, the Edo-Tokyo Museum, Asakusa Temple, the Imperial Palace, NHK Broadcasting Company, a Sumo beya, Kabuki and Bunraku theaters; optional travel to Nikko, Hakone, Mt. Fuji at an extra cost.
Sessions • Fall, spring, winter, yearlong, extended fall and spring terms.
Eligibility Requirements • Minimum age 18; open to freshmen, sophomores, juniors, seniors, graduate students, adults; 2.5 GPA; 1 letter of recommendation; good academic standing at home school; at least 30 quarter credit hours completed; no foreign language proficiency required.
Living Arrangements • Students live in host institution dormitories, host family homes. Quarters are shared with host institution students, students from other programs. Meals are taken on one's own, with host family, in residences, in central dining facility.
Costs (2003-2004) • One term: $5775 for regular semester; $11,550 for extended semester. Yearlong program: $17,325; includes tuition, housing, some meals, insurance, excursions, books and class materials, student support services. $105 application fee. $175 refundable deposit required. Financial aid available for students from sponsoring institution: scholarships, loans.
For More Information • Mr. Mike Anderson, Director, Western Washington University, PO Box 28028, Bellingham, WA 98228-0028; *Phone:* 360-647-0072; *Fax:* 360-647-0736. *E-mail:* kcp@kcp-usa.com. *World Wide Web:* http://wwu.edu/~ipewwu/

TSUKUBA
STATE UNIVERSITY OF NEW YORK AT OSWEGO
UNIVERSITY OF TSUKUBA

Hosted by Tsukuba University
Academic Focus • Business administration/management, cultural studies, economics, history, Japanese, Japanese studies, political science and government.
Program Information • Students attend classes at Tsukuba University. Field trips to the area around Tsukuba, Tokyo.
Sessions • Yearlong.
Eligibility Requirements • Open to sophomores, juniors, seniors; 2.5 GPA; 3 letters of recommendation; good academic standing at home school; language proficiency form; personal study statement; 1 year of college course work in Japanese.

Living Arrangements • Students live in host institution dormitories. Quarters are shared with host institution students, students from other programs. Meals are taken as a group, on one's own, in residences, in central dining facility, in restaurants.

Costs (2003-2004) • Yearlong program: $10,140; includes tuition, housing, all meals, insurance, student support services. $250 nonrefundable deposit required. Financial aid available for students from sponsoring institution: scholarships, loans, Japanese government scholarship open to all participants.

For More Information • Ms. Nefertitti Saheed, Program Specialist, State University of New York at Oswego, 122A Swetman Hall, Oswego, NY 13126; *Phone:* 888-4-OSWEGO; *Fax:* 315-312-2477. *E-mail:* intled@oswego.edu. *World Wide Web:* http://www.oswego.edu/intled/

ZENTSUJI
WHITWORTH COLLEGE
WHITWORTH/SHIKOKU GAKUIN UNIVERSITY EXCHANGE PROGRAM

Hosted by Shikoku Christian College
Academic Focus • Japanese.
Program Information • Students attend classes at Shikoku Christian College. Optional travel at an extra cost.
Sessions • Fall, spring, yearlong.
Eligibility Requirements • Open to sophomores, juniors, seniors, adults; 2.5 GPA; 2 letters of recommendation; 1 year of college course work in Japanese.
Living Arrangements • Students live in host institution dormitories, locally rented apartments. Quarters are shared with host institution students, students from other programs. Meals are taken on one's own, in residences.
Costs (2003-2004) • One term: $13,034. Yearlong program: $26,068; includes tuition, housing, all meals. Financial aid available for students from sponsoring institution: scholarships, loans.
For More Information • Ms. Sue Jackson, Director, Off-Campus Programs, Whitworth College, Center for International and Multicultural Education, 300 West Hawthorne Road, Spokane, WA 99251-2702; *Phone:* 509-777-4596; *Fax:* 509-777-3723. *E-mail:* sjackson@whitworth.edu. *World Wide Web:* http://www.whitworth.edu/

JORDAN
AMMAN
CIEE
CIEE STUDY CENTER AT THE UNIVERSITY OF JORDAN, AMMAN

Hosted by University of Jordan
Academic Focus • Anthropology, Arabic, archaeology, art history, cultural studies, economics, history, literature, political science and government.
Program Information • Students attend classes at University of Jordan. Scheduled travel to Petra, Wadi Rum; field trips to various museums and cultural institutions, Jerash, Um Qais, a Palestinian refugee camp.
Sessions • Fall, spring, yearlong.
Eligibility Requirements • Open to sophomores, juniors, seniors; 2.75 GPA; 2 letters of recommendation; no foreign language proficiency required.
Living Arrangements • Students live in host institution dormitories, locally rented apartments, host family homes. Quarters are shared with host institution students, students from other programs. Meals are taken on one's own, with host family, in residences, in central dining facility.
Costs (2003-2004) • One term: $8100. Yearlong program: $15,795; includes tuition, housing, all meals, insurance, excursions, cultural activities, pre-departure advising, visa fees, optional on-site pick-up.

JORDAN
Amman

$30 application fee. $300 deposit required. Financial aid available for all students: minority student scholarships, non-traditional study grants, travel grants.

For More Information • Ms. Hannah McChesney, Admissions Officer, Europe, Middle East, and Africa, CIEE, 7 Custom House Street, 3rd Floor, Portland, ME 04101; *Phone:* 800-40-STUDY; *Fax:* 207-553-7699. *E-mail:* studyinfo@ciee.org. *World Wide Web:* http://www.ciee.org/isp/

EARLHAM COLLEGE
MIDDLE EAST SEMESTER IN JORDAN

Academic Focus • Arabic, history, literature, political science and government.

Program Information • Faculty members are drawn from the sponsor's U.S. staff and local instructors hired by the sponsor. Field trips to local cultural sites.

Sessions • Spring.

Eligibility Requirements • Open to freshmen, sophomores, juniors, seniors; 2 letters of recommendation; good academic standing at home school; no foreign language proficiency required.

Living Arrangements • Students live in host family homes, a research institute. Meals are taken on one's own, with host family, in residences.

Costs (2004) • One term: contact sponsor for cost. $350 nonrefundable deposit required. Financial aid available for students from sponsoring institution: scholarships, loans.

For More Information • Ms. Kelley Lawson-Khalidi, Director of Middle East Semester in Jordan, Earlham College, Drawer 202, 801 National Road West, Richmond, IN 47374; *Phone:* 765-983-1424; *Fax:* 765-983-1553. *E-mail:* lawsoke@earlham.edu. *World Wide Web:* http://www.earlham.edu/~ipo/offcampus.html

SCHOOL FOR INTERNATIONAL TRAINING, SIT STUDY ABROAD
JORDAN: MODERNIZATION AND SOCIAL CHANGE

Academic Focus • Economics, geography, history, international affairs, Middle Eastern studies, political science and government, social sciences.

Program Information • Faculty members are drawn from the sponsor's U.S. staff and local instructors hired by the sponsor. Field trips to Petra, Aqaba.

Sessions • Fall, spring.

Eligibility Requirements • Open to sophomores, juniors, seniors; 2.5 GPA; 2 letters of recommendation; good academic standing at home school; no foreign language proficiency required.

Living Arrangements • Students live in host family homes, hotels. Meals are taken as a group, on one's own, with host family, in residences, in restaurants.

Costs (2003-2004) • One term: $12,050; includes tuition, housing, all meals, insurance, excursions. $50 application fee. $400 nonrefundable deposit required. Financial aid available for all students: scholarships.

For More Information • School for International Training, SIT Study Abroad, Kipling Road, Brattleboro, VT 05302-0676; *Phone:* 888-272-7881; *Fax:* 802-258-3296. *E-mail:* studyabroad@sit.edu. *World Wide Web:* http://www.sit.edu/studyabroad/

KAZAKHSTAN
ALMATY

ACIE (ACTR/ACCELS)
ACIE–NIS REGIONAL LANGUAGE TRAINING PROGRAM–KAZAKHSTAN

Academic Focus • Cultural studies, Kazakh, language studies, Russian language and literature.

Program Information • Faculty members are local instructors hired by the sponsor.

Sessions • Fall, spring, yearlong.

Eligibility Requirements • Minimum age 18; open to sophomores, juniors, seniors, graduate students, adults; 3 letters of recommendation; good academic standing at home school; 1 year of college course work in Russian or Kazakh.

Living Arrangements • Students live in host institution dormitories, host family homes. Quarters are shared with students from other programs. Meals are taken on one's own, with host family, in residences, in restaurants.

Costs (2002-2003) • One term: contact sponsor for cost. Yearlong program: contact sponsor for cost. $35 application fee. $500 nonrefundable deposit required. Financial aid available for all students: scholarships.

For More Information • Ms. Margaret Stephenson, Russian and Eurasian Program Officer, ACIE (ACTR/ACCELS), 1776 Massachusetts Avenue, NW, Suite 700, Washington, DC 20036; *Phone:* 202-833-7522; *Fax:* 202-833-7523. *E-mail:* outbound@actr.org. *World Wide Web:* http://www.actr.org/

KENYA
CITY TO CITY

THE SCHOOL FOR FIELD STUDIES
KENYA: WILDLIFE ECOLOGY AND MANAGEMENT STUDIES

Held at Center for Wildlife Management Studies, Center for Wildlife Management Studies

Academic Focus • African studies, biological/life sciences, conservation studies, ecology, economics, environmental science/studies, natural resources, wildlife studies.

Program Information • Classes are held on the campus of Center for Wildlife Management Studies (Kilimanjaro Bush Camp), Center for Wildlife Management Studies (Nairobi National Park). Faculty members are drawn from the sponsor's U.S. staff and local instructors hired by the sponsor. Scheduled travel to Tsavo and Amboseli National Parks, the Kimana Wildlife Sanctuary; field trips to the Maasai Mara Game Reserve, Nairobi National Park; optional travel to Tanzania at an extra cost.

Sessions • Fall, spring.

Eligibility Requirements • Minimum age 18; open to freshmen, sophomores, juniors, seniors; course work in biology or ecology; 2.7 GPA; 2 letters of recommendation; personal statement; no foreign language proficiency required.

Living Arrangements • Students live in thatched roof bandas. Quarters are shared with host institution students. Meals are taken as a group, in central dining facility.

Costs (2002-2003) • One term: $13,950; includes tuition, housing, all meals, excursions, lab equipment. $45 application fee. $500 nonrefundable deposit required. Financial aid available for all students: scholarships, loans.

For More Information • Admissions Department, The School for Field Studies, 10 Federal Street, Salem, MA 01970-3853; *Phone:* 800-989-4418; *Fax:* 978-741-3551. *E-mail:* admissions@fieldstudies.org. *World Wide Web:* http://www.fieldstudies.org/

ELDORET

WALLA WALLA COLLEGE
ADVENTIST COLLEGES ABROAD

Hosted by University of Eastern Africa Baraton

Academic Focus • African languages and literature, full curriculum.

Program Information • Students attend classes at University of Eastern Africa Baraton. Scheduled travel; optional travel at an extra cost.

Sessions • Yearlong.

Eligibility Requirements • Minimum age 18; open to freshmen, sophomores, juniors, seniors; 2.5 GPA; good academic standing at home school; minimum 3.0 GPA in Swahili; 1 year of college course work in Swahili.

Living Arrangements • Students live in host institution dormitories. Quarters are shared with host institution students, students from other programs. Meals are taken as a group, in central dining facility.

Costs (2002-2003) • Yearlong program: contact sponsor for cost. $100 nonrefundable deposit required. Financial aid available for all students: scholarships, loans.

For More Information • Mr. Jean-Paul Grimaud, Chair of Modern Language Department, Walla Walla College, 204 South College Avenue, College Place, WA 99324; *Phone:* 509-529-7769; *Fax:* 509-527-2253. *E-mail:* grimje@wwc.edu

MOMBASA

SCHOOL FOR INTERNATIONAL TRAINING, SIT STUDY ABROAD
KENYA: COASTAL CULTURES

Academic Focus • African studies, anthropology, geography, history, political science and government, Swahili, visual and performing arts.

Program Information • Faculty members are drawn from the sponsor's U.S. staff and local instructors hired by the sponsor. Scheduled travel to Zanzibar or Oman (conditions permitting); field trips to a national park, coastal towns, rural areas.

Sessions • Fall, spring.

Eligibility Requirements • Open to sophomores, juniors, seniors; 2.5 GPA; 2 letters of recommendation; good academic standing at home school; no foreign language proficiency required.

Living Arrangements • Students live in host family homes, hotels. Meals are taken as a group, on one's own, with host family, in residences, in restaurants.

Costs (2003-2004) • One term: $12,150; includes tuition, housing, all meals, insurance, excursions, international student ID. $50 application fee. $400 nonrefundable deposit required. Financial aid available for all students: scholarships.

For More Information • School for International Training, SIT Study Abroad, Kipling Road, Brattleboro, VT 05302-0676; *Phone:* 888-272-7881; *Fax:* 802-258-3296. *E-mail:* studyabroad@sit.edu. *World Wide Web:* http://www.sit.edu/studyabroad/

NAIROBI

BAYLOR UNIVERSITY
EAST AFRICA SEMESTER ABROAD

Held at Brackenhurst Baptist International Conference Centre

Academic Focus • African studies, history, literature, religious studies, Swahili.

Program Information • Classes are held on the campus of Brackenhurst Baptist International Conference Centre. Faculty members are drawn from the sponsor's U.S. staff and local instructors hired by the sponsor. Scheduled travel to Serengeti Plains of Tanzania, a homestay with the Maasai, the Rift Valley, a homestay with the Luhya; field trips to temples, churches, mosques, cultural events; optional travel to Mt. Kenya, the coast of Kenya, Mt. Kilimanjaro, game parks at an extra cost.

Sessions • Fall.

Eligibility Requirements • Open to sophomores, juniors, seniors; 3 letters of recommendation; good academic standing at home school; interview (in person or by phone); no foreign language proficiency required.

Living Arrangements • Students live in host family homes, a conference centre. Quarters are shared with host institution students. Meals are taken as a group, with host family, in central dining facility.

Costs (2003-2004) • One term: $12,000 (estimated); includes tuition, housing, all meals, insurance, excursions, international airfare, books and class materials. $500 refundable deposit required. Financial aid available for all students: scholarships, loans.

For More Information • Center for International Education, Baylor University, PO Box 97195, Waco, TX 76798-7195; *Phone:* 254-710-2657; *Fax:* 254-710-1468. *E-mail:* helen_b_miller@baylor.edu. *World Wide Web:* http://www.baylor.edu/international_programs/

COLLEGE OF WOOSTER
WOOSTER IN KENYA

Academic Focus • Economics, health-care management, social sciences, sociology.

Program Information • Faculty members are drawn from the sponsor's U.S. staff and local instructors hired by the sponsor. Scheduled travel to Uganda; field trips to Uganda; optional travel to a destination of student's choice at an extra cost.

Sessions • Fall, program runs every 3 years.

Eligibility Requirements • Open to sophomores, juniors; 2.5 GPA; good academic standing at home school; no foreign language proficiency required.

Living Arrangements • Students live in hotels. Meals are taken on one's own, in restaurants.

Costs (2003) • One term: contact sponsor for cost. $500 nonrefundable deposit required. Financial aid available for students from sponsoring institution: scholarships.

For More Information • Dr. Randy Quaye, Professor of Sociology, College of Wooster, Sociology Department, Wooster, OH 44691; *Phone:* 330-263-2000. *E-mail:* rquaye@wooster.edu. *World Wide Web:* http://www.wooster.edu/ipo/

KALAMAZOO COLLEGE
KALAMAZOO IN KENYA

Hosted by University of Nairobi

Academic Focus • African studies, biological/life sciences, liberal studies, literature, philosophy, social sciences, Swahili, visual and performing arts.

Program Information • Students attend classes at University of Nairobi. Scheduled travel to western Kenya, the Rift Valley; field trips to Machakos; optional travel to Maasai Mara at an extra cost.

Sessions • Fall, yearlong.

Eligibility Requirements • Open to juniors; 2.75 GPA; 2 letters of recommendation; essay; demonstrated interest in African studies; must be a degree-seeking student at an accredited American college or university; no foreign language proficiency required.

Living Arrangements • Students live in host family homes. Meals are taken with host family, in residences.

Costs (2003-2004) • One term: $19,592. Yearlong program: $29,388; includes tuition, housing, all meals, excursions, international airfare. $50 application fee. $300 nonrefundable deposit required. Financial aid available for students from sponsoring institution: scholarships, loans.

For More Information • Dr. Joseph L. Brockington, Director, Center for International Programs, Kalamazoo College, 1200 Academy Street, Kalamazoo, MI 49006; *Phone:* 269-337-7133; *Fax:* 269-337-7400. *E-mail:* cip@kzoo.edu. *World Wide Web:* http://www.kzoo.edu/cip/

ST. LAWRENCE UNIVERSITY
KENYA SEMESTER PROGRAM

Hosted by St. Lawrence University Center

Academic Focus • African studies, anthropology, environmental science/studies, interdisciplinary studies, political science and government, religious studies, sociology, Swahili.

Program Information • Students attend classes at St. Lawrence University Center. Classes are also held on the campus of YMCA. Scheduled travel to northern Tanzania national parks, the Samburu Province, the Rift Valley; optional travel to Mount Kenya at an extra cost.

Sessions • Fall, spring.

Eligibility Requirements • Open to sophomores, juniors, seniors; course work in African studies; 2.8 GPA; 3 letters of recommendation; interview; no foreign language proficiency required.

Living Arrangements • Students live in host family homes, a compound in Nairobi. Meals are taken with host family.

Costs (2003-2004) • One term: $17,870; includes tuition, housing, all meals, excursions. $500 nonrefundable deposit required. Financial aid available for students from sponsoring institution: scholarships, loans.

For More Information • Ms. Sara Hofschulte, Assistant Director, Off-Campus Programs, St. Lawrence University, Center for International and Intercultural Studies, Canton, NY 13617; *Phone:* 315-229-5991; *Fax:* 315-229-5989. *E-mail:* shofschulte@stlawu.edu. *World Wide Web:* http://www.stlawu.edu/ciis/offcampus/

KENYA
Nairobi

SCHOOL FOR INTERNATIONAL TRAINING, SIT STUDY ABROAD
KENYA: DEVELOPMENT, HEALTH, AND SOCIETY

Academic Focus • African studies, anthropology, economics, geography, history, Swahili, visual and performing arts.
Program Information • Faculty members are drawn from the sponsor's U.S. staff and local instructors hired by the sponsor. Scheduled travel to Uganda or Tanzania (conditions permitting); field trips to rural areas, historic sites.
Sessions • Fall, spring.
Eligibility Requirements • Open to sophomores, juniors, seniors; 2.5 GPA; 2 letters of recommendation; good academic standing at home school; no foreign language proficiency required.
Living Arrangements • Students live in host family homes, hotels. Meals are taken as a group, on one's own, with host family, in residences, in restaurants.
Costs (2003-2004) • One term: $12,275; includes tuition, housing, all meals, insurance, excursions, international student ID. $50 application fee. $400 nonrefundable deposit required. Financial aid available for all students: scholarships.
For More Information • School for International Training, SIT Study Abroad, Kipling Road, Brattleboro, VT 05302-0676; *Phone:* 888-272-7881; *Fax:* 802-258-3296. *E-mail:* studyabroad@sit.edu. *World Wide Web:* http://www.sit.edu/studyabroad/

UNIVERSITY OF MINNESOTA
MINNESOTA STUDIES IN INTERNATIONAL DEVELOPMENT (MSID), KENYA

Hosted by University of Nairobi
Academic Focus • African studies, agriculture, anthropology, community service, conservation studies, economics, education, environmental health, environmental science/studies, forestry, health and physical education, international affairs, natural resources, nutrition, public policy, refugee studies, social services, sociology, Swahili, urban/regional planning, wildlife studies, women's studies.
Program Information • Students attend classes at University of Nairobi. Field trips to development projects; optional travel to sites in Kenya at an extra cost.
Sessions • Fall, spring, yearlong.
Eligibility Requirements • Minimum age 19; open to juniors, seniors, graduate students, adults; course work in development studies, area studies, social sciences; 2.5 GPA; 1 letter of recommendation; good academic standing at home school; no foreign language proficiency required.
Living Arrangements • Students live in host family homes. Meals are taken with host family, in residences.
Costs (2004-2005) • One term: contact sponsor for cost. Yearlong program: contact sponsor for cost. $50 application fee. $400 nonrefundable deposit required. Financial aid available for students from sponsoring institution: scholarships, loans.
For More Information • University of Minnesota, Learning Abroad Center, 230 Heller Hall, 271 19th Avenue South, Minneapolis, MN 55455; *Phone:* 612-626-9000; *Fax:* 612-626-8009. *E-mail:* umabroad@umn.edu. *World Wide Web:* http://www.umabroad.umn.edu/

KOREA
SEOUL

DICKINSON COLLEGE
DICKINSON IN SEOUL (SOUTH KOREA)

Hosted by Yonsei University Seoul
Academic Focus • East Asian studies, international affairs, international business, Korean.
Program Information • Students attend classes at Yonsei University Seoul.
Sessions • Fall, spring, yearlong.
Eligibility Requirements • Minimum age 18; open to juniors; 2.8 GPA; 3 letters of recommendation; good academic standing at home school; no foreign language proficiency required.

Living Arrangements • Students live in host institution dormitories.
Costs (2003-2004) • One term: $17,795. Yearlong program: $35,590; includes tuition, housing, all meals, insurance, excursions. $25 application fee. $300 nonrefundable deposit required. Financial aid available for students from sponsoring institution: scholarships, loans.
For More Information • Ms. Karen Peter, Program Manager, Dickinson College, PO Box 1773, Carlisle, PA 17013-2896; *Phone:* 717-245-1341; *Fax:* 717-245-1688. *E-mail:* global@dickinson.edu. *World Wide Web:* http://www.dickinson.edu/global/

EWHA WOMANS UNIVERSITY
DIVISION OF INTERNATIONAL STUDIES (DIS)

Hosted by Ewha Womans University
Academic Focus • Business administration/management, entrepreneurship, international affairs, international business.
Program Information • Students attend classes at Ewha Womans University.
Sessions • Yearlong.
Eligibility Requirements • Minimum age 19; open to precollege students, freshmen, sophomores, juniors, seniors, graduate students, adults; good academic standing at home school; no foreign language proficiency required.
Living Arrangements • Students live in host institution dormitories. Quarters are shared with host institution students, students from other programs. Meals are taken on one's own, in residences, in central dining facility, in restaurants.
Costs (2002-2003) • Yearlong program: $5200; includes tuition, insurance. $70 application fee. Financial aid available for students from sponsoring institution: scholarships, work study.
For More Information • Dr. Chul-Woo Moon, Associate Professor, Ewha Womans University, Division of International Studies, 11-1 Daehyun-dong, Seodaemun-gu, Seoul 120-750, Korea; *Phone:* +82 2-3277-3651; *Fax:* +82 2-365-0942. *E-mail:* is@ewha.ac.kr. *World Wide Web:* http://www.ewha.ac.kr/

EWHA WOMANS UNIVERSITY
GRADUATE SCHOOL OF INTERNATIONAL STUDIES (GSIS)

Hosted by Ewha Womans University
Academic Focus • Advertising and public relations, American studies, area studies, Asian studies, business administration/management, commerce, communication services, communications, economics, entrepreneurship, environmental science/studies, finance, human resources, industrial management, information science, intercultural studies, international affairs, international business, Korean Studies, labor and industrial relations, Latin American studies, law and legal studies, management information systems, marketing, peace and conflict studies, political science and government, women's studies.
Program Information • Students attend classes at Ewha Womans University.
Sessions • Fall, spring.
Eligibility Requirements • Open to seniors, graduate students; 2 letters of recommendation; good academic standing at home school; statement of purpose; study plan; no foreign language proficiency required.
Living Arrangements • Students live in host institution dormitories. Quarters are shared with host institution students, students from other programs. Meals are taken on one's own, in residences, in central dining facility, in restaurants.
Costs (2003-2004) • One term: contact sponsor for cost. $75 application fee. Financial aid available for students from sponsoring institution: scholarships, work study.
For More Information • Dr. Kisuk Cho, Associate Professor, Ewha Womans University, Graduate School of International Studies, 11-1 Daehyun-dong, Seodaemun-gu, Seoul 120-750, Korea; *Phone:* +82 2-3277-3652; *Fax:* +82 2-365-0942. *E-mail:* gsis97@ewha.ac.kr. *World Wide Web:* http://www.ewha.ac.kr/

EWHA WOMANS UNIVERSITY
INTERNATIONAL EXCHANGE AND STUDY ABROAD PROGRAMS (CO-ED)

Hosted by Ewha Womans University
Academic Focus • Full curriculum.
Program Information • Students attend classes at Ewha Womans University. Scheduled travel; field trips to historic and cultural sites; optional travel to tourist attraction sites at an extra cost.
Sessions • Fall, spring, yearlong.
Eligibility Requirements • Open to freshmen, sophomores, juniors, seniors, graduate students, adults; 2.5 GPA; 1 letter of recommendation; good academic standing at home school; no foreign language proficiency required.
Living Arrangements • Students live in host institution dormitories. Quarters are shared with host institution students, students from other programs. Meals are taken on one's own, in residences, in central dining facility.
Costs (2002-2003) • One term: $2600. Yearlong program: contact sponsor for cost; includes tuition, insurance, excursions, lab equipment, international student ID, student support services. $60 application fee.
For More Information • Ms. Jenny Park, International Education Institute, Program Manager, Ewha Womans University, 11-1 Daehyun-dong, Seodaemun-gu, Seoul 120-750, Korea; *Phone:* +82 2-3277-3159; *Fax:* +82 2-364-8019. *E-mail:* iei@ewha.ac.kr. *World Wide Web:* http://www.ewha.ac.kr/

EWHA WOMANS UNIVERSITY
KOREAN LANGUAGE (CO-ED)

Hosted by Ewha Womans University
Academic Focus • Korean.
Program Information • Students attend classes at Ewha Womans University. Scheduled travel; field trips to historic and cultural sites; optional travel to tourist attraction sites at an extra cost.
Sessions • Fall, spring, yearlong.
Eligibility Requirements • Open to freshmen, sophomores, juniors, seniors, graduate students, adults; 2.5 GPA; 1 letter of recommendation; good academic standing at home school; no foreign language proficiency required.
Living Arrangements • Students live in host institution dormitories. Quarters are shared with host institution students, students from other programs. Meals are taken on one's own, in residences, in central dining facility.
Costs (2002-2003) • One term: $2600. Yearlong program: contact sponsor for cost; includes tuition, insurance, excursions, lab equipment, international student ID. $60 application fee.
For More Information • Ms. Jenny Park, International Education Institute, Program Manager, Ewha Womans University, #705 International Education Building, 11-1 Daehyun-dong, Seodaemun-gu, Seoul 120-750, Korea; *Phone:* +82 2-3277-3159; *Fax:* +82 2-364-8019. *E-mail:* iei@ewha.ac.kr. *World Wide Web:* http://www.ewha.ac.kr/

RUTGERS, THE STATE UNIVERSITY OF NEW JERSEY
STUDY ABROAD IN SOUTH KOREA

Hosted by Ewha Womans University
Academic Focus • Accounting.
Program Information • Students attend classes at Ewha Womans University.
Sessions • Fall, spring, yearlong.
Eligibility Requirements • Open to sophomores, juniors, seniors; 3.0 GPA; 2 letters of recommendation; good academic standing at home school; official transcript from each tertiary school attended; no foreign language proficiency required.
Living Arrangements • Students live in host institution dormitories. Quarters are shared with host institution students. Meals are taken on one's own.
Costs (2003-2004) • One term: $6848 for New Jersey residents; $9498 for nonresidents. Yearlong program: $13,197 for New Jersey residents; $18,497 for nonresidents; includes tuition, housing, insurance, student support services. $20 application fee. $750 nonrefundable deposit required. Financial aid available for students from sponsoring institution: scholarships, loans.

For More Information • Ms. Karin Bonello, Regional Coordinator, Rutgers, The State University of New Jersey, 102 College Avenue, New Brunswick, NJ 08901; *Phone:* 732-932-7787; *Fax:* 732-932-8659. *E-mail:* ru_abroad@email.rutgers.edu. *World Wide Web:* http://studyabroad.rutgers.edu/

STONY BROOK UNIVERSITY
EWHA WOMAN'S UNIVERSITY EXCHANGE

Hosted by Ewha Womans University
Academic Focus • Full curriculum.
Program Information • Students attend classes at Ewha Womans University. Optional travel to the DMZ, southern regions at an extra cost.
Sessions • Fall, spring.
Eligibility Requirements • Open to freshmen, sophomores, juniors, seniors; 2.5 GPA; 3 letters of recommendation; good academic standing at home school; essay; transcript; no foreign language proficiency required.
Living Arrangements • Students live in host institution dormitories, locally rented apartments. Quarters are shared with host institution students, students from other programs. Meals are taken as a group, in residences.
Costs • One term: $5000–$6000; includes tuition, housing, all meals, insurance, international airfare, student support services. $200 nonrefundable deposit required. Financial aid available for students from sponsoring institution: loans.
For More Information • Mr. Alfredo Varela, Assistant Dean, Stony Brook University, Study Abroad Office, Melville Library, Room E5340, Stony Brook, NY 11794-3397; *Phone:* 631-632-7030; *Fax:* 631-632-6544. *E-mail:* studyabroad@sunysb.edu. *World Wide Web:* http://www.sunysb.edu/studyabroad/

STONY BROOK UNIVERSITY
SEOUL NATIONAL UNIVERSITY EXCHANGE

Hosted by Seoul National University
Academic Focus • Full curriculum.
Program Information • Students attend classes at Seoul National University.
Sessions • Fall, spring, yearlong.
Eligibility Requirements • Open to seniors, graduate students; 3.0 GPA; 3 letters of recommendation; good academic standing at home school; no foreign language proficiency required.
Living Arrangements • Students live in host institution dormitories, locally rented apartments. Quarters are shared with host institution students. Meals are taken as a group, in residences.
Costs (2002-2003) • One term: $4500–$5500. Yearlong program: $9000–$11,000; includes tuition, housing, some meals, insurance, international airfare. $200 nonrefundable deposit required. Financial aid available for students from sponsoring institution: loans.
For More Information • Mr. Alfredo Varela, Assistant Dean, Stony Brook University, Study Abroad Office, Melville Library, Room E5340, Stony Brook, NY 11794-3397; *Phone:* 631-632-7030; *Fax:* 631-632-6544. *E-mail:* studyabroad@sunysb.edu. *World Wide Web:* http://www.sunysb.edu/studyabroad/

UNIVERSITY AT ALBANY, STATE UNIVERSITY OF NEW YORK
LANGUAGE AND CULTURAL STUDIES IN ENGLISH AT YONSEI UNIVERSITY

Hosted by Yonsei University Seoul
Academic Focus • Anthropology, business administration/management, communications, economics, full curriculum, history, Korean, philosophy, political science and government, sociology.
Program Information • Students attend classes at Yonsei University Seoul. Optional travel to Hong Kong, China at an extra cost.
Sessions • Fall, spring, yearlong.
Eligibility Requirements • Open to sophomores, juniors, seniors; 2.5 GPA; 2 letters of recommendation; good academic standing at home school; fluency in Korean for direct enrollment in host university courses; no foreign language proficiency requirement for all others.
Living Arrangements • Students live in host institution dormitories, locally rented apartments. Quarters are shared with host

institution students, students from other programs. Meals are taken on one's own, in central dining facility, in restaurants.
Costs (2002-2003) • One term: $4613. Yearlong program: $9226; includes housing, all meals, student support services, in-state tuition and fees. $300 nonrefundable deposit required. Financial aid available for students from sponsoring institution: all customary sources.
For More Information • University at Albany, State University of New York, Office of International Education, LI 66, Albany, NY 12222; *Phone:* 518-442-3525; *Fax:* 518-442-3338. *E-mail:* intled@uamail.albany.edu. *World Wide Web:* http://www.albany.edu/intled/

UNIVERSITY STUDIES ABROAD CONSORTIUM
EAST ASIAN AND INTERNATIONAL BUSINESS STUDIES: SEOUL, KOREA

Hosted by Yonsei University Seoul
Academic Focus • East Asian studies, international affairs, international business, Korean.
Program Information • Students attend classes at Yonsei University Seoul.
Sessions • Fall, spring, yearlong.
Eligibility Requirements • Minimum age 18; open to freshmen, sophomores, juniors, seniors; 2.7 GPA; no foreign language proficiency required.
Living Arrangements • Students live in host institution dormitories, locally rented apartments. Quarters are shared with students from other programs. Meals are taken on one's own, in restaurants.
Costs (2005-2006) • One term: $3980. Yearlong program: $7680; includes tuition, insurance. $50 application fee. $150 refundable deposit required. Financial aid available for all students: scholarships, loans.
For More Information • University Studies Abroad Consortium, USAC/323, Reno, NV 89557-0093; *Phone:* 775-784-6569; *Fax:* 775-784-6010. *E-mail:* usac@unr.edu. *World Wide Web:* http://usac.unr.edu/

WHITWORTH COLLEGE
WHITWORTH/SOONG SIL EXCHANGE PROGRAM

Hosted by Soong Sil University Seoul
Academic Focus • Business administration/management, computer science, history, Korean, Korean Studies, political science and government.
Program Information • Students attend classes at Soong Sil University Seoul. Optional travel at an extra cost.
Sessions • Fall, spring, yearlong.
Eligibility Requirements • Open to sophomores, juniors, seniors, adults; 2.5 GPA; 2 letters of recommendation; no foreign language proficiency required.
Living Arrangements • Students live in host institution dormitories, host family homes. Meals are taken with host family, in residences.
Costs (2003-2004) • One term: $13,034. Yearlong program: $26,068; includes tuition, housing, all meals. Financial aid available for students from sponsoring institution: scholarships, loans.
For More Information • Ms. Sue Jackson, Director, Off-Campus Programs, Whitworth College, Center for International and Multicultural Education, 300 West Hawthorne Road, Spokane, WA 99251-2702; *Phone:* 509-777-4596; *Fax:* 509-777-3723. *E-mail:* sjackson@whitworth.edu. *World Wide Web:* http://www.whitworth.edu/

TAEGU

WHITWORTH COLLEGE
WHITWORTH COLLEGE/KEIMYUNG UNIVERSITY EXCHANGE PROGRAM

Hosted by Keimyung University
Academic Focus • Business administration/management, history, Korean, Korean Studies, political science and government, psychology.
Program Information • Students attend classes at Keimyung University. Optional travel at an extra cost.

Sessions • Fall, spring, yearlong.
Eligibility Requirements • Open to sophomores, juniors; 2.5 GPA; 2 letters of recommendation; no foreign language proficiency required.
Living Arrangements • Students live in host institution dormitories, locally rented apartments, host family homes. Meals are taken on one's own, with host family, in residences, in restaurants.
Costs (2003-2004) • One term: $13,034. Yearlong program: $26,068; includes tuition, housing, all meals. Financial aid available for students from sponsoring institution: scholarships, loans.
For More Information • Ms. Sue Jackson, Director, Off-Campus Programs, Whitworth College, Center for International and Multicultural Education, 300 West Hawthorne Road, Spokane, WA 99251-2702; *Phone:* 509-777-4596; *Fax:* 509-777-3723. *E-mail:* sjackson@whitworth.edu. *World Wide Web:* http://www.whitworth.edu/

KYRGYZSTAN

CITY TO CITY
ACIE (ACTR/ACCELS)
ACIE–NIS REGIONAL LANGUAGE TRAINING PROGRAM–KYRGYZSTAN

Hosted by Kyrgyz-Russian Slavic University
Academic Focus • Cultural studies, Kyrgyz, language studies, Russian language and literature.
Program Information • Students attend classes at Kyrgyz-Russian Slavic University (Bishkek).
Sessions • Fall, spring, yearlong.
Eligibility Requirements • Minimum age 18; open to sophomores, juniors, seniors, graduate students, adults; 3 letters of recommendation; good academic standing at home school; 1 year of college course work in Russian or Kyrgyz.
Living Arrangements • Students live in host institution dormitories, locally rented apartments, host family homes. Quarters are shared with students from other programs. Meals are taken on one's own, with host family, in residences, in restaurants.
Costs (2002-2003) • One term: contact sponsor for cost. Yearlong program: contact sponsor for cost. $35 application fee. $500 nonrefundable deposit required. Financial aid available for all students: scholarships.
For More Information • Ms. Margaret Stephenson, Russian and Eurasian Program Officer, ACIE (ACTR/ACCELS), 1776 Massachusetts Avenue, NW, Suite 700, Washington, DC 20036; *Phone:* 202-833-7522; *Fax:* 202-833-7523. *E-mail:* outbound@actr.org. *World Wide Web:* http://www.actr.org/

LATVIA

RIGA
UNIVERSITY OF WISCONSIN–EAU CLAIRE
RIGA, LATVIA

Held at University of Latvia
Academic Focus • Area studies.
Program Information • Classes are held on the campus of University of Latvia. Faculty members are drawn from the sponsor's U.S. staff and local instructors hired by the sponsor. Scheduled travel to Vilnius, Tallinn, St. Petersburg; field trips.
Sessions • Fall.
Eligibility Requirements • Open to sophomores, juniors, seniors; 2.8 GPA; good academic standing at home school; no foreign language proficiency required.
Living Arrangements • Students live in host family homes. Meals are taken with host family, in residences.

Costs (2004-2005) • One term: $5325 for Wisconsin residents (estimated); $6225 for nonresidents; includes tuition, housing, some meals, insurance, excursions, student support services. $30 application fee. $150 nonrefundable deposit required. Financial aid available for all students: loans.

For More Information • Ms. Cheryl Lochner-Wright, Study Abroad Coordinator, University of Wisconsin–Eau Claire, Center for International Education, Eau Claire, WI 54702; *Phone:* 715-836-4411; *Fax:* 715-836-4948. *E-mail:* studyabroad@uwec.edu. *World Wide Web:* http://www.uwec.edu/Cie/

LEBANON
BEIRUT
AMERICAN UNIVERSITY OF BEIRUT
STUDY ABROAD/VISITING STUDENTS

Hosted by American University of Beirut
Academic Focus • Full curriculum.
Program Information • Students attend classes at American University of Beirut. Scheduled travel to Syria, Jordan, Egypt; field trips to destinations within Lebanon, Syria, Jordan, Egypt; optional travel to Syria, Jordan, Egypt at an extra cost.
Sessions • Fall, spring, yearlong.
Eligibility Requirements • Minimum age 18; open to sophomores, juniors, seniors, graduate students, adults; 2.5 GPA; 2 letters of recommendation; good academic standing at home school; no foreign language proficiency required.
Living Arrangements • Students live in host institution dormitories, locally rented apartments. Quarters are shared with host institution students, students from other programs. Meals are taken on one's own, in central dining facility, in restaurants.
Costs (2003) • One term: $10,000. Yearlong program: $20,000; includes tuition, housing, all meals, insurance, international airfare, books and class materials, lab equipment, student support services. $50 application fee. $200 nonrefundable deposit required. Financial aid available for all students: work study.
For More Information • Ms. Julie Millstein, Assistant to the President, American University of Beirut, 3 Dag Hammarskjold Plaza, 8th Floor, New York, NY 10017-2303; *Phone:* 212-583-7600; *Fax:* 212-583-7650. *E-mail:* mills@aub.edu. *World Wide Web:* http://www.aub.edu.lb/

LUXEMBOURG
LUXEMBOURG CITY
MIAMI UNIVERSITY
MIAMI UNIVERSITY JOHN E. DOLIBOIS EUROPEAN CENTER

Hosted by Miami University–John E. Dolibois European Center
Academic Focus • Art history, business administration/management, economics, engineering, English literature, French language and literature, German language and literature, history, liberal studies, marketing, music, political science and government, social sciences.
Program Information • Students attend classes at Miami University–John E. Dolibois European Center. Scheduled travel to Paris, London, Brussels, Eastern European cities; field trips to Trier, Luxembourg; optional travel to Greek Islands at an extra cost.
Sessions • Fall, spring, yearlong.
Eligibility Requirements • Open to sophomores, juniors, seniors; 2.5 GPA; 2 letters of recommendation; good academic standing at home school; good conduct record; essay; interview.
Living Arrangements • Students live in host family homes. Quarters are shared with host institution students. Meals are taken on one's own, in central dining facility, in restaurants.

Costs (2003-2004) • One term: $10,209 for Ohio residents; $14,789 for nonresidents (estimated). Yearlong program: $20,365 for Ohio residents; $29,525 for nonresidents (estimated); includes tuition, housing, some meals, excursions, international airfare, books and class materials, personal expenses, European travel. Financial aid available for students from sponsoring institution: scholarships, loans.

For More Information • Dr. Cordelia Stroinigg, European Center Coordinator, Miami University, Luxembourg Program, MacMillan Hall, Oxford, OH 45056; *Phone:* 513-529-5050; *Fax:* 513-529-5051. *E-mail:* luxembourg@muohio.edu. *World Wide Web:* http://www.muohio.edu/summer/

MADAGASCAR
CITY TO CITY
STONY BROOK UNIVERSITY
FIELD STUDY PROGRAM IN MADAGASCAR

Held at Institute for the Conservation of Tropical Environments
Academic Focus • Anthropology, biological/life sciences, conservation studies, ecology, environmental science/studies, wildlife studies, zoology.
Program Information • Classes are held on the campus of Institute for the Conservation of Tropical Environments (Ranomafana National Park). Faculty members are drawn from the sponsor's U.S. staff and local instructors hired by the sponsor. Scheduled travel to coastal reef of Mozambique Channel, other locations in Madagascar; field trips to Antananarivo; optional travel to Paris at an extra cost.
Sessions • Fall.
Eligibility Requirements • Open to sophomores, juniors, seniors, graduate students; major in a field related to the program's focus; 3.0 GPA; 3 letters of recommendation; good academic standing at home school; enrollment at an accredited college or university; statement of purpose; no foreign language proficiency required.
Living Arrangements • Students live in tents and buildings associated with the biological research foundation. Quarters are shared with host institution students. Meals are taken as a group, in central dining facility.
Costs (2000) • One term: $10,400; includes tuition, housing, all meals, insurance, excursions, international airfare, books and class materials, park entrance fees. $200 nonrefundable deposit required. Financial aid available for students from sponsoring institution: scholarships, loans.
For More Information • Ms. Gretchen Gosnell, Study Abroad Advisor, Stony Brook University, Study Abroad Office, Melville Library, Room E5340, Stony Brook, NY 11794-3397; *Phone:* 631-632-7030; *Fax:* 631-632-6544. *E-mail:* studyabroad@sunysb.edu. *World Wide Web:* http://www.sunysb.edu/studyabroad/

ANTANANARIVO
SCHOOL FOR INTERNATIONAL TRAINING, SIT STUDY ABROAD
MADAGASCAR: CULTURE AND SOCIETY

Academic Focus • Anthropology, economics, French language and literature, geography, history, political science and government, visual and performing arts.
Program Information • Faculty members are drawn from the sponsor's U.S. staff and local instructors hired by the sponsor. Scheduled travel to Ankarana Reserve, Nosy Be, Diego Suarez; field trips to national parks, rural areas.
Sessions • Fall, spring.
Eligibility Requirements • Open to sophomores, juniors, seniors; 2.5 GPA; 2 letters of recommendation; good academic standing at home school; 1.5 years of college course work in French.
Living Arrangements • Students live in host family homes, hotels. Meals are taken as a group, with host family.

MADAGASCAR
Antananarivo

Costs (2003-2004) • One term: $11,975; includes tuition, housing, all meals, insurance, excursions. $50 application fee. $400 nonrefundable deposit required. Financial aid available for all students: scholarships.
For More Information • School for International Training, SIT Study Abroad, Kipling Road, Brattleboro, VT 05302-0676; *Phone:* 888-272-7881; *Fax:* 802-258-3296. *E-mail:* studyabroad@sit.edu. *World Wide Web:* http://www.sit.edu/studyabroad/

FORT DAUPHIN
SCHOOL FOR INTERNATIONAL TRAINING, SIT STUDY ABROAD
MADAGASCAR: ECOLOGY AND CONSERVATION

Academic Focus • African studies, anthropology, biological/life sciences, ecology, environmental science/studies, geography, marine sciences, political science and government, wildlife studies.
Program Information • Faculty members are drawn from the sponsor's U.S. staff and local instructors hired by the sponsor. Scheduled travel to the Spiny Desert, Ranomafana, a rainforest, the barrier reef of Tulear; field trips to conservation areas, research projects.
Sessions • Fall, spring.
Eligibility Requirements • Open to sophomores, juniors, seniors; course work in environmental studies, ecology, biology, or related field; 2.5 GPA; 2 letters of recommendation; good academic standing at home school; 1.5 years of college course work in French.
Living Arrangements • Students live in host family homes, hotels, campsites. Meals are taken as a group, on one's own, with host family, in residences, in restaurants.
Costs (2003-2004) • One term: $12,250; includes tuition, housing, all meals, insurance, excursions. $50 application fee. $400 nonrefundable deposit required. Financial aid available for all students: scholarships.
For More Information • School for International Training, SIT Study Abroad, Kipling Road, Brattleboro, VT 05302-0676; *Phone:* 888-272-7881; *Fax:* 802-258-3296. *E-mail:* studyabroad@sit.edu. *World Wide Web:* http://www.sit.edu/studyabroad/

MALI
BAMAKO
ANTIOCH COLLEGE
ART AND CULTURE IN MALI, WEST AFRICA

Hosted by Institute of National Arts in Bamako
Academic Focus • African languages and literature, African studies, anthropology, art, Bambara, ceramics and pottery, cinematography, crafts, dance, drawing/painting, fine/studio arts, French language and literature, leather working, music, music performance, performing arts, photography, textiles, visual and performing arts.
Program Information • Students attend classes at Institute of National Arts in Bamako. Scheduled travel to Gao, Mopti, Segu, Djenne, Sihy, Dogon County; field trips to destinations within Bamako; optional travel to locations throughout Mali at an extra cost.
Sessions • Fall.
Eligibility Requirements • Minimum age 18; open to freshmen, sophomores, juniors, seniors; 2 letters of recommendation; good academic standing at home school; maturity and cultural sensitivity; 1 year course work in French highly recommended.
Living Arrangements • Students live in host institution dormitories, program-owned houses, host family homes. Quarters are shared with host institution students. Meals are taken as a group, in residences.
Costs (2003) • One term: $12,048; includes tuition, housing, all meals, insurance, excursions, international airfare, international student ID, student support services. $35 application fee. $150 nonrefundable deposit required. Financial aid available for all students: scholarships, loans.

For More Information • Ms. Erin Abrams, Assistant Director/Mali Program Coordinator, Antioch College, 795 Livermore Street, Yellow Springs, OH 45387; *Phone:* 937-769-1015; *Fax:* 937-769-1019. *E-mail:* aea@antioch-college.edu. *World Wide Web:* http://www.antioch-college.edu/aea/

SCHOOL FOR INTERNATIONAL TRAINING, SIT STUDY ABROAD
MALI: GENDER AND DEVELOPMENT

Academic Focus • African studies, anthropology, Bambara, economics, French language and literature, history, political science and government, women's studies.
Program Information • Faculty members are drawn from the sponsor's U.S. staff and local instructors hired by the sponsor. Scheduled travel to Dogon, Timbuktu (conditions permitting), Niger River tours; field trips to rural areas, historic sites.
Sessions • Fall, spring.
Eligibility Requirements • Open to sophomores, juniors, seniors, graduate students; 2.5 GPA; 2 letters of recommendation; good academic standing at home school; 1.5 years of college course work in French.
Living Arrangements • Students live in host family homes, hotels. Meals are taken as a group, on one's own, with host family, in residences, in restaurants.
Costs (2003-2004) • One term: $11,250; includes tuition, housing, all meals, insurance, excursions. $50 application fee. $400 nonrefundable deposit required. Financial aid available for all students: scholarships.
For More Information • School for International Training, SIT Study Abroad, Kipling Road, Brattleboro, VT 05302-0676; *Phone:* 888-272-7881; *Fax:* 802-258-3296. *E-mail:* studyabroad@sit.edu. *World Wide Web:* http://www.sit.edu/studyabroad/

MALTA
MSIDA
UNIVERSITY OF MALTA
ACADEMIC YEAR/SEMESTER ABROAD

Hosted by University of Malta
Academic Focus • Full curriculum.
Program Information • Students attend classes at University of Malta.
Sessions • Fall, spring, yearlong.
Eligibility Requirements • Minimum age 18; open to freshmen, sophomores, juniors, seniors, graduate students, adults; 2.75 GPA; 2 letters of recommendation; good academic standing at home school; no foreign language proficiency required.
Living Arrangements • Students live in host institution dormitories, a university residence. Quarters are shared with host institution students. Meals are taken on one's own, in central dining facility.
Costs (2003-2004) • One term: $4240 (minimum). Yearlong program: $8500 (minimum); includes tuition, housing, all meals, books and class materials, student support services. $104 application fee. $150 nonrefundable deposit required.
For More Information • Ms. Ruth D'Amato, Student Exchange and Welfare Office, University of Malta, International Office, Msida MSD 06, Malta; *Phone:* +356-23402804; *Fax:* +356-21316941. *E-mail:* intexchanges@um.edu.mt. *World Wide Web:* http://www.um.edu.mt/studyabroad/

UNIVERSITY STUDIES ABROAD CONSORTIUM
FULL CURRICULUM STUDIES: MSIDA, MALTA

Hosted by University of Malta
Academic Focus • Full curriculum.
Program Information • Students attend classes at University of Malta.
Sessions • Fall, spring, yearlong.

Eligibility Requirements • Minimum age 18; open to freshmen, sophomores, juniors, seniors, graduate students, adults; 2.7 GPA; no foreign language proficiency required.

Living Arrangements • Students live in host institution dormitories, locally rented apartments. Quarters are shared with host institution students. Meals are taken on one's own, in residences, in central dining facility.

Costs (2005-2006) • One term: $3680. Yearlong program: $6480; includes tuition, insurance, student support services. $50 application fee. $150 refundable deposit required. Financial aid available for all students: scholarships, loans.

For More Information • University Studies Abroad Consortium, USAC/323, Reno, NV 89557-0093; *Phone:* 775-784-6569; *Fax:* 775-784-6010. *E-mail:* usac@unr.edu. *World Wide Web:* http://usac.unr.edu/

MAURITIUS

REDUIT

UNIVERSITY OF MINNESOTA, DULUTH
STUDY IN MAURITIUS

Hosted by University of Mauritius

Academic Focus • Full curriculum.

Program Information • Students attend classes at University of Mauritius.

Sessions • Fall, spring, yearlong.

Eligibility Requirements • Minimum age 18; open to juniors; 3.0 GPA; 1 year college course work in French recommended.

Living Arrangements • Students live in locally rented apartments. Meals are taken on one's own, in residences, in restaurants.

Costs (2003-2004) • One term: $3000. Yearlong program: $6000; includes tuition, insurance. $50 application fee. $500 nonrefundable deposit required. Financial aid available for students from sponsoring institution: scholarships, loans.

For More Information • Ms. Carol Michealson, Program Coordinator, University of Minnesota, Duluth, 110 Cina, 1123 University Drive, Duluth, MN 55812; *Phone:* 218-726-8229; *Fax:* 218-726-7352. *E-mail:* cmicheal@d.umn.edu. *World Wide Web:* http://www.d.umn.edu/ieo/

MEXICO

CITY TO CITY

FLORIDA INTERNATIONAL UNIVERSITY
EXCHANGE PROGRAM–UNIVERSIDAD IBEROAMERICANA DE MEXICO

Hosted by Iberian-American University México

Academic Focus • Full curriculum.

Program Information • Students attend classes at Iberian-American University México (Mexico City).

Sessions • Fall, spring.

Eligibility Requirements • Open to sophomores, juniors, seniors, graduate students, adults; 3.0 GPA; fluency in Spanish.

Living Arrangements • Students live in host institution dormitories. Quarters are shared with students from other programs. Meals are taken on one's own, in central dining facility.

Costs (2003-2004) • One term: $5000; includes housing, all meals, insurance, international airfare, books and class materials, international student ID. $150 application fee. Financial aid available for all students: scholarships, loans.

For More Information • Office of International Studies, Florida International University, University Park Campus–TT100, Miami, FL 33199; *Phone:* 305-348-1913; *Fax:* 305-348-1941. *E-mail:* ois@fiu.edu. *World Wide Web:* http://ois.fiu.edu/

STATE UNIVERSITY OF NEW YORK AT OSWEGO
ITESM: INSTITUTO TECNOLÓGICO Y DE ESTUDIOS SUPERIORES DE MONTERREY

Hosted by Instituto Tecnológico y de Estudios Superiores de Monterrey–Guadalajara Campus, Instituto Tecnológico y de Estudios Superiores de Monterrey–Querétaro Campus, Instituto Tecnológico y de Estudios Superiores de Monterrey–Mexico City Campus, Instituto Tecnológico y de Estudios Superiores de Monterrey–Matzatlan Campus, Instituto Tecnológico y de Estudios Superiores de Monterrey–Monterrey Campus, Instituto Tecnológico y de Estudios Superiores de Monterrey–Morelos Campus

Academic Focus • Full curriculum.

Program Information • Students attend classes at Instituto Tecnológico y de Estudios Superiores de Monterrey-Guadalajara Campus (Zapopan), Instituto Tecnológico y de Estudios Superiores de Monterrey-Querétaro Campus (Querétaro), Instituto Tecnológico y de Estudios Superiores de Monterrey-Mexico City Campus (Mexico City), Instituto Tecnológico y de Estudios Superiores de Monterrey-Matzatlan Campus (Mazatlan), Instituto Tecnológico y de Estudios Superiores de Monterrey-Monterrey Campus (Monterrey), Instituto Tecnológico y de Estudios Superiores de Monterrey-Morelos Campus (Cuernavaca).

Sessions • Fall, spring, yearlong.

Eligibility Requirements • Open to sophomores, juniors, seniors; 2.5 GPA; 3 letters of recommendation; good academic standing at home school; language proficiency form; personal study statement; no foreign language proficiency required.

Living Arrangements • Students live in host institution dormitories, locally rented apartments, host family homes. Quarters are shared with host institution students. Meals are taken on one's own, with host family, in residences, in central dining facility, in restaurants.

Costs (2003-2004) • One term: $2920. Yearlong program: $5840; includes tuition, insurance, student support services. $250 nonrefundable deposit required. Financial aid available for students: home university financial aid, loan processing and scholarships for Oswego students.

For More Information • Ms. Lizette Alvarado, Program Specialist, State University of New York at Oswego, 122A Swetman Hall, Oswego, NY 13126; *Phone:* 888-4-OSWEGO; *Fax:* 315-312-2477. *E-mail:* intled@oswego.edu. *World Wide Web:* http://www.oswego.edu/intled/

UNIVERSITY OF IDAHO
SPANISH AND LATIN AMERICAN STUDIES

Hosted by Instituto Tecnológico y de Estudios Superiores de Monterrey–Toluca Campus, Instituto Tecnológico y de Estudios Superiores de Monterrey–Estado de México Campus, Instituto Tecnológico y de Estudios Superiores de Monterrey–Cuernavaca Campus, Instituto Tecnológico y de Estudios Superiores de Monterrey–Guadalajara Campus, Instituto Tecnológico y de Estudios Superiores de Monterrey–Querétaro Campus, Instituto Tecnológico y de Estudios Superiores de Monterrey–Monterrey Campus, Instituto Tecnológico y de Estudios Superiores de Monterrey–Mexico City Campus, Instituto Tecnológico y de Estudios Superiores de Monterrey–Matzatlan Campus

Academic Focus • Business administration/management, Latin American studies, Mexican studies, Spanish language and literature, tourism and travel.

Program Information • Students attend classes at Instituto Tecnológico y de Estudios Superiores de Monterrey-Toluca Campus (Toluca), Instituto Tecnológico y de Estudios Superiores de Monterrey-Estado de México Campus (Estado de Mexico), Instituto Tecnológico y de Estudios Superiores de Monterrey-Cuernavaca Campus (Temixco), Instituto Tecnológico y de Estudios Superiores de Monterrey-Guadalajara Campus (Zapopan), Instituto Tecnológico y de Estudios Superiores de Monterrey-Querétaro Campus (Querétaro), Instituto Tecnológico y de Estudios Superiores de Monterrey-Monterrey Campus (Monterrey), Instituto Tecnológico y de Estudios Superiores de Monterrey-Mexico City Campus (Mexico City), Instituto Tecnológico y de Estudios Superiores de Monterrey-

Matzatlan Campus (Mazatlan). Field trips to La Silla Mountain, Garria Caves; optional travel to Guanajuato, Mexico City, Zacatecas at an extra cost.

Sessions • Fall, spring, yearlong.

Eligibility Requirements • Open to freshmen, sophomores, juniors, seniors, graduate students, adults; good academic standing at home school; no foreign language proficiency required.

Living Arrangements • Students live in host institution dormitories, locally rented apartments, host family homes. Quarters are shared with host institution students, students from other programs. Meals are taken on one's own, with host family, in residences, in central dining facility.

Costs (2003-2004) • One term: $2500. Yearlong program: $5000; includes tuition, excursions, student support services. $100 application fee. $200 refundable deposit required. Financial aid available for students from sponsoring institution: scholarships, loans.

For More Information • Ms. Amy Bergmann, Advisor, University of Idaho, Room 209, Morrill Hall, Moscow, ID 83844-3013; *Phone:* 208-885-7870; *Fax:* 208-885-2859. *E-mail:* abroad@uidaho.edu. *World Wide Web:* http://www.ets.uidaho.edu/ipo/abroad/

CIUDAD JUÁREZ

EARLHAM COLLEGE
THE BORDER STUDIES PROGRAM IN EL PASO/CIUDAD JUÁREZ

Hosted by Autonomous University of Ciudad Juárez

Academic Focus • International affairs, Latin American studies, liberal studies, Mexican studies, peace and conflict studies, social sciences, Spanish language and literature.

Program Information • Students attend classes at Autonomous University of Ciudad Juárez. Scheduled travel to sites along international border, Chihuahua, far west Texas/southern New Mexico, northern Mexico; field trips to El Paso/Ciudad Juárez region, regional interests/sites, Tarahumara regions, local bi-national/bi-cultural areas; optional travel to Mexico, New Mexico, Texas, the U.S. Southwest at an extra cost.

Sessions • Fall.

Eligibility Requirements • Open to sophomores, juniors, seniors; 2 letters of recommendation; good academic standing at home school; 1 year of college course work in Spanish.

Living Arrangements • Students live in host family homes. Meals are taken on one's own, with host family, in residences.

Costs (2003) • One term: $13,695; includes tuition, housing, all meals, excursions, international student ID, student support services. $350 nonrefundable deposit required. Financial aid available for students from sponsoring institution: scholarships, loans.

For More Information • Ms. Patty Lamson, Director, International Programs, Earlham College, Drawer 202, 801 National Road West, Richmond, IN 47374; *Phone:* 765-983-1424; *Fax:* 765-983-1553. *E-mail:* pattyo@earlham.edu. *World Wide Web:* http://www.earlham.edu/~ipo/offcampus.html

CUERNAVACA

AUGSBURG COLLEGE
CROSSING BORDERS: GENDER AND SOCIAL CHANGE IN MESOAMERICA

Hosted by Universal Centro de Lengua y Communicación Social, Center for Global Education

Academic Focus • Latin American studies, peace and conflict studies, political science and government, religious studies, Spanish language and literature, women's studies.

Program Information • Students attend classes at Universal Centro de Lengua y Communicación Social, Center for Global Education. Scheduled travel to El Salvador, the U.S.-Mexico border; field trips to Mexico City, rural settlements, archaeological/historic sites; optional travel to Acapulco, Manzanillo, Puebla, Tula, Taxco, Mexico City at an extra cost.

Sessions • Fall.

Eligibility Requirements • Open to sophomores, juniors, seniors; 2.5 GPA; 2 letters of recommendation; good academic standing at home school; 0.5 years of college course work in Spanish.

Living Arrangements • Students live in program-owned houses, host family homes. Quarters are shared with host institution students. Meals are taken as a group, with host family, in residences, in central dining facility, in restaurants.

Costs (2004) • One term: sliding fee scale for consortium partners; $13,400 for transfers; includes tuition, housing, all meals, insurance, excursions, some books and class materials. $50 application fee. $500 nonrefundable deposit required. Financial aid available for students from sponsoring institution: scholarships, loans.

For More Information • Ms. Margaret Anderson, Coordinator, Semester Programs Abroad, Augsburg College, 2211 Riverside Avenue, Minneapolis, MN 55454; *Phone:* 800-299-8889; *Fax:* 612-330-1695. *E-mail:* globaled@augsburg.edu. *World Wide Web:* http://www.augsburg.edu/global/

AUGSBURG COLLEGE
SOCIAL AND ENVIRONMENTAL JUSTICE IN LATIN AMERICA

Hosted by Universal Centro de Lengua y Communicación Social, Center for Global Education

Academic Focus • Environmental science/studies, Latin American studies, political science and government, religious studies, Spanish language and literature, women's studies.

Program Information • Students attend classes at Universal Centro de Lengua y Communicación Social, Center for Global Education. Scheduled travel to El Salvador, Guatemala; field trips to Mexico City, rural settlements, archaeological/historic sites; optional travel to Acapulco, Manzanillo, Tula, Taxco, Mexico City at an extra cost.

Sessions • Spring.

Eligibility Requirements • Open to sophomores, juniors, seniors; 2.5 GPA; 2 letters of recommendation; good academic standing at home school; 0.5 years of college course work in Spanish.

Living Arrangements • Students live in program-owned houses, host family homes. Quarters are shared with host institution students. Meals are taken as a group, with host family, in residences, in central dining facility, in restaurants.

Costs (2005) • One term: sliding fee scale for consortium partners; $13,400 for transfers; includes tuition, housing, all meals, insurance, excursions, some books and class materials. $50 application fee. $500 nonrefundable deposit required. Financial aid available for students from sponsoring institution: scholarships, loans.

For More Information • Ms. Margaret Anderson, Coordinator, Semester Programs Abroad, Augsburg College, 2211 Riverside Avenue, Minneapolis, MN 55454; *Phone:* 800-299-8889; *Fax:* 612-330-1695. *E-mail:* globaled@augsburg.edu. *World Wide Web:* http://www.augsburg.edu/global/

AUGSBURG COLLEGE
SOCIAL WORK IN A LATIN AMERICAN CONTEXT

Hosted by Universal Centro de Lengua y Communicación Social, Center for Global Education

Academic Focus • Social work, Spanish language and literature.

Program Information • Students attend classes at Universal Centro de Lengua y Communicación Social, Center for Global Education. Field trips; optional travel at an extra cost.

Sessions • Fall.

Eligibility Requirements • Open to sophomores, juniors, seniors; course work in social work; 2.5 GPA; 2 letters of recommendation; good academic standing at home school; 0.5 years of college course work in Spanish.

Living Arrangements • Students live in program-owned houses, host family homes. Quarters are shared with host institution students. Meals are taken as a group, with host family, in residences, in central dining facility, in restaurants.

Costs (2004) • One term: contact sponsor for cost. $50 application fee. $500 nonrefundable deposit required. Financial aid available for students from sponsoring institution: scholarships, loans.

For More Information • Ms. Margaret Anderson, Coordinator, Semester Programs Abroad, Augsburg College, Center for Global Education, 2211 Riverside Avenue, Minneapolis, MN 55454; *Phone:* 612-330-1159; *Fax:* 612-330-1695. *E-mail:* globaled@augsburg.edu. *World Wide Web:* http://www.augsburg.edu/global/

NICHOLLS STATE UNIVERSITY
STUDY PROGRAM IN MEXICO

Hosted by Nicholls State University–Cuernavaca
Academic Focus • Art, cultural studies, history, Spanish language and literature.
Program Information • Students attend classes at Nicholls State University–Cuernavaca. Field trips to a mountain wool market, Teotihuacán pyramids, the Museum of Anthropology, Xochicalco archaeological zone; optional travel to Acapulco, San Miguel de Allende at an extra cost.
Sessions • Fall, spring, yearlong.
Eligibility Requirements • Minimum age 17; open to precollege students, freshmen, sophomores, juniors, seniors, graduate students, adults; no foreign language proficiency required.
Living Arrangements • Students live in host family homes. Quarters are shared with host institution students. Meals are taken with host family, in residences.
Costs (2003-2004) • One term: $5236. Yearlong program: $10,471; includes tuition, housing, all meals, insurance, books and class materials, lab equipment, student support services, instructional costs. Financial aid available for all students: loans, all customary sources.
For More Information • Ms. Cynthia Webb, Director of Study Programs Abroad, Nicholls State University, PO Box 2080, Thibodaux, LA 70310; *Phone:* 985-448-4440; *Fax:* 985-449-7028. *E-mail:* spab-caw@nicholls.edu. *World Wide Web:* http://www.nicholls.edu/abroad/

STATE UNIVERSITY OF NEW YORK COLLEGE AT BROCKPORT
SPANISH LANGUAGE IMMERSION PROGRAM, CUERNAVACA

Hosted by The Center for Bilingual Multicultural Studies Universidad Internacional
Academic Focus • Cultural studies, Latin American studies, Mexican studies, Spanish language and literature.
Program Information • Students attend classes at The Center for Bilingual Multicultural Studies Universidad Internacional. Field trips to the pyramids of Teotihuacan, Tepoztlán, Cholula, Mexico City; optional travel to Acapulco at an extra cost.
Sessions • Fall, spring, yearlong.
Eligibility Requirements • Minimum age 18; open to sophomores, juniors, seniors; course work in area of internship, if applicable; 2.5 GPA; 2 letters of recommendation; must be at least a second semester sophomore; résumé required for internship option; 1 year college course work in Spanish or the equivalent recommended.
Living Arrangements • Students live in host family homes. Meals are taken with host family, in residences.
Costs (2004-2005) • One term: $7350. Yearlong program: $13,450; includes tuition, housing, some meals, excursions, international student ID, student support services. $350 nonrefundable deposit required. Financial aid available for all students: scholarships, loans, regular financial aid, grants.
For More Information • Dr. John Perry, Director, Office of International Education, State University of New York College at Brockport, 350 New Campus Drive, Brockport, NY 14420; *Phone:* 800-298-SUNY; *Fax:* 585-637-3218. *E-mail:* overseas@brockport.edu. *World Wide Web:* http://www.brockport.edu/studyabroad/

UNIVERSITY OF MINNESOTA
LANGUAGE AND CULTURE IN MEXICO

Hosted by Cemanahuac Educational Community
Academic Focus • History, Mexican studies, Spanish language and literature.
Program Information • Students attend classes at Cemanahuac Educational Community. Scheduled travel to Buena Vista; field trips to Teotihuacán; optional travel to Valley of Calixtlahuaca, Oaxaca at an extra cost.
Sessions • Fall, spring.
Eligibility Requirements • Minimum age 18; open to freshmen, sophomores, juniors, seniors, graduate students, adults; 2.5 GPA; good academic standing at home school; no foreign language proficiency required.
Living Arrangements • Students live in host family homes. Quarters are shared with host institution students. Meals are taken with host family, in residences.

Costs (2004-2005) • One term: contact sponsor for cost. $50 application fee. $400 nonrefundable deposit required. Financial aid available for students from sponsoring institution: scholarships, loans.
For More Information • University of Minnesota, Learning Abroad Center, 230 Heller Hall, 271 19th Avenue South, Minneapolis, MN 55455; *Phone:* 888-700-UOFM; *Fax:* 612-626-8009. *E-mail:* umabroad@umn.edu. *World Wide Web:* http://www.umabroad.umn.edu/

GUADALAJARA
ARCADIA UNIVERSITY
UNIVERSIDAD PANAMERICANA

Hosted by Panamerican University Mexico–Guadalajara Unit
Academic Focus • Cultural studies, literature, political science and government, social sciences, Spanish language and literature, visual and performing arts.
Program Information • Students attend classes at Panamerican University Mexico–Guadalajara Unit. Scheduled travel; field trips.
Sessions • Fall, spring, yearlong.
Eligibility Requirements • Open to sophomores, juniors, seniors; 3.0 GPA; 1 letter of recommendation; Spanish language placement test; proficiency in Spanish for non-language courses.
Living Arrangements • Students live in host family homes. Meals are taken with host family, in residences.
Costs (2003-2004) • One term: $8650-$8950. Yearlong program: $14,120; includes tuition, housing, all meals, insurance, international student ID, student support services, transcripts, pre-departure guide. $35 application fee. $500 nonrefundable deposit required. Financial aid available for all students: scholarships, loans.
For More Information • Arcadia University, Center for Education Abroad, 450 South Easton Road, Glenside, PA 19038-3295; *Phone:* 866-927-2234; *Fax:* 215-572-2174. *E-mail:* cea@arcadia.edu. *World Wide Web:* http://www.arcadia.edu/cea/

COLLEGE CONSORTIUM FOR INTERNATIONAL STUDIES–CENTRAL WASHINGTON UNIVERSITY
PROGRAM IN GUADALAJARA, MEXICO

Hosted by Autonomous University of Guadalajara
Academic Focus • Full curriculum, Spanish language and literature.
Program Information • Students attend classes at Autonomous University of Guadalajara. Field trips to City Center of Guadalajara, markets, Tequila, Mexico City; optional travel to Mexico City, Puerto Vallarta at an extra cost.
Sessions • Fall, spring.
Eligibility Requirements • Minimum age 18; open to freshmen, sophomores, juniors, seniors, graduate students, adults; 2.5 GPA; 2 letters of recommendation; good academic standing at home school; no foreign language proficiency required.
Living Arrangements • Students live in host family homes. Quarters are shared with host institution students, students from other programs. Meals are taken with host family, in residences.
Costs (2004) • One term: $2250; includes tuition, insurance, excursions, student support services, health insurance. $85 application fee. $300 refundable deposit required. Financial aid available for students from sponsoring institution: scholarships, loans.
For More Information • Ms. Katie McCarthy, Study Abroad Advisor, College Consortium for International Studies–Central Washington University, 400 East University Way, Ellensburg, WA 98926-7408; *Phone:* 509-963-3612; *Fax:* 509-963-1558. *E-mail:* goabroad@cwu.edu. *World Wide Web:* http://www.ccisabroad.org/

CULTURAL EXPERIENCES ABROAD (CEA)
STUDY SPANISH LANGUAGE AND LATIN AMERICAN CULTURE IN GUADALAJARA

Hosted by University of Guadalajara
Academic Focus • Art history, civilization studies, cultural studies, drama/theater, economics, film and media studies, history, international business, Latin American literature, Latin American studies, Mexican studies, political science and government, sociology, Spanish language and literature.

MEXICO
Guadalajara

Program Information • Students attend classes at University of Guadalajara. Field trips to Tequila, Tlaquepaque, Lake Chapala, concerts, museums, a cathedral, Zacatecas, Michoacán, Zapopar, Puerto Vallarta; optional travel to other cities in Mexico at an extra cost.

Sessions • Fall, spring, winter, fall quarter, winter quarter, spring quarter.

Eligibility Requirements • Minimum age 18; open to freshmen, sophomores, juniors, seniors, graduate students, adults; 2.5 GPA; 1 letter of recommendation; good academic standing at home school; previous Spanish study recommended.

Living Arrangements • Students live in host institution dormitories, host family homes. Quarters are shared with host institution students, students from other programs. Meals are taken with host family, in residences.

Costs (2003–2004) • One term: $5695–$6995; includes tuition, housing, some meals, excursions, lab equipment, student support services, airport reception, official transcript. $50 application fee. $400 nonrefundable deposit required.

For More Information • Cultural Experiences Abroad (CEA), 1400 East Southern Avenue, Suite B-108, Tempe, AZ 85282-8011; *Phone:* 480-557-7900; *Fax:* 480-557-7926. *E-mail:* petersons@gowithcea. com. *World Wide Web:* http://www.gowithcea.com/

THE INTERNATIONAL PARTNERSHIP FOR SERVICE LEARNING
MEXICO SERVICE–LEARNING

Hosted by Autonomous University of Guadalajara

Academic Focus • Community service, education, international affairs, liberal studies, Mexican studies, social sciences, Spanish language and literature.

Program Information • Students attend classes at Autonomous University of Guadalajara. Field trips to sites around Guadalajara and neighboring villages; optional travel to Mexico City, Guanajuato, Puerto Vallarta at an extra cost.

Sessions • Fall, spring, yearlong.

Eligibility Requirements • Minimum age 18; open to freshmen, sophomores, juniors, seniors, graduate students, adults; 2 letters of recommendation; good academic standing at home school; evidence of maturity, responsibility; 1 year of college course work in Spanish.

Living Arrangements • Students live in host family homes. Meals are taken with host family, in residences.

Costs (2003-2004) • One term: $8600–$8900. Yearlong program: $16,900; includes tuition, housing, some meals, student support services, community service placement. $50 application fee. $250 refundable deposit required. Financial aid available for all students: federal financial aid.

For More Information • Ms. Ilana Golin, Coordinator of Student Programs, The International Partnership for Service Learning, 815 Second Avenue, Suite 315, New York, NY 10017-4594; *Phone:* 212-986-0989; *Fax:* 212-986-5039. *E-mail:* info@ipsl.org. *World Wide Web:* http://www.ipsl.org/

MIDDLEBURY COLLEGE SCHOOLS ABROAD
SCHOOL IN LATIN AMERICA–GUADALAJARA PROGRAM

Hosted by University of Guadalajara

Academic Focus • Full curriculum.

Program Information • Students attend classes at University of Guadalajara. Field trips.

Sessions • Fall, spring, yearlong.

Eligibility Requirements • Open to sophomores, juniors, seniors; 2.7 GPA; 2 letters of recommendation; B average in both Spanish and major; 2.5 years of college course work in Spanish.

Living Arrangements • Students live in host family homes. Meals are taken on one's own, with host family, in residences, in restaurants.

Costs (2004-2005) • One term: $7200. Yearlong program: $14,400; includes tuition. $50 application fee. $300 nonrefundable deposit required. Financial aid available for students from sponsoring institution: scholarships, loans.

For More Information • Mr. Jamie Northrup, University Relations Coordinator, Middlebury College Schools Abroad, Office of Off-Campus Study, Sunderland Language Center, Middlebury, VT 05753;

Phone: 802-443-5745; *Fax:* 802-443-3157. *E-mail:* schoolsabroad@ middlebury.edu. *World Wide Web:* http://www.middlebury.edu/ msa/

STATE UNIVERSITY OF NEW YORK AT PLATTSBURGH
STUDY IN MEXICO, GUADALAJARA

Hosted by University of Guadalajara

Academic Focus • Anthropology, art, art history, biological/life sciences, business administration/management, chemical sciences, communications, computer science, design and applied arts, economics, education, Latin American literature, marketing, philosophy, political science and government, psychology.

Program Information • Students attend classes at University of Guadalajara. Field trips to sites near Guadalajara.

Sessions • Fall, spring, yearlong.

Eligibility Requirements • Minimum age 18; open to sophomores, juniors, seniors; 2.8 GPA; 2 letters of recommendation; good academic standing at home school; SUNY application; essay; transcript; fluency in Spanish.

Living Arrangements • Students live in host institution dormitories, locally rented apartments, host family homes. Quarters are shared with host institution students, students from other programs. Meals are taken on one's own, with host family, in residences, in central dining facility, in restaurants.

Costs (2004-2005) • One term: contact sponsor for cost. Yearlong program: contact sponsor for cost.

For More Information • Ms. Jo Ann Mackie, Study Aborad Coordinator, State University of New York at Plattsburgh, Study Abroad Office, 101 Broad Street, Plattsburgh, NY 12901; *Phone:* 518-564-2321; *Fax:* 518-564-2326. *E-mail:* international@plattsburgh. edu. *World Wide Web:* http://www.plattsburgh.edu/studyabroad/

UNIVERSITY OF COLORADO AT BOULDER
STUDY SPANISH IN MEXICO

Hosted by University of Guadalajara

Academic Focus • Mexican studies, Spanish language and literature.

Program Information • Students attend classes at University of Guadalajara. Optional travel to Mexico City, Oaxaca at an extra cost.

Sessions • Fall, spring.

Eligibility Requirements • Open to freshmen, sophomores, juniors, seniors, graduate students, adults; 2.5 GPA; 2 letters of recommendation; teacher evaluation or Spanish placement test results; maximum 1.5 years of college course work in Spanish.

Living Arrangements • Students live in host family homes. Quarters are shared with students from other programs. Meals are taken with host family.

Costs (2003-2004) • One term: $6940; includes tuition, housing, all meals, insurance, excursions, international airfare, books and class materials, student support services. $400 nonrefundable deposit required. Financial aid available for students from sponsoring institution: scholarships, loans.

For More Information • University of Colorado at Boulder, Office of International Education, UCB 123, Boulder, CO 80309-0123; *Phone:* 303-492-7741; *Fax:* 303-492-5185. *E-mail:* studyabr@colorado. edu. *World Wide Web:* http://www.colorado.edu/OIE/

UNIVERSITY OF IDAHO
SPANISH AND LATIN AMERICAN STUDIES

Hosted by Autonomous University of Guadalajara

Academic Focus • Full curriculum, Mexican studies, Spanish language and literature.

Program Information • Students attend classes at Autonomous University of Guadalajara. Field trips to Lake Chapala, Tequila, Tlaquepaque; optional travel to Mexico City, Guanajuato, Michoacán at an extra cost.

Sessions • Fall, spring, yearlong, intensive language and culture program ends one week earlier than regular program.

Eligibility Requirements • Open to freshmen, sophomores, juniors, seniors, graduate students, adults; good academic standing at home school; fluency in Spanish required for regular program; no foreign language proficiency requirement for Intensive Spanish Program.

Living Arrangements • Students live in locally rented apartments, host family homes. Quarters are shared with host institution students, students from other programs. Meals are taken on one's own, with host family, in residences.

Costs (2003-2004) • One term: $2500. Yearlong program: $4000; includes tuition, excursions, student support services. $100 application fee. $200 refundable deposit required. Financial aid available for students from sponsoring institution: scholarships, loans.

For More Information • Ms. Amy Bergmann, Advisor, University of Idaho, Room 209, Morrill Hall, Moscow, ID 83844-3013; *Phone:* 208-885-7870; *Fax:* 208-885-2859. *E-mail:* abroad@uidaho.edu. *World Wide Web:* http://www.ets.uidaho.edu/ipo/abroad/

GUANAJUATO

CIEE
CIEE STUDY CENTER AT THE UNIVERSITY OF GUANAJUATO, MEXICO

Hosted by University of Guanajuato
Academic Focus • Anthropology, cinematography, history, Spanish language and literature.
Program Information • Students attend classes at University of Guanajuato. Scheduled travel to Mexico City, Michoucán, Zacatecas; field trips to Mexico City, Guadalajara, León.
Sessions • Fall, spring.
Eligibility Requirements • Minimum age 18; open to freshmen, sophomores, juniors, seniors; 2.75 GPA; 1-2 years college coursework in Spanish, depending on course of study.
Living Arrangements • Students live in host family homes. Meals are taken with host family, in residences, in restaurants.
Costs (2004-2005) • One term: $7400; includes tuition, housing, all meals, insurance, excursions, student support services, pre-departure advising, cultural activities. $30 application fee. $300 deposit required. Financial aid available for all students: minority student scholarships, travel grants.
For More Information • Ms. Ellen Whitman, Admissions Officer, Spain and Latin America, CIEE, 7 Custom House Street, 3rd Floor, Portland, ME 04101; *Phone:* 800-40-STUDY; *Fax:* 207-553-7699. *E-mail:* studyinfo@ciee.org. *World Wide Web:* http://www.ciee.org/isp/

INTERNATIONAL STUDIES ABROAD
GUANAJUATO, MEXICO SEMESTER COURSES

Hosted by University of Guanajuato
Academic Focus • Art, economics, history, international business, literature, Spanish language and literature.
Program Information • Students attend classes at University of Guanajuato. Scheduled travel to Michoacán, Puerto Vallarta, Oaxaca, Teotihuacán; field trips to San Miguel de Allende, León, Querétaro, El Rosario Monarch Butterfly Sanctuary (winter).
Sessions • Fall, spring, yearlong.
Eligibility Requirements • Minimum age 18; open to freshmen, sophomores, juniors, seniors, adults; 2.5 GPA; 1 letter of recommendation; good academic standing at home school; transcript; 1 year of college course work in Spanish.
Living Arrangements • Students live in locally rented apartments, host family homes. Quarters are shared with host institution students, students from other programs. Meals are taken with host family.
Costs (2004-2005) • One term: $7300. Yearlong program: $13,500; includes tuition, housing, all meals, insurance, excursions, student support services, laundry service, tutorial assistance, ground transportation, Internet access. $200 deposit required. Financial aid available for all students: scholarships, loans, U.S. federal financial aid.
For More Information • Mr. David Cardena, Mexico Site Specialist, International Studies Abroad, 901 West 24th Street, Austin, TX 78705; *Phone:* 800-580-8826; *Fax:* 512-480-8866. *E-mail:* isa@studiesabroad.com. *World Wide Web:* http://www.studiesabroad.com/

STETSON UNIVERSITY
STUDY ABROAD–GUANAJUATO

Hosted by University of Guanajuato
Academic Focus • Art, Mexican studies, Spanish language and literature.
Program Information • Students attend classes at University of Guanajuato. Field trips to Guadalajara, Michoacán, Mexico City.
Sessions • Fall, spring, yearlong.
Eligibility Requirements • Minimum age 20; open to sophomores, juniors, seniors; 2.5 GPA; 3 letters of recommendation; good academic standing at home school; completed application; 1 year of college course work in Spanish.
Living Arrangements • Students live in host family homes. Quarters are shared with students from other programs. Meals are taken with host family, in residences.
Costs (2002-2003) • One term: $14,025. Yearlong program: $28,050; includes tuition, housing, all meals, insurance, excursions, international airfare, lab equipment. $50 application fee. $200 nonrefundable deposit required. Financial aid available for students from sponsoring institution: scholarships, loans.
For More Information • Ms. Nancy L. Leonard, Director, Stetson University, Center for International Education, Unit 8412, 421 North Woodland Boulevard, Deland, FL 32723-3757; *Phone:* 386-822-8165; *Fax:* 386-822-8167. *E-mail:* nleonard@stetson.edu. *World Wide Web:* http://www.stetson.edu/international/

MÉRIDA

CENTRAL COLLEGE ABROAD
CENTRAL COLLEGE ABROAD IN MÉRIDA, MEXICO

Hosted by Central College in Mérida, Marista University
Academic Focus • Art history, cultural studies, economics, environmental science/studies, history, international business, Mayan studies, Mexican studies, political science and government, psychology, social sciences, Spanish language and literature.
Program Information • Students attend classes at Marista University, Central College in Mérida. Scheduled travel to Chiapas; field trips to Chichen Itzá, Uxmal.
Sessions • Fall, spring, yearlong.
Eligibility Requirements • Minimum age 18; open to freshmen, sophomores, juniors, seniors; 2.5 GPA; 2 letters of recommendation; good academic standing at home school; study abroad approval form; transcript; Student Life endorsement; no foreign language proficiency required.
Living Arrangements • Students live in host family homes, a residence. Quarters are shared with host institution students. Meals are taken as a group, with host family, in residences, in central dining facility.
Costs (2003-2004) • One term: $9990. Yearlong program: $19,980; includes tuition, housing, some meals, excursions, international student ID, student support services. $25 application fee. $350 nonrefundable deposit required. Financial aid available for all students: scholarships.
For More Information • Office of International Education, Central College Abroad, 812 University Street, Pella, IA 50219; *Phone:* 800-831-3629; *Fax:* 641-628-5375. *E-mail:* studyabroad@central.edu. *World Wide Web:* http://www.central.edu/abroad/

INSTITUTE FOR STUDY ABROAD, BUTLER UNIVERSITY
UNIVERSIDATA AUTÓNOMA DE YUCATÁN

Hosted by Autonomous University of Yucatán
Academic Focus • Full curriculum.
Program Information • Students attend classes at Autonomous University of Yucatán. Field trips.
Sessions • Fall, spring, yearlong.
Eligibility Requirements • Open to sophomores, juniors, seniors; 3.0 GPA; 1 letter of recommendation; good academic standing at home school; enrollment at an accredited American college or university; 2 years of college course work in Spanish.
Living Arrangements • Students live in host family homes. Meals are taken with host family.
Costs (2002-2003) • One term: $8650. Yearlong program: $17,300; includes tuition, housing, all meals, excursions, international student

ID, student support services, pre-departure advising, cultural and sporting activities. $40 application fee. $500 deposit required. Financial aid available for all students: scholarships, travel grants.
For More Information • Institute for Study Abroad, Butler University, 1100 West 42nd Street, Suite 305, Indianapolis, IN 46208-3345; *Phone:* 800-858-0229; *Fax:* 317-940-9336. *E-mail:* copa@butler.edu. *World Wide Web:* http://www.ifsa-butler.org/

MICHIGAN STATE UNIVERSITY
MULTIDISCIPLINARY STUDIES IN MÉRIDA

Hosted by Autonomous University of Yucatán
Academic Focus • History, interdisciplinary studies, Mayan studies, Mexican studies, social sciences, Spanish language and literature.
Program Information • Students attend classes at Autonomous University of Yucatán. Field trips to Mayan ruins, the Gulf of Mexico.
Sessions • Spring.
Eligibility Requirements • Minimum age 18; open to freshmen, sophomores, juniors, seniors; 2.75 GPA; good academic standing at home school; approval of faculty directors; 1 year of college course work in Spanish.
Living Arrangements • Students live in host family homes. Meals are taken with host family, in residences.
Costs (2003) • One term: $2900 (estimated); includes housing, all meals, insurance, excursions, student support services. $100 application fee. $200 nonrefundable deposit required. Financial aid available for students from sponsoring institution: scholarships, loans.
For More Information • Ms. Sherry Martinez-Bonilla, Office Assistant, Michigan State University, Office of Study Abroad, 109 International Center, East Lansing, MI 48824-1035; *Phone:* 517-353-8920; *Fax:* 517-432-2082. *E-mail:* marti269@msu.edu. *World Wide Web:* http://studyabroad.msu.edu/

RUTGERS, THE STATE UNIVERSITY OF NEW JERSEY
STUDY ABROAD IN MEXICO

Hosted by Autonomous University of Yucatán
Academic Focus • Full curriculum.
Program Information • Students attend classes at Autonomous University of Yucatán. Scheduled travel to Mexico City, Quintana Roo; field trips to Uxmal, Chichen Itzá.
Sessions • Fall, spring, yearlong.
Eligibility Requirements • Open to sophomores, juniors, seniors; 2.5 GPA; 2 letters of recommendation; 2 years of college course work in Spanish.
Living Arrangements • Students live in host family homes. Quarters are shared with host institution students. Meals are taken on one's own, with host family, in residences.
Costs (2003-2004) • One term: $9771 for New Jersey residents; $12,421 for nonresidents. Yearlong program: $17,253 for New Jersey residents; $22,553 for nonresidents; includes tuition, housing, some meals, insurance, excursions, international student ID. $20 application fee. $750 nonrefundable deposit required. Financial aid available for students from sponsoring institution: scholarships, loans.
For More Information • Ms. Karin Bonello, Regional Coordinator, Rutgers, The State University of New Jersey, 102 College Avenue, New Brunswick, NJ 08901-8543; *Phone:* 732-932-7787; *Fax:* 732-932-8659. *E-mail:* ru_abroad@email.rutgers.edu. *World Wide Web:* http://studyabroad.rutgers.edu/

UNIVERSITY OF FLORIDA
AUTONOMOUS UNIVERSITY OF YUCATÁN

Hosted by Autonomous University of Yucatán
Academic Focus • Full curriculum.
Program Information • Students attend classes at Autonomous University of Yucatán. Field trips to archaeological sites, cultural sites; optional travel to archaeological excavations, ecology field trips, Mayan sites, Caribbean reefs at an extra cost.
Sessions • Fall, spring, yearlong.
Eligibility Requirements • Minimum age 18; open to freshmen, sophomores, juniors, seniors, graduate students; 2.5 GPA; 2 letters of recommendation; good academic standing at home school; transcript; fluency in Spanish.

Living Arrangements • Students live in host family homes. Meals are taken with host family, in residences, in restaurants.
Costs (2003-2004) • One term: contact sponsor for cost. Yearlong program: contact sponsor for cost. $250 refundable deposit required. Financial aid available for students from sponsoring institution: scholarships, loans.
For More Information • Ms. Katrina Gunnels, Study Abroad Services, International Center, University of Florida, 123 Grinter Hall, PO Box 113225, Gainesville, FL 32611-3225; *Phone:* 352-392-5323; *Fax:* 352-392-5575. *E-mail:* studyabroad@ufic.ufl.edu. *World Wide Web:* http://www.ufic.ufl.edu/

UNIVERSITY OF IDAHO
SPANISH AND LATIN AMERICAN STUDIES PROGRAM

Hosted by Autonomous University of Yucatán
Academic Focus • Full curriculum.
Program Information • Students attend classes at Autonomous University of Yucatán.
Sessions • Fall, spring, for direct enrollment students.
Eligibility Requirements • Open to freshmen, sophomores, juniors, seniors, graduate students, adults; good academic standing at home school; 3 years college course work in Spanish for direct enrollment students; no foreign language proficiency requirement for Intensive Spanish session.
Living Arrangements • Students live in host family homes. Quarters are shared with host institution students, students from other programs. Meals are taken with host family, in residences.
Costs (2003-2004) • One term: $2500. Yearlong program: $5000; includes tuition, student support services. $100 application fee. $200 refundable deposit required. Financial aid available for students from sponsoring institution: scholarships, loans.
For More Information • Ms. Amy S. Bergmann, Advisor, University of Idaho, Room 209, Morrill Hall, Moscow, ID 83844-3013; *Phone:* 208-885-4075; *Fax:* 208-885-2859. *E-mail:* abroad@uidaho.edu. *World Wide Web:* http://www.ets.uidaho.edu/ipo/abroad/

UNIVERSITY OF SOUTHERN MISSISSIPPI
UNIVERSITY OF YUCATÁN EXCHANGE PROGRAM

Hosted by Autonomous University of Yucatán
Academic Focus • Anthropology, Spanish language and literature.
Program Information • Students attend classes at Autonomous University of Yucatán. Optional travel to traditional villages (through anthropology courses) at an extra cost.
Sessions • Fall, spring, yearlong.
Eligibility Requirements • Minimum age 18; open to sophomores, juniors, seniors; 2.0 GPA; 2 letters of recommendation; good academic standing at home school; interview; 2.5 years college course work in Spanish (conversational Spanish class is recommended).
Living Arrangements • Students live in locally rented apartments, host family homes. Meals are taken on one's own, with host family, in residences.
Costs (2003-2004) • One term: $2100 for Mississippi residents; $4358 for nonresidents. Yearlong program: $3950 for Mississippi residents; $8466 for nonresidents; includes tuition, student support services. $250 nonrefundable deposit required. Financial aid available for students from sponsoring institution: scholarships, loans.
For More Information • Ms. Holly Buckner, International Programs Coordinator, University of Southern Mississippi, Box 10047, Hattiesburg, MS 39406-0047; *Phone:* 601-266-5624; *Fax:* 601-266-5699. *E-mail:* holly.buckner@usm.edu. *World Wide Web:* http://www.cice.usm.edu/

MEXICO CITY
IBERIAN-AMERICAN UNIVERSITY MÉXICO
JUNIOR YEAR ABROAD

Hosted by Iberian-American University México
Academic Focus • Anthropology, full curriculum, history, international affairs, literature, political science and government, Spanish language and literature.

Program Information • Students attend classes at Iberian-American University México. Field trips to Teotihuacán pyramids, Taxco, Tula, Puebla.

Sessions • Fall, spring, yearlong.

Eligibility Requirements • Minimum age 18; open to juniors, seniors, graduate students, adults; 2.5 GPA; transcript; student visa; no foreign language proficiency required.

Living Arrangements • Students live in host family homes. Quarters are shared with host institution students. Meals are taken on one's own, in residences, in central dining facility, in restaurants.

Costs (2004-2005) • One term: $7500. Yearlong program: $15,000; includes tuition, housing, all meals, excursions, books and class materials, student support services, ID card for library, infirmary, discounts at museums, local transportation, approximately $1000 for personal expenses. $50 application fee.

For More Information • Ms. Catherine Fanning, Assistant Director, Student Exchange Program, Iberian-American University México, Prol. Paseo de la Reforma 880, Col. Lomas de Santa Fe, D.F. 01210, Mexico; *Phone:* +52 55-5950-4243; *Fax:* +52 55-5950-4241. *E-mail:* international@uia.mx. *World Wide Web:* http://www.uia.mx/. Students may also apply through Alma College, Alma, MI 48801-1599; Loyola University New Orleans, 6363 St. Charles Avenue, New Orleans, LA 70118; Pomona College, 333 North College Way, Claremont, CA 91711-6334.

LOYOLA UNIVERSITY NEW ORLEANS
MEXICO PROGRAM

Hosted by Iberian-American University México

Academic Focus • Communications, education, hotel and restaurant management, international affairs, Latin American studies, Mexican studies, political science and government, sociology, Spanish language and literature, visual and performing arts.

Program Information • Students attend classes at Iberian-American University México. Field trips to Tula, Puebla, Teotihuacán, Taxco; optional travel to Cancún, Acapulco, Oaxaca, Guanajuato at an extra cost.

Sessions • Fall, spring, yearlong.

Eligibility Requirements • Minimum age 17; open to precollege students, freshmen, sophomores, juniors, seniors, graduate students, adults; 2.75 GPA; good academic standing at home school; interview.

Living Arrangements • Students live in host family homes. Meals are taken on one's own, with host family, in residences.

Costs (2004-2005) • One term: $10,760–$12,260. Yearlong program: $21,000–$22,000; includes tuition, housing, some meals, insurance, excursions, student support services, student visa. $25 application fee. Financial aid available for all students: scholarships, loans.

For More Information • Dr. Maurice P. Brungardt, Director, Mexico Program, Loyola University New Orleans, 6363 Saint Charles Avenue, New Orleans, LA 70118; *Phone:* 504-865-3537; *Fax:* 504-865-2010. *E-mail:* brungard@loyno.edu. *World Wide Web:* http://www.loyno.edu/cie/

UNIVERSITY OF MIAMI
CENTRO DE INVESTIGACIÓN Y DOCENCIA ECONOMICAS, MEXICO

Hosted by Centro de Investigación y Docencia Económicas

Academic Focus • Business administration/management, economics, international affairs, political science and government.

Program Information • Students attend classes at Centro de Investigación y Docencia Económicas.

Sessions • Fall, spring, yearlong.

Eligibility Requirements • Minimum age 18; open to sophomores, juniors, seniors; 3.0 GPA; 2 letters of recommendation; language evaluation; personal interview; fluency in Spanish.

Living Arrangements • Students live in locally rented apartments, host family homes. Quarters are shared with host institution students, students from other programs. Meals are taken on one's own, with host family, in central dining facility, in restaurants.

Costs (2003-2004) • One term: $12,919. Yearlong program: $25,838; includes tuition, student support services. $40 application fee. $500 nonrefundable deposit required. Financial aid available for students from sponsoring institution: scholarships, loans.

For More Information • Mr. Chris Tingue, Assistant Director, University of Miami, International Education and Exchange Programs, 5050 Brunson Drive, Allen Hall 212, PO Box 248005, Coral Gables, FL 33124-1610; *Phone:* 305-284-3434; *Fax:* 305-284-4235. *E-mail:* ieep@miami.edu. *World Wide Web:* http://www.studyabroad.miami.edu/

UNIVERSITY OF MIAMI
IBEROAMERICANA UNIVERSITY, MEXICO

Hosted by Iberian-American University México

Academic Focus • Business administration/management, economics, education, history, liberal studies, social sciences, Spanish language and literature.

Program Information • Students attend classes at Iberian-American University México.

Sessions • Fall, spring, yearlong.

Eligibility Requirements • Minimum age 18; open to sophomores, juniors, seniors; 3.0 GPA; 2 letters of recommendation; language evaluation; personal interview; 2 years of college course work in Spanish.

Living Arrangements • Students live in locally rented apartments, host family homes. Quarters are shared with host institution students, students from other programs. Meals are taken on one's own, with host family, in central dining facility, in restaurants.

Costs (2003-2004) • One term: $12,919. Yearlong program: $25,838; includes tuition, student support services. $40 application fee. $500 nonrefundable deposit required. Financial aid available for students from sponsoring institution: scholarships, loans.

For More Information • Mr. Chris Tingue, Assistant Director, University of Miami, International Education and Exchange Programs, 5050 Brunson Drive, Allen Hall 212, PO Box 248005, Coral Gables, FL 33124-1610; *Phone:* 305-284-3434; *Fax:* 305-284-4235. *E-mail:* ieep@miami.edu. *World Wide Web:* http://www.studyabroad.miami.edu/

WHITWORTH COLLEGE
WHITWORTH/IBEROAMERICANA UNIVERSITY EXCHANGE PROGRAM

Hosted by Iberian-American University México

Academic Focus • History, Latin American literature, political science and government, Spanish language and literature.

Program Information • Students attend classes at Iberian-American University México. Optional travel to Oaxtepec, Teotihuacán pyramids at an extra cost.

Sessions • Fall, spring, yearlong.

Eligibility Requirements • Open to sophomores, juniors, seniors; 2.5 GPA; 2 letters of recommendation; 2 years of college course work in Spanish.

Living Arrangements • Students live in host family homes. Quarters are shared with students from other programs. Meals are taken with host family, in restaurants.

Costs (2003-2004) • One term: $13,034. Yearlong program: $26,068; includes tuition, housing, all meals. Financial aid available for students from sponsoring institution: scholarships.

For More Information • Ms. Sue Jackson, Director, Off-Campus Programs, Whitworth College, Center for International and Multicultural Education, 300 West Hawthorne Road, Spokane, WA 99251-2702; *Phone:* 509-777-4596; *Fax:* 509-777-3723. *E-mail:* sjackson@whitworth.edu. *World Wide Web:* http://www.whitworth.edu/

MONTERREY
NIAGARA UNIVERSITY
ITESM–MONTERREY, MEXICO

Hosted by Instituto Tecnológico y de Estudios Superiores de Monterrey–Monterrey Campus

Academic Focus • Business administration/management, international business, labor and industrial relations.

Program Information • Students attend classes at Instituto Tecnológico y de Estudios Superiores de Monterrey–Monterrey Campus.

Sessions • Fall, spring.

Eligibility Requirements • Open to sophomores, juniors, seniors; 2 letters of recommendation; good academic standing at home school; 2 years of college course work in Spanish.

Living Arrangements • Students live in host institution dormitories, host family homes. Quarters are shared with host institution students, students from other programs. Meals are taken on one's own, with host family, in residences, in central dining facility.

Costs (2003-2004) • One term: $12,314; includes tuition, housing, all meals, international student ID. Financial aid available for students from sponsoring institution: loans, Pell grants and TAP for qualified New York State residents.

For More Information • Ms. Bernadette Brennen, Assistant to Academic Vice President/Study Abroad Coordinator, Niagara University, Alumni Hall, Niagara University, NY 14109; *Phone:* 716-286-8360; *Fax:* 716-286-8349. *E-mail:* bmb@niagara.edu. *World Wide Web:* http://www.niagara.edu/sap/

STATE UNIVERSITY OF NEW YORK AT PLATTSBURGH
STUDY IN MEXICO, MONTERREY

Hosted by University of Monterrey

Academic Focus • Anthropology, art, art history, biological/life sciences, business administration/management, chemical sciences, communications, computer science, design and applied arts, economics, education, Latin American literature, marketing, philosophy, political science and government, psychology, Spanish language and literature.

Program Information • Students attend classes at University of Monterrey. Field trips to sites near Monterrey.

Sessions • Fall, spring, yearlong.

Eligibility Requirements • Minimum age 18; open to sophomores, juniors, seniors; 2.8 GPA; 2 letters of recommendation; good academic standing at home school; SUNY and UM applications; essay; transcript; 1 year college course work in Spanish for immersion program; fluency in Spanish for direct enrollment.

Living Arrangements • Students live in locally rented apartments, host family homes. Quarters are shared with host institution students, students from other programs. Meals are taken on one's own, with host family, in central dining facility, in restaurants.

Costs (2003-2004) • One term: $4840 for New York residents; nonresidents contact sponsor for cost. Yearlong program: $9680 for New York residents; nonresidents contact sponsor for cost; includes tuition, housing, some meals, insurance, books and class materials, international student ID, student support services. $20 application fee. $350 nonrefundable deposit required. Financial aid available for students from sponsoring institution: scholarships, loans.

For More Information • Ms. Jo Ann Mackie, Study Abroad Coordinator, State University of New York at Plattsburgh, Study Abroad Office, 101 Broad Street, Plattsburgh, NY 12901; *Phone:* 518-564-2321; *Fax:* 518-564-2326. *E-mail:* international@plattsburgh.edu. *World Wide Web:* http://www.plattsburgh.edu/studyabroad/

MORELIA
AHA INTERNATIONAL AN ACADEMIC PROGRAM OF THE UNIVERSITY OF OREGON
THE MIGRATION STUDIES PROGRAM IN MORELIA, MEXICO

Hosted by Latin University of America

Academic Focus • Anthropology, bilingual education, community service, comparative literature, criminal justice, education, full curriculum, Latin American studies, literature, Mexican studies, nutrition, political science and government, social services, sociology, Spanish language and literature, teaching, teaching English as a second language.

Program Information • Students attend classes at Latin University of America. Scheduled travel to Mexico City; field trips to Patzcuaro, Uruapan, Guanajuato.

Sessions • Fall, spring, winter, for direct enrollment, semester corresponds to host institution's calendar.

Eligibility Requirements • Open to sophomores, juniors, seniors, graduate students; 2.7 GPA; 2 letters of recommendation; good academic standing at home school; no foreign language proficiency required.

Living Arrangements • Students live in host family homes. Meals are taken with host family.

Costs (2003-2004) • One term: $3720–$4060; includes tuition, housing, all meals, insurance, excursions, books and class materials, student support services. $50 application fee. $200 refundable deposit required. Financial aid available for all students: scholarships, loans, grants.

For More Information • Ms. Amy Hunter, Associate Director for University Programs, AHA International An Academic Program of the University of Oregon, 741 SW Lincoln Street, Portland, OR 97201; *Phone:* 503-295-7730; *Fax:* 503-295-5969. *E-mail:* mail@aha-intl.org. *World Wide Web:* http://www.aha-intl.org/

KENTUCKY INSTITUTE FOR INTERNATIONAL STUDIES
SEMESTER PROGRAM IN MORELIA, MEXICO

Academic Focus • Latin American studies, Spanish language and literature.

Program Information • Faculty members are drawn from the sponsor's U.S. staff and local instructors hired by the sponsor. Field trips to surrounding areas; optional travel to other areas of Mexico at an extra cost.

Sessions • Fall.

Eligibility Requirements • Minimum age 18; open to sophomores, juniors, seniors, graduate students; 2.5 GPA; 2 letters of recommendation; good academic standing at home school; minimum 3.0 GPA in Spanish; 2 years of college course work in Spanish.

Living Arrangements • Students live in host family homes. Meals are taken with host family, in residences.

Costs (2003) • One term: $4950; includes housing, some meals, excursions, international airfare, international student ID, instructional costs. $150 application fee. Financial aid available for all students: scholarships.

For More Information • Ms. Nancy Martin, Coordinator, Kentucky Institute for International Studies, Murray State University, PO Box 9, Murray, KY 42071-0009; *Phone:* 270-762-3091; *Fax:* 270-762-3434. *E-mail:* kiismsu@murraystate.edu. *World Wide Web:* http://www.kiis.org/

OAXACA
SAINT XAVIER UNIVERSITY
THE OAXACA PROJECT

Academic Focus • Mexican studies, Spanish language and literature.

Program Information • Faculty members are drawn from the sponsor's U.S. staff and local instructors hired by the sponsor. Scheduled travel to Palenque, Veracruz; field trips to Monte Alban, Mitla, monasteries, native markets; optional travel to other areas of Mexico at an extra cost.

Sessions • Fall.

Eligibility Requirements • Open to sophomores, juniors, seniors, adults; good academic standing at home school; no foreign language proficiency required.

Living Arrangements • Students live in locally rented apartments, host family homes, hotels. Quarters are shared with students from other programs. Meals are taken as a group, on one's own, with host family, in residences, in restaurants.

Costs (2003) • One term: $10,400; includes tuition, housing, all meals, excursions, international airfare, books and class materials, student support services, passport fees, laundry service, local transportation. $25 application fee. Financial aid available for all students: loans, some state and federal financial aid.

For More Information • Dr. Olga Vilella, Director, The Oaxaca Project, Saint Xavier University, 3700 West 103rd Street, Chicago, IL 60655; *Phone:* 773-298-3274; *Fax:* 773-779-9061. *E-mail:* vilella@sxu. edu. *World Wide Web:* http://www.sxu.edu/academ/artsci/foreign_languages/oaxaca.htm

SCHOOL FOR INTERNATIONAL TRAINING, SIT STUDY ABROAD
MEXICO: GRASSROOTS DEVELOPMENT, NGO'S AND SOCIAL CHANGE

Academic Focus • Cultural studies, history, Mexican studies, political science and government, social sciences, Spanish language and literature.

Program Information • Faculty members are drawn from the sponsor's U.S. staff and local instructors hired by the sponsor. Scheduled travel to Mexico City, coastal area of Oaxaca, Chiapas; field trips to northern Sierra, San Pablo Etla, community-based projects.

Sessions • Fall, spring.

Eligibility Requirements • Open to sophomores, juniors, seniors; 2.5 GPA; 2 letters of recommendation; good academic standing at home school; 1.5 years of college course work in Spanish.

Living Arrangements • Students live in host family homes, hotels. Meals are taken as a group, on one's own, with host family, in residences, in restaurants.

Costs (2003-2004) • One term: $12,050; includes tuition, housing, all meals, insurance, excursions. $50 application fee. $400 nonrefundable deposit required. Financial aid available for all students: scholarships.

For More Information • School for International Training, SIT Study Abroad, Kipling Road, Brattleboro, VT 05302-0676; *Phone:* 888-272-7881; *Fax:* 802-258-3296. *E-mail:* studyabroad@sit.edu. *World Wide Web:* http://www.sit.edu/studyabroad/

STATE UNIVERSITY OF NEW YORK AT PLATTSBURGH
SUSTAINABLE DEVELOPMENT AND CULTURAL STUDIES IN OAXACA

Hosted by Center for Intercultural Exchange and Dialogue
Academic Focus • Anthropology, cultural studies, social sciences, Spanish language and literature.

Program Information • Students attend classes at Center for Intercultural Exchange and Dialogue. Scheduled travel to cultural sites and communities around Oaxaca; field trips to cultural sites and communities around Oaxaca.

Sessions • Fall.

Eligibility Requirements • Minimum age 18; open to sophomores, juniors, seniors; 2.5 GPA; 2 letters of recommendation; good academic standing at home school; SUNY application; essay; transcripts; intermediate Spanish.

Living Arrangements • Students live in locally rented apartments, host family homes. Meals are taken as a group, on one's own, with host family, in residences, in restaurants.

Costs (2003-2004) • One term: $6809 for New York residents; nonresidents contact sponsor for cost; includes tuition, housing, some meals, insurance, excursions, books and class materials, international student ID, student support services. $20 application fee. $350 nonrefundable deposit required. Financial aid available for students from sponsoring institution: scholarships, loans.

For More Information • Ms. Jo Ann Mackie, Study Abroad Coordinator, State University of New York at Plattsburgh, Study Abroad Office, 101 Broad Street, Plattsburgh, NY 12901; *Phone:* 518-564-2321; *Fax:* 518-564-2326. *E-mail:* international@plattsburgh. edu. *World Wide Web:* http://www.plattsburgh.edu/studyabroad/

WESTERN WASHINGTON UNIVERSITY
SEMESTER IN OAXACA, MEXICO

Hosted by Instituto Tecnológico de Oaxaca, Regional University of the South East Oaxaca, Instituto Welte de Estudios Oaxaquenos
Academic Focus • Anthropology, archaeology, environmental science/studies, history, Spanish language and literature.

Program Information • Students attend classes at Instituto Tecnológico de Oaxaca, Regional University of the South East Oaxaca, Instituto Welte de Estudios Oaxaquenos. Scheduled travel to Mexico City museums, Chiapas communities; field trips to archaeological sites, Monte Alban, indigenous communities.
Sessions • Fall.
Eligibility Requirements • Open to sophomores, juniors, seniors, graduate students; 2.5 GPA; 2 letters of recommendation; good academic standing at home school; statement of purpose; 2 years of college course work in Spanish.
Living Arrangements • Students live in host family homes. Quarters are shared with host institution students. Meals are taken with host family, in residences.
Costs (2003) • One term: $6900; includes tuition, housing, some meals, excursions, lab equipment, student support services. $280 application fee. $280 nonrefundable deposit required. Financial aid available for students from sponsoring institution: loans, grants.
For More Information • Ms. Sandy Ruiz, Program Coordinator, Western Washington University, International Programs and Exchanges, L-7, Bellingham, WA 98225-9046; *Phone:* 360-650-3298; *Fax:* 360-650-6572. *E-mail:* ipewwu@cc.wwu.edu. *World Wide Web:* http://wwu.edu/~ipewwu/

PUEBLA

LOCK HAVEN UNIVERSITY OF PENNSYLVANIA
SEMESTER IN MEXICO

Hosted by University of the Americas–Puebla
Academic Focus • Economics, international affairs, liberal studies, literature, political science and government, Spanish language and literature.
Program Information • Students attend classes at University of the Americas–Puebla.
Sessions • Fall, spring, yearlong.
Eligibility Requirements • Minimum age 18; open to sophomores, juniors, seniors, adults; 2.5 GPA; 3 letters of recommendation; good academic standing at home school; no foreign language proficiency required.
Living Arrangements • Students live in host institution dormitories, locally rented apartments. Quarters are shared with host institution students, students from other programs. Meals are taken on one's own, in central dining facility.
Costs (2002-2003) • One term: $4325 for Pennsylvania residents; $6600 for nonresidents. Yearlong program: $8650 for Pennsylvania residents; $13,200 for nonresidents; includes tuition, housing, fees. $50 application fee. Financial aid available for students from sponsoring institution: scholarships, loans.
For More Information • Dean, Institute for International Studies, Lock Haven University of Pennsylvania, Lock Haven, PA 17745-2390; *Phone:* 570-893-2140; *Fax:* 570-893-2537. *E-mail:* intlstudies_webmonitor@lhup.edu. *World Wide Web:* http://www.lhup.edu/international/goingp/goingplaces_index.htm

UNIVERSITY STUDIES ABROAD CONSORTIUM
SPANISH, LATIN AMERICAN, AND ENGINEERING STUDIES: PUEBLA, MEXICO

Hosted by Iberian-American University Puebla
Academic Focus • Culinary arts, dance, engineering, Latin American studies, sociology, Spanish language and literature.
Program Information • Students attend classes at Iberian-American University Puebla. Field trips to Teotihuacán pyramids, Tlaxcada and Cacaxtla Archeological sites, Cuetzalan and Yohualichan archeological sites, Oaxtapec Aquatic Park; optional travel to Yucatán (fall), central Mexico (spring) at an extra cost.
Sessions • Fall, spring, yearlong.
Eligibility Requirements • Minimum age 18; open to freshmen, sophomores, juniors, seniors; 2.5 GPA; no foreign language proficiency required.
Living Arrangements • Students live in host institution dormitories, host family homes. Quarters are shared with students from other programs. Meals are taken on one's own, in restaurants.

Costs (2005-2006) • One term: $4380. Yearlong program: $7480; includes tuition, housing, insurance, excursions. $50 application fee. $150 refundable deposit required. Financial aid available for all students: scholarships, loans.
For More Information • University Studies Abroad Consortium, USAC/323, Reno, NV 89557-0093; *Phone:* 775-784-6569; *Fax:* 775-784-6010. *E-mail:* usac@unr.edu. *World Wide Web:* http://usac.unr.edu/

VALPARAISO UNIVERSITY
PUEBLA SEMESTER

Hosted by University of the Americas–Puebla
Academic Focus • Cultural studies, sociology, Spanish language and literature.
Program Information • Students attend classes at University of the Americas–Puebla. Scheduled travel to Veracruz, Oaxaca; field trips to Mexico City, Taxco; optional travel to Querétaro, Guanajuato, Acapulco at an extra cost.
Sessions • Spring.
Eligibility Requirements • Minimum age 19; open to sophomores, juniors, seniors; 3.0 GPA; 2 letters of recommendation; 1 year of college course work in Spanish.
Living Arrangements • Students live in host institution dormitories. Quarters are shared with host institution students. Meals are taken on one's own, in central dining facility, in restaurants.
Costs (2004) • One term: $12,859; includes tuition, housing, excursions. $30 application fee. $200 nonrefundable deposit required. Financial aid available for students from sponsoring institution: scholarships, loans.
For More Information • Dr. Hugh McGuigan, Director, International Studies, Valparaiso University, 137 Meier Hall, 1800 Chapel Drive, Valparaiso, IN 46383; *Phone:* 219-464-5333; *Fax:* 219-464-6868. *E-mail:* studyabroad@valpo.edu. *World Wide Web:* http://www.valpo.edu/international/studyabroad.html

PUERTO SAN CARLOS

THE SCHOOL FOR FIELD STUDIES
MEXICO: MARINE MAMMAL CONSERVATION AND COASTAL ECOSYSTEMS STUDIES

Held at Center for Coastal Studies
Academic Focus • Biological/life sciences, conservation studies, ecology, economics, environmental science/studies, Latin American studies, marine sciences, Mexican studies, natural resources.
Program Information • Classes are held on the campus of Center for Coastal Studies. Faculty members are drawn from the sponsor's U.S. staff and local instructors hired by the sponsor. Field trips to La Purisma, Isla Magdalena; optional travel to La Paz, Baja Peninsula at an extra cost.
Sessions • Fall, spring.
Eligibility Requirements • Minimum age 18; open to freshmen, sophomores, juniors, seniors; course work in ecology or biology; 2.7 GPA; 2 letters of recommendation; personal statement; no foreign language proficiency required.
Living Arrangements • Students live in cabin-style accommodations on the waterfront. Quarters are shared with host institution students. Meals are taken as a group, in central dining facility.
Costs (2002-2003) • One term: $13,185; includes tuition, housing, all meals, excursions, lab equipment. $45 application fee. $500 nonrefundable deposit required. Financial aid available for all students: scholarships, loans.
For More Information • Admissions Department, The School for Field Studies, 10 Federal Street, Salem, MA 01970-3853; *Phone:* 800-989-4418; *Fax:* 978-741-3551. *E-mail:* admissions@fieldstudies.org. *World Wide Web:* http://www.fieldstudies.org/

QUERÉTARO

DICKINSON COLLEGE
DICKINSON IN QUERÉTARO (MEXICO)

Hosted by Autonomous University of Querétaro
Academic Focus • Full curriculum.

Program Information • Students attend classes at Autonomous University of Querétaro. Scheduled travel to Mexico City; field trips to neighboring cities.

Sessions • Spring.

Eligibility Requirements • Minimum age 18; open to juniors; 2.8 GPA; 3 letters of recommendation; good academic standing at home school; 2.5 years of college course work in Spanish.

Living Arrangements • Students live in host family homes. Meals are taken with host family, in residences.

Costs (2004) • One term: $17,795; includes tuition, housing, all meals, excursions, student support services. $25 application fee. $300 nonrefundable deposit required. Financial aid available for students from sponsoring institution: scholarships, loans.

For More Information • Ms. Karen Peter, Program Manager, Dickinson College, PO Box 1773, Carlisle, PA 17013-2896; *Phone:* 717-245-1341; *Fax:* 717-245-1688. *E-mail:* global@dickinson.edu. *World Wide Web:* http://www.dickinson.edu/global/

INTERAMERICAN UNIVERSITY STUDIES INSTITUTE
MEXICAN STUDIES

Hosted by Autonomous University of Querétaro

Academic Focus • Art history, literature, Mexican studies, Spanish language and literature.

Program Information • Students attend classes at Autonomous University of Querétaro. Scheduled travel to Michoacán; field trips to Mexico City, Teotihuacán, Pátzcuaro, Guanajuato.

Sessions • Fall, spring.

Eligibility Requirements • Minimum age 18; open to freshmen, sophomores, juniors, seniors, graduate students, adults; course work in Mexican/Latin American Social Sciences; 2.75 GPA; 2 letters of recommendation; good academic standing at home school; 2 brief essays; 1 year of college course work in Spanish.

Living Arrangements • Students live in host family homes. Meals are taken with host family, in residences.

Costs (2003-2004) • One term: $6558–$6904; includes tuition, housing, all meals, excursions, accreditation fee. $50 application fee. $200 nonrefundable deposit required.

For More Information • Ms. Jennifer Jewett, Program Coordinator, Interamerican University Studies Institute, PO Box 10958, Eugene, OR 97440; *Phone:* 800-345-IUSI; *Fax:* 541-686-5947. *E-mail:* office@iusi.org. *World Wide Web:* http://www.iusi.org/

NORTHERN ARIZONA UNIVERSITY
STUDY ABROAD IN MEXICO

Held at Universidad Marista

Academic Focus • Mexican studies, Spanish language and literature.

Program Information • Classes are held on the campus of Universidad Marista. Faculty members are local instructors hired by the sponsor. Scheduled travel to Mexico City, Michoacán; field trips to Lake Patzcuaro, Bernal, San Miguel de Allende.

Sessions • Fall, spring.

Eligibility Requirements • Minimum age 18; open to sophomores, juniors, seniors; 2.5 GPA; 2 letters of recommendation; good academic standing at home school; 0.5 years of college course work in Spanish.

Living Arrangements • Students live in host family homes. Meals are taken with host family, in residences.

Costs (2003-2004) • One term: $6300 for Arizona residents; $7600 for nonresidents; includes tuition, housing, all meals, excursions, international student ID, student support services, airport pick-up in Mexico City. $100 application fee. $250 nonrefundable deposit required. Financial aid available for all students: scholarships, loans.

For More Information • Ms. Marilyn Allen, Study Abroad Advisor, Northern Arizona University, International Office, PO Box 5598, Flagstaff, AZ 86011-5598; *Phone:* 928-523-2409; *Fax:* 928-523-9489. *E-mail:* international.office@nau.edu. *World Wide Web:* http://internationaloffice.nau.edu/

XALAPA
BRETHREN COLLEGES ABROAD
BCA PROGRAM IN XALAPA, MEXICO

Hosted by University of Veracruz

Academic Focus • Full curriculum.

Program Information • Students attend classes at University of Veracruz. Scheduled travel to Mexico City and surrounding area, Yucatán, Puebla, Cholula; field trips to El Tajín, Veracruz.

Sessions • Fall, spring, yearlong.

Eligibility Requirements • Minimum age 18; open to sophomores, juniors, seniors; 2.6 GPA; 3 letters of recommendation; good academic standing at home school; 1 year of college course work in Spanish.

Living Arrangements • Students live in host family homes. Meals are taken on one's own, with host family, in residences, in restaurants.

Costs (2003-2004) • One term: $11,500. Yearlong program: $19,900; includes tuition, housing, all meals, insurance, excursions, international student ID, student support services. $50 application fee. $100 nonrefundable deposit required.

For More Information • Mr. Thomas V. Millington, Senior Program Officer, Brethren Colleges Abroad, PO Box 407, 50 Alpha Drive, Elizabethtown, PA 17022-0407; *Phone:* 717-361-6606; *Fax:* 717-361-6619. *E-mail:* info@bcanet.org. *World Wide Web:* http://www.bcanet.org/

MIDDLEBURY COLLEGE SCHOOLS ABROAD
SCHOOL IN LATIN AMERICA–XALAPA PROGRAM

Hosted by University of Veracruz

Academic Focus • Full curriculum.

Program Information • Students attend classes at University of Veracruz. Field trips.

Sessions • Fall, spring, yearlong.

Eligibility Requirements • Open to sophomores, juniors, seniors; 2.7 GPA; 2 letters of recommendation; B average in both Spanish and major; 2.5 years of college course work in Spanish.

Living Arrangements • Students live in host family homes. Meals are taken on one's own, with host family, in residences.

Costs (2004-2005) • One term: $7200. Yearlong program: $14,400; includes tuition. $50 application fee. $300 nonrefundable deposit required. Financial aid available for students from sponsoring institution: scholarships, loans.

For More Information • Mr. Jamie Northrup, University Relations Coordinator, Middlebury College Schools Abroad, Office of Off-Campus Study, 129 Sunderland Language Center, Middlebury, VT 05753; *Phone:* 802-443-5745; *Fax:* 802-443-3157. *E-mail:* schoolsabroad@middlebury.edu. *World Wide Web:* http://www.middlebury.edu/msa/

MOLDOVA
CHISINAU
ACIE (ACTR/ACCELS)
ACIE–NIS REGIONAL LANGUAGE TRAINING PROGRAM–REPUBLIC OF MOLDOVA

Hosted by Moldova State University

Academic Focus • Cultural studies, language studies.

Program Information • Students attend classes at Moldova State University.

Sessions • Fall, spring, yearlong.

Eligibility Requirements • Minimum age 18; open to sophomores, juniors, seniors, graduate students, adults; 3 letters of recommendation; good academic standing at home school; 1 year of college course work in Russian or Moldovan.

Living Arrangements • Students live in host institution dormitories, locally rented apartments, host family homes. Quarters are shared with students from other programs. Meals are taken on one's own, with host family, in residences, in restaurants.

Costs (2002-2003) • One term: contact sponsor for cost. Yearlong program: contact sponsor for cost. $35 application fee. $500 nonrefundable deposit required. Financial aid available for all students: scholarships.
For More Information • Ms. Margaret Stephenson, Russian and Eurasian Program Officer, ACIE (ACTR/ACCELS), 1776 Massachusetts Avenue, NW, Suite 700, Washington, DC 20036; *Phone:* 202-833-7522; *Fax:* 202-833-7523. *E-mail:* outbound@actr.org. *World Wide Web:* http://www.actr.org/

MONACO
MONTE CARLO
UNIVERSITY OF MIAMI
INTERNATIONAL UNIVERSITY OF MONACO
Hosted by International University of Monaco
Academic Focus • Accounting, business administration/ management, economics, entrepreneurship, finance, international business, marketing, mathematics, Romance languages.
Program Information • Students attend classes at International University of Monaco.
Sessions • Fall, spring, yearlong.
Eligibility Requirements • Minimum age 18; open to sophomores, juniors, seniors; 3.0 GPA; 2 letters of recommendation; good academic standing at home school; college major or minor in business; no foreign language proficiency required.
Living Arrangements • Students live in locally rented apartments, host family homes. Quarters are shared with host institution students, students from other programs. Meals are taken on one's own, with host family, in residences, in restaurants.
Costs (2003-2004) • One term: $12,919. Yearlong program: $25,838; includes tuition, student support services. $40 application fee. $500 nonrefundable deposit required. Financial aid available for students from sponsoring institution: scholarships, loans.
For More Information • Ms. Elyse Resnick, Assistant Director, University of Miami, International Education and Exchange Programs, 5050 Brunson Drive, Allen Hall 212, PO Box 248005, Coral Gables, FL 33124-1610; *Phone:* 305-284-3434; *Fax:* 305-284-4235. *E-mail:* ieep@miami.edu. *World Wide Web:* http://www.studyabroad.miami.edu/

MONGOLIA
ULAANBAATAR
SCHOOL FOR INTERNATIONAL TRAINING, SIT STUDY ABROAD
MONGOLIA: CULTURE AND DEVELOPMENT
Academic Focus • Anthropology, Asian studies, Buddhist studies, economics, geography, history, liberal studies, Mongolian Language, political science and government, religious studies, visual and performing arts.
Program Information • Faculty members are drawn from the sponsor's U.S. staff and local instructors hired by the sponsor. Scheduled travel to Nomad settlements, the Gobi Desert; field trips to cultural historic sites.
Sessions • Fall, spring.
Eligibility Requirements • Open to sophomores, juniors, seniors; 2.5 GPA; 2 letters of recommendation; good academic standing at home school; no foreign language proficiency required.
Living Arrangements • Students live in locally rented apartments, host family homes. Meals are taken as a group, on one's own, with host family, in residences, in central dining facility, in restaurants.

Costs (2003-2004) • One term: $12,675; includes tuition, housing, all meals, insurance, excursions. $50 application fee. $400 nonrefundable deposit required. Financial aid available for all students: scholarships.
For More Information • School for International Training, SIT Study Abroad, Kipling Road, Brattleboro, VT 05302-0676; *Phone:* 888-272-7881; *Fax:* 802-258-3296. *E-mail:* studyabroad@sit.edu. *World Wide Web:* http://www.sit.edu/studyabroad/

MOROCCO
IFRANE
COLLEGE CONSORTIUM FOR INTERNATIONAL STUDIES–MONTANA STATE UNIVERSITY
SEMESTER IN MOROCCO PROGRAM
Hosted by Al Akhawayn University
Academic Focus • Full curriculum.
Program Information • Students attend classes at Al Akhawayn University. Optional travel to Volubilis, Fez, Meknes, Marrakesh, Errachida, Erfoud, Merzouga at an extra cost.
Sessions • Fall, spring, yearlong.
Eligibility Requirements • Open to sophomores, juniors, seniors, graduate students; 2.5 GPA; 2 letters of recommendation; no foreign language proficiency required.
Living Arrangements • Students live in host institution dormitories. Quarters are shared with host institution students. Meals are taken on one's own, in central dining facility, in restaurants.
Costs (2003-2004) • One term: $5400. Yearlong program: $10,800; includes tuition, housing, insurance, student support services, airport pick-up. $200 nonrefundable deposit required. Financial aid available for students from sponsoring institution: scholarships, loans.
For More Information • Study Abroad Advisor, College Consortium for International Studies–Montana State University, 400 Culbertson Hall, Montana State University, Bozeman, MT 59717; *Phone:* 406-994-7151; *Fax:* 406-994-1619. *E-mail:* morocco@montana.edu. *World Wide Web:* http://www.ccisabroad.org/

STATE UNIVERSITY OF NEW YORK AT BINGHAMTON
AL AKHAWAYN UNIVERSITY EXCHANGE PROGRAM
Hosted by Al Akhawayn University
Academic Focus • Full curriculum.
Program Information • Students attend classes at Al Akhawayn University. Field trips to Fez, Azrou.
Sessions • Fall, spring, yearlong.
Eligibility Requirements • Open to sophomores, juniors, seniors, graduate students; 3.0 GPA; 3 letters of recommendation; good academic standing at home school; no foreign language proficiency required.
Living Arrangements • Students live in host institution dormitories. Quarters are shared with host institution students. Meals are taken on one's own, in central dining facility.
Costs (2003-2004) • One term: $9000 for New York residents; $11,000 for nonresidents. Yearlong program: $15,000 for New York residents; $20,000 for nonresidents; includes tuition, housing, all meals, insurance, excursions, international airfare, books and class materials, international student ID, student support services. $250 nonrefundable deposit required. Financial aid available for students from sponsoring institution: scholarships, loans.
For More Information • Dr. Katharine C. Krebs, Director, State University of New York at Binghamton, Office of International Programs, NARC G-1, Binghamton, NY 13902-6000; *Phone:* 607-777-2336; *Fax:* 607-777-2889. *E-mail:* oip@binghamton.edu. *World Wide Web:* http://oip.binghamton.edu/

RABAT

LOCK HAVEN UNIVERSITY OF PENNSYLVANIA
SEMESTER IN MOROCCO

Hosted by Institute for Language and Communications Studies
Academic Focus • Communications, journalism, literature, social sciences.
Program Information • Students attend classes at Institute for Language and Communications Studies.
Sessions • Fall, spring, yearlong.
Eligibility Requirements • Minimum age 18; open to sophomores, juniors, seniors, adults; 2.5 GPA; 3 letters of recommendation; good academic standing at home school; no foreign language proficiency required.
Living Arrangements • Students live in locally rented apartments, host family homes. Meals are taken on one's own, with host family, in residences, in restaurants.
Costs (2002-2003) • One term: $2750 for Pennsylvania residents; $4650 for nonresidents. Yearlong program: $5500 for Pennsylvania residents; $9320 for nonresidents; includes tuition, fees. $50 application fee. Financial aid available for students from sponsoring institution: scholarships, loans.
For More Information • Dean, Institute for International Studies, Lock Haven University of Pennsylvania, Lock Haven, PA 17745-2390; *Phone:* 570-893-2140; *Fax:* 570-893-2537. *E-mail:* intlstudies_webmonitor@lhup.edu. *World Wide Web:* http://www.lhup.edu/international/goingp/goingplaces_index.htm

SCHOOL FOR INTERNATIONAL TRAINING, SIT STUDY ABROAD
MOROCCO CULTURE AND SOCIETY

Academic Focus • Anthropology, Arabic, economics, geography, history, political science and government, visual and performing arts.
Program Information • Faculty members are drawn from the sponsor's U.S. staff and local instructors hired by the sponsor. Scheduled travel to Zagora, Marrakesh, the High Atlas; field trips to historic tours and sites, mosques.
Sessions • Fall, spring.
Eligibility Requirements • Open to sophomores, juniors, seniors; 2.5 GPA; 2 letters of recommendation; good academic standing at home school; background in French is useful.
Living Arrangements • Students live in host family homes, hotels. Meals are taken as a group, on one's own, with host family, in residences, in restaurants.
Costs (2003-2004) • One term: $12,000; includes tuition, housing, all meals, insurance, excursions. $50 application fee. $400 nonrefundable deposit required. Financial aid available for all students: scholarships.
For More Information • School for International Training, SIT Study Abroad, Kipling Road, Brattleboro, VT 05302-0676; *Phone:* 888-272-7881; *Fax:* 802-258-3296. *E-mail:* studyabroad@sit.edu. *World Wide Web:* http://www.sit.edu/studyabroad/

NAMIBIA

OTJIWARONGO
ROUND RIVER CONSERVATION STUDIES
NAMIBIA: NAMIBIA WILDLIFE CONSERVATION PROJECT

Academic Focus • Biological/life sciences, conservation studies, ecology, wildlife studies.
Program Information • Faculty members are drawn from the sponsor's U.S. staff and local instructors hired by the sponsor. Scheduled travel to Skeleton Coast, national parks; field trips to local communities.
Sessions • Fall, spring.

Eligibility Requirements • Minimum age 18; open to freshmen, sophomores, juniors, seniors; 3.0 GPA; 2 letters of recommendation; good academic standing at home school; no foreign language proficiency required.
Living Arrangements • Students live in program-owned houses, remote field camps, a renovated farmhouse. Meals are taken as a group, in central dining facility.
Costs (2003) • One term: $11,500; includes tuition, housing, all meals, excursions, lab equipment, student support services. $50 application fee. $1000 nonrefundable deposit required. Financial aid available for all students: scholarships.
For More Information • Mr. Doug Milek, Student Programs Director, Round River Conservation Studies, 404 North 300 West, #102, Salt Lake City, UT 84103; *Phone:* 801-694-3321. *E-mail:* dougmilek@roundriver.org. *World Wide Web:* http://www.roundriver.org/

WINDHOEK

AUGSBURG COLLEGE
NATION BUILDING, GLOBALIZATION, AND DECOLONIZING THE MIND: SOUTHERN AFRICAN PERSPECTIVES

Hosted by Center for Global Education
Academic Focus • African studies, history, peace and conflict studies, political science and government, religious studies.
Program Information • Students attend classes at Center for Global Education. Scheduled travel to northern and southern Namibia, South Africa; field trips to Walvis Bay, Etosha Game Park; optional travel to the Sossusvlei Sand Dunes, Swapokmund at an extra cost.
Sessions • Fall, spring.
Eligibility Requirements • Open to sophomores, juniors, seniors, adults; 2.5 GPA; 2 letters of recommendation; good academic standing at home school; no foreign language proficiency required.
Living Arrangements • Students live in program-owned houses, host family homes. Quarters are shared with host institution students. Meals are taken as a group, with host family, in residences, in central dining facility, in restaurants.
Costs (2004-2005) • One term: sliding fee scale for consortium partners; $13,400 for transfers; includes tuition, housing, all meals, insurance, excursions, some books and class materials. $50 application fee. $500 nonrefundable deposit required. Financial aid available for students from sponsoring institution: scholarships, loans.
For More Information • Ms. Margaret Anderson, Coordinator, Semester Programs Abroad, Augsburg College, 2211 Riverside Avenue, Minneapolis, MN 55454; *Phone:* 800-299-8889; *Fax:* 612-330-1695. *E-mail:* globaled@augsburg.edu. *World Wide Web:* http://www.augsburg.edu/global/

RUTGERS, THE STATE UNIVERSITY OF NEW JERSEY
STUDY ABROAD IN NAMIBIA

Hosted by University of Namibia
Academic Focus • Full curriculum.
Program Information • Students attend classes at University of Namibia.
Sessions • Spring.
Eligibility Requirements • Open to sophomores, juniors, seniors; 2.5 GPA; 2 letters of recommendation; good academic standing at home school; no foreign language proficiency required.
Living Arrangements • Students live in host institution dormitories. Quarters are shared with students from other programs. Meals are taken on one's own, in residences, in central dining facility.
Costs (2004) • One term: $6790 for New Jersey residents; $9440 for nonresidents; includes tuition, housing, insurance, excursions, student support services. $20 application fee. $750 nonrefundable deposit required. Financial aid available for students from sponsoring institution: scholarships, loans.
For More Information • Ms. Karin Bonello, Regional Coordinator, Rutgers, The State University of New Jersey, 102 College Avenue, New Brunswick, NJ 08901-8543; *Phone:* 732-932-7787; *Fax:* 732-932-8659. *E-mail:* ru_abroad@email.rutgers.edu. *World Wide Web:* http://studyabroad.rutgers.edu/

SANN RESEARCH INSTITUTE
SEMESTER IN NAMIBIA/AFRICA

Hosted by University of Namibia

Academic Focus • Full curriculum.

Program Information • Students attend classes at University of Namibia. Scheduled travel to a wildlife safari (16 days), Himba (Bushmen) community (5 days); field trips to study-related sites.

Sessions • Spring.

Eligibility Requirements • Minimum age 18; open to freshmen, sophomores, juniors, seniors, adults; 2.5 GPA; good health; no foreign language proficiency required.

Living Arrangements • Students live in host institution dormitories. Meals are taken as a group, in central dining facility.

Costs (2004) • One term: $7780; includes tuition, housing, all meals, international airfare. $475 application fee. $500 deposit required.

For More Information • Narayan Shrestha, President, Sann Research Institute, 948 Pearl Street, Boulder, CO 80302; *Phone:* 303-449-4279; *Fax:* 303-440-7328. *E-mail:* info@sannr.com. *World Wide Web:* http://www.sannr.com/

NEPAL
KATHMANDU
CORNELL UNIVERSITY
CORNELL NEPAL STUDY PROGRAM

Held at Cornell Nepal Study Program

Academic Focus • Anthropology, botany, ecology, environmental science/studies, geology, Nepali, Nepali studies, religious studies, social sciences, sociology.

Program Information • Classes are held on the campus of Cornell Nepal Study Program. Faculty members are local instructors hired by the sponsor. Scheduled travel to Nepal, Mustang; field trips to the Himalayan foothills, the Kathmandu Valley, Terai.

Sessions • Fall, spring, yearlong.

Eligibility Requirements • Minimum age 18; open to sophomores, juniors, seniors, graduate students; 3.0 GPA; 2 letters of recommendation; good academic standing at home school; previous Nepali study recommended.

Living Arrangements • Students live in program-owned houses. Quarters are shared with host institution students. Meals are taken as a group, in central dining facility.

Costs (2004-2005) • One term: $17,650. Yearlong program: $35,300; includes tuition, housing, all meals, excursions, student support services, research support. $300 nonrefundable deposit required. Financial aid available for students from sponsoring institution: scholarships, loans.

For More Information • Cornell Abroad, Cornell University, 300 Caldwell Hall, Ithaca, NY 14853-7601; *Phone:* 607-255-6224; *Fax:* 607-255-8700. *E-mail:* cuabroad@cornell.edu. *World Wide Web:* http://www.cuabroad.cornell.edu/

PITZER COLLEGE
PITZER COLLEGE IN NEPAL

Hosted by Tribhuvan University Kathmandu

Academic Focus • Anthropology, art, environmental science/studies, history, Nepali, Nepali studies, political science and government, religious studies, sociology, women's studies.

Program Information • Students attend classes at Tribhuvan University Kathmandu. Scheduled travel to Pokhara, Ghandrung, Chitwan National Park, Terai Region, Simigaun village, Siklis Village; field trips to historic and cultural sites in Kathmandu Valley; optional travel to the Lumbini-Terai region, Solo Khumbu, Eastern Hills, Annapurna Conservation Area at an extra cost.

Sessions • Fall, spring, yearlong.

Eligibility Requirements • Open to sophomores, juniors, seniors; 2.5 GPA; 2 letters of recommendation; good academic standing at home school; independent reading course required of non-Claremont students; no foreign language proficiency required.

Living Arrangements • Students live in host family homes. Meals are taken as a group, with host family, in residences.

Costs (2003-2004) • One term: $18,795. Yearlong program: $37,590; includes tuition, housing, all meals, excursions, international airfare, books and class materials, international student ID, student support services, evacuation insurance. $25 application fee. $500 nonrefundable deposit required. Financial aid available for students from sponsoring institution: scholarships, loans.

For More Information • Ms. Neva Barker, Director of External Studies Admissions, Pitzer College, 1050 North Mills Avenue, Claremont, CA 91711; *Phone:* 909-621-8104; *Fax:* 909-621-0518. *E-mail:* external_studies@pitzer.edu. *World Wide Web:* http://www.pitzer.edu/external_studies/

SANN RESEARCH INSTITUTE
SEMESTER IN NEPAL

Held at Sann Research Institute

Academic Focus • Anthropology, language studies, Nepali, Nepali studies, political science and government, religious studies.

Program Information • Classes are held on the campus of Sann Research Institute. Faculty members are drawn from the sponsor's U.S. staff and local instructors hired by the sponsor. Scheduled travel to villages; field trips to temples, factories in Nepal, museums, historic sites; optional travel to Thailand at an extra cost.

Sessions • Fall, spring.

Eligibility Requirements • Minimum age 17; open to freshmen, sophomores, juniors, seniors, graduate students, adults; 2.5 GPA; good health; no foreign language proficiency required.

Living Arrangements • Students live in host family homes. Quarters are shared with host institution students. Meals are taken with host family, in residences.

Costs (2003-2004) • One term: $7780; includes tuition, housing, all meals, excursions, international airfare, in-transit stay, visa fees, permits. $475 application fee. $500 refundable deposit required.

For More Information • Narayan Shrestha, President, Sann Research Institute, 948 Pearl Street, Boulder, CO 80302; *Phone:* 303-449-4279; *Fax:* 303-440-7328. *E-mail:* info@sannr.com. *World Wide Web:* http://www.sannr.com/

SCHOOL FOR INTERNATIONAL TRAINING, SIT STUDY ABROAD
NEPAL: CULTURE AND DEVELOPMENT

Academic Focus • Anthropology, Buddhist studies, civilization studies, economics, geography, history, liberal studies, Nepali, Nepali studies, political science and government, religious studies, visual and performing arts.

Program Information • Faculty members are drawn from the sponsor's U.S. staff and local instructors hired by the sponsor. Scheduled travel to Middle Hills, Terai, rural Nepal; field trips to festivals, historic sites, temples, monasteries, development sites.

Sessions • Fall, spring.

Eligibility Requirements • Open to sophomores, juniors, seniors; 2.5 GPA; 2 letters of recommendation; good academic standing at home school; no foreign language proficiency required.

Living Arrangements • Students live in host family homes, hotels. Meals are taken as a group, on one's own, with host family, in residences, in central dining facility, in restaurants.

Costs (2003-2004) • One term: $11,350; includes tuition, housing, all meals, insurance, excursions. $50 application fee. $400 nonrefundable deposit required. Financial aid available for all students: scholarships.

For More Information • School for International Training, SIT Study Abroad, Kipling Road, Brattleboro, VT 05302-0676; *Phone:* 888-272-7881; *Fax:* 802-258-3296. *E-mail:* studyabroad@sit.edu. *World Wide Web:* http://www.sit.edu/studyabroad/

UNIVERSITY OF IDAHO
SEMESTER IN NEPAL PROGRAM WITH SERVICE LEARNING

Hosted by Sann Research Institute

Academic Focus • Ecology, Nepali, Nepali studies, photography, political science and government, religious studies.

Program Information • Students attend classes at Sann Research Institute. Scheduled travel to the Himalayas (21-day trek), a village stay; field trips to a wildlife safari, Chitwan National Park.

Sessions • Fall, spring.
Eligibility Requirements • Open to freshmen, sophomores, juniors, seniors, graduate students; good academic standing at home school; no foreign language proficiency required.
Living Arrangements • Students live in host family homes. Quarters are shared with host institution students. Meals are taken with host family, in residences.
Costs (2003-2004) • One term: $5400; includes tuition, housing, all meals, excursions, student support services. $100 application fee. $200 refundable deposit required. Financial aid available for students from sponsoring institution: scholarships, loans.
For More Information • Ms. Amy Bergmann, Advisor, University of Idaho, Room 209, Morrill Hall, Moscow, ID 83844-3013; *Phone:* 208-885-7870; *Fax:* 208-885-2859. *E-mail:* abroad@uidaho.edu. *World Wide Web:* http://www.ets.uidaho.edu/ipo/abroad/

UNIVERSITY OF WISCONSIN–MADISON
COLLEGE YEAR IN NEPAL

Hosted by University of Wisconsin–Madison Program House
Academic Focus • Fine/studio arts, liberal studies, Nepali, performing arts, social sciences, Tibetan.
Program Information • Students attend classes at University of Wisconsin–Madison Program House. Scheduled travel to a Tibetan refugee community; field trips to cultural sites.
Sessions • Yearlong, pre-departure language program also available.
Eligibility Requirements • Open to juniors, seniors; 2.5 GPA; no foreign language proficiency required.
Living Arrangements • Students live in host family homes. Meals are taken as a group, on one's own, in residences, in central dining facility.
Costs (2002-2003) • Yearlong program: $24,800; includes tuition, housing, all meals, insurance, excursions, international airfare, books and class materials, student support services, personal spending, pre-departure expenses, summer school tuition. $100 nonrefundable deposit required. Financial aid available for all students: scholarships, loans.
For More Information • Peer Advisor, University of Wisconsin–Madison, Office of International Studies and Programs, 261 Bascom Hall, 500 Lincoln Drive, Madison, WI 53706; *Phone:* 608-265-6329; *Fax:* 608-262-6998. *E-mail:* peeradvisor@bascom.wisc.edu. *World Wide Web:* http://www.studyabroad.wisc.edu/

POKHARA
MICHIGAN STATE UNIVERSITY
MULTIDISCIPLINARY STUDIES IN NEPAL

Academic Focus • Interdisciplinary studies, natural resources, Nepali studies, social sciences.
Program Information • Faculty members are drawn from the sponsor's U.S. staff and local instructors hired by the sponsor. Scheduled travel to the foothills of the Himalayas, a rainforest; field trips to outlying villages, forests.
Sessions • Spring.
Eligibility Requirements • Minimum age 18; open to freshmen, sophomores, juniors, seniors; 2.5 GPA; good academic standing at home school; approval of faculty director; no foreign language proficiency required.
Living Arrangements • Students live in host family homes. Meals are taken with host family, in residences.
Costs (2002) • One term: $1700 (estimated); includes housing, some meals, insurance, excursions, student support services. $100 application fee. $200 nonrefundable deposit required. Financial aid available for students from sponsoring institution: scholarships, loans.
For More Information • Ms. Sherry Martinez-Bonilla, Office Assistant, Michigan State University, Office of Study Abroad, 109 International Center, East Lansing, MI 48824-1035; *Phone:* 517-353-8920; *Fax:* 517-432-2082. *E-mail:* marti269@msu.edu. *World Wide Web:* http://studyabroad.msu.edu/

NETHERLANDS
AMSTERDAM
CIEE
CIEE STUDY CENTER AT THE UNIVERSITY OF AMSTERDAM, THE NETHERLANDS

Hosted by University of Amsterdam
Academic Focus • Anthropology, art history, communications, Dutch, economics, English literature, European studies, geography, history, international affairs, law and legal studies, liberal studies, literature, political science and government, sociology.
Program Information • Students attend classes at University of Amsterdam. Field trips to Brussels, sites of cultural interest in and around Amsterdam.
Sessions • Fall, spring, yearlong.
Eligibility Requirements • Open to juniors, seniors, graduate students, adults; 3.0 GPA; 2 letters of recommendation; no foreign language proficiency required.
Living Arrangements • Students live in host institution dormitories. Quarters are shared with host institution students. Meals are taken on one's own, in residences, in central dining facility, in restaurants.
Costs (2003-2004) • One term: $8850. Yearlong program: $17,500; includes tuition, housing, insurance, excursions, student support services, cultural activities, pre-departure advising, museum year card, host institution ID card, optional on-site pick-up. $30 application fee. $300 deposit required. Financial aid available for all students: minority student scholarships, travel grants.
For More Information • Ms. Hannah McChesney, Admissions Officer, Europe, Middle East, and Africa, CIEE, 7 Custom House Street, 3rd Floor, Portland, ME 04101; *Phone:* 800-40-STUDY; *Fax:* 207-553-7699. *E-mail:* studyinfo@ciee.org. *World Wide Web:* http://www.ciee.org/isp/

IES, INSTITUTE FOR THE INTERNATIONAL EDUCATION OF STUDENTS
IES–AMSTERDAM

Hosted by Amsterdam School of Music, Gerrit Rietveld Academy School of Art and Design, University of Amsterdam
Academic Focus • Dutch, fine/studio arts, full curriculum, music, social sciences.
Program Information • Students attend classes at Gerrit Rietveld Academy School of Art and Design, University of Amsterdam, Amsterdam School of Music. Scheduled travel to Groningen, Utrecht, Maastricht, The Hague, Haarlem, Antwerp, Brugges, Aachen, Cologne; field trips.
Sessions • Fall, spring, yearlong.
Eligibility Requirements • Minimum age 18; open to sophomores, juniors, seniors, graduate students, adults; 3.0 GPA; 1 letter of recommendation; good academic standing at home school; no foreign language proficiency required.
Living Arrangements • Students live in host institution dormitories, locally rented apartments. Meals are taken on one's own, in residences, in central dining facility, in restaurants.
Costs (2003-2004) • One term: $8800. Yearlong program: $15,840; includes tuition, housing, excursions, student support services, partial insurance coverage. $50 application fee. $500 nonrefundable deposit required. Financial aid available for all students: scholarships, institutional partner need-based grants.
For More Information • International Education Representative, IES, Institute for the International Education of Students, 33 North La Salle Street 15th Floor, Chicago, IL 60602; *Phone:* 800-995-2300; *Fax:* 312-944-1448. *E-mail:* info@iesabroad.org. *World Wide Web:* http://www.IESabroad.org/

MARIST COLLEGE
AMSTERDAM INTERNSHIP PROGRAM

Hosted by Amsterdam School of Business
Academic Focus • Full curriculum.
Program Information • Students attend classes at Amsterdam School of Business.
Sessions • Fall, spring, yearlong.

NETHERLANDS
Amsterdam

Eligibility Requirements • Open to sophomores, juniors, seniors; 2.8 GPA; 2 letters of recommendation; good academic standing at home school; no foreign language proficiency required.

Living Arrangements • Students live in host institution dormitories. Quarters are shared with host institution students. Meals are taken on one's own, in residences, in restaurants.

Costs (2003-2004) • One term: $12,500. Yearlong program: $25,000; includes tuition, housing, insurance, student support services. $35 application fee. $300 nonrefundable deposit required. Financial aid available for students from sponsoring institution: scholarships, loans.

For More Information • Mr. Jerald Z. Thornton, Coordinator, Marist College, 3399 North Road, Poughkeepsie, NY 12601; *Phone:* 845-575-3330; *Fax:* 845-575-3294. *E-mail:* jerre.thornton@marist. edu. *World Wide Web:* http://www.marist.edu/international/

SCHOOL FOR INTERNATIONAL TRAINING, SIT STUDY ABROAD
THE NETHERLANDS: SEXUALITY, GENDER, AND IDENTITY

Academic Focus • Anthropology, bisexual studies, Dutch, geography, history, lesbian studies, liberal studies, sociology, visual and performing arts, women's studies.

Program Information • Faculty members are drawn from the sponsor's U.S. staff and local instructors hired by the sponsor. Scheduled travel to Berlin, London; field trips to Utrecht, The Hague, Northern Ireland.

Sessions • Fall, spring.

Eligibility Requirements • Open to sophomores, juniors, seniors; course work in gender studies or related social science; 2.5 GPA; 2 letters of recommendation; good academic standing at home school; no foreign language proficiency required.

Living Arrangements • Students live in host family homes, hotels. Meals are taken as a group, on one's own, with host family, in residences, in restaurants.

Costs (2003-2004) • One term: $13,400; includes tuition, housing, all meals, insurance, excursions, international student ID. $50 application fee. $400 nonrefundable deposit required. Financial aid available for all students: scholarships.

For More Information • School for International Training, SIT Study Abroad, Kipling Road, Brattleboro, VT 05302-0676; *Phone:* 888-272-7881; *Fax:* 802-258-3296. *E-mail:* studyabroad@sit.edu. *World Wide Web:* http://www.sit.edu/studyabroad/

STATE UNIVERSITY OF NEW YORK COLLEGE AT BUFFALO
AMSTERDAM EXCHANGE

Hosted by Amsterdam School of Business

Academic Focus • Business administration/management, Dutch, economics, French language and literature, German language and literature, Spanish language and literature.

Program Information • Students attend classes at Amsterdam School of Business.

Sessions • Fall, spring, yearlong.

Eligibility Requirements • Open to juniors, seniors; course work in business administration/management, economics; 3.0 GPA; 2 letters of recommendation; no foreign language proficiency required.

Living Arrangements • Students live in locally rented apartments. Quarters are shared with host institution students, students from other programs. Meals are taken on one's own, in residences.

Costs (2003-2004) • One term: $7011 for New York residents; $11,461 for nonresidents. Yearlong program: $13,237 for New York residents; $22,137 for nonresidents; includes tuition, housing, all meals, insurance, international airfare, books and class materials, administrative, passport, and college fees. $10 application fee. $200 nonrefundable deposit required. Financial aid available for students from sponsoring institution: scholarships, loans.

For More Information • Dr. Lee Ann Grace, Director, International Education, State University of New York College at Buffalo, 1300 Elmwood Avenue, Buffalo, NY 14222-1095; *Phone:* 716-878-4620; *Fax:* 716-878-3054. *E-mail:* intleduc@buffalostate.edu. *World Wide Web:* http://www.buffalostate.edu/intnated/

UNIVERSITY OF MIAMI
AMSTERDAM SCHOOL OF BUSINESS

Hosted by Amsterdam School of Business

Academic Focus • Dutch, finance, international business, marketing.

Program Information • Students attend classes at Amsterdam School of Business.

Sessions • Fall, spring, yearlong.

Eligibility Requirements • Minimum age 18; open to sophomores, juniors, seniors; 2 letters of recommendation; good academic standing at home school; no foreign language proficiency required.

Living Arrangements • Students live in host institution dormitories. Quarters are shared with host institution students, students from other programs. Meals are taken on one's own, in residences.

Costs (2003-2004) • One term: $12,919. Yearlong program: $25,838; includes tuition, student support services. $40 application fee. $500 nonrefundable deposit required. Financial aid available for students from sponsoring institution: scholarships, loans.

For More Information • Ms. Elyse Resnick, Assistant Director, University of Miami, International Education and Exchange Programs, 5050 Brunson Drive, Allen Hall 212, PO Box 248005, Coral Gables, FL 33124-1610; *Phone:* 305-284-3434; *Fax:* 305-284-4235. *E-mail:* ieep@miami.edu. *World Wide Web:* http://www.studyabroad. miami.edu/

UNIVERSITY OF MIAMI
CONSERVATORY VON AMSTERDAM

Hosted by Conservatorium von Amsterdam

Academic Focus • Music performance.

Program Information • Students attend classes at Conservatorium von Amsterdam.

Sessions • Fall, spring, yearlong.

Eligibility Requirements • Minimum age 18; open to sophomores, juniors, seniors; major in music; 2 letters of recommendation; good academic standing at home school; audition tape/cd; no foreign language proficiency required.

Living Arrangements • Meals are taken on one's own, in central dining facility, in restaurants.

Costs (2003-2004) • One term: $12,919. Yearlong program: $25,838; includes tuition, student support services. $40 application fee. $500 nonrefundable deposit required. Financial aid available for students from sponsoring institution: scholarships, loans.

For More Information • Ms. Elyse Resnick, Assistant Director, University of Miami, International Education and Exchange Programs, 5050 Brunson Drive, Allen Hall 212, PO Box 248005, Coral Gables, FL 33124-1610; *Phone:* 305-284-3434; *Fax:* 305-284-4235. *E-mail:* ieep@miami.edu. *World Wide Web:* http://www.studyabroad. miami.edu/

LEIDEN
CENTRAL COLLEGE ABROAD
CENTRAL COLLEGE ABROAD IN LEIDEN, THE NETHERLANDS

Hosted by Leiden University, Central College in Leiden, Webster University–Leiden

Academic Focus • Art history, ceramics and pottery, computer science, drawing/painting, Dutch, economics, education, fine/studio arts, history, international affairs, international business, photography, political science and government, psychology, women's studies.

Program Information • Students attend classes at Leiden University, Central College in Leiden, Webster University–Leiden. Scheduled travel to the Frisian Islands, Brussels/Brugge; field trips to Amsterdam, The Hague, Rotterdam, Apeldoorn (Het Loo), Park Hoge Velvwe.

Sessions • Fall, spring, yearlong.

Eligibility Requirements • Minimum age 18; open to sophomores, juniors, seniors, adults; 2.5 GPA; 2 letters of recommendation; good academic standing at home school; study abroad approval form; transcript; Student Life endorsement; no foreign language proficiency required.

Living Arrangements • Students live in host institution dormitories, host family homes. Quarters are shared with host institution students. Meals are taken on one's own, with host family, in residences, in restaurants.
Costs (2003-2004) • One term: $10,387. Yearlong program: $20,774; includes tuition, housing, excursions, international student ID, student support services. $25 application fee. $350 nonrefundable deposit required. Financial aid available for all students: scholarships.
For More Information • Office of International Education, Central College Abroad, 812 University Street, Pella, IA 50219; *Phone:* 800-831-3629; *Fax:* 641-628-5375. *E-mail:* studyabroad@central.edu. *World Wide Web:* http://www.central.edu/abroad/

RUTGERS, THE STATE UNIVERSITY OF NEW JERSEY
STUDY ABROAD IN THE NETHERLANDS

Hosted by Leiden University
Academic Focus • Full curriculum.
Program Information • Students attend classes at Leiden University. Field trips to Amsterdam, The Hague.
Sessions • Fall, spring, yearlong.
Eligibility Requirements • Open to sophomores, juniors, seniors; 3.2 GPA; 2 letters of recommendation; good academic standing at home school; no foreign language proficiency required.
Living Arrangements • Students live in host institution dormitories. Quarters are shared with students from other programs. Meals are taken on one's own, in residences, in central dining facility.
Costs (2003-2004) • One term: $8636 for New Jersey residents; $11,286 for nonresidents. Yearlong program: $16,500 for New Jersey residents; $21,800 for nonresidents; includes tuition, insurance, student support services. $20 application fee. $750 nonrefundable deposit required. Financial aid available for students from sponsoring institution: scholarships, loans.
For More Information • Ms. Karin Bonello, Regional Coordinator, Rutgers, The State University of New Jersey, 102 College Avenue, New Brunswick, NJ 08901-8543; *Phone:* 732-932-7787; *Fax:* 732-932-8659. *E-mail:* ru_abroad@email.rutgers.edu. *World Wide Web:* http://studyabroad.rutgers.edu/

STATE UNIVERSITY OF NEW YORK COLLEGE AT BROCKPORT
LEIDEN UNIVERSITY PROGRAM

Hosted by Leiden University
Academic Focus • Anthropology, archaeology, art history, Asian studies, biological/life sciences, Dutch, education, English, English literature, European studies, history, language studies, law and legal studies, liberal studies, literature, mathematics, medicine, philosophy, political science and government, premedical studies, psychology, public administration, religious studies, sociology, women's studies.
Program Information • Students attend classes at Leiden University. Field trips to sites throughout the Netherlands.
Sessions • Fall, spring, yearlong, 2 spring trimesters.
Eligibility Requirements • Minimum age 18; open to juniors, seniors; course work in area of internship, if applicable; 3.0 GPA; 2 letters of recommendation; good academic standing at home school; ability to do upper-division course work in chosen subject; résumé for internship option; basic knowledge of Dutch recommended.
Living Arrangements • Students live in host institution dormitories. Quarters are shared with host institution students. Meals are taken on one's own, in residences.
Costs (2004-2005) • One term: $10,150 contact sponsor for two-term spring cost. Yearlong program: $16,750; includes tuition, housing, international student ID, student support services. $350 nonrefundable deposit required. Financial aid available for all students: loans, regular financial aid, grants.
For More Information • Dr. John J. Perry, Director, Office of International Education, State University of New York College at Brockport, 350 New Campus Drive, Brockport, NY 14420; *Phone:* 800-298-SUNY; *Fax:* 585-637-3218. *E-mail:* overseas@brockport.edu. *World Wide Web:* http://www.brockport.edu/studyabroad/

WEBSTER UNIVERSITY
WEBSTER UNIVERSITY IN LEIDEN

Hosted by Webster University–Leiden
Academic Focus • Art history, business administration/management, English literature, finance, history, international business, labor and industrial relations, political science and government.
Program Information • Students attend classes at Webster University–Leiden. Optional travel to Amsterdam, bike trips at an extra cost.
Sessions • Fall, spring, yearlong.
Eligibility Requirements • Minimum age 17; open to freshmen, sophomores, juniors, seniors, graduate students, adults; 2.5 GPA; 1 letter of recommendation; good academic standing at home school; no foreign language proficiency required.
Living Arrangements • Students live in host institution dormitories. Quarters are shared with host institution students. Meals are taken as a group, on one's own, in residences, in restaurants.
Costs (2003-2004) • One term: $8240. Yearlong program: $15,980; includes tuition, insurance, international student ID, student support services. $30 application fee. $165 refundable deposit required. Financial aid available for students from sponsoring institution: scholarships, loans.
For More Information • Mr. Mark A. Beirn, Coordinator, Office of Study Abroad, Webster University, 470 East Lockwood Avenue, St. Louis, MO 63119; *Phone:* 314-968-6988; *Fax:* 314-968-5938. *E-mail:* worldview@webster.edu. *World Wide Web:* http://www.webster.edu/intl/sa/

MAASTRICHT
UNIVERSITY OF CONNECTICUT
BUSINESS, ECONOMICS, AND EUROPEAN STUDIES SEMESTER AT MAASTRICHT UNIVERSITY

Hosted by Maastricht University
Academic Focus • Business administration/management, Dutch, economics, history, law and legal studies, political science and government.
Program Information • Students attend classes at Maastricht University. Field trips to The Hague.
Sessions • Fall.
Eligibility Requirements • Open to juniors, seniors; course work in business, economics, or political science; 2.7 GPA; 2 letters of recommendation; no foreign language proficiency required.
Living Arrangements • Students live in host institution dormitories, locally rented apartments. Quarters are shared with students from other programs. Meals are taken on one's own, in residences, in restaurants.
Costs (2002) • One term: $4900; includes tuition, housing, excursions, international student ID. $25 application fee. $350 nonrefundable deposit required. Financial aid available for students from sponsoring institution: scholarships, loans.
For More Information • Mr. Gordon Lustila, Acting Director of Study Abroad Programs, University of Connecticut, 843 Bolton Road, Unit 1207, Storrs, CT 06269-1207; *Phone:* 860-486-5022; *Fax:* 860-486-2976. *E-mail:* sabadm03@uconnvm.uconn.edu. *World Wide Web:* http://studyabroad.uconn.edu/

NIJMEGEN
UNIVERSITY AT ALBANY, STATE UNIVERSITY OF NEW YORK
DIRECT ENROLLMENT AT ARNHEM–NIJMEGEN UNIVERSITY

Hosted by Hogeschool Gelderland
Academic Focus • Dutch, education, language studies, teaching English as a second language.
Program Information • Students attend classes at Hogeschool Gelderland.
Sessions • Fall, spring, yearlong.
Eligibility Requirements • Open to sophomores, juniors, seniors, adults; 2.8 GPA; 2 letters of recommendation; good academic standing at home school; no foreign language proficiency required.
Living Arrangements • Students live in host institution dormitories, locally rented apartments. Quarters are shared with host

institution students. Meals are taken on one's own, in residences, in central dining facility, in restaurants.

Costs (2002-2003) • One term: $5313 for fall term; $5813 for spring. Yearlong program: $11,125; includes housing, all meals, student support services, in-state tuition and fees. $150 nonrefundable deposit required. Financial aid available for students from sponsoring institution: all customary sources.

For More Information • University at Albany, State University of New York, Office of International Education, LI 66, Albany, NY 12222; *Phone:* 518-442-3525; *Fax:* 518-442-3338. *E-mail:* intled@uamail.albany.edu. *World Wide Web:* http://www.albany.edu/intled/

THE HAGUE
UNIVERSITY OF IDAHO
DUTCH BUSINESS PROGRAM

Hosted by Haagse Hogeschool
Academic Focus • Accounting, advertising and public relations, business administration/management, communications, finance, international business, marketing.
Program Information • Students attend classes at Haagse Hogeschool.
Sessions • Fall, spring, yearlong.
Eligibility Requirements • Open to sophomores, juniors, seniors, graduate students; good academic standing at home school; no foreign language proficiency required.
Living Arrangements • Students live in host institution dormitories, locally rented apartments. Quarters are shared with host institution students, students from other programs. Meals are taken on one's own, in residences.
Costs (2003-2004) • One term: $2500. Yearlong program: $5000; includes tuition, student support services. $100 application fee. $200 refundable deposit required. Financial aid available for students from sponsoring institution: scholarships, loans.

For More Information • Ms. Amy Bergmann, Advisor, University of Idaho, Room 209, Morrill Hall, Moscow, ID 83844-3013; *Phone:* 208-885-7870; *Fax:* 208-885-2859. *E-mail:* abroad@uidaho.edu. *World Wide Web:* http://www.ets.uidaho.edu/ipo/abroad/

UNIVERSITY STUDIES ABROAD CONSORTIUM
FULL CURRICULUM STUDIES: THE HAGUE, NETHERLANDS

Hosted by The Hague School of European Studies (HEBO)
Academic Focus • Full curriculum.
Program Information • Students attend classes at The Hague School of European Studies (HEBO).
Sessions • Fall, spring, yearlong.
Eligibility Requirements • Minimum age 18; open to freshmen, sophomores, juniors, seniors; 2.7 GPA; no foreign language proficiency required.
Living Arrangements • Students live in host institution dormitories, locally rented apartments. Quarters are shared with host institution students. Meals are taken on one's own, in restaurants.
Costs (2005-2006) • One term: $2980. Yearlong program: $5680; includes tuition, insurance. $50 application fee. $150 refundable deposit required. Financial aid available for all students: scholarships, loans.

For More Information • University Studies Abroad Consortium, USAC/323, Reno, NV 89557-0093; *Phone:* 775-784-6569; *Fax:* 775-784-6010. *E-mail:* usac@unr.edu. *World Wide Web:* http://usac.unr.edu/

TILBURG

UNIVERSITY AT ALBANY, STATE UNIVERSITY OF NEW YORK
LANGUAGE AND CULTURAL STUDIES IN ENGLISH AT TILBURG UNIVERSITY

Hosted by Tilburg University

Academic Focus • Business administration/management, Dutch, economics, international affairs, language studies, psychology, social sciences.

Program Information • Students attend classes at Tilburg University.

Sessions • Fall, spring, yearlong.

Eligibility Requirements • Minimum age 18; open to sophomores, juniors, seniors; 3.0 GPA; 2 letters of recommendation; good academic standing at home school; no foreign language proficiency required.

Living Arrangements • Students live in host institution dormitories, locally rented apartments. Quarters are shared with host institution students, students from other programs. Meals are taken on one's own, in residences, in restaurants.

Costs (2002-2003) • One term: $5313 for fall term; $5813 for spring. Yearlong program: $11,125; includes housing, all meals, student support services, in-state tuition and fees. $300 nonrefundable deposit required. Financial aid available for students from sponsoring institution: all customary sources.

For More Information • University at Albany, State University of New York, Office of International Education, LI 66, Albany, NY 12222; *Phone:* 518-442-3525; *Fax:* 518-442-3338. *E-mail:* intled@uamail.albany.edu. *World Wide Web:* http://www.albany.edu/intled/

UTRECHT

INTERSTUDY
UTRECHT UNIVERSITY

Hosted by Utrecht University

Academic Focus • Drama/theater, Dutch, English, film and media studies, history, liberal studies, linguistics, literature, social sciences, women's studies.

Program Information • Students attend classes at Utrecht University. Scheduled travel to Bath, Stratford-upon-Avon, Warwick Castle, Oxford, Stonehenge.

Sessions • Fall, spring, yearlong.

Eligibility Requirements • Minimum age 18; open to freshmen, sophomores, juniors, seniors, adults; 3.0 GPA; 2 letters of recommendation; good academic standing at home school; no foreign language proficiency required.

Living Arrangements • Students live in host institution dormitories, locally rented apartments. Quarters are shared with host institution students. Meals are taken on one's own, in residences.

Costs (2003-2004) • One term: $12,250 for fall term; $13,550 for spring. Yearlong program: $22,450; includes tuition, housing, some meals, excursions, international student ID, student support services, Student Union membership, e-mail access, banking facilities, international bank transfers, transcript, cell phone. $35 application fee. $500 nonrefundable deposit required. Financial aid available for all students: scholarships, loans, stipends.

For More Information • InterStudy, Admissions Office, 63 Edward Street, Medford, MA 02155; *Phone:* 800-663-1999; *Fax:* 781-391-7463. *E-mail:* interstudy@interstudy-usa.org. *World Wide Web:* http://www.interstudy.org/

Get a Global Education!

The University Studies Abroad Consortium, with programs in 24 countries, allows students to master languages and study disciplines — including business, fine arts and history — at distinguished, overseas schools. Soak up the vibrant culture and be transformed by the experience of living in a foreign land.

• Summer, semester and yearlong programs • Wide range of academic courses • Internships • Language classes at all levels • Field trips and tours • Small classes • University credit • Scholarships • Housing

UNIVERSITY STUDIES ABROAD CONSORTIUM **USAC**
HTTP://USAC.UNR.EDU•775-784-6569
Your Gateway to the World

UNIVERSITY STUDIES ABROAD CONSORTIUM
FULL CURRICULUM STUDIES: UTRECHT, NETHERLANDS

Hosted by Utrecht University
Academic Focus • Full curriculum.
Program Information • Students attend classes at Utrecht University.
Sessions • Fall, spring, yearlong.
Eligibility Requirements • Minimum age 18; open to freshmen, sophomores, juniors, seniors; 3.0 GPA; no foreign language proficiency required.
Living Arrangements • Students live in locally rented apartments, host family homes. Quarters are shared with host institution students. Meals are taken on one's own, in restaurants.
Costs (2005-2006) • One term: $2980. Yearlong program: $5960; includes tuition, insurance, welcome Dutch course at the James Boswell Institute. $50 application fee. $150 refundable deposit required. Financial aid available for all students: scholarships, loans.
For More Information • University Studies Abroad Consortium, USAC/323, Reno, NV 89557-0093; *Phone:* 775-784-6569; *Fax:* 775-784-6010. *E-mail:* usac@unr.edu. *World Wide Web:* http://usac.unr.edu/

ZWOLLE
DORDT COLLEGE
NETHERLANDS S.P.I.C.E–NETHERLANDS STUDIES PROGRAM IN CONTEMPORARY EUROPE

Hosted by Gereformeerde Hageschool
Academic Focus • Art history, Dutch, history, philosophy, popular culture, religious studies.
Program Information • Students attend classes at Gereformeerde Hageschool. Scheduled travel to Prague, Paris; field trips to museums in Amsterdam, Haarlem, The Hague; optional travel to other European countries at an extra cost.
Sessions • Spring.
Eligibility Requirements • Open to sophomores, juniors, seniors; 2.5 GPA; no foreign language proficiency required.
Living Arrangements • Students live in host family homes. Quarters are shared with host institution students. Meals are taken with host family, in residences.
Costs (2002-2003) • One term: $9500; includes tuition, housing, all meals, excursions, international student ID, student support services. $50 application fee. $350 nonrefundable deposit required. Financial aid available for students from sponsoring institution: scholarships.
For More Information • Dr. Ken Bussema, Director of Off-Campus Programs, Dordt College, 498 4th Avenue, NE, Sioux Center, IA 51250; *Phone:* 712-722-6358; *Fax:* 712-722-4496. *E-mail:* kbussema@dordt.edu. *World Wide Web:* http://www.dordt.edu/academic/programs/offcampus/nspice/

NEW ZEALAND
CITY TO CITY
UNIVERSITY OF IDAHO
NEW ZEALAND STUDIES PROGRAM–MASSEY UNIVERSITY

Hosted by Massey University–Wellington Campus, Massey University–Auckland Campus, Massey University
Academic Focus • Full curriculum.
Program Information • Students attend classes at Massey University–Wellington Campus (Wellington), Massey University–Auckland Campus (Auckland), Massey University (Palmerston North). Optional travel to other destinations in New Zealand at an extra cost.
Sessions • Fall, spring, yearlong, US academic year.
Eligibility Requirements • Open to freshmen, sophomores, juniors, seniors, graduate students, adults; 2.75 GPA; good academic standing at home school.

Living Arrangements • Students live in host institution dormitories, locally rented apartments. Quarters are shared with host institution students, students from other programs. Meals are taken on one's own, in residences, in central dining facility.
Costs (2003-2004) • One term: $4600. Yearlong program: $9200; includes tuition, student support services. $100 application fee. $200 refundable deposit required. Financial aid available for students from sponsoring institution: scholarships, loans.
For More Information • Ms. Amy S. Bergmann, Advisor, University of Idaho, Room 209, Morrill Hall, Moscow, ID 83844-3013; *Phone:* 208-885-7870; *Fax:* 208-885-2859. *E-mail:* abroad@uidaho.edu. *World Wide Web:* http://www.ets.uidaho.edu/ipo/abroad/

AUCKLAND
ARCADIA UNIVERSITY
UNIVERSITY OF AUCKLAND

Hosted by University of Auckland
Academic Focus • Full curriculum.
Program Information • Students attend classes at University of Auckland.
Sessions • Fall, spring, yearlong, US academic year.
Eligibility Requirements • Open to sophomores, juniors, seniors; 3.0 GPA; 1 letter of recommendation.
Living Arrangements • Students live in host institution dormitories. Quarters are shared with host institution students. Meals are taken on one's own, in residences.
Costs (2003-2004) • One term: $8990. Yearlong program: $15,550; includes tuition, housing, insurance, international student ID, student support services, transcript, pre-departure guide. $35 application fee. $500 nonrefundable deposit required. Financial aid available for all students: scholarships, loans.
For More Information • Arcadia University, Center for Education Abroad, 450 South Easton Road, Glenside, PA 19038-3295; *Phone:* 866-927-2234; *Fax:* 215-572-2174. *E-mail:* cea@arcadia.edu. *World Wide Web:* http://www.arcadia.edu/cea/

AUSTRALEARN: NORTH AMERICAN CENTER FOR AUSTRALIAN AND NEW ZEALAND UNIVERSITIES
AUCKLAND UNIVERSITY OF TECHNOLOGY

Hosted by Auckland University of Technology
Academic Focus • Full curriculum.
Program Information • Students attend classes at Auckland University of Technology. Scheduled travel to a pre-trip excursion in Auckland; optional travel to Australia, other parts of New Zealand at an extra cost.
Sessions • Fall, spring, yearlong, alternate year.
Eligibility Requirements • Minimum age 18; open to sophomores, juniors, seniors, graduate students; 2.5 GPA; 1 letter of recommendation; good academic standing at home school.
Living Arrangements • Students live in locally rented apartments. Quarters are shared with host institution students, students from other programs. Meals are taken on one's own, in residences.
Costs (2004) • One term: $9160. Yearlong program: $16,565; includes tuition, housing, insurance, excursions, international student ID, student support services. $30 application fee. $300 deposit required. Financial aid available for all students: scholarships, loans.
For More Information • AustraLearn: North American Center for Australian and New Zealand Universities, 12050 North Pecos Street, Suite 320, Westminster, CO 80234; *Phone:* 800-980-0033; *Fax:* 303-446-5955. *E-mail:* studyabroad@australearn.org. *World Wide Web:* http://www.australearn.org/

AUSTRALEARN: NORTH AMERICAN CENTER FOR AUSTRALIAN AND NEW ZEALAND UNIVERSITIES
UNIVERSITY OF AUCKLAND

Hosted by University of Auckland
Academic Focus • Full curriculum.

Program Information • Students attend classes at University of Auckland. Scheduled travel to a pre-trip excursion in Auckland; optional travel to Australia, other parts of New Zealand at an extra cost.

Sessions • Fall, spring, yearlong, alternate year.

Eligibility Requirements • Minimum age 18; open to sophomores, juniors, seniors, graduate students; 3.0 GPA; 1 letter of recommendation; good academic standing at home school.

Living Arrangements • Students live in locally rented apartments. Quarters are shared with host institution students. Meals are taken on one's own, in residences.

Costs (2004) • One term: $9160. Yearlong program: $16,565; includes tuition, housing, insurance, excursions, student support services. $30 application fee. $300 deposit required. Financial aid available for all students: scholarships, loans.

For More Information • AustraLearn: North American Center for Australian and New Zealand Universities, 12050 North Pecos Street, Suite 320, Westminster, CO 80234; *Phone:* 800-980-0033; *Fax:* 303-446-5955. *E-mail:* studyabroad@australearn.org. *World Wide Web:* http://www.australearn.org/

BOSTON UNIVERSITY
AUCKLAND PROGRAMS

Hosted by University of Auckland

Academic Focus • Full curriculum, geology, liberal studies.

Program Information • Students attend classes at University of Auckland. Scheduled travel to the Cook Islands; optional travel to Sydney, Fiji at an extra cost.

Sessions • Fall, spring.

Eligibility Requirements • Open to juniors, seniors; 3.0 GPA; 2 letters of recommendation; good academic standing at home school; essay; approval of participation; transcript; no foreign language proficiency required.

Living Arrangements • Students live in host institution dormitories. Meals are taken on one's own, in residences.

Costs (2004-2005) • One term: $12,800 for fall term; $14,300 for spring; includes tuition, housing, internship placement. $50 application fee. $400 nonrefundable deposit required. Financial aid available for all students: scholarships, loans.

For More Information • Divison of International Programs, Boston University, 232 Bay State Road, Boston, MA 02215; *Phone:* 617-353-9888; *Fax:* 617-353-5402. *E-mail:* abroad@bu.edu. *World Wide Web:* http://www.bu.edu/abroad/

CENTER FOR INTERNATIONAL STUDIES
UNIVERSITY OF AUCKLAND

Hosted by University of Auckland

Academic Focus • Full curriculum.

Program Information • Students attend classes at University of Auckland. Optional travel at an extra cost.

Sessions • Fall, spring, yearlong.

Eligibility Requirements • Minimum age 18; open to freshmen, sophomores, juniors, seniors, graduate students, adults; 3.0 GPA; 1 letter of recommendation; good academic standing at home school; personal essay.

Living Arrangements • Students live in host institution dormitories, locally rented apartments, program-owned apartments. Quarters are shared with host institution students. Meals are taken on one's own, in residences, in central dining facility, in restaurants.

Costs (2003) • One term: $7800. Yearlong program: $14,000; includes tuition, housing, insurance, international student ID, student support services. $50 application fee. $500 nonrefundable deposit required. Financial aid available for all students: scholarships.

For More Information • Mr. Jeff Palm, Program Director, Center for International Studies, 17 New South Street, #105, Northampton, MA 01060; *Phone:* 413-582-0407; *Fax:* 413-582-0327. *E-mail:* jpalm@cisabroad.com. *World Wide Web:* http://www.cisabroad.com/

IES, INSTITUTE FOR THE INTERNATIONAL EDUCATION OF STUDENTS
IES–AUCKLAND

Hosted by University of Auckland

Academic Focus • Full curriculum.

Program Information • Students attend classes at University of Auckland. Scheduled travel to South Pacific Islands; optional travel to Wellington, southern Alps at an extra cost.

Sessions • Fall, spring, yearlong, calendar year.

Eligibility Requirements • Minimum age 18; open to juniors, seniors, graduate students, adults; 3.0 GPA; 1 letter of recommendation; good academic standing at home school.

Living Arrangements • Students live in host institution dormitories. Meals are taken on one's own, in residences, in central dining facility.

Costs (2004-2005) • One term: contact sponsor for cost. Yearlong program: contact sponsor for cost. $50 application fee. $500 deposit required. Financial aid available for all students: scholarships, institutional partner need-based grants.

For More Information • International Education Representative, IES, Institute for the International Education of Students, 33 North La Salle Street, 15th Floor, Chicago, IL 60602; *Phone:* 800-995-2300; *Fax:* 312-944-1448. *E-mail:* info@iesabroad.org. *World Wide Web:* http://www.IESabroad.org/

INSTITUTE FOR STUDY ABROAD, BUTLER UNIVERSITY
UNIVERSITY OF AUCKLAND

Hosted by University of Auckland

Academic Focus • Full curriculum.

Program Information • Students attend classes at University of Auckland. Scheduled travel to the country (for a weekend).

Sessions • Fall, spring, yearlong, US academic year.

Eligibility Requirements • Open to sophomores, juniors, seniors; 3.0 GPA; 1 letter of recommendation; good academic standing at home school; enrollment at an accredited American college or university.

Living Arrangements • Students live in host institution dormitories. Quarters are shared with host institution students. Meals are taken as a group, on one's own, in residences, in central dining facility.

Costs (2003) • One term: $9475. Yearlong program: $15,575; includes tuition, housing, excursions, international student ID, student support services, cultural and sporting events, pre-departure advising. $40 application fee. $500 nonrefundable deposit required. Financial aid available for all students: scholarships, travel grants.

For More Information • Institute for Study Abroad, Butler University, 1100 West 42nd Street, Suite 305, Indianapolis, IN 46208-3345; *Phone:* 800-858-0229; *Fax:* 317-940-9704. *E-mail:* study-abroad@butler.edu. *World Wide Web:* http://www.ifsa-butler.org/

STATE UNIVERSITY OF NEW YORK AT OSWEGO
SEMESTER AT AUCKLAND UNIVERSITY OF TECHNOLOGY

Hosted by Auckland University of Technology

Academic Focus • Full curriculum.

Program Information • Students attend classes at Auckland University of Technology. Optional travel to Australia, New Zealand, the South Pacific at an extra cost.

Sessions • Fall, spring, yearlong.

Eligibility Requirements • Open to sophomores, juniors, seniors; 2.5 GPA; 3 letters of recommendation; good academic standing at home school; study statement.

Living Arrangements • Students live in host institution dormitories, locally rented apartments. Quarters are shared with host institution students, students from other programs. Meals are taken on one's own, in residences, in restaurants.

Costs (2003-2004) • One term: $6120. Yearlong program: $12,240; includes tuition, insurance, student support services. $250 nonrefundable deposit required. Financial aid available for students: home university financial aid, loan processing and scholarships for Oswego students.

For More Information • Ms. Nefertitti Saheed, Program Specialist, State University of New York at Oswego, 122A Swetman Hall, Oswego, NY 13126; *Phone:* 888-4-OSWEGO; *Fax:* 315-312-2477. *E-mail:* intled@oswego.edu. *World Wide Web:* http://www.oswego.edu/intled/

STUDY AUSTRALIA
STUDY NEW ZEALAND: MASSEY UNIVERSITY–AUCKLAND

Hosted by Massey University–Auckland Campus
Academic Focus • Full curriculum.
Program Information • Students attend classes at Massey University–Auckland Campus. Scheduled travel to Sydney; field trips to the Blue Mountains; optional travel to South Island of New Zealand, Australia, Fiji at an extra cost.
Sessions • Fall, spring, yearlong.
Eligibility Requirements • Minimum age 18; open to freshmen, sophomores, juniors, seniors; 2.5 GPA; good academic standing at home school; enrollment at an accredited American college or university.
Living Arrangements • Students live in host institution dormitories, locally rented apartments, host family homes. Quarters are shared with host institution students, students from other programs. Meals are taken on one's own, in residences, in central dining facility.
Costs (2003) • One term: $7460. Yearlong program: $13,670; includes tuition, housing, insurance, excursions, international student ID, student support services, travel discounts. $500 deposit required. Financial aid available for all students: scholarships, loans.
For More Information • Mr. Chris Shepherd, Director of Programs and Services, Study Australia, 54515 State Road 933 North, Notre Dame, IN 46556-1004; *Phone:* 800-585-9658; *Fax:* 509-357-9457. *E-mail:* info@study-newzealand.com. *World Wide Web:* http://www.study-australia.com/

STUDY AUSTRALIA
UNIVERSITY OF AUCKLAND

Hosted by University of Auckland
Academic Focus • Full curriculum.
Program Information • Students attend classes at University of Auckland. Scheduled travel to Sydney; field trips to the Blue Mountains; optional travel to Hawaii, New Zealand, Tasmania, the Great Barrier Reef at an extra cost.
Sessions • Fall, spring, yearlong.
Eligibility Requirements • Minimum age 18; open to sophomores, juniors, seniors; 3.0 GPA; good academic standing at home school.
Living Arrangements • Students live in host institution dormitories, locally rented apartments, host family homes. Quarters are shared with host institution students, students from other programs. Meals are taken on one's own, in restaurants.
Costs (2003) • One term: $8610. Yearlong program: $15,970; includes tuition, housing, insurance, excursions, student support services. $500 refundable deposit required. Financial aid available for all students: scholarships, loans.
For More Information • Mr. Chris Shepherd, Director of Programs and Services, Study Australia, 54515 State Road 933 North, Notre Dame, IN 46556-1004; *Phone:* 800-585-9638; *Fax:* 509-357-9457. *E-mail:* info@study-australia.com. *World Wide Web:* http://www.study-australia.com/

CANTERBURY

AMERICAN UNIVERSITIES INTERNATIONAL PROGRAMS (AUIP)
LINCOLN UNIVERSITY, NEW ZEALAND

Hosted by Lincoln University
Academic Focus • Full curriculum.
Program Information • Students attend classes at Lincoln University. Optional travel to Fiordland National Park, South Island of New Zealand, Queenstown, Mt. Cook at an extra cost.
Sessions • Fall, spring, yearlong.
Eligibility Requirements • Minimum age 18; open to sophomores, juniors, seniors, graduate students; 2.8 GPA; 2 letters of recommen-

dation; good academic standing at home school; essay; original transcript; no foreign language proficiency required.
Living Arrangements • Students live in host institution dormitories. Quarters are shared with host institution students, students from other programs. Meals are taken as a group, on one's own, in residences, in central dining facility.
Costs (2004) • One term: $7995. Yearlong program: $13,495; includes tuition, housing, some meals, insurance, international student ID, student support services, university fees. $50 application fee. $500 nonrefundable deposit required.
For More Information • Ms. Linda Detling, Program Coordinator, American Universities International Programs (AUIP), PMB 221, 305 West Magnolia Street, Fort Collins, CO 80521; *Phone:* 970-495-0869; *Fax:* 970-484-2082. *E-mail:* info@auip.com. *World Wide Web:* http://www.auip.com/

ST. BONAVENTURE UNIVERSITY
SEMESTER IN NEW ZEALAND

Hosted by Lincoln University
Academic Focus • Accounting, biochemistry, biological/life sciences, business administration/management, communications, finance, full curriculum, international business, liberal studies, marketing, science, tourism and travel.
Program Information • Students attend classes at Lincoln University. Optional travel to Christchurch, Auckland, Australia at an extra cost.
Sessions • Fall, spring, yearlong.
Eligibility Requirements • Minimum age 18; open to sophomores, juniors, seniors, graduate students, adults; 2.5 GPA; 3 letters of recommendation; official transcript; program essay; no foreign language proficiency required.
Living Arrangements • Students live in host institution dormitories. Quarters are shared with host institution students, students from other programs. Meals are taken as a group, on one's own, in residences, in central dining facility.
Costs (2002-2003) • One term: $7750. Yearlong program: $15,500; includes tuition, housing, some meals, airport pick-up. $30 application fee. Financial aid available for students from sponsoring institution: loans.
For More Information • Ms. Alice F. Sayegh, Director, International Studies, St. Bonaventure University, Reilly Center 221B, St. Bonaventure, NY 14778; *Phone:* 716-375-2574; *Fax:* 716-375-7882. *E-mail:* asayegh@sbu.edu. *World Wide Web:* http://www.sbu.edu/intstudies/

CHRISTCHURCH

AUSTRALEARN: NORTH AMERICAN CENTER FOR AUSTRALIAN AND NEW ZEALAND UNIVERSITIES
UNIVERSITY OF CANTERBURY

Hosted by University of Canterbury
Academic Focus • Full curriculum.
Program Information • Students attend classes at University of Canterbury. Scheduled travel to a pre-trip excursion in Auckland; optional travel to Australia, other areas of New Zealand at an extra cost.
Sessions • Fall, spring, yearlong, alternate year.
Eligibility Requirements • Minimum age 18; open to sophomores, juniors, seniors, graduate students; 2.8 GPA; 1 letter of recommendation; good academic standing at home school.
Living Arrangements • Students live in host institution dormitories, locally rented apartments. Meals are taken as a group, on one's own, in residences, in central dining facility.
Costs (2004) • One term: $10,130. Yearlong program: $18,515; includes tuition, housing, all meals, insurance, excursions, international student ID, student support services. $30 application fee. $300 deposit required. Financial aid available for all students: scholarships, loans.
For More Information • AustraLearn: North American Center for Australian and New Zealand Universities, 12050 North Pecos Street, Suite 320, Westminster, CO 80234; *Phone:* 800-980-0033; *Fax:* 303-446-5955. *E-mail:* studyabroad@australearn.org. *World Wide Web:* http://www.australearn.org/

COLLEGE CONSORTIUM FOR INTERNATIONAL STUDIES–MONTANA STATE UNIVERSITY
SEMESTER/YEAR IN NEW ZEALAND

Hosted by University of Canterbury
Academic Focus • Full curriculum.
Program Information • Students attend classes at University of Canterbury. Optional travel to skiing, other outdoor activites at an extra cost.
Sessions • Fall, spring, yearlong.
Eligibility Requirements • Open to sophomores, juniors, seniors, graduate students; 2.75 GPA; 2 letters of recommendation.
Living Arrangements • Students live in host institution dormitories, locally rented apartments, host family homes. Quarters are shared with host institution students. Meals are taken on one's own, in residences, in restaurants.
Costs (2004) • One term: $6820. Yearlong program: $13,640; includes tuition, student support services, transportation from airport. $200 nonrefundable deposit required. Financial aid available for students from sponsoring institution: scholarships, loans.
For More Information • Study Abroad Advisor, College Consortium for International Studies–Montana State University, 400 Culbertson Hall, Montana State University, Bozeman, MT 59717; *Phone:* 406-994-7151; *Fax:* 406-994-1619. *E-mail:* newzealand@montana.edu. *World Wide Web:* http://www.ccisabroad.org/

IES, INSTITUTE FOR THE INTERNATIONAL EDUCATION OF STUDENTS
IES–CHRISTCHURCH

Hosted by University of Canterbury
Academic Focus • Full curriculum.
Program Information • Students attend classes at University of Canterbury. Scheduled travel to South Pacific Islands; optional travel to the Southern Alps, Wellington at an extra cost.
Sessions • Fall, spring, yearlong, calendar year.
Eligibility Requirements • Minimum age 18; open to juniors, seniors, graduate students, adults; 3.0 GPA; 1 letter of recommendation; good academic standing at home school.
Living Arrangements • Students live in host institution dormitories, locally rented apartments. Meals are taken on one's own, in residences.
Costs (2004-2005) • One term: contact sponsor for cost. Yearlong program: contact sponsor for cost. $50 application fee. $500 nonrefundable deposit required. Financial aid available for all students: scholarships, institutional partner need-based grants.
For More Information • International Education Representative, IES, Institute for the International Education of Students, 33 North La Salle Street, 15th Floor, Chicago, IL 60602; *Phone:* 800-995-2300; *Fax:* 312-944-1448. *E-mail:* info@iesabroad.org. *World Wide Web:* http://www.IESabroad.org/

INSTITUTE FOR STUDY ABROAD, BUTLER UNIVERSITY
UNIVERSITY OF CANTERBURY

Hosted by University of Canterbury
Academic Focus • Full curriculum.
Program Information • Students attend classes at University of Canterbury. Scheduled travel to the country (for a weekend).
Sessions • Fall, spring, yearlong, US academic year.
Eligibility Requirements • Open to sophomores, juniors, seniors; 3.0 GPA; 1 letter of recommendation; good academic standing at home school; enrollment at an accredited American or Canadian college or university.

NEW ZEALAND
Christchurch

Living Arrangements • Students live in host institution dormitories, locally rented apartments. Quarters are shared with host institution students, students from other programs. Meals are taken on one's own, in residences.

Costs (2003) • One term: $8975. Yearlong program: $14,975; includes tuition, housing, excursions, international student ID, student support services, cultural and sporting events, pre-departure advising. $40 application fee. $500 nonrefundable deposit required. Financial aid available for all students: scholarships, travel grants.

For More Information • Institute for Study Abroad, Butler University, 1100 West 42nd Street, Suite 305, Indianapolis, IN 46208-3345; *Phone:* 800-858-0229; *Fax:* 317-940-9704. *E-mail:* study-abroad@butler.edu. *World Wide Web:* http://www.ifsa-butler.org/

STATE UNIVERSITY OF NEW YORK COLLEGE AT BROCKPORT
UNIVERSITY OF CANTERBURY PROGRAM

Hosted by University of Canterbury
Academic Focus • Full curriculum.
Program Information • Students attend classes at University of Canterbury. Field trips.
Sessions • Fall, spring, yearlong.
Eligibility Requirements • Minimum age 18; open to juniors, seniors; 2.8 GPA; 2 letters of recommendation; good academic standing at home school; demonstrated ability to do upper-division work in the subjects chosen.
Living Arrangements • Students live in host institution dormitories, halls of residence. Quarters are shared with host institution students. Meals are taken as a group, on one's own, in residences, in central dining facility.
Costs (2003-2004) • One term: $8350. Yearlong program: $15,350; includes tuition, housing, excursions, international student ID, student support services, meals in halls of residence. $350 nonrefundable deposit required. Financial aid available for all students: scholarships, loans, regular financial aid, grants.
For More Information • Dr. John Perry, Director, Office of International Education, State University of New York College at Brockport, 350 New Campus Drive, Brockport, NY 14420; *Phone:* 800-298-SUNY; *Fax:* 585-637-3218. *E-mail:* overseas@brockport.edu. *World Wide Web:* http://www.brockport.edu/studyabroad/

UNIVERSITY OF IDAHO
NEW ZEALAND STUDIES PROGRAM–LINCOLN UNIVERSITY

Hosted by Lincoln University
Academic Focus • Full curriculum.
Program Information • Students attend classes at Lincoln University. Optional travel to local attractions at an extra cost.
Sessions • Fall, spring, yearlong, US academic year.
Eligibility Requirements • Open to freshmen, sophomores, juniors, seniors, graduate students, adults; 2.75 GPA; good academic standing at home school.
Living Arrangements • Students live in host institution dormitories, locally rented apartments. Quarters are shared with host institution students, students from other programs. Meals are taken on one's own, in residences, in central dining facility.
Costs (2003-2004) • One term: $7000. Yearlong program: $14,000; includes tuition, housing, some meals, student support services. $100 application fee. $200 refundable deposit required. Financial aid available for students from sponsoring institution: scholarships, loans.
For More Information • Ms. Amy S. Bergmann, Advisor, University of Idaho, Room 209, Morrill Hall, Moscow, ID 83844-3013; *Phone:* 208-885-7870; *Fax:* 208-885-2859. *E-mail:* abroad@uidaho.edu. *World Wide Web:* http://www.ets.uidaho.edu/ipo/abroad/

UNIVERSITY OF WISCONSIN–STEVENS POINT
SEMESTER IN NEW ZEALAND

Hosted by University of Canterbury
Academic Focus • Environmental science/studies, geography, natural resources, political science and government.

Program Information • Students attend classes at University of Canterbury. Scheduled travel to Tahiti; field trips to Milford Sound, Mount Cook, Fox Glacier; optional travel to the Cook Islands at an extra cost.
Sessions • Spring.
Eligibility Requirements • Minimum age 18; open to sophomores, juniors, seniors; 2.25 GPA; 3 letters of recommendation; good academic standing at home school.
Living Arrangements • Students live in host family homes. Meals are taken with host family.
Costs (2003-2004) • One term: $9000 for Wisconsin residents; $14,250 for nonresidents; includes tuition, housing, excursions, books and class materials. $15 application fee. $250 nonrefundable deposit required. Financial aid available for all students: work study, loans.
For More Information • Mr. Mark Koepke, Associate Director, University of Wisconsin–Stevens Point, International Programs, 208 Collins, Stevens Point, WI 54481; *Phone:* 715-346-2717; *Fax:* 715-349-3591. *E-mail:* intlprog@uwsp.edu. *World Wide Web:* http://www.uwsp.edu/studyabroad/

DUNEDIN
AHA INTERNATIONAL AN ACADEMIC PROGRAM OF THE UNIVERSITY OF OREGON
AHA AT THE UNIVERSITY OF OTAGO

Hosted by University of Otago
Academic Focus • Biological/life sciences, economics, environmental health, environmental science/studies, full curriculum, geography, geology, journalism, marketing, mathematics, music, natural resources, nutrition, Pacific studies, physics, science, tourism and travel.
Program Information • Students attend classes at University of Otago.
Sessions • Fall, spring, yearlong.
Eligibility Requirements • Open to sophomores, juniors, seniors, graduate students, adults; 2 letters of recommendation; good academic standing at home school; transcripts; no foreign language proficiency required.
Living Arrangements • Students live in host institution dormitories, locally rented apartments. Quarters are shared with host institution students. Meals are taken on one's own, in central dining facility, in restaurants.
Costs (2004) • One term: $5180. Yearlong program: $10,360; includes tuition, insurance, international student ID, student support services. $50 application fee. $200 refundable deposit required.
For More Information • Ms. Carlotta Troy, Associate Director for University Programs, AHA International An Academic Program of the University of Oregon, 741 SW Lincoln Street, Portland, OR 97201; *Phone:* 503-295-7730; *Fax:* 503-295-5969. *E-mail:* mail@aha-intl.org. *World Wide Web:* http://www.aha-intl.org/

ALMA COLLEGE
PROGRAM OF STUDIES IN NEW ZEALAND

Hosted by University of Otago
Academic Focus • Full curriculum.
Program Information • Students attend classes at University of Otago.
Sessions • Fall, spring.
Eligibility Requirements • Minimum age 18; open to sophomores, juniors, seniors; 3.0 GPA; 2 letters of recommendation; good academic standing at home school.
Living Arrangements • Students live in host institution dormitories, locally rented apartments. Quarters are shared with host institution students. Meals are taken on one's own, in central dining facility, in restaurants.
Costs (2002-2003) • One term: $8250; includes tuition, housing, some meals, insurance, international student ID, student support services. $50 application fee. $200 refundable deposit required. Financial aid available for all students: scholarships.
For More Information • Ms. Julie Elenbaas, Office Coordinator, Alma College, 614 West Superior Street, Alma, MI 48801-1599; *Phone:* 989-463-7055; *Fax:* 989-463-7126. *World Wide Web:* http://international.alma.edu/

ARCADIA UNIVERSITY
UNIVERSITY OF OTAGO

Hosted by University of Otago
Academic Focus • Full curriculum.
Program Information • Students attend classes at University of Otago.
Sessions • Fall, spring, yearlong, US academic year.
Eligibility Requirements • Open to sophomores, juniors, seniors; 3.0 GPA; 1 letter of recommendation.
Living Arrangements • Students live in host institution dormitories, locally rented apartments, program-owned apartments. Quarters are shared with host institution students. Meals are taken as a group, on one's own, in residences.
Costs (2003-2004) • One term: $8990. Yearlong program: $15,250 for Australian academic year; $15,550 for US academic year; includes tuition, housing, insurance, international student ID, student support services, transcript, pre-departure guide. $35 application fee. $500 nonrefundable deposit required. Financial aid available for all students: scholarships, loans.
For More Information • Arcadia University, Center for Education Abroad, 450 South Easton Road, Glenside, PA 19038-3295; *Phone:* 866-927-2234; *Fax:* 215-572-2174. *E-mail:* cea@arcadia.edu. *World Wide Web:* http://www.arcadia.edu/cea/

AUSTRALEARN: NORTH AMERICAN CENTER FOR AUSTRALIAN AND NEW ZEALAND UNIVERSITIES
UNIVERSITY OF OTAGO

Hosted by University of Otago
Academic Focus • Full curriculum.
Program Information • Students attend classes at University of Otago. Scheduled travel to a pre-trip excursion in Auckland; optional travel to Australia, other areas of New Zealand at an extra cost.
Sessions • Fall, spring, yearlong, alternate year.
Eligibility Requirements • Minimum age 18; open to sophomores, juniors, seniors, graduate students; 3.0 GPA; 1 letter of recommendation; good academic standing at home school.
Living Arrangements • Students live in host institution dormitories, locally rented apartments. Quarters are shared with host institution students. Meals are taken on one's own, in residences, in central dining facility.
Costs (2004) • One term: $9620. Yearlong program: $17,290; includes tuition, housing, all meals, insurance, excursions, international student ID, student support services. $30 application fee. $300 deposit required. Financial aid available for all students: scholarships, loans.
For More Information • AustraLearn: North American Center for Australian and New Zealand Universities, 12050 North Pecos Street, Suite 320, Westminster, CO 80234; *Phone:* 800-980-0033; *Fax:* 303-446-5955. *E-mail:* studyabroad@australearn.org. *World Wide Web:* http://www.australearn.org/

BRETHREN COLLEGES ABROAD
BCA PEACE AND JUSTICE PROGRAM IN DUNEDIN, NEW ZEALAND

Hosted by University of Otago
Academic Focus • Aboriginal studies, full curriculum.
Program Information • Students attend classes at University of Otago. Field trips.
Sessions • Fall, spring, yearlong.
Eligibility Requirements • Minimum age 18; open to sophomores, juniors, seniors; 3.0 GPA; 3 letters of recommendation; good academic standing at home school.
Living Arrangements • Students live in host institution dormitories. Meals are taken on one's own, in residences, in central dining facility.
Costs (2003-2004) • One term: $11,500. Yearlong program: $19,900; includes tuition, housing, all meals, excursions, international student ID, student support services. $50 application fee. $100 nonrefundable deposit required.
For More Information • Ms. Natalya Latysheva-Derova, Program Officer, Brethren Colleges Abroad, 50 Alpha Drive, Elizabethtown, PA 17022; *Phone:* 866-222-6188; *Fax:* 717-361-6619. *E-mail:* info@bcanet.org. *World Wide Web:* http://www.bcanet.org/

INSTITUTE FOR STUDY ABROAD, BUTLER UNIVERSITY
UNIVERSITY OF OTAGO

Hosted by University of Otago
Academic Focus • Full curriculum.
Program Information • Students attend classes at University of Otago. Scheduled travel to the country (for a weekend).
Sessions • Fall, spring, yearlong, US academic year.
Eligibility Requirements • Open to sophomores, juniors, seniors; 3.0 GPA; 1 letter of recommendation; good academic standing at home school; enrollment at an accredited American college or university.
Living Arrangements • Students live in locally rented apartments. Quarters are shared with host institution students. Meals are taken on one's own, in residences.
Costs (2003) • One term: $9475. Yearlong program: $15,275; includes tuition, housing, excursions, international student ID, student support services, cultural and sporting events, pre-departure advising. $40 application fee. $500 nonrefundable deposit required. Financial aid available for all students: scholarships, travel grants.
For More Information • Institute for Study Abroad, Butler University, 1100 West 42nd Street, Suite 305, Indianapolis, IN 46208-3345; *Phone:* 800-858-0229; *Fax:* 317-940-9704. *E-mail:* study-abroad@butler.edu. *World Wide Web:* http://www.ifsa-butler.org/

STATE UNIVERSITY OF NEW YORK AT OSWEGO
UNIVERSITY OF OTAGO

Hosted by University of Otago
Academic Focus • Full curriculum.
Program Information • Students attend classes at University of Otago. Optional travel to Australia, New Zealand, the South Pacific at an extra cost.
Sessions • Fall, spring, yearlong.
Eligibility Requirements • Open to sophomores, juniors, seniors; 3.0 GPA; 3 letters of recommendation; good academic standing at home school; written statement on purpose of study overseas.
Living Arrangements • Students live in host institution dormitories, locally rented apartments. Quarters are shared with host institution students, students from other programs. Meals are taken on one's own, in residences, in central dining facility.
Costs (2003-2004) • One term: $5520. Yearlong program: $11,040; includes tuition, insurance, student support services. $250 nonrefundable deposit required. Financial aid available for students: home university financial aid, loan processing and scholarships for Oswego students.
For More Information • Ms. Nefertitti Saheed, Program Specialist, State University of New York at Oswego, 122A Swetman Hall, Oswego, NY 13126; *Phone:* 888-4-OSWEGO; *Fax:* 315-312-2477. *E-mail:* intled@oswego.edu. *World Wide Web:* http://www.oswego.edu/intled/

HAMILTON

AMERICAN UNIVERSITIES INTERNATIONAL PROGRAMS (AUIP)
WAIKATO UNIVERSITY, NEW ZEALAND

Hosted by University of Waikato
Academic Focus • Full curriculum.
Program Information • Students attend classes at University of Waikato. Optional travel to Fiordland National Park, South Island of New Zealand, Queenstown, Mt. Cook at an extra cost.
Sessions • Fall, spring, yearlong.
Eligibility Requirements • Minimum age 18; open to sophomores, juniors, seniors, adults; 2.8 GPA; 2 letters of recommendation; essay; original transcript.
Living Arrangements • Students live in host institution dormitories, locally rented apartments. Quarters are shared with host institution students, students from other programs. Meals are taken as a group, on one's own, in residences, in central dining facility.
Costs (2003) • One term: $6795. Yearlong program: $13,090; includes tuition, housing, all meals, insurance, student support

services, advising at host institution, university fees. $50 application fee. $500 nonrefundable deposit required.

For More Information • Ms. Linda Detling, Program Coordinator, American Universities International Programs (AUIP), PMB 221, 305 West Magnolia Street, Fort Collins, CO 80521; *Phone:* 970-495-0869; *Fax:* 970-484-2028. *E-mail:* info@auip.com. *World Wide Web:* http://www.auip.com/

AUSTRALEARN: NORTH AMERICAN CENTER FOR AUSTRALIAN AND NEW ZEALAND UNIVERSITIES
UNIVERSITY OF WAIKATO

Hosted by University of Waikato
Academic Focus • Full curriculum.
Program Information • Students attend classes at University of Waikato. Scheduled travel to the Great Barrier Reef and Aboriginal Cultural Park (pre-trip excursion); optional travel to Australia and other parts of New Zealand at an extra cost.
Sessions • Fall, spring, yearlong, alternate year.
Eligibility Requirements • Minimum age 18; open to sophomores, juniors, seniors, graduate students; 2.5 GPA; 1 letter of recommendation; good academic standing at home school.
Living Arrangements • Students live in host institution dormitories, locally rented apartments. Quarters are shared with host institution students. Meals are taken on one's own, in residences, in central dining facility.
Costs (2004) • One term: $9185. Yearlong program: $16,535; includes tuition, housing, all meals, insurance, excursions, international student ID, student support services. $30 application fee. $300 deposit required. Financial aid available for all students: scholarships, loans.
For More Information • AustraLearn: North American Center for Australian and New Zealand Universities, 12050 North Pecos Street, Suite 320, Westminster, CO 80234; *Phone:* 800-980-0033; *Fax:* 303-446-5955. *E-mail:* studyabroad@australearn.org. *World Wide Web:* http://www.australearn.org/

COLLEGE CONSORTIUM FOR INTERNATIONAL STUDIES–MONTANA STATE UNIVERSITY
SEMESTER/YEAR IN NEW ZEALAND

Hosted by University of Waikato
Academic Focus • Full curriculum.
Program Information • Students attend classes at University of Waikato. Optional travel to beaches, mountains, limestone caves, thermal pools, many cultural activities, skiing at an extra cost.
Sessions • Fall, spring, yearlong.
Eligibility Requirements • Open to sophomores, juniors, seniors; 2.5 GPA; 2 letters of recommendation.
Living Arrangements • Students live in host institution dormitories, locally rented apartments. Quarters are shared with host institution students. Meals are taken on one's own, in residences, in central dining facility, in restaurants.
Costs (2004) • One term: $5920. Yearlong program: $11,840; includes tuition, student support services, airport pick-up. $200 nonrefundable deposit required. Financial aid available for students from sponsoring institution: scholarships, loans.
For More Information • Study Abroad Advisor, College Consortium for International Studies–Montana State University, 400 Culbertson Hall, Montana State University, Bozeman, MT 59717; *Phone:* 406-994-7151; *Fax:* 406-994-1619. *E-mail:* newzealand@montana.edu. *World Wide Web:* http://www.ccisabroad.org/

SCHOOL FOR INTERNATIONAL TRAINING, SIT STUDY ABROAD
NEW ZEALAND: BIODIVERSITY AND CONSERVATION

Academic Focus • Biological/life sciences, conservation studies, ecology, environmental science/studies, ethnic studies, marine sciences, natural resources, wildlife studies.
Program Information • Faculty members are drawn from the sponsor's U.S. staff and local instructors hired by the sponsor. Scheduled travel to Christchurch, Milford Sound, Otaga Peninsula; field trips to conservation areas, forest and marine reserves, farms.

Sessions • Fall, spring.
Eligibility Requirements • Open to sophomores, juniors, seniors; course work in environmental studies, biology, ecology, or related field; 2.5 GPA; 2 letters of recommendation; good academic standing at home school; no foreign language proficiency required.
Living Arrangements • Students live in host family homes, hotels. Meals are taken as a group, on one's own, with host family, in residences, in restaurants.
Costs (2003-2004) • One term: $12,825; includes tuition, housing, all meals, insurance, excursions. $50 application fee. $400 nonrefundable deposit required. Financial aid available for all students: scholarships.
For More Information • School for International Training, SIT Study Abroad, Kipling Road, Brattleboro, VT 05302-0676; *Phone:* 888-272-7881; *Fax:* 802-258-3296. *E-mail:* studyabroad@sit.edu. *World Wide Web:* http://www.sit.edu/studyabroad/

STATE UNIVERSITY OF NEW YORK AT OSWEGO
UNIVERSITY OF WAIKATO

Hosted by University of Waikato
Academic Focus • Full curriculum.
Program Information • Students attend classes at University of Waikato. Optional travel to Australia, New Zealand, the South Pacific at an extra cost.
Sessions • Fall, spring, yearlong.
Eligibility Requirements • Open to sophomores, juniors, seniors; 2.5 GPA; 3 letters of recommendation; good academic standing at home school; program study statement.
Living Arrangements • Students live in host institution dormitories, locally rented apartments. Quarters are shared with host institution students. Meals are taken on one's own, in central dining facility, in restaurants.
Costs (2003-2004) • One term: $5620. Yearlong program: $11,240; includes tuition, insurance, student support services. $250 nonrefundable deposit required. Financial aid available for students: home university financial aid, loan processing and scholarships for Oswego students.
For More Information • Ms. Nefertitti Saheed, Program Specialist, State University of New York at Oswego, 122A Swetman Hall, Oswego, NY 13126; *Phone:* 888-4-OSWEGO; *Fax:* 315-312-2477. *E-mail:* intled@oswego.edu. *World Wide Web:* http://www.oswego.edu/intled/

UNIVERSITY STUDIES ABROAD CONSORTIUM
FULL CURRICULUM STUDIES: HAMILTON, NEW ZEALAND

Hosted by University of Waikato
Academic Focus • Full curriculum.
Program Information • Students attend classes at University of Waikato.
Sessions • Fall, spring, yearlong.
Eligibility Requirements • Minimum age 18; open to freshmen, sophomores, juniors, seniors, graduate students, adults; 2.5 GPA.
Living Arrangements • Students live in host institution dormitories, locally rented apartments. Quarters are shared with host institution students. Meals are taken on one's own, in residences, in central dining facility.
Costs (2005-2006) • One term: $4980. Yearlong program: $9680; includes tuition, insurance, student support services. $50 application fee. $150 refundable deposit required. Financial aid available for all students: scholarships, loans.
For More Information • University Studies Abroad Consortium, USAC/323, Reno, NV 89557-0093; *Phone:* 775-784-6569; *Fax:* 775-784-6010. *E-mail:* usac@unr.edu. *World Wide Web:* http://usac.unr.edu/

KAIAUA
UNIVERSITY OF NEW HAMPSHIRE
ECOQUEST NEW ZEALAND

Hosted by Ecoquest New Zealand

Academic Focus • Biological/life sciences, botany, conservation studies, ecology, economics, environmental science/studies, fisheries studies, forestry, geography, international affairs, marine sciences, natural resources, political science and government, public policy, social sciences, wildlife studies, zoology.
Program Information • Students attend classes at Ecoquest New Zealand. Scheduled travel to various destinations on North and South Islands; field trips to Auckland, Hamilton, Coromandel regions.
Sessions • Fall, spring.
Eligibility Requirements • Open to juniors, seniors; course work in natural sciences, social sciences; 2.5 GPA; 2 letters of recommendation; good academic standing at home school; high level of physical fitness; teamwork skills.
Living Arrangements • Students live in host institution dormitories, overnight facilities (education centers, parks, research stations). Quarters are shared with host institution students. Meals are taken as a group, in residences.
Costs (2004-2005) • One term: $12,850; includes tuition, housing, all meals, excursions, books and class materials, lab equipment, student support services, in-country program travel. $35 application fee. $850 nonrefundable deposit required. Financial aid available for all students: scholarships, loans.
For More Information • Ms. Donna M. Dowal, UNH-EcoQuest Admissions Director, University of New Hampshire, Department of Natural Resources, 215 James Hall, Durham, NH 03824; *Phone:* 603-862-2036; *Fax:* 603-862-4976. *E-mail:* ecoquest@unh.edu. *World Wide Web:* http://www.unh.edu/

PALMERSTON NORTH

AUSTRALEARN: NORTH AMERICAN CENTER FOR AUSTRALIAN AND NEW ZEALAND UNIVERSITIES
MASSEY UNIVERSITY

Hosted by Massey University
Academic Focus • Full curriculum.
Program Information • Students attend classes at Massey University. Scheduled travel to a pre-trip excursion in Auckland; optional travel to Australia, other parts of New Zealand at an extra cost.
Sessions • Fall, spring, yearlong, alternate year.
Eligibility Requirements • Minimum age 18; open to sophomores, juniors, seniors, graduate students; 2.75 GPA; 1 letter of recommendation; good academic standing at home school.
Living Arrangements • Students live in host institution dormitories, locally rented apartments. Quarters are shared with host institution students, students from other programs. Meals are taken on one's own, in central dining facility.
Costs (2004) • One term: $9725. Yearlong program: $17,395; includes tuition, housing, insurance, excursions, student support services. $30 application fee. $300 deposit required. Financial aid available for all students: scholarships, loans.
For More Information • AustraLearn: North American Center for Australian and New Zealand Universities, 12050 North Pecos Street, Suite 320, Westminster, CO 80234; *Phone:* 800-9800033; *Fax:* 303-4465955. *E-mail:* studyabroad@australearn.org. *World Wide Web:* http://www.australearn.org/

INSTITUTE FOR STUDY ABROAD, BUTLER UNIVERSITY
MASSEY UNIVERSITY

Hosted by Massey University
Academic Focus • Full curriculum.
Program Information • Students attend classes at Massey University. Scheduled travel to the country (for a weekend).
Sessions • Fall, spring, yearlong, US academic year.
Eligibility Requirements • Open to sophomores, juniors, seniors; 3.0 GPA; 1 letter of recommendation; enrollment at an accredited American college or university.
Living Arrangements • Students live in locally rented apartments. Quarters are shared with host institution students. Meals are taken on one's own, in residences.

Costs (2003) • One term: $8375. Yearlong program: $13,975; includes tuition, housing, excursions, international student ID, student support services, cultural and sporting events, pre-departure advising. $40 application fee. $500 deposit required. Financial aid available for all students: scholarships, travel grants.
For More Information • Institute for Study Abroad, Butler University, 1100 West 42nd Street, Suite 305, Indianapolis, IN 46208-3345; *Phone:* 800-858-0229; *Fax:* 317-940-9704. *E-mail:* study-abroad@butler.edu. *World Wide Web:* http://www.ifsa-butler.org/

STUDY AUSTRALIA
MASSEY UNIVERSITY–PALMERSTON NORTH

Hosted by Massey University
Academic Focus • Full curriculum.
Program Information • Students attend classes at Massey University. Scheduled travel to Sydney; field trips to the Blue Mountains; optional travel to South Island of New Zealand, Australia, Fiji at an extra cost.
Sessions • Fall, spring, yearlong.
Eligibility Requirements • Minimum age 18; open to freshmen, sophomores, juniors, seniors; 2.5 GPA; good academic standing at home school; enrollment at an accredited American college or university.
Living Arrangements • Students live in host institution dormitories, locally rented apartments, host family homes. Quarters are shared with host institution students, students from other programs. Meals are taken on one's own, in residences, in central dining facility.
Costs (2003) • One term: $7460. Yearlong program: $13,670; includes tuition, housing, insurance, excursions, travel discounts. $500 deposit required. Financial aid available for all students: scholarships, loans.
For More Information • Mr. Chris Shepherd, Director of Programs and Services, Study Australia, 54515 State Road 933 North, Notre Dame, IN 46556-1004; *Phone:* 800-585-9658; *Fax:* 509-357-9457. *E-mail:* info@study-newzealand.com. *World Wide Web:* http://www.study-australia.com/

WELLINGTON

ARCADIA UNIVERSITY
VICTORIA UNIVERSITY OF WELLINGTON

Hosted by Victoria University of Wellington
Academic Focus • Full curriculum.
Program Information • Students attend classes at Victoria University of Wellington.
Sessions • Fall, spring, yearlong, US academic year.
Eligibility Requirements • Open to sophomores, juniors, seniors; 3.0 GPA; 1 letter of recommendation.
Living Arrangements • Students live in host institution dormitories, locally rented apartments. Quarters are shared with host institution students. Meals are taken as a group, on one's own, in residences.
Costs (2003-2004) • One term: $8390. Yearlong program: $13,900 for Australian academic year; $14,200 for US academic year; includes tuition, housing, insurance, international student ID, student support services, transcript, pre-departure guide. $35 application fee. $500 nonrefundable deposit required. Financial aid available for all students: scholarships, loans.
For More Information • Arcadia University, Center for Education Abroad, 450 South Easton Road, Glenside, PA 19038-3295; *Phone:* 866-927-2234; *Fax:* 215-572-2174. *E-mail:* cea@arcadia.edu. *World Wide Web:* http://www.arcadia.edu/cea/

AUSTRALEARN: NORTH AMERICAN CENTER FOR AUSTRALIAN AND NEW ZEALAND UNIVERSITIES
VICTORIA UNIVERSITY OF WELLINGTON

Hosted by Victoria University of Wellington
Academic Focus • Full curriculum.

NEW ZEALAND
Wellington

Program Information • Students attend classes at Victoria University of Wellington. Scheduled travel to a pre-trip excursion in Auckland; optional travel to Australia, other areas of New Zealand at an extra cost.
Sessions • Fall, spring, yearlong, alternate year.
Eligibility Requirements • Minimum age 18; open to sophomores, juniors, seniors, graduate students; 2.7 GPA; 1 letter of recommendation; good academic standing at home school.
Living Arrangements • Students live in host institution dormitories, locally rented apartments. Quarters are shared with host institution students. Meals are taken on one's own, in residences, in central dining facility.
Costs (2004) • One term: $9915. Yearlong program: $18,070; includes tuition, housing, all meals, insurance, excursions, international student ID, student support services. $30 application fee. $300 deposit required. Financial aid available for all students: scholarships, loans.
For More Information • AustraLearn: North American Center for Australian and New Zealand Universities, 12050 North Pecos Street, Suite 320, Westminster, CO 80234; *Phone:* 800-980-0033; *Fax:* 303-446-5955. *E-mail:* studyabroad@australearn.org. *World Wide Web:* http://www.australearn.org/

CENTER FOR INTERNATIONAL STUDIES
VICTORIA UNIVERSITY OF WELLINGTON

Hosted by Victoria University of Wellington
Academic Focus • Full curriculum.
Program Information • Students attend classes at Victoria University of Wellington. Optional travel at an extra cost.
Sessions • Fall, spring, yearlong.
Eligibility Requirements • Minimum age 18; open to sophomores, juniors, seniors, graduate students, adults; 2.75 GPA; 1 letter of recommendation; good academic standing at home school; personal essay.
Living Arrangements • Students live in host institution dormitories, locally rented apartments, program-owned apartments. Quarters are shared with host institution students, students from other programs. Meals are taken on one's own, in residences, in central dining facility.
Costs (2003) • One term: $7290–$8050. Yearlong program: $12,460–$14,440; includes tuition, housing, insurance, international student ID, student support services. $50 application fee. $500 nonrefundable deposit required. Financial aid available for all students: scholarships.
For More Information • Mr. Jeff Palm, Program Director, Center for International Studies, 17 New South Street, #105, Northampton, MA 01060; *Phone:* 413-582-0407; *Fax:* 413-582-0327. *E-mail:* jpalm@cisabroad.com. *World Wide Web:* http://www.cisabroad.com/

INSTITUTE FOR STUDY ABROAD, BUTLER UNIVERSITY
VICTORIA UNIVERSITY OF WELLINGTON

Hosted by Victoria University of Wellington
Academic Focus • Full curriculum.
Program Information • Students attend classes at Victoria University of Wellington. Scheduled travel to the country (for a weekend); optional travel to local cultural and sporting events, local wilderness areas and coastal areas.
Sessions • Fall, spring, yearlong, US academic year.
Eligibility Requirements • Open to sophomores, juniors, seniors; 2.7 GPA; 1 letter of recommendation; good academic standing at home school; enrollment at an accredited American or Canadian college or university.
Living Arrangements • Students live in host institution dormitories, locally rented apartments. Quarters are shared with host institution students, students from other programs. Meals are taken as a group, on one's own, in residences, in central dining facility, in restaurants.
Costs (2003) • One term: $8675. Yearlong program: $12,875; includes tuition, housing, excursions, international student ID, student support services, cultural and sporting events, pre-departure advising. $40 application fee. $500 nonrefundable deposit required. Financial aid available for all students: scholarships, travel grants.

For More Information • Institute for Study Abroad, Butler University, 1100 West 42nd Street, Suite 305, Indianapolis, IN 46208-3345; *Phone:* 800-858-0229; *Fax:* 317-940-9704. *E-mail:* study-abroad@butler.edu. *World Wide Web:* http://www.ifsa-butler.org/

STATE UNIVERSITY OF NEW YORK AT NEW PALTZ
STUDY ABROAD IN WELLINGTON, NEW ZEALAND

Hosted by Victoria University of Wellington
Academic Focus • Full curriculum.
Program Information • Students attend classes at Victoria University of Wellington.
Sessions • Fall, spring, yearlong.
Eligibility Requirements • Minimum age 18; open to sophomores, juniors, seniors; 2.75 GPA; 2 letters of recommendation.
Living Arrangements • Students live in host institution dormitories. Quarters are shared with host institution students, students from other programs. Meals are taken on one's own, in residences.
Costs (2003-2004) • One term: $5937 for New York residents; $6092 for nonresidents. Yearlong program: $11,874 for New York residents; $12,184 for nonresidents; includes tuition, insurance, administrative fee. $25 application fee. $300–$600 nonrefundable deposit required. Financial aid available for students from sponsoring institution: scholarships, loans.
For More Information • Center for International Programs, State University of New York at New Paltz, 75 South Manheim Boulevard, Suite 9, New Paltz, NY 12561; *Phone:* 845-257-3125; *Fax:* 845-257-3129. *E-mail:* international@newpaltz.edu. *World Wide Web:* http://www.newpaltz.edu/studyabroad/

STUDY AUSTRALIA
STUDY NEW ZEALAND: MASSEY UNIVERSITY–WELLINGTON

Hosted by Massey University–Wellington Campus
Academic Focus • Full curriculum.
Program Information • Students attend classes at Massey University–Wellington Campus. Scheduled travel to Sydney; field trips to the Blue Mountains; optional travel to South Island of New Zealand, Australia, Fiji at an extra cost.
Sessions • Fall, spring, yearlong.
Eligibility Requirements • Minimum age 18; open to freshmen, sophomores, juniors, seniors; 2.5 GPA; good academic standing at home school; enrollment at an accredited American college or university.
Living Arrangements • Students live in host institution dormitories, locally rented apartments, host family homes. Quarters are shared with host institution students, students from other programs. Meals are taken on one's own, in residences, in central dining facility.
Costs (2003) • One term: $7460. Yearlong program: $13,670; includes tuition, housing, insurance, excursions, international student ID, student support services, travel discounts. $500 deposit required. Financial aid available for all students: scholarships, loans.
For More Information • Mr. Chris Shepherd, Director of Programs and Services, Study Australia, 54515 State Road 933 North, Notre Dame, IN 46556-1004; *Phone:* 800-585-9658; *Fax:* 509-357-9457. *E-mail:* info@study-newzealand.com. *World Wide Web:* http://www.study-australia.com/

NICARAGUA
MANAGUA
AUGSBURG COLLEGE
SUSTAINABLE DEVELOPMENT AND SOCIAL CHANGE IN CENTRAL AMERICA

Hosted by Center for Global Education
Academic Focus • Economics, history, interdisciplinary studies, Latin American studies, peace and conflict studies, religious studies, Spanish language and literature.

Program Information • Students attend classes at Center for Global Education. Scheduled travel to Guatemala, El Salvador, Nicaragua; field trips; optional travel at an extra cost.
Sessions • Fall, spring.
Eligibility Requirements • Open to sophomores, juniors, seniors; course work in economics (1 course); 2.5 GPA; 2 letters of recommendation; good academic standing at home school; 0.5 years of college course work in Spanish.
Living Arrangements • Students live in program-owned houses, host family homes, hotels, guest houses. Quarters are shared with host institution students. Meals are taken as a group, with host family, in central dining facility, in restaurants.
Costs (2004-2005) • One term: sliding fee scale for consortium partners; $13,400 for transfers; includes tuition, housing, all meals, insurance, excursions, international student ID, some books and class materials. $50 application fee. $500 nonrefundable deposit required. Financial aid available for students from sponsoring institution: scholarships, loans.
For More Information • Mr. Margaret Anderson, Coordinator, Semester Programs Abroad, Augsburg College, 2211 Riverside Avenue, Minneapolis, MN 55454; *Phone:* 800-299-8889; *Fax:* 612-330-1695. *E-mail:* globaled@augsburg.edu. *World Wide Web:* http://www.augsburg.edu/global/

SCHOOL FOR INTERNATIONAL TRAINING, SIT STUDY ABROAD
NICARAGUA: REVOLUTION, TRANSFORMATION, AND CIVIL SOCIETY

Academic Focus • Anthropology, cultural studies, Latin American studies, political science and government, sociology, Spanish language and literature, women's studies.
Program Information • Faculty members are drawn from the sponsor's U.S. staff and local instructors hired by the sponsor. Scheduled travel to Havana, Matagalpa or Estelli, the South Atlantic Autonomous Region; field trips to León, El Crucero.
Sessions • Fall, spring.
Eligibility Requirements • Open to sophomores, juniors, seniors; 2.5 GPA; 2 letters of recommendation; good academic standing at home school; 1.5 years of college course work in Spanish.
Living Arrangements • Students live in host family homes, hotels. Meals are taken as a group, with host family, in residences, in restaurants.
Costs (2003-2004) • One term: $12,025; includes tuition, housing, all meals, insurance, excursions. $50 application fee. $400 nonrefundable deposit required. Financial aid available for all students: scholarships.
For More Information • School for International Training, SIT Study Abroad, Kipling Road, Brattleboro, VT 05302-0676; *Phone:* 888-272-7881; *Fax:* 802-258-3296. *E-mail:* studyabroad@sit.edu. *World Wide Web:* http://www.sit.edu/studyabroad/

NIGER
NIAMEY
BOSTON UNIVERSITY
NIAMEY LANGUAGE AND LIBERAL ARTS PROGRAM

Held at Universty Abdou Moumouni
Academic Focus • African languages and literature, African studies, community service, economics, French language and literature, Hausa, performing arts, philosophy, political science and government, Zarma.
Program Information • Classes are held on the campus of Universty Abdou Moumouni. Faculty members are local instructors hired by the sponsor. Scheduled travel to Burkina Faso, Benin; field trips to Balayara Outdoor Market, Parc W (national park), a Peace Corps Village.
Sessions • Fall, spring, yearlong.
Eligibility Requirements • Open to sophomores, juniors, seniors, adults; 3.0 GPA; 2 letters of recommendation; good academic

standing at home school; essay; approval of participation; transcript; 1 year of college course work in French.
Living Arrangements • Students live in the Centre de Formation des Cadres d'Alphabetisation. Quarters are shared with host institution students. Meals are taken as a group, in residences.
Costs (2004-2005) • One term: $19,834. Yearlong program: $39,668; includes tuition, housing, all meals, excursions, international airfare, medical evacuation insurance. $50 application fee. $400 nonrefundable deposit required. Financial aid available for all students: scholarships, loans.
For More Information • Division of International Programs, Boston University, 232 Bay State Road, Boston, MA 02215; *Phone:* 617-353-9888; *Fax:* 617-353-5402. *E-mail:* abroad@bu.edu. *World Wide Web:* http://www.bu.edu/abroad/

NORTHERN IRELAND
See also England, Ireland, Scotland, and Wales.

CITY TO CITY
ARCADIA UNIVERSITY
UNIVERSITY OF ULSTER

Hosted by University of Ulster, University of Ulster at Belfast, University of Ulster at Jordanstown, University of Ulster, Magee College
Academic Focus • Asian studies, business administration/management, communications, computer science, drama/theater, English, environmental science/studies, history, international business, Irish studies, mathematics, nursing, peace and conflict studies, social sciences.
Program Information • Students attend classes at University of Ulster (Coleraine), University of Ulster at Belfast (Belfast), University of Ulster at Jordanstown (Newtownabbey), University of Ulster, Magee College (Londonderry). Scheduled travel to sites within Northern Ireland.
Sessions • Fall, spring, yearlong, fall semester.
Eligibility Requirements • Open to sophomores, juniors, seniors; 3.0 GPA; 1 letter of recommendation; previous study in chosen field.
Living Arrangements • Students live in program-owned apartments, host family homes. Quarters are shared with host institution students, students from other programs. Meals are taken on one's own, in residences.
Costs (2003-2004) • One term: $9590–$9790. Yearlong program: $14,950; includes tuition, housing, insurance, international student ID, student support services, pre-departure guide, transcripts. $35 application fee. $500 nonrefundable deposit required. Financial aid available for all students: scholarships, loans.
For More Information • Arcadia University, Center for Education Abroad, 450 South Easton Road, Glenside, PA 19038-3295; *Phone:* 866-927-2234; *Fax:* 215-572-2174. *E-mail:* cea@arcadia.edu. *World Wide Web:* http://www.arcadia.edu/cea/

EARLHAM COLLEGE
PEACE STUDIES PROGRAM IN NORTHERN IRELAND

Academic Focus • History, international affairs, liberal studies, peace and conflict studies, political science and government, social sciences.
Program Information • Faculty members are local instructors hired by the sponsor. Scheduled travel to Dublin; field trips to Ballycastle and Antrim Coast, Portrush, various sites in Northern Ireland; optional travel to Armagh, Mourne Mountains at an extra cost.
Sessions • Spring.

Eligibility Requirements • Minimum age 18; open to sophomores, juniors, seniors; 2 letters of recommendation; good academic standing at home school.

Living Arrangements • Students live in host family homes. Meals are taken on one's own, with host family, in residences.

Costs (2003) • One term: $14,352; includes tuition, housing, all meals, excursions, international student ID, student support services. $350 nonrefundable deposit required. Financial aid available for students from sponsoring institution: scholarships, loans.

For More Information • Ms. Jennifer Lewis, Program Associate, International Programs, Earlham College, Drawer 202, 801 National Road West, Richmond, IN 47374; *Phone:* 765-983-1424; *Fax:* 765-983-1553. *E-mail:* ipo@earlham.edu. *World Wide Web:* http://www.earlham.edu/~ipo/offcampus.html

HIGHER EDUCATION CONSORTIUM FOR URBAN AFFAIRS (HECUA)
NORTHERN IRELAND: DEMOCRACY AND SOCIAL CHANGE

Hosted by University of Ulster

Academic Focus • Community service, ethics, history, interdisciplinary studies, Irish studies, liberal studies, peace and conflict studies, political science and government, public policy, social sciences, social services, sociology, women's studies.

Program Information • Students attend classes at University of Ulster (Coleraine). Classes are also held on the campus of Glencree Centre for Reconciliation (Dublin, Ireland). Scheduled travel to the Glencree Centre for Reconciliation in the Republic of Ireland, Belfast internship; field trips to government and nongovernment organizations working in education, human rights, and conflict resolution.

Sessions • Spring.

Eligibility Requirements • Open to sophomores, juniors, seniors, graduate students, adults; 2.5 GPA; 1 letter of recommendation; good academic standing at home school.

Living Arrangements • Students live in host institution dormitories, host family homes. Quarters are shared with host institution students. Meals are taken on one's own, in residences.

Costs (2003) • One term: $12,100; includes tuition, housing, all meals, insurance, excursions, student support services. $75 application fee. $400 nonrefundable deposit required. Financial aid available for all students: scholarships.

For More Information • Mr. Michael Eaton, Director of Admissions and Student Services, Higher Education Consortium for Urban Affairs (HECUA), 2233 University Avenue West, Suite 210, St. Paul, MN 55114-1629; *Phone:* 800-554-1089; *Fax:* 651-659-9421. *E-mail:* info@hecua.org. *World Wide Web:* http://www.hecua.org/

STATE UNIVERSITY OF NEW YORK AT BINGHAMTON
UNIVERSITY OF ULSTER EXCHANGE

Hosted by University of Ulster, Magee College, University of Ulster, University of Ulster at Jordanstown, University of Ulster at Belfast

Academic Focus • Biological/life sciences, communications, design and applied arts, economics, environmental science/studies, full curriculum, history, international affairs, Irish studies, literature, peace and conflict studies, political science and government, public policy, sociology.

Program Information • Students attend classes at University of Ulster, Magee College (Londonderry), University of Ulster (Coleraine), University of Ulster at Jordanstown (Newtownabbey), University of Ulster at Belfast (Belfast). Field trips to historic and scenic sites, cultural sites.

Sessions • Fall, spring, yearlong.

Eligibility Requirements • Open to sophomores, juniors, seniors, graduate students; 3.0 GPA; 2 letters of recommendation; good academic standing at home school.

Living Arrangements • Students live in host institution dormitories, locally rented apartments. Quarters are shared with host institution students. Meals are taken on one's own, in residences, in central dining facility, in restaurants.

Costs (2002-2003) • One term: $8500 for New York residents; $12,000 for nonresidents. Yearlong program: $14,000 for New York residents; $19,500 for nonresidents; includes tuition, housing, all meals, insurance, excursions, international airfare, books and class

materials, international student ID. $250 nonrefundable deposit required. Financial aid available for students from sponsoring institution: scholarships, loans.

For More Information • Dr. Katharine C. Krebs, Director, State University of New York at Binghamton, Office of International Programs, NARC G-1, Binghamton, NY 13902-6000; *Phone:* 607-777-2336; *Fax:* 607-777-2889. *E-mail:* oip@binghamton.edu. *World Wide Web:* http://oip.binghamton.edu/

BELFAST

ARCADIA UNIVERSITY
THE QUEEN'S UNIVERSITY OF BELFAST

Hosted by Queen's University Belfast

Academic Focus • Agriculture, economics, engineering, liberal studies, science, social sciences.

Program Information • Students attend classes at Queen's University Belfast. Scheduled travel to sites within Northern Ireland.

Sessions • Fall, spring, yearlong, fall semester.

Eligibility Requirements • Open to sophomores, juniors, seniors; 3.0 GPA; 1 letter of recommendation.

Living Arrangements • Students live in host institution dormitories, program-owned apartments, host family homes. Quarters are shared with host institution students, students from other programs. Meals are taken on one's own, in residences, in central dining facility.

Costs (2003-2004) • One term: $9990–$10,490. Yearlong program: $17,190; includes tuition, housing, insurance, international student ID, student support services, pre-departure guide, transcripts. $35 application fee. $500 nonrefundable deposit required. Financial aid available for all students: scholarships, loans.

For More Information • Arcadia University, Center for Education Abroad, 450 South Easton Road, Glenside, PA 19038-3295; *Phone:* 866-927-2234; *Fax:* 215-572-2174. *E-mail:* cea@arcadia.edu. *World Wide Web:* http://www.arcadia.edu/cea/

INSTITUTE FOR STUDY ABROAD, BUTLER UNIVERSITY
QUEEN'S UNIVERSITY BELFAST

Hosted by Queen's University Belfast

Academic Focus • Full curriculum.

Program Information • Students attend classes at Queen's University Belfast. Field trips to Killarney, Delphi, sites in Northern Ireland, Dublin.

Sessions • Fall, spring, yearlong.

Eligibility Requirements • Open to sophomores, juniors, seniors; 3.0 GPA; 1 letter of recommendation; good academic standing at home school.

Living Arrangements • Students live in host institution dormitories. Quarters are shared with host institution students, students from other programs. Meals are taken on one's own, in residences, in central dining facility, in restaurants.

Costs (2002-2003) • One term: $9775. Yearlong program: $15,875; includes tuition, housing, excursions, international student ID, student support services, family visit, cultural and sporting events, pre-departure advising. $40 application fee. $500 nonrefundable deposit required. Financial aid available for all students: scholarships, travel grants.

For More Information • Institute for Study Abroad, Butler University, 1100 West 42nd Street, Suite 305, Indianapolis, IN 46208-3345; *Phone:* 800-858-0229; *Fax:* 317-940-9704. *E-mail:* study-abroad@butler.edu. *World Wide Web:* http://www.ifsa-butler.org/

INSTITUTE FOR STUDY ABROAD, BUTLER UNIVERSITY
UNIVERSITY OF ULSTER–BELFAST

Hosted by University of Ulster at Belfast

Academic Focus • Design and applied arts, fine/studio arts.

Program Information • Students attend classes at University of Ulster at Belfast. Field trips to Delphi, Killarney, destinations within Northern Ireland, Dublin.

Sessions • Fall, spring, yearlong.

Eligibility Requirements • Open to sophomores, juniors, seniors; 3.0 GPA; 1 letter of recommendation; good academic standing at home school; enrollment at an accredited American college or university.

Living Arrangements • Students live in host institution dormitories, locally rented apartments. Quarters are shared with host institution students, students from other programs. Meals are taken on one's own, in residences, in restaurants.

Costs (2002-2003) • One term: $8775. Yearlong program: $14,175; includes tuition, housing, excursions, international student ID, student support services, family visit, cultural and sporting events, pre-departure advising. $40 application fee. $500 nonrefundable deposit required. Financial aid available for all students: scholarships, travel grants.

For More Information • Institute for Study Abroad, Butler University, 1100 West 42nd Street, Suite 305, Indianapolis, IN 46208-3345; *Phone:* 800-858-0229; *Fax:* 317-940-9704. *E-mail:* study-abroad@butler.edu. *World Wide Web:* http://www.ifsa-butler.org/

INTERSTUDY
QUEEN'S UNIVERSITY OF BELFAST

Hosted by Queen's University Belfast

Academic Focus • Accounting, agriculture, ancient history, anthropology, architecture, art history, biochemistry, biological/life sciences, Celtic studies, classics and classical languages, drama/theater, economics, English, geography, law and legal studies, music, philosophy, political science and government, psychology, social sciences, women's studies.

Program Information • Students attend classes at Queen's University Belfast. Scheduled travel to Bath, Stratford-upon-Avon, Warwick Castle, Oxford, Stonehenge.

Sessions • Fall, spring, yearlong, early start Irish culture session.

Eligibility Requirements • Minimum age 18; open to freshmen, sophomores, juniors, seniors, adults; 3.0 GPA; good academic standing at home school.

Living Arrangements • Students live in host institution dormitories. Quarters are shared with host institution students. Meals are taken on one's own, in residences.

Costs (2003-2004) • One term: $10,675 for fall term; $11,650 for spring. Yearlong program: $19,795; includes tuition, housing, some meals, excursions, international student ID, student support services. $35 application fee. $500 nonrefundable deposit required. Financial aid available for all students: scholarships, loans.

For More Information • InterStudy, Admissions Office, 63 Edward Street, Medford, MA 02155; *Phone:* 800-663-1999; *Fax:* 781-391-7463. *E-mail:* interstudy@interstudy-usa.org. *World Wide Web:* http://www.interstudy.org/

NORTH AMERICAN INSTITUTE FOR STUDY ABROAD
STUDY IN NORTHERN IRELAND

Hosted by Queen's University Belfast

Academic Focus • Full curriculum.

Program Information • Students attend classes at Queen's University Belfast. Optional travel at an extra cost.

Sessions • Fall, spring, yearlong.

Eligibility Requirements • Minimum age 18; open to sophomores, juniors, seniors; 3.0 GPA; 2 letters of recommendation; good academic standing at home school.

Living Arrangements • Students live in host institution dormitories, locally rented apartments, host family homes. Quarters are shared with host institution students. Meals are taken on one's own, in residences, in central dining facility, in restaurants.

Costs (2003-2004) • One term: $9000. Yearlong program: $17,000; includes tuition, housing, insurance, international student ID, student support services, transcripts. $50 application fee. $500 nonrefundable deposit required. Financial aid available for all students: scholarships.

For More Information • Dr. Michael Currid, Director, North American Institute for Study Abroad, 129 Mill Street, Danville, PA 17821; *Phone:* 570-275-5099; *Fax:* 570-275-1644. *E-mail:* naisa@naisa.com. *World Wide Web:* http://www.naisa.com/

NORTH AMERICAN INSTITUTE FOR STUDY ABROAD
STUDY IN NORTHERN IRELAND

Hosted by University of Ulster at Belfast

Academic Focus • Art, design and applied arts, graphic design/illustration.

Program Information • Students attend classes at University of Ulster at Belfast. Optional travel at an extra cost.

Sessions • Fall, spring, yearlong.

Eligibility Requirements • Minimum age 18; open to sophomores, juniors, seniors; 3.0 GPA; 2 letters of recommendation; good academic standing at home school.

Living Arrangements • Students live in host institution dormitories, host family homes. Quarters are shared with host institution students. Meals are taken on one's own, with host family, in residences, in central dining facility, in restaurants.

Costs (2003-2004) • One term: $8500. Yearlong program: $16,000; includes tuition, housing, international student ID, student support services, transcripts. $50 application fee. $500 nonrefundable deposit required. Financial aid available for all students: scholarships.

For More Information • Dr. Michael Currid, Director, North American Institute for Study Abroad, 129 Mill Street, Danville, PA 17821; *Phone:* 570-275-5099; *Fax:* 570-275-1644. *E-mail:* naisa@naisa.com. *World Wide Web:* http://www.naisa.com/

QUEEN'S UNIVERSITY BELFAST
STUDY ABROAD

Hosted by Queen's University Belfast

Academic Focus • Anthropology, drama/theater, English literature, European studies, history, Irish literature, Irish studies, peace and conflict studies, political science and government, social sciences, women's studies.

Program Information • Students attend classes at Queen's University Belfast.

Sessions • Fall, spring, yearlong.

Eligibility Requirements • Open to sophomores, juniors, seniors; 3.0 GPA.

Living Arrangements • Students live in host institution dormitories, locally rented apartments, program-owned houses. Quarters are shared with host institution students, students from other programs. Meals are taken as a group, on one's own, in residences, in central dining facility.

Costs (2003-2004) • One term: £2900. Yearlong program: £5800; includes tuition.

For More Information • Queen's University Belfast, International Office, Belfast BT7 1NN, Northern Ireland; *Phone:* +44 28-9033 5088; *Fax:* +44 28-9033 5089. *E-mail:* international@qub.ac.uk. *World Wide Web:* http://www.qub.ac.uk/ilo/studyabroad/frame.htm. Students may also apply through Arcadia University, Center for Education Abroad, 450 South Easton Road, Glenside, PA 19038-3295; Butler University, Institute for Study Abroad, 1100 West 42nd Street, Suite 305, Indianapolis, IN 46208-3345; InterStudy USA, 63 Edward Street, Medford, MA 02155.

THE UNIVERSITY OF NORTH CAROLINA AT CHAPEL HILL
STUDY ABROAD AT UNIVERSITY OF ULSTER

Hosted by University of Ulster

Academic Focus • Full curriculum.

Program Information • Students attend classes at University of Ulster.

Sessions • Fall, spring, yearlong.

Eligibility Requirements • Open to sophomores, juniors, seniors, graduate students, adults; 3.0 GPA; 2 letters of recommendation; good academic standing at home school; essay; transcript.

Living Arrangements • Students live in host institution dormitories, locally rented apartments. Quarters are shared with host institution students. Meals are taken on one's own, in residences, in central dining facility.

Costs (2003-2004) • One term: $7796 for fall term; $11,789 for spring. Yearlong program: $16,300; includes tuition, housing, some meals, insurance, study abroad fee. $100 application fee. $500

nonrefundable deposit required. Financial aid available for students from sponsoring institution: scholarships, loans.

For More Information • Study Abroad Office, The University of North Carolina at Chapel Hill, 201 Porthole Building, CB 3130, Chapel Hill, NC 27599-3130; *Phone:* 919-962-7002; *Fax:* 919-962-2262. *E-mail:* abroad@unc.edu. *World Wide Web:* http://studyabroad.unc.edu/

COLERAINE

INSTITUTE FOR STUDY ABROAD, BUTLER UNIVERSITY
UNIVERSITY OF ULSTER–COLERAINE

Hosted by University of Ulster
Academic Focus • Full curriculum.
Program Information • Students attend classes at University of Ulster. Field trips to Delphi, Killarney, sites within Northern Ireland, Dublin.
Sessions • Fall, spring, yearlong.
Eligibility Requirements • Open to sophomores, juniors, seniors; 3.0 GPA; 1 letter of recommendation; good academic standing at home school; enrollment at an accredited American college or university.
Living Arrangements • Students live in host institution dormitories, locally rented apartments. Quarters are shared with host institution students, students from other programs. Meals are taken on one's own, in residences, in central dining facility, in restaurants.
Costs (2002-2003) • One term: $8775. Yearlong program: $14,175; includes tuition, housing, excursions, international student ID, student support services, family visit, cultural and sporting events, pre-departure advising. $40 application fee. $500 nonrefundable deposit required. Financial aid available for all students: scholarships, travel grants.
For More Information • Institute for Study Abroad, Butler University, Institute for Study Abroad, 1100 West 42nd Street, Suite 305, Indianapolis, IN 46208-3345; *Phone:* 800-858-0229; *Fax:* 317-940-9704. *E-mail:* study-abroad@butler.edu. *World Wide Web:* http://www.ifsa-butler.org/

NORTH AMERICAN INSTITUTE FOR STUDY ABROAD
STUDY IN NORTHERN IRELAND

Hosted by University of Ulster
Academic Focus • Full curriculum.
Program Information • Students attend classes at University of Ulster. Optional travel at an extra cost.
Sessions • Fall, spring, yearlong.
Eligibility Requirements • Minimum age 18; open to sophomores, juniors, seniors; 3.0 GPA; 2 letters of recommendation; good academic standing at home school.
Living Arrangements • Students live in host institution dormitories, locally rented apartments, host family homes. Quarters are shared with host institution students. Meals are taken on one's own, with host family, in residences, in central dining facility, in restaurants.
Costs (2003-2004) • One term: $8500. Yearlong program: $17,000; includes tuition, housing, international student ID, student support services, transcripts. $50 application fee. $500 nonrefundable deposit required. Financial aid available for all students: scholarships.
For More Information • Dr. Michael Currid, Director, North American Institute for Study Abroad, 129 Mill Street, Danville, PA 17821; *Phone:* 570-275-5099; *Fax:* 570-275-1644. *E-mail:* naisa@naisa.com. *World Wide Web:* http://www.naisa.com/

DERRY

BRETHREN COLLEGES ABROAD
BCA PEACE AND JUSTICE PROGRAM IN DERRY, NORTHERN IRELAND

Hosted by University of Ulster, Magee College
Academic Focus • Full curriculum, peace and conflict studies.

Program Information • Students attend classes at University of Ulster, Magee College. Field trips.
Sessions • Fall, spring, yearlong.
Eligibility Requirements • Minimum age 18; open to sophomores, juniors, seniors; 3.0 GPA; 3 letters of recommendation; good academic standing at home school.
Living Arrangements • Students live in host institution dormitories. Meals are taken on one's own, in residences, in restaurants.
Costs (2003-2004) • One term: $11,500. Yearlong program: $19,900; includes tuition, housing, all meals, insurance, excursions, international student ID, student support services. $50 application fee. $100 nonrefundable deposit required.
For More Information • Ms. Natalya Latysheva-Derova, Program Officer, Brethren Colleges Abroad, 50 Alpha Drive, Elizabethtown, PA 17022; *Phone:* 866-222-6188; *Fax:* 717-361-6619. *E-mail:* info@bcanet.org. *World Wide Web:* http://www.bcanet.org/

LONDONDERRY

INSTITUTE FOR STUDY ABROAD, BUTLER UNIVERSITY
UNIVERSITY OF ULSTER–MAGEE

Hosted by University of Ulster, Magee College
Academic Focus • Full curriculum.
Program Information • Students attend classes at University of Ulster, Magee College. Field trips to Delphi, Killarney, sites within Northern Ireland, Dublin.
Sessions • Fall, spring, yearlong.
Eligibility Requirements • Open to sophomores, juniors, seniors; 3.0 GPA; 1 letter of recommendation; good academic standing at home school; enrollment at an accredited American college or university.
Living Arrangements • Students live in host institution dormitories, locally rented apartments. Quarters are shared with host institution students, students from other programs. Meals are taken on one's own, in residences, in central dining facility, in restaurants.
Costs (2002-2003) • One term: $8775. Yearlong program: $14,175; includes tuition, housing, excursions, international student ID, student support services, family visit, cultural and sporting events, pre-departure advising. $40 application fee. $500 nonrefundable deposit required. Financial aid available for all students: scholarships, travel grants.
For More Information • Institute for Study Abroad, Butler University, 1100 West 42nd Street, Suite 305, Indianapolis, IN 46208-3345; *Phone:* 800-858-0229; *Fax:* 317-940-9704. *E-mail:* study-abroad@butler.edu. *World Wide Web:* http://www.ifsa-butler.org/

NORTH AMERICAN INSTITUTE FOR STUDY ABROAD
STUDY IN NORTHERN IRELAND

Hosted by University of Ulster, Magee College
Academic Focus • Full curriculum.
Program Information • Students attend classes at University of Ulster, Magee College. Optional travel at an extra cost.
Sessions • Fall, spring, yearlong.
Eligibility Requirements • Minimum age 18; open to sophomores, juniors, seniors; 3.0 GPA; 2 letters of recommendation; good academic standing at home school.
Living Arrangements • Students live in host institution dormitories, host family homes. Quarters are shared with host institution students. Meals are taken on one's own, with host family, in residences, in central dining facility, in restaurants.
Costs (2003-2004) • One term: $9000. Yearlong program: $17,000; includes tuition, housing, international student ID, student support services, transcripts. $50 application fee. $500 nonrefundable deposit required. Financial aid available for all students: scholarships.
For More Information • Dr. Michael Currid, Director, North American Institute for Study Abroad, 129 Mill Street, Danville, PA 17821; *Phone:* 570-275-5099; *Fax:* 570-275-1644. *E-mail:* naisa@naisa.com. *World Wide Web:* http://www.naisa.com/

NEWTOWNABBEY

INSTITUTE FOR STUDY ABROAD, BUTLER UNIVERSITY
UNIVERSITY OF ULSTER–JORDANSTOWN

Academic Focus • Full curriculum.

Program Information • Field trips to Delphi, Killarney, destinations in Northern Ireland, Dublin.

Sessions • Fall, spring, yearlong.

Eligibility Requirements • Open to sophomores, juniors, seniors; 3.0 GPA; 1 letter of recommendation; good academic standing at home school; enrollment at an accredited American college or university.

Living Arrangements • Students live in host institution dormitories, locally rented apartments. Quarters are shared with host institution students, students from other programs. Meals are taken on one's own, in residences, in central dining facility.

Costs (2002-2003) • One term: $8775. Yearlong program: $14,175; includes tuition, housing, excursions, international student ID, student support services, family visit, cultural and sporting events, pre-departure advising. $40 application fee. $500 nonrefundable deposit required. Financial aid available for all students: scholarships, travel grants.

For More Information • Institute for Study Abroad, Butler University, 1100 West 42nd Street, Suite 305, Indianapolis, IN 46208-3345; *Phone:* 800-858-0229; *Fax:* 317-940-9704. *E-mail:* study-abroad@butler.edu. *World Wide Web:* http://www.ifsa-butler.org/

NORTH AMERICAN INSTITUTE FOR STUDY ABROAD
STUDY IN NORTHERN IRELAND

Hosted by University of Ulster at Jordanstown

Academic Focus • Full curriculum.

Program Information • Students attend classes at University of Ulster at Jordanstown. Optional travel at an extra cost.

Sessions • Fall, spring, yearlong.

Eligibility Requirements • Minimum age 18; open to sophomores, juniors, seniors; 3.0 GPA; 2 letters of recommendation; good academic standing at home school.

Living Arrangements • Students live in host institution dormitories, locally rented apartments, host family homes. Quarters are shared with host institution students. Meals are taken on one's own, with host family, in residences, in central dining facility, in restaurants.

Costs (2001-2002) • One term: $9000. Yearlong program: $17,000; includes tuition, housing, insurance, international student ID, student support services, transcripts. $50 application fee. $500 nonrefundable deposit required. Financial aid available for all students: scholarships.

For More Information • Dr. Michael Currid, Director, North American Institute for Study Abroad, 129 Mill Street, Danville, PA 17821; *Phone:* 570-275-5099; *Fax:* 570-275-1644. *E-mail:* naisa@naisa.com. *World Wide Web:* http://www.naisa.com/

NORWAY

BERGEN

UNIVERSITY AT ALBANY, STATE UNIVERSITY OF NEW YORK
DIRECT ENROLLMENT AT THE UNIVERSITY OF BERGEN

Hosted by University of Bergen

Academic Focus • Full curriculum, liberal studies, mathematics, Norwegian, Scandinavian studies, science, social sciences.

Program Information • Students attend classes at University of Bergen.

Sessions • Fall, spring, yearlong.

Eligibility Requirements • Open to sophomores, juniors, seniors, graduate students; 3.0 GPA; 2 letters of recommendation; good academic standing at home school; foreign language requirement dependent on track chosen.

Living Arrangements • Students live in host institution dormitories, locally rented apartments. Meals are taken on one's own, in residences, in restaurants.

Costs (2003-2004) • One term: $5872. Yearlong program: $11,745; includes housing, all meals, student support services, in-state tuition and fees. $150 nonrefundable deposit required. Financial aid available for students from sponsoring institution: all customary sources.

For More Information • University at Albany, State University of New York, Office of International Education, LI 66, Albany, NY 12222; *Phone:* 518-442-3525; *Fax:* 518-442-3338. *E-mail:* intled@uamail.albany.edu. *World Wide Web:* http://www.albany.edu/intled/

BODO

BODO REGIONAL UNIVERSITY
STUDY ABROAD AT BODO

Hosted by Bodo Regional University

Academic Focus • Full curriculum.

Program Information • Students attend classes at Bodo Regional University. Field trips; optional travel to Lofoten Islands at an extra cost.

Sessions • Fall, spring, yearlong.

Eligibility Requirements • Minimum age 18; open to freshmen, sophomores, juniors, seniors, graduate students, adults; good academic standing at home school; no foreign language proficiency required.

Living Arrangements • Students live in host institution dormitories, program-owned apartments. Quarters are shared with host institution students. Meals are taken on one's own, in residences.

Costs (2004) • One term: NKr600. Yearlong program: NKr1200; includes tuition, student support services.

For More Information • Ms. Monica Herman Brobakk, International Coordinator, Bodo Regional University, 8049 Bodo, Norway; *Phone:* +47-7551 7803; *Fax:* +47-7551 7551. *E-mail:* admission@hibo.no. *World Wide Web:* http://www.hibo.no/

MOSS

UNIVERSITY OF NORTH DAKOTA
UND–AMERICAN COLLEGE OF NORWAY–STUDY IN NORWAY

Hosted by American College of Norway

Academic Focus • Area studies, art, communications, history, international business, Norwegian, political science and government, sociology.

Program Information • Students attend classes at American College of Norway. Scheduled travel to Lillehammer, Scandinavian sites; field trips to Oslo, Norwegian sites, Denmark; optional travel to Europe at an extra cost.

Sessions • Fall, spring, yearlong.

Eligibility Requirements • Minimum age 18; open to freshmen, sophomores, juniors, seniors; 2.5 GPA; 2 letters of recommendation; good academic standing at home school; no foreign language proficiency required.

Living Arrangements • Students live in host institution dormitories. Quarters are shared with host institution students. Meals are taken as a group, in residences, in central dining facility.

Costs (2002-2003) • One term: $7900. Yearlong program: $15,800; includes tuition, housing, all meals, international airfare, books and class materials, student support services, fees. $25 application fee. $100 refundable deposit required. Financial aid available for all students: scholarships, loans.

For More Information • Mr. Raymond Lagasse, Assistant Director for Education Abroad, University of North Dakota, Box 7901, Grand Forks, ND 58202-7109; *Phone:* 701-777-2938; *Fax:* 701-777-4773. *E-mail:* raymond.lagasse@mail.uivd.nodak.edu. *World Wide Web:* http://www.und.nodak.edu/dept/oip/. Students may also apply through American College of Norway, Sortunveien 22, 1513 Moss, Norway.

OSLO

HIGHER EDUCATION CONSORTIUM FOR URBAN AFFAIRS (HECUA)
SCANDINAVIAN URBAN STUDIES TERM

Hosted by University of Oslo

Academic Focus • Art history, economics, environmental science/studies, interdisciplinary studies, international affairs, liberal studies, literature, Norwegian, political science and government, public policy, Scandinavian studies, social sciences, sociology, urban studies.

Program Information • Students attend classes at University of Oslo. Scheduled travel to Stockholm, Tallinn; field trips to government offices, agencies, galleries, performances in Oslo, homestays and projects in other parts of Norway, a walk and sleep in the woods.

Sessions • Fall.

Eligibility Requirements • Open to sophomores, juniors, seniors, graduate students, adults; 2.5 GPA; 1 letter of recommendation; good academic standing at home school; no foreign language proficiency required.

Living Arrangements • Students live in host institution dormitories, host family homes. Quarters are shared with host institution students. Meals are taken on one's own, in residences.

Costs (2003) • One term: $12,100; includes tuition, housing, all meals, insurance, excursions, student support services. $75 application fee. $400 nonrefundable deposit required. Financial aid available for all students: scholarships.

For More Information • Mr. Michael Eaton, Director of Admissions and Student Services, Higher Education Consortium for Urban Affairs (HECUA), 2233 University Avenue West, Suite 210, St. Paul, MN 55114-1629; *Phone:* 800-554-1089; *Fax:* 651-659-9421. *E-mail:* info@hecua.org. *World Wide Web:* http://www.hecua.org/

UNIVERSITY STUDIES ABROAD CONSORTIUM
FULL-CURRICULUM STUDIES: OSLO, NORWAY

Hosted by University of Oslo

Academic Focus • Full curriculum.

Program Information • Students attend classes at University of Oslo. Field trips.

Sessions • Fall, spring, yearlong.

Eligibility Requirements • Minimum age 18; open to juniors, seniors, graduate students, adults; 3.0 GPA; good academic standing at home school; no foreign language proficiency required.

Living Arrangements • Students live in host institution dormitories. Quarters are shared with host institution students. Meals are taken on one's own, in residences, in central dining facility.

Costs (2005-2006) • One term: $3980. Yearlong program: $6980; includes tuition, insurance. $50 application fee. $150 refundable deposit required. Financial aid available for all students: scholarships.

For More Information • University Studies Abroad Consortium, USAC/323, Reno, NV 89557-0093; *Phone:* 775-784-6569; *Fax:* 775-784-6010. *E-mail:* usac@unr.edu. *World Wide Web:* http://usac.unr.edu/

PANAMA

PANAMA CITY

FLORIDA STATE UNIVERSITY
PANAMA: PANAMA CITY PROGRAM

Hosted by Florida State University–Panama Campus

Academic Focus • Cultural studies, ecology, full curriculum, Spanish language and literature.

Program Information • Students attend classes at Florida State University–Panama Campus. Field trips to the Panama Canal, snorkeling.

Sessions • Fall, spring, yearlong, application deadlines differ for internship applicants.

Eligibility Requirements • Open to freshmen, sophomores, juniors, seniors, graduate students; 2.5 GPA; good academic standing at home school; no foreign language proficiency required.

Living Arrangements • Students live in duplexes (3-4 bedrooms). Quarters are shared with host institution students. Meals are taken on one's own, in residences, in restaurants.

Costs (2002-2003) • One term: $5690. Yearlong program: $11,380; includes tuition, housing, insurance, excursions, international student ID, student support services, program T-shirt. $50 application fee. $500 nonrefundable deposit required. Financial aid available for students from sponsoring institution: scholarships, work study, loans.

For More Information • International Programs, Florida State University, A5500 University Center, Tallahassee, FL 32306-2420; *Phone:* 850-644-3272; *Fax:* 850-644-8817. *E-mail:* intprog@www.fsu.edu. *World Wide Web:* http://www.international.fsu.edu/. Students may also apply through Florida State University Panama Branch, Center Cultural Chino, Panama Boulevard, El Dorado, Panama City, Panama.

SCHOOL FOR INTERNATIONAL TRAINING, SIT STUDY ABROAD
PANAMA: DEVELOPMENT AND CONSERVATION

Academic Focus • Conservation studies, ecology, environmental science/studies, Latin American studies, Spanish language and literature.

Program Information • Faculty members are drawn from the sponsor's U.S. staff and local instructors hired by the sponsor. Scheduled travel to Bocas del Toro Archipelago, Darien Province Rainforest, Barú Volcano; field trips to Canal Zone, tropical ecology and conservation research institutes.

Sessions • Fall, spring.

Eligibility Requirements • Open to sophomores, juniors, seniors; course work in environmental studies, ecology, biology, or related field; 2.5 GPA; 2 letters of recommendation; good academic standing at home school; 1.5 years of college course work in Spanish.

Living Arrangements • Students live in host institution dormitories, host family homes. Meals are taken as a group, on one's own, with host family, in residences, in restaurants.

Costs (2003-2004) • One term: $12,550; includes tuition, housing, all meals, insurance, excursions. $50 application fee. $400 nonrefundable deposit required. Financial aid available for all students: scholarships.

For More Information • School for International Training, SIT Study Abroad, Kipling Road, Brattleboro, VT 05302-0676; *Phone:* 888-272-7881; *Fax:* 802-258-3296. *E-mail:* studyabroad@sit.edu. *World Wide Web:* http://www.sit.edu/studyabroad/

PERU

CITY TO CITY

PROWORLD SERVICE CORPS
PROWORLD SERVICE CORPS

Hosted by Peruvian University of Applied Sciences

Academic Focus • Community service, environmental science/studies, Latin American literature, Latin American studies, public policy, Quechua, social sciences, social work, Spanish language and literature.

Program Information • Students attend classes at Peruvian University of Applied Sciences (Lima). Scheduled travel to Machu Picchu, Bolivia, Lake Titicaca; field trips to Machu Picchu, Incan ruins, Glacier Lakes; optional travel to a rainforest, Peruvian coast at an extra cost.

Sessions • Fall, spring.

Eligibility Requirements • Minimum age 18; open to freshmen, sophomores, juniors, seniors, graduate students; good academic standing at home school; desire to learn and help others; no foreign language proficiency required.

Living Arrangements • Students live in host family homes. Quarters are shared with host institution students. Meals are taken with host family, in residences.

Costs (2003) • One term: $8750; includes tuition, housing, all meals, insurance, excursions, books and class materials, lab equipment, international student ID, student support services. $50 application fee. $200 refundable deposit required. Financial aid available for all students: scholarships.

For More Information • Mr. Nick Bryngelson, Director of Operations, ProWorld Service Corps, PO Box 21121, Billings, MT 59104-1121; *Phone:* 877-733-7378; *Fax:* 406-252-3973. *E-mail:* nick@proworldsc.org. *World Wide Web:* http://properu.org/

CUSCO

ALMA COLLEGE
ALMA IN PERU (CUSCO)

Hosted by Academia Latinoamericana

Academic Focus • Cultural studies, Spanish language and literature.

Program Information • Students attend classes at Academia Latinoamericana. Field trips to Pipon, Pisac, Chinchero; optional travel to Machu Picchu, the Temple of the Sun at an extra cost.

Sessions • Fall, spring, winter, yearlong, fall and winter semesters.

Eligibility Requirements • Minimum age 18; open to sophomores, juniors, seniors, graduate students, adults; 2.5 GPA; 2 letters of recommendation; no foreign language proficiency required.

Living Arrangements • Students live in host family homes. Meals are taken with host family, in residences.

Costs (2002-2003) • One term: $6300. Yearlong program: $11,600; includes tuition, housing, some meals, insurance, excursions, books and class materials, international student ID, student support services. $50 application fee. $200 refundable deposit required. Financial aid available for all students: scholarships.

For More Information • Ms. Julie Elenbaas, Office Coordinator, Alma College, 614 West Superior Street, Alma, MI 48801-1599; *Phone:* 989-463-7055; *Fax:* 989-463-7126. *E-mail:* intl_studies@alma.edu. *World Wide Web:* http://international.alma.edu/

LIMA

COLLEGE CONSORTIUM FOR INTERNATIONAL STUDIES–TOMPKINS-CORTLAND COMMUNITY COLLEGE-STATE UNIVERSITY OF NEW YORK
SEMESTER IN PERU–SPANISH LANGUAGE/ADVERTISING AND PUBLICITY

Hosted by Instituto Peruano de Publicidad

Academic Focus • Advertising and public relations, Latin American studies, Spanish language and literature.

Program Information • Students attend classes at Instituto Peruano de Publicidad. Scheduled travel to historic sites; field trips to museums, galleries, historic sites; optional travel to Machu Picchu, beach areas, Cuzco at an extra cost.

Sessions • Fall, spring.

Eligibility Requirements • Minimum age 18; open to freshmen, sophomores, juniors, seniors, adults; 2.5 GPA; 3 letters of recommendation; foreign language requirement dependent on track chosen.

Living Arrangements • Students live in locally rented apartments, hotels. Quarters are shared with host institution students, students from other programs. Meals are taken on one's own, in residences.

Costs (2004) • One term: $3815; includes tuition, some meals, insurance, excursions, books and class materials, student support services. $200 nonrefundable deposit required. Financial aid available for students from sponsoring institution: scholarships, loans.

For More Information • Mr. Miguel Angel Piery, Coordinator of Study Abroad Programs, College Consortium for International Studies–Tompkins-Cortland Community College-State University of New York, PO Box 139, Dryden, NY 13053; *Phone:* 607-844-8211; *Fax:* 607-844-6543. *E-mail:* pierym@sunytccc.edu. *World Wide Web:* http://www.ccisabroad.org/

UNIVERSITY OF VIRGINIA
PROGRAM IN PERU

Hosted by Pontifical Catholic University of Peru

Academic Focus • Full curriculum.

Program Information • Students attend classes at Pontifical Catholic University of Peru. Field trips to museums, archaeological sites; optional travel to Cuzco, Machu Picchu, the Amazon forest at an extra cost.

Sessions • Fall.

Eligibility Requirements • Open to freshmen, sophomores, juniors, seniors, graduate students, adults; 2.8 GPA; 1 letter of recommendation; no foreign language proficiency required.

Living Arrangements • Students live in host family homes. Meals are taken with host family, in residences.

Costs (2004) • One term: $7400; includes tuition, housing, all meals, excursions, books and class materials, student support services, transport from Lima airport to host home. $200 application fee. Financial aid available for students from sponsoring institution: scholarships, loans, delayed payment schedule.

For More Information • Mr. Jorge Secada, Director, University of Virginia Program in Perú, University of Virginia, International Studies Office, 208 Minor Hall, UVA, PO Box 400165, Charlottesville, VA 22904-4165; *Phone:* 434-924-6918; *Fax:* 434-924-6927. *E-mail:* jes2f@virginia.edu. *World Wide Web:* http://www.virginia.edu/iso/

PHILIPPINES

LOS BAÑOS

MICHIGAN STATE UNIVERSITY
MULTIDISCIPLINARY STUDIES IN THE PHILIPPINES

Hosted by University of the Philippines at Los Baños

Academic Focus • Agriculture, forestry, natural resources, social sciences.

Program Information • Students attend classes at University of the Philippines at Los Baños.

Sessions • Fall, spring, internship.

Eligibility Requirements • Minimum age 18; open to sophomores, juniors, seniors; 2.5 GPA; good academic standing at home school; faculty approval; interview; no foreign language proficiency required.

Living Arrangements • Students live in host institution dormitories, locally rented apartments. Quarters are shared with host institution students. Meals are taken on one's own, in central dining facility, in restaurants.

Costs (2002-2003) • One term: $4000 (estimated); includes housing, all meals, insurance, excursions, international airfare, books and class materials, student support services. $100 application fee. Financial aid available for students from sponsoring institution: scholarships, loans.

For More Information • Ms. Sherry Martinez-Bonilla, Office Assistant, Michigan State University, Office of Study Abroad, 109 International Center, East Lansing, MI 48824-1035; *Phone:* 517-353-8920; *Fax:* 517-432-2082. *E-mail:* marti269@msu.edu. *World Wide Web:* http://studyabroad.msu.edu/

MANILA

THE INTERNATIONAL PARTNERSHIP FOR SERVICE LEARNING
PHILIPPINES SERVICE–LEARNING

Hosted by Trinity College

Academic Focus • Asian studies, community service, international affairs, liberal studies, Pacific studies, social sciences.

Program Information • Students attend classes at Trinity College. Field trips to sites around Manila, Baguio; optional travel at an extra cost.

Sessions • Fall, spring, yearlong.

Eligibility Requirements • Minimum age 18; open to freshmen, sophomores, juniors, seniors, graduate students, adults; 2 letters of

PHILIPPINES
Manila

recommendation; good academic standing at home school; evidence of maturity, responsibility; no foreign language proficiency required.
Living Arrangements • Students live in host institution dormitories, locally rented apartments. Quarters are shared with host institution students. Meals are taken on one's own, in central dining facility.
Costs (2003-2004) • One term: $8200. Yearlong program: $15,900; includes tuition, housing, some meals. $50 application fee. $250 refundable deposit required. Financial aid available for all students: scholarships, federal financial aid.
For More Information • Ms. Ilana Golin, Coordinator of Student Programs, The International Partnership for Service Learning, 815 Second Avenue, Suite 315, New York, NY 10017-4594; *Phone:* 212-986-0989; *Fax:* 212-986-5039. *E-mail:* info@ipsl.org. *World Wide Web:* http://www.ipsl.org/

POLAND
KRAKOW

ACADEMIC PROGRAMS INTERNATIONAL (API)
(API)–KRAKOW, POLAND

Hosted by Jagiellonian University
Academic Focus • Art history, biological/life sciences, European studies, history, Polish, Polish studies, religious studies, science.
Program Information • Students attend classes at Jagiellonian University. Scheduled travel to Budapest; field trips to Gdansk, Ojców National Park, Auschwitz, the Wieliczka Salt Mine, Warsaw, Zakopane.
Sessions • Fall, spring, yearlong.
Eligibility Requirements • Minimum age 18; open to freshmen, sophomores, juniors, seniors, graduate students, adults; 2.75 GPA; 1 letter of recommendation; good academic standing at home school; official transcript from home university; no foreign language proficiency required.
Living Arrangements • Students live in host institution dormitories, locally rented apartments, host family homes. Quarters are shared with host institution students. Meals are taken on one's own, with host family, in residences, in central dining facility, in restaurants.
Costs (2004-2005) • One term: $8800–$9000. Yearlong program: $17,400; includes tuition, housing, insurance, excursions, student support services, airport pick-up, ground transportation. $150 nonrefundable deposit required. Financial aid available for all students: scholarships.
For More Information • Ms. Jennifer C. Allen, Director, Academic Programs International (API), 107 East Hopkins, San Marco, TX 78666; *Phone:* 800-844-4124; *Fax:* 512-392-8420. *E-mail:* api@academicintl.com. *World Wide Web:* http://www.academicintl.com/

CENTRAL EUROPEAN EDUCATION AND CULTURAL EXCHANGE (CEECE)
CEECE IN KRAKOW POLAND

Hosted by Jagiellonian University
Academic Focus • Central European studies, Eastern European studies, Polish, Polish studies.
Program Information • Students attend classes at Jagiellonian University. Field trips to the Tatra mountains, Zakopane, Auschwitz, Birkenau; optional travel to Berlin, Vienna, Budapest, Prague, Munich at an extra cost.
Sessions • Fall, spring, yearlong.
Eligibility Requirements • Minimum age 18; open to freshmen, sophomores, juniors, seniors, graduate students, adults; 2.0 GPA; good academic standing at home school; no foreign language proficiency required.
Living Arrangements • Students live in host institution dormitories. Quarters are shared with host institution students. Meals are taken on one's own, in central dining facility, in restaurants.
Costs (2004) • One term: $7999. Yearlong program: $13,998; includes tuition, housing, excursions, books and class materials,

student support services, transport pass, pre-paid cell phone. $300 refundable deposit required. Financial aid available for all students: home university financial aid.
For More Information • Mr Eric Molengraf, Executive Director, Central European Education and Cultural Exchange (CEECE), 2956 Florence Drive, Grand Rapids, MI 49418; *Phone:* 800-352-9845. *E-mail:* info@ceece.org. *World Wide Web:* http://www.ceece.org/

LEXIA INTERNATIONAL
LEXIA IN KRAKOW

Hosted by Jagiellonian University
Academic Focus • Anthropology, area studies, art, art history, Central European studies, civilization studies, comparative history, cultural studies, drawing/painting, Eastern European studies, economics, environmental science/studies, ethnic studies, film and media studies, fine/studio arts, geography, history, interdisciplinary studies, international affairs, international business, liberal studies, literature, music, music history, music performance, peace and conflict studies, philosophy, Polish, Polish studies, political science and government, psychology, religious studies, Slavic languages, social sciences, sociology, urban studies.
Program Information • Students attend classes at Jagiellonian University. Field trips to Warsaw, Gdansk, Auschwitz, Birkenau, Berlin, Prague.
Sessions • Fall, spring, yearlong.
Eligibility Requirements • Minimum age 18; open to sophomores, juniors, seniors, graduate students, adults; 2.5 GPA; 2 letters of recommendation; no foreign language proficiency required.
Living Arrangements • Students live in host institution dormitories, host family homes. Quarters are shared with host institution students. Meals are taken on one's own, with host family, in residences, in central dining facility, in restaurants.
Costs (2002-2003) • One term: $9450. Yearlong program: $18,350; includes tuition, housing, some meals, insurance, excursions, student support services, computer access, transcript. $35 application fee. $300 refundable deposit required. Financial aid available for all students: scholarships, work study.
For More Information • Lexia International, 23 South Main Street, Hanover, NH 03755; *Phone:* 800-775-3942; *Fax:* 603-643-9899. *E-mail:* info@lexiaintl.org. *World Wide Web:* http://www.lexiaintl.org/

UNIVERSITY OF WISCONSIN–STEVENS POINT
SEMESTER IN EAST CENTRAL EUROPE: KRAKOW, POLAND

Hosted by Jagiellonian University
Academic Focus • Art history, geography, history, Polish, Polish studies, political science and government.
Program Information • Students attend classes at Jagiellonian University. Scheduled travel to Hungary, Czech and Slovakian Republics, Germany, Austria; field trips to Auschwitz, Zakopane, Warsaw, Gdansk.
Sessions • Fall.
Eligibility Requirements • Minimum age 18; open to freshmen, sophomores, juniors, seniors, adults; 2.25 GPA; 3 letters of recommendation; good academic standing at home school; no foreign language proficiency required.
Living Arrangements • Students live in host institution dormitories, locally rented apartments. Quarters are shared with host institution students, students from other programs. Meals are taken as a group, in central dining facility.
Costs (2003-2004) • One term: $5700 for Wisconsin residents; $13,000 for nonresidents (estimated); includes tuition, housing, all meals, excursions, international airfare, books and class materials. $15 application fee. $150 nonrefundable deposit required. Financial aid available for all students: scholarships, work study, loans.
For More Information • Mr. Mark Koepke, Associate Director, University of Wisconsin–Stevens Point, International Programs Office, Stevens Point, WI 54481; *Phone:* 715-346-2717; *Fax:* 715-346-3591. *E-mail:* intlprog@uwsp.edu. *World Wide Web:* http://www.uwsp.edu/studyabroad/

LUBLIN

LOCK HAVEN UNIVERSITY OF PENNSYLVANIA
SEMESTER IN POLAND

Hosted by Maria Curie Sklodowska University Lublin
Academic Focus • Cultural studies, economics, history, Polish, Polish studies.
Program Information • Students attend classes at Maria Curie Sklodowska University Lublin. Field trips.
Sessions • Spring.
Eligibility Requirements • Minimum age 18; open to sophomores, juniors, seniors, adults; 2.5 GPA; 3 letters of recommendation; good academic standing at home school; no foreign language proficiency required.
Living Arrangements • Students live in hotels. Quarters are shared with students from other programs. Meals are taken in central dining facility.
Costs (2003) • One term: $5450 for Pennsylvania residents; $7360 for nonresidents; includes tuition, housing, all meals, fees. $50 application fee. Financial aid available for all students: scholarships, loans.
For More Information • Dean, Institute for International Studies, Lock Haven University of Pennsylvania, Lock Haven, PA 17745-2390; *Phone:* 570-893-2140; *Fax:* 570-893-2537. *E-mail:* intlstudies_webmonitor@lhup.edu. *World Wide Web:* http://www.lhup.edu/international/goingp/goingplaces_index.htm

WARSAW

CIEE
CIEE STUDY CENTER AT THE WARSAW SCHOOL OF ECONOMICS, POLAND

Hosted by Warsaw School of Economics
Academic Focus • Central European studies, economics, finance, history, international business, Jewish studies, literature, marketing, Polish, political science and government, popular culture, sociology.
Program Information • Students attend classes at Warsaw School of Economics. Scheduled travel to Krakow, Auschwitz; field trips to Warsaw museums, sites of cultural interest in and around Warsaw.
Sessions • Fall, spring.
Eligibility Requirements • Open to sophomores, juniors, seniors, graduate students, adults; 2.75 GPA; 2 letters of recommendation; no foreign language proficiency required.
Living Arrangements • Students live in host institution dormitories. Quarters are shared with host institution students. Meals are taken on one's own, in central dining facility, in restaurants.
Costs (2003-2004) • One term: $8100; includes tuition, housing, insurance, excursions, books and class materials, student support services, cultural activities, pre-departure advisers, optional on-site pick-up. $30 application fee. $300 deposit required. Financial aid available for all students: minority student scholarships, non-traditional study scholarships, travel grants.
For More Information • Ms. Hannah McChesney, Admissions Officer Europe, Middle East, and Africa, CIEE, 7 Custom House Street, 3rd Floor, Portland, ME 04101; *Phone:* 800-40-STUDY; *Fax:* 207-553-7699. *E-mail:* studyinfo@ciee.org. *World Wide Web:* http://www.ciee.org/isp/

PORTUGAL

COIMBRA

UNIVERSITY OF WISCONSIN–MADISON
COIMBRA, PORTUGAL

Hosted by University of Coimbra
Academic Focus • Portuguese, Portuguese studies, social sciences.
Program Information • Students attend classes at University of Coimbra. Field trips to Lisbon, Oporto.
Sessions • Fall, spring, yearlong.

Eligibility Requirements • Open to juniors, seniors; 2 letters of recommendation; minimum 2.5 GPA overall; minimum 3.0 GPA in Portuguese; 1 year of college course work in Portuguese.
Living Arrangements • Students live in host institution dormitories, locally rented apartments. Quarters are shared with host institution students, students from other programs. Meals are taken on one's own, in residences.
Costs (2003-2004) • One term: $8800 for Wisconsin residents; $12,050 for nonresidents. Yearlong program: $14,350 for Wisconsin residents $19,040 for nonresidents; includes tuition, housing, all meals, insurance, excursions, international airfare, books and class materials, student support services. $100 nonrefundable deposit required. Financial aid available for students from sponsoring institution: scholarships, loans.
For More Information • Peer Advisor, University of Wisconsin–Madison, International Academic Programs, 261 Bascom, 500 Lincoln Drive, Madison, WI 53706; *Phone:* 608-265-6329; *Fax:* 608-262-6998. *E-mail:* peeradvisor@bascom.wisc.edu. *World Wide Web:* http://www.studyabroad.wisc.edu/

PUERTO RICO

PONCE

RIDER UNIVERSITY
STUDY ABROAD IN PUERTO RICO

Hosted by Pontifical Catholic University of Puerto Rico
Academic Focus • Bilingual education, Puerto Rican studies, Spanish language and literature.
Program Information • Students attend classes at Pontifical Catholic University of Puerto Rico.
Sessions • Fall, spring, yearlong.
Eligibility Requirements • Open to sophomores, juniors, seniors; 2.5 GPA; 1 letter of recommendation; good academic standing at home school; 2 years of college course work in Spanish.
Living Arrangements • Students live in host institution dormitories, locally rented apartments, host family homes. Quarters are shared with host institution students. Meals are taken on one's own, in residences, in central dining facility, in restaurants.
Costs (2001-2002) • One term: $8995. Yearlong program: $17,990; includes tuition, student support services, administrative fees. $35 application fee. $300 refundable deposit required. Financial aid available for students from sponsoring institution: regular financial aid.
For More Information • Dr. Joseph E. Nadeau, Director of Study Abroad, Rider University, 2083 Lawrenceville Road, Lawrenceville, NJ 08648; *Phone:* 609-896-5314; *Fax:* 609-895-5670. *E-mail:* nadeau@rider.edu. *World Wide Web:* http://www.rider.edu/academic/uwp/index.htm

SAN JUAN

STATE UNIVERSITY OF NEW YORK AT OSWEGO
UNIVERSITY OF PUERTO RICO–RIO PIEDRAS

Hosted by University of Puerto Rico Rio Piedras
Academic Focus • Full curriculum.
Program Information • Students attend classes at University of Puerto Rico Rio Piedras.
Sessions • Fall, spring, yearlong.
Eligibility Requirements • Open to sophomores, juniors, seniors; 2.5 GPA; 3 letters of recommendation; good academic standing at home school; language proficiency form; personal study statement; 2 years of college course work in Spanish.
Living Arrangements • Students live in host institution dormitories. Quarters are shared with host institution students. Meals are taken on one's own, in residences, in central dining facility, in restaurants.
Costs (2003-2004) • One term: $3020. Yearlong program: $6040; includes tuition, housing, student support services. $250 nonrefund-

able deposit required. Financial aid available for students: home university financial aid, loan processing and scholarships for Oswego students.

For More Information • Ms. Lizette Alvarado, Program Specialist, State University of New York at Oswego, 122A Swetman Hall, Oswego, NY 13126; *Phone:* 888-4-OSWEGO; *Fax:* 315-312-2477. *E-mail:* intled@oswego.edu. *World Wide Web:* http://www.oswego. edu/intled/

UNIVERSITY AT ALBANY, STATE UNIVERSITY OF NEW YORK
DIRECT ENROLLMENT AT THE UNIVERSITY OF THE SACRED HEART

Hosted by University of the Sacred Heart

Academic Focus • Biological/life sciences, business administration/ management, communications, education, full curriculum, history, Latin American studies, liberal studies, social sciences, Spanish language and literature.

Program Information • Students attend classes at University of the Sacred Heart.

Sessions • Fall, spring, yearlong.

Eligibility Requirements • Open to sophomores, juniors, seniors, adults; 2 letters of recommendation; good academic standing at home school; advanced college course work in Spanish or the equivalent.

Living Arrangements • Students live in host institution dormitories, locally rented apartments. Meals are taken on one's own.

Costs (2002-2003) • One term: $5243. Yearlong program: $10,486; includes housing, all meals, student support services, in-state tuition and fees. $15 application fee. $150 nonrefundable deposit required. Financial aid available for students from sponsoring institution: all customary sources.

For More Information • University at Albany, State University of New York, Office of International Education, LI 66, Albany, NY 12222; *Phone:* 518-442-3525; *Fax:* 518-442-3338. *E-mail:* intled@ uamail.albany.edu. *World Wide Web:* http://www.albany.edu/intled/

RUSSIA

CITY TO CITY
ACIE (ACTR/ACCELS)
ACIE–NIS REGIONAL LANGUAGE TRAINING PROGRAM– RUSSIA

Academic Focus • Cultural studies, language studies.

Program Information • Faculty members are local instructors hired by the sponsor.

Sessions • Fall, spring, yearlong.

Eligibility Requirements • Minimum age 18; open to sophomores, juniors, seniors, graduate students, adults; 3 letters of recommendation; good academic standing at home school; 1 year of college course work in Russian.

Living Arrangements • Students live in host institution dormitories, locally rented apartments, host family homes. Quarters are shared with students from other programs. Meals are taken on one's own, with host family, in residences, in restaurants.

Costs (2002-2003) • One term: contact sponsor for cost. Yearlong program: contact sponsor for cost. $35 application fee. $500 nonrefundable deposit required. Financial aid available for all students: scholarships.

For More Information • Ms. Margaret Stephenson, Russian and Eurasian Program Officer, ACIE (ACTR/ACCELS), 1776 Massachusetts Avenue, NW, Suite 700, Washington, DC 20036; *Phone:* 202-833-7522; *Fax:* 202-833-7523. *E-mail:* outbound@actr.org. *World Wide Web:* http://www.actr.org/

IRKUTSK
MIDDLEBURY COLLEGE SCHOOLS ABROAD
SCHOOL IN RUSSIA–IRKUTSK PROGRAM

Hosted by Irkutsk State University

Academic Focus • Anthropology, environmental science/studies, history, linguistics, Russian language and literature.

Program Information • Students attend classes at Irkutsk State University. Scheduled travel to Mongolia; field trips to Lake Baikal, Listvyanka, Ulan-Ude.

Sessions • Fall, spring, yearlong.

Eligibility Requirements • Open to sophomores, juniors, seniors; 2.7 GPA; 2 letters of recommendation; minimum grade of B in Russian and in major; 2 years of college course work in Russian.

Living Arrangements • Students live in host family homes. Meals are taken with host family, in residences.

Costs (2004-2005) • One term: $11,440. Yearlong program: $21,940; includes tuition, housing, some meals, insurance, excursions, international airfare, student support services, visa fees, deorientation. $50 application fee. $300 nonrefundable deposit required. Financial aid available for students from sponsoring institution: scholarships, loans.

For More Information • Mr. Jamie Northrup, University Relations Coordinator, Middlebury College Schools Abroad, Office of Off-Campus Study, Sunderland Language Center, Middlebury, VT 05753; *Phone:* 802-443-5745; *Fax:* 802-443-3157. *E-mail:* schoolsabroad@ middlebury.edu. *World Wide Web:* http://www.middlebury.edu/ msa/

KEMEROVO
LOCK HAVEN UNIVERSITY OF PENNSYLVANIA
SEMESTER IN RUSSIA

Hosted by Kemerovo State University

Academic Focus • Art, history, Russian language and literature, Russian studies.

Program Information • Students attend classes at Kemerovo State University.

Sessions • Fall, spring, yearlong.

Eligibility Requirements • Minimum age 18; open to sophomores, juniors, seniors; 2.5 GPA; 3 letters of recommendation; good academic standing at home school; no foreign language proficiency required.

Living Arrangements • Students live in host institution dormitories, locally rented apartments. Quarters are shared with host institution students. Meals are taken in central dining facility.

Costs (2002-2003) • One term: $5450 for Pennsylvania residents; $7360 for nonresidents. Yearlong program: $10,900 for Pennsylvania residents; $14,720 for nonresidents; includes tuition, housing, all meals, fees. $50 application fee. Financial aid available for students from sponsoring institution: scholarships, loans.

For More Information • Dean, Institute for International Studies, Lock Haven University of Pennsylvania, Lock Haven, PA 17745-2390; *Phone:* 570-893-2140; *Fax:* 570-893-2537. *E-mail:* intlstudies_webmonitor@lhup.edu. *World Wide Web:* http://www. lhup.edu/international/goingp/goingplaces_index.htm

KRASNODAR
ASSOCIATED COLLEGES OF THE MIDWEST
ACM RUSSIA PROGRAM

Hosted by Kuban State University

Academic Focus • Art, economics, history, literature, religious studies, Russian language and literature, Russian studies.

Program Information • Students attend classes at Kuban State University. Scheduled travel to Moscow, St. Petersburg; field trips to Sochi, Taman.

Sessions • Fall.

Eligibility Requirements • Open to sophomores, juniors, seniors; 3 letters of recommendation; good academic standing at home school; 1 year of college course work in Russian.

Living Arrangements • Students live in host family homes. Meals are taken on one's own, with host family, in residences.

Costs (2003) • One term: contact sponsor for cost. $400 nonrefundable deposit required.

For More Information • Program Associate, Russia Program, Associated Colleges of the Midwest, 205 West Wacker Drive, Suite 1300, Chicago, IL 60606; *Phone:* 312-263-5000; *Fax:* 312-263-5879. *E-mail:* acm@acm.edu. *World Wide Web:* http://www.acm.edu/

MOSCOW

ACIE (ACTR/ACCELS)
ACIE (ACTR) ADVANCED RUSSIAN LANGUAGE AND AREA STUDIES PROGRAM IN MOSCOW

Hosted by International University in Moscow
Academic Focus • Russian language and literature, Russian studies.
Program Information • Students attend classes at International University in Moscow. Scheduled travel to Gaden Ring, St. Petersburg, Kazan, Sochi; field trips to museums, churches, historic sites.
Sessions • Fall, spring, yearlong.
Eligibility Requirements • Minimum age 18; open to sophomores, juniors, seniors, graduate students, adults; 3 letters of recommendation; good academic standing at home school; 2 years of college course work in Russian.
Living Arrangements • Students live in host institution dormitories, host family homes. Meals are taken on one's own, with host family, in residences, in central dining facility, in restaurants.
Costs (2002-2003) • One term: contact sponsor for cost. Yearlong program: contact sponsor for cost. $35 application fee. $500 nonrefundable deposit required. Financial aid available for all students: scholarships.
For More Information • Ms. Margaret Stephenson, Russian and Eurasian Program Officer, ACIE (ACTR/ACCELS), 1776 Massachusetts Avenue, NW, Suite 700, Washington, DC 20036; *Phone:* 202-833-7522; *Fax:* 202-833-7523. *E-mail:* outbound@actr.org. *World Wide Web:* http://www.actr.org/

ACIE (ACTR/ACCELS)
ACIE (ACTR) BUSINESS RUSSIAN LANGUAGE AND INTERNSHIP PROGRAM IN MOSCOW

Hosted by International University in Moscow
Academic Focus • Area studies, international business, Russian language and literature.
Program Information • Students attend classes at International University in Moscow.
Sessions • Fall, spring, yearlong.
Eligibility Requirements • Minimum age 18; open to sophomores, juniors, seniors, graduate students, adults; 3 letters of recommendation; good academic standing at home school; 1 year of college course work in Russian.
Living Arrangements • Students live in host institution dormitories, host family homes. Meals are taken on one's own, with host family, in residences, in central dining facility, in restaurants.
Costs (2002-2003) • One term: contact sponsor for cost. Yearlong program: contact sponsor for cost. $35 application fee. $500 nonrefundable deposit required. Financial aid available for all students: scholarships.
For More Information • Ms. Margaret Stephenson, Russian and Eurasian Program Officer, ACIE (ACTR/ACCELS), 1776 Massachusetts Avenue, NW, Suite 700, Washington, DC 20036; *Phone:* 202-833-7522; *Fax:* 202-833-7523. *E-mail:* outbound@actr.org. *World Wide Web:* http://www.actr.org/

ACIE (ACTR/ACCELS)
ACIE (ACTR) INDIVIDUALIZED RUSSIAN LANGUAGE TRAINING PROGRAM IN MOSCOW

Hosted by International University in Moscow
Academic Focus • History, political science and government, Russian language and literature, Russian studies.
Program Information • Students attend classes at International University in Moscow. Scheduled travel; field trips.
Sessions • Fall, spring, yearlong.

Eligibility Requirements • Minimum age 18; open to sophomores, juniors, seniors, graduate students, adults; 3 letters of recommendation; good academic standing at home school; no foreign language proficiency required.
Living Arrangements • Students live in host institution dormitories, host family homes. Meals are taken on one's own, with host family, in residences, in central dining facility, in restaurants.
Costs (2002-2003) • One term: contact sponsor for cost. Yearlong program: contact sponsor for cost. $35 application fee. $500 nonrefundable deposit required. Financial aid available for all students: scholarships.
For More Information • Ms. Margaret Stephenson, Russian and Eurasian Program Officer, ACIE (ACTR/ACCELS), 1776 Massachusetts Avenue, NW, Suite 700, Washington, DC 20036; *Phone:* 202-833-7522; *Fax:* 202-833-7523. *E-mail:* outbound@actr.org. *World Wide Web:* http://www.actr.org/

COLLEGE CONSORTIUM FOR INTERNATIONAL STUDIES–TRUMAN STATE UNIVERSITY
TRUMAN IN MOSCOW

Hosted by Moscow Academy for the Humanities and Social Sciences
Academic Focus • Russian language and literature, Russian studies.
Program Information • Students attend classes at Moscow Academy for the Humanities and Social Sciences. Scheduled travel to Saint Petersburg; field trips to Moscow, the Golden Ring; optional travel to Siberia, Kiev, the Volga region at an extra cost.
Sessions • Fall, spring, yearlong.
Eligibility Requirements • Minimum age 18; open to sophomores, juniors, seniors, graduate students, adults; 2.5 GPA; 3 letters of recommendation; good academic standing at home school; no foreign language proficiency required.
Living Arrangements • Students live in host institution dormitories, host family homes. Quarters are shared with students from other programs. Meals are taken as a group, with host family, in residences, in central dining facility.
Costs (2004-2005) • One term: $5500. Yearlong program: $11,000; includes tuition, housing, all meals, insurance, excursions, student support services, visa fees. $300 nonrefundable deposit required. Financial aid available for students from sponsoring institution: scholarships, loans.
For More Information • Center for International Education Abroad, College Consortium for International Studies, Truman State University, Kirk Building 114, Kirksville, MO 63501; *Phone:* 660-785-4076; *Fax:* 660-785-7473. *E-mail:* ciea@truman.edu. *World Wide Web:* http://www.ccisabroad.org/

DICKINSON COLLEGE
DICKINSON IN MOSCOW (RUSSIA)

Hosted by Russian State University for the Humanities
Academic Focus • Russian language and literature, Russian studies.
Program Information • Students attend classes at Russian State University for the Humanities. Field trips.
Sessions • Fall, spring, yearlong.
Eligibility Requirements • Minimum age 18; open to juniors; 2.8 GPA; 3 letters of recommendation; good academic standing at home school; fluency in Russian.
Living Arrangements • Students live in host family homes. Meals are taken with host family, in residences.
Costs (2003-2004) • One term: $17,795. Yearlong program: $35,590; includes tuition, housing, all meals, excursions, student support services. $25 application fee. $300 nonrefundable deposit required. Financial aid available for students from sponsoring institution: scholarships, loans.
For More Information • Ms. Karen Peter, Program Manager, Dickinson College, PO Box 1773, Carlisle, PA 17013-2896; *Phone:* 717-245-1341; *Fax:* 717-245-1688. *E-mail:* global@dickinson.edu. *World Wide Web:* http://www.dickinson.edu/global/

RUSSIA
Moscow

THE INTERNATIONAL PARTNERSHIP FOR SERVICE LEARNING
RUSSIA SERVICE–LEARNING

Hosted by GRINT Centre for Education
Academic Focus • Russian language and literature, Russian studies, social sciences, Spanish language and literature.
Program Information • Students attend classes at GRINT Centre for Education. Scheduled travel to St. Petersburg, Tver (a provincial Russian town), Golden Ring towns; field trips to weekly theater, music, or circus performances; optional travel at an extra cost.
Sessions • Fall, spring, yearlong.
Eligibility Requirements • Minimum age 18; open to freshmen, sophomores, juniors, seniors, graduate students, adults; 2 letters of recommendation; good academic standing at home school; evidence of maturity, responsibility; no foreign language proficiency required.
Living Arrangements • Students live in host institution dormitories, host family homes, hostels or Institute of Youth. Quarters are shared with host institution students, students from other programs. Meals are taken on one's own, with host family, in residences.
Costs (2003-2004) • One term: $8600. Yearlong program: $15,800; includes tuition, housing, service placement and supervision. $50 application fee. $250 refundable deposit required. Financial aid available for all students: federal financial aid.
For More Information • Ms. Ilana Golin, Coordinator of Student Programs, The International Partnership for Service Learning, 815 Second Avenue, Suite 315, New York, NY 10017-4594; *Phone:* 212-986-0989; *Fax:* 212-986-5039. *E-mail:* info@ipsl.org. *World Wide Web:* http://www.ipsl.org/

MIDDLEBURY COLLEGE SCHOOLS ABROAD
SCHOOL IN RUSSIA–MOSCOW PROGRAM

Hosted by Russian State University for the Humanities
Academic Focus • History, liberal studies, linguistics, literature, Russian language and literature, social sciences.
Program Information • Students attend classes at Russian State University for the Humanities. Scheduled travel to St. Petersburg, Irkutsk, Baltics; field trips to Nizhnii Novgorod, Pskov, Suzdal; optional travel to Irkutsk, Europe, Baltics at an extra cost.
Sessions • Fall, spring, yearlong.
Eligibility Requirements • Open to sophomores, juniors, seniors, graduate students; 2.7 GPA; 2 letters of recommendation; good academic standing at home school; minimum grade of B in Russian; 2 years of college course work in Russian.
Living Arrangements • Students live in host family homes. Quarters are shared with host institution students. Meals are taken with host family, in residences.
Costs (2004-2005) • One term: $11,440. Yearlong program: $21,940; includes tuition, housing, some meals, insurance, excursions, international airfare, student support services, visa fees, language assessment, deorientation. $50 application fee. $300 nonrefundable deposit required. Financial aid available for students from sponsoring institution: scholarships, loans.
For More Information • Mr. Jamie Northrup, University Relations Coordinator, Middlebury College Schools Abroad, Office of Off-Campus Study, Sunderland Language Center, Middlebury, VT 05753; *Phone:* 802-443-5745; *Fax:* 802-443-3157. *E-mail:* schoolsabroad@middlebury.edu. *World Wide Web:* http://www.middlebury.edu/msa/

MONTCLAIR STATE UNIVERSITY
THE MOSCOW STATE CONSERVATORY

Hosted by The Moscow State Conservatory
Academic Focus • Music, music performance, Russian language and literature.
Program Information • Students attend classes at The Moscow State Conservatory. Field trips.
Sessions • Fall, spring, yearlong.
Eligibility Requirements • Minimum age 18; open to sophomores, juniors, seniors, graduate students, adults; course work in music; 3.0 GPA; 2 letters of recommendation; good academic standing at home school; completed application; curriculum vitae; no foreign language proficiency required.

Living Arrangements • Students live in host institution dormitories. Quarters are shared with host institution students, students from other programs. Meals are taken on one's own, in central dining facility.
Costs (2003-2004) • One term: $5000. Yearlong program: $10,000; includes tuition, housing, student support services. $300 application fee. $300 nonrefundable deposit required. Financial aid available for students from sponsoring institution: scholarships, loans.
For More Information • Ms. Tracy Hogan, Study Abroad Advisor, Montclair State University, Global Education Center, 22 Normal Avenue, Upper Montclair, NJ 07043; *Phone:* 973-655-4483; *Fax:* 973-655-7687. *E-mail:* hogant@mail.montclair.edu. *World Wide Web:* http://www.montclair.edu/international.shtml

O'NEILL NATIONAL THEATER INSTITUTE
O'NEILL MOSCOW ART THEATER SEMESTER

Held at Moscow Art Theatre
Academic Focus • Dance, design and applied arts, drama/theater, Russian language and literature, Russian studies.
Program Information • Classes are held on the campus of Moscow Art Theatre. Faculty members are local instructors hired by the sponsor. Scheduled travel to St. Petersburg; field trips.
Sessions • Fall, spring.
Eligibility Requirements • Minimum age 18; open to sophomores, juniors, seniors, graduate students, adults; major in theater studies; course work in theater; 2 letters of recommendation; good academic standing at home school; résumé; interview; essay; no foreign language proficiency required.
Living Arrangements • Students live in host institution dormitories, host family homes. Quarters are shared with host institution students. Meals are taken as a group, in central dining facility.
Costs (2004) • One term: $14,200; includes tuition, housing, all meals, excursions, international airfare, all cultural events. $40 application fee. $800 nonrefundable deposit required. Financial aid available for all students: scholarships.
For More Information • Kato McNickle, Director of College Relations and International Programs, O'Neill National Theater Institute, 305 Great Neck Road, Waterford, CT 06385; *Phone:* 860-443-7139; *Fax:* 860-443-9653. *E-mail:* kjmcn@conncoll.edu. *World Wide Web:* http://nti.conncoll.edu/

STETSON UNIVERSITY
STUDY ABROAD–MOSCOW

Hosted by Moscow State University
Academic Focus • Russian language and literature.
Program Information • Students attend classes at Moscow State University. Field trips to St. Petersburg.
Sessions • Fall, spring, yearlong.
Eligibility Requirements • Minimum age 20; open to sophomores, juniors, seniors; 2.5 GPA; 3 letters of recommendation; good academic standing at home school; completed application; 2 years of college course work in Russian.
Living Arrangements • Students live in host institution dormitories, host family homes. Quarters are shared with host institution students, students from other programs. Meals are taken on one's own, in residences, in central dining facility.
Costs (2002-2003) • One term: $14,025. Yearlong program: $28,050; includes tuition, housing, all meals, insurance, excursions, international airfare, international student ID, student support services. $50 application fee. $200 nonrefundable deposit required. Financial aid available for students from sponsoring institution: scholarships, loans.
For More Information • Ms. Nancy L. Leonard, Director, Stetson University, Center for International Education, Unit 8412, 421 North Woodland Boulevard, Deland, FL 32723-3757; *Phone:* 386-822-8165; *Fax:* 386-822-8167. *E-mail:* nleonard@stetson.edu. *World Wide Web:* http://www.stetson.edu/international/

UNIVERSITY AT ALBANY, STATE UNIVERSITY OF NEW YORK
LANGUAGE AND CULTURAL STUDIES AT MOSCOW STATE UNIVERSITY

Hosted by Moscow State University

Academic Focus • Communications, comparative literature, intercultural studies, Russian language and literature, Russian studies.
Program Information • Students attend classes at Moscow State University. Scheduled travel to St. Petersburg.
Sessions • Fall, spring, yearlong.
Eligibility Requirements • Minimum age 18; open to freshmen, sophomores, juniors, seniors, graduate students, adults; 2.7 GPA; 2 letters of recommendation; good academic standing at home school; no foreign language proficiency required.
Living Arrangements • Students live in host institution dormitories. Quarters are shared with students from other programs. Meals are taken on one's own, in residences, in central dining facility, in restaurants.
Costs (2002-2003) • One term: $7513. Yearlong program: $15,026; includes housing, all meals, excursions, student support services, in-state tuition and fees. $300 nonrefundable deposit required. Financial aid available for students from sponsoring institution: all customary sources.
For More Information • University at Albany, State University of New York, Office of International Education, LI 66, Albany, NY 12222; *Phone:* 518-442-3525; *Fax:* 518-442-3338. *E-mail:* intled@uamail.albany.edu. *World Wide Web:* http://www.albany.edu/intled/

NOVGOROD

STATE UNIVERSITY OF NEW YORK COLLEGE AT BROCKPORT
INTERNSHIPS: RUSSIA

Academic Focus • Full curriculum.
Eligibility Requirements • Minimum age 18; open to juniors, seniors; 2.5 GPA; 2 letters of recommendation; good academic standing at home school; basic knowledge of Russian recommended.
Living Arrangements • Students live in host institution dormitories, host family homes. Meals are taken on one's own, with host family, in residences, in restaurants.
Costs (2003-2004) • One term: $6350; includes tuition, housing, some meals, international student ID, student support services. $350 nonrefundable deposit required. Financial aid available for all students: scholarships, loans, grants.
For More Information • Dr. John J. Perry, Director, Office of International Education, State University of New York College at Brockport, 3102 Morgan III, Brockport, NY 14420; *Phone:* 585-395-2119; *Fax:* 585-637-3218. *E-mail:* overseas@brockport.edu. *World Wide Web:* http://www.brockport.edu/studyabroad/

ST. PETERSBURG

ACIE (ACTR/ACCELS)
ACIE (ACTR) ADVANCED RUSSIAN LANGUAGE AND AREA STUDIES PROGRAM IN ST. PETERSBURG
Hosted by Russian State Pedagogical University
Academic Focus • Russian language and literature, Russian studies.
Program Information • Students attend classes at Russian State Pedagogical University. Scheduled travel to Moscow, Golden Ring, Sochi; field trips to museums, churches, historic sites.
Sessions • Fall, spring, yearlong.
Eligibility Requirements • Minimum age 18; open to sophomores, juniors, seniors, graduate students, adults; 3 letters of recommendation; good academic standing at home school; 2 years of college course work in Russian.
Living Arrangements • Students live in host institution dormitories, host family homes. Meals are taken on one's own, with host family, in residences, in central dining facility, in restaurants.
Costs (2002-2003) • One term: contact sponsor for cost. Yearlong program: contact sponsor for cost. $35 application fee. $500 nonrefundable deposit required. Financial aid available for all students: scholarships.
For More Information • Ms. Margaret Stephenson, Russian and Eurasian Program Officer, ACIE (ACTR/ACCELS), 1776 Massachusetts Avenue, NW, Suite 700, Washington, DC 20036; *Phone:* 202-833-7522; *Fax:* 202-833-7523. *E-mail:* outbound@actr.org. *World Wide Web:* http://www.actr.org/

ACIE (ACTR/ACCELS)
ACIE (ACTR) BUSINESS RUSSIAN LANGUAGE AND INTERNSHIP PROGRAM IN ST. PETERSBURG
Hosted by Russian State Pedagogical University
Academic Focus • Area studies, international business, Russian language and literature.
Program Information • Students attend classes at Russian State Pedagogical University. Optional travel to Moscow, Baltics at an extra cost.
Sessions • Fall, spring, yearlong.
Eligibility Requirements • Minimum age 18; open to sophomores, juniors, seniors, graduate students, adults; 3 letters of recommendation; good academic standing at home school; 1 year of college course work in Russian.
Living Arrangements • Students live in host institution dormitories, host family homes. Meals are taken on one's own, with host family, in residences, in central dining facility, in restaurants.
Costs (2002-2003) • One term: contact sponsor for cost. Yearlong program: contact sponsor for cost. $35 application fee. $500 nonrefundable deposit required. Financial aid available for all students: scholarships.
For More Information • Ms. Margaret Stephenson, Russian and Eurasian Program Officer, ACIE (ACTR/ACCELS), 1776 Massachusetts Avenue, NW, Suite 700, Washington, DC 20036; *Phone:* 202-833-7522; *Fax:* 202-833-7523. *E-mail:* outbound@actr.org. *World Wide Web:* http://www.actr.org/

ACIE (ACTR/ACCELS)
ACIE (ACTR) INDIVIDUALIZED RUSSIAN LANGUAGE TRAINING PROGRAM IN ST. PETERSBURG
Hosted by Saint Petersburg State University, Russian State Pedagogical University
Academic Focus • International business, Russian language and literature, Russian studies.
Program Information • Students attend classes at Saint Petersburg State University, Russian State Pedagogical University. Scheduled travel; field trips.
Sessions • Fall, spring, yearlong.
Eligibility Requirements • Minimum age 18; open to sophomores, juniors, seniors, graduate students, adults; 3 letters of recommendation; good academic standing at home school; no foreign language proficiency required.
Living Arrangements • Students live in host institution dormitories, host family homes. Meals are taken on one's own, with host family, in residences, in central dining facility, in restaurants.
Costs (2002-2003) • One term: contact sponsor for cost. Yearlong program: contact sponsor for cost. $35 application fee. $500 nonrefundable deposit required. Financial aid available for all students: scholarships.
For More Information • Ms. Margaret Stephenson, Russian and Eurasion Program Officer, ACIE (ACTR/ACCELS), 1776 Massachusetts Avenue, NW, Suite 700, Washington, DC 20036; *Phone:* 202-833-7522; *Fax:* 202-833-7523. *E-mail:* outbound@actr.org. *World Wide Web:* http://www.actr.org/

AMERICAN INSTITUTE FOR FOREIGN STUDY (AIFS)
ST. PETERSBURG STATE POLYTECHNIC UNIVERSITY
Hosted by Saint Petersburg State Polytechnic University
Academic Focus • Art history, history, literature, political science and government, Russian language and literature, Russian studies.
Program Information • Students attend classes at Saint Petersburg State Polytechnic University. Scheduled travel to London; field trips to Moscow.
Sessions • Fall, spring, yearlong.
Eligibility Requirements • Minimum age 17; open to freshmen, sophomores, juniors, seniors; 2.5 GPA; 1 letter of recommendation; good academic standing at home school; no foreign language proficiency required.
Living Arrangements • Students live in host institution dormitories, host family homes. Quarters are shared with host institution students. Meals are taken on one's own, with host family, in residences, in central dining facility.
Costs (2004-2005) • One term: $8995. Yearlong program: $16,490; includes tuition, housing, excursions, books and class materials,

RUSSIA
St. Petersburg

student support services, round-trip airfare, 2-day London stopover. $75 application fee. $350 nonrefundable deposit required. Financial aid available for all students: scholarships.

For More Information • Mr. David Mauro, Admissions Advisor, American Institute For Foreign Study (AIFS), 9 West Broad Street, Stamford, CT 06902-3788; *Phone:* 800-727-2437 Ext. 5163; *Fax:* 203-399-5597. *E-mail:* dmauro@aifs.com. *World Wide Web:* http://www.aifsabroad.com/

BOWLING GREEN STATE UNIVERSITY
RUSSIAN LANGUAGE AND CULTURE PROGRAM

Hosted by Saint Petersburg State University

Academic Focus • Russian language and literature, Russian studies.

Program Information • Students attend classes at Saint Petersburg State University. Scheduled travel to Vladimir, Pskov, Novgorod; field trips to Moscow; optional travel to Novgorod, Moscow, Golden Ring at an extra cost.

Sessions • Fall, spring, yearlong.

Eligibility Requirements • Minimum age 18; open to sophomores, juniors, seniors, graduate students, adults; 2 letters of recommendation; 3 years of college course work in Russian.

Living Arrangements • Students live in host family homes. Meals are taken with host family, in residences.

Costs (2003-2004) • One term: $3000 for Ohio residents; $4080 for nonresidents. Yearlong program: $6000 for Ohio residents; $8160 for nonresidents; includes tuition, housing, all meals, excursions, books and class materials, international student ID, student support services. $126 application fee. Financial aid available for students: scholarships.

For More Information • Dr. Irina Stakhanova, Director, Bowling Green State University, Department of German, Russian, and East Asian Languages, Bowling Green, OH 43403-0219; *Phone:* 419-372-2268; *Fax:* 419-372-2571. *E-mail:* irina@bgnet.bgsu.edu. *World Wide Web:* http://www.bgsu.edu/. Students may also apply through St. Petersburg Universitatskaya, Nabereznaya, Leitenanta Shmidta 11, St. Petersburg 199034, Russia.

CIEE
CIEE STUDY CENTER AT ST. PETERSBURG STATE UNIVERSITY, RUSSIA–RUSSIAN AREA STUDIES PROGRAM

Hosted by Saint Petersburg State University

Academic Focus • History, political science and government, Russian language and literature, Russian studies.

Program Information • Students attend classes at Saint Petersburg State University. Scheduled travel to Moscow; field trips to Pskov, Tallinn, Valaam, Novgorod, cultural interest sites in St. Petersburg.

Sessions • Fall, spring.

Eligibility Requirements • Open to sophomores, juniors, seniors, graduate students, adults; 2.75 GPA; 2 letters of recommendation; good academic standing at home school; no foreign language proficiency required.

Living Arrangements • Students live in host institution dormitories, host family homes. Meals are taken on one's own, with host family, in residences, in central dining facility, in restaurants.

Costs (2003-2004) • One term: $8500; includes tuition, housing, all meals, insurance, excursions, books and class materials, student support services, visa fees, cultural activities, pre-departure advising, optional on-site pick-up. $30 application fee. $300 deposit required. Financial aid available for all students: minority student scholarships, non-traditional study scholarships, travel grants.

For More Information • Ms. Hannah McChesney, Admissions Officer, Europe, Middle East, and Africa, CIEE, 7 Custom House Street, 3rd Floor, Portland, ME 04101; *Phone:* 800-40-STUDY; *Fax:* 207-553-7699. *E-mail:* studyinfo@ciee.org. *World Wide Web:* http://www.ciee.org/isp/

CIEE
CIEE STUDY CENTER AT ST. PETERSBURG STATE UNIVERSITY, RUSSIA–RUSSIAN LANGUAGE PROGRAM

Hosted by Saint Petersburg State University

Academic Focus • History, political science and government, Russian language and literature, Russian studies.

Program Information • Students attend classes at Saint Petersburg State University. Scheduled travel to Moscow; field trips to Pskov, Tallinn, Valaam, cultural interest sites in St. Petersburg, Novgorod.

Sessions • Fall, spring, yearlong.

Eligibility Requirements • Open to sophomores, juniors, seniors, graduate students, adults; 2.75 GPA; 2 letters of recommendation; good academic standing at home school; 2 years of college course work in Russian.

Living Arrangements • Students live in host institution dormitories, host family homes. Quarters are shared with host institution students. Meals are taken on one's own, with host family, in residences, in central dining facility, in restaurants.

Costs (2003-2004) • One term: $8700. Yearlong program: $17,500; includes tuition, housing, all meals, insurance, student support services, visa fees, cultural activities, pre-departure advising, optional on-site pick-up. $30 application fee. $300 deposit required. Financial aid available for all students: minority student scholarships, non-traditional study scholarships, travel grants.

For More Information • Ms. Hannah McChesney, Admissions Officer, Europe, Middle East, and Africa, CIEE, 7 Custom House Street, 3rd Floor, Portland, ME 04101; *Phone:* 800-40-STUDY; *Fax:* 207-553-7699. *E-mail:* studyinfo@ciee.org. *World Wide Web:* http://www.ciee.org/isp/

COLBY COLLEGE
COLBY IN ST. PETERSBURG

Hosted by Saint Petersburg Classical School

Academic Focus • Russian language and literature, Russian studies.

Program Information • Students attend classes at Saint Petersburg Classical School. Scheduled travel to Moscow, Baltic countries, Novgorod; field trips to Peterhof, Pushkin.

Sessions • Fall, spring.

Eligibility Requirements • Open to sophomores, juniors; 2.7 GPA; 2 letters of recommendation; good academic standing at home school; 3 years of college course work in Russian.

Living Arrangements • Students live in host family homes. Meals are taken with host family, in residences.

Costs (2002-2003) • One term: $17,900; includes tuition, housing, all meals, insurance, excursions, international airfare, student support services. $500 nonrefundable deposit required. Financial aid available for students from sponsoring institution: scholarships.

For More Information • Ms. Martha J. Denney, Director, Off-Campus Study, Colby College, Waterville, ME 04901; *Phone:* 207-872-3648; *Fax:* 207-872-3061. *E-mail:* mjdenney@colby.edu. *World Wide Web:* http://www.colby.edu/off-campus/

DUKE UNIVERSITY
DUKE IN ST. PETERSBURG

Held at Saint Petersburg University

Academic Focus • Film and media studies, Russian language and literature, Russian studies.

Program Information • Classes are held on the campus of Saint Petersburg University. Faculty members are local instructors hired by the sponsor. Scheduled travel to Moscow, Baltic states.

Sessions • Fall, spring, yearlong.

Eligibility Requirements • Minimum age 18; open to sophomores, juniors; 3.0 GPA; 2 letters of recommendation; good academic standing at home school; 2 years of college course work in Russian.

Living Arrangements • Students live in host institution dormitories, locally rented apartments, host family homes. Quarters are shared with students from other programs. Meals are taken as a group, on one's own, in residences, in central dining facility.

Costs (2003-2004) • One term: $14,237. Yearlong program: $28,000; includes tuition, housing, excursions. $2000 nonrefundable deposit required. Financial aid available for students from sponsoring institution: scholarships, loans, institutional grants.

For More Information • Dr. Edna Andrews, Professor, Department of Slavic Languages and Literature, Duke University, 314 Languages Building, Box 90259, Durham, NC 27708-0259; *Phone:* 919-660-3140; *Fax:* 919-660-3141. *E-mail:* eda@duke.edu. *World Wide Web:* http://www.aas.duke.edu/study_abroad/

SCHOOL FOR INTERNATIONAL TRAINING, SIT STUDY ABROAD
RUSSIA: ETHNIC AND CULTURAL STUDIES

Academic Focus • Anthropology, Eastern European studies, ethnic studies, geography, history, political science and government, Russian language and literature, Russian studies, social sciences, sociology.

Program Information • Faculty members are drawn from the sponsor's U.S. staff and local instructors hired by the sponsor. Scheduled travel to Irkutsk, Tuva, Moscow; field trips to museums, Buddhist temples, rural areas.

Sessions • Fall, spring.

Eligibility Requirements • Open to sophomores, juniors, seniors; 2.5 GPA; 2 letters of recommendation; good academic standing at home school; no foreign language proficiency required.

Living Arrangements • Students live in host institution dormitories, host family homes, hotels. Meals are taken as a group, on one's own, with host family, in residences, in central dining facility, in restaurants.

Costs (2003-2004) • One term: $12,225; includes tuition, housing, all meals, insurance, excursions, international student ID. $50 application fee. $400 nonrefundable deposit required. Financial aid available for all students: scholarships.

For More Information • School for International Training, SIT Study Abroad, Kipling Road, Brattleboro, VT 05302-0676; *Phone:* 888-272-7881; *Fax:* 802-258-3296. *E-mail:* studyabroad@sit.edu. *World Wide Web:* http://www.sit.edu/studyabroad/

STONY BROOK UNIVERSITY
STONY BROOK ABROAD: ST. PETERSBURG

Hosted by Saint Petersburg University

Academic Focus • Eastern European studies, history, Russian language and literature, Russian studies.

Program Information • Students attend classes at Saint Petersburg University.

Sessions • Fall, spring.

Eligibility Requirements • Open to juniors; 2.5 GPA; 3 letters of recommendation; good academic standing at home school; 2 years of college course work in Russian.

Living Arrangements • Students live in host institution dormitories, locally rented apartments, program-owned apartments, host family homes. Meals are taken on one's own, with host family, in residences, in central dining facility.

Costs (2000-2001) • One term: $5500; includes tuition, housing, some meals, books and class materials. $200 nonrefundable deposit required. Financial aid available for students from sponsoring institution: loans.

For More Information • Ms. Gretchen Gosnell, Study Abroad Advisor, Stony Brook University, Study Abroad Office, Melville Library, Room E5340, Stony Brook, NY 11794-3397; *Phone:* 631-632-7030; *Fax:* 631-632-6544. *E-mail:* studyabroad@sunysb.edu. *World Wide Web:* http://www.sunysb.edu/studyabroad/

VLADIMIR

ACIE (ACTR/ACCELS)
ACIE (ACTR) ADVANCED RUSSIAN LANGUAGE PROGRAM IN VLADIMIR

Held at Moscow University for Small Business Management, Vladimir Campus

Academic Focus • Russian language and literature, Russian studies.

Program Information • Classes are held on the campus of Moscow University for Small Business Management, Vladimir Campus. Faculty members are local instructors hired by the sponsor. Scheduled travel; field trips.

Sessions • Fall, spring, yearlong.

Eligibility Requirements • Minimum age 18; open to sophomores, juniors, seniors, graduate students, adults; 3 letters of recommendation; good academic standing at home school; 1 year of college course work in Russian.

Living Arrangements • Students live in host family homes. Meals are taken on one's own, with host family, in residences, in restaurants.

Costs (2000-2001) • One term: $7250. Yearlong program: $12,450; includes tuition, housing, some meals, insurance, excursions, international airfare, books and class materials, student support services, visa processing fees. $35 application fee. $500 nonrefundable deposit required. Financial aid available for all students: scholarships.

For More Information • Russian and Eurasian Program Officer, ACIE (ACTR/ACCELS), 1776 Massachusetts Avenue, NW, Suite 700, Washington, DC 20036; *Phone:* 202-833-7522; *Fax:* 202-833-7523. *E-mail:* outbound@actr.org. *World Wide Web:* http://www.actr.org/

YAROSLAVL

MIDDLEBURY COLLEGE SCHOOLS ABROAD
SCHOOL IN RUSSIA–YAROSLAVL PROGRAM

Hosted by Yaroslavl State University

Academic Focus • Economics, history, liberal studies, linguistics, literature, Russian language and literature, social sciences.

Program Information • Students attend classes at Yaroslavl State University. Scheduled travel to St. Petersburg, Nizhnii Novgorod, Baltics, Moscow; field trips to Sergiev Posad, Pskov, Suzdal, Moscow; optional travel to St. Petersburg, Europe, Voronezh, Moscow at an extra cost.

Sessions • Fall, spring, yearlong.

Eligibility Requirements • Open to sophomores, juniors, seniors; 2.7 GPA; 2 letters of recommendation; good academic standing at home school; minimum grade of B in Russian; 2 years of college course work in Russian.

Living Arrangements • Students live in host family homes. Quarters are shared with host institution students. Meals are taken on one's own, with host family, in residences.

Costs (2004-2005) • One term: $11,440. Yearlong program: $21,940; includes tuition, housing, some meals, insurance, excursions, international airfare, student support services, visa fees, language assessment, deorientation. $50 application fee. $300 nonrefundable deposit required. Financial aid available for students from sponsoring institution: scholarships, loans.

For More Information • Mr. Jamie Northrup, University Relations Coordinator, Middlebury College Schools Abroad, Office of Off-Campus Study, Sunderland Language Center, Middlebury, VT 05753; *Phone:* 802-443-5745; *Fax:* 802-443-3157. *E-mail:* schoolsabroad@middlebury.edu. *World Wide Web:* http://www.middlebury.edu/msa/

SCOTLAND

See also England, Ireland, Northern Ireland, and Wales.

ABERDEEN

ALMA COLLEGE
PROGRAM OF STUDIES IN ABERDEEN, SCOTLAND

Hosted by University of Aberdeen

Academic Focus • Biological/life sciences, business administration/management, chemical sciences, English, mathematics, philosophy, political science and government, psychology.

Program Information • Students attend classes at University of Aberdeen. Field trips to the River Dee, the Scottish Highlands, Dunnotter Castle, Stonehaven.

Sessions • Fall, spring, yearlong.

Eligibility Requirements • Minimum age 18; open to sophomores, juniors, seniors, adults; 3.0 GPA; 2 letters of recommendation; good academic standing at home school; no foreign language proficiency required.

Living Arrangements • Students live in host institution dormitories, locally rented apartments, program-owned apartments. Quarters are shared with host institution students, students from other programs. Meals are taken as a group, on one's own, in residences, in central dining facility.

Costs (2002-2003) • One term: $9000. Yearlong program: $18,600; includes tuition, housing, all meals, insurance, excursions, international student ID, student support services. $50 application fee. $200 refundable deposit required. Financial aid available for all students: scholarships.

For More Information • Ms. Julie Elenbaas, Office Coordinator, Alma College, 614 West Superior Street, Alma, MI 48801-1599; *Phone:* 989-463-7055; *Fax:* 989-463-7126. *E-mail:* intl_studies@alma.edu. *World Wide Web:* http://international.alma.edu/

ARCADIA UNIVERSITY
UNIVERSITY OF ABERDEEN

Hosted by University of Aberdeen

Academic Focus • Art history, biological/life sciences, chemical sciences, engineering, English literature, liberal studies, religious studies, social sciences.

Program Information • Students attend classes at University of Aberdeen.

Sessions • Fall, spring, yearlong, fall semester.

Eligibility Requirements • Open to sophomores, juniors, seniors; 3.0 GPA; 1 letter of recommendation.

Living Arrangements • Students live in host institution dormitories. Quarters are shared with host institution students, students from other programs. Meals are taken on one's own, in residences.

Costs (2003-2004) • One term: $10,250–$10,990. Yearlong program: $17,990; includes tuition, housing, insurance, international student ID, student support services, pre-departure guide, transcripts. $35 application fee. $500 nonrefundable deposit required. Financial aid available for all students: scholarships, loans.

For More Information • Arcadia University, Center for Education Abroad, 450 South Easton Road, Glenside, PA 19038-3295; *Phone:* 866-927-2234; *Fax:* 215-572-2174. *E-mail:* cea@arcadia.edu. *World Wide Web:* http://www.arcadia.edu/cea/

NORTH AMERICAN INSTITUTE FOR STUDY ABROAD
STUDY IN SCOTLAND

Hosted by University of Aberdeen

Academic Focus • Full curriculum.

Program Information • Students attend classes at University of Aberdeen.

Sessions • Fall, spring, yearlong.

Eligibility Requirements • Minimum age 18; open to sophomores, juniors, seniors; 3.0 GPA; good academic standing at home school.

Living Arrangements • Students live in host institution dormitories, locally rented apartments, host family homes. Quarters are shared with host institution students. Meals are taken on one's own, in residences, in central dining facility, in restaurants.

Costs (2003-2004) • One term: $9500. Yearlong program: $18,000; includes tuition, housing, international student ID, student support services, transcripts. $50 application fee. $500 nonrefundable deposit required. Financial aid available for all students: scholarships.

For More Information • Dr. Michael Currid, Director, North American Institute for Study Abroad, 129 Mill Street, Danville, PA 17821; *Phone:* 570-275-5099; *Fax:* 570-275-1644. *E-mail:* naisa@naisa.com. *World Wide Web:* http://www.naisa.com/

WABASH COLLEGE
THE SCOTLAND PROGRAM AT THE UNIVERSITY OF ABERDEEN

Hosted by University of Aberdeen

Academic Focus • Full curriculum.

Program Information • Students attend classes at University of Aberdeen. Field trips to the Highlands, Edinburgh, Grampian castles and gardens.

Sessions • Fall, spring, yearlong.

Eligibility Requirements • Minimum age 18; open to sophomores, juniors, seniors; 3.0 GPA; 2 letters of recommendation; good academic standing at home school; essay.

Living Arrangements • Students live in host institution dormitories. Quarters are shared with host institution students. Meals are taken on one's own, in residences.

Costs (2003-2004) • One term: $9600. Yearlong program: $16,000; includes tuition, housing, excursions, student support services, re-entry support, transcript service. $500 nonrefundable deposit required.

For More Information • Ms. Edith C. Dallinger, Director, Wabash College, The Scotland Program, Box 352, Crawfordsville, IN 47933; *Phone:* 765-361-6410; *Fax:* 765-361-6470. *E-mail:* scotland@wabash.edu. *World Wide Web:* http://www.wabash.edu/scot/

DUNDEE
COLLEGE CONSORTIUM FOR INTERNATIONAL STUDIES–BROOKDALE COMMUNITY COLLEGE
UNIVERSITY OF DUNDEE–PROGRAM IN SCOTLAND

Hosted by University of Dundee

Academic Focus • Full curriculum.

Program Information • Students attend classes at University of Dundee. Optional travel to Edinburgh, Glasgow, St. Andrews, the Highlands, London at an extra cost.

Sessions • Fall, spring, yearlong.

Eligibility Requirements • Minimum age 18; open to freshmen, sophomores, juniors, seniors; 3.0 GPA; 3 letters of recommendation; transcript; essay; 15 college credits.

Living Arrangements • Students live in host institution dormitories, program-owned apartments, program-owned houses. Quarters are shared with host institution students. Meals are taken on one's own, in residences, in central dining facility.

Costs (2004-2005) • One term: $6870. Yearlong program: $13,740; includes tuition, insurance, lab equipment, student support services, e-mail access, fees, airport pick-up. $35 application fee. Financial aid available for students from sponsoring institution: scholarships, loans.

For More Information • College Consortium for International Studies–Brookdale Community College, 2000 P Street, NW, Suite 503, Washington, DC 20036; *Phone:* 800-543-6956; *Fax:* 202-223-0999. *E-mail:* info@ccisabroad.org. *World Wide Web:* http://www.ccisabroad.org/. Students may also apply through Brookdale Community College, International Center, 765 Newman Springs Road, Lincroft, NJ 07738-1597.

NORTH AMERICAN INSTITUTE FOR STUDY ABROAD
STUDY IN SCOTLAND

Hosted by University of Dundee

Academic Focus • Full curriculum.

Program Information • Students attend classes at University of Dundee. Optional travel at an extra cost.

Sessions • Fall, spring, yearlong.

Eligibility Requirements • Minimum age 18; open to sophomores, juniors, seniors; 3.0 GPA; 2 letters of recommendation; good academic standing at home school.

Living Arrangements • Students live in host family homes. Quarters are shared with host institution students. Meals are taken on one's own, in residences, in central dining facility, in restaurants.

Costs (2003-2004) • One term: $9000–$9500. Yearlong program: $17,500; includes tuition, housing, international student ID, student support services, transcripts. $50 application fee. $500 nonrefundable deposit required. Financial aid available for all students: scholarships.

For More Information • Dr. Michael Currid, Director, North American Institute for Study Abroad, 129 Mill Street, Danville, PA 17821; *Phone:* 570-275-5099; *Fax:* 570-275-1644. *E-mail:* naisa@naisa.com. *World Wide Web:* http://www.naisa.com/

STATE UNIVERSITY OF NEW YORK AT NEW PALTZ
STUDY ABROAD IN DUNDEE, SCOTLAND: DUNDEE UNIVERSITY

Hosted by University of Dundee

Academic Focus • Full curriculum.

Program Information • Students attend classes at University of Dundee.
Sessions • Fall, spring, yearlong.
Eligibility Requirements • Minimum age 18; open to sophomores, juniors, seniors; 2.5 GPA; 2 letters of recommendation; good academic standing at home school.
Living Arrangements • Students live in host institution dormitories, locally rented apartments, program-owned apartments. Quarters are shared with host institution students. Meals are taken on one's own, in residences, in restaurants.
Costs (2003-2004) • One term: $6300 for New York residents; $6454 for nonresidents. Yearlong program: $12,600 for New York residents; $12,908 for nonresidents; includes tuition, insurance, student support services. $25 application fee. $300 nonrefundable deposit required. Financial aid available for students from sponsoring institution: scholarships, loans.
For More Information • Center for International Programs, State University of New York at New Paltz, 75 South Manheim Boulevard, Suite 9, New Paltz, NY 12561; *Phone:* 845-257-3125; *Fax:* 845-257-3129. *E-mail:* international@newpaltz.edu. *World Wide Web:* http://www.newpaltz.edu/studyabroad/

EDINBURGH

AMERICAN UNIVERSITIES INTERNATIONAL PROGRAMS (AUIP)
EDINBURGH, SCOTLAND PROGRAM

Hosted by University of Edinburgh
Academic Focus • Archaeology, art history, business administration/management, health and physical education, literature, parks and recreation, political science and government, Scottish studies, tourism and travel.
Program Information • Students attend classes at University of Edinburgh. Scheduled travel to Outdoor Pursuits (week-long outdoor recreational program in The Highlands); field trips to art galleries, theatre, museums, archaeological sites, cultural activities.
Sessions • Spring.
Eligibility Requirements • Minimum age 18; open to sophomores, juniors, seniors, graduate students, adults; 2.5 GPA; 2 letters of recommendation; good academic standing at home school; personal statement; original transcript.
Living Arrangements • Students live in host institution dormitories. Quarters are shared with host institution students, students from other programs. Meals are taken on one's own, in central dining facility.
Costs (2003) • One term: $6695; includes tuition, housing, some meals, insurance, excursions, student support services, Outdoor Pursuits course. $50 application fee. $500 nonrefundable deposit required.
For More Information • Ms. Linda Detling, Program Coordinator, American Universities International Programs (AUIP), PMB 221, 305 West Magnolia Street, Fort Collins, CO 80521; *Phone:* 970-495-0869; *Fax:* 970-484-2028. *E-mail:* info@auip.com. *World Wide Web:* http://www.auip.com/

ARCADIA UNIVERSITY
SCOTTISH PARLIAMENTARY INTERNSHIP

Hosted by University of Edinburgh
Academic Focus • Political science and government.
Program Information • Students attend classes at University of Edinburgh.
Sessions • Fall, spring.
Eligibility Requirements • Open to juniors, seniors; 3.0 GPA; 1 letter of recommendation.
Living Arrangements • Students live in host institution dormitories, locally rented apartments. Quarters are shared with host institution students, students from other programs. Meals are taken on one's own, in residences.
Costs (2003-2004) • One term: $12,390; includes tuition, housing, insurance, international student ID, student support services, pre-departure guide, transcript. $35 application fee. $500 nonrefundable deposit required. Financial aid available for all students: scholarships, loans.
For More Information • Arcadia University, Center for Education Abroad, 450 South Easton Road, Glenside, PA 19038-3295; *Phone:*

866-927-2234; *Fax:* 215-572-2174. *E-mail:* cea@arcadia.edu. *World Wide Web:* http://www.arcadia.edu/cea/

ARCADIA UNIVERSITY
UNIVERSITY OF EDINBURGH

Hosted by University of Edinburgh
Academic Focus • Biological/life sciences, engineering, English literature, history, liberal studies, religious studies, social sciences, visual and performing arts.
Program Information • Students attend classes at University of Edinburgh.
Sessions • Fall, spring, yearlong, spring semester.
Eligibility Requirements • Open to sophomores, juniors, seniors; 3.0 GPA; 1 letter of recommendation; minimum 3.3 GPA for engineering; minimum 3.4 GPA for English.
Living Arrangements • Students live in host institution dormitories, locally rented apartments. Quarters are shared with host institution students, students from other programs. Meals are taken as a group, on one's own, in residences.
Costs (2003-2004) • One term: $9250–$12,190. Yearlong program: $19,390; includes tuition, housing, insurance, international student ID, student support services, pre-departure guide, transcripts. $35 application fee. $500 nonrefundable deposit required. Financial aid available for all students: scholarships, loans.
For More Information • Arcadia University, Center for Education Abroad, 450 South Easton Road, Glenside, PA 19038-3295; *Phone:* 866-927-2234; *Fax:* 215-572-2174. *E-mail:* cea@arcadia.edu. *World Wide Web:* http://www.arcadia.edu/cea/

CENTER FOR INTERNATIONAL STUDIES
NAPIER UNIVERSITY

Hosted by Napier University
Academic Focus • Full curriculum.
Program Information • Students attend classes at Napier University. Field trips to Edinburgh; optional travel to Scotland at an extra cost.
Sessions • Fall, spring, yearlong.
Eligibility Requirements • Minimum age 18; open to sophomores, juniors, seniors, graduate students, adults; 2.5 GPA; 1 letter of recommendation; good academic standing at home school; personal essay.
Living Arrangements • Students live in program-owned apartments. Quarters are shared with host institution students, students from other programs. Meals are taken on one's own, in residences, in central dining facility, in restaurants.
Costs (2003-2004) • One term: $8100. Yearlong program: $14,300; includes tuition, housing, excursions, international student ID, student support services, airport reception. $50 application fee. $500 nonrefundable deposit required. Financial aid available for all students: scholarships.
For More Information • Mr. Jeff Palm, Program Director, Center for International Studies, 17 New South Street, #105, Northampton, MA 01060; *Phone:* 413-582-0407; *Fax:* 413-582-0327. *E-mail:* jpalm@cisabroad.com. *World Wide Web:* http://www.cisabroad.com/

INSTITUTE FOR STUDY ABROAD, BUTLER UNIVERSITY
UNIVERSITY OF EDINBURGH

Hosted by University of Edinburgh
Academic Focus • Full curriculum.
Program Information • Students attend classes at University of Edinburgh. Field trips to London, the Isle of Arran, Iona, Skye.
Sessions • Fall, spring, yearlong, spring term for social sciences.
Eligibility Requirements • Open to juniors, seniors; 3.0 GPA; 1 letter of recommendation; good academic standing at home school; enrollment at an accredited American college or university.
Living Arrangements • Students live in host institution dormitories, locally rented apartments. Quarters are shared with host institution students, students from other programs. Meals are taken as a group, on one's own, in residences, in central dining facility.
Costs (2002-2003) • One term: $8775 for fall term; $11,275 for spring ($11,475 with internship). Yearlong program: $18,375 ($20,675 with internship); includes tuition, housing, excursions,

international student ID, student support services, family visit, cultural and sporting events, pre-departure advising. $40 application fee. $500 nonrefundable deposit required. Financial aid available for all students: scholarships, travel grants.

For More Information • Institute for Study Abroad, Butler University, 1100 West 42nd Street, Suite 305, Indianapolis, IN 46208-3345; *Phone:* 800-858-0229; *Fax:* 317-940-9704. *E-mail:* study-abroad@butler.edu. *World Wide Web:* http://www.ifsa-butler.org/

NORTHERN ILLINOIS UNIVERSITY
ACADEMIC INTERNSHIPS IN EDINBURGH, SCOTLAND

Hosted by University of Edinburgh
Academic Focus • History, political science and government, Scottish studies.
Program Information • Students attend classes at University of Edinburgh. Optional travel at an extra cost.
Sessions • Fall, spring.
Eligibility Requirements • Open to juniors, seniors; 3.0 GPA; 2 letters of recommendation; good academic standing at home school; essay; résumé.
Living Arrangements • Students live in locally rented apartments, host family homes. Quarters are shared with host institution students. Meals are taken with host family, in residences, in restaurants.
Costs (2003-2004) • One term: $8125; includes tuition, housing, some meals, insurance, internship placement. $45 application fee. $800 refundable deposit required. Financial aid available for students from sponsoring institution: scholarships, regular financial aid.
For More Information • Ms. Clare Foust, Program Assistant, Northern Illinois University, Study Abroad Office, Williston Hall 417, DeKalb, IL 60115-2854; *Phone:* 815-753-0420; *Fax:* 815-753-0825. *E-mail:* niuabroad@niu.edu. *World Wide Web:* http://www.niu.edu/niuabroad/

QUEEN MARGARET UNIVERSITY COLLEGE
STUDY ABROAD

Hosted by Queen Margaret University College
Academic Focus • Advertising and public relations, biological/life sciences, business administration/management, communications, drama/theater, film and media studies, French language and literature, German language and literature, health and physical education, hotel and restaurant management, management information systems, marketing, nursing, nutrition, psychology, social sciences, speech pathology, tourism and travel.
Program Information • Students attend classes at Queen Margaret University College.
Sessions • Fall.
Eligibility Requirements • Minimum age 18; open to precollege students, freshmen, sophomores, juniors, seniors, adults; 3.0 GPA; 2 letters of recommendation; good academic standing at home school.
Living Arrangements • Students live in locally rented apartments, program-owned apartments. Quarters are shared with host institution students. Meals are taken on one's own, in residences, in central dining facility, in restaurants.
Costs (2002) • One term: $4950–$5250; includes tuition. Financial aid available for all students: work study.
For More Information • Mr. P. Whitelaw, Head of the International Office, Queen Margaret University College, Clerwood Terrace, Corstorphine Campus, Edinburgh EH 12 8TS, Scotland; *Phone:* +44 131-317-3760; *Fax:* +44 131-317-3256. *E-mail:* international@qmuc.ac.uk. *World Wide Web:* http://www.qmuc.ac.uk/

STATE UNIVERSITY OF NEW YORK COLLEGE AT BROCKPORT
QUEEN MARGARET UNIVERSITY COLLEGE PROGRAM

Hosted by Queen Margaret University College
Academic Focus • Full curriculum.

Program Information • Students attend classes at Queen Margaret University College. Field trips to the London weekend program.
Sessions • Fall, yearlong.
Eligibility Requirements • Minimum age 18; open to juniors, seniors; 3.0 GPA; 2 letters of recommendation; good academic standing at home school; ability to do upper-division work in the subjects chosen.
Living Arrangements • Students live in host institution dormitories. Quarters are shared with host institution students. Meals are taken on one's own, in residences, in central dining facility.
Costs (2003-2004) • One term: $10,025. Yearlong program: $18,325; includes tuition, housing, excursions, international student ID, student support services. $350 nonrefundable deposit required. Financial aid available for all students: scholarships, loans, regular financial aid, grants.
For More Information • Dr. John Perry, Director, Office of International Education, State University of New York College at Brockport, 350 New Campus Drive, Brockport, NY 14420; *Phone:* 800-298-SUNY; *Fax:* 585-637-3218. *E-mail:* overseas@brockport.edu. *World Wide Web:* http://www.brockport.edu/studyabroad/

UNIVERSITY OF MIAMI
UNIVERSITY OF EDINBURGH, SCOTLAND

Hosted by University of Edinburgh
Academic Focus • Area studies, biological/life sciences, English literature, history, philosophy, Scottish studies, social sciences.
Program Information • Students attend classes at University of Edinburgh.
Sessions • Yearlong.
Eligibility Requirements • Minimum age 18; open to sophomores, juniors; 3.5 GPA; 2 letters of recommendation; official transcript; essay.
Living Arrangements • Students live in host institution dormitories. Quarters are shared with host institution students. Meals are taken on one's own, in residences, in central dining facility.
Costs (2003-2004) • Yearlong program: $25,838; includes tuition, housing, all meals. $40 application fee. $500 nonrefundable deposit required. Financial aid available for students from sponsoring institution: scholarships, loans.
For More Information • Ms. Elyse Resnick, Assistant Director, University of Miami, International Education and Exchange Programs, 5050 Brunson Drive, Allen Hall 212, PO Box 248005, Coral Gables, FL 33124-1610; *Phone:* 305-284-3434; *Fax:* 305-284-4235. *E-mail:* ieep@miami.edu. *World Wide Web:* http://www.studyabroad.miami.edu/

FINDHORN
LIVING ROUTES–STUDY ABROAD IN ECOVILLAGES
LIVING ROUTES–SCOTLAND: SELF AND COMMUNITY AT FINDHORN

Hosted by Findhorn Community
Academic Focus • Agriculture, art, community service, conservation studies, creative writing, ecology, environmental health, environmental science/studies, interdisciplinary studies, peace and conflict studies, social sciences.
Program Information • Students attend classes at Findhorn Community. Scheduled travel to the Isle of Erraid; field trips to the Findhorn River, the Caledonian Forest.
Sessions • Fall, spring.
Eligibility Requirements • Minimum age 18; open to sophomores, juniors, seniors, adults; 2.5 GPA; 2 letters of recommendation; good academic standing at home school.
Living Arrangements • Students live in locally rented apartments. Quarters are shared with host institution students. Meals are taken as a group, in residences, in central dining facility.
Costs (2003-2004) • One term: $10,750; includes tuition, housing, all meals, excursions, student support services. $50 application fee. $800 nonrefundable deposit required. Financial aid available for all students: scholarships.
For More Information • Dr. Daniel Greenberg, Director, Living Routes–Study Abroad in Ecovillages, 79 South Pleasant Street, Suite

302, Amherst, MA 01002; *Phone:* 888-515-7333; *Fax:* 413-259-1256. *E-mail:* programs@livingroutes.org. *World Wide Web:* http://www.LivingRoutes.org/

GLASGOW
ARCADIA UNIVERSITY
GLASGOW SCHOOL OF ART

Hosted by Glasgow School of Art
Academic Focus • Architecture, art history, crafts, design and applied arts, fine/studio arts.
Program Information • Students attend classes at Glasgow School of Art.
Sessions • Fall, spring, yearlong.
Eligibility Requirements • Open to sophomores, juniors, seniors; 3.0 GPA; 1 letter of recommendation; 10-12 slides of recent work.
Living Arrangements • Students live in host institution dormitories, locally rented apartments. Quarters are shared with host institution students, students from other programs. Meals are taken on one's own, in residences.
Costs (2003-2004) • One term: $9575–$15,290. Yearlong program: $20,990; includes tuition, housing, insurance, international student ID, student support services, pre-departure guide, transcripts. $35 application fee. $500 nonrefundable deposit required. Financial aid available for all students: scholarships, loans.
For More Information • Arcadia University, Center for Education Abroad, 450 South Easton Road, Glenside, PA 19038-3295; *Phone:* 866-927-2234; *Fax:* 215-572-2174. *E-mail:* cea@arcadia.edu. *World Wide Web:* http://www.arcadia.edu/cea/

ARCADIA UNIVERSITY
UNIVERSITY OF GLASGOW

Hosted by University of Glasgow
Academic Focus • Biological/life sciences, engineering, liberal studies, social sciences, visual and performing arts.
Program Information • Students attend classes at University of Glasgow.
Sessions • Fall, spring, yearlong, pre-session.
Eligibility Requirements • Open to sophomores, juniors, seniors; 3.0 GPA; 1 letter of recommendation.
Living Arrangements • Students live in host institution dormitories. Quarters are shared with host institution students, students from other programs. Meals are taken as a group, on one's own, in residences, in central dining facility.
Costs (2003-2004) • One term: $8550–$11,190 ($1990 for pre-session). Yearlong program: $17,790; includes tuition, housing, insurance, international student ID, student support services, pre-departure guide, transcripts. $35 application fee. $500 nonrefundable deposit required. Financial aid available for all students: scholarships, loans.
For More Information • Arcadia University, Center for Education Abroad, 450 South Easton Road, Glenside, PA 19038-3295; *Phone:* 866-927-2234; *Fax:* 215-572-2174. *E-mail:* cea@arcadia.edu. *World Wide Web:* http://www.arcadia.edu/cea/

INSTITUTE FOR STUDY ABROAD, BUTLER UNIVERSITY
GLASGOW SCHOOL OF ART

Hosted by Glasgow School of Art
Academic Focus • Architecture, art history, ceramics and pottery, design and applied arts, drawing/painting, textiles.
Program Information • Students attend classes at Glasgow School of Art. Field trips to London, the Isle of Arran, the Isle of Iona, or the Isle of Skye.
Sessions • Fall, spring, yearlong.
Eligibility Requirements • Open to juniors, seniors; major in fine arts; course work in studio art; 3.0 GPA; 1 letter of recommendation; good academic standing at home school; enrollment at an accredited American college or university; portfolio.
Living Arrangements • Students live in host institution dormitories, locally rented apartments. Quarters are shared with host institution students. Meals are taken on one's own, in residences, in restaurants.

Costs (2002-2003) • One term: $9275 for fall term; $14,275 for spring. Yearlong program: $19,775; includes tuition, housing, excursions, international student ID, student support services, family visit, cultural and sporting events, pre-departure advising. $40 application fee. $500 nonrefundable deposit required. Financial aid available for all students: scholarships, travel grants.
For More Information • Institute for Study Abroad, Butler University, 1100 West 42nd Street, Suite 305, Indianapolis, IN 46208-3345; *Phone:* 800-858-0229; *Fax:* 317-940-9704. *E-mail:* study-abroad@butler.edu. *World Wide Web:* http://www.ifsa-butler.org/

INSTITUTE FOR STUDY ABROAD, BUTLER UNIVERSITY
UNIVERSITY OF GLASGOW

Hosted by University of Glasgow
Academic Focus • Full curriculum.
Program Information • Students attend classes at University of Glasgow. Field trips to London, the Isle of Arran, Iona, Skye.
Sessions • Fall, spring, yearlong, early start fall session.
Eligibility Requirements • Open to juniors, seniors; 3.0 GPA; 1 letter of recommendation; good academic standing at home school; enrollment at an accredited American college or university.
Living Arrangements • Students live in host institution dormitories, locally rented apartments. Quarters are shared with host institution students, students from other programs. Meals are taken as a group, on one's own, in residences, in central dining facility.
Costs (2002-2003) • One term: $8375 for fall term; $9,975 for spring ($10,475 with early start session). Yearlong program: $16,975 ($19,225 with early start session); includes tuition, housing, excursions, international student ID, student support services, family visit, cultural and sporting events, pre-departure advising. $40 application fee. $500 nonrefundable deposit required. Financial aid available for all students: scholarships, travel grants.
For More Information • Institute for Study Abroad, Butler University, 1100 West 42nd Street, Suite 305, Indianapolis, IN 46208-3345; *Phone:* 800-858-0229; *Fax:* 317-940-9704. *E-mail:* study-abroad@butler.edu. *World Wide Web:* http://www.ifsa-butler.org/

THE INTERNATIONAL PARTNERSHIP FOR SERVICE LEARNING
SCOTLAND SERVICE–LEARNING

Hosted by University of Glasgow
Academic Focus • Community service, international affairs, liberal studies, social sciences.
Program Information • Students attend classes at University of Glasgow. Optional travel to Edinburgh, London, Dublin at an extra cost.
Sessions • Fall, spring, yearlong.
Eligibility Requirements • Minimum age 18; open to freshmen, sophomores, juniors, seniors, graduate students, adults; 2 letters of recommendation; good academic standing at home school; evidence of maturity, responsibility.
Living Arrangements • Students live in host institution dormitories, program-owned apartments. Quarters are shared with host institution students. Meals are taken on one's own, in residences.
Costs (2003-2004) • One term: $9100. Yearlong program: $17,800; includes tuition, service placement and supervision. $50 application fee. $250 refundable deposit required. Financial aid available for all students: federal financial aid.
For More Information • Ms. Ilana Golin, Coordinator of Student Programs, The International Partnership for Service Learning, 815 Second Avenue, Suite 315, New York, NY 10017-4594; *Phone:* 212-986-0989; *Fax:* 212-986-5039. *E-mail:* info@ipsl.org. *World Wide Web:* http://www.ipsl.org/

LOCK HAVEN UNIVERSITY OF PENNSYLVANIA
SEMESTER IN GLASGOW

Hosted by Glasgow Caledonian University
Academic Focus • Business administration/management, communications, economics, engineering, fashion merchandising, hospitality services, management information systems, mathematics, psychology, social sciences.
Program Information • Students attend classes at Glasgow Caledonian University.
Sessions • Fall, spring, yearlong.
Eligibility Requirements • Minimum age 18; open to sophomores, juniors, seniors, adults; 2.5 GPA; 3 letters of recommendation; good academic standing at home school.
Living Arrangements • Students live in host institution dormitories, locally rented apartments. Meals are taken on one's own.
Costs (2002-2003) • One term: $2750 for Pennsylvania residents; $4650 for nonresidents. Yearlong program: $5500 for Pennsylvania residents; $9275 for nonresidents; includes tuition, fees. $50 application fee. Financial aid available for students from sponsoring institution: scholarships, loans.
For More Information • Dean, Institute for International Studies, Lock Haven University of Pennsylvania, Lock Haven, PA 17745-2390; *Phone:* 570-893-2140; *Fax:* 570-893-2537. *E-mail:* intlstudies_webmonitor@lhup.edu. *World Wide Web:* http://www.lhup.edu/international/goingp/goingplaces_index.htm

NORTH AMERICAN INSTITUTE FOR STUDY ABROAD
STUDY IN SCOTLAND

Hosted by University of Strathclyde
Academic Focus • Full curriculum.
Program Information • Students attend classes at University of Strathclyde.
Sessions • Fall, spring, yearlong.
Eligibility Requirements • Minimum age 18; open to sophomores, juniors, seniors; 3.0 GPA; 2 letters of recommendation; good academic standing at home school.
Living Arrangements • Students live in host institution dormitories, locally rented apartments. Quarters are shared with host institution students. Meals are taken on one's own, in residences, in central dining facility, in restaurants.
Costs (2003-2004) • One term: $9000–$9500. Yearlong program: $17,500; includes tuition, housing, international student ID, student support services, transcripts. $50 application fee. $500 nonrefundable deposit required. Financial aid available for all students: scholarships.
For More Information • Dr. Michael Currid, Director, North American Institute for Study Abroad, 129 Mill Street, Danville, PA 17821; *Phone:* 570-275-5099; *Fax:* 570-275-1644. *E-mail:* naisa@naisa.com. *World Wide Web:* http://www.naisa.com/

NORTH AMERICAN INSTITUTE FOR STUDY ABROAD
STUDY IN SCOTLAND

Hosted by Glasgow Caledonian University
Academic Focus • Full curriculum.
Program Information • Students attend classes at Glasgow Caledonian University.
Sessions • Fall, spring, yearlong.
Eligibility Requirements • Minimum age 18; open to sophomores, juniors, seniors; 3.0 GPA; 2 letters of recommendation; good academic standing at home school.
Living Arrangements • Students live in host institution dormitories, locally rented apartments, host family homes. Quarters are shared with host institution students. Meals are taken on one's own, with host family, in residences, in central dining facility, in restaurants.
Costs (2003-2004) • One term: $9000–$9500. Yearlong program: $18,000; includes tuition, housing, international student ID, student support services, transcripts. $50 application fee. $500 nonrefundable deposit required. Financial aid available for all students: scholarships.
For More Information • Dr. Michael Currid, Director, North American Institute for Study Abroad, 129 Mill Street, Danville, PA 17821; *Phone:* 570-275-5099; *Fax:* 570-275-1644. *E-mail:* naisa@naisa.com. *World Wide Web:* http://www.naisa.com/

NORTH AMERICAN INSTITUTE FOR STUDY ABROAD
STUDY IN SCOTLAND

Hosted by University of Glasgow
Academic Focus • Full curriculum.
Program Information • Students attend classes at University of Glasgow.
Sessions • Fall, spring, yearlong.
Eligibility Requirements • Minimum age 18; open to sophomores, juniors, seniors; 3.0 GPA; 2 letters of recommendation; good academic standing at home school.
Living Arrangements • Students live in host institution dormitories, locally rented apartments, host family homes. Quarters are shared with host institution students. Meals are taken on one's own, with host family, in residences, in central dining facility, in restaurants.
Costs (2003-2004) • One term: $9000–$9500. Yearlong program: $17,500; includes tuition, housing, international student ID, student support services, transcripts. $50 application fee. $500 nonrefundable deposit required. Financial aid available for all students: scholarships.
For More Information • Dr. Michael Currid, Director, North American Institute for Study Abroad, 129 Mill Street, Danville, PA 17821; *Phone:* 570-275-5099; *Fax:* 570-275-1644. *E-mail:* naisa@naisa.com. *World Wide Web:* http://www.naisa.com/

RUTGERS, THE STATE UNIVERSITY OF NEW JERSEY
STUDY ABROAD IN SCOTLAND: GLASGOW

Hosted by University of Glasgow
Academic Focus • Full curriculum.
Program Information • Students attend classes at University of Glasgow. Field trips to London, Stonehenge, Oxford.
Sessions • Fall, spring, yearlong.
Eligibility Requirements • Open to sophomores, juniors, seniors; 3.0 GPA; 2 letters of recommendation; good academic standing at home school.
Living Arrangements • Students live in host institution dormitories. Quarters are shared with students from other programs. Meals are taken on one's own, in residences, in central dining facility.
Costs (2003-2004) • One term: $11,743–$14,924 for New Jersey residents; $14,393–$17,574 for nonresidents. Yearlong program: $19,686 for New Jersey residents; $24,986 for nonresidents; includes tuition, insurance, excursions, student support services. $20 application fee. $750 nonrefundable deposit required. Financial aid available for students from sponsoring institution: scholarships, loans.
For More Information • Ms. Karin Bonello, Regional Coordinator, Rutgers, The State University of New Jersey, 102 College Avenue, New Brunswick, NJ 08901-8543; *Phone:* 732-932-7787; *Fax:* 732-932-8659. *E-mail:* ru_abroad@email.rutgers.edu. *World Wide Web:* http://studyabroad.rutgers.edu/

STATE UNIVERSITY OF NEW YORK COLLEGE AT BROCKPORT
UNIVERSITY OF STRATHCLYDE PROGRAM

Hosted by University of Strathclyde
Academic Focus • Full curriculum.
Program Information • Students attend classes at University of Strathclyde. Field trips to the London weekend program.
Sessions • Fall, spring, yearlong.
Eligibility Requirements • Minimum age 18; open to juniors, seniors; 3.0 GPA; 2 letters of recommendation; good academic standing at home school; ability to do upper-division coursework in chosen area of study.
Living Arrangements • Students live in host institution dormitories. Quarters are shared with host institution students. Meals are taken on one's own, in residences.
Costs (2003-2004) • One term: $9950. Yearlong program: $18,550; includes tuition, housing, excursions, international student ID, student support services. $350 nonrefundable deposit required. Financial aid available for all students: scholarships, loans, regular financial aid, grants.

For More Information • Dr. John J. Perry, Director, Office of International Education, State University of New York College at Brockport, 350 New Campus Drive, Brockport, NY 14420; *Phone:* 800-298-SUNY; *Fax:* 585-637-3218. *E-mail:* overseas@brockport.edu. *World Wide Web:* http://www.brockport.edu/studyabroad/

TRUMAN STATE UNIVERSITY
UNIVERSITY OF STRATHCLYDE, GLASGOW, SCOTLAND

Hosted by University of Strathclyde
Academic Focus • Full curriculum.
Program Information • Students attend classes at University of Strathclyde. Optional travel at an extra cost.
Sessions • Fall, spring, yearlong.
Eligibility Requirements • Open to sophomores, juniors, seniors, graduate students; 2.7 GPA; 2 letters of recommendation; good academic standing at home school; no foreign language proficiency required.
Living Arrangements • Students live in program-owned apartments. Quarters are shared with students from other programs. Meals are taken on one's own, in residences.
Costs (2003-2004) • One term: $6000. Yearlong program: $12,000; includes tuition, insurance. $200 nonrefundable deposit required. Financial aid available for students from sponsoring institution: loans.
For More Information • Truman State University, Center for International Education Abroad, Kirk Building, 120, Kirksville, MO 63501; *Phone:* 660-785-4076; *Fax:* 660-785-7473. *E-mail:* ciea@truman.edu. *World Wide Web:* http://www2.truman.edu/ciea/

UNIVERSITY AT ALBANY, STATE UNIVERSITY OF NEW YORK
DIRECT ENROLLMENT AT THE UNIVERSITY OF GLASGOW

Hosted by University of Glasgow
Academic Focus • Full curriculum.
Program Information • Students attend classes at University of Glasgow.
Sessions • Fall, spring, yearlong.
Eligibility Requirements • Open to juniors, seniors, adults; 2.8 GPA; 2 letters of recommendation; good academic standing at home school.
Living Arrangements • Students live in host institution dormitories. Quarters are shared with host institution students, students from other programs. Meals are taken on one's own, in residences, in central dining facility, in restaurants.
Costs (2002-2003) • One term: $7970. Yearlong program: $15,940; includes housing, all meals, student support services, in-state tuition and fees. $150 nonrefundable deposit required. Financial aid available for students from sponsoring institution: all customary sources.
For More Information • University at Albany, State University of New York, Office of International Education, LI 66, Albany, NY 12222; *Phone:* 518-442-3525; *Fax:* 518-442-3338. *E-mail:* intled@uamail.albany.edu. *World Wide Web:* http://www.albany.edu/intled/

UNIVERSITY OF GLASGOW
STUDY ABROAD PROGRAMME

Hosted by Glasgow School of Art, University of Glasgow
Academic Focus • Full curriculum.
Program Information • Students attend classes at Glasgow School of Art, University of Glasgow. Field trips to archaelogical and historic sites.
Sessions • Fall, spring, yearlong, fall term.
Eligibility Requirements • Minimum age 18; open to precollege students, sophomores, juniors, seniors; 3.0 GPA; 2 letters of recommendation; good academic standing at home school; brief statement in support of application.
Living Arrangements • Students live in host institution dormitories, program-owned apartments, program-owned houses. Quarters are shared with host institution students, students from other programs. Meals are taken on one's own, in residences.
Costs (2003-2004) • One term: £2500–£3750. Yearlong program: £7500; includes tuition, student support services.
For More Information • Ms. Colette McGowan, Study Abroad Coordinator, University of Glasgow, Student Recruitment and

Admissions Service, No 1 The Square, Glasgow G12 8QQ, Scotland; *Phone:* +44 141-330-6516; *Fax:* +44 141-330-4045. *E-mail:* c.mcgowan@admin.gla.ac.uk. *World Wide Web:* http://www.gla.ac.uk/studying/studyabroad/

UNIVERSITY OF MIAMI
UNIVERSITY OF GLASGOW, SCOTLAND

Hosted by University of Glasgow
Academic Focus • Art history, biological/life sciences, economics, English, Gaelic, history, political science and government, psychology, Scottish studies, Welsh.
Program Information • Students attend classes at University of Glasgow.
Sessions • Fall, spring, yearlong.
Eligibility Requirements • Minimum age 18; open to sophomores, juniors; 3.0 GPA; 2 letters of recommendation; official transcripts; essay.
Living Arrangements • Students live in host institution dormitories. Quarters are shared with host institution students. Meals are taken on one's own, in residences, in central dining facility.
Costs (2003-2004) • One term: $12,919. Yearlong program: $25,838; includes tuition, student support services. $40 application fee. $500 nonrefundable deposit required. Financial aid available for students from sponsoring institution: scholarships, loans.
For More Information • Ms. Elyse Resnick, Assistant Director, University of Miami, International Education and Exchange Programs, 5050 Brunson Drive, Allen Hall 212, PO Box 248005, Coral Gables, FL 33124-1610; *Phone:* 305-284-3434; *Fax:* 305-284-4235. *E-mail:* ieep@miami.edu. *World Wide Web:* http://www.studyabroad.miami.edu/

UNIVERSITY OF STRATHCLYDE
STUDY ABROAD–STRATHCLYDE

Hosted by University of Strathclyde
Academic Focus • Business administration/management, education, engineering, science, Scottish studies, social sciences.
Program Information • Students attend classes at University of Strathclyde. Optional travel to the Isle of Skye, the Isle of Mull, Braemar, Carbisdale Castle at an extra cost.
Sessions • Fall, spring, yearlong.
Eligibility Requirements • Minimum age 18; open to juniors, seniors; 3.0 GPA.
Living Arrangements • Students live in host institution apartments. Quarters are shared with host institution students. Meals are taken on one's own, in residences.
Costs (2003-2004) • One term: £3810–£4875. Yearlong program: £7620–£9750; includes tuition, student support services. Financial aid available for all students: loans.
For More Information • Ms. Michelle Stewart, International Liaison Manager, University of Strathclyde, International Office, 50 George Street, Glasgow G1 1QE, Scotland; *Phone:* +44 141-548-2593; *Fax:* +44 141-552-7493. *E-mail:* m.stewart@mis.strath.ac.uk. *World Wide Web:* http://www.strath.ac.uk/. Students may also apply through International Student Exchange Program, (ISEP), 3222 N Street, NW, Suite 400, Washington, DC 20036; State University of New York at Brockport, Office of International Education, 350 New Campus Drive, Brockport, NY 14420.

GREENOCK
COLLEGE CONSORTIUM FOR INTERNATIONAL STUDIES–BROOKDALE COMMUNITY COLLEGE
JAMES WATT COLLEGE–PROGRAM IN SCOTLAND

Hosted by James Watt College
Academic Focus • Accounting, biomedical sciences, business administration/management, communications, computer science, design and applied arts, electrical engineering, European studies, finance, French language and literature, German language and literature, health and physical education, hospitality services, hotel and restaurant management, information science, journalism, liberal studies, science, social sciences, tourism and travel.

Program Information • Students attend classes at James Watt College. Field trips to Glasgow, Stirling, Edinburgh, Loch Lomond; optional travel to the Highlands, Glasgow, Edinburgh at an extra cost.
Sessions • Fall, spring, winter, yearlong.
Eligibility Requirements • Minimum age 18; open to freshmen, sophomores, juniors, seniors; 2.5 GPA; 3 letters of recommendation; essay; transcript; visa for internship; completion of 15 credits prior to application.
Living Arrangements • Students live in host institution dormitories. Quarters are shared with host institution students, students from other programs. Meals are taken on one's own, in residences, in central dining facility.
Costs (2004-2005) • One term: $6000. Yearlong program: $18,000; includes tuition, housing, insurance, excursions, student support services, fees, e-mail access, airport pick-up. $35 application fee. Financial aid available for students from sponsoring institution: scholarships, loans.
For More Information • College Consortium for International Studies, 2000 P Street, NW, Suite 503, Washington, DC 20036; *Phone:* 800-453-6956; *Fax:* 202-223-0999. *E-mail:* info@ccisabroad.org. *World Wide Web:* http://www.ccisabroad.org/. Students may also apply through Brookdale Community College, International Center, 765 Newman Springs Road, Lincroft, NJ 07738-1597.

ST. ANDREWS
INSTITUTE FOR STUDY ABROAD, BUTLER UNIVERSITY
UNIVERSITY OF ST. ANDREWS

Hosted by University of St. Andrews
Academic Focus • Full curriculum.
Program Information • Students attend classes at University of St. Andrews. Field trips to London, the Isle of Arran, the Isle of Iona, the Isle of Skye.
Sessions • Fall, spring, yearlong.
Eligibility Requirements • Open to juniors, seniors; 3.2 GPA; 2 letters of recommendation; good academic standing at home school; enrollment at an accredited American college or university.
Living Arrangements • Students live in host institution dormitories, locally rented apartments. Quarters are shared with host institution students, students from other programs. Meals are taken as a group, on one's own, in residences, in central dining facility.
Costs (2002-2003) • One term: $10,975. Yearlong program: $18,375; includes tuition, housing, excursions, international student ID, student support services, family visit, cultural and sporting events, pre-departure advising. $40 application fee. $500 nonrefundable deposit required. Financial aid available for all students: scholarships, travel grants.
For More Information • Institute for Study Abroad, Butler University, 1100 West 42nd Street, Suite 305, Indianapolis, IN 46208-3345; *Phone:* 800-858-0229; *Fax:* 317-940-9704. *E-mail:* study-abroad@butler.edu. *World Wide Web:* http://www.ifsa-butler.org/

INTERSTUDY
UNIVERSITY OF ST. ANDREWS

Hosted by University of St. Andrews
Academic Focus • Anthropology, art history, biological/life sciences, business administration/management, chemical sciences, classics and classical languages, computer science, economics, English, environmental science/studies, European studies, history, international affairs, linguistics, mathematics, music, philosophy, physics, psychology, science, social sciences.
Program Information • Students attend classes at University of St. Andrews. Scheduled travel to Bath, Stratford-upon-Avon, Warwick Castle, Oxford, Stonehenge.
Sessions • Fall, spring, yearlong.
Eligibility Requirements • Minimum age 18; open to freshmen, sophomores, juniors, seniors, adults; 3.0 GPA; 2 letters of recommendation; good academic standing at home school.
Living Arrangements • Students live in host institution dormitories, locally rented apartments. Quarters are shared with host institution students. Meals are taken on one's own, in residences.

Costs (2003-2004) • One term: $12,350 for fall term; $12,975 for spring. Yearlong program: $21,250; includes tuition, housing, some meals, excursions, international student ID, student support services, Student Union membership, e-mail access, banking facilities, international bank transfers, transcript, cell phone. $35 application fee. $500 nonrefundable deposit required. Financial aid available for all students: scholarships, loans, stipends.

For More Information • InterStudy, Admissions Office, 63 Edward Street, Medford, MA 02155; *Phone:* 800-663-1999; *Fax:* 781-391-7463. *E-mail:* interstudy@interstudy-usa.org. *World Wide Web:* http://www.interstudy.org/

RUTGERS, THE STATE UNIVERSITY OF NEW JERSEY
STUDY ABROAD IN SCOTLAND: ST. ANDREWS, SCOTLAND

Hosted by University of St. Andrews
Academic Focus • Full curriculum.
Program Information • Students attend classes at University of St. Andrews. Field trips to London, Stonehenge, Oxford.
Sessions • Fall, spring, yearlong.
Eligibility Requirements • Open to juniors, seniors; 3.0 GPA; 2 letters of recommendation; good academic standing at home school.
Living Arrangements • Students live in host institution dormitories. Quarters are shared with host institution students. Meals are taken on one's own, in residences, in central dining facility.
Costs (2003-2004) • One term: $11,790–$12,795 for New Jersey residents; $14,440–$15,445 for nonresidents. Yearlong program: $19,891 for New Jersey residents; $25,191 for nonresidents; includes tuition, insurance, excursions. $20 application fee. $750 nonrefundable deposit required. Financial aid available for students from sponsoring institution: scholarships, loans.
For More Information • Ms. Karin Bonello, Regional Coordinator, Rutgers, The State University of New Jersey, 102 College Avenue, New Brunswick, NJ 08901-8543; *Phone:* 732-932-7787; *Fax:* 732-932-8659. *E-mail:* ru_abroad@email.rutgers.edu. *World Wide Web:* http://studyabroad.rutgers.edu/

STATE UNIVERSITY OF NEW YORK COLLEGE AT BROCKPORT
UNIVERSITY OF ST. ANDREWS PROGRAM

Hosted by University of St. Andrews
Academic Focus • Full curriculum.
Program Information • Students attend classes at University of St. Andrews. Field trips to the London weekend program.
Sessions • Fall, spring, yearlong.
Eligibility Requirements • Minimum age 18; open to juniors, seniors, graduate students; 3.0 GPA; 2 letters of recommendation; good academic standing at home school; ability to do upper-division course work in chosen subject.
Living Arrangements • Students live in host institution dormitories. Quarters are shared with host institution students. Meals are taken on one's own, in residences.
Costs (2003-2004) • One term: $10,550 for fall term; $12,000 for spring. Yearlong program: $20,700; includes tuition, housing, excursions, international student ID, student support services. $350 nonrefundable deposit required. Financial aid available for all students: scholarships, loans, regular financial aid, grants.
For More Information • Dr. John J. Perry, Director, Office of International Education, State University of New York College at Brockport, 350 New Campus Drive, Brockport, NY 14420; *Phone:* 800-298-SUNY; *Fax:* 585-637-3218. *E-mail:* overseas@brockport.edu. *World Wide Web:* http://www.brockport.edu/studyabroad/

UNIVERSITY STUDIES ABROAD CONSORTIUM
FULL CURRICULUM STUDIES: ST. ANDREWS, SCOTLAND

Hosted by University of St. Andrews
Academic Focus • Full curriculum.
Program Information • Students attend classes at University of St. Andrews.
Sessions • Fall, spring, yearlong.
Eligibility Requirements • Minimum age 18; open to sophomores, juniors, seniors, graduate students, adults; 3.3 GPA.

Living Arrangements • Students live in host institution dormitories. Quarters are shared with host institution students. Meals are taken on one's own, in residences, in central dining facility.
Costs (2005-2006) • One term: $9980. Yearlong program: $19,780; includes tuition, insurance, student support services. $50 application fee. $150 refundable deposit required. Financial aid available for all students: scholarships, loans.
For More Information • University Studies Abroad Consortium, USAC/323, Reno, NV 89557-0093; *Phone:* 775-784-6569; *Fax:* 775-784-6010. *E-mail:* usac@unr.edu. *World Wide Web:* http://usac.unr.edu/

STIRLING
ARCADIA UNIVERSITY
UNIVERSITY OF STIRLING

Hosted by University of Stirling
Academic Focus • Biological/life sciences, film and media studies, history, social sciences, visual and performing arts.
Program Information • Students attend classes at University of Stirling.
Sessions • Fall, spring, yearlong.
Eligibility Requirements • Open to sophomores, juniors, seniors; 3.0 GPA; 1 letter of recommendation.
Living Arrangements • Students live in host institution dormitories. Quarters are shared with host institution students. Meals are taken on one's own, in residences, in central dining facility.
Costs (2003-2004) • One term: $10,590. Yearlong program: $17,490; includes tuition, housing, insurance, international student ID, student support services, transcripts, pre-departure guide. $35 application fee. $500 nonrefundable deposit required. Financial aid available for all students: scholarships, loans.
For More Information • Arcadia University, Center for Education Abroad, 450 South Easton Road, Glenside, PA 19038-3295; *Phone:* 866-927-2234; *Fax:* 215-572-2174. *E-mail:* cea@arcadia.edu. *World Wide Web:* http://www.arcadia.edu/cea/

CENTER FOR INTERNATIONAL STUDIES
UNIVERSITY OF STIRLING

Hosted by University of Stirling
Academic Focus • Full curriculum.
Program Information • Students attend classes at University of Stirling. Optional travel at an extra cost.
Sessions • Fall, spring, yearlong.
Eligibility Requirements • Minimum age 18; open to freshmen, sophomores, juniors, seniors, graduate students, adults; 2.5 GPA; 1 letter of recommendation; good academic standing at home school; personal essay.
Living Arrangements • Students live in locally rented apartments, program-owned apartments. Quarters are shared with host institution students, students from other programs. Meals are taken as a group, on one's own, in residences, in central dining facility, in restaurants.
Costs (2003-2004) • One term: $8400. Yearlong program: $14,900; includes tuition, housing, insurance, international student ID, student support services. $50 application fee. $500 nonrefundable deposit required. Financial aid available for all students: scholarships.
For More Information • Mr. Jeff Palm, Program Director, Center for International Studies, 17 New South Street, #105, Northampton, MA 01060; *Phone:* 413-582-0407; *Fax:* 413-582-0327. *E-mail:* jpalm@cisabroad.com. *World Wide Web:* http://www.cisabroad.com/

COLLEGE CONSORTIUM FOR INTERNATIONAL STUDIES–BROOKDALE COMMUNITY COLLEGE
UNIVERSITY OF STIRLING–PROGRAM IN SCOTLAND

Hosted by University of Stirling
Academic Focus • Full curriculum.

Program Information • Students attend classes at University of Stirling. Field trips to Trossachs, Loch Lomond, St. Andrews; optional travel to Glasgow, Edinburgh, the Highlands, London at an extra cost.

Sessions • Fall, spring, yearlong.

Eligibility Requirements • Minimum age 18; open to freshmen, sophomores, juniors, seniors; 3.0 GPA; 3 letters of recommendation; transcript; essay; 15 college credits.

Living Arrangements • Students live in host institution dormitories, program-owned apartments, program-owned houses. Quarters are shared with host institution students, students from other programs. Meals are taken on one's own, in residences, in central dining facility.

Costs (2004-2005) • One term: $6700. Yearlong program: $13,400; includes tuition, insurance, excursions, student support services, e-mail access, fees, airport pick-up. $35 application fee. Financial aid available for students from sponsoring institution: scholarships, loans.

For More Information • College Consortium for International Studies–Brookdale Community College, 2000 P Street, NW, Suite 503, Washington, DC 20036; *Phone:* 800-453-6956; *Fax:* 202-223-0999. *E-mail:* info@ccisabroad.org. *World Wide Web:* http://www.ccisabroad.org/

INSTITUTE FOR STUDY ABROAD, BUTLER UNIVERSITY
UNIVERSITY OF STIRLING

Hosted by University of Stirling

Academic Focus • Full curriculum.

Program Information • Students attend classes at University of Stirling. Field trips to London, the Isle of Arran, the Isle of Skye.

Sessions • Fall, spring, yearlong.

Eligibility Requirements • Open to juniors, seniors; 3.0 GPA; 1 letter of recommendation; good academic standing at home school; enrollment at an accredited American college or university; no foreign language proficiency required.

Living Arrangements • Students live in host institution dormitories, locally rented apartments. Quarters are shared with host institution students. Meals are taken on one's own, in residences.

Costs (2002-2003) • One term: $9775. Yearlong program: $15,875; includes tuition, housing, excursions, international student ID, student support services, family visit, cultural and sporting events, pre-departure advising. $40 application fee. $500 nonrefundable deposit required. Financial aid available for all students: scholarships, travel grants.

For More Information • Institute for Study Abroad, Butler University, 1100 West 42nd Street, Suite 305, Indianapolis, IN 46208-3345; *Phone:* 800-858-0229; *Fax:* 317-940-9704. *E-mail:* study-abroad@butler.edu. *World Wide Web:* http://www.ifsa-butler.org/

NORTH AMERICAN INSTITUTE FOR STUDY ABROAD
STUDY IN SCOTLAND

Hosted by University of Stirling

Academic Focus • Full curriculum.

Program Information • Students attend classes at University of Stirling.

Sessions • Fall, spring, yearlong.

Eligibility Requirements • Minimum age 18; open to sophomores, juniors, seniors; 3.0 GPA; good academic standing at home school.

Living Arrangements • Students live in host institution dormitories, locally rented apartments, host family homes. Quarters are shared with host institution students. Meals are taken on one's own, in residences, in central dining facility, in restaurants.

Costs (2003-2004) • One term: $9500. Yearlong program: $17,500; includes tuition, housing, international student ID, student support services, transcripts. $50 application fee. $500 nonrefundable deposit required. Financial aid available for all students: scholarships.

For More Information • Dr. Michael Currid, Director, North American Institute for Study Abroad, 129 Mill Street, Danville, PA 17821; *Phone:* 570-275-5099; *Fax:* 570-275-1644. *E-mail:* naisa@naisa.com. *World Wide Web:* http://www.naisa.com/

STATE UNIVERSITY OF NEW YORK COLLEGE AT BROCKPORT
UNIVERSITY OF STIRLING PROGRAM

Hosted by University of Stirling

Academic Focus • Full curriculum.

Program Information • Students attend classes at University of Stirling. Field trips to the London weekend program.

Sessions • Fall, spring, yearlong.

Eligibility Requirements • Minimum age 18; open to juniors, seniors; 3.0 GPA; 2 letters of recommendation; ability to do upper-division course work in chosen subject.

Living Arrangements • Students live in host institution dormitories. Quarters are shared with host institution students. Meals are taken on one's own, in residences.

Costs (2003-2004) • One term: $9950. Yearlong program: $18,550; includes tuition, housing, excursions, international student ID, student support services. $350 nonrefundable deposit required. Financial aid available for all students: loans, regular financial aid, grants.

For More Information • Dr. John J. Perry, Director, Office of International Education, State University of New York College at Brockport, 350 New Campus Drive, Brockport, NY 14420; *Phone:* 800-298-SUNY; *Fax:* 585-637-3218. *E-mail:* overseas@brockport.edu. *World Wide Web:* http://www.brockport.edu/studyabroad/

UNIVERSITY OF STIRLING
STUDY ABROAD

Hosted by University of Stirling

Academic Focus • Accounting, biological/life sciences, business administration/management, English literature, environmental science/studies, film and media studies, finance, fisheries studies, history, human resources, journalism, liberal studies, marine sciences, marketing, nursing, philosophy, political science and government, psychology, religious studies, Scottish studies, sociology, sports management, tourism and travel.

Program Information • Students attend classes at University of Stirling.

Sessions • Fall, spring, yearlong.

Eligibility Requirements • Minimum age 18; open to freshmen, sophomores, juniors, seniors; 3.0 GPA; 1 letter of recommendation; good academic standing at home school.

Living Arrangements • Students live in program-owned apartments, residences owned by the university. Quarters are shared with host institution students. Meals are taken on one's own, in residences, in central dining facility.

Costs (2003-2004) • One term: £6200. Yearlong program: £12,400; includes tuition, housing, all meals, books and class materials, lab equipment, student support services, local transportation, some personal expenses. Financial aid available for all students: loans.

For More Information • Ms. Wendy Reid, Assistant Recruitment and Admissions Officer, University of Stirling, Stirling FK9 4LA, Scotland; *Phone:* +44 178-646-7040; *Fax:* +44 178-646-6800. *E-mail:* study-abroad@stir.ac.uk. *World Wide Web:* http://www.stir.ac.uk/. Students may also apply through Butler University, Institute for Study Abroad, 1100 West 42nd Street, Indianapolis, IN 46208-3345; Arcadia University, Center for Education Abroad, 450 South Easton Road, Glenside, PA 19038-3295; State University of New York at Brockport, Office of International Education, 350 New Campus Drive, Brockport, NY 14420; University Studies Abroad Consortium, University of Nevada, Reno/323, Reno, NV 89557.

UNIVERSITY STUDIES ABROAD CONSORTIUM
FULL CURRICULUM STUDIES IN STIRLING, SCOTLAND

Hosted by University of Stirling

Academic Focus • Full curriculum.

Program Information • Students attend classes at University of Stirling. Optional travel to Edinburgh, the Britannia Tour, St. Andrew's, Falkland Palas, lochs, glens at an extra cost.

Sessions • Fall, spring, yearlong.

Eligibility Requirements • Minimum age 18; open to freshmen, sophomores, juniors, seniors, graduate students, adults; 2.8 GPA.

Living Arrangements • Students live in host institution dormitories. Quarters are shared with host institution students. Meals are taken on one's own, in residences, in central dining facility, in restaurants.

Costs (2005-2006) • One term: $6980. Yearlong program: $13,680; includes tuition, insurance, student support services. $50 application fee. $150 refundable deposit required. Financial aid available for all students: scholarships, loans.

For More Information • University Studies Abroad Consortium, USAC/323, Reno, NV 89557-0093; *Phone:* 775-784-6569; *Fax:* 775-784-6010. *E-mail:* usac@unr.edu. *World Wide Web:* http://usac. unr.edu/

SENEGAL

DAKAR

BELOIT COLLEGE
SENEGAL PROGRAM

Hosted by University Cheikh Anta Diop of Dakar
Academic Focus • African studies, French language and literature, Wolof.
Program Information • Students attend classes at University Cheikh Anta Diop of Dakar. Optional travel to other parts of Senegal, west Africa at an extra cost.
Sessions • Fall, spring, yearlong.
Eligibility Requirements • Open to sophomores, juniors, seniors; 4 letters of recommendation; evidence of preparation to study in Senegal; 3 years of college course work in French.
Living Arrangements • Students live in host family homes. Meals are taken with host family, in residences.
Costs (2002-2003) • One term: $14,232. Yearlong program: contact sponsor for cost; includes tuition, housing, all meals. $100 nonrefundable deposit required. Financial aid available for all students: loans.
For More Information • Office of International Education, Beloit College, 700 College Street, Beloit, WI 53511; *Phone:* 608-363-2269; *Fax:* 608-363-2689. *E-mail:* oie@beloit.edu. *World Wide Web:* http://www.beloit.edu/~oie/

CIEE
CIEE STUDY CENTER AT THE BAOBAB CENTER, DAKAR, SENEGAL

Hosted by Baobab Center, University Cheikh Anta Diop of Dakar
Academic Focus • African studies, community service, cultural studies, French language and literature, history, social sciences, Wolof.
Program Information • Students attend classes at University Cheikh Anta Diop of Dakar, Baobab Center. Field trips to Gorée Island, Lac Rose, Saint-Louis.
Sessions • Fall, spring, yearlong.
Eligibility Requirements • Open to sophomores, juniors, seniors; 2.75 GPA; 2 letters of recommendation; no foreign language proficiency required.
Living Arrangements • Students live in host family homes. Meals are taken with host family, in residences.
Costs (2003-2004) • One term: $8700. Yearlong program: $15,250; includes tuition, housing, all meals, insurance, excursions, student support services, cultural activities, pre-departure advising, membership to the French Cultural Center, optional on-site pick-up. $30 application fee. $300 deposit required. Financial aid available for all students: minority student scholarships, non-traditional study scholarships, travel grants.
For More Information • Ms. Hannah McChesney, Admissions Officer, Europe, Middle East, and Africa, CIEE, 7 Custom House Street, 3rd Floor, Portland, ME 04101; *Phone:* 800-40-STUDY; *Fax:* 207-553-7699. *E-mail:* studyinfo@ciee.org. *World Wide Web:* http://www.ciee.org/isp/

KALAMAZOO COLLEGE
KALAMAZOO IN SENEGAL

Hosted by University Cheikh Anta Diop of Dakar
Academic Focus • African studies, French language and literature, liberal studies, literature, social sciences, Wolof.
Program Information • Students attend classes at University Cheikh Anta Diop of Dakar. Scheduled travel to Saint-Louis, Yoff.
Sessions • Fall, yearlong.
Eligibility Requirements • Open to juniors; 2.75 GPA; 2 letters of recommendation; essay; demonstrated interest in African studies; must be a degree-seeking student at an accredited American college or university; 2 years of college course work in French.
Living Arrangements • Students live in program-owned houses, host family homes. Meals are taken as a group, with host family, in residences.
Costs (2003-2004) • One term: $19,592. Yearlong program: $29,388; includes tuition, housing, all meals, excursions, international airfare. $50 application fee. $300 nonrefundable deposit required. Financial aid available for students from sponsoring institution: scholarships, loans.
For More Information • Dr. Joseph L. Brockington, Director, Center for International Programs, Kalamazoo College, 1200 Academy Street, Kalamazoo, MI 49006; *Phone:* 269-337-7133; *Fax:* 269-337-7400. *E-mail:* cip@kzoo.edu. *World Wide Web:* http://www. kzoo.edu/cip/

MICHIGAN STATE UNIVERSITY
FRANKOPHONE STUDIES IN DAKAR

Hosted by University Cheikh Anta Diop of Dakar
Academic Focus • Full curriculum.
Program Information • Students attend classes at University Cheikh Anta Diop of Dakar. Scheduled travel to Saint-Louis; field trips to Pink Lake, Gorée Island, Joal-Gadiouth, Banjul, Fatick.
Sessions • Spring.
Eligibility Requirements • Minimum age 18; open to juniors, seniors, graduate students; 3.0 GPA; good academic standing at home school; 1 year college course work in French required; 2 years recommended.
Living Arrangements • Students live in host family homes. Meals are taken with host family, in residences.
Costs (2003) • One term: $6300; includes tuition, housing, all meals, insurance, excursions, international airfare, books and class materials, student support services. $100 application fee. $200 deposit required. Financial aid available for all students: scholarships, loans.
For More Information • Ms. Sherry Martinez-Bonilla, Office Assistant, Michigan State University, Office of Study Abroad, 109 International Center, East Lansing, MI 48824-1035; *Phone:* 517-353-8920; *Fax:* 517-432-2082. *E-mail:* marti269@msu.edu. *World Wide Web:* http://studyabroad.msu.edu/

SCHOOL FOR INTERNATIONAL TRAINING, SIT STUDY ABROAD
SENEGAL: ARTS AND CULTURE

Academic Focus • African studies, anthropology, art history, French language and literature, visual and performing arts, Wolof.
Program Information • Faculty members are drawn from the sponsor's U.S. staff and local instructors hired by the sponsor. Scheduled travel to Saint-Louis, Lac Rose, eastern Senegal; field trips to Gorée Island, the Dakar area.
Sessions • Fall, spring.
Eligibility Requirements • Open to sophomores, juniors, seniors; 2.5 GPA; 2 letters of recommendation; good academic standing at home school; 1.5 years of college course work in French.
Living Arrangements • Students live in host family homes. Meals are taken as a group, on one's own, with host family, in residences, in restaurants.
Costs (2003-2004) • One term: $12,075; includes tuition, housing, all meals, insurance, excursions. $50 application fee. $400 nonrefundable deposit required. Financial aid available for all students: scholarships.
For More Information • School for International Training, SIT Study Abroad, Kipling Road, Brattleboro, VT 05302-0676; *Phone:* 888-272-7881; *Fax:* 802-258-3296. *E-mail:* studyabroad@sit.edu. *World Wide Web:* http://www.sit.edu/studyabroad/

SENEGAL
Dakar

UNIVERSITY OF MINNESOTA
MINNESOTA STUDIES IN INTERNATIONAL DEVELOPMENT (MSID), SENEGAL

Hosted by West African Research Center

Academic Focus • African studies, agriculture, anthropology, community service, conservation studies, economics, education, environmental health, environmental science/studies, French language and literature, international affairs, public policy, social sciences, social services, urban/regional planning, Wolof, women's studies.

Program Information • Students attend classes at West African Research Center. Field trips to development projects, Senegal; optional travel to sites in Senegal at an extra cost.

Sessions • Fall, spring, yearlong.

Eligibility Requirements • Minimum age 19; open to juniors, seniors, graduate students, adults; course work in development studies, area studies, social sciences; 2.5 GPA; 2 letters of recommendation; good academic standing at home school; 2 years of college course work in French.

Living Arrangements • Students live in host family homes. Meals are taken with host family, in residences.

Costs (2004-2005) • One term: contact sponsor for cost. Yearlong program: contact sponsor for cost. $50 application fee. $400 nonrefundable deposit required. Financial aid available for students from sponsoring institution: scholarships, loans.

For More Information • University of Minnesota, Learning Abroad Center, 230 Heller Hall, 271 19th Avenue South, Minneapolis, MN 55455; *Phone:* 612-626-9000; *Fax:* 612-626-8009. *E-mail:* umabroad@umn.edu. *World Wide Web:* http://www.umabroad.umn.edu/

WELLS COLLEGE
PROGRAM IN DAKAR

Hosted by WARE, ACI Baobab Center, University Cheikh Anta Diop of Dakar

Academic Focus • African studies, art, French language and literature, history, literature, music, sociology, Wolof, women's studies.

Program Information • Students attend classes at University Cheikh Anta Diop of Dakar, ACI Baobab Center, WARE. Field trips to St. Louis, Gorée Island, Touba.

Sessions • Spring.

Eligibility Requirements • Minimum age 19; open to juniors, seniors, graduate students, adults; 2.8 GPA; 2 letters of recommendation; good academic standing at home school; 2.5 years of college course work in French.

Living Arrangements • Students live in host family homes. Meals are taken as a group, on one's own, with host family, in residences, in central dining facility.

Costs (2005) • One term: $10,150; includes tuition, housing, all meals, excursions, international airfare, international student ID, student support services, local transportation, some class materials. $55 application fee. $1000 refundable deposit required. Financial aid available for students from sponsoring institution: scholarships, loans.

For More Information • Dr. Lydie J. Haenlin, Program Director, Wells College, Main Street, Aurora, NY 13026; *Phone:* 315-364-3308; *Fax:* 315-364-3257. *E-mail:* dakar@wells.edu. *World Wide Web:* http://www.wells.edu/academic/ac2d.htm

SAINT-LOUIS

UNIVERSITY OF WISCONSIN–MADISON
SAINT-LOUIS, SENEGAL

Hosted by Gaston Berger University of Saint-Louis

Academic Focus • Economics, French language and literature, liberal studies, political science and government, social sciences, Wolof.

Program Information • Students attend classes at Gaston Berger University of Saint-Louis. Field trips to Dakar.

Sessions • Yearlong.

Eligibility Requirements • Open to juniors, seniors, graduate students; 2.5 GPA; 2 letters of recommendation; minimum 3.0 GPA in French; 2 years of college course work in French.

Living Arrangements • Students live in host institution dormitories, locally rented apartments. Quarters are shared with host institution students. Meals are taken on one's own, in central dining facility.

Costs (2002-2003) • Yearlong program: $14,300 for Wisconsin residents; $18,400 for nonresidents; includes tuition, housing, all meals, insurance, international airfare, books and class materials, student support services, local transportation, personal expenses. $100 nonrefundable deposit required. Financial aid available for students from sponsoring institution: scholarships, loans.

For More Information • Peer Advisor, University of Wisconsin-Madison, Office of International Studies and Programs, 261 Bascom Hall, 500 Lincoln Drive, Madison, WI 53706; *Phone:* 608-265-6329; *Fax:* 608-262-6998. *E-mail:* peeradvisor@bascom.wisc.edu. *World Wide Web:* http://www.studyabroad.wisc.edu/

SINGAPORE
SINGAPORE

UNIVERSITY OF MIAMI
NANYANG TECHNOLOGICAL UNIVERSITY

Hosted by Nanyang Technological University

Academic Focus • Business administration/management, education, engineering, science.

Program Information • Students attend classes at Nanyang Technological University.

Sessions • Fall, spring, yearlong.

Eligibility Requirements • Minimum age 18; open to sophomores, juniors, seniors; 3.0 GPA; 2 letters of recommendation; good academic standing at home school; no foreign language proficiency required.

Living Arrangements • Students live in host institution dormitories. Quarters are shared with host institution students. Meals are taken on one's own, in central dining facility.

Costs (2003-2004) • One term: $12,919. Yearlong program: $25,838; includes tuition, student support services. $40 application fee. $500 nonrefundable deposit required. Financial aid available for students from sponsoring institution: scholarships, loans.

For More Information • Ms. Glenda Hayley, Assistant Director, University of Miami, International Education and Exchange Programs, 5050 Brunson Drive, Allen Hall 212, PO Box 248005, Coral Gables, FL 33124-1610; *Phone:* 305-284-3434; *Fax:* 305-284-4235. *E-mail:* ieep@miami.edu. *World Wide Web:* http://www.studyabroad.miami.edu/

SLOVAKIA
BRATISLAVA

ACIE (ACTR/ACCELS)
ACIE (ACCELS) SLOVAK LANGUAGE PROGRAMS

Hosted by Comenius University in Bratislava

Academic Focus • Slavic languages.

Program Information • Students attend classes at Comenius University in Bratislava.

Sessions • Fall, spring, yearlong.

Eligibility Requirements • Minimum age 18; open to freshmen, sophomores, juniors, seniors, graduate students, adults; 3 letters of recommendation; good academic standing at home school; 1 year of college course work in Slovak.

Living Arrangements • Students live in host institution dormitories, locally rented apartments. Quarters are shared with students from other programs. Meals are taken on one's own, in residences, in central dining facility.

Costs (2002-2003) • One term: contact sponsor for cost. Yearlong program: contact sponsor for cost. $35 application fee. $500 nonrefundable deposit required. Financial aid available for all students: scholarships.
For More Information • Nurhan Kocaoglu, Russian and Eurasian Program Manager, ACIE (ACTR/ACCELS), 1776 Massachusetts Avenue, NW, Suite 700, Washington, DC 20036; Phone: 202-833-7522; Fax: 202-833-7523. E-mail: outbound@actr.org. World Wide Web: http://www.actr.org/

SOUTH AFRICA

CITY TO CITY

ORGANIZATION FOR TROPICAL STUDIES
OTS UNDERGRADUATE SEMESTER ABROAD IN SOUTH AFRICA

Held at Kruger National Park
Academic Focus • African studies, biological/life sciences, conservation studies, ecology, environmental science/studies.
Program Information • Classes are held on the campus of Kruger National Park (South Africa). Faculty members are drawn from the sponsor's U.S. staff and local instructors hired by the sponsor. Scheduled travel to Cape Town; field trips to other national parks (Nylsvley).
Sessions • Spring.
Eligibility Requirements • Open to sophomores, juniors, seniors; course work in biology; 2 letters of recommendation; good academic standing at home school.
Living Arrangements • Students live in rest camps at national parks. Meals are taken as a group, in central dining facility.
Costs (2004) • One term: $17,300; includes tuition, housing, all meals, excursions, books and class materials, lab equipment. $1000 nonrefundable deposit required. Financial aid available for all students: scholarships.
For More Information • Mr. Rodney J. Vargas, Undergraduate Program Officer, Organization for Tropical Studies, Box 90630, Duke University/OTS, Durham, NC 27708-0630; Phone: 919-684-5574; Fax: 919-684-5661. E-mail: nao@duke.edu. World Wide Web: http://www.ots.duke.edu/

ALICE

INTERSTUDY
UNIVERSITY OF FORT HARE

Hosted by University of Fort Hare
Academic Focus • African languages and literature, agriculture, anthropology, archaeology, art, botany, communications, economics, education, English literature, history, law and legal studies, mathematics, music, philosophy, political science and government, religious studies, sociology, zoology.
Program Information • Students attend classes at University of Fort Hare. Scheduled travel to game reserves, elephant parks, history tours; optional travel to Zimbabwe, game parks, Namibia, Botswana, Cape Town at an extra cost.
Sessions • Fall, spring, yearlong.
Eligibility Requirements • Minimum age 18; open to freshmen, sophomores, juniors, seniors, graduate students, adults; 2.5 GPA; 2 letters of recommendation; good academic standing at home school.
Living Arrangements • Students live in host institution dormitories. Quarters are shared with host institution students. Meals are taken as a group, in central dining facility.
Costs (2003-2004) • One term: $8175. Yearlong program: $14,650; includes tuition, housing, some meals, excursions, international student ID, student support services, Student Union membership, e-mail access, banking facilities, international bank transfers, transcript, visa processing, cell phones. $35 application fee. $500 nonrefundable deposit required. Financial aid available for all students: scholarships, loans, stipends.

For More Information • InterStudy, Admissions Office, 63 Edward Street, Medford, MA 02155; Phone: 800-663-1999; Fax: 781-391-7463. E-mail: interstudy@interstudy-usa.org. World Wide Web: http://www.interstudy.org/

BELLVILLE

INTERSTUDY
UNIVERSITY OF THE WESTERN CAPE

Hosted by University of Western Cape
Academic Focus • Anthropology, botany, business administration/management, chemical sciences, computer science, economics, environmental science/studies, geography, history, international affairs, liberal studies, linguistics, mathematics, nursing, philosophy, political science and government, psychology, science, zoology.
Program Information • Students attend classes at University of Western Cape. Scheduled travel to game reserves, elephant parks, historic tours; optional travel to Zimbabwe, game parks, Namibia, Botswana, Cape Town at an extra cost.
Sessions • Fall, spring, yearlong.
Eligibility Requirements • Minimum age 18; open to freshmen, sophomores, juniors, seniors, graduate students, adults; 2.5 GPA; 2 letters of recommendation; good academic standing at home school.
Living Arrangements • Students live in host institution dormitories, locally rented apartments. Quarters are shared with host institution students. Meals are taken as a group, on one's own, in residences, in central dining facility.
Costs (2003-2004) • One term: $8350. Yearlong program: $15,625; includes tuition, housing, some meals, excursions, international student ID, student support services, Student Union membership, e-mail access, banking facilities, international bank transfers, transcript, visa processing, cell phone. $35 application fee. $500 nonrefundable deposit required. Financial aid available for all students: scholarships, loans, stipends.
For More Information • InterStudy, Admissions Office, 63 Edward Street, Medford, MA 02155; Phone: 800-663-1999; Fax: 781-391-7463. E-mail: interstudy@interstudy-usa.org. World Wide Web: http://www.interstudy.org/

BLOEMFONTEIN

INTERSTUDY
UNIVERSITY OF THE FREE STATE

Hosted by University of the Orange Free State
Academic Focus • Accounting, African studies, agriculture, anthropology, business administration/management, communications, economics, environmental science/studies, fine/studio arts, history, law and legal studies, music, nursing, political science and government, psychology, religious studies, science, sociology.
Program Information • Students attend classes at University of the Orange Free State. Scheduled travel to game reserves, elephant parks, historic tours; optional travel to Zimbabwe, game parks, Namibia, Botswana, Cape Town at an extra cost.
Sessions • Fall, spring, yearlong.
Eligibility Requirements • Minimum age 18; open to freshmen, sophomores, juniors, seniors, graduate students, adults; 2.7 GPA; 2 letters of recommendation; good academic standing at home school.
Living Arrangements • Students live in host institution dormitories. Quarters are shared with host institution students. Meals are taken as a group, on one's own, in residences, in central dining facility.
Costs (2003-2004) • One term: $8675. Yearlong program: $15,425; includes tuition, housing, some meals, excursions, international student ID, student support services, Student Union membership, e-mail access, banking facilities, international bank transfers, transcript, visa processing, cell phone. $35 application fee. $500 nonrefundable deposit required. Financial aid available for all students: scholarships, loans, stipends.
For More Information • InterStudy, Admissions Office, 63 Edward Street, Medford, MA 02155; Phone: 800-663-1999; Fax: 781-391-7463. E-mail: interstudy@interstudy-usa.org. World Wide Web: http://www.interstudy.org/

CAPE TOWN

CIEE
CIEE STUDY CENTER AT THE UNIVERSITY OF CAPE TOWN, SOUTH AFRICA

Hosted by University of Cape Town
Academic Focus • Full curriculum.
Program Information • Students attend classes at University of Cape Town. Field trips to Cape Peninsula, Robben Island.
Sessions • Fall, spring, yearlong.
Eligibility Requirements • Open to juniors, seniors, graduate students, adults; course work in African studies; 3.0 GPA; 2 letters of recommendation; no foreign language proficiency required.
Living Arrangements • Students live in host institution dormitories, locally rented apartments. Quarters are shared with host institution students. Meals are taken on one's own, in central dining facility, in restaurants.
Costs (2003-2004) • One term: $9800. Yearlong program: $17,500; includes tuition, housing, all meals, insurance, excursions, student support services, pre-departure advising, cultural activities, visa fees, optional on-site pick-up. $30 application fee. $300 deposit required. Financial aid available for all students: minority student scholarships, non-traditional study grants, travel grants.
For More Information • Ms. Hannah McChesney, Admissions Officer, Europe, Middle East, and Africa, CIEE, 7 Custom House Street, 3rd Floor, Portland, ME 04101; *Phone:* 800-40-STUDY; *Fax:* 207-553-7699. *E-mail:* studyinfo@ciee.org. *World Wide Web:* http://www.ciee.org/isp/

INTERSTUDY
UNIVERSITY OF CAPE TOWN

Hosted by University of Cape Town
Academic Focus • Anthropology, botany, business administration/management, chemical sciences, computer science, economics, environmental science/studies, geography, history, international affairs, law and legal studies, liberal studies, linguistics, mathematics, music, nursing, philosophy, political science and government, science.
Program Information • Students attend classes at University of Cape Town. Scheduled travel to game reserves, elephant parks, historic tours; optional travel to Zimbabwe, game parks, Namibia, Botswana, Cape Town at an extra cost.
Sessions • Fall, spring, yearlong.
Eligibility Requirements • Minimum age 18; open to freshmen, sophomores, juniors, seniors, graduate students, adults; 3.0 GPA; 2 letters of recommendation; good academic standing at home school.
Living Arrangements • Students live in host institution dormitories, locally rented apartments. Quarters are shared with host institution students. Meals are taken as a group, on one's own, in residences, in central dining facility.
Costs (2003-2004) • One term: $8950. Yearlong program: $16,690; includes tuition, housing, some meals, excursions, international student ID, student support services, Student Union membership, e-mail access, banking facilities, international bank transfers, transcript, visa processing, cell phones. $35 application fee. $500 nonrefundable deposit required. Financial aid available for all students: scholarships, loans, stipends.
For More Information • InterStudy, Admissions Office, 63 Edward Street, Medford, MA 02155; *Phone:* 800-663-1999; *Fax:* 781-391-7463. *E-mail:* interstudy@interstudy-usa.org. *World Wide Web:* http://www.interstudy.org/

LEXIA INTERNATIONAL
LEXIA IN CAPE TOWN

Hosted by University of Western Cape
Academic Focus • African languages and literature, African studies, anthropology, area studies, art, art history, civilization studies, comparative history, cultural studies, drawing/painting, economics, environmental science/studies, ethnic studies, film and media studies, fine/studio arts, geography, history, interdisciplinary studies, international affairs, international business, liberal studies, literature, music, music history, music performance, peace and conflict studies, philosophy, political science and government, psychology, religious studies, social sciences, sociology, urban studies, Xhosa.
Program Information • Students attend classes at University of Western Cape. Field trips to Cape of Good Hope, the wine route, a peninsula tour, game parks, wildlife reserves.
Sessions • Fall, spring, yearlong.
Eligibility Requirements • Minimum age 18; open to sophomores, juniors, seniors, graduate students, adults; 2.5 GPA; 2 letters of recommendation; no foreign language proficiency required.
Living Arrangements • Students live in host institution dormitories, host family homes. Quarters are shared with host institution students. Meals are taken on one's own, with host family, in residences, in central dining facility.
Costs (2003-2004) • One term: $10,950. Yearlong program: $20,550; includes tuition, housing, some meals, insurance, excursions, international student ID, student support services, computer access, transcript. $35 application fee. $300 refundable deposit required. Financial aid available for all students: scholarships, work study.
For More Information • Lexia International, 23 South Main Street, Hanover, NH 03755; *Phone:* 800-775-3942; *Fax:* 603-643-9899. *E-mail:* info@lexiaintl.org. *World Wide Web:* http://www.lexiaintl.org/

SCHOOL FOR INTERNATIONAL TRAINING, SIT STUDY ABROAD
SOUTH AFRICA: MULTICULTURALISM AND SOCIAL CHANGE

Academic Focus • Anthropology, economics, ethnic studies, history, intercultural studies, literature, music, political science and government, visual and performing arts, Xhosa.
Program Information • Faculty members are drawn from the sponsor's U.S. staff and local instructors hired by the sponsor. Scheduled travel to the Umfolozi Game Reserve, Durban, Johannesburg; field trips to natural reserves, historic sites.
Sessions • Fall, spring.
Eligibility Requirements • Open to sophomores, juniors, seniors; 2.5 GPA; 2 letters of recommendation; good academic standing at home school; no foreign language proficiency required.
Living Arrangements • Students live in host family homes, hotels. Meals are taken as a group, on one's own, with host family, in residences, in restaurants.
Costs (2003-2004) • One term: $12,300; includes tuition, housing, all meals, insurance, excursions. $50 application fee. $400 nonrefundable deposit required. Financial aid available for all students: scholarships.
For More Information • School for International Training, SIT Study Abroad, Kipling Road, Brattleboro, VT 05302-0676; *Phone:* 888-272-7881; *Fax:* 802-258-3296. *E-mail:* studyabroad@sit.edu. *World Wide Web:* http://www.sit.edu/studyabroad/

UNIVERSITY AT ALBANY, STATE UNIVERSITY OF NEW YORK
DIRECT ENROLLMENT AT THE UNIVERSITY OF CAPE TOWN

Hosted by University of Cape Town
Academic Focus • African studies, full curriculum.
Program Information • Students attend classes at University of Cape Town. Field trips to Cape of Good Hope, Robben Island.
Sessions • Fall, spring, yearlong, University of Cape Town academic year.
Eligibility Requirements • Open to sophomores, juniors, seniors, graduate students; 3.0 GPA; 2 letters of recommendation; good academic standing at home school; no foreign language proficiency required.
Living Arrangements • Students live in locally rented apartments. Quarters are shared with students from other programs. Meals are taken on one's own, in residences, in restaurants.
Costs (2003-2004) • One term: $6985. Yearlong program: $13,968; includes housing, all meals, student support services, in-state tuition and fees. $150 nonrefundable deposit required. Financial aid available for students from sponsoring institution: all customary sources.
For More Information • University at Albany, State University of New York, Office of International Education, LI 66, Albany, NY 12222; *Phone:* 518-442-3525; *Fax:* 518-442-3338. *E-mail:* intled@uamail.albany.edu. *World Wide Web:* http://www.albany.edu/intled/

DURBAN
INTERSTUDY
UNIVERSITY OF NATAL AT DURBAN

Hosted by University of Natal
Academic Focus • Accounting, architecture, business administration/management, chemical sciences, computer science, economics, education, engineering, environmental science/studies, geology, law and legal studies, music, nursing, physics, political science and government.
Program Information • Students attend classes at University of Natal. Scheduled travel to game reserves, elephant parks, historic tours; optional travel to Zimbabwe, game parks, Namibia, Botswana, Cape Town at an extra cost.
Sessions • Fall, spring, yearlong.
Eligibility Requirements • Minimum age 18; open to freshmen, sophomores, juniors, seniors, graduate students, adults; 3.0 GPA; 2 letters of recommendation; good academic standing at home school.
Living Arrangements • Students live in host institution dormitories. Quarters are shared with host institution students. Meals are taken as a group, on one's own, in residences.
Costs (2003-2004) • One term: $8995. Yearlong program: $16,150; includes tuition, housing, some meals, excursions, international student ID, student support services, Student Union membership, e-mail access, banking facilities, international bank transfers, transcript, visa processing, cell phones. $35 application fee. $500 nonrefundable deposit required. Financial aid available for all students: scholarships, loans, stipends.
For More Information • InterStudy, Admissions Office, 63 Edward Street, Medford, MA 02155; *Phone:* 800-663-1999; *Fax:* 781-391-7463. *E-mail:* interstudy@interstudy-usa.org. *World Wide Web:* http://www.interstudy.org/

MICHIGAN STATE UNIVERSITY
MULTIDISCIPLINARY STUDIES IN DURBAN

Hosted by University of Durban Westville
Academic Focus • Full curriculum.
Program Information • Students attend classes at University of Durban Westville.
Sessions • Fall, spring, yearlong.
Eligibility Requirements • Minimum age 18; open to juniors, seniors, graduate students; course work in African studies (recommended); 3.0 GPA; good academic standing at home school; faculty approval; no foreign language proficiency required.
Living Arrangements • Students live in host institution dormitories. Quarters are shared with host institution students. Meals are taken on one's own, in residences, in central dining facility, in restaurants.
Costs (2002-2003) • One term: $6218 (estimated). Yearlong program: $10,936 (estimated); includes tuition, housing, all meals, insurance, excursions, international airfare, books and class materials, student support services. $100 application fee. $200 nonrefundable deposit required. Financial aid available for all students: scholarships, loans.
For More Information • Ms. Sherry Martinez-Bonilla, Office Assistant, Michigan State University, Office of Study Abroad, 109 International Center, East Lansing, MI 48824-1035; *Phone:* 517-353-8920; *Fax:* 517-432-2082. *E-mail:* marti269@msu.edu. *World Wide Web:* http://studyabroad.msu.edu/

SCHOOL FOR INTERNATIONAL TRAINING, SIT STUDY ABROAD
SOUTH AFRICA: RECONCILIATION AND DEVELOPMENT

Academic Focus • Anthropology, education, geography, history, peace and conflict studies, political science and government, Zulu.
Program Information • Faculty members are drawn from the sponsor's U.S. staff and local instructors hired by the sponsor. Scheduled travel to Cape Town, Western Cape; field trips to Johannesburg, Soweto, Pretoria.
Sessions • Fall, spring.
Eligibility Requirements • Open to sophomores, juniors, seniors; 2.5 GPA; 2 letters of recommendation; good academic standing at home school; no foreign language proficiency required.

Living Arrangements • Students live in host family homes, hotels. Meals are taken as a group, on one's own, with host family, in residences, in restaurants.
Costs (2003-2004) • One term: $12,300; includes tuition, housing, all meals, insurance, excursions. $50 application fee. $400 nonrefundable deposit required. Financial aid available for all students: scholarships.
For More Information • School for International Training, SIT Study Abroad, Kipling Road, Brattleboro, VT 05302-0676; *Phone:* 888-272-7881; *Fax:* 802-258-3296. *E-mail:* studyabroad@sit.edu. *World Wide Web:* http://www.sit.edu/studyabroad/

UNIVERSITY AT ALBANY, STATE UNIVERSITY OF NEW YORK
DIRECT ENROLLMENT AT THE UNIVERSITY OF NATAL, DURBAN OR PIETERMARITZBURG

Hosted by University of Natal, University of Natal
Academic Focus • Full curriculum.
Program Information • Students attend classes at University of Natal, University of Natal. Optional travel to game parks, battle sites at an extra cost.
Sessions • Fall, spring, yearlong, University of Natal academic year.
Eligibility Requirements • Open to sophomores, juniors, seniors, graduate students; 3.0 GPA; 2 letters of recommendation; good academic standing at home school; no foreign language proficiency required.
Living Arrangements • Students live in host institution dormitories. Meals are taken on one's own, in residences, in central dining facility.
Costs (2003-2004) • One term: $4739. Yearlong program: $9429; includes housing, all meals, student support services, in-state tuition and fees. $150 nonrefundable deposit required. Financial aid available for students from sponsoring institution: all customary sources.
For More Information • University at Albany, State University of New York, Office of International Education, LI 66, Albany, NY 12222; *Phone:* 518-442-3525; *Fax:* 518-442-3338. *E-mail:* intled@uamail.albany.edu. *World Wide Web:* http://www.albany.edu/intled/

GRAHAMSTOWN
INTERSTUDY
RHODES UNIVERSITY

Hosted by Rhodes University
Academic Focus • Accounting, African languages and literature, art, biochemistry, botany, business administration/management, computer science, drama/theater, economics, education, environmental health, history, journalism, law and legal studies, mathematics, music, philosophy, social sciences, sociology, statistics, zoology.
Program Information • Students attend classes at Rhodes University. Scheduled travel to game reserves, elephant parks, historic tours; optional travel to Zimbabwe, game parks, Botswana, Namibia, Cape Town at an extra cost.
Sessions • Fall, spring, yearlong.
Eligibility Requirements • Minimum age 18; open to freshmen, sophomores, juniors, seniors, graduate students, adults; 3.0 GPA; 2 letters of recommendation; good academic standing at home school.
Living Arrangements • Students live in host institution dormitories. Quarters are shared with host institution students. Meals are taken as a group, in residences, in central dining facility.
Costs (2003-2004) • One term: $8355. Yearlong program: $14,675; includes tuition, housing, some meals, excursions, international student ID, student support services, Student Union membership, e-mail access, banking facilities, international bank transfers, transcript, visa processing, cell phones. $35 application fee. $500 nonrefundable deposit required. Financial aid available for all students: scholarships, loans, stipends.
For More Information • InterStudy, Admissions Office, 63 Edward Street, Medford, MA 02155; *Phone:* 800-663-1999; *Fax:* 781-391-7463. *E-mail:* interstudy@interstudy-usa.org. *World Wide Web:* http://www.interstudy.org/

JOHANNESBURG

INTERSTUDY
UNIVERSITY OF WITWATERSRAND

Hosted by University of the Witwatersrand

Academic Focus • Accounting, African languages and literature, African studies, archaeology, architecture, art, art history, biochemistry, botany, classics and classical languages, drama/theater, economics, electrical engineering, English, geology, history, international affairs, linguistics, mathematics, mechanical engineering, nursing, philosophy, physics, political science and government, psychology, sociology.

Program Information • Students attend classes at University of the Witwatersrand. Scheduled travel to game reserves, elephant parks, historic tours; optional travel to Zimbabwe, game parks, Namibia, Botswana, Cape Town at an extra cost.

Sessions • Fall, spring, yearlong.

Eligibility Requirements • Minimum age 18; open to freshmen, sophomores, juniors, seniors, graduate students, adults; 3.0 GPA; 2 letters of recommendation; good academic standing at home school.

Living Arrangements • Students live in host institution dormitories, locally rented apartments. Quarters are shared with host institution students. Meals are taken as a group, on one's own, in residences, in central dining facility.

Costs (2003-2004) • One term: $9725. Yearlong program: $16,795; includes tuition, housing, some meals, excursions, international student ID, student support services, Student Union membership, e-mail access, banking facilities, international bank transfers, transcript, visa processing, cell phones. $35 application fee. $500 nonrefundable deposit required. Financial aid available for all students: scholarships, loans, stipends.

For More Information • InterStudy, Admissions Office, 63 Edward Street, Medford, MA 02155; *Phone:* 800-663-1999; *Fax:* 781-391-7463. *E-mail:* interstudy@interstudy-usa.org. *World Wide Web:* http://www.interstudy.org/

PIETERMARITZBURG

INTERSTUDY
UNIVERSITY OF NATAL AT PIETERMARITZBURG

Hosted by University of Natal

Academic Focus • Agriculture, business administration/management, communications, environmental science/studies, law and legal studies, mathematics, psychology, social sciences.

Program Information • Students attend classes at University of Natal. Scheduled travel to game reserves, elephant parks, historic tours; optional travel to Zimbabwe, game parks, Namibia, Botswana, Cape Town at an extra cost.

Sessions • Fall, spring, yearlong.

Eligibility Requirements • Minimum age 18; open to freshmen, sophomores, juniors, seniors, graduate students, adults; 3.0 GPA; 2 letters of recommendation; good academic standing at home school.

Living Arrangements • Students live in host institution dormitories. Quarters are shared with host institution students. Meals are taken on one's own, in residences, in central dining facility.

Costs (2003-2004) • One term: $8850. Yearlong program: $15,925; includes tuition, housing, some meals, excursions, international student ID, student support services, Student Union membership, e-mail access, banking facilities, international bank transfers, transcript, visa processing, cell phones. $35 application fee. $500 nonrefundable deposit required. Financial aid available for all students: scholarships, loans, stipends.

For More Information • InterStudy, Admissions Office, 63 Edward Street, Medford, MA 02155; *Phone:* 800-663-1999; *Fax:* 781-391-7463. *E-mail:* interstudy@interstudy-usa.org. *World Wide Web:* http://www.interstudy.org/

RUTGERS, THE STATE UNIVERSITY OF NEW JERSEY
STUDY ABROAD IN SOUTH AFRICA

Hosted by University of Natal

Academic Focus • Full curriculum.

Program Information • Students attend classes at University of Natal. Optional travel to Cape Town at an extra cost.

Sessions • Fall, spring, yearlong.

Eligibility Requirements • Open to sophomores, juniors, seniors; 2.5 GPA; 2 letters of recommendation; good academic standing at home school; official transcript from each tertiary school attended.

Living Arrangements • Students live in host institution dormitories, locally rented apartments. Quarters are shared with host institution students. Meals are taken on one's own, in residences.

Costs (2003-2004) • One term: $6837 for New Jersey residents; $9487 for nonresidents. Yearlong program: $12,494 for New Jersey residents; $17,794 for nonresidents; includes tuition, housing, insurance, student support services. $20 application fee. $750 nonrefundable deposit required. Financial aid available for students from sponsoring institution: scholarships, loans.

For More Information • Ms. Karin Bonello, Regional Coordinator, Rutgers, The State University of New Jersey, 102 College Avenue, New Brunswick, NJ 08901-8543; *Phone:* 732-932-7787; *Fax:* 732-932-8659. *E-mail:* ru_abroad@email.rutgers.edu. *World Wide Web:* http://studyabroad.rutgers.edu/

PORT ELIZABETH

INTERSTUDY
UNIVERSITY OF PORT ELIZABETH

Hosted by University of Port Elizabeth

Academic Focus • Accounting, architecture, biochemistry, botany, business administration/management, economics, education, environmental science/studies, geography, law and legal studies, liberal studies, music, nursing, physics, psychology, science, social sciences, zoology.

Program Information • Students attend classes at University of Port Elizabeth. Scheduled travel to game reserves, elephant parks, historic tours; optional travel to Zimbabwe, game parks, Namibia, Botswana, Cape Town at an extra cost.

Sessions • Fall, spring, yearlong.

Eligibility Requirements • Minimum age 18; open to freshmen, sophomores, juniors, seniors, graduate students, adults; 2.5 GPA; 2 letters of recommendation; good academic standing at home school.

Living Arrangements • Students live in host institution dormitories, locally rented apartments. Quarters are shared with host institution students. Meals are taken as a group, on one's own, in residences, in central dining facility.

Costs (2003-2004) • One term: $7750. Yearlong program: $13,950; includes tuition, housing, some meals, excursions, international student ID, student support services, Student Union membership, e-mail access, banking facilities, international bank transfers, transcript, visa processing, cell phones. $35 application fee. $500 nonrefundable deposit required. Financial aid available for all students: scholarships, loans, stipends.

For More Information • InterStudy, Admissions Office, 63 Edward Street, Medford, MA 02155; *Phone:* 800-663-1999; *Fax:* 781-391-7463. *E-mail:* interstudy@interstudy-usa.org. *World Wide Web:* http://www.interstudy.org/

SCHOOL FOR INTERNATIONAL TRAINING, SIT STUDY ABROAD
SOUTH AFRICA: PUBLIC HEALTH AND PUBLIC POLICY

Academic Focus • Public health, Xhosa.

Program Information • Faculty members are local instructors hired by the sponsor. Scheduled travel; field trips.

Sessions • Fall, spring.

Eligibility Requirements • Open to sophomores, juniors, seniors; 2.5 GPA; no foreign language proficiency required.

Living Arrangements • Students live in locally rented apartments, host family homes. Meals are taken with host family, in residences.

Costs (2004-2005) • One term: contact sponsor for cost. $50 application fee. $400 nonrefundable deposit required. Financial aid available for all students: scholarships.

For More Information • School for International Training, SIT Study Abroad, Kipling Road, Brattleboro, VT 05302-0676; *Phone:* 888-272-7881; *Fax:* 802-258-3296. *E-mail:* studyabroad@sit.edu. *World Wide Web:* http://www.sit.edu/studyabroad/

PRETORIA

INTERSTUDY
UNIVERSITY OF PRETORIA

Hosted by University of Pretoria
Academic Focus • African languages and literature, agriculture, biological/life sciences, business administration/management, computer science, dance, drama/theater, economics, education, engineering, English, law and legal studies, music, nursing, nutrition, political science and government, psychology, public administration, religious studies.
Program Information • Students attend classes at University of Pretoria. Scheduled travel to game reserves, elephant parks, historic tours; optional travel to Zimbabwe, game parks, Namibia, Botswana, Cape Town at an extra cost.
Sessions • Fall, spring, yearlong.
Eligibility Requirements • Minimum age 18; open to freshmen, sophomores, juniors, seniors, graduate students, adults; 2.7 GPA; 2 letters of recommendation; good academic standing at home school.
Living Arrangements • Students live in host institution dormitories, locally rented apartments. Quarters are shared with host institution students. Meals are taken as a group, on one's own, in residences, in central dining facility.
Costs (2003-2004) • One term: $8725. Yearlong program: $15,450; includes tuition, housing, some meals, excursions, international student ID, student support services, Student Union membership, e-mail access, banking facilities, international bank transfers, transcript, visa processing, cell phones. $35 application fee. $500 nonrefundable deposit required. Financial aid available for all students: scholarships, loans, stipends.
For More Information • InterStudy, Admissions Office, 63 Edward Street, Medford, MA 02155; *Phone:* 800-663-1999; *Fax:* 781-391-7463. *E-mail:* interstudy@interstudy-usa.org. *World Wide Web:* http://www.interstudy.org/

STELLENBOSCH

AMERICAN INSTITUTE FOR FOREIGN STUDY (AIFS)
UNIVERSITY OF STELLENBOSCH

Hosted by University of Stellenbosch
Academic Focus • African studies, business administration/management, drama/theater, literature, political science and government, religious studies.
Program Information • Students attend classes at University of Stellenbosch. Scheduled travel to London, a Garden Route Tour; field trips to Robben Island, Cape Town, Cape of Good Hope.
Sessions • Fall, spring, yearlong.
Eligibility Requirements • Minimum age 17; open to sophomores, juniors, seniors; 2.5 GPA; 1 letter of recommendation; good academic standing at home school; at least second semester sophomore status.
Living Arrangements • Students live in host institution dormitories, host family homes. Meals are taken on one's own, in residences, in central dining facility.
Costs (2004-2005) • One term: $10,495. Yearlong program: $18,890; includes tuition, housing, all meals, insurance, excursions, international airfare, student support services. $75 application fee. $350 nonrefundable deposit required. Financial aid available for all students: scholarships.
For More Information • Mr. David Mauro, Admissions Advisor, American Institute For Foreign Study (AIFS), 9 West Broad Street, Stamford, CT 06902-3788; *Phone:* 800-727-2437 Ext. 5163; *Fax:* 203-399-5597. *E-mail:* dmauro@aifs.com. *World Wide Web:* http://www.aifsabroad.com/

INTERSTUDY
UNIVERSITY OF STELLENBOSCH

Hosted by University of Stellenbosch
Academic Focus • African languages and literature, African studies, ancient history, biochemistry, botany, business administration/management, conservation studies, drama/theater, Dutch, economics, engineering, English, history, international affairs, journalism, law and legal studies, music, philosophy, political science and government, psychology, religious studies, sociology, Spanish studies.
Program Information • Students attend classes at University of Stellenbosch. Scheduled travel to game reserves, elephant parks, historic tours; optional travel to Zimbabwe, game parks, Namibia, Botswana, Cape Town at an extra cost.
Sessions • Fall, spring, yearlong.
Eligibility Requirements • Minimum age 18; open to freshmen, sophomores, juniors, seniors, graduate students, adults; 2.5 GPA; 2 letters of recommendation; good academic standing at home school; no foreign language proficiency required.
Living Arrangements • Students live in host institution dormitories, locally rented apartments. Quarters are shared with host institution students. Meals are taken as a group, on one's own, in residences, in central dining facility.
Costs (2003-2004) • One term: $8125. Yearlong program: $13,775; includes tuition, housing, some meals, excursions, international student ID, student support services, Student Union membership, e-mail access, banking facilities, international bank transfers, transcript, visa processing, discount airfare, cell phones. $35 application fee. $500 nonrefundable deposit required. Financial aid available for all students: scholarships, loans, stipends.
For More Information • InterStudy, Admissions Office, 63 Edward Street, Medford, MA 02155; *Phone:* 800-663-1999; *Fax:* 781-391-7463. *E-mail:* interstudy@interstudy-usa.org. *World Wide Web:* http://www.interstudy.org/

SPAIN

CITY TO CITY
BOSTON UNIVERSITY
BURGOS LANGUAGE AND LIBERAL ARTS PROGRAM

Hosted by University of Burgos
Academic Focus • Full curriculum, Spanish studies.
Program Information • Students attend classes at University of Burgos (Burgos).
Sessions • Spring, yearlong.
Eligibility Requirements • Open to sophomores, juniors, seniors, adults; 3.0 GPA; 2 letters of recommendation; good academic standing at home school; essay; writing sample in Spanish; approval of participation; transcript; 2.5 years of college course work in Spanish.
Living Arrangements • Students live in host institution dormitories. Meals are taken on one's own, in residences, in restaurants.
Costs (2004-2005) • One term: $14,834. Yearlong program: $39,668; includes tuition, housing, all meals, excursions, international airfare, limited reimbursement for cultural activities and local transportation. $50 application fee. $400 nonrefundable deposit required. Financial aid available for all students: scholarships, work study, loans.
For More Information • Division of International Programs, Boston University, 232 Bay State Road, Boston, MA 02215; *Phone:* 617-353-9888; *Fax:* 617-353-5402. *E-mail:* abroad@bu.edu. *World Wide Web:* http://www.bu.edu/abroad/

EF INTERNATIONAL LANGUAGE SCHOOLS
SPANISH IN BARCELONA

Hosted by EF Escuela Internacional de Español (Barcelona)
Academic Focus • Spanish language and literature.
Program Information • Students attend classes at EF Escuela Internacional de Español (Barcelona). Field trips to Picasso museums, the Doll Museum, Sagrada Familia Cathedral; optional travel to Madrid, Seville, Costa Brava, the Pyrenees at an extra cost.
Sessions • Program length 2 to 52 weeks, year-round.
Eligibility Requirements • Minimum age 16; open to precollege students, freshmen, sophomores, juniors, seniors, graduate students, adults; no foreign language proficiency required.

Living Arrangements • Students live in host institution dormitories, host family homes. Quarters are shared with host institution students. Meals are taken with host family, in residences.

Costs (2004-2005) • One term: contact sponsor for cost. Yearlong program: contact sponsor for cost. $125 application fee. Financial aid available for all students: scholarships.

For More Information • Ms. Katie Mahon, Director of Admissions, EF International Language Schools, One Education Street, Cambridge, MA 02141; *Phone:* 800-992-1892; *Fax:* 800-590-1125. *E-mail:* ils@ef.com. *World Wide Web:* http://www.ef.com/

FLORIDA INTERNATIONAL UNIVERSITY
UNIVERSITY AUTONOMA DE ESPAÑA

Hosted by Autonomous University of Barcelona, Autonomous University of Madrid

Academic Focus • Full curriculum.

Program Information • Students attend classes at Autonomous University of Barcelona (Barcelona), Autonomous University of Madrid (Madrid).

Sessions • Fall, spring.

Eligibility Requirements • Open to sophomores, juniors, seniors, graduate students, adults; 3.0 GPA; fluency in Spanish.

Living Arrangements • Students live in host institution dormitories. Meals are taken on one's own, in central dining facility.

Costs (2003-2004) • One term: $5000; includes some meals, insurance, international airfare, books and class materials, international student ID. $150 application fee. Financial aid available for all students: scholarships, loans.

For More Information • Office of International Studies, Florida International University, University Park Campus–TT100, Miami, FL 33199; *Phone:* 305-348-1913; *Fax:* 305-348-1941. *E-mail:* ois@fiu.edu. *World Wide Web:* http://ois.fiu.edu/

ALCALÁ DE HENARES
BOWLING GREEN STATE UNIVERSITY
ACADEMIC YEAR ABROAD (AYA) IN SPAIN

Hosted by University of Alcalá de Henares

Academic Focus • Spanish language and literature, Spanish studies.

Program Information • Students attend classes at University of Alcalá de Henares. Scheduled travel to Andalucía, Barcelona, Granada; field trips to Cáceres, Madrid, Segovia, Salamanca.

Sessions • Fall, spring, yearlong.

Eligibility Requirements • Open to freshmen, sophomores, juniors, seniors, graduate students, adults; good academic standing at home school; minimum 3.0 GPA in Spanish, 2.5 GPA overall; 2 years of college course work in Spanish.

Living Arrangements • Students live in host family homes. Quarters are shared with host institution students. Meals are taken with host family, in residences.

Costs (2002-2003) • One term: $6722 for Ohio residents; $10,036 for nonresidents. Yearlong program: $13,244 for Ohio residents; $19,872 for nonresidents; includes tuition, housing, all meals, insurance, excursions, application and program fees. $170 nonrefundable deposit required. Financial aid available for students from sponsoring institution: scholarships, loans.

For More Information • Ms. Cynthia Phelps Whipple, Director, AYA Spain, Bowling Green State University, Department of Romance Languages, Bowling Green, OH 43403; *Phone:* 419-372-8053; *Fax:* 419-372-7332. *E-mail:* ayaspain@bgnet.bsgu.edu. *World Wide Web:* http://www.bgsu.edu/

CIEE
CIEE STUDY CENTER AT THE UNIVERSITY OF ALCALÁ, SPAIN

Hosted by University of Alcalá de Henares

Academic Focus • Geography, history, international affairs, international business, literature, political science and government, Spanish language and literature, Spanish studies.
Program Information • Students attend classes at University of Alcalá de Henares. Scheduled travel to Andalucía, Galicia; field trips to Toledo, Cuenca, El Escorial, Segovia, Salamanca, Barcelona, Andalusia.
Sessions • Fall, spring, yearlong.
Eligibility Requirements • Minimum age 18; open to sophomores, juniors, seniors, adults; good academic standing at home school; personal essay in Spanish; 2 references (1 from language instructor); minimum 2.75 GPA overall, minimum 3.0 GPA in most recent Spanish class; 2.5 years of college course work in Spanish.
Living Arrangements • Students live in host institution dormitories, host family homes. Quarters are shared with host institution students. Meals are taken with host family, in residences, in central dining facility.
Costs (2004-2005) • One term: $8850. Yearlong program: $15,250; includes tuition, housing, all meals, insurance, excursions, student support services, cultural activities, pre-departure advising. $30 application fee. $300 deposit required. Financial aid available for all students: minority student scholarships, travel grants.
For More Information • Ms. Ellen Whitman, Admissions Officer, Spain and Latin America, CIEE, 7 Custom House Street, 3rd Floor, Portland, ME 04101; *Phone:* 800-40-STUDY; *Fax:* 207-553-7699. *E-mail:* studyinfo@ciee.org. *World Wide Web:* http://www.ciee.org/isp/

LANGUAGE STUDIES ABROAD, INC.
LSA ALCALÁ, SPAIN
Hosted by LSA Alcala
Academic Focus • Full curriculum.
Program Information • Students attend classes at LSA Alcala.
Sessions • 2 weeks or longer throughout the year.

Eligibility Requirements • Minimum age 18; open to freshmen, sophomores, juniors, seniors, graduate students, adults; no foreign language proficiency required.
Living Arrangements • Students live in host institution dormitories, locally rented apartments, host family homes. Quarters are shared with host institution students. Meals are taken with host family.
Costs (2004) • One term: contact sponsor for cost. $100 application fee. $100 nonrefundable deposit required.
For More Information • Student Service Representative, Language Studies Abroad, Inc., 1801 Highway 50 East, Suite I, Carson City, NV 89701; *Phone:* 800-424-5522; *Fax:* 775-883-2266. *E-mail:* info@languagestudiesabroad.com. *World Wide Web:* http://www.languagestudiesabroad.com/

SKIDMORE COLLEGE
SKIDMORE IN ALCALÁ
Hosted by Skidmore Program Center, University of Alcalá de Henares
Academic Focus • Anthropology, art history, business administration/management, drama/theater, economics, education, history, philosophy, Spanish language and literature, Spanish studies.
Program Information • Students attend classes at University of Alcalá de Henares, Skidmore Program Center. Scheduled travel; field trips.
Sessions • Fall, spring, yearlong.
Eligibility Requirements • Open to juniors; 3.0 GPA; 2 letters of recommendation; good academic standing at home school; 2.5 years college course work in Spanish or the equivalent.
Living Arrangements • Students live in host family homes. Meals are taken with host family, in residences.
Costs (2003-2004) • One term: contact sponsor for cost. Yearlong program: contact sponsor for cost. $25 application fee. $350

nonrefundable deposit required. Financial aid available for students from sponsoring institution: scholarships, loans.
For More Information • Office of International Programs, Skidmore College, 815 North Broadway, Starbuck Center, Saratoga Springs, NY 12866; *Phone:* 518-580-5355; *Fax:* 518-580-5359. *E-mail:* oip@skidmore.edu. *World Wide Web:* http://www.skidmore.edu/internationalprograms/

ALICANTE

CENTER FOR STUDY ABROAD (CSA)
SPANISH LANGUAGE AND CULTURE, ALICANTE–UNIVERSITY OF ALICANTE

Hosted by University of Alicante
Academic Focus • Spanish language and literature, Spanish studies.
Program Information • Students attend classes at University of Alicante. Optional travel to Barcelona, Valencia, Granada.
Sessions • Fall, spring, yearlong.
Eligibility Requirements • Minimum age 18; open to precollege students, freshmen, sophomores, juniors, seniors, graduate students, adults; no foreign language proficiency required.
Living Arrangements • Students live in host institution dormitories, host family homes. Quarters are shared with host institution students. Meals are taken on one's own, with host family, in residences.
Costs (2003-2004) • One term: contact sponsor for cost. Yearlong program: contact sponsor for cost. $45 application fee.
For More Information • Ms. Alima K. Virtue, Program Director, Center for Study Abroad (CSA), 325 Washington Avenue South, #93, Kent, WA 98032; *Phone:* 206-726-1498; *Fax:* 253-850-0454. *E-mail:* info@centerforstudyabroad.com. *World Wide Web:* http://www.centerforstudyabroad.com/

CIEE
CIEE CENTER AT THE UNIVERSITY OF ALICANTE, SPAIN–LANGUAGE AND CULTURE PROGRAM

Hosted by University of Alicante
Academic Focus • Anthropology, conservation studies, history, political science and government, Spanish language and literature, women's studies.
Program Information • Students attend classes at University of Alicante. Field trips to Madrid, Barcelona, Salmanca, Granada, Mallorca, Valencia, Tunisia, Brussels, Portugal; optional travel to Valencia, the Iberian Peninsula, the Mediterranean Rim at an extra cost.
Sessions • Fall, spring.
Eligibility Requirements • Minimum age 18; open to sophomores, juniors, seniors; 2.75 GPA; 2 letters of recommendation; 3 years of college course work in Spanish.
Living Arrangements • Students live in host family homes. Meals are taken with host family, in residences.
Costs (2004-2005) • One term: $8850; includes tuition, housing, all meals, insurance, excursions, student support services, cultural activities, pre-departure advising. $30 application fee. $300 deposit required. Financial aid available for all students: minority student scholarships, travel/study grants.
For More Information • Ms. Ellen Whitman, Admissions Officer, Spain and Latin America, CIEE, 7 Custom House Street, 3rd Floor, Portland, ME 04101; *Phone:* 800-40-STUDY; *Fax:* 207-553-7699. *E-mail:* studyinfo@ciee.org. *World Wide Web:* http://www.ciee.org/isp/

CIEE
CIEE STUDY CENTER AT THE UNIVERSITY OF ALICANTE, SPAIN–LANGUAGE IN CONTEXT PROGRAM

Hosted by University of Alicante
Academic Focus • Accounting, art history, commerce, comparative literature, economics, environmental science/studies, history, human resources, international affairs, Spanish language and literature.
Program Information • Students attend classes at University of Alicante. Field trips to Madrid, Barcelona, Salamanca, Granada,

Mallorca, Valencia, Tunisia, Brussels, Portugal; optional travel to the Valencia region, the Iberian Peninsula, the Mediterranean Rim at an extra cost.
Sessions • Fall, spring.
Eligibility Requirements • Minimum age 18; open to sophomores, juniors, seniors; 2.75 GPA; 0.5 years of college course work in Spanish.
Living Arrangements • Students live in host family homes. Meals are taken with host family, in residences.
Costs (2004-2005) • One term: $8850; includes tuition, housing, all meals, insurance, excursions, student support services, cultural activities, pre-departure advising. $30 application fee. $300 deposit required. Financial aid available for all students: minority student scholarships, travel grants.
For More Information • Ms. Ellen Whitman, Admissions Officer, Spain and Latin America, CIEE, 7 Custom House Street, 3rd Floor, Portland, ME 04101; *Phone:* 800-40-STUDY; *Fax:* 207-553-7699. *E-mail:* studyinfo@ciee.org. *World Wide Web:* http://www.ciee.org/isp/

CIEE
CIEE STUDY CENTER AT THE UNIVERSITY OF ALICANTE, SPAIN–LIBERAL ARTS PROGRAM

Hosted by University of Alicante
Academic Focus • Full curriculum.
Program Information • Students attend classes at University of Alicante. Scheduled travel to Santiago de Compostela, Tunisia; field trips to Valencia, Mallorca, Barcelona, Muro de Alcoy, Granada, Madrid; optional travel to Santiago de Compostela, Granada, Madrid, Mallorca, Tunisia at an extra cost.
Sessions • Fall, spring, yearlong.
Eligibility Requirements • Minimum age 18; open to sophomores, juniors, seniors, graduate students, adults; 2.75 GPA; 2 letters of recommendation; personal essay; 2 years of college course work in Spanish.
Living Arrangements • Students live in host family homes. Meals are taken with host family, in residences.
Costs (2004-2005) • One term: $8850. Yearlong program: $15,250; includes tuition, housing, all meals, insurance, excursions, student support services, e-mail access, cultural activities, pre-departure advising. $30 application fee. $300 deposit required. Financial aid available for all students: minority student scholarships, travel grants.
For More Information • Ms. Ellen Whitman, Admissions Officer, Spain and Latin America, CIEE, 7 Custom House Street, 3rd Floor, Portland, ME 04101; *Phone:* 800-40-STUDY; *Fax:* 207-553-7699. *E-mail:* studyinfo@ciee.org. *World Wide Web:* http://www.ciee.org/isp/

CULTURAL EXPERIENCES ABROAD (CEA)
STUDY SPANISH LANGUAGE AND CULTURE IN ALICANTE

Hosted by University of Alicante
Academic Focus • Civilization studies, Spanish language and literature, Spanish studies.
Program Information • Students attend classes at University of Alicante. Field trips to Valencia, Granada, Barcelona, Costa Blanca.
Sessions • Fall, spring, winter, intensive month sessions also available in January and September.
Eligibility Requirements • Minimum age 18; open to freshmen, sophomores, juniors, seniors, graduate students; 2.5 GPA; 1 letter of recommendation; good academic standing at home school; previous Spanish study recommended.
Living Arrangements • Students live in locally rented apartments, host family homes. Quarters are shared with students from other programs. Meals are taken on one's own, with host family, in residences.
Costs (2003-2004) • One term: $6695–$6995; includes tuition, housing, some meals, insurance, excursions, student support services. $50 application fee. $400 nonrefundable deposit required.
For More Information • Cultural Experiences Abroad (CEA), 1400 East Southern Avenue, Suite B-108, Tempe, AZ 85282-8011; *Phone:* 480-557-7900; *Fax:* 480-557-7926. *E-mail:* petersons@gowithcea.com. *World Wide Web:* http://www.gowithcea.com/

UNIVERSITY OF MIAMI
UNIVERSITY OF ALICANTE

Hosted by University of Alicante
Academic Focus • Economics, liberal studies, political science and government, social sciences, Spanish language and literature.
Program Information • Students attend classes at University of Alicante. Optional travel at an extra cost.
Sessions • Fall, spring, yearlong.
Eligibility Requirements • Minimum age 18; open to sophomores, juniors, seniors; 3.0 GPA; 2 letters of recommendation; language evaluation; personal interview; fluency in Spanish.
Living Arrangements • Students live in locally rented apartments, host family homes. Quarters are shared with host institution students, students from other programs. Meals are taken on one's own, with host family, in residences, in restaurants.
Costs (2003–2004) • One term: $12,919. Yearlong program: $25,838; includes tuition, student support services. $40 application fee. $500 nonrefundable deposit required. Financial aid available for students from sponsoring institution: scholarships, loans.
For More Information • Mr. Chris Tingue, Assistant Director, University of Miami, International Education and Exchange Programs, 5050 Brunson Drive, Allen Hall 212, PO Box 248005, Coral Gables, FL 33124-1610; *Phone:* 305-284-3434; *Fax:* 305-284-4235. *E-mail:* ieep@miami.edu. *World Wide Web:* http://www.studyabroad.miami.edu/

UNIVERSITY STUDIES ABROAD CONSORTIUM
SPANISH STUDIES: ALICANTE, SPAIN

Hosted by University of Alicante
Academic Focus • Art history, culinary arts, dance, economics, history, political science and government, Spanish language and literature, Spanish studies, tourism and travel.
Program Information • Students attend classes at University of Alicante. Field trips to Gaudalest, Calpe, Valencia, Cabo San Antonio, Savea, Granada; optional travel to Madrid at an extra cost.
Sessions • Fall, spring, yearlong.
Eligibility Requirements • Minimum age 18; open to freshmen, sophomores, juniors, seniors, graduate students, adults; 2.5 GPA; no foreign language proficiency required.
Living Arrangements • Students live in locally rented apartments, host family homes. Quarters are shared with host institution students. Meals are taken on one's own, with host family, in residences, in restaurants.
Costs (2005–2006) • One term: $7470. Yearlong program: $12,680; includes tuition, some meals, insurance, excursions, student support services. $50 application fee. $150 refundable deposit required. Financial aid available for all students: scholarships, loans.
For More Information • University Studies Abroad Consortium, USAC/323, Reno, NV 89557-0093; *Phone:* 775-784-6569; *Fax:* 775-784-6010. *E-mail:* usac@unr.edu. *World Wide Web:* http://usac.unr.edu/

BARCELONA
ACADEMIC PROGRAMS INTERNATIONAL (API)
(API)–UNIVERSITY AUTONOMA OF BACELONA, SPAIN

Hosted by Autonomous University of Barcelona
Academic Focus • Business administration/management, economics, international affairs, international business, marketing, political science and government, Spanish language and literature, Spanish studies.
Program Information • Students attend classes at Autonomous University of Barcelona. Scheduled travel to Madrid, Mallorca, Seville; field trips to Toledo, El Escorial, Figueres, Costa Brava, the Pyrnees Mountains, Andoria.
Sessions • Fall, spring.
Eligibility Requirements • Minimum age 18; open to freshmen, sophomores, juniors, seniors, graduate students, adults; 2.75 GPA; 1 letter of recommendation; good academic standing at home school; official transcript from home university; no foreign language proficiency required.

Living Arrangements • Students live in host institution dormitories, locally rented apartments, host family homes. Quarters are shared with host institution students. Meals are taken on one's own, with host family, in residences, in restaurants.
Costs (2004) • One term: $7800; includes tuition, housing, all meals, insurance, excursions, student support services, airport pick-up, ground transportation. $150 nonrefundable deposit required. Financial aid available for all students: scholarships.
For More Information • Ms. Jennifer C. Allen, Director, Academic Programs International (API), 107 East Hopkins, San Marcos, TX 78666; *Phone:* 800-844-4124; *Fax:* 512-392-8420. *E-mail:* api@academicintl.com. *World Wide Web:* http://www.academicintl.com/

ACADEMIC PROGRAMS INTERNATIONAL (API)
(API)–UNIVERSITY OF BARCELONA, SPAIN

Hosted by University of Barcelona
Academic Focus • Art history, civilization studies, economics, film and media studies, geography, history, international business, Spanish language and literature, Spanish studies.
Program Information • Students attend classes at University of Barcelona. Scheduled travel to Madrid, Mallorca, Seville; field trips to Toledo, El Escorial, Girona, Figueres, Costa Brava, Mallorca, Seville, the Pyrenees, Andorra.
Sessions • Fall, spring, yearlong.
Eligibility Requirements • Minimum age 18; open to freshmen, sophomores, juniors, seniors, graduate students, adults; 2.75 GPA; 1 letter of recommendation; good academic standing at home school; official transcript from home university; 2 years of college course work in Spanish.
Living Arrangements • Students live in host institution dormitories, locally rented apartments, host family homes. Quarters are shared with host institution students. Meals are taken with host family, in residences.
Costs (2004–2005) • One term: $7900. Yearlong program: $14,800; includes tuition, housing, all meals, insurance, excursions, student support services, airport pick-up, ground transportation. $150 nonrefundable deposit required. Financial aid available for all students: scholarships.
For More Information • Ms. Jennifer C. Allen, Director, Academic Programs International (API), 107 East Hopkins, San Marcos, TX 78666; *Phone:* 800-844-4124; *Fax:* 512-392-8420. *E-mail:* api@academicintl.com. *World Wide Web:* http://www.academicintl.com/

BRETHREN COLLEGES ABROAD
BCA PROGRAM IN BARCELONA, SPAIN

Hosted by University of Barcelona
Academic Focus • Full curriculum.
Program Information • Students attend classes at University of Barcelona. Scheduled travel to Madrid, Toledo, Córdoba, Sevilla, Granada, Segovia, Avila; field trips to Poblet, Ampurias, Besalú, Olot, Gerona.
Sessions • Fall, spring, yearlong.
Eligibility Requirements • Minimum age 18; open to sophomores, juniors, seniors, graduate students, adults; 2.6 GPA; 3 letters of recommendation; good academic standing at home school; 2 years of college course work in Spanish.
Living Arrangements • Students live in host family homes. Meals are taken with host family, in residences, in restaurants.
Costs (2003–2004) • One term: $11,500. Yearlong program: $19,900; includes tuition, housing, all meals, insurance, excursions, international student ID, student support services. $50 application fee. $100 nonrefundable deposit required.
For More Information • Mr. Thomas V. Millington, Senior Program Officer for Spain, Brethren Colleges Abroad, 50 Alpha Drive, Elizabethtown, PA 17022-0407; *Phone:* 717-361-6600; *Fax:* 717-361-6619. *E-mail:* info@bcanet.org. *World Wide Web:* http://www.bcanet.org/

CIEE
CIEE STUDY CENTER AT THE UNIVERSITAT POMPEU FABRA, BARCELONA, SPAIN: BUSINESS AND CULTURE PROGRAM

Hosted by Pompeu Fabra University

Academic Focus • Art, business administration/management, Catalan, economics, European studies, history, marketing, political science and government, Spanish language and literature, Spanish studies.

Program Information • Students attend classes at Pompeu Fabra University. Scheduled travel to Cuenca, Madrid, Mallorca, the Pyranees, Zaragoza, Valencia, Spain's northern coast; field trips to Montserrat, Figueras, Ampurias, Cadaqués, Gerona, Tarragona, Penedés.

Sessions • Fall, spring, yearlong.

Eligibility Requirements • Minimum age 18; open to sophomores, juniors, seniors; 3.0 GPA.

Living Arrangements • Students live in host family homes. Meals are taken with host family, in residences.

Costs (2004-2005) • One term: $10,950. Yearlong program: contact sponsor for cost; includes tuition, housing, all meals, insurance, excursions, on-site airport meet-and-greet. $30 application fee. Financial aid available for all students: scholarships, travel grants, minority student scholarships.

For More Information • Ms. Ellen Whitman, Admissions Officer, Spain and Latin America, CIEE, 7 Custom House Street, 3rd Floor, Portland, ME 04101; *Phone:* 800-40-STUDY; *Fax:* 207-553-7699. *E-mail:* ewhitman@ciee.org. *World Wide Web:* http://www.ciee.org/isp/

CIEE
CIEE STUDY CENTER AT UNIVERSITAT POMPEU FABRA, BARCELONA, SPAIN: LIBERAL ARTS PROGRAM

Hosted by Pompeu Fabra University

Academic Focus • Art history, business administration/management, Catalan, economics, history, international affairs, law and legal studies, marketing, political science and government, Spanish language and literature.

Program Information • Students attend classes at Pompeu Fabra University. Scheduled travel to Cuenca, Madrid, Mallorca, the Pyranees, Zaragoza, Valencia, north coast; field trips to Montserrat, Figueras, Ampurias, Cadgués, Gerona, Terragara, Penedés.

Sessions • Fall, spring, yearlong.

Eligibility Requirements • Minimum age 18; open to juniors, seniors; 3.0 GPA; 4 semesters of college course work in Spanish for fall term; 5 semesters for spring.

Living Arrangements • Students live in host institution dormitories, host family homes. Quarters are shared with host institution students, students from other programs. Meals are taken on one's own, with host family, in residences, in restaurants.

Costs (2004-2005) • One term: $10,950. Yearlong program: $19,900; includes tuition, housing, some meals, insurance, excursions, on-site airport meet-and-greet. $30 application fee. $300 deposit required. Financial aid available for all students: scholarships, minority student scholarships, travel grants.

For More Information • Ms. Ellen Whitman, Admissions Officer, Spain and Latin America, CIEE, 7 Custom House Street, 3rd Floor, Portland, ME 04101; *Phone:* 800-40-STUDY; *Fax:* 207-553-7699. *E-mail:* ewhitman@ciee.org. *World Wide Web:* http://www.ciee.org/isp/

CULTURAL EXPERIENCES ABROAD (CEA)
STUDY SPANISH LANGUAGE AND CULTURE IN BARCELONA

Hosted by University of Barcelona

Academic Focus • Ancient history, art history, comparative history, cultural studies, economics, geography, history, Latin American studies, literature, political science and government, Spanish language and literature.

Program Information • Students attend classes at University of Barcelona. Field trips to Monserrat, Tarragona, Penedés, Girona, Figueres, Cadaques.

Sessions • Fall, spring, yearlong, fall quarter II.

Eligibility Requirements • Minimum age 18; open to freshmen, sophomores, juniors, seniors, graduate students; 2.5 GPA; 1 letter of recommendation; good academic standing at home school; previous Spanish study recommended.

Living Arrangements • Students live in host institution dormitories, locally rented apartments, program-owned apartments. Quarters are shared with host institution students, students from other programs. Meals are taken as a group, on one's own, in residences.

Costs (2003-2004) • One term: $7995–$8995. Yearlong program: $16,695; includes tuition, housing, some meals, insurance, excursions, student support services. $50 application fee. $400 nonrefundable deposit required.

For More Information • Cultural Experiences Abroad (CEA), 1400 East Southern Avenue, Suite B-108, Tempe, AZ 85282-8011; *Phone:* 480-557-7900; *Fax:* 480-557-7926. *E-mail:* petersons@gowithcea.com. *World Wide Web:* http://www.gowithcea.com/

IES, INSTITUTE FOR THE INTERNATIONAL EDUCATION OF STUDENTS
IES–BARCELONA

Hosted by Institute for the International Education of Students (IES)–Barcelona, University Pompeu Fabra, Barcelona

Academic Focus • Art history, business administration/management, communications, economics, environmental science/studies, history, international business, literature, political science and government, Spanish language and literature.

Program Information • Students attend classes at University Pompeu Fabra, Barcelona, Institute for the International Education of Students (IES)–Barcelona. Scheduled travel to Mallorca; field trips to Girona, Figueres; optional travel to south of France, the Pyrenees at an extra cost.

Sessions • Fall, spring, yearlong.

Eligibility Requirements • Minimum age 18; open to sophomores, juniors, seniors, graduate students, adults; 3.0 GPA; 1 letter of recommendation; good academic standing at home school; no foreign language proficiency required.

Living Arrangements • Students live in host institution dormitories, locally rented apartments, host family homes. Meals are taken on one's own, with host family, in residences.

Costs (2003-2004) • One term: $11,350. Yearlong program: $20,430; includes tuition, housing, some meals, excursions, student support services, partial insurance coverage. $50 application fee. $500 nonrefundable deposit required. Financial aid available for all students: scholarships, institutional partner need-based grants.

For More Information • International Education Representative, IES, Institute for the International Education of Students, 33 North La Salle Street, 15th Floor, Chicago, IL 60602; *Phone:* 800-995-2300; *Fax:* 312-944-1448. *E-mail:* info@iesabroad.org. *World Wide Web:* http://www.IESabroad.org/

INTERNATIONAL STUDIES ABROAD
BARCELONA, SPAIN: SEMESTER/YEAR: HISPANIC STUDIES

Held at Pompeu Fabra University

Academic Focus • Art history, geography, history, Spanish language and literature, Spanish studies.

Program Information • Classes are held on the campus of Pompeu Fabra University. Faculty members are drawn from the sponsor's U.S. staff. Scheduled travel to Toledo, Madrid; field trips to Madrid, Valencia, Girona, Figueres, Barcelona, Sitges, Valle de Boi, El Escorial; optional travel to Sevilla at an extra cost.

Sessions • Fall, spring, yearlong.

Eligibility Requirements • Minimum age 18; open to freshmen, sophomores, juniors, seniors, graduate students, adults; 2.5 GPA; 1 letter of recommendation; good academic standing at home school; 2 letters of recommendation if GPA is lower than 2.5; no foreign language proficiency required.

Living Arrangements • Meals are taken with host family, in residences.

Costs (2003-2004) • One term: $8500. Yearlong program: $16,000; includes tuition, housing, all meals, insurance, excursions, student support services, excursion transportation, Internet access. $200 deposit required. Financial aid available for all students: scholarships, loans, U.S. federal financial aid via consortium agreement.

For More Information • Spain Site Specialist, International Studies Abroad, 901 West 24th Street, Austin, TX 78705; *Phone:* 800-580-8826; *Fax:* 512-480-8866. *E-mail:* isa@studiesabroad.com. *World Wide Web:* http://www.studiesabroad.com/

INTERNATIONAL STUDIES ABROAD
BARCELONA, SPAIN: SEMESTER/YEAR: HISPANIC STUDIES

Hosted by University of Barcelona

Academic Focus • Art history, geography, history, Spanish language and literature, Spanish studies.

Program Information • Students attend classes at University of Barcelona. Scheduled travel to Madrid, Toledo; field trips to Valle de Boi, Valencia, Girona, Sitges, Figueres, Barcelona; optional travel to Sevilla at an extra cost.

Sessions • Fall, spring, yearlong, extended fall term.

Eligibility Requirements • Minimum age 18; open to freshmen, sophomores, juniors, seniors, graduate students, adults; 2.5 GPA; 1 letter of recommendation; good academic standing at home school; 2 letters of recommendation if GPA is lower than 2.5; 1 year of college course work in Spanish.

Living Arrangements • Students live in locally rented apartments, host family homes. Meals are taken with host family, in residences.

Costs (2004-2005) • One term: $7400–$8000. Yearlong program: $14,500; includes tuition, housing, all meals, insurance, excursions, student support services, excursion transportation, Internet access. $200 deposit required. Financial aid available for all students: scholarships, loans, U.S. federal financial aid via consortium agreement.

For More Information • Spain Site Specialist, International Studies Abroad, 901 West 24th Street, Austin, TX 78705; *Phone:* 800-580-8826; *Fax:* 512-480-8866. *E-mail:* isa@studiesabroad.com. *World Wide Web:* http://www.studiesabroad.com/

INTERNATIONAL STUDIES ABROAD
BARCELONA, SPAIN–SPANISH LANGUAGE AND CULTURE PLUS ECONOMICS

Hosted by Pompeu Fabra University

Academic Focus • Art history, civilization studies, history, Spanish language and literature, Spanish studies.

Program Information • Students attend classes at Pompeu Fabra University. Scheduled travel to Madrid, Toledo; field trips to Valencia, Valle de Boi, El Escorial, Sitges, Girona, Figueres; optional travel to San Sebastián, Sevilla at an extra cost.

Sessions • Fall, spring, yearlong.

Eligibility Requirements • Minimum age 18; open to freshmen, sophomores, juniors, seniors, graduate students, adults; 2.5 GPA; 1 letter of recommendation; good academic standing at home school; transcript; no foreign language proficiency required.

Living Arrangements • Students live in locally rented apartments, host family homes. Quarters are shared with host institution students, students from other programs. Meals are taken with host family, in residences.

Costs (2004-2005) • One term: $8500. Yearlong program: $16,000; includes tuition, housing, all meals, insurance, excursions, student support services, excursion transportation, Internet access. $200 nonrefundable deposit required. Financial aid available for all students: scholarships, work study, federal financial aid.

For More Information • Spain Site Specialist, International Studies Abroad, 901 West 24th Street, Austin, TX 78705; *Phone:* 800-580-8826; *Fax:* 512-480-8866. *E-mail:* isa@studiesabroad.com. *World Wide Web:* http://www.studiesabroad.com/

KNOX COLLEGE
BARCELONA PROGRAM

Hosted by Knox College Program in Barcelona at University of Barcelona

Academic Focus • Art history, Catalan, film and media studies, full curriculum, history, political science and government, Spanish language and literature, Spanish studies.

Program Information • Students attend classes at Knox College Program in Barcelona at University of Barcelona. Scheduled travel to Valencia, Seville, Granada, Córdoba, Madrid, Toledo; field trips to Ampurias, St. Pere de Roda, Figueres, Montserrat, Girona, Poblet, Besalú, Basque country.

SPAIN
Barcelona

Sessions • Fall, spring, winter, yearlong.
Eligibility Requirements • Open to sophomores, juniors, seniors; 2.5 GPA; 4 letters of recommendation; good academic standing at home school; parental consent if under 21; 2 years of college course work in Spanish.
Living Arrangements • Students live in host family homes. Meals are taken with host family.
Costs (2004-2005) • One term: $10,189 ; $20,377 for two terms. Yearlong program: $30,566; includes tuition, housing, all meals, insurance, excursions, student support services, 14-day trip through Spain, 2 travel allowances of $200. $650 nonrefundable deposit required. Financial aid available for all students: scholarships, loans.
For More Information • Prof. Tim Foster, Campus Director, Program in Barcelona, Knox College, Box 224, 2 East South Street, Galesburg, IL 61401-4999; *Phone:* 309-341-7331; *Fax:* 309-341-7824. *E-mail:* barcelona@knox.edu. *World Wide Web:* http://www.knox.edu/offcampus/

STATE UNIVERSITY OF NEW YORK AT OSWEGO
UNIVERSITY OF BARCELONA

Hosted by University of Barcelona
Academic Focus • Art history, Catalan, European studies, film and media studies, geography, history, Spanish language and literature, Spanish studies.
Program Information • Students attend classes at University of Barcelona. Field trips to the coast of Spain, cities near Barcelona.
Sessions • Fall, spring, yearlong.
Eligibility Requirements • Open to sophomores, juniors, seniors; 2.5 GPA; 3 letters of recommendation; good academic standing at home school; language proficiency form; personal study statement; 1 year of college course work in Spanish.

Living Arrangements • Students live in locally rented apartments, host family homes. Meals are taken on one's own, with host family, in residences, in restaurants.
Costs (2003-2004) • One term: $7120. Yearlong program: $14,640; includes tuition, housing, all meals, insurance, excursions, student support services. $250 nonrefundable deposit required. Financial aid available for students: home university financial aid, loan processing and scholarships for Oswego students.
For More Information • Ms. Lizette Alvarado, Program Specialist, State University of New York at Oswego, 122A Swetman Hall, Oswego, NY 13126; *Phone:* 888-4-OSWEGO; *Fax:* 315-312-2477. *E-mail:* intled@oswego.edu. *World Wide Web:* http://www.oswego.edu/intled/

BILBAO
UNIVERSITY STUDIES ABROAD CONSORTIUM
BUSINESS, SPANISH, AND AREA STUDIES; MBA: BILBAO, SPAIN

Hosted by University of the Basque Country
Academic Focus • Art history, business administration/management, culinary arts, cultural studies, dance, economics, finance, history, international business, marketing, political science and government, Spanish language and literature, Spanish studies, teaching.
Program Information • Students attend classes at University of the Basque Country. Field trips to Northern Spain, Bizkaia, San Sebastián, France, the Pyrenees, Pamplona, Saint Jean Pied de Port; optional travel to Madrid at an extra cost.
Sessions • Fall, spring, yearlong.

Get a Global Education!

Christian: Australia, Chile and Costa Rica
Logan: Costa Rica and Spain

The University Studies Abroad Consortium, with programs in 24 countries, allows students to master languages and study disciplines — including business, fine arts and history — at distinguished, overseas schools. Soak up the vibrant culture and be transformed by the experience of living in a foreign land.

• Summer, semester and yearlong programs • Wide range of academic courses • Internships • Language classes at all levels • Field trips and tours • Small classes • University credit • Scholarships • Housing

UNIVERSITY STUDIES ABROAD CONSORTIUM **USAC**
HTTP://USAC.UNR.EDU • 775-784-6569
Your Gateway to the World

Eligibility Requirements • Minimum age 18; open to freshmen, sophomores, juniors, seniors, graduate students, adults; 2.5 GPA; no foreign language proficiency required.
Living Arrangements • Students live in locally rented apartments, host family homes. Quarters are shared with host institution students. Meals are taken on one's own, with host family, in residences, in restaurants.
Costs (2005-2006) • One term: $4980. Yearlong program: $8760; includes tuition, some meals, insurance, excursions, student support services. $50 application fee. $150 refundable deposit required. Financial aid available for all students: scholarships, loans.
For More Information • University Studies Abroad Consortium, USAC/323, Reno, NV 89557-0093; *Phone:* 775-784-6569; *Fax:* 775-784-6010. *E-mail:* usac@unr.edu. *World Wide Web:* http://usac.unr.edu/

CÁCERES

MICHIGAN STATE UNIVERSITY
SPANISH LANGUAGE, LITERATURE, AND CULTURE IN CÁCERES

Hosted by University of Extremadura
Academic Focus • Spanish language and literature, Spanish studies.
Program Information • Students attend classes at University of Extremadura. Field trips to surrounding areas, Madrid.
Sessions • Spring.
Eligibility Requirements • Minimum age 18; open to freshmen, sophomores, juniors, seniors; 2.75 GPA; good academic standing at home school; faculty approval; 3 years of college course work in Spanish.
Living Arrangements • Students live in host family homes. Meals are taken with host family, in residences.
Costs (2003) • One term: $3100 (estimated); includes housing, all meals, insurance, excursions, student support services. $100 application fee. $200 nonrefundable deposit required. Financial aid available for students from sponsoring institution: scholarships, loans.
For More Information • Ms. Sherry Martinez-Bonilla, Office Assistant, Michigan State University, Office of Study Abroad, 109 International Center, East Lansing, MI 48824-1035; *Phone:* 517-353-8920; *Fax:* 517-432-2082. *E-mail:* marti269@msu.edu. *World Wide Web:* http://studyabroad.msu.edu/

GETAFE

MIDDLEBURY COLLEGE SCHOOLS ABROAD
SCHOOL IN SPAIN—GETAFE PROGRAM

Hosted by University Carlos III, Madrid
Academic Focus • Full curriculum.
Program Information • Students attend classes at University Carlos III, Madrid. Field trips to Segovia, La Granja, Toledo, Chinchón; optional travel to Cataluña, Valencia, Galicia, Barcelona at an extra cost.
Sessions • Fall, spring, yearlong.
Eligibility Requirements • Open to sophomores, juniors, seniors; 2.7 GPA; 2 letters of recommendation; B average in both Spanish and major; 2.5 years college course work in Spanish, including at least 1 content course at the 300-level.
Living Arrangements • Students live in locally rented apartments, host family homes. Meals are taken on one's own, with host family, in residences, in restaurants.
Costs (2004-2005) • One term: $7200. Yearlong program: $14,400; includes tuition, student support services. $50 application fee. $300 nonrefundable deposit required. Financial aid available for students from sponsoring institution: scholarships, loans.
For More Information • Mr. Jamie Northrup, University Relations Coordinator, Middlebury College Schools Abroad, Office of Off-Campus Study, Sunderland Language Center, Middlebury, VT 05753; *Phone:* 802-443-5745; *Fax:* 802-443-3157. *E-mail:* schoolsabroad@middlebury.edu. *World Wide Web:* http://www.middlebury.edu/msa/

GRANADA

ACADEMIC PROGRAMS INTERNATIONAL (API)
(API)–GRANADA, SPAIN

Hosted by University of Granada
Academic Focus • Art history, civilization studies, communications, European studies, geography, history, international business, Islamic studies, Latin American studies, political science and government, sociology, Spanish language and literature, Spanish studies.
Program Information • Students attend classes at University of Granada. Scheduled travel to Madrid, Seville; field trips to Toledo, El Escorial, Las Alpujarras, Cádiz, Seville, Cabo de Gata, Nerja.
Sessions • Fall, spring, yearlong, fall A1, B1, C1; spring A1; spring B, C; year A1, B1, C1.
Eligibility Requirements • Minimum age 18; open to freshmen, sophomores, juniors, seniors, adults; 2.75 GPA; 1 letter of recommendation; good academic standing at home school; official transcript from home university; no foreign language proficiency required.
Living Arrangements • Students live in host institution dormitories, locally rented apartments, host family homes. Quarters are shared with host institution students. Meals are taken on one's own, with host family, in residences, in restaurants.
Costs (2004-2005) • One term: $5900–$7600. Yearlong program: $11,200–$13,500; includes tuition, housing, all meals, insurance, excursions, student support services, airport pick-up, ground transportation. $150 nonrefundable deposit required. Financial aid available for all students: scholarships.
For More Information • Ms. Jennifer C. Allen, Director, Academic Programs International (API), 107 East Hopkins, San Marcos, TX 78666; *Phone:* 800-844-4124; *Fax:* 512-392-8420. *E-mail:* api@academicintl.com. *World Wide Web:* http://www.academicintl.com/

AMERICAN INSTITUTE FOR FOREIGN STUDY (AIFS)
UNIVERSITY OF GRANADA

Hosted by University of Granada
Academic Focus • Anthropology, art history, economics, geography, history, literature, music, political science and government, sociology, Spanish language and literature.
Program Information • Students attend classes at University of Granada. Scheduled travel to London; field trips to Madrid, Avila, Segovia, Salamanca, Seville, Córdoba; optional travel to Morocco at an extra cost.
Sessions • Fall, spring, yearlong.
Eligibility Requirements • Minimum age 17; open to freshmen, sophomores, juniors, seniors; 2.5 GPA; 1 letter of recommendation; good academic standing at home school; no foreign language proficiency required.
Living Arrangements • Students live in host family homes. Meals are taken with host family, in residences.
Costs (2004-2005) • One term: $10,995. Yearlong program: $19,790; includes tuition, housing, all meals, insurance, excursions, international student ID, student support services, one-way airfare, 2-day London stopover. $75 application fee. $350 nonrefundable deposit required. Financial aid available for students: scholarships.
For More Information • Mr. David Mauro, Admissions Advisor, American Institute For Foreign Study (AIFS), 9 West Broad Street, Stamford, CT 06902-3788; *Phone:* 800-727-2437 Ext. 5163; *Fax:* 203-399-5597. *E-mail:* dmauro@aifs.com. *World Wide Web:* http://www.aifsabroad.com/

CENTRAL COLLEGE ABROAD
CENTRAL COLLEGE ABROAD IN GRANADA, SPAIN

Hosted by University of Granada
Academic Focus • Anthropology, art history, community service, economics, ethics, geography, history, international affairs, international business, music history, philosophy, political science and government, psychology, Spanish language and literature, teaching English as a second language.
Program Information • Students attend classes at University of Granada. Scheduled travel to Madrid, Seville, Toledo; field trips to Córdoba, Gibraltar, Alhambra, Guadix.

SPAIN
Granada

Sessions • Fall, spring, yearlong.
Eligibility Requirements • Minimum age 18; open to sophomores, juniors, seniors, adults; 2.5 GPA; 2 letters of recommendation; good academic standing at home school; study abroad approval form; transcript; Student Life endorsement; no foreign language proficiency required.
Living Arrangements • Students live in host family homes. Meals are taken with host family, in residences.
Costs (2002-2003) • One term: $9600 for fall term; $9975 for spring. Yearlong program: $18,200; includes tuition, housing, all meals, excursions, international student ID, student support services. $25 application fee. $350 nonrefundable deposit required. Financial aid available for all students: scholarships.
For More Information • Office of International Education, Central College Abroad, 812 University Street, Pella, IA 50219; *Phone:* 800-831-3629; *Fax:* 641-628-5375. *E-mail:* studyabroad@central.edu. *World Wide Web:* http://www.central.edu/abroad/

CULTURAL EXPERIENCES ABROAD (CEA)
STUDY SPANISH LANGUAGE AND CULTURE IN GRANADA
Hosted by University of Granada
Academic Focus • Ancient history, anthropology, art history, comparative history, cultural studies, economics, geography, history, international affairs, international business, liberal studies, linguistics, music history, political science and government, Spanish language and literature, translation.
Program Information • Students attend classes at University of Granada. Field trips to Córdoba, Seville, La Alpujarras, Cazorla, Cabo de Gata, Nerja.
Sessions • Fall, spring, yearlong.
Eligibility Requirements • Minimum age 18; open to freshmen, sophomores, juniors, seniors, graduate students; 2.5 GPA; 1 letter of recommendation; good academic standing at home school; previous Spanish study recommended.
Living Arrangements • Students live in host institution dormitories, locally rented apartments, program-owned apartments, host family homes. Quarters are shared with host institution students, students from other programs. Meals are taken with host family, in residences.
Costs (2004) • One term: $6995–$7995. Yearlong program: $14,495–$14,995; includes tuition, housing, some meals, insurance, excursions, student support services. $50 application fee. $400 nonrefundable deposit required.
For More Information • Cultural Experiences Abroad (CEA), 1400 East Southern Avenue, Suite B-108, Tempe, AZ 85282-8011; *Phone:* 480-557-7900; *Fax:* 480-557-7926. *E-mail:* petersons@gowithcea.com. *World Wide Web:* http://www.gowithcea.com/

INTERNATIONAL STUDIES ABROAD
GRANADA, SPAIN–HISPANIC STUDIES
Hosted by University of Granada
Academic Focus • Art history, cultural studies, geography, history, literature, political science and government, Spanish language and literature.
Program Information • Students attend classes at University of Granada. Scheduled travel to Toledo, Madrid; field trips to Córdoba, El Escorial, Sevilla, Las Alpujarras, Valencia; optional travel at an extra cost.
Sessions • Fall, spring, yearlong.
Eligibility Requirements • Minimum age 18; open to precollege students, freshmen, sophomores, juniors, seniors, graduate students; adults; 2.5 GPA; 1 letter of recommendation; good academic standing at home school; transcript; 2.5 years of college course work in Spanish.
Living Arrangements • Students live in locally rented apartments, host family homes, hotels. Quarters are shared with host institution students, students from other programs. Meals are taken with host family, in residences.
Costs (2004-2005) • One term: $7600. Yearlong program: $13,500; includes tuition, housing, all meals, insurance, excursions, student support services, tutoring, ground transportation, laundry service, Internet access. $200 deposit required. Financial aid available for all students: scholarships, loans, U.S. federal financial aid.
For More Information • Spain Site Specialist, International Studies Abroad, 901 West 24th Street, Austin, TX 78705; *Phone:* 800-580-

8826; *Fax:* 512-480-8866. *E-mail:* isa@studiesabroad.com. *World Wide Web:* http://www.studiesabroad.com/

INTERNATIONAL STUDIES ABROAD
GRANADA, SPAIN, INTENSIVE SPANISH LANGUAGE
Hosted by University of Granada
Academic Focus • Cultural studies, Spanish language and literature.
Program Information • Students attend classes at University of Granada. Scheduled travel to Toledo, Madrid; field trips to Córdoba, Seville, El Escorial, La Alpujarras, Valencia; optional travel at an extra cost.
Sessions • Fall, spring.
Eligibility Requirements • Minimum age 18; open to precollege students, freshmen, sophomores, juniors, seniors, adults; 2.5 GPA; 1 letter of recommendation; good academic standing at home school; transcripts; 1 year college course work in Spanish for upper-division courses.
Living Arrangements • Students live in locally rented apartments, host family homes. Quarters are shared with host institution students. Meals are taken with host family, in residences.
Costs (2004-2005) • One term: $5900; includes tuition, housing, all meals, insurance, excursions, student support services, ground transportation, laundry service, tutoring, Internet access. $200 deposit required. Financial aid available for all students: scholarships, loans, U.S. federal financial aid.
For More Information • Spain Site Specialist, International Studies Abroad, 901 West 24th Street, Austin, TX 78705; *Phone:* 800-580-8826; *Fax:* 512-480-8866. *E-mail:* isa@studiesabroad.com. *World Wide Web:* http://www.studiesabroad.com/

INTERNATIONAL STUDIES ABROAD
GRANADA, SPAIN–SPANISH LANGUAGE AND CULTURE
Hosted by University of Granada
Academic Focus • Art history, civilization studies, geography, history, Spanish language and literature, Spanish studies.
Program Information • Students attend classes at University of Granada. Field trips to Córdoba, El Escorial, Sevilla, Las Alpujarras, Valencia; optional travel at an extra cost.
Sessions • Fall, spring.
Eligibility Requirements • Minimum age 18; open to precollege students, freshmen, sophomores, juniors, seniors, graduate students, adults; 2.5 GPA; 1 letter of recommendation; good academic standing at home school; transcript; 1.5 years of college course work in Spanish.
Living Arrangements • Students live in locally rented apartments, host family homes, hotels. Quarters are shared with host institution students, students from other programs. Meals are taken with host family, in residences.
Costs (2004-2005) • One term: $7600; includes tuition, housing, all meals, insurance, excursions, student support services, laundry service, ground transportation, tutors, Internet access. $200 deposit required. Financial aid available for all students: scholarships, loans, U.S. federal financial aid.
For More Information • Spain Site Specialist, International Studies Abroad, 901 West 24th Street, Austin, TX 78705; *Phone:* 800-580-8826; *Fax:* 512-480-8866. *E-mail:* isa@studiesabroad.com. *World Wide Web:* http://www.studiesabroad.com/

SCHOOL FOR INTERNATIONAL TRAINING, SIT STUDY ABROAD
SPAIN: CULTURAL STUDIES AND THE ARTS
Academic Focus • Cultural studies, economics, geography, history, political science and government, Spanish language and literature, visual and performing arts.
Program Information • Faculty members are drawn from the sponsor's U.S. staff and local instructors hired by the sponsor. Scheduled travel to Barcelona, Madrid, Seville; field trips to national parks, medieval cities, cathedrals, Alhambra.
Sessions • Fall, spring.
Eligibility Requirements • Open to sophomores, juniors, seniors; 2.5 GPA; 2 letters of recommendation; good academic standing at home school; 2 years of college course work in Spanish.

Living Arrangements • Students live in host family homes, hotels. Meals are taken as a group, on one's own, with host family, in residences, in restaurants.

Costs (2003–2004) • One term: $12,750; includes tuition, housing, all meals, insurance, excursions. $50 application fee. $400 nonrefundable deposit required. Financial aid available for all students: scholarships.

For More Information • School for International Training, SIT Study Abroad, Kipling Road, Brattleboro, VT 05302-0676; *Phone:* 888-272-7881; *Fax:* 802-258-3296. *E-mail:* studyabroad@sit.edu. *World Wide Web:* http://www.sit.edu/studyabroad/

SCHOOL FOR INTERNATIONAL TRAINING, SIT STUDY ABROAD
SPAIN: INTENSIVE LANGUAGE AND CULTURE

Academic Focus • Economics, geography, history, political science and government, Spanish language and literature, visual and performing arts.

Program Information • Faculty members are drawn from the sponsor's U.S. staff and local instructors hired by the sponsor. Scheduled travel to Barcelona, Segovia, Madrid, Seville; field trips to monasteries, castles, museums.

Sessions • Fall, spring.

Eligibility Requirements • Open to sophomores, juniors, seniors; 2.5 GPA; 2 letters of recommendation; good academic standing at home school; no foreign language proficiency required.

Living Arrangements • Students live in host family homes, hotels. Meals are taken as a group, on one's own, with host family, in residences, in restaurants.

Costs (2003–2004) • One term: $12,750; includes tuition, housing, all meals, insurance, excursions, international student ID. $50 application fee. $400 nonrefundable deposit required. Financial aid available for all students: scholarships.

For More Information • School for International Training, SIT Study Abroad, Kipling Road, Brattleboro, VT 05302-0676; *Phone:* 888-272-7881; *Fax:* 802-258-3296. *E-mail:* studyabroad@sit.edu. *World Wide Web:* http://www.sit.edu/studyabroad/

SEVEN CONTINENTS' EXCHANGE PROGRAMS
SEVEN CONTINENTS' EXCHANGE PROGRAMS AT THE UNIVERSITY OF GRANADA, SPAIN

Hosted by University of Granada

Academic Focus • Full curriculum.

Program Information • Students attend classes at University of Granada. Scheduled travel to Córdoba, Montilla, Seville, Jerez; field trips to the coast, mountains, historic monuments in Andalucia, bullfights, wine and cuisine tours; optional travel to Morocco, Portugal, other destinations in Spain at an extra cost.

Sessions • Fall, spring, winter, yearlong.

Eligibility Requirements • Minimum age 16; open to precollege students, freshmen, sophomores, juniors, seniors, graduate students, adults; no foreign language proficiency requirement for intensive language programs; intermediate level Spanish required for all other courses.

Living Arrangements • Students live in locally rented apartments, host family homes. Meals are taken on one's own, with host family, in restaurants.

Costs (2002–2003) • One term: $6975. Yearlong program: $14,050; includes tuition, housing, all meals, excursions, lab equipment, student support services, travel and lodging for excursions, certificates. $250 nonrefundable deposit required. Financial aid available for all students: scholarships, travel vouchers.

For More Information • Mr. Domenico M. Verne, President/Director, Seven Continents' Exchange Programs, 671 East Beverwyck, Suite 1, Paramus, NJ 07653-8163; *Phone:* 201-444-8687; *Fax:* 201-444-8687. *E-mail:* 7continents@arborea.cjb.net. *World Wide Web:* http://www.mediterranean-heritage.org/7continents/. Students may also apply through Mediterranean World Heritage Association, Bruselas 11, 3G, 18008 Granada, Spain.

UNIVERSITY OF CONNECTICUT
SPANISH LANGUAGE AND SOCIETY IN GRANADA

Hosted by University of Granada

Academic Focus • Liberal studies, literature, Spanish language and literature.

Program Information • Students attend classes at University of Granada. Scheduled travel to Madrid; field trips to Seville, Córdoba.

Sessions • Fall, spring, yearlong.

Eligibility Requirements • Open to sophomores, juniors, seniors; 2.5 GPA; 3 letters of recommendation; good academic standing at home school; 2 years of college course work in Spanish.

Living Arrangements • Students live in host family homes. Meals are taken with host family, in residences.

Costs (2003–2004) • One term: $8090 for Connecticut residents or consortium members; $9405 for all others. Yearlong program: $15,945 for Connecticut residents or consortium members; $18,575 for all others; includes tuition, housing, all meals, insurance, excursions, international student ID, fees, one-way airfare. $25 application fee. $350 nonrefundable deposit required. Financial aid available for students from sponsoring institution: scholarships, loans.

For More Information • Mr. Gordon Lustila, Acting Director of Study Abroad Programs, University of Connecticut, 843 Bolton Road, Unit 1207, Storrs, CT 06269-1207; *Phone:* 860-486-5022; *Fax:* 860-486-2976. *E-mail:* sabadm03@uconnvm.uconn.edu. *World Wide Web:* http://studyabroad.uconn.edu/

UNIVERSITY OF DELAWARE
FALL SEMESTER IN GRANADA, SPAIN

Hosted by University of Granada

Academic Focus • Art history, history, political science and government, Spanish language and literature, Spanish studies.

Program Information • Students attend classes at University of Granada. Scheduled travel to Madrid; field trips to Toledo, Seville, Córdoba; optional travel to Europe at an extra cost.

Sessions • Fall.

Eligibility Requirements • Open to freshmen, sophomores, juniors, seniors, adults; 2.8 GPA; 2 letters of recommendation; 2 courses beyond intermediate Spanish.

Living Arrangements • Students live in host family homes. Meals are taken with host family, in residences.

Costs (2003) • One term: contact sponsor for cost. $200 nonrefundable deposit required. Financial aid available for all students: scholarships.

For More Information • Center for International Studies, University of Delaware, 186 South College Avenue, Newark, DE 19716-1450; *Phone:* 888-831-4685; *Fax:* 302-831-6042. *E-mail:* studyabroad@udel.edu. *World Wide Web:* http://www.udel.edu/studyabroad/

UNIVERSITY OF DELAWARE
SPRING SEMESTER IN GRANADA

Hosted by University of Granada

Academic Focus • Art history, communications, history, music, political science and government, Spanish language and literature.

Program Information • Students attend classes at University of Granada. Scheduled travel to Madrid, Seville; field trips to the Prado art museum, Sierra Nevada, Toledo; optional travel to Europe.

Sessions • Spring.

Eligibility Requirements • Open to freshmen, sophomores, juniors, seniors, adults; 2.0 GPA; 2 letters of recommendation; no foreign language proficiency required.

Living Arrangements • Students live in host family homes. Meals are taken on one's own, with host family, in residences.

Costs (2003) • One term: contact sponsor for cost. $200 nonrefundable deposit required. Financial aid available for all students: scholarships.

For More Information • Center for International Studies, University of Delaware, 186 South College Avenue, Newark, DE 19716-1450; *Phone:* 888-831-4685; *Fax:* 302-831-6042. *E-mail:* studyabroad@udel.edu. *World Wide Web:* http://www.udel.edu/studyabroad/

UNIVERSITY OF MIAMI
UNIVERSITY OF GRANADA

Hosted by University of Granada

Academic Focus • Art history, biological/life sciences, history, sociology, Spanish language and literature.

SPAIN
Granada

Program Information • Students attend classes at University of Granada.
Sessions • Fall, spring, yearlong.
Eligibility Requirements • Minimum age 18; open to sophomores, juniors, seniors; 3.0 GPA; 2 letters of recommendation; language evaluation; personal interview; fluency in Spanish.
Living Arrangements • Students live in host institution dormitories, locally rented apartments, host family homes. Quarters are shared with host institution students, students from other programs. Meals are taken as a group, on one's own, with host family, in residences, in central dining facility, in restaurants.
Costs (2003-2004) • One term: $12,919. Yearlong program: $25,838; includes tuition, student support services. $40 application fee. $500 nonrefundable deposit required. Financial aid available for students from sponsoring institution: scholarships, loans.
For More Information • Mr. Chris Tingue, Assistant Director, University of Miami, International Education and Exchange Programs, 5050 Brunson Drive, Allen Hall 212, PO Box 248005, Coral Gables, FL 33124-1610; *Phone:* 305-284-3434; *Fax:* 305-284-4235. *E-mail:* ieep@miami.edu. *World Wide Web:* http://www.studyabroad.miami.edu/

LAS PALMAS
UNIVERSITY AT ALBANY, STATE UNIVERSITY OF NEW YORK
DIRECT ENROLLMENT AT THE UNIVERSITY OF LAS PALMAS

Hosted by University of Las Palmas
Academic Focus • Business administration/management, economics, education, engineering, full curriculum, marine sciences, mathematics, psychology, sociology, Spanish language and literature.
Program Information • Students attend classes at University of Las Palmas.
Sessions • Fall, spring, yearlong.
Eligibility Requirements • Open to juniors, seniors, graduate students, adults; 3.0 GPA; 2 letters of recommendation; good academic standing at home school; 2.5 years college course work in Spanish or the equivalent.
Living Arrangements • Students live in host institution dormitories, locally rented apartments. Meals are taken on one's own.
Costs (2002-2003) • One term: $6513. Yearlong program: $13,026; includes housing, all meals, student support services, in-state tuition and fees. $150 nonrefundable deposit required. Financial aid available for students from sponsoring institution: all customary sources.
For More Information • University at Albany, State University of New York, Office of International Education, LI 66, Albany, NY 12222; *Phone:* 518-442-3525; *Fax:* 518-442-3338. *E-mail:* intled@uamail.albany.edu. *World Wide Web:* http://www.albany.edu/intled/

LEÓN
STONY BROOK UNIVERSITY
STONY BROOK ABROAD: LEÓN, SPAIN

Hosted by University of León
Academic Focus • Liberal studies, social sciences, Spanish language and literature, Spanish studies.
Program Information • Students attend classes at University of León. Optional travel to Madrid, other locations in Spain, Morocco at an extra cost.
Sessions • Fall, spring, yearlong.
Eligibility Requirements • Open to juniors, seniors, graduate students; 2.5 GPA; 3 letters of recommendation; statement of purpose; 2 years of college course work in Spanish.
Living Arrangements • Students live in host institution dormitories, locally rented apartments, host family homes. Quarters are shared with host institution students, students from other programs. Meals are taken on one's own, with host family, in residences, in central dining facility.
Costs (2002-2003) • One term: contact sponsor for cost. Yearlong program: contact sponsor for cost. $200 nonrefundable deposit

required. Financial aid available for students from sponsoring institution: scholarships, loans, grants, TAP awards for New York State residents.
For More Information • Ms. Gretchen Gosnell, Study Abroad Advisor, Stony Brook University, Study Abroad Office, Melville Library, Room E5340, Stony Brook, NY 11794-3397; *Phone:* 631-632-7030; *Fax:* 631-632-6544. *E-mail:* studyabroad@sunysb.edu. *World Wide Web:* http://www.sunysb.edu/studyabroad/

LOGROÑO
MIDDLEBURY COLLEGE SCHOOLS ABROAD
SCHOOL IN SPAIN–LOGROÑO PROGRAM

Hosted by University of La Rioja
Academic Focus • Full curriculum.
Program Information • Students attend classes at University of La Rioja.
Sessions • Fall, spring, yearlong.
Eligibility Requirements • Open to sophomores, juniors, seniors; 2.7 GPA; 2 letters of recommendation; B average in both Spanish and major; 2.5 years college course work in Spanish, including at least 1 content course at the 300-level.
Living Arrangements • Students live in host institution dormitories, locally rented apartments, host family homes. Quarters are shared with host institution students. Meals are taken on one's own, with host family, in residences, in central dining facility, in restaurants.
Costs (2004-2005) • One term: $7200. Yearlong program: $14,400; includes tuition, student support services. $50 application fee. $300 nonrefundable deposit required. Financial aid available for students from sponsoring institution: scholarships, loans.
For More Information • Mr. Jamie Northrup, University Relations Coordinator, Middlebury College Schools Abroad, Office of Off-Campus Study, Sunderland Language Center, Middlebury, VT 05753; *Phone:* 802-443-5745; *Fax:* 802-443-3157. *E-mail:* schoolsabroad@middlebury.edu. *World Wide Web:* http://www.middlebury.edu/msa/

MADRID
ACADEMIC PROGRAMS INTERNATIONAL (API)
(API)–MADRID ENGLISH PROGRAM, SPAIN

Hosted by Suffolk University Madrid Campus
Academic Focus • Art, biological/life sciences, business administration/management, communications, computer science, economics, full curriculum, history, international business, marketing, mathematics, philosophy, political science and government, science, sociology, Spanish language and literature, Spanish studies.
Program Information • Students attend classes at Suffolk University Madrid Campus. Scheduled travel to Santander, Bilbao, Seville; field trips to El Escorial, Toledo, Segovia, Salamanca, Barcelona, Granada; optional travel to Lisbon, Rome, Paris.
Sessions • Fall, spring, yearlong.
Eligibility Requirements • Minimum age 18; open to sophomores, juniors, seniors; 2.75 GPA; 1 letter of recommendation; good academic standing at home school; official transcript from home university; no foreign language proficiency required.
Living Arrangements • Students live in host institution dormitories, locally rented apartments, host family homes. Quarters are shared with host institution students. Meals are taken on one's own, with host family, in central dining facility, in restaurants.
Costs (2004-2005) • One term: $10,500. Yearlong program: $19,900; includes tuition, housing, all meals, insurance, excursions, student support services, airport pick-up, ground transportation. $150 nonrefundable deposit required. Financial aid available for all students: scholarships.
For More Information • Ms. Jennifer C. Allen, Director, Academic Programs International (API), 107 East Hopkins, San Marcos, TX 78666; *Phone:* 800-844-4124; *Fax:* 512-392-8420. *E-mail:* api@academicintl.com. *World Wide Web:* http://www.academicintl.com/

ACADEMIC PROGRAMS INTERNATIONAL (API)
(API)–MADRID, SPAIN

Hosted by Complutense University of Madrid

Academic Focus • Art history, civilization studies, communications, dance, European studies, film and media studies, geography, history, international business, Latin American studies, music, Spanish language and literature, Spanish studies.

Program Information • Students attend classes at Complutense University of Madrid. Scheduled travel to Seville; field trips to Toledo, Salamanca, Segovia, Santander, Barcelona, Granada; optional travel to Rome, Paris, Lisbon.

Sessions • Fall, spring, yearlong, spring A1 term; spring B term.

Eligibility Requirements • Minimum age 18; open to freshmen, sophomores, juniors, seniors, adults; 2.75 GPA; 1 letter of recommendation; good academic standing at home school; official transcript from home university; no foreign language proficiency required.

Living Arrangements • Students live in host institution dormitories, host family homes. Quarters are shared with host institution students. Meals are taken on one's own, with host family, in residences, in restaurants.

Costs (2004-2005) • One term: $6900–$11,600. Yearlong program: $13,900–$17,500; includes tuition, housing, all meals, insurance, excursions, student support services, airport pick-up, ground transportation. $150 nonrefundable deposit required. Financial aid available for all students: scholarships.

For More Information • Ms. Jennifer C. Allen, Director, Academic Programs International (API), 107 East Hopkins, San Marcos, TX 78666; *Phone:* 800-844-4124; *Fax:* 512-392-8420. *E-mail:* api@academicintl.com. *World Wide Web:* http://www.academicintl.com/

ACADEMIC YEAR ABROAD
ACADEMIC YEAR ABROAD: MADRID CONSORTIUM

Hosted by Complutense University of Madrid, University Carlos III, Madrid

Academic Focus • Full curriculum.

Program Information • Students attend classes at Complutense University of Madrid, University Carlos III, Madrid. Scheduled travel to Sevilla, Barcelona; field trips to Salamanca, Cadiz, Basque country, Toledo, Cuenca, Córdoba.

Sessions • Fall, spring, yearlong.

Eligibility Requirements • Open to juniors, seniors, graduate students; 3.0 GPA; 3 letters of recommendation; good academic standing at home school; language evaluation; letter of recommendation; statement of purpose in Spanish; 2 years of college course work in Spanish.

Living Arrangements • Students live in host institution dormitories, locally rented apartments, host family homes. Meals are taken on one's own, with host family, in residences, in central dining facility.

Costs (2004-2005) • One term: $10,800. Yearlong program: $18,900; includes tuition, housing, insurance, excursions, international student ID, student support services, cultural activities, commuter rail tickets, most meals, advising. $30 application fee. $500 refundable deposit required. Financial aid available for all students: scholarships, loans, consortium agreement for financial aid.

For More Information • Dr. Anthony M. Cinquemani, Director, Academic Year Abroad, PO Box 67, Red Hook, NY 12571; *Phone:* 845-758-9655; *Fax:* 845-758-1588. *E-mail:* aya@ayabroad.com. *World Wide Web:* http://www.ayabroad.com/. Students may also apply through Universidad Carlos III, Edificio López Aranguren, 28903 Getafe, Madrid, Spain.

SPAIN
Madrid

ACCENT INTERNATIONAL CONSORTIUM FOR ACADEMIC PROGRAMS ABROAD
SEMESTER IN MADRID WITH CITY COLLEGE OF SAN FRANCISCO

Hosted by Complutense University of Madrid

Academic Focus • Art history, Spanish language and literature, Spanish studies.

Program Information • Students attend classes at Complutense University of Madrid. Scheduled travel to Barcelona; field trips to Avila, Segovia, El Escorial, Toledo.

Sessions • Spring.

Eligibility Requirements • Minimum age 18; open to freshmen, sophomores, juniors, seniors, graduate students, adults; no foreign language proficiency required.

Living Arrangements • Students live in locally rented apartments, host family homes. Quarters are shared with host institution students, students from other programs. Meals are taken on one's own, in residences.

Costs (2004) • One term: $5350; includes housing, excursions, international student ID, student support services. $250 nonrefundable deposit required.

For More Information • ACCENT International Consortium for Academic Programs Abroad, 870 Market Street, Suite 1026, San Francisco, CA 94102; *Phone:* 415-835-3744; *Fax:* 415-835-3749. *E-mail:* info@accentintl.com. *World Wide Web:* http://www.accentintl.com/. Students may also apply through City College of San Francisco, Study Abroad Office, Box A-71, 50 Phelan Avenue, San Francisco, CA 94112.

ALMA COLLEGE
PROGRAM OF STUDIES IN MADRID, SPAIN

Hosted by ENFOREX–Spanish in the Spanish World

Academic Focus • Art history, business administration/management, history, Spanish language and literature.

Program Information • Students attend classes at ENFOREX–Spanish in the Spanish World. Field trips to Avila, Segovia, Toledo, Valle de los Caídos.

Sessions • Fall, winter, yearlong, fall and winter semesters.

Eligibility Requirements • Minimum age 18; open to sophomores, juniors, seniors, adults; 2.5 GPA; 2 letters of recommendation; good academic standing at home school; no foreign language proficiency required.

Living Arrangements • Students live in host family homes. Quarters are shared with host institution students, students from other programs. Meals are taken on one's own, with host family, in residences.

Costs (2003-2004) • One term: $7785–$9200. Yearlong program: $13,850–$16,950; includes tuition, housing, all meals, excursions, books and class materials, student support services, Metro pass, e-mail access. $50 application fee. $200 refundable deposit required. Financial aid available for all students: scholarships.

For More Information • Ms. Julie Elenbaas, Office Coordinator, Alma College, 614 West Superior Street, Alma, MI 48801-1599; *Phone:* 989-463-7055; *Fax:* 989-463-7126. *E-mail:* intl_studies@alma.edu. *World Wide Web:* http://international.alma.edu/

AMERICAN UNIVERSITY
SEMESTER IN MADRID

Hosted by University of Alcalá de Henares

Academic Focus • Film and media studies, history, international affairs, political science and government, Spanish language and literature, Spanish studies.

Program Information • Students attend classes at University of Alcalá de Henares. Scheduled travel to Andalucía, Cataluña; field trips to Toledo, El Escorial, Salamanca.

Sessions • Spring.

Eligibility Requirements • Open to sophomores, juniors, seniors, graduate students; 2.75 GPA; 1 letter of recommendation; second semester sophomore status; recommendation of advisor; 2 years of college course work in Spanish.

Living Arrangements • Students live in host family homes. Meals are taken with host family, in residences.

Costs (2003) • One term: $17,659; includes tuition, housing, some meals, excursions, books and class materials, international student ID, student support services. $35 application fee. $300 nonrefundable deposit required. Financial aid available for all students: scholarships, loans.

For More Information • Dr. David C. Brown, Dean, Washington Semester and World Capitals Programs, American University, Tenley Campus–Constitution Building, Washington, DC 20016-8083; *Phone:* 800-424-2600; *Fax:* 202-895-4960. *E-mail:* travel@american.edu. *World Wide Web:* http://www.worldcapitals.american.edu/

BENTLEY COLLEGE
STUDY ABROAD PROGRAM IN MADRID, SPAIN

Hosted by Suffolk University–Madrid Campus

Academic Focus • Accounting, advertising and public relations, communications, economics, history, international affairs, mathematics, Spanish language and literature, Spanish studies, statistics.

Program Information • Students attend classes at Suffolk University–Madrid Campus. Scheduled travel to El Escorial, Segovia, Toledo, Avila, Salamanca, Andalucía; optional travel.

Sessions • Fall, spring.

Eligibility Requirements • Open to sophomores, juniors, seniors; 1 letter of recommendation; good academic standing at home school; essays; minimum 3.0 GPA for internship students, minimum 2.7 GPA for all others; 1 year of college course work in Spanish.

Living Arrangements • Students live in host family homes. Quarters are shared with students from other programs. Meals are taken with host family, in residences.

Costs (2003-2004) • One term: $16,600; includes tuition, housing, all meals, excursions, international student ID, student support services. $35 application fee. $500 nonrefundable deposit required. Financial aid available for students from sponsoring institution: scholarships, loans.

For More Information • Ms. Jennifer Aquino, Assistant Director, International Center, Bentley College, 175 Forest Street, Waltham, MA 02452; *Phone:* 781-891-3474; *Fax:* 781-891-2819. *E-mail:* study_abroad@bentley.edu. *World Wide Web:* http://ecampus.bentley.edu/dept/sa/

BOSTON UNIVERSITY
MADRID PROGRAMS

Hosted by Autonomous University of Madrid

Academic Focus • Civilization studies, liberal studies, social sciences, Spanish language and literature, Spanish studies.

Program Information • Students attend classes at Autonomous University of Madrid. Classes are also held on the campus of Instituto Internacional en España. Scheduled travel to Granada, Seville, Córdoba; field trips to Segovia, Toledo.

Sessions • Fall, spring, yearlong.

Eligibility Requirements • Open to freshmen, sophomores, juniors, seniors, adults; 3.0 GPA; 2 letters of recommendation; good academic standing at home school; essay; writing sample in Spanish; approval of participation; transcript; 1 year of college course work in Spanish.

Living Arrangements • Students live in host family homes. Meals are taken on one's own, with host family, in residences, in restaurants.

Costs (2004-2005) • One term: $19,834. Yearlong program: $39,668; includes tuition, housing, all meals, excursions, international airfare, limited reimbursement for cultural activities and local transportation. $50 application fee. $400 nonrefundable deposit required. Financial aid available for all students: scholarships, work study, loans.

For More Information • Division of International Programs, Boston University, 232 Bay State Road, Boston, MA 02215; *Phone:* 617-353-9888; *Fax:* 617-353-5402. *E-mail:* abroad@bu.edu. *World Wide Web:* http://www.bu.edu/abroad/

CENTER FOR INTERNATIONAL STUDIES
SUFFOLK UNIVERSITY, MADRID

Hosted by Suffolk University–Madrid Campus

Academic Focus • Full curriculum.

Program Information • Students attend classes at Suffolk University–Madrid Campus. Scheduled travel to Italy, France; field trips to Seville, Barcelona; optional travel to Europe at an extra cost.

Sessions • Fall, spring, yearlong.

Eligibility Requirements • Minimum age 18; open to freshmen, sophomores, juniors, seniors, adults; 2.5 GPA; 1 letter of recommendation; good academic standing at home school; personal essay; no foreign language proficiency required.

Living Arrangements • Students live in host institution dormitories, program-owned apartments, host family homes. Quarters are shared with host institution students. Meals are taken on one's own, in residences, in central dining facility, in restaurants.

Costs (2003-2004) • One term: $10,400. Yearlong program: $19,800; includes tuition, housing, some meals, excursions, international student ID, student support services, 1-2 week intensive Spanish course at the beginning of the semester. $50 application fee. $500 nonrefundable deposit required. Financial aid available for all students: scholarships.

For More Information • Mr. Jeff Palm, Program Director, Center for International Studies, 17 New South Street, #105, Northampton, MA 01060; *Phone:* 413-582-0407; *Fax:* 413-582-0327. *E-mail:* jpalm@cisabroad.com. *World Wide Web:* http://www.cisabroad.com/

CENTER FOR STUDY ABROAD (CSA)
UNIVERSITY COMPLUTENSE MADRID (SPAIN)

Hosted by Complutense University of Madrid

Academic Focus • Spanish language and literature, Spanish studies.

Program Information • Students attend classes at Complutense University of Madrid. Optional travel.

Sessions • Fall, spring, winter, yearlong.

Eligibility Requirements • Minimum age 17; open to precollege students, freshmen, sophomores, juniors, seniors, graduate students, adults; no foreign language proficiency required.

Living Arrangements • Quarters are shared with students from other programs. Meals are taken on one's own, in residences, in central dining facility, in restaurants.

Costs (2003-2004) • One term: contact sponsor for cost. Yearlong program: contact sponsor for cost. $45 application fee.

For More Information • Ms. Alima K. Virtue, Program Director, Center for Study Abroad (CSA), 325 Washington Avenue South, #93, Kent, WA 98032; *Phone:* 206-726-1498; *Fax:* 253-850-0454. *E-mail:* info @centerforstudyabroad.com. *World Wide Web:* http://www.centerforstudyabroad.com/

CIEE
CIEE STUDY CENTER AT THE UNIVERSIDAD CARLOS III DE MADRID, SPAIN

Hosted by University Carlos III, Madrid

Academic Focus • Economics, journalism, political science and government, sociology, Spanish language and literature.

Program Information • Students attend classes at University Carlos III, Madrid. Scheduled travel to points of interest in the Madrid metropolitan area and historical sites in Spain; field trips to points of interest in the Madrid metropolitan area and historical sites in Spain.

Sessions • Fall, spring, yearlong.

Eligibility Requirements • Minimum age 18; open to sophomores, juniors, seniors; minimum 2.75 GPA overall, minimum 3.0 GPA in most recent Spanish class; 3 years of college course work in Spanish.

Living Arrangements • Students live in host family homes. Meals are taken with host family, in residences.

Costs (2005-2006) • One term: contact sponsor for cost. Yearlong program: contact sponsor for cost. $30 application fee. $300 deposit required. Financial aid available for all students: scholarships, travel grants, minority student scholarships.

For More Information • Ms. Ellen Whitman, Admissions Officer, Spain and Latin America, CIEE, 7 Custom House Street, 3rd Floor, Portland, ME 04101; *Phone:* 800-40-STUDY; *Fax:* 207-553-7699. *E-mail:* ewhitman@ciee.org. *World Wide Web:* http://www.ciee.org/isp/

CITY COLLEGE OF SAN FRANCISCO
SEMESTER IN MADRID

Hosted by Complutense University of Madrid

Academic Focus • Art history, Spanish language and literature, Spanish studies.

Program Information • Students attend classes at Complutense University of Madrid. Scheduled travel to Barcelona; field trips to Segovia, Avila, El Escorial, Valle de los Caídos.

Sessions • Spring.

Eligibility Requirements • Minimum age 18; open to freshmen, sophomores, juniors, seniors, adults; 2.0 GPA; good academic standing at home school; no foreign language proficiency required.

Living Arrangements • Students live in program-owned apartments, host family homes. Quarters are shared with host institution students. Meals are taken on one's own, with host family, in residences, in restaurants.

Costs (2005) • One term: $5300–$6450; includes housing, some meals, insurance, excursions, international student ID, student support services. $250 nonrefundable deposit required. Financial aid available for students from sponsoring institution: scholarships, loans.

For More Information • Ms. Jill Heffron, Study Abroad Coordinator, City College of San Francisco, 50 Phelan Avenue, Box C212, San Francisco, CA 94112; *Phone:* 415-239-3778; *Fax:* 415-239-3804. *E-mail:* studyabroad@ccsf.edu. *World Wide Web:* http://www.ccsf.edu/studyabroad/. Students may also apply through ACCENT, 870 Market Street, Suite 1026, San Francisco, CA 94102.

CULTURAL EXPERIENCES ABROAD (CEA)
STUDY SPANISH LANGUAGE AND CULTURE IN MADRID

Hosted by Complutense University of Madrid

Academic Focus • Art history, geography, history, philosophy, sociology, Spanish language and literature, Spanish studies.

Program Information • Students attend classes at Complutense University of Madrid. Field trips to Salamanca, Avila, Segovia, Toledo, Córdoba, Burgos.

Sessions • Fall, spring, winter, yearlong, alternate fall and spring terms.

Eligibility Requirements • Minimum age 18; open to freshmen, sophomores, juniors, seniors, graduate students; 2.5 GPA; 1 letter of recommendation; good academic standing at home school; previous Spanish study recommended.

Living Arrangements • Students live in locally rented apartments, program-owned apartments, host family homes. Quarters are shared with students from other programs. Meals are taken with host family.

Costs (2003-2004) • One term: $7395–$8695. Yearlong program: $14,790–$16,495; includes tuition, housing, some meals, insurance, excursions, student support services. $50 application fee. $400 nonrefundable deposit required.

For More Information • Cultural Experiences Abroad (CEA), 1400 East Southern Avenue, Suite B-108, Tempe, AZ 85282-8011; *Phone:* 480-557-7900; *Fax:* 480-557-7926. *E-mail:* petersons@gowithcea.com. *World Wide Web:* http://www.gowithcea.com/

DUKE UNIVERSITY
DUKE IN MADRID

Hosted by Universidad San Pablo

Academic Focus • Full curriculum.

Program Information • Students attend classes at Universidad San Pablo. Field trips to various sites in Spain.

Sessions • Fall, spring, yearlong.

Eligibility Requirements • Open to sophomores, juniors, seniors; 2 letters of recommendation; good academic standing at home school; 2.5 years of college course work in Spanish.

Living Arrangements • Students live in host family homes. Meals are taken with host family, in residences.

Costs (2003-2004) • One term: $15,938. Yearlong program: $31,876; includes tuition, housing, all meals, excursions, student support services, program activities. $1000 nonrefundable deposit required. Financial aid available for students from sponsoring institution: scholarships, loans.

For More Information • Dr. Amanda Kelso, Associate Director, Duke University, Office of Study Abroad, 2016 Campus Drive, Box 90057, Durham, NC 27708-0057; *Phone:* 919-684-2174; *Fax:* 919-684-3083. *E-mail:* amanda.kelso@duke.edu. *World Wide Web:* http://www.aas.duke.edu/study_abroad/

FOUNDATION FOR INTERNATIONAL EDUCATION
MADRID STUDY PROGRAM

Hosted by Universidad Europea de Madrid

Academic Focus • Art history, drama/theater, history, political science and government, Spanish language and literature, Spanish studies.

Program Information • Students attend classes at Universidad Europea de Madrid. Field trips to Salamanca, Toledo.

Sessions • Fall, spring.

Eligibility Requirements • Minimum age 18; open to sophomores, juniors, seniors; 2.75 GPA; advisor's approval; no foreign language proficiency required.

Living Arrangements • Students live in locally rented apartments. Quarters are shared with host institution students. Meals are taken on one's own, in residences, in central dining facility, in restaurants.

Costs (2003-2004) • One term: $9110 for fall term; $9430 for spring; includes tuition, housing, some meals, insurance, excursions, books and class materials, student support services, UEM transcript, membership of UEM University. $500 deposit required.

For More Information • Ms. Erika Richards, Director of Program Development, Foundation for International Education, PBM 326, 5 Bessom Street, Marblehead, MA 01945; *Phone:* 781-631-6153. *E-mail:* studyabroad@fie.co.uk. *World Wide Web:* http://www.fie.org.uk/

THE GEORGE WASHINGTON UNIVERSITY
GW MADRID STUDY CENTER

Hosted by Autonomous University of Madrid

Academic Focus • Art, drama/theater, economics, history, international affairs, political science and government, Spanish language and literature.

Program Information • Students attend classes at Autonomous University of Madrid. Scheduled travel to Granada, Seville, Extremadura, Andalucía; field trips to Toledo, Salamanca, Segovia; optional travel to San Sebastián, Barcelona at an extra cost.

Sessions • Fall, spring, yearlong.

Eligibility Requirements • Minimum age 19; open to sophomores, juniors, seniors; 3.0 GPA; 2 letters of recommendation; good academic standing at home school; 1 year of college course work in Spanish.

Living Arrangements • Students live in host family homes. Meals are taken with host family, in residences.

Costs (2003-2004) • One term: $20,395. Yearlong program: $40,790; includes tuition, housing, all meals, excursions, student support services. $300 nonrefundable deposit required. Financial aid available for students from sponsoring institution: scholarships, loans.

For More Information • Ms. Kari McGriff, Assistant Director, The George Washington University, Office for Study Abroad, 812 20th Street, Washington, DC 20052-0001; *Phone:* 202-994-1649; *Fax:* 202-994-9133. *E-mail:* studyabr@gwu.edu. *World Wide Web:* http://www.gwu.edu/~studyabr/

HAMILTON COLLEGE
ACADEMIC YEAR IN SPAIN

Hosted by Centro Universitario de Estudios Hispanicos

Academic Focus • Anthropology, art, drama/theater, literature, political science and government, sociology, Spanish language and literature, translation.

Program Information • Students attend classes at Centro Universitario de Estudios Hispanicos. Scheduled travel to Barcelona, Santiago de Compostela, Mallorca, Andalucía; field trips to Toledo, La Mancha, La Rioja, Salamanca, Avila, Segovia, Extremadura, Cataluña.

Sessions • Fall, spring, yearlong.

Eligibility Requirements • Open to freshmen, sophomores, juniors, seniors; 3.0 GPA; 3 letters of recommendation; good academic standing at home school; pledge to speak only Spanish while enrolled in the program; 2.5 years of college course work in Spanish.

Living Arrangements • Students live in host family homes. Quarters are shared with host institution students. Meals are taken with host family, in residences.

Costs (2003-2004) • One term: $17,400. Yearlong program: $33,300; includes tuition, housing, all meals, excursions, interna-

tional airfare, student support services, group entertainment. $25 application fee. $500 deposit required. Financial aid available for all students: scholarships, work study.

For More Information • Ms. Gena Hasburgh, Coordinator, Hamilton College Programs Abroad, Hamilton College, 198 College Hill Road, Clinton, NY 13323; *Phone:* 315-859-4201; *Fax:* 315-859-4969. *E-mail:* ghasburgh@hamilton.edu. *World Wide Web:* http://www.hamilton.edu/academics/programs_abroad/. Students may also apply through Swarthmore College, 500 College Avenue, Swarthmore, PA 19081; Williams College, Williamstown, MA 01267.

MORE ABOUT THE PROGRAM

The goal of the Hamilton College Academic Year in Spain (HCAYS) is to offer academic standards that are truly commensurate with those of the best U.S. colleges and universities. This entails a strictly enforced Spanish-only rule, an academic and cultural agreement with the Madrid University of San Pablo while free from the Spanish university bureaucracy, very small classes and selection of some of the best professors from Spanish academia, recruitment of students from U.S. institutions of the highest caliber (including those who have joined an informal affiliation with the HCAYS—Swarthmore, Williams, Amherst, and Haverford), and a varied and rich curriculum (including credit-bearing internships). The program also includes special 10-day orientation sessions in the beachside villages of Comillas (fall) and Nerja (spring); an extensive, professionally guided series of cultural excursions throughout Spain; and the strong support (and minimal interference) of a trusting home institution administration. Students receive truly personalized treatment—the size of the group is limited to about 45. Spanish families for lodging are chosen with great care and given special attention by both the Director-in-Residence and the Program Assistant. The role of the Director is full-time and includes the organization of many activities that are designed to create an atmosphere of caring and a spirit of flexibility with regard to the individual needs of each program participant.

Motivated first-year students, sophomores, and juniors with language skills that are equivalent to 5th-semester college level are encouraged to apply.

IES, INSTITUTE FOR THE INTERNATIONAL EDUCATION OF STUDENTS
IES-MADRID

Hosted by Institute for the International Education of Students (IES)–Madrid, Complutense University of Madrid

Academic Focus • Art history, business administration/management, drama/theater, economics, European studies, film and media studies, fine/studio arts, history, international affairs, marketing, political science and government, Spanish language and literature.

Program Information • Students attend classes at Complutense University of Madrid, Institute for the International Education of Students (IES)–Madrid. Scheduled travel to Córdoba, Seville, Mérida; field trips to Segovia; optional travel to Barcelona, Trujillo, Cáceres, Toledo, Granada, Galicia at an extra cost.

Sessions • Fall, spring, yearlong.

Eligibility Requirements • Minimum age 18; open to sophomores, juniors, seniors, graduate students, adults; 3.0 GPA; 1 letter of recommendation; good academic standing at home school; 2 years of college course work in Spanish.

Living Arrangements • Students live in host institution dormitories, locally rented apartments, host family homes. Meals are taken on one's own, with host family, in residences, in central dining facility.

Costs (2003-2004) • One term: $11,300. Yearlong program: $20,340; includes tuition, housing, some meals, excursions, student support services, partial insurance coverage. $50 application fee. $500 nonrefundable deposit required. Financial aid available for all students: scholarships, institutional partner need-based grants.

For More Information • International Education Representative, IES, Institute for the International Education of Students, 33 North LaSalle Street, 15th Floor, Chicago, IL 60602; *Phone:* 800-995-2300; *Fax:* 312-944-1448. *E-mail:* info@iesabroad.org. *World Wide Web:* http://www.IESabroad.org/

INTERNATIONAL STUDIES ABROAD
MADRID, SPAIN–HISPANIC STUDIES

Hosted by Complutense University of Madrid
Academic Focus • Art history, history, Spanish language and literature, Spanish studies.
Program Information • Students attend classes at Complutense University of Madrid. Field trips to Granada, Segovia, Salamanca, Toledo, Sevilla, El Escorial, Avila, La Granja; optional travel.
Sessions • Fall, spring, yearlong.
Eligibility Requirements • Minimum age 18; open to freshmen, sophomores, juniors, seniors, graduate students, adults; 2.5 GPA; 1 letter of recommendation; good academic standing at home school; transcript; 2 years of college course work in Spanish.
Living Arrangements • Students live in locally rented apartments, host family homes. Meals are taken with host family, in residences.
Costs (2004-2005) • One term: $7975. Yearlong program: $13,500; includes tuition, housing, all meals, insurance, excursions, student support services, laundry service, excursion transportation, Internet access. $200 deposit required. Financial aid available for all students: scholarships, loans, U.S. federal financial aid.
For More Information • Spain Site Specialist, International Studies Abroad, 901 West 24th Street, Austin, TX 78705; *Phone:* 800-580-8826; *Fax:* 512-480-8866. *E-mail:* isa@studiesabroad.com. *World Wide Web:* http://www.studiesabroad.com/

INTERNATIONAL STUDIES ABROAD
MADRID, SPAIN, LANGUAGE AND CULTURE

Hosted by Complutense University of Madrid
Academic Focus • Art history, cinematography, history, international business, music, philosophy, Spanish language and literature, Spanish studies.
Program Information • Students attend classes at Complutense University of Madrid. Field trips to Granada, Segovia, Salamanca, Toledo, Sevilla, El Escorial, La Granja, Avila; optional travel at an extra cost.
Sessions • Fall, spring, winter.
Eligibility Requirements • Minimum age 18; open to freshmen, sophomores, juniors, seniors, graduate students, adults; 2.5 GPA; 1 letter of recommendation; good academic standing at home school; transcript; minimum 2.5 GPA or 2 letters of recommendation; 1 year college course work in Spanish for upper-division courses.
Living Arrangements • Students live in locally rented apartments, host family homes. Quarters are shared with host institution students. Meals are taken with host family, in residences.
Costs (2004-2005) • One term: $6600 for one trimester; $11,000 for two trimesters; includes tuition, housing, all meals, insurance, excursions, student support services, laundry service, Internet access, excursion transportation. $200 deposit required. Financial aid available for all students: scholarships, loans, U.S. federal financial aid via consortium agreement.
For More Information • Spain Site Specialist, International Studies Abroad, 901 West 24th Street, Austin, TX 78705; *Phone:* 800-580-8826; *Fax:* 512-480-8866. *E-mail:* isa@studiesabroad.com. *World Wide Web:* http://www.studiesabroad.com/

INTERNATIONAL STUDIES ABROAD
MADRID, SPAIN, STUDIES WITH SPANIARDS

Hosted by Complutense University of Madrid
Academic Focus • Art history, cinematography, geography, history, international business, music, philosophy, political science and government, Spanish language and literature, Spanish studies.
Program Information • Students attend classes at Complutense University of Madrid. Field trips to Granada, Segovia, Salamanca, Toledo, Sevilla, El Escorial, Avila, La Granja; optional travel at an extra cost.
Sessions • Fall, spring, yearlong.
Eligibility Requirements • Minimum age 18; open to freshmen, sophomores, juniors, seniors, graduate students, adults; 2.75 GPA; 1

letter of recommendation; good academic standing at home school; transcript; minimum 2.5 GPA or 2 letters of recommendation; 2.5 years of college course work in Spanish.
Living Arrangements • Students live in host family homes. Quarters are shared with host institution students, students from other programs. Meals are taken with host family, in residences.
Costs (2004-2005) • One term: $8550. Yearlong program: $14,650; includes tuition, housing, all meals, insurance, excursions, student support services, excursion transportation. $200 deposit required. Financial aid available for all students: scholarships, loans, U.S. federal financial aid.
For More Information • Ms. Jennifer Acosta, Spain Site Specialist, International Studies Abroad, 901 West 24th Street, Austin, TX 78705; *Phone:* 800-580-8826; *Fax:* 512-480-8866. *E-mail:* isa@studiesabroad.com. *World Wide Web:* http://www.studiesabroad.com/

LYCOMING COLLEGE
SEMESTER STUDY ABROAD (SPAIN)

Hosted by Tandem
Academic Focus • Art history, history, international business, Spanish language and literature, Spanish studies.
Program Information • Students attend classes at Tandem. Scheduled travel; field trips; optional travel at an extra cost.
Sessions • Fall, spring.
Eligibility Requirements • Open to sophomores, juniors, seniors; 2.5 GPA; 1 letter of recommendation; good academic standing at home school; 2 years of college course work in Spanish.
Living Arrangements • Students live in host family homes. Quarters are shared with students from other programs. Meals are taken with host family, in residences.
Costs (2003-2004) • One term: $8250; includes tuition, housing, all meals, excursions, books and class materials, student support services. $300 refundable deposit required.
For More Information • Dr. Barbara Buedel, Coordinator of Study Abroad Program, Lycoming College, Campus Box 2, 700 College Place, Williamsport, PA 17701-5192; *Phone:* 570-321-4210; *Fax:* 570-321-4389. *E-mail:* buedel@lycoming.edu. *World Wide Web:* http://www.lycoming.edu/

MARIST COLLEGE
SPANISH INTERNSHIP AND LANGUAGE PROGRAM

Hosted by Complutense University of Madrid
Academic Focus • Liberal studies, Spanish language and literature, Spanish studies.
Program Information • Students attend classes at Complutense University of Madrid. Scheduled travel to Seville, Córdoba, Granada; field trips to El Escorial, Segovia, Madrid environs, Toledo.
Sessions • Fall, spring, yearlong.
Eligibility Requirements • Open to sophomores, juniors, seniors; 2.8 GPA; 2 letters of recommendation; good academic standing at home school; 2 years of college course work in Spanish.
Living Arrangements • Students live in host family homes. Meals are taken with host family.
Costs (2003-2004) • One term: $12,500. Yearlong program: $25,000; includes tuition, housing, all meals, insurance, excursions, student support services, internship. $35 application fee. $300 nonrefundable deposit required. Financial aid available for students from sponsoring institution: scholarships, loans.
For More Information • Ms. Carol Toufali, Coordinator, Marist Abroad Program, Marist College, 3399 North Road, Poughkeepsie, NY 12601-1387; *Phone:* 845-575-3330; *Fax:* 845-575-3294. *E-mail:* international@marist.edu. *World Wide Web:* http://www.marist.edu/international/

MARQUETTE UNIVERSITY
MARQUETTE UNIVERSITY STUDY CENTER AT THE UNIVERSIDAD COMPLUTENSE DE MADRID

Hosted by Complutense University of Madrid
Academic Focus • Art history, drama/theater, economics, geography, history, international business, philosophy, political science and government, religious studies, Spanish language and literature, Spanish studies.

SPAIN
Madrid

Program Information • Students attend classes at Complutense University of Madrid. Scheduled travel to Barcelona, Asturias, Valencia; field trips to Córdoba, Extremadura, Galicia, Granada, Segovia, Sevilla, Toledo.

Sessions • Fall, spring, yearlong.

Eligibility Requirements • Open to sophomores, juniors, seniors; 2.75 GPA; 3 letters of recommendation; good academic standing at home school; minimum 3.0 GPA in Spanish; 2 college courses beyond intermediate Spanish.

Living Arrangements • Students live in host family homes. Quarters are shared with students from other programs. Meals are taken with host family, in residences.

Costs (2004-2005) • One term: $8710. Yearlong program: $17,420; includes tuition, excursions, student support services. $25 application fee. $150 nonrefundable deposit required. Financial aid available for all students: loans.

For More Information • Ms. Kristen Michelson, Study Abroad Coordinator, Marquette University, Study Center in Madrid, Marquette Hall 208, PO Box 1881, Milwaukee, WI 53201-1881; *Phone:* 414-288-7059; *Fax:* 414-288-5521. *E-mail:* madrid@marquette.edu. *World Wide Web:* http://www.marquette.edu/studyabroad/

MIDDLEBURY COLLEGE SCHOOLS ABROAD
SCHOOL IN SPAIN–MADRID PROGRAM

Held at Middlebury School in Spain, Sede Prim

Academic Focus • Art history, civilization studies, ecology, economics, film and media studies, history, political science and government, Spanish language and literature, Spanish studies.

Program Information • Classes are held on the campus of Middlebury School in Spain, Sede Prim. Faculty members are local instructors hired by the sponsor. Field trips to Segovia, Toledo, La Granja, Chinchón; optional travel to Cataluña, Valencia, Galicia, Barcelona at an extra cost.

Sessions • Fall, spring, yearlong.

Eligibility Requirements • Open to sophomores, juniors, seniors, graduate students; 2.7 GPA; 2 letters of recommendation; B average in both Spanish and major; 2.5 years college course work in Spanish, including at least 1 content course at the 300-level.

Living Arrangements • Students live in locally rented apartments, host family homes. Meals are taken on one's own, with host family, in residences, in restaurants.

Costs (2004-2005) • One term: $7200. Yearlong program: $14,400; includes tuition, excursions, student support services. $50 application fee. $300 nonrefundable deposit required. Financial aid available for students from sponsoring institution: scholarships, loans.

For More Information • Mr. Jamie Northrup, University Relations Coordinator, Middlebury College Schools Abroad, Office of Off-Campus Study, Sunderland Language Center, Middlebury, VT 05753; *Phone:* 802-443-5745; *Fax:* 802-443-3157. *E-mail:* schoolsabroad@middlebury.edu. *World Wide Web:* http://www.middlebury.edu/msa/

NEW YORK UNIVERSITY
NYU IN MADRID

Hosted by NYU Center, Autonomous University of Madrid

Academic Focus • Art history, civilization studies, cultural studies, drama/theater, film and media studies, fine/studio arts, Latin American studies, political science and government, social sciences, Spanish language and literature.

Program Information • Students attend classes at Autonomous University of Madrid, NYU Center. Field trips to Toledo, Segovia, Almagro, Salamanca, Avila, Cáceres, Trujillo.

Sessions • Fall, spring, yearlong.

Eligibility Requirements • Open to sophomores, juniors, seniors; 3.0 GPA; 1 letter of recommendation; good academic standing at home school; transcripts; personal statement; foreign language requirement dependent on track chosen.

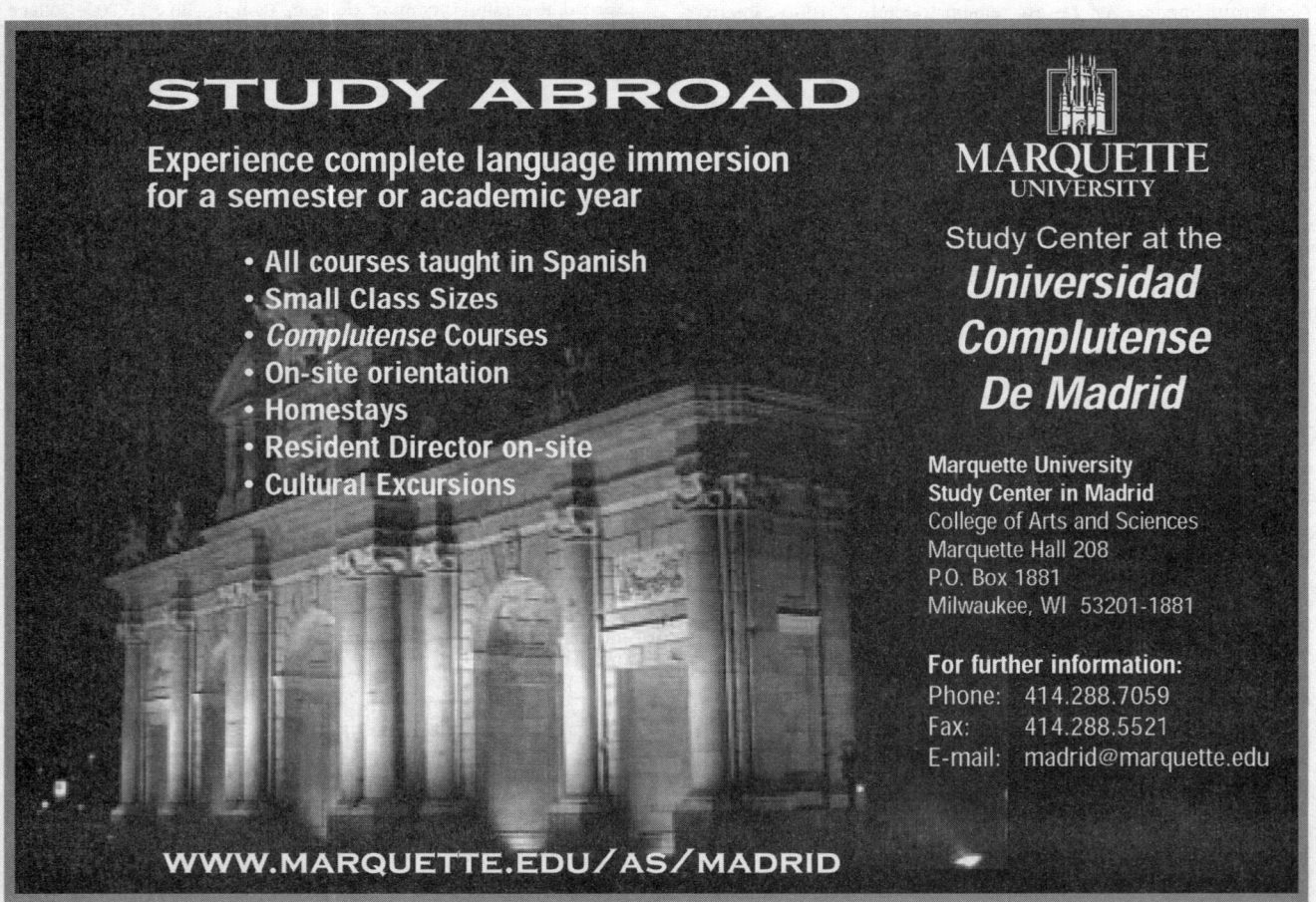

Living Arrangements • Students live in locally rented apartments, host family homes. Quarters are shared with host institution students. Meals are taken on one's own, with host family, in residences, in restaurants.

Costs (2003-2004) • One term: $14,248. Yearlong program: $28,495; includes tuition, excursions, student support services. $25 application fee. $300 nonrefundable deposit required. Financial aid available for all students: scholarships, loans.

For More Information • Office of Study Abroad Admissions, New York University, 7 East 12th Street, 6th Floor, New York, NY 10003; *Phone:* 212-998-4433; *Fax:* 212-995-4103. *E-mail:* studyabroad@nyu.edu. *World Wide Web:* http://www.nyu.edu/studyabroad/

NORTHERN ILLINOIS UNIVERSITY
ACADEMIC INTERNSHIPS IN MADRID, SPAIN

Hosted by Antonio de Nebrija University

Academic Focus • Art history, history, political science and government, social services, urban/regional planning.

Program Information • Students attend classes at Antonio de Nebrija University. Optional travel at an extra cost.

Sessions • Fall, spring.

Eligibility Requirements • Open to juniors, seniors; 3.0 GPA; 2 letters of recommendation; good academic standing at home school; application essay in Spanish; résumé; 3 years of college course work in Spanish.

Living Arrangements • Students live in host family homes. Quarters are shared with students from other programs. Meals are taken on one's own, with host family, in residences.

Costs (2003-2004) • One term: $8425; includes tuition, housing, some meals, insurance, internship placement. $45 application fee. $800 refundable deposit required. Financial aid available for students from sponsoring institution: regular financial aid.

For More Information • Ms. Clare Foust, Program Assistant, Northern Illinois University, Study Abroad Office, Williston Hall 417, DeKalb, IL 60115-2854; *Phone:* 815-753-0420; *Fax:* 815-753-0825. *E-mail:* niuabroad@niu.edu. *World Wide Web:* http://www.niu.edu/niuabroad/

RIDER UNIVERSITY
STUDY ABROAD IN SPAIN

Hosted by Antonio de Nebrija University, Complutense University of Madrid

Academic Focus • International affairs, international business, Spanish language and literature, Spanish studies.

Program Information • Students attend classes at Antonio de Nebrija University, Complutense University of Madrid.

Sessions • Fall, spring, yearlong.

Eligibility Requirements • Open to sophomores, juniors, seniors; 2.5 GPA; 1 letter of recommendation; good academic standing at home school; 1-2 years college course work in Spanish, depending on course of study.

Living Arrangements • Students live in host family homes. Quarters are shared with students from other programs. Meals are taken on one's own, with host family, in central dining facility, in restaurants.

Costs (2001-2002) • One term: $8995. Yearlong program: $17,990; includes tuition, student support services, administrative fees. $35 application fee. $300 refundable deposit required. Financial aid available for students from sponsoring institution: regular financial aid.

For More Information • Dr. Joseph E. Nadeau, Director of Study Abroad, Rider University, 2083 Lawrenceville Road, Lawrenceville, NJ 08648; *Phone:* 609-896-5314; *Fax:* 609-895-5670. *E-mail:* nadeau@rider.edu. *World Wide Web:* http://www.rider.edu/academic/uwp/index.htm

ST. LAWRENCE UNIVERSITY
SPAIN PROGRAM

Held at Complutense University of Madrid

Academic Focus • Art history, drama/theater, economics, environmental science/studies, history, political science and government, sociology, Spanish language and literature, women's studies.

Program Information • Classes are held on the campus of Complutense University of Madrid. Faculty members are drawn from the sponsor's U.S. staff and local instructors hired by the sponsor. Scheduled travel to Córdoba, Seville, Granada, Barcelona, Picos de Europa, Salamanca; field trips to El Escorial, Segovia, Toledo.

Sessions • Fall, spring, yearlong.

Eligibility Requirements • Open to sophomores, juniors, seniors; 2.8 GPA; 3 letters of recommendation; statement on how this study fits into student's overall academic training; 3 years of college course work in Spanish.

Living Arrangements • Students live in host institution dormitories, host family homes. Meals are taken with host family, in residences.

Costs (2003-2004) • One term: $17,870. Yearlong program: $35,740; includes tuition, housing, all meals, insurance, excursions, lab equipment, ticket reimbursement to cultural activities. $500 nonrefundable deposit required. Financial aid available for students from sponsoring institution: scholarships, loans.

For More Information • Ms. Sara Hofschulte, Assistant Director, Off-Campus Programs, St. Lawrence University, Center for International and Intercultural Studies, Canton, NY 13617; *Phone:* 315-229-5991; *Fax:* 315-229-5989. *E-mail:* shofschulte@stlawu.edu. *World Wide Web:* http://www.stlawu.edu/ciis/offcampus/

SAINT LOUIS UNIVERSITY, MADRID CAMPUS
SAINT LOUIS UNIVERSITY, MADRID CAMPUS

Hosted by Saint Louis University Madrid Campus

Academic Focus • Arabic, biological/life sciences, business administration/management, communications, engineering, English, fine/studio arts, French language and literature, German language and literature, liberal studies, mathematics, physical sciences, Portuguese, social sciences, Spanish language and literature.

Program Information • Students attend classes at Saint Louis University Madrid Campus. Scheduled travel to Spain, Europe, North Africa; field trips to Segovia, Salamanca, El Escorial, Cuenca, Galicia, Balearic Islands, Toledo, Canary Islands, Pyrenees; optional travel to sites in Spain and other areas of Europe, north Africa at an extra cost.

Sessions • Fall, spring, yearlong.

Eligibility Requirements • Minimum age 17; open to precollege students, freshmen, sophomores, juniors, seniors, graduate students, adults; 3.0 GPA; transcripts; 1 year of college course work in Spanish.

Living Arrangements • Students live in host institution dormitories, locally rented apartments, program-owned apartments, host family homes. Quarters are shared with host institution students. Meals are taken as a group, on one's own, with host family, in residences.

Costs (2003-2004) • One term: $7405. Yearlong program: $14,810; includes tuition, student support services, computer services. $45 application fee. $100 nonrefundable deposit required. Financial aid available for all students: scholarships, work study, loans.

For More Information • Ms. Phyllis Chaney, Director of Admission, Saint Louis University, Madrid Campus, Avda Del Valle, 34, 28003 Madrid, Spain; *Phone:* +34 91-554-5858; *Fax:* +34 91-554-6202. *E-mail:* chaneyp@spmail.slu.edu. *World Wide Web:* http://spain.slu.edu/

SCHILLER INTERNATIONAL UNIVERSITY
STUDY ABROAD, UNDERGRADUATE AND GRADUATE PROGRAMS

Hosted by Schiller International University

Academic Focus • Computer science, economics, English, European studies, history, interdisciplinary studies, international affairs, international business, marketing, political science and government, Spanish language and literature.

Program Information • Students attend classes at Schiller International University. Field trips to Segovia, Toledo, Avila; optional travel to France, Germany, Italy, England, the Netherlands at an extra cost.

Sessions • Fall, spring, yearlong.

Eligibility Requirements • Minimum age 17; open to freshmen, sophomores, juniors, seniors, graduate students; 2.0 GPA; no foreign language proficiency required.

Living Arrangements • Students live in locally rented apartments, host family homes. Quarters are shared with host institution students, students from other programs. Meals are taken on one's own, in residences, in restaurants.

SPAIN
Madrid

Costs (2003-2004) • One term: €6200. Yearlong program: €12,250; includes tuition, lab equipment, student support services, activity fee, liability deposit. €500 nonrefundable deposit required. Financial aid available for all students: scholarships, loans, federal grants, Exchange Student Scholarship Award, graduate assistantship.
For More Information • Ms. Kamala Dontamsetti, Admissions Office, Florida Campus, Schiller International University, 453 Edgewater Drive, Dunedin, FL 34698; *Phone:* 727-736-5082 Ext. 240; *Fax:* 727-734-0359. *E-mail:* admissions@schiller.edu. *World Wide Web:* http://www.schiller.edu/

SKIDMORE COLLEGE
SKIDMORE IN MADRID

Hosted by Skidmore Program Center, Autonomous University of Madrid
Academic Focus • Anthropology, art, art history, business administration/management, dance, economics, education, English literature, fine/studio arts, geography, history, Islamic studies, language studies, law and legal studies, literature, music, philosophy, political science and government, psychology, Spanish studies, women's studies.
Program Information • Students attend classes at Autonomous University of Madrid, Skidmore Program Center. Scheduled travel to Segovia, Andalucía; field trips to Mérida, Extremadura, Toledo, La Rioja.
Sessions • Spring, yearlong.
Eligibility Requirements • Open to juniors; 3.0 GPA; 2 letters of recommendation; good academic standing at home school; 2.5 years college course work in Spanish or the equivalent.
Living Arrangements • Students live in host family homes. Meals are taken with host family, in residences.
Costs (2003-2004) • One term: contact sponsor for cost. Yearlong program: contact sponsor for cost. $25 application fee. $350 nonrefundable deposit required. Financial aid available for students from sponsoring institution: scholarships, loans.
For More Information • Office of International Programs, Skidmore College, 815 North Broadway, Starbuck Center, Saratoga Springs, NY 12866; *Phone:* 518-580-5355; *Fax:* 518-580-5359. *E-mail:* oip@skidmore.edu. *World Wide Web:* http://www.skidmore.edu/internationalprograms/

SOUTHERN METHODIST UNIVERSITY
SMU IN SPAIN

Hosted by José Ortega y Gasset Foundation
Academic Focus • Art history, history, international business, political science and government, religious studies, Spanish language and literature.
Program Information • Students attend classes at José Ortega y Gasset Foundation. Scheduled travel to Toledo, Andalucía, Barcelona; field trips to Avila.
Sessions • Fall, spring, yearlong.
Eligibility Requirements • Open to sophomores, juniors, seniors; 2.7 GPA; 2 letters of recommendation; good academic standing at home school; essay; personal interview; 1.5 years of college course work in Spanish.
Living Arrangements • Students live in host family homes. Quarters are shared with host institution students. Meals are taken with host family, in residences.
Costs (2002-2003) • One term: $15,744. Yearlong program: $29,488; includes tuition, housing, some meals, excursions, student support services, lodging on excursions. $40 application fee. $500 nonrefundable deposit required. Financial aid available for students from sponsoring institution: scholarships, loans.
For More Information • Ms. Karen Westergaard, Associate Director, Southern Methodist University, International Office, PO Box 750391, Dallas, TX 75275-0391; *Phone:* 214-768-2338; *Fax:* 214-768-1051. *E-mail:* intlpro@mail.smu.edu. *World Wide Web:* http://www.smu.edu/studyabroad/

SPRINGFIELD COLLEGE
SPRING SEMESTER IN SPAIN, ALCALÁ

Hosted by University of Alcalá de Henares
Academic Focus • Spanish language and literature, Spanish studies.

Program Information • Students attend classes at University of Alcalá de Henares. Scheduled travel to Cisneros; field trips to the Prado, Toledo, Avila, Segovia, Granada; optional travel to Barcelona at an extra cost.
Sessions • Spring.
Eligibility Requirements • Minimum age 18; open to freshmen, sophomores, juniors, seniors; 2.5 GPA; good academic standing at home school; 2 letters of recommendation (1 general, 1 language); 3.0 GPA in Spanish; 1 term college course work in Spanish or 2 years of high school Spanish.
Living Arrangements • Students live in host institution dormitories, host family homes. Quarters are shared with students from other programs. Meals are taken on one's own, with host family, in residences, in central dining facility, in restaurants.
Costs (2004) • One term: $13,500; includes tuition, housing, some meals, insurance, excursions, books and class materials, lab equipment, international student ID, student support services, voucher for airfare. $500 nonrefundable deposit required. Financial aid available for students from sponsoring institution: loans.
For More Information • Dr. Joyce L. Szewczynski, Program Director, Spain, Springfield College, 263 Alden Street, Springfield, MA 01109; *Phone:* 413-748-3665; *Fax:* 413-748-3347. *E-mail:* jszewczy@spfldcol.edu. Students may also apply through Antiguo Colegio de los Irlandeses, c/o Escritorios, 4, E28801 Alcala de Henares, Madr, Spain.

SYRACUSE UNIVERSITY
BUSINESS ADMINISTRATION SEMESTER ABROAD IN SPAIN

Hosted by Syracuse University Center–Madrid
Academic Focus • Business administration/management, economics, finance, liberal studies, marketing, Spanish language and literature.
Program Information • Students attend classes at Syracuse University Center–Madrid. Scheduled travel to Frankfurt, Paris, Geneva, Amsterdam (Eurovision); field trips to Barcelona, El Escorial, Avila, Segovia, Valle de los Caídos.
Sessions • Fall, spring, yearlong.
Eligibility Requirements • Open to sophomores, juniors, seniors; 2 letters of recommendation; good academic standing at home school; home school approval; no foreign language proficiency required.
Living Arrangements • Students live in host family homes. Meals are taken with host family, in residences.
Costs (2004-2005) • One term: $19,430. Yearlong program: $38,860; includes tuition, housing, some meals, excursions, lab equipment, international student ID, student support services, traveling seminar and one-way airfare. $50 application fee. $450 nonrefundable deposit required. Financial aid available for all students: scholarships, work study, loans, tuition differential grants.
For More Information • Mr. James Buschman, Senior Associate Director, Syracuse University, 106 Walnut Place, Syracuse, NY 13244-4170; *Phone:* 315-443-3471; *Fax:* 315-443-4593. *E-mail:* suabroad@syr.edu. *World Wide Web:* http://suabroad.syr.edu/

SYRACUSE UNIVERSITY
MADRID PROGRAM

Hosted by Polytechnic University of Madrid, Syracuse University Center–Madrid, Autonomous University of Madrid
Academic Focus • Anthropology, biological/life sciences, business administration/management, communications, economics, engineering, English, finance, fine/studio arts, geography, history, information science, liberal studies, political science and government, Spanish language and literature, women's studies.
Program Information • Students attend classes at Polytechnic University of Madrid, Syracuse University Center–Madrid, Autonomous University of Madrid. Scheduled travel to Toledo, Seville, Córdoba, Granada, Barcelona, La Costa Brava, Palma de Mallorca, Valencia, Frankfurt, Amsterdam, Paris; field trips to Barcelona, El Escorial, Avila, Segovia, Valle de los Caídos.
Sessions • Fall, spring, yearlong.
Eligibility Requirements • Open to sophomores, juniors, seniors; 2 letters of recommendation; good academic standing at home school; home school approval; no foreign language proficiency required.
Living Arrangements • Students live in host family homes. Meals are taken with host family, in residences.

Costs (2004-2005) • One term: $19,430. Yearlong program: $38,860; includes tuition, housing, some meals, excursions, lab equipment, international student ID, one-way airfare, traveling seminar. $50 application fee. $450 nonrefundable deposit required. Financial aid available for all students: scholarships, work study, loans, tuition differential grants.

For More Information • Mr. James Buschman, Senior Associate Director, Syracuse University, 106 Walnut Place, Syracuse, NY 13244-4170; *Phone:* 315-443-3471; *Fax:* 315-443-4593. *E-mail:* suabroad@syr.edu. *World Wide Web:* http://suabroad.syr.edu/

TUFTS UNIVERSITY
TUFTS IN MADRID

Hosted by University of Alcalá de Henares, Autonomous University of Madrid

Academic Focus • Full curriculum.

Program Information • Students attend classes at University of Alcalá de Henares, Autonomous University of Madrid. Scheduled travel to Castile, Extremadura, Andalucía; field trips.

Sessions • Fall, spring, yearlong.

Eligibility Requirements • Open to juniors, seniors; 3.0 GPA; 2 letters of recommendation; good academic standing at home school; 3 years of college course work in Spanish.

Living Arrangements • Students live in host family homes. Meals are taken with host family, in residences.

Costs (2004-2005) • One term: $19,657. Yearlong program: $39,314; includes tuition, housing, all meals, excursions, student support services, monthly transportation pass, all cultural activities. $40 application fee. $350 nonrefundable deposit required. Financial aid available for students from sponsoring institution: scholarships, work study, loans.

For More Information • Ms. Melanie Armstrong, Program and Marketing Coordinator, Tufts Programs Abroad, Tufts University, Dowling Hall, Medford, MA 02155-7084; *Phone:* 617-627-2000; *Fax:* 617-627-3971. *E-mail:* melanie.armstrong@tufts.edu. *World Wide Web:* http://ase.tufts.edu/studyabroad/

UNIVERSITY AT ALBANY, STATE UNIVERSITY OF NEW YORK
LANGUAGE AND CULTURAL STUDIES AT THE INTERNATIONAL INSTITUTE

Held at International Institute

Academic Focus • Art history, community service, film and media studies, history, Latin American studies, linguistics, Spanish language and literature, Spanish studies.

Program Information • Classes are held on the campus of International Institute. Faculty members are local instructors hired by the sponsor. Scheduled travel to Andalucía, Seville; field trips to Segovia, Toledo.

Sessions • Fall, spring, yearlong.

Eligibility Requirements • Open to sophomores, juniors, seniors, adults; 2 letters of recommendation; good academic standing at home school; survey of Spanish literature recommended; 2.5 years college course work in Spanish or the equivalent.

Living Arrangements • Students live in locally rented apartments, host family homes. Quarters are shared with host institution students, students from other programs. Meals are taken with host family, in residences.

Costs (2002-2003) • One term: $10,278 for fall term; $10,443 for spring. Yearlong program: $20,721; includes housing, all meals, excursions, student support services, in-state tuition and fees, study abroad differential. $150 nonrefundable deposit required. Financial aid available for students from sponsoring institution: all customary sources.

For More Information • University at Albany, State University of New York, Office of International Education, LI 66, Albany, NY 12222; *Phone:* 518-442-3525; *Fax:* 518-442-3338. *E-mail:* intled@uamail.albany.edu. *World Wide Web:* http://www.albany.edu/intled/

SPAIN
Madrid

UNIVERSITY OF MARYLAND, COLLEGE PARK
MARYLAND IN SPAIN

Hosted by University of Alcalá de Henares
Academic Focus • International business, Spanish language and literature, Spanish studies.
Program Information • Students attend classes at University of Alcalá de Henares. Field trips to Segovia, El Escorial, Toledo.
Sessions • Spring.
Eligibility Requirements • Open to sophomores, juniors, seniors; 1 letter of recommendation; minimum 2.75 GPA overall, minimum 3.0 GPA in Spanish courses; 2 years of college course work in Spanish.
Living Arrangements • Students live in host institution dormitories, locally rented apartments, host family homes. Quarters are shared with host institution students, students from other programs. Meals are taken on one's own, with host family, in residences, in central dining facility.
Costs (2004) • One term: $3919; includes tuition, excursions, student support services, athletic facilities, cinema trips, advising. $50 application fee. $500 nonrefundable deposit required. Financial aid available for students from sponsoring institution: scholarships.
For More Information • Ms. Samantha Brandauer, Study Abroad Advisor, University of Maryland, College Park, 3125 Mitchell Building, College Park, MD 20742-5215; *Phone:* 301-314-7746; *Fax:* 301-314-9347. *E-mail:* studyabr@deans.umd.edu. *World Wide Web:* http://www.umd.edu/studyabroad/

UNIVERSITY OF ROCHESTER
INTERNSHIPS IN EUROPE–SPAIN

Hosted by Antonio de Nebrija University
Academic Focus • Art administration, art history, business administration/management, communications, film and media studies, political science and government, social sciences, Spanish language and literature, tourism and travel.
Program Information • Students attend classes at Antonio de Nebrija University.
Sessions • Fall, spring.
Eligibility Requirements • Open to juniors, seniors; 3.0 GPA; 2 letters of recommendation; good academic standing at home school; 2 years of college course work in Spanish.
Living Arrangements • Students live in locally rented apartments, host family homes. Meals are taken on one's own, with host family, in residences, in restaurants.
Costs (2003) • One term: $9900; includes tuition, housing, some meals, student support services. $30 application fee. $300 nonrefundable deposit required. Financial aid available for students from sponsoring institution: scholarships, loans.
For More Information • Ms. Jacqueline Levine, Study Abroad Director, University of Rochester, Center for Study Abroad, PO Box 270376, Lattimore 206, Rochester, NY 14627-0376; *Phone:* 585-275-7532; *Fax:* 585-461-5131. *E-mail:* abroad@mail.rochester.edu. *World Wide Web:* http://www.rochester.edu/college/study-abroad/

UNIVERSITY STUDIES ABROAD CONSORTIUM
SPANISH STUDIES: MADRID, SPAIN

Hosted by University Rey Juan Carlos
Academic Focus • Art history, culinary arts, dance, economics, ethnic studies, history, political science and government, Spanish language and literature, Spanish studies, teaching.
Program Information • Students attend classes at University Rey Juan Carlos. Field trips to El Escorial, Segovia, Cuenca, Avila, Salamanca, La Mancha.
Sessions • Fall, spring, yearlong.
Eligibility Requirements • Minimum age 18; open to freshmen, sophomores, juniors, seniors, graduate students, adults; 2.5 GPA; no foreign language proficiency required.
Living Arrangements • Students live in locally rented apartments, host family homes. Quarters are shared with host institution students. Meals are taken on one's own, with host family, in residences, in central dining facility, in restaurants.
Costs (2005-2006) • One term: $7670. Yearlong program: $12,680; includes tuition, some meals, insurance, excursions, student support services. $50 application fee. $150 refundable deposit required. Financial aid available for all students: scholarships, loans.

For More Information • University Studies Abroad Consortium, USAC/323, Reno, NV 89557-0093; *Phone:* 775-784-6569; *Fax:* 775-784-6010. *E-mail:* usac@unr.edu. *World Wide Web:* http://usac.unr.edu/

VANDERBILT UNIVERSITY
VANDERBILT IN SPAIN

Hosted by Complutense University of Madrid
Academic Focus • Art history, civilization studies, social sciences, Spanish language and literature, Spanish studies.
Program Information • Students attend classes at Complutense University of Madrid. Field trips to Alicante, Córdoba, Andalucía, Seville.
Sessions • Fall, spring, yearlong.
Eligibility Requirements • Open to sophomores, juniors, seniors; 2.7 GPA; 1 letter of recommendation; good academic standing at home school; personal essay; 2 years of college course work in Spanish.
Living Arrangements • Students live in host family homes. Quarters are shared with host institution students. Meals are taken with host family, in residences.
Costs (2003-2004) • One term: $16,360. Yearlong program: $32,720; includes tuition, housing, all meals, excursions. $200 nonrefundable deposit required. Financial aid available for students from sponsoring institution: scholarships, loans.
For More Information • Mr. Gary Johnston, Director of Study Abroad Programs, Vanderbilt University, Study Abroad Office, Box 1573, Station B, Nashville, TN 37235-1573; *Phone:* 615-343-3139; *Fax:* 615-343-5774. *E-mail:* gary.w.johnston@vanderbilt.edu. *World Wide Web:* http://www.vanderbilt.edu/studyabroad/

VASSAR COLLEGE AND WESLEYAN UNIVERSITY
VASSAR–WESLEYAN PROGRAM IN MADRID

Hosted by University Carlos III, Madrid, University Carlos III, Madrid
Academic Focus • Art history, film and media studies, history, Latin American literature, political science and government, sociology, Spanish language and literature.
Program Information • Students attend classes at University Carlos III, Madrid, University Carlos III, Madrid. Scheduled travel; field trips to Salamanca, Seville, Andalucía, Barcelona.
Sessions • Fall, spring, yearlong.
Eligibility Requirements • Open to sophomores, juniors, seniors; 3.0 GPA; 1 letter of recommendation; 2 years college course work in Spanish for fall semester or year-long session; 2.5 years for spring semester.
Living Arrangements • Students live in host family homes. Meals are taken with host family, in residences.
Costs (2002-2003) • One term: $18,000 for fall semester; $16,800 for spring. Yearlong program: $34,800; includes tuition, housing, all meals, excursions, international airfare, student support services. $25 application fee. $200 nonrefundable deposit required. Financial aid available for students from sponsoring institution: scholarships, work study, loans.
For More Information • Ms. Gail Winter, Assistant Director, Vassar College and Wesleyan University, Office of International Studies, Wesleyan University, Middletown, CT 06459-0400; *Phone:* 860-685-2550; *Fax:* 860-685-2551. *E-mail:* gwinter@wesleyan.edu. *World Wide Web:* http://www.wesleyan.edu/ois/

MÁLAGA
DICKINSON COLLEGE
DICKINSON IN MÁLAGA (SPAIN)

Hosted by Dickinson Center, University of Málaga
Academic Focus • Spanish language and literature, Spanish studies.
Program Information • Students attend classes at Dickinson Center, University of Málaga. Scheduled travel to Jerez/Coto Donana, Valencia, Lisbon; field trips to Madrid, Córdoba, Seville, Granada; optional travel to Morocco, Barcelona at an extra cost.
Sessions • Fall, yearlong.

Eligibility Requirements • Minimum age 18; open to juniors; 2.8 GPA; 3 letters of recommendation; good academic standing at home school; fluency in Spanish.

Living Arrangements • Students live in host family homes. Meals are taken with host family, in residences.

Costs (2003-2004) • One term: $17,795. Yearlong program: $35,590; includes tuition, housing, all meals, excursions. $25 application fee. $300 nonrefundable deposit required. Financial aid available for students from sponsoring institution: scholarships, work study, loans.

For More Information • Ms. Karen Peter, Program Manager, Dickinson College, PO Box 1773, Carlisle, PA 17013-2896; *Phone:* 717-245-1341; *Fax:* 717-245-1688. *E-mail:* global@dickinson.edu. *World Wide Web:* http://www.dickinson.edu/global/

MURCIA

UNIVERSITY OF MIAMI
UNIVERSIDAD DE MURCIA

Hosted by University of Murcia

Academic Focus • Art history, biological/life sciences, history, sociology, Spanish language and literature.

Program Information • Students attend classes at University of Murcia.

Sessions • Fall, spring, yearlong.

Eligibility Requirements • Minimum age 18; open to sophomores, juniors, seniors; 3.0 GPA; 2 letters of recommendation; language evaluation; personal interview; fluency in Spanish.

Living Arrangements • Students live in host institution dormitories, locally rented apartments, host family homes. Quarters are shared with host institution students, students from other programs. Meals are taken as a group, on one's own, with host family, in residences, in central dining facility, in restaurants.

Costs (2003-2004) • One term: $12,919. Yearlong program: $25,838; includes tuition, student support services. $40 application fee. $500 nonrefundable deposit required. Financial aid available for students from sponsoring institution: scholarships, loans.

For More Information • Mr. Chris Tingue, Assistant Director, University of Miami, International Education and Exchange Programs, 5050 Brunson Drive, Allen Hall 212, PO Box 248005, Coral Gables, FL 33124-1610; *Phone:* 305-284-3434; *Fax:* 305-284-4235. *E-mail:* ieep@miami.edu. *World Wide Web:* http://www.studyabroad.miami.edu/

OVIEDO

AHA INTERNATIONAL AN ACADEMIC PROGRAM OF THE UNIVERSITY OF OREGON
OVIEDO, SPAIN: NORTHWEST COUNCIL ON STUDY ABROAD (NCSA)

Hosted by University of Oviedo

Academic Focus • Art history, European studies, history, Latin American literature, Romance languages, Spanish language and literature, Spanish studies.

Program Information • Students attend classes at University of Oviedo. Scheduled travel to Barcelona, Toledo, Santiago de Compostela, La Coruña; field trips to Oviedo museums, local pre-Romanesque and Celtic architectural sites, Covadonga, Gijón.

Sessions • Fall, spring, yearlong.

Eligibility Requirements • Open to sophomores, juniors, seniors; 2 letters of recommendation; good academic standing at home school; 1 year of college course work in Spanish.

Living Arrangements • Students live in host family homes. Meals are taken with host family.

Costs (2003-2004) • One term: $5600 for fall quarter; $8000 for spring semester. Yearlong program: $13,263; includes tuition, housing, all meals, insurance, excursions, books and class materials, international student ID, student support services. $50 application fee. $200 refundable deposit required. Financial aid available for students: scholarships, loans.

For More Information • Ms. Carlotta Troy, Associate Director for University Programs, AHA International An Academic Program of the University of Oregon, 741 SW Lincoln Street, Portland, OR 97201;

Phone: 503-295-7730; *Fax:* 503-295-5969. *E-mail:* mail@aha-intl.org. *World Wide Web:* http://www.aha-intl.org/

STATE UNIVERSITY OF NEW YORK AT NEW PALTZ
STUDY ABROAD IN OVIEDO, SPAIN

Hosted by University of Oviedo

Academic Focus • Cultural studies, Spanish language and literature, Spanish studies.

Program Information • Students attend classes at University of Oviedo.

Sessions • Fall, spring, yearlong.

Eligibility Requirements • Minimum age 18; open to sophomores, juniors, seniors; 2.5 GPA; 2 letters of recommendation; good academic standing at home school; 2 years of college course work in Spanish.

Living Arrangements • Students live in locally rented apartments. Quarters are shared with host institution students, students from other programs. Meals are taken on one's own, in residences, in restaurants.

Costs (2003-2004) • One term: $2798 for New York residents; $5928 for nonresidents. Yearlong program: $5598 for New York residents; $11,858 for nonresidents; includes tuition, insurance, administrative fee. $25 application fee. $300–$600 nonrefundable deposit required. Financial aid available for students from sponsoring institution: scholarships, loans.

For More Information • Center for International Programs, State University of New York at New Paltz, 75 South Manheim Boulevard, Suite 9, New Paltz, NY 12561; *Phone:* 845-257-3125; *Fax:* 845-257-3129. *E-mail:* international@newpaltz.edu. *World Wide Web:* http://www.newpaltz.edu/studyabroad/

PALMA DE MALLORCA

VANDERBILT UNIVERSITY
VANDERBILT IN SPAIN–PALMA DE MALLORCA

Hosted by University of the Balearic Islands

Academic Focus • Full curriculum.

Program Information • Students attend classes at University of the Balearic Islands. Field trips to Barcelona, the Iberian Peninsula.

Sessions • Yearlong.

Eligibility Requirements • Open to sophomores, juniors, seniors; 3.0 GPA; 1 letter of recommendation; good academic standing at home school; minimum B average in Spanish; personal essay; 2 years of college course work in Spanish.

Living Arrangements • Students live in host family homes. Meals are taken with host family, in residences.

Costs (2003-2004) • Yearlong program: $32,000; includes tuition, housing, all meals, excursions, student support services. $200 nonrefundable deposit required. Financial aid available for students from sponsoring institution: scholarships, loans.

For More Information • Mr. Gary Johnston, Director of Study Abroad Programs, Vanderbilt University, Study Abroad Office, Box 1573, Station B, Nashville, TN 37235-1573; *Phone:* 615-343-3139; *Fax:* 615-343-5774. *E-mail:* gary.w.johnston@vanderbilt.edu. *World Wide Web:* http://www.vanderbilt.edu/studyabroad/

RONDA

UNIVERSITY OF KANSAS
SPRING SEMESTER IN SPAIN: RONDA

Hosted by University of Málaga

Academic Focus • Spanish language and literature, Spanish studies.

Program Information • Students attend classes at University of Málaga. Scheduled travel to Madrid, Toledo, Córdoba, Consuegra; optional travel at an extra cost.

Sessions • Spring.

Eligibility Requirements • Minimum age 18; open to freshmen, sophomores, juniors, seniors; 2.5 GPA; 2 letters of recommendation; good academic standing at home school; high school transcripts if student has no college Spanish; short autobiography; statement of purpose; 0.5 years of college course work in Spanish.

Living Arrangements • Students live in host family homes. Meals are taken with host family, in residences.
Costs (2003-2004) • One term: $6825; includes tuition, housing, all meals, student support services, use of some instructional materials. $38 application fee. $300 nonrefundable deposit required. Financial aid available for students from sponsoring institution: scholarships, loans.
For More Information • Ms. Angela Dittrich, Assistant Director, University of Kansas, Office of Study Abroad, Lippincott Hall, 1410 Jayhawk Boulevard, Room 108, Lawrence, KS 66045-7515; *Phone:* 785-864-3742; *Fax:* 785-864-5040. *E-mail:* osa@ku.edu. *World Wide Web:* http://www.ku.edu/~osa/

SAGUNTO

WALLA WALLA COLLEGE
ADVENTIST COLLEGES ABROAD

Hosted by Colegio Adventist de Sagunto
Academic Focus • Full curriculum, Spanish language and literature.
Program Information • Students attend classes at Colegio Adventist de Sagunto. Scheduled travel to Zaragoza, Castilla, Andorra, Andalucía; optional travel at an extra cost.
Sessions • Yearlong.
Eligibility Requirements • Minimum age 18; open to freshmen, sophomores, juniors, seniors; 2.5 GPA; 3 letters of recommendation; good academic standing at home school; minimum 3.0 GPA in Spanish; 1 year of college course work in Spanish.
Living Arrangements • Students live in host institution dormitories. Quarters are shared with host institution students, students from other programs. Meals are taken as a group, in central dining facility.
Costs (2002-2003) • Yearlong program: contact sponsor for cost. $100 nonrefundable deposit required. Financial aid available for all students: scholarships, loans.
For More Information • Mr. Jean-Paul Grimaud, Chair of Modern Language Department, Walla Walla College, 204 South College Avenue, College Place, WA 99324; *Phone:* 509-529-7769; *Fax:* 509-527-2253. *E-mail:* grimje@wwc.edu

SALAMANCA

ACADEMIC PROGRAMS INTERNATIONAL (API)
(API)–SALAMANCA, SPAIN

Hosted by University of Salamanca
Academic Focus • Art, art history, bilingual education, civilization studies, communications, economics, European studies, geography, history, international business, law and legal studies, linguistics, philosophy, psychology, Spanish language and literature, Spanish studies, teaching.
Program Information • Students attend classes at University of Salamanca. Scheduled travel to Madrid; field trips to Toledo, El Escorial, Segovia, Santander, Bilbao, Barcelona, Granada, Seville, Avila; optional travel to Rome, Paris, Lisbon.
Sessions • Fall, spring, yearlong, alternate term and year dates also available.
Eligibility Requirements • Minimum age 18; open to freshmen, sophomores, juniors, seniors, graduate students, adults; 2.75 GPA; 1 letter of recommendation; good academic standing at home school; official transcript from home university; no foreign language proficiency required.
Living Arrangements • Students live in host institution dormitories, locally rented apartments, host family homes. Quarters are shared with host institution students, students from other programs. Meals are taken with host family, in residences.
Costs (2004-2005) • One term: $6250–$10,600. Yearlong program: $12,900–$18,000; includes tuition, housing, all meals, insurance, excursions, student support services, airport pick-up, ground transportation. $150 nonrefundable deposit required. Financial aid available for all students: scholarships.
For More Information • Ms. Jennifer C. Allen, Director, Academic Programs International (API), 107 East Hopkins, San Marcos, TX 78666; *Phone:* 800-844-4124; *Fax:* 512-392-8420. *E-mail:* api@academicintl.com. *World Wide Web:* http://www.academicintl.com/

AMERICAN INSTITUTE FOR FOREIGN STUDY (AIFS)
UNIVERSITY OF SALAMANCA

Hosted by University of Salamanca
Academic Focus • Art history, economics, geography, history, literature, political science and government, sociology, Spanish language and literature.
Program Information • Students attend classes at University of Salamanca. Scheduled travel to Seville, Granada, Costa del Sol, Córdoba; field trips to Segovia, Toledo, Galicia.
Sessions • Fall, spring, yearlong.
Eligibility Requirements • Minimum age 17; open to freshmen, sophomores, juniors, seniors; 2.5 GPA; 1 letter of recommendation; good academic standing at home school; 1 year of college course work in Spanish.
Living Arrangements • Students live in host family homes. Meals are taken with host family, in residences.
Costs (2004-2005) • One term: $10,995. Yearlong program: $19,790; includes tuition, housing, all meals, insurance, excursions, student support services, one-way airfare, 2-day London stopover. $75 application fee. $350 nonrefundable deposit required. Financial aid available for all students: scholarships.
For More Information • Mr. David Mauro, Admissions Advisor, American Institute For Foreign Study (AIFS), 9 West Broad Street, Stamford, CT 06902-3788; *Phone:* 800-727-2437 Ext. 5163; *Fax:* 203-399-5597. *E-mail:* dmauro@aifs.com. *World Wide Web:* http://www.aifsabroad.com/

AUGUSTA STATE UNIVERSITY
SALAMANCA PROGRAM–ACADEMIC YEAR

Hosted by University of Salamanca
Academic Focus • Spanish language and literature.
Program Information • Students attend classes at University of Salamanca. Scheduled travel to Seville, Córdoba, Barcelona, Madrid; field trips to Avila, Toledo, Segovia; optional travel to Portugal, various student-chosen sites at an extra cost.
Sessions • Fall, spring, spring session II.
Eligibility Requirements • Minimum age 18; open to freshmen, sophomores, juniors, seniors; 2.5 GPA; 2 letters of recommendation; good academic standing at home school; minimum 3.0 GPA in Spanish; 1.5 years of college course work in Spanish.
Living Arrangements • Students live in host family homes. Quarters are shared with host institution students. Meals are taken with host family, in residences.
Costs (2005) • One term: $6300–$6600; includes tuition, housing, all meals, insurance, excursions, international airfare, books and class materials, student support services, laundry service while in Salamanca. $200 nonrefundable deposit required. Financial aid available for students from sponsoring institution: scholarships, loans.
For More Information • Dr. Jana Sandarg, Program Director, Augusta State University, Department of Languages, Literature and Communications, Augusta, GA 30904-2200; *Phone:* 706-737-1500; *Fax:* 706-667-4770. *E-mail:* jsandarg@dug.edu. *World Wide Web:* http://www.aug.edu/langlitcom/foreign/spanish/salamanca/

MORE ABOUT THE PROGRAM

Former participants in the program say, "Salamanca is the greatest possible college town. Don't go anywhere else!" This program gives more for the money than other programs, even with the $250 out-of-state fee. Students learn Spanish, culture, and customs by living with a family. Classes are taught by faculty members at the University of Salamanca, not professors from the States or local institutes. There are excursions to Madrid, Toledo, Segovia, Seville, Avila, Granada, and Barcelona.

Program price includes airfare from Atlanta (students can deduct $850 if arranging their own airfare), tuition, books, housing, laundry, all meals, insurance, and excursions. Alternate departure or return dates are available. Predeparture orientation is provided.

CENTER FOR CULTURAL INTERCHANGE
COLLEGE ABROAD–UNIVERSITY OF SALAMANCA

Hosted by University of Salamanca
Academic Focus • Spanish language and literature.
Program Information • Students attend classes at University of Salamanca. Field trips to cultural activities, guided tours, museum visits.
Sessions • Yearlong.
Eligibility Requirements • Minimum age 18; open to juniors, seniors, graduate students, adults; 2.75 GPA; 1 letter of recommendation; good academic standing at home school; 2 years of college course work in Spanish.
Living Arrangements • Students live in host institution dormitories, locally rented apartments, host family homes. Quarters are shared with host institution students, students from other programs. Meals are taken on one's own, with host family, in residences.
Costs (2003) • Yearlong program: $4680; includes tuition, housing, some meals, insurance, excursions, student support services, activities. $500 nonrefundable deposit required. Financial aid available for students from sponsoring institution: scholarships.
For More Information • Ms. Jacqui Metcalf, Outbound Programs Director, Center for Cultural Interchange, 17 North Second Avenue, St. Charles, IL 60174; *Phone:* 888-ABROAD1; *Fax:* 630-377-2307. *E-mail:* info@cci-exchange.com. *World Wide Web:* http://www.cci-exchange.com/

CENTER FOR STUDY ABROAD (CSA)
SPANISH LANGUAGE AND CULTURE, SALAMANCA–UNIVERSITY OF SALAMANCA

Hosted by University of Salamanca
Academic Focus • Spanish language and literature, Spanish studies.
Program Information • Students attend classes at University of Salamanca. Optional travel at an extra cost.
Sessions • Fall, spring, winter, yearlong.
Eligibility Requirements • Minimum age 17; open to precollege students, freshmen, sophomores, juniors, seniors, graduate students, adults; no foreign language proficiency required.
Living Arrangements • Students live in host institution dormitories, host family homes. Quarters are shared with students from other programs. Meals are taken on one's own, with host family, in residences, in central dining facility.
Costs (2003-2004) • One term: contact sponsor for cost. Yearlong program: contact sponsor for cost. $45 application fee.
For More Information • Ms. Alima K. Virtue, Program Director, Center for Study Abroad (CSA), 325 Washington Avenue South, #93, Kent, WA 98032; *Phone:* 206-726-1498; *Fax:* 253-850-0454. *E-mail:* info@centerforstudyabroad.com. *World Wide Web:* http://www.centerforstudyabroad.com/

COLBY COLLEGE
COLBY IN SALAMANCA

Hosted by University of Salamanca
Academic Focus • Art history, economics, history, law and legal studies, psychology, sociology, Spanish language and literature, Spanish studies.
Program Information • Students attend classes at University of Salamanca. Scheduled travel to Asturias, Valencia, Sevilla; field trips to Ciudad Rodrigo, Madrid, Andalucía.
Sessions • Fall, spring, yearlong.
Eligibility Requirements • Open to freshmen, juniors, seniors; course work in Spanish (at least one advanced composition course and a literature course); 3.0 GPA; 2 letters of recommendation; good academic standing at home school; fluency in Spanish.
Living Arrangements • Students live in locally rented apartments, host family homes. Quarters are shared with host institution students. Meals are taken on one's own, with host family, in residences, in restaurants.
Costs (2002-2003) • One term: $17,900. Yearlong program: $35,800; includes tuition, housing, all meals, insurance, excursions, international airfare, student support services. $500 nonrefundable deposit required. Financial aid available for students from sponsoring institution: scholarships, loans.
For More Information • Ms. Martha J. Denney, Director, Off-Campus Study, Colby College, Waterville, ME 04901; *Phone:*

207-872-3648; *Fax:* 207-872-3061. *E-mail:* mjdenney@colby.edu. *World Wide Web:* http://www.colby.edu/off-campus/

CULTURAL EXPERIENCES ABROAD (CEA)
STUDY SPANISH LANGUAGE AND CULTURE IN SALAMANCA

Hosted by University of Salamanca
Academic Focus • Art history, economics, geography, history, international affairs, linguistics, sociology, Spanish studies.
Program Information • Students attend classes at University of Salamanca. Field trips to Avila, Madrid, Segovia, Toledo, Cuenca.
Sessions • Fall, spring, winter, yearlong.
Eligibility Requirements • Minimum age 18; open to freshmen, sophomores, juniors, seniors, graduate students; 2.5 GPA; previous Spanish study recommended.
Living Arrangements • Students live in host family homes. Meals are taken with host family.
Costs (2003-2004) • One term: contact sponsor for cost. Yearlong program: contact sponsor for cost. $50 application fee. $400 nonrefundable deposit required.
For More Information • Cultural Experiences Abroad (CEA), 1400 East Southern Avenue, Suite B-108, Tempe, AZ 85282-8011; *Phone:* 480-557-7900; *Fax:* 480-557-7926. *E-mail:* petersons@gowithcea.com. *World Wide Web:* http://www.gowithcea.com/

EMORY UNIVERSITY
SEMESTER IN SALAMANCA, SPAIN

Hosted by University of Salamanca
Academic Focus • Anthropology, cultural studies, full curriculum, psychology, Spanish language and literature.
Program Information • Students attend classes at University of Salamanca. Scheduled travel; field trips to Granada, Córdoba, Segovia, Avila, Santiago, Barcelona, Toledo, Sevilla.
Sessions • Fall, spring, Hispanic Culture Course.
Eligibility Requirements • Open to sophomores, juniors, seniors; 3.0 GPA; 2 letters of recommendation; good academic standing at home school; 3 years college course work in Spanish for regular university courses; no foreign language proficiency requirement for beginners.
Living Arrangements • Students live in locally rented apartments, host family homes. Meals are taken on one's own, with host family, in residences, in restaurants.
Costs (2003-2004) • One term: $16,700 ; $17,300 for Hispanic Culture Course; includes tuition, housing, some meals, insurance, excursions, student support services. $300 refundable deposit required. Financial aid available for students from sponsoring institution.
For More Information • Ms. Cornelia Lindenau, Study Abroad Advisor, Emory University, 1385 Oxford Road, Atlanta, GA 30322; *Phone:* 404-727-2240; *Fax:* 404-727-6724. *E-mail:* culinde@emory.edu

IES, INSTITUTE FOR THE INTERNATIONAL EDUCATION OF STUDENTS
IES–SALAMANCA

Hosted by Institute for the International Education of Students (IES)–Salamanca, University of Salamanca
Academic Focus • Full curriculum.
Program Information • Students attend classes at University of Salamanca, Institute for the International Education of Students (IES)–Salamanca. Scheduled travel to Portugal; field trips to Toledo, Madrid, Segovia, El Escorial; optional travel to Barcelona at an extra cost.
Sessions • Fall, spring, yearlong.
Eligibility Requirements • Minimum age 18; open to sophomores, juniors, seniors, graduate students, adults; 3.0 GPA; 1 letter of recommendation; good academic standing at home school; 2 years of college course work in Spanish.
Living Arrangements • Students live in host institution dormitories, host family homes. Meals are taken on one's own, with host family, in residences, in central dining facility.
Costs (2003-2004) • One term: $10,600. Yearlong program: $19,080; includes tuition, housing, some meals, excursions, student support services, partial insurance coverage. $50 application fee.

SPAIN
Salamanca

$500 nonrefundable deposit required. Financial aid available for all students: scholarships, institutional partner need-based grants.

For More Information • International Education Representative, IES, Institute for the International Education of Students, 33 North LaSalle Street, 15th Floor, Chicago, IL 60602; *Phone:* 800-995-2300; *Fax:* 312-944-1448. *E-mail:* info@iesabroad.org. *World Wide Web:* http://www.IESabroad.org/

INTERNATIONAL STUDIES ABROAD
SALAMANCA, SPAIN–HISPANIC STUDIES

Hosted by University of Salamanca

Academic Focus • Art history, cinematography, economics, geography, history, political science and government, Spanish language and literature, Spanish studies.

Program Information • Students attend classes at University of Salamanca. Scheduled travel to Madrid, Toledo; field trips to Segovia, El Escorial, Avila, Granada, Sevilla; optional travel at an extra cost.

Sessions • Fall, spring, yearlong.

Eligibility Requirements • Minimum age 18; open to precollege students, freshmen, sophomores, juniors, seniors, graduate students, adults; 2.5 GPA; 1 letter of recommendation; good academic standing at home school; transcript; 2 years of college course work in Spanish.

Living Arrangements • Students live in locally rented apartments, host family homes, hotels. Quarters are shared with host institution students, students from other programs. Meals are taken with host family, in residences.

Costs (2004-2005) • One term: $5900–$8100. Yearlong program: $12,500; includes tuition, housing, all meals, insurance, excursions, student support services, tutoring, ground transportation, laundry service, Internet access. $200 deposit required. Financial aid available for all students: scholarships, loans, U.S. federal financial aid.

For More Information • Spain Site Specialist, International Studies Abroad, 901 West 24th Street, Austin, TX 78705; *Phone:* 800-580-8826; *Fax:* 512-480-8866. *E-mail:* isa@studiesabroad.com. *World Wide Web:* http://www.studiesabroad.com/

INTERNATIONAL STUDIES ABROAD
SALAMANCA, SPAIN: LANGUAGE AND CULTURE TRIMESTER/YEAR

Hosted by University of Salamanca

Academic Focus • Art, cultural studies, geography, history, literature, Spanish language and literature.

Program Information • Students attend classes at University of Salamanca. Scheduled travel to Madrid, Toledo; field trips to Segovia, El Escorial, Avila, La Granja, Granada, Sevilla; optional travel at an extra cost.

Sessions • Fall, spring, winter.

Eligibility Requirements • Minimum age 18; open to precollege students, freshmen, sophomores, juniors, seniors, adults; 2.5 GPA; 1 letter of recommendation; good academic standing at home school; transcript; no foreign language proficiency required.

Living Arrangements • Students live in locally rented apartments, host family homes. Quarters are shared with students from other programs. Meals are taken with host family, in residences.

Costs (2004-2005) • One term: $5900 for one trimester; $10,500 for back to back trimesters; includes tuition, housing, all meals, insurance, excursions, student support services, tutorial assistance, ground transportation, laundry service, Internet access. $200 deposit required. Financial aid available for all students: scholarships, loans, U.S. federal financial aid.

For More Information • Spain Site Specialist, International Studies Abroad, 901 West 24th Street, Austin, TX 78705; *Phone:* 800-580-8826; *Fax:* 512-480-8866. *E-mail:* isa@studiesabroad.com. *World Wide Web:* http://www.studiesabroad.com/

INTERNATIONAL STUDIES ABROAD
SALAMANCA, SPAIN, STUDY WITH SPANIARDS

Hosted by University of Salamanca

Academic Focus • Accounting, art history, commerce, economics, finance, geography, history, international business, law and legal studies, Spanish language and literature.

Program Information • Students attend classes at University of Salamanca. Scheduled travel to Madrid, Toledo; field trips to Segovia, El Escorial, Avila, Sevilla, Granada; optional travel at an extra cost.

Sessions • Fall, spring, yearlong, fall term II.

Eligibility Requirements • Minimum age 18; open to precollege students, freshmen, sophomores, juniors, seniors, graduate students, adults; 2.75 GPA; 1 letter of recommendation; good academic standing at home school; transcript; 3 years of college course work in Spanish.

Living Arrangements • Students live in locally rented apartments, host family homes, hotels. Quarters are shared with host institution students, students from other programs. Meals are taken with host family, in residences.

Costs (2003-2004) • One term: $7975–$8675. Yearlong program: $12,500; includes tuition, housing, all meals, insurance, excursions, tutorial assistance, ground transportation, Internet access. $200 deposit required. Financial aid available for all students: scholarships, loans, U.S. federal financial aid via consortium agreement.

For More Information • Spain Site Specialist, International Studies Abroad, 901 West 24th Street, Austin, TX 78705; *Phone:* 800-580-8826; *Fax:* 512-480-8866. *E-mail:* isa@studiesabroad.com. *World Wide Web:* http://www.studiesabroad.com/

JAMES MADISON UNIVERSITY
SEMESTER IN SALAMANCA

Hosted by University of Salamanca

Academic Focus • Art, art history, economics, international business, literature, political science and government, Spanish language and literature, Spanish studies.

Program Information • Students attend classes at University of Salamanca. Scheduled travel to Toledo, Segovia, Seville; field trips to Barcelona, Granada, Madrid, Santillana del Mar.

Sessions • Fall, spring.

Eligibility Requirements • Minimum age 18; open to sophomores, juniors, seniors; 2.8 GPA; 1 letter of recommendation; good academic standing at home school; 2 years of college course work in Spanish.

Living Arrangements • Students live in host family homes. Quarters are shared with host institution students. Meals are taken with host family, in residences.

Costs (2003-2004) • One term: $8367 for Virginia residents; $12,478 for nonresidents; includes tuition, housing, some meals, excursions, books and class materials. $400 nonrefundable deposit required. Financial aid available for students from sponsoring institution: scholarships, work study, loans.

For More Information • Mr. Felix Wang, Director, James Madison University, Office of International Programs, MSC 5731, 1077 South Main Street, Harrisonburg, VA 22807; *Phone:* 540-568-6419; *Fax:* 540-568-3310. *E-mail:* studyabroad@jmu.edu. *World Wide Web:* http://www.jmu.edu/international/

STATE UNIVERSITY OF NEW YORK COLLEGE AT CORTLAND
SALAMANCA

Hosted by University of Salamanca

Academic Focus • Spanish language and literature.

Program Information • Students attend classes at University of Salamanca. Scheduled travel to Andalucía (spring only); field trips to Segovia, Toledo, El Escorial, Avila, Peña de Francia, Alberca; optional travel to Seville, Paris, Morocco, other European cities at an extra cost.

Sessions • Fall, spring, yearlong, spring trimester.

Eligibility Requirements • Minimum age 18; open to freshmen, sophomores, juniors, seniors, graduate students; 2.5 GPA; 2 letters of recommendation; good academic standing at home school; 0.5 years of college course work in Spanish.

Living Arrangements • Students live in host family homes. Quarters are shared with students from other programs. Meals are taken with host family, in residences.

Costs (2003-2004) • One term: $7500 for fall term; $5500 for one spring trimester. Yearlong program: contact sponsor for cost; includes tuition, housing, all meals, insurance, excursions, international airfare, books and class materials, international student ID, student support services, passport and visa fees, cell phone package.

$20 application fee. $250 nonrefundable deposit required. Financial aid available for students from sponsoring institution: scholarships, loans.

For More Information • Ms. Liz Kopp, Assistant Director, Office of International Programs, State University of New York College at Cortland, PO Box 2000, Cortland, NY 13045; *Phone:* 607-753-2209; *Fax:* 607-753-5989. *E-mail:* cortlandabroad@cortland.edu. *World Wide Web:* http://www.studyabroad.com/suny/cortland/

SAN SEBASTIAN
TRUMAN STATE UNIVERSITY
BUSINESS PROGRAM IN SPAIN

Hosted by University of Deusto

Academic Focus • Basque studies, finance, international business, marketing, Spanish studies.

Program Information • Students attend classes at University of Deusto.

Sessions • Fall, spring, yearlong.

Eligibility Requirements • Open to sophomores, juniors, seniors, graduate students; course work in business; 3.0 GPA; fluency in Spanish.

Living Arrangements • Students live in locally rented apartments. Quarters are shared with host institution students, students from other programs. Meals are taken on one's own, in residences.

Costs (2003-2004) • One term: $3000 for Missouri residents; $4500 for nonresidents. Yearlong program: $6000 for Missouri residents; $9000 for nonresidents; includes tuition, insurance. $200 nonrefundable deposit required. Financial aid available for students from sponsoring institution: scholarships, loans.

For More Information • Mr. Patrick Lecaque, Director, Truman State University, Center for International Education Abroad, Kirk Building, 120, Kirksville, MO 63501; *Phone:* 660-785-4076; *Fax:* 660-785-7473. *E-mail:* ciea@truman.edu. *World Wide Web:* http://www2.truman.edu/ciea/

UNIVERSITY STUDIES ABROAD CONSORTIUM
SPANISH AND BASQUE STUDIES: SAN SEBASTIAN, SPAIN

Hosted by University of the Basque Country–San Sebastian Campus

Academic Focus • Anthropology, art history, Basque studies, culinary arts, cultural studies, dance, economics, film and media studies, history, political science and government, Spanish language and literature, Spanish studies, teaching.

Program Information • Students attend classes at University of the Basque Country–San Sebastian Campus. Field trips to France, Basque provinces: Bizkaia, Gipukoa, Alaba, the Pyrenees; optional travel to Madrid at an extra cost.

Sessions • Fall, spring, yearlong.

Eligibility Requirements • Minimum age 18; open to freshmen, sophomores, juniors, seniors, graduate students, adults; 2.5 GPA; no foreign language proficiency required.

Living Arrangements • Students live in locally rented apartments, program-owned apartments, host family homes. Quarters are shared with host institution students. Meals are taken on one's own, with host family, in residences.

Costs (2005-2006) • One term: $7470. Yearlong program: $12,680; includes tuition, some meals, insurance, excursions, student support services. $50 application fee. $150 refundable deposit required. Financial aid available for all students: scholarships, loans.

For More Information • University Studies Abroad Consortium, USAC/323, Reno, NV 89557-0093; *Phone:* 775-784-6569; *Fax:* 775-784-6010. *E-mail:* usac@unr.edu. *World Wide Web:* http://usac.unr.edu/

SANTANDER
INTERNATIONAL STUDIES ABROAD
SANTANDER, SPAIN–STUDIES WITH SPANIARDS

Hosted by University of Cantabria

Academic Focus • Business administration/management, economics, geography, history, psychology, Spanish studies.

Program Information • Students attend classes at University of Cantabria. Scheduled travel to Madrid, Toledo; field trips to San Sabastián, El Escorial, Potes, Picos de Europa, Comillas, Bilbao; optional travel at an extra cost.

Sessions • Fall, spring.

Eligibility Requirements • Minimum age 18; open to freshmen, sophomores, juniors, seniors, graduate students, adults; 2.75 GPA; 1 letter of recommendation; good academic standing at home school; transcript; 3 years of college course work in Spanish.

Living Arrangements • Students live in locally rented apartments, host family homes. Quarters are shared with host institution students, students from other programs. Meals are taken with host family, in residences.

Costs (2004-2005) • One term: $17,350; includes tuition, housing, all meals, insurance, excursions, student support services, excursion transportation, Internet access. $200 deposit required. Financial aid available for all students: scholarships, work study, U.S. federal financial aid.

For More Information • Spain Site Specialist, International Studies Abroad, 901 West 24th Street, Austin, TX 78705; *Phone:* 800-580-8826; *Fax:* 572-480-8866. *E-mail:* isa@studiesabroad.com. *World Wide Web:* http://www.studiesabroad.com/

UNIVERSITY OF MIAMI
UNIVERSITY OF CANTABRIA

Hosted by University of Cantabria

Academic Focus • Engineering, liberal studies, social sciences, telecommunications.

Program Information • Students attend classes at University of Cantabria.

Sessions • Fall, spring, yearlong.

Eligibility Requirements • Minimum age 18; open to sophomores, juniors, seniors; 3.0 GPA; 2 letters of recommendation; language evaluation; personal interview; fluency in Spanish.

Living Arrangements • Students live in host institution dormitories, locally rented apartments, host family homes. Quarters are shared with host institution students, students from other programs. Meals are taken on one's own, with host family, in residences, in restaurants.

Costs (2003-2004) • One term: $12,919. Yearlong program: $25,838; includes tuition, student support services. $40 application fee. $500 nonrefundable deposit required. Financial aid available for students from sponsoring institution: scholarships, loans.

For More Information • Mr. Chris Tingue, Assistant Director, University of Miami, International Education and Exchange Programs, 5050 Brunson Drive, Allen Hall 212, PO Box 248005, Coral Gables, FL 33124-1610; *Phone:* 305-284-3434; *Fax:* 305-284-4235. *E-mail:* ieep@miami.edu. *World Wide Web:* http://www.studyabroad.miami.edu/

THE UNIVERSITY OF NORTH CAROLINA AT CHARLOTTE
SEMESTER IN SPAIN

Hosted by University of Cantabria

Academic Focus • Art history, geography, history, literature, Spanish language and literature.

Program Information • Students attend classes at University of Cantabria. Scheduled travel to Madrid, Toledo; field trips to regional field sites.

Sessions • Fall.

Eligibility Requirements • Minimum age 18; open to sophomores, juniors, seniors; 2.5 GPA; 3 letters of recommendation; good academic standing at home school; 2 years of college course work in Spanish.

Living Arrangements • Students live in host family homes. Meals are taken with host family, in residences.

Costs (2003) • One term: $7200; includes tuition, housing, all meals, insurance, excursions, international airfare, student support services, laundry service. $10 application fee. $110 refundable deposit required. Financial aid available for students from sponsoring institution: scholarships, loans.

For More Information • Mr. Brad Sekulich, Assistant Director, Office of Education Abroad, The University of North Carolina at Charlotte, 9201 University City Boulevard, Charlotte, NC 28223-

0001; *Phone:* 704-687-2464; *Fax:* 704-687-3168. *E-mail:* edabroad@email.uncc.edu. *World Wide Web:* http://www.uncc.edu/edabroad/

THE UNIVERSITY OF NORTH CAROLINA AT CHARLOTTE
SEMESTER IN SPAIN

Hosted by University of Cantabria
Academic Focus • Art history, geography, history, literature, Spanish language and literature.
Program Information • Students attend classes at University of Cantabria. Scheduled travel to Madrid, Toledo; field trips.
Sessions • Spring.
Eligibility Requirements • Minimum age 18; open to sophomores, juniors, seniors; 2.5 GPA; 3 letters of recommendation; good academic standing at home school; 2 years of college course work in Spanish.
Living Arrangements • Students live in host family homes. Meals are taken with host family, in residences.
Costs (2004) • One term: $7200; includes tuition, housing, all meals, insurance, excursions, international airfare, student support services, laundry service. $10 application fee. $110 refundable deposit required. Financial aid available for students from sponsoring institution: scholarships, loans.
For More Information • Mr. Brad Sekulich, Assistant Director, Office of Education Abroad, The University of North Carolina at Charlotte, 9201 University City Boulevard, Charlotte, NC 28223-0001; *Phone:* 704-687-2464; *Fax:* 704-687-3168. *E-mail:* edabroad@email.uncc.edu. *World Wide Web:* http://www.uncc.edu/edabroad/

SANTIAGO DE COMPOSTELA

UNIVERSITY OF KANSAS
SEMESTER IN SPAIN, SANTIAGO DE COMPOSTELA

Hosted by University of Santiago de Compostela
Academic Focus • Art history, civilization studies, liberal studies, Spanish language and literature, Spanish studies.
Program Information • Students attend classes at University of Santiago de Compostela. Scheduled travel to Madrid, El Escorial, Andalucía; field trips.
Sessions • Fall, spring, yearlong.
Eligibility Requirements • Minimum age 18; open to sophomores, juniors, seniors; 2.75 GPA; 2 letters of recommendation; good academic standing at home school; minimum 3.0 GPA in Spanish; 2.5 years of college course work in Spanish.
Living Arrangements • Students live in locally rented apartments. Quarters are shared with host institution students. Meals are taken on one's own, in residences, in restaurants.
Costs (2003-2004) • One term: $7120. Yearlong program: $13,290; includes tuition, housing, excursions, administrative fees, medical evacuation and repatriation insurance. $38 application fee. $300 nonrefundable deposit required. Financial aid available for students from sponsoring institution: scholarships, loans.
For More Information • Ms. Angela Dittrich, Assistant Director, University of Kansas, Office of Study Abroad, Lippincott Hall, 1410 Jayhawk Boulevard, Room 108, Lawrence, KS 66045-7515; *Phone:* 785-864-3742; *Fax:* 785-864-5040. *E-mail:* osa@ku.edu. *World Wide Web:* http://www.ku.edu/~osa/

UNIVERSITY OF MIAMI
SANTIAGO DE COMPOSTELA

Hosted by University of Santiago de Compostela
Academic Focus • Business administration/management, international affairs, liberal studies, political science and government, social sciences, Spanish language and literature, telecommunications.
Program Information • Students attend classes at University of Santiago de Compostela.
Sessions • Fall, spring, yearlong.
Eligibility Requirements • Minimum age 18; open to sophomores, juniors, seniors; 3.0 GPA; 2 letters of recommendation; language evaluation; personal interview; fluency in Spanish.

Living Arrangements • Students live in host institution dormitories. Quarters are shared with host institution students, students from other programs. Meals are taken on one's own, in residences, in restaurants.
Costs (2003-2004) • One term: $12,919. Yearlong program: $25,838; includes tuition, student support services. $40 application fee. $500 nonrefundable deposit required. Financial aid available for students from sponsoring institution: scholarships, loans.
For More Information • Mr. Chris Tingue, Assistant Director, University of Miami, International Education and Exchange Programs, 5050 Brunson Drive, Allen Hall 212, PO Box 248005, Coral Gables, FL 33124-1610; *Phone:* 305-284-3434; *Fax:* 305-284-4235. *E-mail:* ieep@miami.edu. *World Wide Web:* http://www.studyabroad.miami.edu/

SEGOVIA

AHA INTERNATIONAL AN ACADEMIC PROGRAM OF THE UNIVERSITY OF OREGON
SEGOVIA, SPAIN: MIDWEST CONSORTIUM FOR STUDY ABROAD (MCSA)

Hosted by AHA Segovia Center
Academic Focus • Art history, cultural studies, European studies, international affairs, political science and government, Romance languages, Spanish language and literature, Spanish studies.
Program Information • Students attend classes at AHA Segovia Center. Scheduled travel to Santiago de Compostela, Asturias, Barcelona; field trips to the Route of the Castles, museums in Madrid including El Prado, Sofia Reina, Toledo, Salamanca, La Granja.
Sessions • Fall, winter, yearlong.
Eligibility Requirements • Open to sophomores, juniors, seniors, adults; 2 letters of recommendation; good academic standing at home school; 2 years of college course work in Spanish.
Living Arrangements • Students live in host family homes. Meals are taken with host family, in residences.
Costs (2003-2004) • One term: $6960. Yearlong program: $13,800; includes tuition, housing, all meals, insurance, excursions, books and class materials, international student ID, student support services. $50 application fee. $200 refundable deposit required. Financial aid available for students: scholarships, loans, home institution financial aid.
For More Information • Ms. Carlotta Troy, Associate Director for University Programs, AHA International An Academic Program of the University of Oregon, 741 SW Lincoln Street, Portland, OR 97201; *Phone:* 503-295-7730; *Fax:* 503-295-5969. *E-mail:* mail@aha-intl.org. *World Wide Web:* http://www.aha-intl.org/

KENTUCKY INSTITUTE FOR INTERNATIONAL STUDIES
SEMESTER PROGRAM IN SEGOVIA, SPAIN

Academic Focus • Art, cultural studies, literature, philosophy, Spanish language and literature, Spanish studies.
Program Information • Faculty members are drawn from the sponsor's U.S. staff and local instructors hired by the sponsor. Field trips to surrounding points of interest; optional travel to other areas of Spain, surrounding European countries at an extra cost.
Sessions • Spring.
Eligibility Requirements • Minimum age 18; open to sophomores, juniors, seniors, graduate students; 2.5 GPA; 2 letters of recommendation; minimum 3.0 GPA in Spanish; 2 years of college course work in Spanish.
Living Arrangements • Students live in host family homes. Meals are taken with host family, in residences.
Costs (2003) • One term: $5950; includes housing, some meals, insurance, excursions, international airfare, international student ID, student support services, instructional costs. $150 application fee. Financial aid available for all students: scholarships.
For More Information • Ms. Nancy Martin, Coordinator, Kentucky Institute for International Studies, Murray State University, PO Box 9, Murray, KY 42071-0009; *Phone:* 270-762-3091; *Fax:* 270-762-3434. *E-mail:* kiismsu@murraystate.edu. *World Wide Web:* http://www.kiis.org/

MIDDLEBURY COLLEGE SCHOOLS ABROAD
SCHOOL IN SPAIN–SEGOVIA PROGRAM

Hosted by University SEK
Academic Focus • Full curriculum.
Program Information • Students attend classes at University SEK.
Sessions • Fall, spring, yearlong.
Eligibility Requirements • Open to sophomores, juniors, seniors; 2.7 GPA; 2 letters of recommendation; B average in both Spanish and major; 2.5 years college course work in Spanish, including at least 1 content course at the 300-level.
Living Arrangements • Students live in host institution dormitories, locally rented apartments, host family homes. Quarters are shared with host institution students. Meals are taken on one's own, with host family, in residences, in central dining facility, in restaurants.
Costs (2004-2005) • One term: $7200. Yearlong program: $14,400; includes tuition, student support services. $50 application fee. $300 nonrefundable deposit required. Financial aid available for students from sponsoring institution: scholarships, loans.
For More Information • Mr. Jamie Northrup, University Relations Coordinator, Middlebury College Schools Abroad, Office of Off-Campus Study, Sunderland Language Center, Middlebury, VT 05753; *Phone:* 802-443-5745; *Fax:* 803-443-3157. *E-mail:* schoolsabroad@middlebury.edu. *World Wide Web:* http://www.middlebury.edu/msa/

SEVILLE
ACADEMIC PROGRAMS INTERNATIONAL (API)
(API)–SEVILLE ENGLISH PROGRAM, SPAIN

Hosted by Pablo de Olavide University

Academic Focus • Business administration/management, economics, full curriculum, history, human resources, marketing, political science and government, religious studies, science, social sciences.
Program Information • Students attend classes at Pablo de Olavide University. Scheduled travel to Madrid; field trips to Toledo, El Escorial, Granada, Córdoba, Cadiz, Jerez, Extremadura; optional travel to Rome, Lisbon, Paris at an extra cost.
Sessions • Fall, spring, yearlong.
Eligibility Requirements • Minimum age 18; open to sophomores, juniors, seniors; 2.75 GPA; 1 letter of recommendation; good academic standing at home school; official transcript from home university; no foreign language proficiency required.
Living Arrangements • Students live in host institution dormitories, locally rented apartments, host family homes. Quarters are shared with host institution students. Meals are taken on one's own, with host family, in residences, in restaurants.
Costs (2004-2005) • One term: $7400. Yearlong program: $13,600; includes tuition, housing, all meals, insurance, excursions, student support services, airport pick-up, ground transportation. $150 nonrefundable deposit required. Financial aid available for all students: scholarships.
For More Information • Ms. Jennifer C. Allen, Director, Academic Programs International (API), 107 East Hopkins, San Marcos, TX 78666; *Phone:* 800-844-4124; *Fax:* 512-392-8420. *E-mail:* api@academicintl.com. *World Wide Web:* http://www.academicintl.com/

ACADEMIC PROGRAMS INTERNATIONAL (API)
(API)–SEVILLE, SPAIN

Hosted by University of Seville
Academic Focus • Art history, civilization studies, commerce, cultural studies, economics, education, geography, history, interna-

SPAIN
Seville

tional business, Islamic studies, Latin American studies, marketing, political science and government, Spanish language and literature, Spanish studies, teaching.

Program Information • Students attend classes at University of Seville. Scheduled travel to Madrid; field trips to Toledo, Granada, El Escorial, Cádiz, Jerez, Córdoba, Extremadura; optional travel to Paris, Rome, Lisbon at an extra cost.

Sessions • Fall, spring, yearlong, fall B, H terms; spring B, H terms; year B, H terms.

Eligibility Requirements • Minimum age 18; open to freshmen, sophomores, juniors, seniors, adults; 2.75 GPA; 1 letter of recommendation; good academic standing at home school; official transcript from home university; 2 years of college course work in Spanish.

Living Arrangements • Students live in host institution dormitories, locally rented apartments, host family homes. Quarters are shared with host institution students. Meals are taken with host family, in residences.

Costs (2004-2005) • One term: $7200–$7500. Yearlong program: $13,000–$13,800; includes tuition, housing, all meals, insurance, excursions, student support services, airport pick-up, ground transportation. $150 nonrefundable deposit required. Financial aid available for all students: scholarships.

For More Information • Ms. Jennifer C. Allen, Director, Academic Programs International (API), 107 East Hopkins, San Marcos, TX 78666; *Phone:* 800-844-4124; *Fax:* 512-392-8420. *E-mail:* api@academicintl.com. *World Wide Web:* http://www.academicintl.com/

THE CENTER FOR CROSS CULTURAL STUDY
INTENSIVE INTERMEDIATE PROGRAM IN SPANISH LANGUAGE AND CULTURE IN SEVILLE, SPAIN

Hosted by The Center for Cross Cultural Study

Academic Focus • Civilization studies, dance, Spanish language and literature, Spanish studies.

Program Information • Students attend classes at The Center for Cross Cultural Study. Field trips to Granada, Córdoba, Italica, Mérida, Cáceres, Trujillo, Cadiz, La Rábida.

Sessions • Fall, spring.

Eligibility Requirements • Minimum age 16; open to precollege students, freshmen, sophomores, juniors, seniors, adults; 1 letter of recommendation; good academic standing at home school; minimum 3.0 GPA in Spanish; 1 year of college course work in Spanish.

Living Arrangements • Students live in host institution dormitories, host family homes. Quarters are shared with host institution students. Meals are taken as a group, with host family, in residences, in central dining facility.

Costs (2004-2005) • One term: $8990; includes tuition, housing, all meals, insurance, excursions, student support services, laundry service, activities, study tours, e-mail account. $50 application fee. $300 nonrefundable deposit required. Financial aid available for all students: scholarships.

For More Information • Dr. Judith M. Ortiz, Director, U.S., The Center for Cross Cultural Study, Department PY, 446 Main Street, Amherst, MA 01002-2314; *Phone:* 800-377-2621; *Fax:* 413-256-1968. *E-mail:* petersons@cccs.com. *World Wide Web:* http://www.cccs.com/

THE CENTER FOR CROSS CULTURAL STUDY
UPPER DIVISION SPANISH STUDIES PROGRAM IN SEVILLE, SPAIN

Hosted by The Center for Cross Cultural Study

Academic Focus • Anthropology, art history, business administration/management, civilization studies, dance, economics, film and media studies, history, international business, marketing, political science and government, sociology, Spanish language and literature, Spanish studies, teaching English as a second language.

Program Information • Students attend classes at The Center for Cross Cultural Study. Field trips to Granada, Córdoba, La Rabida, Italica, Cádiz, Cáceres, Trujillo.

Sessions • Fall, spring, yearlong.

Eligibility Requirements • Minimum age 16; open to precollege students, freshmen, sophomores, juniors, seniors, graduate students, adults; 1 letter of recommendation; good academic standing at home school; minimum 3.0 GPA in Spanish; 2 years of college course work in Spanish.

Living Arrangements • Students live in host institution dormitories, host family homes. Quarters are shared with host institution students. Meals are taken as a group, with host family, in residences, in central dining facility.

Costs (2004-2005) • One term: $8990. Yearlong program: $17,455; includes tuition, housing, all meals, insurance, excursions, student support services, activities, study tours, laundry service, e-mail account. $50 application fee. $300 nonrefundable deposit required. Financial aid available for all students: scholarships.

For More Information • Dr. Judith M. Ortiz, Director, U.S., The Center for Cross Cultural Study, Department PY, 446 Main Street, Amherst, MA 01002-2314; *Phone:* 800-377-2621; *Fax:* 413-256-1968. *E-mail:* petersons@cccs.com. *World Wide Web:* http://www.cccs.com/

CIEE
CIEE STUDY CENTER AT THE UNIVERSITY OF SEVILLE, SPAIN–ADVANCED LIBERAL ARTS PROGRAM

Hosted by Pablo de Olavide University, University of Seville

Academic Focus • Full curriculum.

Program Information • Students attend classes at Pablo de Olavide University, University of Seville. Field trips to Córdoba, Ronda, Italica, Granada.

Sessions • Fall, spring, yearlong.

Eligibility Requirements • Minimum age 18; open to sophomores, juniors, seniors, graduate students, adults; 3.0 GPA; good academic standing at home school; personal essay in Spanish; 2 references (1 from language instructor); 3 years of college course work in Spanish.

Living Arrangements • Students live in host family homes. Meals are taken with host family, in residences.

Costs (2004-2005) • One term: $8850. Yearlong program: $15,250; includes tuition, housing, all meals, insurance, excursions, student support services, cultural activities, pre-departure advising. $30 application fee. $300 deposit required. Financial aid available for all students: minority student scholarships, travel grants.

For More Information • Ms. Ellen Whitman, Admissions Officer, Spain and Latin America, CIEE, 7 Custom House Street, 3rd Floor, Portland, ME 04101; *Phone:* 800-40-STUDY; *Fax:* 207-553-7699. *E-mail:* studyinfo@ciee.org. *World Wide Web:* http://www.ciee.org/isp/

CIEE
CIEE STUDY CENTER AT THE UNIVERSITY OF SEVILLE, SPAIN–BUSINESS AND SOCIETY PROGRAM

Hosted by University of Seville

Academic Focus • Area studies, art history, business administration/management, economics, European studies, finance, history, international business, management information systems, marketing, political science and government, Spanish language and literature, Spanish studies.

Program Information • Students attend classes at University of Seville. Field trips to Granada, the Gonzalez Byass sherry winery, Cruz Campo, a glass manufacturing factory, Spanish National Television; optional travel.

Sessions • Fall, spring, yearlong.

Eligibility Requirements • Minimum age 18; open to sophomores, juniors, seniors, graduate students, adults; course work in business; 2.75 GPA; good academic standing at home school; personal essay; 2 references (1 from language instructor); 2.5 years of college course work in Spanish.

Living Arrangements • Students live in host family homes. Meals are taken with host family, in residences.

Costs (2004-2005) • One term: $9000. Yearlong program: $15,250; includes tuition, housing, all meals, insurance, excursions, student support services. $30 application fee. $300 deposit required. Financial aid available for all students: minority student scholarships, travel grants.

For More Information • Ms. Ellen Whitman, Admissions Officer, Spain and Latin America, CIEE, 7 Custom House Street, 3rd Floor, Portland, ME 04101; *Phone:* 800-40-STUDY; *Fax:* 207-553-7699. *E-mail:* studyinfo@ciee.org. *World Wide Web:* http://www.ciee.org/isp/

CIEE

CIEE STUDY CENTER AT THE UNIVERSITY OF SEVILLE, SPAIN–LANGUAGE AND SOCIETY PROGRAM

Hosted by University of Seville
Academic Focus • Art history, cultural studies, history, literature, political science and government, Spanish language and literature.
Program Information • Students attend classes at University of Seville. Field trips to Córdoba, Carmona, Granada, Italica, Ronda, Extremadura.
Sessions • Fall, spring.
Eligibility Requirements • Minimum age 18; open to freshmen, sophomores, juniors, seniors, graduate students, adults; 2.75 GPA; 2 letters of recommendation; good academic standing at home school; personal essay; 2 references (1 from language instructor); 1.5 years of college course work in Spanish.
Living Arrangements • Students live in host family homes. Meals are taken with host family, in residences.
Costs (2004-2005) • One term: $8850; includes tuition, housing, all meals, insurance, excursions, student support services, cultural activities, pre-departure advising. $30 application fee. $300 deposit required. Financial aid available for all students: minority student scholarships, travel grants.
For More Information • Ms. Ellen Whitman, Admissions Officer, Spain and Latin America, CIEE, 7 Custom House Street, 3rd Floor, Portland, ME 04101; *Phone:* 800-40-STUDY; *Fax:* 207-553-7699. *E-mail:* studyinfo@ciee.org. *World Wide Web:* http://www.ciee.org/isp/

CIEE

CIEE STUDY CENTER AT THE UNIVERSITY OF SEVILLE, SPAIN–LIBERAL ARTS PROGRAM

Hosted by University of Seville
Academic Focus • Full curriculum.

Program Information • Students attend classes at University of Seville. Field trips to Córdoba, Ronda, Italica, Granada.
Sessions • Fall, spring, yearlong.
Eligibility Requirements • Minimum age 18; open to sophomores, juniors, seniors, graduate students, adults; 2.75 GPA; good academic standing at home school; personal essay in Spanish; 2 references (1 from language instructor); 2.5 years of college course work in Spanish.
Living Arrangements • Students live in host family homes. Meals are taken with host family, in residences.
Costs (2004-2005) • One term: $8850. Yearlong program: $15,250; includes tuition, housing, all meals, insurance, excursions, student support services. $30 application fee. $300 deposit required. Financial aid available for all students: minority student scholarships.
For More Information • Ms. Ellen Whitman, Admissions Officer, Spain and Latin America, CIEE, 7 Custom House Street, 3rd Floor, Portland, ME 04101; *Phone:* 800-40-STUDY; *Fax:* 207-553-7699. *E-mail:* studyinfo@ciee.org. *World Wide Web:* http://www.ciee.org/isp/

CIEE

CIEE STUDY CENTER AT UNIVERSIDAD PABLO DE OLAVIDE, SEVILLE, SPAIN: INTERNATIONAL BUSINESS AND LANGUAGE PROGRAM

Hosted by Pablo de Olavide University
Academic Focus • Economics, finance, management information systems, marketing, Spanish language and literature.
Program Information • Students attend classes at Pablo de Olavide University. Scheduled travel to Granada, Córdoba, Carmona, Extremadura, Itálica, Ronda; field trips to Granada, Carmona, Extremadura, Itálica, Ronda, Córdoba.
Eligibility Requirements • Minimum age 18; open to sophomores, juniors, seniors; 2.75 GPA.

Living Arrangements • Students live in host institution dormitories, host family homes. Quarters are shared with host institution students. Meals are taken as a group, on one's own, with host family, in residences, in restaurants.

Costs (2005) • One term: contact sponsor for cost. $30 application fee. $300 deposit required. Financial aid available for all students: scholarships, minority scholarships, travel grants.

For More Information • Ms. Ellen Whitman, Admissions Officer, Spain and Latin America, CIEE, 7 Custom House Street, 3rd Floor, Portland, ME 04101; *Phone:* 800-553-7699; *Fax:* 207-553-7699. *E-mail:* ewhitman@ciee.org. *World Wide Web:* http://www.ciee.org/isp/

CIEE

CIEE STUDY CENTER IN SEVILLE, SPAIN: TEACHING DEVELOPMENT PROGRAM

Hosted by Pablo de Olavide University, University of Seville
Academic Focus • Bilingual education, education, social sciences, Spanish language and literature.

Program Information • Students attend classes at Pablo de Olavide University, University of Seville. Scheduled travel to Granada, Córdoba, Carmona, Extremadura, Itálica, Ronda; field trips to Granada, Córdoba, Carmona, Extremadura, Itálica, Ronda.

Sessions • Fall, spring, yearlong.

Eligibility Requirements • Minimum age 18; open to sophomores, juniors, seniors; 2.75 GPA; 2.5 years of college course work in Spanish.

Living Arrangements • Students live in host institution dormitories, locally rented apartments, host family homes. Quarters are shared with host institution students. Meals are taken as a group, on one's own, with host family, in residences, in restaurants.

Costs (2005-2006) • One term: contact sponsor for cost. Yearlong program: contact sponsor for cost. $30 application fee. $300 deposit

required. Financial aid available for all students: scholarships, minority scholarships, travel grants.

For More Information • Ms. Ellen Whitman, Admissions Officer, Latin America and Spain, CIEE, 7 Custom House Street, 3rd Floor, Portland, ME 04101; *Phone:* 800-40-STUDY; *Fax:* 207-553-7699. *E-mail:* ewhitman@ciee.org. *World Wide Web:* http://www.ciee.org/isp/

COLLEGE CONSORTIUM FOR INTERNATIONAL STUDIES–BROWARD COMMUNITY COLLEGE AND ST. BONAVENTURE UNIVERSITY

SEMESTER IN SPAIN

Hosted by Institute of International Studies, University of Seville

Academic Focus • Anthropology, art history, economics, European studies, history, international affairs, international business, Latin American studies, liberal studies, political science and government, social sciences, Spanish language and literature, Spanish studies.

Program Information • Students attend classes at Institute of International Studies, University of Seville. Field trips to Córdoba, Granada, Gibraltar, Jerez; optional travel to Madrid, Morocco, Portugal at an extra cost.

Sessions • Fall, spring, yearlong.

Eligibility Requirements • Minimum age 18; open to freshmen, sophomores, juniors, seniors, graduate students, adults; 2.5 GPA; 3 letters of recommendation; good academic standing at home school; no foreign language proficiency required.

Living Arrangements • Students live in host family homes. Quarters are shared with host institution students. Meals are taken on one's own, with host family, in residences, in restaurants.

Costs (2004-2005) • One term: $7490. Yearlong program: $15,280; includes tuition, housing, all meals, insurance, excursions, student support services. Financial aid available for students from sponsoring institution: scholarships.

For More Information • College Consortium for International Studies, 2000 P Street, NW, Suite 503, Washington, DC 20036; *Phone:* 800-453-6956; *Fax:* 202-223-0999. *E-mail:* info@ccisabroad. org. *World Wide Web:* http://www.ccisabroad.org/

CULTURAL EXPERIENCES ABROAD (CEA)
STUDY SPANISH LANGUAGE AND CULTURE IN SEVILLE

Hosted by Pablo de Olavide University

Academic Focus • Art history, business administration/management, economics, history, human resources, international affairs, Latin American literature, linguistics, marketing, political science and government, religious studies, sociology, Spanish language and literature, Spanish studies.

Program Information • Students attend classes at Pablo de Olavide University. Field trips to Granada, Cadiz, Córdoba, Jerez, Aracena.

Sessions • Fall, spring, yearlong.

Eligibility Requirements • Minimum age 18; open to freshmen, sophomores, juniors, seniors, graduate students; 2.5 GPA; 1 letter of recommendation; good academic standing at home school; no foreign language proficiency required.

Living Arrangements • Students live in program-owned apartments, host family homes. Meals are taken on one's own, with host family, in residences.

Costs (2003-2004) • One term: $7995–$8195. Yearlong program: $14,995; includes tuition, housing, some meals, insurance, excursions, student support services. $50 application fee. $400 nonrefundable deposit required.

For More Information • Cultural Experiences Abroad (CEA), 1400 East Southern Avenue, Suite B-108, Tempe, AZ 85282-8011; *Phone:* 480-557-7900; *Fax:* 480-557-7926. *E-mail:* petersons@gowithcea. com. *World Wide Web:* http://www.gowithcea.com/

CULTURAL EXPERIENCES ABROAD (CEA)
STUDY SPANISH LANGUAGE AND CULTURE IN SEVILLE

Hosted by University of Seville

Academic Focus • Anthropology, archaeology, art history, economics, geography, history, international affairs, Latin American literature, linguistics, music, political science and government, sociology, Spanish language and literature, Spanish studies.

Program Information • Students attend classes at University of Seville. Field trips to Granada, Cadiz, Córdoba, Jerez, Arauna.

Sessions • Fall, spring, yearlong.

Eligibility Requirements • Minimum age 18; open to freshmen, sophomores, juniors, seniors, graduate students; 2.5 GPA; 1 letter of recommendation; good academic standing at home school; 2.5 years of college course work in Spanish.

Living Arrangements • Students live in program-owned apartments, host family homes. Quarters are shared with students from other programs. Meals are taken on one's own, with host family, in residences.

Costs (2003-2004) • One term: $7995. Yearlong program: $14,495; includes tuition, housing, some meals, insurance, excursions, student support services. $50 application fee. $400 nonrefundable deposit required.

For More Information • Cultural Experiences Abroad (CEA), 1400 East Southern Avenue, Suite B-108, Tempe, AZ 85282-8011; *Phone:* 480-557-7900; *Fax:* 480-557-7926. *E-mail:* petersons@gowithcea. com. *World Wide Web:* http://www.gowithcea.com/

GEORGE MASON UNIVERSITY
SEVILLA SEMESTER

Hosted by Institute of International Studies

Academic Focus • Full curriculum.

Program Information • Students attend classes at Institute of International Studies. Field trips to cultural sites.

Sessions • Fall, spring.

Eligibility Requirements • Minimum age 18; open to freshmen, sophomores, juniors, seniors, adults; 2.5 GPA; good academic standing at home school; 1 year of college course work in Spanish.

Living Arrangements • Students live in host family homes. Quarters are shared with host institution students.

Costs (2003-2004) • One term: contact sponsor for cost. $75 application fee. Financial aid available for students from sponsoring institution: scholarships, loans.

For More Information • Program Officer, Center for Global Education, George Mason University, 235 Johnson Center, 4400 University Drive, Fairfax, VA 22030; *Phone:* 703-993-2154; *Fax:* 703-993-2153. *E-mail:* cge@gmu.edu. *World Wide Web:* http://www. gmu.edu/departments/cge/

INSTITUTO SEVILLANO DE ESTUDIOS Y PRACTICAS (ISEPS)
INSTITUTO SEVILLANO DE ESTUDIOS Y PRACTICAS (ISEPS)

Hosted by University of Seville

Academic Focus • Full curriculum.

Program Information • Students attend classes at University of Seville. Field trips to cultural and natural sites, resorts; optional travel to cultural and natural sites, resorts at an extra cost.

Sessions • Fall, spring, yearlong.

Eligibility Requirements • Open to sophomores, juniors, seniors, graduate students, adults; 3.0 GPA; good academic standing at home school; 1 year of college course work in Spanish.

Living Arrangements • Students live in host family homes. Quarters are shared with host institution students. Meals are taken with host family, in residences.

Costs (2003-2004) • One term: $6800. Yearlong program: $12,500; includes tuition, housing, all meals, insurance, excursions, international student ID, student support services, cell phone, special activities. $50 application fee.

For More Information • Chilton E. Harper, Director for Campus and Institutional Relations, Instituto Sevillano de Estudios y Practicas (ISEPS), 6795 SW 132 Avenue, #107, Miami, FL 33183; *Phone:* 305-733-4073; *Fax:* +34 95-423-1123. *E-mail:* info@sevillestudies. com. *World Wide Web:* http://www.sevillestudies.com/

INTERNATIONAL STUDIES ABROAD
SEVILLA BUSINESS AND ECONOMICS

Hosted by University of Seville

Academic Focus • Economics, international business, marketing.

Program Information • Students attend classes at University of Seville. Scheduled travel to Madrid, Toledo; field trips to Granada, Salamanca, Ronda, El Escorial, Córdoba, Cáceres; optional travel at an extra cost.

Sessions • Fall, spring, yearlong.

Eligibility Requirements • Minimum age 18; open to freshmen, sophomores, juniors, seniors, graduate students, adults; 2.5 GPA; 1 letter of recommendation; good academic standing at home school; 2 letters of recommendation if GPA is lower than 2.5; 2 years of college course work in Spanish.

Living Arrangements • Students live in locally rented apartments, host family homes, hotels. Meals are taken with host family, in residences.

Costs (2004-2005) • One term: $6800. Yearlong program: $12,700; includes tuition, housing, all meals, insurance, excursions, student support services, ground transportation, Internet access. $200 deposit required. Financial aid available for all students: scholarships, loans, U.S. federal financial aid via consortium agreement.

For More Information • Spain Site Specialist, International Studies Abroad, 901 West 24th Street, Austin, TX 78705; *Phone:* 800-580-8826; *Fax:* 512-480-8866. *E-mail:* isa@studiesabroad.com. *World Wide Web:* http://www.studiesabroad.com/

INTERNATIONAL STUDIES ABROAD
SEVILLA LANGUAGE AND CULTURE PROGRAM

Hosted by International University 'Menéndez Pelayo'–Seville

Academic Focus • Business administration/management, civilization studies, marketing, Spanish language and literature.

Program Information • Students attend classes at International University 'Menéndez Pelayo'–Seville. Scheduled travel to Madrid, Toledo; field trips to Granada, Salamanca, Ronda, El Escorial, Córdoba, Cáceres; optional travel at an extra cost.

Sessions • Fall, spring.

Eligibility Requirements • Minimum age 18; open to freshmen, sophomores, juniors, seniors, graduate students, adults; 2.5 GPA; 1 letter of recommendation; good academic standing at home school; transcript; 1 year college course work in Spanish for upper-division courses.

Living Arrangements • Students live in locally rented apartments, host family homes. Quarters are shared with host institution students, students from other programs. Meals are taken with host family, in residences.

Costs (2004-2005) • One term: $6600; includes tuition, housing, all meals, insurance, excursions, books and class materials, student support services, excursion transportation, Internet access. $200 deposit required. Financial aid available for all students: scholarships, loans, U.S. federal financial aid.

For More Information • Spain Site Specialist, International Studies Abroad, 901 West 24th Street, Austin, TX 78705; *Phone:* 800-580-8826; *Fax:* 512-480-8866. *E-mail:* isa@studiesabroad.com. *World Wide Web:* http://www.studiesabroad.com/

INTERNATIONAL STUDIES ABROAD
SEVILLE, SPAIN, HUMANITIES

Hosted by University of Seville

Academic Focus • Art history, cultural studies, geography, history, literature, Spanish language and literature.

Program Information • Students attend classes at University of Seville. Scheduled travel to Toledo, Madrid; field trips to Córdoba, Granada, Salamanca, Ronda, El Escorial, Cáceres; optional travel at an extra cost.

Sessions • Fall, spring, yearlong.

Eligibility Requirements • Minimum age 18; open to freshmen, sophomores, juniors, seniors, adults; 2.5 GPA; 1 letter of recommendation; good academic standing at home school; transcript; 2 years of college course work in Spanish.

Living Arrangements • Students live in locally rented apartments, host family homes, hotels. Quarters are shared with host institution students. Meals are taken with host family, in residences.

Costs (2004-2005) • One term: $7600. Yearlong program: $13,250; includes tuition, housing, all meals, insurance, excursions, student support services, ground transportation, laundry service, tutoring. $200 deposit required. Financial aid available for all students: scholarships, loans, U.S. federal financial aid.

For More Information • Spain Site Specialist, International Studies Abroad, 901 West 24th Street, Austin, TX 78705; *Phone:* 800-580-8826; *Fax:* 512-480-8866. *E-mail:* isa@studiesabroad.com. *World Wide Web:* http://www.studiesabroad.com/

NIAGARA UNIVERSITY
SEVILLE, SPAIN

Hosted by The Center for Cross Cultural Study

Academic Focus • Spanish language and literature.

Program Information • Students attend classes at The Center for Cross Cultural Study. Scheduled travel; field trips; optional travel at an extra cost.

Sessions • Fall, spring, winter.

Eligibility Requirements • Open to juniors, seniors; 2.5 GPA; 2 letters of recommendation; 2 years of college course work in Spanish.

Living Arrangements • Students live in locally rented apartments, host family homes. Quarters are shared with host institution students, students from other programs. Meals are taken on one's own, with host family, in residences, in restaurants.

Costs (2003-2004) • One term: $12,314; includes tuition, housing, all meals, excursions, student support services. Financial aid available for students from sponsoring institution: Pell grants and TAP for qualified New York State residents.

For More Information • Dr. Ana Spitzmeser, Chair, Foreign Language Department, Niagara University, St. Vincents Hall, Niagara University, NY 14109; *Phone:* 716-286-8211; *Fax:* 716-286-8349. *E-mail:* ams@niagara.edu. *World Wide Web:* http://www.niagara.edu/sap/

NICHOLLS STATE UNIVERSITY
STUDY PROGRAM IN SEVILLE, SPAIN

Hosted by Nicholls State University–Seville

Academic Focus • Art, cultural studies, history, Spanish language and literature.

Program Information • Students attend classes at Nicholls State University-Seville. Field trips to bullfights, Isla Cristina (fishing village); optional travel to the beach, sporting events, film sessions, horseback riding.

Sessions • Fall, spring, yearlong.

Eligibility Requirements • Minimum age 17; open to precollege students, freshmen, sophomores, juniors, seniors, graduate students, adults; no foreign language proficiency required.

Living Arrangements • Students live in host family homes. Quarters are shared with host institution students. Meals are taken with host family, in residences.

Costs (2003-2004) • One term: $5441. Yearlong program: $10,881; includes tuition, housing, some meals, insurance, books and class materials, lab equipment, student support services, instructional costs. Financial aid available for all students: loans, all customary sources.

For More Information • Ms. Cynthia Webb, Director of Study Programs Abroad, Nicholls State University, PO Box 2080, Thibodaux, LA 70310; *Phone:* 985-448-4440; *Fax:* 985-449-7028. *E-mail:* spab-caw@nicholls.edu. *World Wide Web:* http://www.nicholls.edu/abroad/

STATE UNIVERSITY OF NEW YORK AT NEW PALTZ
STUDY ABROAD IN SEVILLE, SPAIN

Hosted by University of Seville

Academic Focus • Cultural studies, history, political science and government, Spanish language and literature, Spanish studies, theater management.

Program Information • Students attend classes at University of Seville. Scheduled travel to Córdoba, Granada; field trips to Granada, Córdoba, La Costa Del Sol, Andalucía.

Sessions • Fall, spring, yearlong.

Eligibility Requirements • Minimum age 18; open to juniors, seniors; 2.5 GPA; 2 letters of recommendation; good academic standing at home school; 2 years of college course work in Spanish.

Living Arrangements • Students live in locally rented apartments. Quarters are shared with host institution students. Meals are taken on one's own, in residences, in restaurants.

Costs (2003-2004) • One term: $7098 for New York residents; $10,229 for nonresidents. Yearlong program: $14,196 for New York residents; $20,458 for nonresidents; includes tuition, housing, all meals, insurance, excursions, books and class materials, student support services, administrative fee. $25 application fee. $300–$600 nonrefundable deposit required. Financial aid available for students from sponsoring institution: scholarships, loans.

For More Information • Center for International Programs, State University of New York at New Paltz, 75 South Manheim Boulevard, Suite 9, New Paltz, NY 12561; *Phone:* 845-257-3125; *Fax:* 845-257-3129. *E-mail:* international@newpaltz.edu. *World Wide Web:* http://www.newpaltz.edu/studyabroad/

SWEET BRIAR COLLEGE
JUNIOR YEAR IN SPAIN

Hosted by University of Seville

Academic Focus • Full curriculum.

Program Information • Students attend classes at University of Seville. Field trips to Córdoba, Granada, Carmona, Jerez de la Frontera, Lagos, Portugal.

Sessions • Fall, spring, yearlong.

Eligibility Requirements • Minimum age 18; open to juniors; 3.0 GPA; 2 letters of recommendation; enrollment at an accredited four-year college or university; 2.5 years college course work in Spanish or the equivalent.

Living Arrangements • Students live in host family homes. Quarters are shared with host institution students. Meals are taken with host family, in residences.

Costs (2004-2005) • One term: $14,500 for fall semester; $15,400 for spring. Yearlong program: $24,500; includes tuition, housing, all meals, insurance, excursions, international airfare, international student ID, student support services, books and class materials for orientation period. $50 application fee. $500 refundable deposit required. Financial aid available for all students: scholarships.

For More Information • Dr. Lynn McGovern, Director, Junior Year in Spain, Sweet Briar College, Sweet Briar, VA 24595; *Phone:* 434-381-6281; *Fax:* 434-381-6293. *E-mail:* jys@sbc.edu

TRINITY CHRISTIAN COLLEGE
SEMESTER IN SPAIN

Held at Trinity Christian College
Academic Focus • Spanish language and literature, Spanish studies.
Program Information • Classes are held on the campus of Trinity Christian College. Faculty members are local instructors hired by the sponsor. Field trips to Córdoba, Granada, Toledo, Jerez, Italica, Ronda, Aracena.
Sessions • Fall, spring, yearlong.
Eligibility Requirements • Minimum age 18; open to freshmen, sophomores, juniors, seniors, graduate students, adults; 2.5 GPA; 2 letters of recommendation; good academic standing at home school; good health; no foreign language proficiency required.
Living Arrangements • Students live in host family homes. Quarters are shared with host institution students. Meals are taken with host family, in residences.
Costs (2004-2005) • One term: $9000. Yearlong program: $18,000; includes tuition, housing, all meals, insurance, excursions, books and class materials, student support services, laundry service and linens. $40 application fee. $100 nonrefundable deposit required. Financial aid available for all students: loans, governmental grants.
For More Information • Ms. Debra Veenstra, Semester in Spain, SIS Program Coordinator, Trinity Christian College, 6601 West College Drive, Palos Heights, IL 60463-1768; *Phone:* 800-748-0087; *Fax:* 708-239-3986. *E-mail:* spain@trnty.edu. *World Wide Web:* http://www.semesterinspain.org/

THE UNIVERSITY OF NORTH CAROLINA AT CHAPEL HILL
UNC YEAR AT SEVILLA–LANGUAGE, SOCIETY, AND CULTURAL STUDIES PROGRAM

Hosted by Estudios Universitarios y Superiores de Andalucía (EUSA)
Academic Focus • Art, communications, film and media studies, history, international business, nutrition, Spanish language and literature, Spanish studies.
Program Information • Students attend classes at Estudios Universitarios y Superiores de Andalucía (EUSA). Field trips to Córdoba, Granada.
Sessions • Fall, spring, yearlong.
Eligibility Requirements • Open to freshmen, sophomores, juniors, seniors; 2.7 GPA; 2 letters of recommendation; good academic standing at home school; 2 years college course work in Spanish or the equivalent.
Living Arrangements • Students live in host family homes. Meals are taken with host family, in residences.
Costs (2003-2004) • One term: $5275 for North Carolina residents; $7025 for nonresidents. Yearlong program: $9050 for North Carolina residents; $12,550 for nonresidents; includes tuition, housing, all meals, insurance, excursions, student support services. $500 nonrefundable deposit required. Financial aid available for all students: scholarships.
For More Information • Dr. Larry King, Director, The University of North Carolina at Chapel Hill, UNC-Year at Sevilla, Department of Romance Languages and Literatures, CB# 3170, 238 Dey Hall, Chapel Hill, NC 27599-3170; *Phone:* 919-962-5078; *Fax:* 919-962-5457. *E-mail:* sevi@unc.edu. *World Wide Web:* http://studyabroad.unc.edu/

Goodbye dorm life, Hola Spain.

You'll fit right in at Semester in Spain.

FALL, SPRING, SUMMER OR JANUARY TERMS
Receive 16 credits for semester study, or 4-8 credits for Summer/January study. A discount is available to students who study for a full year.

BEGINNING, INTERMEDIATE OR ADVANCED SPANISH CLASSES
Experience a home stay, which includes all meals and laundry. Take excursions to Toledo, Cordoba and the ocean. Have fun and build your fluency in Spanish in beautiful Seville—your location in Spain.

Semester in Spain
A PROGRAM OF TRINITY CHRISTIAN COLLEGE

Order an application by calling: 800.748.0087
Email: spain@trnty.edu
Web: www.semesterinspain.org

Semester in Spain
6601 West College Drive
Department PR
Palos Heights, IL 60463

ACADEMIC QUALITY - FAITH OPPORTUNITIES - IMMERSION EXPERIENCE

THE UNIVERSITY OF NORTH CAROLINA AT CHAPEL HILL

UNC YEAR AT SEVILLA PROGRAM IN ADVANCED HISPANIC STUDIES

Hosted by University of Seville

Academic Focus • Full curriculum.

Program Information • Students attend classes at University of Seville. Field trips to Granada, Córdoba.

Sessions • Fall, spring.

Eligibility Requirements • Open to freshmen, sophomores, juniors, seniors; 2.7 GPA; 2 letters of recommendation; good academic standing at home school; 3 years college course work in Spanish or the equivalent.

Living Arrangements • Students live in host family homes. Meals are taken with host family, in residences.

Costs (2003-2004) • One term: $5275 for North Carolina residents; $7025 for nonresidents; includes tuition, housing, all meals, insurance, excursions, student support services. $500 nonrefundable deposit required. Financial aid available for all students: scholarships.

For More Information • Dr. Larry King, Director, The University of North Carolina at Chapel Hill, UNC-Year at Sevilla, Department of Romance Languages, CB# 3170, 238 Dey Hall, Chapel Hill, NC 27599-3710; *Phone:* 919-962-5078; *Fax:* 919-962-5457. *E-mail:* sevi@unc.edu. *World Wide Web:* http://studyabroad.unc.edu/

THE UNIVERSITY OF NORTH CAROLINA AT CHAPEL HILL

UNC YEAR AT SEVILLA PROGRAM IN SPECIALIZED AREA STUDIES

Hosted by University of Seville

Academic Focus • Full curriculum.

Program Information • Students attend classes at University of Seville. Field trips to Granada, Córdoba.

Sessions • Fall, spring, yearlong.

Eligibility Requirements • Open to freshmen, sophomores, juniors, seniors; 3.0 GPA; 2 letters of recommendation; good academic standing at home school; 3 years college course work in Spanish or the equivalent.

Living Arrangements • Students live in host family homes. Meals are taken with host family, in residences.

Costs (2003-2004) • One term: $5275 for North Carolina residents; $7025 for nonresidents. Yearlong program: $9050 for North Carolina residents; $12,550 for nonresidents; includes tuition, housing, all meals, insurance, excursions, student support services. $500 nonrefundable deposit required. Financial aid available for all students: scholarships.

For More Information • Dr. Larry King, Director, The University of North Carolina at Chapel Hill, UNC-Year at Sevilla, Department of Romance Language, CB 3170, 238 Dey Hall, Chapel Hill, NC 27599-3170; *Phone:* 919-962-5078; *Fax:* 919-962-5457. *E-mail:* sevi@unc.edu. *World Wide Web:* http://studyabroad.unc.edu/

UNIVERSITY OF WISCONSIN–PLATTEVILLE

SEVILLE STUDY CENTER

Hosted by Spanish American Institute of International Education

Academic Focus • Art history, business administration/management, geography, history, political science and government, sociology, Spanish language and literature, Spanish studies.

Program Information • Students attend classes at Spanish American Institute of International Education. Field trips to Córdoba, Matalascanas, museums, galleries, churches, Jerez, Ronda, historic sites in and around Seville; optional travel to Salamanca, Portugal, Granada at an extra cost.

Sessions • Fall, spring, yearlong.
Eligibility Requirements • Minimum age 18; open to freshmen, sophomores, juniors, seniors; 2.5 GPA; 2 letters of recommendation; good academic standing at home school; no foreign language proficiency required.
Living Arrangements • Students live in host family homes. Meals are taken on one's own, with host family, in residences, in restaurants.
Costs (2004-2005) • One term: $7895 for Wisconsin and Minnesota residents; $8495 for nonresidents. Yearlong program: $15,790 for Wisconsin and Minnesota residents; $16,990 for nonresidents; includes tuition, housing, some meals, insurance, excursions, books and class materials, international student ID, student support services. $25 application fee. $400 nonrefundable deposit required. Financial aid available for all students: loans, federal/state grants, scholarships for Platteville students.
For More Information • Ms. Donna Anderson, Director, University of Wisconsin–Platteville, Institute for Study Abroad Programs, 111 Royce Hall, 1 University Plaza, Platteville, WI 53818-3099; *Phone:* 800-342-1725; *Fax:* 608-342-1736. *E-mail:* studyabroad@uwplatt.edu. *World Wide Web:* http://www.uwplatt.edu/~studyabroad/

WELLS COLLEGE
SEVILLA PROGRAM

Hosted by University of Seville
Academic Focus • Anthropology, art history, cultural studies, literature, political science and government, Spanish language and literature.
Program Information • Students attend classes at University of Seville. Scheduled travel to Madrid, Segovia, El Escorial, Toledo, Córdoba, Granada, Málaga, Marbella, Barcelona, Zaragoza; field trips to Córdoba, Ronda, Italica, Jerez; optional travel to Cadiz, Sierra Nevada, Lisboa at an extra cost.
Sessions • Fall, spring, yearlong.

Eligibility Requirements • Open to sophomores, juniors; 2.7 GPA; 2 letters of recommendation; 2 years of college course work in Spanish.
Living Arrangements • Students live in locally rented apartments, host family homes. Quarters are shared with host institution students. Meals are taken on one's own, with host family, in residences.
Costs (2004-2005) • One term: $8800 for fall term; $9800 for spring. Yearlong program: $17,500; includes tuition, housing, all meals, excursions, international airfare, international student ID, student support services. $35 application fee. $1000 refundable deposit required. Financial aid available for students from sponsoring institution: scholarships, loans.
For More Information • Dr. Miguel Gil, Director, Sevilla Program, Wells College, Foreign Languages and Literatures Department, Aurora, NY 13026; *Phone:* 315-364-3280; *Fax:* 315-364-3257. *E-mail:* mgil@wells.edu. *World Wide Web:* http://www.wells.edu/academic/ac2d.htm

TOLEDO
ARCADIA UNIVERSITY
LA FUNDACION JOSÉ ORTEGA Y GASSET

Hosted by Fundación José Ortega y Gasset
Academic Focus • Liberal studies, social sciences, Spanish language and literature.
Program Information • Students attend classes at Fundación José Ortega y Gasset. Scheduled travel; field trips; optional travel at an extra cost.
Sessions • Fall, spring, yearlong.
Eligibility Requirements • Open to sophomores, juniors, seniors; 3.0 GPA; 1 letter of recommendation; Spanish proficiency test; 2 years of college course work in Spanish.

Living Arrangements • Students live in host institution dormitories, host family homes. Quarters are shared with host institution students, students from other programs. Meals are taken as a group, in central dining facility.
Costs (2003-2004) • One term: $9990. Yearlong program: $17,990; includes tuition, housing, all meals, insurance, international student ID, student support services, transcript, pre-departure guide. $35 application fee. $500 nonrefundable deposit required. Financial aid available for all students: scholarships, loans.
For More Information • Arcadia University, Center for Education Abroad, 450 South Easton Road, Glenside, PA 19038-3295; *Phone:* 866-927-2234; *Fax:* 215-572-2174. *E-mail:* cea@arcadia.edu. *World Wide Web:* http://www.arcadia.edu/cea/

KENTUCKY INSTITUTE FOR INTERNATIONAL STUDIES
SEMESTER PROGRAM IN TOLEDO, SPAIN

Hosted by University of Castilla-La Mancha
Academic Focus • Spanish language and literature, Spanish studies.
Program Information • Students attend classes at University of Castilla-La Mancha. Field trips to Madrid, Sierra de San Vicente, La Mancha; optional travel at an extra cost.
Sessions • Fall.
Eligibility Requirements • Minimum age 18; open to sophomores, juniors, seniors, graduate students; minimum 2.5 GPA overall; minimum 3.0 GPA in Spanish; 2.5 years of college course work in Spanish.
Living Arrangements • Students live in host institution dormitories. Meals are taken in residences.
Costs (2002) • One term: $5950; includes housing, some meals, insurance, excursions, international airfare, international student ID, student support services. $150 application fee. Financial aid available for all students: scholarships.

For More Information • Ms. Nancy Martin, Coordinator, Kentucky Institute for International Studies, Murray State University, PO Box 9, Murray, KY 42071-0009; *Phone:* 270-762-3423; *Fax:* 270-762-3434. *E-mail:* kiismsu@murraystate.edu. *World Wide Web:* http://www.kiis.org/

UNIVERSITY OF MINNESOTA
INTERNATIONAL PROGRAM IN TOLEDO

Hosted by Fundación José Ortega y Gasset
Academic Focus • Anthropology, archaeology, art history, drama/theater, economics, European studies, film and media studies, history, interdisciplinary studies, Latin American studies, political science and government, Spanish language and literature, Spanish studies, women's studies.
Program Information • Students attend classes at Fundación José Ortega y Gasset. Field trips to the route of Don Quixote, Madrid, El Escorial, Segovia, Aranjuez, Cúenca; optional travel to Andalucía, Avila, Salamanca at an extra cost.
Sessions • Fall, spring, yearlong.
Eligibility Requirements • Minimum age 18; open to freshmen, sophomores, juniors, seniors, graduate students, adults; 2.5 GPA; good academic standing at home school; 2 years of college course work in Spanish.
Living Arrangements • Students live in host family homes, the Residencia San Juan de la Penitencia. Quarters are shared with host institution students, students from other programs. Meals are taken as a group, with host family, in residences, in central dining facility.
Costs (2004-2005) • One term: contact sponsor for cost. Yearlong program: contact sponsor for cost. $50 application fee. $400 nonrefundable deposit required. Financial aid available for students from sponsoring institution: scholarships, loans.
For More Information • University of Minnesota, Learning Abroad Center, 230 Heller Hall, 271 19th Avenue South, Minneapolis, MN

55455; *Phone:* 612-626-9000; *Fax:* 612-626-8009. *E-mail:* umabroad@umn.edu. *World Wide Web:* http://www.umabroad.umn.edu/. Students may also apply through Centro de Estudios Internacionales, Fundación Ortega y Gasset, Callejón de San Justo, S/N, 45001 Toledo, Spain.

VALENCIA

FLORIDA INTERNATIONAL UNIVERSITY
UNIVERSITY OF VALENCIA, SPAIN

Hosted by University of Valencia
Academic Focus • Full curriculum.
Program Information • Students attend classes at University of Valencia.
Sessions • Fall, spring.
Eligibility Requirements • Open to sophomores, juniors, seniors, graduate students; 3.0 GPA; 2 years of college course work in Spanish.
Living Arrangements • Students live in locally rented apartments.
Costs (2004) • One term: $5000; includes housing, all meals, international airfare, books and class materials, student support services. $150 application fee. Financial aid available for students from sponsoring institution: scholarships, loans.
For More Information • Office of International Studies, Florida International University, University Park Campus-TT100, Miami, FL 33199; *Phone:* 305-348-1913; *Fax:* 305-348-1941. *E-mail:* ois@fiu.edu. *World Wide Web:* http://ois.fiu.edu/

FLORIDA STATE UNIVERSITY
SPAIN: VALENCIA PROGRAM

Hosted by Florida State University–Spain Study Center
Academic Focus • Art, civilization studies, liberal studies, mathematics, music, Spanish language and literature.

Program Information • Students attend classes at Florida State University–Spain Study Center. Scheduled travel to Madrid, Barcelona; field trips to Granada, Córdoba, Sevilla.
Sessions • Fall, spring, application deadlines differ for internship applicants.
Eligibility Requirements • Open to freshmen, sophomores, juniors, seniors; 2.5 GPA; good academic standing at home school; pre-departure course in Spanish recommended.
Living Arrangements • Students live in host institution dormitories. Quarters are shared with host institution students. Meals are taken as a group, on one's own, in residences, in central dining facility, in restaurants.
Costs (2002-2003) • One term: $7500; includes tuition, housing, some meals, insurance, excursions, international student ID, student support services, program T-shirt or cap. $50 application fee. $500 nonrefundable deposit required. Financial aid available for students from sponsoring institution: scholarships, work study, loans.
For More Information • International Programs, Florida State University, A5500 University Center, Tallahassee, FL 32306-2420; *Phone:* 850-644-3272; *Fax:* 850-644-8817. *E-mail:* intprog@www.fsu.edu. *World Wide Web:* http://www.international.fsu.edu/

INSTITUTE OF SPANISH STUDIES
SEMESTER ABROAD IN VALENCIA, SPAIN

Hosted by Institute of Spanish Studies
Academic Focus • Civilization studies, geography, history, literature, Spanish language and literature.
Program Information • Students attend classes at Institute of Spanish Studies. Field trips to Peñiscola, Sagunto, beaches; optional travel to Barcelona, Mallorca at an extra cost.
Sessions • Fall, spring, yearlong.
Eligibility Requirements • Open to juniors, seniors, graduate students, adults; 2.5 GPA; 2 letters of recommendation; 2 years of college course work in Spanish.

Living Arrangements • Students live in host family homes. Quarters are shared with host institution students. Meals are taken with host family.

Costs (2004-2005) • One term: $6800. Yearlong program: $13,100; includes tuition, housing, all meals, insurance, excursions, student support services. $600 refundable deposit required.

For More Information • Mr. Arturo Sanchez, Director, Institute of Spanish Studies, El Bachiller 13, 46010 Valencia, Spain; *Phone:* +34 96-369-6168; *Fax:* +34 96-361-5189. *E-mail:* arturo@spanish-studies.com. *World Wide Web:* http://www.spanish-studies.com/. Students may also apply through Longwood College, International Affairs, 201 High Street, Farmville, VA 23909.

INTERNATIONAL STUDIES ABROAD
COURSES IN ENGLISH AND SPANISH LANGUAGE

Hosted by Polytechnic University of Valencia

Academic Focus • Economics, engineering, fine/studio arts, management information systems, Spanish language and literature.

Program Information • Students attend classes at Polytechnic University of Valencia. Scheduled travel to Madrid, Toledo; field trips to El Escorial, Barcelona, Granada; optional travel at an extra cost.

Sessions • Fall, spring, yearlong.

Eligibility Requirements • Minimum age 18; open to freshmen, sophomores, juniors, seniors, graduate students, adults; 2.5 GPA; 1 letter of recommendation; good academic standing at home school; transcript; no foreign language proficiency required.

Living Arrangements • Students live in locally rented apartments, host family homes. Quarters are shared with host institution students, students from other programs. Meals are taken with host family, in residences.

Costs (2004-2005) • One term: $6900. Yearlong program: $12,200; includes tuition, housing, some meals, insurance, excursions, student support services, tutoring, laundry service. $200 deposit required. Financial aid available for all students: scholarships, work study, loans, federal financial aid.

For More Information • Spain Site Specialist, International Studies Abroad, 901 West 24th Street, Austin, TX 78705; *Phone:* 800-580-8876; *Fax:* 512-480-8866. *E-mail:* isa@studiesabroad.com. *World Wide Web:* http://www.studiesabroad.com/

INTERNATIONAL STUDIES ABROAD
SPANISH LANGUAGE AND LITERATURE

Hosted by University of Valencia

Academic Focus • Spanish language and literature.

Program Information • Students attend classes at University of Valencia. Scheduled travel to Madrid, Toledo; field trips to Granada, Barcelona, El Escorial; optional travel at an extra cost.

Sessions • Fall, spring, yearlong.

Eligibility Requirements • Minimum age 18; open to freshmen, sophomores, juniors, seniors, graduate students, adults; 2.5 GPA; 1 letter of recommendation; good academic standing at home school; transcript; no foreign language proficiency required.

Living Arrangements • Students live in locally rented apartments, host family homes. Quarters are shared with host institution students, students from other programs. Meals are taken with host family, in residences.

Costs (2004-2005) • One term: $6400. Yearlong program: $12,200; includes tuition, housing, some meals, insurance, excursions, student support services, tutoring, laundry service. $200 deposit required. Financial aid available for all students: scholarships, work study, federal financial aid.

For More Information • Spain Site Specialist, International Studies Abroad, 901 West 24th Street, Austin, TX 78705; *Phone:* 800-580-8876; *Fax:* 512-480-8866. *E-mail:* isa@studiesabroad.com. *World Wide Web:* http://www.studiesabroad.com/

NORTHERN ARIZONA UNIVERSITY
STUDY ABROAD IN SPAIN

Hosted by University of Valencia

Academic Focus • Full curriculum, Spanish studies.

Program Information • Students attend classes at University of Valencia. Field trips to sites in the surrounding areas.

Sessions • Fall, spring, yearlong.

Eligibility Requirements • Minimum age 18; open to sophomores, juniors, seniors, graduate students, adults; 2.5 GPA; 2 letters of recommendation; good academic standing at home school; minimum 2.75 GPA in Spanish; 2 years of college course work in Spanish.

Living Arrangements • Students live in host institution dormitories, locally rented apartments. Quarters are shared with host institution students. Meals are taken as a group, on one's own, in residences, in central dining facility.

Costs (2003-2004) • One term: $4500 for Arizona residents; $6033 for nonresidents. Yearlong program: $9000 for Arizona residents; $12,066 for nonresidents; includes tuition, excursions, international student ID, student support services. $100 application fee. Financial aid available for all students: scholarships, loans.

For More Information • International Office, Northern Arizona University, PO Box 5598, Flagstaff, AZ 86011-5598; *Phone:* 928-523-2409; *Fax:* 928-523-9489. *E-mail:* international.office@nau.edu. *World Wide Web:* http://internationaloffice.nau.edu/

RUTGERS, THE STATE UNIVERSITY OF NEW JERSEY
STUDY ABROAD IN SPAIN

Hosted by University of Valencia

Academic Focus • Full curriculum.

Program Information • Students attend classes at University of Valencia. Scheduled travel to Castile, Andalucía; field trips to Madrid, Barcelona.

Sessions • Spring, yearlong.

Eligibility Requirements • Open to sophomores, juniors, seniors; 2.5 GPA; 2 letters of recommendation; good academic standing at home school; 2 years of college course work in Spanish.

Living Arrangements • Students live in host institution dormitories. Quarters are shared with host institution students. Meals are taken on one's own, in central dining facility.

Costs (2003-2004) • One term: $10,204 for New Jersey residents; $12,854 for nonresidents. Yearlong program: $19,203 for New Jersey residents; $24,503 for nonresidents; includes tuition, housing, some meals, insurance, excursions, student support services. $20 application fee. $750 nonrefundable deposit required. Financial aid available for students from sponsoring institution: scholarships, loans.

For More Information • Ms. Karin Bonello, Regional Coordinator, Rutgers, The State University of New Jersey, 102 College Avenue, New Brunswick, NJ 08901-8543; *Phone:* 732-932-7787; *Fax:* 732-932-8659. *E-mail:* ru_abroad@email.rutgers.edu. *World Wide Web:* http://studyabroad.rutgers.edu/

UNIVERSITY AT ALBANY, STATE UNIVERSITY OF NEW YORK
DIRECT ENROLLMENT AT THE POLYTECHNIC UNIVERSITY OF VALENCIA

Hosted by Polytechnic University of Valencia

Academic Focus • Agriculture, architecture, business administration/management, cartography, computer science, engineering, fine/studio arts, full curriculum, science, telecommunications.

Program Information • Students attend classes at Polytechnic University of Valencia.

Sessions • Fall, spring, yearlong.

Eligibility Requirements • Open to juniors, seniors, graduate students; 3.0 GPA; 2 letters of recommendation; good academic standing at home school; 2.5 years college course work in Spanish or the equivalent.

Living Arrangements • Students live in host institution dormitories, locally rented apartments. Meals are taken on one's own.

Costs (2002-2003) • One term: $6513. Yearlong program: $13,026; includes housing, all meals, student support services, in-state tuition and fees. $150 nonrefundable deposit required. Financial aid available for students from sponsoring institution: all customary sources.

For More Information • University at Albany, State University of New York, Office of International Education, LI 66, Albany, NY 12222; *Phone:* 518-442-3525; *Fax:* 518-442-3338. *E-mail:* intled@uamail.albany.edu. *World Wide Web:* http://www.albany.edu/intled/

UNIVERSITY AT ALBANY, STATE UNIVERSITY OF NEW YORK
LANGUAGE AND CULTURAL STUDIES IN ENGLISH AT THE AIP LANGUAGE INSTITUTE

Hosted by A.I.P. Language Institute

Academic Focus • Art history, film and media studies, history, international affairs, international business, liberal studies, Spanish language and literature, Spanish studies.

Program Information • Students attend classes at A.I.P. Language Institute. Scheduled travel to Morocco; field trips to Peñíscola, Morella, Ibiza; optional travel to Madrid, Barcelona at an extra cost.

Sessions • Fall, spring, yearlong.

Eligibility Requirements • Open to sophomores, juniors, seniors, adults; 2.5 GPA; 2 letters of recommendation; good academic standing at home school; no foreign language proficiency required.

Living Arrangements • Students live in host family homes. Meals are taken with host family, in residences.

Costs (2002-2003) • One term: $8383 for fall term; $8523 for spring. Yearlong program: $16,906; includes housing, all meals, excursions, student support services, in-state tuition and fees, Madrid/Valencia transfer. $150 nonrefundable deposit required. Financial aid available for students from sponsoring institution: all customary sources.

For More Information • University at Albany, State University of New York, Office of International Education, LI 66, Albany, NY 12222; *Phone:* 518-442-3525; *Fax:* 518-442-3338. *E-mail:* intled@uamail.albany.edu. *World Wide Web:* http://www.albany.edu/intled/

VALLADOLID

UNIVERSITY OF WISCONSIN–STEVENS POINT
SEMESTER IN SPAIN

Hosted by University of Valladolid

Academic Focus • Cultural studies, economics, history, literature, Spanish language and literature.

Program Information • Students attend classes at University of Valladolid. Scheduled travel to Madrid; field trips to Toledo, Salamanca; optional travel to France, Africa, Italy at an extra cost.

Sessions • Spring.

Eligibility Requirements • Open to sophomores, juniors, seniors; 2.5 GPA; 3 letters of recommendation; good academic standing at home school; 2 years of college course work in Spanish.

Living Arrangements • Students live in host institution dormitories, locally rented apartments, host family homes. Quarters are shared with host institution students, students from other programs. Meals are taken on one's own, with host family, in residences, in central dining facility, in restaurants.

Costs (2003-2004) • One term: $5300 for Wisconsin residents; $10,500 for nonresidents (estimated); includes tuition, housing, all meals, excursions, international airfare, books and class materials. $15 application fee. $150 nonrefundable deposit required. Financial aid available for all students: scholarships, work study, loans.

For More Information • Mr. Mark Koepke, Associate Director, University of Wisconsin–Stevens Point, International Programs

Office, Stevens Point, WI 54481; *Phone:* 715-346-2717; *Fax:* 715-346-3591. *E-mail:* intlprog@uwsp.edu. *World Wide Web:* http://www.uwsp.edu/studyabroad/

VIC

UNIVERSITY OF NORTH CAROLINA AT WILMINGTON
SEMESTER IN SPAIN

Hosted by University of Vic
Academic Focus • Political science and government, Spanish language and literature, Spanish studies, translation.
Program Information • Students attend classes at University of Vic. Field trips to attractions in and around Barcelona, museums, exhibitions, the Pyrenees mountains; optional travel to Madrid, other European sites at an extra cost.
Sessions • Spring.
Eligibility Requirements • Minimum age 19; open to sophomores, juniors, seniors, graduate students, adults; 2.75 GPA; 2 letters of recommendation; good academic standing at home school; 2 years of college course work in Spanish.
Living Arrangements • Students live in host institution dormitories. Quarters are shared with host institution students. Meals are taken on one's own, in residences.
Costs (2002-2003) • One term: $6800; includes tuition, housing, all meals, insurance, excursions, student support services. $200 nonrefundable deposit required. Financial aid available for students from sponsoring institution: scholarships, loans.
For More Information • Ms. Elizabeth A. Adams, Education Abroad Coordinator, Office of International Programs, University of North Carolina at Wilmington, 601 South College Road, Wilmington, NC 28403; *Phone:* 910-962-3685; *Fax:* 910-962-4053. *E-mail:* adamse@uncw.edu. *World Wide Web:* http://www.uncw.edu/intprogs/

ZARAGOZA

UNIVERSITY OF IDAHO
SEMESTER IN ZARAGOZA PROGRAM

Hosted by University of Zaragoza
Academic Focus • Full curriculum.
Program Information • Students attend classes at University of Zaragoza.
Sessions • Fall, spring, yearlong.
Eligibility Requirements • Open to sophomores, juniors, seniors, graduate students; good academic standing at home school; fluency in Spanish.
Living Arrangements • Students live in host institution dormitories, locally rented apartments. Quarters are shared with host institution students, students from other programs. Meals are taken on one's own, in residences, in central dining facility.
Costs (2003-2004) • One term: $2500. Yearlong program: $5000; includes tuition, student support services. $100 application fee. $200 refundable deposit required. Financial aid available for students from sponsoring institution: scholarships, loans.
For More Information • Ms. Amy Bergmann, Advisor, University of Idaho, Room 209, Morrill Hall, Moscow, ID 83844-3013; *Phone:* 208-885-7870; *Fax:* 208-885-2859. *E-mail:* abroad@uidaho.edu. *World Wide Web:* http://www.ets.uidaho.edu/ipo/abroad/

SWEDEN

GÖTEBORG

CORNELL UNIVERSITY
CORNELL SWEDISH PRACTICUM IN CHILDHOOD, FAMILY, AND SOCIAL POLICY
Held at University of Göteborg

Academic Focus • Education, political science and government, public policy, social sciences, social services, sociology, Swedish studies.
Program Information • Classes are held on the campus of University of Göteborg. Faculty members are local instructors hired by the sponsor. Scheduled travel to Stockholm; field trips to the Swedish coastline.
Sessions • Spring.
Eligibility Requirements • Minimum age 18; open to juniors, seniors; 3.0 GPA; 2 letters of recommendation; good academic standing at home school; experience working with children; 0.5 years of college course work in Swedish.
Living Arrangements • Students live in host institution dormitories. Quarters are shared with host institution students. Meals are taken on one's own, in residences.
Costs (2005) • One term: $17,650; includes tuition, housing, excursions, international airfare, student support services. $300 nonrefundable deposit required. Financial aid available for students from sponsoring institution: scholarships, loans.
For More Information • Cornell Abroad, Cornell University, 300 Caldwell Hall, Ithaca, NY 14853-7601; *Phone:* 607-255-6224; *Fax:* 607-255-8700. *E-mail:* cuabroad@cornell.edu. *World Wide Web:* http://www.cuabroad.cornell.edu/

UNIVERSITY AT ALBANY, STATE UNIVERSITY OF NEW YORK
DIRECT ENROLLMENT AT GÖTEBORG UNIVERSITY

Hosted by University of Göteborg
Academic Focus • Art, business administration/management, economics, liberal studies, Scandinavian studies, science, social sciences, Swedish.
Program Information • Students attend classes at University of Göteborg.
Sessions • Fall, spring, yearlong.
Eligibility Requirements • Open to sophomores, juniors, seniors, graduate students; 3.0 GPA; 2 letters of recommendation; good academic standing at home school; foreign language requirement dependent on track chosen.
Living Arrangements • Students live in host institution dormitories, locally rented apartments. Meals are taken on one's own, in residences.
Costs (2003-2004) • One term: $5828. Yearlong program: $11,655; includes housing, all meals, student support services, in-state tuition and fees. $150 nonrefundable deposit required. Financial aid available for students from sponsoring institution: all customary sources.
For More Information • University at Albany, State University of New York, Office of International Education, LI 66, Albany, NY 12222; *Phone:* 518-442-3525; *Fax:* 518-442-3338. *E-mail:* intled@uamail.albany.edu. *World Wide Web:* http://www.albany.edu/intled/

JÖNKÖPING

NORTHERN ARIZONA UNIVERSITY
STUDY ABROAD IN SWEDEN

Hosted by Jönköping International Business School
Academic Focus • Business administration/management, engineering, entrepreneurship.
Program Information • Students attend classes at Jönköping International Business School. Optional travel at an extra cost.
Sessions • Fall, spring, yearlong.
Eligibility Requirements • Minimum age 18; open to sophomores, juniors, seniors; major in business/management, engineering; 2.5 GPA; 2 letters of recommendation; no foreign language proficiency required.
Living Arrangements • Students live in host institution dormitories. Quarters are shared with host institution students. Meals are taken on one's own, in residences.
Costs (2003-2004) • One term: $1754 for Arizona residents; $6014 for nonresidents. Yearlong program: $3508 for Arizona residents; $12,028 for nonresidents; includes tuition, international student ID, fees. $100 application fee. Financial aid available for all students: scholarships, loans, Pell grants, Supplemental Educational Opportunity Grant (SEOG).

For More Information • Ms. Marilyn Allen, Advisor, Northern Arizona University, PO Box 5598, Flagstaff, AZ 86011-5598; *Phone:* 928-523-2409; *Fax:* 928-523-9489. *E-mail:* international.office@nau. edu. *World Wide Web:* http://internationaloffice.nau.edu/

KARLSTAD
KARLSTAD UNIVERSITY
STUDY IN ENGLISH

Hosted by Karlstad University

Academic Focus • Area studies, biological/life sciences, business administration/management, chemical sciences, communications, computer science, economics, education, information science, marketing, mathematics, physics, political science and government.
Program Information • Students attend classes at Karlstad University.
Sessions • Fall, spring, yearlong.
Eligibility Requirements • Open to juniors, seniors; 1 letter of recommendation; good academic standing at home school; at least one year of academic study in a relevant area; no foreign language proficiency required.
Living Arrangements • Students live in host institution dormitories, locally rented apartments, host institution apartments. Quarters are shared with host institution students. Meals are taken on one's own, in central dining facility.
Costs (2002-2003) • One term: $3700. Yearlong program: $7500; includes housing, all meals, books and class materials, spending money. $800 nonrefundable deposit required.
For More Information • Mr. Michael Cooper, Director of International Relations, Karlstad University, 651 88 Karlstad, Sweden; *Phone:* +46 54-7001385; *Fax:* +46 54-83-32-70. *E-mail:* michael.cooper@kau.se. *World Wide Web:* http://www.kau.se/

LULEÅ
UNIVERSITY OF IDAHO
SEMESTER IN SWEDEN

Hosted by Luleå University

Academic Focus • Business administration/management, computer science, education, engineering, geology, music, political science and government, social sciences.
Program Information • Students attend classes at Luleå University. Field trips to other areas in Sweden, a traditional market at Jokkmok, mines, ski trips; optional travel to Vasa at an extra cost.
Sessions • Fall, spring, yearlong.
Eligibility Requirements • Open to juniors, seniors, graduate students; good academic standing at home school; no foreign language proficiency required.
Living Arrangements • Students live in host institution dormitories, locally rented apartments, program-owned apartments. Quarters are shared with host institution students, students from other programs. Meals are taken on one's own, in residences, in central dining facility.
Costs (2003-2004) • One term: $2500. Yearlong program: $5000; includes tuition, student support services. $100 application fee. $200 refundable deposit required. Financial aid available for students from sponsoring institution: scholarships, loans.
For More Information • Ms. Amy Bergmann, Advisor, University of Idaho, Room 209, Morrill Hall, Moscow, ID 83844-3013; *Phone:* 208-885-7870; *Fax:* 208-885-2859. *E-mail:* abroad@uidaho.edu. *World Wide Web:* http://www.ets.uidaho.edu/ipo/abroad/

LUND
ISU PROGRAMS–FOLKUNIVERSITETET
STUDY IN SWEDEN

Hosted by ISU Programs–Folkuniversitetet
Academic Focus • Swedish.
Program Information • Students attend classes at ISU Programs–Folkuniversitetet.
Sessions • Fall, spring, yearlong.
Eligibility Requirements • Minimum age 18; open to freshmen, sophomores, juniors, seniors, graduate students, adults; 2.7 GPA;

good academic standing at home school; high school diploma; no foreign language proficiency required.
Living Arrangements • Students live in host institution dormitories, locally rented apartments, host family homes. Quarters are shared with host institution students, students from other programs. Meals are taken on one's own, in residences.
Costs (2003-2004) • One term: Sk23,200. Yearlong program: Sk43,200; includes tuition, books and class materials, student support services. Sk60 application fee.
For More Information • Ms. Jenny Nilsson, ISU Course Coordinator, ISU Programs–Folkuniversitetet, Box 2116, 220 02 Lund, Sweden; *Phone:* +46 46-19-77-72; *Fax:* +46 46-97-008. *E-mail:* isu.lund@folkuniversitetet.se. *World Wide Web:* http://www. tolkuniversitetet.se/isu/

ÖREBRO
NORTHERN ARIZONA UNIVERSITY
STUDY ABROAD IN SWEDEN

Hosted by Högskolani Örebro
Academic Focus • Business administration/management, communications, education, liberal studies, political science and government, Swedish.
Program Information • Students attend classes at Högskolani Örebro.
Sessions • Fall, spring, yearlong.
Eligibility Requirements • Minimum age 18; open to sophomores, juniors, seniors; 2.5 GPA; 2 letters of recommendation; good academic standing at home school; no foreign language proficiency required.
Living Arrangements • Students live in host institution dormitories, locally rented apartments. Quarters are shared with students from other programs. Meals are taken on one's own, in central dining facility, in restaurants.
Costs (2003-2004) • One term: $1754 for Arizona residents; $6014 for nonresidents. Yearlong program: $3508 for Arizona residents; $12,028 for nonresidents; includes tuition, international student ID, fees. $100 application fee. Financial aid available for all students: scholarships, loans, Pell grants, Supplemental Educational Opportunity Grant (SEOG).
For More Information • Ms. Marilyn Allen, Advisor, Northern Arizona University, PO Box 5598, Flagstaff, AZ 86011-5598; *Phone:* 928-523-2409; *Fax:* 928-523-9489. *E-mail:* international.office@nau. edu. *World Wide Web:* http://internationaloffice.nau.edu/

STOCKHOLM
SWEDISH PROGRAM
SWEDISH PROGRAM

Hosted by Stockholm University
Academic Focus • Art, art history, comparative history, comparative literature, creative writing, economics, education, environmental science/studies, film and media studies, international affairs, literature, political science and government, psychology, public policy, sociology, Swedish, Swedish studies, women's studies.
Program Information • Students attend classes at Stockholm University. Scheduled travel to an Archipelago boat tour, Rattvik, Mora, Leksand; field trips to government agencies, museums, companies; optional travel to Gotland at an extra cost.
Sessions • Fall, spring, yearlong.
Eligibility Requirements • Open to sophomores, juniors, seniors; 2 letters of recommendation; good academic standing at home school; no foreign language proficiency required.
Living Arrangements • Students live in host institution dormitories, locally rented apartments, host family homes. Quarters are shared with host institution students. Meals are taken on one's own, with host family, in residences.
Costs (2003-2004) • One term: $17,775. Yearlong program: $33,525; includes tuition, housing, all meals, excursions, student support services. $35 application fee. $750 nonrefundable deposit required. Financial aid available for all students: scholarships.
For More Information • Dr. Kenneth Wagner, Executive Director, The Swedish Program, Swedish Program, Hamilton College, 198 College Hill Road, Clinton, NY 13323; *Phone:* 315-737-0123; *Fax:* 315-737-0127. *E-mail:* swedishprg@aol.com. *World Wide Web:* http://www.swedishprogram.org/

UPPSALA

UNIVERSITY OF MIAMI
UPPSALA UNIVERSITY, SWEDEN

Hosted by Uppsala University
Academic Focus • Economics, peace and conflict studies, political science and government, sociology, Swedish studies.
Program Information • Students attend classes at Uppsala University.
Sessions • Fall, spring, yearlong.
Eligibility Requirements • Minimum age 18; open to sophomores, juniors, seniors; 3.0 GPA; 2 letters of recommendation; good academic standing at home school; essay; official transcript; no foreign language proficiency required.
Living Arrangements • Students live in host institution dormitories. Quarters are shared with host institution students, students from other programs. Meals are taken on one's own, in residences.
Costs (2003-2004) • One term: $12,979. Yearlong program: $25,838; includes tuition. $40 application fee. $500 nonrefundable deposit required. Financial aid available for students from sponsoring institution: scholarships, loans.
For More Information • Ms. Elyse Resnick, Assistant Director, University of Miami, International Education and Exchange Programs, 5050 Brunson Drive, Allen Hall 212, PO Box 248005, Coral Gables, FL 33124-1610; *Phone:* 305-284-3434; *Fax:* 305-284-4235. *E-mail:* ieep@miami.edu. *World Wide Web:* http://www.studyabroad.miami.edu/

VÄXJÖ

UNIVERSITY OF IDAHO
SEMESTER IN SWEDEN

Hosted by Växjö University

Academic Focus • Biological/life sciences, business administration/management, communications, computer science, education, human resources, political science and government, Swedish, Swedish studies.
Program Information • Students attend classes at Växjö University. Field trips to cultural sites near Växjö; optional travel to mainland Europe at an extra cost.
Sessions • Fall, spring, yearlong.
Eligibility Requirements • Open to sophomores, juniors, seniors; good academic standing at home school; no foreign language proficiency required.
Living Arrangements • Students live in host institution dormitories, locally rented apartments, host family homes. Quarters are shared with host institution students, students from other programs. Meals are taken on one's own, with host family, in residences, in central dining facility.
Costs (2003-2004) • One term: $2500. Yearlong program: $5000; includes tuition, student support services. $100 application fee. $200 refundable deposit required. Financial aid available for students from sponsoring institution: scholarships, loans.
For More Information • Ms. Amy Bergmann, Advisor, University of Idaho, Room 209, Morrill Hall, Moscow, ID 83844-3013; *Phone:* 208-885-7870; *Fax:* 208-885-2859. *E-mail:* abroad@uidaho.edu. *World Wide Web:* http://www.ets.uidaho.edu/ipo/abroad/

UNIVERSITY STUDIES ABROAD CONSORTIUM
FULL CURRICULUM STUDIES: VÄXJÖ, SWEDEN

Hosted by Växjö University
Academic Focus • Full curriculum.
Program Information • Students attend classes at Växjö University. Field trips.
Sessions • Fall, spring, yearlong.

SWEDEN
Växjö

Eligibility Requirements • Minimum age 18; open to freshmen, sophomores, juniors, seniors, graduate students, adults; 3.0 GPA; no foreign language proficiency required.
Living Arrangements • Students live in host institution dormitories, host family homes. Quarters are shared with host institution students, students from other programs. Meals are taken on one's own, with host family, in residences, in restaurants.
Costs (2005-2006) • One term: $3980. Yearlong program: $6980; includes tuition, insurance, student support services. $50 application fee. $150 refundable deposit required. Financial aid available for all students: scholarships, loans.
For More Information • University Studies Abroad Consortium, USAC/323, Reno, NV 89557-0093; *Phone:* 775-784-6569; *Fax:* 775-784-6010. *E-mail:* usac@unr.edu. *World Wide Web:* http://usac.unr.edu/

SWITZERLAND
FRIBOURG
AMERICAN COLLEGE PROGRAM AT THE UNIVERSITY OF FRIBOURG
AMERICAN COLLEGE PROGRAM AT THE UNIVERSITY OF FRIBOURG

Hosted by American College Program at the University of Fribourg
Academic Focus • Full curriculum.
Program Information • Students attend classes at American College Program at the University of Fribourg. Scheduled travel to Zurich, Lucerne, Interlaken, Pilatus; field trips to Gstaad, Lausanne, Geneva, Bern, Montreux; optional travel to Paris, Berlin at an extra cost.
Sessions • Fall, spring, yearlong.
Eligibility Requirements • Open to sophomores, juniors, seniors; 3.0 GPA; 2 letters of recommendation; good academic standing at home school; 2 years of college course work in French or German.
Living Arrangements • Students live in host institution dormitories, host family homes. Quarters are shared with host institution students. Meals are taken on one's own, with host family, in residences, in restaurants.
Costs (2004-2005) • One term: $8900. Yearlong program: $16,900; includes tuition, housing, some meals, insurance, excursions, international airfare, international student ID, student support services, 4-week intensive language practicum. $500 nonrefundable deposit required. Financial aid available for all students: scholarships.
For More Information • Mr. Andrej N. Lushnycky, Executive Director, American College Program at the University of Fribourg, Avenue de Beauregard 13, Case Postal 102, 1701 Fribourg, Switzerland; *Phone:* +41 26-300-8190; *Fax:* +41 26-300-9690. *E-mail:* acp@unifr.ch. *World Wide Web:* http://www.unifr.ch/acp/

GENEVA
BOSTON UNIVERSITY
GENEVA INTERNSHIP PROGRAM

Hosted by University of Geneva
Academic Focus • Full curriculum.
Program Information • Students attend classes at University of Geneva.
Sessions • Spring.
Eligibility Requirements • Open to juniors, seniors; 3.0 GPA; 2 letters of recommendation; good academic standing at home school; essay; approval of participation; transcript; no foreign language proficiency required.

Living Arrangements • Students live in host institution dormitories. Meals are taken on one's own, in residences.
Costs (2005) • One term: $18,084; includes tuition, housing, excursions, international airfare, books and class materials, internship placement. $50 application fee. $400 nonrefundable deposit required. Financial aid available for all students: scholarships, loans.
For More Information • Division of International Programs, Boston University, 232 Bay State Road, Boston, MA 02215; *Phone:* 617-353-9888; *Fax:* 617-353-5402. *E-mail:* abroad@bu.edu. *World Wide Web:* http://www.bu.edu/abroad/

KENT STATE UNIVERSITY
GENEVA SEMESTER

Hosted by Kent State University–John Knox International Center
Academic Focus • Economics, French language and literature, international affairs, international business.
Program Information • Students attend classes at Kent State University–John Knox International Center. Scheduled travel to Brussels, Brugge, Strasbourg, The Hague; field trips to Bern; optional travel.
Sessions • Fall, spring.
Eligibility Requirements • Minimum age 18; open to sophomores, juniors, seniors; 2.5 GPA; 2 letters of recommendation; good academic standing at home school; no foreign language proficiency required.
Living Arrangements • Students live in host institution dormitories, host family homes. Quarters are shared with host institution students. Meals are taken as a group, in central dining facility.
Costs (2002-2003) • One term: $7869 for Ohio residents; $14,781 for nonresidents; includes tuition, some meals, insurance, excursions, international airfare, books and class materials, international student ID, student support services, Eurail pass. $30 application fee. $1000 refundable deposit required. Financial aid available for students from sponsoring institution: scholarships, loans.
For More Information • Dr. Alan Coe, Assistant Director, Center for International and Comparative Programs, Kent State University, PO Box 5190, Kent, OH 44242-0001; *Phone:* 330-672-7980; *Fax:* 330-672-4025. *E-mail:* acoe@kent.edu. *World Wide Web:* http://www.kent.edu/cicp/geneva/

SCHOOL FOR INTERNATIONAL TRAINING, SIT STUDY ABROAD
SWITZERLAND: INTERNATIONAL STUDIES, ORGANIZATIONS, AND SOCIAL JUSTICE

Academic Focus • Economics, European studies, French language and literature, international affairs, peace and conflict studies, political science and government, refugee studies.
Program Information • Faculty members are drawn from the sponsor's U.S. staff and local instructors hired by the sponsor. Scheduled travel to Lugano, Bern, Paris; field trips to United Nations headquarters, International Red Cross Museum, international organizations.
Sessions • Fall, spring.
Eligibility Requirements • Open to sophomores, juniors, seniors; course work in international relations, government, or another relevant academic discipline; 2.5 GPA; 2 letters of recommendation; good academic standing at home school; no foreign language proficiency required.
Living Arrangements • Students live in host family homes, hotels. Meals are taken as a group, on one's own, with host family, in residences, in restaurants.
Costs (2003-2004) • One term: $13,650; includes tuition, housing, all meals, insurance, excursions, international student ID. $50 application fee. $400 nonrefundable deposit required. Financial aid available for all students: scholarships.
For More Information • School for International Training, SIT Study Abroad, Kipling Road, Brattleboro, VT 05302-0676; *Phone:* 888-272-7881; *Fax:* 802-258-3296. *E-mail:* studyabroad@sit.edu. *World Wide Web:* http://www.sit.edu/studyabroad/

SMITH COLLEGE
JUNIOR YEAR IN GENEVA

Hosted by Smith College Center, University of Geneva

Academic Focus • Anthropology, art history, economics, European studies, French language and literature, French studies, history, international affairs, political science and government, social sciences.

Program Information • Students attend classes at Smith College Center, University of Geneva. Scheduled travel to the Loire Valley, Burgundy, Paris; field trips to the Geneva region, Basel, Lyon.

Sessions • Yearlong.

Eligibility Requirements • Open to juniors, seniors; 3.0 GPA; 3 letters of recommendation; good academic standing at home school; fluency in French.

Living Arrangements • Students live in host institution dormitories. Quarters are shared with host institution students. Meals are taken on one's own, in residences, in central dining facility.

Costs (2004-2005) • Yearlong program: $39,814; includes tuition, housing, all meals, insurance, excursions, books and class materials. $35 application fee. $300 refundable deposit required. Financial aid available for students from sponsoring institution: scholarships, loans.

For More Information • Office for International Study, Smith College, Clark Hall 305, Northampton, MA 01063; *Phone:* 413-585-4905; *Fax:* 413-585-4906. *E-mail:* studyabroad@smith.edu. *World Wide Web:* http://www.smith.edu/studyabroad/

WEBSTER UNIVERSITY
WEBSTER UNIVERSITY IN GENEVA

Hosted by Webster University–Geneva

Academic Focus • Business administration/management, human resources, international business, labor and industrial relations, marketing, political science and government, refugee studies.

Program Information • Students attend classes at Webster University–Geneva. Field trips to skiing, hiking; optional travel at an extra cost.

Sessions • Fall, spring, yearlong.

Eligibility Requirements • Minimum age 17; open to sophomores, juniors, seniors, graduate students, adults; 2.5 GPA; 1 letter of recommendation; good academic standing at home school; no foreign language proficiency required.

Living Arrangements • Students live in host institution dormitories. Quarters are shared with host institution students, students from other programs. Meals are taken as a group, on one's own, in residences, in central dining facility, in restaurants.

Costs (2003-2004) • One term: $8240. Yearlong program: $15,980; includes tuition, insurance, international student ID, student support services. $30 application fee. $165 refundable deposit required. Financial aid available for students from sponsoring institution: scholarships, loans.

For More Information • Mr. Mark A. Beirn, Coordinator, Office of Study Abroad, Webster University, 470 East Lockwood Avenue, St. Louis, MO 63119; *Phone:* 314-968-6988; *Fax:* 314-968-5938. *E-mail:* worldview@webster.edu. *World Wide Web:* http://www.webster.edu/intl/sa/

LAUSANNE
UNIVERSITY OF MIAMI
UNIVERSITÉ DE LAUSANNE

Hosted by University of Lausanne

Academic Focus • Full curriculum.

Program Information • Students attend classes at University of Lausanne.

Sessions • Spring, yearlong.

SWITZERLAND
Lausanne

Eligibility Requirements • Minimum age 18; open to sophomores, juniors, seniors; 3.0 GPA; 2 letters of recommendation; good academic standing at home school; 3 years college course work in French or near fluency.

Living Arrangements • Students live in host institution dormitories. Quarters are shared with host institution students. Meals are taken on one's own, in central dining facility, in restaurants.

Costs (2003-2004) • One term: $12,919. Yearlong program: $25,838; includes tuition, student support services. $40 application fee. $500 nonrefundable deposit required. Financial aid available for students from sponsoring institution: scholarships, loans.

For More Information • Ms. Diane Mahin, Study Abroad Advisor, University of Miami, International Education and Exchange Programs, 5050 Brunson Drive, Allen Hall 212, PO Box 248005, Coral Gables, FL 33124-1610; *Phone:* 305-284-3434; *Fax:* 305-284-4235. *E-mail:* ieep@miami.edu. *World Wide Web:* http://www.studyabroad.miami.edu/

LEYSIN
SCHILLER INTERNATIONAL UNIVERSITY AMERICAN COLLEGE OF SWITZERLAND
STUDY ABROAD PROGRAM, UNDERGRADUATE AND GRADUATE PROGRAM, LEYSIN CAMPUS

Hosted by Schiller International University American College of Switzerland

Academic Focus • Art, computer science, economics, English, French language and literature, history, hotel and restaurant management, international affairs, international business, mathematics, political science and government, social sciences.

Program Information • Students attend classes at Schiller International University American College of Switzerland. Scheduled travel to Florence; field trips to Gruyère, Lausaune, Vevey, Geneva; optional travel to France, Germany, Italy at an extra cost.

Sessions • Fall, spring, yearlong.

Eligibility Requirements • Minimum age 17; open to freshmen, sophomores, juniors, seniors, graduate students; 2.0 GPA; no foreign language proficiency required.

Living Arrangements • Students live in host institution dormitories, locally rented apartments, hotels. Quarters are shared with host institution students, students from other programs. Meals are taken as a group, on one's own, in residences, in central dining facility.

Costs (2002-2003) • One term: SwF20,600. Yearlong program: SwF51,200; includes tuition, housing, all meals, lab equipment, student support services. SwF1000 nonrefundable deposit required. Financial aid available for all students: scholarships, loans, Exchange Student Scholarship Award, federal grants, graduate assistantship.

For More Information • Ms. Kamala Dontamsetti, Admissions Office, Florida Campus, Schiller International University American College of Switzerland, 453 Edgewater Drive, Dunedin, FL 34698; *Phone:* 727-736-5082 Ext. 240; *Fax:* 727-734-0359. *E-mail:* admissions@schiller.edu. *World Wide Web:* http://www.schiller.edu/

LUGANO
COLLEGE CONSORTIUM FOR INTERNATIONAL STUDIES–EMPIRE STATE COLLEGE OF THE STATE UNIVERSITY OF NEW YORK
SEMESTER PROGRAM IN SWITZERLAND

Hosted by Franklin College Switzerland

Academic Focus • Full curriculum.

Program Information • Students attend classes at Franklin College Switzerland. Optional travel to Italy, France, Germany, Greece, Eastern Europe, Asia, Africa at an extra cost.

Sessions • Fall, spring, yearlong.

Eligibility Requirements • Minimum age 18; open to freshmen, sophomores, juniors, seniors; 2.5 GPA; 3 letters of recommendation; good academic standing at home school; essay; no foreign language proficiency required.

Living Arrangements • Students live in program-owned apartments. Quarters are shared with host institution students. Meals are taken on one's own, in residences, in central dining facility, in restaurants.

Costs (2003-2004) • One term: $13,500 (estimated) plus mandatory Swiss health insurance. Yearlong program: $27,000; includes tuition, housing, student support services, student activity and administrative fees, academic travel. $300 nonrefundable deposit required. Financial aid available for students from sponsoring institution: loans, Pell grants, TAP for New York State residents.

For More Information • Dr. Kenneth Abrams, Director for International Programs, College Consortium for International Studies, 28 Union Avenue, Saratoga Springs, NY 12866; *Phone:* 518-587-2100 Ext. 231; *Fax:* 518-580-0287. *E-mail:* international@esc.edu. *World Wide Web:* http://www.ccisabroad.org/

FRANKLIN COLLEGE SWITZERLAND
FRANKLIN COLLEGE SWITZERLAND

Hosted by Franklin College Switzerland

Academic Focus • Full curriculum.

Program Information • Students attend classes at Franklin College Switzerland. Scheduled travel to Rome, southern Italy, London, Madrid, Barcelona, Paris, Brussels, Strasbourg, Prague, Budapest, Greece; field trips to Milan, Torino, Lugano and environs; optional travel to Florence, Munich, Venice, Zurich, Geneva, Nice, Paris, Rome at an extra cost.

Sessions • Fall, spring, yearlong.

Eligibility Requirements • Minimum age 18; open to freshmen, sophomores, juniors, seniors, adults; 2.5 GPA; 1 letter of recommendation; good academic standing at home school; no foreign language proficiency required.

Living Arrangements • Students live in host institution dormitories, program-owned apartments. Quarters are shared with host institution students. Meals are taken in residences, in central dining facility.

Costs (2004-2005) • One term: $17,985. Yearlong program: $35,970; includes tuition, housing, some meals, insurance, 2-week academic travel trip each semester. $50 application fee. $300 nonrefundable deposit required. Financial aid available for all students: scholarships, work study, loans.

For More Information • Ms. Karen Ballard, Director of Admissions, Franklin College Switzerland, U.S. Office, Suite 411, 91-31 Queens Boulevard, Elmhurst, NY 11378-5506; *Phone:* 718-335-6800; *Fax:* 718-385-6733. *E-mail:* info@fc.edu. *World Wide Web:* http://www.fc.edu/. Students may also apply through CCIS–State University of New York Empire State College, International Programs, 320 Broadway, Saratoga Springs, NY 12866.

MORE ABOUT THE PROGRAM

Franklin College is located in Lugano, Switzerland, overlooking Italy to the south and the foothills of the Swiss Alps to the north. Famous for its scenic beauty and its mild Mediterranean climate, Lugano is an ideal base from which to explore Europe. Franklin College is a 4-year liberal arts college that offers B.A. degrees in a variety of majors and has a full range of courses available for study abroad students. A special feature of the program is the 2-week Academic Travel Program each semester. Students travel with their professors to destinations in Eastern and Western Europe, Asia, Africa, and South America.

NEUCHÂTEL
IHTTI SCHOOL OF HOTEL MANAGEMENT NEUCHÂTEL
BA (HONS) IN INTERNATIONAL HOSPITALITY AND TOURISM MANAGEMENT

Hosted by IHTTI School of Hotel Management Neuchâtel

Academic Focus • Hospitality services, hotel and restaurant management.

Program Information • Students attend classes at IHTTI School of Hotel Management Neuchâtel. Field trips to Swiss companies.

Sessions • Fall, spring.

Eligibility Requirements • Minimum age 18; open to precollege students, freshmen, sophomores, juniors, seniors, graduate students; good academic standing at home school; no foreign language proficiency required.

Living Arrangements • Students live in program-owned houses. Quarters are shared with host institution students. Meals are taken as a group, in central dining facility.

Costs (2002-2003) • One term: SwF25,000; includes tuition, housing, all meals, insurance, excursions, books and class materials, lab equipment, international student ID, student support services. SwF500 application fee. SwF500 refundable deposit required.

For More Information • Ms. Maria Baks, Head of Admission, IHTTI School of Hotel Management Neuchâtel, St. Alban-Anlage 64, PO Box IM 4006, CH-4006 Basel, Switzerland; *Phone:* +4161-3123094; *Fax:* +4161-3126035. *E-mail:* headoffice@ihtti.ch. *World Wide Web:* http://www.ihtti.ch/

TANZANIA

ARUSHA

SCHOOL FOR INTERNATIONAL TRAINING, SIT STUDY ABROAD
TANZANIA: WILDLIFE ECOLOGY AND CONSERVATION

Academic Focus • African studies, anthropology, biological/life sciences, conservation studies, ecology, environmental science/ studies, Swahili, wildlife studies.

Program Information • Faculty members are drawn from the sponsor's U.S. staff and local instructors hired by the sponsor. Scheduled travel to Ngorongoro Crater, Serengeti, a Maasai village; field trips to national parks, conservation areas.

Sessions • Fall, spring.

Eligibility Requirements • Open to sophomores, juniors, seniors; course work in environmental studies, ecology, biology, or related field; 2.5 GPA; 2 letters of recommendation; good academic standing at home school; no foreign language proficiency required.

Living Arrangements • Students live in host family homes, hotels, campsites. Meals are taken as a group, on one's own, with host family, in residences, in restaurants.

Costs (2003-2004) • One term: $12,775; includes tuition, housing, all meals, insurance, excursions. $50 application fee. $400 nonrefundable deposit required. Financial aid available for all students: scholarships.

For More Information • School for International Training, SIT Study Abroad, Kipling Road, Brattleboro, VT 05302-0676; *Phone:* 888-272-7881; *Fax:* 802-258-3296. *E-mail:* studyabroad@sit.edu. *World Wide Web:* http://www.sit.edu/studyabroad/

DAR ES SALAAM

ASSOCIATED COLLEGES OF THE MIDWEST
ACM NATION BUILDING AND DEVELOPMENT IN AFRICA PROGRAM

Hosted by University of Dar Es Salaam

Academic Focus • African languages and literature, anthropology, economics, history, political science and government, Swahili.

Program Information • Students attend classes at University of Dar Es Salaam. Scheduled travel; field trips to Bagamoyo, Zanzibar; optional travel to Mt. Kilimanjaro, Zanzibar, Mount Meru Game Preserve, Pemba at an extra cost.

Sessions • Spring.

Eligibility Requirements • Open to sophomores, juniors, seniors; 3 letters of recommendation; good academic standing at home school; no foreign language proficiency required.

Living Arrangements • Students live in host institution dormitories, host family homes. Meals are taken with host family, in residences.

Costs (2004) • One term: contact sponsor for cost. $400 nonrefundable deposit required.

For More Information • Ms. Whitney Kidd, Program Associate, ACM Zimbabwe Program, Associated Colleges of the Midwest, 205 West Wacker Drive, Suite 1300, Chicago, IL 60606; *Phone:* 312-263-5000; *Fax:* 312-263-5879. *E-mail:* acm@acm.edu. *World Wide Web:* http://www.acm.edu/

ASSOCIATED COLLEGES OF THE MIDWEST
ACM TANZANIA PROGRAM

Hosted by University of Dar Es Salaam

Academic Focus • Anthropology, archaeology, biological/life sciences, ecology, environmental science/studies, geology, Swahili, zoology.

Program Information • Students attend classes at University of Dar Es Salaam. Scheduled travel to Olduvai, Serengeti, Ngorongoro, Laetoli; field trips to Bagamoyo, Zanzibar; optional travel to Zanzibar, Mount Kilimanjaro, Mount Meru Game Preserve, Pemba at an extra cost.

Sessions • Fall.

Eligibility Requirements • Open to sophomores, juniors, seniors; 3 letters of recommendation; good academic standing at home school; no foreign language proficiency required.

Living Arrangements • Students live in host institution dormitories, host family homes, a tent encampment. Meals are taken on one's own, with host family, in residences, in central dining facility.

Costs (2004) • One term: contact sponsor for cost. $400 nonrefundable deposit required.

For More Information • Ms. Whitney Kidd, Program Associate, ACM Tanzania Program, Associated Colleges of the Midwest, 205 West Wacker Drive, Suite 1300, Chicago, IL 60606; *Phone:* 312-263-5000; *Fax:* 312-263-5879. *E-mail:* acm@acm.edu. *World Wide Web:* http://www.acm.edu/

BROWN UNIVERSITY
BROWN IN TANZANIA

Hosted by University of Dar Es Salaam

Academic Focus • Full curriculum.

Program Information • Students attend classes at University of Dar Es Salaam. Field trips to Dar es Salaam and surrounding area.

Sessions • Fall, yearlong.

Eligibility Requirements • Open to juniors, seniors; 3.0 GPA; 2 letters of recommendation; good academic standing at home school; demonstrated academic interest in Africa; no foreign language proficiency required.

Living Arrangements • Students live in host institution dormitories. Quarters are shared with host institution students. Meals are taken in residences, in central dining facility.

Costs (2004-2005) • One term: $15,336. Yearlong program: $30,672; includes tuition, housing, excursions, international student ID, living allowance, language course. $250 nonrefundable deposit required. Financial aid available for students from sponsoring institution: scholarships, loans.

For More Information • Ms. Mell Bolen, Director, Brown University, Office of International Programs, Box 1973, Providence, RI 02912-1973; *Phone:* 401-863-3555; *Fax:* 401-863-3311. *E-mail:* oip_office@brown.edu. *World Wide Web:* http://www.brown.edu/OIP/

UNIVERSITY OF FLORIDA
UNIVERSITY OF DAR ES SALAAM

Hosted by University of Dar Es Salaam

Academic Focus • Full curriculum.

Program Information • Students attend classes at University of Dar Es Salaam. Field trips to local cultural excursions; optional travel to Tanzania, East Africa at an extra cost.

Sessions • Yearlong.

Eligibility Requirements • Minimum age 18; open to freshmen, sophomores, juniors, seniors, graduate students, adults; course work in African studies (2 courses); 2.5 GPA; 2 letters of recommendation; good academic standing at home school; no foreign language proficiency required.

Living Arrangements • Students live in host institution dormitories, locally rented apartments. Quarters are shared with host institution students. Meals are taken as a group, on one's own, in central dining facility.

Costs (2003-2004) • Yearlong program: contact sponsor for cost. $500 application fee. Financial aid available for students from sponsoring institution: scholarships, loans.

For More Information • Mr. Martin McKellar, International Center, University of Florida, Overseas Studies, 123 Grinter Hall, PO Box

TANZANIA
Dar es Salaam

113225, Gainesville, FL 32611-3225; *Phone:* 352-392-5323 Ext. 701; *Fax:* 352-392-5575. *E-mail:* studyabroad@ufic.ufl.edu. *World Wide Web:* http://www.ufic.ufl.edu/

ZANZIBAR

SCHOOL FOR INTERNATIONAL TRAINING, SIT STUDY ABROAD
TANZANIA: ZANZIBAR COASTAL ECOLOGY

Academic Focus • African studies, anthropology, biological/life sciences, conservation studies, ecology, environmental science/studies, marine sciences, Swahili.
Program Information • Faculty members are drawn from the sponsor's U.S. staff and local instructors hired by the sponsor. Scheduled travel to a Marine Park, Chole Island, Bagamoyo, Mafia Island; field trips to surrounding islands.
Sessions • Fall, spring.
Eligibility Requirements • Open to sophomores, juniors, seniors; course work in environmental studiies, ecology, biology, or related field; 2.5 GPA; 2 letters of recommendation; good academic standing at home school; no foreign language proficiency required.
Living Arrangements • Students live in host family homes, hotels, campsites. Meals are taken as a group, on one's own, with host family, in residences, in restaurants.
Costs (2003-2004) • One term: $12,650; includes tuition, housing, all meals, insurance, excursions. $50 application fee. $400 nonrefundable deposit required. Financial aid available for all students: scholarships.
For More Information • School for International Training, SIT Study Abroad, Kipling Road, Brattleboro, VT 05302-0676; *Phone:* 888-272-7881; *Fax:* 802-258-3296. *E-mail:* studyabroad@sit.edu. *World Wide Web:* http://www.sit.edu/studyabroad/

THAILAND

CITY TO CITY
WEBSTER UNIVERSITY
WEBSTER UNIVERSITY–THAILAND

Hosted by Webster University–Thailand
Academic Focus • Full curriculum.
Program Information • Students attend classes at Webster University–Thailand (Cha-am). Field trips to King's summer palaces and temples in Phetchaburi province.
Sessions • Fall, spring, yearlong.
Eligibility Requirements • Open to sophomores, juniors, seniors, graduate students; 2.5 GPA; 1 letter of recommendation; good academic standing at home school; no foreign language proficiency required.
Living Arrangements • Students live in locally rented apartments. Quarters are shared with host institution students. Meals are taken as a group, on one's own, in central dining facility, in restaurants.
Costs (2003-2004) • One term: $8240. Yearlong program: $15,980; includes tuition, housing, insurance, international student ID, student support services. $30 application fee. $165 refundable deposit required. Financial aid available for students from sponsoring institution: scholarships, loans.
For More Information • Mr. Mark A. Beirn, Coordinator, Office of Study Abroad, Webster University, 470 East Lockwood Avenue, St. Louis, MO 63119; *Phone:* 800-984-6857; *Fax:* 314-968-5938. *E-mail:* worldview@webster.edu. *World Wide Web:* http://www.webster.edu/intl/sa/

BANGKOK
MICHIGAN STATE UNIVERSITY
MULTIDISCIPLINARY STUDIES AT THE AIT IN BANGKOK

Hosted by Asian Institute of Technology
Academic Focus • Agriculture, Brazilian studies, social sciences.

Program Information • Students attend classes at Asian Institute of Technology. Scheduled travel to Chang Mai, Phuket; field trips.
Sessions • Spring.
Eligibility Requirements • Minimum age 18; open to juniors, seniors; 2.5 GPA; good academic standing at home school; no foreign language proficiency required.
Living Arrangements • Students live in host institution dormitories, hotels. Meals are taken in residences, in central dining facility, in restaurants.
Costs (2003) • One term: $1800; includes housing, some meals, insurance, excursions. $100 application fee. $200 nonrefundable deposit required. Financial aid available for students from sponsoring institution: scholarships, loans.
For More Information • Ms. Sherry Martinez-Bonilla, Office Assistant, Michigan State University, 109 International Center, East Lansing, MI 48824-1035; *Phone:* 517-432-8920; *Fax:* 517-432-2082. *E-mail:* marti269@msu.edu. *World Wide Web:* http://studyabroad.msu.edu/

SANN RESEARCH INSTITUTE
SEMESTER IN THAILAND

Hosted by Eastern Asia University
Academic Focus • Full curriculum.
Program Information • Students attend classes at Eastern Asia University. Field trips to historic places and temples; optional travel to Phuket Islands at an extra cost.
Sessions • Fall, spring.
Eligibility Requirements • Minimum age 18; open to freshmen, sophomores, juniors, seniors; 2.5 GPA; good health; no foreign language proficiency required.
Living Arrangements • Students live in host institution dormitories. Meals are taken as a group, in central dining facility, in restaurants.
Costs (2003-2004) • One term: $7780; includes tuition, housing, all meals, international airfare. $475 application fee. $500 refundable deposit required.
For More Information • Narayan Shrestha, President, Sann Research Institute, 948 Pearl Street, Boulder, CO 80302; *Phone:* 303-449-4279; *Fax:* 303-440-7328. *E-mail:* info@sannr.com. *World Wide Web:* http://www.sannr.com/

UNIVERSITY STUDIES ABROAD CONSORTIUM
BUSINESS AND SOUTHEAST ASIAN STUDIES: BANGKOK, THAILAND

Hosted by Rangsit University
Academic Focus • Accounting, Asian studies, business administration/management, economics, finance, hospitality services, hotel and restaurant management, international business, marketing, music, philosophy, political science and government, Thai, tourism and travel.
Program Information • Students attend classes at Rangsit University. Optional travel to Huahin, Ayutthaya, Kanchanaburi, Rayong at an extra cost.
Sessions • Fall, spring, yearlong.
Eligibility Requirements • Minimum age 18; open to freshmen, sophomores, juniors, seniors, graduate students, adults; 2.5 GPA; no foreign language proficiency required.
Living Arrangements • Students live in host institution dormitories, locally rented apartments. Quarters are shared with host institution students. Meals are taken on one's own, in central dining facility, in restaurants.
Costs (2005-2006) • One term: $2980. Yearlong program: $4980; includes tuition, insurance, excursions, student support services. $50 application fee. $150 refundable deposit required. Financial aid available for all students: scholarships, loans.
For More Information • University Studies Abroad Consortium, USAC/323, Reno, NV 89557-0093; *Phone:* 775-784-6569; *Fax:* 775-784-6010. *E-mail:* usac@unr.edu. *World Wide Web:* http://usac.unr.edu/

CHIANG MAI

COLLEGE OF WOOSTER
WOOSTER IN THAILAND

Held at Payap University
Academic Focus • Religious studies.
Program Information • Classes are held on the campus of Payap University. Faculty members are drawn from the sponsor's U.S. staff and local instructors hired by the sponsor. Optional travel to a destination of student's choice at an extra cost.
Sessions • Fall, program runs every 3 years.
Eligibility Requirements • Open to sophomores, juniors; 2.5 GPA; good academic standing at home school; no foreign language proficiency required.
Living Arrangements • Students live in host institution dormitories. Quarters are shared with host institution students. Meals are taken on one's own, in restaurants.
Costs (2003) • One term: contact sponsor for cost. $500 nonrefundable deposit required. Financial aid available for students from sponsoring institution: scholarships.
For More Information • Dr. Ishwar Harris, Professor of Religious Studies, College of Wooster, Religious Studies Department, Wooster, OH 44691; *Phone:* 330-263-2000. *E-mail:* iharris@wooster.edu. *World Wide Web:* http://www.wooster.edu/ipo/

THE INTERNATIONAL PARTNERSHIP FOR SERVICE LEARNING
THAILAND SERVICE–LEARNING

Hosted by Payap University
Academic Focus • History, political science and government, social sciences, Thai.
Program Information • Students attend classes at Payap University. Field trips to Bangkok, mountain towns, villages of hill tribes; optional travel at an extra cost.
Sessions • Fall, spring, yearlong.
Eligibility Requirements • Minimum age 18; open to freshmen, sophomores, juniors, seniors, graduate students, adults; 2 letters of recommendation; good academic standing at home school; evidence of maturity, responsibility; no foreign language proficiency required.
Living Arrangements • Students live in host institution dormitories, guest houses. Quarters are shared with host institution students, students from other programs. Meals are taken on one's own, in central dining facility.
Costs (2003-2004) • One term: $9500. Yearlong program: $18,700; includes tuition, housing, some meals, excursions, student support services, service placement and supervision. $50 application fee. $250 refundable deposit required. Financial aid available for all students: federal financial aid.
For More Information • Ms. Ilana Golin, Coordinator of Student Programs, The International Partnership for Service Learning, 815 Second Avenue, Suite 315, Suite 315, New York, NY 10017-4594; *Phone:* 212-986-0989; *Fax:* 212-986-5039. *E-mail:* info@ipsl.org. *World Wide Web:* http://www.ipsl.org/

KALAMAZOO COLLEGE
DEVELOPMENT STUDIES IN THAILAND

Hosted by Chiang Mai University
Academic Focus • Conservation studies, environmental science/studies, sociology, Thai.
Program Information • Students attend classes at Chiang Mai University. Scheduled travel to the Mekong region; field trips to the Mekong region; optional travel at an extra cost.
Sessions • Fall.
Eligibility Requirements • Open to juniors; 2.75 GPA; 2 letters of recommendation; interest in development studies; no foreign language proficiency required.
Living Arrangements • Students live in host institution dormitories, host family homes. Meals are taken on one's own, in residences.
Costs (2003) • One term: $19,592; includes tuition, housing, all meals, excursions, international airfare. $50 application fee. $300 nonrefundable deposit required. Financial aid available for students from sponsoring institution: scholarships, loans.
For More Information • Dr. Joseph L. Brockington, Director, Center for International Programs, Kalamazoo College, 1200 Academy Street, Kalamazoo, MI 49006; *Phone:* 269-337-7133; *Fax:* 269-337-7400. *E-mail:* cip@kzoo.edu. *World Wide Web:* http://www.kzoo.edu/cip/

LEXIA INTERNATIONAL
LEXIA IN CHIANG MAI

Hosted by Payap University
Academic Focus • Anthropology, area studies, art, art history, Asian studies, Buddhist studies, civilization studies, cultural studies, drawing/painting, economics, environmental science/studies, ethnic studies, film and media studies, fine/studio arts, geography, history, interdisciplinary studies, international affairs, international business, liberal studies, literature, music, music history, music performance, peace and conflict studies, philosophy, political science and government, psychology, religious studies, social sciences, sociology, Thai, urban studies.
Program Information • Students attend classes at Payap University. Field trips to Chiang Rai, Bangkok.
Sessions • Fall, spring, yearlong.
Eligibility Requirements • Minimum age 18; open to sophomores, juniors, seniors, graduate students, adults; 2.5 GPA; 2 letters of recommendation; no foreign language proficiency required.
Living Arrangements • Students live in host institution dormitories, host family homes. Quarters are shared with host institution students. Meals are taken on one's own, with host family, in residences.
Costs (2003-2004) • One term: $9950. Yearlong program: $18,550; includes tuition, housing, insurance, excursions, international student ID, student support services, transcript, computer access. $35 application fee. $300 nonrefundable deposit required. Financial aid available for all students: scholarships, work study.
For More Information • Lexia International, 23 South Main Street, Hanover, NH 03755; *Phone:* 800-775-3942; *Fax:* 603-643-9899. *E-mail:* info@lexiaintl.org. *World Wide Web:* http://www.lexiaintl.org/

UNIVERSITY OF WISCONSIN–MADISON
COLLEGE YEAR IN THAILAND

Hosted by Chiang Mai University
Academic Focus • Art history, education, environmental science/studies, liberal studies, religious studies, social sciences, Thai.
Program Information • Students attend classes at Chiang Mai University. Field trips to other academic institutions, historic sites.
Sessions • Fall, yearlong, pre-departure language program also available.
Eligibility Requirements • Open to juniors, seniors; 2.5 GPA; good academic standing at home school; no foreign language proficiency required.
Living Arrangements • Students live in host institution dormitories, locally rented apartments, host family homes. Meals are taken on one's own, in residences, in central dining facility.
Costs (2003-2004) • One term: $15,600 for Wisconsin residents; $16,600 for nonresidents. Yearlong program: $21,000 for Wisconsin residents; $22,000 for nonresidents; includes tuition, housing, all meals, insurance, international airfare, books and class materials, student support services, personal spending, pre-departure expenses, summer school (for spring term students). $100 nonrefundable deposit required. Financial aid available for all students: scholarships, loans.
For More Information • Peer Advisor, University of Wisconsin–Madison, Office of International Studies and Programs, 261 Bascom Hall, 500 Lincoln Drive, Madison, WI 53706; *Phone:* 608-265-6329; *Fax:* 608-262-6998. *E-mail:* peeradvisor@bascom.wisc.edu. *World Wide Web:* http://www.studyabroad.wisc.edu/

WHITWORTH COLLEGE
WHITWORTH/PAYAP UNIVERSITY EXCHANGE PROGRAM

Hosted by Payap University
Academic Focus • Cultural studies, Thai.
Program Information • Students attend classes at Payap University. Optional travel at an extra cost.
Sessions • Fall, spring, yearlong.

THAILAND
Chiang Mai

Eligibility Requirements • Open to sophomores, juniors, seniors, adults; 2.5 GPA; 2 letters of recommendation; 1 year of college course work in Thai.

Living Arrangements • Students live in host institution dormitories, locally rented apartments. Quarters are shared with host institution students. Meals are taken in central dining facility.

Costs (2003-2004) • One term: $13,034. Yearlong program: $26,068; includes tuition, housing, all meals. Financial aid available for students from sponsoring institution: scholarships, loans.

For More Information • Ms. Sue Jackson, Director, Off-Campus Programs, Whitworth College, Center for International and Multicultural Education, 300 West Hawthorne Road, Spokane, WA 99251-2702; *Phone:* 509-777-4596; *Fax:* 509-777-3723. *E-mail:* sjackson@whitworth.edu. *World Wide Web:* http://www.whitworth.edu/

KHON KAEN
CIEE
CIEE STUDY CENTER AT KHON KAEN UNIVERSITY, THAILAND

Hosted by Khon Kaen University

Academic Focus • Asian studies, Buddhist studies, environmental health, environmental science/studies, interdisciplinary studies, literature, social work, Thai.

Program Information • Students attend classes at Khon Kaen University. Scheduled travel to Khmer ruins, the Mekong River, natural parks, Chiang Mai, village stays; field trips to museums, festivals, villages.

Sessions • Fall, spring.

Eligibility Requirements • Open to sophomores, juniors, seniors, graduate students, adults; 2.75 GPA; 2 letters of recommendation; good academic standing at home school; community service experience recommended; no foreign language proficiency required.

Living Arrangements • Students live in off-campus rental units. Quarters are shared with host institution students. Meals are taken on one's own, in central dining facility, in restaurants.

Costs (2004-2005) • One term: $9600 for fall term; contact sponsor for spring cost; includes tuition, housing, insurance, excursions, student support services, visa fees, cultural activities, pre-departure advising, transportation from Bangkok to Khon Kaen. $30 application fee. $300 deposit required. Financial aid available for all students: scholarships, minority student scholarships, travel grants.

For More Information • Mr. Adam Rubin, Admissions Officer, Asia Pacific, CIEE, 7 Custom House Street, 3rd Floor, Portland, ME 04101; *Phone:* 800-40-STUDY; *Fax:* 207-553-7699. *E-mail:* studyinfo@ciee.org. *World Wide Web:* http://www.ciee.org/isp/

TRINIDAD AND TOBAGO
TUNAPUNA
PACIFIC LUTHERAN UNIVERSITY
TRINIDAD AND TOBAGO: CULTURE, CREATIVITY, AND COMPLEXITY IN THE CARIBBEAN

Hosted by University of the West Indies, St. Augustine Campus

Academic Focus • Full curriculum.

Program Information • Students attend classes at University of the West Indies, St. Augustine Campus. Scheduled travel to Tobago; field trips to cultural events related to Carnival.

Sessions • Spring.

Eligibility Requirements • Open to sophomores, juniors, seniors; 3.0 GPA; 2 letters of recommendation; good academic standing at home school; no foreign language proficiency required.

Living Arrangements • Students live in locally rented apartments. Quarters are shared with host institution students. Meals are taken as a group, in residences.

Costs (2002-2003) • One term: $11,000; includes tuition, housing, some meals, excursions, international airfare, international student ID, student support services. $300 nonrefundable deposit required. Financial aid available for students from sponsoring institution: scholarships, loans.

For More Information • Ms. Janet Moore, Director, Off-Campus Programs, Pacific Lutheran University, Wang Center for International Programs, Tacoma, WA 98447; *Phone:* 253-535-7629; *Fax:* 253-535-8752. *E-mail:* moorejg@plu.edu. *World Wide Web:* http://www.plu.edu/~inpr/

TUNISIA
SFAX
LOCK HAVEN UNIVERSITY OF PENNSYLVANIA
SEMESTER IN TUNISIA

Hosted by University of Sfax for the South

Academic Focus • Arabic, French language and literature, Islamic studies, social sciences.

Program Information • Students attend classes at University of Sfax for the South.

Sessions • Fall, yearlong.

Eligibility Requirements • Minimum age 18; open to sophomores, juniors, seniors, adults; 2.5 GPA; 3 letters of recommendation; good academic standing at home school; transcript; no foreign language proficiency required.

Living Arrangements • Students live in host institution dormitories, host family homes. Quarters are shared with host institution students. Meals are taken as a group, in central dining facility.

Costs (2002-2003) • One term: $5450 for Pennsylvania residents; $7360 for nonresidents. Yearlong program: $10,900 for Pennsylvania residents; $14,720 for nonresidents; includes tuition, all meals, excursions, fees. $50 application fee. Financial aid available for students from sponsoring institution: scholarships, loans.

For More Information • Dean, Institute of International Studies, Lock Haven University of Pennsylvania, Lock Haven, PA 17745-2390; *Phone:* 570-893-2140; *Fax:* 570-893-2537. *E-mail:* intlstudies_webmonitor@lhup.edu. *World Wide Web:* http://www.lhup.edu/international/goingp/goingplaces_index.htm

TURKEY
CITY TO CITY
ASSOCIATED COLLEGES OF THE SOUTH
GLOBAL PARTNERS SEMESTER IN TURKEY

Hosted by Middle East Technical University, Bilkent University, Istanbul Technical University

Academic Focus • Full curriculum.

Program Information • Students attend classes at Middle East Technical University (Ankara), Bilkent University (Ankara), Istanbul Technical University (Istanbul). Scheduled travel to Ephesus, Troy, Pergamon; field trips to sites in Istanbul; optional travel at an extra cost.

Sessions • Fall.

Eligibility Requirements • Open to sophomores, juniors, seniors; 2.5 GPA; 2 letters of recommendation; good academic standing at home school; no foreign language proficiency required.

Living Arrangements • Students live in host institution dormitories. Quarters are shared with host institution students. Meals are taken on one's own, in central dining facility.

Costs (2003) • One term: $10,000; includes tuition, housing, some meals, excursions. $500 nonrefundable deposit required.

For More Information • Ms. Terese E. Wise, Director of International Programs, Associated Colleges of the South, 1975 Century Boulevard, Suite 10, Atlanta, GA 30345-3316; *Phone:* 404-636-9533; *Fax:* 404-636-9558. *E-mail:* twise@colleges.org. *World Wide Web:* http://www.colleges.org/~international/

ANKARA

CIEE
CIEE STUDY CENTER ANKARA, TURKEY

Hosted by Bilkent University, Middle East Technical University
Academic Focus • Full curriculum.
Program Information • Students attend classes at Bilkent University, Middle East Technical University. Field trips to Cappadocia, Konya, Nemrut Dag.
Sessions • Fall, spring, yearlong.
Eligibility Requirements • Open to sophomores, juniors, seniors, graduate students, adults; 2.75 GPA; 2 letters of recommendation; no foreign language proficiency required.
Living Arrangements • Students live in host institution dormitories. Quarters are shared with host institution students, students from other programs. Meals are taken on one's own, in central dining facility, in restaurants.
Costs (2003-2004) • One term: $7900. Yearlong program: $15,405; includes tuition, housing, insurance, excursions, student support services, pre-departure advising and handbook, cultural activities, optional on-site pick-up. $30 application fee. $300 deposit required. Financial aid available for all students: loans, minority student scholarships, non-traditional study grants, travel grants.
For More Information • Ms. Hannah McChesney, Admissions Officer, Europe, Middle East, and Africa, CIEE, 7 Custom House Street, 3rd Floor, Portland, ME 04101; *Phone:* 800-40-STUDY; *Fax:* 207-553-7699. *E-mail:* studyinfo@ciee.org. *World Wide Web:* http://www.ciee.org/isp/

PITZER COLLEGE
PITZER COLLEGE IN TURKEY

Hosted by Middle East Technical University
Academic Focus • Area studies, full curriculum, Turkish, Turkish studies.
Program Information • Students attend classes at Middle East Technical University. Scheduled travel to Cappadocia, Southeast Anatolia, the GAP region; field trips to Istanbul, Konya; optional travel to Cyprus, Greece at an extra cost.
Sessions • Fall, spring, yearlong.
Eligibility Requirements • Open to sophomores, juniors, seniors; course work in area studies; 2.5 GPA; 2 letters of recommendation; good academic standing at home school; no foreign language proficiency required.
Living Arrangements • Students live in host family homes. Meals are taken on one's own, with host family, in residences.
Costs (2002-2003) • One term: $18,795. Yearlong program: $37,590; includes tuition, housing, all meals, excursions, international airfare, international student ID, student support services, evacuation insurance. $25 application fee. $500 nonrefundable deposit required. Financial aid available for students from sponsoring institution: scholarships, loans.
For More Information • Ms. Neva Barker, Director of External Studies Admissions, Pitzer College, 1050 North Mills Avenue, Claremont, CA 91711; *Phone:* 909-621-8104; *Fax:* 909-621-0518. *E-mail:* external_studies@pitzer.edu. *World Wide Web:* http://www.pitzer.edu/external_studies/

ISTANBUL

BELOIT COLLEGE
TURKEY PROGRAM

Hosted by Marmara University
Academic Focus • Business administration/management, economics, international affairs, Turkish studies.
Program Information • Students attend classes at Marmara University. Field trips; optional travel to Greece, eastern Central Europe at an extra cost.

Sessions • Spring.
Eligibility Requirements • Open to sophomores, juniors, seniors; 4 letters of recommendation; evidence of preparation to study in Turkey; no foreign language proficiency required.
Living Arrangements • Students live in host institution dormitories. Meals are taken on one's own, in restaurants.
Costs (2003) • One term: $14,232; includes tuition, housing, all meals, excursions. $100 nonrefundable deposit required. Financial aid available for all students: loans.
For More Information • Office of International Education, Beloit College, 700 College Street, Beloit, WI 53511; *Phone:* 608-363-2269; *Fax:* 608-363-2689. *E-mail:* oie@beloit.edu. *World Wide Web:* http://www.beloit.edu/~oie/

STATE UNIVERSITY OF NEW YORK AT BINGHAMTON
BOSPHORUS UNIVERSITY EXCHANGE PROGRAM

Hosted by Bosphorus University
Academic Focus • Full curriculum.
Program Information • Students attend classes at Bosphorus University. Field trips to Istanbul and environs.
Sessions • Fall, spring, yearlong.
Eligibility Requirements • Open to freshmen, sophomores, juniors, seniors, graduate students; 3.0 GPA; 2 letters of recommendation; no foreign language proficiency required.
Living Arrangements • Students live in host institution dormitories, locally rented apartments. Quarters are shared with host institution students. Meals are taken on one's own, in residences, in central dining facility.
Costs (2003-2004) • One term: $7000 for New York residents; $9200 for nonresidents. Yearlong program: $13,000 for New York residents; $17,400 for nonresidents; includes tuition, housing, all meals, insurance, excursions, international airfare, books and class materials, student support services. $250 nonrefundable deposit required. Financial aid available for students from sponsoring institution: scholarships, loans.
For More Information • Dr. Katharine C. Krebs, Director, State University of New York at Binghamton, Office of International Programs, NARC G-1, Binghamton, NY 13902-6000; *Phone:* 607-777-2336; *Fax:* 607-777-2889. *E-mail:* oip@binghamton.edu. *World Wide Web:* http://oip.binghamton.edu/

UNIVERSITY OF MIAMI
ISTANBUL TECHNICAL UNIVERSITY

Hosted by Istanbul Technical University
Academic Focus • Architecture, engineering, mechanical engineering, urban/regional planning.
Program Information • Students attend classes at Istanbul Technical University.
Sessions • Fall, spring, yearlong.
Eligibility Requirements • Minimum age 18; open to sophomores, juniors, seniors; major in engineering, architecture; 3.0 GPA; 2 letters of recommendation; good academic standing at home school; essay; no foreign language proficiency required.
Living Arrangements • Students live in host institution dormitories. Quarters are shared with host institution students, students from other programs. Meals are taken on one's own, in central dining facility, in restaurants.
Costs (2003-2004) • One term: $12,919. Yearlong program: $25,838; includes tuition. $40 application fee. $500 nonrefundable deposit required. Financial aid available for students from sponsoring institution: scholarships, loans.
For More Information • Ms. Carol Lazzeri, Associate Dean and Director, University of Miami, International Education and Exchange Programs, PO Box 248005, 5050 Brunson Drive, Allen Hall #212, Coral Gables, FL 33124-1610; *Phone:* 305-284-3434; *Fax:* 305-284-4235. *E-mail:* ieep@miami.edu. *World Wide Web:* http://www.studyabroad.miami.edu/

TURKMENISTAN
Ashgabat

TURKMENISTAN
ASHGABAT
ACIE (ACTR/ACCELS)
ACIE–NIS REGIONAL LANGUAGE TRAINING PROGRAM–TURKMENISTAN

Hosted by various institutions
Academic Focus • Cultural studies, language studies, Turkmen.
Program Information • Students attend classes at various institutions.
Sessions • Fall, spring, yearlong.
Eligibility Requirements • Minimum age 18; open to sophomores, juniors, seniors, graduate students, adults; 3 letters of recommendation; good academic standing at home school; 1 year of college course work in Russian or Turkmen.
Living Arrangements • Students live in host institution dormitories, locally rented apartments, host family homes. Quarters are shared with students from other programs. Meals are taken on one's own, with host family, in residences, in restaurants.
Costs (2002-2003) • One term: contact sponsor for cost. Yearlong program: contact sponsor for cost. $35 application fee. $500 nonrefundable deposit required. Financial aid available for all students: scholarships.
For More Information • Ms. Margaret Stephenson, Russian and Eurasian Program Officer, ACIE (ACTR/ACCELS), 1776 Massachusetts Avenue, NW, Suite 700, Washington, DC 20036; *Phone:* 202-833-7522; *Fax:* 202-833-7523. *E-mail:* outbound@actr.org. *World Wide Web:* http://www.actr.org/

TURKS AND CAICOS ISLANDS
SOUTH CAICOS
THE SCHOOL FOR FIELD STUDIES
BRITISH WEST INDIES: MARINE RESOURCE STUDIES

Held at Center for Marine Resource Studies
Academic Focus • Biological/life sciences, conservation studies, ecology, economics, environmental science/studies, fisheries studies, marine sciences, natural resources.
Program Information • Classes are held on the campus of Center for Marine Resource Studies. Faculty members are drawn from the sponsor's U.S. staff and local instructors hired by the sponsor. Optional travel to nearby Caribbean Islands at an extra cost.
Sessions • Fall, spring.
Eligibility Requirements • Minimum age 18; open to freshmen, sophomores, juniors, seniors; course work in biology or ecology; 2.7 GPA; 2 letters of recommendation; scuba certification (if student wishes to participate in scuba diving); personal statement; no foreign language proficiency required.
Living Arrangements • Students live in a waterfront residence. Quarters are shared with host institution students. Meals are taken as a group, in central dining facility.
Costs (2002-2003) • One term: $13,185; includes tuition, housing, all meals, lab equipment. $45 application fee. $500 nonrefundable deposit required. Financial aid available for all students: scholarships, loans.
For More Information • Admissions Department, The School for Field Studies, 10 Federal Street, Salem, MA 01970-3853; *Phone:* 800-989-4418; *Fax:* 978-741-3551. *E-mail:* admissions@fieldstudies.org. *World Wide Web:* http://www.fieldstudies.org/

THE SCHOOL FOR FIELD STUDIES
TURKS AND CAICOS ISLANDS

Hosted by Center for Marine Resource Studies
Academic Focus • Biological/life sciences, ecology, marine sciences.
Program Information • Students attend classes at Center for Marine Resource Studies. Optional travel to Grand Turk, Salt Cay.
Sessions • Fall, spring.
Eligibility Requirements • Minimum age 16; open to freshmen, sophomores, juniors, seniors; 2 letters of recommendation; good academic standing at home school.
Living Arrangements • Students live in a field station (former hotel). Quarters are shared with host institution students. Meals are taken as a group, in central dining facility.
Costs (2004-2005) • One term: $13,000–$14,000; includes tuition, housing, all meals, lab equipment, student support services, some excursions, emergency evacuation insurance. $45 application fee. $650 deposit required. Financial aid available for all students: scholarships, loans.
For More Information • Ms. Coleen Cusick, Admissions Counselor, The School for Field Studies, 10 Federal Street, Suite 24, Salem, MA 01970-3876; *Phone:* 978-741-3544; *Fax:* 978-741-3551. *E-mail:* admissions@fieldstudies.org. *World Wide Web:* http://www.fieldstudies.org/

UGANDA
KAMPALA
SCHOOL FOR INTERNATIONAL TRAINING, SIT STUDY ABROAD
UGANDA: DEVELOPMENT STUDIES

Academic Focus • African studies, anthropology, community service, economics, geography, history, sociology, Swahili.
Program Information • Faculty members are drawn from the sponsor's U.S. staff and local instructors hired by the sponsor. Scheduled travel to Ruwenzori, Jinja, western Uganda; field trips to Entebbe, rural areas, development projects.
Sessions • Fall, spring.
Eligibility Requirements • Open to sophomores, juniors, seniors; 2.5 GPA; 2 letters of recommendation; good academic standing at home school; background in development studies or related field recommended; no foreign language proficiency required.
Living Arrangements • Students live in host family homes, hotels. Meals are taken as a group, on one's own, with host family, in residences, in restaurants.
Costs (2003-2004) • One term: $11,900; includes tuition, housing, all meals, insurance, excursions. $50 application fee. $400 nonrefundable deposit required. Financial aid available for all students: scholarships.
For More Information • School for International Training, SIT Study Abroad, Kipling Road, Brattleboro, VT 05302-0676; *Phone:* 888-272-7881; *Fax:* 802-258-3296. *E-mail:* studyabroad@sit.edu. *World Wide Web:* http://www.sit.edu/studyabroad/

UKRAINE
CITY TO CITY
ACIE (ACTR/ACCELS)
ACIE–NIS REGIONAL LANGUAGE TRAINING PROGRAM–UKRAINE

Hosted by Ivan Franko National University of L'viv, Kiev 'Taras Scevchenko' University
Academic Focus • Cultural studies, language studies, Ukrainian.

Program Information • Students attend classes at Ivan Franko National University of L'viv (L'viv), Kiev 'Taras Scevchenko' University (Kiev). Optional travel at an extra cost.
Sessions • Fall, spring, yearlong.
Eligibility Requirements • Minimum age 18; open to sophomores, juniors, seniors, graduate students, adults; 3 letters of recommendation; good academic standing at home school; 1 year of college course work in Russian or Ukrainian.
Living Arrangements • Students live in host institution dormitories, host family homes. Quarters are shared with students from other programs. Meals are taken on one's own, with host family, in residences, in central dining facility, in restaurants.
Costs (2002-2003) • One term: contact sponsor for cost. Yearlong program: contact sponsor for cost. $35 application fee. $500 nonrefundable deposit required. Financial aid available for all students: scholarships.
For More Information • Ms. Margaret Stephenson, Russian and Eurasian Program Officer, ACIE (ACTR/ACCELS), 1776 Massachusetts Avenue, NW, Suite 700, Washington, DC 20036; *Phone:* 202-833-7522; *Fax:* 202-833-7523. *E-mail:* outbound@actr.org. *World Wide Web:* http://www.actr.org/

CHERNIVTSI
LOCK HAVEN UNIVERSITY OF PENNSYLVANIA
SEMESTER IN UKRAINE

Hosted by Yuriy Fedkovych Chernivtsi National University
Academic Focus • English literature, language studies, Russian language and literature, Ukrainian, Ukrainian studies.
Program Information • Students attend classes at Yuriy Fedkovych Chernivtsi National University.
Sessions • Fall, spring, yearlong.
Eligibility Requirements • Minimum age 18; open to sophomores, juniors; 2.5 GPA; 3 letters of recommendation; good academic standing at home school; transcript; no foreign language proficiency required.
Living Arrangements • Students live in host institution dormitories, locally rented apartments. Quarters are shared with host institution students. Meals are taken in central dining facility.
Costs (2002-2003) • One term: $5450 for Pennsylvania residents; $7360 for nonresidents. Yearlong program: $10,900 for Pennsylvania residents; $14,720 for nonresidents; includes tuition, housing, all meals, fees. $50 application fee. Financial aid available for students from sponsoring institution: scholarships, loans.
For More Information • Dean, Institute for International Studies, Lock Haven University of Pennsylvania, Lock Haven, PA 17745-2390; *Phone:* 570-893-2140; *Fax:* 570-893-2537. *E-mail:* intlstudies_webmonitor@lhup.edu. *World Wide Web:* http://www.lhup.edu/international/goingp/goingplaces_index.htm

UNITED ARAB EMIRATES
DUBAI
AMERICAN INTERCONTINENTAL UNIVERSITY
AMERICAN UNIVERSITY IN DUBAI

Hosted by American University in Dubai
Academic Focus • Advertising and public relations, Arabic, art, business administration/management, commercial art, communications, design and applied arts, engineering, fine/studio arts, information science, intercultural studies, interior design, international business, liberal studies, marketing, Middle Eastern studies, photography.

Program Information • Students attend classes at American University in Dubai. Optional travel to other Middle East destinations at an extra cost.
Sessions • Fall, spring, winter, yearlong.
Eligibility Requirements • Open to freshmen, sophomores, juniors, seniors, graduate students, adults; good academic standing at home school; advisor/dean and study abroad office approval; college transcripts; no foreign language proficiency required.
Living Arrangements • Students live in host institution dormitories. Quarters are shared with host institution students. Meals are taken on one's own, in central dining facility.
Costs (2004-2005) • One term: $5240. Yearlong program: $15,720; includes tuition, housing, fees. $150 refundable deposit required. Financial aid available for all students: scholarships, loans.
For More Information • American InterContinental University, Study Abroad Programs, 3150 West Higgins Road, Suite 105, Hoffman Estates, IL 60195; *Phone:* 800-255-6839; *Fax:* 847-885-8422. *E-mail:* studyabroad@aiuniv.edu. *World Wide Web:* http://www.studyabroad.aiuniv.edu/

URUGUAY
MONTEVIDEO
MIDDLEBURY COLLEGE SCHOOLS ABROAD
SCHOOL IN LATIN AMERICA–URUGUAY PROGRAM

Hosted by ORT University of Uruguay, University of the Republic of Montevideo, Catholic University of Uruguay 'Dámaso A Larrañaga'
Academic Focus • Full curriculum.
Program Information • Students attend classes at ORT University of Uruguay, University of the Republic of Montevideo, Catholic University of Uruguay 'Dámaso A Larrañaga'. Field trips.
Sessions • Fall, spring, yearlong.
Eligibility Requirements • Open to sophomores, juniors, seniors; 2.7 GPA; 2 letters of recommendation; 2.5 years college course work in Spanish, including 1 content course at the 300-level.
Living Arrangements • Students live in host institution dormitories, host family homes. Meals are taken with host family.
Costs (2004-2005) • One term: $7200. Yearlong program: $14,400; includes tuition, student support services. $50 application fee. $300 nonrefundable deposit required. Financial aid available for students from sponsoring institution: scholarships, loans.
For More Information • Mr. Jamie Northrup, University Relations Coordinator, Middlebury College Schools Abroad, Office of Off-Campus Study, Sunderland Language Center, Middlebury, VT 05753; *Phone:* 802-443-5745; *Fax:* 802-443-3157. *E-mail:* schoolsabroad@middlebury.edu. *World Wide Web:* http://www.middlebury.edu/msa/

STATE UNIVERSITY OF NEW YORK AT PLATTSBURGH
LATIN AMERICAN SOUTHERN CONE PROGRAMS, MONTEVIDEO, WITH MIDDLEBURY COLLEGE

Hosted by Catholic University of Uruguay 'Dámaso A Larrañaga'
Academic Focus • Full curriculum.
Program Information • Students attend classes at Catholic University of Uruguay 'Dámaso A Larrañaga'. Field trips to neighborhoods of Montevideo; optional travel to Buenos Aires, Brazil, Punta del Este, Iguazú Falls at an extra cost.
Sessions • Fall, spring, yearlong, South American academic year.
Eligibility Requirements • Minimum age 18; open to sophomores, juniors, seniors, graduate students, adults; 2.5 GPA; 3 letters of recommendation; intermediate-level Spanish.
Living Arrangements • Students live in host family homes. Meals are taken on one's own, with host family, in residences, in restaurants.
Costs (2003-2004) • One term: New York residents contact sponsor for cost; $6,995 for nonresidents. Yearlong program: New York residents contact sponsor for cost; $12,995 for nonresidents;

includes tuition. $20 application fee. $200 nonrefundable deposit required. Financial aid available for all students: scholarships, loans.
For More Information • Ms. Liz Ross, C.V. Starr-Middlebury School in Latin America, State University of New York at Plattsburgh, Middlebury College, Middlebury, VT 05753; *Phone:* 802-443-5745. *E-mail:* schoolsabroad@middlebury.edu. *World Wide Web:* http://www.plattsburgh.edu/studyabroad/

U.S. VIRGIN ISLANDS

ST. THOMAS

STATE UNIVERSITY OF NEW YORK AT NEW PALTZ

STUDY ABROAD IN THE U.S. VIRGIN ISLANDS–ST. THOMAS

Hosted by University of the Virgin Islands
Academic Focus • Full curriculum.
Program Information • Students attend classes at University of the Virgin Islands.
Sessions • Fall, spring, yearlong.
Eligibility Requirements • Minimum age 18; open to sophomores, juniors, seniors; 2.5 GPA; 2 letters of recommendation; good academic standing at home school.
Living Arrangements • Students live in host institution dormitories. Quarters are shared with host institution students. Meals are taken on one's own, in central dining facility.
Costs (2003-2004) • One term: $5383 for New York residents; $8968 for nonresidents. Yearlong program: $10,766 for New York residents; $17,937 for nonresidents; includes tuition, housing, all meals, insurance, administrative fee. $25 application fee. $300–$600 nonrefundable deposit required. Financial aid available for students from sponsoring institution: scholarships, loans.
For More Information • Center for International Programs, State University of New York at New Paltz, 75 South Manheim Boulevard, Suite 9, New Paltz, NY 12561; *Phone:* 845-257-3125; *Fax:* 845-257-3129. *E-mail:* international@newpaltz.edu. *World Wide Web:* http://www.newpaltz.edu/studyabroad/

UZBEKISTAN

TASHKENT

ACIE (ACTR/ACCELS)

ACIE–NIS REGIONAL LANGUAGE TRAINING PROGRAM–UZBEKISTAN

Hosted by Samarkand Institute of Language, Institute of World Languages
Academic Focus • Cultural studies, language studies, Russian language and literature, Uzbek.
Program Information • Students attend classes at Samarkand Institute of Language, Institute of World Languages.
Sessions • Fall, spring, yearlong.
Eligibility Requirements • Minimum age 18; open to sophomores, juniors, seniors, graduate students, adults; 3 letters of recommendation; good academic standing at home school; 1 year of college course work in Russian or Uzbek.
Living Arrangements • Students live in host institution dormitories, locally rented apartments, host family homes. Quarters are shared with students from other programs. Meals are taken on one's own, with host family, in residences, in restaurants.
Costs (2002-2003) • One term: contact sponsor for cost. Yearlong program: contact sponsor for cost. $35 application fee. $500 nonrefundable deposit required. Financial aid available for all students: scholarships.

For More Information • Ms. Margaret Stephenson, Russian and Eurasian Program Officer, ACIE (ACTR/ACCELS), 1776 Massachusetts Avenue, NW, Suite 700, Washington, DC 20036; *Phone:* 202-833-7522; *Fax:* 202-833-7523. *E-mail:* outbound@actr.org. *World Wide Web:* http://www.actr.org/

VENEZUELA

MÉRIDA

LONGWOOD UNIVERSITY

STUDY ABROAD IN VENEZUELA

Hosted by VEN-USA–Institute of International Studies and Modern Languages
Academic Focus • International business, Latin American literature, Latin American studies, Spanish language and literature.
Program Information • Students attend classes at VEN-USA–Institute of International Studies and Modern Languages. Scheduled travel to student-chosen locations; field trips to the Andes Mountains; optional travel to Caribbean countries at an extra cost.
Sessions • Fall, spring.
Eligibility Requirements • Minimum age 18; open to sophomores, juniors, seniors, adults; 2.5 GPA; 2 years of college course work in Spanish.
Living Arrangements • Students live in host family homes. Meals are taken with host family, in residences.
Costs (2002-2003) • One term: $6000 for Virginia residents; includes tuition, housing, all meals, excursions, social and cultural events, transportation from airport to program site. $250 nonrefundable deposit required. Financial aid available for students from sponsoring institution: scholarships.
For More Information • Dr. John F. Reynolds, Director, International Affairs Program, Longwood University, International Affairs, 201 High Street, Farmville, VA 23909-1899; *Phone:* 434-395-2172; *Fax:* 434-395-2141. *E-mail:* jreynold@longwood.edu. *World Wide Web:* http://www.longwood.edu/

PITZER COLLEGE

PITZER COLLEGE IN VENEZUELA

Hosted by University of the Andes Mérida
Academic Focus • Environmental science/studies, fine/studio arts, Latin American studies, Spanish language and literature.
Program Information • Students attend classes at University of the Andes Mérida. Scheduled travel to Coro/La Vela, Canaima (Angel Falls); field trips to Caracas, Las Llanos, Morrocoy National Park; optional travel to Aruba at an extra cost.
Sessions • Fall, spring, yearlong.
Eligibility Requirements • Open to sophomores, juniors, seniors; course work in area studies; 2.5 GPA; 2 letters of recommendation; good academic standing at home school; 1 year of college course work in Spanish.
Living Arrangements • Students live in host family homes. Meals are taken with host family, in residences.
Costs (2003-2004) • One term: $18,795. Yearlong program: $37,590; includes tuition, housing, all meals, excursions, international airfare, international student ID, student support services, evacuation insurance. $25 application fee. $500 nonrefundable deposit required. Financial aid available for students from sponsoring institution: scholarships, loans.
For More Information • Ms. Neva Barker, Director of External Studies Admissions, Pitzer College, 1050 North Mills Avenue, Claremont, CA 91711; *Phone:* 909-621-8104; *Fax:* 909-621-0518. *E-mail:* external_studies@pitzer.edu. *World Wide Web:* http://www.pitzer.edu/external_studies/

STATE UNIVERSITY OF NEW YORK COLLEGE AT CORTLAND

CORTLAND/MÉRIDA

Hosted by VEN-USA–Institute of International Studies and Modern Languages

Academic Focus • Anthropology, botany, civilization studies, communications, ecology, film and media studies, geography, interdisciplinary studies, international affairs, international business, Latin American studies, social sciences, sociology, teaching English as a second language.

Program Information • Students attend classes at VEN-USA–Institute of International Studies and Modern Languages. Field trips to businesses, health centers, orphanages, schools, local sites, the Andes Mountains; optional travel to beaches of the Caribbean, Margarita Island, Los Llanos, Amazonas region, Canaima at an extra cost.

Sessions • Fall, spring, yearlong.

Eligibility Requirements • Minimum age 18; open to sophomores, juniors, seniors, graduate students, adults; 2.5 GPA; 3 letters of recommendation; good academic standing at home school; 0.5 years of college course work in Spanish.

Living Arrangements • Students live in host family homes. Meals are taken with host family, in residences.

Costs (2000-2001) • One term: $5550. Yearlong program: $10,000; includes tuition, housing, some meals, insurance, international airfare, books and class materials, student support services, passport and visa fees, some field trips. $20 application fee. $250 nonrefundable deposit required. Financial aid available for students from sponsoring institution: scholarships, loans.

For More Information • Liz Kopp, Assistant Director, Office of International Programs, State University of New York College at Cortland, PO Box 2000, Cortland, NY 13045; *Phone:* 607-753-2209; *Fax:* 607-753-5989. *E-mail:* studyabroad@cortland.edu. *World Wide Web:* http://www.studyabroad.com/suny/cortland/

UNIVERSITY OF MINNESOTA
STUDY ABROAD IN VENEZUELA

Hosted by VEN-USA–Institute of International Studies and Modern Languages

Academic Focus • Botany, civilization studies, ecology, history, international business, Latin American studies, literature, political science and government, science, Spanish language and literature, teaching English as a second language.

Program Information • Students attend classes at VEN-USA–Institute of International Studies and Modern Languages.

Sessions • Fall, spring, yearlong.

Eligibility Requirements • Minimum age 18; open to freshmen, sophomores, juniors, seniors, graduate students, adults; 2.5 GPA; good academic standing at home school; no foreign language proficiency required.

Living Arrangements • Students live in host family homes. Quarters are shared with host institution students. Meals are taken with host family, in residences.

Costs (2004-2005) • One term: contact sponsor for cost. Yearlong program: contact sponsor for cost. $50 application fee. $400 nonrefundable deposit required. Financial aid available for students from sponsoring institution: scholarships, loans.

For More Information • University of Minnesota, Learning Abroad Center, 230 Heller Hall, 271 19th Avenue South, Minneapolis, MN 55455; *Phone:* 888-700-UOFM; *Fax:* 612-626-8009. *E-mail:* umabroad@umn.edu. *World Wide Web:* http://www.umabroad.umn.edu/. Students may also apply through Venusa, C.P.S.A., Institute of International Studies, 6542 Hypoluxo Road, PMB #324, Lake Worth, FL 33467.

VIETNAM

DA NANG

STATE UNIVERSITY OF NEW YORK COLLEGE AT BROCKPORT
THE BROCKPORT VIETNAM PROGRAM

Hosted by School of Politics, Duy Tan University, Da Nang University

Academic Focus • Cultural studies, history, international business, political science and government, social services, social work, teaching English as a second language, Vietnamese.

Program Information • Students attend classes at Da Nang University, Duy Tan University, School of Politics. Field trips to Ho Chi Minh City, Hanoi, various locations in and around Da Nang.

Sessions • Fall, spring.

Eligibility Requirements • Minimum age 18; open to juniors, seniors, graduate students; 2.5 GPA; 2 letters of recommendation; a willingness both to study and provide community services in Vietnam; basic knowledge of Vietnamese recommended.

Living Arrangements • Students live in program-owned houses. Meals are taken as a group, in residences.

Costs (2003-2004) • One term: $8175; includes tuition, housing, all meals, excursions, international student ID, student support services, laundry service, interpreter services. $350 nonrefundable deposit required. Financial aid available for all students: scholarships, loans, regular financial aid, grants.

For More Information • Dr. John Perry, Director, Office of International Education, State University of New York College at Brockport, 350 New Campus Drive, Brockport, NY 14420; *Phone:* 800-298-SUNY; *Fax:* 585-637-3218. *E-mail:* overseas@brockport.edu. *World Wide Web:* http://www.brockport.edu/studyabroad/

HANOI
CIEE
CIEE STUDY CENTER AT VIETNAM NATIONAL UNIVERSITY

Hosted by Vietnam National University

Academic Focus • Art, Asian studies, comparative history, cultural studies, economics, history, literature, Vietnamese.

Program Information • Students attend classes at Vietnam National University. Scheduled travel to Ho Chi Minh City, Hue, Nha Trang, Da Lat, Cambodia; field trips to temple festivals outside Hanoi, museums, monuments, cultural performances, Ha Long Bay.

Sessions • Fall, spring, yearlong.

Eligibility Requirements • Open to freshmen, sophomores, juniors, seniors, graduate students, adults; course work in Asian studies (1 course); 2.75 GPA; 2 letters of recommendation; good academic standing at home school; no foreign language proficiency required.

Living Arrangements • Students live in host institution dormitories, a guest house for foreign students. Meals are taken on one's own, in central dining facility, in restaurants.

Costs (2004-2005) • One term: $8850. Yearlong program: $15,800; includes tuition, housing, insurance, excursions, student support services, visa fees. $30 application fee. $300 deposit required. Financial aid available for all students: scholarships, minority student scholarships, travel grants.

For More Information • Mr. Adam Rubin, Admissions Officer, Asia Pacific, CIEE, 7 Custom House Street, 3rd Floor, Portland, ME 04101; *Phone:* 800-40-STUDY; *Fax:* 207-553-7699. *E-mail:* studyinfo@ciee.org. *World Wide Web:* http://www.ciee.org/isp/

HO CHI MINH CITY
SCHOOL FOR INTERNATIONAL TRAINING, SIT STUDY ABROAD
VIETNAM: CULTURE AND DEVELOPMENT

Academic Focus • Anthropology, Buddhist studies, East Asian studies, economics, geography, history, liberal studies, political science and government, religious studies, Vietnamese, visual and performing arts.

Program Information • Faculty members are drawn from the sponsor's U.S. staff and local instructors hired by the sponsor. Scheduled travel to Hanoi, Da Nang, Nha Trang, Hue; field trips to religious and historic sites, museums, art exhibits.

Sessions • Fall, spring.

Eligibility Requirements • Open to sophomores, juniors, seniors; 2.5 GPA; 2 letters of recommendation; good academic standing at home school; no foreign language proficiency required.

Living Arrangements • Students live in host family homes, hotels. Meals are taken as a group, on one's own, with host family, in residences, in restaurants.

Costs (2003-2004) • One term: $12,050; includes tuition, housing, all meals, insurance, excursions. $50 application fee. $400 nonrefundable deposit required. Financial aid available for all students: scholarships.

VIETNAM
Ho Chi Minh City

For More Information • School for International Training, SIT Study Abroad, Kipling Road, Brattleboro, VT 05302-0676; *Phone:* 888-272-7881; *Fax:* 802-258-3296. *E-mail:* studyabroad@sit.edu. *World Wide Web:* http://www.sit.edu/studyabroad/

WALES

See also England, Ireland, Northern Ireland, and Scotland.

ABERYSTWYTH
BRETHREN COLLEGES ABROAD
BCA PEACE AND JUSTICE PROGRAM IN ABERYSTWYTH, WALES

Hosted by University of Wales–Aberystwyth
Academic Focus • Full curriculum, peace and conflict studies, political science and government.
Program Information • Students attend classes at University of Wales–Aberystwyth. Field trips.
Sessions • Fall, spring, yearlong.
Eligibility Requirements • Minimum age 18; open to sophomores, juniors, seniors; 3.0 GPA; 1 letter of recommendation; good academic standing at home school.
Living Arrangements • Students live in host institution dormitories. Meals are taken on one's own, in residences, in central dining facility, in restaurants.
Costs (2003-2004) • One term: $11,500. Yearlong program: $19,900; includes tuition, housing, all meals, insurance, excursions, international student ID, student support services. $50 application fee. $100 nonrefundable deposit required.
For More Information • Ms. Natalya Latysheva-Derova, Program Officer, Brethren Colleges Abroad, 50 Alpha Drive, Elizabethtown, PA 17022; *Phone:* 866-222-6188; *Fax:* 717-361-6619. *E-mail:* info@bcanet.org. *World Wide Web:* http://www.bcanet.org/

BANGOR
ARCADIA UNIVERSITY
UNIVERSITY OF WALES, BANGOR

Hosted by University of Wales–University College of North Wales Bangor
Academic Focus • Biological/life sciences, business administration/management, engineering, liberal studies, religious studies, social sciences, Welsh studies.
Program Information • Students attend classes at University of Wales–University College of North Wales Bangor.
Sessions • Fall, spring, yearlong.
Eligibility Requirements • Open to sophomores, juniors, seniors; 3.0 GPA; 1 letter of recommendation.
Living Arrangements • Students live in host institution dormitories. Quarters are shared with host institution students. Meals are taken on one's own, in residences.
Costs (2003-2004) • One term: $10,490–$11,290. Yearlong program: $18,190; includes tuition, housing, insurance, international student ID, student support services, pre-departure guide, transcripts. $35 application fee. $500 nonrefundable deposit required. Financial aid available for all students: scholarships, loans.
For More Information • Arcadia University, Center for Education Abroad, 450 South Easton Road, Glenside, PA 19038-3295; *Phone:* 866-927-2234; *Fax:* 215-572-2174. *E-mail:* cea@arcadia.edu. *World Wide Web:* http://www.arcadia.edu/cea/

NORTH AMERICAN INSTITUTE FOR STUDY ABROAD
STUDY IN WALES

Hosted by University of Wales–University College of North Wales Bangor
Academic Focus • Full curriculum.
Program Information • Students attend classes at University of Wales–University College of North Wales Bangor.
Sessions • Fall, spring, yearlong.
Eligibility Requirements • Minimum age 18; open to sophomores, juniors, seniors; 3.0 GPA; 2 letters of recommendation; good academic standing at home school.
Living Arrangements • Students live in host institution dormitories, locally rented apartments. Quarters are shared with host institution students. Meals are taken on one's own, in residences, in central dining facility, in restaurants.
Costs (2003-2004) • One term: $9000–$9500. Yearlong program: $18,000; includes tuition, housing, international student ID, student support services, transcripts. $50 application fee. $500 nonrefundable deposit required. Financial aid available for all students: scholarships.
For More Information • Dr. Michael Currid, Director, North American Institute for Study Abroad, 129 Mill Street, Danville, PA 17821; *Phone:* 570-275-5099; *Fax:* 570-275-1644. *E-mail:* naisa@naisa.com. *World Wide Web:* http://www.naisa.com/

CARMARTHEN
CENTRAL COLLEGE ABROAD
CENTRAL COLLEGE ABROAD IN CARMARTHEN, WALES

Hosted by Trinity College
Academic Focus • Archaeology, art, art history, Celtic studies, communications, computer science, creative writing, drama/theater, education, English, environmental science/studies, health and physical education, history, literature, political science and government, religious studies, sports management, tourism and travel, Welsh, Welsh studies.
Program Information • Students attend classes at Trinity College. Scheduled travel to Wales, Ireland, London; field trips to Cardiff, St. David's Cathedral, Gower Peninsula, Pembroke Castle, Tenby, Haye on Wye, Castell Henllys Celtic Village, Big Pit Coal Mine; optional travel to Stonehenge, Stratford-upon-Avon, Ireland, Bath, Scotland, Liverpool at an extra cost.
Sessions • Fall, spring, yearlong.
Eligibility Requirements • Minimum age 18; open to freshmen, sophomores, juniors, seniors; 2.5 GPA; 2 letters of recommendation; good academic standing at home school; study abroad approval form; transcript; Student Life endorsement.
Living Arrangements • Students live in host institution dormitories. Quarters are shared with host institution students. Meals are taken in central dining facility.
Costs (2003-2004) • One term: $11,850. Yearlong program: $23,700; includes tuition, housing, some meals, excursions, international student ID, student support services. $25 application fee. $350 nonrefundable deposit required. Financial aid available for all students: scholarships.
For More Information • Office of International Education, Central College Abroad, 812 University Street, Pella, IA 50219; *Phone:* 800-831-3629; *Fax:* 641-628-5375. *E-mail:* studyabroad@central.edu. *World Wide Web:* http://www.central.edu/abroad/

SWANSEA
ARCADIA UNIVERSITY
UNIVERSITY OF WALES, SWANSEA

Hosted by University of Wales–University College of Swansea
Academic Focus • American studies, computer science, engineering, international business, language studies, science, Welsh.
Program Information • Students attend classes at University of Wales–University College of Swansea.
Sessions • Fall, spring, yearlong, pre-session.
Eligibility Requirements • Open to precollege students, sophomores, juniors, seniors; 3.0 GPA; 1 letter of recommendation.

Living Arrangements • Students live in host institution dormitories, host family homes. Quarters are shared with host institution students, students from other programs. Meals are taken on one's own, in residences.
Costs (2003-2004) • One term: $9290 for fall term; $10,790 for spring semester ($1500 for pre-session). Yearlong program: $17,490; includes tuition, housing, insurance, international student ID, student support services, pre-departure guide, transcripts. $35 application fee. $500 nonrefundable deposit required. Financial aid available for all students: scholarships, loans.
For More Information • Arcadia University, Center for Education Abroad, 450 South Easton Road, Glenside, PA 19038-3295; *Phone:* 866-927-2234; *Fax:* 215-572-2174. *E-mail:* cea@arcadia.edu. *World Wide Web:* http://www.arcadia.edu/cea/

INTERSTUDY
UNIVERSITY OF WALES AT SWANSEA

Hosted by University of Wales–University College of Swansea
Academic Focus • American studies, biological/life sciences, chemical sciences, classics and classical languages, computer science, economics, education, electrical engineering, engineering, English, French language and literature, German language and literature, history, international business, language studies, law and legal studies, mathematics, music, philosophy, physics, political science and government, psychology, social services.
Program Information • Students attend classes at University of Wales–University College of Swansea. Scheduled travel to Bath, Stratford-upon-Avon, Warwick Castle, Oxford, Stonehenge.
Sessions • Fall, spring, yearlong, early start British culture session.
Eligibility Requirements • Minimum age 18; open to freshmen, sophomores, juniors, seniors, adults; 3.0 GPA; 2 letters of recommendation; good academic standing at home school.
Living Arrangements • Students live in host institution dormitories. Quarters are shared with host institution students. Meals are taken on one's own, in residences.
Costs (2003-2004) • One term: $10,650 for fall term; $12,125 for spring term; $500 for early start session. Yearlong program: $19,950; includes tuition, housing, some meals, excursions, international student ID, student support services, Student Union membership, e-mail access, banking facilities, international bank transfers, transcript, cell phone. $35 application fee. $500 nonrefundable deposit required. Financial aid available for all students: scholarships, loans, stipends.
For More Information • InterStudy, Admissions Office, 63 Edward Street, Medford, MA 02155; *Phone:* 800-663-1999; *Fax:* 781-391-7463. *E-mail:* interstudy@interstudy-usa.org. *World Wide Web:* http://www.interstudy.org/

NORTH AMERICAN INSTITUTE FOR STUDY ABROAD
STUDY IN WALES

Hosted by University of Wales–University College of Swansea
Academic Focus • Full curriculum.
Program Information • Students attend classes at University of Wales–University College of Swansea.
Sessions • Fall, spring, yearlong.
Eligibility Requirements • Minimum age 18; open to sophomores, juniors, seniors; 3.0 GPA; 2 letters of recommendation; good academic standing at home school.
Living Arrangements • Students live in host institution dormitories, locally rented apartments. Quarters are shared with host institution students. Meals are taken on one's own, in residences, in central dining facility, in restaurants.
Costs (2003-2004) • One term: $9000–$9500. Yearlong program: $18,000; includes tuition, housing, insurance, international student ID, student support services, transcripts. $50 application fee. $500 nonrefundable deposit required. Financial aid available for all students: scholarships.
For More Information • Dr. Michael Currid, Director, North American Institute for Study Abroad, 129 Mill Street, Danville, PA 17821; *Phone:* 570-275-5099; *Fax:* 570-275-1644. *E-mail:* naisa@naisa.com. *World Wide Web:* http://www.naisa.com/

UNIVERSITY AT ALBANY, STATE UNIVERSITY OF NEW YORK
DIRECT ENROLLMENT AT THE UNIVERSITY OF SWANSEA

Hosted by University of Wales–University College of Swansea
Academic Focus • Full curriculum.
Program Information • Students attend classes at University of Wales–University College of Swansea.
Sessions • Fall, spring, yearlong.
Eligibility Requirements • Open to sophomores, juniors, seniors, graduate students, adults; 3.0 GPA; 2 letters of recommendation; good academic standing at home school.
Living Arrangements • Students live in host institution dormitories. Quarters are shared with host institution students, students from other programs. Meals are taken on one's own, in residences, in central dining facility, in restaurants.
Costs (2002-2003) • One term: $6038 for fall term; $7,188 for spring. Yearlong program: $13,226; includes housing, all meals, student support services, in-state tuition and fees. $150 nonrefundable deposit required. Financial aid available for students from sponsoring institution: all customary sources.
For More Information • University at Albany, State University of New York, Office of International Education, LI 66, Albany, NY 12222; *Phone:* 518-442-3525; *Fax:* 518-442-3338. *E-mail:* intled@uamail.albany.edu. *World Wide Web:* http://www.albany.edu/intled/

UNIVERSITY OF NORTH CAROLINA AT WILMINGTON
NORTH CAROLINA SEMESTER IN SWANSEA

Hosted by University of Wales–University College of Swansea
Academic Focus • Full curriculum.
Program Information • Students attend classes at University of Wales–University College of Swansea. Field trips to attractions around Swansea, Stonehenge, Bath, Salisbury, Cardiff, north Wales; optional travel to London, Edinburgh, Bath, Bristol at an extra cost.
Sessions • Spring.
Eligibility Requirements • Minimum age 18; open to sophomores, juniors, seniors, adults; 2.8 GPA; 2 letters of recommendation; good academic standing at home school; minimum 3.0 GPA in major; internship application; résumé; internship objectives statement (if applicable).
Living Arrangements • Students live in host institution dormitories. Quarters are shared with host institution students. Meals are taken on one's own, in residences, in central dining facility, in restaurants.
Costs (2003) • One term: $6059; includes tuition, housing, insurance, excursions, student support services, local bus pass. $200 nonrefundable deposit required. Financial aid available for students from sponsoring institution: scholarships, loans.
For More Information • Ms. Elizabeth A. Adams, Education Abroad Coordinator, Office of International Programs, University of North Carolina at Wilmington, 601 South College Road, Wilmington, NC 28403; *Phone:* 910-962-3685; *Fax:* 910-962-4053. *E-mail:* adamse@uncw.edu. *World Wide Web:* http://www.uncw.edu/intprogs/

WESTERN SAMOA

APIA
SCHOOL FOR INTERNATIONAL TRAINING, SIT STUDY ABROAD
SAMOA: PACIFIC ISLANDS STUDIES

Academic Focus • Anthropology, economics, geography, history, liberal studies, political science and government, Samoan, social sciences, sociology, visual and performing arts.

WESTERN SAMOA
Apia

Program Information • Faculty members are drawn from the sponsor's U.S. staff and local instructors hired by the sponsor. Scheduled travel to American Samoa or Fiji, Savai'i Island, rural U'polu; field trips to a rainforest, historic sites, museums.

Sessions • Fall, spring.

Eligibility Requirements • Open to sophomores, juniors, seniors; 2.5 GPA; 2 letters of recommendation; good academic standing at home school; no foreign language proficiency required.

Living Arrangements • Students live in host institution dormitories, host family homes, hotels. Meals are taken as a group, on one's own, with host family, in residences, in central dining facility, in restaurants.

Costs (2003-2004) • One term: $12,725; includes tuition, housing, all meals, insurance, excursions. $50 application fee. $400 nonrefundable deposit required. Financial aid available for all students: scholarships.

For More Information • School for International Training, SIT Study Abroad, Kipling Road, Brattleboro, VT 05302-0676; *Phone:* 888-272-7881; *Fax:* 802-258-3296. *E-mail:* studyabroad@sit.edu. *World Wide Web:* http://www.sit.edu/studyabroad/

INDEXES

Field of Study

ART HISTORY, CRITICISM, AND CONSERVATION

COMPUTER SCIENCE

CONSERVATION AND NATURAL RESOURCES

ECONOMICS

ENGLISH LITERATURE

FINANCE

FINE/STUDIO ARTS

Costa Rica

Associated Colleges of the Midwest, ACM Tropical Field
  Research 150

Ecuador

College Consortium for International Studies–College of
  Staten Island/CUNY and Brookdale Community College,
  Program in Quito, Ecuador 166

England

Dickinson College, Dickinson Science Program in Norwich
  (England) 215

Kingston University, American Visiting Student Programme. 180

Ireland

University College Cork–National University of Ireland,
  Cork, Visiting Student Program in Science 296

Israel

Tel Aviv University, Lowy School for Overseas
  Students/Semester or Year Abroad 310

Nepal

Cornell University, Cornell Nepal Study Program 370

New Zealand

AHA International An Academic Program of the University
  of Oregon, AHA at the University of Otago 380

Boston University, Auckland Programs 377

South Africa

InterStudy, University of Natal at Durban 413

InterStudy, University of Witwatersrand 414

Sweden

University of Idaho, Semester in Sweden 458

Tanzania

Associated Colleges of the Midwest, ACM Tanzania Program 463

GERMANIC LANGUAGES AND LITERATURES

Austria

AHA International An Academic Program of the University
  of Oregon, Program in Vienna, Austria: Midwest
  Consortium for Study Abroad and Northwest Council on
  Study Abroad 117

American Institute For Foreign Study (AIFS), University of
  Salzburg 116

Bentley College, Study Abroad Program in Vienna, Austria . 117

Bowling Green State University, Academic Year Abroad in
  Austria 116

Central College Abroad, Central College Abroad in Vienna,
  Austria 118

College Consortium for International Studies–Miami Dade
  College and Truman State University, Semester in
  Austria 116

European Heritage Institute, Academic Year at the
  University of Vienna, Austria 118

IES, Institute for the International Education of Students,
  IES–Vienna 118

Longwood University, Study Abroad in Salzburg 116

Nicholls State University, Nicholls State University in
  Vienna, Austria 118

Northern Illinois University, European, Communication, and
  Business Studies 116

Rider University, Study Abroad in Austria 115

St. Lawrence University, Vienna Austria Program 119

State University of New York at Binghamton, Graz Program 115

University of New Orleans, Innsbruck Academic Year
  Abroad 115

The University of North Carolina at Chapel Hill, Study
  Abroad at Vienna University of Economics and Business
  Administration 119

University of Redlands, Salzburg Semester 117

Walla Walla College, Adventist Colleges Abroad 115

Belgium

Bentley College, Business Program Abroad in Belgium 121

Canada

State University of New York at Plattsburgh, Study in
  Canada, Montreal (Concordia) 128

Czech Republic

New York University, NYU in Prague 159

England

InterStudy, Goldsmiths College, University of London 196

InterStudy, King's College, University of London 197

InterStudy, Queen Mary and Westfield College, University of
  London 197

InterStudy, University of Essex 176

Long Island University, Friends World Program–European
  Center-London 198

University of Kent, Junior Year Abroad in Canterbury 175

University of Sheffield, Study Abroad Programme 222

France

Syracuse University, European Program in Strasbourg 261

Syracuse University, International Relations Program in
  Strasbourg 262

Tufts University, Tufts in Paris 258

Germany

Acadia University, Trent University, Brook University and
  University of British Columbia, Canadian Year in
  Freiburg 269

AHA International An Academic Program of the University
  of Oregon, Program in Cologne, Germany 268

Alma College, Program of Studies in Germany 272

American University, Semester in Berlin 265

Antioch College, Antioch in Tübingen 277

Boston University, Dresden Engineering and Science
  Program 269

Boston University, Dresden Music Studies Program 269

College Consortium for International Studies–Ocean County
  College and St. Ambrose University, Business/Liberal Arts
  in Germany 271

Columbia University, Berlin Consortium for German Studies 266

Duke University, Duke in Berlin 266

IES, Institute for the International Education of Students,
  IES–Freiburg, European Union 270

Kentucky Institute for International Studies, Semester
  Program in Regensburg, Germany 275

Lexia International, Lexia in Berlin 266

Lock Haven University of Pennsylvania, Semester in
  Germany 275

Loyola University New Orleans, Loyola in Berlin 267

Murray State University, Semester in Regensburg 275

Nicholls State University, Nicholls State in Germany 270

Northern Arizona University, German Intensive Language
  Program 277

Northern Arizona University, Study Abroad in Germany 279

Northern Arizona University, Study Abroad in Germany 272

St. Cloud State University, German Studies—Language 272

Schiller International University, Study Abroad
  Undergraduate and Graduate Programs 271

School for International Training, SIT Study Abroad, Central
  Europe: Nationalism, Ethnicity, and Culture 267

Scripps College, Scripps College in Germany 272

Smith College, Junior Year in Hamburg 271

State University of New York at Oswego, University of
  Osnabrück 275

University of Colorado at Boulder, Regensburg Program . . . 275

University of Connecticut, Baden-Württemberg Exchange
  Program 265

University of Connecticut, Regensburg Exchange: Business,
  Computer Science, and Engineering Work/Study Abroad
  Program 276

University of Delaware, Spring Semester in Bayreuth,
  Germany 265

University of Miami, University of Tübingen, Germany 278

University of Wisconsin-Eau Claire, Institute for German
  Language and Culture 278

University of Wisconsin-Madison, Academic Year in
  Freiburg, Germany 270

University of Wisconsin-Stevens Point, Semester in
  Germany: Magdeburg 273

FIELD OF STUDY
Interdisciplinary Studies

MATHEMATICS

SOCIAL SCIENCES, GENERAL

WOMEN'S STUDIES

Program Sponsors

ART UNDER ONE ROOF

ASSOCIATED COLLEGES IN CHINA

ASSOCIATED COLLEGES OF THE MIDWEST

ASSOCIATED COLLEGES OF THE SOUTH

ASSOCIATED KYOTO PROGRAM

AUGSBURG COLLEGE

AUGUSTA STATE UNIVERSITY

AUSTRALEARN: NORTH AMERICAN CENTER FOR AUSTRALIAN AND NEW ZEALAND UNIVERSITIES

AUSTRALIAN NATIONAL UNIVERSITY

BATH SPA UNIVERSITY COLLEGE

BAYLOR UNIVERSITY

BELOIT COLLEGE

BEMIDJI STATE UNIVERSITY

BEN-GURION UNIVERSITY OF THE NEGEV

BENTLEY COLLEGE

Host Institutions